T0231160

Software Application Development

*A Visual C++®,
MFC, and STL
Tutorial*

CHAPMAN & HALL/CRC
COMPUTER and INFORMATION SCIENCE SERIES

Series Editor: Sartaj Sahni

Software Application Development

A Visual C++®,
MFC, and STL
Tutorial

Bud Fox
Zhang Wenzu
Tan May Ling

CRC Press
Taylor & Francis Group
Boca Raton London New York

CRC Press is an imprint of the
Taylor & Francis Group, an **informa** business

A CHAPMAN & HALL BOOK

MATLAB® and Simulink® are trademarks of The MathWorks, Inc. and are used with permission. The MathWorks does not warrant the accuracy of the text or exercises in this book. This book's use or discussion of MATLAB® and Simulink® software or related products does not constitute endorsement or sponsorship by The MathWorks of a particular pedagogical approach or particular use of the MATLAB® and Simulink® software.

CRC Press
Taylor & Francis Group
6000 Broken Sound Parkway NW, Suite 300
Boca Raton, FL 33487-2742

First issued in hardback 2018

© 2013 by Taylor & Francis Group, LLC
CRC Press is an imprint of Taylor & Francis Group, an Informa business

No claim to original U.S. Government works

ISBN-13: 978-1-4665-1100-2 (pbk)
ISBN-13: 978-1-138-46845-0 (hbk)

This book contains information obtained from authentic and highly regarded sources. Reasonable efforts have been made to publish reliable data and information, but the author and publisher cannot assume responsibility for the validity of all materials or the consequences of their use. The authors and publishers have attempted to trace the copyright holders of all material reproduced in this publication and apologize to copyright holders if permission to publish in this form has not been obtained. If any copyright material has not been acknowledged please write and let us know so we may rectify in any future reprint.

Except as permitted under U.S. Copyright Law, no part of this book may be reprinted, reproduced, transmitted, or utilized in any form by any electronic, mechanical, or other means, now known or hereafter invented, including photocopying, microfilming, and recording, or in any information storage or retrieval system, without written permission from the publishers.

For permission to photocopy or use material electronically from this work, please access www.copyright.com (http://www.copyright.com/) or contact the Copyright Clearance Center, Inc. (CCC), 222 Rosewood Drive, Danvers, MA 01923, 978-750-8400. CCC is a not-for-profit organization that provides licenses and registration for a variety of users. For organizations that have been granted a photocopy license by the CCC, a separate system of payment has been arranged.

Trademark Notice: Product or corporate names may be trademarks or registered trademarks, and are used only for identification and explanation without intent to infringe.

Visit the Taylor & Francis Web site at
http://www.taylorandfrancis.com

and the CRC Press Web site at
http://www.crcpress.com

Contents

PART I   User Interaction

PART II *Model Computation and Data*

Preface

One night as I sat at my small kitchen table, I had a great flash of awareness. It changed my life. I suddenly realized that everything that would happen to me for the rest of my life was going to be up to me. No one else was ever going to help me. No one was coming to the rescue. I was responsible.

Brian Tracy [1]

A TUTORIAL

This book has been written as a set of steps that can be followed to develop a Visual C++ demonstration application addressing the main features of Windows-based applications provided for by Visual C++ 6.0 and later editions of C++. The step-by-step instructions show how the development of an application is progressive and that careful consideration is required upon implementation, since all decisions will affect the structure and maintainability of the software at later stages. The software developed here is titled DiagramEng. It is a block-diagram-based engineering application used to model and simulate dynamical systems and is similar to what one may encounter in control engineering. The mathematics and computer code has intentionally been kept simple and easy-to-understand, and the detailed explanations clarify the underlying concepts and problems encountered. All computer code is included in this learn-by-example approach. Once the developer has gone through this extensive tutorial, he or she would be aptly prepared for real-world Visual C++ software application development and be ready to take the next developmental step forward.

WRITE IT DOWN

Always be sure to think on paper. Write things down. There is something that happens between the brain and the hand when you write. You get a greater sense of clarity and understanding with regard to the issues involved.

Brian Tracy [1]

Software development starts with turning off the screen, putting the keyboard aside, and writing ideas down with a pen on paper. Reactionary behavior is then replaced by thoughtfulness and peace of mind, allowing ideas to surface and flow from one problem to the next. Diagrams are drawn, text is used to explain the desired software functionality, key nouns and verbs are highlighted, candidate classes are identified, and header files may be written, and these then form an initial basic design.

To implement all the necessary application functionality, write every idea down on paper first, plan the software development steps, discuss them with colleagues, formulate them as instructions, and then finally code them in easy-to-understand and easy-to-remember progressive actions.

PREREQUISITES

The prerequisites to be able to follow the instructions in this book are enthusiasm and hard work. The reader should also have an understanding of how to program in C/C++, and this may be developed by working through texts similar to "Teach Yourself C++ in 21 Days" [2] and "Teach Yourself C++ in 24 Hours" [3]. However, as this book is a tutorial on Visual C++ software demonstration application development, the reader is encouraged to read and work through Chapters 1 through 8 and 10 through 13 of "Teach Yourself Visual C++ 6 in 21 Days" [4]. These chapters cover the essential fundamentals of using the Microsoft® Visual C++ 6.0 and Visual Studio™ 6.0 Development

System (integrated development environment [IDE]) [5], and provide instructions on how the user can build Visual C++ applications similar to the Windows-based applications ubiquitous in modern personal computing environments.

However, if the reader would prefer to simply start with the material in this text, *Software Application Development: A Visual C++®, MFC, and STL Tutorial*, then that is certainly possible, since the instructions herein are detailed, progressive, complete, and supported by many figures, tables, and error-resolving notes. Moreover, the source code, including all source and header files necessary to compile, link, and run the software application is included; nothing is omitted.

Additional materials are available for download from http://www.crcpress.com/product/isbn/9781466511002

MATLAB ® is a registered trademark of The MathWorks, Inc. For product information, please contact:

The MathWorks, Inc.
3 Apple Hill Drive
Natick, MA, 01760-2098 USA
Tel: 508-647-7000
Fax: 508-647-7001
E-mail: info@mathworks.com
Web: www.mathworks.com

Microsoft products for which there exist trademarks is presented here:
http://www.microsoft.com/about/legal/en/us/intellectualProperty/Trademarks/EN-US.aspx

Acknowledgments

We would like to acknowledge the following people and organizations that have directly or indirectly influenced the content of this book:

- The Institute of High Performance Computing (IHPC) [6]—for supporting the Interactive Engineering Research Group through the duration of the project
- Dr. Zsolt Szabo (IHPC)—for providing useful guidelines about computation of nonlinear systems using the Newton method
- Dr. Wang Binfang (IHPC)—for her advice concerning various implementation issues throughout the software development process
- Jeanne, Chow Hui Hsien (IHPC)—for her enthusiastic and friendly computer systems support
- Wayne, Lee Choon Hiang (IHPC)—for his efficient computer systems support and willingness to help proactively whenever problems arose
- Evelyn Lau (Director, Science and Engineering Research Council [7] Shared Services)—for her encouragement towards people development.
- Sharon Ee Chew Suan (Director, IHPC Corporate Services)—for her encouragement towards people development and its implementation within IHPC.
- Microsoft Corporation—for Visual C++ 6.0, Visual Studio 6.0, Windows-based applications, and the Microsoft Developer Network (MSDN) [8] for a valuable source of information on software development, Microsoft Foundation Classes (MFC), and the Standard Template Library (STL)
- The MathWorks—for two very powerful, useful, high-level software applications, MATLAB® and SIMULINK® [9], that have been an inspiration to us and have provided us with an example and standard of interactive mathematical modeling and computation software.
- Jesse J. Pepper and Daniel Paull (Think Bottom Up Pty. Ltd. [10])—for their helpful insight into improving the developed software application DiagramEng
- Dr. Roy M. Howard (Curtin University of Technology)—for his insight concerning the classification of signals and systems
- Professor Leslie S. Jennings (The University of Western Australia)—for his important input concerning the computation of nonlinear systems using Newton's method
- Professor David J. Lilja (University of Minnesota)—for his thoughtful comments toward improving the manuscript
- Professor Albert Y. Zomaya (The University of Sydney)—for his input toward professional publication
- Professor Michael A. Small (The University of Western Australia)—for his feedback concerning improvement of the manuscript
- Assistant Professor Karl Erik Birgersson (National University of Singapore)—for his enthusiasm and helpful suggestions in making the book a valuable teaching aid for academics introducing the discipline of computer science to students
- Project manager Arunkumar Aranganathan (SPi Global)—for overseeing the production, including typesetting and editing of the text.

We would sincerely like to thank Ms Randi Cohen, acquisitions editor, Computer Science, Chapman & Hall/CRC Press, for her belief in the subject matter; persistence and patience with legal, business and administration issues; efficiency in communication; and tireless hard work in managing the acquisition, production and promotion of this book that shares the software development process in detail with the reader.

REFERENCES

1. Tracy, B., *Goals: How to Get Everything You Want – Faster than You Ever Thought Possible*, Berrett-Koehler, San Francisco, CA, 2004.
2. Liberty, J., *Teach Yourself C++ in 21 Days*, SAMS Publishing, Indianapolis, IN, 2001.
3. Liberty, J. and Horvath, D. B., *Teach Yourself C++ in 24 Hours*, SAMS Publishing, Indianapolis, IN, 2005.
4. Chapman, D., *Teach Yourself Visual C++ 6 in 21 Days*, SAMS Publishing, Indianapolis, IN, 1998.
5. Microsoft Visual C++ 6.0, Microsoft® Visual Studio™ 6.0 Development System, Professional Edition, Microsoft Corporation, 1998.
6. Institute of High Performance Computing, www.ihpc.a-star.edu.sg
7. Science and Engineering Research Council, www.a-star.edu.sg
8. Microsoft Developer Network Library Visual Studio 6.0, Microsoft® Visual Studio™ 6.0 Development System, Microsoft Corporation, 1998.
9. The MathWorks Inc., www.mathworks.com
10. Think Bottom Up, Pty. Ltd., www.thinkbottomup.com.au/site

Introduction

Most often, people start something new, only to give up at the very beginning. The sense of shame encroaches and leaves the entrant to a field feeling overwhelmed, where failure appears inevitable. All that is needed is a thorough tutorial from which one may learn by example and move forward. This book is that tutorial!

LOST, DIRECTIONLESS, AND AVOIDING THE START

Many books have been published on C/C++, Visual C++, and object-oriented analysis and design, conveying language constructs, usage of specific features, and organizing program structure and execution control. However, often the software developer reads whole books or refers to certain sections of texts recommended by their peers and is left saying:

"Now, what the hell am I supposed to do with all this stuff?"

Often there is frustration, a lack of fulfillment, and a feeling of being left behind the crowd. The worst thing that can then happen is to avoid the area of work in which one is left feeling deficient. The solution is to improve one's knowledge and skills to a point where one feels capable and useful and is equal to any task that is asked of oneself. The key is to make a start and to follow through to completion, regardless of destructive criticism from others and even self-criticism.

This book, *Software Application Development: A Visual C++®, MFC, and STL Tutorial*, is designed to lead the reader through a demonstration application software development project from start to finish, covering design and implementation in C/C++ and Visual C++, and allow the developer to be able to reproduce the software that is presented. All the code to compile, link, and run the software is included; nothing is omitted. This mechanism of teaching by example is designed to allow the developer to experience a real-world software development cycle and shows the importance of making a start, to break the perfectionism barrier, and quite simply "get some points on the board." This book has been written by software engineers, for software engineers, and for those who need to get going, to get something working, to get something up and running, and to keep pushing forward allowing the design and software to evolve as greater operational complexity is relentlessly introduced.

CONTENTS

The text is structured in a progressive manner: a software application idea is introduced, a design method ensues, a preliminary Win32 Console Application is written, and then the actual Visual C++ coding commences. Thereafter, code modules are added incrementally, problems are encountered, and methods to solve them are suggested and implemented. Each step of the development procedure is engaging and rewarding: it involves the reader and provides instructions to move from one step to the next at a smooth pace. It is similar to following a recipe for making a coffee cake.

The following is a brief description of the material covered in each chapter of the book: it is designed to convey to the reader in a brief manner all the steps to be expected toward developing the end software product titled, DiagramEng. There are three main parts in this book: (1) User Interaction, (2) Model Computation and Data, and (3) Refinement.

Part I consists of Chapters 1 through 17 and provides instructions to first design the software and then discusses key graphical interface elements and user-interaction sequences. Menus, toolbars, dialog windows, controls, string conversion, blocks, connections, item movement, and presentation are all thoroughly covered to allow the user to set up and draw a model diagram containing feedback loops that represent a real-world engineering problem.

Part II, Model Computation and Data, consists of Chapters 18 through 25 and leads the reader carefully through the preparation and implementation of block-based data operations and a Newton-method-based nonlinear equation solver to compute a system model containing feedback/algebraic loops that represent a set of simultaneous equations. Six key examples are explored and graphical output displayed, confirming the underlying physics of the problems concerned. Finally, serialization is performed to allow the user to save and restore system model data and save graphical output data.

Part III, Refinement, consisting of Chapters 26 through 34, completes the software development process, firstly by reviewing what remaining functionality is to be added and then implementing the necessary features typically found in Windows-based applications, including printing and print preview, a scrolling view, editing actions, annotations, diagnostic information, and the presentation of a help-related document, before finalizing the project.

PART I: USER INTERACTION

Chapter 1, Object-Oriented Analysis and Design, presents a discussion of the initial software application idea and introduces certain software design principles to get the development going. Requirements are discussed and use case narratives, scenarios, and conversations are introduced to describe the basic user actions and system responsibilities concerning software function and behavior. A noun and verb analysis is made that then leads to an object analysis involving candidate, responsibilities, and collaborators (CRC) cards and their content. Preliminary class structure diagrams are then drawn, and finally a Win32 Console Application is provided that reflects the basic class structure and allows the user to witness object construction and destruction through a console window.

Chapter 2, Initial Graphical User Interface, commences the Visual C++ application development and allows the user to get graphical user interface (GUI) entities functioning interactively. Menus and toolbars are added to the GUI, and event-handler functions are associated with their entries and buttons, respectively. A block library dialog window is then added to the project to allow the addition of blocks to a diagram model. Block construction functionality is introduced in preparation for constructing individual diagram-based blocks. Finally, a function is added that allows a pointer-to-CDiagramEngDoc to be retrieved from outside the CDiagramEngView class, allowing access to the document associated with a view.

Chapter 3, Constructing Blocks, provides instructions to the developer to merge a Win32 Console application with the initial Visual C++ application, providing the essential structure of the DiagramEng application. Particular block-based classes are then derived from the base CBlock class and, upon construction, are added to the system model. Drawing of the individual block types is performed through a virtual function, where, based on the derived run-time type of a pointer-to-CBlock, the appropriate block-drawing method is called.

Chapter 4, Constructing Block Ports, shows the reader how block port objects are constructed and set up, and then added to the block's vector of input and/or output ports. The drawing of ports involves iterating through the block's vectors of input and/or output ports, and the port-drawing method of the CPort class called to display the port on a side-face of the block, based on a port positioning angle.

Chapter 5, Constructing Connections, adds connections, designed to retain signal-based data, to the project, that involve, in their initial form, both a head and tail point. The drawing of connections, including a connection-based arrow head indicating the direction of signal flow, is performed through the use of mouse-button-based event-handler functions. The connections are added to and retrieved from a list of connections retained by a system model.

Chapter 6, Moving Blocks and Connections, introduces a CRectTracker object used to perform the movement of blocks and connection objects, including their head, tail, and bend points. Bend points may be inserted in a connection object via an entry on the Context menu and allow branching of signal flow within a model diagram. The connection head and tail end points can be snapped and unsnapped to and from block input and output ports, respectively, where the tail point can also emanate from another connection's bend point. Finally, the deletion of individual connection-based bend points and whole connection objects is implemented.

Chapter 7, Automatic Block Placement, addresses placement of blocks on the palette by comparing two possible methods. Blocks are automatically placed in an array-like manner, horizontally and vertically, in the earliest available position on the palette, such that they are sufficiently spaced apart.

Chapter 8, Connection-Based Bend Points, explores the implementation of functionality concerning a *primary* connection's bend points to which other, *secondary* connections may be attached and remain connected. The deletion of bend points, to which other connections are attached, requires the disconnection of *secondary* connection tail points prior to *primary* connection-based bend point deletion. The automatic connection of connection end points to ports and bend points allows the user to simultaneously draw connections and link diagram entities together. In addition, the deletion of a block invokes automatic disconnection of any connected objects from the block ports.

Chapter 9, Block Dialog Windows, adds block-based dialog windows to the project that may be used to enter block-specific parameters by double-left-clicking the block. To add dialog window-based functionality for each block type, six key steps are pursued: (1) insertion of a dialog window resource and all necessary controls, (2) creation of a class for the dialog window, (3) attachment of variables to the dialog window controls, (4) the addition of functionality to the dialog window buttons, (5) the addition of functionality to initialize the class variables, and (6) the addition of an overriding block dialog window parameter input function to each derived block class that creates an instance of the appropriate block dialog window.

Chapter 10, Conversion of String Input to Double Data, details all the steps required to transform CString user input, entered through a block's parameter-input dialog window, to double member data. The steps involve stripping a string of unwanted leading and trailing characters, determining the number of rows and columns of input data, and conversion of the string into a matrix or vector. The Constant, Gain, Integrator and Transfer Function blocks all require string processing.

Chapter 11, Moving Multiple Items, introduces the simultaneous movement of multiple diagram entities, including blocks and connection objects, through the use of a CRectTracker object and a rectangular rubber-band tracking region. The user can circumscribe the items, followed by left-clicking within the region and subsequently drag the entities to another location on the palette.

Chapter 12, Addition of a Tree View Control, discusses the addition of a Tree View control for the display of a block directory tree, the leaves of which may be double-clicked to add blocks to a system model. The key steps involve adding a dialog resource, attaching a class to the dialog, attaching a variable to the dialog window control to be used to display Tree View items, performing of initialization, and the adding of icons for the Tree View leaves. Finally, the docking of the Tree dialog window to the Main frame is performed manually according to a nine-step procedure, since the CTreeDialog class is inherited from the CDialog base class rather than the CDialogBar class.

Chapter 13, A Review of Menu and Toolbar-Based Functionality—Part 1, reviews the existing menu and toolbar-based functionality to determine the necessary features to be added and involve (1) the Main frame–based and Child frame–based menus and (2) the Main frame, Common Blocks, and Common Operations toolbars.

Chapter 14, Context Menu Extension, pursues the extension of the Context menu to allow the user to easily delete multiple grouped items using a CRectTracker object and to set block and numerical solver properties through a Set Properties entry that invokes the corresponding entity-specific dialog window and updates user input to the appropriate class.

Chapter 15, Setting Port Properties, introduces a port properties dialog window to allow the user to specifically configure block input and output ports via an entry on the Context menu. The number of input ports for the Sum and Divide blocks may be adjusted via their corresponding block dialog parameter input windows. The drawing of block ports, depending on their connection status, and the drawing of port signs, is also added. Finally, the mechanism to delete a port via an entry on the Context menu is implemented.

Chapter 16, Key-Based Item Movement, provides instructions for adding functionality for the keyboard-based, fine-scale movement of blocks and connection-based bend points to the project. An entry is added to the Context menu whose event-handler function sets a flag-like member variable used to control four possible movement-related states: no movement, recording of the address of the diagram entity to be moved, moving a block, and moving a bend point.

Chapter 17, Reversing Block Direction, presents a method to reverse the orientation of a block and its ports, such that diagrams can be drawn in a more flexible manner with connections, denoting the path of signal flow, being able to be drawn entering a block in both the forward and reverse directions: this allows the correct drawing of feedback loops.

PART II: MODEL COMPUTATION AND DATA

Chapter 18, Model Validation, discusses the process of validating a model in preparation for model computation and checks the following: (1) the existence of at least one source block and one output block in the model, (2) the connection status of block ports, and (3) the connectivity of model connections to block input and output ports. Errors detected at the model validation stage are presented flashing in red, and this is done through the usage of a device context and the setting of its attributes at the stage of drawing the system model. Finally, functionality is added to prevent the user from connecting more than one head or tail point to an input or output port.

Chapter 19, Non-Feedback-Based Signal Propagation, clarifies the difference between direct signal propagation, used for models that do not contain feedback loops, and a simultaneous-equations-based approach, used for models that contain a feedback or algebraic loop, where the output of a block depends on the input, yet that very input depends, usually indirectly, on the same block's output. To determine whether a model contains a feedback loop, a node-arc connectivity matrix is constructed and a recursive function used to build possible tours through the model diagram that either end in an output block, denoting the absence of a loop, or a repeated block/node, signifying the presence of a loop. In addition, a direct signal propagation function is added to the system model class, and data-operation functions are added to the derived block classes that operate on input signals and generate output signal data.

Chapter 20, Graph Drawing, leads the developer through the process of adding a graph-drawing window to graphically display the numerical data stored in an output block. Six incremental steps are taken to add the graph-drawing-related functionality to the project: (1) structure is added to display an empty view window associated with the output block, (2) existing classes are supplemented with methods and variables to access the output block's numerical data, (3) data is initially plotted as a text string in the view window, (4) numerical data is plotted as graphical curves in the view window, (5) button-based functionality is added to the output block's dialog window to allow the user to display output in a variety of forms, and (6) an output block and its related view window are properly deleted.

Chapter 21, Block Operations, adds key block-based data-operation functions that operate on input signals and generate dimensionally consistent output signals. Block operations are finalized for the Derivative and Integrator (Continuous) blocks; the Divide, Gain, and Sum (Math Operations) blocks; the Output (Sink) block; and the Constant, Linear Function, and Signal Generator (Source) blocks.

Chapter 22, Preparation for Feedback-Based Signal Propagation, makes the necessary preparations to the software structure through the introduction of member methods and variables for the computation of a model containing feedback or algebraic loops. In general, a system of nonlinear equations of the form, $F(x(t)) = x(t) - f(x(t)) = 0$, is to be constructed, where $F(x(t))$ is the generalized system vector, $x(t)$ is the generalized output signal vector, and $f(x(t))$ is the generalized block operation function vector. A solution or root, $x_r(t)$, to the system is sought using a Newton-method-based solver, which is a vector of system signals at the current time-step $t \in [t_0, t_f]$, where t_0 and t_f are the initial and final time points of the simulation, respectively. In addition, functionality is added to allow the user to set the initial output signals of a block if required. Finally, a method to terminate a simulation prematurely is added using message-related functions.

Chapter 23, Feedback-Based Signal Propagation, implements a Newton-method-based solver to compute a system of nonlinear equations representing a model with feedback loops to determine the output signal vectors of all diagram blocks at each time point of the simulation. Six problem types involving feedback loops are explored to test the accuracy of the nonlinear solver: (1) a linear problem, (2) a first order linear ordinary differential equation, (3) a second order linear ordinary differential equation representing a mechanical/electrical problem transformed into the state-space equations, (4) a coupled linear system, (5) the Lotka–Volterra system consisting of two coupled first order nonlinear differential equations representing population dynamics, and (6) the nonlinear dynamical Lorenz equations used to model the atmosphere, showing chaotic dynamical motion on the strange attractor set.

Chapter 24, Placing an Edit Box on a Toolbar, demonstrates how a read-only Edit box control, created using a pointer-to-CEdit variable, may be placed on a toolbar that allows the user to dynamically see the simulation time, t (s), of a running experiment and then the total execution time, t_{exe} (s), at the end of the simulation. The Edit box control is updated through a chain of function calls that begins in the signal propagation functions of the system model class.

Chapter 25, Serialization, extends the application by implementing serialization, i.e., the writing and reading of key class data, to and from a file, using the output ("ofstream") and input ("ifstream") file stream objects, respectively. Event-handler functions are added to the Main frame–based and Child frame–based windows to initiate the serialization process, through, e.g., the Save and Save As (File) menu entries. The system model data, including block-based and connection-based data, are written to and read from a simple text file that contains string identifiers organizing the output. In addition, changes are made to the project such that the initial output signal of a multiply/divide block, which forms a loop-repeated node in a feedback loop, can also be serialized. Finally, the output block is extended to allow the user to save numerical data to a specified output file.

PART III: REFINEMENT

Chapter 26, A Review of Menu and Toolbar-Based Functionality—Part 2, assesses the remaining Child frame–based menu functionality that is to be added to the DiagramEng project to allow the user to perform efficient modeling and simulation. The key menus identified, for which final details are to be added, are File, Edit, View, Model, Format, Tools, and Help.

Chapter 27, Printing and Print Preview, clarifies the printing and print preview processes involved in Windows-based applications. A mapping mode is used to define both the transformation from page-space units into device-space units and the axes orientations. The window and viewport rectangles, together with the extent and origin setting functions, define the mapping from the window to the viewport. In addition, a scaling is used in the transformation and is typically based on the ratio of the screen and printer device capacities. Three key CView-based methods to which functionality is added are OnBeginPrinting(), to set the maximum number of pages to be printed; OnPrepareDC(), to prepare the device context and set mapping modes; and OnDraw(), to perform a transformation and scaling between the window and viewport rectangles before drawing the model diagram.

Chapter 28, Implementing a Scroll View, indicates the changes required to the application to implement a scrolling view, including deriving the original CView-based class from CScrollView. However, with the introduction of a scrolling view, a conversion is required to be made between device points and logical points and vice versa, given a change in the scroll position, and the functions affected are numerous. The automatic fitting of the viewport scale to the physical window allows the user to shrink or enlarge the diagram to fit the window exactly in one view. Zooming in and out of a view displaying the model diagram is also implemented through a scaling of diagram entity geometry, and finally, a mechanism to reset the default diagram geometry is implemented.

Chapter 29, Edit Menu, provides the instructions to add functionality for the Undo, Redo, Cut, Copy, Paste, and Select All entries of the Edit menu. A clipboard object is introduced and used to make copies of blocks and connections upon selection of the Cut and Copy entries of the Edit menu. Upon pasting of diagram entities, the contents of the clipboard lists are merged with the corresponding lists of the system model. The copying of objects is performed using a class copy constructor. The undoing and redoing of editing actions involves creating a list of system model pointers used to record their addresses, and saving or retrieving the addresses of system models to and from the list. The copying of system models is performed using a class copy constructor, and the class assignment operator is used to assign the system model retrieved from the list to the system model object of the CDocument-derived class. Updating of the user interface is also implemented, indicating the applicability of the appropriate undoing or redoing editing action.

Chapter 30, Annotations, completes the diagram editing process by adding an annotation class and functionality that allows the user to annotate a system model through the use of an annotation dialog invoked from the Context menu. A list of the available system fonts is displayed in the dialog window, and font creation is performed for the CFont member annotation class-based variable. Annotations are displayed on the screen as individual system-model-based entities, and may be moved, edited, and deleted: in addition, they may be shown or hidden via an entry under the Format menu. The Cut, Copy, and Paste Edit menu-based actions require the introduction of an annotation class copy constructor, and the Undo and Redo actions require changes to be made to existing functions. Finally, the serialization of the annotation class data is performed and existing methods augmented to cater for a system-model-based annotation list.

Chapter 31, Tools Menu, adds the functionality required to present diagnostic information, via a dialog window, to the user concerning memory usage information. Two key structures are used: (1) PROCESS_MEMORY_COUNTERS contains memory statistics for a process and (2) MEMORYSTATUS retains information about the current state of the system physical and virtual memory [1]. The "working set size" is an important statistic that denotes the physical memory used by a process—here the DiagramEng application itself.

Chapter 32, Help Menu, provides instructions to display a portable document format (PDF) Help-like document named, "UsingDiagramEng.pdf", explaining how the DiagramEng application is to be used for block diagram–based mathematical modeling and engineering simulation. A process is to be created, requiring a complete command line argument, which is a concatenation of the executable file name, "Acrobat.exe", the file path of the PDF document, and its name "UsingDiagramEng.pdf". The topics covered in the Help document include menus, toolbars, examples, and forms of output.

Chapter 33, Finalizing the Project, finalizes the software development process and involves the following: (1) disabling of non-functional elements, (2) checking the application for memory leaks using a Debug-build configuration of the application followed by running the program with a debugger and observing the Debug output window for memory leak messages, and (3) preparing the final Open Source and executable code by including any required modules in the Release-build configuration of the application.

Chapter 34, Conclusion, briefly reviews the entire software development process, summarizing all the design and implementation steps taken to arrive at the final DiagramEng demonstration application prototype to be used for block-diagram-based, applied mathematics-oriented engineering simulation. Mistakes made, lessons learned, and suggestions for improving the software are provided so that the passionate developer may extend the application to solve specific engineering problems of interest.

REFERENCE

1. Microsoft Developer Network Library Visual Studio 6.0, Microsoft® Visual Studio™ 6.0 Development System, Microsoft Corporation, 1998.

Authors

Dr. Bud FOX received his BSc (Hons) in applied mathematics (1996) and his PhD, majoring in electrical and electronic engineering (2000), from The University of Western Australia. He has been working for the Institute of High Performance Computing (IHPC) (http://www.ihpc.a-star.edu.sg) in Singapore since 2003 and is currently a senior research engineer in the Engineering Software Group, pursuing research in interactive engineering. His other areas of interest include computational multibody dynamics, operations research, parallel computing, and software development. He has published numerous conference and IEEE and ASME journal articles and is the coauthor of the book titled *Constrained Dynamics Computations: Models and Case Studies* (ISBN: 981-02-4368-5).

Dr. FOX has been engaged in computer programming since 1990 and has used the following languages and applications: C/C++, Visual C++, Fortran, MATLAB®, Message Passing Interface (MPI), Open Multi-Processing (OpenMP), and X-Windows. He has written a UNIX-based software application in the area of computational multibody dynamics titled "Multibody System," involving Basic Linear Algebra Subprograms (BLAS), C, Linear Algebra Package (LAPACK), Livermore Solver of Ordinary Differential Equations with Automatic Method Switching and Root Finding (LSODAR), and X-Windows.

Dr. FOX has contributed the following titles to the IHPC Open Source Software Downloads website, http://software.ihpc.a-star.edu.sg/software.html:

- "RobotSearch"—Software for the exploration of multirobot social group-based search algorithms. OS: MS Windows XP, Software Platform: MATLAB (and Octave).
- "ACO-ILS-SA"—Software for operations research work involving Ant Colony Optimization (ACO), Iterated Local Search (ILS), and Simulated Annealing (SA). OS: IBM Unix AIX, Software Platform: C.

Dr. FOX has tutored first year university applied mathematics and statistics students and third year university computer systems engineering students. He recognizes that students and practitioners require all the underlying fine detail in order to make complex applied-mathematics-oriented software development projects work as designed. Hence, the tutorial-like nature of this book will lead the reader through all the difficult aspects of a software project, including compilation and run-time error–resolving notes and information on the importance and effective use of the debugger. The book is designed to be practically helpful and is written by software developers, for software developers.

Dr. Wenzu ZHANG received his BSc (Hons) in mechanical engineering (1985) from the Wuhan University of Hydraulic and Electrical Engineering, his MSc in computer graphics and computer-aided design (1989), and his PhD, majoring in intelligent manufacturing (1993), from the Huazhong University of Science and Technology (HUST), China. He joined HUST in 1993 as a lecturer and then as an associate professor. Thereafter, from 1997, he worked at the National University of Singapore as a research fellow. He has been an employee of IHPC since 1999 as a senior research engineer and then as a research scientist, and is currently in the Engineering Software Group, pursuing research in interactive engineering and electronic design automation (EDA). He has interests in computer graphics, interactive technology, numerical algorithms, and software development for electronic packaging simulation.

Dr. Zhang brings a wealth of modern Visual C++ software development experience, acquired from more than ten large-scale, well-capitalized, software development projects conducted throughout more than ten years of service at IHPC, which were completed to increase productivity for multinational engineering companies operating in Singapore.

Ms. May Ling TAN received her BSc in computational science and physics (1999) from the National University of Singapore (NUS) and her MSc in high performance computation for engineered systems (2002) from the Singapore-MIT Alliance. She has worked at the Singaporean Defence Science Organization (DSO) National Laboratories from 1999 to 2001 as a simulation software engineer and from 2002 to 2006 as an operations analyst. She has been working at IHPC since 2007 and is currently a research officer in the Engineering Software Group.

Ms TAN is an excitingly energetic, interactive engineering software developer with a passion for delivering practical, easy-to-use, and intuitive Visual C++ software applications for the purpose of increasing productivity of scientists and engineers working in industrial and research environments. She has additional interests in computer graphics, computer games, operations research, algorithm development, and interactive and intuitive interfaces for portable devices.

Part I

User Interaction

INTRODUCTION

There are three main parts to the book that organize the contained chapters into developmental themes: (1) User Interaction, (2) Model Computation and Data, and (3) Refinement. Part I consists of Chapters 1 through 17, and presents material to instruct the user on how to interactively draw a diagram representing a system of equations that describe a mathematical model that will ultimately be computed. Initially, the software application is designed, leading to a class structure representing the key components of the modeling environment, including the application, document, and view classes, and those of the system model representing, blocks, ports, connections, and signals. Then typical graphical user interface (GUI) features are added, including menus, toolbars, dialog windows, controls, and mouse-based actions, which allow the user to construct blocks joined by connections on the palette that may be organized as desired. The assigning of data values to diagram entity attributes is facilitated through a dialog and its associated class working in conjunction with the class of the underlying entity. The net result of Part I is that a block diagram model, with user-specified data attributes, may be drawn, which represents a system of equations that may be validated and then computed in Part II.

The developer should read each chapter of instructions at least once, prior to commencing the implementation, in order to gain a broader perspective of the developmental steps and to know what results to expect. In addition, the chapters are tutorial-like in nature and hence involve numerous numbered lists that should be followed in an ordered and progressive, step-by-step manner to implement each application feature. Significant explanatory detail is added for each set of steps, and all code modules are carefully explained to lead the developer through the entire developmental procedure. The aim of the instruction is to present the material at a fast but easy-to-follow pace, and to engage and educate the developer.

1

1 Object-Oriented Analysis and Design

1.1 INTRODUCTION

At the initial stage of the development procedure, an object-oriented analysis and design phase is required to aid in expressing what it is that the final software application should accomplish. This may involve considering various resources, including *Object-Oriented Analysis and Design with Applications* by Booch et al. [1] and *Object Design—Roles, Responsibilities, and Collaborations* by Wirfs-Brock and McKean [2], for examples of structured and methodical approaches to initial design and to decide upon an analysis and design approach that is suitable.

The design method that was chosen toward the current Visual C++ demonstration application development consisted of the following steps, some of which are covered in Ref. [2]:

1. Background research on the type of application to be developed
2. Requirements of the intended software application concerning scope and function
3. General use case narratives describing the general workings of the target application
4. Use case scenarios and conversations involving user actions and system responsibilities
5. A noun and verb analysis of the key items and actions concerning the application scope
6. Object analysis involving candidate, responsibilities, and collaborators (CRC) cards
7. Preliminary diagrams reflecting the initial class structure
8. Basic header and source files implementing the intentionally bare class structure

Once the key classes and objects are defined, a hierarchical class diagram may be drawn to succinctly and visually present the key classes and their association relationships. A preliminary program involving a basic set of source and header files organizing and implementing the class structure may then be written, e.g., as a Win32 Console Application, to express the initial set of ideas about how the program should function. This includes basic member methods, variables, and data structures to manage the flow of information throughout the program: this is intentionally very brief and concerns only the developer's initial structure, rather than any additional system-provided structure and is designed to be exploratory in nature.

However, after the coding has begun, there are numerous unforeseen changes that need to be made to both the class structure and the manner in which data are managed within and between classes. It was found that the production of diagrams had only limited use, but the overall planning process involving the aforementioned steps including brief diagrams forces the developer to think through as many stages of the design and development process as possible, before the commencement of the implementation of the greater Visual C++ application.

The Visual C++ demonstration application development pursued here has been performed under tight time constraints, and this forced the development to continually move forward according to the initial software design. Various changes were made as the project evolved, but in general once the initial class structure was decided upon, the project then grew upon that foundation. In addition, as the current development is a Microsoft Visual C++® 6.0 [3] multiple document interface (MDI) application, the Microsoft Foundation Classes (MFC) were used and involved the key provided classes [4]:

1. CDocument—class that manages the underlying data of the application
2. CMDIChildWnd—class that processes messages for the CView class
3. CMDIFrameWnd—class that provides the main frame window for all user interaction
4. CView—class that presents visual elements through the graphical user interface (GUI)
5. CWinApp—class responsible for receiving event messages

The current chapter pursues a Win32 Console Application, named ControlEng, and Chapter 2 involves the setting up of the Visual C++ application, titled DiagramEng. Then, in Chapter 3, the Visual C++ and the Win32 Console applications are merged, laying the initial class foundation, in preparation for adding further block-diagram-based engineering objects to the project.

1.2   BACKGROUND RESEARCH

The intended software application to be built is a block-diagram-based engineering application, allowing the user to draw block-based diagrams on a palette, to organize program and engineering work flow, to perform scientific experiments, and to model and compute control engineering problems. The interested reader should consult *Modern Control Engineering* by Ogata [5], *Getting Started with Simulink*® 6 [6], and *Simulink*® 6, Using Simulink® [7], for examples of typical modeling, simulation, and control engineering problems and their diagrammatic representations.

The intended application should facilitate modeling and simulation and support the computation of linear and nonlinear systems. It should also provide for the hierarchical modeling of systems and their related subsystems in block-diagram form. A GUI should allow the user to interact with the application in an intuitive manner and be consistent with typical Microsoft Windows-based [8] applications, involving, e.g., menus, toolbars, dialog windows, a Tree View control, mouse and keyboard interaction, and be user-friendly in operation.

The general aim here is to build a demonstration application prototype that incorporates common features that may be found in typical control engineering applications, e.g., "Simulink®" [7]. Hence, the aforementioned references concerning control engineering in general, and Refs. [6] and [7] in particular, are useful in guiding the archetypical functionality desired of the block-diagram-based engineering tool designed here, titled DiagramEng.

1.3   SOFTWARE REQUIREMENTS

The software requirements, as briefly presented in the following, are a general description of the purpose of the software and its intended use, and they provide an overview of what the demonstration application should allow the user to accomplish.

> The block-diagram-based engineering software application prototype, DiagramEng, should allow a mathematician, simulation scientist and control engineer, the means to organize and conduct mathematical equation representation, model building and experimental simulation, and basic control engineering, on a palette, using a visual block-diagram style involving model blocks and signal flow lines, connecting input/output (I/O) ports, to be able to determine and visualize the states of a system at each simulation time-step.

In addition, the software application should allow the user to model and compute a selection of archetypical scientific problems from the domains of mathematics, physics, and control engineering, e.g.:

1. Linear and nonlinear equations
2. Differential equations
3. Newtonian mechanical dynamics problems (mass–spring–damper systems)

4. Electrical circuit problems (resistor–inductor–capacitor [RLC] circuits)
5. Control systems with proportional, integral, and derivative (PID) control action

The requirements specification is a general overview of what the application should allow the user to perform, and this guideline is then explored in detail in the following sections concerning use case narratives, scenarios, and conversations, which reveal more specific functionality and behavior to be brought together toward the initial class design.

1.4 GENERAL USE CASE NARRATIVES

A range of methods are introduced in Ref. [2] to facilitate the developer in designing software including "narratives", "scenarios", and "conversations". A use case is "a behaviourally related sequence of transactions in a dialogue with the system" [2]. Use case narratives are a general overview of how the software should function in a typical operation including general capabilities: they describe general facilities in a paragraph or two of natural language [2].

The use case narrative may be extended from the software requirements to provide a slightly more detailed perspective of the intended use of the software toward a specific end. The following use case narrative describes the general action that a user would take in using the software application.

The DiagramEng software application should allow an engineer to model and compute basic engineering problems using a visual workflow style involving model blocks and signal flow lines, to determine and visualize system states. The GUI including menus, toolbars, a Tree View control and a drawing palette, should allow the user to drag blocks and connectors from various block or functional libraries onto the palette, to completely represent the system being modeled. Typical blocks to be used in model building may include: constant, derivative, gain, integrator, output, signal generator, sum, and the transfer function block. The user should be able to create systems and subsystems through block grouping, to form an hierarchical system model, and be able to subsequently compute the system states over a specified time frame using toolbar-based commands.

This narrative provides a brief indication of the typical system components and user actions in interacting with the system to model and compute a block-diagram-based engineering model. The next step is to analyze various use case scenarios and list user actions and the corresponding system responsibilities.

1.5 USE CASE SCENARIOS AND CONVERSATIONS

A use case scenario describes a specific path that a user may take to perform a task [2]. The conversation describes the interactions between the user and the software application as a dialog [2]. The typical types of scenarios that may be analyzed for the proposed block-diagram-based engineering application are as follows:

1. Starting the software application and performing basic file actions.
   a. Initiating the application
   b. Creating a new model file
   c. Opening an existing model file
   d. Saving a model file
2. Building models using a GUI
   a. Adding a function block to a model
   b. Editing a function block's parameters
   c. Moving a function block by a drag-and-drop action
   d. Adding a connection line between two blocks on the drawing palette
   e. Editing and adjusting a connection

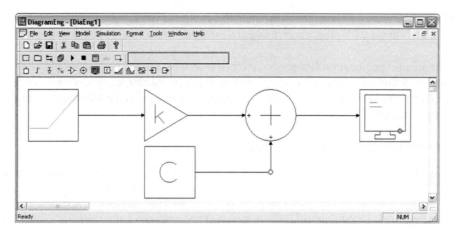

FIGURE 1.1   A block diagram representing a linear equation model, $f(x) = mx + c$.

3. Simulating models
   a. Simulating the current model
   b. Visualizing simulation results
   c. Pausing and resuming a simulation

Here, just one example will be analyzed that of building a simple linear function model using some basic blocks. Consider the modeling of the equation of a line, $y = mx + c$, where the dependent variable $y = f(x)$, x is the independent variable, m is the gradient, and c, a constant, is the y intercept. The blocks that are required to model this equation are constant, gain, linear function generator, output, and sum. The typical block diagram that the developer may draw (with pen on paper initially) to assist in the development process is shown in Figure 1.1: this diagram has actually been drawn with the to-be-developed, DiagramEng, Visual C++ application discussed in the following chapters.

A very brief but logical scenario for the construction of the block diagram model of this linear equation and its computation may be simply recorded in a numbered list. It could be more expressive, but here just the essential details are required and, when presented in a listed form, makes the conversion to a conversation, as presented in Table 1.1, easier.

1.5.1 Scenario

The scenario for the construction of a linear mathematical model and execution of its simulation:

1. User invokes the software application by double-clicking on the application icon.
2. System presents a model editor and a block library.
3. User navigates the block library for the required blocks.
4. System presents all available blocks through the block library.
5. User selects–moves–releases blocks from the block library to the model editor workspace palette.
6. System allows clearly visible placement of blocks on the model editor palette.
7. User double clicks each block on the palette in an attempt to assign values/parameters/ properties.
8. System spawns a dialog window, on a double-click event, with all necessary fields allowing user input.

TABLE 1.1

A Conversation Listing the Interactions between the User and the Software, for Building the Linear Equation Model

No.	User Actions	System Responsibilities
1.	User invokes the software application by double-clicking on the application icon.	System presents a model editor and a block library.
2.	User navigates the block library for the required blocks.	System presents all available blocks through the block library.
3.	User selects–moves–releases blocks from the block library to the model editor workspace palette.	System allows clearly visible placement of blocks on the model editor palette.
4.	User double clicks each block on the palette in an attempt to assign values/parameters/properties.	System spawns a dialog window, on a double-click event, with all necessary fields allowing user input.
5.	User enters data and clicks "OK" to update the system.	System checks, warns, and if OK, assigns values to variables as appropriate.
6.	User clicks the output port of a block and drags a mouse cursor to the input port of another block.	System generates an arrow on output-port-click and draws a connector to the cursor and then to the input port.
7.	User checks the model by clicking the "check model" button.	System recognizes connections/signals, checks for invalid loops, and builds the equivalent mathematical equation representation.
8.	User views the actual mathematical equations in the system-refreshed "check model" dialog window and clicks "OK".	System accepts user's acknowledgment that the equations are in the correct form and are to be computed.
9.	User clicks "start simulation" on the model editor's menu bar or toolbar button.	System simulates the model by performing appropriate mathematical operations as specified by the mathematical blocks.
10.	User double clicks an "output" block to view the output.	System presents a window displaying graphical and/or numerical results.

9. User enters data and clicks "OK" to update the system.
10. System checks, warns, and if OK, assigns values to variables as appropriate.
11. User clicks the output port of a block and drags a mouse cursor to the input port of another block.
12. System generates an arrow on output-port-click and draws a connector to the cursor and then to the input port.
13. User checks the model by clicking the "check model" button.
14. System recognizes connections/signals, checks for invalid loops, and builds the equivalent mathematical equation representation.
15. User views the actual mathematical equations in the system-refreshed "check model" dialog window and clicks "OK".
16. System accepts user's acknowledgment that the equations are in the correct form and are to be computed.

17. User clicks "start simulation" on the model editor's menu bar or toolbar button.
18. System simulates the model by performing appropriate mathematical operations as specified by the mathematical blocks.
19. User double clicks an "output" block to view the output.
20. System presents a window displaying graphical and/or numerical results.

1.5.2 CONVERSATION

The conversation shown in Table 1.1 divides the interactions between the user and the software application into user actions and the related system responsibilities.

Table 1.1 divides the user actions and system responsibilities for clarity and is helpful in identifying the nouns and verbs used to describe the interactive process in a typical usage operation: this then leads to possible candidate classes.

1.6 NOUN AND VERB ANALYSIS

A listing of nouns and verbs concerning a typical user-system operational path is useful in identifying candidate classes, objects, member variables, and member methods, in preparation for writing a simple application consisting of brief source and header files to organize data structures and class relationships. From the previous scenario and conversation (Table 1.1), the following list of key nouns and related nouns (Table 1.2), and key verbs and nouns affected by those verbs (Table 1.3), may be formed.

Now, these nouns and verbs may be organized into a set of CRC cards to simply organize initial ideas about possible classes, their responsibilities, and their collaborators. It is expected that the initial structure will be changed as the development process evolves, but a start needs to be made somewhere, and this candidate set of nouns and verbs helps clarify what appears to be important, at least at present.

1.7 OBJECT ANALYSIS

CRC cards allow candidate objects and roles and their responsibilities and collaborators to be visualized and shuffled around to arrive at a preliminary class structure. The CRC cards that are formed from the previous use case scenario and accompanying noun and verb analysis are shown in Table 1.4. It should be noted that Tables 1.2 and 1.3 provide a sample of the nouns and verbs relevant to the application, but

---

TABLE 1.2
Key Nouns and Related Nouns, Extracted from the Use Case Scenario

Nouns (Key)	Nouns (Related)
Block	Constant, data, Derivative, dialog window values/parameters/ properties, Gain, input/output data (e.g., numerical results), Integrator, Linear Function Generator, Output, Sum, variables.
Block library	Directory structure, icons
Connector	Arrow, mouse cursor, line
Mathematical equation	Display of equations in a dialog window by the system
Model	System model on the canvas, i.e., the block diagram
Model editor	Button, canvas, context menu, menu bar, status bar, toolbar
Port	Input port, output port, port multiplicity
Signal	Connections (linking) blocks

TABLE 1.3

Key Verbs and the Nouns Affected, Extracted from the Use Case Scenario

Verbs (Key)	Nouns Affected
Assign	Variables/values/parameters/properties to a block
Build	Math equations (from model)
Check and Warn	Model
Click	Port, context menu, button of model editor menu bar, toolbar
Double-click	Block, connector
Generate/Draw	Connector (from output to input port), port
Navigate	Block library, model and sub-models represented by block(s)
Present/Display	Model editor, block library, block to show numerical graphical output
Refresh	Dialog window (with math equations or graphical output)
Select–move–release	Block, connector, port
Simulate	Model represented by connections adjoining blocks
Spawn	Dialog window
Update	Block, model

---

when the developer thinks in more general terms, more may come to mind, and some may be omitted: there need not be a one-to-one correspondence between nouns and verbs and what appears on the cards.

This initial set of candidate classes, responsibilities, and collaborators allows the developer to explore the relationships between the various entities of the project, and assists in organizing hierarchical object relationships in a preliminary class design. It may not be known at the current stage where some of the candidate classes fit in, if at all, in the whole structure, but it provides ideas as to how a first step toward coding may be taken. It is assumed at this stage that this preliminary design will change substantially, but it is an important step to take toward a more stable structure.

1.8 PRELIMINARY CLASS DIAGRAM

At this stage, the developer aims to create some kind of a class structure from the relationships between the candidate classes identified in the previous step concerning CRC card generation. The following key classes (listed in alphabetical order) were decided upon as being quite central to the project: CBlock, CBlockLib, CBlockShape, CConnection, CModelEditor, CPort, CSignal, and CSystemModel. Note how this actually differs from the CRC cards in particular, but in general it captures the essence of what it required. The classes that were omitted for now are ComputeEngine, NumericalMethod, and Solver: these will be addressed later at the signal propagation and system model computation/simulation stage of the Visual C++, DiagramEng, project.

The CBlock class is the base class from which other specific block classes are derived, e.g., CConstantBlock (`class CConstantBlock:public CBlock`). Its main member variables are a CBlockShape object, vectors of input and output port addresses, (`vector<CPort*>`), and a pointer to the CSystemModel in which the block is contained. CBlockShape is not shown in the CRC cards, but it was decided that each diagram block should be defined by some shape parameters, and these should be contained in a block-shape (CBlockShape) class (see the following).

A CBlockLib class is anticipated to organize or classify the types of blocks available for use into key groups, e.g., Continuous, Math Operations, Sink, Source, and Subsystem blocks. A Tree View

TABLE 1.4

CRC Cards for the Initial Object Analysis Listed in Alphabetical Order

Object	Responsibilities	Collaborators
Block	BlockPropertiesParameters	SystemModel
	BlockIOPort	BlockLibrary
	BlockDlgWnd	Signal
	BlockAssignParameters	
	GetListOfInputPorts	
	GetListOfOutputPorts	
BlockLibrary	BrowseLibraryStructure	Block
	DisplayDirStructure	ModelEditor
	DisplayDirBlocks	
	BlockDragDrop	
ComputeEngine	Compile	SystemModel
	Link	ModelEditor
	Simulate/Compute	Solver
	SingularityDetection	
	SourceCodeGeneration	
Connection	GetState	Signal
	GetFromPort	
	GetToPort	
	Update	
ModelEditor	Palette	Block
	ContextMenu	SystemModel
	MenuBar	BlockLibrary
	StatusBar	ComputeEngine
	ToolBar	Signal
	BlockBind	
	BlockDragDrop	
NumericalMethod	ComputeSysState	ComputeEngine
	ComputeTimeStepSize	
Port	GetName	Block
	SetName	Signal
	GetPosn	
	SetPosn	
	GetParameters	
	SetParameters	
	KnowsItsBlock	
	TransferSignal	
Signal	ConnectIOPorts	Block
	CreateBranchLine	Connection
	CreateSignalLine	Port
	DetermineTimeStep	SystemModel
		ModelEditor

TABLE 1.4 (continued)
CRC Cards for the Initial Object Analysis Listed
in Alphabetical Order

Object	Responsibilities	Collaborators
Solver	SelectNumericalMethod	SystemModel
	RecordStates	ModelEditor
		ComputeEngine
SystemModel	ModelPropertiesParameters	Block
	BlockIOPortConnectivity	ModelEditor
	ModelContextMenu	Signal
	CreateBlockSubsystem	
	GroupBlocks	

control is expected to be used in the actual implementation to present the block groups in folders and their associated blocks as the individual tree leaves.

A CBlockShape class, contained within the CBlock class, is required to encapsulate the geometrical information of a block, e.g., its width, height, and primitive shape: an ellipse, rectangle, or triangle. The CBlock and CBlockShape classes would then be closely associated as far as setting up basic block properties is concerned.

A CConnection object is the signal flow line that connects various block ports together. Hence, the main CConnection class member variables are a reference-from port of type pointer-to-CPort, a reference-to port of type pointer-to-CPort, and a signal of type pointer-to-CSignal that are propagated along the connection itself. Hence, the CConnection and CSignal classes are closely related.

The model editor facilitates the drawing of a block diagram using the GUI. In the Win32 Console Application that follows, the CModelEditor class is absent as no GUI is explored. Hence, it is envisaged that this class may not actually exist, but rather be represented by the Visual C++ MFC-based GUI-specific classes, i.e., CDocument, CMDIChildWnd, CMDIFrameWnd, CView, and CWinApp, all working together.

An input/output port, represented by the CPort class, is associated with the block upon which it resides and to which connection objects are connected. Some blocks consist of only input ports, e.g., the Output block used for graphical display, others consist of only output ports, e.g., the Constant block and function generation blocks, and the rest consist of both input and output ports, e.g., the Gain and Sum blocks. The main member variables of the CPort class are its name, position, shape, and a reference to the block to which it belongs, of type pointer-to-CBlock.

The CSignal class is used to model a signal that acts like an electrical pulse and is propagated down a wire, where the wire may be considered as the connection object. At this stage, the only member variable for the CSignal class is its name. However, other types of signals may be derived from this base CSignal class, e.g., double, matrix, and vector signals, represented by CDoubleSignal, CMatrixSignal, and CVectorSignal respectively. This class will be revisited at the system model compilation stage, when signals are propagated down a connection from one block port to another: for now, its details are sparse, and it may even be appropriate to make it very simple, allowing the signal to be the more general, matrix, data structure only.

The actual block diagram model, or system model, is represented by the CSystemModel class and, at this stage, contains a block list, a list of pointers-to-CBlock (list<CBlock*> m_lstBlock), and a connection list, a list of pointers-to-CConnection (list<CConnection*> m_lstConnection). In the ControlEng Win32 Console Application presented in Appendix A, the

TABLE 1.5

Class Containment Relationships Organized in Five Levels

Class Level 1	Level 2	Level 3	Level 4	Level 5
CModelEditor				
	CSystemModel			
		CBlock		
			CBlockShape	
			CPort	
				CBlock *p
			CSystemModel *p	
		CConnection		
			CPort	
				CBlock *p
			CSignal	
	CBlockLib			
		CBlock		
			CBlockShape	
			CPort	
				CBlock *p
			CSystemModel *p	

The classes highlighted in bold are of particular interest toward generating an initial working program, elements shaded are pointers.

"system_model" object, of type CSystemModel, is the main object in the program, as it contains the lists of other entities, i.e., blocks and connections. However, in the DiagramEng Visual C++ application discussed later, the CDiagramEngDoc class, which is responsible for holding the document object and all the necessary data structures, has as a member variable, the "m_SystemModel" object of type CSystemModel. For now, CSystemModel objects can be considered to hold the whole block diagram model representing the engineering problem.

Once the main classes have been decided upon, a hierarchical structure is required to organize them in a coherent and manageable fashion to cater for extension as the project grows. Table 1.5 presents an initial class structure with five levels of containment. Two main hierarchies exist: (1) CSystemModel and (2) CBlockLib. The former involves the structure to manage all system model entities, which are used to build a block diagram representing the modeled system. The latter concerns the classification of block entities in a directory-like structure for ease of managing the available drawing entities. The "*p" notation signifies a pointer-to-Class to remind the developer that the contained class has a mechanism of referring to its parent class. Figure 1.2 is a class association tree diagram that reflects the structure in Table 1.5. Here, the left branch of the tree emanating from CModelEditor is of particular interest toward generating an initial working program.

It is interesting to note that the block library structure shown in the right branch of Figure 1.2 is actually completely ignored for now, indicating that the data structure represented by the left branch of the tree is more important. These types of organizational patterns are typical of a design procedure and indicate where attention should be focused. In Chapter 3, the class association diagram will be revisited and refined specifically for the conjoining of the Win32 Console Application, ControlEng, and the Visual C++ application, DiagramEng.

Now that an initial association structure is in place, any class inheritance (`class CDerived public CBase`) relationships should be listed as shown in Table 1.6: here only the CBlock, CBlockLib, and CSignal classes appear to have derived classes. The remaining classes, at least at this stage, do not appear to be parent classes from which other classes may be derived.

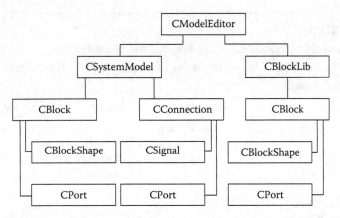

FIGURE 1.2 Initial class association relationships for block diagram model building: the left tree is of particular interest and the right tree will be considered later.

TABLE 1.6
Derived Classes (Inheritance) for the CBlock,
CBlockLib, and CSignal Base Classes

CBlock	CBlockLib	CSignal
CConstantBlock	CCtsBlockDir	CDoubleSignal
CDerivativeBlock	CMathOpsBlockDir	CMatrixSignal
CDivideBlock	CSinkBlockDir	CVectorSignal
CGainBlock	CSourceBlockDir	
CIntegratorBlock	CSubsystemBlockDir	
CLinearFnBlock		
COutputBlock		
CSignalGeneratorBlock		
CSubsystemBlock		
CSubsystemInBlock		
CSubsystemOutBlock		
CSumBlock		
CTransferFnBlock		

1.9 BASIC PROGRAM IMPLEMENTING THE CLASS STRUCTURE

The initial class structure appears to be satisfactory at present, but to really check whether it is sensible or not, a small test program was desired to get a better understanding of how to organize the project. At this stage, a Win32 Console Application, named ControlEng, was written to simply organize the data structures in preparation to contain the actual model. However, later, a Visual C++ application will be required to allow the user to interact with the data structures through the MFC-provided classes introduced earlier (in alphabetical order): CDocument, CMDIChildWnd, CMDIFrameWnd, CView, and CWinApp. The ControlEng application is composed of header and source header files containing the declaration and definition of classes, respectively: Table 1.7 lists the files and their contained classes.

The actual source ("filename.cpp") and header ("filename.h") files used to get an initial working Win32 Console Application are provided in alphabetical order in Appendix A (header files are shown first). The reader can port this code in an application titled, e.g., ControlEng, denoting

TABLE 1.7

ControlEng Win32 Console Application Header Files and Contained Classes in Order of Appearance in the Actual Header Files

Block.h	ControlEng.h	Signal.h	SystemModel.h
CBlockShape	No class definition	CSignal	CSystemModel
CPort		CDoubleSignal	
CBlock		CMatrixSignal	
CConstantBlock		CVectorSignal	
CDerivativeBlock		CConnection	
CDivideBlock			
CGainBlock			
CIntegratorBlock			
CLinearFnBlock			
COutputBlock			
CSignalGeneratorBlock			
CSubsystemBlock			
CSubsystemInBlock			
CSubsystemOutBlock			
CSumBlock			
CTransferFnBlock			

```
"C:\BudFox\C++\Work\Diagram Eng Project\DiagramEng (01 preliminary)\ControlEng\Debug...

main()
PrepareControlEng()
CSystemModel::CSystemModel()
CBlockShape::CBlockShape()
CBlock::CBlock()
CPort::CPort()
CBlock::CBlock(), n_vecInputPorts item = 004919A0
CPort::GetName()
CBlock::CBlock(), n_vecInputPorts item name = actual_port_name
CPort::CPort()
CBlock::CBlock(), n_vecOutputPorts item = 00491890
CPort::GetName()
CBlock::CBlock(), n_vecOutputPorts item name = actual_port_name
CSystemModel::CSystemModel(), n_lstBlock item = 004919F0
CBlock::GetName()
CSystemModel::CSystemModel(), n_lstBlock item name = actual_block_name
CConnection::CConnection()
CSignal::CSignal()
CDoubleSignal::CDoubleSignal()
CSystemModel::CSystemModel(), n_lstConnection item = 00491770
CConnection::GetSignal()
CSignal::GetName()
CSystemModel::CSystemModel(), signal_name = actual_signal_name
CSystemModel::~CSystemModel()
CBlock::~CBlock()
CPort::~CPort()
CPort::~CPort()
CBlockShape::~CBlockShape()
CConnection::~CConnection()
Press any key to continue_
```

FIGURE 1.3 Console-based output concerning basic object construction and destruction for the Win32 Console Application, ControlEng.

"control engineering," distinct from the DiagramEng Visual C++ application to be developed in the following chapters, and compile and run the executable, to see simple constructor and destructor statements being displayed in an output console window as shown in Figure 1.3. The developer will notice that the following objects are constructed (listed in the order of their construction): CSystemModel, CBlockShape, CBlock, CPort, CConnection, and CSignal.

1.10 SUMMARY

To make a start with the software development process, initial background research is necessary to understand the problem that is to be solved and the requirements of the application to be developed. Then, use case narratives, scenarios, and conversations can be written down to determine the typical user actions and system responsibilities. A noun and verb analysis is then used to identify the candidate objects in the domain of the problem, and CRC cards may be used to list the possible objects, their responsibilities, and collaborators and identify their interrelationships. Preliminary diagrams reflecting the initial class structure may then be drawn, and basic header files can be used to capture all the preliminary class definitions. A Win32 Console Application may be written to simply show that objects can be constructed and destructed properly. This is done in anticipation of porting the code into a MDI Visual C++ application later and need not be perfect, but simply presents an initial expression of exploratory ideas allowing the developer to make insightful preliminary mistakes. The developer can rest assured that the design and implementation will change as it evolves, and it is impossible to foresee a perfectly stable structure from the outset: the key is to simply make a start.

REFERENCES

1. Booch, G., Maksimchuk, R. A., Engle, M. W., Young, B. J., Conallen, J., and Houston, K. A., *Object-Oriented Analysis and Design with Applications*, 3rd edn., Pearson Education, Boston, MA, 2007.
2. Wirfs-Brock, R. and McKean, A., *Object Design: Roles, Responsibilities and Collaborations*, Addison Wesley, Boston, MA, 2003.
3. Microsoft Visual C++® 6.0, Microsoft® Visual Studio™ 6.0 Development System, Professional Edition, Microsoft Corporation, 1998.
4. Chapman, D., *Teach Yourself Visual C++ 6 in 21 Days*, Sams Publishing, Indianapolis, IN, 1998.
5. Ogata, K., *Modern Control Engineering*, 4th edn., Prentice Hall, Upper Saddle River, NJ, 2002, http://www.mathworks.com/
6. *Getting Started with Simulink® 6*, MATLAB® & Simulink®, The MathWorks, Natick, MA, 2007, http:// www.mathworks.com/
7. *Simulink® 6, Using Simulink®*, MATLAB® & Simulink®, The MathWorks, Natick, MA, 2007.
8. Microsoft Corporation, www.microsoft.com/en/us/default.aspx

2 Initial Graphical User Interface

2.1 INTRODUCTION

The previous chapter discussed the design of the software application and presented typical use case scenarios detailing user interaction and system responsibilities. The next step involves the implementation of an initial graphical user interface to display typical Window-based application features, such as child windows, menus with entries, and toolbars with buttons. The Microsoft Visual C++® 6.0, Microsoft® Visual Studio™ 6.0 Development System [1] (integrated development environment [IDE]), allows the developer to easily set up the interactive features of the application and the key topics covered here are the Application Wizard, menus, icons, toolbars, dialog windows, and attaching functionality to the menu entries and toolbar buttons.

2.2 APPLICATION WIZARD

The Application Wizard (AppWizard) of the IDE [1] allows the developer to easily set up a new Microsoft Visual C++ 6.0 [1] application depending on the type of functional support that is required. The following steps indicate how the current multiple document interface (MDI), Microsoft Foundation Class (MFC)-based application, titled, DiagramEng, is set up:

1. Create a new "MFC AppWizard (exe)" project with the name, DiagramEng.
2. On step 1 of the AppWizard select "Multiple documents".
3. Use the default settings for steps 2 and 3, retaining support for ActiveX Controls.
4. On step 4 of the AppWizard, click the Advanced button: use "txt" as the three-letter file extension to denote a project text file, named, e.g., "project.txt".
5. Choose the default settings on step 5.
6. Finally, on step 6 of the AppWizard, leave the base class as CView* and select Finish.

The AppWizard will then present a summary of the setup steps in a dialog window titled, "New Project Information" including a summary of the classes to be created: upon clicking OK, the developer is then taken to the newly constructed project ready to start adding features to the application.

2.3 MENUS

The application, once set up, has two key menus: (1) the Main frame-based menu, with ID, IDR_MAINFRAME, available when no child window is open and (2) the Child frame-based menu, with sample ID, IDR_CHILDMENU, intended for the child window only and relates to documents that the user works on. Tables 2.1 and 2.2 show the Main frame and Child frame menus and their menu entries. Table 2.3 shows the Child frame-based menu augmented with the intended entries to be added shown in italics, for the DiagramEng application being built. The new menus for the Child window frame to be inserted to the right of the View menu are as follows: Model, Simulation, Format, and Tools. Table 2.4 shows the specific menu entry objects, properties, and settings. The developer will notice that the ID, ID_EDIT_SELECTALL, is used, rather than, e.g., ID_EDIT_SELECT_ALL: this is the case since the latter is a system default ID, and using it in conjunction

---

* Later in the project a Scrolling View will be implemented using the CScrollView base class: but leave CView as the base class for now, as specific conversion instructions will be provided later.

TABLE 2.1
Main Frame–Based Menus Provided by the Development Environment

File	View	Help
New	Toolbar	About DiagramEng
Open	Status bar	
Print Setup …		
Recent File		
Exit		

TABLE 2.2
Child Frame–Based Menus Provided by the Development Environment

File	Edit	View	Window	Help
New	Undo	Toolbar	New Window	About DiagramEng
Open …	Cut	Statusbar	Cascade	
Close	Copy		Tile	
Save	Paste		Arrange Icons	
Save As …			(previous files)	
Print				
Print Preview				
Print Setup				
Recent File				
Exit				

TABLE 2.3
DiagramEng Child Frame–Based Menu Items to be Added by the Developer, Shown in Italics

File	Edit	View	Model	Simulation	Format	Tools	Window	Help
New	Cut	Toolbar	*Build Model*	*Start*	*Show*	*Diagnostic*	New	About
Open	Copy	Status	*Build*	*Stop*	*Annotations*	*Info.*	Window	DiagramEng
Close	Paste	Bar	*Subsystem*	*Numerical*			Cascade	*Using*
Save	*Delete*	*Auto Fit*		*Solver*			Tile	*DiagramEng*
Save	*Select All*	*Diagram*					Arrange	
As	*Add*	*Zoom In*					Icons	
Print	*Multiple*	*Zoom*					*Close All*	
Print	*Blocks*	*Out*					*Documents*	
Setup							(previous	
Recent							files)	
File								
Exit								

TABLE 2.4

Child Frame–Based Menu Entry Objects, IDs, Captions, Prompts (Status Bar and Tooltips)[a], and Settings

Object	Property	Setting
Edit/Delete	ID	ID_EDIT_DELETE
	Caption	&Delete
	Prompts	Delete the selection\nDelete
Edit/Select All	ID	ID_EDIT_SELECTALL
	Caption	Select &All
	Prompts	Selection of all content\nSelect All
Edit/Add Multiple Blocks	ID	ID_EDIT_ADD_MULTI_BLOCKS
	Caption	Add &Multiple Blocks
	Prompts	Add multiple blocks\nAdd Multiple Blocks
View/Auto Fit Diagram	ID	ID_VIEW_AUTO_FIT_DIAGRAM
	Caption	Auto Fit Diagram
	Prompts	Auto fit diagram to view\nAuto Fit Diagram
View/Zoom In	ID	ID_VIEW_ZOOM_IN
	Caption	Zoom &In
	Prompts	Zoom in to detail\nZoom In
View/Zoom Out	ID	ID_VIEW_ZOOM_OUT
	Caption	Zoom &Out
	Prompts	Zoom out of detail\nZoom Out
Model/Build Model	ID	ID_MODEL_BUILD
	Caption	&Build Model
	Prompts	Build model\nBuild Model
Model/Build Subsystem	ID	ID_MODEL_BUILD_SUBSYS
	Caption	Build &Subsystem
	Prompts	Build model subsystem\nBuild Subsystem
Simulation/Start	ID	ID_SIM_START
	Caption	S&tart
	Prompts	Start simulation\nStart Simulation
Simulation/Stop	ID	ID_SIM_STOP
	Caption	Sto&p
	Prompts	Stop simulation\nStop Simulation
Simulation/Numerical Solver	ID	ID_SIM_NUM_SOLVER
	Caption	&Numerical Solver
	Prompts	Numerical solver settings\nNumerical Solver Settings
Format/Show Annotations	ID	ID_FORMAT_SHOW_ANNOTATIONS
	Caption	&Show Annotations
	Prompts	Show annotations\nShow Annotations
Tools/Diagnostic Info.	ID	ID_TOOLS_DIAGNOSTIC_INFO
	Caption	Dia&gnostic Info.
	Prompts	Diagnostic information\nDiagnostic Information

(*continued*)

TABLE 2.4 (continued)
Child Frame–Based Menu Entry Objects, IDs, Captions, Prompts
(Status Bar and Tooltips)[a], and Settings

Object	Property	Setting
Window/Close All Documents	ID	ID_WND_CLOSE_ALL_DOCS
	Caption	&Close All Documents
	Prompts	Close all documents\nClose All Documents
Help/Using DiagramEng	ID	ID_HELP_USING_DIAENG
	Caption	&Using DiagramEng
	Prompts	Using diagram engineering\nUsing DiagramEng

[a] The developer should be aware that the Prompts property field involves both the status bar and tooltips text, where the two are separated by the "\n" characters (Tables 2.4 through 2.7).

with user-defined functionality would override its default-context-based operation. Hence, insert the additional menu items in the project according to Tables 2.3 and 2.4.

2.4 APPLICATION ICON

The application icon is a graphic that appears when running the application or upon selection of the About entry under the Help menu. The Application Wizard provides a default application icon, as shown in Figure 2.1a (32 × 32 pixels) and c (16 × 16 pixels). However, the developer can add both the small and large icons as follows:

1. Go to the resources tab of the workspace pane and select the Icon menu.
2. Double-click IDR_MAINFRAME to view both the 16 × 16 (pixel) and 32 × 32 (pixel) icons.
3. Redesign the icons to reflect the nature of the application, as shown, e.g., in Figure 2.1b and d.

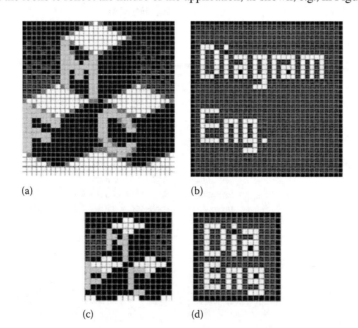

(a)   (b)

(c)   (d)

FIGURE 2.1 Application icons (units denote pixel dimensions): (a) MFC (32 × 32), (b) DiagramEng (32 × 32), (c) MFC (16 × 16), and (d) DiagramEng (16 × 16).

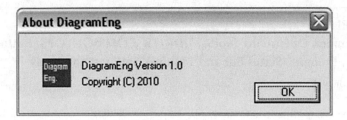

FIGURE 2.2 The DiagramEng application icon shown upon the About DiagramEng dialog window.

Then, upon selecting, About DiagramEng, under the Help menu, the dialog window shown in Figure 2.2 will appear, displaying the application icon.

2.5 TOOLBARS

Toolbars are bars usually found beneath the drop-down menus that contain button-based graphical icons representing application operations that are associated with a frame, e.g., the Main frame or Child frame, and relate to the underlying document. An example of the Main frame-based Standard toolbar is shown in Figure 2.3, with the default icons: New, Open, Save, Cut, Copy, Paste, Print, and About. The enabled buttons (New, Open, and About) relate to Main frame-based functionality, and the disabled items become enabled when a Child window is present, since these relate to the underlying child document-based content.

2.5.1 INSERTING A COMMON OPERATIONS TOOLBAR

The common operations that are to be performed by the DiagramEng application involve typical user-interaction sequences in the modeling and computation of engineering systems represented by equations. The following instructions indicate how a new toolbar representing the common application operations is constructed.

1. Right-click on the toolbar folder and select Insert Toolbar from the pop-up menu.
2. Draw icons on the toolbar to represent the functionality, which is to be provided by the corresponding menus: see Table 2.5 and Figure 2.4 as a guide.
3. Invoke the properties dialog and enter the ID and prompts of the corresponding menu entry whose associated functionality is to be triggered by the toolbar button.
4. Finally, right-click on the toolbar and change the toolbar ID via the properties dialog to a descriptive name: e.g., IDR_TB_COMMON_OPS, denoting the ID of the Common Operations toolbar resource.

The developer will notice that the final toolbar button named Track Multiple Items is not associated with a menu entry: the details for this will be described later when moving multiple items on the palette, in Chapter 11.

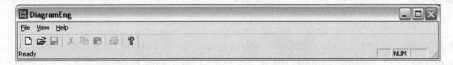

FIGURE 2.3 Main frame-based Standard toolbar provided by default, with buttons: New, Open, Save, Cut, Copy, Paste, Print, and About.

TABLE 2.5

Common Operations Toolbar (IDR_TB_COMMON_OPS) Buttons: IDs, Prompts (Status Bar and Tooltips), Settings, and Icons

Button and Corresponding Menu Entry	Property	Setting	Icon
Edit/Select All	ID	ID_EDIT_SELECTALL	
	Prompts	Selection of all contentnSelect All	
Edit/Add Multiple Blocks	ID	ID_EDIT_ADD_MULTI_BLOCKS	
	Prompts	Add multiple blocksnAdd Multiple Blocks	
View/Auto Fit Diagram	ID	ID_VIEW_AUTO_FIT_DIAGRAM	
	Prompts	Auto fit diagram to viewnAuto Fit Diagram	
Model/Build	ID	ID_MODEL_BUILD	
	Prompts	Build modelnBuild Model	
Simulation/Start	ID	ID_SIM_START	
	Prompts	Start simulationnStart Simulation	
Simulation/Stop	ID	ID_SIM_STOP	
	Prompts	Stop simulationnStop Simulation	
Simulation/Numerical Solver	ID	ID_SIM_NUM_SOLVER	
	Prompts	Numerical solver settingsnNumerical Solver Settings	
Format/Show Annotations	ID	ID_FORMAT_SHOW_ ANNOTATIONS	
	Prompts	Show annotationsnShow Annotations	
(No menu)/Track Multiple Items	ID	ID_INIT_TRACK_MULTIPLE_ ITEMS	
	Prompts	Initiate tracking of multiple itemsnTrack Multiple Items	

FIGURE 2.4 The Common Operations and Common Blocks toolbars docked to the left side of the Main frame window.

2.5.2 INSERTING A COMMON BLOCKS TOOLBAR

The Common Operations toolbar allows the user to perform various operations on an existing document. Similarly, a Common Blocks toolbar will allow the user to add common model blocks to the document when drawing a model diagram. The following instructions indicate the steps to construct a new Common Blocks toolbar.

1. Right-click on the toolbar folder and select Insert Toolbar from the pop-up menu.
2. Right-click on the toolbar and change the toolbar ID via the properties dialog to a descriptive name: e.g., IDR_TB_COMMON_BLOCKS, denoting the ID of the Common Blocks toolbar resource.

TABLE 2.6

Common Blocks Toolbar (IDR_TB_COMMON_OPS) Buttons: IDs, Prompts (Status Bar and Tooltips), Settings, and Icons

Object group and block	Property	Setting	Icon
Continuous/Derivative Block	ID	ID_BLOCK_CTS_DERIVATIVE	
	Prompts	Continuous blocks: Derivative BlocknDerivative Block	
Continuous/Integrator Block	ID	ID_BLOCK_CTS_INTEGRATOR	
	Prompts	Continuous blocks: Integrator BlocknIntegrator Block	
Continuous/TransferFn Block	ID	ID_BLOCK_CTS_TRANSFERFN	
	Prompts	Continuous blocks: TransferFn BlocknTransferFn Block	
Math Operations/Divide Block	ID	ID_BLOCK_MATHOPS_DIVIDE	
	Prompts	Math operations blocks: Divide BlocknDivide Block	
Math Operations/Gain Block	ID	ID_BLOCK_MATHOPS_GAIN	
	Prompts	Math operations blocks: Gain BlocknGain Block	
Math Operations/Sum Block	ID	ID_BLOCK_MATHOPS_SUM	
	Prompts	Math operations blocks: Sum BlocknSum Block	
Sink/Output Block	ID	ID_BLOCK_SINK_OUTPUT	
	Prompts	Sink blocks: Ouput BlocknOutput Block	
Sink/SubsystemOut Block	ID	ID_BLOCK_SUBSYS_SUBSYSOUT	
	Prompts	Sink blocks: SubsystemOut BlocknOutput Block	
Source/Constant Block	ID	ID_BLOCK_SOURCE_CONST	
	Prompts	Source blocks: Constant BlocknConstant Block	
Source/LinearFn Block	ID	ID_BLOCK_SOURCE_LINEARFN	
	Prompts	Source blocks: LinearFn BlocknLinearFn Block	
Source/SignalGenerator Block	ID	ID_BLOCK_SOURCE_SIGNALGEN	
	Prompts	Source blocks: SignalGenerator BlocknSignalGenerator Block	
Source/SubsystemIn Block	ID	ID_BLOCK_SUBSYS_SUBSYSIN	
	Prompts	Source blocks: SubsystemIn BlocknSubsystemIn Block	
Subsystem/Subsystem Block	ID	ID_BLOCK_SUBSYS_SUBSYS	
	Prompts	Subsystem blocks: Subsystem BlocknSubsystem Block	

3. Draw icons on the toolbar to represent the block-based functionality as shown in Table 2.6, which will also be made available by clicking on the corresponding blocks of a to-be-added block library dialog window and later a block library Tree View directory.
4. Invoke the properties dialog and enter the ID and prompts for the buttons representing the blocks.
5. Place separators on the toolbar where desired and check to see that they appear upon application execution.

2.5.3 ATTACHING THE TOOLBARS TO THE APPLICATION FRAME

Now that the properties of both the Common Operations and Common Blocks toolbars have been assigned, the toolbars need to be created and docked to the application Main window frame. The following instructions indicate how this is performed and follow (in part) those provided by Chapman, in particular, Listing 12.1 of Ref. [2].

1. Add a protected member variable of type CToolBar to the CMainFrame class to hold the Common Operations toolbar, named "m_wndTBCommonOps".
2. Add a protected member variable of type CToolBar, to the CMainFrame class to hold the Common Blocks toolbar with name, "m_wndTBCommonBlocks".

3. Add code to the `OnCreate()` function of the CMainFrame class to add the toolbars and attach them to the frame, as shown in bold in the following: the developer will notice the "DiagramEng (start)" and "DiagramEng (end)" comments surrounding DiagramEng-specific code introduced by the current instructions.

```
int CMainFrame::OnCreate(LPCREATESTRUCT lpCreateStruct)
{
    if (CMDIFrameWnd::OnCreate(lpCreateStruct) == -1)
        return -1;

    if (!m_wndToolBar.CreateEx(this, TBSTYLE_FLAT, WS_CHILD | WS_VISIBLE |
        CBRS_TOP
    | CBRS_GRIPPER | CBRS_TOOLTIPS | CBRS_FLYBY | CBRS_SIZE_DYNAMIC) ||
!m_wndToolBar.LoadToolBar(IDR_MAINFRAME) )
    {
        TRACE0("Failed to create toolbar\n");
        return -1;     // fail to create
    }

    // DiagramEng (start)

    // -- CREATE THE CommonOps TOOLBAR /////////////////////////////////////
    // NOTE: 'this' is the ptr to the parent frame wnd to which the
        toolbar will be attached.
    // CreateEx creates the toolbar
    // LoadToolBar loads the toolbar specified by the ID
    if(!m_wndTBCommonOps.CreateEx(this, TBSTYLE_FLAT, WS_CHILD |
        WS_VISIBLE | CBRS_TOP | CBRS_GRIPPER | CBRS_TOOLTIPS |
            CBRS_FLYBY | CBRS_SIZE_DYNAMIC) ||
                !m_wndTBCommonOps.LoadToolBar(IDR_TB_COMMON_OPS) )
    {
        // Failed to create msg.
        TRACE0("Failed to create toolbar\n");
        return -1;
    }
    // -- END CREATION OF CommonOps TOOLBAR

    // -- CREATE THE CommonBlocks TOOLBAR //////////////////////////////////
    // NOTE: 'this' is the ptr to the parent frame wnd to which the
        toolbar will be attached.
    // CreateEx creates the toolbar
    // LoadToolBar loads the toolbar specified by the ID
    if(!m_wndTBCommonBlocks.CreateEx(this, TBSTYLE_FLAT, WS_CHILD |
        WS_VISIBLE | CBRS_TOP | CBRS_GRIPPER | CBRS_TOOLTIPS |
            CBRS_FLYBY | CBRS_SIZE_DYNAMIC) ||
                !m_wndTBCommonBlocks.LoadToolBar(IDR_TB_COMMON_BLOCKS) )
    {
        // Failed to create msg.
        TRACE0("Failed to create toolbar\n");
        return -1;
    }
    // -- END CREATION OF CommonBlocks TOOLBAR

    // DiagramEng (end)

    if (!m_wndStatusBar.Create(this) ||
    !m_wndStatusBar.SetIndicators(indicators,
      sizeof(indicators)/sizeof(UINT)) )
```

```
{
    TRACE0("Failed to create status bar\n");
    return -1;   // fail to create
}
// TODO: Delete these three lines if you don't want the toolbar to
// be dockable
m_wndToolBar.EnableDocking(CBRS_ALIGN_ANY);

// DiagramEng (start)
// -- ENABLE DOCKING OF TOOLBARS

// Enable docking for the Common Ops toolbar (IDR_TB_COMMON_OPS)
// NOTE: enables the toolbar for docking with the frame wnd.
m_wndTBCommonOps.EnableDocking(CBRS_ALIGN_ANY);

// Enable docking for the Common Blocks toolbar (IDR_TB_COMMON_BLOCKS)
// NOTE: enables the toolbar for docking with the frame wnd.
m_wndTBCommonBlocks.EnableDocking(CBRS_ALIGN_ANY);

// DiagramEng (end)

EnableDocking(CBRS_ALIGN_ANY);      // called for the frame wnd.
DockControlBar(&m_wndToolBar);      // frame wnd fn passed & of toolbar
  var. physically docks the toolbar to the frame wnd.

// DiagramEng (start)
// -- DOCK TOOLBARS
// Dock the Common Ops toolbar.
DockControlBar(&m_wndTBCommonOps);

// Dock the Common Blocks toolbar.
DockControlBar(&m_wndTBCommonBlocks);

// DiagramEng (end)

    return 0;
}
```

Rebuild the application by selecting Rebuild All from the Build menu to obtain the toolbars docked to the left hand side of the window as shown in Figure 2.4: if no functionality has been associated with the toolbar buttons (as will actually be the case since this is to be added later), then they will appear in a disabled state.

2.5.4 Controlling the Toolbar Visibility

Now that both the Common Operations (IDR_TB_COMMON_OPS) and Common Blocks (IDR_TB_COMMON_BLOCKS) toolbars have been docked to the Main window frame, their visibility may be controlled using the options under the View menu. Hence, add two menu entries under the View menu to toggle the visibility of the toolbars with the properties and settings shown in Table 2.7.

Add an event-handler function, to the CMainFrame class, for the UPDATE_COMMAND_UI event message of the ID_VIEW_TB_COMMON_OPS menu entry. Edit the code as shown in the following to set the tick-like check mark (✓) next to the View menu entry denoting whether the corresponding toolbar is visible or not (see also Listing 12.2 of Ref. [2]).

```
void CMainFrame::OnUpdateViewTbCommonOps(CCmdUI* pCmdUI)
{
    // TODO: Add your command update UI handler code here

    // DiagramEng (start)
```

TABLE 2.7

Menu Entry, Object ID, Caption, Prompts (Status Bar and Tooltips), and Settings

Object	Property	Setting
View/Common Ops. Toolbar	ID	ID_VIEW_TB_COMMON_OPS
	Caption	&Common Ops. Toolbar
	Prompts	Common operations toolbar\nCommon Ops. Toolbar
View/Common Blocks Toolbar	ID	ID_VIEW_TB_COMMON_BLOCKS
	Caption	&Common Blocks Toolbar
	Prompts	Common blocks toolbar\nCommon Blocks Toolbar

```
    // Check the status of the Common Ops. Toolbar (IDR_TB_COMMON_OPS)
    // NOTE: get style of toolbar and mask out for the WS_VISIBLE style
      flag.
    // If the flag is in the current toolbar style, then the toolbar is
      visible.
    // The SetCheck() allows checking and unchecking the toolbar MENU
      entry (in the View menu here).
    pCmdUI->SetCheck(((m_wndTBCommonOps.GetStyle() & WS_VISIBLE) != 0));

    // DiagramEng (end)
}
```

Add an event-handler function, to the CMainFrame class, for the COMMAND event message of the ID_VIEW_TB_COMMON_OPS menu entry. Edit the code as shown in the following to show or hide the toolbar (see also Listing 12.3 of Ref. [2]).

```
void CMainFrame::OnViewTbCommonOps()
{
    // TODO: Add your command handler code here
    // DiagramEng (start)
    BOOL bShow;

    // Check state of Common Ops. toolbar
    bShow = ((m_wndTBCommonOps.GetStyle() & WS_VISIBLE) != 0);

    // Switch state
    // NOTE: & of toolbar, bool show/hide toolbar, delay showing toolbar
      (FALSE => no delay)
    ShowControlBar(&m_wndTBCommonOps, !bShow, FALSE);

    // Recalculate Layout
    RecalcLayout();

    // DiagramEng (end)
}
```

Add an event-handler function to the CMainFrame class, for the UPDATE_COMMAND_UI event message of the ID_VIEW_TB_COMMON_BLOCKS menu entry. Edit the code as shown in the following, to set the check mark (✓) next to the View menu entry denoting the visibility of the corresponding toolbar.

```
void CMainFrame::OnUpdateViewTbCommonBlocks(CCmdUI* pCmdUI)
{
    // TODO: Add your command update UI handler code here

    // DiagramEng (start)

    // Check the status of the Common Blocks Toolbar (IDR_TB_COMMON_BLOCKS)
    // NOTE: get style of toolbar and mask out for the WS_VISIBLE style
       flag.
    // If the flag is in the current toolbar style, then the toolbar is
       visible.
    // The SetCheck() allows checking and unchecking the toolbar MENU
       entry (in the View menu here).
    pCmdUI->SetCheck(((m_wndTBCommonBlocks.GetStyle() & WS_VISIBLE) != 0));

    // DiagramEng (end)
}
```

Add an event-handler function to the CMainFrame class, for the COMMAND event message of the ID_VIEW_TB_COMMON_BLOCKS menu entry. Edit the code as shown in the following to show or hide the toolbar.

```
void CMainFrame::OnViewTbCommonBlocks()
{
    // TODO: Add your command handler code here

    // DiagramEng (start)
    BOOL bShow;

    // Check state of Common Ops. toolbar
    bShow = ((m_wndTBCommonBlocks.GetStyle() & WS_VISIBLE) != 0);
    // Switch state
    // NOTE: & of toolbar, bool show/hide toolbar, delay showing toolbar
       (FALSE => no delay)
    ShowControlBar(&m_wndTBCommonBlocks, !bShow, FALSE);

    // Recalculate Layout
    RecalcLayout();

    // DiagramEng (end)
}
```

Now the Common Ops. Toolbar and Common Blocks Toolbar entries under the View menu may be selected to show or hide the corresponding toolbar.

2.5.5 ADD EVENT-HANDLER FUNCTIONS FOR THE MENU ENTRIES

Simple event-handler functions may be added for the COMMAND event messages for all the added menu entries as shown in Table 2.8. The Common Operations toolbar buttons share the same object IDs as those of the menu items: hence, the functionality caters for both the menu items and the toolbar buttons (except for the Track Multiple Items button that does not have a corresponding menu entry and will be covered in a later chapter).

1. Navigate to the Menu folder in the Workspace pane and double-click the IDR_CHILDMENU to make the menu visible.
2. Right-click the editor area (right hand side) and select the ClassWizard from the pop-up menu.

TABLE 2.8

Menu Entry Objects, IDs, Classes, and COMMAND Event-Handler Functions

Object	ID	Class	COMMAND Event-Handler
Edit/Delete	ID_EDIT_DELETE	CDiagramEngDoc	OnEditDelete()
Edit/Select All	ID_EDIT_SELECTALL	CDiagramEngDoc	OnEditSelectAll()
Edit/Add Multiple Blocks	ID_EDIT_ADD_MULTI_BLOCKS	CDiagramEngDoc	OnEditAddMultipleBlocks()
View/Auto Fit Diagram	ID_VIEW_AUTO_FIT_DIAGRAM	CDiagramEngView	OnViewAutoFitDiagram()
View/Zoom In	ID_VIEW_ZOOM_IN	CDiagramEngView	OnViewZoomIn()
View/Zoom Out	ID_VIEW_ZOOM_OUT	CDiagramEngView	OnViewZoomOut()
Model/Build Model	ID_MODEL_BUILD	CDiagramEngDoc	OnModelBuild()
Model/Build Subsystem	ID_MODEL_BUILD_SUBSYS	CDiagramEngDoc	OnModelBuildSubsystem()
Simulation/Start	ID_SIM_START	CDiagramEngDoc	OnSimStart()
Simulation/Stop	ID_SIM_STOP	CDiagramEngDoc	OnSimStop()
Simulation/Numerical Solver	ID_SIM_NUM_SOLVER	CDiagramEngDoc	OnSimNumericalSolver()
Format/Show Annotations	ID_FORMAT_SHOW_ANNOTATIONS	CDiagramEngDoc	OnFormatShowAnnotations()
Tools/Diagnostic Info.	ID_TOOLS_DIAGNOSTIC_INFO	CDiagramEngDoc	OnToolsDiagnosticInfo()
Window/Close All Documents	ID_WND_CLOSE_ALL_DOCS	CDiagramEngDoc	OnWndCloseAllDocs()
Help/Using DiagramEng	ID_HELP_USING_DIAENG	CDiagramEngDoc	OnHelpUsingDiagramEng()

3. Select as the class name either CDiagramEngDoc for Document-based action or CDiagramEngView for purely View-based action: almost all of the event-handler functions relate to the underlying document; hence, CDiagramEngDoc is prevalent.

4. Find the IDs for which functionality should be added for the COMMAND event message, e.g., ID_EDIT_DELETE.

5. Select the ID, highlight COMMAND, and click Add Function to add the event-handler function.

6. Omit adding the event-handler function for the UPDATE_COMMAND_UI event message, since no updating of the UI is necessary here (although it was necessary to place a check mark next to the menu entry "View/Common Ops. Toolbar", as explained earlier).

7. Add event-handler functions for all the IDs presented in Table 2.4: the menu object, ID, class, and the corresponding function are listed in Table 2.8.

8. Place a simple message box in each event-handler function to check its operation on menu entry and toolbar button selection. For example, for the Delete entry of the Edit menu, the event-handler function CDiagramEngDoc::OnEditDelete() displays a simple message. This can be done for all the remaining menu entries.

```
void CDiagramEngDoc::OnEditDelete()
{
    // TODO: Add your command handler code here

    // DiagramEng (start)
    CString sMsg;        // string to be displayed
    UINT nType = MB_OK;  // style of msg. box
    UINT nIDhelp = 0;    // help context ID for the msg: 0 indicates the
      app's default help context will be used
```

```
    // Display a msg.
    sMsg.Format("\n CDiagramEngDoc::OnEditDelete()\n\n");
    AfxMessageBox(sMsg, nType, nIDhelp);

    // DiagramEng (end)
}
```

The developer may prefer to simply use a one-line statement, rather than declare three local variables, for the message-box-based display as follows: `AfxMessageBox("\n message content\n",` `MB_OK,  0)`, where the arguments, "message content", "MB_OK", and "0", represent the message to be displayed, the style of the message box and the help context ID of the message, respectively [3].

2.5.6 ADD EVENT-HANDLER FUNCTIONS FOR THE COMMON BLOCKS TOOLBAR BUTTONS

Event-handler functions may now be added for the buttons on the Common Blocks toolbar that, at this stage, display a simple message: more functional detail will be added to these later.

1. Right-click the editor area (right hand side) and select the ClassWizard from the pop-up menu.
2. Select as the class name, CDiagramEngDoc, for document-based action, since all of the event-handler functions relate to inserting blocks in the system model held by the underlying document.
3. Find the IDs of the buttons for which functionality should be added for the COMMAND event message, e.g., ID_BLOCK_CTS_DERIVATIVE, etc.
4. Select the ID, highlight COMMAND, and click Add Function to add the event-handler function.

TABLE 2.9
Common Blocks Toolbar Buttons, IDs, Classes, and the Corresponding Functions

Toolbar Buttons and Their Block Groups	ID	Class	COMMAND Event-Handler
Continuous/Derivative Block	ID_BLOCK_CTS_DERIVATIVE	CDiagramEngDoc	OnBlockCtsDerivative()
Continuous/Integrator Block	ID_BLOCK_CTS_INTEGRATOR	CDiagramEngDoc	OnBlockCtsIntegrator()
Continuous/TransferFn Block	ID_BLOCK_CTS_TRANSFERFN	CDiagramEngDoc	OnBlockCtsTransferfn()
Math Operations/Divide Block	ID_BLOCK_MATHOPS_DIVIDE	CDiagramEngDoc	OnBlockMathopsDivide()
Math Operations/Gain Block	ID_BLOCK_MATHOPS_GAIN	CDiagramEngDoc	OnBlockMathopsGain()
Math Operations/Sum Block	ID_BLOCK_MATHOPS_SUM	CDiagramEngDoc	OnBlockMathopsSum()
Sink/Output Block	ID_BLOCK_SINK_OUTPUT	CDiagramEngDoc	OnBlockSinkOutput()
Sink/SubsystemOut Block	ID_BLOCK_SUBSYS_SUBSYSOUT	(see Subsys)	(see Subsys)
Source/Constant Block	ID_BLOCK_SOURCE_CONST	CDiagramEngDoc	OnBlockSourceConst()
Source/LinearFn Block	ID_BLOCK_SOURCE_LINEARFN	CDiagramEngDoc	OnBlockSourceLinearfn()
Source/SignalGenerator Block	ID_BLOCK_SOURCE_SIGNALGEN	CDiagramEngDoc	OnBlockSourceSignalgen()
Source/SubsystemIn Block	ID_BLOCK_SUBSYS_SUBSYSIN	(see Subsys)	(see Subsys)
Subsystem/Subsystem	ID_BLOCK_SUBSYS_SUBSYS	CDiagramEngDoc	OnBlockSubsysSubsys()
Subsystem/SubsystemIn	ID_BLOCK_SUBSYS_SUBSYSIN	CDiagramEngDoc	OnBlockSubsysSubsysin()
Subsystem/SubsystemOut	ID_BLOCK_SUBSYS_SUBSYSOUT	CDiagramEngDoc	OnBlockSubsysSubsysout()

5. Omit adding the event-handler function for the UPDATE_COMMAND_UI event message, since no updating of the UI is necessary here.
6. Add event-handlers for all the IDs in Table 2.9, showing the toolbar button objects, IDs, classes, and the corresponding functions.
7. Place a simple `AfxMessageBox()` call in each event-handler function to check its operation on menu entry and toolbar button selection. For example, the Derivative block, a type of continuous mathematical operation block, has a COMMAND event-handler function named "`OnBlockCtsDerivative()`" as shown in the following. All other functions will have a similar appearance.

```
void CDiagramEngDoc::OnBlockCtsDerivative()
{
    // TODO: Add your command handler code here

    // DiagramEng (start)
    AfxMessageBox("\n CDiagramEngDoc::OnBlockCtsDerivative()\n\n",
      MB_OK, 0);

    // DiagramEng (end)
}
```

2.6   BLOCK LIBRARY DIALOG WINDOW

A dialog window, often called a dialog box or dialog resource, typically has controls on it, e.g., edit boxes, check boxes, and buttons, that are used to present information to the user and allow user input to either update parameter values to the underlying code or invoke specific functional behavior.

2.6.1   INSERT A NEW DIALOG RESOURCE

The Common Blocks toolbar will eventually allow the user to add blocks to the diagram model by clicking on the appropriate toolbar button. Another method to add blocks is through the use of either a Tree View directory listing or a dialog window. Here, instructions are provided for adding a dialog window containing check boxes and buttons (Figure 2.5) that is used to add blocks to the model.

1. Go to the ResourceView of the Workspace pane.
2. Right-click on Dialog and insert dialog: IDD_DIALOG1 will appear in the Dialog directory. Rename it to reflect the nature of the dialog window, e.g., IDD_BLOCKLIBDLG, for the Block Library Dialog window. (This is not a directory listing but rather a standard dialog window.)
3. Leave the Cancel button on the dialog, but delete the OK button, as this will be replaced with a Close button.
4. Add controls desired from the controls toolbar, e.g., static text and additional buttons as indicated in Table 2.10, to create the dialog window shown in Figure 2.5.

5. The title "Dialog" will appear (when the executable runs) in the actual title portion of the pane. Right-click on the top of the Dialog window to change the title-properties of the dialog window to reflect the purpose of the window: e.g., "Block Library Dialog".
6. Add maximize and minimize buttons and scroll bars to the Block Library Dialog window if desired: select the dialog window, right click on the dialog to access the dialog properties, select the styles tab, and activate the maximize and minimize buttons.

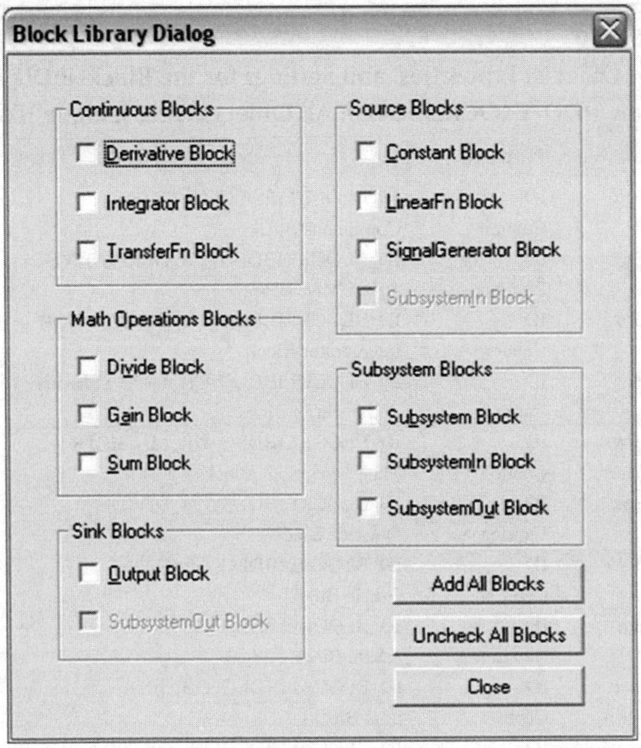

FIGURE 2.5   Block Library Dialog window showing check boxes for all model block types.

7. Specify the control tab order: choose Layout/Tab Order and click the numbers in the desired order and then choose Layout/Tab Order to return to the layout editor.
8. Check mnemonics: right-click on the dialog window and click check mnemonics (leave duplicates if they represent the same dialog control).

The Block Library Dialog window is shown with all group boxes and their relevant check boxes. Two check boxes are repeated: i.e., Subsystem Out (Sink Blocks) and Subsystem In (Source Blocks). The primary versions of these are found in the Subsystem Blocks group box. However, the IDs for the repeated check boxes will link to the same event-handler function if enabled. These check boxes may be disabled altogether, as shown, in which case they would serve as an implicit comment to the user that they may be considered as Sink/Source blocks, but are found in the Subsystem Blocks group box.

2.6.2   ATTACH A CLASS TO THE DIALOG WINDOW

Now that the dialog resource exists, a class is to be attached to it such that the user selections made through the dialog may be interpreted and used to ultimately add blocks to the diagram model. The actual dialog object will be declared in the OnEditAddMultipleBlocks() function of the CDiagramEngDoc class given in the following. Attach the class to the dialog as follows:

1. Select the IDD_BLOCKLIBDLG resource from the ResourceView tab on the Workspace pane, to show the corresponding dialog window in the editor area (Figure 2.5), and right-click on the dialog to invoke the ClassWizard.
2. A message box appears with the content: "IDD_BLOCKLIBDLG is a new resource. Since it is a dialog resource you probably want to create a new class for it. You can also select an existing class." The option (1) to create a new class or (2) to select and existing class is provided. Create a new class with the name CBlockLibDlg and base class CDialog.

TABLE 2.10

Dialog Objects, Properties, and Settings for the BlockLibDlg Dialog Window (IDD_BLOCKLIBDLG): All Objects Have Unique IDs

Object	Property	Setting
Group Box	ID	ID_BLOCKLIBDLG_GB_CTS
	Caption	Continuous Blocks
Check Box	ID	ID_BLOCKLIBDLG_CB_DERIVATIVE
	Caption	&Derivative Block
Check Box	ID	ID_BLOCKLIBDLG_CB_INTEGRATOR
	Caption	Inte&grator Block
Check Box	ID	ID_BLOCKLIBDLG_CB_TRANSFERFN
	Caption	&TransferFn Block
Group Box	ID	ID_BLOCKLIBDLG_GB_MATHOPS
	Caption	Math Operations Blocks
Check Box	ID	ID_BLOCKLIBDLG_CB_DIVIDE
	Caption	Di&vide Block
Check Box	ID	ID_BLOCKLIBDLG_CB_GAIN
	Caption	G&ain Block
Check Box	ID	ID_BLOCKLIBDLG_CB_SUM
	Caption	&Sum Block
Group Box	ID	ID_BLOCKLIBDLG_GB_SINK
	Caption	Sink Blocks
Check Box	ID	ID_BLOCKLIBDLG_CB_OUTPUT
	Caption	&Output Block
Check Box	ID	ID_BLOCKLIBDLG_CB_SUBSYSOUT2
	Caption	SubsystemO&ut Block
Group Box	ID	ID_BLOCKLIBDLG_GB_SOURCE
	Caption	Source Blocks
Check Box	ID	ID_BLOCKLIBDLG_CB_CONST
	Caption	&Constant Block
Check Box	ID	ID_BLOCKLIBDLG_CB_LINEARFN
	Caption	&LinearFn Block
Check Box	ID	ID_BLOCKLIBDLG_CB_SIGNALGEN
	Caption	Sig&nalGenerator Block
Check Box	ID	ID_BLOCKLIBDLG_CB_SUBSYSIN2
	Caption	Subsystem&In Block
Group Box	ID	ID_BLOCKLIBDLG_GB_SUBSYS
	Caption	Subsystem Blocks
Check Box	ID	ID_BLOCKLIBDLG_CB_SUBSYS
	Caption	Su&bsystem Block
Check Box	ID	ID_BLOCKLIBDLG_CB_SUBSYSIN
	Caption	Subsystem&In Block
Check Box	ID	ID_BLOCKLIBDLG_CB_SUBSYSOUT
	Caption	SubsystemO&ut Block
Button	ID	ID_BLOCKLIBDLG_BTN_ADDALLBLOCKS
	Caption	Add All Blocks
Button	ID	ID_BLOCKLIBDLG_BTN_UNCHECKALLBLOCKS
	Caption	Uncheck All Blocks
Button	ID	IDCANCEL (default provided setting)
	Caption	Close

2.6.3 Menu Entry and Toolbar Button Event-Handling Functions

The ID (ID_EDIT_ADD_MULTI_BLOCKS) of the Edit menu entry, Add Multiple Blocks, to show the block dialog window, and the same ID of the corresponding toolbar button, can be used to invoke the Block Library Dialog window (since at present the directory structure Tree View-based block listing has not yet been added to the project). Edit the CDiagramEngDoc::OnEdit AddMultipleBlocks() function as shown in the following to create a CBlockLibDlg object, "oDlg": this will require the header file of the CBlockLibDlg class, i.e., "BlockLibDlg.h" to be included at the top of the "DiagramEngDoc.cpp" source file, i.e., #include "BlockLibDlg.h".

```
void CDiagramEngDoc::OnEditAddMultipleBlocks()
{
    // TODO: Add your command handler code here

    // DiagramEng (start)

    // Local var declaration
    int display_item = 1;  // used to display msg box or dlg wnd.

    // Display a msg.
    if(display_item == 0)
    {
        AfxMessageBox("\n CDiagramEngDoc::OnEditAddMultipleBlocks()\n",
            MB_OK, 0);
    }
    else if(display_item == 1)
    {
        CBlockLibDlg oDlg;  // create a dlg obj. of class CBlockLibDlg :
            public CDialog

        // Return val of DoModal() fn of ancestor class CDialog is
            checked to determine which btn was clicked.
        if(oDlg.DoModal() == IDOK)
        {
            //AfxMessageBox("\n CDiagramEngDoc::OnEditAddMultipleBlocks()\n,"
                MB_OK, 0);
        }
    }
    // DiagramEng (end)
}
```

At present, the OnEditAddMultipleBlocks() function simply instantiates a CBlockLibDlg object, "oDlg" and uses the DoModal() function to display it to the user. The user can then select various fields of the dialog window and click the appropriate buttons to add blocks to the model.

2.6.4 Attach Variables to the Controls

The Block Library Dialog window has all objects in place, but variables now need to be associated with the check box controls as follows:

1. Open the ClassWizard and select the member variables tab.
2. Select the class name to be CBlockLibDlg, since variables to be added relate to the dialog window controls.
3. Select the ID of the control to which a variable should be added, click Add Variable, and specify the details as shown in Table 2.11: the category and type for all check box variables are value and Boolean, respectively.

TABLE 2.11

Dialog Window Control IDs, Variable Names, Categories, and Types, for the IDD_BLOCKLIBDLG (Dialog Window) Resource

Control	Variable Name	Category	Type
ID_BLOCKLIBDLG_CB_DERIVATIVE	m_bChkBoxDerivativeBlock	Value	BOOL
ID_BLOCKLIBDLG_CB_INTEGRATOR	m_bChkBoxIntegratorBlock	Value	BOOL
ID_BLOCKLIBDLG_CB_TRANSFERFN	m_bChkBoxTransferFnBlock	Value	BOOL
ID_BLOCKLIBDLG_CB_DIVIDE	m_bChkBoxDivideBlock	Value	BOOL
ID_BLOCKLIBDLG_CB_GAIN	m_bChkBoxGainBlock	Value	BOOL
ID_BLOCKLIBDLG_CB_SUM	m_bChkBoxSumBlock	Value	BOOL
ID_BLOCKLIBDLG_CB_OUTPUT	m_bChkBoxOutputBlock	Value	BOOL
ID_BLOCKLIBDLG_CB_SUBSYSOUT2	m_bChkBoxSubsysOut2Block	Value	BOOL
ID_BLOCKLIBDLG_CB_CONST	m_bChkBoxConstBlock	Value	BOOL
ID_BLOCKLIBDLG_CB_LINEARFN	m_bChkBoxLinearFnBlock	Value	BOOL
ID_BLOCKLIBDLG_CB_SIGNALGEN	m_bChkBoxSignalGenBlock	Value	BOOL
ID_BLOCKLIBDLG_CB_SUBSYSIN2	m_bChkBoxSubsysIn2Block	Value	BOOL
ID_BLOCKLIBDLG_CB_SUBSYS	m_bChkBoxSubsysBlock	Value	BOOL
ID_BLOCKLIBDLG_CB_SUBSYSIN	m_bChkBoxSubsysInBlock	Value	BOOL
ID_BLOCKLIBDLG_CB_SUBSYSOUT	m_bChkBoxSubsysOutBlock	Value	BOOL

2.6.5 ADD FUNCTIONALITY FOR THE BLOCK LIBRARY DIALOG BUTTONS

Functionality now needs to be added for the Block Library Dialog window buttons, Add All Blocks, Uncheck All Blocks and Cancel, to add blocks to the diagram model, uncheck selected blocks or cancel the operation, respectively. Hence, add event-handler functions for the three buttons on the Block Library Dialog window as shown in Table 2.12. The "Cancel" button event-handler function OnCancel() calls CDialog::OnCancel(), and hence, no new functionality needs to be added here. Display an Afx message box (AfxMessageBox()) for the OnBlocklibdlgBtnAddallblocks() and OnBlocklibdlgBtnUncheckallblocks() functions as discussed earlier to confirm that they may be invoked correctly.

2.6.5.1 Disable Duplicate Check Boxes

The Block Library Dialog window shown in Figure 2.5 has two check boxes that are disabled. The disabling may be initialized by either selecting the Disabled option of the General tab of the Check Box Properties dialog for the control concerned, or explicitly calling EnableWindow(FALSE) for

TABLE 2.12

Block Library Dialog Resource Button Objects, IDs, Classes, and Event-Handler Functions

Button	ID	Class	COMMAND Event-Handler
Add All Blocks	ID_BLOCKLIBDLG_BTN_ ADDALLBLOCKS	CBlockLibDlg	OnBlocklibdlgBtnAddallblocks()
Uncheck All Blocks	ID_BLOCKLIBDLG_BTN_ UNCHECKALLBLOCKS	CBlockLibDlg	OnBlocklibdlgBtnUncheckallblocks()
Cancel	IDCANCEL (default)	CBlockLibDlg	OnCancel()

the dialog control item, from within the OnInitDialog() function of the CBlockLibDlg class. The latter is performed as follows:

1. Invoke the ClassWizard and click on the "Message Maps" tab: the "Class Name" is CBlockLibDlg.
2. Click on the CBlockLibDlg under "Object IDs".
3. Select the WM_INITDIALOG message under the "Messages" section.
4. Click Add Function to add the initialization function named CBlockLibDlg::OnInitDialog(): the initialization cannot be done within the constructor, since the constructor can only handle variable initialization, not dialog function-call-based initialization.
5. Edit the CBlockLibDlg::OnInitDialog() function and disable the duplicated check boxes with IDs, "ID_BLOCKLIBDLG_CB_SUBSYSIN2" and "ID_BLOCKLIBDLG_CB_SUBSYSOUT2".

```
BOOL CBlockLibDlg::OnInitDialog()
{
    CDialog::OnInitDialog();

    // TODO: Add extra initialization here

    // DiagramEng (start)

    // Disable the duplicate check boxes
    GetDlgItem(ID_BLOCKLIBDLG_CB_SUBSYSOUT2)->EnableWindow(FALSE); // False
        disables the control
    GetDlgItem(ID_BLOCKLIBDLG_CB_SUBSYSIN2)->EnableWindow(FALSE); // False
        disables the control

    // DiagramEng (end)

    return TRUE;   // return TRUE unless you set the focus to a control
                   // EXCEPTION: OCX Property Pages should return FALSE
}
```

2.6.5.2 Add All Blocks

The OnBlocklibdlgBtnAddallblocks() function is called when the user clicks the Add All Blocks button on the Block Library Dialog window: the function then determines which blocks have been selected and proceeds to call a block-construction function to construct the relevant blocks. Edit the function as shown to do the following: (1) call UpdateData(TRUE) to update the variable values with the dialog window control values, (2) get a pointer to the current document, "pDoc", of type CDiagramEngDoc, and (3) filter the Boolean check box-related values calling the ConstructBlock() function using the document pointer, passing an enumerated type argument indicating the type of block to be constructed. In addition, do the following:

1. Declare the enumerated type variable at the top of the "DiagramEngDoc.h" header file, after the "#endif // _MSC_VER > 1000" line, as follows: enum EBlockType {eConstBlock, eDerivativeBlock, eDivideBlock, eGainBlock, eIntegratorBlock, eLinearFnBlock, eOutputBlock, eSignalGenBlock, eSubsysBlock, eSubsysInBlock, eSubsysOutBlock, eSumBlock, eTransferFnBlock}
2. Include the "DiagramEngDoc.h" header file at the top of the "BlockLibDlg.cpp" source file, since the CBlockLibDlg-based member function uses the enumerated type, "EBlockType".

```
void CBlockLibDlg::OnBlocklibdlgBtnAddallblocks()
{
    // TODO: Add your control notification handler code here

    // DiagramEng (start)
    CString sMsg;                  // string to be displayed
    UINT nType = MB_OK;            // style of msg. box
    UINT nIDhelp = 0;              // help context ID for the msg.
    EBlockType e_block_type;       // enum block type defined in
      DiagramEngDoc.cpp
    CDiagramEngDoc *pDoc = NULL;   // declare pDoc to be a ptr to
      CDiagramEngDoc.

    // -- Display a msg. box
    sMsg.Format("\n CBlockLibDlg::OnBlocklibdlgBtnAddallblocks()\n\n");
    AfxMessageBox(sMsg, nType, nIDhelp);

    // -- Update the dlg. wnd. control vals. to the vars.
    UpdateData(TRUE);

    // -- Check to see if no check boxes were checked and inform the
      user: then return. (blocks listed in alpha order).
    if(!m_bChkBoxConstBlock && !m_bChkBoxDerivativeBlock &&
       !m_bChkBoxDivideBlock && !m_bChkBoxGainBlock &&
       !m_bChkBoxIntegratorBlock && !m_bChkBoxLinearFnBlock &&
       !m_bChkBoxOutputBlock && !m_bChkBoxSignalGenBlock &&
       !m_bChkBoxSubsysBlock && !m_bChkBoxSubsysInBlock &&
       !m_bChkBoxSubsysOutBlock && !m_bChkBoxSumBlock &&
       !m_bChkBoxTransferFnBlock)
    {
        sMsg.Format("\n CBlockLibDlg::OnBlocklibdlgBtnAddallblocks()\n No
          blocks selected.\n\n");
        AfxMessageBox(sMsg, nType, nIDhelp);
        return;  // return now since no blocks were checked.
    }

    // -- Get a ptr to document, i.e. pDoc.
    // This can be done calling CDiagramEngView::GetDocument().
    // However, from within the Dlg class, in the absence of a View obj.,
      a global fn is rqd that returns pDoc.
    // This global fn header is declared in DiagramEngDoc.h and defined
      in DiagramEngDoc.cpp

    pDoc = GetDocumentGlobalFn();

    // Invoke a general block creation fn passing an enum EBlockType var.
    if(m_bChkBoxConstBlock)
    {
        e_block_type = eConstBlock;
        pDoc->ConstructBlock(e_block_type);
    }
    if(m_bChkBoxDerivativeBlock)
    {
        e_block_type = eDerivativeBlock;
        pDoc->ConstructBlock(e_block_type);
    }
    if(m_bChkBoxDivideBlock)
    {
```

```
            e_block_type = eDivideBlock;
            pDoc->ConstructBlock(e_block_type);
        }
        if(m_bChkBoxGainBlock)
        {
            e_block_type = eGainBlock;
            pDoc->ConstructBlock(e_block_type);
        }
        if(m_bChkBoxIntegratorBlock)
        {
            e_block_type = eIntegratorBlock;
            pDoc->ConstructBlock(e_block_type);
        }
        if(m_bChkBoxLinearFnBlock)
        {
            e_block_type = eLinearFnBlock;
            pDoc->ConstructBlock(e_block_type);
        }
        if(m_bChkBoxOutputBlock)
        {
            e_block_type = eOutputBlock;
            pDoc->ConstructBlock(e_block_type);
        }
        if(m_bChkBoxSignalGenBlock)
        {
            e_block_type = eSignalGenBlock;
            pDoc->ConstructBlock(e_block_type);
        }
        if(m_bChkBoxSubsysBlock)
        {
            e_block_type = eSubsysBlock;
            pDoc->ConstructBlock(e_block_type);
        }
        if(m_bChkBoxSubsysInBlock)
        {
            e_block_type = eSubsysInBlock;
            pDoc->ConstructBlock(e_block_type);
        }
        if(m_bChkBoxSubsysOutBlock)
        {
            e_block_type = eSubsysOutBlock;
            pDoc->ConstructBlock(e_block_type);
        }
        if(m_bChkBoxSumBlock)
        {
            e_block_type = eSumBlock;
            pDoc->ConstructBlock(e_block_type);
        }
        if(m_bChkBoxTransferFnBlock)
        {
            e_block_type = eTransferFnBlock;
            pDoc->ConstructBlock(e_block_type);
        }

    // DiagramEng (end)
}
```

The developer will have noticed the call to ConstructBlock() called upon the pointer-to-CDiagramEngDoc, "pDoc". Hence, add a public member function to the CDiagramEngDoc class with the prototype, int CDiagramEngDoc::ConstructBlock(EBlockType e_block_type), and edit it as shown in the following to use a *switch* statement to call the appropriate block construction function. At present, no blocks are actually constructed (the calls are commented out), but this will completed in a following chapter.

```cpp
int CDiagramEngDoc::ConstructBlock(EBlockType e_block_type)
{
    // General ConstructBlock() fn which calls specific block
      construction fns.
    CString sMsg;          // string to be displayed
    UINT nType = MB_OK;  // style of msg. box
    UINT nIDhelp = 0;    // help context ID for the msg.

    // -- Display a msg. box
    sMsg.Format("\n CDiagramEngDoc::ConstructBlock()\n\n");
    AfxMessageBox(sMsg, nType, nIDhelp);

    // -- Filter out the approp. partic. block consturction fn. to be called

    switch(e_block_type)
    {
    case eConstBlock:
        //ConstructConstantBlock();
        break;

    case eDerivativeBlock:
        //ConstructDerivativeBlock();
        break;

    case eDivideBlock:
        //ConstructDivideBlock();
        break;

    case eGainBlock:
        //ConstructGainBlock();
        break;

    case eIntegratorBlock:
        //ConstructIntegratorBlock();
        break;

    case eLinearFnBlock:
        //ConstructLinearFnBlock();
        break;

    case eOutputBlock:
        //ConstructOutputBlock();
        break;

    case eSignalGenBlock:
        //ConstructSignalGeneratorBlock();
        break;

    case eSubsysBlock:
        //ConstructSubsystemBlock();
        break;

    case eSubsysInBlock:
        //ConstructSubsystemInBlock();
        break;
```

```
    case eSubsysOutBlock:
        //ConstructSubsystemOutBlock();
        break;

    case eSumBlock:
        //ConstructSumBlock();
        break;

    case eTransferFnBlock:
        //ConstructTransferFnBlock();
        break;

    default:
        // Inform user of switch default
        sMsg.Format("\n CDiagramEngDoc::ConstructBlock(): switch default\
          n\n");
        AfxMessageBox(sMsg, nType, nIDhelp);
        break;
    }
    return 0; // return int for error checking
}
```

Finally, in the CBlockLibDlg::OnBlocklibdlgBtnAddallblocks() function given earlier, the calls to CDiagramEngDoc::ConstructBlock() are made via the pointer-to-CDiagramEngDoc, "pDoc". Now, the View class function, CDiagramEngView::GetDocument(), returns a pointer-to-CDiagramEngDoc, but unfortunately this cannot be called from within the CBlockLibDlg function, OnBlocklibdlgBtnAddallblocks(). So a new global function needs to be manually inserted to return a pointer-to-CDiagramEngDoc, yielding a pointer to the active document in a similar manner to the View class version, CDiagramEngView::GetDocument(). Hence, perform the following:

1. Add a new function prototype in the "DiagramEngDoc.h" header file after the CDiagramEngDoc class definition: CDiagramEngDoc* GetDocumentGlobalFn(void).
2. Place the actual function in the "DiagramEngDoc.cpp" source file, after the ConstructBlock() function as shown in the following.

```
CDiagramEngDoc* GetDocumentGlobalFn(void)
{
    // Get a pointer to the main frame window
    CMDIFrameWnd *pFrame = (CMDIFrameWnd*)AfxGetApp()->m_pMainWnd;

    // Get the active MDI child window.
    CMDIChildWnd *pChild = (CMDIChildWnd*)pFrame->GetActiveFrame();

    // Get the active document associated with the active child window
    CDiagramEngDoc *pDoc = (CDiagramEngDoc*)pChild->GetActiveDocument();

    // Return the pDoc
    if(pDoc != NULL)
    {
        return pDoc;
    }

    // If pDoc != NULL then it would have already been returned, o/wise
      return NULL.
    return NULL;
}
```

The GetDocumentGlobalFn() returns the address of the active document that contains the complete data structure for a system model, including its list of blocks and connections. The first line gets a pointer to the Main frame window and assigns it to the pointer-to-CMDIFrameWnd, "pFrame". Then, using this pointer, a pointer to the active MDI Child window, "pChild", is obtained via the call to GetActiveFrame(). The active document associated with the active Child window is then retrieved using the "pChild" pointer and the call to GetActiveDocument() and is assigned to the pointer-to-CDiagramEngDoc, "pDoc". Finally, if "pDoc" is not NULL, it is returned; otherwise, NULL is explicitly returned.

Note that instead of using "AfxGetApp()->m_pMainWnd" given earlier, the alternative "theApp.m_pMainWnd" could have been used. However, in this case, the application, "theApp", would need to be accessed from within the "DiagramEngDoc.cpp" file, although it is declared in the "DiagramEng.cpp" file. Hence, if this is preferred (and here it is not implemented), place the statement "extern CDiagramEngApp theApp"; at the top of the "DiagramEngDoc.cpp" file, as follows, to allow its use within the GetDocumentGlobalFn().

```
// theApp needs to be accessed from within the DiagramEngDoc.cpp file,
  although it's declared in the DiagramEng.cpp file.
// It is used in the fn GetDocumentGlobalFn() below.
extern CDiagramEngApp theApp;
```

This global GetDocumentGlobalFn() will be used extensively throughout the project, since on numerous occasions, CDiagramEngDoc functions are required to be called from outside of CDiagramEngView functions, within which CDiagramEngView::GetDocument()could otherwise be called.

2.6.5.3 Uncheck All Blocks

Finally, the last button event-handler function OnBlocklibdlgBtnUncheckallblocks() may be edited as shown in the following to reset all Boolean check boxes to the unchecked FALSE state and then UpdateData(FALSE) called to update the variable values to the dialog window controls.

```
void CBlockLibDlg::OnBlocklibdlgBtnUncheckallblocks()
{
    // TODO: Add your control notification handler code here

    // DiagramEng (start)

    //AfxMessageBox("\n CBlockLibDlg::OnBlocklibdlgBtnUncheckallblock
      s()\n", MB_OK, 0);

    // Mark all the check boxes as unchecked
    m_bChkBoxConstBlock = FALSE;
    m_bChkBoxDerivativeBlock = FALSE;
    m_bChkBoxDivideBlock = FALSE;
    m_bChkBoxGainBlock = FALSE;
    m_bChkBoxIntegratorBlock = FALSE;
    m_bChkBoxLinearFnBlock = FALSE;
    m_bChkBoxOutputBlock = FALSE;
    m_bChkBoxSignalGenBlock = FALSE;
    m_bChkBoxSubsysBlock = FALSE;
    m_bChkBoxSubsysInBlock = FALSE;
    m_bChkBoxSubsysIn2Block = FALSE;
    m_bChkBoxSubsysOutBlock = FALSE;
    m_bChkBoxSubsysOut2Block = FALSE;
```

```
m_bChkBoxSumBlock = FALSE;
m_bChkBoxTransferFnBlock = FALSE;

UpdateData(FALSE);   // FALSE => var vals updated to the dlg. wnd.

// DiagramEng (end)
}
```

2.7 ADD FUNCTIONALITY TO THE COMMON BLOCKS TOOLBAR BUTTONS

Now that functionality has been added for the `OnBlocklibdlgBtnAddallblocks()`
method, a similar internal operation needs to be added for functions associated with the common blocks toolbar buttons: i.e., on button selection, the button-based event-handler function is
called, and the appropriate EBlockType enumerated value is set and the `ConstructBlock()`
function called to construct the block. An example of this is shown in the following for the
Derivative block of the Continuous Blocks group: the remaining event-handler functions may be
edited in a similar manner.

```
void CDiagramEngDoc::OnBlockCtsDerivative()
{
    // TODO: Add your command handler code here

    // DiagramEng (start)
    //AfxMessageBox("\n CDiagramEngDoc::OnBlockCtsDerivative()\n", MB_OK, 0);

    // Invoke a general block creation fn passing an enum EBlockType var.
    EBlockType e_block_type = eDerivativeBlock; // enum block type
       defined in DiagramEngDoc.cpp
    ConstructBlock(e_block_type);
    // DiagramEng (end)
}
```

2.8 SUMMARY

The Application Wizard [1] is used to set up an MFC-based MDI Windows application, named
DiagramEng. Menus are added to the GUI to allow selection of operations relating to the underlying document. A Common Operations toolbar and a Common Blocks toolbar are set up under
the default toolbar, and event-handler functions are associated with the toolbar buttons and corresponding menu entries. A Block Library Dialog window is constructed in preparation for adding a selection of blocks to the model, and variables are attached to the controls of the dialog
window. A `ConstructBlock()` function is added that will ultimately invoke the constructor
of the appropriate derived-block class to construct a model block: this function is called from
`OnBlocklibdlgBtnAddallblocks()` and the event-handler functions for the Common
Blocks toolbar buttons. An important global function named `GetDocumentGlobalFn()`
is introduced, which allows a pointer-to-CDiagramEngDoc to be obtained from a scope outside the View class: the View class has its own `GetDocument()` function to retrieve a
pointer-to-CDiagramEngDoc.

REFERENCES

1. The Microsoft Visual C++® 6.0, Microsoft® Visual Studio™ 6.0 Development System, Professional
   Edition, Microsoft Corporation, 1998.
2. Chapman, D., *Teach Yourself Visual C++ 6 in 21 Days*, Sams Publishing, Indianapolis, IN, 1998.
3. Microsoft Developer Network Library Visual Studio 6.0, Microsoft® Visual Studio™ 6.0 Development
   System, Microsoft Corporation, 1998.

3 Constructing Blocks

3.1 INTRODUCTION

The ControlEng Win32 Console Application developed in Chapter 1 involved brief class declarations and definitions for the classes shown in the following class hierarchical diagram (Figure 3.1). The key association relationships between the objects/classes are (1) "Generalization," modeling the "is-a" relationship, used for class derivation, shown by the arrowhead ($\rightarrow$) notation and (2) "Composition," modeling the "has-a" or "containment" relationship, illustrated by the diamond-head ($\blacklozenge$) notation.

The developer may rebuild and rerun the ControlEng application (see Appendix A for the code) to see the construction of the following objects (in order): CSystemModel, CBlockShape, CBlock, CPort, CConnection, and CSignal. Now the ControlEng Win32 Console Application project material needs to be merged with the DiagramEng Visual C++ [1] (initial GUI) application built in Chapter 2.

3.2 MERGING THE WIN32 CONSOLE APPLICATION WITH THE VISUAL C++ APPLICATION

To merge the ControlEng Win32 Console Application project with the DiagramEng Visual C++ application, the following steps need to be taken: (1) backup, (2) copy, (3) transfer files, (4) add files, (5) add a variable, and (6) display construction.

Step 1: First, make a backup of the initial DiagramEng Visual C++ application that may be located, e.g., in a directory of the following structure (the ellipsis denotes a preceding general structure reflecting the developer's account):

```
"...\Diagram Eng Project\DiagramEng (Initial GUI)\DiagramEng"
```

Step 2: Now copy the initial DiagramEng Visual C++ application from the following sample location

```
"...\Diagram Eng Project\DiagramEng (Initial GUI)\DiagramEng"
```

into a new directory, indicating that the GUI will have the aforementioned class structure defined in the ControlEng Win32 Console Application, inserted within it, e.g.,

```
"...\Diagram Eng Project\DiagramEng (GUI + classes)\DiagramEng"
```

Step 3: Copy the source and header files, "Block.h/cpp", "SystemModel.h/cpp", and "Signal.h/cpp", from the ControlEng Win32 Console Application, located, e.g., in the following directory

```
"...\Diagram Eng Project\DiagramEng (preliminary)\ControlEng"
```

to the location of the new DiagramEng Visual C++ application with the current GUI and the to-be-added classes

```
"...\Diagram Eng Project\DiagramEng (GUI + classes)\DiagramEng"
```

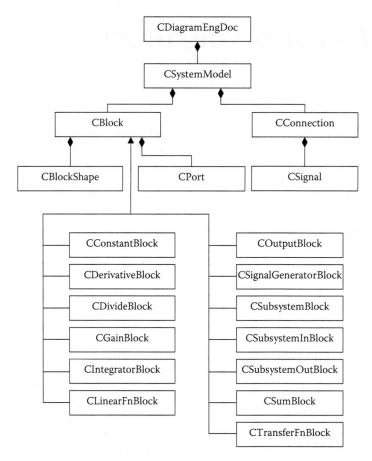

FIGURE 3.1 Class hierarchical diagram showing association relationships: generalization (→) and composition (♦).

Note that here the source and header files, "ControlEng.cpp" and "ControlEng.h", respectively, are omitted, since they constitute the main line of the ControlEng Win32 Console Application, and this main line will be assumed by a main() function that calls a WinMain() function but is not visible via the IDE [1] in the DiagramEng Visual C++ application.

Step 4: Add the copied-and-pasted files ("Block.h/cpp", "SystemModel.h/cpp", and "Signal.h/cpp") to the DiagramEng project by first selecting the menu entry, Project/Add To Project/Files, and then navigating to the current project directory, found, e.g., at the following location

```
"...\Diagram Eng Project\DiagramEng (GUI + classes)\DiagramEng"
```

and select the (recently copied) files to be added, i.e., "Block.h/cpp", "SystemModel.h/cpp", and "Signal.h/cpp". As a result, the following files and their contained classes exist in the new DiagramEng Visual C++ project as shown in Table 3.1.

Now compile the code without declaring a CSystemModel variable to check the compilation. The compiler yields the following error:

```
"unexpected end of file while looking for precompiled header directive".
```

The compiler looks for the directive: #include "stdafx.h". If #include "stdafx.h" is not present in the newly added source files, add this directive at the very top of the file before all other #include statements. See the following code excerpt as an example. The reason for this compilation error is

TABLE 3.1

Combined DiagramEng Source Files (.cpp), Header Files (.h), and Classes, Augmented with the ControlEng Files and Classes

DiagramEng Files	DiagramEng Classes
BlockLibDlg.cpp/h	CBlockLibDlg
ChildFrm.cpp/h	CChildFrame
DiagramEng.cpp/h	CDiagramEngApp
DiagramEng.rc	NA
DiagramEngDoc.cpp/h	CDiagramEngDoc
DiagramEngView.cpp/h	CDiagramEngView
MainFrm.cpp/h	CMainFrame
Resource.h	NA
StdAfx.cpp/h	NA

ControlEng Files	ControlEng Classes
Block.cpp/h	CBlockShape, CPort, CBlock, CConstantBlock, CDerivativeBlock, CGainBlock, CIntegratorBlock, CLinearFnBlock, COutputBlock, CSignalGeneratorBlock, CSubsystemBlock, CSubsystemInBlock, CSubsystemOutBlock, CSumBlock, CTransferFnBlock
Signal.cpp/h	CSignal, CDoubleSignal, CMatrixSignal, CVectorSignal, CConnection
SystemModel.cpp/h	CSystemModel

due to the fact that the inclusion of the precompiled header is set through the Application Wizard when creating a new Visual C++ application. However, Application Framework, or "Afx" support, was not present for the Win32 Console Application, ControlEng.

```
// Title: Block.cpp
// Purpose: Contains all Block related code.

#include "stdafx.h"        // rqd. for precompiled header info.
#include <iostream>
#include <string.h>
#include <vector>
#include <list>
using namespace std;
#include "Block.h"
#include "SystemModel.h"  // rqd. since Block() destr potentially deletes
  a ptr-to-CSystemModel(m_pSubSystemModel)
```

Step 5: Add a private member variable to the CDiagramEngDoc class, specifying the type as CSystemModel and the name as "m_SystemModel". Compile the code again. Error messages concerning <vector> and <list> appear. These may be resolved by inserting #include <vector>, #include <list>, and "using namespace std" (to avoid having to use the prefix "std::") in the source and header files where appropriate, as shown in the code excerpts ("Block.cpp") and ("Block.h").

```
// Title: Block.h

#ifndef BLOCK_H
    #define BLOCK_H      // inclusion guard

    #include <vector>    // rqd. for vector (below)
    using namespace std;
    ...
#endif
```

Step 6: Now to display the object construction statements that were printed through the use of "cout" statements in the Console window of the ControlEng Win32 Console Application, `AfxMessageBox()` calls may be used as shown in the following code excerpt in the CSystemModel constructor.

```
// Message Box
CString sMsg;             // main msg string
CString sMsgTemp;         // temp msg string
UINT nType = MB_OK;       // style of msg. box
UINT nIDhelp = 0;         // help context ID for the msg.

sMsgTemp.Format("\n CSystemModel::CSystemModel()\n");
sMsg += sMsgTemp;
AfxMessageBox(sMsg, nType, nIDhelp);
```

Alternatively, if a one-line statement is preferred, without the need to declare additional variables, then the following may be used instead: `AfxMessageBox("\n CSystemModel:: CSystemModel()\n,"` `MB_OK, 0)`.

Now when the code is built and run, a message box appears indicating that a CSystemModel object has been constructed, including all its contained member objects, i.e., a list of CBlock pointers and a list of CConnection pointers. CBlock contains a CBlockShape object and a vector of CPort pointers, and CConnection contains pointers to CPort and CSignal, as is reflected by the class association diagram shown in Figure 3.1. Once the construction is shown to work as expected, the `AfxMessageBox()` calls may be commented out.

3.3   MODIFYING PROGRAM STRUCTURE FOR BLOCK CONSTRUCTION

The process of constructing a block and placing it into the block list involves four evolving stages: (1) preliminary changes to the existing code, (2) introduction of a new `CBlock()` constructor, (3) adding a constructed block to the block list, and (4) checking that all objects were constructed properly. The developer may need to be patient in implementing the changes required when working through these steps: some of the changes become redundant by the end of the process, e.g., when progressing from a `CBlock()` constructor that takes no arguments, to one that takes three arguments. The final code provided presents the end result, but the process of arriving at that result is still insightful and worth pursuing.

3.3.1   PRELIMINARY CHANGES

The preliminary changes that need to be made to the existing code involve (1) the CSystemModel class, (2) the block construction code, and (3) the CBlock class. The changes are at times somewhat laborious, but the end result is an easier-to-understand and easier-to-work-with structure.

3.3.1.1   Class CSystemModel

The first change to be made concerns the CSystemModel class. Comment out the block construction that already exists in the `CSystemModel()` constructor to leave only initialization of the following: "m_strModelName", "t_start", and "t_stop" as shown in the following. This involves changing the character array, "model_name", to the CString variable "m_strModelName".

In addition, the `GetName()` member function should also be changed to a constant function with prototype, `CString GetModelName(void) const`, as shown in the following to return the CString member variable, "m_strModelName". Finally, a new function can be added with the prototype, void SetModelName(CString name), as shown, to set the member variable.

```
CSystemModel::CSystemModel(void)
{
    m_strModelName = "model_name";
    t_start = 0.0;                              // sim start time
    t_stop = 10.0;
}

CString CSystemModel::GetModelName(void) const
{
    return m_strModelName;
}

void CSystemModel::SetModelName(CString name)
{
    m_strModelName = name;
}
```

Later in the development, more changes will be made to the CSystemModel class and new member variables added when required.

3.3.1.2   Block Construction Code

Blocks are added to the system model by either clicking a Common Blocks toolbar button or the Add All Blocks button of the Block Library Dialog window. The event-handler functions for the toolbar buttons were introduced in the previous chapter, e.g., CDiagramEngDoc::OnBlockCts Derivative(). The event-handler function for the Add All Blocks button is CBlockLibDlg:: OnBlocklibdlgBtnAddallblocks(). All the event-handler functions here call ConstructBlock(e_block_type) (upon a pointer-to-CDiagramEngDoc), where the ConstructBlock() function has a *switch* statement involving particular block construction calls. The first case of the *switch* statement concerns the construction of a Constant block via the to-be-introduced function, ConstructConstantBlock().

Hence, add a public member function to the CDiagramEngDoc class with the prototype, void CDiagramEngDoc::ConstructConstantBlock(void), and call this function from within the *switch* statement of the ConstructBlock() function as shown in bold in the following. The calls were already in place from the previous chapter, but were commented out, since the block-construction functions had not been added to the project.

```
int CDiagramEngDoc::ConstructBlock(EBlockType e_block_type)
{
    ...
    switch(e_block_type)
    {
    case eConstBlock:
        ConstructConstantBlock();
        break;
    ...
    case eTransferFnBlock:
        //ConstructTransferFnBlock();
        break;

    default:
        // Inform user of switch default
        sMsg.Format("\n CDiagramEngDoc::ConstructBlock(): switch
          default\n\n");
```

```
            AfxMessageBox(sMsg, nType, nIDhelp);
            break;
    }

    return 0;    // return int for error checking
}
```

Edit the `CDiagramEngDoc::ConstructConstantBlock()` function as shown in the following, to setup constructor arguments in preparation to construct a Constant block. The arguments are the address of the parent, CSystemModel object of the block, the CPoint, block position, "block_posn", and the EBlockShape, block shape, "e_blk_shape". The CSystemModel will be obtained shortly using a function named `GetSystemModel()`, the block position can be set to (1,1), and the block shape is "e_rectangle".

```
void CDiagramEngDoc::ConstructConstantBlock()
{
    // NOTE
    // CConstantBlock : public CBlock
    // CBlock contains a m_BlockShape obj. of type CBlockShape
    // Hence rqe. constructor args for CConstantBlock and CBlock.

    CPoint block_posn;

    //AfxMessageBox("\n CDiagramEngDoc::ConstructConstantBlock()\n",
      MB_OK, 0);

    // Constructor args. for CBlock
    block_posn.x = 1;
    block_posn.y = 1;
    // AssignBlockPosition(block_posn);

    // Constructor args. for CBlockShape
    EBlockShape e_block_shape = e_rectangle;

    // Construct a new constant block
    //CBlock *p_block = new CConstantBlock();
    CBlock *p_block = new CConstantBlock(&(GetSystemModel()), block_posn,
      e_block_shape);

    // Add the new block to the system model block list.
    GetSystemModel().GetBlockList().push_back(p_block);
}
```

3.3.1.3 Class CBlock

Edit the original `CBlock()` constructor and comment out the Port construction, as this will be done elsewhere, to leave only initialization of the following arguments: "m_strBlockName" and "m_pSubSystemModel". The developer will notice that "block_name", used in the original Win32 Console application code, is changed to "m_strBlockName", i.e., the declaration "char *block_name" is now "CString m_strBlockName". The deletion of the "block_name" character array in the destructor can now also be removed. In addition, make the following changes:

1. Remove the "double block_position [2]" member declaration in the CBlock class, and replace this with "CPoint m_ptBlockPosition" by adding a new private member variable.
2. Remove the "double geometry [3]" member variable statement in the CBlockShape class, and replace this with two new member variables: "double m_dBlockWidth" and "EBlockDirection m_eBlockDirection". Modify the "Block.h" header file and change "EDirection" to "EBlockDirection" for clarity, as shown in the following.

```
// Title: Block.h

#ifndef BLOCK_H
    #define BLOCK_H                     // inclusion guard

    #include <vector>                   // rqd. for vector (below)
    using namespace std;

    // User defined consts/vars.
    const double PI = 3.14159265359;  // pi in radians (rounded)

    // User defined types
    enum EBlockShape {e_ellipse, e_rectangle, e_triangle}; // block
      shapes
    enum EBlockDirection {e_left, e_right, e_up, e_down};  // block
      direction (triangle specific)
    enum EIntegrationMethod {e_Euler, e_RungeKutta};        // integration
      schemes, (Euler) 1st and (RK) 4th order
    enum EMultAction {e_element_wise, e_mat_x_input, e_input_x_mat,
      e_divide};                   // multiplication action, form and order
    enum EOutputDataFormat {e_dep_var, e_dep_and_indep_var};  // form of
      output: dependent and independent vars
    enum EPortID {e_left_arrow, e_up_arrow, e_right_arrow, e_down_arrow};
      // left '<', up '^', right '>', and, down 'v'
    enum ESignalForm {e_sine, e_cosine, e_square, e_sawtooth, e_random};
      // form of signal/wave
    enum EUnits {e_m, e_s, e_kg, e_radians, e_hertz, e_radians_per_sec};
      // units

    // BlockShape
    class CBlockShape
    {
    public:
        void SetBlockWidth(double blk_width);
        double GetBlockHeight(void) const;
        void SetBlockHeight(double blk_height);
        EBlockDirection GetBlockDirection() const;
        double GetBlockWidth() const;
        EBlockShape GetBlockShapeType() const;
        void SetBlockShapeType(EBlockShape e_blk_shape);
        CBlockShape(void);
        ~CBlockShape(void);

    private:
        double m_dBlockHeight;
        double m_dBlockWidth;
        EBlockDirection m_eBlockDirection;
        EBlockShape m_eBlockShape;
    };
    ...

    // Block
    class CSystemModel; // predefining CSystemModel as it's rqd. by
      CBlock, additionally CSystemModel rqes. CBlock
    class CBlock
    {
    public:
        CBlock(void);
        ~CBlock(void);
```

```
        // Accessor methods
        char* GetName(void);

    private:
        CPoint m_ptBlockPosition;           // ordered pair denoting
            (x,y) location of CofM of block
        CString m_strBlockName;             // block name
        CBlockShape m_BlockShape;           // member obj of type
            CBlockShape
        vector<CPort*> m_vecInputPorts;     // vector of ptrs to CPort
        vector<CPort*> m_vecOutputPorts;    // vector of ptrs to CPort
        CSystemModel *m_pParentSystemModel; // ptr to parent system model
        CSystemModel *m_pSubSystemModel;    // ptr = NULL => no contained
            system/sub model, ptr != NULL => system model
    };
    ...

#endif
```

3.3.2 Introduce a New CBlock Constructor

In the particular block construction functions, e.g., `ConstructConstantBlock()` given earlier, a three-argument constructor is called, and the base CBlock class constructor is to be called via member initialization passing in the same three arguments. Hence, add a new constructor function to the CBlock class with the following prototype, `CBlock::CBlock(CSystemModel *pParentSystemModel, CPoint blk_posn, EBlockShape e_blk_shape)` and member initialization: `m_ptBlockPosition(blk_posn)`. The body of the constructor has the same initialization as the original `CBlock()` constructor (i.e., initialization of "m_strBlockName" and "m_pSubSystemModel") with the addition of the lines shown in bold in the following.

   Note that the `CBlockShape::SetBlockShapeType()` member function of class CBlockShape is being called by the CBlock constructor to initialize the contained "m_BlockShape" object's "m_eBlockShape" variable. The EBlockDirection "m_eBlockDirection" variable is set to a default "e_right" value in the `CBlockShape()` constructor and is not passed as a constructor argument, as shown in the code that follows.

```
CBlock::CBlock(CSystemModel *pParentSystemModel, CPoint blk_posn,
  EBlockShape e_blk_shape):
m_ptBlockPosition(blk_posn)
{
    // Init
    //block_name = new char[32];
    //strcpy(block_name, "actual_block_name");
    m_BlockShape.SetBlockShapeType(e_blk_shape);   // block shape:
      ellipse, rectangle, triangle
    m_strBlockName = "actual_block_name";
    m_pParentSystemModel = pParentSystemModel;     // ptr to parent
      system model.
    m_pSubSystemModel = NULL; // ptr to a possibly CONTAINED SUB MODEL:
      ptr = NULL => no contained system model, ptr = !NULL => system
      model
    pen_color = RGB(0,0,255);  // red = RGB(255,0,0), green = RGB(0,255,0),
      blue = RGB(0,0,255), Black = RGB(0,0,0), White = (255,255,255)
    pen_width = 1;             // 1 = v. thin, 8 = thin, 16 = medium, 24 =
      thick, 32 = v. thick. (mults. of 8)
}
```

```
CBlockShape::CBlockShape(void)
{
    m_eBlockDirection = e_right;        // default direc is to the right.
    m_dBlockWidth = (GetDocumentGlobalFn()->GetDeltaLength())*2.0;
    m_dBlockHeight = m_dBlockWidth;
}
```

The developer will have noticed the call to set the block shape type in the CBlock() constructor given earlier. Hence, add a public member function to the CBlockShape class with the prototype, void CBlockShape::SetBlockShapeType(EBlockShape e_blk_shape), and edit it as shown.

```
void CBlockShape::SetBlockShapeType(EBlockShape e_blk_shape)
{
    m_eBlockShape = e_blk_shape;
}
```

Now add a new constructor function to the CConstantBlock class with prototype, CConstantBlock::CConstantBlock(CSystemModel *pParentSystemModel, CPoint blk_posn, EBlockShape e_blk_shape), and member initialization: CBlock(pParentSystemModel, blk_posn, e_blk_shape), as shown in the following code (the constructor has an empty body for now).

```
CConstantBlock::CConstantBlock(CSystemModel *pParentSystemModel, CPoint
  blk_posn, EBlockShape e_blk_shape):
CBlock(pParentSystemModel, blk_posn, e_blk_shape)
{
    // empty for now
}
```

For completeness, add a public constant accessor method to the CBlock class to retrieve a pointer to the parent system model to which the block belongs, with the following prototype: CSystemModel *CBlock::GetParentSystemModel(void) const. Edit the code as shown in the following. This function is not used until later in the project, but it is useful to keep in mind that a block can "know" its parent system model.

```
CSystemModel* CBlock::GetParentSystemModel() const
{
    // Return the parent system model that contains the list of blocks
      and connections
    return m_pParentSystemModel;
}
```

Finally, a new Constant block can be constructed from within the CDiagramEngDoc:: ConstructConstantBlock() function as introduced earlier, by the line:

```
CBlock *p_block = new CConstantBlock(&(GetSystemModel()), block_posn,
  e_block_shape);
```

3.3.3 ADD A CONSTRUCTED BLOCK TO THE BLOCK LIST

Now that the Constant block has been constructed, it needs to be added to the system model's block list in the ConstructConstantBlock() function, by using two function calls: GetSystemModel() followed by GetBlockList().

Hence, add a public member function to the CDiagramEngDoc class to get the contained system model object with prototype, CSystemModel &CDiagramEngDoc:: GetSystemModel(void). Note that a reference-to-CSystemModel is being returned and make sure the header file has the appropriate reference (&) notation. Edit the code as shown in the following.

```
CSystemModel &CDiagramEngDoc::GetSystemModel()
{
    return m_SystemModel;
}
```

Now add a public member function to the CSystemModel class to get the contained block list, with prototype, list<CBlock*> &GetBlockList(void), and edit the code as shown in the following. The ClassWizard indicates that "Template declarations or definitions cannot be added", so use "int &" as the return type, then manually change the source and header files to have the following definition: list<CBlock*> &GetBlockList(void).

```
list<CBlock*>& CSystemModel::GetBlockList()
{
    return m_lstBlock;
}
```

Now these two functions may be successively called to retrieve the system model and then the model's block list, before adding the block to the end of the list, as shown in bold in the following code.

```
void CDiagramEngDoc::ConstructConstantBlock()
{
    // NOTE
    // CConstantBlock : public CBlock
    // CBlock contains a m_BlockShape obj. of type CBlockShape
    // Hence rqe. constructor args for CConstantBlock and CBlock.

    CPoint block_posn;

    //AfxMessageBox("\n CDiagramEngDoc::ConstructConstantBlock()\n",
      MB_OK, 0);

    // Constructor args. for CBlock
    AssignBlockPosition(block_posn);

    // Constructor args. for CBlockShape
    EBlockShape e_block_shape = e_rectangle;

    // Construct a new constant block
    //CBlock *p_block = new CConstantBlock();
    CBlock *p_block = new CConstantBlock(&(GetSystemModel()), block_posn,
      e_block_shape);

    // Add the new block to the system model block list.
    GetSystemModel().GetBlockList().push_back(p_block);
}
```

Build and run the project: there will likely be a bug on program termination. Hence, do the following:

- Make the CBlock() destructor virtual, i.e., write virtual ~CBlock(); in the "Block.h" file, as upon destruction, a derived block object, e.g., CConstantBlock is being destroyed, not a CBlock object.
- Check the original ~CBlock() destructor, and make sure that what is being destroyed was actually constructed in the newly created CBlock(CSystemModel *pParentSystemModel, CPoint blk_posn, EBlockShape e_blk_shape) constructor taking three arguments. If something was omitted, then add all things that were constructed in the original CBlock() constructor to the new constructor taking three arguments (this was indicated earlier and should not actually be a problem here).

Now upon running the code, there should be no erroneous operation, but the object construction needs to be checked to be certain.

3.3.4 CHECK OBJECT CONSTRUCTION

A function now needs to be written to check that all constructed objects were done so properly, and this should be reported in a simple message box (for now). Hence, add a new public member function to the CDiagramEngDoc class with the prototype, void CDiagramEngDoc::CheckSystemModel(void), and edit the code as follows.

```
void CDiagramEngDoc::CheckSystemModel()
{
    int n_in_ports = 0;
    int n_out_ports = 0;

    // -- Message box vars.
    CString sMsg;           // main msg string
    CString sMsgTemp;       // temp msg string
    UINT nType = MB_OK;     // style of msg. box
    UINT nIDhelp = 0;       // help context ID for the msg.

    sMsgTemp.Format("\n CDiagramEngDoc::CheckSystemModel()\n");
    sMsg += sMsgTemp;

    // -- Block list vars.
    list<CBlock*> blk_list;
    list<CBlock*>::iterator it_blk;   // iterator for list of CBlock-ptrs

    blk_list = GetSystemModel().GetBlockList();

    // -- Check Block List
    for(it_blk = blk_list.begin(); it_blk != blk_list.end(); it_blk++)
    {
        sMsgTemp.Format("%s:",(*it_blk)->GetBlockName());
        sMsg += sMsgTemp;

        // Get the vectors of input and output ports and determine their
          sizes.
        //n_in_ports = (*it_blk)->GetVectorOfInputPorts().size();
        //n_out_ports = (*it_blk)->GetVectorOfOutputPorts().size();

        //sMsgTemp.Format(" n_in_ports = %d, n_out_ports = %d\n",
          n_in_ports, n_out_ports);
        //sMsg += sMsgTemp;
    }
    AfxMessageBox(sMsg, nType, nIDhelp);
}
```

The developer will notice the call to GetBlockName() given earlier. Hence, change the CBlock member function with prototype, char *CBlock::GetName(void), to the constant member function with prototype, CString CBlock::GetBlockName() const, to make it clear that it is the block name, "m_strBlockName" of type CString, that is being retrieved. For completeness, add a new public member function to the CBlock class with the prototype, void CBlock::SetBlockName(CString blk_name), and set the CBlock member variable "m_strBlockName" to the incoming argument as follows.

```
void CBlock::SetBlockName(CString blk_name)
{
    m_strBlockName = blk_name;
}
```

Now, in the CConstantBlock() constructor, call SetBlockName ("constant_block") in the body of the code: this sets the name of the CConstantBlock object to "constant_block", so identification of it in the block list is possible.

```
CConstantBlock::CConstantBlock(CSystemModel *pParentSystemModel, CPoint
  blk_posn, EBlockShape e_blk_shape):
CBlock(pParentSystemModel, blk_posn, e_blk_shape)
{
    SetBlockName("constant_block");
}
```

Now upon repeated selection of the Constant Block button on the Common Blocks toolbar, additional CConstantBlock objects will be added to the block list. This will then be evident through the message box output displayed by the CheckSystemModel() function.

In addition, make the function call to CDiagramEngDoc::CheckSystemModel() from within the CDiagramEngDoc::ConstructBlock(), directly after the *switch* statement: this reduces the need to place the CheckSystemModel() function in every individual block construction function.

Finally, add the statement SetModifiedFlag(TRUE) just after the *switch* statement in the CDiagramEngDoc::ConstructBlock() function: this causes the document to be marked as having been modified and prompts the user to save the document upon closing or exiting the application. This will be discussed in more depth in Chapter 25.

3.4 DRAWING OF PRIMITIVE BLOCK SHAPES

The drawing of blocks stored in the block list involves several steps: (1) general drawing functionality, (2) drawing an ellipse block, (3) drawing a rectangle block, (4) drawing a triangle block, (5) automatic assignment of block position, (6) construction of a Gain block, and (7) construction of a Sum block. The construction of a rectangular Constant block was already performed in the previous section.

3.4.1 General Drawing Functionality

The general drawing functionality to be provided here involves augmenting the CDiagramEngView::OnDraw() method, adding a DrawSystemModel() method to the CSystemModel class and adding a DrawBlock() method to the CBlock class.

Edit the CDiagramEngView::OnDraw() function to retrieve the system model using GetSystemModel() and then draw the system model by calling DrawSystemModel() as shown in bold in the following.

```
void CDiagramEngView::OnDraw(CDC* pDC)
{
    CDiagramEngDoc* pDoc = GetDocument();
    ASSERT_VALID(pDoc);
    // TODO: add draw code for native data here

    // Draw the system model
    pDoc->GetSystemModel().DrawSystemModel(pDC);
}
```

Now add a new public member function to the CSystemModel class with the prototype: void CSystemModel::DrawSystemModel(CDC *pDC). Edit the function as shown in the following to iterate through the block list calling DrawBlock() on the pointer-to-CBlock.

```
void CSystemModel::DrawSystemModel(CDC *pDC)
{
    // Iterates through the SystemModel lists drawing the stored entities.

    // -- Draw Blocks
    list<CBlock*>::iterator it_blk;      // local iterator
    list<CBlock*> blk_list;              // local block list

    blk_list = GetBlockList();

    // Iterate through the list
    for(it_blk = blk_list.begin(); it_blk != blk_list.end(); it_blk++)
    {
        (*it_blk)->DrawBlock(pDC);       // DrawBlock() called on the
        ptr-to-CBlock
    }
    // -- Draw Connections (to do)
    /*list<CConnection*>::iterator it_con; // local iterator
    list<CConnection*> con_list;  // local connection list

    con_list = GetConnectionList();

    // Iterate through the list
    for(it_con = con_list.begin(); it_con != con_list.end(); it_con++)
    {
    (*it_con)->DrawConnection(pDC);
    }
    */
}
```

Now, add a new public member function to the CBlock class with the prototype: void CBlock::DrawBlock(CDC *pDC). This function will be made virtual and needs to be overridden later, but for now edit it as follows. Its contents will be commented out later.

```
void CBlock::DrawBlock(CDC *pDC)
{
    // WARNING! THIS FN WILL BE MADE VIRTUAL AND IS TO BE OVERRIDDEN BY
      ALL DERIVED CLASSES THAT DRAW OBJS.

    EBlockShape e_blk_shape; // enum block shape: ellipse, rectangle,
      triangle.

    //AfxMessageBox("\n CBlock::DrawBlock()\n", MB_OK, 0);

    // Get the EBlockShape of the current block via the member obj.
      CBlockShape m_BlockShape;
    e_blk_shape = m_BlockShape.GetBlockShapeType();

    switch(e_blk_shape)
    {
    case e_ellipse:
        DrawEllipseBlock(pDC);
        break;

    case e_rectangle:
        DrawRectangleBlock(pDC);
        break;
```

```
      case e_triangle:
         DrawTriangleBlock(pDC);
         break;

      default:
         // Inform user of switch default
         DrawRectangleBlock(pDC);
         //AfxMessageBox("\n CBlock::DrawBlock(), switch(e_blk_shape)
           default case\n", MB_OK, 0);
         break;
      }// end switch
}
```

The developer will notice the call to GetBlockShapeType() in the DrawBlock() function given earlier. Hence, add a public constant member function to the CBlockShape class with the prototype: EBlockShape CBlockShape::GetBlockShapeType(void) const. Edit this function as follows.

```
EBlockShape CBlockShape::GetBlockShapeType() const
{
    return m_eBlockShape;
}
```

3.4.2 DRAWING AN ELLIPSE BLOCK

To draw an Ellipse block, used in the drawing of a Sum block, add a new public member function to the CBlock class with prototype: void CBlock::DrawEllipseBlock(CDC *pDC). Edit the function as follows.

```
void CBlock::DrawEllipseBlock(CDC *pDC)
{
    // Note: pDC is a ptr to the device context of "Class Device Context"
      (CDC)
    double l_width = m_BlockShape.GetBlockWidth();
    CPoint bottom_right;
    CPoint top_left;

    // Create a pen
    CPen lpen(PS_SOLID, m_iPenWidth, m_iPenColor);

    // Set the new pen as the drawing obj.
    CPen *pOldPen = pDC->SelectObject(&lpen);

    // Draw the ellipse
    top_left.x = (int)(m_ptBlockPosition.x - l_width*0.5);
    top_left.y = (int)(m_ptBlockPosition.y - l_width*0.5);
    bottom_right.x = (int)(m_ptBlockPosition.x + l_width*0.5);
    bottom_right.y = (int)(m_ptBlockPosition.y + l_width*0.5);
    pDC->Ellipse(top_left.x, top_left.y, bottom_right.x, bottom_right.y);

    // Reset the prev. pen
    pDC->SelectObject(pOldPen);
}
```

The developer will notice that the block width is obtained by a call to GetBlockWidth(). Hence, add a public constant member function to the CBlockShape class, with the prototype: double CBlockShape::GetBlockWidth(void) const. Edit the function as shown in the following.

```
double CBlockShape::GetBlockWidth() const
{
    return m_dBlockWidth;
}
```

The developer will also see that a pen is created using the statement: CPen lpen(PS_SOLID, m_iPenWidth, m_iPenColor). Because "m_iPenWidth" and "m_iPenColor" are new integer variables, they must be added (privately) to the CBlock class. Default initialization of the "m_iPenWidth" and "m_iPenColor" member variables can be done in the CBlock constructor, i.e., "m_iPenWidth = 1", and "m_iPenColor = RGB(0,0,255)".

In addition, the following constant functions need to be added to the CBlock class, int GetPenWidth() const and int GetPenColor() const, to return the "m_iPenWidth" and "m_iPenColor" variable values, respectively. Edit these functions as follows.

```
int CBlock::GetPenWidth() const
{
    return m_iPenWidth;
}
int CBlock::GetPenColor() const
{
    return m_iPenColor;
}
```

Note that as "m_iPenWidth" and "m_iPenColor" are both member variables of CBlock, then GetPenWidth() and GetPenColor() do not need to be called prior to the pen creation statement given earlier, since DrawEllipseBlock() is itself a member function of the CBlock class: these accessor functions are added for possible future use.

Note also that the new pen is set as the drawing object as follows, i.e., CPen *pOldPen = pDC->SelectObject(&lpen). The Microsoft Developer Network (MSDN) Library Help feature indicates that the return type of the SelectObject() function is a "pointer to the object being replaced" [2]: i.e., "pOldPen" holds a pointer to the previous pen. Later, after all drawing is completed using the new "lpen" object, the old pen is restored through the call: pDC->SelectObject(pOldPen).

3.4.3 Drawing a Rectangle Block

The rectangle shape is most commonly used in block drawing, since all but the Sum and Gain blocks are rectangular. Add a new public member function to the CBlock class with prototype: void CBlock::DrawRectangleBlock(CDC *pDC). Edit this function as shown.

```
void CBlock::DrawRectangleBlock(CDC *pDC)
{
    // Note: pDC is a ptr to the device context of "Class Device Context"
      (CDC)
    CPoint top_left;       // top left cnr. of rectangle
    CPoint top_right;      // top right cnr. of rectangle
    CPoint bottom_right;   // bottom right cnr. of rectangle
    CPoint bottom_left;    // bottom left cnr. of rectangle
    double l_width = m_BlockShape.GetBlockWidth();

    // Assign vals to the cnr. pts.
    top_left.x = m_ptBlockPosition.x - l_width*0.5;
    top_left.y = m_ptBlockPosition.y - l_width*0.5;
    top_right.x = m_ptBlockPosition.x + l_width*0.5;
```

```
top_right.y = m_ptBlockPosition.y - l_width*0.5;
bottom_right.x = m_ptBlockPosition.x + l_width*0.5;
bottom_right.y = m_ptBlockPosition.y + l_width*0.5;
bottom_left.x = m_ptBlockPosition.x - l_width*0.5;
bottom_left.y = m_ptBlockPosition.y + l_width*0.5;

// Create a pen
CPen lpen(PS_SOLID, pen_width, pen_color);

// Set the new pen as the drawing obj.
CPen *pOldPen = pDC->SelectObject(&lpen);

// Draw the rectangle (clockwise)
pDC->MoveTo(top_left);
pDC->LineTo(top_right);
pDC->LineTo(bottom_right);
pDC->LineTobottom_left);
pDC->LineTo(top_left);

// Reset the prev. pen
pDC->SelectObject(pOldPen);
}
```

3.4.4 DRAWING A TRIANGLE BLOCK

The triangle shape is used for the display of only the triangular Gain block. Add a new public member function to the CBlock class with the prototype: void CBlock::DrawTriangleBlock(CDC *pDC). Edit the code as shown in the following to draw the triangle using the block's position, "m_ptBlockPosition", and the direction, "e_triangle_direction", in which the block is oriented.

```
void CBlock::DrawTriangleBlock(CDC *pDC)
{
    // Note: pDC is a ptr to the device context of "Class Device Context"
      (CDC)
    CPoint A;      // vertex A of the equilateral triangle.
    CPoint B;      // vertex B of the equilateral triangle that points in
      the direc of m_eBlockDirection.
    CPoint C;      // vertex C of the equilateral triangle.
    double d;      // opp side length of a subtriangle with hypotenuse h,
      and base length l_width*0.5.
    double h;      // hypotenuse of a subtriangle with opp. side length
      d, and base length l_width*0.5.
    double length; // length of side of triangle
    double width = m_BlockShape.GetBlockWidth(); // equilateral triangle
      side length
    EBlockDirection e_triangle_direc = m_BlockShape.GetBlockDirection();
      // direction of vertex B

    // Assign vals to subtriangle paras d and h.
    length = 1.0*width;        // length of side of triangle
    d = length*0.2887;         // d = (length*0.5)*tan(30)
    h = length*0.5773;         // h = (length*0.5)*(1/cos(30))

    // Get A, B, and C vertices given triangle block direc.
    switch(e_triangle_direc)
    {
    case e_left:    // vertex B pts. to the left
        A.x = m_ptBlockPosition.x + d;
        A.y = m_ptBlockPosition.y + length*0.5;
```

```
        B.x = m_ptBlockPosition.x - h;
        B.y = m_ptBlockPosition.y;
        C.x = m_ptBlockPosition.x + d;
        C.y = m_ptBlockPosition.y - length*0.5;
        break;
    case e_up:        // vertex B pts. up
        A.x = m_ptBlockPosition.x - length*0.5;
        A.y = m_ptBlockPosition.y + d;
        B.x = m_ptBlockPosition.x;
        B.y = m_ptBlockPosition.y - h;
        C.x = m_ptBlockPosition.x + length*0.5;
        C.y = m_ptBlockPosition.y + d;
        break;
    case e_right:  // vertex B pts. to the right
        A.x = m_ptBlockPosition.x - d;
        A.y = m_ptBlockPosition.y - length*0.5;
        B.x = m_ptBlockPosition.x + h;
        B.y = m_ptBlockPosition.y;
        C.x = m_ptBlockPosition.x - d;
        C.y = m_ptBlockPosition.y + length*0.5;
        break;
    case e_down:    // vertex B pts. down
        A.x = m_ptBlockPosition.x + length*0.5;
        A.y = m_ptBlockPosition.y - d;
        B.x = m_ptBlockPosition.x;
        B.y = m_ptBlockPosition.y + h;
        C.x = m_ptBlockPosition.x - length*0.5;
        C.y = m_ptBlockPosition.y - d;
        break;
    default:          // assign same values as for e_right assuming default
      direc. vertex B pointing to the right.
        A.x = m_ptBlockPosition.x - d;
        A.y = m_ptBlockPosition.y - length*0.5;
        B.x = m_ptBlockPosition.x + h;
        B.y = m_ptBlockPosition.y;
        C.x = m_ptBlockPosition.x - d;
        C.y = m_ptBlockPosition.y + length*0.5;
        break;
    }// end switch

    // Create a pen
    CPen lpen(PS_SOLID, pen_width, pen_color);

    // Set the new pen as the drawing obj.
    CPen *pOldPen = pDC->SelectObject(&lpen);

    // Draw the triangle (A to B to C)
    pDC->MoveTo(A);
    pDC->LineTo(B);
    pDC->LineTo(C);
    pDC->LineTo(A);

    // Reset the prev. pen
    pDC->SelectObject(pOldPen);
}
```

Figure 3.2 shows an equilateral triangle representing the Gain block, with vertices, *A*, *B*, and *C*, where vertex *B* points in the direction in which the block is oriented: here to the right. The center

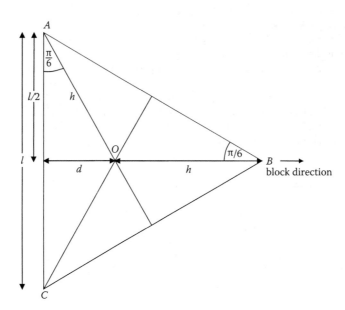

FIGURE 3.2   A triangle block of side length, l, where h, is the hypotenuse of a subtriangle, with opposite side length d, and base length, $l/2$.

of the block, denoted O, defining the block's position, "m_ptBlockPosition", is considered to be that where the three side bisectors intersect. The triangle has a side length, l, where h is the hypotenuse of a subtriangle, with opposite side length d, and base length $l/2$. The "length", "d", and "h" arguments in the code correspond to l, d, and h in Figure 3.2, respectively, where l is the default block width, $d = (l/2)\tan(\pi/6)$ and $h = l/2 \cos(\pi/6)$.

The developer will also notice the call to GetBlockDirection() to get the direction in which the triangle block is facing. Hence, add a new public constant member function to the CBlockShape class, with prototype: EBlockDirection CBlockShape::GetBlockDirection(void) const. Edit this function as follows.

```
EBlockDirection CBlockShape::GetBlockDirection() const
{
    return m_eBlockDirection;
}
```

Finally, add the call UpdateAllViews(NULL) to the CDiagramEngDoc::Construct Block() function after the CheckSystemModel() call. This will automatically call CDiagramEngView::OnDraw(), which calls CSystemModel::DrawSystemModel() to draw the blocks on the palette.

3.4.5 Automatic Assignment of Block Position

To perform automatic placement of blocks on the palette, the block width, "m_dBlockWidth", is required to set the block position, "m_ptBlockPosition". However, as the variable "m_dBlockWidth", is a member of the CBlockShape class, which itself is contained in the CBlock class, then it cannot be available prior to the block's very own construction (this is a "chicken-egg" problem). Hence, an explicit assignment of the block width is required in the CBlockShape() constructor body.

```
CBlockShape::CBlockShape(void)
{
    m_eBlockDirection = e_right;      // default direc is to the right.
```

```
    m_dBlockWidth = (GetDocumentGlobalFn()->GetDeltaLength())*2.0;
    m_dBlockHeight = m_dBlockWidth;
}
```

Here, a call to GetDocumentGlobalFn() is made followed by GetDeltaLength() to get the standard default length increment, "m_dDeltaLength", of the CDiagramEngDoc class used to gauge sizes of GUI elements and user-interaction processes. Hence, add a private double member variable to the CDiagramEngDoc class with name, "m_dDeltaLength", and initialize it in the CDiagramEngDoc constructor as shown in the following.

```
CDiagramEngDoc::CDiagramEngDoc()
{
    // TODO: add one-time construction code here

    // DiagramEng (start)
    m_dDeltaLength = 50.0;
    // DiagramEng (end)
}
```

Now add a public constant accessor method to the CDiagramEngDoc class with the prototype, double CDiagramEngDoc::GetDeltaLength(void) const, and edit it as shown in the following to simply return the member variable.

```
double CDiagramEngDoc::GetDeltaLength() const
{
    return m_dDeltaLength;
}
```

Since GetDocumentGlobalFn() returns a pointer-to-CDiagramEngDoc, upon which the GetDeltaLength() function is called, include the "DiagramEngDoc.h" header file beneath the inclusion of the "SystemModel.h" header file, near the top of "Block.cpp", i.e., #include "DiagramEngDoc.h".

Finally, to automatically assign the block position, add a public member function to the CDiagramEngDoc class with the prototype, void CDiagramEngDoc::AssignBlockPosition (CPoint &block_posn), and edit the code as follows.

```
void CDiagramEngDoc::AssignBlockPosition(CPoint &block_posn)
{
    int n_blocks;
    int n_blks_in_row = 10;
double height = 2.0*m_dDeltaLength;
    double width = 2.0*m_dDeltaLength;
    double left_spacing = 0.2*width;
    double blk_spacing = 0.2*width;
    double top_spacing = 0.2*width;

    // Assign block_posn
    n_blocks = GetSystemModel().GetBlockList().size();

    block_posn.x = left_spacing + (n_blocks%n_blks_in_row)*(width +
      blk_spacing) + 0.5*width;      // CofM of block at width*0.5
    block_posn.y = top_spacing + (n_blocks/n_blks_in_row)*(height +
      blk_spacing) + 0.5*height;     // CofM of block at height*0.5
}
```

This `AssignBlockPosition()` function call should be made in all block construction functions that require it in a similar manner to its use in the `ConstructConstantBlock()` function.

3.5 COMPLETING BLOCK CONSTRUCTION

The ellipse, rectangle and triangle block-shape types are used, e.g., in the drawing of Sum, Constant, and Gain blocks, respectively. In an earlier section, the construction of a Constant block was performed: here, block construction is completed, first for the triangular Gain block and then for the elliptical Sum block, followed by all the remaining blocks. The primitive block shapes may be drawn on the palette, and, in the following section, the detailed block graphics will be displayed.

3.5.1 CONSTRUCTION OF A GAIN BLOCK

To construct a Gain block, the `CDiagramEngDoc::ConstructGainBlock()` function is to be completed and then called from within the `CDiagramEngDoc::ConstructBlock()` method. In addition, as for the construction of the Constant block introduced earlier, a new three-argument constructor function is required whose arguments completely define the CBlock-derived block.

First, add a public member function to the CDiagramEngDoc class with prototype, void `CDiagramEngDoc::ConstructGainBlock(void)`, and edit the function as follows.

```
void CDiagramEngDoc::ConstructGainBlock()
{
    CPoint block_posn;

    //AfxMessageBox("\n CDiagramEngDoc::ConstructGainBlock()\n", MB_OK, 0);

    // Constructor args. for CBlock
    AssignBlockPosition(block_posn);

    // Constructor args. for CBlockShape
    EBlockShape e_block_shape = e_triangle;

    // Construct a new constant block
    //CBlock *p_block = new CGainBlock();
    CBlock *p_block = new CGainBlock(&(GetSystemModel()), block_posn,
      e_block_shape);

    // Add the new block to the system model block list.
    GetSystemModel().GetBlockList().push_back(p_block);
}
```

Now, `ConstructGainBlock()` needs to be called from within the *switch* statement inside the function `CDiagramEngDoc::ConstructBlock()`, in a similar manner to `ConstructConstantBlock()`: i.e., uncomment the appropriate line of code to allow the call.

Finally, add a new constructor function to the CGainBlock class with prototype, `CGainBlock(CSystemModel *pParentSystemModel, CPoint blk_posn, EBlockShape e_blk_shape)`, and member initialization: `CBlock(pParentSystemModel, blk_posn, e_blk_shape)`. Add the statement, `SetBlockName("gain_block")`, within the constructor, as shown in the following.

```
CGainBlock::CGainBlock(CSystemModel *pParentSystemModel, CPoint blk_posn,
  EBlockShape e_blk_shape):
CBlock(pParentSystemModel, blk_posn, e_blk_shape)
{
    SetBlockName("gain_block");
}
```

3.5.2 CONSTRUCTION OF A SUM BLOCK

To construct a Sum block, the CDiagramEngDoc::ConstructSumBlock() function is to be completed and then called from with the CDiagramEngDoc::ConstructBlock() method. In addition, as for the construction of the Gain block introduced earlier, a new three-argument constructor function is required whose arguments completely define the CBlock-derived block.

First, add a public member function to the CDiagramEngDoc class with the prototype, void CDiagramEngDoc::ConstructSumBlock(void), and edit the function as follows.

```
void CDiagramEngDoc::ConstructSumBlock()
{
    CPoint block_posn;

    //AfxMessageBox("\n CDiagramEngDoc::ConstructSumBlock()\n", MB_OK, 0);

    // Constructor args. for CBlock
    AssignBlockPosition(block_posn);

    // Constructor args. for CBlockShape
    EBlockShape e_block_shape = e_ellipse;

    // Construct a new constant block
    //CBlock *p_block = new CSumBlock();
    CBlock *p_block = new CSumBlock(&(GetSystemModel()), block_posn,
      e_block_shape);

    // Add the new block to the system model block list.
    GetSystemModel().GetBlockList().push_back(p_block);
}
```

Now, ConstructSumBlock() needs to be called from within the *switch* statement inside the function CDiagramEngDoc::ConstructBlock().

Finally, add a new constructor function to the CSumBlock class with prototype, CSumBlock::CSumBlock(CSystemModel *pParentSystemModel, CPoint blk_posn, EBlockShape e_blk_shape), and member initialization: CBlock(pParentSystemModel, blk_posn, e_blk_shape). Add the statement, SetBlockName("sum_block"), within the constructor as shown in the following.

```
CSumBlock::CSumBlock(CSystemModel *pParentSystemModel, CPoint blk_posn,
  EBlockShape e_blk_shape):
CBlock(pParentSystemModel, blk_posn, e_blk_shape)
{
    SetBlockName("sum_block");
}
```

"At last a confirmation!" Upon building and running the application and clicking on a Constant, Gain, or Sum block toolbar button, the blocks appear on the palette as shown in Figure 3.3. Blocks are automatically assigned positions to fill up to 10 places per row: across the rows and down the

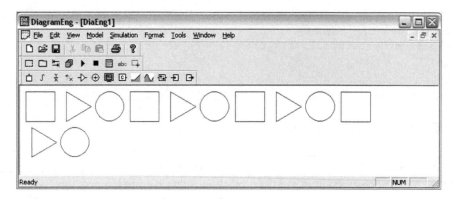

FIGURE 3.3   Constant, Gain, and Sum blocks (repeated) placed in automatically assigned positions.

columns as if they were in a matrix. Here, the Constant, Gain, and Sum blocks are repeatedly pressed one after the other to show the automatic display action.

3.5.3 CONSTRUCTION OF ALL REMAINING BLOCKS

The Constant, Gain, and Sum blocks have been constructed as indicated by the instructions given earlier, by introducing a new three-argument constructor for the CBlock-derived block, adding a particular block-construction function to the CDiagramEngDoc class and then calling this function from within the ConstructBlock() function. The remaining CBlock-derived blocks to be constructed, and their respective classes are indicated in alphabetical order in Table 3.2: particular instructions for block construction follow.

3.5.3.1 Construction of a Derivative Block

Add a public member function to the CDiagramEngDoc class, with the prototype, void CDiagram EngDoc::ConstructDerivativeBlock(void), and edit the function as follows.

TABLE 3.2
Blocks to Be Constructed and Drawn

Block Name	Class Name	Construction Status
Constant	CConstantBlock	☑
Derivative	CDerivativeBlock	☒
Divide	CDivideBlock	☒
Gain	CGainBlock	☑
Integrator	CIntegratorBlock	☒
Linear Function	CLinearFnBlock	☒
Output	COutputBlock	☒
Signal Generator	CSignalGeneratorBlock	☒
Subsystem	CSubsystemBlock	☒
Subsystem In	CSubsystemInBlock	☒
Subsystem Out	CSubsystemOutBlock	☒
Sum	CSumBlock	☑
Transfer Function	CTransferFnBlock	☒

The symbols ☑ and ☒ denote whether a block has been constructed thus
   far or not, respectively.

```
void CDiagramEngDoc::ConstructDerivativeBlock()
{
    CPoint block_posn;

    //AfxMessageBox("\n CDiagramEngDoc::ConstructDerivativeBlock()\n",
      MB_OK, 0);

    // Constructor args. for CBlock
    AssignBlockPosition(block_posn);

    // Constructor args. for CBlockShape
    EBlockShape e_block_shape = e_rectangle;

    // Construct a new derivative block
    //CBlock *p_block = new CDerivativeBlock();
    CBlock *p_block = new CDerivativeBlock(&(GetSystemModel()),
      block_posn, e_block_shape);

    // Add the new block to the system model block list.
    GetSystemModel().GetBlockList().push_back(p_block);
}
```

Add a new constructor function to the CDerivativeBlock class, with prototype, CDerivative Block::CDerivativeBlock(CSystemModel *pParentSystemModel, CPoint blk_posn, EBlockShape e_blk_shape), and member initialization: CBlock(pParentSystemModel, blk_posn, e_blk_shape). Edit the function as shown.

```
CDerivativeBlock::CDerivativeBlock(CSystemModel *pParentSystemModel,
  CPoint blk_posn, EBlockShape e_blk_shape):
CBlock(pParentSystemModel, blk_posn, e_blk_shape)
{
    SetBlockName("derivative_block");
}
```

3.5.3.2 Construction of a Divide Block

Add a public member function to the CDiagramEngDoc class, with prototype, void CDiagramEngDoc::ConstructDivideBlock(void), and edit the function as follows.

```
void CDiagramEngDoc::ConstructDivideBlock()
{
    CPoint block_posn;

    //AfxMessageBox("\n CDiagramEngDoc::ConstructDivideBlock()\n",
      MB_OK, 0);

    // Constructor args. for CBlock
    AssignBlockPosition(block_posn);

    // Constructor args. for CBlockShape
    EBlockShape e_block_shape = e_rectangle;

    // Construct a new divide block
    //CBlock *p_block = new CDivideBlock();
    CBlock *p_block = new CDivideBlock(&(GetSystemModel()), block_posn,
      e_block_shape);

    // Add the new block to the system model block list.
    GetSystemModel().GetBlockList().push_back(p_block);
}
```

Add a new constructor function to the CDivideBlock class with prototype, CDivideBlock:: CDivideBlock(CSystemModel *pParentSystemModel, CPoint blk_posn, EBlock Shape   e_blk_shape), and member initialization, CBlock(pParentSystemModel, blk_posn, e_blk_shape). Edit the function as shown.

```
CDivideBlock::CDivideBlock(CSystemModel *pParentSystemModel, CPoint
  blk_posn, EBlockShape e_blk_shape):
CBlock(pParentSystemModel, blk_posn, e_blk_shape)
{
    SetBlockName("divide_block");
}
```

3.5.3.3   Construction of an Integrator Block

Add a public member function to the CDiagramEngDoc class with prototype, void CDiagramEngDoc::ConstructIntegratorBlock(void), and edit the function as follows.

```
void CDiagramEngDoc::ConstructIntegratorBlock()
{
    CPoint block_posn;

    //AfxMessageBox("\n CDiagramEngDoc::ConstructIntegratorBlock()\n",
      MB_OK, 0);

    // Constructor args. for CBlock
    AssignBlockPosition(block_posn);

    // Constructor args. for CBlockShape
    EBlockShape e_block_shape = e_rectangle;

    // Construct a new integrator block
    //CBlock *p_block = new CIntegratorBlock();
    CBlock *p_block = new CIntegratorBlock(&(GetSystemModel()),
      block_posn, e_block_shape);

    // Add the new block to the system model block list.
    GetSystemModel().GetBlockList().push_back(p_block);
}
```

Add a new constructor function to the CIntegratorBlock class with prototype, CIntegratorBlock::CIntegratorBlock(CSystemModel *pParentSystemModel, CPoint blk_posn, EBlockShape e_blk_shape), and member initialization: CBlock (pParentSystemModel, blk_posn, e_blk_shape). Edit the function as shown.

```
CIntegratorBlock::CIntegratorBlock(CSystemModel *pParentSystemModel,
  CPoint blk_posn, EBlockShape e_blk_shape):
CBlock(pParentSystemModel, blk_posn, e_blk_shape)
{
    SetBlockName("integrator_block");
}
```

3.5.3.4   Construction of a Linear Function Block

Add a public member function to the CDiagramEngDoc class with prototype, void CDiagramEngDoc::ConstructLinearFnBlock(void), and edit the function as follows.

```
void CDiagramEngDoc::ConstructLinearFnBlock()
{
    CPoint block_posn;
```

```
    //AfxMessageBox("\n CDiagramEngDoc::ConstructLinearFnBlock()\n",
      MB_OK, 0);

    // Constructor args. for CBlock
    AssignBlockPosition(block_posn);

    // Constructor args. for CBlockShape
    EBlockShape e_block_shape = e_rectangle;

    // Construct a new linear fn block
    //CBlock *p_block = new CLinearFnBlock();
    CBlock *p_block = new CLinearFnBlock(&(GetSystemModel()), block_posn,
      e_block_shape);

    // Add the new block to the system model block list.
    GetSystemModel().GetBlockList().push_back(p_block);
}
```

Add a new constructor function to the CLinearFnBlock class with prototype, CLinearFnBlock::
CLinearFnBlock(CSystemModel *pParentSystemModel, CPoint blk_posn,
EBlockShape e_blk _shape), and member initialization: CBlock(pParentSystemModel,
blk_posn, e_blk_shape). Edit the function as shown.

```
CLinearFnBlock::CLinearFnBlock(CSystemModel *pParentSystemModel, CPoint
  blk_posn, EBlockShape e_blk_shape):
CBlock(pParentSystemModel, blk_posn, e_blk_shape)
{
    SetBlockName("linear_fn_block");
}
```

3.5.3.5 Construction of an Output Block

Add a public member function to the CDiagramEngDoc class with prototype, void CDiagram
EngDoc::ConstructOutputBlock(void), and edit the function as shown in the following.

```
void CDiagramEngDoc::ConstructOutputBlock()
{
    CPoint block_posn;

    //AfxMessageBox("\n CDiagramEngDoc::ConstructOutputBlock()\n",
      MB_OK, 0);

    // Constructor args. for CBlock
    AssignBlockPosition(block_posn);

    // Constructor args. for CBlockShape
    EBlockShape e_block_shape = e_rectangle;

    // Construct a new output block
    //CBlock *p_block = new COutputBlock();
    CBlock *p_block = new COutputBlock(&(GetSystemModel()), block_posn,
      e_block_shape);

    // Add the new block to the system model block list.
    GetSystemModel().GetBlockList().push_back(p_block);
}
```

Add a new constructor function to the COutputBlock class with prototype, COutputBlock::
COutputBlock(CSystemModel *pParentSystemModel, CPoint blk_posn,
EBlockShape e_blk_shape), and member initialization: CBlock(pParentSystemModel,
blk_posn, e_blk_shape). Edit the constructor as shown.

```
COutputBlock::COutputBlock(CSystemModel *pParentSystemModel, CPoint
  blk_posn, EBlockShape e_blk_shape):
CBlock(pParentSystemModel, blk_posn, e_blk_shape)
{
    SetBlockName("output_block");
}
```

3.5.3.6   Construction of a Signal Generator Block

Add a public member function to the CDiagramEngDoc class with prototype, void CDiagramEngDoc::ConstructSignalGeneratorBlock(void), and edit the function as shown in the following.

```
void CDiagramEngDoc::ConstructSignalGeneratorBlock()
{
    CPoint block_posn;

    //AfxMessageBox("\n CDiagramEngDoc::ConstructSignalGeneratorBlock()\n",
      MB_OK, 0);

    // Constructor args. for CBlock
    AssignBlockPosition(block_posn);

    // Constructor args. for CBlockShape
    EBlockShape e_block_shape = e_rectangle;

    // Construct a new signal generator block
    //CBlock *p_block = new CSignalGeneratorBlock();
    CBlock *p_block = new CSignalGeneratorBlock(&(GetSystemModel()),
      block_posn, e_block_shape);

    // Add the new block to the system model block list.
    GetSystemModel().GetBlockList().push_back(p_block);
}
```

Add a new constructor function to the CSignalGeneratorBlock class with prototype, CSignalGeneratorBlock::CSignalGeneratorBlock(CSystemModel *pParentSystemModel, CPoint blk_posn, EBlockShape e_blk_shape), and member initialization: CBlock(pParentSystemModel, blk_posn, e_blk_shape). Edit the constructor as shown.

```
CSignalGeneratorBlock::CSignalGeneratorBlock(CSystemModel
  *pParentSystemModel, CPoint blk_posn, EBlockShape e_blk_shape):
CBlock(pParentSystemModel, blk_posn, e_blk_shape)
{
    SetBlockName("signal_generator_block");
}
```

3.5.3.7   Construction of a Subsystem Block

Add a public member function to the CDiagramEngDoc class with prototype, void CDiagramEngDoc::ConstructSubsystemBlock(void), and edit the code as follows.

```
void CDiagramEngDoc::ConstructSubsystemBlock()
{
    CPoint block_posn;

    //AfxMessageBox("\n CDiagramEngDoc::ConstructSubsystemBlock()\n",
      MB_OK, 0);
```

```
    // Constructor args. for CBlock
    AssignBlockPosition(block_posn);
    // Constructor args. for CBlockShape
    EBlockShape e_block_shape = e_rectangle;

    // Construct a new subsystem block
    //CBlock *p_block = new CSubsystemBlock();
    CBlock *p_block = new CSubsystemBlock(&(GetSystemModel()),
      block_posn, e_block_shape);

    // Add the new block to the system model block list.
    GetSystemModel().GetBlockList().push_back(p_block);
}
```

Add a new constructor function to the CSubsystemBlock class with prototype, CSubsystemBlock::CSubsystemBlock(CSystemModel *pParentSystemModel, CPoint blk_posn, EBlockShape e_blk_shape), and member initialization: CBlock(pParentSystemModel, blk_posn, e_blk_shape). Edit the constructor as shown.

```
CSubsystemBlock::CSubsystemBlock(CSystemModel *pParentSystemModel, CPoint
  blk_posn, EBlockShape e_blk_shape):
CBlock(pParentSystemModel, blk_posn, e_blk_shape)
{
    SetBlockName("subsystem_block");
}
```

3.5.3.8   Construction of a Subsystem in Block

Add a public member function to the CDiagramEngDoc class with prototype, void CDiagramEngDoc::ConstructSubsystemInBlock(void), and edit the function as follows.

```
void CDiagramEngDoc::ConstructSubsystemInBlock()
{
    CPoint block_posn;

    //AfxMessageBox("\n CDiagramEngDoc::ConstructSubsystemInBlock()\n",
      MB_OK, 0);

    // Constructor args. for CBlock
    AssignBlockPosition(block_posn);

    // Constructor args. for CBlockShape
    EBlockShape e_block_shape = e_rectangle;

    // Construct a new subsystem in block
    //CBlock *p_block = new CSubsystemInBlock();
    CBlock *p_block = new CSubsystemInBlock(&(GetSystemModel()),
      block_posn, e_block_shape);

    // Add the new block to the system model block list.
    GetSystemModel().GetBlockList().push_back(p_block);
}
```

Add a new constructor function to the CSubsystemInBlock class with prototype, CSubsystemInBlock::CSubsystemInBlock(CSystemModel *pParentSystemModel, CPoint blk_posn, EBlockShape e_blk_shape), and member initialization: CBlock(pParentSystemModel, blk_posn, e_blk_shape). Edit the constructor as shown.

```
CSubsystemInBlock::CSubsystemInBlock(CSystemModel *pParentSystemModel,
  CPoint blk_posn, EBlockShape e_blk_shape):
CBlock(pParentSystemModel, blk_posn, e_blk_shape)
{
    SetBlockName("subsystem_in_block");
}
```

3.5.3.9   Construction of a Subsystem out Block

Add a public member function to the CDiagramEngDoc class with prototype, void CDiagramEngDoc::ConstructSubsystemOutBlock(void), and edit the function as follows.

```
void CDiagramEngDoc::ConstructSubsystemOutBlock()
{
    CPoint block_posn;

    //AfxMessage.Box("\n CDiagramEngDoc::ConstructSubsystemOutBlock()\n",
      MB_OK, 0);

    // Constructor args. for CBlock
    AssignBlockPosition(block_posn);

    // Constructor args. for CBlockShape
    EBlockShape e_block_shape = e_rectangle;

    // Construct a new subsystem out block
    //CBlock *p_block = new CSubsystemOutBlock();
    CBlock *p_block = new CSubsystemOutBlock(&(GetSystemModel()),
      block_posn, e_block_shape);

    // Add the new block to the system model block list.
    GetSystemModel().GetBlockList().push_back(p_block);
}
```

Add a new constructor function to the CSubsystemOutBlock class with prototype, CSubsystemOutBlock::CSubsystemOutBlock(CSystemModel *pParentSystemModel, CPoint blk_posn, EBlockShape e_blk_shape), and member initialization: CBlock(pParentSystemModel, blk_posn, e_blk_shape). Edit the constructor as shown in the following.

```
CSubsystemOutBlock::CSubsystemOutBlock(CSystemModel *pParentSystemModel,
  CPoint blk_posn, EBlockShape e_blk_shape):
CBlock(pParentSystemModel, blk_posn, e_blk_shape)
{
    SetBlockName("subsystem_out_block");
}
```

3.5.3.10   Construction of a Transfer Function Block

Add a public member function to the CDiagramEngDoc class with prototype, void CDiagramEngDoc::ConstructTransferFnBlock(void), and edit the function as shown in the following.

```
void CDiagramEngDoc::ConstructTransferFnBlock()
{
    CPoint block_posn;

    //AfxMessageBox("\n CDiagramEngDoc::ConstructTransferFnBlock()\n",
      MB_OK, 0);

    // Constructor args. for CBlock
    AssignBlockPosition(block_posn);
```

```
    // Constructor args. for CBlockShape
    EBlockShape e_block_shape = e_rectangle;

    // Construct a new transfer fn block
    //CBlock *p_block = new CTransferFnBlock();
    CBlock *p_block = new CTransferFnBlock(&(GetSystemModel()), block_posn,
      e_block_shape);

    // Add the new block to the system model block list.
    GetSystemModel().GetBlockList().push_back(p_block);
}
```

Add a new constructor function to the CTransferFnBlock class with prototype, CTransferFnBlock::CTransferFnBlock(CSystemModel *pParentSystemModel, CPoint blk_posn, EBlockShape e_blk_shape), and member initialization: CBlock(pParentSystemModel, blk_posn, e_blk_shape). Edit the constructor as shown.

```
CTransferFnBlock::CTransferFnBlock(CSystemModel *pParentSystemModel,
CPoint blk_posn, EBlockShape e_blk_shape):
CBlock(pParentSystemModel, blk_posn, e_blk_shape)
{
    SetBlockName("transfer_fn_block");
}
```

Finally, all the particular block-construction methods may be called from within CDiagramEngDoc:: ConstructBlock() function as shown in the following.

```
int CDiagramEngDoc::ConstructBlock(EBlockType e_block_type)
{
    // General ConstructBlock() fn which calls specific block
      construction fns.
    CString sMsg;           // string to be displayed
    UINT nType = MB_OK;     // style of msg. box
    UINT nIDhelp = 0;       // help context ID for the msg.

    // -- Display a msg. box
    sMsg.Format("\n CDiagramEngDoc::ConstructBlock()\n\n");
    AfxMessageBox(sMsg, nType, nIDhelp);

    // -- Filter out the approp. partic. block construction fn. to
      be called

    switch(e_block_type)
    {
    case eConstBlock:
        ConstructConstantBlock();
        break;

    case eDerivativeBlock:
        ConstructDerivativeBlock();
        break;

    case eDivideBlock:
        ConstructDivideBlock();
        break;

    case eGainBlock:
        ConstructGainBlock();
        break;
```

```
    case eIntegratorBlock:
        ConstructIntegratorBlock();
        break;

    case eLinearFnBlock:
        ConstructLinearFnBlock();
        break;

    case eOutputBlock:
        ConstructOutputBlock();
        break;

    case eSignalGenBlock:
        ConstructSignalGeneratorBlock();
        break;

    case eSubsysBlock:
        ConstructSubsystemBlock();
        break;

    case eSubsysInBlock:
        ConstructSubsystemInBlock();
        break;

    case eSubsysOutBlock:
        ConstructSubsystemOutBlock();
        break;

    case eSumBlock:
        ConstructSumBlock();
        break;

    case eTransferFnBlock:
        ConstructTransferFnBlock();
        break;

    default:
        // Inform user of switch default
        sMsg.Format("\n CDiagramEngDoc::ConstructBlock(): switch
         default\n\n");
        AfxMessageBox(sMsg, nType, nIDhelp);
        break;
    }

    SetModifiedFlag(TRUE);       // prompt the user to save after adding a
      block to the system model
    CheckSystemModel();          // check the syste model
    UpdateAllViews(NULL);        // this fn calls OnDraw to redraw the
      system model.
    return 0;                    // return int for error checking
}
```

3.5.3.11 Check Construction of System Model

Now after all blocks are constructed, the system model is checked with the call to CDiagramEngDoc::CheckSystemModel() from within the CDiagramEngDoc::ConstructBlock() function (after the *switch* statement). Figure 3.4 shows the CheckSystemModel()-based message box dialog confirming correct block construction: the blocks are displayed in the order of their appearance on the Common Blocks toolbar.

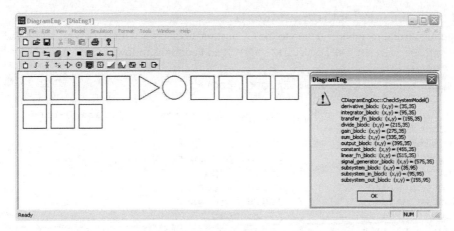

FIGURE 3.4 Primitive drawing functionality with the `CheckSystemModel()`-based message box dialog to check for correct block construction.

3.6 DRAWING BLOCK GRAPHICAL DETAIL

The primitive ellipse, rectangle, and triangle block shapes, thus far, have been drawn for the appropriate blocks based on the enumerated type variable, "m_eBlockShape", that is examined in the *switch* statement of the existing function, `CBlock::DrawBlock()`. Now, individual block-specific detail is required to be added to these primitive shapes. Hence, it appears appropriate to make the base class CBlock member function, `DrawBlock()`, virtual. This virtual `DrawBlock()` function should be overridden in each of the CBlock-derived classes, i.e., in each of the classes listed in Table 3.2 concerning blocks to be constructed and drawn. Then, a chaining to the base class functions, `DrawEllipseBlock()`, `DrawRectangleBlock()`, and `DrawTriangleBlock()`, may be performed to obtain the primitive shapes: ellipse, rectangle, and triangle, respectively.

3.6.1 IMPLEMENTING FUNCTIONALITY TO DRAW DETAIL

The drawing of the diagram on the palette is performed by `CSystemModel::DrawSystemModel()`, in particular through a looping of the statement `(*it_blk)->DrawBlock()` through the model's block list, and, based on the derived runtime type of the pointer-to-CBlock, the correct derived-class-overriding `DrawBlock()` function is called.

In order to implement the desired drawing mechanism, the following preliminary steps should be made:

1. Make the existing CBlock member function `DrawBlock(CDC *pDC)` virtual, i.e., use the prototype, `virtual void CBlock::DrawBlock(CDC *pDC)`, in the CBlock class declaration.
2. Finally, comment out the internals of the existing `CBlock::DrawBlock()` function so that it performs no action for now, as shown in the following code.

```
void CBlock::DrawBlock(CDC *pDC)
{
    // WARNING! THIS FN HAS BEEN MADE VIRTUAL AND IS TO BE OVERRIDDEN BY
        ALL DERIVED CLASSES THAT DRAW OBJS.
    // Old internals used to be here.
}
```

3.6.1.1 `CConstantBlock::DrawBlock()`

Add a public virtual member function to the CConstantBlock class with prototype, `virtual void CConstantBlock::DrawBlock(CDC *pDC)`, and edit it as follows.

```
void CConstantBlock::DrawBlock(CDC *pDC)
{
    // Note: pDC is a ptr to the device context of "Class Device
      Context" (CDC)
        int i;
    int n_pts = 55;       // no. of pts in pt array
    int pen_color;        // color of pen
    int pen_width;        // width of pen
    double degree;        // angle in degrees
    double pi = PI;       // pi rounded
    double radian;        // andgle in radians
    double radius;        // radius in.t.o. width
    double width;         // width of block
    CPoint pt_array[55];  // array of pts
    CPoint blk_posn;      // local blk_posn var. that is assigned
     m_ptBlockPosition of CBlock

    //AfxMessageBox("\n CConstantBlock::DrawBlock()\n", MB_OK, 0);

    // Get CBlock and CBlockShape vars.
    blk_posn = GetBlockPosition();
    width = GetBlockShape().GetBlockWidth();

    // Assign vals to pt_array
    radius = 0.20*width;

    for(i=0;i<n_pts;i++)
    {
        degree = i*5 + 45; // arc steps of 5 degrees
        radian = (pi/180)*degree;
        pt_array[i].x = radius*cos(radian);
        pt_array[i].y = radius*sin(radian);
    }

    // Add blk posn to pts.
    for(i=0;i<n_pts;i++)
    {
        pt_array[i].x = blk_posn.x + pt_array[i].x;
        pt_array[i].y = blk_posn.y + pt_array[i].y;
    }

    // Chain up to CBlock for primitive drawing
    CBlock::DrawRectangleBlock(pDC);

    // Create a pen
    pen_width = GetPenWidth();
    pen_color = GetPenColor();
    CPen lpen(PS_SOLID, pen_width, pen_color);

    // Set the new pen as the drawing obj.
    CPen *pOldPen = pDC->SelectObject(&lpen);

    // Draw the letter "C"
    pDC->MoveTo(pt_array[0]);
    for(i=1; i<n_pts; i++)
```

```
    {
        pDC->LineTo(pt_array[i]);
    }
    // Reset the prev. pen
    pDC->SelectObject(pOldPen);
}
```

The developer will have noticed the use of the functions `GetBlockPosition()` and `GetBlockShape()` to obtain the block position and shape, respectively. Hence, add a new public constant member function to the `CBlock()` class, as shown in the following, with the prototype, `CPoint CBlock::GetBlockPosition(void) const`, that returns a CPoint object.

```
CPoint CBlock::GetBlockPosition() const
{
    return m_ptBlockPosition;
}
```

In addition, add a new public member function to the `CBlock()` class with the prototype, `CBlockShape &CBlock::GetBlockShape(void)`, that returns a reference-to-a-CBlock-Shape object, i.e., the contained, "m_BlockShape", object: this is then used in the call to obtain the block width. Edit the function as shown.

```
CBlockShape &CBlock::GetBlockShape()
{
    return m_BlockShape;      // return a ref-to-a-CBlockShape obj.
      m_BlockShape (contained obj. of CBlock)
}
```

Finally, test that a CConstantBlock object can in fact be drawn by running the program and inserting only one Constant block in the system model's block list: this consists of a rectangle block, drawn from within the function, `CBlock::DrawRectangleBlock()`, and the letter "C," drawn from within the function, `CConstantBlock::DrawBlock()`.

3.6.1.2 `CGainBlock::DrawBlock()`

Add a public virtual member function to the CGainBlock class with the prototype, `virtual void CGainBlock::DrawBlock(CDC *pDC)`, and edit it as follows.

```
void CGainBlock::DrawBlock(CDC *pDC)
{
    // Note: pDC is a ptr to the device context of "Class Device
      Context" (CDC)
    int pen_color;                    // color of pen
    int pen_width;                    // width of pen
    CPoint A;                         // top pt. of letter "k"
    CPoint B;                         // middle pt. of letter "k"
    CPoint C;                         // lower pt. of letter "k"
    CPoint D;                         // upper right pt. of letter "k"
    CPoint E;                         // central pt. of letter "k"
    CPoint F;                         // lower right pt of letter "k"
    CPoint blk_posn;                  // local blk_posn var. that is assigned
      m_ptBlockPosition of CBlock
    double width;                      // width of block
```

```
//AfxMessageBox("\n CGainBlock::DrawBlock()\n", MB_OK, 0);

// Get CBlock and CBlockShape vars.
blk_posn = GetBlockPosition();
width = GetBlockShape().GetBlockWidth();

// Assign vals to pts relative to central pt. E of the letter "k"
E.x = blk_posn.x - 0.02*width; // was at blk_posn.x - 0.035
E.y = blk_posn.y + 0.02*width; // was at blk_posn.y + 0.035
A.x = E.x - 0.055*width;
A.y = E.y - 0.23*width;
B.x = A.x;
B.y = E.y + 0.035*width;
C.x = A.x;
C.y = E.y + 0.145*width;
D.x = E.x + 0.1*width;
D.y = E.y - 0.090*width;
F.x = E.x + 0.135*width;
F.y = C.y;

// Chain up to CBlock for primitive drawing
CBlock::DrawTriangleBlock(pDC);

// Create a pen
pen_width = GetPenWidth();
pen_color = GetPenColor();
CPen lpen(PS_SOLID, pen_width, pen_color);

// Set the new pen as the drawing obj.
CPen *pOldPen = pDC->SelectObject(&lpen);

// Draw the letter "C" from lower 4 o'clock posn to upper 2 o'clock
  posn (clockwise)
pDC->MoveTo(A);
pDC->LineTo(C);
pDC->MoveTo(D);
pDC->LineTo(B);
pDC->MoveTo(E);
pDC->LineTo(F);

// Reset the prev. pen
pDC->SelectObject(pOldPen);
}
```

Test that a CGainBlock can in fact be drawn by running the program and inserting only one Gain block in the system model's block list: this consists of a triangle block, drawn from within the function, CBlock::DrawTriangleBlock(), and the letter "K," denoting the gain constant, drawn from within the function, CGainBlock::DrawBlock().

3.6.1.3 CSumBlock::DrawBlock()

Add a public virtual member function to the CSumBlock class with the prototype, virtual void CSumBlock::DrawBlock(CDC *pDC), and edit it as follows.

```
void CSumBlock::DrawBlock(CDC *pDC)
{
    // Note: pDC is a ptr to the device context of "Class Device
      Context" (CDC)
    int pen_color;        // color of pen
```

```
      int pen_width;          // width of pen
      CPoint left;            // left pt. of char "+"
      CPoint right;           // right pt. of char "+"
      CPoint up;              // upper pt. of char "+"
      CPoint down;            // lower pt. of char "+"
      CPoint blk_posn;        // local blk_posn var. that is assigned
        m_ptBlockPosition of CBlock
      double plus_size;       // size of plus sign strokes
      double width;           // width of block

      //AfxMessageBox("\n CSumBlock::DrawBlock()\n", MB_OK, 0);

      // Get CBlock and CBlockShape vars.
      blk_posn = GetBlockPosition();
      width = GetBlockShape().GetBlockWidth();

      // Assign vals to the cnr. pts.
      plus_size = 0.2;
      left.x = blk_posn.x - plus_size*width;
      left.y = blk_posn.y;
      right.x = blk_posn.x + plus_size*width;
      right.y = blk_posn.y;
      up.x = blk_posn.x;
      up.y = blk_posn.y - plus_size*width;
      down.x = blk_posn.x;
      down.y = blk_posn.y + plus_size*width;

      // Chain up to CBlock for primitive drawing
      CBlock::DrawEllipseBlock(pDC);

      // Create a pen
      pen_width = GetPenWidth();
      pen_color = GetPenColor();
      CPen lpen(PS_SOLID, pen_width, pen_color);

      // Set the new pen as the drawing obj.
      CPen *pOldPen = pDC->SelectObject(&lpen);

      // Draw the letter "C" from lower 4 o'clock posn to upper 2 o'clock
        posn (clockwise)
      pDC->MoveTo(left);
      pDC->LineTo(right);
      pDC->MoveTo(up);
      pDC->LineTo(down);

      // Reset the prev. pen
      pDC->SelectObject(pOldPen);
}
```

Test that a CSumBlock can be drawn by running the program and adding a Sum block to the system model's block list: this consists of an ellipse block, drawn from within the function, CBlock::DrawEllipseBlock(), and the character "+," denoting summation, drawn from within the function, CSumBlock::DrawBlock().

3.6.1.4 CDerivativeBlock::DrawBlock()

Add a public virtual member function to the CDerivativeBlock class, with the prototype, virtual void CDerivativeBlock::DrawBlock(CDC *pDC), and edit it as follows.

```
void CDerivativeBlock::DrawBlock(CDC *pDC)
{
```

```
// Note: pDC is a ptr to the device context of "Class Device
  Context" (CDC)
int pen_color;          // color of pen
int pen_width;          // width of pen
double width;           // width of block
CPoint blk_posn;        // local blk_posn var. that is assigned
  m_ptBlockPosition of CBlock
CPoint bottom_left;     // derivative box
CPoint bottom_right;
CPoint dot_top_left;    // derivative dot
CPoint dot_bottom_right;
CPoint top_left;        // derivative box
CPoint top_right;

//AfxMessageBox("\n CDerivativeBlock::DrawBlock()\n", MB_OK, 0);

// Get CBlock and CBlockShape vars.
blk_posn = GetBlockPosition();
width = GetBlockShape().GetBlockWidth();

// Assign vals to graphics pts.
top_left.x = blk_posn.x - 0.2*width;
top_left.y = blk_posn.y - 0.25*width;
top_right.x = blk_posn.x + 0.2*width;
top_right.y = top_left.y;
bottom_right.x = top_right.x;
bottom_right.y = blk_posn.y + 0.35*width;
bottom_left.x = top_left.x;
bottom_left.y = bottom_right.y;

// Chain up to CBlock for primitive drawing
CBlock::DrawRectangleBlock(pDC);

// Create a pen
pen_width = GetPenWidth();
pen_color = GetPenColor();
CPen lpen(PS_SOLID, pen_width, pen_color);

// Set the new pen as the drawing obj.
CPen *pOldPen = pDC->SelectObject(&lpen);

// Draw the derivative box
pDC->MoveTo(top_left);
pDC->LineTo(top_right);
pDC->LineTo(bottom_right);
pDC->LineTo(bottom_left);
pDC->LineTo(top_left);

// Draw the dot (above the derivative box)
dot_top_left.x = (int)(blk_posn.x - 0.05*width);
dot_top_left.y = (int)(blk_posn.y - 0.40*width);
dot_bottom_right.x = (int)(blk_posn.x + 0.05*width);
dot_bottom_right.y = (int)(blk_posn.y - 0.30*width);
pDC->Ellipse(dot_top_left.x, dot_top_left.y, dot_bottom_right.x,
  dot_bottom_right.y);

// Declare and create the brush, and fill in the ellipse
CBrush lSolidBrush(pen_color);
CBrush *pOldBrush = pDC->SelectObject(&lSolidBrush);
pDC->Ellipse(dot_top_left.x, dot_top_left.y, dot_bottom_right.x,
  dot_bottom_right.y);
```

```
    // Reset the prev. pen and brush
    pDC->SelectObject(pOldPen);
    pDC->SelectObject(pOldBrush);
}
```

3.6.1.5 CDivideBlock::DrawBlock()

Add a public virtual member function to the CDivideBlock class, with the prototype, virtual void CDivideBlock::DrawBlock(CDC *pDC), and edit it as follows.

```
void CDivideBlock::DrawBlock(CDC *pDC)
{
    // Note: pDC is a ptr to the device context of "Class Device Context"
      (CDC)
    int pen_color;              // color of pen
    int pen_width;              // width of pen
    double width;               // width of block
    CPoint pt[8];               // pts of line segments used to draw
      "divide", "multiply", and "line-separator" symbols.
    CPoint blk_posn;            // local blk_posn var. that is assigned
      m_ptBlockPosition of CBlock
    CPoint lower_dot_top_left;  // lower dot used in divide sign
    CPoint lower_dot_bottom_right;
    CPoint upper_dot_top_left;  // upper dot used in divide sign
    CPoint upper_dot_bottom_right;

    //AfxMessageBox("\n CDivideBlock::DrawBlock()\n", MB_OK, 0);

    // Get CBlock and CBlockShape vars.
    blk_posn = GetBlockPosition();
    width = GetBlockShape().GetBlockWidth();

    // Assign vals to "divide" sign vinculum end pts.
    pt[0].x = blk_posn.x - 0.35*width;
    pt[0].y = blk_posn.y - 0.25*width;
    pt[1].x = blk_posn.x - 0.05*width;
    pt[1].y = pt[0].y;

    // Assign vals to "multiply (X)" sign line segment end pts.
    pt[2].x = blk_posn.x + 0.05*width;
    pt[2].y = blk_posn.y + 0.05*width;
    pt[3].x = blk_posn.x + 0.35*width;
    pt[3].y = blk_posn.y + 0.35*width;

    pt[4].x = pt[3].x;
    pt[4].y = pt[2].y;
    pt[5].x = pt[2].x;
    pt[5].y = pt[3].y;

    // Assign vals to the "line separator" symbol bw the "divide" and
      "multiply" signs
    pt[6].x = blk_posn.x - 0.25*width;
    pt[6].y = blk_posn.y + 0.20*width;
    pt[7].x = blk_posn.x + 0.20*width;
    pt[7].y = blk_posn.y - 0.25*width;

    // Assign vals to ellipse-bounding rectangles for upper and lower dots
    upper_dot_top_left.x = (int)(blk_posn.x - 0.24*width);
    upper_dot_top_left.y = (int)(blk_posn.y - 0.40*width);
    upper_dot_bottom_right.x = (int)(blk_posn.x - 0.16*width);
    upper_dot_bottom_right.y = (int)(blk_posn.y - 0.32*width);
```

```
    lower_dot_top_left.x = (int)(upper_dot_top_left.x);
    lower_dot_top_left.y = (int)(blk_posn.y - 0.18*width);
    lower_dot_bottom_right.x = (int)(upper_dot_bottom_right.x);
    lower_dot_bottom_right.y = (int)(blk_posn.y - 0.10*width);

    // Chain up to CBlock for primitive drawing
    CBlock::DrawRectangleBlock(pDC);

    // Create a pen
    pen_width = GetPenWidth();
    pen_color = GetPenColor();
    CPen lpen(PS_SOLID, pen_width, pen_color);

    // Set the new pen as the drawing obj.
    CPen *pOldPen = pDC->SelectObject(&lpen);

    // Draw the vinculum of the "divide" sign.
    pDC->MoveTo(pt[0]);
    pDC->LineTo(pt[1]);

    // Draw the line segments of the "multiply (X)" sign.
    pDC->MoveTo(pt[2]);
    pDC->LineTo(pt[3]);
    pDC->MoveTo(pt[4]);
    pDC->LineTo(pt[5]);

    // Draw the line segment separating the "divide" and "multiply"
      signs.
    pen_color = RGB(120,120,120);     // set the color to grey
    CPen lnew_pen(PS_SOLID, pen_width, pen_color);  // create a new pen
      with the new color
    pDC->SelectObject(&lnew_pen);     // select the new pen
    pDC->MoveTo(pt[6]);
    pDC->LineTo(pt[7]);

    // Draw the upper and lower dots
    pDC->SelectObject(&lpen);              // select the old pen using
      "&lpen".
    pDC->Ellipse(upper_dot_top_left.x, upper_dot_top_left.y,
      upper_dot_bottom_right.x, upper_dot_bottom_right.y);
    pDC->Ellipse(lower_dot_top_left.x, lower_dot_top_left.y,
      lower_dot_bottom_right.x, lower_dot_bottom_right.y);

    // Declare and create the brush, and fill in the ellipses (dots)
    pen_color = GetPenColor();         // get the blue color again
    CBrush lSolidBrush(pen_color);  // create a brush with the pen
      color
    CBrush *pOldBrush = pDC->SelectObject(&lSolidBrush);
    pDC->Ellipse(upper_dot_top_left.x, upper_dot_top_left.y,
      upper_dot_bottom_right.x, upper_dot_bottom_right.y);
    pDC->Ellipse(lower_dot_top_left.x, lower_dot_top_left.y,
      lower_dot_bottom_right.x, lower_dot_bottom_right.y);

    // Reset the prev. pen and brush
    pDC->SelectObject(pOldPen);
    pDC->SelectObject(pOldBrush);
}
```

3.6.1.6 `CIntegratorBlock::DrawBlock()`

Add a public virtual member function to the CIntegratorBlock class, with the prototype, `virtual void CIntegratorBlock::DrawBlock(CDC *pDC)`, and edit it as follows.

```
void CIntegratorBlock::DrawBlock(CDC *pDC)
{
    // Note: pDC is a ptr to the device context of "Class Device
      Context" (CDC)
    int i;
    int k;
    int pen_color;      // color of pen
    int pen_width;      // width of pen
    double width;       // width of block
    CPoint pt_array[25]; // array of CPoint
    CPoint blk_posn;     // local blk_posn var. that is assigned
      m_ptBlockPosition of CBlock
    CPoint upper_dot_top_left; // upper dot used for integrator sign
    CPoint upper_dot_bottom_right;
    CPoint lower_dot_top_left; // lower dot used for integrator sign
    CPoint lower_dot_bottom_right;

    //AfxMessageBox("\n CIntegratorBlock::DrawBlock()\n", MB_OK, 0);

    // Get CBlock and CBlockShape vars.
    blk_posn = GetBlockPosition();
    width = GetBlockShape().GetBlockWidth();

    // Assign vals to integral sign pts. (upper right portion of integral
      sign)
    pt_array[0].x = 0.10*width;
    pt_array[0].y = -0.37*width;
    pt_array[1].x = 0.08*width;
    pt_array[1].y = -0.37*width;
    pt_array[2].x = 0.06*width;
    pt_array[2].y = -0.365*width;
    pt_array[3].x = 0.045*width;
    pt_array[3].y = -0.355*width;
    pt_array[4].x = 0.035*width;
    pt_array[4].y = -0.34*width;
    pt_array[5].x = 0.02*width;
    pt_array[5].y = -0.325*width;
    pt_array[6].x = 0.015*width;
    pt_array[6].y = -0.305*width;
    pt_array[7].x = 0.005*width;
    pt_array[7].y = -0.29*width;
    pt_array[8].x = 0.0025*width;
    pt_array[8].y = -0.27*width;
    pt_array[9].x = 0.00125*width;
    pt_array[9].y = -0.25*width;
    pt_array[10].x = 0.001*width;
    pt_array[10].y = -0.225*width;
    pt_array[11].x = 0.00*width;
    pt_array[11].y = -0.2*width;
    pt_array[12].x = 0.00*width;
    pt_array[12].y = 0.00*width;
```

```
// Assign vals to the lower left portion of integral sign
  (symmetry)
k = 11;
for(i=0; i<12; i++)
{
    pt_array[i+13].x = -pt_array[k].x;
    pt_array[i+13].y = -pt_array[k].y;
    k-;
}

// Add the blk_posn to the pts.
for(i=0; i<25; i++)
{
    pt_array[i].x = blk_posn.x + pt_array[i].x;
    pt_array[i].y = blk_posn.y + pt_array[i].y;
}

// Assign vals to ellipse-bounding rectangles for upper and lower
  dot-end-pts of integral sign
upper_dot_top_left.x = (int)(blk_posn.x + 0.08*width);
upper_dot_top_left.y = (int)(blk_posn.y - 0.40*width);
upper_dot_bottom_right.x = (int)(blk_posn.x + 0.18*width);
upper_dot_bottom_right.y = (int)(blk_posn.y - 0.30*width);

lower_dot_top_left.x = (int)(blk_posn.x - 0.18*width);
lower_dot_top_left.y = (int)(blk_posn.y + 0.30*width);
lower_dot_bottom_right.x = (int)(blk_posn.x -0.08*width);
lower_dot_bottom_right.y = (int)(blk_posn.y + 0.40*width);

// Chain up to CBlock for primitive drawing
CBlock::DrawRectangleBlock(pDC);

// Create a pen
pen_width = GetPenWidth();
pen_color = GetPenColor();
CPen lpen(PS_SOLID, pen_width, pen_color);

// Set the new pen as the drawing obj.
CPen *pOldPen = pDC->SelectObject(&lpen);

// Draw all pts of integral sign.
pDC->MoveTo(pt_array[0]);
for(i=0; i<25; i++)
{
    pDC->LineTo(pt_array[i]);
}

// Draw the upper and lower dots
pDC->Ellipse(upper_dot_top_left.x, upper_dot_top_left.y,
  upper_dot_bottom_right.x, upper_dot_bottom_right.y);
pDC->Ellipse(lower_dot_top_left.x, lower_dot_top_left.y,
  lower_dot_bottom_right.x, lower_dot_bottom_right.y);

// Declare and create the brush, and fill in the ellipses (dots)
CBrush lSolidBrush(pen_color);
CBrush *pOldBrush = pDC->SelectObject(&lSolidBrush);
pDC->Ellipse(upper_dot_top_left.x, upper_dot_top_left.y,
  upper_dot_bottom_right.x, upper_dot_bottom_right.y);
pDC->Ellipse(lower_dot_top_left.x, lower_dot_top_left.y,
  lower_dot_bottom_right.x, lower_dot_bottom_right.y);
```

```
        // Reset the prev. pen and brush
        pDC->SelectObject(pOldPen);
        pDC->SelectObject(pOldBrush);
}
```

3.6.1.7 CLinearFnBlock::DrawBlock()

Add a public virtual member function to the CLinearFnBlock class with the prototype, virtual void CLinearFnBlock::DrawBlock(CDC *pDC), and edit it as follows.

```
void CLinearFnBlock::DrawBlock(CDC *pDC)
{
        // Note: pDC is a ptr to the device context of "Class Device Context"
          (CDC)
        int pen_color;      // color of pen
        int pen_width;      // width of pen
        CPoint A;           // pt. on curve graphic.
        CPoint B;
        CPoint C;
        CPoint blk_posn;    // local blk_posn var. that is assigned
          m_ptBlockPosition of CBlock
        double width;       // width of block

        //AfxMessageBox("\n CLinearFnBlock::DrawBlock()\n", MB_OK, 0);

        // Get CBlock and CBlockShape vars.
        blk_posn = GetBlockPosition();
        width = GetBlockShape().GetBlockWidth();

        // Assign vals to graphics pts.
        A.x = blk_posn.x - 0.47*width;
        A.y = blk_posn.y + 0.25*width;
        B.x = blk_posn.x - 0.1*width;
        B.y = A.y;
        C.x = blk_posn.x + 0.5*width;
        C.y = blk_posn.y - 0.4*width;

        // Chain up to CBlock for primitive drawing
        CBlock::DrawRectangleBlock(pDC);

        // Create a pen
        pen_width = GetPenWidth();

        //pen_color = GetPenColor();
        pen_color = RGB(0,255,0);
        CPen lpen(PS_SOLID, pen_width, pen_color);

        // Set the new pen as the drawing obj.
        CPen *pOldPen = pDC->SelectObject(&lpen);

        // Draw the linear fn. graphic curve
        pDC->MoveTo(A);
        pDC->LineTo(B);
        pDC->LineTo(C);

        // Reset the prev. pen
        pDC->SelectObject(pOldPen);
}
```

3.6.1.8 `COutputBlock::DrawBlock()`

Add a public virtual member function to the COutputBlock class with the prototype, `virtual void COutputBlock::DrawBlock(CDC *pDC)`, and edit it as follows.

```
void COutputBlock::DrawBlock(CDC *pDC)
{
    // Note: pDC is a ptr to the device context of "Class Device Context"
      (CDC)
    int i;
    int pen_color;          // color of pen
    int pen_width;          // width of pen
    double width;           // width of block
    CPoint blk_posn;        // local blk_posn var. that is assigned
      m_ptBlockPosition of CBlock
    CPoint dot_top_left;    // green dot top left
    CPoint dot_bottom_right; // green dot bottom right
    CPoint pt_array[20];    // array of CPoint

    //AfxMessageBox("\n COutputBlock::DrawBlock()\n", MB_OK, 0);

    // Get CBlock and CBlockShape vars.
    blk_posn = GetBlockPosition();
    width = GetBlockShape().GetBlockWidth();

    // Assign vals to graphic pts.

    // Outer box pts
    pt_array[0].x = -0.4*width;
    pt_array[0].y = -0.4*width;
    pt_array[1].x = 0.4*width;
    pt_array[1].y = pt_array[0].y;
    pt_array[2].x = pt_array[1].x;
    pt_array[2].y = 0.3*width;
    pt_array[3].x = pt_array[0].x;
    pt_array[3].y = pt_array[2].y;

    // Inner box pts
    pt_array[4].x = -0.35*width;
    pt_array[4].y = -0.35*width;
    pt_array[5].x = 0.35*width;
    pt_array[5].y = pt_array[4].y;
    pt_array[6].x = pt_array[5].x;
    pt_array[6].y = 0.25*width;
    pt_array[7].x = pt_array[4].x;
    pt_array[7].y = pt_array[6].y;

    // Stand pts
    pt_array[8].x = -0.1*width;
    pt_array[8].y = 0.3*width;
    pt_array[9].x = 0.1*width;
    pt_array[9].y = pt_array[8].y;
    pt_array[10].x = pt_array[9].x;
    pt_array[10].y = 0.37*width;
    pt_array[11].x = pt_array[8].x;
    pt_array[11].y = pt_array[10].y;
    pt_array[12].x = -0.2*width;
    pt_array[12].y = pt_array[11].y;
    pt_array[13].x = 0.2*width;
    pt_array[13].y = pt_array[12].y;
```

```
pt_array[14].x = pt_array[13].x;
pt_array[14].y = 0.45*width;
pt_array[15].x = pt_array[12].x;
pt_array[15].y = pt_array[14].y;

// Pseudo text pts.
// Line 1
pt_array[16].x = -0.3*width;
pt_array[16].y = -0.25*width;
pt_array[17].x = -0.15*width;
pt_array[17].y = pt_array[16].y;

// Line 2
pt_array[18].x = -0.3*width;
pt_array[18].y = -0.175*width;
pt_array[19].x = -0.05*width;
pt_array[19].y = pt_array[18].y;

// Add the blk_posn to the pts.
for(i=0; i<20; i++)
{
    pt_array[i].x = blk_posn.x + pt_array[i].x;
    pt_array[i].y = blk_posn.y + pt_array[i].y;
}

// Assign vals to ellipse-bounding rectangles for green dot
dot_top_left.x = (int)(blk_posn.x + 0.25*width);
dot_top_left.y = (int)(blk_posn.y + 0.25*width);
dot_bottom_right.x = (int)(blk_posn.x + 0.35*width);
dot_bottom_right.y = (int)(blk_posn.y + 0.35*width);

// Chain up to CBlock for primitive drawing
CBlock::DrawRectangleBlock(pDC);

// Create a pen
pen_width = GetPenWidth();
pen_color = GetPenColor();
CPen lpen(PS_SOLID, pen_width, pen_color);

// Set the new pen as the drawing obj.
CPen *pOldPen = pDC->SelectObject(&lpen);

// Draw all pts of the monitor graphic.
// Outer bounding box
pDC->MoveTo(pt_array[0]);
for(i=1; i<4; i++)
{
    pDC->LineTo(pt_array[i]);
}
pDC->LineTo(pt_array[0]);

// Inner bounding box
/*pDC->MoveTo(pt_array[4]);
for(i=4; i<8; i++)
{
    pDC->LineTo(pt_array[i]);
}
pDC->LineTo(pt_array[4]);
*/

// Stand box
pDC->MoveTo(pt_array[8]);
```

```
    for(i=9; i<11; i++)
    {
        pDC->LineTo(pt_array[i]);
    }
    pDC->LineTo(pt_array[13]);
    for(i=14; i<16; i++)
    {
        pDC->LineTo(pt_array[i]);
    }
    pDC->LineTo(pt_array[12]);
    pDC->LineTo(pt_array[11]);
    pDC->LineTo(pt_array[8]);

    // Pseudo text pts
    pen_color = RGB(120,120,120);
    CPen lnew_pen(PS_SOLID, pen_width, pen_color);
    pDC->SelectObject(&lnew_pen);

    pDC->MoveTo(pt_array[16]);
    pDC->LineTo(pt_array[17]);
    pDC->MoveTo(pt_array[18]);
    pDC->LineTo(pt_array[19]);

    // Declare and create the brush, and fill in the ellipse: green dot
    pDC->SelectObject(&lpen);
    pen_color = RGB(0, 255,0);
    CBrush lSolidBrush(pen_color);
    CBrush *pOldBrush = pDC->SelectObject(&lSolidBrush);
    pDC->Ellipse(dot_top_left.x, dot_top_left.y, dot_bottom_right.x,
      dot_bottom_right.y);

    // Reset the prev. pen and brush
    pDC->SelectObject(pOldPen);
    pDC->SelectObject(pOldBrush);
}
```

3.6.1.9 `CSignalGeneratorBlock::DrawBlock()`

Add a public virtual member function to the CSignalGeneratorBlock class with the prototype, virtual void CSignalGeneratorBlock::DrawBlock(CDC *pDC), and edit it as follows.

```
void CSignalGeneratorBlock::DrawBlock(CDC *pDC)
{
    // Note: pDC is a ptr to the device context of "Class Device Context"
      (CDC)
        int i;
    int pen_color;      // color of pen
    int pen_width;      // width of pen
    double pi = PI;     // pi rounded
    double width;       // width of block
    double degree;      // angle theta in degrees
    double radian;      // angle theta in radians
    CPoint fn1[361];    // function 1 of theta (sin)
    CPoint fn2[361];    // function 2 of theta (cos)
    CPoint blk_posn;    // local blk_posn var. that is assigned
     m_ptBlockPosition of CBlock

    //AfxMessageBox("\n CSignalGeneratorBlock::DrawBlock()\n", MB_OK, 0);

    // Get CBlock and CBlockShape vars.
```

```
blk_posn = GetBlockPosition();
width = GetBlockShape().GetBlockWidth();
// Generate functional eval of pts for sine and cosine curves
for(i=0; i<361; i++)
{
    degree = i;
    radian = (pi/180)*degree;

    fn1[i].x = ((degree - 180)/360)*width; // ((degree - 180)/360)
      scales the angle val bw. [-0.5,0.5]
    fn1[i].y = sin(radian)*(-0.4)*width;    // (-0.4)*width scales
      the curve the right way around
    fn2[i].x = ((degree - 180)/360)*width;  // ((degree - 180)/360)
      scales the angle val bw. [-0.5,0.5]
    fn2[i].y = cos(radian)*(-0.4)*width;    // (-0.4)*width scales the
      curve the right way around
}

// Add the blk_posn to the pts.
for(i=0; i<361; i++)
{
    fn1[i].x = blk_posn.x + fn1[i].x;
    fn1[i].y = blk_posn.y + fn1[i].y;
    fn2[i].x = blk_posn.x + fn2[i].x;
    fn2[i].y = blk_posn.y + fn2[i].y;
}

// Chain up to CBlock for primitive drawing
CBlock::DrawRectangleBlock(pDC);

// Create a pen
pen_width = GetPenWidth();
//pen_color = GetPenColor();
pen_color = RGB(0,255,0);       // green
CPen lpen(PS_SOLID, pen_width, pen_color);

// Create a new pen
pen_color = RGB(255,0,0);       // red
CPen lnew_pen(PS_SOLID, pen_width, pen_color);

// Set the new pen as the drawing obj.
CPen *pOldPen = pDC->SelectObject(&lpen);

// Draw the sine curve
pDC->MoveTo(fn1[0]);
for(i=1; i<361; i++)
{
    pDC->LineTo(fn1[i]);
}

// Draw the cosine curve
pDC->SelectObject(&lnew_pen); // select the pen that's red.
pDC->MoveTo(fn2[0]);
for(i=1; i<361; i++)
{
    pDC->LineTo(fn2[i]);
}

// Reset the prev. pen
pDC->SelectObject(pOldPen);
}
```

3.6.1.10 CSubsystemBlock::DrawBlock()

Add a public virtual member function to the CSubsystemBlock class, with the prototype, virtual void CSubsystemBlock::DrawBlock(CDC *pDC), and edit it as follows.

```
void CSubsystemBlock::DrawBlock(CDC *pDC)
{
    // Note: pDC is a ptr to the device context of "Class Device Context"
      (CDC)
    int i;
    int pen_color;          // color of pen
    int pen_width;          // width of pen
    double width;           // width of block
    CPoint pt_array[18];    // array of CPoints to draw the block
      graphics
    CPoint blk_posn;        // local blk_posn var. that is assigned
      m_ptBlockPosition of CBlock

    //AfxMessageBox("\n CSubsystemBlock::DrawBlock()\n", MB_OK, 0);

    // Get CBlock and CBlockShape vars.
    blk_posn = GetBlockPosition();
    width = GetBlockShape().GetBlockWidth();

    // Pt arrays coords.
    pt_array[0].x = -0.4*width;
    pt_array[0].y = -0.4*width;
    pt_array[1].x = -0.1*width;
    pt_array[1].y = pt_array[0].y;
    pt_array[2].x = pt_array[1].x;
    pt_array[2].y = -0.1*width;
    pt_array[3].x = pt_array[0].x;
    pt_array[3].y = pt_array[2].y;
    pt_array[4].x = 0.1*width;
    pt_array[4].y = 0.1*width;
    pt_array[5].x = 0.4*width;
    pt_array[5].y = pt_array[4].y;
    pt_array[6].x = pt_array[5].x;
    pt_array[6].y = 0.4*width;
    pt_array[7].x = pt_array[4].x;
    pt_array[7].y = pt_array[6].y;
    pt_array[8].x = -0.1*width;
    pt_array[8].y = -0.25*width;
    pt_array[9].x = 0.25*width;
    pt_array[9].y = pt_array[8].y;
    pt_array[10].x = pt_array[9].x;
    pt_array[10].y = 0.1*width;
    pt_array[11].x = 0.1*width;
    pt_array[11].y = 0.25*width;
    pt_array[12].x = -0.25*width;
    pt_array[12].y = pt_array[11].y;
    pt_array[13].x = pt_array[12].x;
    pt_array[13].y = -0.1*width;
    pt_array[14].x = pt_array[0].x;
    pt_array[14].y = -0.25*width;
    pt_array[15].x = -0.5*width;
    pt_array[15].y = pt_array[14].y;
    pt_array[16].x = pt_array[5].x;
    pt_array[16].y = 0.25*width;
```

```
        pt_array[17].x = 0.5*width;
        pt_array[17].y = pt_array[16].y;

        // Add the blk_posn to the pts*width.
        for(i=0; i<18; i++)
        {
            pt_array[i].x = blk_posn.x + pt_array[i].x;
            pt_array[i].y = blk_posn.y + pt_array[i].y;
        }

        // Chain up to CBlock for primitive drawing
        CBlock::DrawRectangleBlock(pDC);

        // Create a pen
        pen_width = GetPenWidth();
        pen_color = GetPenColor();
        CPen lpen(PS_SOLID, pen_width, pen_color);

        // Create a new pen
        pen_color = RGB(0,255,0);        // green
        CPen lnew_pen(PS_SOLID, pen_width, pen_color);

        // Set the new pen as the drawing obj.
        CPen *pOldPen = pDC->SelectObject(&lpen);

        // Draw the i/o blocks
        pDC->MoveTo(pt_array[0]);
        for(i=1; i<4; i++)
        {
            pDC->LineTo(pt_array[i]);
        }
        pDC->LineTo(pt_array[0]);
        pDC->MoveTo(pt_array[4]);
        for(i=4; i<8; i++)
        {
            pDC->LineTo(pt_array[i]);
        }
        pDC->LineTo(pt_array[4]);

        // Draw the connecting wires
        pDC->SelectObject(&lnew_pen);        // select the pen that's red.
        pDC->MoveTo(pt_array[8]);
        pDC->LineTo(pt_array[9]);
        pDC->LineTo(pt_array[10]);

        pDC->MoveTo(pt_array[11]);
        pDC->LineTo(pt_array[12]);
        pDC->LineTo(pt_array[13]);

        pDC->MoveTo(pt_array[14]);
        pDC->LineTo(pt_array[15]);

        pDC->MoveTo(pt_array[16]);
        pDC->LineTo(pt_array[17]);

        // Reset the prev. pen
        pDC->SelectObject(pOldPen);
}
```

3.6.1.11 CSubsystemInBlock::DrawBlock()

Add a public virtual member function to the CSubsystemInBlock class with the prototype, virtual void CSubsystemInBlock::DrawBlock(CDC *pDC), and edit it as follows.

```
void CSubsystemInBlock::DrawBlock(CDC *pDC)
{
    // Note: pDC is a ptr to the device context of "Class Device Context"
      (CDC)
    int i;
    int pen_color;         // color of pen
    int pen_width;         // width of pen
    double width;          // width of block
    CPoint pt_array[18];   // array of CPoints to draw the block graphics
    CPoint blk_posn;       // local blk_posn var. that is assigned
      m_ptBlockPosition of CBlock

    //AfxMessageBox("\n CSubsystemInBlock::DrawBlock()\n", MB_OK, 0);

    // Get CBlock and CBlockShape vars.
    blk_posn = GetBlockPosition();
    width = GetBlockShape().GetBlockWidth();

    // Pt arrays coords.
    pt_array[0].x = -0.4*width;
    pt_array[0].y = -0.4*width;
    pt_array[1].x = -0.1*width;
    pt_array[1].y = pt_array[0].y;
    pt_array[2].x = pt_array[1].x;
    pt_array[2].y = -0.1*width;
    pt_array[3].x = pt_array[0].x;
    pt_array[3].y = pt_array[2].y;
    pt_array[4].x = 0.1*width;
    pt_array[4].y = 0.1*width;
    pt_array[5].x = 0.4*width;
    pt_array[5].y = pt_array[4].y;
    pt_array[6].x = pt_array[5].x;
    pt_array[6].y = 0.4*width;
    pt_array[7].x = pt_array[4].x;
    pt_array[7].y = pt_array[6].y;
    pt_array[8].x = -0.1*width;
    pt_array[8].y = -0.25*width;
    pt_array[9].x = 0.25*width;
    pt_array[9].y = pt_array[8].y;
    pt_array[10].x = pt_array[9].x;
    pt_array[10].y = 0.1*width;
    pt_array[11].x = 0.1*width;
    pt_array[11].y = 0.25*width;
    pt_array[12].x = -0.25*width;
    pt_array[12].y = pt_array[11].y;

    // modified from CSubsystemBlock::DrawBlock() to be on side of
      "input" triangle
    pt_array[13].x = pt_array[12].x;
    pt_array[13].y = -(0.1+0.075)*width;
    // end modification

    pt_array[14].x = pt_array[0].x;
    pt_array[14].y = -0.25*width;
    pt_array[15].x = -0.5*width;
    pt_array[15].y = pt_array[14].y;
    pt_array[16].x = pt_array[5].x;
    pt_array[16].y = 0.25*width;
```

```
pt_array[17].x = 0.5*width;
pt_array[17].y = pt_array[16].y;

// Add the blk_posn to the pts*width.
for(i=0; i<18; i++)
{
    pt_array[i].x = blk_posn.x + pt_array[i].x;
    pt_array[i].y = blk_posn.y + pt_array[i].y;
}

// Chain up to CBlock for primitive drawing
CBlock::DrawRectangleBlock(pDC);

// Create a pen
pen_width = GetPenWidth();
//pen_color = GetPenColor();
pen_color = RGB(180,180,180);
CPen lpen(PS_SOLID, pen_width, pen_color);

// Create a new pen
pen_color = RGB(0,255,0);
CPen lnew_pen(PS_SOLID, pen_width, pen_color);

// Set the new pen as the drawing obj.
CPen *pOldPen = pDC->SelectObject(&lpen);

// Draw the i/o blocks
pDC->MoveTo(pt_array[0]);
/*for(i=1; i<4; i++)
{
    pDC->LineTo(pt_array[i]);
}
pDC->LineTo(pt_array[0]);
*/

pDC->MoveTo(pt_array[4]);
for(i=4; i<8; i++)
{
    pDC->LineTo(pt_array[i]);
}
pDC->LineTo(pt_array[4]);

// Draw the connecting wires
pDC->MoveTo(pt_array[8]);
pDC->LineTo(pt_array[9]);
pDC->LineTo(pt_array[10]);
pDC->MoveTo(pt_array[11]);
pDC->LineTo(pt_array[12]);
pDC->LineTo(pt_array[13]);

pDC->MoveTo(pt_array[16]);
pDC->LineTo(pt_array[17]);

// Draw the input graphics denoted by green
pDC->SelectObject(&lnew_pen);
pDC->MoveTo(pt_array[0]);
pDC->LineTo(pt_array[8]);
pDC->LineTo(pt_array[3]);
pDC->LineTo(pt_array[0]);
pDC->MoveTo(pt_array[14]);
pDC->LineTo(pt_array[15]);
```

```
    // Reset the prev. pen
    pDC->SelectObject(pOldPen);
}
```

3.6.1.12 `CSubsystemOutBlock::DrawBlock()`

Add a public virtual member function to the CSubsystemOutBlock class with the prototype, `virtual void CSubsystemOutBlock::DrawBlock(CDC *pDC)`, and edit it as follows.

```
void CSubsystemOutBlock::DrawBlock(CDC *pDC)
{
    // Note: pDC is a ptr to the device context of "Class Device Context"
      (CDC)
        int i;
    int pen_color;          // color of pen
    int pen_width;          // width of pen
    double width;           // width of block
    CPoint pt_array[18];    // array of CPoints to draw the block
      graphics
    CPoint blk_posn;        // local blk_posn var. that is assigned
      m_ptBlockPosition of CBlock

    //AfxMessageBox("\n CSubsystemOutBlock::DrawBlock()\n", MB_OK, 0);

    // Get CBlock and CBlockShape vars.
    blk_posn = GetBlockPosition();
    width = GetBlockShape().GetBlockWidth();

    // Pt arrays coords.
    pt_array[0].x = -0.4*width;
    pt_array[0].y = -0.4*width;
    pt_array[1].x = -0.1*width;
    pt_array[1].y = pt_array[0].y;
    pt_array[2].x = pt_array[1].x;
    pt_array[2].y = -0.1*width;
    pt_array[3].x = pt_array[0].x;
    pt_array[3].y = pt_array[2].y;
    pt_array[4].x = 0.1*width;
    pt_array[4].y = 0.1*width;
    pt_array[5].x = 0.4*width;
    pt_array[5].y = pt_array[4].y;
    pt_array[6].x = pt_array[5].x;
    pt_array[6].y = 0.4*width;
    pt_array[7].x = pt_array[4].x;
    pt_array[7].y = pt_array[6].y;
    pt_array[8].x = -0.1*width;
    pt_array[8].y = -0.25*width;
    pt_array[9].x = 0.25*width;
    pt_array[9].y = pt_array[8].y;

    // modified from CSubsystemBlock::DrawBlock() to be on side of
      "output" triangle
    pt_array[10].x = pt_array[9].x;
    pt_array[10].y = (0.1+0.075)*width;
    // end modification

    pt_array[11].x = 0.1*width;
    pt_array[11].y = 0.25*width;
    pt_array[12].x = -0.25*width;
```

```
pt_array[12].y = pt_array[11].y;
pt_array[13].x = pt_array[12].x;
pt_array[13].y = -0.1*width;
pt_array[14].x = pt_array[0].x;
pt_array[14].y = -0.25*width;
pt_array[15].x = -0.5*width;
pt_array[15].y = pt_array[14].y;
pt_array[16].x = pt_array[5].x;
pt_array[16].y = 0.25*width;
pt_array[17].x = 0.5*width;
pt_array[17].y = pt_array[16].y;

// Add the blk_posn to the pts*width.
for(i=0; i<18; i++)
{
    pt_array[i].x = blk_posn.x + pt_array[i].x;
    pt_array[i].y = blk_posn.y + pt_array[i].y;
}

// Chain up to CBlock for primitive drawing
CBlock::DrawRectangleBlock(pDC);

// Create a pen
pen_width = GetPenWidth();
//pen_color = GetPenColor();
pen_color = RGB(180,180,180);
CPen lpen(PS_SOLID, pen_width, pen_color);

// Create a new pen
pen_color = RGB(0,255,0);
CPen lnew_pen(PS_SOLID, pen_width, pen_color);

// Set the new pen as the drawing obj.
CPen *pOldPen = pDC->SelectObject(&lpen);

// Draw the i/o blocks
pDC->MoveTo(pt_array[0]);
for(i=1; i<4; i++)
{
    pDC->LineTo(pt_array[i]);
}
pDC->LineTo(pt_array[0]);

/*pDC->MoveTo(pt_array[4]);
for(i=4; i<8; i++)
{
    pDC->LineTo(pt_array[i]);
}
pDC->LineTo(pt_array[4]);
*/

// Draw the connecting wires
pDC->MoveTo(pt_array[8]);
pDC->LineTo(pt_array[9]);
pDC->LineTo(pt_array[10]);
pDC->MoveTo(pt_array[11]);
pDC->LineTo(pt_array[12]);
pDC->LineTo(pt_array[13]);

pDC->MoveTo(pt_array[14]);
pDC->LineTo(pt_array[15]);
```

```
pDC->MoveTo(pt_array[16]);
pDC->LineTo(pt_array[17]);

// Draw the output graphics denoted by green
pDC->SelectObject(&lnew_pen);
pDC->MoveTo(pt_array[4]);
pDC->LineTo(pt_array[16]);
pDC->LineTo(pt_array[7]);
pDC->LineTo(pt_array[4]);
pDC->MoveTo(pt_array[16]);
pDC->LineTo(pt_array[17]);

// Reset the prev. pen
pDC->SelectObject(pOldPen);
}
```

3.6.1.13   `CTransferFnBlock::DrawBlock()`

Add a public virtual member function to the CTransferFnBlock class, with the prototype, `virtual void CTransferFnBlock::DrawBlock(CDC *pDC)`, and edit it as follows.

```
void CTransferFnBlock::DrawBlock(CDC *pDC)
{
    // Note: pDC is a ptr to the device context of "Class Device Context"
      (CDC)
        int i;
    int pen_color;        // color of pen
    int pen_width;        // width of pen
    CPoint pt_array[10];  // pt. on curve graphic.
    CPoint blk_posn;      // local blk_posn var. that is assigned
      m_ptBlockPosition of CBlock
    double width;         // width of block

    //AfxMessageBox("\n CTransferFnBlock::DrawBlock()\n", MB_OK, 0);

    // Get CBlock and CBlockShape vars.
    blk_posn = GetBlockPosition();
    width = GetBlockShape().GetBlockWidth();

    // Assign vals to graphics pts.
    // Letter Y
    pt_array[0].x = -0.15*width;
    pt_array[0].y = -0.4*width;
    pt_array[1].x = 0.15*width;
    pt_array[1].y = pt_array[0].y;
    pt_array[2].x = 0.0;
    pt_array[2].y = -0.2*width;
    pt_array[3].x = 0.0;
    pt_array[3].y = -0.05*width;

    // Letter X
    pt_array[4].x = -0.15*width;
    pt_array[4].y = 0.05*width;
    pt_array[5].x = 0.15*width;
    pt_array[5].y = 0.4*width;
    pt_array[6].x = pt_array[5].x;
    pt_array[6].y = pt_array[4].y;
    pt_array[7].x = pt_array[4].x;
    pt_array[7].y = pt_array[5].y;
```

```
    // Vinculum
    pt_array[8].x = -0.2*width;
    pt_array[8].y = 0.0;
    pt_array[9].x = 0.2*width;
    pt_array[9].y = 0.0;

    // Add the blk_posn to the pts*width.
    for(i=0; i<10; i++)
    {
        pt_array[i].x = blk_posn.x + pt_array[i].x;
        pt_array[i].y = blk_posn.y + pt_array[i].y;
    }

    // Chain up to CBlock for primitive drawing
    CBlock::DrawRectangleBlock(pDC);

    // Create a pen
    pen_width = GetPenWidth();
    pen_color = GetPenColor();
    CPen lpen(PS_SOLID, pen_width, pen_color);

    // Set the new pen as the drawing obj.
    CPen *pOldPen = pDC->SelectObject(&lpen);

    // Draw the transfer fn. graphic curve
    pDC->MoveTo(pt_array[0]);
    pDC->LineTo(pt_array[2]);
    pDC->MoveTo(pt_array[1]);
    pDC->LineTo(pt_array[2]);
    pDC->MoveTo(pt_array[2]);
    pDC->LineTo(pt_array[3]);

    pDC->MoveTo(pt_array[4]);
    pDC->LineTo(pt_array[5]);
    pDC->MoveTo(pt_array[6]);
    pDC->LineTo(pt_array[7]);

    pDC->MoveTo(pt_array[8]);
    pDC->LineTo(pt_array[9]);

    // Reset the prev. pen
    pDC->SelectObject(pOldPen);
}
```

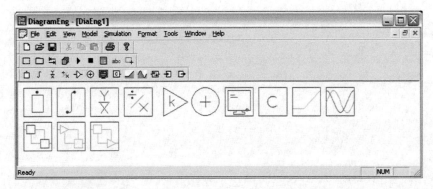

FIGURE 3.5 All blocks available from the Common Blocks toolbar presented in the form of primitive shapes with block-specific graphics.

3.6.2 DISPLAY OF BLOCK GRAPHICS

Now the user may build and run the application: after all blocks are added to the system model block list, the `DrawSystemModel()` function iterates through the block list calling `(*it_blk)->DrawBlock (pDC)`, which calls the correct derived block's `DrawBlock()` member method. The output should appear as shown: here the blocks are added in the same order as they appear on the Common Blocks toolbar (Figure 3.5).

3.7 SUMMARY

The Win32 Console application, ControlEng, is merged with the initial Visual C++ application, DiagramEng, to result in an application whose structure is presented in a class hierarchical diagram (Figure 3.1) showing the association relationships between the classes of the project. Changes are made to the CBlock and CBlock-derived class constructors in preparation for the complete construction of concrete blocks. The `ConstructBlock()` method of the CDiagramEngDoc class calls the particular block-construction functions in which a block is constructed and added to the system model block list: thereafter, the system model is checked for correctness. The `DrawBlock()` function of the base CBlock class is then made virtual, and overriding methods to draw specific block graphics are provided for each of the derived blocks, where a chaining to the base class is made for the drawing of the primitive ellipse, rectangle, and triangle shapes.

REFERENCES

1. Microsoft Visual C++® 6.0, Microsoft® Visual Studio™ 6.0 Development System, Professional Edition, Microsoft Corporation, 1998.
2. Microsoft Developer Network Library Visual Studio 6.0, Microsoft® Visual Studio™ 6.0 Development System, Microsoft Corporation, 1998.

4 Constructing Block Ports

4.1 INTRODUCTION

In Chapter 3, blocks were constructed, added to the system model, and then drawn with specific block-defining graphics on the palette. However, at this stage, no block input or output ports have been constructed, and hence, they are not visible on the block icons. Ports are particular to the blocks upon which they reside and hence should be constructed within the derived block class constructor and their properties set prior to their insertion into the block-based vectors of input or output ports.

The structure of the present chapter is centered around the manner in which ports are to be drawn on a block and predominantly involves the CPort, CBlock, CBlock-derived, and CBlockShape classes. Initially, the mathematical details concerning determining a port's position on a face of a block using a location-defining position angle are introduced. Then, the necessary additions and alterations are made to the CPort, CBlock, CBlock-derived, and CBlockShape classes to construct and set the properties of the input and output ports. Finally, the drawing of ports is implemented by adding drawing-related code to the CBlock and CPort classes.

The instructions here could be presented in a function-by-function approach, where changes are made to successive functions in the order that a developer may make them if coding one step at a time. However, here, a class-centric approach is taken to convey the material in a more structured manner. It may not be entirely clear as to why individual changes are being made to certain classes and their member methods and variables until the collective process is completed: in this case, the developer is encouraged to read the whole chapter first prior to adding code to the project.

4.2 BLOCK-BASED PORT POSITION

The position of a port on the boundary of an ellipse, rectangle, or triangle block may be determined by specifying the port position angle, $\theta \in [0, 2\pi]$, with respect to the horizontal x axis, of a local block-based coordinate system with x and y axes pointing (positively) to the right and to the top of the page, respectively. However, as the global screen coordinate system has its x and y axes pointing to the right and to the bottom of the page, respectively, when determining the port positions with respect to the (global) screen coordinate system, either subtracting or adding the local y component has the effect of moving the port upward or downward on the screen, respectively.

4.2.1 PORTS ON AN ELLIPSE BLOCK

Consider Figure 4.1, illustrating an ellipse block with width w, port position angle θ, and radius $r = w/2$. To determine the x and y coordinates of a port on the boundary of an ellipse block with respect to the (global) screen coordinate system, one only needs to determine the cosine and sine of the port position angle θ and perform the following calculation:

$$x_{\text{port}} = x_{\text{block}} + r\cos(\theta) \tag{4.1a}$$

$$y_{\text{port}} = y_{\text{block}} - r\sin(\theta) \tag{4.1b}$$

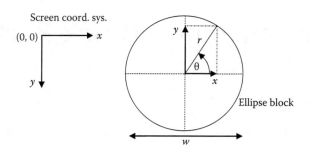

FIGURE 4.1   An ellipse block showing a port location vector of length r at an angle θ.

4.2.2   PORTS ON A RECTANGLE BLOCK

To determine the x and y coordinates of a port on the boundary of the rectangle block, a critical angle $\theta_{crit} = \tan^{-1}(h/w)$ is determined to partition the angular domain to facilitate computation, where h and w are the rectangle block height and width, respectively, and r is the length of the port position vector, as shown in Figure 4.2. For the purpose of writing C++ code, the development that follows is divided into five angular domains: $\theta \in [0, \theta_{crit}]$, $\theta \in (\theta_{crit}, \pi - \theta_{crit})$, $\theta \in [\pi - \theta_{crit}, \pi + \theta_{crit}]$, $\theta \in (\pi + \theta_{crit}, 2\pi - \theta_{crit})$, and $\theta \in [2\pi - \theta_{crit}, 2\pi]$.

For $\theta \in [0, \theta_{crit}]$, the local body coordinates of a port located on the boundary of the rectangle block are $x = w/2$ and $y = r \sin(\theta)$, where $\cos(\theta) = w/2r, \Rightarrow r = w/2 \cos(\theta)$. Hence,

$$x_{port} = x_{block} + \frac{w}{2} \tag{4.2a}$$

$$y_{port} = y_{block} - r \sin(\theta) \tag{4.2b}$$

For $\theta \in (\theta_{crit}, \pi - \theta_{crit})$, the local body coordinates of a port located on the boundary of the rectangle block are $x = r \cos(\theta)$ and $y = h/2$, where $\sin(\theta) = h/2r, \Rightarrow r = h/2 \sin(\theta)$. Hence,

$$x_{port} = x_{block} + r \cos(\theta) \tag{4.3a}$$

$$y_{port} = y_{block} - \frac{h}{2} \tag{4.3b}$$

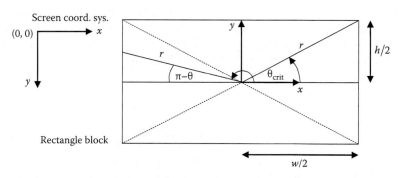

FIGURE 4.2   A rectangle block showing a port location vector of length r at an angle θ.

For $\theta \in [\pi - \theta_{crit}, \pi + \theta_{crit}]$, the local body coordinates of a port located on the boundary of the rectangle block are $x = -w/2$ and $y = r\sin(\theta)$, where $\cos(\pi - \theta) = w/2r, \Rightarrow r = -w/2\cos(\theta)$. Hence,

$$x_{port} = x_{block} - \frac{w}{2} \tag{4.4a}$$

$$y_{port} = y_{block} - r\sin(\theta) \tag{4.4b}$$

For $\theta \in (\pi + \theta_{crit}, 2\pi - \theta_{crit})$, the local body coordinates of a port located on the boundary of the rectangle block are $x = r\cos(\theta)$ and $y = -h/2$, where $\sin(\theta - \pi) = h/2r, \Rightarrow r = -h/2\sin(\theta)$. Hence,

$$x_{port} = x_{block} + r\cos(\theta) \tag{4.5a}$$

$$y_{port} = y_{block} + \frac{h}{2} \tag{4.5b}$$

For $\theta \in [2\pi - \theta_{crit}, 2\pi]$, the local body coordinates of a port located on the boundary of the rectangle block are $x = w/2$ and $y = r\sin(\theta)$, where $\cos(2\pi - \theta) = w/2r, \Rightarrow r = w/2\cos(\theta)$. Hence,

$$x_{port} = x_{block} + \frac{w}{2} \tag{4.6a}$$

$$y_{port} = y_{block} - r\sin(\theta) \tag{4.6b}$$

4.2.3 PORTS ON A TRIANGLE BLOCK

The gain block makes use of an equilateral triangle that may point to the left or right depending on the direction of connection/signal flow. The port position angle, θ, is used to locate the position of the ports on the exterior boundary of the triangle and is measured anticlockwise from the horizontal x axis about the block center, where the positive x and y axes point to the right and up, respectively, as indicated in Figure 4.3: the center of the triangle is where the three side bisectors intersect.

To determine the x and y coordinates of the port located on the boundary of the triangle block, elementary geometry is used as follows. The hypotenuse h of the subtriangle with opposite side length d and adjacent side length $w/2$ is

$$h = \frac{w/2}{\cos(\pi/6)} = \frac{w}{\sqrt{3}} \tag{4.7}$$

where w is the block width and the opposite side length

$$d = \left(\frac{w}{2}\right)\tan\left(\frac{\pi}{6}\right) \tag{4.8}$$

For the purpose of writing C++ code, the development that follows is divided into three angular domains: $\theta \in [0, 2\pi/3)$, $\theta \in [2\pi/3, 4\pi/3]$, and $\theta \in (4\pi/3, 2\pi]$.

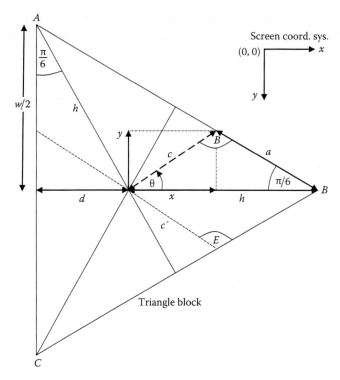

FIGURE 4.3   A triangle block showing a port location vector of length c or c' at an angle θ.

For $\theta \in [0, 2\pi/3)$, the law of sines allows one to determine the length of the side length c, i.e.,

$$\frac{\sin(B)}{h} = \frac{\sin(\pi/6)}{c} \tag{4.9a}$$

$$\Rightarrow c = \frac{h}{2\sin(5\pi/6 - \theta)} \tag{4.9b}$$

where the denominator is nonzero for $\theta \in [0, 2\pi/3)$. The x and y components, with respect to the local triangle coordinate system, of the port on the boundary of the block, are $x = c\cos(\theta)$ and $y = c\sin(\theta)$, and hence, the global port position is

$$x_{\text{port}} = x_{\text{block}} + c\cos(\theta) \tag{4.10a}$$

$$y_{\text{port}} = y_{\text{block}} - c\sin(\theta) \tag{4.10b}$$

For $\theta \in [2\pi/3, 4\pi/3]$, the x and y components of the port located on the boundary of the block are, $x = -d$ and $y = d\tan(\pi - \theta)$, where $\pi - \theta \neq \pm\pi/2$ for $\theta \in [2\pi/3, 4\pi/3]$, and hence, the global port position is

$$x_{\text{port}} = x_{\text{block}} - d \tag{4.11a}$$

$$y_{\text{port}} = y_{\text{block}} - d\tan(\pi - \theta) \tag{4.11b}$$

For $\theta \in (4\pi/3, 2\pi]$, the law of sines allows one to determine the length of the side length c', i.e.,

$$\frac{\sin(E)}{h} = \frac{\sin(\pi/6)}{c'} \tag{4.12a}$$

$$\Rightarrow c' = \frac{h}{2\sin(\theta - 7\pi/6)} \tag{4.12b}$$

where the denominator is nonzero for $\theta \in (4\pi/3, 2\pi]$. The local x and y components of the position of the port on the boundary of the block are $x = c' \cos(\theta)$ and $y = c' \sin(\theta)$, and hence, the global port position is

$$x_{\text{port}} = x_{\text{block}} + c' \cos(\theta) \tag{4.13a}$$

$$y_{\text{port}} = y_{\text{block}} - c' \sin(\theta) \tag{4.13b}$$

A similar analysis may be performed for a triangle block facing to the left rather than to the right (as pictured earlier). For the purpose of writing C++ code, the development that follows is divided into four angular domains: $\theta \in [0, \pi/3]$, $\theta \in (\pi/3, \pi]$, $\theta \in [\pi, 5\pi/3)$, and $\theta \in [5\pi/3, 2\pi]$.

For $\theta \in [0, \pi/3]$, the x and y components of a port located on the boundary of the block are $x = d$ and $y = d \tan(\theta)$, and hence, the global port position is

$$x_{\text{port}} = x_{\text{block}} + d \tag{4.14a}$$

$$y_{\text{port}} = y_{\text{block}} - d \tan(\theta) \tag{4.14b}$$

For $\theta \in (\pi/3, \pi]$, the law of sines allows one to determine the length of the side length c, i.e.,

$$\frac{\sin(B)}{h} = \frac{\sin(\pi/6)}{c} \tag{4.15a}$$

$$\Rightarrow c = \frac{h}{2\sin(\theta - \pi/6)} \tag{4.15b}$$

where the denominator is nonzero for $\theta \in (\pi/3, \pi]$. The x and y components, with respect to the local triangle coordinate system, of the position of the port on the boundary of the block are $x = c \cos(\theta)$ and $y = c \sin(\theta)$, and hence, the global port position is

$$x_{\text{port}} = x_{\text{block}} + c \cos(\theta) \tag{4.16a}$$

$$y_{\text{port}} = y_{\text{block}} - c \sin(\theta) \tag{4.16b}$$

For $\theta \in [\pi, 5\pi/3)$, the law of sines allows one to determine the length of the side length c', i.e.,

$$\frac{\sin(E)}{h} = \frac{\sin(\pi/6)}{c'} \tag{4.17a}$$

$$\Rightarrow c' = \frac{h}{2\sin(11\pi/6 - \theta)} \tag{4.17b}$$

where the denominator is nonzero for $\theta \in [\pi, 5\pi/3)$. The local x and y components of the position of the port on the boundary of the block are $x = c' \cos(\theta)$ and $y = c' \sin(\theta)$, and hence, the global port position is

$$x_{\text{port}} = x_{\text{block}} + c' \cos(\theta) \tag{4.18a}$$

$$y_{\text{port}} = y_{\text{block}} - c' \sin(\theta) \tag{4.18b}$$

For $\theta \in [5\pi/3, 2\pi]$, the x and y components of the port located on the boundary of the block are $x = d$ and $y = d \tan(2\pi - \theta)$, and hence, the global port position is

$$x_{\text{port}} = x_{\text{block}} + d \tag{4.19a}$$

$$y_{\text{port}} = y_{\text{block}} + d \tan(2\pi - \theta) \tag{4.19b}$$

The implementation that follows is structured to support the setting up of a port whose location is defined by a positioning angle, as described earlier: the developer should keep this general idea in mind.

4.3   CHANGING THE CPORT CLASS

The changes and additions that need to be made to the CPort class, to calculate the port position and setup port properties, involve its member variables and methods, including the CPort constructor.

4.3.1   CPORT MEMBER VARIABLES

At present, a placeholder variable of type double, named "port_position", exists in the CPort class declaration: this should be deleted and replaced with a private CPoint variable, named "m_ptPortPosition". This will hold the (x, y) position of the port in generalized coordinates, i.e., with respect to the upper left corner of the screen, rather than in relative coordinates, with respect to the center point of the block.

In addition, the port name, recorded in the character array, "port_name", should be changed to the more convenient CString type variable, "m_strPortName".

In the earlier discussion, the port position angle is used to determine the local port position on the side face of a block, which in turn is used to determine the port's generalized coordinates with respect to the upper left corner of the screen. Hence, add a private double member variable to the CPort class to hold the port position angle, named "m_dPortPositionAngle".

Finally, in the Win32 Console Application code, the enumerated type, "EPortID", was used to identify the nature of a port. Now that this identification has become clear, in that it should reflect the direction or the arrow-head-like port icon, "EPortID" should be replaced with "EPortArrowDirection" throughout the code. In addition, the CPort member variable, "e_port_id", can be changed to "m_ePortArrowDirec" wherever it appears, for ease of interpretation.

4.3.2 CPORT MEMBER METHODS

There are numerous CPort member methods that need to be added to the project to facilitate the calculation of the port position given a location-defining angle, as described in Section 4.3.1.

4.3.2.1 Accessor Methods

Add a public constant member function to the CPort class, with the prototype, CPoint CPort::GetPortPosition(void) const, to return the port position, "m_ptPortPosition", introduced earlier and edit the function as follows.

```
CPoint CPort::GetPortPosition() const
{
    return m_ptPortPosition;
}
```

Add a public member function to the CPort class to set the port position, with the prototype, void CPort::SetPortPosition(CPoint port_posn), and edit the function as shown.

```
void CPort::SetPortPosition(CPoint port_posn)
{
    m_ptPortPosition = port_posn;
}
```

The original Win32 Console Application had a GetName() member method of the CPort class. However, to make it clear that it is the port name that is to be retrieved, delete the existing, GetName() method, and replace it with a new CPort public constant member function with the prototype, CString CPort::GetPortName(void) const, and edit it as follows.

```
CString CPort::GetPortName() const
{
    return m_strPortName;
}
```

Now, add a public member function to the CPort class to set the port name, with prototype, void CPort::SetPortName(CString name), and edit it as follows.

```
void CPort::SetPortName(CString name)
{
    m_strPortName = name;
}
```

The port position angle variable, "m_ptPortPositionAngle", used to define the position of a port on the side face of a block requires its own accessor functions. Hence, add a public constant member function to the CPort class to get the port position angle, with prototype, double CPort::GetPortPositionAngle(void) const, and edit the code as follows.

```
double CPort::GetPortPositionAngle() const
{
    // Port position angle
    return m_dPortPositionAngle;
}
```

Add a public member function to the CPort class to set the port position angle, with prototype, `void CPort::SetPortPositionAngle(angle)`, and edit the code as shown.

```
void CPort::SetPortPositionAngle(double angle)
{
    // Set the angle w.r.t. the horizontal x-axis that the port should be
      located at, on the bndy of the block.
    m_dPortPositionAngle = angle;
}
```

The "m_ePortArrowDirection" member variable introduced earlier, specifying the enumerated-type-based direction of the port, is to be accessed. Hence, add a new public constant member function to the CPort class, with prototype, `EPortArrowDirection CPort::GetPortArrowDirection (void) const`, and edit it as follows.

```
EPortArrowDirection CPort::GetPortArrowDirection() const
{
    return m_ePortArrowDirec;
}
```

Finally, for completeness, add a new public member method to the CPort class with the prototype, `void CPort::SetPortArrowDirection(EPortArrowDirection arrow_direc)`, and edit it as follows.

```
void CPort::SetPortArrowDirection(EPortArrowDirection arrow_direc)
{
    m_ePortArrowDirec = arrow_direc;
}
```

4.3.2.2 Calculate Port Position

The mathematical discussion presented earlier indicated how a block's port position, measured with respect to the global coordinate system, may be determined using the port position angle, "m_dPortPositionAngle": this is performed using a position calculation function. Hence, add a public member function to the CPort class, with prototype, `CPoint CPort::CalculatePortPosition(void)`, and edit the code as shown in the following.

```
CPoint CPort::CalculatePortPosition()
{
    int count;   // no. of times 360 divides into m_dPortPositionAngle.
    double c;    // length of ray from triangle CM to port posn on bndy of
      triangle.
    double d;    // opp. side length of a subtriangle with hypotenuse h,
      and adjacent side length width/2.
    double eps = 0.0087;   // epsilon value (radians) to allow setting of
      angle at 2*pi; (0.0087 radians = 0.5 degrees)
    double h;              // hypotenuse of a subtriangle with opp. side
      length d, and adjacent side length width/2.
    double height = m_rRefToBlock.GetBlockShape().GetBlockHeight();
    double pi = PI;
    double r;              // length of port posn vector.
    double theta;          // m_dPortPositionAngle converted to an angle
      in radians.
```

```
double theta_crit;     // critical theta value used to determine
  port_posn.x and port_posn.y
double width = m_rRefToBlock.GetBlockShape().GetBlockWidth();
CPoint blk_posn = m_rRefToBlock.GetBlockPosition();
CPoint port_posn;
EBlockDirection e_blk_direc = m_rRefToBlock.GetBlockShape().
  GetBlockDirection();
EBlockShape e_blk_shape = m_rRefToBlock.GetBlockShape().
  GetBlockShapeType();

CString sMsg;          // main msg string
UINT nType = MB_OK;    // style of msg. box
UINT nIDhelp = 0;      // help context ID for the msg.

// Convert port position angle into domain [0,360]
if(m_dPortPositionAngle > 360.00)
{
    count = int(m_dPortPositionAngle/360.00);
    m_dPortPositionAngle = m_dPortPositionAngle - count*360.00;
}
if(m_dPortPositionAngle < 0.00)
{
    count = int(fabs(m_dPortPositionAngle/360.00));
    m_dPortPositionAngle = m_dPortPositionAngle +
      (count + 1)*360.00;
}

// Convert port position angle from degrees into radians
theta = m_dPortPositionAngle*pi/180.00;

//sMsg.Format("\n CPort::CalculatePortPosition(),
  m_dPortPositionAngle = %lf, theta = %3.15lf, 2*pi+eps = %3.15lf\n",
  m_dPortPositionAngle, theta, 2*pi+eps);
//AfxMessageBox(sMsg, nType, nIDhelp);

// Switch upon shape
switch(e_blk_shape)
{
case e_ellipse:

    port_posn.x = blk_posn.x + 0.5*width*cos(theta);
    port_posn.y = blk_posn.y - 0.5*width*sin(theta);
    break;

case e_rectangle:      // rectangle caters for squares (width = height)
  and rectangles (width != height)

    theta_crit = atan(height/width); // atan2(y,x) = arctangent of y/x

    if((theta >= 0) && (theta <= theta_crit))
    {
        r = width/(2*cos(theta));
        port_posn.x = blk_posn.x + width*0.5;
        port_posn.y = blk_posn.y - r*sin(theta);
    }
    if((theta > theta_crit) && (theta < (pi - theta_crit)))
    {
        r = height/(2*sin(theta));
        port_posn.x = blk_posn.x + r*cos(theta);
        port_posn.y = blk_posn.y - height*0.5;
    }
```

```
    if((theta >= (pi - theta_crit)) && (theta <= (pi + theta_crit)))
    {
        r = -width/(2*cos(theta));
        port_posn.x = blk_posn.x - width*0.5;
        port_posn.y = blk_posn.y - r*sin(theta);
    }
    if((theta > (pi + theta_crit)) && (theta < (2*pi - theta_crit)))
    {
        r = -height/(2*sin(theta));
        port_posn.x = blk_posn.x + r*cos(theta);
        port_posn.y = blk_posn.y + height*0.5;
    }
    if((theta >= (2*pi - theta_crit)) && (theta <= (2*pi + eps)))
    {
        r = width/(2*cos(theta));
        port_posn.x = blk_posn.x + width*0.5;
        port_posn.y = blk_posn.y - r*sin(theta);
    }
    break;

case e_triangle:

    // Get lengths of subtriangle sides: hypotenuse h, opp. side
    //   length d., and base side length width/2.
    d = (width/2)*tan(pi/6);
    h = width/sqrt(3);

    if(e_blk_direc == e_right)      // triangle pointing to the right.
    {
        if((theta >= 0) && (theta < 2*pi/3))
        {
            c = h/(2*sin(5*pi/6 - theta));    // length of ray from
              CM to port posn on bndy of triangle.
            port_posn.x = blk_posn.x + c*cos(theta);
            port_posn.y = blk_posn.y - c*sin(theta);
        }
        if((theta >= 2*pi/3) && (theta <= 4*pi/3))
        {
            port_posn.x = blk_posn.x - d;
            port_posn.y = blk_posn.y - d*tan(pi - theta);
        }
        if((theta > 4*pi/3) && (theta <= (2*pi + eps)))
        {
            c = h/(2*sin(theta - 7*pi/6));
            port_posn.x = blk_posn.x + c*cos(theta);
            port_posn.y = blk_posn.y - c*sin(theta);
        }
    }
    else if(e_blk_direc == e_left)    // triangle pointing to the
      left.
    {
        if((theta >= 0) && (theta <= pi/3))
        {
            port_posn.x = blk_posn.x + d;
            port_posn.y = blk_posn.y - d*tan(theta);
        }
        if((theta > pi/3) && (theta <= pi))
```

```
                {
                    c = h/(2*sin(theta - pi/6));           // length of ray
                        from CM to port posn on bndy of triangle.
                    port_posn.x = blk_posn.x + c*cos(theta);
                    port_posn.y = blk_posn.y - c*sin(theta);
                }
                if((theta > pi) && (theta < 5*pi/3))
                {
                    c = h/(2*sin(11*pi/6 - theta));
                    port_posn.x = blk_posn.x + c*cos(theta);
                    port_posn.y = blk_posn.y - c*sin(theta);
                }
                if((theta >= 5*pi/3) && (theta <= (2*pi + eps)))
                {
                    port_posn.x = blk_posn.x + d;
                    port_posn.y = blk_posn.y + d*tan(2*pi - theta);
                }
            }
        else
            {
                // Print msg.
                sMsg.Format("\n CPort::CalculatePortPosition()\n e_blk_direc
                    for triangles should be e_left or e_right only!");
            AfxMessageBox(sMsg, nType, nIDhelp);
        }
        break;

        default:
        // no code for now
        break;
        }// end switch

    // Set port position within CalculatePortPosition() to prevent an
        additional call.
    SetPortPosition(port_posn);

    return port_posn;
}
```

The developer will notice, in the previous code, the use of the constant double value, "PI", to set the numerical value of π. Hence, add the definition of this constant to the "Block.h" header file as shown in the following (the ellipsis, "…", denotes omitted, unchanged code).

```
// Title: Block.h

#ifndef BLOCK_H
    #define BLOCK_H                        // inclusion guard

    #include <vector>                      // rqd. for vector (below)

    using namespace std;

    // User defined consts/vars.
    const double PI = 3.14159265359; // pi in radians (rounded)

    // User defined types
    ...
#endif
```

In addition, search for all occurrences of "pi" in the code and initialize, "pi = PI", in place of any numerical initialization that may be present. Note that, "PI" is in radians, and code using trigonometric functions will require arguments in radians.

After the variable declaration section, the port position angle, θ, represented by, "m_dPortPositionAngle", has its domain bounded, such that $\theta \in [0, 2\pi]$, to allow the user setting up the port to specify any value of the angle. The developer will notice the use of the function, "double fabs(double x)", to obtain the floating point absolute value of the operand: this is used since the argument is a floating point number. If an integer-valued argument is used, then the function, "int abs(int x)", should be used instead: these two versions of the absolute value function should not be confused.

The main *switch* statement concerns the block shape: an ellipse, a rectangle, or a triangle. Thereafter, the port position is determined with respect to the global screen coordinate system, where the mathematical details reflect those provided earlier. The developer will notice that the triangular Gain block can be oriented to the right (default) or left (although the enumerated type EBlockDirection, does cater for the additional "up" and "down" directions, these are not considered here: the interested reader may add this functionality if desired). Finally, after the *switch* statement, a call to SetPortPosition() is made to set the port position member variable, "m_ptPortPosition".

The developer will notice that an epsilon value, $\varepsilon = 0.0087^c = 0.5°$, was added to the domain-checking code for the rectangle block for the port position angle $\theta \in [2\pi - \theta_{crit}, 2\pi + \varepsilon]$ and the right and left facing triangle blocks for the port position angle, $\theta \in [4\pi/3, 2\pi + \varepsilon]$ and $\theta \in [5\pi/3, 2\pi + \varepsilon]$, respectively. This was done to allow setting of the angle at 360.00° rather than 0.00° if desired by the user. Finally, when testing the code, the developer may choose values of θ in all critical subdomains and on the domain boundaries specified in the earlier mathematical development.

4.3.2.3   CPort Constructor

The CPort constructor may now be altered to be of the form shown in the following, where the member variables, "m_strPortName", "m_ptPortPosition", and "m_ePortArrowDirec", are explicitly set with default values, and the reference-to-CBlock, "m_rRefToBlock", is set via member initialization (as introduced earlier). Later in the development, the name of the port will be used, where appropriate, to denote the port sign, e.g., when using a Divide or Sum block, but, for now, it can assume the CPort-based placeholder identity, "actual_port_name".

```
CPort::CPort(CBlock &block_ref):
m_rRefToBlock(block_ref)    // must init the m_rRefToBlock rather than
  assign on CPort obj. creation
{
    // Init
    m_strPortName = "actual_port_name";
    m_ptPortPosition.x = 0.0;             // generalized coords not rel.
      coords.
    m_ptPortPosition.y = 0.0;             // generalized coords not rel.
      coords.
    m_ePortArrowDirec = e_right_arrow;    // in general port arrows point
      to the right.
}
```

4.4   AUGMENTING THE CBLOCK CLASS

A block has a vector of input and output, "m_vecInputPorts" and "m_vecOutputPorts", respectively, and these are of type, "vector<CPort*>", i.e., they contain pointer-to-CPort objects, effectively, the addresses of the ports. The developer will recall from Chapter 3 that the

`CSystemModel::GetBlockList()` function returns the system model's block list by reference: this idea is used here when retrieving the vectors of input and output ports of the block.

Hence, add a public member function to the CBlock class with the prototype, `vector<CPort*> &CBlock::GetVectorOfInputPorts()`, to return "m_vecInputPorts" by reference. The ClassWizard indicates that, "Template declarations or definitions cannot be added.", so change the return type to be "int &", i.e., a reference-to-integer, then manually change the source and header files to have the aforementioned definition. Edit the code as follows.

```
vector<CPort*> &CBlock::GetVectorOfInputPorts()
{
    return m_vecInputPorts;
}
```

Add a public member function to the CBlock class with the prototype, `vector<CPort*> &CBlock::GetVectorOfOutputPorts()`, to return "m_vecOutputPorts" by reference, and edit the code as follows.

```
vector<CPort*> &CBlock::GetVectorOfOutputPorts()
{
    return m_vecOutputPorts;
}
```

Make sure the "Block.h" header file has the correct function prototypes for the recently added accessor functions, i.e., the return type is "`vector<CPort*> &`".

4.5   AUGMENTING THE CBLOCKSHAPE CLASS

The `CPort::CalculatePortPostion()` function introduced earlier and the `DrawPort()` function to be introduced in the following port-drawing section make use of CBlockShape functions to retrieve variables denoting the block shape. The CBlockShape class is amended as follows to include a new member variable and member accessor functions.

First, add a private member variable of type double, to the CBlockShape class named "m_dBlockHeight": this accompanies the "m_dBlockWidth" variable already present. Now add a public constant member function to the CBlockShape class, to get the member variable, "m_dBlockHeight", with the prototype, `double CBlockShape::GetBlockHeight(void) const`, and edit the function as shown.

```
double CBlockShape::GetBlockHeight() const
{
    // Return the member var m_dBlockHeight
    return m_dBlockHeight;
}
```

Add a public member function to the CBlockShape class, to set the variable, "m_dBlockHeight", with prototype, `void CBlockShape::SetBlockHeight(double blk_height)`, and edit the code as follows.

```
void CBlockShape::SetBlockHeight(double blk_height)
{
    // Set the member var m_dBlockHeight
    m_dBlockHeight = blk_height;
}
```

The developer should make sure that the width member variable, "m_dBlockWidth", also has the relevant accessor methods. The `GetBlockWidth()` function was introduced in Chapter 3, but for convenience, it is repeated here.

```
double CBlockShape::GetBlockWidth() const
{
    return m_dBlockWidth;
}
```

Add a public member function to the CBlockShape class to set the block width, with prototype, void CBlockShape::SetBlockWidth(double blk_width), and edit the code as follows.

```
void CBlockShape::SetBlockWidth(double blk_width)
{
    // Set the member var m_dBlockWidth
    m_dBlockWidth = blk_width;
}
```

Finally, make sure that the width and height member variables are correctly set in the CBlockShape constructor function as shown in the following.

```
CBlockShape::CBlockShape(void)
{
    m_eBlockDirection = e_right;          // default direc is to the right.
    m_dBlockWidth = (GetDocumentGlobalFn()->GetDeltaLength())*2.0;
    m_dBlockHeight = m_dBlockWidth;
}
```

4.6   DERIVED-BLOCK CONSTRUCTORS

Now that the underlying structure has been added to the CPort, CBlock, and CBlockShape classes, a CPort object may be instantiated from within a CBlock-derived block constructor and then set up before being added to the appropriate block-based vector of input or output ports.

4.6.1   CConstantBlock CONSTRUCTOR

Chapter 3 provided the CBlock-derived block constructor functions for all the blocks on the Common Blocks toolbar. Here, the CConstantBlock constructor is augmented as shown in the following, to construct a CPort object using the CPort constructor, where the "this" pointer is dereferenced to access the block object and used to set the "m_rRefToBlock" variable of the CPort class (see the previous CPort constructor).

In addition, the developer will notice that the output port name "output_port" is replaced with "_", denoting that there is no mathematical sign applicable to the output port. The names used for the input ports are "×", "/", "+", and "−", corresponding to the multiplication, division, addition, and subtraction operations, respectively. An example of names being set for both the input and output ports may be found in the CSumBlock constructor in Section 4.6.3.

```
CConstantBlock::CConstantBlock(CSystemModel *pParentSystemModel, CPoint
  blk_posn, EBlockShape e_blk_shape):
CBlock(pParentSystemModel, blk_posn, e_blk_shape)
{
    SetBlockName("constant_block");

    // Create an output port
    CPort *p_output_port = new CPort(*this);

    // Set port properties
    p_output_port->SetPortName("_");
    p_output_port->SetPortPositionAngle(0.0);             // port posn angle
      0 degrees, i.e. right side.
```

```
    p_output_port->CalculatePortPosition();
    p_output_port->SetPortArrowDirection(e_right_arrow);

    // Add the port to the vector of ports
    GetVectorOfOutputPorts().push_back(p_output_port);
}
```

The developer will notice that the accessor functions introduced earlier are used to set the port name, position angle, and arrow direction. The CalculatePortPosition() function does not require arguments, since as it is a function of the CPort class, it has access to the class member variables: in particular, "m_dPortPositionAngle", as shown in the function definition provided earlier. Finally, after the port has been constructed and set up, it is added to the vector of output ports that are retrieved by the CBlock function, GetVectorOfOutputPorts().

4.6.2   CHECK THE SYSTEM MODEL

The CheckSystemModel() function of the CDiagramEngDoc class was used in Chapter 3 to check the construction of blocks added to the system model's block list. This function is now augmented as shown in bold in the following to simply display the number of input and output ports on a block.

```
void CDiagramEngDoc::CheckSystemModel()
{
    int n_in_ports = 0;
    int n_out_ports = 0;

    // -- Message box vars.
    CString sMsg;            // main msg string
    CString sMsgTemp;        // temp msg string
    UINT nType = MB_OK;      // style of msg. box
    UINT nIDhelp = 0;        // help context ID for the msg.

    sMsgTemp.Format("\n CDiagramEngDoc::CheckSystemModel()\n");
    sMsg += sMsgTemp;

    // -- Block list vars.
    list<CBlock*> blk_list;
    list<CBlock*>::iterator it_blk;   // iterator for list of CBlock-ptrs

    blk_list = GetSystemModel().GetBlockList();

    // -- Check Block List
    for(it_blk = blk_list.begin(); it_blk != blk_list.end(); it_blk++)
    {
        sMsgTemp.Format(" %s: ",(*it_blk)->GetBlockName());
        sMsg += sMsgTemp;

        // Get the vectors of input and output ports and determine their
         sizes.
        n_in_ports = (*it_blk)->GetVectorOfInputPorts().size();
        n_out_ports = (*it_blk)->GetVectorOfOutputPorts().size();

        sMsgTemp.Format(" n_in_ports = %d, n_out_ports = %d\n",
          n_in_ports, n_out_ports);
        sMsg += sMsgTemp;
    }
    AfxMessageBox(sMsg, nType, nIDhelp);
}
```

FIGURE 4.4 `CheckSystemModel()` displays a message box showing the block type and the number of input and output ports: here, a Constant Block is constructed with no input ports and one output port.

Compile and run the code to check the numbers of input and output ports for the block concerned (here a Constant block): the following message box indicates that the numbers of input and output ports are zero and one, respectively (Figure 4.4).

4.6.3 AUGMENTING THE REMAINING BLOCK CONSTRUCTORS

Now that the CConstantBlock constructor function has been shown to work, wherein a CPort object is constructed and added to the vector of output ports, the remaining block construction functions should be augmented in a similar manner, to first construct a port, set its properties, and then to add it to the appropriate vector. Table 4.1 lists the CBlock-derived block classes, the default port position angles, and port arrow directions used in block construction: "right" and "up" denote "e_right_arrow" and "e_up_arrow", respectively. Input and output ports are named (at least at this stage in the project) "input_port" and "output_port", respectively.

An example of a block with multiple input ports and an output port is the Sum block, whose constructor function is provided in the following for convenience. The developer can model the remaining block constructors of the classes listed in Table 4.1, using this example.

TABLE 4.1
CBlock-Derived Block Classes Whose Constructors Should Be Augmented to Construct Ports with the Following Settings

Class Name	Input Port θ	Port Direction	Output Port θ	Port Direction
CConstantBlock	NA	NA	0.0	Right
CDerivativeBlock	180.0	Right	0.0	Right
CDivideBlock	150.0, 210.0	Right, Right	0.0	Right
CGainBlock	180.0	Right	0.0	Right
CIntegratorBlock	180.0	Right	0.0	Right
CLinearFnBlock	NA	NA	0.0	Right
COutputBlock	180.0	Right	NA	NA
CSignalGeneratorBlock	NA	NA	0.0	Right
CSubsystemBlock	180.0	Right	0.0	Right
CSubsystemInBlock	NA	NA	0.0	Right
CSubsystemOutBlock	180.0	Right	NA	NA
CSumBlock	180.0, 270.0	Right, Up	0.0	Right
CTransferFnBlock	180.0	Right	0.0	Right

NA, not applicable.

```
CSumBlock::CSumBlock(CPoint blk_posn, EBlockShape e_blk_shape):
CBlock(blk_posn, e_blk_shape)
{
    SetBlockName("sum_block");

    // Create input and output ports
    CPort *p_input_port1 = new CPort(*this);
    CPort *p_input_port2 = new CPort(*this);
    CPort *p_output_port = new CPort(*this);

    // Set the port names
    p_input_port1->SetPortName("+");
    p_input_port2->SetPortName("+");
    p_output_port->SetPortName("_");

    // Set the port posns.
    p_input_port1->SetPortPositionAngle(180.0);    // port on left side
      at 180.0
    p_input_port1->CalculatePortPosition();
    p_input_port2->SetPortPositionAngle(270.0); // port below at 270.0
    p_input_port2->CalculatePortPosition();
    p_output_port->SetPortPositionAngle(0.0);      // port on right side
      at 0.0
    p_output_port->CalculatePortPosition();

    // Set the port arrow directions
    p_input_port1->SetPortArrowDirection(e_right_arrow);
    p_input_port2->SetPortArrowDirection(e_up_arrow);
    p_output_port->SetPortArrowDirection(e_right_arrow);

    // Add the port to the vector of ports
    GetVectorOfInputPorts().push_back(p_input_port1);
    GetVectorOfInputPorts().push_back(p_input_port2);
    GetVectorOfOutputPorts().push_back(p_output_port);
}
```

4.7 DRAWING PORTS

Now that input and output ports have been constructed and added to their block-based input and output port vectors, these may be drawn via a call to `CBlock::DrawBlockPorts()` (note the plural, "ports") from within the particular derived-block-overriding `DrawBlock()` function. For example, `CConstantBlock::DrawBlock()` calls `DrawBlockPorts()` of the CBlock class, and inside `CBlock::DrawBlockPorts()` the vector of input and output ports may be obtained and iterated over, and `CPort::DrawPort()` (note the singular, "port") may be called to draw the particular vector-based port. The general steps involved to draw block ports are as follows.

1. Call `CBlock::DrawBlockPorts()`
2. Add `CBlock::DrawBlockPorts()`
3. Add `CPort::DrawPort()`

4.7.1 CALL `CBlock::DrawBlockPorts()`

The CBlock-derived block classes all have an overriding virtual `DrawBlock()` member method in which derived-block-specific drawing functionality is provided, as introduced in Chapter 3. Now that a block's ports can be constructed, they can be drawn via a call to `DrawBlockPorts()`, from within the derived block's `DrawBlock()` function.

Augment all the CBlock-derived blocks' virtual `DrawBlock()` functions, with a call to the to-be-added CBlock-based `DrawBlockPorts()` method, as shown in the following code excerpt. Here, the `CConstantBlock::DrawBlock()` function performs all its drawing, before finally calling the base class `DrawBlockPorts()` function, passing in the pointer-to-Class-Device-Context argument. The ellipsis ("…") denotes omitted but unchanged code from Chapter 3.

```
void CConstantBlock::DrawBlock(CDC *pDC)
{
    // Note: pDC is a ptr to the device context of "Class Device
      Context" (CDC)
    int i;
    ...

    // Reset the prev. pen
    ...

    // Draw block ports
    DrawBlockPorts(pDC);
}
```

The call to DrawBlockPorts() shown earlier in bold needs to be made to all overriding virtual `DrawBlock()` functions of all CBlock-derived classes, as listed in Table 4.1.

4.7.2 ADD `CBlock::DrawBlockPorts()`

Now that the call to `DrawBlockPorts()` has been made within the overriding `DrawBlock()` functions, it needs to be added to the CBlock base class. Hence, add a public member function to the CBlock class with the prototype, void `CBlock::DrawBlockPorts(CDC *pDC)`, and edit it as shown in the following.

```
void CBlock::DrawBlockPorts(CDC *pDC)
{
    vector<CPort*>::iterator it_port;    // vector iterator.

    //AfxMessageBox("\n CBlock::DrawBlockPorts()\n", MB_OK, 0);

    // Iterate through vec of input ports
    for(it_port = m_vecInputPorts.begin(); it_port != m_vecInputPorts.
      end(); it_port++)
    {
        (*it_port)->DrawPort(pDC);          // call CPort::DrawPort()
    }

    // Iterate through vec of output ports
    for(it_port = m_vecOutputPorts.begin(); it_port != m_vecOutputPorts.
      end(); it_port++)
    {
        (*it_port)->DrawPort(pDC);          // call CPort::DrawPort()
    }
}
```

4.7.3 ADD `CPort::DrawPort()`

The function `CBlock::DrawBlockPorts()` iterates over the vectors of input and output ports, "m_vecInputPorts" and "m_vecOutputPorts", respectively, calling `DrawPort()` upon the pointer-to-CPort object. Hence, add a public member function to the CPort class, with the prototype, void `CPort::DrawPort(CDC *pDC)`, and edit the function as shown.

```
void CPort::DrawPort(CDC *pDC)
{
    int i;
    int brush_color;        // local brush color
    int pen_color;          // local pen color
    int pen_width;          // local pen width
    int shift_left = 0;     // shift left arrow port graphic
    int shift_up = 0;       // shift up arrow port graphic
    int shift_right = 0;    // shift right arrow port graphic
    int shift_down = 0;     // shift down arrow port graphic
    double d;               // half the length of the longest port
      triangle side
    double width;           // block width
    CPoint pt_array[3];     // array of pts to draw the port graphic
    CString sMsg;           // main msg string
    UINT nType = MB_OK;     // style of msg. box
    UINT nIDhelp = 0;       // help context ID for the msg.

    // Msg. box
    sMsg.Format("\n CPort::DrawPort(), m_ePortArrowDirec = %d\n,"
      m_ePortArrowDirec);
    //AfxMessageBox(sMsg, nType, nIDhelp);

    // Get block width using the m_rRefToBlock
    width = m_rRefToBlock.GetBlockShape().GetBlockWidth();
    d = 0.05*width;  // d as a percentage of block width

    // Switch on EPortArrowDirection m_ePortArrowDirec
    switch(m_ePortArrowDirec)
    {
    case e_left_arrow:
        pt_array[0].x = m_ptPortPosition.x + 0.5*d;
        pt_array[0].y = m_ptPortPosition.y + d;
        pt_array[1].x = m_ptPortPosition.x - 0.5*d;
        pt_array[1].y = m_ptPortPosition.y;
        pt_array[2].x = pt_array[0].x;
        pt_array[2].y = m_ptPortPosition.y - d;

        // Shift pts as desired
        if(shift_left)
        {
            for(i=0;i<3;i++)
            {
                pt_array[i].x = pt_array[i].x - 0.5*d;
            }
        }
        break;

    case e_up_arrow:
        pt_array[0].x = m_ptPortPosition.x - d;
        pt_array[0].y = m_ptPortPosition.y + 0.5*d;
        pt_array[1].x = m_ptPortPosition.x;
        pt_array[1].y = m_ptPortPosition.y - 0.5*d;
        pt_array[2].x = m_ptPortPosition.x + d;
        pt_array[2].y = pt_array[0].y;

        // Shift pts as desired
        if(shift_up)
```

```
        {
        for(i=0;i<3;i++)
        {
            pt_array[i].y = pt_array[i].y + 0.5*d;
        }
    }
    break;

    case e_right_arrow:
        pt_array[0].x = m_ptPortPosition.x - 0.5*d;
        pt_array[0].y = m_ptPortPosition.y - d;
        pt_array[1].x = m_ptPortPosition.x + 0.5*d;
        pt_array[1].y = m_ptPortPosition.y;
        pt_array[2].x = pt_array[0].x;
        pt_array[2].y = m_ptPortPosition.y + d;

        // Shift pts as desired
        if(shift_right)
        {
            for(i=0;i<3;i++)
            {
                pt_array[i].x = pt_array[i].x + 0.5*d;
            }
        }
        break;

    case e_down_arrow:
        pt_array[0].x = m_ptPortPosition.x + d;
        pt_array[0].y = m_ptPortPosition.y - 0.5*d;
        pt_array[1].x = m_ptPortPosition.x;
        pt_array[1].y = m_ptPortPosition.y + 0.5*d;
        pt_array[2].x = m_ptPortPosition.x - d;
        pt_array[2].y = pt_array[0].y;

        // Shift pts as desired
        if(shift_down)
        {
            for(i=0;i<3;i++)
            {
                pt_array[i].y = pt_array[i].y - 0.5*d;
            }
        }
        break;

    default:
        // Use e_right_arrow case
        pt_array[0].x = m_ptPortPosition.x - 0.5*d;
        pt_array[0].y = m_ptPortPosition.y - d;
        pt_array[1].x = m_ptPortPosition.x + 0.5*d;
        pt_array[1].y = m_ptPortPosition.y;
        pt_array[2].x = m_ptPortPosition.x - 0.5*d;
        pt_array[2].y = m_ptPortPosition.y + d;

        // Shift pts as desired
        if(shift_right)
        {
            for(i=0;i<3;i++)
```

```
            {
                pt_array[i].x = pt_array[i].x + 0.5*d;
            }
        }
        break;
    }// end switch

    // -- FILL THE TRIANGULAR PORT POLYGON
    // Create a brush
    brush_color = RGB(200,200,200);    // White = RGB(255,255,255),
        Black = RGB(0,0,0)
    CBrush NewBrush(brush_color);      // create a new brush using the
        brush_color
    CBrush *pBrush;                    // declare a ptr-to-CBrush (for
        resetting below)

    // Select the new brush
    pBrush = pDC->SelectObject(&NewBrush);

    // Fill the polygon
    pDC->Polygon(pt_array, 3);         // 3 vertices of triangle stored in
        pt_array enclose polygon region

    // Reset the old brush
    pDC->SelectObject(pBrush);

    // -- DRAW THE BORDER OF THE TRIANGULAR PORT POLYGON
    // Set a new pen color for the border only
    pen_color = RGB(0,0,0);            // White = RGB(255,255,255), Black =
        RGB(0,0,0)
    pen_width = 1;

    // Create the pen
    CPen lpen(PS_SOLID, pen_width, pen_color);

    // Select the pen as the drawing obj.
    // The value returned by SelectObject() is a ptr to the obj. being
        replaced, i.e. an old-pen-ptr.
    CPen *pOldPen = pDC->SelectObject(&lpen);

    // Draw the arrow/triangle (clockwise)
    pDC->MoveTo(pt_array[0]);
    pDC->LineTo(pt_array[1]);
    pDC->LineTo(pt_array[2]);
    pDC->LineTo(pt_array[0]);

    // Reset the prev. pen
    pDC->SelectObject(pOldPen);
}
```

The developer will notice that the length, "d", used in the code, represents half the length of the hypotenuse of a right-angled triangle used to draw a port, where the 90° vertex ("pt_array[1]" given earlier) points in the intended direction of the port (left, up, right, or down) as shown in Figure 4.5. The center of the port lies in the middle of this right-angled triangle, such that the port intersects the block face upon which it resides, clearly displaying the intended signal flow direction.

4.7.4 DISPLAY OF BLOCK PORTS

Now that all block CBlock-derived block constructors can create their input and output ports and place them in the respective port vectors, "m_vecInputPorts" and "m_vecOutputPorts",

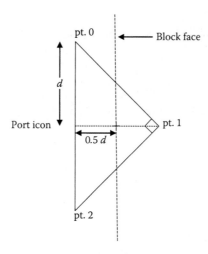

FIGURE 4.5   Block port graphic intersecting the block face and pointing to the right.

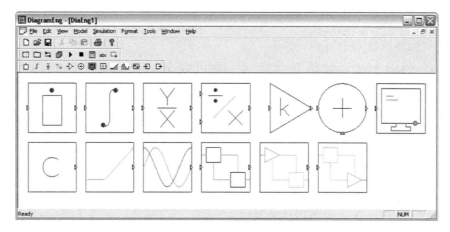

FIGURE 4.6   Derived blocks with default port settings as specified in their constructors.

they may be drawn via the virtual overriding DrawBlock() method, which invokes the base CBlock class' DrawBlockPorts() method, which in turn iterates through the aforementioned vectors calling DrawPort() upon a pointer-to-CPort. On building and then running the DiagramEng application and adding all the blocks available on the Common Blocks toolbar on the palette, the output should appear as shown in Figure 4.6: here, the default block ports are shaded in gray where the direction of the port arrow indicates the direction of signal flow into and/or out of the block.

4.8   SUMMARY

The construction of block-based ports first involved a mathematical discussion of the mechanism to place ports, based on a port position angle, on the side face of an elliptical-, rectangular-, or triangular-shaped block. CPort-based member variables and methods were added in preparation for calculating the port position, through a `CalculatePortPosition()` function, to determine the location of a port with respect to the generalized screen-based coordinate system. The CBlock and CBlockShape classes were also extended to aid correct derived-block construction. Sample CBlock-derived block constructors, i.e., the CConstantBlock and the CSumBlock, were provided, showing how CPort objects are to be constructed and set up prior to their addition in the block-based port vectors, "m_vecInputPorts" and "m_vecOutputPorts". Finally, the drawing of ports involved the derived block's `DrawBlock()` method invoking the base class `CBlock::DrawBlockPorts()` function, which in turn iterates through the vectors of input and output ports calling `CPort::DrawPort()` to draw the arrow-head-like ports.

5 Constructing Connections

5.1 INTRODUCTION

Connection objects are used to connect and transfer signal data between model blocks. A connection involves a tail and a head point, including an arrowhead that indicates the direction of signal flow. Appendix B presents a single document interface application that allows a user to simply draw lines with arrowheads attached, on the screen using the mouse. The developer is encouraged to read this material that is actually based on the work of Chapman [1], before commencing the development presented herein to extend the DiagramEng project.

5.2 ADDING CONNECTIONS TO THE DiagramEng PROJECT

The drawing of connections has been shown to work for the structurally simple Exp10 project, presented in Appendix B, involving the main classes: CExp10App, CExp10Doc, CExp10View, and CConnection. In the DiagramEng project, the CDiagramEngDoc class contains a "m_SystemModel" object of type CSystemModel, which itself contains the connection list, "list<CConnection*> m_lstConnection": it also contains the familiar block list, "list<CBlock*> m_lstBlock", discussed in previous chapters. Hence, there is an extra level of structure that needs to be taken into consideration: i.e., some of the functions that appeared in the CExp10Doc class of the Exp10 project (Appendix B) will appear in the CSystemModel class of the DiagramEng project, since the latter class directly has, as a member object, the connection list, "m_lstConnection".

The general steps to add CConnection objects to the DiagramEng project are listed as follows, where specific details are presented in the sections that follow.

1. Augment the CConnection class
2. Add a function to add the connection to the list
3. Add a function to get the connection list
4. Add an OnLButtonDown() function
5. Add an OnMouseMove() function
6. Add an OnLButtonUp() function
7. Draw connections
8. Build and run the application

5.2.1 AUGMENT THE CConnection CLASS

The CConnection class should be augmented to accommodate for model connections. Change the existing private (double-typed) member variables of the CConnection class, named, "start_pt" and "end_pt", to two CPoint members, "m_ptFrom" and "m_ptTo", respectively. In addition, add a new public constructor to the CConnection class with the prototype, CConnection::CConnection(CPoint ptFrom, CPoint ptTo), and edit the function as shown in the following to construct a CConnection object using the starting and ending points, "ptFrom" and "ptTo", respectively.

```
CConnection::CConnection(CPoint ptFrom, CPoint ptTo)
{
    // Init. member vars.
    m_ptFrom = ptFrom;              // pt from which connection is drawn
    m_ptTo = ptTo;                  // pt to which connection is drawn
    m_pRefFromPort = NULL;          // from-port ref.
    m_pRefToPort = NULL;            // to-port ref.
    m_pSignal = new CDoubleSignal;  // contained ptr-to-CSignal init. to
        NULL.
}
```

An aside: the developer will notice that, at present, a new CSignal-based object is created and its address assigned to "m_pSignal". This may change later depending on the CSignal-based class structure that is finally used for signal propagation purposes.

5.2.2 ADD A FUNCTION TO ADD THE CONNECTION TO THE LIST

CConnection objects need to be stored in a list of connections, i.e., the private "list<CConnection*> m_lstConnection" that is present in the CSystemModel class. Hence, add a public member function to the CSystemModel class to add the connection to the list, with the prototype, void CSystemModel::AddConnection(CPoint ptFrom, CPoint ptTo), and edit the function as shown.

```
void CSystemModel::AddConnection(CPoint ptFrom, CPoint ptTo)
{
    CString sMsg;           // main msg string
    UINT nType = MB_OK;     // style of msg. box
    UINT nIDhelp = 0;       // help context ID for the msg.

    // Print msg.
    sMsg.Format("\n CSystemModel::AddConnection(), from (%d,%d) to
        (%d,%d)\n", ptFrom.x, ptFrom.y, ptTo.x, ptTo.y);
    //AfxMessageBox(sMsg, nType, nIDhelp);

    // Create a new CConnection obj.
    CConnection *pCon = new CConnection(ptFrom, ptTo);

    // Add the new connection to the connection list
    m_lstConnection.push_back(pCon);

    // Get a ptr. to the doc. to call the CDocument member fn.
      SetModifiedFlag(), and mark the doc. as modified (TRUE).
    GetDocumentGlobalFn()->SetModifiedFlag(TRUE);
}
```

The AddConnection() function creates the connection using the CConnection constructor taking two CPoint arguments and adds it to the list of connections, "m_lstConnection".

5.2.3 ADD A FUNCTION TO GET THE CONNECTION LIST

Add a public member function to the CSystemModel class to get the connection list by reference, with prototype, list<CConnection*> &CSystemModel::GetConnectionList(void). This function works in a similar way to the CSystemModel::GetBlockList() method. The warning "Template declarations or definitions cannot be added" is presented. Hence, use an "int &" return type and then manually alter the function prototype declaration in "SystemModel.h" and definition in "SystemModel.cpp", to return the connection list by reference. Edit the function as shown.

```
list<CConnection*> &CSystemModel::GetConnectionList()
{
    // Return the connection list by reference
    return m_lstConnection;
}
```

5.2.4 ADD AN OnLButtonDown() FUNCTION

The user can draw a connection on the palette by clicking the left mouse button and moving the mouse pointer and then releasing the left button. Hence, these events should have functions associated with them. To add functionality to the left-button-down event, invoke the ClassWizard, choose CDiagramEngView as the class, WM_LBUTTONDOWN as the event message, and add the event-handler function, with the prototype: CDiagramEngView::OnLButtonDown(UINT nFlags, CPoint point). Edit the function to set the previous point, "m_ptPrevPos", and origin point, "m_ptOrigin", as shown.

```
void CDiagramEngView::OnLButtonDown(UINT nFlags, CPoint point)
{
    // TODO: Add your message handler code here and/or call default

    // DiagramEng (start)

    // Capture the mouse so no other apps. can get it.
    SetCapture();

    // Save the pt that the cursor is at, upon left-btn-down, i.e. init
      member var with incoming CPoint var.
    m_ptPrevPos = point;  // Init the prev. pt, to be used in
     OnMouseMove(), to the current point
    m_ptOrigin = point;   // Init the origin of the ensuing line, to be
      drawn in OnMouseMove(), to be the starting pt.

    // DiagramEng (end)

    CView::OnLButtonDown(nFlags, point);
}
```

The developer will notice that this function uses the member variables "m_ptPrevPos" and "m_ptOrigin" to be used in the following OnMouseMove() and OnLButtonUp() functions. Hence, add these two private CPoint member variables to the CDiagramEngView class.

5.2.5 ADD AN OnMouseMove() FUNCTION

Functionality is now added to the mouse movement event that takes place after the left-button-down event. Invoke the ClassWizard and select CDiagramEngView as the class and add an event-handler function with prototype, CDiagramEngView::OnMouseMove(UINT nFlags, CPoint point), for the WM_MOUSEMOVE event message: edit the function as shown in the following.

```
void CDiagramEngView::OnMouseMove(UINT nFlags, CPoint point)
{
    // TODO: Add your message handler code here and/or call default

    // DiagramEng (start)
```

```
    // Check to see if the left mouse btn. is down
    if((nFlags & MK_LBUTTON) == MK_LBUTTON)
    {
        // Check to see if mouse is captured
        if(GetCapture() == this)   // If what has been captured is the
          obj. upon which the present fn is called.
        {
            // Get the device context
            CClientDC dc(this);

            // Reverse the pixel color from the original pt to the prev pt.
            // SetROP2() sets the current foreground mix mode.
            dc.SetROP2(R2_NOT);    // R2_NOT => pixel is the inverse of
              the screen color

            // Declare a CConnection obj in order to call
              DrawConnection()
            CConnection con_obj1(m_ptOrigin, m_ptPrevPos);
            con_obj1.DrawConnection(&dc);
            //dc.MoveTo(m_ptOrigin);
            //dc.LineTo(m_ptPrevPos);

            // Declare a CConnection obj in order to call DrawConnection()
            // Draw the current stretch of line (but don't save it until
              OnLButtonUp().
            CConnection con_obj2(m_ptOrigin, point);
            con_obj2.DrawConnection(&dc);
            //dc.MoveTo(m_ptOrigin);
            //dc.LineTo(point);

            // Save the current pt (point) as the prev. pt (m_ptPrevPos)
              of the CView class.
            m_ptPrevPos = point;
        }
    }

    // DiagramEng (end)

    CView::OnMouseMove(nFlags, point);
}
```

The OnMouseMove() function declares two local objects of class CConnection, where the to-be-added DrawConnection() function is called on those objects. The first CConnection object, "con_obj1", is used to effectively erase the previous line drawn on a prior call to the OnMouseMove() function: otherwise, it would remain on the screen. This is performed by reversing the color, using SetROP2(R2_NOT) and overdrawing the old line defined by the points: "m_ptOrigin" and "m_ptPrevPos". The second CConnection object, "con_obj2", defining the present connection line, with the starting and ending points, "m_ptOrigin" and "point", respectively, is drawn as normal, with DrawConnection(). Finally, the current mouse cursor point, "point", is assigned to "m_ptPrevPos" to make a record of what will become the previous point, to be subsequently used when overdrawing the line on the next entry into the OnMouseMove() function.

5.2.6 ADD AN OnLButtonUp() FUNCTION

The left-button-up event signifies the end of the connection-drawing process, at which time the drawn connection should be added to the list of connections. Hence, invoke the ClassWizard and choose CDiagramEngView as the class, select WM_LBUTTONUP as the event message and add an event-handler function with the prototype, void CDiagramEngView::OnLButtonUp(UINT nFlags, CPoint point), and edit the function as shown.

```
void CDiagramEngView::OnLButtonUp(UINT nFlags, CPoint point)
{
    // TODO: Add your message handler code here and/or call default

    // DiagramEng (start)

    // Check to see mouse has been captured
    if(GetCapture() == this) // if what has been captured is the obj.
      that the "this" ptr. is pointing to.
    {
        // Add the connection to the connection list
        GetDocument()->GetSystemModel().AddConnection(m_ptOrigin, point);

        // Make the document redraw itself using either Invalidate(TRUE)
          or UpdateAllViews(NULL)
        //Invalidate(TRUE);
        GetDocument()->UpdateAllViews(NULL);

        // Release the capture so other apps. can have access to the
          mouse.
        ReleaseCapture();
    }

    // DiagramEng (end)

    CView::OnLButtonUp(nFlags, point);
}
```

The developer will note that GetSystemModel() is called upon the pointer-to-CDiagramEngDoc, obtained via GetDocument(), and then AddConnection(), a member function of the CSystemModel class introduced earlier, is called to add the connection to the list. To make the document redraw itself, UpdateAllViews() is called on the pointer-to-CDiagramEngDoc. In fact, UpdateAllViews() calls CView::OnUpdate() and allows the view to update its display to reflect the modifications made to the view's document [2].

5.2.7 DRAW CONNECTIONS

The CView-based CDiagramEngView class has an OnDraw() function that is called by the framework to render an image of the document [2]. Hence, augment the CDiagramEngView::OnDraw() function, with a call to DrawSystemModel() made via the membership operator upon the "m_SystemModel" object returned by GetSystemModel().

```
void CDiagramEngView::OnDraw(CDC* pDC)
{
    CDiagramEngDoc* pDoc = GetDocument();
    ASSERT_VALID(pDoc);
    // TODO: add draw code for native data here

    // DiagramEng (start)
    pDoc->GetSystemModel().DrawSystemModel(pDC);
    // DiagramEng (end)
}
```

`DrawSystemModel()` then iterates over the list of blocks, "m_lstBlock" and connections (with arrowheads) "m_lstConnection", calling `DrawBlock()` and `DrawConnection()`, respectively, as shown in the following.

```
void CSystemModel::DrawSystemModel(CDC *pDC)
{
    // Iterates through the SystemModel lists drawing the stored
      entities.

    // -- Draw Blocks
    list<CBlock*>::iterator it_blk;       // local iterator
    list<CBlock*> blk_list;               // local block list

    blk_list = GetBlockList();

    // Iterate through the list
    for(it_blk = blk_list.begin(); it_blk != blk_list.end(); it_blk++)
    {
        (*it_blk)->DrawBlock(pDC);        // DrawBlock() called on the
          ptr-to-CBlock
    }

    // -- Draw Connections (to do)
    list<CConnection*>::iterator it_con; // local iterator
    list<CConnection*> con_list;          // local connection list

    con_list = GetConnectionList();

    // Iterate through the list
    for(it_con = con_list.begin(); it_con != con_list.end(); it_con++)
    {
        (*it_con)->DrawConnection(pDC);
    }
}
```

The `DrawSystemModel()` function provided earlier calls the `DrawConnection()` function to draw each individual connection. Hence, add a public member function to the CConnection class with the prototype, `void CConnection::DrawConnection(CDC *pDC)`, and edit it as shown to draw the connection.

```
void CConnection::DrawConnection(CDC *pDC)
{
    int pen_color = RGB(0,0,0);           // White = RGB(255,255,255),
      Black = RGB(0,0,0).
    int pen_width = 1;                    // pen width

    // Create the pen
    CPen lpen(PS_SOLID, pen_width, pen_color);

    // Select the pen as the drawing obj.
    // The value returned by SelectObject() is a ptr to the obj. being
      replaced, i.e. an old-pen-ptr.
    CPen *pOldPen = pDC->SelectObject(&lpen);

    // Draw connection line
    pDC->MoveTo(m_ptFrom);
    pDC->LineTo(m_ptTo);
```

```
    // Reset the prev. pen
    pDC->SelectObject(pOldPen);

    // Draw arrow head
    DrawArrowHead(pDC);
}
```

The developer will notice the call to DrawArrowHead() made earlier to draw the connection line's arrowhead. Hence, add a public member function to the CConnection class with the prototype, void CConnection::DrawArrowHead(CDC *pDC), and edit the function as shown in the following. Note the width of the arrowhead is fixed for all block sizes. In addition, include the "math.h" header file, using #include <math.h>, at the top of the source file, "Signal.cpp", holding all CConnection and CSignal-related code, since the mathematical functions, sin() and cos(), are used.

```
void CConnection::DrawArrowHead(CDC *pDC)
{
    int pen_color = RGB(0,0,0);   // pen color: White = RGB(255,255,255),
      Black = RBF(0,0,0)
    int pen_width = 1;            // pen width
    double d;                     // opp. side length of subtriangle with
      hypotenuse h and base side length
length/2.
    double dDeltaLength;          // std ref delta length
    double h;                     // hypotenuse of subtriangle with opp.
      side length d and base side length
length/2.
    double length;               // a fraction of a std ref delta length
    double length_u;             // length of vector u
    double length_v;             // length of vector v
    double theta;                // angle of ith body rotated positively
      clockwise w.r.t. the global screen coord
sys. X axis.
    double u[2];                  // one of two vectors used to determined
      angle theta
    double v[2];                  // one of two vectors used to determined
      angle theta: the unit vector [1,0]
    CBrush *pBrush = NULL;        // a ptr to brush
    CPoint A;                     // vertex in anticlock direc from
      pointing vertex B of arrowhead
    CPoint B;                     // vertex of arrowhead pointing in direc
      of arrow (m_ptTo)
    CPoint C;                     // vertex in clock direc from pointing
      vertex B of arrowhead
    CPoint vertices[3];           // vertices array to hold triangle
      vertices
    CString sMsg;                 // main msg string
    UINT nType = MB_OK;           // style of msg. box
    UINT nIDhelp = 0;             // help context ID for the msg.

    // Set length
    dDeltaLength = GetDocumentGlobalFn()->GetDeltaLength();
    length = 0.15*dDeltaLength;

    // Assign lengths to arrowhead (triangle) paras.
    d = 0.2887*length;
    h = 0.5773*length;
```

```cpp
    // Print msg.
    sMsg.Format("\n CConnection::DrawArrowHead(), d = %lf, h = %lf\n", d, h);
    //AfxMessageBox(sMsg, nType, nIDhelp);

    // Length of vecs u and v
    v[0] = 1.0;                    // x cmpt. of unit vector [1,0]
    v[1] = 0.0;                    // y cmpt. of unit vector [1,0]
    u[0] = m_ptTo.x - m_ptFrom.x; // length in x direc of connection vector
    u[1] = m_ptTo.y - m_ptFrom.y; // length in y direc of connection vector

    length_u = sqrt(pow(u[0],2) + pow(u[1],2));
    length_v = sqrt(pow(v[0],2) + pow(v[1],2));

    // Angle between vecs u and v
    theta = acos((u[0]*v[0] + u[1]*v[1])/(length_u*length_v));
    if(u[1] < 0)
    {
        theta = -theta;            // negate theta if y-cmpt of u < 0, since
            acos result is an element from [0,pi] radians ONLY (non-neg).
    }

    // Global position vecs of arrowhead triangle vertices
    A.x = m_ptTo.x + long(cos(theta)*(-(h+d)) - sin(theta)*(-length*0.5));
    A.y = m_ptTo.y + long(sin(theta)*(-(h+d)) + cos(theta)*(-length*0.5));
    B.x = m_ptTo.x;
    B.y = m_ptTo.y;
    C.x = m_ptTo.x + long(cos(theta)*(-(h+d)) - sin(theta)*(length*0.5));
    C.y = m_ptTo.y + long(sin(theta)*(-(h+d)) + cos(theta)*(length*0.5));

    // Create the pen
    CPen lpen(PS_SOLID, pen_width, pen_color);

    // Select the pen as the drawing obj.
    // The value returned by SelectObject() is a ptr to the obj. being
      replaced, i.e. an old-pen-ptr.
    CPen *pOldPen = pDC->SelectObject(&lpen);

    // Draw arrowhead
    pDC->MoveTo(A);
    pDC->LineTo(B);
    pDC->LineTo(C);
    pDC->LineTo(A);

    // Prepare for filling the polygon
    CBrush NewBrush(RGB(0,0,0)); // create a new brush

    vertices[0] = A;
    vertices[1] = B;
    vertices[2] = C;

    // Select the new brush
    pBrush = pDC->SelectObject(&NewBrush);

    // Fill the polygon
    pDC->Polygon(vertices, 3);

    // Reset the prev. pen and brush
    pDC->SelectObject(pOldPen);
    pDC->SelectObject(pBrush);
}
```

The developer will have noticed that since `GetDocumentGlobalFn()` returns a pointer-to-CDiagramEngDoc, upon which the `GetDeltaLength()` function is called, the "DiagramEngDoc.h" header file needs to be included beneath the inclusion of the "Signal.h" header file, near the top of "Signal.cpp", i.e., #include "DiagramEngDoc.h".

In addition, the developer will recall that the previous code simply implements the mathematical derivation provided in Appendix B, concerning the geometrical method of determining the position vectors of the arrowhead vertices to draw the connection-based arrowhead in the appropriate direction and with the correct angular orientation.

5.2.8 BUILD AND RUN THE PROJECT

Building the project presents the following compilation error: " 'SetModifiedFlag': undeclared identifier". This occurs since the `SetModifiedFlag()` function is a member function of the CDocument class, and here the usage of it is in the `CSystemModel::AddConnection()` function, not in a function belonging to the CDiagramEngDoc class, which is itself derived publicly from CDocument. Hence, either the call to `SetModifiedFlag()` should be relocated to a CDiagramEngDoc class member function after the document has changed or the `GetDocumentGlobalFn()` function should be called to get a pointer-to-CDiagramEngDoc, and then `SetModifiedFlag(TRUE)` should be called on the document pointer. Augment the `CSystemModel::AddConnection()` function with the following code (as actually shown earlier).

```
// Get a ptr. to the doc. to call the CDocument member fn.
  SetModifiedFlag(), and mark the doc. as modified (TRUE).
GetDocumentGlobalFn()->SetModifiedFlag(TRUE);
```

Now upon running the application and drawing on the palette, the document is labeled as having been modified, and a message box appears upon closing or exiting the application, prompting the user to save changes to the document.

Finally, the user may now draw both blocks and connections on the palette as shown in Figure 5.1. However, at this stage, the connections do not connect/snap to the block ports but simply lie in a disconnected state. In future, functionality will be added to the project to allow the user to attach connection head and tail points, to block input and output ports, respectively.

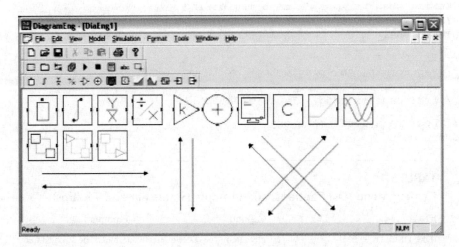

FIGURE 5.1 Blocks, block ports, and connection objects, with arrowheads pointing in the correct direction, drawn on the palette.

5.3   CONTEXT MENU

A Context menu is invoked by a right-mouse-button-down event, where the CPoint, "point", location of the cursor where the click occurred, is used, contextually, to invoke specific action concerning the selected diagram entity. A Context menu is to be added to the project that will allow the user to delete diagram entities or set item properties, through, e.g., a dialog window. Later in the project, more entries and associated functionality will be added to allow the user to perform modeling and simulation activities in an easy-to-use an intuitive manner.

5.3.1   INSERT A CONTEXT MENU

The instructions here, concerning the implementation of a Context menu, have been adapted from Chapters 6 (pp. 108–118) and 11 (pp. 236–239) of Ref. [1].

A new menu may be added to the project by right-clicking the Menu folder of the Resource View tab of the workspace pane and selecting Insert Menu: the ID should be set to IDR_CONTEXTMENU, denoting the Context menu. The top-level menu caption should be a single space: " ", causing the first entry to appear in the drop-down part of the menu. Add the menu entries listed in Table 5.1 (in alphabetical order), including their IDs, captions, and prompts.

5.3.2   ADD AN EVENT-HANDLER FUNCTION FOR THE CONTEXT MENU

A function needs to be added to load the Context menu, display its contents to the user, and record the CPoint, "point", of the right-mouse-button-down event at which the menu was invoked. Hence, invoke the ClassWizard, select the CDiagramEngView class, and add an event-handler function for the WM_CONTEXTMENU event message, with prototype, void CDiagramEngView::OnContextMenu(CWnd *pWnd, CPoint point), and edit the function as shown.

```
void CDiagramEngView::OnContextMenu(CWnd* pWnd, CPoint point)
{
    // TODO: Add your message handler code here

    // DiagramEng (start)

    CPoint ptClient;       // used to store the converted screen pt coords
      to the client coord sys.
    CString sMsg;          // main msg string
    UINT nType = MB_OK;    // style of msg. box
    UINT nIDhelp = 0;      // help context ID for the msg.

    // Print msg.
    //sMsg.Format("\n CDiagramEngView::OnContextMenu(), point (x,y) =
      (%d,%d)\n", point.x, point.y);
    //AfxMessageBox(sMsg, nType, nIDhelp);

    // Declare a local menu obj.
    CMenu menu;
```

TABLE 5.1

Context Menu IDs, Captions, and Prompts (Status Bar and Tooltips)

ID	Caption	Prompts
IDM_DELETE_ITEM	&Delete Item	Delete selected item\nDelete selected item
IDM_SET_ITEM_PROPERTIES	&Set Properties	Set item properties\nSet item properties

---

```
    // Load the context menu
    menu.LoadMenu(IDR_CONTEXTMENU);

    // Get the first sub-menu (the actual context menu has a 'space' to
      diff. it from std. menus).
    CMenu *pContextMenu = menu.GetSubMenu(0);

    // Display the context menu for the user
    pContextMenu->TrackPopupMenu(TPM_LEFTALIGN + TPM_RIGHTBUTTON +
      TPM_TOPALIGN, point.x, point.y, this, NULL);

    // Set the m_ptContextMenu var in the doc class first converting the
      Screen coord to the Client coord
    ptClient = point;                   // make a copy of the screen coord
    ScreenToClient(&ptClient);    // overwrite the screen coord with the
      client coord
    GetDocument()->SetContextMenuPoint(ptClient);   // set the client
      coord in the CDiagramEngDoc class.

    // DiagramEng (end)
}
```

Initially, the menu is loaded by declaring a CMenu object and then calling LoadMenu() upon the object specifying the ID of the menu to be loaded, i.e., IDR_CONTEXTMENU. Thereafter, the first submenu is obtained and used to display the Context menu to the user via a call to TrackPopupMenu(). Finally, the point at which the Context menu was invoked is recorded.

5.3.3 SET THE CONTEXT MENU POINT

At the end of the OnContextMenu() function provided earlier, a call to SetContextMenuPoint() is made, where the CPoint argument passed, is that at which the Context menu was invoked. A record of this point is necessary, since it is used to determine the diagram entity selected, by a right-mouse-button-down action, and then the appropriate context-based function called. For example, if an item were to be deleted, or to have its properties set, then the point at which a menu selection is made would be compared to the location of the diagram entity, to determine the applicability of the operation for the item.

Note also that the "point" screen coordinate is converted into the client coordinate, "ptClient", through a call to ScreenToClient() passing the address of the screen coordinate to have it overwritten with the client coordinate.

Hence, add a private member variable to the CDiagramEngDoc class, of type CPoint, named, "m_ptContextMenu", to record the point at which the Context menu is invoked. Add a public accessor function to the CDiagramEngDoc class with the prototype, void CDiagram EngDoc::SetContextMenuPoint(CPoint point), and edit the function as follows.

```
void CDiagramEngDoc::SetContextMenuPoint(CPoint point)
{
    // Assign the View's p.oint at which the context menu is invoked, to
      the Doc's copy.
    m_ptContextMenu = point;
}
```

5.3.4 ATTACH EVENT-HANDLER FUNCTIONS FOR THE CONTEXT MENU ENTRIES

Event-hander functions now need to be attached to the Context menu entries, specified by their IDs, as presented in Table 5.1, to delete a diagram item or set its properties.

5.3.4.1   Item Deletion

Invoke the ClassWizard, choose CDiagramEngDoc as the class, and select IDM_DELETE_ITEM, as the object ID. Add a function to the Command message, naming it `OnDeleteItem()`, and edit the code as shown.

```
void CDiagramEngDoc::OnDeleteItem()
{
    // TODO: Add your command handler code here

    // DiagramEng (start)
    int item_deleted = 0;

    // Delete a block
    item_deleted = DeleteBlock();
    if(item_deleted == 1)
    {
        return;
    }

    // DiagramEng (end)
}
```

The diagram-based items to be deleted may be numerous, and each item type will have its own deletion function: here, `DeleteBlock()` is called to perform block deletion where the integer variable, "item_deleted", denotes whether an entity was deleted. Hence, add a public member function to the CDiagramEngDoc class with the prototype, `int CDiagramEngDoc::DeleteBlock(void)`, and edit the code as shown.

```
int CDiagramEngDoc::DeleteBlock()
{
    int count = 0;          // counter
    int delete_blk = 0;     // blk deletion flag
    double dist;            // Euclidean dist bw. block posn and point posn.
    double width;           // block width
    CPoint blk_posn;        // block posn.
    CPoint point;           // local point var.
    CString sMsg;           // main msg string
    UINT nType = MB_OK;     // style of msg. box
    UINT nIDhelp = 0;       // help context ID for the msg.
    list<CBlock*>::iterator it_blk;          // iterator
    list<CBlock*>::iterator it_er = NULL;    // element to erase

    // Get the point at which the context menu was invoked
    point = m_ptContextMenu;                 // init a local copy.

    // Print msg.
    //sMsg.Format("\n CDiagramEngDoc::DeleteBlock(), point (x,y) =
      (%d,%d)\n", point.x, point.y);
    //AfxMessageBox(sMsg, nType, nIDhelp);

    // Get a copy of the blk_list in the system model
    list<CBlock*> &blk_list = GetSystemModel().GetBlockList(); // MUST BE
      A REFERENCE!

    // Iterate through the list to find which item to delete.
    for(it_blk = blk_list.begin(); it_blk != blk_list.end(); it_blk++)
    {
        blk_posn = (*it_blk)->GetBlockPosition();
        width = (*it_blk)->GetBlockShape().GetBlockWidth();
```

```
        dist = sqrt(pow((blk_posn.x - point.x),2) + pow((blk_posn.y -
          point.y),2));
        if(dist <= 0.8*width*0.5)
        {
            //sMsg.Format("\n CDiagramEngDoc::DeleteBlock(), blk(x,y) =
              (%d,%d), point(x,y) = (%d,%d)\n", blk_posn.x, blk_posn.y,
               point.x, point.y);
            //AfxMessageBox(sMsg, nType, nIDhelp);

            // Record which block to erase
            delete_blk = 1;
            it_er = it_blk;
            break;
        }
    }

    // Delete the item in the list
    if(delete_blk == 1)
    {
        delete *it_er;           // delete actual block pointed to by it_er
        blk_list.erase(it_er);  // delete element at offset it_er in list
          (that held the block)

        count = m_SystemModel.GetBlockList().size();
        //sMsg.Format("\n CDiagramEngDoc::DeleteBlock(), size = %d\n",
          count);
        //AfxMessageBox(sMsg, nType, nIDhelp);
    }
    // Set as modified and redraw the doc.
    SetModifiedFlag(TRUE);       // set the doc. as having been modified to
      prompt user to save
    UpdateAllViews(NULL);        // indicate that sys. should redraw.

    // Return a flag indicating whether an item was deleted
    return delete_blk;
}
```

The DeleteBlock() function iterates through the list of blocks to determine whether the mouse cursor point, "point", or equivalently, the Context menu point, "m_ptContextMenu", was over a block: a block deletion flag, "delete_blk", is used to denote whether a block is to be deleted. This is then checked in the following conditional statement: "if(delete_blk == 1)". The iterator "it_er" should not be used in the *if* statement as follows, "if(it_er != NULL)", since it could be nonnull, but a block may not have been marked for deletion: in that case, a block would be deleted erroneously. Hence, an integer or Boolean flag should be used rather than a pointer.

GetBlockList() returns a reference: hence, "blk_list" should be preceded with an ampersand "&" upon its declaration, and in this case its simultaneous assignment. This block-list-reference then refers to the "m_lstBlock" member variable in the CSystemModel class: so whatever happens to "blk_list" locally in DeleteBlock() will then be reflected at the CSystemModel-class level in "m_lstBlock".

Upon deletion of a block in the list, "blk_list", or effectively in the CSystemModel list, "m_lstBlock", the iterator "it_er" should be dereferenced (*it_er) and "delete" called to delete the block pointed to by "it_er". Thereafter, erase(it_er) is called to delete the element in the list at offset "it_er" that held the block. This ensures proper deletion of what is in the list and that the size of the list is reduced by one. This may be verified as shown by calling size() upon the block list.

5.3.4.2 Set Item Properties

A function now needs to be added for the Set Item Properties entry on the Context menu. Hence, invoke the ClassWizard, choose CDiagramEngDoc as the class, and select IDM_SET_ ITEM_PROPERTIES as the object ID. Add a function to the Command message, naming it OnSetItemProperties() and edit the code as shown. For now, this function takes no action and will be completed later.

```
void CDiagramEngView::OnSetItemProperties()
{
    // TODO: Add your command handler code here

    // DiagramEng (start)
    // DiagramEng (end)
}
```

5.3.5 System Model–Based Object Deletion

Finally, now that a list of blocks, "m_lstBlock", and a list of connections, "m_lstConnection", exist in the CSystemModel class, these need to be deleted when a CSystemModel object is destroyed. Hence, edit the CSystemModel destructor as shown in the following to call the relevant member deletion functions.

```
CSystemModel::~CSystemModel(void)
{
    // Delete block list
    DeleteBlockList();

    // Delete connection list
    DeleteConnectionList();
}
```

Now, add a public member function to the CSystemModel class with the prototype, void CSystemModel::DeleteBlockList(void), and edit the function as shown.

```
void CSystemModel::DeleteBlockList()
{
    list<CBlock*>::iterator it_blk;

    // Delete block list
    for(it_blk = m_lstBlock.begin(); it_blk != m_lstBlock.end(); it_blk++)
    {
        delete (*it_blk);        // delete what it_blk is pointing to:
          i.e. deref the it_blk ptr and delete the ptr-to-CBlock.
    }
    m_lstBlock.clear();
}
```

In addition, add a public member function to the CSystemModel class with the prototype, void CSystemModel::DeleteConnectionList(void), and edit the function as shown in the following.

```
void CSystemModel::DeleteConnectionList()
{
    list<CConnection*>::iterator it_con;
```

```
    // Delete connection list
    for(it_con = m_lstConnection.begin(); it_con != m_lstConnection.
      end(); it_con++)
    {
        delete (*it_con);  // delete what it_conn is pointing to:
           i.e. deref the it_conn ptr and delete the ptr-to-CConnection.
    }
    m_lstConnection.clear();
}
```

Further functionality, concerning the deletion of drawing objects, e.g., blocks, and connections, will be added in later sections. In addition, the setting of item properties, selected with the right mouse button, will be added through the use of dialog windows.

5.4   SUMMARY

Initially, an exploration is made in Appendix B to construct and draw connection objects with attached arrowheads that indicate the direction of intended signal flow. The mathematical derivation of the global position vectors of the arrowhead vertices shows that the arrowhead will be correctly oriented with a change in orientation of the connection object.

The CConnection class was augmented by the following: (1) providing a new constructor function taking two CPoint arguments defining the connection object, (2) introducing a function to add a connection to the list, "m_lstConnection", and (3) adding a method to retrieve the connection list by reference. Event-handler functions were added to the CView-derived class to set the points of the connection (OnLButtonDown()), to dynamically draw the connection (OnMouseMove()) and to add the connection to the list (OnLButtonUp()). The actual drawing of connections is initiated by the CView-based OnDraw() method, which calls the DrawSystemModel() function that iterates through the list of blocks and connections calling DrawBlock() and DrawConnection() upon the appropriate pointers, wherein the latter, DrawArrowHead(), is called to draw the connection-based arrowhead.

A Context menu is introduced and the point at which it is invoked is stored in the CDiagramEngDoc class, such that event-handler functions, associated with the menu entries, may use it to contextually determine the appropriate action to take upon the selected diagram object. Item deletion (OnDeleteItem()) and CSystemModel object destruction are also added to the project.

REFERENCES

1. Chapman, D., *Teach Yourself Visual C++ 6 in 21 Days*, Sams Publishing, Indianapolis, IN, 1998.
2. Microsoft Developer Network Library Visual Studio 6.0, Microsoft® Visual Studio™ 6.0 Development System, Microsoft Corporation, 1998.

6 Moving Blocks and Connections

6.1 INTRODUCTION

At present, both blocks and simple connections may be drawn on the palette but they cannot be interactively moved by the user or connected together to form a system model. Here, an object of the CRectTracker class is instantiated and used to move a diagram item [1]. The topics presented include the moving of blocks and connection-based head, tail, and bend points, the snapping and unsnapping of connection end points to and from block ports, inserting and deleting connection-based bend points, and the deletion of whole connection objects.

6.2 MOVING BLOCKS

The movement of blocks and connections involves the creation of a CRectTracker object that may be used, through its member methods, to reposition a diagram entity, interactively selected using the mouse, on the palette.

6.2.1 CRectTracker CLASS

The CRectTracker class is provided by the Microsoft Visual C++® 6.0, Microsoft® Visual Studio™ 6.0 Development System (integrated development environment [IDE]) [2] and may be used to display, move, and resize a GUI item [1]. More specifically, the CRectTracker class provides a user interface between rectangular items in an application and the user by providing a variety of display styles [1].

Introduce a CRectTracker object to the DiagramEng project by adding a private member variable to the CDiagramEngDoc class, of type, CRectTracker, named "m_RectTracker". Include the header file, "afxext.h", i.e., #include "afxext.h", at the top of the "DiagramEngDoc.cpp" source file, since it declares the CRectTracker class members and methods.

Add a public constant accessor function to the CDiagramEngDoc class, with the prototype, CRectTracker CDiagramEngDoc::GetRectTracker(void) const, to return the "m_RectTracker" object, and edit the function as follows:

```
CRectTracker CDiagramEngDoc::GetRectTracker() const
{
    // Return the CRectTracker member var.
    return m_RectTracker;
}
```

6.2.2 AUGMENTING THE OnLButtonDown() FUNCTION

The CDiagramEngView::OnLButtonDown() function currently captures the mouse and initializes two CPoint member variables with the mouse cursor, CPoint "point", argument, as indicated as follows.

```
void CDiagramEngView::OnLButtonDown(UINT nFlags, CPoint point)
{
    // TODO: Add your message handler code here and/or call default
```

```
    // DiagramEng (start)

    // Capture the mouse so no other apps. can get it.
    SetCapture();

    // Save the pt that the cursor is at, upon left-btn-down,
      i.e. init member var with incoming CPoint var.
    m_ptPrevPos = point;   // Init the prev. pt, to be used in
      OnMouseMove(), to the current point
    m_ptOrigin = point;    // Init the origin of the ensuing line,
      to be drawn in OnMouseMove(), to be the starting pt.

    // DiagramEng (end)

    CView::OnLButtonDown(nFlags, point);
}
```

New functionality needs to be added to this function to differentiate between two actions
triggered by a left-mouse-button click event: (1) the tracking or moving of a block or connection object (see TrackItem()) or (2) the construction of a connection object. Hence, modify
the CDiagramEngView::OnLButtonDown() function as shown in bold in the following,
such that upon a left-mouse-button-down event, either a CRectTracker object is used (within
TrackItem()), or a connection constructed, depending on the returned value of the tracker
flag, "tracker_flag".

```
void CDiagramEngView::OnLButtonDown(UINT nFlags, CPoint point)
{
    // TODO: Add your message handler code here and/or call default

    // DiagramEng (start)
    int tracker_flag;           // 0 => no tracker and hence a connector,
      1 => tracker and hence no connector

    //AfxMessageBox("\n CDiagramEngView::OnLButtondown()\n", MB_OK, 0);

    // Assume an item is being tracked: if so tracker_flag = 1, if not:
      tracker_flag = 0.
    tracker_flag = GetDocument()->TrackItem(point, this);   // this is a
      ptr-to-CWnd, i.e. CWnd *pWnd.

    // If nothing was tracked, i.e. tracker_flag = 0, then record points
      to draw and construct a connector.
    if(tracker_flag == 0)
    {
        // Capture the mouse so no other apps. can get it.
        SetCapture();

        // Save the pt that the cursor is at, upon left-btn-down,
          i.e. init member var with incoming CPoint var.
        m_ptPrevPos = point;   // Init the prev. pt, to be used in
          OnMouseMove(), to the current point
        m_ptOrigin = point;    // Init the origin of the ensuing line,
          to be drawn in OnMouseMove(), to be the starting pt.
    }

    // DiagramEng (end)

    CView::OnLButtonDown(nFlags, point);
}
```

6.2.3   MOVING A BLOCK

The developer will have noticed the call to `TrackItem()` in the `OnLButtonDown()` function mentioned earlier that is used to move a diagram entity on the palette. Hence, add a new public member function to the CDiagramEngDoc class with the prototype, `int CDiagramEngDoc:: TrackItem(CPoint point, CWnd *pWnd)`, and edit the function as shown in the following.

```
int CDiagramEngDoc::TrackItem(CPoint point, CWnd *pWnd)
{
    int tracker_flag = 0;

    tracker_flag = TrackBlock(point, pWnd);

    // Return flag indicating if an item was tracked: 0 => not tracked,
      1 => tracked.
    return tracker_flag;
}
```

The `TrackItem()` function is the main function that processes various item tracking calls, e.g., the tracking of blocks and connection-based head, tail, and bend points (to be added later). The flag-like variable, "tracker_flag", indicates whether an item was tracked (1) or not (0).

In the `OnLButtonDown()` function shown earlier, `TrackItem(point, this)` is called passing in the CPoint argument, "point", which is the current mouse cursor position, and the "this" pointer, pointing to the object upon which the function is called, i.e., a pointer-to-CWnd. These variables are then used in the various item tracking actions.

Now, add a public member function to the CDiagramEngDoc class with prototype, `int CDiagramEngDoc::TrackBlock(CPoint point, CWnd *pWnd)`, passing in the CPoint and pointer-to-CWnd arguments, and edit it as shown in the following.

```
int CDiagramEngDoc::TrackBlock(CPoint point, CWnd *pWnd)
{
    int delta;                  // integer increment
    int tracker_flag = 0;
    double blk_width;
    double dist;
    CPoint bottom_right;
    CPoint top_left;
    CPoint blk_posn;
    list<CBlock*>::iterator it_blk;
    list<CBlock*> blk_list = GetSystemModel().GetBlockList();

    // Iterate through block list
    for(it_blk = blk_list.begin(); it_blk != blk_list.end(); it_blk++)
    {
        blk_posn = (*it_blk)->GetBlockPosition();
        blk_width = (*it_blk)->GetBlockShape().GetBlockWidth();
        dist = sqrt(pow(blk_posn.x - point.x,2) +
          pow(blk_posn.y - point.y,2));

        // If the block is clicked
        if(dist <= 0.5*blk_width*0.5)
        {
            delta = (int)(blk_width*0.5);
            top_left.x = blk_posn.x - delta;
            top_left.y = blk_posn.y - delta;
            bottom_right.x = blk_posn.x + delta;
            bottom_right.y = blk_posn.y + delta;
```

```
        // Set the rect tracker's position
        m_RectTracker.m_rect.SetRect(top_left.x, top_left.y,
          bottom_right.x, bottom_right.y);

        // Track the mouse's position till left mouse button up
        tracker_flag = m_RectTracker.Track(pWnd, point, TRUE);
          // 0 => item not tracked, 1 => item was tracked

        // Get the new tracker position and update the new block
          position with the tracker position
        blk_posn = m_RectTracker.m_rect.CenterPoint();
        (*it_blk)->SetBlockPosition(blk_posn);

        // Set flags
        SetModifiedFlag(TRUE);     // set the doc. as having been
          modified to prompt user to save
        UpdateAllViews(NULL);      // indicate that sys. should redraw.
        break;
      }
   }

   // Return flag indicating if an item was tracked: 0 => not tracked,
     1 => tracked.
   return tracker_flag;
}
```

The `TrackBlock()` function iterates through the list of blocks and determines whether a block is selected by the user through a left-button-down event. If the point at which the click occurred is sufficiently close to the block, then the CRectTracker object, "m_RectTracker" is set up, using `SetRect()` and then tracked using `Track()`, whereupon release of the left mouse button, the movement action is terminated and the block position updated using `SetBlockPosition()`. If the left-button-down event is not sufficiently close to a block, then the action is deemed to have taken place over white space on the palette and the drawing of a connection object intended.

6.2.4 SET BLOCK POSITION

The developer will have noticed in the `TrackItem()` function provided earlier, the call to `SetBlockPosition()` to update the block's position with the center point of the tracking rectangle. Hence, add a public member function to the CBlock class with the prototype, `void CBlock::SetBlockPosition(CPoint blk_posn)`, and edit the function as follows:

```
void CBlock::SetBlockPosition(CPoint blk_posn)
{
    vector<CPort*>::iterator it_port;     // vector iterator.

    // Set the member var. to the incoming value.
    m_ptBlockPosition = blk_posn;

    // Calculate the position of the ports associated with this block since
      its position has moved by iterating through the vector of i/o ports.

    // Iterate through vec of input ports
    for(it_port = m_vecInputPorts.begin(); it_port != m_vecInputPorts.end();
      it_port++)
    {
        (*it_port)->CalculatePortPosition();
    }
```

```
    // Iterate through vec of output ports
    for(it_port = m_vecOutputPorts.begin(); it_port != m_vecOutputPorts.end();
      it_port++)
    {
        (*it_port)->CalculatePortPosition();
    }
}
```

Initially, the CPoint member variable, "m_ptBlockPosition", is updated with the incoming argument, and then the vectors of input and output ports are iterated over and the port positions recalculated due to the change in the position of the block on which they reside.

6.3   MOVING CONNECTION END POINTS

Blocks can be conveniently moved using a CRectTracker object as shown in the `TrackBlock()` function provided earlier: now connection-based end points, i.e., the head and tail points, are to be moved in a similar manner. In addition, the head and tail points are to be snapped and unsnapped, to and from, block input and output ports, respectively.

6.3.1   MOVE A CONNECTION END POINT

Augment the `TrackItem()` function as shown in bold in the following with a call to `TrackConnectionEndPoint()` to initiate the tracking of a connection-based end point.

```
int CDiagramEngDoc::TrackItem(CPoint point, CWnd *pWnd)
{
    int tracker_flag = 0;

    tracker_flag = TrackBlock(point, pWnd);
    if(tracker_flag != 0)
    {
        return tracker_flag;
    }

    tracker_flag = TrackConnectionEndPoint(point, pWnd);
    if(tracker_flag != 0)
    {
        return tracker_flag;
    }

    // Return flag indicating if an item was tracked: 0 => not tracked,
    1 => tracked.
    return tracker_flag;
}
```

Now add a public member function to the CDiagramEngDoc class, with the prototype, int CDiagramEngDoc::TrackConnectionEndPoint(CPoint point, CWnd *pWnd), and edit the function as shown.

```
int CDiagramEngDoc::TrackConnectionEndPoint(CPoint point, CWnd *pWnd)
{
    int delta = (int)(0.25*m_dDeltaLength);        // integer increment
    int tracker_flag = 0;
    double disc_r = 0.1*m_dDeltaLength;
    double dist_to_tail;
```

```
double dist_to_head;
CPoint bottom_right;
CPoint head_pt;
CPoint tail_pt;
CPoint top_left;
list<CConnection*>::iterator it_con;
list<CConnection*> con_list = GetSystemModel().GetConnectionList();

// Iterate through connection list
for(it_con = con_list.begin(); it_con != con_list.end(); it_con++)
{
    // Get tail and head points of connection
    tail_pt = (*it_con)->GetConnectionPointTail();
    head_pt = (*it_con)->GetConnectionPointHead();

    // Determine Euclidean dist bw point and tail and head pts
    dist_to_tail = sqrt(pow(tail_pt.x - point.x,2) +
      pow(tail_pt.y - point.y,2));
    dist_to_head = sqrt(pow(head_pt.x - point.x,2) +
      pow(head_pt.y - point.y,2));

    // If the tail pt is clicked
    if(dist_to_tail <= disc_r)
    {
        top_left.x = tail_pt.x - delta;
        top_left.y = tail_pt.y - delta;
        bottom_right.x = tail_pt.x + delta;
        bottom_right.y = tail_pt.y + delta;

        // Set the rect tracker's position
        m_RectTracker.m_rect.SetRect(top_left.x, top_left.y,
          bottom_right.x, bottom_right.y);

        // Track the mouse's position till left mouse button up
        tracker_flag = m_RectTracker.Track(pWnd, point, TRUE);
          // 0 => item not tracked, 1 => item was tracked

        // Get the new tracker position and update the new connection
        //   end pt position with the tracker position
        tail_pt = m_RectTracker.m_rect.CenterPoint();
        (*it_con)->SetConnectionPointTail(tail_pt);

        // Set flags
        SetModifiedFlag(TRUE);    // set the doc. as having been
          modified to prompt user to save
        UpdateAllViews(NULL);     // indicate that sys. should redraw.
        break;
    }

    // If the head pt is clicked
    if(dist_to_head <= disc_r)
    {
        top_left.x = head_pt.x - delta;
        top_left.y = head_pt.y - delta;
        bottom_right.x = head_pt.x + delta;
        bottom_right.y = head_pt.y + delta;

        // Set the rect tracker's position
        m_RectTracker.m_rect.SetRect(top_left.x, top_left.y,
          bottom_right.x, bottom_right.y);
```

```
        // Track the mouse's position till left mouse button up
        tracker_flag = m_RectTracker.Track(pWnd, point, TRUE);
          // 0 => item not tracked, 1 => item was tracked

        // Get the new tracker position and update the new connection
          end pt position with the tracker position
        head_pt = m_RectTracker.m_rect.CenterPoint();
        (*it_con)->SetConnectionPointHead(head_pt);

        // Set flags
        SetModifiedFlag(TRUE);    // set the doc. as having been
          modified to prompt user to save
        UpdateAllViews(NULL);     // indicate that sys. should redraw.
        break;
    }

  }// end for

  // Return flag indicating if an item was tracked: 0 => not tracked,
    1 => tracked.
  return tracker_flag;
}
```

The `TrackConnectionEndPoint()` function iterates through the list of connections, retrieves the head and tail points, and then determines whether they were selected. Then, as in the `TrackBlock()` function provided earlier, the CRectTracker object, "m_RectTracker", is set up using `SetRect()` and tracking performed using `Track()`, before the CPoint end point objects are updated through calls to `SetConnectionPointHead()` and/or `SetConnectionPointTail()`.

For ease of identification, modify the CConnection class such that "m_ptFrom" is renamed "m_ptTail" and "m_ptTo" is renamed "m_ptHead", since the connection object is more explicitly defined through head, tail, and bend points. Then search throughout the code for all occurrences of "m_ptFrom" and "m_ptTo" and change these accordingly.

Add a public constant member function to the CConnection class with prototype, `CPoint CConnection::GetConnectionPointHead(void)` const, to return the connection head point, "m_ptHead", and edit the code as shown.

```
CPoint CConnection::GetConnectionPointHead() const
{
    // Return head point.
    return m_ptHead;
}
```

Add a public constant member function to the CConnection class with prototype, `CPoint CConnection::GetConnectionPointTail(void)` const, to return the connection tail point, "m_ptTail", and edit the code as shown.

```
CPoint CConnection::GetConnectionPointTail() const
{
    // Return tail point.
    return m_ptTail;
}
```

Add a public member function to the CConnection class with the prototype, `void CConnection::SetConnectionPointHead(CPoint new_pt)`, and edit the code as shown to set the connection head point.

```
void CConnection::SetConnectionPointHead(CPoint new_pt)
{
    // Assign the member var the new pt.
    m_ptHead = new_pt;
}
```

Add a public member function to the CConnection class with the prototype void CConnection::SetConnectionPointTail(CPoint new_pt), and edit the code as shown to set the connection tail point.

```
void CConnection::SetConnectionPointTail(CPoint new_pt)
{
    // Assign the member var the new pt.
    m_ptTail = new_pt;
}
```

6.3.2   SNAP CONNECTION END POINTS TO A PORT

The connection head and tail end points may be moved with the CRectTracker object, "m_RectTracker". However, immediately after movement, these connection-based head and tail end points should be compared to the block input and output port positions, respectively, to determine whether they are close enough to be conveniently snapped to the port. If so, end point positions should be updated with the port positions, and, whenever a block is subsequently moved, and hence its ports, the connection end points should be redrawn to their new port positions. If a connection is snapped to a port and then later dragged off the port, then there needs to be an unsnapping or disassociation of that connection's end point from the port to which it was previously snap-connected.

6.3.2.1   Augment `TrackConnectionEndPoint()`

Navigate to the previously introduced, TrackConnectionEndPoint(), function, and declare two port pointers-to-CPort, i.e., CPort *from_port and CPort *to_port and assign them both to NULL. Now add the statements shown in bold, to the conditional section for both the head and tail points, to result in the following code: the ellipsis denotes omitted but unchanged code provided earlier.

```
int CDiagramEngDoc::TrackConnectionEndPoint(CPoint point, CWnd *pWnd)
{
    int delta = (int)(0.25*m_dDeltaLength);      // integer increment
    ...
    CPort *from_port = NULL;
    CPort *to_port = NULL;
    ...
    for(it_con = con_list.begin(); it_con != con_list.end(); it_con++)
    {
        ...
        if(dist_to_tail <= disc_r)
        {
            ...
            tail_pt = m_RectTracker.m_rect.CenterPoint();

            // Check to snap connector to port
            if( (*it_con)->GetRefFromPort() == NULL)
            {
                from_port = SnapConnectionTailPointToPort(tail_pt);
                // tail_pt passed by ref. and may be updated.
```

```
            if(from_port != NULL)
            {
                (*it_con)->SetRefFromPort(from_port);
            }
        }
        (*it_con)->SetConnectionPointTail(tail_pt);
        ...
        break;
    }

    // If the head pt is clicked
    if(dist_to_head <= disc_r)
    {
        ...
        head_pt = m_RectTracker.m_rect.CenterPoint();

        // Check to snap connector to port
        if((*it_con)->GetRefToPort() == NULL)
        {
            to_port = SnapConnectionHeadPointToPort(head_pt);
            // head_pt passed by ref. and may be updated.
            if(to_port != NULL)
            {
                (*it_con)->SetRefToPort(to_port);
            }
        }

        (*it_con)->SetConnectionPointHead(head_pt);
        ...
        break;
    }

    }// end for

    // Return flag indicating if an item was tracked: 0 => not tracked,
      1 => tracked.
    return tracker_flag;
}
```

The developer will have noticed the two calls to get the reference-from-port, "m_pRefFromPort" and reference-to-port, "m_pRefToPort", in the previous code. Hence, add a public member function to the CConnection class with the prototype, CPort *CConnection::GetRefFromPort(void), and edit it as shown.

```
CPort* CConnection::GetRefFromPort()
{
    return m_pRefFromPort;
}
```

Add a public member function to the CConnection class with the prototype, CPort *CConnection:: GetRefToPort(void), and edit it as shown.

```
CPort* CConnection::GetRefToPort()
{
    return m_pRefToPort;
}
```

In addition, add a public member function to the CConnection class to set the reference-from-port, with the prototype, void CConnection::SetRefFromPort(CPort *from_port), and edit it as shown.

```
void CConnection::SetRefFromPort(CPort *from_port)
{
    m_pRefFromPort = from_port;
}
```

Add a public member function to the CConnection class to set the reference-to-port, with the prototype, void CConnection::SetRefToPort(CPort *to_port), and edit it as shown.

```
void CConnection::SetRefToPort(CPort *to_port)
{
    m_pRefToPort = to_port;
}
```

Now, to snap the connection-based head and tail points to their respective input and output ports, two more functions are required, as called in the TrackConnectionEndPoint() function provided earlier. Hence, add a public member function to the CDiagramEngDoc class, with the prototype, CPort *CDiagramEngDoc::SnapConnectionTailPointToPort(CPoint &tail_pt), and edit it as shown.

```
CPort* CDiagramEngDoc::SnapConnectionTailPointToPort(CPoint &tail_pt)
{
    // Passing in a point by reference, and returning a prt-to-CPort
      "m_pRefFromPort".
    double disc_r = 0.1*m_dDeltaLength;
    double dist_to_port;
    CPoint port_posn;
    list<CBlock*>::iterator it_blk;
    list<CBlock*> blk_list = GetSystemModel().GetBlockList();
    vector<CPort*> vec_output_ports;
    vector<CPort*>::iterator it_port;

    // Iterate through block list
    for(it_blk = blk_list.begin(); it_blk != blk_list.end(); it_blk++)
    {
        vec_output_ports = (*it_blk)->GetVectorOfOutputPorts();
        for(it_port = vec_output_ports.begin(); it_port !=
          vec_output_ports.end(); it_port++)
        {
            port_posn = (*it_port)->GetPortPosition();
            dist_to_port = sqrt(pow(tail_pt.x - port_posn.x,2) +
            pow(tail_pt.y - port_posn.y,2));

            if(dist_to_port <= disc_r)
            {
                tail_pt = port_posn;
                return (*it_port);      // return CPort*, i.e. a from_port
            }
        }
    }

    // Return 0 if no "m_pRefFromPort" returned earlier
    return 0;
}
```

A connection-based tail point is to be snapped to an output port. Hence, the SnapConnectionTailPointToPort() function simply iterates through the list of blocks, obtains the vector of output ports, and compares the port position with the tail point position: if they are coincident, the iterator "it_port" is dereferenced to access the pointer-to-CPort, equivalently, the address of the port, which is returned.

Add a public member function to the CDiagramEngDoc class, with the prototype, CPort *CDiagramEngDoc::SnapConnectionHeadPointToPort(CPoint &head_pt), and edit it as shown.

```
CPort* CDiagramEngDoc::SnapConnectionHeadPointToPort(CPoint &head_pt)
{
    // Passing in a point by reference, and returning a prt-to-CPort
      "m_pRefToPort".
    double disc_r = 0.1*m_dDeltaLength;
    double dist_to_port;
    CPoint port_posn;
    list<CBlock*>::iterator it_blk;
    list<CBlock*> blk_list = GetSystemModel().GetBlockList();
    vector<CPort*> vec_input_ports;
    vector<CPort*>::iterator it_port;

    // Iterate through block list
    for(it_blk = blk_list.begin(); it_blk != blk_list.end(); it_blk++)
    {
        vec_input_ports = (*it_blk)->GetVectorOfInputPorts();
        for(it_port = vec_input_ports.begin(); it_port !=
          vec_input_ports.end(); it_port++)
        {
            port_posn = (*it_port)->GetPortPosition();
            dist_to_port = sqrt(pow(head_pt.x - port_posn.x,2) +
              pow(head_pt.y - port_posn.y,2));

            if(dist_to_port <= disc_r)
            {
                head_pt = port_posn;
                return (*it_port);      // return CPort*, i.e. a to_port
            }
        }
    }
    // Return 0 if no "m_pRefToPort" returned earlier
    return 0;
}
```

This function operates in a similar manner to the previous one, but here, as a head point is to be attached to an input port, the vector of input ports is iterated over and the position of the port compared to that of the head point: if they are coincident, the address of the input port is returned.

6.3.2.2 Augment SetBlockPosition()

Now that the connection-based head and tail end points are snapped to the ports, these must then remain connected should a block, and hence the block's ports, be moved. In order for this to happen, the CBlock::SetBlockPosition() function needs to be augmented to calculate the connection end point positions based on the new port positions. Hence, modify the SetBlockPosition() function as shown in bold in the following to call both UpdateConnectionPointHead() and UpdateConnectionPointTail(), to update the connection-based head and tail points to the block's ports.

```
void CBlock::SetBlockPosition(CPoint blk_posn)
{
    vector<CPort*>::iterator it_port;     // vector iterator.

    // Set the member var. to the incoming value.
    m_ptBlockPosition = blk_posn;

    // Calculate the position of the ports associated with this block
      since its position has moved by iterating through the vector
      of i/o ports.

    // Iterate through vec of input ports
    for(it_port = m_vecInputPorts.begin(); it_port != m_vecInputPorts.end();
      it_port++)
    {
        // Calculate the new port position
        (*it_port)->CalculatePortPosition();        // deref the iterator
          to get the ptr-to-CPort obj.

        // Update any connection head end point associated with the port.
        m_pParentSystemModel->UpdateConnectionPointHead(*it_port);
          // deref the iterator to get the ptr-to-CPort obj.
    }
    // Iterate through vec of output ports
    for(it_port = m_vecOutputPorts.begin(); it_port != m_vecOutputPorts.end();
      it_port++)
    {
        // Calculate the new port position
        (*it_port)->CalculatePortPosition();        // deref the iterator
          to get the ptr-to-CPort obj.

        // Update any connection tail end point associated with the port.
        m_pParentSystemModel->UpdateConnectionPointTail(*it_port);
          // deref the iterator to get the ptr-to-CPort obj.
    }
}
```

The developer will notice that the update functions are called on the pointer-to-parent-system-model, "m_pParentsystemModel": a member variable of the CBlock class. If this pointer member variable were not present, then the system model object, "m_SystemModel", would have to be retrieved explicitly, by first calling GetDocumentGlobalFn(), followed by GetSystemModel(), which would require the inclusion of the "DiagramEngDoc.h" header file at the top of the "Block.cpp" source file. The power of the pointer, "m_pParentSystemModel", is particularly important here: a block can "know" the model to which it belongs quite easily.

Finally, to update the head and tail points to the ports to which they are snap-associated, two new functions need to be added to the CSystemModel class that iterate through the connection list, "m_lstConnection", retrieve the port-reference-variable, i.e., the port address, and compare this to the pointer-to-CPort argument, "port", passed into the function.

Add a public member function to the CSystemModel class, with the prototype, void CSystemModel::UpdateConnectionPointHead(CPort *port), and edit it as shown.

```
void CSystemModel::UpdateConnectionPointHead(CPort *port)
{
    list<CConnection*>::iterator it_con;

    // Iterate through the list of connections to check for connection
      end pt. updating due to port associations
```

```
    for(it_con = m_lstConnection.begin(); it_con != m_lstConnection.
      end(); it_con++)
    {
        if( (*it_con)->GetRefToPort() == port)    // if m_pRefToPort =
          current port address
        {
            (*it_con)->SetConnectionPointHead(port->GetPortPosition());
        }
    }
}
```

Add a public member function to the CSystemModel class, with the prototype, void CSystemModel::UpdateConnectionPointTail(CPort *port), and edit it as shown.

```
void CSystemModel::UpdateConnectionPointTail(CPort *port)
{
    list<CConnection*>::iterator it_con;

    // Iterate through the list of connections to check for connection
      end pt. updating due to port associations
    for(it_con = m_lstConnection.begin(); it_con != m_lstConnection.end();
      it_con++)
    {
        if( (*it_con)->GetRefFromPort() == port) // if m_pRefFromPort =
          current port address
        {
            (*it_con)->SetConnectionPointTail(port->GetPortPosition());
        }
    }
}
```

6.3.3 Unsnap Connection End Points from a Port

Blocks may be placed on a diagram, connections are constructed by a click–drag–release action on the palette, connection tail and head end points may be moved to the block output and input ports respectively, and then they are automatically snapped to their respective ports when within a disc of radius r from the eligible port. Then, when the blocks are moved, the connection end points remain affixed to their ports. However, when a connection end point is dragged away from its block port, it appears to be detached, but if the block to which it was previously connected is then moved, the detached connection end point suddenly snaps back to the port, regardless of its distance from the port concerned.

To prevent this reattachment of detached connection end points, the connection's pointer-to-CPort member variables, "m_pRefFromPort" and "m_pRefToPort", must be reassigned to nullity upon detachment, or equivalently when the connection end points are moved, regardless of how far they are moved away from the port. The logic here is that if a connection end point was attached to a port and hence has a non-null "m_pRefFromPort" or "m_pRefToPort", then any attempt to move the connection end point away from the port is regarded as an intention by the user to break the connection to the port.

Hence, in the TrackConnectionEndPoint() function, an *else* clause is added to both the "tail_pt" and "head_pt" parts of the code, wherein SetRefFromPort(NULL) and SetRefToPort(NULL) are called, respectively, as shown in bold in the following: otherwise, there are no further alterations (the ellipsis denotes omitted, yet unchanged code).

```cpp
int CDiagramEngDoc::TrackConnectionEndPoint(CPoint point, CWnd *pWnd)
{
    int delta = (int)(0.25*m_dDeltaLength);       // integer increment
    ...

    for(it_con = con_list.begin(); it_con != con_list.end(); it_con++)
    {
        ...

        if(dist_to_tail <= disc_r)
        {
            ...

            // Check to snap connector to port
            if( (*it_con)->GetRefFromPort() == NULL)
            {
                from_port = SnapConnectionTailPointToPort(tail_pt);
                  // tail_pt passed by ref. and may be updated.
                if(from_port != NULL)
                {
                    (*it_con)->SetRefFromPort(from_port);
                }
            }
            else    // If already a ref-from-port, then the intention on
              moving the end pt. is to break the assoc. with the port.
            {
                (*it_con)->SetRefFromPort(NULL);
            }
            (*it_con)->SetConnectionPointTail(tail_pt);
            ...
            break;
        }
        // If the head pt is clicked
        if(dist_to_head <= disc_r)
        {
            ...

            head_pt = m_RectTracker.m_rect.CenterPoint();

            // Check to snap connector to port
            if( (*it_con)->GetRefToPort() == NULL)
            {
                to_port = SnapConnectionHeadPointToPort(head_pt);
                  // head_pt passed by ref. and may be updated.
                if(to_port != NULL)
                {
                    (*it_con)->SetRefToPort(to_port);
                }
            }
            else    // If already a ref-to-port, then the intention on
              moving the end pt. is to break the assoc. with the port.
            {
                (*it_con)->SetRefToPort(NULL);
            }
            (*it_con)->SetConnectionPointHead(head_pt);
            ...
            break;
        }
    }// end for
```

```
    // Return flag indicating if an item was tracked: 0 => not tracked,
      1 => tracked.
    return tracker_flag;
}
```

6.4   INSERTING AND MOVING CONNECTION-BASED BEND POINTS

A bend point is a point on a connection line where the angle of the line may change and is used to facilitate the drawing of orderly diagrams, in particular, those with feedback loops. It is placed manually on an existing connection by right-clicking the mouse to invoke the Context menu and selecting, Insert Bend Point. If the mouse cursor is located close enough to the line, then a bend point will be placed at the point specified. The general steps to implement the bend point insertion functionality are as follows, where specific details are provided in the following sections.

1. Augment the Context menu with an Insert Bend Point operation
2. Drawing a connection with head, tail, and bend points
3. Moving a connection-based bend point

6.4.1   AUGMENT THE CONTEXT MENU WITH AN INSERT BEND POINT OPERATION

Navigate to the Menu Designer and select the menu with ID: IDR_CONTEXT_MENU. Drag the blank entry at the bottom of the Context menu list, i.e., the entry below Set Properties, and place this in between Delete Item and Set Properties. Add the menu entry listed in Table 6.1, with the ID, IDM_INSERT_BEND_POINT, named Insert Bend Point.

To attach functionality to the event message for the new entry, invoke the ClassWizard: if the dialog box shown in Figure 6.1 appears, just click cancel and ignore this message for now.

Select the class name to be CDiagramEngDoc and choose the object ID: IDM_INSERT_BEND_POINT. Add a function to the Command message, naming it OnInsertBendPoint() and edit the code as shown.

```
void CDiagramEngDoc::OnInsertBendPoint()
{
    // TODO: Add your command handler code here

    // DiagramEng (start)
    double delta_x;
    double delta_y;
    double eps = 1.0*m_dDeltaWidth;
    double gradient;
    double y_val;
    CPoint current_pt;
    CPoint head_pt;
    CPoint point = m_ptContextMenu;
    CPoint prev_pt;
```

TABLE 6.1

Context Menu Entries, IDs, Captions, and Prompts (Status Bar and Tooltips)

ID	Caption	Prompt
IDM_DELETE_ITEM	&Delete Item	Delete selected item\nDelete selected item
IDM_INSERT_BEND_POINT	&Insert Bend Point	Insert bend point\nInsert bend point
IDM_SET_ITEM_PROPERTIES	&Set Properties	Set item properties\nSet item properties

---

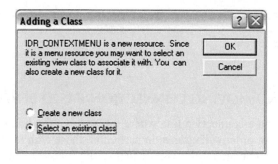

FIGURE 6.1 Adding a Class dialog window as a result of an attempt to attach an event-handler function to a Context menu entry.

```cpp
CPoint tail_pt;
list<CConnection*> &con_list = GetSystemModel().GetConnectionList();
list<CConnection*>::iterator it_con;
list<CPoint> local_pts_list;
list<CPoint>::iterator it_loc;
list<CPoint>::iterator it_pt;
list<CPoint>::iterator temp_it;
CString sMsg;                        // string to be displayed
UINT nType = MB_OK;                  // style of msg. box
UINT nIDhelp = 0;                    // help context ID for the msg.

// Iterate through all connections
for(it_con = con_list.begin(); it_con != con_list.end(); it_con++)
{
    // Get the bend points list
    list<CPoint> &bend_pts_list = (*it_con)-
      >GetConnectionBendPointsList();
    local_pts_list = bend_pts_list;

    // Augment the bend points list with the Connection's tail_pt and
      head_pt.
    head_pt = (*it_con)->GetConnectionPointHead();
    tail_pt = (*it_con)->GetConnectionPointTail();
    local_pts_list.push_front(tail_pt);
    local_pts_list.push_back(head_pt);

    //sMsg.Format("\n CDiagramEngDoc::OnInsertBendPoint(),
      local_pts_list.size() = %d\n", local_pts_list.size());
    //AfxMessageBox(sMsg, nType, nIDhelp);

    // Iterate through points making up this connection after the
      tail pt.
    prev_pt = tail_pt;
    temp_it = local_pts_list.begin();
    temp_it++;

    for(it_pt = temp_it; it_pt != local_pts_list.end(); it_pt++)
    {
        current_pt = *it_pt;

        // Consider a vertical connection line segment
        if(current_pt.x == prev_pt.x)
        {
            // Check to see if mouse point is on the vertical
              connection line segment in the x domain
```

```
            if(abs(point.x - prev_pt.x) <= eps)
            {
                // Check to see if mouse point is on the vertical
                   connection line segment in the y domain
                if( (point.y >= min(prev_pt.y, current_pt.y)) &&
                    (point.y <= max(prev_pt.y, current_pt.y)) )
                {
                    // Create a bend pt.
                    it_loc = it_pt;
                    local_pts_list.insert(it_loc, point);

                    // Placed bend pt on line segment so quit
                       searching line segments in bw connection pts
                    break;
                }
            }
        }
        else // Consider a non-vertical connection, line segment equ.
          of line: y - y0 = ((y1-y0)/(x1-x0))*(x - x0);
        {
            // Check to see if mouse point is on the connection line
               segment in the x domain
            if( (point.x >= min(prev_pt.x, current_pt.x)) &&
                (point.x <= max(prev_pt.x, current_pt.x)) )
            {
                delta_x = (double)(current_pt.x - prev_pt.x);
                delta_y = (double)(current_pt.y - prev_pt.y);
                gradient = delta_y/delta_x;
                y_val = gradient*(point.x - prev_pt.x) + prev_pt.y;

                // Check to see if mouse point is on the connection
                   line segment in the y domain
                if( (point.y >= min(prev_pt.y, current_pt.y)) &&
                    (point.y <= max(prev_pt.y, current_pt.y)) )
                {
                    // Check to see if mouse point is close enough to
                       the line in the y domain
                    if(abs(point.y - y_val) <= eps)
                    {
                        // Create a bend pt.
                        it_loc = it_pt;
                        local_pts_list.insert(it_loc, point);

                        // Placed bend pt on line segment so
                           quit searching line segments in bw
                           connection pts
                        break;
                    }
                }
            }
        }

        // Update the previous pt.
        prev_pt = *it_pt;

}// end for it_pt

// Update the bend points list
local_pts_list.pop_front();      // take off the tail_pt
```

```
          local_pts_list.pop_back();      // take off the head_pt
          (*it_con)->SetConnectionBendPointsList(local_pts_list);
      }// end for it_con

      // Redraw the doc. (since the connections have been modified)
      UpdateAllViews(NULL);

      // DiagramEng (end)
}
```

The function works as follows: the list of connections is iterated over, the current connection's bend point list is retrieved, the tail and head points are augmented to the bend point list, if the mouse cursor point is on the connection line connecting two consecutive points, a bend point is inserted between them, and, finally, the bend points list is updated. Two line segments are considered: an approximately vertical connection-line segment and a nonvertical connection-line segment. Elementary linear geometry is used to determine whether the point, at which the Context menu is invoked, lies on the line.

The developer will have noticed the usage of a bend-point list in the previous code, to which the head and tail points are added, prior to the iteration of all connection-based points. Hence, add a private member variable to the CConnection class that is a list of CPoint objects, i.e., "list<CPoint> m_lstBendPoints". The ClassWizard will complain with the message: "Template declarations or definitions cannot be added." Hence, change the type to integer, and then manually change the declaration in the "Signal.h" header file.

Note that in the function OnInsertBendPoint(), to update the member variable "m_lstBendPoints" of class CConnection, the assignment "bend_pts_list = local_pts_list" would be incorrect, since this would just pass the address of the "local_pts_list" to the "bend_pts_list". Hence, an accessor method is required to pass the "local_pts_list", containing the bend points for the current connection, and perform explicit assignment of the member variable "m_lstBendPoints" within the accessor function.

Hence, first, add a public accessor function to the CConnection class to return the list, "m_lstBendPoints" by reference, with the prototype, list<CPoint>& CConnection:: GetConnectionBendPointsList(void): again, use "int &" as the return type, and then manually change the declaration in the "Signal.h" header file, and the definition in the "Signal. cpp" source file. Edit the function as follows.

```
list<CPoint>& CConnection::GetConnectionBendPointsList()
{
    // Return connection's bend points list
    return m_lstBendPoints;
}
```

Then, add a public accessor function to the CConnection class to set the bend points list, "m_lstBendPoints", by passing in a list<CPoint> argument, with the prototype, void CConnection::SetConnectionBendPointsList(list<CPoint> bend_pts_ list): again, use "int &" as the incoming argument type, and then manually change the declaration in the "Signal.h" header file, and the definition in the "Signal.cpp" source file. Edit the function as follows.

```
void CConnection::SetConnectionBendPointsList(list<CPoint> bend_pts_list)
{
    // Assign the incoming var. to the member var.
    m_lstBendPoints = bend_pts_list;
}
```

Finally add, #include <list>, followed by using namespace std; within the inclusion guard portion of the code, in the "Signal.h" header file, and do the same at the top of the "Signal. cpp" source file. At this point, the code should compile; however, no bend point is visible as it has not yet been drawn.

6.4.2   Drawing a Connection with Head, Tail, and Bend Points

The existing CConnection::DrawConnection() function draws a connection from (CPoint) "m_ptTail" to (CPoint) "m_ptHead" and then draws the arrowhead in the direction from the tail to the head point. This function now needs to be modified, given the possible introduction of bend points by the user.

6.4.2.1   DrawConnection()

Edit the DrawConnection() function as indicated in the following, to perform the following actions: (1) initialize all local variables, (2) move to the tail point, (3) draw lines connecting all points from the tail point, through the bend points and finally to the head point, (4) draw an ellipse around each bend point, and (5) draw an arrowhead in the direction from the tail point or final bend point, to the head point.

```
void CConnection::DrawConnection(CDC *pDC)
{
    int pen_color = RGB(0,0,0);   // White = RGB(255,255,255),
      Black = RGB(0,0,0).
    int pen_width = 1;            // pen width
    double dDeltaLength;          // std default reference delta length
    double length;                // length of side of rectangle bounding
      ellipse
    CPoint bend_pt;               // temp pt. to hold bend pt.
    CPoint bottom_right;          // bottom right cnr. coord. of rectangle
      bounding ellipse
    CPoint final_pt = m_ptTail;   // init as tail pt. in case there are no
      bend pts.
    CPoint top_left;              // top left cnr. coord. of rectangle
      bounding ellipse
    list<CPoint>::iterator it_pt;

    // Set length
    dDeltaLength = GetDocumentGlobalFn()->GetDeltaLength();
    length = 0.2*dDeltaLength;

    // Create the pen
    CPen lpen(PS_SOLID, pen_width, pen_color);

    // Select the pen as the drawing obj.
    // The value returned by SelectObject() is a ptr to the obj. being
      replaced, i.e. an old-pen-ptr.
    CPen *pOldPen = pDC->SelectObject(&lpen);

    // Move to the tail pt.
    pDC->MoveTo(m_ptTail);

    // Iterate through the bend pts. drawing lines bw. them.
    for(it_pt = m_lstBendPoints.begin(); it_pt != m_lstBendPoints.end();
      it_pt++)
    {
        // Draw a line to the bend pt.
        pDC->LineTo(*it_pt);
```

```
        // Set the current bend pt. as the pt prior to the head_pt: used
          for DrawArrowHead().
        final_pt = *it_pt;
    }

    // Line to head pt.
    pDC->LineTo(m_ptHead);

    // Iterate through the bend pts. drawing ellipses at each pt.
    for(it_pt = m_lstBendPoints.begin(); it_pt != m_lstBendPoints.end();
      it_pt++)
    {
        // Draw an ellipse about the bend pt.
        bend_pt = *it_pt;
        top_left.x = (int)(bend_pt.x - length*0.5);
        top_left.y = (int)(bend_pt.y - length*0.5);
        bottom_right.x = (int)(bend_pt.x + length*0.5);
        bottom_right.y = (int)(bend_pt.y + length*0.5);
        pDC->Ellipse(top_left.x, top_left.y, bottom_right.x,
          bottom_right.y);
    }

    // Reset the prev. pen
    pDC->SelectObject(pOldPen);

    // Draw arrowhead
    DrawArrowHead(pDC, final_pt, m_ptHead);
}
```

6.4.2.2 Amend `DrawArrowHead()`

The original `DrawArrowHead()` function had only the one CDC *pDC argument. However, with the possibility of the arrowhead being drawn from either the tail point, or from the final bend point, to the head point, the existing `DrawArrowHead()` function should be augmented to take three arguments to result in the new function prototype: void CConnection::DrawArrowHead(CDC *pDC, CPoint tail, CPoint head). Edit the new `DrawArrowHead()` function as shown in bold in the following, by changing its declaration in the "Signal.h" header file, and its definition in the "Signal.cpp" source file, and replace occurrences of "m_ptHead" and "m_ptTail" with "head" and "tail," respectively, in the body of the function, to match the arguments in the header.

```
void CConnection::DrawArrowHead(CDC *pDC, CPoint tail, CPoint head)
{
    int pen_color = RGB(0,0,0);     // pen color:
      White = RGB(255,255,255), Black = RBF(0,0,0)
    int pen_width = 1;              // pen width
    double d;                       // opp. side length of subtriangle
      with hypotenuse h and base side length length/2.
    double dDeltaLength;            // std ref delta length
    double h;                       // hypotenuse of subtriangle with opp.
      side length d and base side length length/2.
    double length;                  // a fraction of a std ref delta
      length
    double length_u;                // length of vector u
    double length_v;                // length of vector v
    double theta;                   // angle of ith body rotated
      positively clockwise w.r.t. the global screen coord sys. X axis.
    double u[2];                    // one of two vectors used to
      determined angle theta
```

```
double v[2];                        // one of two vectors used to
  determined angle theta: the unit vector [1,0]
CBrush *pBrush = NULL;               // a ptr to brush
CPoint A;                           // vertex in anticlock direc from
  pointing vertex B of arrowhead
CPoint B;                           // vertex of arrowhead pointing in
  direc of arrow (m_ptTo)
CPoint C;                           // vertex in clock direc from pointing
  vertex B of arrowhead
CPoint vertices[3];                 // vertices array to hold triangle
  vertices
CString sMsg;                       // main msg string
UINT nType = MB_OK;                 // style of msg. box
UINT nIDhelp = 0;                   // help context ID for the msg.

// Set length
dDeltaLength = GetDocumentGlobalFn()->GetDeltaLength();
length = 0.15*dDeltaLength;

// Assign lengths to arrowhead (triangle) paras.
d = 0.2887*length;
h = 0.5773*length;

// Print msg.
sMsg.Format("\n CConnection::DrawArrowHead(), d = %lf, h = %lf\n", d, h);
//AfxMessageBox(sMsg, nType, nIDhelp);

// Length of vecs u and v
v[0] = 1.0;                 // x cmpt. of unit vector [1,0]
v[1] = 0.0;                 // y cmpt. of unit vector [1,0]
u[0] = head.x - tail.x;     // length in x direc of connection vector
u[1] = head.y - tail.y;     // length in y direc of connection vector

length_u = sqrt(pow(u[0],2) + pow(u[1],2));
length_v = sqrt(pow(v[0],2) + pow(v[1],2));

// Angle between vecs u and v
theta = acos((u[0]*v[0] + u[1]*v[1])/(length_u*length_v));
if(u[1] < 0)
{
    theta = -theta; // negate theta if y-cmpt of u < 0, since acos
      result is an element from [0,pi] radians ONLY (non-neg).
}

// Global position vecs of arrowhead triangle vertices
A.x = head.x + long(cos(theta)*(-(h+d)) - sin(theta)*(-length*0.5));
A.y = head.y + long(sin(theta)*(-(h+d)) + cos(theta)*(-length*0.5));
B.x = head.x;
B.y = head.y;
C.x = head.x + long(cos(theta)*(-(h+d)) - sin(theta)*(length*0.5));
C.y = head.y + long(sin(theta)*(-(h+d)) + cos(theta)*(length*0.5));

// Create the pen
CPen lpen(PS_SOLID, pen_width, pen_color);

// Select the pen as the drawing obj.
// The value returned by SelectObject() is a ptr to the obj. being
  replaced, i.e. an old-pen-ptr.
CPen *pOldPen = pDC->SelectObject(&lpen);
```

```
    // Draw arrowhead
    pDC->MoveTo(A);
    pDC->LineTo(B);
    pDC->LineTo(C);
    pDC->LineTo(A);

    // Prepare for filling the polygon
    CBrush NewBrush(RGB(0,0,0));      // create a new brush

    vertices[0] = A;
    vertices[1] = B;
    vertices[2] = C;

    // Select the new brush
    pBrush = pDC->SelectObject(&NewBrush);

    // Fill the polygon
    pDC->Polygon(vertices, 3);

    // Reset the prev. pen and brush
    pDC->SelectObject(pOldPen);
    pDC->SelectObject(pBrush);
}
```

6.4.2.3 Interaction Problem Concerning Invisible Connections

There is a slight problem concerning the adding of a connection. The flow of control to add the connection is as follows: (1) on the left-button-down event, the start point of the connection line is initialized, (2) on the mouse-move event, a line is drawn to the mouse cursor from the start point, and (3) on the left-button-up event, the start and end points of the connection line are passed into the AddConnection() function.

If the user touches the left mouse button and does not drag the mouse, then although a connection is automatically added to the model (upon left-button-up), it will be invisible, since the points of the left-button-down and left-button-up events are the same, or so close that they are indistinguishable, so no line or arrow is visibly present. The context under which the user performs various operations should be made clear by the software application, and the functional behavior of the software should also be user-friendly and intuitive.

To solve this problem for now, requires altering the AddConnection() function to not permit the user to add connection lines of a length $l < l_{min}$, where l_{min} is the minimum permitted connection length. Make the following changes to the AddConnection() function as shown in the following and add #include <math.h> at the top of "SystemModel.cpp" since the square root, sqrt(), and power, pow(), mathematical functions are being used.

```
void CSystemModel::AddConnection(CPoint ptFrom, CPoint ptTo)
{
    double con_length;      // length of connection
    double dDeltaLength;    // std def delta length
    double min_length;      // min connection length
    CString sMsg;           // main msg string
    CString sMsgTemp;       // temp msg string
    UINT nType = MB_OK;     // style of msg. box
    UINT nIDhelp = 0;       // help context ID for the msg.

    // Print msg.
    //sMsg.Format("\n CSystemModel::AddConnection(), from (%d,%d) to
      (%d,%d)\n", ptFrom.x, ptFrom.y, ptTo.x, ptTo.y);
    //AfxMessageBox(sMsg, nType, nIDhelp);
```

```
// Set min length
dDeltaLength = GetDocumentGlobalFn()->GetDeltaLength();
min_length = 0.5*dDeltaLength;

// Check to make sure that connection is greater than the rqd. min.
  connection length.
con_length = sqrt(pow(((ptFrom.x - ptTo.x),2) +
  pow(((ptFrom.y - ptTo.y),2));
if(con_length < min_length)
{
    sMsgTemp.Format("\n CSystemModel::AddConnection()\n");
    sMsg += sMsgTemp;
    sMsgTemp.Format("Connection line from point (%d, %d) to point
      (%d, %d).\n", ptFrom.x, ptFrom.y, ptTo.x, ptTo.y);
    sMsg += sMsgTemp;
    sMsgTemp.Format("Connection length = %lf < %lf = min_length. \n",
      con_length, min_length);
    sMsg += sMsgTemp;
    sMsgTemp.Format("Add new connection >= min_length.\n");
    sMsg += sMsgTemp;
    AfxMessageBox(sMsg, nType, nIDhelp);
    return;
}

// Create a new CConnection obj.
CConnection *pCon = new CConnection(ptFrom, ptTo);

// Add the new connection to the connection list
m_lstConnection.push_back(pCon);

// Get a ptr. to the doc. to call the CDocument member fn.
  SetModifiedFlag(), and mark the doc. as modified (TRUE).
GetDocumentGlobalFn()->SetModifiedFlag(TRUE);
}
```

When the user runs the program and attempts to place a connection with length, $l < l_{min}$, the message box shown in Figure 6.2 appears reporting the start and end points of the connection, the connection length and that the connection was not constructed: the AfxMessageBox() calls may be commented out later.

6.4.3 Moving a Connection-Based Bend Point

The objects that may be moved using the CRectTracker object, "m_RectTracker", are blocks and connection-based head and tail points. Functionality is now added to the project to allow the user to move connection-based bend points. This is achieved by editing the TrackItem() function of the CDiagramEngDoc class with bend-point-tracking related code and adding an additional TrackConnectionBendPoint() function to the CDiagramEngDoc class.

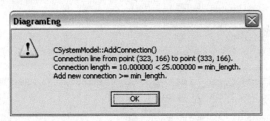

FIGURE 6.2 Diagnostic warning indicating an invalid length for the connection object.

Hence, add code to the `TrackItem()` function as shown in bold in the following to call `TrackConnectionBendPoint()` and check the returned value of the flag-like "tracker_flag" variable.

```
int CDiagramEngDoc::TrackItem(CPoint point, CWnd *pWnd)
{
    int tracker_flag = 0;

    // Track block
    tracker_flag = TrackBlock(point, pWnd);
    if(tracker_flag != 0)
    {
        return tracker_flag;
    }

    // Track connection end point
    tracker_flag = TrackConnectionEndPoint(point, pWnd);
    if(tracker_flag != 0)
    {
        return tracker_flag;
    }

    // Track connection bend point
    tracker_flag = TrackConnectionBendPoint(point, pWnd);
    if(tracker_flag != 0)
    {
        return tracker_flag;
    }

    // Return flag indicating if an item was tracked: 0 => not tracked,
      1 => tracked.
    return tracker_flag;
}
```

Now, add a public member function to the CDiagramEngDoc class with the prototype, `int CDiagramEngDoc::TrackConnectionBendPoint(CPoint point, CWnd *pWnd)`, and edit the function as shown in the following. The developer will notice that there are two *for* loops: the first iterates through the list of connections in the current diagram, and the second iterates through all the bend points on the current connection. The conditional statement checks to see whether the bend point has actually been selected, i.e., if the cursor position at the left-button-down event is within a disc of radius *r* of the center of the bend point.

```
int CDiagramEngDoc::TrackConnectionBendPoint(CPoint point, CWnd *pWnd)
{
    int delta = (int)(0.25*m_dDeltaLength); // integer increment
    int tracker_flag = 0;
    double disc_r = 0.25*m_dDeltaLength;
    double dist;
    CPoint bend_pt;
    CPoint bottom_right;
    CPoint top_left;
    list<CConnection*>::iterator it_con;
    list<CConnection*> con_list = GetSystemModel().GetConnectionList();
    list<CPoint>::iterator it_pt;

    // Iterate through connection list
    for(it_con = con_list.begin(); it_con != con_list.end(); it_con++)
```

```
    {
        // Get connection bend pts.
        list<CPoint> &bend_pts_list = (*it_con)-
          >GetConnectionBendPointsList();

        // Iterate through all bend pts. for this connection
        for(it_pt = bend_pts_list.begin(); it_pt != bend_pts_list.end();
          it_pt++)
        {
            bend_pt = *it_pt;

            // Determine Euclidean dist bw mouse point and connection
              bend pt.
            dist = sqrt(pow(bend_pt.x - point.x,2) +
              pow(bend_pt.y - point.y,2));

            // If the bend pt is clicked
            if(dist <= disc_r)
            {
                // Assign rectangle setting values
                top_left.x = bend_pt.x - delta;
                top_left.y = bend_pt.y - delta;
                bottom_right.x = bend_pt.x + delta;
                bottom_right.y = bend_pt.y + delta;

                // Set the rect tracker's position
                m_RectTracker.m_rect.SetRect(top_left.x, top_left.y,
                  bottom_right.x, bottom_right.y);

                // Track the mouse's position till left mouse button up
                tracker_flag = m_RectTracker.Track(pWnd, point, TRUE);
                  // 0 => item not tracked, 1 => item was tracked

                // Get the new tracker position and update the connection
                  bend pt position with the tracker position
                *it_pt = m_RectTracker.m_rect.CenterPoint();

                // Set flags
                SetModifiedFlag(TRUE);          // set the doc. as having
                  been modified to prompt user to save
                UpdateAllViews(NULL);           // indicate that sys. should
                  redraw.
                break;

            }// end if dist
        }// end for it_pt
    }// end for it_con

    return tracker_flag;
}
```

Now, upon running the program, connection-based bend points may be inserted using the Context menu and moved using the mouse. Figure 6.3 shows that mathematical models may now be interactively drawn with all items aligned: (a) a linear function involving the Linear Function, Gain, Constant, Sum, and Output blocks, and (b) a differential equation being integrated, involving the Signal Generator, Sum, Integrator, and Output blocks, using a branch/bend point to allow the drawing of a feedback loop.

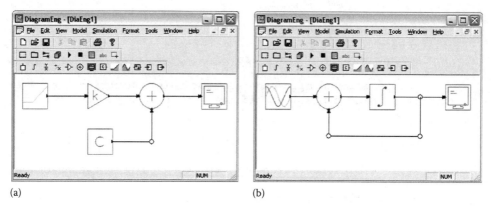

(a)   (b)

FIGURE 6.3   System models: (a) a linear equation representation and (b) a differential equation representation.

6.5   DELETION OF CONNECTIONS AND BEND POINTS

Now that connections and their bend points exist, a mechanism is required to allow the user to remove selected bend points on a particular connection object and also an entire connection and all its contained bend points.

6.5.1   DELETION OF A BEND POINT

Bend points are inserted via right-clicking on a connection line and choosing Insert Bend Point from the Context menu. Here, functionality is added to allow the user to right-click on a connection line bend point, and upon choosing Delete Item from the Context menu, the correct item, i.e., the bend point, should be deleted. This works in a similar way to right-clicking on a block and choosing Delete Item from the Context menu to delete a block, via a call to DeleteBlock(). Hence, augment the OnDeleteItem() function as shown in the following to call the to-be-added DeleteConnectionBendPoint() method.

```
void CDiagramEngDoc::OnDeleteItem()
{
    // TODO: Add your command handler code here

    // DiagramEng (start)
    int item_deleted = 0;

    // Delete a block
    item_deleted = DeleteBlock();
    if(item_deleted == 1)
    {
        return;
    }

    // Delete a connection bend point
    item_deleted = DeleteConnectionBendPoint();
    if(item_deleted == 1)
    {
        return;
    }

    // DiagramEng (end)
}
```

Now add a public member function to the CDiagramEngDoc class to delete a connection-based bend point, with the prototype, int CDiagramEngDoc::DeleteConnectionBendPoint (void), and edit the code as shown in the following.

```
int CDiagramEngDoc::DeleteConnectionBendPoint()
{
    int count = 0;                          // counter
    int delete_bp = 0;                      // bend pt. deletion flag
    double dist;                            // Euclidean dist bw. bend
      pt. posn and mouse point posn.
    double disc_r = 0.8*m_dDeltaLength*0.5; // disc or radius r
    CPoint bend_pt_posn;                    // bend pt. posn.
    CPoint point;                           // local point var.
    CString sMsg;                           // main msg string
    UINT nType = MB_OK;                     // style of msg. box
    UINT nIDhelp = 0;                       // help context ID for
      the msg.
    list<CConnection*>::iterator it_con;    // connection iterator
    list<CPoint>::iterator it_pt;           // bend pt iterator
    list<CPoint>::iterator it_er = NULL;    // erase iterator
      (element to erase)

    // Get the point at which the context menu was invoked
    point = m_ptContextMenu;                // init a local copy.

    // Print msg.
    //sMsg.Format("\n CDiagramEngDoc::DeleteConnectionBendPoint(), point
      (x,y) = (%d,%d)\n", point.x, point.y);
    //AfxMessageBox(sMsg, nType, nIDhelp);

    // Get a copy of the bend_pts_list in the system model
    list<CConnection*> &con_list = GetSystemModel().GetConnectionList();
      // MUST BE A REFERENCE!

    // Iterate through the connection list
    for(it_con = con_list.begin(); it_con != con_list.end(); it_con++)
    {
        // Get the bend points list
        list<CPoint> &bend_pts_list = (*it_con)-
          >GetConnectionBendPointsList();

        // Iterate through the bend pts. list
            delete_bp = 0;     // init delete_bp = 0 since, at present no
              bend_pt is to be deleted
        for(it_pt = bend_pts_list.begin(); it_pt != bend_pts_list.end();
          it_pt++)
        {
            bend_pt_posn = *it_pt;

            // Check whether mouse cursor within disc_r of bend pt.
            dist = sqrt(pow((bend_pt_posn.x - point.x),2) +
              pow((bend_pt_posn.y - point.y),2));
            if(dist <= disc_r)
            {
                //sMsg.Format("\n CDiagramEngDoc::
                  DeleteConnectionBendPoint(), blk(x,y) = (%d,%d),
                  point(x,y) = (%d,%d)\n", blk_posn.x, blk_posn.y,
                  point.x, point.y);
                //AfxMessageBox(sMsg, nType, nIDhelp);
```

```
                // Record which block to erase
                delete_bp = 1;
                it_er = it_pt;
                break;
            }
        }// end for it_pt

        // Delete the item in the list
        if(delete_bp == 1)
        {
            bend_pts_list.erase(it_er);    // delete element at offset
              it_er in list (that held the bend pt)

            count = (*it_con)->GetConnectionBendPointsList().size();
            //sMsg.Format("\n CDiagramEngDoc::DeleteConnectionBendPoint(),
              size = %d\n", count);
            //AfxMessageBox(sMsg, nType, nIDhelp);
        }

    }// end for it_con

    // Set as modified and redraw the doc.
    SetModifiedFlag(TRUE); // set the doc. as having been modified to
      prompt user to save
    UpdateAllViews(NULL);   // indicate that sys. should redraw.

    // Return a flag indicating whether an item was deleted
    return delete_bp;
}
```

Note that "break" is required in the first distance-checking conditional (*if*) statement if the mouse cursor position was close enough to a bend point. This is so, since after the bend point is found, the *for* loop concerning bend points for the particular connection should be terminated. Note also that *delete* should not be called to delete the CPoint object, i.e., the statement, "delete (*it_pt)" is not required in the second conditional (*if*) statement in the DeleteConnectionBendPoint() function: "erase(it_er)" will suffice.

6.5.2 DELETION OF A CONNECTION

A connection consists of at least a tail point and a head point, and any bend points, if they have been inserted, using the Context menu, by the user. Deletion of a connection line should be achieved by right-clicking on the connection's head point and choosing Delete Item from the Context menu. The CDiagramEngDoc::OnDeleteItem() function then calls, DeleteBlock(), DeleteConnectionBendPoint(), and DeleteConnection(), to determine the proximity of the point at which the Context menu was invoked, i.e., "m_ptContextMenu", to the item being examined for deletion, i.e., blocks, bend points, and whole connections, respectively.

The user can also right-click on approximately the midpoint of any of the line segments connected by the tail point, bend points, and the head point, and choose, Delete Item, from the Context menu: depending on the proximity of the mouse cursor to the midpoint of the connection line segment, the connection will be deleted. The problem with the latter method is that the midpoint of a connection line segment is not clearly visible, but the head point marked clearly by an arrowhead allows a more accurate positioning of the mouse cursor to delete the connection. Hence, in the following code, the developer will notice that the midpoint-based bend point deletion method has been commented out, but the developer is free to choose the preferred method.

Hence, add a new section to the OnDeleteItem() function, as shown in bold in the following, that calls DeleteConnection().

```
void CDiagramEngDoc::OnDeleteItem()
{
    // TODO: Add your command handler code here

    // DiagramEng (start)
    int item_deleted = 0;

    // Delete a block
    item_deleted = DeleteBlock();
    if(item_deleted == 1)
    {
        return;
    }

    // Delete a connection bend point
    item_deleted = DeleteConnectionBendPoint();
    if(item_deleted == 1)
    {
        return;
    }

    // Delete a connection line
    item_deleted = DeleteConnection();
    if(item_deleted == 1)
    {
        return;
    }

    // DiagramEng (end)
}
```

Now add a public member function to the CDiagramEngDoc class with the prototype, int CDiagramEngDoc::DeleteConnection(void), and edit the code as shown.

```
int CDiagramEngDoc::DeleteConnection()
{
    int delete_con = 0;
    double disc_r = 0.5*m_dDeltaLength;
    double dist;
    CPoint current_pt;
    CPoint head_pt;
    CPoint midpoint;
    CPoint point = m_ptContextMenu;
    CPoint prev_pt;
    CPoint tail_pt;
    list<CConnection*> &con_list = GetSystemModel().
      GetConnectionList();
    list<CConnection*>::iterator it_con;
    list<CConnection*>::iterator it_er;
    list<CPoint> local_pts_list;
    list<CPoint>::iterator it_pt;
    list<CPoint>::iterator temp_it;
    CString sMsg;         // string to be displayed
    UINT nType = MB_OK;   // style of msg. box
    UINT nIDhelp = 0;     // help context ID for the msg.
```

```
// Iterate through all connections
for(it_con = con_list.begin(); it_con != con_list.end(); it_con++)
{
    // Get the bend points list
    list<CPoint> &bend_pts_list = (*it_con)-
      >GetConnectionBendPointsList();
    local_pts_list = bend_pts_list;

    // Augment the bend points list with the Connection's tail_pt
      and head_pt.
    head_pt = (*it_con)->GetConnectionPointHead();
    tail_pt = (*it_con)->GetConnectionPointTail();
    local_pts_list.push_front(tail_pt);
    local_pts_list.push_back(head_pt);

    //sMsg.Format("\n CDiagramEngDoc::DeleteConnection(),
      local_pts_list.size() = %d\n", local_pts_list.size());
    //AfxMessageBox(sMsg, nType, nIDhelp);

    // Iterate through points making up this connection after the
      tail pt.
    prev_pt = tail_pt;
    temp_it = local_pts_list.begin();
    temp_it++;

    // -- Delete connection object based on clicking the midpoint of
      a line segment
    /*for(it_pt = temp_it; it_pt != local_pts_list.end(); it_pt++)
    {
        current_pt = *it_pt;

        // Calculate the midpoint of the line segment bounded by
          connection line pts.
        midpoint.x = (current_pt.x + prev_pt.x)/2;
        midpoint.y = (current_pt.y + prev_pt.y)/2;

        // Calculate dist of mouse cursor pt. from midpoint
        dist = sqrt(pow((midpoint.x - point.x),2) +
          pow((midpoint.y - point.y),2));

        // If mouse cursor is in the ngbd of the midpoint
        if(dist <= disc_r)
        {
            // Record which connection to erase
            delete_con = 1;
            it_er = it_con;
            break;
        }

        // Update the previous pt.
        prev_pt = *it_pt;

    }// end for it_pt
    */

    // -- Delete connection object based on clicking on the head
      point only.
    // Calculate dist of mouse cursor pt. from head point
    dist = sqrt(pow((head_pt.x - point.x),2) +
      pow((head_pt.y - point.y),2));
```

```
        // If mouse cursor is in the ngbd of the head point
        if(dist <= disc_r)
        {
            // Record which connection to erase
            delete_con = 1;
            it_er = it_con;
            break;
        }
    }// end for it_con

    // Delete the connection in the list
    if(delete_con == 1)
    {
        // Disconnect all tail points from all the bend points on this
          connection.
        //DisconnectTailPointsFromBendPoints(*it_er);

        delete *it_er;                // delete actual connection pointed to
          by it_er
        con_list.erase(it_er);        // delete element at offset it_er in
          list (that held the connection)

        //count = m_SystemModel.GetBlockList().size();
        //sMsg.Format("\n CDiagramEngDoc::DeleteConnection(), size =
          %d\n", count);
        //AfxMessageBox(sMsg, nType, nIDhelp);
    }

    // Set as modfied and redraw the doc.
    SetModifiedFlag(TRUE);            // set the doc. as having been modified
      to prompt user to save
    UpdateAllViews(NULL);            // indicate that sys. should redraw.

    // Return a flag indicating whether an item was deleted
    return delete_con;
}
```

The developer will notice the introduction of a new function, named `DisconnectTailPointsFromBendPoints()` that is to be added later in order to disconnect any *secondary* connection tail points from a *primary* connection's bend points. For example, in Figure 6.3b, the *primary* connection joining the Integrator and Output blocks has a bend point, to which a *secondary* connection, forming a feedback loop to the Sum block, is attached. The call to this function is commented out at present, since the functionality to attach a *secondary* connection's tail point to a *primary* connection's bend point has not yet been added to the project. This will be added in Chapter 8.

6.6 SUMMARY

The movement of items, including blocks, connection objects and their head, tail, and bend points, is performed using a CRectTracker object and its related functions, SetRect(), Track(), and CenterPoint(). Connection-based end points, i.e., head and tail points, can then be moved and snapped to block input and output ports, respectively. Functionality to unsnap the end points is then added to allow the user to disassociate or break the connection from the ports to which the connection may be attached. Bend points were then inserted on a connection line, using an entry on the Context menu, and moved or tracked with the CRectTracker object. An interaction problem concerning the left-button-down action, resulting in invisible connections, was also resolved. Finally, the deletion of connection-based bend points and whole connection objects was implemented.

REFERENCES

1. Microsoft Developer Network Library Visual Studio 6.0, Microsoft® Visual Studio™ 6.0 Development System, Microsoft Corporation, 1998.
2. Microsoft Visual C++® 6.0, Microsoft® Visual Studio™ 6.0 Development System, Professional Edition, Microsoft Corporation, 1998.

7 Automatic Block Placement

7.1 INTRODUCTION

Currently, upon clicking the Common Blocks toolbar, the bottom toolbar shown in Figure 7.1, the OnBlock*GroupName*() command-event message handling function of the CDiagramEngDoc class is called, where *Group* represents either of the Continuous, Math Operations, Sink, Source, and Subsystem group classifications, and *Name* represents the particular name of the block: e.g., OnBlockSourceConst() is the command-event message handling function for the clicking of the Constant block toolbar button, representing the Constant block of the Source group. This function then calls ConstructBlock() that filters an enumerated type to call the particular block construction function, e.g., ConstructConstantBlock(). However, prior to calling the block's actual constructor, an automatic position assignment function, AssignBlockPosition() is called to automatically determine the position of the block to be placed on the palette. This was initially used in the developmental process to avoid unnecessary interactive complexity.

The software developer may choose between three different courses of action to take here: (1) retain the existing automatic block placement functionality provided by AssignBlockPosition(), (2) enhance the AssignBlockPosition() function with more flexible block positioning, or (3) introduce an interactive mechanism such that if the CDiagramEngDoc::ConstructBlock() function is invoked via a particular toolbar button command-event message handling function, then the position of the block will be that of the mouse pointer upon a subsequent left-button-down event to locate the block on the palette.

The following first set of instructions concern option three given earlier and indicate how the new interactive point-based block-position-assignment mechanism may be implemented if desired. However, this does require significant alteration, and it was decided that option two given earlier, concerning the implementation of an enhanced AssignBlockPosition() function, would be preferable (see Section 7.3).

7.2 HYPOTHETICAL INTERACTIVE BLOCK POSITIONING

Listed in the following are the steps that would be taken to implement interactive functionality to select a block on the Common Blocks toolbar and then click the desired location on the palette to specify the block's position. The interested developer may like to pursue this approach; however, substantial changes to the program structure are required.

Step 1: Add two private member variables to the CDiagramEngDoc class: the first, an integer with the name, "m_BtnClick" and the second, an EBlockType enumerated type with the name, "m_eBlockType".

Step 2: Add three public accessor member methods to the CDiagramEngDoc class with the following prototypes:

1. int CDiagramEngDoc::GetButtonClick(void) to return, "m_BtnClick".
2. void CDiagramEngDoc::SetButtonClick(int click), to set, "m_BtnClick".
3. EBlockType CDiagramEngDoc::GetBlockType(void), to return, "m_eBlockType".

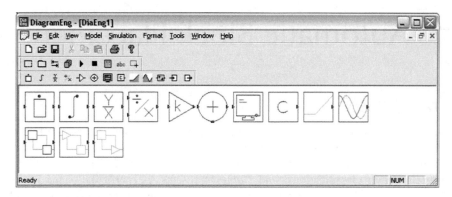

FIGURE 7.1 The Main-frame-based toolbar (top), Common Ops. toolbar (middle), and the Common Blocks toolbar (bottom) of the DiagramEng application used to add blocks to the model.

Step 3: Edit the CDiagramEngDoc toolbar button command-event handler functions, e.g., OnBlockSourceConst(), as follows:

1. Set the "m_eBlockType" variable with the type of the block that needs to be constructed, e.g., "eConstBlock".
2. Set the "m_BtnClick" variable with the value "1" indicating that a button was clicked.
3. Comment out the call, "pDoc->ConstructBlock(e_block_type)", as an extended version of this would be performed in the CDiagramEngView::OnLButtonDown() function.

Step 4: Edit the OnLButtonDown() function as shown in the following hypothetical code excerpt. First, the value of the "m_BtnClick" variable is retrieved using the statement: GetDocument()->GetButtonClick(). Then, the value of the "m_eBlockType" variable is obtained: GetDocument()->GetBlockType(). Finally, the ConstructBlock(m_eBlockType, point) is called, passing in both the existing EBlockType variable and the new mouse position, CPoint, "point" variable. The passing of the variable "m_eBlockType" from OnLButtonDown() is somewhat excessive, since the variable "m_eBlockType" and the function ConstructBlock() both belong to the CDiagramEngDoc class: but this is done here to conform to the existing structure, since a Block Library Dialog window may be used (see the following).

```
void CDiagramEngView::OnLButtonDown(UINT nFlags, CPoint point)
{
    // TODO: Add your message handler code here and/or call default

    // DiagramEng (start)
    int tracker_flag;      // 0 => no tracker and hence a connector, 1 =>
      tracker and hence no connector

    // Check to see whether toolbar button has been clicked.
    if(GetDocument()->GetButtonClick() == 1)
    {
        ConstructBlock(GetDocument()->GetBlockType(), point);
        GetDocument()->SetButtonClick(0);
    }
    else
    {
        // Assume an item is being tracked: if so tracker_flag = 1, if
          not: tracker_flag = 0.
```

```
        tracker_flag = GetDocument()->TrackItem(point, this); // this is
          a ptr-to-CWnd, i.e. CWnd *pWnd.

        // If nothing was tracked, i.e. tracker_flag = 0, then record
          points to draw and construct a connector.
        if(tracker_flag == 0)
        {
            // Capture the mouse so no other apps. can get it.
            SetCapture();

            // Save the pt that the cursor is at, upon left-btn-down,
              i.e. init member var with incoming CPoint var.
            m_ptPrevPos = point;    // Init the prev. pt, to be used in
              OnMouseMove(), to the current point
            m_ptOrigin = point;     // Init the origin of the ensuing
              line, to be drawn in OnMouseMove(), to be the starting pt.
        }
    }
    // DiagramEng (end)

    CView::OnLButtonDown(nFlags, point);
}
```

Step 5: Amend the `ConstructBlock()` function as follows: (1) change the formal parameter list to take two arguments, the EBlockType and CPoint variables, i.e., `ConstructBlock(EBlockType e_block_type, CPoint point)`, and (2) pass the CPoint "point" variable into the `ConstructParticularBlock()` functions, where *Particular* denotes the particular block construction function: e.g., for the Constant block construction function, `ConstructConstantBlock(point)` should be called. This will require changing the parameter lists of these *Particular* functions to take the CPoint, "point", argument.

Step 6: Comment out the `AssignBlockPosition()` call in the `ConstructParticularBlock()` functions, since the block position is now that of the "point" variable, i.e., the mouse cursor location that is passed into the function `ConstructParticularBlock()`. Assign to the local variable, "block_posn", the incoming CPoint argument, i.e., "block_posn = point". The block will then be constructed correctly.

However, there is a slight additional complication: if the user decides to add blocks to the palette using the Block Library Dialog window as shown in Figure 7.2, then the Add All Blocks button will be used, and the `CBlockLibDlg::OnBlocklibdlgBtnAddallblocks()` command event message handling function is invoked. Within this function, `ConstructBlock()` is called passing in the enumerated type EBlockType argument. However, if the *interactive* changes mentioned earlier were to have been made, then the call to `ConstructBlock()` would have to take both the enumerated type argument and a CPoint block-position argument. In this case, to have both the interactive mouse-based positioning as a result of toolbar button usage, and the automatic block position assignment functionality of `AssignBlockPosition()`, a local CPoint block-position, "block_posn", variable would need to be declared within the Add All Blocks function, `CBlockLibDlg::OnBlocklibdlgBtnAddallblocks()`, and the call `pDoc->GetBlockPosition(block_posn)` would need to be made to retrieve the block position. Then the call `pDoc->ConstructBlock(e_block_type, block_posn)` would pass the necessary variables to the `ConstructParticularBlock()` functions for correct ensuing block construction.

These alterations can be made, but it appears to be a lot of work for the additional interactive flexibility of being able to click a toolbar button and then click the palette at the desired location for

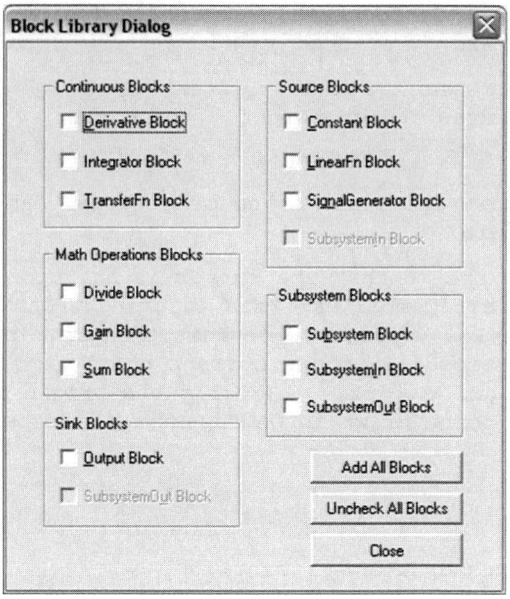

FIGURE 7.2   Block Library Dialog window used to add blocks to the project.

initial block placement: in fact, on implementation, there may be other unforeseen difficulties. The disadvantage of clicking a button and then clicking the palette is that an additional mouse-button click is required per toolbar button click, for block placement. The alternative is to simply click the toolbar button and for the block to be positioned automatically without overlapping any existing blocks on the palette: it is the automatic nonoverlapping behavior that should be augmented to the `AssignBlockPosition()` function as discussed later, since it requires no structural changes to the project.

7.3   ACTUAL IMPROVED AUTOMATIC BLOCK POSITIONING

The original `AssignBlockPosition()` function places the blocks in consecutive rows of 10 columns across the screen regardless of whether they overlap any existing blocks. The modifications here place the blocks in the earliest available trial block position $T_{bp}(x_i, y_i)$, where (x_i, y_i) denote the column and row location: x_i is the x coordinate of the ith block chosen in step-sizes equal to the block width plus an intermediate lateral spacing, across the palette window in increasing value towards the right, and y_i is the y coordinate of the ith block chosen in row-step-sizes equal to the block height plus an intermediate vertical spacing, increasing in value downward (consistent with the positive direction of the screen coordinate system).

The automatic positioning algorithm uses three essential loops: (1) the *while* loop iterates until a suitable trial block position that does not overlap with any existing blocks is found, (2) the first *for* loop iterates over a suitably large number of potential trial block positions (row and column locations) where the number should be greater than the number of existing blocks in the current system model block list, and (3) the second *for* loop iterates over the list of blocks checking that the distance between the trial block position and the existing block positions is large enough to prevent an overlap. Augment the `AssignBlockPosition()` function as shown in the following and build the application. Then, upon running the program, if blocks are deleted from the block list using the Delete Item entry of the Context menu, and new blocks inserted, these will be placed in the earliest available space from the top of the palette downward (see Figure 7.3a through d).

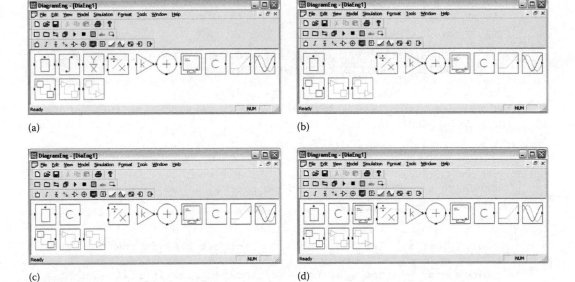

FIGURE 7.3 Automatic block placement: (a) blocks added to system model, (b) two blocks deleted, (c) a constant block added (earliest available position), and (d) an output block added (second available position).

```
void CDiagramEngDoc::AssignBlockPosition(CPoint &block_posn)
{
    int i;
    int large_no_of_blocks = 500;
    int n_blocks;
    int n_blks_in_row = 10;
    int posn_found = 0;
    int too_close = 0;
    double dist = 0.0;
    double dist_crit;
    double height = 2.0*m_dDeltaLength;
    double width = 2.0*m_dDeltaLength;
    double left_spacing = 0.2*width;
    double blk_spacing = 0.2*width;
    double top_spacing = 0.2*width;
    //static int n_blks_static = 0;
    CPoint blk_posn;
    CPoint trial_blk_posn;
    list<CBlock*>::iterator it_blk;
    CString sMsg;          // main msg string
    UINT nType = MB_OK;    // style of msg. box
    UINT nIDhelp = 0;      // help context ID for the msg.

    //sMsg.Format("\n CDiagramEngDoc::AssignBlockPosition(), i = %d\n", i);
    //AfxMessageBox(sMsg, nType, nIDhelp);

    // -- ASSIGN BLOCK POSITION IN THE NEXT ROW/COL POSN.
    //n_blocks = GetSystemModel().GetBlockList().size();
    /*n_blocks = n_blks_static;
    n_blks_static++;

    block_posn.x = left_spacing + (n_blocks%n_blks_in_row)*(width +
        blk_spacing) + 0.5*width;      // CofM of block at width*0.5
```

```
    block_posn.y = top_spacing + (n_blocks/n_blks_in_row)*(height +
      blk_spacing) + 0.5*height;    // CofM of block at height*0.5
    */

    // -- ASSIGN BLOCK POSITION FLEXIBLY (TO NOT OVERLAP EXISTING BLOCKS)
       IN THE EARLIEST AVAILABLE ROW/COL POSN.

    // Get a copy of the blk_list in the system model
    list<CBlock*> &blk_list = GetSystemModel().GetBlockList();    // MUST
      BE A REFERENCE!

    dist_crit = width + blk_spacing;
    n_blocks = blk_list.size();

    // Check to see whether there are no blocks: if so, set the first
      block and return.
    if(n_blocks == 0)
    {
        block_posn.x = left_spacing + (n_blocks%n_blks_in_row)*(width +
          blk_spacing) + 0.5*width;    // CofM of block at width*0.5
        block_posn.y = top_spacing + (n_blocks/n_blks_in_row)*(height +
          blk_spacing) + 0.5*height;    // CofM of block at height*0.5
        return;
    }

    // While not suitable row/col position has been found
    while(posn_found == 0)
    {
        // Iterate through the potential row/col positions, trying each
          one against existing block positions
        for(i=0; i<large_no_of_blocks; i++)
        {
            trial_blk_posn.x = left_spacing + (i%n_blks_in_row)*(width +
              blk_spacing) + 0.5*width;    // CofM of block at width*0.5
            trial_blk_posn.y = top_spacing + (i/n_blks_in_row)*(height +
              blk_spacing) + 0.5*height;   // CofM of block at height*0.5

            // Iterate through the existing blocks to get the distance
              from the trial temp_block_posn.
            too_close = 0;
            for(it_blk = blk_list.begin(); it_blk != blk_list.end();
              it_blk++)
            {
                blk_posn = (*it_blk)->GetBlockPosition();

                // Check the distance bw. trial posn and block posn
                dist = sqrt(pow((blk_posn.x - trial_blk_posn.x),2) +
                  pow((blk_posn.y - trial_blk_posn.y),2));

                if(dist < dist_crit)
                {
                    too_close = 1;    // if too close, then get another
                      trial_blk_posn
                    break;
                }
            }// end for it
```

```
                if(too_close == 0)
                {
                    posn_found = 1;
                    block_posn = trial_blk_posn;
                    break;
                }
        }// end for i
    }// end while
}
```

7.4   SUMMARY

Two different methods are presented for the placement of blocks on the palette: (1) a hypothetical interactive block positioning method and (2) an improved automatic block positioning method. The former method would place a selected block at the (user-defined) point of a mouse-click left-button-down event on the palette. The latter process places blocks in an array, across the rows and down the columns, in the earliest available position on the palette such that the blocks are sufficiently spaced apart. The second method was implemented since it required the fewest changes to the existing program structure.

8 Connection-Based Bend Points

8.1 INTRODUCTION

The movement of blocks with connection-based head and tail points attached to input and output ports was introduced in Chapter 6. Connection tail points can not only be connected to a block output port but also to another connection's bend point to allow the formation of a feedback loop in a model diagram. The topics covered here are (1) the attachment of a *secondary* connection's tail point to a *primary* connection's bend point, (2) the deletion of a bend point to which a *secondary* connection is attached, (3) the deletion of a whole connection with bend points to which other connections are attached, (4) the insertion of multiple bend points, (5) automatic attachment of connection end points to ports and bend points upon initial construction, and (6) the deletion of blocks with attached connections.

8.2 ATTACHING A CONNECTION TAIL POINT TO A BEND POINT

Bend points may be added to a connection object using the Context menu and selecting Insert Bend Point as discussed in Chapter 6. However, at present, connection head and tail points can only be snap-connected to block input and output ports, respectively. Hence, functionality needs to be added to allow the snap-connection of a *secondary* connection's tail point to a *primary* connection's bend point (see Figure 8.1) and for the tail point position to be updated when the bend point is moved.

The developer will recall that the two functions concerning end point and bend point movement or tracking are `TrackConnectionEndPoint()` and `TrackConnectionBendPoint()`, respectively: the former allows movement of the end point and snaps it to the appropriate port if sufficiently close, and the latter simply allows movement of the connection bend point, but no snapping to a location is necessary.

The following code excerpt, in particular that shown in bold, concerning the tail point is found in the `TrackConnectionEndPoint()` function.

```
int CDiagramEngDoc::TrackConnectionEndPoint(CPoint point, CWnd *pWnd)
{
    ...
    // If the tail pt is clicked
    if(dist_to_tail <= disc_r)
    {
        top_left.x = tail_pt.x - delta;
        top_left.y = tail_pt.y - delta;
        bottom_right.x = tail_pt.x + delta;
        bottom_right.y = tail_pt.y + delta;

        // Set the rect tracker's position
        m_RectTracker.m_rect.SetRect(top_left.x, top_left.y,
          bottom_right.x, bottom_right.y);

        // Track the mouse's position till left mouse button up
        tracker_flag = m_RectTracker.Track(pWnd, point, TRUE);
        // 0 => item not tracked, 1 => item was tracked
```

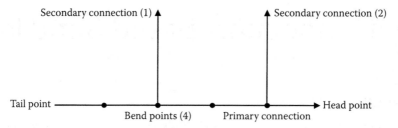

FIGURE 8.1 *Primary* connection with four bend points to which two *secondary* connection tail end points are attached.

```
// Get the new tracker position and update the new connection end
  pt position with the tracker position
tail_pt = m_RectTracker.m_rect.CenterPoint();

// Check to snap connector to port
if((*it_con)->GetRefFromPort() == NULL)  // If not already a
  ref_from port
{
    from_port = SnapConnectionTailPointToPort(tail_pt);
     // tail_pt passed by ref. and may be updated.
    if(from_port != NULL)
    {
        (*it_con)->SetRefFromPort(from_port);
    }
}
else  // If already a ref-from-port, then the intention on moving
  the end pt. is to break the assoc. with the port.
{
    (*it_con)->SetRefFromPort(NULL);
}
(*it_con)->SetConnectionPointTail(tail_pt);

// Set flags
SetModifiedFlag(TRUE);    // set the doc. as having been modified
  to prompt user to save
UpdateAllViews(NULL);     // indicate that sys. should redraw.
break;
    }
    ...
}
```

First, a check is made to determine whether the connection object has a reference-from-port, if not, then an attempt is made to snap the tail point to an output port, and if this is successful, the "from_port" is set to be the output port from which the tail point then emanates, and the tail point position is adjusted to be that of the output port position.

Later, if the block to which the connection object is attached is moved, the connection object tail point associated with the block's output port moves when the block and hence its port moves. The TrackBlock() function allows the user to move a block to a different position, and inside this function a call to SetBlockPosition() is made, wherein the vector of input and output ports are iterated over and the ports repositioned according to the block movement. However, after the ports have been positioned, a call is made to UpdateConnectionPointHead() and UpdateConnectionPointTail(). In these functions if the reference-to-port variable, "m_pRefToPort" and reference-from-port variable, "m_pRefFromPort", match the input pointer-to-CPort argument, then the head and tail points are assigned the input and output port positions, respectively.

The development to attach a connection tail point to a bend point and allow the tail point to subsequently move when the bend point to which it is attached is moved is very similar to the attachment of a connection tail point to a block output port described earlier. The general steps to perform this attachment are provided in the following list, while specific details are provided in the ensuing sections:

1. Amend the `TrackConnectionEndPoint()` function.
2. Add member variables and methods to the CConnection class.
3. Add a `SnapConnectionTailPointToBendPoint()` function.
4. Resolve a problem concerning the connection tail point.

8.2.1 AMEND THE `TrackConnectionEndPoint()` FUNCTION

Amend the `CDiagramEngDoc::TrackConnectionEndPoint()` function inserting the new code (shown in bold) to check whether a connection tail point can be snapped to a connection bend point below the code concerning the snapping of a connection tail point to a block output port (done previously). This will require the declaration of a local pointer-to-CPoint variable named "from_point" initially assigned to NULL, also shown in bold.

```
int CDiagramEngDoc::TrackConnectionEndPoint(CPoint point, CWnd *pWnd)
{
    int delta = (int)(0.25*m_dDeltaLength);   // integer increment
    int tracker_flag = 0;
    …
    CPoint bottom_right;
    CPoint *from_point = NULL;
    CPoint head_pt;
    CPoint tail_pt;
    CPoint top_left;
    CPort *from_port = NULL;
    CPort *to_port = NULL;
    …

    // If the tail pt is clicked
    if(dist_to_tail <= disc_r)
    {
        top_left.x = tail_pt.x - delta;
        top_left.y = tail_pt.y - delta;
        bottom_right.x = tail_pt.x + delta;
        bottom_right.y = tail_pt.y + delta;

        // Set the rect tracker's position
        m_RectTracker.m_rect.SetRect(top_left.x, top_left.y,
          bottom_right.x, bottom_right.y);

        // Track the mouse's position till left mouse button up
        tracker_flag = m_RectTracker.Track(pWnd, point, TRUE);
          // 0 => item not tracked, 1 => item was tracked

        // Get the new tracker position and update the new connection end
          pt position with the tracker position
        tail_pt = m_RectTracker.m_rect.CenterPoint();

        // Check to snap connector to port
        if((*it_con)->GetRefFromPort() == NULL)      // If not already a
          ref_from port
```

```
            {
                from_port = SnapConnectionTailPointToPort(tail_pt);
                  // tail_pt passed by ref. and may be updated.
                if(from_port != NULL)
                {
                    (*it_con)->SetRefFromPort(from_port);
                }
            }
        else // If already a ref-from-port, then the intention on moving the
          end pt. is to break the assoc. with the port.
        {
            (*it_con)->SetRefFromPort(NULL);
        }
        (*it_con)->SetConnectionPointTail(tail_pt);

        // Check to snap connector to bend point
        if((*it_con)->GetRefFromPoint() == NULL)  // If not already a
          ref_from point
        {
            from_point = SnapConnectionTailPointToBendPoint(tail_pt);
              // tail_pt passed by ref. and may be updated.
            if(from_point != NULL)
            {
                (*it_con)->SetRefFromPoint(from_point);
            }
        }
        else    // If already a ref-from-point, then the intention on moving
          the end pt. is to break the assoc. with the point.
        {
            (*it_con)->SetRefFromPoint(NULL);
        }
        (*it_con)->SetConnectionPointTail(tail_pt);

        // Set flags
        SetModifiedFlag(TRUE);   // set the doc. as having been modified to
          prompt user to save
        UpdateAllViews(NULL);    // indicate that sys. should redraw.
        break;
        }
        ...
}
```

The outer loop iterates through all connection objects, and the first *if* statement checks to see whether the current connection object has a valid reference-from-port variable, "m_pRefFromPoint". If so (*else*), then any tracking movement applied to the connection tail point is an intention to break the connection from an existing bend point, and hence the "m_pRefFromPoint" is set to NULL. However, if there is no bend point reference (*if*), then an attempt is made to snap the tail point to a connection bend point through the call to SnapConnectionTailPointToBendPoint(). The return value from this function is the address of the bend point, i.e., "m_pRefFromPoint", to which the tail point is to be attached, and the new tail point position is updated since it is passed by reference as an argument.

8.2.2 ADD MEMBER VARIABLES AND METHODS TO THE **CConnection** CLASS

The aforementioned code requires the addition of a private member variable to the CConnection class to hold the address of the bend point to which the connection tail point should be attached, and accessor methods to get and set the value of this variable. Hence, add a private member variable to the CConnection class of type pointer-to-CPoint (CPoint *), with name "m_pRefFromPoint".

Add a public accessor method to the CConnection class with the prototype CPoint *GetRefFromPoint(void) to return the "m_pRefFromPoint" member variable, and edit the code as shown.

```
CPoint* CConnection::GetRefFromPoint()
{
    return m_pRefFromPoint;
}
```

Add a public accessor method to the CConnection class with the prototype void SetRefFromPoint(CPoint *from_pt) to set the "m_pRefFromPoint" member variable, and edit the code as shown.

```
void CConnection::SetRefFromPoint(CPoint *from_pt)
{
    m_pRefFromPoint = from_pt;
}
```

8.2.3 ADD A `SnapConnectionTailPointToBendPoint()` FUNCTION

In the function TrackConnectionEndPoint() mentioned earlier, a check is made to see whether the connection tail end point can be snapped to a block port through the function call to SnapConnectionTailPointToPort(). In addition, a similar attempt is made to snap the connection tail end point to an existing connection bend point through the call to SnapConnectionTailPointToBendPoint(). Hence, add a public member function to the CDiagramEngDoc class with the prototype CPoint *CDiagramEngDoc::SnapConnection TailPointToBendPoint(CPoint &tail_pt), and edit the code as shown.

```
CPoint* CDiagramEngDoc::SnapConnectionTailPointToBendPoint(CPoint &tail_pt)
{
    // Passing in a point by reference, and returning a prt-to-CPoint
      "m_pRefFromPoint".
    double disc_r = 0.1*m_dDeltaLength;
    double dist_to_bend_pt;
    CPoint bend_pt;
    list<CConnection*>::iterator it_con;
    list<CConnection*> con_list = GetSystemModel().GetConnectionList();
    list<CPoint>::iterator it_pt;

    // Iterate through connection list
    for(it_con = con_list.begin(); it_con != con_list.end(); it_con++)
    {
        // Get the bend points list for this partic. connection obj.
        list<CPoint> &bend_pts_list = (*it_con)-
          >GetConnectionBendPointsList();

        // Iterate through the bend points list
        for(it_pt = bend_pts_list.begin(); it_pt != bend_pts_list.end();
          it_pt++)
        {
            bend_pt = *it_pt;
            dist_to_bend_pt = sqrt(pow(tail_pt.x - bend_pt.x,2) +
              pow(tail_pt.y - bend_pt.y,2));
```

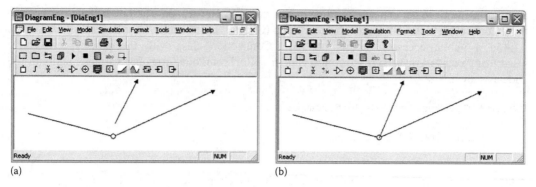

(a)   (b)

FIGURE 8.2   Snapping of a connection tail point to another connection's bend point: (a) moving connection tail point toward the bend point and (b) snapping the tail point to the bend point.

```
        if(dist_to_bend_pt <= disc_r)
        {
            tail_pt = bend_pt;
            return &(*it_pt);      // return the address of the bend_pt
        }
      }
    }

    // Return 0 if no "m_pRefFromPoint" returned earlier
    return 0;
}
```

The code may be compiled and run, and a connection tail point may be snapped to a connection bend point as shown in Figure 8.2.

8.2.4 Problem Concerning the Connection Tail Point

However, at present if the bend point to which a tail end point is snapped is moved, the tail end point does not move with the bend point. But this is confusing, since in the function SnapConnectionTailPointToBendPoint() as shown earlier, what is returned is the address of the bend point. Then in the function TrackConnectionEndPoint() the following lines of code set the "from_point" of the connection object to the address of the bend point to which the tail is attached and hence from which it emanates.

```
int CDiagramEngDoc::TrackConnectionEndPoint(CPoint point, CWnd *pWnd)
{
    ...
    // Check to snap connector to bend point
    if( (*it_con)->GetRefFromPoint() == NULL) // If not already a ref_from
      point
    {
        from_point = SnapConnectionTailPointToBendPoint(tail_pt);
         // tail_pt passed by ref. and may be updated.
        if(from_point != NULL)
        {
            (*it_con)->SetRefFromPoint(from_point);
        }
    }
```

```
    else // If already a ref-from-point, then the intention on moving the
        end pt. is to break the assoc. with the point.
    {
        (*it_con)->SetRefFromPoint(NULL);
    }
    (*it_con)->SetConnectionPointTail(tail_pt);
    ...
}
```

In the function `TrackConnectionBendPoint()`, only the CPoint position of the bend point is updated, but because the bend point and the connection tail end point that is snapped to that bend point share the same address, any motion applied to the bend point should also apply to the tail end point.

The problem lies in drawing the connection object. If the "m_pRefFromPoint" of the connection object is NULL, i.e., if the connection end point is not associated with a bend point, then a connection line should be drawn from the tail point. If, however, the "m_pRefFromPoint" is not NULL, then the connection tail end point must be associated with a connection bend point from which it emanates, and hence the connection line should be drawn from the "m_pRefFromPoint". Edit the initial part of the function `DrawConnection()` as shown. (Later in the development the changes to the `DrawConnection()` function will be supplemented, but the process is worth pursuing.)

```
void CConnection::DrawConnection(CDC *pDC)
{
    int pen_color = RGB(0,0,0);    // White = RGB(255,255,255),
      Black = RGB(0,0,0).
    ...
    // The value returned by SelectObject() is a ptr to the obj. being
      replaced, i.e. an old-pen-ptr.
    CPen *pOldPen = pDC->SelectObject(&lpen);

    if(m_pRefFromPoint != NULL)
    {
        // Move to the bend_point to which the tail point is connected
          (if it's connected)
        pDC->MoveTo(*m_pRefFromPoint);
    }
    else
    {
        // Move to the tail pt.
        pDC->MoveTo(m_ptTail);
    }

    // Iterate through the bend pts. drawing lines bw. them.
    ...
}
```

There is still a problem: the "m_pRefFromPoint" should be initialized in the `CConnection()` constructor to be NULL. Hence edit the constructor as follows:

```
CConnection::CConnection(CPoint ptFrom, CPoint ptTo)
{
    // Init. member vars.
    m_ptTail = ptFrom;         // pt from which connection is drawn
    m_ptHead = ptTo;           // pt to which connection is drawn
    m_pRefFromPoint = NULL;    // not connected to a bend point initially
```

```
    m_pRefFromPort = NULL;     // from-port ref.
    m_pRefToPort = NULL;       // to-port ref.
    m_pSignal = new CSignal;   // contained ptr-to-CSignal
}
```

Now, when the code is compiled and run, the tail point of one connection may be snapped to a bend point of another, and when the bend point is moved, the tail point moves with the bend point as shown in Figure 8.3.

In addition, in the DrawConnection() function, the call to DrawArrowHead(pDC, final_pt, m_ptHead) uses the "final_pt" and the "m_ptHead" to determine the angular orientation of the arrowhead. The developer will recall that "final_pt" is either the tail point or the final bend point on the connection object prior to the head point. However, when a tail point is connected to another connection object's bend point, the tail point position must be updated if the bend point to which it is attached is moved. Hence, code should be added that explicitly sets the value of the CConnection member variable, "m_ptTail".

Hence, add a public member function to the CSystemModel class with the prototype void CSystemModel::UpdateConnectionPointTailToBendPoint(CPoint *bend_pt), and edit it as shown in the following:

```
void CSystemModel::UpdateConnectionPointTailToBendPoint(CPoint *bend_pt)
{
    list<CConnection*>::iterator it_con;

    // Iterate through the list of connections
    for(it_con = m_lstConnection.begin(); it_con != m_lstConnection.
      end(); it_con++)
    {
        // If current connection tail point is associated with another
          connection's bend point
        if( (*it_con)->GetRefFromPoint() == bend_pt)
        {
            // Update the tail point (member variable) with the new bend
              point position.
            (*it_con)->SetConnectionPointTail(*bend_pt);
        }
    }
}
```

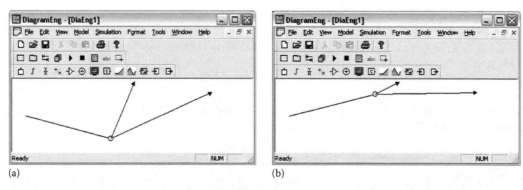

(a)   (b)

FIGURE 8.3 Movement of a tail point with a bend point: (a) tail point connected to a bend point and (b) tail point moves with the moving bend point.

Now, make a call from within the `TrackConnectionBendPoint()` function to update the connection tail end point given its association to another connection's bend point, i.e., add the code after getting the new tracker position, and before the setting of flags, as shown in bold in the following:

```
int CDiagramEngDoc::TrackConnectionBendPoint(CPoint point, CWnd *pWnd)
{
    ...
    // If the bend pt is clicked
    if(dist <= disc_r)
    {
        // Assign rectangle setting values
        top_left.x = bend_pt.x - delta;
        top_left.y = bend_pt.y - delta;
        bottom_right.x = bend_pt.x + delta;
        bottom_right.y = bend_pt.y + delta;

        // Set the rect tracker's position
        m_RectTracker.m_rect.SetRect(top_left.x, top_left.y,
          bottom_right.x, bottom_right.y);

        // Track the mouse's position till left mouse button up
        tracker_flag = m_RectTracker.Track(pWnd, point, TRUE);
          // 0 => item not tracked, 1 => item was tracked

        // Get the new tracker position and update the connection bend pt
          position with the tracker position
        *it_pt = m_RectTracker.m_rect.CenterPoint();

        // Update any connection's tail point if it was connected to this
          bend point
        m_SystemModel.UpdateConnectionPointTailToBendPoint(&(*it_pt));

        // Set flags
        SetModifiedFlag(TRUE);           // set the doc. as having been
          modified to prompt user to save
        UpdateAllViews(NULL);            // indicate that sys. should redraw.
        break;
    }// end if dist
    ...
}
```

Hence, the code that was altered (shown in bold in the following) in the `DrawConnection()` function to take into consideration any connection tail points that may have been associated with a connection bend point, i.e.,

```
void CConnection::DrawConnection(CDC *pDC)
{
    int pen_color = RGB(0,0,0);    // White = RGB(255,255,255),
      Black = RGB(0,0,0).
    ...
    // The value returned by SelectObject() is a ptr to the obj. being
      replaced, i.e. an old-pen-ptr.
    CPen *pOldPen = pDC->SelectObject(&lpen);

    if(m_pRefFromPoint != NULL)
    {
        // Move to the bend_point to which the tail point is connected
          (if it's connected)
```

```
        pDC->MoveTo(*m_pRefFromPoint);
    }
    else
    {
        // Move to the tail pt.
        pDC->MoveTo(m_ptTail);
    }
    ...
}
```

can now be replaced with the following single line (shown in bold), since now the CConnection member variable "m_ptTail" has been updated explicitly using the call to the function UpdateConnectionPointTailToBendPoint(). The redundant code is commented out.

```
void CConnection::DrawConnection(CDC *pDC)
{
    int pen_color = RGB(0,0,0); // White = RGB(255,255,255),
      Black = RGB(0,0,0).
    int pen_width = 1;          // pen width
    double dDeltaLength;        // std default reference delta length
    double length;              // length of side of rectangle bounding
      ellipse
    CPoint bend_pt;             // temp pt. to hold bend pt.
    CPoint bottom_right;        // bottom right cnr. coord. of rectangle
      bounding ellipse
    CPoint final_pt = m_ptTail; // init as tail pt. in case there are no
      bend pts.
    CPoint top_left;            // top left cnr. coord. of rectangle
      bounding ellipse
    list<CPoint>::iterator it_pt;

    // Set length
    dDeltaLength = GetDocumentGlobalFn()->GetDeltaLength();
    length = 0.2*dDeltaLength;

    // Create the pen
    CPen lpen(PS_SOLID, pen_width, pen_color);

    // Select the pen as the drawing obj.
    // The value returned by SelectObject() is a ptr to the obj. being
      replaced, i.e. an old-pen-ptr.
    CPen *pOldPen = pDC->SelectObject(&lpen);

    /*if(m_pRefFromPoint != NULL)
    {
        // Move to the bend_point to which the tail point is connected
          (if it's connected)
        pDC->MoveTo(*m_pRefFromPoint);
    }
    else
    {
        // Move to the tail pt.
        pDC->MoveTo(m_ptTail);
    }*/

    // Move to the tail pt. (m_ptTail always updated so can use just this
      line rather than the above).
    pDC->MoveTo(m_ptTail);
```

```
    // Iterate through the bend pts. drawing lines bw. them.
    for(it_pt = m_lstBendPoints.begin(); it_pt != m_lstBendPoints.end();
      it_pt++)
    {
        // Draw a line to the bend pt.
        pDC->LineTo(*it_pt);

        // Set the current bend pt. as the pt prior to the head_pt: used
          for DrawArrowHead().
        final_pt = *it_pt;
    }
    // Line to head pt.
    pDC->LineTo(m_ptHead);

    // Iterate through the bend pts. drawing ellipses at each pt.
    for(it_pt = m_lstBendPoints.begin(); it_pt != m_lstBendPoints.end();
      it_pt++)
    {
        // Draw an ellipse about the bend pt.
        bend_pt = *it_pt;
        top_left.x = (int)(bend_pt.x - length*0.5);
        top_left.y = (int)(bend_pt.y - length*0.5);
        bottom_right.x = (int)(bend_pt.x + length*0.5);
        bottom_right.y = (int)(bend_pt.y + length*0.5);
        pDC->Ellipse(top_left.x, top_left.y, bottom_right.x,
          bottom_right.y);
    }
    // Reset the prev. pen
    pDC->SelectObject(pOldPen);

    // Draw arrowhead
    DrawArrowHead(pDC, final_pt, m_ptHead);
}
```

These changes do not reflect a perfect design. This may be a suboptimal workaround, but allows the code to continue to evolve in a consistent manner, i.e., consistent with previous design decisions.

8.3 DELETION OF A BEND POINT TO WHICH A CONNECTION IS ATTACHED

The current state of the `DeleteConnectionBendPoint()` function allows simple deletion of a bend point from the existing connection line. However, now with the additional complexity of the possibility of a *secondary* connection's tail point being attached to a *primary* connection's bend point, a check is required to determine whether the reference-from-point, "m_pRefFromPoint", of the *secondary* connection is the bend point of another *primary* connection object. The following changes are necessary:

1. Add a public member function to the CDiagramEngDoc class with the prototype: `void   CDiagramEngDoc::DisconnectTailPointFromBendPoint(CPoint *bend_pt)`.
2. Add a call to this function from within the `DeleteConnectionBendPoint()` function as shown in the *if* statement concerning bend point deletion in bold:

```
int CDiagramEngDoc::DeleteConnectionBendPoint()
{
    ...
    // Delete the item in the list
```

```
    if(delete_bp == 1)
    {
        // Unsnap any tail points connected to this bend point prior to
          delete bend point
        DisconnectTailPointFromBendPoint(&(*it_er)); // pass address of
          the bend_pt

        // Delete element at offset it_er in list (that held the bend pt)
        bend_pts_list.erase(it_er);

        count = (*it_con)->GetConnectionBendPointsList().size();
        //sMsg.Format("\n CDiagramEngDoc::DeleteConnectionBendPoint(),
          size = %d\n", count);
        //AfxMessageBox(sMsg, nType, nIDhelp);
    }
    ...
}
```

3. Edit the `DisconnectTailPointFromBendPoint()` function as shown in the following:

```
void CDiagramEngDoc::DisconnectTailPointFromBendPoint(CPoint *bend_pt)
{
    list<CConnection*>::iterator it_con;

    // Get the connection list
    list<CConnection*> &con_list = GetSystemModel().
      GetConnectionList();// MUST BE A REFERENCE!

    // Iterate through the connections
    for(it_con = con_list.begin(); it_con != con_list.end(); it_con++)
    {
        // If the connection tail pt. was attached to the bend pt.
        if((*it_con)->GetRefFromPoint() == bend_pt)
        {
            // Set the tail pt. to NULL since the bend pt. will be deleted.
            (*it_con)->SetRefFromPoint(NULL);
        }
    }
}
```

The code was compiled and run, but when a bend point was deleted the program crashed. A break point was set using the debugger to be at the first "for(it_con)" loop of the `DeleteConnectionBendPoint()` function as shown in the following:

```
int CDiagramEngDoc::DeleteConnectionBendPoint()
{
    ...
    // Iterate through the connection list
    for(it_con = con_list.begin(); it_con != con_list.end(); it_con++)
    {
        ...
    }
    ...
}
```

It was noticed that the delete-bend-point flag, "delete_bp", was not set to zero prior to the "for(it_pt)" loop, and hence if a bend point was deleted in one iteration of this loop, causing the "delete_bp" flag

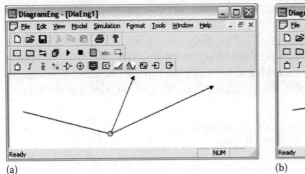 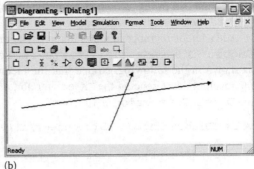

(a)   (b)

FIGURE 8.4 Deletion of a bend point to which a tail end point is attached: (a) a *secondary* connection's tail end point attached to a *primary* connection's bend point and (b) a disconnected tail end point after bend point deletion.

to be set to 1, then in subsequent iterations, more delete points would be marked for deletion even if they did not exist in the bend points list, "m_lstBendPoints". Hence, "delete_bp = 0" was inserted prior to the "for(it_pt)" loop as shown in bold in the following:

```
int CDiagramEngDoc::DeleteConnectionBendPoint()
{
    ...
    // Iterate through the connection list
    for(it_con = con_list.begin(); it_con != con_list.end(); it_con++)
    {
        // Get the bend points list
        list<CPoint> &bend_pts_list = (*it_con)-
          >GetConnectionBendPointsList();

        // Iterate through the bend pts. list
        delete_bp = 0;       // init delete_bp = 0 since, at present no
          bend_pt is to be deleted
        for(it_pt = bend_pts_list.begin(); it_pt != bend_pts_list.end();
          it_pt++)
        {
            ...
        }
    }
    ...
}
```

Now if the code is compiled and run, a bend point may be deleted from the connection line object and the tail point that was connected to this bend point, simply disconnects, as shown in Figure 8.4.

8.4 DELETION OF A CONNECTION WITH A BEND POINT TO WHICH A CONNECTION IS ATTACHED

The previous section concerned the deletion of only a bend point on a *primary* connection line to which another *secondary* connection's tail point was attached. The next step concerning deletion of bend points is the deletion of the whole *primary* connection object, including all its bend points to which other *secondary* connection tail points may be attached. This requires amending the DeleteConnection() function with a call to iterate over the *primary* connection object and examine its bend points for any tail point attachments. If there are *secondary* connection tail points attached to the bend points, then these need to be disconnected prior to deleting the *primary* connection.

Add a public member function to the CDiagramEngDoc class with prototype void CDiagram EngDoc::DisconnectTailPointsFromBendPoints(CConnection *con), and edit it as shown in the following. Notice that the incoming argument is of type pointer-to-CConnection: the result of dereferencing the "it_er" iterator, or equivalently, the "it_con" iterator (see the following DeleteConnection() function).

```
void CDiagramEngDoc::DisconnectTailPointsFromBendPoints(CConnection *con)
{
    list<CPoint>::iterator it_pt;

    list<CPoint> &bend_pts_list = con->GetConnectionBendPointsList();

    for(it_pt = bend_pts_list.begin(); it_pt != bend_pts_list.end();
      it_pt++)
    {
        // Unsnap any tail points connected to this bend point prior to
          delete bend point
        DisconnectTailPointFromBendPoint(&(*it_pt)); // pass address of
          the bend_pt
    }
}
```

In the *if* statement concerning deletion of the connection from the connection list in the DeleteConnection() function below, make a call to the newly added function DisconnectTailPointsFromBendPoints() as shown in bold. Here the iterator "it_er" itself is dereferenced ("*it_er"), passing the pointer-to-CConnection object to the disconnecting function: this is the case since "it_er" was assigned "it_con" in the prior loop concerning the connection list, and dereferencing the "it_con" iterator yields the item stored in the connection list, i.e., the pointer-to-CConnection object.

```
int CDiagramEngDoc::DeleteConnection()
{
    ...
    // Delete the connection in the list
    if(delete_con == 1)
    {
        // Disconnect all tail points from all the bend points on this
          connection.
        DisconnectTailPointsFromBendPoints(*it_er);

        delete *it_er;          // delete actual connection pointed to by
          it_er
        con_list.erase(it_er);  // delete element at offset it_er in list
          (that held the connection)

        //count = m_SystemModel.GetBlockList().size();
        //sMsg.Format("\n CDiagramEngDoc::DeleteBlock(), size = %d\n",
          count);
        //AfxMessageBox(sMsg, nType, nIDhelp);
    }
    ...
}
```

Now upon compiling and running the code, a *primary* connection object, with a bend point to which a tail point of a *secondary* connection is attached, may be deleted, disconnecting the tail point, as shown in Figure 8.5.

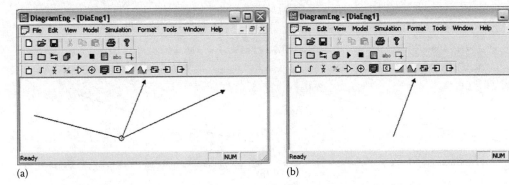

FIGURE 8.5 Deletion of a *primary* connection to which a tail point is attached: (a) a tail point connected to a *primary* connection's bend point and (b) the disconnected tail point after the whole *primary* connection object, to which it was attached, is deleted.

8.5 PROBLEM CONCERNING THE INSERTION OF BEND POINTS

At present bend points may be inserted on a connection line object (Figure 8.6a) and the tail points of other connections may be attached to the bend points (Figure 8.6b). The bend points may then be moved, and as expected the tail points remain connected and move with them (Figure 8.6c). If another bend point is inserted just prior to the head point of the connection (Figure 8.6d) and the other bend points are moved, then the tail points connected to these bend points move accordingly (Figure 8.6e). However, if a bend point is inserted just after the tail point of the main connection line (Figure 8.6f) and this new bend point to which no connections are attached is then moved, then the tail point of the connection attached to the next bend point suddenly jumps to the first bend point (Figure 8.6g). In addition, if the third bend point is then moved (Figure 8.6h), the tail point of the connection that appears to be attached to it does not move with it but is in fact unintentionally disconnected.

The problem here lies in the insertion of a bend point earlier in the list than any of those already present, e.g., between the tail point and the first bend point, or between existing bend points. However, if the bend point is placed between the last bend point in the list and the following head point, then there is no problem.

In the function, `CDiagramEngDoc::OnInsertBendPoint()`, first introduced in Section 6.4, the list of connections is iterated over in the outer *for* loop, and the list of bend points for each connection object is then iterated over in the inner *for* loop. If the mouse cursor lies on the line segment from the previous point to the current point, then a bend point is inserted between the previous and current points. However, two mistakes have been made: (1) a local points list, "local_pts_list", is made up of the tail point of the current connection object, its bend points, and finally its head point, and then the new bend point is placed in this local list, and (2) this "local_pts_list" is then used to overwrite the bend points list "m_lstBendPoints" of the connection object via the call to the function `SetConnectionBendPointsList(local_pts_list)`. This overwriting then disorders the sequence of bend points.

The solution to this problem is to rewrite parts of the `OnInsertBendPoint()` function to (1) make use of the connection's actual bend points list "m_lstBendPoints", since this is already obtained by reference through the call to `GetConnectionBendPointsList()` and (2) not overwrite the connection's bend points list, "m_lstBendPoints", with a local points list, since this disorders the sequence of bend points. The former fix, using a bend-points-list reference, obviates the need for the latter, i.e., the list-overwrite.

The new function provided in the following implements the solution: (1) first, an iteration is made through the list of connections in the model, (2) then a check is made to determine if

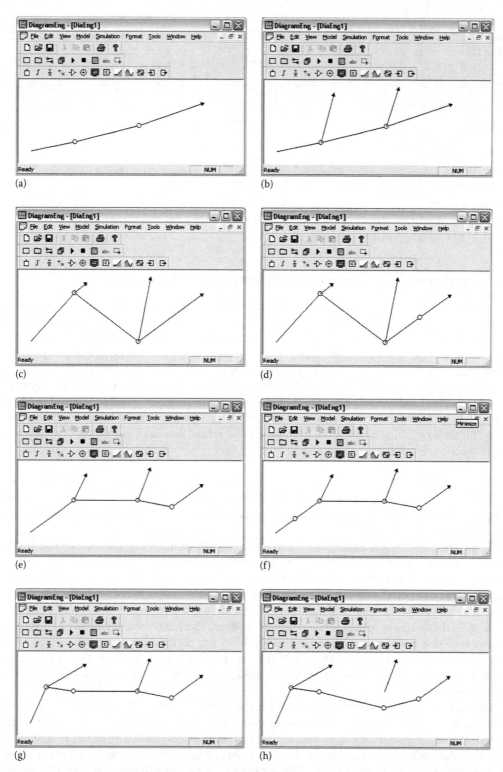

FIGURE 8.6 A problem of inserting a bend point: (a) bend points on a connection, (b) connections attached to bend points, (c) bend points moved, (d) bend point inserted prior to the head, (e) bend points moved, (f) bend point inserted just after the tail, (g) bend point moved inducing an unintentional jump of connectivity, and (h) an unintentional disconnection of a connection object from its bend point.

there are any bend points on the current connection, if not then bend point insertion would be between the connection's tail point and head point, (3) if there are bend points, then bend point insertion would be between either the tail point and the first bend point, or between subsequent bend points, and (4) finally, (if there are bend points) a check is made to determine whether a bend point should be placed between the connection's final existing bend point and its head point. Break statements are required to avoid unnecessary checks and potentially incorrect bend point placement.

```
void CDiagramEngDoc::OnInsertBendPoint()
{
    // TODO: Add your command handler code here

    // DiagramEng (start)
    int inserted;
    int point_on_line;
    CPoint current_pt;
    CPoint head_pt;
    CPoint point = m_ptContextMenu;
    CPoint prev_pt;
    CPoint tail_pt;
    list<CConnection*> &con_list = GetSystemModel().
     GetConnectionList();
    list<CConnection*>::iterator it_con;
    list<CPoint>::iterator it_pt;

    // -- ITERATE THROUGH ALL CONNECTIONS
    for(it_con = con_list.begin(); it_con != con_list.end(); it_con++)
    {
        inserted = 0;
        // Get the bend points list
        list<CPoint> &bend_pts_list = (*it_con)-
          >GetConnectionBendPointsList();

        // Get the Connection's tail_pt and head_pt.
        head_pt = (*it_con)->GetConnectionPointHead();
        tail_pt = (*it_con)->GetConnectionPointTail();
        prev_pt = tail_pt;

        // -- IF THERE ARE NO BEND POINTS ON THIS CONNECTION
        if(bend_pts_list.size() == 0)
        {
            current_pt = head_pt;
            point_on_line = 0;
            point_on_line = CheckPointOnLineSegment(prev_pt, current_pt,
              point);

            if(point_on_line == 1)
            {
                // Create a bend pt. at the front of the list.
                bend_pts_list.push_front(point);
                inserted = 1;
                break; // THIS BREAK EXITS THE it_con LOOP
            }
        }
        else    // -- IF THERE ARE BEND POINTS ON THIS CONNECTION
        {
            prev_pt = tail_pt;
```

```
            // -- ITERATE THROUGH THIS CONNECTION'S bend_pts_list
            for(it_pt = bend_pts_list.begin(); it_pt != bend_pts_list.end();
              it_pt++)
            {
                current_pt = *it_pt;
                point_on_line = 0;
                point_on_line = CheckPointOnLineSegment(prev_pt,
                  current_pt, point);

                if(point_on_line == 1)
                {
                    // Create a bend pt. prior to it_pt
                    bend_pts_list.insert(it_pt, point);
                    inserted = 1;
                    break; // THIS BREAK EXITS THE it_pt LOOP
                }

                // Update the previous pt.
                prev_pt = *it_pt;

            }// end for it_pt

            // If a bend point was inserted, then break from the it_con loop
            if(inserted == 1)
            {
                break;
            }

            // -- NOW CHECK IF BEND POINT IS TO BE INSERTED BW FINAL BEND
            //    POINT AND HEAD POINT.
            current_pt = head_pt;
            point_on_line = 0;
            point_on_line = CheckPointOnLineSegment(prev_pt, current_pt,
              point);

            if(point_on_line == 1)
            {
                // Create a new bend pt. after the (thus far) final
                //   bend_pt in the list.
                bend_pts_list.push_back(point);
                inserted = 1;
                break; // THIS BREAK EXITS THE it_con LOOP
            }

        }// end size() != 0
    }// end for it_con

    // Set as modified and redraw the doc. (since the connections have
    //   been modified)
    SetModifiedFlag(TRUE);      // set the doc. as having been modified to
      prompt user to save
    UpdateAllViews(NULL);       // redraw the doc.

    // DiagramEng (end)
}
```

This function separates the bend-point-insertion logic into two main parts: a connection with no bend points and a connection with bend points. A check is made to determine whether the mouse cursor, denoting the bend point position, lies on the line segment, and this test is performed through a new function call to CheckPointOnLineSegment().

Hence, add a new public member function to the CDiagramEngDoc class, with the prototype int CDiagramEngDoc::CheckPointOnLineSegment(CPoint prev_pt, CPoint current_pt, CPoint point), and edit it as shown in the following:

```
int CDiagramEngDoc::CheckPointOnLineSegment(CPoint prev_pt, CPoint
  current_pt, CPoint point)
{
    int point_on_line = 0;
    double delta_x;
    double delta_y;
    double eps = 0.20*m_dDeltaLength;
    double gradient;
    double y_val;
    CString sMsg;             // main msg string
    CString sMsg1;            // substring
    UINT nType = MB_OK;       // style of msg. box
    UINT nIDhelp = 0;         // help context ID for the msg.

    // Message
    /*sMsg.Format("CheckPointOnLineSegment, eps = %lf", eps);
    sMsg1.Format("\n prev_pt = (%d,%d), point = (%d,%d),
      current_pt = (%d,%d)\n", prev_pt.x, prev_pt.y, point.x, point.y,
      current_pt.x, current_pt.y);
    sMsg += sMsg1;
    AfxMessageBox(sMsg, nType, nIDhelp);
    */

    // -- CONSIDER A VERTICAL OR NEAR VERTICAL CONNECTION LINE SEGMENT
    if(abs(current_pt.x - prev_pt.x) <= eps)
    {
        // Check to see if mouse point is on the vertical connection line
          segment in the x domain
        if( (point.x >= (min(prev_pt.x, current_pt.x) - 0.5*eps)) &&
          (point.x <= (max(prev_pt.x, current_pt.x) + 0.5*eps)) )
        {
            // Check to see if mouse point is on the vertical connection
              line segment in the y domain
            if( (point.y >= min(prev_pt.y, current_pt.y)) &&
              (point.y <= max(prev_pt.y, current_pt.y)) )
            {
                // Point lies on line segment
                point_on_line = 1;
            }
        }
    }
    else // -- CONSIDER A NON-VERTICAL CONNECTION LINE SEGMENT: equ. of
      line: y - y0 = ( (y1-y0)/(x1-x0) )*(x - x0);
    {
        // Check to see if mouse point is on the connection line segment
          in the x domain
        if( (point.x >= min(prev_pt.x, current_pt.x)) &&
          (point.x <= max(prev_pt.x, current_pt.x)) )
        {
            delta_x = (double)(current_pt.x - prev_pt.x);
            delta_y = (double)(current_pt.y - prev_pt.y);
            gradient = delta_y/delta_x;
            y_val = gradient*(point.x - prev_pt.x) + prev_pt.y;
```

```
        // Check to see if mouse point is close enough to the line in
           the y domain
        if(fabs(point.y - y_val) <= eps)
        {
            // Point lies on line segment
            point_on_line = 1;
        }
    }
}// end if line segment

// Return flag indicating whether point lies on line segment: (0) pt.
   not on line, (1) pt. on line
return point_on_line;
}
```

The developer may compare the original OnInsertBendPoint() function introduced in Section 6.4 with the aforementioned function, noting that the function CheckPointOnLineSegment() extracts the point-on-line-segment test for clarity and to avoid repetition. Finally, now that there is no need for the SetConnectionBendPointsList() function, this may be deleted from the "Signal.cpp" source and "Signal.h" header files. Now when a bend point is inserted or deleted, no spurious side effects result.

In addition, the user will notice that the integer, abs(), and double, fabs(), forms of the absolute value function are used in the aforementioned code, in the statements, "if(abs(current_pt.x − prev_pt.x) <= eps)" and "if(fabs(point.y − y_val) <= eps)", respectively: these should not be confused.

8.6　AUTOMATIC ATTACHMENT OF CONNECTION END POINTS UPON INITIAL CONSTRUCTION

At present the user can draw connection objects on the palette beside block ports or near existing bend points of another connection. However, after the initial connection is drawn, the user must then perform a secondary action and drag the connection end points, i.e., the head and tail points, over an input/output port or a bend point to snap the connection end point to the port or bend point. This is cumbersome, since it requires two actions, a drawing followed by an attachment of a connection, and is not intuitive in the sense that the user may want to directly connect two different blocks' ports together. Here, functionality is added to the project to perform an automatic snapping of connection end points just after initial connection construction. The three steps to add this mechanism are as follows.

First, add code to the CDiagramEngView::OnLButtonUp() function to attempt an initial snap of the connection end point by calling the (to be added) CDiagramEngDoc function SnapConnectionEndPointsAfterInitialConstruction(), as shown in bold in the following:

```
void CDiagramEngView::OnLButtonUp(UINT nFlags, CPoint point)
{
    // TODO: Add your message handler code here and/or call default

    // DiagramEng (start)
    int valid = 0;                  // validity of connection object (length)

    // Check to see if mouse has been captured
    if(GetCapture() == this)     // if what has been captured is the obj.
       that the "this" ptr. is pointing to.
    {
        // Add the connection to the connection list
        valid = GetDocument()->GetSystemModel().AddConnection(m_ptOrigin,
           point);
```

```
        if(valid)
        {
            // Attempt snapping of connection end points to ports or
              bend points
            GetDocument()->SnapConnectionEndPointsAfterInitial
              Construction();
        }

        // Make the document redraw itself using either Invalidate(TRUE)
          or UpdateAllViews(NULL)
        //Invalidate(TRUE);
        GetDocument()->UpdateAllViews(NULL);

        // Release the capture so other apps. can have access to the
          mouse.
        ReleaseCapture();
    }

    // DiagramEng (end)

    CView::OnLButtonUp(nFlags, point);
}
```

The valid flag is "0" if the drawn connection is not of a suitable length and "1" otherwise, whereupon a snapping of the connection's end points is attempted for the newly constructed connection object.

Second, the developer will notice the conditional action ("if(valid)") taken upon the returned value ("valid") from the AddConnection() function. Hence, alter the CSystemModel::AddConnection() function to return a value indicating whether the drawn connection is valid, i.e., whether it is long enough to be deemed an intended connection object, as shown in bold in the following. The new prototype is then int CSystemModel::AddConnection (CPoint ptFrom, CPoint ptTo) and this is to be updated in the "SystemModel.h" header file.

```
int CSystemModel::AddConnection(CPoint ptFrom, CPoint ptTo)
{
    int valid = 0; // validity of connection: (0) not long enough,
        (1) long enough
    double con_length;      // length of connection
    double dDeltaLength;    // std def delta length
    double min_length;      // min connection length
    CString sMsg;           // main msg string
    CString sMsgTemp;       // temp msg string
    UINT nType = MB_OK;     // style of msg. box
    UINT nIDhelp = 0;       // help context ID for the msg.

    // Print msg.
    //sMsg.Format("\n CSystemModel::AddConnection(), from (%d,%d) to
        (%d,%d)\n", ptFrom.x, ptFrom.y, ptTo.x, ptTo.y);
    //AfxMessageBox(sMsg, nType, nIDhelp);

    // Set min length
    dDeltaLength = GetDocumentGlobalFn()->GetDeltaLength();
    min_length = 0.5*dDeltaLength;

    // Check to make sure that connection is greater than the rqd. min.
      connection length.
    con_length = sqrt(pow((ptFrom.x - ptTo.x),2) +
      pow((ptFrom.y - ptTo.y),2));
```

```
    if(con_length < min_length)
    {
        sMsgTemp.Format("\n CSystemModel::AddConnection()\n");
        sMsg += sMsgTemp;
        sMsgTemp.Format("Connection line from point (%d, %d) to point
          (%d, %d).\n", ptFrom.x, ptFrom.y, ptTo.x, ptTo.y);
        sMsg += sMsgTemp;
        sMsgTemp.Format("Connection length = %lf < %lf = min_length. \n",
          con_length, min_length);
        sMsg += sMsgTemp;
        sMsgTemp.Format("Add new connection >= min_length.\n");
        sMsg += sMsgTemp;
        //AfxMessageBox(sMsg, nType, nIDhelp);

        valid = 0;    // connection not long enough
        return valid;
    }
    else
    {
        valid = 1;    // connection long enough

        // Create a new CConnection obj.
        CConnection *pCon = new CConnection(ptFrom, ptTo);

        // Add the new connection to the connection list
        m_lstConnection.push_back(pCon);

        // Get a ptr. to the doc. to call the CDocument member fn.
          SetModifiedFlag(), and mark the doc. as modified (TRUE).
        GetDocumentGlobalFn()->SetModifiedFlag(TRUE);
    }

    return valid;
}
```

Third, add the `SnapConnectionEndPointsAfterInitialConstruction()` function to the CDiagramEngDoc class, with the prototype `void CDiagramEngDoc::SnapConnection EndPointsAfterInitialConstruction(void)`. Edit the function as shown to iterate over the list of connections and attempt a snap of the end points to ports and bend points.

```
void CDiagramEngDoc::SnapConnectionEndPointsAfterInitialConstruction()
{
    int modified = 0;          // flag indicating whether drawing is
      modified
    CPoint head_pt;            // connection head point
    CPoint tail_pt;            // connection tail point
    CPoint *from_point = NULL; // connection from point
    CPort *from_port = NULL;   // connection from port
    CPort *to_port = NULL;     // connection to port
    list<CConnection*>::iterator it_con;
    list<CConnection*> con_list = GetSystemModel().GetConnectionList();

    // -- ITERATE THROUGH SYSTEM MODEL'S CONNECTION LIST
    for(it_con = con_list.begin(); it_con != con_list.end(); it_con++)
    {
        // Get tail and head points of connection
        tail_pt = (*it_con)->GetConnectionPointTail();
        head_pt = (*it_con)->GetConnectionPointHead();
```

```
        // CHECK TO SNAP TAIL POINT TO PORT
        if((*it_con)->GetRefFromPort() == NULL) // If not already a
          ref_from port
        {
            from_port = SnapConnectionTailPointToPort(tail_pt);
              // tail_pt passed by ref. and may be updated.
            if(from_port != NULL)
            {
                (*it_con)->SetRefFromPort(from_port);
                modified = 1;
            }
        }
        (*it_con)->SetConnectionPointTail(tail_pt);

        // CHECK TO SNAP TAIL POINT TO BEND POINT
        if((*it_con)->GetRefFromPoint() == NULL)  // If not already a
          ref_from point
        {
            from_point = SnapConnectionTailPointToBendPoint(tail_pt);
              // tail_pt passed by ref. and may be updated.
            if(from_point != NULL)
            {
                (*it_con)->SetRefFromPoint(from_point);
                modified = 1;
            }
        }
        (*it_con)->SetConnectionPointTail(tail_pt);

        // CHECK TO SNAP HEAD POINT TO PORT
        if((*it_con)->GetRefToPort() == NULL)   // If not already a ref_to
          port
        {
            to_port = SnapConnectionHeadPointToPort(head_pt); // head_pt
              passed by ref. and may be updated.
            if(to_port != NULL)
            {
                (*it_con)->SetRefToPort(to_port);
                modified = 1;
            }
        }
        (*it_con)->SetConnectionPointHead(head_pt);

    }// end for

    // Set flags
    if(modified)
    {
        //SetModifiedFlag(TRUE); // DO NOT SET MODIFIED TO TRUE SINCE IT
          IS UNNEC AND INTERFERES WITH OTHER FNS
        UpdateAllViews(NULL);    // indicate that sys. should redraw.
    }

    return;
}
```

The SnapConnectionEndPointsAfterInitialConstruction() iterates over the connection list and attempts to snap (1) a connection tail point to an output port, (2) a connection tail point to a bend point on an existing connection, and (3) a connection head point to an input port. The three conditional clauses test whether the end point in question has a "from port", "from point", or "to port", and if not, a snapping to the desired port or point and a setting of the connection's state is performed.

Now the user can draw connections linking ports of different blocks directly in one action and also have the tail point of a connection directly snap to an existing bend point; the only requirement is that the end points are suitably close to the port or bend point to which they are to be snapped.

8.7   DELETION OF BLOCKS WITH ATTACHED CONNECTIONS

The previous discussion concerning the deletion of a connection line with bend points to which other connections may be attached involved the function `DeleteConnection()`, which iterates through the system model's connection list and calls `DisconnectTailPointsFromBendPoints()` to disconnect the tail points of connections attached to the bend points of the main connection object that is to be deleted. Inside the latter function, the main connection object's bend-points list is iterated through and the call to `DisconnectTailPointFromBendPoint()` is made to set the reference-from-point of an attached connection to NULL, hence disassociating a tail point from the bend point that would be deleted when deleting its parent (the whole main *primary*) connection.

The `DeleteBlock()` function thus far simply iterates through the list of blocks and determines which block is to be deleted. Then in the conditional section of this function shown in the following code, the block is deleted.

```
int CDiagramEngDoc::DeleteBlock()
{
    ...
    // Delete the item in the list
    if(delete_blk == 1)
    {
        // Delete block
        delete *it_er;          // delete actual block pointed to by it_er
        blk_list.erase(it_er);  // delete element at offset it_er in list
          (that held the block)
        count = m_SystemModel.GetBlockList().size();
        //sMsg.Format("\n CDiagramEngDoc::DeleteBlock(), size = %d\n",
          count);
        //AfxMessageBox(sMsg, nType, nIDhelp);
    }
    ...
}
```

However, if connection head or tail points, i.e., end points, are connected to the block's input or output ports, then these connection objects' reference-to-port and reference-from-port port variables, need to be reassigned to NULL prior to block deletion. The previous code is then modified as shown in the following (in bold) to call the `DisconnectEndPointFromPorts()` function, passing in a pointer-to-CBlock ("it_er" is assigned "it_blk" if the block is to be deleted), to disconnect the connection object's head and tail (end) points from the block's ports to which they may be associated.

```
int CDiagramEngDoc::DeleteBlock()
{
    ...
    // Delete the item in the list
    if(delete_blk == 1)
    {
        // Dereference block's ports (allowing previously connected
          connections to be reassigned to new ports)
        DisconnectEndPointsFromPorts(*it_er);
```

```
            // Delete block
            delete *it_er;           // delete actual block pointed to by it_er
            blk_list.erase(it_er); // delete element at offset it_er in list
              (that held the block)

            count = m_SystemModel.GetBlockList().size();
            //sMsg.Format("\n CDiagramEngDoc::DeleteBlock(), size = %d\n",
              count);
            //AfxMessageBox(sMsg, nType, nIDhelp);
    }
    ...
}
```

Hence, add a public member function to the CDiagramEngDoc class taking a pointer-to-CBlock argument with the prototype void DisconnectEndPointsFromPorts(CBlock *block), and edit it as shown in the following (note the plural "Ports" in the function name):

```
void CDiagramEngDoc::DisconnectEndPointsFromPorts(CBlock *block)
{
    vector<CPort*>::iterator it_port;

    // Get vector of input ports
    vector<CPort*> &vec_of_input_ports = block->GetVectorOfInputPorts();

    // Get vector of output ports
    vector<CPort*> &vec_of_output_ports = block-
      >GetVectorOfOutputPorts();

    // Iterate through the vector of output ports
    for(it_port = vec_of_output_ports.begin(); it_port
      != vec_of_output_ports.end(); it_port++)
    {
        DisconnectEndPointFromPort(*it_port);
    }
    // Iterate through the vector of input ports
    for(it_port = vec_of_input_ports.begin(); it_port
      != vec_of_input_ports.end(); it_port++)
    {
        DisconnectEndPointFromPort(*it_port);
    }
}
```

In this function the vector of input and output ports are iterated over, and the function DisconnectEndPointFromPort() is called to disconnect the tail or head point associated with the pointer-to-CPort argument that is passed (note the singular "Port" used in the function name). Hence, add a public member function to the CDiagramEngDoc class taking the aforementioned pointer-to-CPort argument, i.e., void DisconnectEndPointFromPort(CPort *port), and edit the function as shown.

```
void CDiagramEngDoc::DisconnectEndPointFromPort(CPort *port)
{
    list<CConnection*>::iterator it_con;

    // Get the connection list
    list<CConnection*> &con_list = GetSystemModel().GetConnectionList();
      // MUST BE A REFERENCE!
    // Iterate through the connections
```

```
for(it_con = con_list.begin(); it_con != con_list.end(); it_con++)
{
    // If the connection end point was attached to the block's port.
    if((*it_con)->GetRefFromPort() == port)
    {
        // Set the ref from port to NULL
        (*it_con)->SetRefFromPort(NULL);
    }

    // If the connection end point was attached to the block's port.
    if((*it_con)->GetRefToPort() == port)
    {
        // Set the ref to port to NULL
        (*it_con)->SetRefToPort(NULL);
    }
}
}
```

All the system model's connections are iterated over, and if the reference-from-port or reference-to-port (port reference) matches that passed in ("port"), i.e., the one from which the connection end point should be disconnected, then the reference-from-port or reference-to-port is set to NULL. This disconnects the connection head or tail points, i.e., end points, from the port of the block that is to be deleted.

8.8   SUMMARY

Branch points are bend points on a *primary* connection object that may have other *secondary* connection tail points attached to them. To attach a connection tail point to a bend point, various modifications and additions were made to the project, including the introduction of the functions: GetRefFromPoint(), SetRefFromPoint(), of the CConnection class and CDiagramEngDoc::SnapConnectionTailPointToBendPoint(). The UpdateConnectionPointTailToBendPoint() function was required to keep the connection emanating from a bend point, attached to the moving bend point. The deletion of a bend point to which a *secondary* connection is attached required a disconnecting of the tail point first, using the CDiagramEngDoc::DisconnectTail PointFromBendPoint() function. The deletion of a whole *primary* connection line containing bend points to which another *secondary* connection's tail point is attached required a similar CDiagramEngDoc function named DisconnectTailPointsFromBendPoints() to perform a disconnection prior to deletion. A problem concerning the insertion of bend points was resolved using the CDiagramEngDocOnInsertBendPoint() and CheckPointOnLineSegment() functions. The automatic connection of connection end points to ports and bend points, allowing the direct connection of block ports, was performed by the CDiagramEngDoc::SnapConnectionEndPointsAfterInitialConstruction() function. Finally, the deletion of a block requires any connection that may be attached to its ports to first be disconnected. This was performed using the CDiagramEngDoc functions DisconnectEndPointsFromPorts(), to iterate through the vector of input and output ports, and DisconnectEndPointFromPort(), to perform the disconnection from the actual port.

9 Block Dialog Windows

9.1 INTRODUCTION

Blocks may be placed on the palette, and connections may be drawn to connect the blocks together. However, before a simulation can be initiated, block parameters need to be set using a dialog window, and the values of these variables need to be updated to the underlying code. Double-left-clicking on any of the blocks should invoke the block dialog window for that particular block and clicking the OK button should update the entered data to the program variables. The following step-by-step instructions indicate how functionality can be added to the code to allow block parameter values to be assigned to a block via a dialog window invoked upon double-left-clicking a block.

9.2 PROCESSING A LEFT-BUTTON-DOUBLE-CLICK EVENT

The left-button-double-click event is used to invoke the block-related dialog window to be used to enter data for a model block. Add functionality for this event by invoking the MFC ClassWizard, choose CDiagramEngView as the class name, select the WM_LBUTTONDBLCLK message, add the event-handler function, OnLButtonDblClk(), to the CDiagramEngView class, and edit it as follows.

```
void CDiagramEngView::OnLButtonDblClk(UINT nFlags, CPoint point)
{
    // TODO: Add your message handler code here and/or call default

    // DiagramEng (start)
    int dbl_click_flag = 0;

    // Assume that a block is being double-clicked: if so
    //   dbl_click_flag = 1, if not, dlb_click_flag = 0.
    dbl_click_flag = GetDocument()->DoubleLeftClickBlock(point);
    // DiagramEng (end)

    CView::OnLButtonDblClk(nFlags, point);
}
```

The developer will notice the call to the CDiagramEngDoc-based method, DoubleLeftClickBlock(), to process the document-based double-left-click action. Hence, add a member function to the CDiagramEngDoc class with prototype, int CDiagramEngDoc::DoubleLeftClickBlock(CPoint point), and edit the function as shown in the following code. At this stage upon double-left-clicking a block, a simple message appears indicating that a block has been successfully double-clicked.

```
int CDiagramEngDoc::DoubleLeftClickBlock(CPoint point)
{
    int dbl_click_flag = 0;   // if block double-clicked flag = 1, else
        flag = 0.
    double blk_width;         // block width
    double dist;              // dist bw mouse click and CM of block.
    CPoint blk_posn;          // block posn.
    list<CBlock*>::iterator it_blk;
```

```
    // Get a copy of the blk_list in the system model
    list<CBlock*> &blk_list = GetSystemModel().GetBlockList();
      // MUST BE A REFERENCE!

    // Iterate through block list
    for(it_blk = blk_list.begin(); it_blk != blk_list.end(); it_blk++)
    {
        blk_posn = (*it_blk)->GetBlockPosition();
        blk_width = (*it_blk)->GetBlockShape().GetBlockWidth();
        dist = sqrt(pow(blk_posn.x - point.x,2) +
          pow(blk_posn.y - point.y,2));

        // If the block is clicked
        dbl_click_flag = 0;   // reset to zero
        if(dist <= 0.8*blk_width*0.5)
        {
            // Print a msg. that block double-clicked
            AfxMessageBox("\n CDiagramEngDoc::DoubleLeftClickBlock()\n",
              MB_OK, 0);

            // Invoke the block-related dialog wnd para setting fn
            //(*it_blk)->BlockDlgWndParameterInput();

            // Since this block has been double-clicked, then break
            dbl_click_flag = 1;
            break;
        }
    }// end for

    return dbl_click_flag;
}
```

The developer will notice that the call "(*it_blk)->BlockDlgWndParameterInput()" has been commented out at this stage as the block-based dialog window parameter input function has not yet been added to the project. This line may be uncommented after the function is added for the classes concerned and the proper block dialog window will be presented upon double-left-clicking a block on the palette.

9.3   ADDING DIALOG WINDOWS TO ACCEPT USER INPUT

A dialog window allows the user to interactively set various block parameters by selecting dialog controls, e.g., check boxes and radio buttons, and entering input data, using, e.g., edit boxes, that are then updated to the program variables. The dialog window presents default values initially and then upon subsequent block double-click events the current state of the program variables is shown. Two classes are used for each block: the derived CBlock class itself, which represents the block's parameters, and the derived CDialog class, which is used to display the block's parameters to the user in a dialog window. For example, the Constant block is modeled using a CConstantBlock class derived from CBlock, and the dialog mechanism is provided through a CConstantBlockDialog class, derived from CDialog.

The general procedure for adding dialog windows for the derived CBlock classes is separated into six logical steps:

1. Insert a new dialog window and add necessary controls.
2. Attach a class to the dialog window.
3. Attach variables to the dialog window controls.
4. Add functionality to the dialog window buttons.
5. Add functionality to initialize variables.
6. Add the overriding BlockDlgWndParameterInput() function to the derived block class.

TABLE 9.1

The Derived Block Classes and Their Corresponding Derived Dialog Classes

No.	Derived Block Class (Base Class: CBlock)	Dialog Class (Base Class: CDialog)
1	CConstantBlock	CConstantBlockDialog
2	CDerivativeBlock	CDerivativeBlockDialog
3	CDivideBlock	CDivideBlockDialog
4	CGainBlock	CGainBlockDialog
5	CIntegratorBlock	CIntegratorBlockDialog
6	CLinearFnBlock	CLinearFnBlockDialog
7	COutputBlock	COutputBlockDialog
8	CSignalGeneratorBlock	CSignalGeneratorBlockDialog
9	CSubsystemBlock	CSubsystemBlockDialog
10	CSubsystemInBlock	CSubsystemInBlockDialog
11	CSubsystemOutBlock	CSubsystemOutBlockDialog
12	CSumBlock	CSumBlockDialog
13	CTransferFnBlock	CTransferFnBlockDialog

All the block classes derived from the base CBlock class and their corresponding dialog classes derived from the base CDialog class are shown in Table 9.1: the aforementioned six-step procedure needs to be performed for all CBlock-derived classes as detailed in the instructions that follow.

9.3.1 CONSTANT BLOCK DIALOG

The following six steps indicate how dialog-window-based functionality is implemented for the Constant block and involves two key classes: CConstantBlock and CConstantBlockDialog.

9.3.1.1 Insert a New Dialog Window and Add Controls

Insert a new dialog by going to the ResourceView of the Workspace pane and right-clicking on Dialog and choosing Insert Dialog: IDD_DIALOG1 will appear in the Dialog directory. Rename it by right-clicking on the dialog window itself to activate the Dialog Properties window, and change the ID to reflect the nature of the dialog window, e.g., IDD_CONSTANT_BLK_DLG, for the Constant block dialog window. Leave the OK and Cancel buttons on the dialog and add controls from the controls toolbar, as indicated in Table 9.2, and place them on the dialog window, as shown in Figure 9.1.

The title Dialog will appear when the executable runs in the actual title portion of the pane. Right click on the top of the Dialog window to change the title properties of the dialog window to reflect the purpose of the window, e.g., ConstantBlockDialog.

Add maximize and minimize buttons to the ConstantBlockDialog, by right-clicking on the dialog to access the dialog properties, select the styles tab, and turn on the maximize and minimize buttons.

Specify the control tab order: choose Layout/Tab Order and click the numbers in the desired order. Check mnemonics by right-clicking on the dialog window and clicking check mnemonics (leave duplicates if they represent the same dialog control).

9.3.1.2 Attach a Class to the Dialog Window

Select the IDD_CONSTANT_BLK_DLG resource from the ResourceView tab on the Workspace pane to show the corresponding dialog window in the editor area and right click on the dialog box to invoke

TABLE 9.2

Constant Block Dialog Window Controls

Object	Property	Setting
Static Text	ID	ID_CONSTANT_BLK_DLG_TXT
	Caption	Enter constant &value/vector/matrix:
Edit Box	ID	ID_CONSTANT_BLK_DLG_VALUE
	Multiline	Checked
	Horizontal scroll	Checked
	Vertical scroll	Checked
	Want return	Checked
Button	ID	ID_CONSTANT_BLK_DLG_BTN_OK
	Caption	&OK
Button	ID	IDCANCEL
	Caption	&Cancel

FIGURE 9.1   ConstantBlockDialog window showing the controls as specified in Table 9.2.

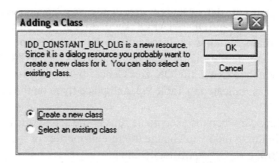

FIGURE 9.2   Adding a Class dialog window for the IDD_CONSTANT_BLK_DLG resource.

the ClassWizard. A message box appears (Figure 9.2) with the content: "IDD_CONSTANT_BLK_DLG is a new resource. Since it is a dialog resource you probably want to create a new class for it. You can also select an existing class." Create a new class with the name CConstantBlockDialog and base class CDialog.

9.3.1.3 Attach Variables to the Dialog Window Controls

Open the ClassWizard and select the Member Variables tab, select the class name to be CConstantBlockDialog, since variables to be added relate to dialog window controls. Select the

TABLE 9.3

Dialog Window Controls, Variable Name, Category, and Type for the IDD_CONSTANT_BLK_DLG Resource

Control	Variable Name	Category	Type
ID_CONSTANT_BLK_DLG_VALUE	m_strConstValue	Value	CString

ID of the control to which a variable should be added, click Add Variable, and specify the details as shown in Table 9.3.

Add a private member variable to the CConstantBlock class of the same CString type and name, "m_strConstValue", since this variable will be updated with the value of that of the dialog class. The other variables "scalar_const", "vector_const", and "matrix_const" of the CConstantBlock class may be consolidated into one (double) variable "m_dConstMatrix" since all numerical data will be treated as double-type matrices in future for consistency reasons.

9.3.1.4 Add Functionality to the Dialog Window Buttons

The two buttons for the IDD_CONSTANT_BLK_DLG dialog window are OK and Cancel. Add an event-handler function for the OK button as shown in Table 9.4, but leave the current event-handler function for the Cancel button as OnCancel(), since this already calls the CDialog::OnCancel() function, so no new code is required. Edit the OnConstantBlkDlgBtnOk() function as shown in the following to call UpdateData(), where the Boolean argument indicates whether the dialog box is being initialized (FALSE) or data are being retrieved (TRUE) [1]: here TRUE implies that the dialog window control values are updated to the underlying dialog class variable values.

```
void CConstantBlockDialog::OnConstantBlkDlgBtnOk()
{
    // TODO: Add your control notification handler code here

    // DiagramEng (start)

    //AfxMessageBox("\n CConstantBlockDialog::OnConstantBlkDlgBtnOk()\n",
      MB_OK, 0);

    // Update variable values with the Dlg Wnd control values
    UpdateData(TRUE);

    // Close the dialog wnd with OnOK()
    OnOK();

    // DiagramEng (end)
}
```

TABLE 9.4

Objects, IDs, Class, and Event-Handler Functions for the Constant Block Dialog Buttons

Object	ID	Class	COMMAND Event Handler
OK button	ID_CONSTANT_BLK_DLG_BTN_OK	CConstantBlockDialog	OnConstantBlkDlgBtnOk()
Cancel button	IDCANCEL (default)	CDialog	OnCancel()

9.3.1.5 Add Functionality to Initialize Variables

Dialog window parameters may be set via the `OnInitDialog()` message handling function associated with the WM_INITDIALOG message for the particular dialog class. This is convenient if the user wants to display a dialog window that provides default values or settings that must appear every time the dialog window is invoked. For example, if various check boxes should appear cleared, or default messages are to be placed in edit boxes prompting user action, or if controls are to be visible but disabled, then the `OnInitDialog()` function can be used to provide this consistent, default display.

However, if a dialog window is to be used to obtain user input and also reflect the current state of the variables of its class, e.g., the ConstantBlockDialog window may be required to show the constant variable value of the CConstantBlockDialog class associated with the CConstantBlock class, then the `OnInitDialog()` function could be used, but it would be necessary to obtain a reference to the class whose member variables it should display. Instead of using the `OnInitDialog()` function, an alternative approach is adopted here and involves the following steps:

1. Initialize member variables of the CBlock-derived class in the class constructor.
2. Create a dialog object in the `BlockDlgWndParameterInput()` function.
3. Assign the variables values from the CBlock-derived class to the CDialog-derived class.

Then, if the dialog window variable values are changed, these are updated to the derived CBlock class's variables in the `BlockDlgWndParameterInput()` function. If the dialog window is closed and later reopened, the correct CBlock-derived class' member values are reflected in the dialog window.

The member variable of the CConstantBlock and CConstantBlockDialog classes is the CString "m_strConstValue" (the name is shared for convenience). Initialize this variable in the CConstantBlock constructor as shown in bold in the following code.

```
CConstantBlock::CConstantBlock(CSystemModel *pParentSystemModel, CPoint
  blk_posn, EBlockShape e_blk_shape):
CBlock(pParentSystemModel, blk_posn, e_blk_shape)
{
    SetBlockName("constant_block");

    // Set the constant scalar/vector/matrix CString value.
    m_strConstValue = "1";

    // Create an output port
    CPort *p_output_port = new CPort(*this);

    // Set port properties
    p_output_port->SetPortName("_");   // "_" indicates no sign operation
      performed on the output signal
    p_output_port->SetPortPositionAngle(0.0); // port posn angle
      0 degrees, i.e. right side.
    p_output_port->CalculatePortPosition();
    p_output_port->SetPortArrowDirection(e_right_arrow);

    // Add the port to the vector of ports
    GetVectorOfOutputPorts().push_back(p_output_port);
}
```

9.3.1.6 Add the Overriding `BlockDlgWndParameterInput()` Function

Firstly add a virtual public member function to the CBlock class with the prototype: `virtual void CBlock::BlockDlgWndParameterInput(void)`. This is to be overridden by all derived block classes providing their own version of the function. Hence, make a comment in the function that the function is to be overridden; otherwise leave the function empty as shown in the following code.

```
void CBlock::BlockDlgWndParameterInput()
{
    // VIRTUAL FN to be OVERRIDDEN by each DERIVED Block class.
    // This is done, so the correct BlockDlgWndParameterInput() fn is
      called,
    // based on the run time type of the ptr-to-CBlock, within the block
      list.
}
```

Add a public member method to the CConstantBlock class with prototype: void CConstantBlock::BlockDlgWndParameterInput(void). A dialog window needs to be constructed within this function and displayed to allow the user to set the Constant block parameters. In fact the developer may like to make the function virtual, as a reminder that it is an overriding function, although this is not strictly required. Edit the CConstantBlock::BlockDlgWndPara meterInput() function as shown in the following code. This will require the header file of the CConstantBlockDialog class to be included at the top of the "Block.cpp" source file, i.e., add #include "ConstantBlockDialog.h".

```
void CConstantBlock::BlockDlgWndParameterInput()
{
    CString sMsg;          // string to be displayed
    UINT nType = MB_OK;    // style of msg. box
    UINT nIDhelp = 0;      // help context ID for the msg.

    // Create a dlg obj. of class CConstantBlockDialog : public CDialog
    CConstantBlockDialog oDlg;

    // Set the dialog class vars using the block class vars
    oDlg.m_strConstValue = m_strConstValue;

    // Return val of DoModal() fn of ancestor class CDialog is checked to
      determine which btn was clicked.
    if(oDlg.DoModal() == IDOK)
    {
        // Assign CConstantBlockDialog variable values to CConstantBlock
          variable values.
        m_strConstValue = oDlg.m_strConstValue;
        // Print msg with variable value.
        sMsg.Format("\n CConstantBlock::BlockDlgWndParameterInput(),
          string = %s\n", m_strConstValue);
        AfxMessageBox(sMsg, nType, nIDhelp);
    }
}
```

The developer will notice that first the CConstantBlock variable "m_strConstValue" is written to the CConstantBlockDialog variable which is then subsequently displayed. Then, in the conditional "if(oDlg.DoModal() == IDOK)" section, the dialog window input, recorded in the CConstantBlockDialog "oDlg.m_strConstValue" dialog window variable is assigned to the associated CConstantBlock-based "m_strConstValue" class variable.

Note also that upon compilation of the code, the following error is reported: "error C2065: 'IDD_CONSTANT_BLK_DLG': undeclared identifier"! To resolve this, add #include "Resource.h" at the top of the "ConstantBlockDialog.h" header file as shown in bold in the following.

```
#if !defined(AFX_CONSTANTBLOCKDIALOG_H__EAFC2435_59E6_4653_
  B7C0_5C7B656D7064__INCLUDED_)
#define AFX_CONSTANTBLOCKDIALOG_H__EAFC2435_59E6_4653_B7C0_5C7B656D7064__
  INCLUDED_

#if _MSC_VER > 1000
#pragma once
#endif // _MSC_VER > 1000

#include "Resource.h"  // rqd. since resources are used to build the dlg.
  wnd.

// ConstantBlockDialog.h : header file
//

/////////////////////////////////////////////////////////////////////////
// CConstantBlockDialog dialog

class CConstantBlockDialog : public CDialog
{
...
};

//{{AFX_INSERT_LOCATION}}
// Microsoft Visual C++ will insert additional declarations immediately
  before the previous line.

#endif // !defined(AFX_CONSTANTBLOCKDIALOG_H__EAFC2435_59E6_4653_
  B7C0_5C7B656D7064__INCLUDED_)
```

9.3.1.7   Combined Left-Button-Down and Left-Button-Double-Click Problem

A runtime error occurred! If the user places a Constant block on the palette and then double-clicks the block, invoking the CConstantBlockDialog window, strangely a connector seems to be drawn from the block position toward the OK button of the block-parameter-input dialog window, as shown in Figure 9.3a. If the user then moves the ConstantBlockDialog window away, the connector is clearly visible, as shown in Figure 9.3b.

What has happened is that although a double-click event has occurred, the left button has still been pressed down and released: i.e., both left-button-down and left-button-up events have also occurred. In addition, upon left-button-up, the mouse pointer has been snapped to the OK button. This position is far enough away from the point at which the left-button-down event occurred (upon the block), that a connector is deemed to have been intended: If the distance is very small then a connector would be judged to have not been intended by the user. As a result the connector is drawn, although erroneously.

To avoid this problem, the properties for the ConstantBlockDialog, IDD_CONSTANT_BLK_DLG resource, need to be changed. If the user navigates to the ResourceView and invokes the properties dialog for the OK button on the IDD_CONSTANT_BLK_DLG resource, then the "Default button" check box will be visibly selected, as shown in Figure 9.4. If this is unchecked, then double-clicking on the block on the palette will not result in a connector being unintentionally drawn.

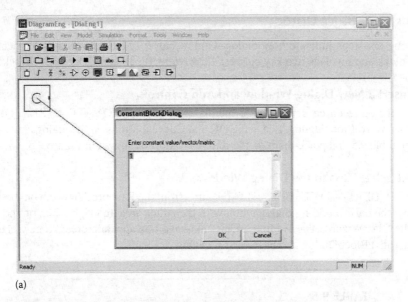

FIGURE 9.3 (a) A connector is drawn from the block position to the location of the OK button on the ConstantBlockDialog window. (b) Connector erroneously drawn to where the OK button was on the dialog window.

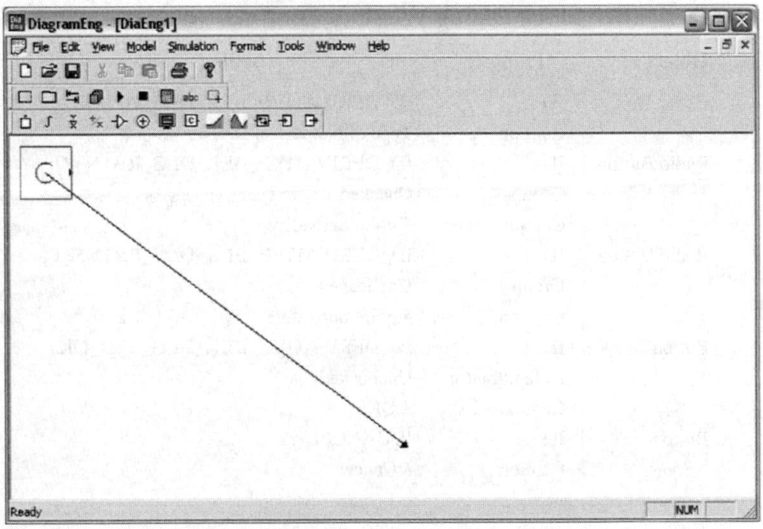

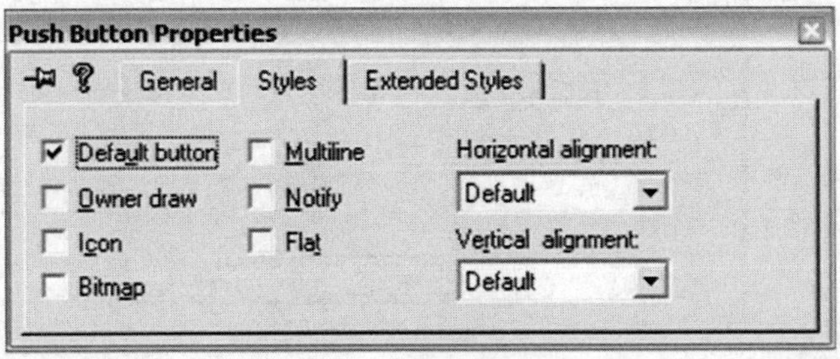

FIGURE 9.4 Properties dialog for the OK button on the IDD_CONSTANT_BLK_DLG resource shows the "Default button" option unintentionally checked: this should be unchecked.

9.3.2 DERIVATIVE BLOCK DIALOG

The following six steps indicate how dialog-window-based functionality is implemented for the Derivative block and involves two key classes: CDerivativeBlock and CDerivativeBlockDialog.

9.3.2.1 Insert a New Dialog Window and Add Controls

Insert a new dialog resource: set the ID of the dialog to IDD_DERIVATIVE_BLK_DLG and the caption to DerivativeBlockDialog. Leave the OK and Cancel buttons on the dialog, and add controls as shown in Table 9.5 and place them on the dialog window as shown in Figure 9.5.

9.3.2.2 Attach a Class to the Dialog Window

Select the IDD_DERIVATIVE_BLK_DLG resource from the ResourceView tab on the Workspace pane to show the corresponding dialog window in the editor area and right click on the dialog box to invoke the ClassWizard. The Adding a Class message box appears: create a new class with the name CDerivativeBlockDialog and base class CDialog.

TABLE 9.5
Derivative Block Dialog Window Controls

Object	Property	Setting
Group Box	ID	ID_DERIVATIVE_BLK_DLG_GPBOX
	Caption	Type of Numerical Derivative df/dt
Radio Button	ID	ID_DERIVATIVE_BLK_DLG_RBTN3PT
	Group	Checked
	Caption	3 point derivative
Radio Button	ID	ID_DERIVATIVE_BLK_DLG_RBTN5PT
	Group	Unchecked
	Caption	5 point derivative
Button	ID	ID_DERIVATIVE_BLK_DLG_BTN_OK
	Default button	Unchecked
	Caption	&OK
Button	ID	IDCANCEL
	Caption	&Cancel

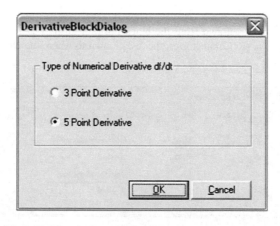

FIGURE 9.5   DerivativeBlockDialog window showing the controls as specified in Table 9.5.

TABLE 9.6

Dialog Window Controls, Variable Name, Category, and Type for the IDD_DERIVATIVE_BLK_DLG Resource

Control	Variable Name	Category	Type
ID_DERIVATIVE_BLK_DLG_RBTN3PT	m_iDerivativeMethod	Value	int

9.3.2.3 Attach Variables to the Dialog Window Controls

Open the ClassWizard, select the Member Variables tab, and choose the class name to be CDerivativeBlockDialog, since variables to be added relate to dialog window controls. Select the ID of the control to which a variable should be added, click Add Variable, and specify the details as shown in Table 9.6. Note that only one variable will be added to the "checked" radio button: the other button in the group will be numbered sequentially.

Now add a private member variable to the CDerivativeBlock class of the same integer type and name, i.e., "m_iDerivativeMethod", since this variable will be updated with the value of that of the dialog class.

9.3.2.4 Add Functionality to the Dialog Window Buttons

The two buttons for the IDD_DERIVATIVE_BLK_DLG dialog window are OK and Cancel. Add an event-handler function for the OK button as shown in Table 9.7. Leave the current event-handler function for the Cancel button, since this already calls the CDialog::OnCancel() function, so no new code is required. Edit the OnDerivativeBlkDlgBtnOk() function as shown in the following.

```
void CDerivativeBlockDialog::OnDerivativeBlkDlgBtnOk()
{
    // TODO: Add your control notification handler code here
    // DiagramEng (start)

    //AfxMessageBox("\n CDerivativeBlockDialog::OnDerivativeBlkDlgBtn
      Ok()\n", MB_OK, 0);

    // Update variable values with the Dlg Wnd control values
    UpdateData(TRUE);

    // Close the dialog wnd with OnOK()
    OnOK();

    // DiagramEng (end)
}
```

TABLE 9.7

Objects, IDs, Class, and Event-Handler Functions for the Derivative Block Dialog Buttons

Object	ID	Class	COMMAND Event Handler
OK button	ID_DERIVATIVE_BLK_DLG_BTN_OK	CDerivativeBlockDialog	OnDerivativeBlkDlgBtnOk()
Cancel button	IDCANCEL (default)	CDialog	OnCancel()

9.3.2.5   Add Functionality to Initialize Variables

The member variable of the CDerivativeBlock and CDerivativeBlockDialog classes is the integer "m_iDerivativeMethod" (the name is shared for convenience). Initialize this variable in the CDerivativeBlock constructor as shown in the following code: the ellipsis "…" denotes omitted but unchanged code.

```
CDerivativeBlock::CDerivativeBlock(CSystemModel *pParentSystemModel,
  CPoint blk_posn, EBlockShape e_blk_shape):
CBlock(pParentSystemModel, blk_posn, e_blk_shape)
{
    ...
    // Set the derivative method
    m_iDerivativeMethod = 1;  // (0) Euler, (1) Runge-Kutta
    ...
}
```

9.3.2.6   Add the Overriding `BlockDlgWndParameterInput()` Function

Add a public member function to the CDerivativeBlock class with prototype, void CDerivativeBlock::BlockDlgWndParameterInput(void), and edit it as shown in the following code. The header file for the CDerivativeBlockDialog class is required by the CDerivativeBlock function; hence, add #include "DerivativeBlockDialog.h" at the top of the "Block. cpp" source file.

```
void CDerivativeBlock::BlockDlgWndParameterInput()
{
    CString  sMsg;        // string to be displayed
    UINT nType = MB_OK;   // style of msg. box
    UINT nIDhelp = 0;     // help context ID for the msg.

    // Create a dialog object. of class CDerivativeBlockDialog : public
      CDialog
    CDerivativeBlockDialog oDlg;

    // Set the dialog class vars using the block class vars
    oDlg.m_iDerivativeMethod = m_iDerivativeMethod;

    // Return val of DoModal() fn of ancestor class CDialog is checked to
      determine which btn was clicked.
    if(oDlg.DoModal() == IDOK)
    {
        // Assign CDerivativeBlockDialog variable values to
          CDerivativeBlock variable values.
        m_iDerivativeMethod = oDlg.m_iDerivativeMethod;

        // Print msg with variable value.
        sMsg.Format("\n CDerivativeBlock::BlockDlgWndParameterInput(),
          m_iDerivativeMethod = %d\n", m_iDerivativeMethod);
        AfxMessageBox(sMsg, nType, nIDhelp);
    }
}
```

9.3.3   Divide Block Dialog

The following six steps indicate how dialog-window-based functionality is implemented for the Divide block and involves two key classes: CDivideBlock and CDivideBlockDialog.

9.3.3.1   Insert a New Dialog Window and Add Controls

Insert a new dialog resource: set the ID of the dialog to IDD_DIVIDE_BLK_DLG and the caption to DivideBlockDialog. Leave the OK and Cancel buttons on the dialog. Add controls as shown in Table 9.8 and place them on the dialog window as shown in Figure 9.6.

9.3.3.2   Attach a Class to the Dialog Window

Select the IDD_DIVIDE_BLK_DLG resource from the ResourceView tab on the Workspace pane to show the corresponding dialog window in the editor area and right click on the dialog box to

TABLE 9.8
Divide Block Dialog Window Controls

Object	Property	Setting
Static Text	ID	ID_DIVIDE_BLK_DLG_TXT_NMULTS
	Caption	Number of multiplication inputs:
Static Text	ID	ID_DIVIDE_BLK_DLG_TXT_NDIVIDES
	Caption	Number of divide inputs:
Edit Box	ID	ID_DIVIDE_BLK_DLG_EB_NMULTS
Edit Box	ID	ID_DIVIDE_BLK_DLG_EB_NDIVIDES
Group Box	ID	ID_DIVIDE_BLK_DLG_GPBOX
	Caption	Type of Multiplication/Division
Radio Button	ID	ID_DIVIDE_BLK_DLG_RBTN_ELEMENT
	Group	Checked
	Caption	Elemental
Radio Button	ID	ID_DIVIDE_BLK_DLG_RBTN_MATRIX
	Group	Unchecked
	Caption	Matrix
Button	ID	ID_DIVIDE_BLK_DLG_BTN_OK
	Default button	Unchecked
	Caption	&OK
Button	ID	IDCANCEL
	Caption	&Cancel

FIGURE 9.6   DivideBlockDialog window showing the controls as specified in Table 9.8.

TABLE 9.9

Dialog Window Controls, Variable Name, Category, and Type for the IDD_DIVIDE_BLK_DLG Resource

Control	Variable Name	Category	Type	Min. Value	Max. Value
ID_DIVIDE_BLK_DLG_EB_NMULTS	m_iNMultiplyInputs	Value	int	0	1000
ID_DIVIDE_BLK_DLG_EB_NDIVIDES	m_iNDivideInputs	Value	int	0	1000
ID_DIVIDE_BLK_DLG_RBTN_ELEMENT	m_iMultType	Value	int		

invoke the ClassWizard. The familiar Adding a Class message box appears: create a new class with the name CDivideBlockDialog and base class CDialog.

9.3.3.3   Attach Variables to the Dialog Window Controls

Open the ClassWizard, select the Member Variables tab, choose the class name to be CDivideBlockDialog, select the ID of the control to which a variable should be added, click Add Variable, and specify the details as shown in Table 9.9. Note that only one variable will be added to the "checked" radio button: the other button in the group will be numbered sequentially.

Replace the (previous) placeholder variable "e_mult_action" of the CDivideBlock class with the integer member variable "m_iMultType": This is done so that the CDivideBlock and CDivideBlockDialog classes share the same names for their member variables.

9.3.3.4   Add Functionality to the Dialog Window Buttons

The two buttons for the IDD_DIVIDE_BLK_DLG dialog window are OK and Cancel. Add an event-handler function for the OK button as shown in Table 9.10. Leave the current event-handler function for the Cancel button, since this already calls the `CDialog::OnCancel()` function, so no new code is required. Edit the `OnDivideBlkDlgBtnOk()` function as shown in the following.

```
void CDivideBlockDialog::OnDivideBlkDlgBtnOk()
{
    // TODO: Add your control notification handler code here

    // DiagramEng (start)

    //AfxMessageBox("\n CDivideBlockDialog::OnDivideBlkDlgBtnOk()\n",
      MB_OK, 0);

    // Update variable values with the Dlg Wnd control values
    UpdateData(TRUE);

    // Close the dialog wnd with OnOK()
    OnOK();

    // DiagramEng (end)
}
```

TABLE 9.10

Objects, IDs, Class, and Event-Handler Functions for the Divide Block Dialog Buttons

Object	ID	Class	COMMAND Event Handler
OK button	ID_DIVIDE_BLK_DLG_BTN_OK	CDivideBlockDialog	OnDivideBlkDlgBtnOk()
Cancel button	IDCANCEL (default)	CDialog	OnCancel()

9.3.3.5   Add Functionality to Initialize Variables

The member variables of the CDivideBlock and CDivideBlockDialog classes are "m_iNDivideInputs", "m_iNMultiplyInputs", and "m_iMultType". Initialize these variables in the CDivideBlock constructor as shown in the following code.

```
CDivideBlock::CDivideBlock(CSystemModel *pParentSystemModel,
  CPoint blk_posn, EBlockShape e_blk_shape):
CBlock(pParentSystemModel, blk_posn, e_blk_shape)
{
    ...
    // Set the Divide block member vars
    m_iNMultiplyInputs = 1;
    m_iNDivideInputs = 1;
    m_iMultType = 1;
    ...
}
```

9.3.3.6   Add the Overriding `BlockDlgWndParameterInput()` Function

Add a public member function to the CDivideBlock class with prototype, void CDivideBlock::BlockDlgWndParameterInput(void), and edit the function as shown in the following code. The header file for the CDivideBlockDialog class is required by the CDivideBlock function; hence, add #include "DivideBlockDialog.h" at the top of the "Block.cpp" source file.

```
void CDivideBlock::BlockDlgWndParameterInput()
{
    int n_inputs = 0;      // number of input ports
    CString sMsg;          // string to be displayed
    CString sMsgTemp;      // temp string msg.
    UINT nType = MB_OK;    // style of msg. box
    UINT nIDhelp = 0;      // help context ID for the msg.

    // Create a dialog object. of class CDivideBlockDialog : public CDialog
    CDivideBlockDialog oDlg;

    // Set the dialog class vars using the block class vars
    oDlg.m_iMultType = m_iMultType;
    oDlg.m_iNDivideInputs = m_iNDivideInputs;
    oDlg.m_iNMultiplyInputs = m_iNMultiplyInputs;

    // While less than two input ports get user input
    while(n_inputs < 2)
    {
        // Return val of DoModal() fn of ancestor class CDialog is
        // checked to determine which btn was clicked.
        if(oDlg.DoModal() == IDOK)
        {
            // Assign CDivideBlockDialog variable values to CDivideBlock
            // variable values.
            m_iNDivideInputs = oDlg.m_iNDivideInputs;
            m_iNMultiplyInputs = oDlg.m_iNMultiplyInputs;
            m_iMultType = oDlg.m_iMultType;

            // Print msg with variable value.
            //sMsg.Format("\n CDivideBlock::BlockDlgWndParameterInput(),
            //  m_iMultType = %d\n", m_iMultType);
            //AfxMessageBox(sMsg, nType, nIDhelp);
        }
```

```
// Check input for correctness and warn user if approp.
n_inputs = m_iNDivideInputs + m_iNMultiplyInputs;

if(n_inputs < 2)
{
    sMsgTemp.Format("\n CDivideBlock::BlockDlgWndParameter
      Input()\n");
    sMsg += sMsgTemp;
    sMsgTemp.Format(" No. of input ports = %d\n", n_inputs);
    sMsg += sMsgTemp;
    sMsgTemp.Format(" Two or more input ports are required!\n");
    sMsg += sMsgTemp;
    AfxMessageBox(sMsg, nType, nIDhelp);
    sMsg.Format(""); // reset the msg since within a while loop
}
    }
}
```

9.3.4   GAIN BLOCK DIALOG

The following familiar six steps indicate how dialog-window-based functionality is implemented for the Gain block and involves two key classes: CGainBlock and CGainBlockDialog.

9.3.4.1   Insert a New Dialog Window and Add Controls

Insert a new dialog resource: set the ID of the dialog to IDD_GAIN_BLK_DLG and the caption to GainBlockDialog. Leave the OK and Cancel buttons on the dialog. Add controls as provided in Table 9.11 and place them on the dialog window as shown in Figure 9.7.

9.3.4.2   Attach a Class to the Dialog Window

Select the IDD_GAIN_BLK_DLG resource from the ResourceView tab on the Workspace pane to show the corresponding dialog window in the editor area and right click on the dialog box to invoke the ClassWizard. The Adding a Class message box appears: create a new class with the name CGainBlockDialog and base class CDialog.

9.3.4.3   Attach Variables to the Dialog Window Controls

Open the ClassWizard, select the Member Variables tab, choose the class name to be CGainBlockDialog, select the ID of the control to which a variable should be added, click Add Variable, and specify the details as shown in Table 9.12. Note that only one variable will be added to the "checked" radio button: the others in the group will be numbered sequentially.

Now replace the previous placeholder variable "e_mult_action" of the CGainBlock class, with the integer variable "m_iGainType": now the definition of the enumerated type, EMultAction, may be removed from the "Block.h" header file as it is no longer required. The other variables "matrix_gain", "scalar_gain", and "vector_gain" of the CGainBlock class may be consolidated into one variable, "m_dGainMatrix", since all numerical data will be treated as double-typed matrices in future for consistency reasons. However, add a new private CString variable to the CGainBlock class, "m_strGainValue"; this holds the gain input. The variable names of the CGainBlockDialog class are the same as those of the CGainBlock class: this is done for convenience.

9.3.4.4   Add Functionality to the Dialog Window Buttons

The two buttons for the IDD_GAIN_BLK_DLG dialog window are OK and Cancel. Add an event-handler function for the OK button as shown in Table 9.13. Leave the current event-handler

TABLE 9.11
Gain Block Dialog Window Controls

Object	Property	Setting
Static Text	ID	ID_GAIN_BLK_DLG_TXT_GAIN
	Caption	Enter gain constant/vector/matrix:
Edit Box	ID	ID_GAIN_BLK_DLG_EB_GAIN
	Multiline	Checked
	Horizontal scroll	Checked
	Vertical scroll	Checked
	Want return	Checked
Group Box	ID	ID_GAIN_BLK_DLG_GPBOX
	Caption	Type of Gain
Radio Button	ID	ID_GAIN_BLK_DLG_RB_ELEMENT
	Group	Checked
	Caption	Elemental
Radio Button	ID	ID_GAIN_BLK_DLG_RB_GAIN_INPUT
	Group	Unchecked
	Caption	Gain*Input
Radio Button	ID	ID_GAIN_BLK_DLG_RB_INPUT_GAIN
	Group	Unchecked
	Caption	Input*Gain
Button	ID	ID_GAIN_BLK_DLG_BTN_OK
	Default button	Unchecked
	Caption	&OK
Button	ID	IDCANCEL
	Caption	&Cancel

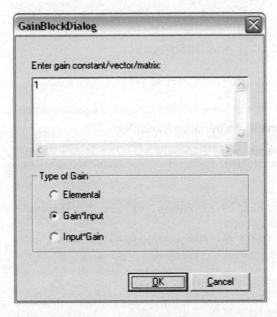

FIGURE 9.7 GainBlockDialog window showing the controls as specified in Table 9.11.

TABLE 9.12

Dialog Window Controls, Variable Name, Category, and Type for the IDD_GAIN_BLK_DLG Resource

Control	Variable Name	Category	Type
ID_GAIN_BLK_DLG_EB_GAIN	m_strGainValue	Value	CString
ID_GAIN_BLK_DLG_RBTN_ELEMENT	m_iGainType	Value	int

TABLE 9.13

Objects, IDs, Class, and Event-Handler Functions for the Gain Block Dialog Buttons

Object	ID	Class	COMMAND Event Handler
OK button	ID_GAIN_BLK_DLG_BTN_OK	CGainBlockDialog	OnGainBlkDlgBtnOk()
Cancel button	IDCANCEL (default)	CDialog	OnCancel()

function for the Cancel button, since this already calls the `CDialog::OnCancel()` function, so no new code is required. Edit the `OnGainBlkDlgBtnOk()` function as shown in the following.

```
void CGainBlockDialog::OnGainBlkDlgBtnOk()
{
    // TODO: Add your control notification handler code here

    // DiagramEng (start)

    //AfxMessageBox("\n CGainBlockDialog::OnGainBlkDlgBtnOk()n", MB_OK, 0);

    // Update variable values with the Dlg Wnd control values
    UpdateData(TRUE);

    // Close the dialog wnd with OnOK()
    OnOK();

    // DiagramEng (end)
}
```

9.3.4.5   Add Functionality to Initialize Variables

The member variables of the CGainBlock and CGainBlockDialog classes are "m_iGainType" and "m_strGainValue". Initialize these variables in the CGainBlock constructor as shown in the following code.

```
CGainBlock::CGainBlock(CSystemModel *pParentSystemModel, CPoint blk_posn,
  EBlockShape e_blk_shape):
CBlock(pParentSystemModel, blk_posn, e_blk_shape)
{
    ...
    // Set the Gain block member vars.
    m_iGainType = 1;
    m_strGainValue = "1";
    ...
}
```

9.3.4.6 Add the Overriding `BlockDlgWndParameterInput()` Function

Add a public member function to the CGainBlock class with prototype, void CGainBlock::BlockDlgWndParameterInput(void), and edit the function as shown in the following code. The header file for the CGainBlockDialog class is required by the CGainBlock function; hence, add #include "GainBlockDialog.h" at the top of the "Block.cpp" source file.

```
void CGainBlock::BlockDlgWndParameterInput()
{
    CString sMsg;            // string to be displayed
    UINT nType = MB_OK;     // style of msg. box
    UINT nIDhelp = 0;       // help context ID for the msg.

    // Create a dialog object. of class CGainBlockDialog : public CDialog
    CGainBlockDialog oDlg;

    // Set the dialog class vars using the block class vars
    oDlg.m_iGainType = m_iGainType;
    oDlg.m_strGainValue = m_strGainValue;

    // Return val of DoModal() fn of ancestor class CDialog is checked to
      determine which btn was clicked.
    if(oDlg.DoModal() == IDOK)
    {
        // Assign CGainBlockDialog variable values to CGainBlock variable
          values.
        m_strGainValue = oDlg.m_strGainValue;
        m_iGainType = oDlg.m_iGainType;

        // Print msg with variable value.
        sMsg.Format("\n CGainBlock::BlockDlgWndParameterInput(),
          m_strGainValue = %s\n", m_strGainValue);
        AfxMessageBox(sMsg, nType, nIDhelp);
    }
}
```

9.3.5 Integrator Block Dialog

The following six steps indicate how dialog-window-based functionality is implemented for the Integrator block and involves two key classes: CIntegratorBlock and CIntegratorBlockDialog.

9.3.5.1 Insert a New Dialog Window and Add Controls

Insert a new dialog resource: set the ID of the dialog to IDD_INTEGRATOR_BLK_DLG and the caption to IntegratorBlockDialog. Leave the OK and Cancel buttons on the dialog. Add controls as provided in Table 9.14 and place them on the dialog window as shown in Figure 9.8.

9.3.5.2 Attach a Class to the Dialog Window

Select the IDD_INTEGRATOR_BLK_DLG resource from the ResourceView tab on the Workspace pane to show the corresponding dialog window in the editor area and right click on the dialog box to invoke the ClassWizard. The Adding a Class message box appears: create a new class with the name CIntegratorBlockDialog and base class CDialog.

9.3.5.3 Attach Variables to the Dialog Window Controls

Open the ClassWizard, select the Member Variables tab, choose the class name to be CIntegratorBlockDialog, select the ID of the control to which a variable should be added, click Add Variable, and specify the details as shown in Table 9.15.

TABLE 9.14

Integrator Block Dialog Window Controls

Object	Property	Setting
Static Text	ID	ID_INTEGRATOR_BLK_DLG_TXT_NOTE
	Caption	IntegratorBlockDialog controls initial condition vector input!\nNumericalSolverDialog controls numerical method variable input!
	Sunken	Checked
Static Text	ID	ID_INTEGRATOR_BLK_DLG_TXT_IC
	Caption	Initial Condition Vector:
Edit Box	ID	ID_INTEGRATOR_BLK_DLG_EB_IC
	Multiline	Checked
	Horizontal scroll	Checked
	Vertical scroll	Checked
	Want return	Checked
Button	ID	ID_INTEGRATOR_BLK_DLG_BTN_OK
	Default button	Unchecked
	Caption	&OK
Button	ID	IDCANCEL
	Caption	&Cancel

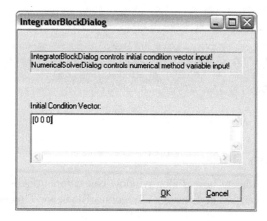

FIGURE 9.8   IntegratorBlockDialog window showing the controls as specified in Table 9.14.

TABLE 9.15

Dialog Window Controls, Variable Name, Category, and Type for the IDD_INTEGRATOR_BLK_DLG Resource

Control	Variable Name	Category	Type
ID_INTEGRATOR_BLK_DLG_EB_IC	m_strICVector	Value	CString

Remove the previous placeholder variable "e_integration_method" of the CIntegratorBlock class, since the CSystemModel class will hold a CString variable named "m_strIntegrationMethod" used to specify the integration method when working with the NumericalSolverDialog window. Hence, the enumerated type EIntegrationMethod may also be removed from the "Block.h" header file, as it is no longer required. The initial condition vector "ic_vector" of the CIntegratorBlock

TABLE 9.16

Objects, IDs, Class, and Event-Handler Functions for the Integrator Block Dialog Buttons

Object	ID	Class	COMMAND Event Handler
OK button	ID_INTEGRATOR_BLK_DLG_BTN_OK	CIntegratorBlockDialog	OnIntegratorBlkDlgBtnOk()
Cancel button	IDCANCEL (default)	CDialog	OnCancel()

class may be left there for now as it may be used in future as a double-typed vector variable. However, add a new private CString variable to the CIntegratorBlock class, "m_strICVector"; this holds the initial condition vector for the integration process as a CString object. The variable names of the CIntegratorBlockDialog and the CIntegratorBlock classes are the same for convenience.

9.3.5.4 Add Functionality to the Dialog Window Buttons

The two buttons for the IDD_INTEGRATOR_BLK_DLG dialog window are OK and Cancel. Add an event-handler function for the OK button as shown in Table 9.16. Leave the current event-handler function for the Cancel button, since this already calls the CDialog::OnCancel() function, so no new code is required. Edit the OnIntegratorBlkDlgBtnOk() function as shown in the following.

```
void CIntegratorBlockDialog::OnIntegratorBlkDlgBtnOk()
{
    // TODO: Add your control notification handler code here

    // DiagramEng (start)

    //AfxMessageBox("\n CIntegratorBlockDialog::OnIntegratorBlkDlgBtn
      Ok()\n", MB_OK, 0);

    // Update variable values with the Dlg Wnd control values
    UpdateData(TRUE);

    // Close the dialog wnd with OnOK()
    OnOK();

    // DiagramEng (end)
}
```

9.3.5.5 Add Functionality to Initialize Variables

The member variable of the CIntegratorBlock and CIntegratorBlockDialog classes is "m_strICVector". Initialize this variable in the CIntegratorBlock constructor as shown in the following code.

```
CIntegratorBlock::CIntegratorBlock(CSystemModel *pParentSystemModel,
  CPoint blk_posn, EBlockShape e_blk_shape):
CBlock(pParentSystemModel, blk_posn, e_blk_shape)
{
    ...
    // Set the Integrator block member var.
    m_strICVector = "[0 0 0]";
    ...
}
```

9.3.5.6　Add the Overriding `BlockDlgWndParameterInput()` Function

Add a public member function to the CIntegratorBlock class with prototype, void CIntegratorBlock::BlockDlgWndParameterInput(void), and edit it as shown in the following code. The header file for the CIntegratorBlockDialog class is required by the CIntegratorBlock function; hence, add #include "IntegratorBlockDialog.h", at the top of the "Block. cpp" source file.

```
void CIntegratorBlock::BlockDlgWndParameterInput()
{
    CString sMsg;            // string to be displayed
    UINT nType = MB_OK;     // style of msg. box
    UINT nIDhelp = 0;        // help context ID for the msg.

    // Create a dialog object. of class CIntegratorBlockDialog : public
        CDialog
    CIntegratorBlockDialog oDlg;

    // Set the dialog class vars using the block class vars
    oDlg.m_strICVector = m_strICVector;

    // Return val of DoModal() fn of ancestor class CDialog is checked to
        determine which btn was clicked.
    if(oDlg.DoModal() == IDOK)
    {
        // Assign CIntegratorBlockDialog variable values to
            CIntegratorBlock variable values.
        m_strICVector = oDlg.m_strICVector;

        // Print msg with variable value.
        sMsg.Format("\n CIntegratorBlock::BlockDlgWndParameterInput(),
            m_strICVector = %s\n", m_strICVector);
        AfxMessageBox(sMsg, nType, nIDhelp);
    }
}
```

9.3.6　Linear Function Block Dialog

The following six steps indicate how dialog-window-based functionality is implemented for the Linear Function block and involves two key classes: CLinearFnBlock and CLinearFnBlockDialog.

9.3.6.1　Insert a New Dialog Window and Add Controls

Insert a new dialog resource: set the ID of the dialog to IDD_LINEARFN_BLK_DLG and the caption to LinearFnBlockDialog. Leave the OK and Cancel buttons on the dialog. Add controls as provided in Table 9.17 and place them on the dialog window as shown in Figure 9.9.

Mathematicians and engineers familiar with the *Simulink*® application, developed by *The MathWorks* [2], will notice similarities between the Linear Function block dialog introduced here and the Ramp Source Block Parameters dialog of *Simulink*. However, here the final time of the linear function source signal is used to denote the end of signal activation, after which the function is constant, maintaining its final value. This behavior is explained in more detail in Chapter 21.

9.3.6.2　Attach a Class to the Dialog Window

Select the IDD_LINEARFN_BLK_DLG resource from the ResourceView tab on the Workspace pane, to show the corresponding dialog window in the editor area and right click on the dialog box to invoke the ClassWizard. The Adding a Class message box appears: create a new class named CLinearFnBlockDialog with base class CDialog.

TABLE 9.17
Linear Function Block Dialog Window Controls

Object	Property	Setting
Group Box	ID	ID_LINEARFN_BLK_DLG_GPBOX
	Caption	Linear Function Parameters
Static Text	ID	ID_LINEARFN_BLK_DLG_TXT_TINIT
	Caption	Initial Time:
Edit Box	ID	ID_LINEARFN_BLK_DLG_EB_TINIT
Static Text	ID	ID_LINEARFN_BLK_DLG_TXT_TFINAL
	Caption	Final Time:
Edit Box	ID	ID_LINEARFN_BLK_DLG_EB_TFINAL
Static Text	ID	ID_LINEARFN_BLK_DLG_TXT_VINIT
	Caption	Initial Value:
Edit Box	ID	ID_LINEARFN_BLK_DLG_EB_VINIT
Static Text	ID	ID_LINEARFN_BLK_DLG_TXT_DERIV
	Caption	Derivative:
Edit Box	ID	ID_LINEARFN_BLK_DLG_EB_DERIV
Button	ID	ID_LINEARFN_BLK_DLG_BTN_OK
	Default button	Unchecked
	Caption	&OK
Button	ID	IDCANCEL
	Caption	&Cancel

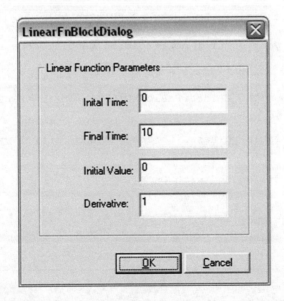

FIGURE 9.9 LinearFnBlockDialog window showing the controls as specified in Table 9.17.

9.3.6.3 Attach Variables to the Dialog Window Controls

Open the ClassWizard, select the Member Variables tab, choose the class name to be CLinearFnBlockDialog, select the ID of the control to which a variable should be added, click Add Variable, and specify the details as shown in Table 9.18.

Replace the previous placeholder double variables "fn_derivative", "signal_init_val", and "t_signal_start", of the CLinearFnBlock class, with the double variables "m_dDerivative",

TABLE 9.18

Dialog Window Controls, Variable Name, Category, and Type for the IDD_LINEARFN_BLK_DLG Resource

Control	Variable Name	Category	Type
ID_LINEARFN_BLK_DLG_EB_TINIT	m_dTimeInit	Value	double
ID_LINEARFN_BLK_DLG_EB_TFINAL	m_dTimeFinal	Value	double
ID_LINEARFN_BLK_DLG_EB_VINIT	m_dValueInit	Value	double
ID_LINEARFN_BLK_DLG_EB_DERIV	m_dDerivative	Value	double

"m_dValueInit", and "m_dTimeInit", respectively. In addition, a new private double variable should be added to the CLinearFnBlock class, i.e., "m_dTimeFinal": this holds the final time value at which the signal is considered to act. The variable names of the CLinearFnBlockDialog class are the same as those of the CLinearFnBlock class for convenience.

9.3.6.4 Add Functionality to the Dialog Window Buttons

The two buttons for the IDD_LINEARFN_BLK_DLG dialog window are OK and Cancel. Add an event-handler function for the OK button as shown in Table 9.19. Leave the current event-handler function for the Cancel button, since this already calls the CDialog::OnCancel() function, so no new code is required. Edit the OnLinearFnBlkDlgBtnOk() function as shown in the following.

```
void CLinearFnBlockDialog::OnLinearFnBlkDlgBtnOk()
{
    // TODO: Add your control notification handler code here

    // DiagramEng (start)

    //AfxMessageBox("\n CLinearFnBlockDialog::OnLinearFnBlkDlgBtnOk
      ()\n", MB_OK, 0);

    // Update variable values with the Dlg Wnd control values
    UpdateData(TRUE);

    // Close the dialog wnd with OnOK()
    OnOK();

    // DiagramEng (end)
}
```

TABLE 9.19

Objects, IDs, Class, and Event-Handler Functions for the Linear Function Block Dialog Buttons

Object	ID	Class	COMMAND Event Handler
OK button	ID_LINEARFN_BLK_DLG_BTN_OK	CLinearFnBlockDialog	OnLinearFnBlkDlgBtnOk()
Cancel button	IDCANCEL (default)	CDialog	OnCancel()

9.3.6.5   Add Functionality to Initialize Variables

The member variables of the CLinearFnBlock and CLinearFnBlockDialog classes are "m_dTimeInit", "m_dTimeFinal", "m_dValueInit", and "m_dDerivative". Initialize these variables in the CLinearFnBlock constructor as shown in the following code.

```
CLinearFnBlock::CLinearFnBlock(CSystemModel *pParentSystemModel,
  CPoint blk_posn, EBlockShape e_blk_shape):
CBlock(pParentSystemModel, blk_posn, e_blk_shape)
{
    …
    // Set the LinearFnBlock member vars.
    m_dTimeInit = 0.0;
    m_dTimeFinal = 10.0;
    m_dValueInit = 0.0;
    m_dDerivative = 1.0;
    …

}
```

9.3.6.6   Add the Overriding `BlockDlgWndParameterInput()` Function

Add a public member function to the CLinearFnBlock class with prototype, void CLinearFnBlock::BlockDlgWndParameterInput(void), and edit the function as shown in the following code. The header file for the CLinearFnBlockDialog class is required by the CLinearFnBlock function; hence, add #include "LinearFnBlockDialog.h", at the top of the "Block.cpp" source file.

```
void CLinearFnBlock::BlockDlgWndParameterInput()
{
    CString sMsg;         // string to be displayed
    UINT nType = MB_OK;   // style of msg. box
    UINT nIDhelp = 0;     // help context ID for the msg.

    // Create a dialog object. of class CLinearFnBlockDialog : public
      CDialog
    CLinearFnBlockDialog oDlg;

    // Set the dialog class vars using the block class vars
    oDlg.m_dDerivative = m_dDerivative;
    oDlg.m_dTimeFinal = m_dTimeFinal;
    oDlg.m_dTimeInit = m_dTimeInit;
    oDlg.m_dValueInit = m_dValueInit;

    // Return val of DoModal() fn of ancestor class CDialog is checked to
      determine which btn was clicked.
    if(oDlg.DoModal() == IDOK)
    {
        // Assign CLinearFnBlockDialog variable values to CLinearFnBlock
          variable values.
        m_dDerivative = oDlg.m_dDerivative;
        m_dTimeInit = oDlg.m_dTimeInit;
        m_dTimeFinal = oDlg.m_dTimeFinal;
        m_dValueInit = oDlg.m_dValueInit;
```

```
          // Print msg with variable value.
          sMsg.Format("\n CLinearFnBlock::BlockDlgWndParameterInput(),
            m_dDerivative = %lf\n", m_dDerivative);
          AfxMessageBox(sMsg, nType, nIDhelp);
      }
  }
```

9.3.7   Output Block Dialog

The following six steps indicate how dialog-window-based functionality is implemented for the Output block and involves two key classes: COutputBlock and COutputBlockDialog.

9.3.7.1   Insert a New Dialog Window and Add Controls

Insert a new dialog resource: set the ID of the dialog to IDD_OUTPUT_BLK_DLG and the caption to OutputBlockDialog. Leave the OK and Cancel buttons on the dialog. Add controls as provided in Table 9.20 and place them on the dialog window as shown in Figure 9.10.

9.3.7.2   Attach a Class to the Dialog Window

Select the IDD_OUTPUT_BLK_DLG resource from the ResourceView tab on the Workspace pane, to show the corresponding dialog window in the editor area and right click on the dialog box to invoke the ClassWizard. The Adding a Class message box appears: create a new class with the name COutputBlockDialog and base class CDialog.

TABLE 9.20

Output Block Dialog Window Controls

Object	Property	Setting
Group Box	ID	ID_OUTPUT_BLK_DLG_GPBOXNOT
	Caption	Textual Output Settings
Radio Button	ID	ID_OUTPUT_BLK_DLG_RB_STDNOT
	Group	Checked
	Caption	Standard notation
Radio Button	ID	ID_OUTPUT_BLK_DLG_RB_SCINOT
	Group	Unchecked
	Caption	Scientific notation
Group Box	ID	ID_OUTPUT_BLK_DLG_GPBOXTPTS
	Caption	Graphical Output Settings
Radio Button	ID	ID_OUTPUT_BLK_DLG_RB_TPTS
	Group	Checked
	Caption	Show time points
Radio Button	ID	ID_OUTPUT_BLK_DLG_RB_NOTPTS
	Group	Unchecked
	Caption	Hide time points
Button	ID	ID_OUTPUT_BLK_DLG_BTN_OK
	Default button	Unchecked
	Caption	&OK
Button	ID	IDCANCEL
	Caption	&Cancel

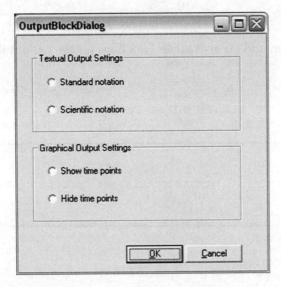

FIGURE 9.10 OutputBlockDialog window showing the controls as specified in Table 9.20.

TABLE 9.21

Dialog Window Controls, Variable Name, Category, and Type for the IDD_OUTPUT_BLK_DLG Resource

Control	Variable Name	Category	Type
ID_OUTPUT_BLK_DLG_RB_STDNOT	m_iNotation	Value	int
ID_OUTPUT_BLK_DLG_RB_TPTS	m_iTimePtDisplay	Value	int

9.3.7.3 Attach Variables to the Dialog Window Controls

Open the ClassWizard, select the Member Variables tab, choose the class name to be COutputBlockDialog, select the ID of the control to which a variable should be added, click Add Variable and specify the details as shown in Table 9.21.

Add two private integer variables, "m_iNotation" and "m_iTimePtDisplay", to the COutputBlock class: these are the same name and type of those in the COutputDialog class for convenience. Remove the other placeholder variables, "t_start", "t_stop", "file_name", and "e_data_format", and also the definition of the EOutputDataFormat enumerated type, as these will no longer been required.

9.3.7.4 Add Functionality to the Dialog Window Buttons

The two buttons for the IDD_OUTPUT_BLK_DLG dialog window are OK and Cancel. Add an event-handler function for the OK button as shown in Table 9.22. Leave the current event-handler function for the Cancel button, since this already calls the CDialog::OnCancel() function, so no new code is required. Edit the OnOutputBlkDlgBtnOk() function as shown in the following.

```
void COutputBlockDialog::OnOutputBlkDlgBtnOk()
{
    // TODO: Add your control notification handler code here

    // DiagramEng (start)
```

TABLE 9.22

Objects, IDs, Class, and Event-Handler Functions for the Output Block Dialog Buttons

Object	ID	Class	COMMAND Event Handler
OK button	ID_OUTPUT_BLK_DLG_BTN_OK	COutputBlockDialog	OnOutputBlkDlgBtnOk()
Cancel button	IDCANCEL (default)	CDialog	OnCancel()

```
    //AfxMessageBox("\n COutputBlockDialog::OnOutputBlkDlgBtnOk()\n",
      MB_OK, 0);

    // Update variable values with the Dlg Wnd control values
    UpdateData(TRUE);

    // Close the dialog wnd with OnOK()
    OnOK();

    // DiagramEng (end)
}
```

9.3.7.5 Add Functionality to Initialize Variables

The common member variables of the COutputBlock and COutputBlockDialog classes are "m_iNotation" and "m_iTimePtDisplay". Initialize these variables in the COutputBlock constructor as shown in the following code.

```
COutputBlock::COutputBlock(CSystemModel *pParentSystemModel, CPoint
  blk_posn, EBlockShape e_blk_shape):
CBlock(pParentSystemModel, blk_posn, e_blk_shape)
{
    ...
    // Set COutputBlock member var.
    m_iNotation = 0;
    m_iTimePtDisplay = 0;
    ...
}
```

9.3.7.6 Add the Overriding `BlockDlgWndParameterInput()` Function

Add a public member function to the COutputBlock class with prototype, void COutputBlock:: BlockDlgWndParameterInput(void), and edit the function as shown in the following code. The header file for the COutputBlockDialog class is required by the COutputBlock function; hence, add #include "OutputBlockDialog.h" at the top of the "Block.cpp" source file.

```
void COutputBlock::BlockDlgWndParameterInput()
{
    CString sMsg;        // string to be displayed
    UINT nType = MB_OK;  // style of msg. box
    UINT nIDhelp = 0;    // help context ID for the msg.

    // Create a dialog object. of class COutputBlockDialog : public
      CDialog
    COutputBlockDialog oDlg;
```

```
    // Set the dialog class vars using the block class vars
    oDlg.m_iNotation = m_iNotation;
    oDlg.m_iTimePtDisplay = m_iTimePtDisplay;

    // Return val of DoModal() fn of ancestor class CDialog is checked to
      determine which btn was clicked.
    if(oDlg.DoModal() == IDOK)
    {
        // Assign COutputBlockDialog variable values to COutputBlock
          variable values.
        m_iNotation = oDlg.m_iNotation;
        m_iTimePtDisplay = oDlg.m_iTimePtDisplay;

        // Print msg with variable value.
        sMsg.Format("\n COutputBlock::BlockDlgWndParameterInput(),
          m_iNotation = %d\n'', m_iNotation);
        AfxMessageBox(sMsg, nType, nIDhelp);
    }
}
```

9.3.8   SIGNAL GENERATOR BLOCK DIALOG

The following six steps indicate how dialog-window-based functionality is implemented for the Signal Generator block and involves two key classes: CSignalGeneratorBlock and CSignalGeneratorBlockDialog.

9.3.8.1   Insert a New Dialog Window and Add Controls

Insert a new dialog resource: set the ID of the dialog to IDD_SIGNALGEN_BLK_DLG and the caption to SignalGeneratorBlockDialog. Leave the OK and Cancel buttons on the dialog. Add controls as provided in Table 9.23 and place them on the dialog window as shown Figure 9.11.

Mathematicians and engineers familiar with the *Simulink* application, developed by *The MathWorks* [2], will notice similarities between the Signal Generator block dialog introduced here and the SigGen Source Block Parameters dialog of *Simulink*. However, here the phase field is introduced and allows the user to set the phase of the source sinusoidal signal: otherwise, the necessary fundamental mathematical properties for signal specification are present. The behavior of the Signal Generator block will be discussed in more detail in Chapter 21.

9.3.8.2   Attach a Class to the Dialog Window

Select the IDD_SIGNALGEN_BLK_DLG resource from the ResourceView tab on the Workspace pane to show the corresponding dialog window in the editor area and right click on the dialog box to invoke the ClassWizard. The Adding a Class message box appears: create a new class with the name CSignalGeneratorBlockDialog and base class CDialog.

9.3.8.3   Attach Variables to the Dialog Window Controls

Open the ClassWizard, select the Member Variables tab, choose the class name to be CSignalGeneratorBlockDialog, select the ID of the control to which a variable should be added, click Add Variable, and specify the details as shown in Table 9.24.

Change the existing CSignalGeneratorBlock placeholder double-typed "amplitude" and "frequency" variables to "m_dAmplitude" and "m_dFrequency", respectively. In addition, replace the "e_signal_form" and "e_units" variables with "m_strFnType" and "m_strUnits", respectively. Now the enumerated types, EUnits and ESignalForm, may be removed from the "Block.h" header file as they are no longer required. Finally add the double "m_dPhase" variable to the CSignalGeneratorBlock class. The variables in the CSignalGeneratorBlock and CSignalGeneratorBlockDialog classes share the same names for convenience.

TABLE 9.23
Signal Generator Block Dialog Window Controls

Object	Property	Setting
Group Box	ID	ID_SIGNALGEN_BLK_DLG_GB_PARAS
	Caption	Signal Generator Function Parameters
Static Text	ID	ID_SIGNALGEN_BLK_DLG_TXT_FN
	Caption	Function Type:
Static Text	ID	ID_SIGNALGEN_BLK_DLG_TXT_AMP
	Caption	Amplitude:
Static Text	ID	ID_SIGNALGEN_BLK_DLG_TXT_FREQ
	Caption	Frequency:
Static Text	ID	ID_SIGNALGEN_BLK_DLG_TXT_PHASE
	Caption	Phase:
Static Text	ID	ID_SIGNALGEN_BLK_DLG_TXT_UNITS
	Caption	Domain Units:
Combo Box	ID	ID_SIGNALGEN_BLK_DLG_CB_FN
	Data	Random
		Sine
		Square
Combo Box	ID	ID_SIGNALGEN_BLK_DLG_CB_UNITS
	Data	Hz
		rad/s
Edit Box	ID	ID_SIGNALGEN_BLK_DLG_EB_AMP
Edit Box	ID	ID_SIGNALGEN_BLK_DLG_EB_FREQ
Edit Box	ID	ID_SIGNALGEN_BLK_DLG_EB_PHASE
Button	ID	ID_SIGNALGEN_BLK_DLG_BTN_OK
	Default button	Unchecked
	Caption	&OK
Button	ID	IDCANCEL
	Caption	&Cancel

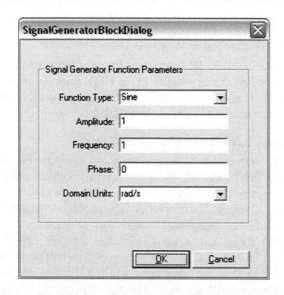

FIGURE 9.11 SignalGeneratorBlockDialog window showing the controls as specified in Table 9.23.

TABLE 9.24

Dialog Window Controls, Variable Name, Category, and Type for the IDD_SIGNALGEN_BLK_DLG Resource

Control	Variable Name	Category	Type
ID_SIGNALGEN_BLK_DLG_CB_FN	m_strFnType	Value	CString
ID_SIGNALGEN_BLK_DLG_EB_AMP	m_dAmplitude	Value	double
ID_SIGNALGEN_BLK_DLG_EB_FREQ	m_dFrequency	Value	double
ID_SIGNALGEN_BLK_DLG_EB_PHASE	m_dPhase	Value	double
ID_SIGNALGEN_BLK_DLG_CB_UNITS	m_strUnits	Value	CString

TABLE 9.25

Objects, IDs, Class, and Event-Handler Functions for the Signal Generator Block Dialog Buttons

Object	ID	Class	COMMAND Event Handler
OK button	ID_SIGNALGEN_BLK_DLG_BTN_OK	CSignalGeneratorBlockDialog	OnSignalGeneratorBlkDlgBtnOk()
Cancel button	IDCANCEL (default)	CDialog	OnCancel()

9.3.8.4 Add Functionality to the Dialog Window Buttons

The two buttons for the IDD_SIGNALGEN_BLK_DLG dialog window are OK and Cancel. Add an event-handler function for the OK button as shown in Table 9.25. Leave the current event-handler function for the Cancel button, since this already calls the `CDialog::OnCancel()` function, so no new code is required. Edit the `OnSignalGeneratorBlkDlgBtnOk()` function as shown in the following.

```
void CSignalGeneratorBlockDialog::OnSignalGeneratorBlkDlgBtnOk()
{
    // TODO: Add your control notification handler code here

    // DiagramEng (start)

    //AfxMessageBox("\n CSignalGeneratorBlockDialog::OnSignalGeneratorBlk
      DlgBtnOk()\n", MB_OK, 0);

    // Update variable values with the Dlg Wnd control values
    UpdateData(TRUE);

    // Close the dialog wnd with OnOK()
    OnOK();

    // DiagramEng (end)
}
```

9.3.8.5 Add Functionality to Initialize Variables

The common member variables of the CSignalGeneratorBlock and CSignalGeneratorBlockDialog classes are "m_strFnType", "m_dAmplitude", "m_dFrequency", "m_dPhase", and "m_strUnits". Initialize these variables in the CSignalGeneratorBlock constructor as shown in the following code.

```
CSignalGeneratorBlock::CSignalGeneratorBlock(CSystemModel
  *pParentSystemModel, CPoint blk_posn, EBlockShape e_blk_shape):
CBlock(pParentSystemModel, blk_posn, e_blk_shape)
```

```
{
    ...
    // Init. member vars.
    m_strFnType = "Sine";
    m_dAmplitude = 1.0;
    m_dFrequency = 1.0;
    m_dPhase = 0.0;
    m_strUnits = "rad/s";
    ...
}
```

9.3.8.6 Add the Overriding `BlockDlgWndParameterInput()` Function

Add a public member function to the CSignalGeneratorBlock class with proto-type, void CSignalGeneratorBlock::BlockDlgWndParameterInput(void), and edit the function as shown in the following code. The header file for the CSignalGeneratorBlockDialog class is required by the CSignalGeneratorBlock function; hence, add #include "SignalGeneratorBlockDialog.h" at the top of the "Block.cpp" source file.

```
void CSignalGeneratorBlock::BlockDlgWndParameterInput()
{
    CString sMsg;          // string to be displayed
    UINT nType = MB_OK;    // style of msg. box
    UINT nIDhelp = 0;      // help context ID for the msg.

    // Create a dialog object. of class CSignalGeneratorBlockDialog :
      public CDialog
    CSignalGeneratorBlockDialog oDlg;

    // Set the dialog class vars using the block class vars
    oDlg.m_strFnType = m_strFnType;
    oDlg.m_dAmplitude = m_dAmplitude;
    oDlg.m_dFrequency = m_dFrequency;
    oDlg.m_dPhase = m_dPhase;
    oDlg.m_strUnits = m_strUnits;

    // Return val of DoModal() fn of ancestor class CDialog is checked to
      determine which btn was clicked.
    if(oDlg.DoModal() == IDOK)
    {
        // Assign CSignalGeneratorBlockDialog variable values to
          CSignalGeneratorBlock variable values.
        m_strFnType = oDlg.m_strFnType;
        m_dAmplitude = oDlg.m_dAmplitude;
        m_dFrequency = oDlg.m_dFrequency;
        m_dPhase = oDlg.m_dPhase;
        m_strUnits = oDlg.m_strUnits;

        // Print msg with variable value.
        sMsg.Format("\n CSignalGeneratorBlock::BlockDlgWndParameterInput(),
          m_strFnType = %s\n", m_strFnType);
        AfxMessageBox(sMsg, nType, nIDhelp);
    }
}
```

9.3.9 SUBSYSTEM BLOCK DIALOG

The following six steps indicate how dialog-window-based functionality is implemented for the Subsystem block and involves two key classes: CSubsystemBlock and CSubsystemBlockDialog.

9.3.9.1 Insert a New Dialog Window and Add Controls

Insert a new dialog resource: set the ID of the dialog to IDD_SUBSYS_BLK_DLG and the caption to SubsystemBlockDialog. Leave the OK and Cancel buttons on the dialog. Add controls as provided in Table 9.26 and place them on the dialog window as shown in Figure 9.12.

9.3.9.2 Attach a Class to the Dialog Window

Select the IDD_SUBSYS_BLK_DLG resource from the ResourceView tab on the Workspace pane to show the corresponding dialog window in the editor area and right click on the dialog box to

TABLE 9.26
Subsystem Block Dialog Window Controls

Object	Property	Setting
Group Box	ID	ID_SUBSYS_BLK_DLG_IN
	Caption	SubsystemIn Parameters
Group Box	ID	ID_SUBSYS_BLK_DLG_OUT
	Caption	SubsystemOut Parameters
Static Text	ID	ID_SUBSYS_BLK_DLG_TXT_INPUT
	Caption	Name of Input Port:
Static Text	ID	ID_SUBSYS_BLK_DLG_TXT_OUTPUT
	Caption	Name of Output Port:
Edit Box	ID	ID_SUBSYS_BLK_DLG_EB_INPUT
Edit Box	ID	ID_SUBSYS_BLK_DLG_EB_OUTPUT
Button	ID	ID_SUBSYS_BLK_DLG_BTN_OK
	Default button	Unchecked
	Caption	&OK
Button	ID	IDCANCEL
	Caption	&Cancel

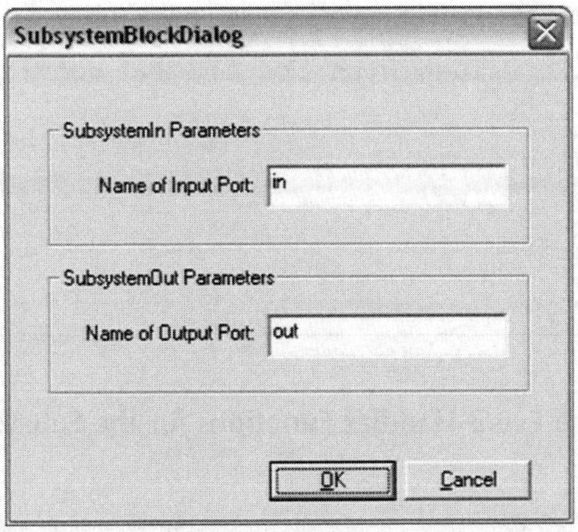

FIGURE 9.12 SubsystemBlockDialog window showing the controls as specified in Table 9.26.

TABLE 9.27

Dialog Window Controls, Variable Name, Category, and Type for the IDD_SUBSYS_BLK_DLG Resource

Control	Variable Name	Category	Type
ID_SUBSYS_BLK_DLG_EB_INPUT	m_strInputPortName	Value	CString
ID_SUBSYS_BLK_DLG_EB_OUTPUT	m_strOutputPortName	Value	CString

invoke the ClassWizard. The Adding a Class message box appears: create a new class with the name CSubsystemBlockDialog and base class CDialog.

9.3.9.3 Attach Variables to the Dialog Window Controls

Open the ClassWizard, select the Member Variables tab, choose the class name to be CSubsystemBlockDialog, select the ID of the control to which a variable should be added, click Add Variable, and specify the details as shown in Table 9.27.

Change the existing CSubsystemBlock character array placeholder variables "port_signal_label_1" and "port_signal_label_2" to CString variables "m_strInputPortName" and "m_strOutputPortName", respectively. In addition, remove the two integer variables "port_number_label_1" and "port_number_label_2". The variables in the CSubsystemBlock and CSubsystemBlockDialog classes share the same names for convenience.

9.3.9.4 Add Functionality to the Dialog Window Buttons

The two buttons for the IDD_SUBSYS_BLK_DLG dialog window are OK and Cancel. Add an event-handler function for the OK button as shown in Table 9.28. Leave the current event-handler function for the Cancel button, since this already calls the `CDialog::OnCancel()` function, so no new code is required. Edit the `OnSubsystemBlkDlgBtnOk()` function as shown in the following.

```
void CSubsystemBlockDialog::OnSubsystemBlkDlgBtnOk()
{
    // TODO: Add your control notification handler code here

    // DiagramEng (start)

    //AfxMessageBox("\n CSubsystemBlockDialog::OnSubsystemBlkDlgBt
      nOk()\n", MB_OK, 0);

    // Update variable values with the Dlg Wnd control values
    UpdateData(TRUE);

    // Close the dialog wnd with OnOK()
    OnOK();

    // DiagramEng (end)
}
```

TABLE 9.28

Objects, IDs, Class, and Event-Handler Functions for the Subsystem Block Dialog Buttons

Object	ID	Class	COMMAND Event Handler
OK button	ID_SUBSYS_BLK_DLG_BTN_OK	CSubsystemBlockDialog	OnSubsystemBlkDlgBtnOk()
Cancel button	IDCANCEL (default)	CDialog	OnCancel()

9.3.9.5   Add Functionality to Initialize Variables

The common member variables of the CSubsystemBlock and CSubsystemBlockDialog classes are: "m_strInputPortName" and "m_strOutputPortName". Initialize these variables in the CSubsystemBlock constructor as shown in the following code.

```
CSubsystemBlock::CSubsystemBlock(CSystemModel *pParentSystemModel, CPoint
  blk_posn, EBlockShape e_blk_shape):
CBlock(pParentSystemModel, blk_posn, e_blk_shape)
{
    ...
    // Assign init values to the CString vars.
    m_strInputPortName = "input port name";
    m_strOutputPortName = "output port name";
    ...
}
```

9.3.9.6   Add the Overriding `BlockDlgWndParameterInput()` Function

Add a public member function to the CSubsystemBlock class with prototype, `void CSubsystemBlock::BlockDlgWndParameterInput(void)`, and edit the function as shown in the following code. The header file for the CSubsystemBlockDialog class is required by the CSubsystemBlock function; hence, add #include "SubsystemBlockDialog.h", at the top of the "Block.cpp" source file.

```
void CSubsystemBlock::BlockDlgWndParameterInput()
{
    CString sMsg;          // string to be displayed
    UINT nType = MB_OK;    // style of msg. box
    UINT nIDhelp = 0;      // help context ID for the msg.

    // Create a dialog object. of class CSubsystemBlockDialog : public
      CDialog
    CSubsystemBlockDialog oDlg;

    // Set the dialog class vars using the block class vars
    oDlg.m_strInputPortName = m_strInputPortName;
    oDlg.m_strOutputPortName = m_strOutputPortName;

    // Return val of DoModal() fn of ancestor class CDialog is checked to
      determine which btn was clicked.
    if(oDlg.DoModal() == IDOK)
    {
        // Assign CSubsystemBlockDialog variable values to
          CSubsystemBlock variable values.
        m_strInputPortName = oDlg.m_strInputPortName;
        m_strOutputPortName = oDlg.m_strOutputPortName;

        // Print msg with variable value.
        sMsg.Format("\n CSubsystemBlock::BlockDlgWndParameterInput(),
          ports: %s, %s\n", m_strInputPortName, m_strOutputPortName);
        AfxMessageBox(sMsg, nType, nIDhelp);
    }
}
```

9.3.10   SUBSYSTEM IN BLOCK DIALOG

The following six steps indicate how dialog-window-based functionality is implemented for the Subsystem In Block and involves two key classes: CSubsystemIn Block and CSubsystemIn BlockDialog.

9.3.10.1   Insert a New Dialog Window and Add Controls

Insert a new dialog resource: set the ID of the dialog to IDD_SUBSYSIN_BLK_DLG and the caption to SubsystemInBlockDialog. Leave the OK and Cancel buttons on the dialog. Add controls as provided in Table 9.29 and place them on the dialog window as shown in Figure 9.13.

9.3.10.2   Attach a Class to the Dialog Window

Select the IDD_SUBSYSIN_BLK_DLG resource from the ResourceView tab on the Workspace pane to show the corresponding dialog window in the editor area and right click on the dialog box to invoke the ClassWizard. The Adding a Class message box appears: create a new class with the name CSubsystemInBlockDialog and base class CDialog.

9.3.10.3   Attach Variables to the Dialog Window Controls

Open the ClassWizard, select the Member Variables tab, choose the class name to be CSubsystemInBlockDialog, select the ID of the control to which a variable should be added, click Add Variable, and specify the details as shown in Table 9.30.

TABLE 9.29

Subsystem In Block Dialog Window Controls

Object	Property	Setting
Static Text	ID	ID_SUBSYSIN_BLK_DLG_TXT_INPUT
	Caption	Name of Input Port:
Edit Box	ID	ID_SUBSYSIN_BLK_DLG_EB_INPUT
Button	ID	ID_SUBSYSIN_BLK_DLG_BTN_OK
	Default button	Unchecked
	Caption	&OK
Button	ID	IDCANCEL
	Caption	&Cancel

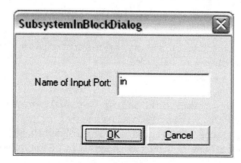

FIGURE 9.13   SubsytemInBlockDialog window showing the controls as specified in Table 9.29.

TABLE 9.30

Dialog Window Controls, Variable Name, Category, and Type for the IDD_SUBSYSIN_BLK_DLG Resource

Control	Variable Name	Category	Type
ID_SUBSYSIN_BLK_DLG_EB_INPUT	m_strInputPortName	Value	CString

TABLE 9.31

Objects, IDs, Class, and Event-Handler Functions for the Subsystem In Block Dialog Buttons

Object	ID	Class	COMMAND Event Handler
OK button	ID_SUBSYSIN_BLK_DLG_BTN_OK	CSubsystemInBlockDialog	OnSubsystemInBlkDlgBtnOk()
Cancel button	IDCANCEL (default)	CDialog	OnCancel()

Modify the CSubsystemInBlock class member variables: remove the integer variable, "port_number_label" and change the existing character array placeholder variable, "port_signal_label", to a CString variable, "m_strInputPortName". The "m_strInputPortName" variable in the CSubsystemInBlock and CSubsystemInBlockDialog classes shares the same name for convenience.

9.3.10.4 Add Functionality to the Dialog Window Buttons

The two buttons for the IDD_SUBSYSIN_BLK_DLG dialog window are OK and Cancel. Add an event-handler function for the OK button as shown in Table 9.31. Leave the current event-handler function for the Cancel button, since this already calls the CDialog::OnCancel() function, so no new code is required. Edit the OnSubsystemInBlkDlgBtnOk() function as shown in the following.

```
void CSubsystemInBlockDialog::OnSubsysInBlkDlgBtnOk()
{
    // TODO: Add your control notification handler code here

    // DiagramEng (start)

    //AfxMessageBox("\n CSubsystemInBlockDialog::OnSubsystemInBlkDlgBtn
      Ok()\n", MB_OK, 0);

    // Update variable values with the Dlg Wnd control values
    UpdateData(TRUE);

    // Close the dialog wnd with OnOK()
    OnOK();

    // DiagramEng (end)
}
```

9.3.10.5 Add Functionality to Initialize Variables

The common member variable of the CSubsystemInBlock and CSubsystemInBlockDialog classes is "m_strInputPortName". Initialize this variable in the CSubsystemInBlock constructor as shown in the following code.

```
CSubsystemInBlock::CSubsystemInBlock(CSystemModel *pParentSystemModel,
  CPoint blk_posn, EBlockShape e_blk_shape):
CBlock(pParentSystemModel, blk_posn, e_blk_shape)
{
    ...
    // Init. the member CString var.
    m_strInputPortName = "input port name";
    ...
}
```

9.3.10.6 Add the Overriding `BlockDlgWndParameterInput()` Function

Add a public member function to the CSubsystemInBlock class, with the prototype, void CSubsystemInBlock::BlockDlgWndParameterInput(void), and edit the function as shown in the following. The header file for the CSubsystemInBlockDialog class is required by the CSubsystemInBlock function; hence, add #include "SubsystemInBlockDialog.h", at the top of the "Block.cpp" source file.

```
void CSubsystemInBlock::BlockDlgWndParameterInput()
{
    CString sMsg;           // string to be displayed
    UINT nType = MB_OK;     // style of msg. box
    UINT nIDhelp = 0;       // help context ID for the msg.

    // Create a dialog object. of class CSubsystemInBlockDialog : public
      CDialog
    CSubsystemInBlockDialog oDlg;

    // Set the dialog class var using the block class var
    oDlg.m_strInputPortName = m_strInputPortName;

    // Return val of DoModal() fn of ancestor class CDialog is checked to
      determine which btn was clicked.
    if(oDlg.DoModal() == IDOK)
    {
        // Assign CSubsystemInBlockDialog variable values to
          CSubsystemInBlock variable values.
        m_strInputPortName = oDlg.m_strInputPortName;

        // Print msg with variable value.
        sMsg.Format("\n CSubsystemInBlock::BlockDlgWndParameterInput(),
          port: %s\n", m_strInputPortName);
        AfxMessageBox(sMsg, nType, nIDhelp);
    }
}
```

9.3.11 SUBSYSTEM OUT BLOCK DIALOG

The following six steps indicate how dialog-window-based functionality is implemented for the Subsystem Out block and involves two key classes: CSubsystemOutBlock and CSubsystemOutBlockDialog.

9.3.11.1 Insert a New Dialog Window and Add Controls

Insert a new dialog resource: set the ID of the dialog to IDD_SUBSYSOUT_BLK_DLG and the caption to SubsystemOutBlockDialog. Leave the OK and Cancel buttons on the dialog. Add controls as provided in Table 9.32 and place them on the dialog window as shown in Figure 9.14.

9.3.11.2 Attach a Class to the Dialog Window

Select the IDD_SUBSYSOUT_BLK_DLG resource from the ResourceView tab on the Workspace pane to show the corresponding dialog window in the editor area and right click on the dialog box to invoke the ClassWizard. The Adding a Class message box appears: create a new class with the name CSubsystemOutBlockDialog and base class CDialog.

TABLE 9.32

Subsystem Out Block Dialog Window Controls

Object	Property	Setting
Static Text	ID	ID_SUBSYSOUT_BLK_DLG_TXT_OUTPUT
	Caption	Name of Output Port:
Edit Box	ID	ID_SUBSYSOUT_BLK_DLG_EB_OUTPUT
Button	ID	ID_SUBSYSOUT_BLK_DLG_BTN_OK
	Default button	Unchecked
	Caption	&OK
Button	ID	IDCANCEL
	Caption	&Cancel

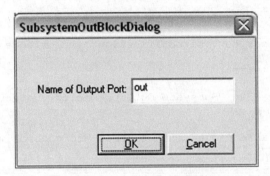

FIGURE 9.14 SubsytemOutBlockDialog window showing the controls as specified in Table 9.32.

TABLE 9.33

Dialog Window Controls, Variable Name, Category, and Type for the IDD_SUBSYSOUT_BLK_DLG Resource

Control	Variable Name	Category	Type
ID_SUBSYSOUT_BLK_DLG_EB_OUTPUT	m_strOutputPortName	Value	CString

9.3.11.3 Attach Variables to the Dialog Window Controls

Open the ClassWizard, select the Member Variables tab, choose the class name to be CSubsystemOutBlockDialog, select the ID of the control to which a variable should be added, click Add Variable, and specify the details as shown in Table 9.33.

Modify the CSubsystemOutBlock class member variables: remove the integer variable, "port_number_label", and change the existing character array placeholder variable, "port_signal_label", to a CString variable, "m_strOutputPortName". The variable in the CSubsystemOutBlock and CSubsystemOutBlockDialog classes share the same names for convenience.

9.3.11.4 Add Functionality to the Dialog Window Buttons

The two buttons for the IDD_SUBSYSOUT_BLK_DLG dialog window are OK and Cancel. Add an event-handler function for the OK button as shown in Table 9.34. Leave the current event-handler function for the Cancel button, since this already calls the CDialog::OnCancel() function,

TABLE 9.34

Objects, IDs, Class, and Event-Handler Functions for the Subsystem Out Block Dialog Buttons

Object	ID	Class	COMMAND Event Handler
OK button	ID_SUBSYSOUT_BLK_DLG_BTN_OK	CSubsystemOutBlockDialog	OnSubsystemOutBlkDlgBtnOk()
Cancel button	IDCANCEL (default)	CDialog	OnCancel()

so no new code is required. Edit the `OnSubsystemOutBlkDlgBtnOk()` function as shown in the following.

```
void CSubsystemOutBlockDialog::OnSubsysOutBlkDlgBtnOk()
{
    // TODO: Add your control notification handler code here

    // DiagramEng (start)

    //AfxMessageBox("\n CSubsystemOutBlockDialog::OnSubsystemOutBlkDlgBtn
      Ok()\n", MB_OK, 0);

    // Update variable values with the Dlg Wnd control values
    UpdateData(TRUE);

    // Close the dialog wnd with OnOK()
    OnOK();

    // DiagramEng (end)
}
```

9.3.11.5 Add Functionality to Initialize Variables

The common member variable of the CSubsystemOutBlock and CSubsystemOutBlockDialog classes is "m_strOutputPortName". Initialize this variable in the CSubsystemOutBlock constructor as shown in the following code.

```
CSubsystemOutBlock::CSubsystemOutBlock(CSystemModel *pParentSystemModel,
  CPoint blk_posn, EBlockShape e_blk_shape):
CBlock(pParentSystemModel, blk_posn, e_blk_shape)
{
    ...
    // Init. the member CString var.
    m_strOutputPortName = "output port name";
    ...
}
```

9.3.11.6 Add the Overriding `BlockDlgWndParameterInput()` Function

Add a public member function to the CSubsystemOutBlock class with prototype, `void CSubsystemOutBlock::BlockDlgWndParameterInput(void)`, and edit the function as shown in the following code. The header file for the CSubsystemOutBlockDialog class is required by the CSubsystemOutBlock function; hence, add #include "SubsystemOutBlockDialog.h", at the top of the "Block.cpp" source file.

```
void CSubsystemOutBlock::BlockDlgWndParameterInput()
{
    CString sMsg;           // string to be displayed
    UINT nType = MB_OK;     // style of msg. box
    UINT nIDhelp = 0;       // help context ID for the msg.

    // Create a dialog object. of class CSubsystemOutBlockDialog : public
      CDialog
    CSubsystemOutBlockDialog oDlg;

    // Set the dialog class var using the block class var
    oDlg.m_strOutputPortName = m_strOutputPortName;

    // Return val of DoModal() fn of ancestor class CDialog is checked to
      determine which btn was clicked.
    if(oDlg.DoModal() == IDOK)
    {
        // Assign CSubsystemOutBlockDialog variable values to
          CSubsystemOutBlock variable values.
        m_strOutputPortName = oDlg.m_strOutputPortName;

        // Print msg with variable value.
        sMsg.Format("\n CSubsystemOutBlock::BlockDlgWndParameterInput(),
          port: %s\n", m_strOutputPortName);
        AfxMessageBox(sMsg, nType, nIDhelp);
    }
}
```

9.3.11.7 Synchronizing the Subsystem-Related Block Values

The three subsystem-related blocks are Subsystem, Subsystem In, and Subsystem Out, where the latter two blocks' dialog windows display the CString variables, "m_strInputPortName" and "m_strOutputPortName", respectively: both of these variables should also be reflected on the Subsystem block dialog window. This can only happen if a Subsystem block contains the Subsystem In and Subsystem Out blocks. At present this containment relationship has not been implemented, but in future when this is done, it will be possible to make changes to the input parameters of the subsystem blocks, and for these changes to be updated for the blocks concerned.

9.3.12 SUM BLOCK DIALOG

The following six steps indicate how dialog-window-based functionality is implemented for the Sum block and involves two key classes: CSumBlock and CSumBlockDialog.

9.3.12.1 Insert a New Dialog Window and Add Controls

Insert a new dialog resource: set the ID of the dialog to IDD_SUM_BLK_DLG and the caption to SumBlockDialog. Leave the OK and Cancel buttons on the dialog. Add controls as provided in Table 9.35 and place them on the dialog window as shown in Figure 9.15.

9.3.12.2 Attach a Class to the Dialog Window

Select the IDD_SUM_BLK_DLG resource from the ResourceView tab on the Workspace pane to show the corresponding dialog window in the editor area and right click on the dialog box to invoke the ClassWizard. The Adding a Class message box appears: create a new class with the name CSumBlockDialog and base class CDialog.

TABLE 9.35
Sum Block Dialog Window Controls

Object	Property	Setting
Static Text	ID	ID_SUM_BLK_DLG_TXT_NPLUS
	Caption	Number of addition inputs:
Edit Box	ID	ID_SUM_BLK_DLG_EB_NPLUS
Static Text	ID	ID_SUM_BLK_DLG_TXT_NMINUS
	Caption	Number of subtraction inputs:
Edit Box	ID	ID_SUM_BLK_DLG_EB_NMINUS
Button	ID	ID_SUM_BLK_DLG_BTN_OK
	Default button	Unchecked
	Caption	&OK
Button	ID	IDCANCEL
	Caption	&Cancel

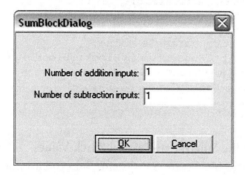

FIGURE 9.15   SumBlockDialog window showing the controls as specified in Table 9.35.

9.3.12.3   Attach Variables to the Dialog Window Controls

Open the ClassWizard, select the Member Variables tab, choose the class name to be CSumBlockDialog, select the ID of the control to which a variable should be added, click Add Variable, and specify the details as shown in Table 9.36.

Modify the CSumBlock class member variables: change the existing integer placeholder variables, "no_of_plus_inputs" and "no_of_minus_inputs", to "m_iNAddInputs" and "m_iNSubtractInputs", respectively. The variables in the CSumBlock and CSumBlockDialog classes share the same names for convenience.

9.3.12.4   Add Functionality to the Dialog Window Buttons

The two buttons for the IDD_SUM_BLK_DLG dialog window are OK and Cancel. Add an event-handler function for the OK button as shown in Table 9.37. Leave the current event-handler

TABLE 9.36
Dialog Window Controls, Variable Name, Category, and Type for the IDD_SUM_BLK_DLG Resource

Control	Variable Name	Category	Type	Min Value	Max Value
ID_SUM_BLK_DLG_EB_NPLUS	m_iNAddInputs	Value	int	0	1000
ID_SUM_BLK_DLG_EB_NMINUS	m_iNSubtractInputs	Value	int	0	1000

TABLE 9.37

Objects, IDs, Class, and Event-Handler Functions for the Sum Block Dialog Buttons

Object	ID	Class	COMMAND Event Handler
OK button	ID_SUM_BLK_DLG_BTN_OK	CSumBlockDialog	OnSumBlkDlgBtnOk()
Cancel button	IDCANCEL (default)	CDialog	OnCancel()

function for the Cancel button, since this already calls the CDialog::OnCancel() function, so no new code is required. Edit the OnSumBlkDlgBtnOk() function as shown in the following.

```
void CSumBlockDialog::OnSumBlkDlgBtnOk()
{
    // TODO: Add your control notification handler code here

    // DiagramEng (start)

    //AfxMessageBox("\n CSumBlockDialog::OnSumBlkDlgBtnOk()\n", MB_OK, 0);

    // Update variable values with the Dlg Wnd control values
    UpdateData(TRUE);

    // Close the dialog wnd with OnOK()
    OnOK();

    // DiagramEng (end)
}
```

9.3.12.5 Add Functionality to Initialize Variables

The common member variables of the CSumBlock and CSumBlockDialog classes are "m_iNAddInputs" and "m_iNSubtractInputs". Initialize these variables in the CSumBlock constructor as shown in the following code.

```
CSumBlock::CSumBlock(CSystemModel *pParentSystemModel, CPoint blk_posn,
    EBlockShape e_blk_shape) :
CBlock(pParentSystemModel, blk_posn, e_blk_shape)
{
    ...
    // Init. the integer vars.
    m_iNAddInputs = 1;
    m_iNSubtractInputs = 1;
    ...
}
```

9.3.12.6 Add the Overriding `BlockDlgWndParameterInput()` Function

Add a public member function to the CSumBlock class with prototype, void CSumBlock:: BlockDlgWndParameterInput(void), and edit the function as shown in the following code. The header file for the CSumBlockDialog class is required by the CSumBlock function; hence, add #include "SumBlockDialog.h", at the top of the "Block.cpp" source file.

```
void CSumBlock::BlockDlgWndParameterInput()
{
    int n_inputs = 0;        // number of input ports
    CString sMsg;            // string to be displayed
    CString sMsgTemp;        // temp string msg.
    UINT nType = MB_OK;      // style of msg. box
    UINT nIDhelp = 0;        // help context ID for the msg.

    // Create a dialog object. of class CSumBlockDialog : public CDialog
    CSumBlockDialog oDlg;

    // Set the dialog class var using the block class var
    oDlg.m_iNAddInputs = m_iNAddInputs;
    oDlg.m_iNSubtractInputs = m_iNSubtractInputs;

    // While less than two input ports get user input
    while(n_inputs < 2)
    {
        // Return val of DoModal() fn of ancestor class CDialog is
          checked to determine which btn was clicked.
        if(oDlg.DoModal() == IDOK)
        {
            // Assign CSumBlockDialog variable values to CSumBlock
              variable values.
            m_iNAddInputs = oDlg.m_iNAddInputs;
            m_iNSubtractInputs = oDlg.m_iNSubtractInputs;

            // Print msg with variable value.
            //sMsg.Format("\n CSumBlock::BlockDlgWndParameterInput(),
              m_iNAddInputs = %d, m_iNSubractInputs = %d\n",
              m_iNAddInputs, m_iNSubtractInputs);
            //AfxMessageBox(sMsg, nType, nIDhelp);
        }

        // Check input for correctness and warn user if approp.
        n_inputs = m_iNAddInputs + m_iNSubtractInputs;

        if(n_inputs < 2)
        {
            sMsgTemp.Format("\n CSumBlock::BlockDlgWndParameter
              Input()\n");
            sMsg += sMsgTemp;
            sMsgTemp.Format(" No. of input ports = %d\n", n_inputs);
            sMsg += sMsgTemp;
            sMsgTemp.Format(" Two or more input ports are required!\n");
            sMsg += sMsgTemp;
            AfxMessageBox(sMsg, nType, nIDhelp);
            sMsg.Format("");    // reset the msg since within a while loop
        }
    }
}
```

9.3.13   TRANSFER FUNCTION BLOCK DIALOG

The following six steps indicate how dialog-window-based functionality is implemented for the Transfer Function block and involves two key classes: CTransferFnBlock and CTransferFnBlockDialog.

9.3.13.1 Insert a New Dialog Window and Add Controls

Insert a new dialog resource: set the ID of the dialog to IDD_TRANSFERFN_BLK_DLG and the caption to TransferFnBlockDialog. Leave the OK and Cancel buttons on the dialog. Add controls as provided in Table 9.38 and place them on the dialog window as shown in Figure 9.16.

The developer will notice that the numerator and denominator coefficients are to be specified in decreasing powers of s, where $s = \sigma + j\omega$ is a complex variable used in the expression of the Laplace transform, $L[f(t)] = F(s) = B(s)/A(s)$, of a time-dependent function, $f(t)$, where $B(s)$ and $A(s)$ are polynomials in s [3]. The interested reader should consult the work of Ogata [3], Chapter 2, The Laplace Transform, for examples concerning finding the partial-fraction expansion and zeros, poles, and gain of $B(s)/A(s)$ using MATLAB® [4].

9.3.13.2 Attach a Class to the Dialog Window

Select the IDD_TRANSFERFN_BLK_DLG resource from the ResourceView tab on the Workspace pane to show the corresponding dialog window in the editor area and right click on the dialog box to invoke the ClassWizard. The Adding a Class message box appears: create a new class with the name CTransferFnBlockDialog and base class CDialog.

TABLE 9.38
Transfer Function Block Dialog Window Controls

Object	Property	Setting
Static Text	ID	ID_TRANSFERFN_BLK_DLG_TXT_NUMER
	Caption	Numerator coefficients (in decreasing powers of s):
Edit Box	ID	ID_TRANSFERFN_BLK_DLG_EB_NUMER
Static Text	ID	ID_TRANSFERFN_BLK_DLG_TXT_DENOM
	Caption	Denominator coefficients (in decreasing powers of s):
Edit Box	ID	ID_TRANSFERFN_BLK_DLG_EB_DENOM
Button	ID	ID_TRANSFERFN_BLK_DLG_BTN_OK
	Default button	Unchecked
	Caption	&OK
Button	ID	IDCANCEL
	Caption	&Cancel

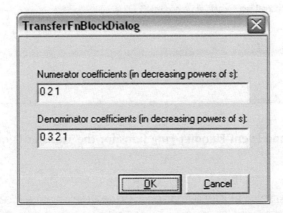

FIGURE 9.16 TransferFnBlockDialog window showing the controls as specified in Table 9.38.

TABLE 9.39

Dialog Window Controls, Variable Name, Category, and Type for the IDD_TRANSFERFN_BLK_DLG Resource

Control	Variable Name	Category	Type
ID_TRANSFERFN_BLK_DLG_EB_NUMER	m_strNumerCoeffs	Value	CString
ID_TRANSFERFN_BLK_DLG_EB_DENOM	m_strDenomCoeffs	Value	CString

9.3.13.3   Attach Variables to the Dialog Window Controls

Open the ClassWizard, select the Member Variables tab, choose the class name to be CTransferFnBlockDialog, select the ID of the control to which a variable should be added, click Add Variable, and specify the details as shown in Table 9.39.

Add two new CString variables to the CTransferFnBlock class: "m_strNumerCoeffs" and "m_strDenomCoeffs" to hold the numerator and denominator coefficients, respectively. The existing, "numer_coeffs_vec" and "denom_coeffs_vec", pointer-to-double variables may be retained since they may be used later. The variables in the CTransferFnBlock and CTransferFnBlockDialog classes share the same names for convenience.

9.3.13.4   Add Functionality to the Dialog Window Buttons

The two buttons for the IDD_TRANSFERFN_BLK_DLG dialog window are OK and Cancel. Add an event-handler function for the OK button as shown in Table 9.40. Leave the current event-handler function for the Cancel button, since this already calls the CDialog::OnCancel() function, so no new code is required. Edit the OnTransferFnBlkDlgBtnOk() function as shown in the following.

```
void CTransferFnBlockDialog::OnTransferFnBlkDlgBtnOk()
{
    // TODO: Add your control notification handler code here

    // DiagramEng (start)

    //AfxMessageBox("\n CTransferFnBlockDialog::OnTransferFnBlkDlgBtn
      Ok()\n", MB_OK, 0);

    // Update variable values with the Dlg Wnd control values
    UpdateData(TRUE);

    // Close the dialog wnd with OnOK()
    OnOK();

    // DiagramEng (end)
}
```

TABLE 9.40

Objects, IDs, Class, and Event-Handler Functions for the Transfer Function Block Dialog Buttons

Object	ID	Class	COMMAND Event Handler
OK button	ID_TRANSFERFN_BLK_DLG_BTN_OK	CTransferFnBlockDialog	OnTransferFnBlkDlgBtnOk()
Cancel button	IDCANCEL (default)	CDialog	OnCancel()

9.3.13.5   Add Functionality to Initialize Variables

The common member variables of the CTransferFnBlock and CTransferFnBlockDialog classes are "m_strNumerCoeffs" and "m_strDenomCoeffs". Initialize these variables in the CTransferFnBlock constructor as shown in the following code.

```
CTransferFnBlock::CTransferFnBlock(CSystemModel *pParentSystemModel,
  CPoint blk_posn, EBlockShape e_blk_shape):
CBlock(pParentSystemModel, blk_posn, e_blk_shape)
{
    ...
    // Init. the CString member vars.
    m_strNumerCoeffs = "0 2 1";
    m_strDenomCoeffs = "0 3 2 1";
    ...
}
```

9.3.13.6   Add the Overriding `BlockDlgWndParameterInput()` Function

Add a public member function to the CTransferFnBlock class with prototype, void CTransferFnBlock::BlockDlgWndParameterInput(void), and edit the function as shown in the following code. The header file for the CTransferFnBlockDialog class is required by the CTransferFnBlock function; hence, add #include "TransferFnBlockDialog.h", at the top of the "Block.cpp" source file.

```
void CTransferFnBlock::BlockDlgWndParameterInput()
{
    CString sMsg;        // string to be displayed
    UINT nType = MB_OK; // style of msg. box
    UINT nIDhelp = 0;    // help context ID for the msg.

    // Create a dialog object. of class CTransferFnBlockDialog : public
      CDialog
    CTransferFnBlockDialog oDlg;

    // Set the dialog class vars using the block class vars
    oDlg.m_strNumerCoeffs = m_strNumerCoeffs;
    oDlg.m_strDenomCoeffs = m_strDenomCoeffs;

    // Return val of DoModal() fn of ancestor class CDialog is checked to
      determine which btn was clicked.
    if(oDlg.DoModal() == IDOK)
    {
        // Assign CTransferFnBlockDialog variable values to
          CTransferFnBlock variable values.
        m_strNumerCoeffs = oDlg.m_strNumerCoeffs;
        m_strDenomCoeffs = oDlg.m_strDenomCoeffs;

        // Print msg with variable value.
        sMsg.Format("\n CTransferFnBlock::BlockDlgWndParameterInput(),
          m_strNumerCoeffs = %s, m_strDenomCoeffs = %s\n",
          m_strNumerCoeffs, m_strDenomCoeffs);
        AfxMessageBox(sMsg, nType, nIDhelp);
    }
}
```

9.4 SUMMARY

Blocks placed on the palette can be double-clicked in order to generate a dialog window to allow the user to enter block-based parameters. A function titled `CDiagramEngView:: OnLButtonDblClk()` is added to process double-left-click events and this calls a `CDiagramEngDoc::DoubleLeftClickBlock()` method which in turn calls a CBlock-derived `BlockDlgWndParameterInput()` function for the clicked block to accept block parameter input. To add dialog window based functionality, six key steps are required: (1) insert a new dialog window and add controls, (2) attach a class to the dialog window, (3) attach variables to the dialog window controls, (4) add functionality to the dialog window buttons, (5) add functionality to initialize the variables, and (6) add the overriding `BlockDlgWndParameterInput()` function to the derived block class.

REFERENCES

1. Microsoft Developer Network Library Visual Studio 6.0, Microsoft® Visual Studio™ 6.0 Development System, Microsoft Corporation, 1998.
2. Simulink® 6, Using Simulink, MATLAB® SIMULINK®, The MathWorks Inc., Natick, MA, 2007.
3. Ogata, K., *Modern Control Engineering*, 4th edn., Prentice Hall, Upper Saddle River, NJ, 2002.
4. MATLAB®, The MathWorks Inc., Natick, MA, 2007.

10 Conversion of String Input to Double Data

10.1 INTRODUCTION

The Constant, Gain, Integrator, and Transfer Function blocks all require user input of numerical values, for the constant (scalar, vector, or matrix), gain multiplier (scalar, vector, or matrix), initial condition vector, and numerator and denominator coefficient vectors, respectively. The user input is entered via the block dialog windows and is processed by the class' `BlockDlgWndParameterInput()` function described in the previous chapter. At present, the numerical input is read in as a CString value from the dialog window and stored in the associated block class' CString data member. For example, the initial condition vector is recorded in the CString variable, "m_strICVector", of the CIntegratorBlockDialog and CIntegratorBlock classes. This CString value now needs to be converted to the equivalent numerical (double) representation and stored in the block class.

10.2 CONVERSION OF CString INPUT STRINGS TO DOUBLE MEMBER DATA

The user may enter data via the block-based dialog windows to represent scalar values, vectors, or matrices, using a space (" ") or a comma (",") to denote a separation between values and a semicolon (";") to denote the end of a row. For example, a row vector may be entered in any of the following forms, "[1.01 2.02 3.03]", "[1, 2, 3]", or "1 2 3", and a column vector as follows, "[1; 2; 3]". In addition, a matrix may be entered in any of the following forms: "[1.0 2.0 3.0; 4.01 5.05 6.06; 7 8 9]", "[1, 2, 3; 4, 5, 6; .7, .8, 0.9]", or "1 2 3; 4 5 6; 7 8 9". Furthermore, if the user enters erroneous input, for example, a matrix with an inconsistent number of rows and columns, "[1 2 3; 4 5]", then the software should detect and report the problem to the user to correct the input. Finally, nonessential, nonnumeric characters preceding and trailing the string are to be automatically stripped from the input. This approach allows the user significant freedom and flexibility in entering data via the dialog windows but does require additional features in the software to accommodate for this input.

Initial experiments on the conversion of a CString string value to the corresponding double value were performed using a Win32 Console Application titled StringToDouble: the function-call tree, representing the flow of execution, is shown in Table 10.1.

The starting CString is initialized in `PrepareStringToDouble()` and then passed to `ConvertStringToDouble()` to be converted from a CString value into a matrix of double values. This is performed by converting the CString into a pointer-to-char and stripping the string of unwanted leading and trailing characters (`StripInputString()`). Thereafter, the (double) data dimensions, i.e., the number of rows ("nrows") and columns ("ncols"), are determined using either `DetermineDataDimsByStrpbrk()` or `DetermineDataDimsByStrtok()`, which makes predominant use of the `strpbrk()` and `strtok()` functions, respectively (see Table 10.2). A string matrix is used to record the rows of input data, whose size is set using the number of rows ("nrows") and the maximum row (string) length. The `atof()` "ASCII to floating number" function is used to convert the string values into double values, which are then stored in a double matrix and passed back to the calling environment by `ConvertStringMatrixToDoubleMatrix()`.

In the current DiagramEng project, a similar process is required: the CString class member variable used to record user input is required to be converted into its corresponding double-valued matrix or vector. However, as the converted matrix has memory allocated for it within the

TABLE 10.1

Function-Call Tree of the StringToDouble Application Showing Functions Used in Converting a CString to Double Values

Level 0	Level 1	Level 2	Level 3
main()			
	PrepareStringToDouble()		
		ConvertStringToDouble()	
			StripInputString()
			DetermineDataDimsByStrpbrk()
			DetermineDataDimsByStrtok()
			ConvertStringMatrixToDoubleMatrix()

TABLE 10.2

Common String Handling/Conversion Functions

String Function	Description
double atof(const char *s)	ASCII to floating number conversion: the string "s" is converted to a double value
char *strcpy(char *s1, const char *s2)	The string "s2" is copied into string "s1" including the "\0" terminator, given sufficient space in "s1"
size_t strlen(const char *s)	The length of string "s", not including the "\0" terminator, is returned
char *strncpy(char *s1, const char *s2, size_t n)	The first "n" characters from "s2" are copied into "s1". If strlen(s2) $\geq n$, then no "\0" terminator will be written in "s1"
char *strpbrk(const char *s1, const char *s2)	The address of the first character in "s1" that matches the character(s) in "s2" is returned; otherwise, NULL is returned
char *strtok(char *s1, const char *s2)	The address of a character group or token in "s1" separated by separators in "s2" is returned. The first separator is overwritten with a NULL character. Further calls with "s1" = NULL return the address of the next separated character group or token

Source: Kelley, A. and Pohl, I., *A Book On C: Programming in C*, 2nd edn., Benjamin Cummings, Redwood City, CA, 1990.

`ConvertStringMatrixToDoubleMatrix()` function, the matrix dimensions, in particular, the number of rows, are required for memory deallocation purposes in the destructor. Hence, new integer member variables need to be added to the CConstantBlock and CGainBlock classes to retain the size of their two-dimensional double datatype, as indicated in the instructions that follow. The CIntegratorBlock and CTransferFnBlock classes use one-dimensional double vectors but still require the addition of integer member variables, although memory management is somewhat easier.

Various string handling functions are used in the code excerpts that follow, to convert strings of type CString, to double data. A brief explanation of the common string handling functions used is made here for clarity: this material follows closely the work of Kelley and Pohl [1].

The following general steps are required to add functionality to the DiagramEng project to allow the conversion of CString input to double member data:

1. Add a global `ConvertStringToDouble()` function.
2. Add a global `StripInputString()` function.

3. Add a global `DetermineDataDimsByStrpbrk()` or `DetermineDataDimsBy Strtok()` function.
4. Add a global `ConvertStringMatrixToDoubleMatrix()` function.
5. Add global diagnostic printing functions.

10.2.1 ADD A GLOBAL `ConvertStringToDouble()` FUNCTION

Add a new global function to the "DiagramEngDoc.cpp" source file, with the following proto-type: `double **ConvertStringToDouble(CString string, int &nrows, int &ncols)`. Place the declaration in the "DiagramEngDoc.h" header file under the "Global Functions" section (where the function `GetDocumentGlobalFn()` may be found) as shown in the following.

```
// DiagramEngDoc.h : interface of the CDiagramEngDoc class
//
/////////////////////////////////////////////////////////////////////

#if !defined(AFX_DIAGRAMENGDOC_H__9DA8C218_5A85_4AB4_B77B_A9F8FF828990__
  INCLUDED_)
#define AFX_DIAGRAMENGDOC_H__9DA8C218_5A85_4AB4_B77B_A9F8FF828990__
  INCLUDED_

#include "SystemModel.h"   // Added by ClassView
#if _MSC_VER > 1000
#pragma once
#endif // _MSC_VER > 1000
…
// Global Functions
CDiagramEngDoc* GetDocumentGlobalFn(void);
double **ConvertStringToDouble(CString string, int &nrows, int &ncols);
char *StripInputString(char *input_str);
int DetermineDataDimsByStrpbrk(char *in_str, int &nrows, int &ncols,
  int &max_row_length);
int DetermineDataDimsByStrtok(char *in_str, int &nrows, int &ncols,
  int &max_row_length);
double **ConvertStringMatrixToDoubleMatrix(char **str_matrix, int nrows,
  int ncols);
int PrintMatrix(double **M, int nrows, int ncols);
int PrintMatrix(int **M, int nrows, int ncols);
int PrintVector(double *v, int ncols);
int PrintVector(int *v, int ncols);

/////////////////////////////////////////////////////////////////////

//{{AFX_INSERT_LOCATION}}
// Microsoft Visual C++ will insert additional declarations immediately
  before the previous line.
#endif // !defined(AFX_DIAGRAMENGDOC_H__9DA8C218_5A85_4AB4_B77B_
  A9F8FF828990__INCLUDED_)
```

Edit the `ConvertStringToDouble()` function as shown in the following to perform the key actions described previously: the various functions called herein are introduced in the sections that follow.

```
double **ConvertStringToDouble(CString string, int &nrows, int &ncols)
{
    int i;                          // row i
    int cnt = 0;                    // counter used
```

```
int dim_flag = 0;                    // flag to control determining of
  data dims: (0) strpbrk(), (1) strtok()
int max_row_length = 0;              // max row length
int str_length = 0;                  // length of input string
int valid = 0;                       // validity of consistency of number
  of cols.
char *ptr_char = NULL;               // ptr-to-char holds base address of
  first char of a poss gp. of chars.
char *input_str = NULL;              // input string declared as an array
  of chars
char **str_matrix = NULL;            // str matrix of size nrows, no. of
  rows, by str_length no. of char. cols
char *stripped_str = NULL;           // input_str after preceding and
  trailing unwanted chars removed
char *stripped_str_copy = NULL;      // copy of stripped string
double **d_matrix = NULL;            // double matrix

// GET THE INITIAL LENGTH OF THE STRING using the GetLength() member
  function
// WARNING! THIS DOES NOT INCLUDE THE NULL TERMINATOR: HENCE ADD ONE
  TO THE LENGTH (see below).
str_length = string.GetLength();

// -- MEMORY ALLOC
input_str = new char[str_length+1]; // add one to the str_length to
  cater for the null terminator.

// CONVERT the original CString into a CHAR ARRAY typecasting CString
  to a long pointer-to-constant character string.
strcpy(input_str, LPCTSTR(string));

// STRIP UNNEC CHARS FROM STRING
stripped_str = StripInputString(input_str);  // memory for stripped
  str allocated within StripInputString()

if(stripped_str == NULL)
{
    delete [] input_str;            // delete the input_str that had
      memory just allocated to it
    return NULL;
}

// -- MEMORY ALLOC (Delete memory for stripped_str along with
  stripped_str_copy.)
stripped_str_copy = new char[strlen(stripped_str)+1];  // add one to
  the str_length to cater for the null terminator.

// DETERMINE INPUT DATA DIMENSIONS
// Need to copy the stripped string since strtok() is called inside
  DetermineInputDataDimensions() and this modifies
// the input string: hence pass in stripped_str_copy instead of
  stripped_str.
strcpy(stripped_str_copy, stripped_str);
if(dim_flag == 0)
{
    valid = DetermineDataDimsByStrpbrk(stripped_str_copy, nrows,
      ncols, max_row_length);
}
else
```

```
{
    valid = DetermineDataDimsByStrtok(stripped_str_copy, nrows,
      ncols, max_row_length);
}

// -- BUILD THE STRING MATRIX
// -- MEMORY ALLOC
str_matrix = new char *[nrows];      // input string matrix
for(i=0; i<nrows; i++)
{
    str_matrix[i] = new char[max_row_length + 1];  // allocate an
      array of chars, return & to str_Matrix[i]
}

// Get the first TOKEN/SET-OF-CHARS/ROW-OF-DATA of stripped_str,
  up until the first delimiter/SEPARATOR ";"
// The address of the first character of the token is returned.
// The character immediately following the token is overwritten
  with the NULL character.
ptr_char = strtok(stripped_str, ";");

// Record the rows
while(ptr_char != NULL)      // while not at the end of the original
  string (denoted by NULL)
{
    strcpy(str_matrix[cnt], ptr_char);

    // -- GET THE NEXT TOKEN/SET-OF-CHARS/ROW-OF-DATA
    // NOTE! - "Subsequent calls with the first string = NULL,
      return the base address of a string supplied
    // by the system that contains the NEXT token." [Kelley & Pohl]
    // Hence, find the next set of chars from the prev end pt (NULL)
      as a result of using strtok(),
    // to the next delimiter ";", i.e. get the next row of
      characters, where the base address of the first char,
    // is returned to ptr_char.
    ptr_char = strtok(NULL, ";");

    cnt++;             // increment the row cnt.
}

// EXTRACT THE STRING DATA OUT OF THE STRING MATRIX AND CONVERT IT TO
  A DOUBLE MATRIX
if(valid == 0)      // inconsistent no. of cols per row
{
    nrows = 0;
    ncols = 0;
    d_matrix = NULL;
}
else if(valid == 1) // consistent no. of cols per row
{
    d_matrix = ConvertStringMatrixToDoubleMatrix(str_matrix, nrows,
      ncols);
}

// MEMORY DELETE
// Note: memory for stripped_str is only allocated when return value
  of StripInputString() is not NULL.
delete [] input_str; // original input str
```

```
delete [] stripped_str;           // stripped_str memory allocated in
   StripInputString()
delete [] stripped_str_copy;      // copy of stripped string

for(i=0; i<nrows; i++)
{
    delete [] str_matrix[i];
}
delete [] str_matrix;

return d_matrix;
}
```

The `ConvertStringToDouble()` function initially typecasts the CString variable into a character array and then copies it into the input string variable, "input_str", of type pointer-to-char. Then the input string is stripped of potentially unnecessary user-entered characters at the front or back of the string. The stripped string is then copied before being passed into the `DetermineDataDimsByStrpbrk()` or `DetermineDataDimsByStrtok()` functions, since both make use of a `strtok()` call that alters the input string argument. The number of rows and columns of data, including whether the data is valid, and the maximum row length are returned by the latter functions before memory is allocated for a string matrix, "str_matrix", to hold the rows of string input data. A `strtok()` call is used to extract the rows of string data separated by a semicolon (";"), and these are stored in the "str_matrix". Finally, if there is a consistent number of columns for each row of data (valid = 1), `ConvertStringMatrixToDoubleMatrix()` is called to convert the two-dimensional matrix of pointers-to-char to a two-dimensional matrix of pointers-to-double; otherwise, (valid = 0) "d_matrix" is set to NULL, and the number of rows and columns is set to zero.

10.2.2 ADD A GLOBAL `StripInputString()` FUNCTION

Add a global function to the "DiagramEngDoc.cpp" source file with the following prototype: `char *StripInputString(char *input_str)`. Place the declaration in the "DiagramEngDoc.h" header file under the "Global Functions" section and edit the code as shown in the following.

```
char *StripInputString(char *input_str)
{
    int length = 0;               // length of stripped string
    int number_present = 0;       // flag indicating whether a number is
        present in the string
    char *ptr_begin = NULL;       // the base address of the new char array
        beginning at a number of decimal point
    char *ptr_char = NULL;        // a ptr to the next number in the array
    char *ptr_end = NULL;         // a ptr to the position just after the
        last number in the array
    char *ptr_str = input_str;    // a ptr to the str being searched
        incrementally one character at a time
    char *stripped_str = NULL;    // the new string with unnec. chars
        removed.
    CString sMsg;                 // main msg string
    CString sMsgTemp;             // temp msg string
    UINT nType = MB_OK;           // style of msg. box
    UINT nIDhelp = 0;             // help context ID for the msg.

    // GET THE NEW CHAR ARRAY BEGINNING AT THE FIRST MINUS SIGN, NUMBER,
       OR DECIMAL POINT
    ptr_begin = strpbrk(input_str, "-0123456789.");
```

```
// Check that the string contains at least a number or a decimal
  point: if not return NULL.
if(ptr_begin == NULL)
{
    sMsgTemp.Format("\n StripInputString()\n");
    sMsg += sMsgTemp;
    sMsgTemp.Format("\n Incomplete data!\n Please enter numerical
      data.\n");
    sMsg += sMsgTemp;
    //AfxMessageBox(sMsg, nType, nIDhelp);
    return NULL;
}

// GET THE NEW CHAR ARRAY BEGINNING JUST AFTER THE LAST NUMBER
ptr_char = ptr_str;          // initialize the ptr_char to ptr_str.
while(ptr_char != NULL)
{
    ptr_char = strpbrk(ptr_str, "0123456789");   // get the next
      number

    // Check for presence of a number
    if(ptr_char != NULL)
    {
        ptr_end = ptr_char;
        number_present = 1;
    }
    else if(ptr_char == NULL)
    {
        ptr_end = ptr_end + 1;
    }

    // Increment the ptr to the next char. of the string
    ptr_str++;
}

// It the string does not contain a number display msg. and return NULL.
if(number_present == 0)
{
    sMsgTemp.Format("\n StripInputString()\n");
    sMsg += sMsgTemp;
    sMsgTemp.Format("\n Incomplete data!\n Please enter numerical
      data.\n");
    sMsg += sMsgTemp;
    //AfxMessageBox(sMsg, nType, nIDhelp);
    return NULL;
}

// BUILD THE STRIPPED INPUT_STR
length = strlen(ptr_begin) - strlen(ptr_end); // get distance bw.
  ptr_begin and ptr_end

// -- MEMORY ALLOC
stripped_str = new char[length + 1];

// Copy ptr_begin into the new stripped string.
strncpy(stripped_str, ptr_begin, length);  // ptr_begin is larger
  than stripped_str, hence no NULL is placed at the end
stripped_str[length] = '\0';  // manually add the NULL in the last
  entry at offset length.
```

```
// -- MEMORY DELETE
// Note: deletion of stripped_str should take place in the calling
   environ.

return stripped_str;
}
```

The `StripInputString()` function extracts only the meaningful numerical data from the string entered by the user: it strips away unnecessary characters leading and trailing the string, e.g., "[", "]", ";", ":", etc. Initially the first number, minus sign, or decimal point is found using `strpbrk()`, and the pointer returned denotes the start of the string. Then the string is traversed (ptr_str++) updating the end point recorded in "ptr_end", with the position one beyond the last number found. The length of valid data is determined by taking the difference in the string lengths of "ptr_begin" and "ptr_end", and a stripped string is formed using `strncpy()`. However, since the string, "ptr_begin", is longer than "stripped_str", which is constructed to be of size "length + 1", no NULL ("0") character is placed at the end of "stripped_str" automatically: this must then be manually performed as shown. The stripped string is returned, and the responsibility for deleting the memory is that of the calling environment, i.e., `ConvertStringToDouble()`.

10.2.3 ADD A GLOBAL DATA-DIMENSION-DETERMINING FUNCTION

Add either of the following two global functions or both, if desired, to the "DiagramEngDoc.cpp" source file with the following prototypes.

1. int DetermineDataDimsByStrpbrk(char *in_str, int &nrows, int &ncols, int &max_row_length)
2. int DetermineDataDimsByStrtok(char *in_str, int &nrows, int &ncols, int &max_row_length)

Place their declarations in the "DiagramEngDoc.h" header file under the "Global Functions" section and edit these functions as shown in the following. The user may select which of these two functions is desired in the `ConvertStringToDouble()` function by setting the data-dimension-determining flag-like variable, "dim_flag", accordingly.

```
int DetermineDataDimsByStrpbrk(char *in_str, int &nrows, int &ncols, int
&max_row_length)
{
    int ncols_ref = 0;      // reference no. of cols.
    int valid = 0;          // validity of consistency of no. of cols
      per row.
    char *pch1 = NULL;      // ptr to char
    char *pch2 = NULL;      // ptr to char
    char *ptr_row = NULL;   // ptr to the start of each row
    char *ptr_str = NULL;   // string being search for no. of cols,
      i.e. the row being searched.

    // Get the first row
    ptr_row = strtok(in_str, ";");

    // Init. vars.
    max_row_length = 0;
    nrows = 0;

    // -- ITERATE OVER ALL ROWS
    while(ptr_row != NULL)
```

```
{
    ncols = 1;

    // -- ITERATE OVER ALL COLS
    ptr_str = ptr_row;

    // While the address of the next no. or decimal pt. is not NULL
    while( (pch1 = strpbrk(ptr_str, "0123456789.") ) != NULL)
    {
        // Advance the ptr_str by one.
        ptr_str = pch1 + 1;

        // Get the address of the next number or decimal pt.
        pch2 = strpbrk(ptr_str, "0123456789.");

        // If the address of the next no. is greater than one space
        //  away, then white space intervened.
        if( (pch2 != NULL) && (pch2 > (pch1 + 1)) )
        {
            ncols++;
        }
    }

    // Increment nrows
    nrows++;

    // Check the consistency of ncols.
    if(nrows == 1)
    {
        ncols_ref = ncols;
        valid = 1;
    }
    else if(ncols != ncols_ref)
    {
        AfxMessageBox("\n DetermineDataDimsByStrpbrk(): Inconsistent
          number of columns\n", MB_OK, 0);
        valid = 0;
    }

    // Record the max row length for memory alloc purposes
    if(strlen(ptr_row) >= max_row_length)
    {
        max_row_length = strlen(ptr_row);
    }

    // Get the new row
    ptr_row = strtok(NULL, ";");
}

    return valid;
}
```

The DetermineDataDimsByStrpbrk() function uses a nested strtok() function call and two strpbrk() calls. The initial strtok() call obtains a pointer to the beginning of a row of character data or token separated by a semicolon (";"): if a row is present, then "nrows" is incremented. While there is a valid row of data, the two strpbrk() function calls return pointers-to-char denoting the address/location of numbers or a decimal point in the row. A column is deemed to have been traversed if the difference between the locations of successive numbers or a decimal point is at least one (empty space); hence, "ncols" is incremented. The maximum row length is determined in order to allocate memory for the string matrix in the ConvertStringToDouble() function.

```
int DetermineDataDimsByStrtok(char *in_str, int &nrows, int &ncols,
  int &max_row_length)
{
    int ncols_ref = 0;        // reference no. of cols.
    int row_length;           // length of row
    int total_length = 0;     // accumulated sum of row lengths
    int valid = 0;            // validity of consistency of no. of cols
      per row.
    char *ptr_row = NULL;     // ptr holding the base address of the row
    char *ptr_element = NULL;// ptr holding the base address of the
      element within a row
    char *ptr_str_temp_copy = NULL; // ptr to a temp string
    char *str_temp = NULL;          // temp char array
    char *str_temp_copy = NULL;     // copy of str_temp used since
      str_temp is altered by strtok()

    // -- MEMORY ALLOC
    str_temp = new char[strlen(in_str) + 1];      // allocate the length
      of the string plus one to hold the '\0' char.
    str_temp_copy = new char[strlen(in_str) + 1]; // allocate the length
      of the string plus one to hold the '\0' char.

    // Copy in_str into str_temp and str_temp_copy
    strcpy(str_temp, in_str);
    strcpy(str_temp_copy, in_str);

    // Assign the base address of str_temp_copy to ptr_str_temp_copy.
    ptr_str_temp_copy = str_temp_copy;

    ptr_row = strtok(str_temp, ";"); // get the first row separated by ";"

    // ITERATE OVER ALL THE ROWS
    nrows = 1;
    while(ptr_row != NULL)
    {
        row_length = strlen(ptr_row);
        total_length += row_length + 1; // one is added here to cater
          for the ";"

        ncols = 1;

        ptr_element = strtok(ptr_row, " ");    // get element separated
          by " " on the current row

        while(ptr_element != NULL)
        {
            ptr_element = strtok(NULL, " ");   // get the next element
              separated by " " on the current row

            if(ptr_element != NULL)
            {
                ncols++;
            }
        }

        // Check the consistency of ncols.
        if(nrows == 1)
        {
            ncols_ref = ncols;
            valid = 1;
        }
```

```
            else if(ncols != ncols_ref)
            {
                //AfxMessageBox("\n DetermineDataDimsByStrtok(): Inconsistent
                  number of columns\n", MB_OK, 0);
                valid = 0;
            }

            // Record the max row length for memory alloc purposes
            if(row_length >= max_row_length)
            {
                max_row_length = row_length;
            }

            // Advance the position of the ptr to the beginning of the next row
            ptr_str_temp_copy = ptr_str_temp_copy + row_length + 1;
              // oneis added to cater for the ";"

            // Exit if looping has traversed to the end of the original
              string
            if(total_length >= strlen(in_str))
            {
                break;
            }
            // Copy what is pointed to by ptr_str_temp_copy, i.e. the next
              row onwards, into str_temp.
            strcpy(str_temp, ptr_str_temp_copy);

            // Obtain the next row separated by ";"
            ptr_row = strtok(str_temp, ";");

            if(ptr_row != NULL)
            {
                nrows++;
            }
        }

        // MEMORY DELETE
        delete [] str_temp;
        delete [] str_temp_copy;

        return valid;
}
```

The DetermineDataDimsByStrtok() function uses nested strtok() function calls. Initially the address of the first row of character data, or token, is obtained and returned in "ptr_row". Then within the outer *while* loop, strtok() is called again to obtain a pointer to an element ("ptr_element") in the particular row. In the inner *while* loop, strtok() is successively called extracting each element separated by white space (" ") from where the previous NULL character was placed. However, since strtok() is nested in two locations, the NULL sentinel cannot be used in the outer *while* loop, as it is in the inner loop. Hence, the next row of data, separated by a semicolon ";", needs to be obtained from a string containing only the remaining rows of the original string, "in_str". The beginning of this string is defined to be the sum of the row lengths thus far, including one space per row for the row-ending semicolon. The number of rows and columns is incremented as long as valid (nonNULL) pointers-to-char are returned by strtok().

10.2.4 ADD A GLOBAL ConvertStringMatrixToDoubleMatrix() FUNCTION

Add a global function to the "DiagramEngDoc.cpp" source file with the following proto-type: double **ConvertStringMatrixToDoubleMatrix(char **str_matrix, int nrows, int ncols). Place the declaration in the "DiagramEngDoc.h" header file under the "Global Functions" section and edit the code as shown in the following.

```
double **ConvertStringMatrixToDoubleMatrix(char **str_matrix, int nrows,
  int ncols)
{
    int i;                      // row i
    int j;                      // col j
    int valid = 1;              // confirm the no. of cols of data per row.
      (assume valid to begin with)
    char *ptr_char = NULL;      // ptr-to-char holds base address of first
      char of a poss gp. of chars.
    double **d_matrix = NULL; // input matrix of chars converted to
      doubles

    // MEMORY ALLOCATION
    d_matrix = new double *[nrows];
    for(i=0; i<nrows; i++)
    {
        d_matrix[i] = new double[ncols]; // allocate an array of doubles,
          return & to matrix[i] }
    }

    // Iterate over the number of rows.
    for(i=0; i<nrows; i++)
    {
        ptr_char = strtok(str_matrix[i], " ");  // extract the character
          of the current row separated by " " (space).

        // Iterate across the cols for this partic. row.
        j = 0;
        while(ptr_char != NULL)  // while not at the end of the current
          row of chars.
        {
            d_matrix[i][j] = atof(ptr_char);  // convert the char to a
              double and place in the double array.

            ptr_char = strtok(NULL, " ");       // extract the subsequent
              char of the current row separated by " " (space).

            j++;                     // increment the col cnt
        }

        if(j != ncols)          // if the no. of times the loop was
          iterated is not equal to the number of cols, print error msg.
        {
            AfxMessageBox("\n ConvertStringMatrixToDoubleMatrix():
              Inconsistent number of columns\n", MB_OK, 0);
            valid = 0;
        }
    }

    return d_matrix;
}
```

The ConvertStringMatrixToDoubleMatrix() function initially allocates memory for a double matrix of size "nrows" by "ncols". However, the developer will notice that memory is not deleted in this function, but rather the double matrix, and its dimensions, are passed back to the calling environment, i.e., to ConvertStringToDouble(). Hence, the responsibility for deleting the matrix with "nrows" number of rows will be the destructor of the class whose member variable of the form "double **matrix" was assigned the returned matrix or the function in which the returned matrix was assigned.

The character data are extracted from each row of data, using strtok(), which returns the address (a pointer-to-char) of the (next) token, character, or group of characters, separated by white space (" "). This array of ASCII character(s), or string, is then converted to a double type using the "ASCII to floating number" conversion function atof().

10.2.5 ADD GLOBAL DIAGNOSTIC PRINTING FUNCTIONS

Add a function to print a matrix to the project with the prototype, int PrintMatrix(double **M, int nrows, int ncols), and place the declaration in the "DiagramEngDoc.h" header file. Place the function definition in the "DiagramEngDoc.cpp" source file and edit it as follows.

```
int PrintMatrix(double **M, int nrows, int ncols)
{
    int i;
    int j;
    CString sMsg;          // main msg string
    CString sMsgTemp;      // temp msg string
    UINT nType = MB_OK;    // style of msg. box
    UINT nIDhelp = 0;      // help context ID for the msg.

    // If the matrix is NULL then return.
    if(M == NULL)
    {
        return 1;
    }

    sMsgTemp.Format("\n PrintMatrix()\n");
    sMsg += sMsgTemp;

    // Print Matrix
    sMsgTemp.Format("\n");
    sMsg += sMsgTemp;

    for(i=0; i<nrows; i++)
    {
        for(j=0; j<ncols; j++)
        {
            //sMsgTemp.Format(" %-10.3e", M[i][j]); // left adjusted,
              total width 10, 3 decimal places, exponential notation
            sMsgTemp.Format(" %lf", M[i][j]);  // standard double
              formatting
            sMsg += sMsgTemp;
        }
        sMsgTemp.Format("\n");
        sMsg += sMsgTemp;
    }
    sMsgTemp.Format("\n");
    sMsg += sMsgTemp;

    // Display msg. box
    AfxMessageBox(sMsg, nType, nIDhelp);

    return 0;
}
```

Add a function to print a vector to the project with the prototype, `int PrintVector(double *v, int ncols)`, and place the declaration in the "DiagramEngDoc.h" header file. Place the function definition in the "DiagramEngDoc.cpp" source file and edit it as shown.

```
int PrintVector(double *v, int ncols)
{
    int i;
    CString sMsg;          // main msg string
    CString sMsgTemp;      // temp msg string
    UINT nType = MB_OK;    // style of msg. box
    UINT nIDhelp = 0;      // help context ID for the msg.

    // If the vector is NULL then return.
    if(v == NULL)
    {
        return 1;
    }

    sMsgTemp.Format("\n PrintVector()\n");
    sMsg += sMsgTemp;

    // Print Vector
    sMsgTemp.Format("\n");
    sMsg += sMsgTemp;

    for(i=0; i<ncols; i++)
    {
        //sMsgTemp.Format(" %-10.3e", v[i]); // left adjusted, total
            width 10, 3 decimal places, exponential notation
        sMsgTemp.Format(" %lf", v[i]);        // standard double
            formatting
        sMsg += sMsgTemp;
    }
    sMsgTemp.Format("\n");
    sMsg += sMsgTemp;

    // Display msg. box
    AfxMessageBox(sMsg, nType, nIDhelp);

    return 0;
}
```

10.3   AUGMENTING THE CBlock-DERIVED CLASSES

Now that the functionality for the conversion of string to double data has been added, the CBlock-derived classes, CConstantBlock, CGainBlock, CIntegratorBlock, and CTransferFnBlock, need to be augmented with member variables, functions, and additional code.

10.3.1   AUGMENT THE **CConstantBlock** CLASS

Add two new private integer member variables to the CConstantBlock class with names, "m_iNrows" and "m_iNcols", to be assigned the dimensions of the double matrix returned by `ConvertStringToDouble()`.

Now augment the `BlockDlgWndParameterInput()` function as shown in the following to delete the possibly existing data, convert the input string to a double matrix, and check for correct user input.

```cpp
void CConstantBlock::BlockDlgWndParameterInput()
{
    int i;
    int input = 0;       // input: (0) incomplete, (1) complete
    CString  sMsg;        // string msg. to be displayed
    CString sMsgTemp;     // temp string msg.
    UINT nType = MB_OK;  // style of msg. box
    UINT nIDhelp = 0;    // help context ID for the msg.

    // Create a dlg obj. of class CConstantBlockDialog : public CDialog
    CConstantBlockDialog oDlg;

    // Set the dialog class vars using the block class vars
    oDlg.m_strConstValue = m_strConstValue;

    // While input not correct
    while(input == 0)
    {
        // Return val of DoModal() fn of ancestor class CDialog is
        //  checked to determine which btn was clicked.
        if(oDlg.DoModal() == IDOK)
        {
            // Assign CConstantBlockDialog variable values to
            //  CConstantBlock variable values.
            m_strConstValue = oDlg.m_strConstValue;
            // Print msg with variable value.
            //sMsg.Format("\n CConstantBlock::BlockDlgWndParameterIn
              put(), string = %s\n", m_strConstValue);
            //AfxMessageBox(sMsg, nType, nIDhelp);
        }

        // DELETE POSSIBLY EXISTING MATRIX
        // Delete the input data matrix whose memory was allocated in
        //  ConvertStringMatrixToDoubleMatrix()
        if(m_dConstMatrix != NULL)
        {
            for(i=0; i<m_iNrows; i++)
            {
                delete [] m_dConstMatrix[i];
            }
            delete [] m_dConstMatrix;
        }

        // Convert the input string into a double matrix.
        m_dConstMatrix = ConvertStringToDouble(m_strConstValue, m_iNrows,
          m_iNcols);
        //PrintMatrix(m_dConstMatrix, m_iNrows, m_iNcols);

        // Check validity of input
        if(m_dConstMatrix == NULL)
        {
            sMsgTemp.Format("\n WARNING!: Incorrect constant scalar/
              vector/matrix input. \n");
```

```
            sMsg += sMsgTemp;
            sMsgTemp.Format("\n Please enter consistent numerical
              data. \n");
            sMsg += sMsgTemp;
            AfxMessageBox(sMsg, nType, nIDhelp);
            sMsg.Format("");    // reset the msg since within a while loop
        }
        else
        {
            input = 1;
        }
    }
}
```

Augment the CConstantBlock destructor to delete the memory allocated for the two-dimensional double array, "m_dConstMatrix", (on block deletion) as shown in the following.

```
CConstantBlock::~CConstantBlock(void)
{
    int i;

    // MEMORY DEALLOCATION

    // Delete the input data matrix whose memory was allocated in
      ConvertStringMatrixToDoubleMatrix()
    if(m_dConstMatrix != NULL)
    {
        for(i=0; i<m_iNrows; i++)
        {
            delete [] m_dConstMatrix[i];
        }
        delete [] m_dConstMatrix;
        m_dConstMatrix = NULL;
    }
    // Reset member vars.
    m_iNrows = 0;
    m_iNcols = 0;
}
```

Finally, augment the CConstantBlock constructor to set the member variable, "m_dConstMatrix", given the CString value defined earlier, "m_strConstValue". This is done so that the block has a default starting value. This also prevents erroneous memory deletion in the destructor in the event that the pointer was not assigned to NULL. The ellipsis denotes omitted but unchanged code from before (as usual).

```
CConstantBlock::CConstantBlock(CSystemModel *pParentSystemModel, CPoint
  blk_posn, EBlockShape e_blk_shape):
CBlock(pParentSystemModel, blk_posn, e_blk_shape)
{
    ...
    // Initialize m_dConstMatrix to have the default numerical value of
      the CString arg. (a non-NULL value).
    // If a Constant block were to be deleted, then memory would be
      deleted correctly.
    m_dConstMatrix = ConvertStringToDouble(m_strConstValue, m_iNrows,
      m_iNcols);
}
```

10.3.2 AUGMENT THE **CGainBlock** CLASS

Add two new private integer member variables to the CGainBlock class, with the names, "m_iNrows" and "m_iNcols", to be assigned the dimensions of the double matrix returned by ConvertStringToDouble().

Augment the BlockDlgWndParameterInput() function as shown in the following to delete the possibly existing data, convert the input string to a double matrix, and check for correct user input.

```
void CGainBlock::BlockDlgWndParameterInput()
{
    int i;
    int input = 0;       // input: (0) incomplete, (1) complete
    CString  sMsg;       // string msg. to be displayed
    CString sMsgTemp;    // temp string msg.
    UINT nType = MB_OK;  // style of msg. box
    UINT nIDhelp = 0;    // help context ID for the msg.

    // Create a dialog object. of class CGainBlockDialog : public CDialog
    CGainBlockDialog oDlg;

    // Set the dialog class vars using the block class vars
    oDlg.m_iGainType = m_iGainType;
    oDlg.m_strGainValue = m_strGainValue;

    // While input not correct
    while(input == 0)
    {
        // Return val of DoModal() fn of ancestor class CDialog is
          checked to determine which btn was clicked.
        if(oDlg.DoModal() == IDOK)
        {
            // Assign CGainBlockDialog variable values to CGainBlock
              variable values.
            m_strGainValue = oDlg.m_strGainValue;
            m_iGainType = oDlg.m_iGainType;

            // Print msg with variable value.
            //sMsg.Format("\n CGainBlock::BlockDlgWndParameterInput(),
              m_strGainValue = %s\n", m_strGainValue);
            //AfxMessageBox(sMsg, nType, nIDhelp);
        }

        // DELETE POSSIBLY EXISTING MATRIX
        // Delete the input data matrix whose memory was allocated in
          ConvertStringMatrixToDoubleMatrix()
        if(m_dGainMatrix != NULL)
        {
            for(i=0; i<m_iNrows; i++)
            {
                delete [] m_dGainMatrix[i];
            }
            delete [] m_dGainMatrix;
        }

        // Convert the input string into a double matrix.
        m_dGainMatrix = ConvertStringToDouble(m_strGainValue, m_iNrows,
          m_iNcols);
        //PrintMatrix(m_dGainMatrix, m_iNrows, m_iNcols);
```

```
        // Check validity of input
        if(m_dGainMatrix == NULL)
        {
            sMsgTemp.Format("\n WARNING!: Incorrect gain scalar/vector/
              matrix input. \n");
            sMsg += sMsgTemp;
            sMsgTemp.Format("\n Please enter consistent
              numerical data. \n");
            sMsg += sMsgTemp;
            AfxMessageBox(sMsg, nType, nIDhelp);
            sMsg.Format(""); // reset the msg since within a while loop
        }
        else
        {
        input = 1;
        }
    }
}
```

Augment the CGainBlock destructor to delete the memory allocated for the two-dimensional double array, "m_dGainMatrix" (upon block deletion), as shown in the following.

```
CGainBlock::~CGainBlock(void)
{
    int i;

    // MEMORY DEALLOCATION

    // Delete the input data matrix whose memory was allocated in
      ConvertStringMatrixToDoubleMatrix()
    if(m_dGainMatrix != NULL)
    {
        for(i=0; i<m_iNrows; i++)
        {
            delete [] m_dGainMatrix[i];
        }
        delete [] m_dGainMatrix;
        m_dGainMatrix = NULL;
    }
    // Reset member vars.
    m_iNrows = 0;
    m_iNcols = 0;
}
```

Augment the CGainBlock constructor to set the member variable, "m_dGainMatrix", given the CString value, "m_strGainValue", defined earlier. This is done so that the block has a default starting value.

```
CGainBlock::CGainBlock(CSystemModel *pParentSystemModel, CPoint blk_posn,
  EBlockShape e_blk_shape):
CBlock(pParentSystemModel, blk_posn, e_blk_shape)
{
    ...
    // Initialize m_dGainMatrix to have the default numerical value of
      the CString arg. (a non-NULL value).
```

```
    // If a Gain block were to be deleted, then memory would be deleted
       correctly.
    m_dGainMatrix = ConvertStringToDouble(m_strGainValue, m_iNrows,
       m_iNcols);
}
```

10.3.3 AUGMENT THE CIntegratorBlock CLASS

Add three new private integer member variables to the CIntegratorBlock class, "m_iNrows", "m_iNcols", and "m_iLength", to be assigned the size properties of the initial condition vector. The method of this assignment differs to the previous functions, since the one-dimensional initial condition vector is not a two-dimensional array. In addition, change the existing class placeholder member variable, "ic_vector", to "m_dICVector".

Augment the BlockDlgWndParameterInput() function as shown in the following to delete the possibly existing data, convert the input string to a double vector, and check for correct user input.

```
void CIntegratorBlock::BlockDlgWndParameterInput()
{
    int input = 0;          // input: (0) incomplete, (1) complete
    CString  sMsg;          // string msg. to be displayed
    CString sMsgTemp;       // temp string msg.
    UINT nType = MB_OK;     // style of msg. box
    UINT nIDhelp = 0;       // help context ID for the msg.

    // Create a dialog object. of class CIntegratorBlockDialog : public
       CDialog
    CIntegratorBlockDialog oDlg;

    // Set the dialog class vars using the block class vars
    oDlg.m_strICVector = m_strICVector;

    // While input not correct
    while(input == 0)
    {
        // Return val of DoModal() fn of ancestor class CDialog is
          checked to determine which btn was clicked.
        if(oDlg.DoModal() == IDOK)
        {
            // Assign CIntegratorBlockDialog variable value to
              CIntegratorBlock variable value.
            m_strICVector = oDlg.m_strICVector;

            // Print msg with variable value.
            //sMsg.Format("\n CIntegratorBlock::BlockDlgWndParameter
              Input(), m_strICVector = %s\n", m_strICVector);
            //AfxMessageBox(sMsg, nType, nIDhelp);
        }

        // DELETE POSSIBLY EXISTING VECTOR
        // Delete the initial condition vector whose memory was allocated
          in ConvertStringToDoubleVector()
        if(m_dICVector != NULL)
        {
            delete [] m_dICVector;
        }
```

```
    // Convert the input string into a double vector
    m_dICVector = ConvertStringToDoubleVector(m_strICVector,
      m_iNrows, m_iNcols);
    //PrintVector(m_dICVector, m_iLength);

    // Check validity of input
    if(m_dICVector == NULL)
    {
        sMsgTemp.Format("\n WARNING!: Incorrect initial condition
          vector input. \n");
        sMsg += sMsgTemp;
        sMsgTemp.Format("\n Please enter numerical vector data. \n");
        sMsg += sMsgTemp;
        AfxMessageBox(sMsg, nType, nIDhelp);
        sMsg.Format("");  // reset the msg since within a while loop
    }
    else
    {
        input = 1;
    }
  }
}
```

The `BlockDlgWndParameterInput()` function is simply augmented with the call to `ConvertStringToDoubleVector()`, passing in the dialog window-based input CString argument to be converted to a vector of double values. If there is an error in the conversion, a NULL pointer is returned.

Now add a new public member function to the CIntegratorBlock class with the following prototype, `double *ConvertStringToDoubleVector(CString string, int &nrows, int &ncols)`, and edit this function as shown in the following.

```
double *CIntegratorBlock::ConvertStringToDoubleVector(CString string, int
  &nrows, int &ncols)
{
    int i;
    double *ICVector = NULL;   // temporary initial condition vector
    double **matrix = NULL;    // matrix returned by
      ConvertStringToDouble()
    CString  sMsg;             // string to be displayed
    CString sMsgTemp;          // temp string
    UINT nType = MB_OK;        // style of msg. box
    UINT nIDhelp = 0;          // help context ID for the msg.

    //sMsgTemp.Format("\n ConvertStringToDoubleVector()\n");
    //sMsg += sMsgTemp;
    //AfxMessageBox(sMsg, nType, nIDhelp);

    // Convert the input string into a double matrix
    matrix = ConvertStringToDouble(string, nrows, ncols);

    // Check if matrix is NULL
    if(matrix == NULL)
    {
        return NULL;
    }

    // Assign the dimensions of the vector to the member vars.
    m_iNrows = nrows;
    m_iNcols = ncols;
```

```
if(ncols >= nrows)
{
    m_iLength = ncols;
}
else
{
    m_iLength = nrows;
}

// Check the dimensions of the input matrix
if(((nrows >= 1) && (ncols == 1)) || ((nrows == 1) && (ncols >= 1)))
{
    // MEMORY ALLOCATION
    ICVector = new double[m_iLength];

    // Copy the double matrix into the initial condition vector
    if(ncols >= nrows)
    {
        for(i=0; i<ncols; i++)
        {
            ICVector[i] = matrix[0][i];   // zeroth row, m_iNcols
        }
    }
    else if(nrows >= ncols)
    {
        for(i=0; i<m_iNrows; i++)
        {
            ICVector[i] = matrix[i][0];    // m_iNrows, zeroth col.
        }
    }
}
else if((nrows == 0) && (ncols == 0))
{
    sMsgTemp.Format("\n CIntegratorBlock::ConvertStringToDouble
      Vector()\n");
    sMsg += sMsgTemp;
    sMsgTemp.Format("\n Size of initial condition vector is zero!\n");
    sMsg += sMsgTemp;
    sMsgTemp.Format("\n Re-enter initial condition vector.\n");
    sMsg += sMsgTemp;
    AfxMessageBox(sMsg, nType, nIDhelp);

    // Assign NULL indicating that something is wrong
    ICVector = NULL;
}
else
{
    sMsgTemp.Format("\n CIntegratorBlock::ConvertStringToDouble
      Vector()\n");
    sMsg += sMsgTemp;
    sMsgTemp.Format("\n Dimensions of initial condition vector are
      that of a matrix!\n");
    sMsg += sMsgTemp;
    sMsgTemp.Format("\n nrows = %d, ncols = %d\n", nrows, ncols);
    sMsg += sMsgTemp;
    sMsgTemp.Format("\n Re-enter initial condition vector.\n");
    sMsg += sMsgTemp;
    AfxMessageBox(sMsg, nType, nIDhelp);
```

```
        // Assign NULL indicating that something is wrong
        ICVector = NULL;
    }

    // MEMORY DELETE
    // Delete the input data matrix whose memory was allocated in
      ConvertStringMatrixToDoubleMatrix()
    // Note: if matrix = NULL, then fn already returns NULL and hence
      memory not deleted as expected.
    for(i=0; i<m_iNrows; i++)
    {
        delete [] matrix[i];
    }
    delete [] matrix;

    return ICVector;
}
```

The ConvertStringToDoubleVector() function is required since the initial condition vector
is to be recorded as a vector and not as a matrix. However, a call to ConvertStringToDouble()
is initially made to obtain the input string conversion in matrix form: if the matrix is NULL, then the
function returns NULL and no memory is erroneously deallocated. If the matrix contains valid entries,
then the size of the matrix is checked to determine whether it is a vector or not, and if so, the matrix
entries are assigned to the vector: if not, a warning message is displayed and "ICVector = NULL" is
returned.

Augment the CIntegratorBlock destructor to delete the memory allocated for the "m_dICVector"
array as shown in the following. Memory will not be erroneously deallocated if the ICVector could
not be constructed properly resulting in it being NULL.

```
CIntegratorBlock::~CIntegratorBlock(void)
{
// Delete the initial condition vector whose memory was allocated in
  ConvertStringToDoubleVector()
    if(m_dICVector != NULL)
    {
        delete [] m_dICVector;
        m_dICVector = NULL;
    }
}
```

Augment the CIntegratorBlock constructor to set the member variable, "m_dICVector", given
the CString value, "m_strICVector", defined earlier. This is done so that the block has a default
starting value.

```
CIntegratorBlock::CIntegratorBlock(CSystemModel *pParentSystemModel,
  CPoint blk_posn, EBlockShape e_blk_shape) :
CBlock(pParentSystemModel, blk_posn, e_blk_shape)
{
    ...
    // Initialize m_dICVector to have the default numerical value of the
      CString arg. (a non-NULL value).
    // If an Integrator block were to be deleted, then memory would be
      deleted correctly.
    m_dICVector = ConvertStringToDoubleVector(m_strICVector, m_iNrows,
      m_iNcols);
}
```

10.3.4 AUGMENT THE **CTransferFnBlock** CLASS

Add two new private integer member variables to the CTransferFnBlock class, with names, "m_iLengthNumer" and "m_iLengthDenom", to be assigned the length of the vector of numerator and denominator coefficients, respectively. Change the existing class placeholder member variables, "numerator_coeffs_vec" and "denominator_coeffs_vec", to "m_dNumerVector" and "m_dDenomVector", respectively.

Augment the BlockDlgWndParameterInput() function as shown in the following to delete the possibly existing data, convert the input strings to double vectors, and check for correct user input.

```
void CTransferFnBlock::BlockDlgWndParameterInput()
{
    int input = 0;       // input: (0) incomplete, (1) complete
    CString  sMsg;       // string msg. to be displayed
    CString sMsgTemp;    // temp string msg.
    UINT nType = MB_OK;  // style of msg. box
    UINT nIDhelp = 0;    // help context ID for the msg.

    // Create a dialog object. of class CTransferFnBlockDialog : public
      CDialog
    CTransferFnBlockDialog oDlg;

    // Set the dialog class vars using the block class vars
    oDlg.m_strNumerCoeffs = m_strNumerCoeffs;
    oDlg.m_strDenomCoeffs = m_strDenomCoeffs;

    // While input not correct
    while(input == 0)
    {
        // Return val of DoModal() fn of ancestor class CDialog is
          checked to determine which btn was clicked.
        if(oDlg.DoModal() == IDOK)
        {
            // Assign CTransferFnBlockDialog variable values to
              CTransferFnBlock variable values.
            m_strNumerCoeffs = oDlg.m_strNumerCoeffs;
            m_strDenomCoeffs = oDlg.m_strDenomCoeffs;

            // Print msg with variable value.
            //sMsg.Format("\n CTransferFnBlock::BlockDlgWndParameter
              Input(), m_strNumerCoeffs = %s, m_strDenomCoeffs = %s\n",
              m_strNumerCoeffs, m_strDenomCoeffs);
            //AfxMessageBox(sMsg, nType, nIDhelp);
        }

        // DELETE POSSIBLY EXISTING VECTORS
        // Delete the coeff vectors whose memory was allocated in
          ConvertStringToDoubleVector()
        if(m_dNumerVector != NULL)
        {
            delete [] m_dNumerVector;
        }

        if(m_dDenomVector != NULL)
        {
            delete [] m_dDenomVector;
        }
```

```
    // Convert the input strings into double vectors
    m_dNumerVector = ConvertStringToDoubleVector(m_strNumerCoeffs,
      m_iLengthNumer);
    //PrintVector(m_dNumerVector, m_iLengthNumer);

    m_dDenomVector = ConvertStringToDoubleVector(m_strDenomCoeffs,
      m_iLengthDenom);
    //PrintVector(m_dDenomVector, m_iLengthDenom);

    // Check validity of input
    if(m_dNumerVector == NULL || m_dDenomVector == NULL)
    {
        sMsgTemp.Format("\n WARNING!: Incorrect coefficient vector
          input. \n");
        sMsg += sMsgTemp;

        if(m_dNumerVector == NULL)
        {
            sMsgTemp.Format("\n Please enter correct numerator
              coefficient vector data. \n");
            sMsg += sMsgTemp;
        }
        if(m_dDenomVector == NULL)
        {
            sMsgTemp.Format("\n Please enter correct denominator
              coefficient vector data. \n");
            sMsg += sMsgTemp;
        }

        AfxMessageBox(sMsg, nType, nIDhelp);
        sMsg.Format("");    // reset the msg since within a while loop
    }
    else
    {
        input = 1;
    }
    }
}
```

The `BlockDlgWndParameterInput()` function is augmented with calls to `ConvertStringToDoubleVector()`, passing in the dialog window-based input CString arguments, to be converted to vectors of double values. If there is an error in the conversion, NULL pointers are returned.

Add a new public member function to the CTransferFnBlock class with the following prototype, `double *ConvertStringToDoubleVector(CString string, int &length)`, and edit this function as shown in the following.

```
double *CTransferFnBlock::ConvertStringToDoubleVector(CString string,
  int &length)
{
    int i;
    int nrows = 0;              // no. of rows of data
    int ncols = 0;              // no. of cols of data
    double *coeff_vector = NULL; // temporary coefficient vector
    double **matrix = NULL;     // matrix returned by
      ConvertStringToDouble()
    CString sMsg;               // string to be displayed
```

```
CString sMsgTemp;                   // temp string
UINT nType = MB_OK;                 // style of msg. box
UINT nIDhelp = 0;                   // help context ID for the msg.

// Convert the input string into a double matrix
matrix = ConvertStringToDouble(string, nrows, ncols);

// Check if matrix is NULL
if(matrix == NULL)
{
    return NULL;
}

// Assign the length of the vector to the member var.
if(ncols >= nrows)
{
    length = ncols;
}
else
{
    length = nrows;
}

// Check the dimensions of the input matrix
if(((nrows >= 1) && (ncols == 1)) || ((nrows == 1) && (ncols >= 1)))
{
    // MEMORY ALLOCATION
    coeff_vector = new double[length];

    // Copy the double matrix into the vector of coefficients
    if(ncols >= nrows)
    {
        for(i=0; i<ncols; i++)
        {
            coeff_vector[i] = matrix[0][i]; // zeroth row, m_iNcols
        }
    }
    else if(nrows >= ncols)
    {
        for(i=0; i<nrows; i++)
        {
            coeff_vector[i] = matrix[i][0]; // m_iNrows, zeroth col.
        }
    }
}
else if((nrows == 0) && (ncols == 0))
{
    sMsgTemp.Format("\n CTransferFnBlock::ConvertStringToDouble
      Vector()\n");
    sMsg += sMsgTemp;
    sMsgTemp.Format("\n Size of coefficient vector is zero!\n");
    sMsg += sMsgTemp;
    sMsgTemp.Format("\n Re-enter coefficient vector.\n");
    sMsg += sMsgTemp;
    AfxMessageBox(sMsg, nType, nIDhelp);

    // Assign NULL indicating that something is wrong
    coeff_vector = NULL;
}
```

```
        else
        {
            sMsgTemp.Format("\n CTransferFnBlock::ConvertStringToDouble
              Vector()\n");
            sMsg += sMsgTemp;
            sMsgTemp.Format("\n Dimensions of coefficient vector are that of
              a matrix!\n");
            sMsg += sMsgTemp;
            sMsgTemp.Format("\n nrows = %d, ncols = %d\n", nrows, ncols);
            sMsg += sMsgTemp;
            sMsgTemp.Format("\n Re-enter coefficient vector.\n");
            sMsg += sMsgTemp;
            AfxMessageBox(sMsg, nType, nIDhelp);

            // Assign NULL indicating that something is wrong
            coeff_vector = NULL;
        }

        // MEMORY DELETE
        // Delete the input data matrix whose memory was allocated in
          ConvertStringMatrixToDoubleMatrix()
        // Note: if matrix = NULL, then fn already returns NULL and hence
          memory not deleted as expected.
        for(i=0; i<nrows; i++)
        {
            delete [] matrix[i];
        }
        delete [] matrix;

        return coeff_vector;
}
```

The `ConvertStringToDoubleVector()` function operates in a similar manner to that described earlier for the CIntegratorBlock class. It differs in the function prototype, where only the length argument is a member variable as the number of rows and columns is not required, and a coefficient vector, "coeff_vector", is returned and subsequently assigned to either the numerator or denominator coefficient vector "m_dNumerVector" or "m_dDenomVector", respectively.

Augment the CTransferFnBlock destructor to delete the memory allocated for the "m_dNumerVector" and "m_dDenomVector" arrays as shown in the following. Memory will not be erroneously deallocated if either of the vectors could not be constructed properly resulting in their value being NULL.

```
CTransferFnBlock::~CTransferFnBlock(void)
{
    // Delete the coefficient vector whose memory was allocated in
      ConvertStringToDoubleVector()
    if(m_dNumerVector != NULL)
    {
        delete [] m_dNumerVector;
        m_dNumerVector = NULL;
    }

    if(m_dDenomVector != NULL)
    {
        delete [] m_dDenomVector;
        m_dDenomVector = NULL;
    }
}
```

Augment the CTransferFnBlock constructor to set the member variables, "m_dNumerVector" and "m_dDenomVector", given the CString values defined earlier, i.e., "m_strNumerCoeffs" and "m_strDenomCoeffs", respectively. This is done so that the block has default starting values.

```
CTransferFnBlock::CTransferFnBlock(CSystemModel *pParentSystemModel,
  CPoint blk_posn, EBlockShape e_blk_shape):
CBlock(pParentSystemModel, blk_posn, e_blk_shape)
{
    ...
    // Initialize m_dNumerVector and m_dDenomVector to have the default
      numerical values of the CString args. (non-NULL values).
    // If a TransferFn block were to be deleted, then memory would be
      deleted correctly.
    m_dNumerVector = ConvertStringToDoubleVector(m_strNumerCoeffs,
      m_iLengthNumer);
    m_dDenomVector = ConvertStringToDoubleVector(m_strDenomCoeffs,
      m_iLengthDenom);
}
```

Now upon running the code, data may be entered for each of the four block objects of type, CConstantBlock, CGainBlock, CIntegratorBlock, and CTransferFnBlock, where the values are converted into a matrix or vector of double values as appropriate. This input then forms the initial data of the block that is used in signal propagation (to be introduced later).

10.4 SUMMARY

The conversion of CString input strings to double member data is performed by using various global and class-specific functions. The ConvertStringToDouble() function converts a CString value into double values. A StripInputString() function strips the input string of unwanted leading and trailing characters. The data dimensions, i.e., the number of rows and columns of matrix values, are determined using either a DetermineDataDimsByStrpbrk() function or a DetermineDataDimsByStrtok() function, which makes predominant use of the strpbrk() and strtok() functions, respectively. The ConvertStringMatrixToDoubleMatrix() function then converts the string data to double matrix data. A ConvertStringToDoubleVector() function is also used to convert string data to a double vector if a vector is required. The classes that required modification to cater for string input are CConstantBlock, CGainBlock, CIntegratorBlock, and CTransferFnBlock.

REFERENCE

1. Kelley, A. and Pohl, I., *A Book On C: Programming in C*, 2nd edn., Benjamin Cummings, Redwood City, CA, 1990.

11 Moving Multiple Items

11.1 INTRODUCTION

Many different types of items may be moved together by first circumscribing them with what is called a "rubber band" and then moving the whole rubber-band-enclosed group together. This is performed using a CRectTracker object and determining whether the enclosed region of the rubber band intersects or contains items on the palette, e.g., blocks, connection bend points, and connection end points, and then updating the positions of the items to be translated by the same amount as the center point of the whole rectangular rubber band region.

The process of tracking or moving of multiple items using a CRectTracker object first involves initiating the procedure using either a keyboard key or a toolbar button, followed by multiple invocation of a to-be-introduced TrackMultipleItems() function, where, on the first entry, a rubber band is created and, on a subsequent entry, the circumscribed items may be moved. The key topics presented here are as follows:

1. Edit the TrackItem() function to call TrackMultipleItems().
2. Add a TrackMultipleItems() function to the CDiagramEngDoc class.
3. Add a function for a "key down" event to the CDiagramEngView class.
4. Add key-flag-based members to the CDiagramEngDoc class.
5. Flow of control in the TrackMultipleItems() function.
6. Add a toolbar button to activate tracking of multiple items.

11.2 EDIT THE TrackItem() FUNCTION TO CALL TrackMultipleItems()

The tracking of multiple items can occur if the user first presses the "T" key and then clicks the left mouse button on the palette to describe a rubber band region containing the items to be moved. Hence, add the conditional clause to the TrackItem() function as shown in bold in the following, calling TrackMultipleItems() only if the correct key-character-based flag has been set.

```
int CDiagramEngDoc::TrackItem(CPoint point, CWnd *pWnd)
{
    int tracker_flag = 0;

    // Track block
    tracker_flag = TrackBlock(point, pWnd);
    if(tracker_flag != 0)
    {
        return tracker_flag;   // Return from the function since an item
        was tracked
    }

    // Track connection end point
    tracker_flag = TrackConnectionEndPoint(point, pWnd);
    if(tracker_flag != 0)
    {
        return tracker_flag;   // Return from the function since an item
        was tracked
    }
```

```
    // Track connection bend point
    tracker_flag = TrackConnectionBendPoint(point, pWnd);
    if(tracker_flag != 0)
    {
        return tracker_flag; // Return from the function since an item
            was tracked
    }

    // Track multiple items
    if(m_iKeyFlagTrack == 1)
    {
        tracker_flag = TrackMultipleItems(point, pWnd);

        if(tracker_flag !=0)
        {
            return tracker_flag;  // Return from the function since an
                item was tracked
        }
    }
    else
    {
        tracker_flag = 0;
    }

    // Return flag indicating if an item was tracked: 0 => not tracked,
        1 => tracked.
    return tracker_flag;
}
```

The developer will notice that the flag-like variable, "tracker_flag", is returned from the `TrackMultipleItems()` function denoting whether an item was actually moved, as is the case for all diagram entity movement functions shown.

11.3   ADD A `TrackMultipleItems()` FUNCTION TO CDiagramEngDoc

The `TrackMultipleItems()` function allows the creation of a rubber band to enclose a region of items on the palette, and then after defining this region, the enclosed items may be selected by left-clicking the interior of the bounded region (rubber band), and all contained items may be moved, i.e., translated, to a new location. The function has three main conditional clauses: (1) if a rubber band has not been created, then it is to be (initially) created; (2) if a rubber band has been created but a left-click event subsequently occurs outside the rubber band region, then the region containing items cannot be moved, so no movement action is taken; and (3) if a rubber band has been created and a left-click event subsequently occurs inside the rubber band region, then the region containing items can be translated to a new location, and the positions of the contained items are updated accordingly.

Hence, add a public member function to the CDiagramEngDoc class with the prototype, `int CDiagramEngDoc::TrackMultipleItems(CPoint point, CWnd *pWnd)`, and edit it as shown.

```
int CDiagramEngDoc::TrackMultipleItems(CPoint point, CWnd *pWnd)
{
    int intersected = 0;
    int item_tracked = 0;
    int manual_rect = 1;
    int tracker_flag = 0;
    double blk_width;
```

```
double delta = 0.25*m_dDeltaLength;
static CPoint tracker_init; // require tracker_init for else clause
  on re-entry of OnLButtonDown
CPoint bend_pt;
CPoint blk_posn;
CPoint delta_posn;
CPoint head_pt;
CPoint tail_pt;
CRectTracker temp_tracker;
list<CBlock*> &blk_list = GetSystemModel().GetBlockList();
list<CBlock*>::iterator it_blk;
list<CConnection*>::iterator it_con;
list<CConnection*> &con_list = GetSystemModel().GetConnectionList();
list<CPoint>::iterator it_pt;
CClientDC dc(pWnd);

// -- IF A RUBBER BAND HAS NOT BEEN CREATED, THEN CREATE IT.
if(m_iRubberBandCreated == 0)
{
    // Create a rubber band
    m_RectTracker.TrackRubberBand(pWnd, point, TRUE);
    m_RectTracker.m_rect.NormalizeRect();
    tracker_init = m_RectTracker.m_rect.CenterPoint();

    // Create a temporary rectangle indicating where the initial
      CRectTracker rectangle was.
    // This is done, since the temporary CRectTracker rectangle
      disappears upon fn exit.
    if(manual_rect) // Manually create a red, dotted lined rectangle
    {
        CPen lpen(PS_DOT, 1, RGB(255,0,0));         // create a pen
        CPen *pOldPen = dc.SelectObject(&lpen);   // create a copy
        dc.SetROP2(R2_NOTXORPEN);          // make the rectangle
          transparent
        dc.Rectangle(m_RectTracker.m_rect.TopLeft().x,
          m_RectTracker.m_rect.TopLeft().y, m_RectTracker.m_rect.
          BottomRight().x, m_RectTracker.m_rect.BottomRight().y);
          // create the rectangle using the m_RectTracker object
          coords.
        dc.SelectObject(pOldPen);  // reset the old pen
    }
    else    // Use the default black dotted lined rectangle
    {
        m_RectTracker.m_nStyle = CRectTracker::dottedLine;
        m_RectTracker.Draw(&dc);
    }

    // Set flags.
    m_iRubberBandCreated = 1; // rubber band state is active
    tracker_flag = 1;          // tracking of multiple items has
      commenced
    return tracker_flag;
}

// -- IF A RUBBER BAND HAS BEEN CREATED, BUT LEFT-CLICK OUTSIDE OF
  ENCLOSING REGION, THEN END TRACK ACTION.
else if((m_RectTracker.HitTest(point) == CRectTracker::hitNothing)
  && (m_iRubberBandCreated == 1))
```

```
{
    m_iRubberBandCreated = 0;  // end the rubber band state
    SetKeyFlagTrack(0);        // reset the key-based track flag since
      tracking aborted
    tracker_flag = 0;          // tracking did not occur
    return tracker_flag;
}

// -- IF A RUBBER BAND HAS BEEN CREATED, AND LEFT-CLICK INSIDE
  ENCLOSING REGION, THEN POSSIBLY MOVE ITEMS.
else if((m_RectTracker.HitTest(point) != CRectTracker::hitNothing)
  && (m_iRubberBandCreated == 1))
{
    // Create a temp tracker since m_RectTracker will have its coords
      updated when the rubber band is moved.
    temp_tracker = m_RectTracker;

    // -- ITERATE THROUGH BLOCKS
    for(it_blk = blk_list.begin(); it_blk != blk_list.end(); it_blk++)
    {
        // BLOCK
        blk_posn = (*it_blk)->GetBlockPosition();
        blk_width = (*it_blk)->GetBlockShape().GetBlockWidth();

        // Determine if item lies within rubber band
        intersected = DetermineCurrentAndIntersectRects(temp_tracker,
          blk_posn, (blk_width*0.5));
        if(intersected)
        {
            if(item_tracked == 0)
            {
                // Determine the tracker's change in position
                item_tracked = DetermineTrackerDeltaPosition(pWnd,
                  point, tracker_init, delta_posn);
            }

            // Update the block posn.
            (*it_blk)->SetBlockPosition(blk_posn + delta_posn);

            // Set flags
            SetModifiedFlag(TRUE); // set the doc. as having been
              modified to prompt user to save
            UpdateAllViews (NULL); // indicate that sys. should
              redraw.
        }
    }// end for it_blk

    // -- ITERATE THROUGH ALL CONNECTIONS (of this model)
    for(it_con = con_list.begin(); it_con != con_list.end();
      it_con++)
    {
        // TAIL POINT
        tail_pt = (*it_con)->GetConnectionPointTail();

        // Determine if item lies within rubber band
        intersected = DetermineCurrentAndIntersectRects(temp_tracker,
          tail_pt, delta);
        if(intersected)
```

```
{
    if(item_tracked == 0)
    {
        // Determine the tracker's change in position
        item_tracked = DetermineTrackerDeltaPosition(pWnd,
          point, tracker_init, delta_posn);
    }
    // Check if the TAIL POINT is NOT CONNECTED to a PORT or
      a BEND POINT: if so move it.
    if( ( (*it_con)->GetRefFromPort() == NULL) &&
      ((*it_con)->GetRefFromPoint() == NULL))
    {
        // Update tail pt. posn.
        (*it_con)->SetConnectionPointTail(tail_pt + delta_posn);

        // Set flags
        SetModifiedFlag(TRUE); // set the doc. as having been
          modified to prompt user to save
        UpdateAllViews(NULL);  // indicate that sys. should
          redraw.
    }
}

// HEAD POINT
head_pt = (*it_con)->GetConnectionPointHead();

// Determine if item lies within rubber band
intersected = DetermineCurrentAndIntersectRects(temp_tracker,
  head_pt, delta);
if(intersected)
{
    if(item_tracked == 0)
    {
        // Determine the tracker's change in position
        item_tracked = DetermineTrackerDeltaPosition(pWnd,
          point, tracker_init, delta_posn);
    }

    // Check if the HEAD POINT is NOT CONNECTED to a PORT:
      if so move it.
    if( (*it_con)->GetRefToPort() == NULL)
    {
        // Update head pt. posn.
        (*it_con)->SetConnectionPointHead(head_pt + delta_posn);

        // Set flags
        SetModifiedFlag(TRUE); // set the doc. as having been
          modified to prompt user to save
        UpdateAllViews(NULL); // indicate that sys. should
          redraw.
    }
}
// -- ITERATE THROUGH ALL BEND POINTS FOR THIS CONNECTION

list<CPoint> &bend_pts_list = (*it_con)-
  >GetConnectionBendPointsList();

for(it_pt = bend_pts_list.begin(); it_pt != bend_pts_list.
  end(); it_pt++)
```

```
        {
            // BEND POINT
            bend_pt = *it_pt;

            // Determine if item lies within rubber band
            intersected = DetermineCurrentAndIntersectRects(temp_tracker,
              bend_pt, delta);
            if(intersected)
            {
                if(item_tracked == 0)
                {
                    // Determine the tracker's change in position
                    item_tracked = DetermineTrackerDeltaPosition(pWnd,
                      point, tracker_init, delta_posn);
                }

                // Update the connection bend pt posn.
                *it_pt = *it_pt + delta_posn;

                // Update any connection's tail point if it was
                  connected to this bend point
                m_SystemModel.UpdateConnectionPointTailToBendPoint
                  (&(*it_pt));

                // Set flags
                SetModifiedFlag(TRUE); // set the doc. as having been
                  modified to prompt user to save
                UpdateAllViews(NULL);  // indicate that sys. should
                  redraw.
            }
        }// end for it_pt
    }// end for it_con

    // Set flags
    m_iRubberBandCreated = 0; // end the rubber band state
    SetKeyFlagTrack(0);       // reset the key-based track flag since
      tracking aborted

    if(item_tracked == 0)      // if no item was tracked
    {
        tracker_flag = 0;
        return tracker_flag;
    }
    else    // if an item was tracked
    {
        tracker_flag = 1;
        return tracker_flag;
    }
}

// Return the tracker_flag
return tracker_flag;
}
```

The `TrackMultipleItems()` function uses a variable named "m_iRubberBandCreated" to determine whether or not a rubber band has been created. Since the `TrackMultipleItems()` function is entered twice, firstly to create the rubber band and secondly to check that a subsequent left-click event has occurred within the previously created rubber band region, the "m_iRubberBandCreated" variable cannot be local, but rather needs to be a class member variable. Hence, add the private integer member variable, "m_iRubberBandCreated", to the CDiagramEngDoc class and initialize it to zero in the CDiagramEngDoc class' constructor, as shown in the following.

```
CDiagramEngDoc::CDiagramEngDoc()
{
    // TODO: add one-time construction code here
    // DiagramEng (start)
    m_iRubberBandCreated = 0;
    m_dDeltaLength = 50.0;
    // DiagramEng (end)
}
```

The developer will also notice two often-used function calls within the TrackMultipleItems() function, i.e., DetermineCurrentAndIntersectRects() and DetermineTrackerDeltaPosition(). DetermineCurrentAndIntersectRects() determines the rectangle coordinates of the current graphic item on the palette, e.g., a block, connection end point, or connection bend point, and the rectangle coordinates of its intersection with the rubber band: this is used to determine whether the current item lies within the rubber band region. DetermineTrackerDeltaPosition() is used to determine the change in position (translation) of the rubber band region through the initial and final positions of the center point of the "m_RectTracker" object.

11.3.1 ADD THE DetermineCurrentAndIntersectRects() FUNCTION

Add a public member function to the CDiagramEngDoc class with the prototype int Determine CurrentAndIntersectRects(CRectTracker temp_tracker, CPoint item_posn, double delta) and edit the code as shown.

```
int CDiagramEngDoc::DetermineCurrentAndIntersectRects(CRectTracker
  temp_tracker, CPoint item_posn, double delta)
{
    int intersected = 0;
    CPoint bottom_right;
    CPoint top_left;
    CRect current_rect;
    CRect intersect_rect;

    // Determine the coordinates of the item
    top_left.x = (int)(item_posn.x - delta);
    top_left.y = (int)(item_posn.y - delta);
    bottom_right.x = (int)(item_posn.x + delta);
    bottom_right.y = (int)(item_posn.y + delta);

    // Determine the current and intersect rectangles
    current_rect.SetRect(top_left.x, top_left.y, bottom_right.x,
      bottom_right.y);
    intersect_rect.IntersectRect(temp_tracker.m_rect, current_rect);

    // Check whether the item lies within the rubber band region,
    //  i.e. it intersects.
    if(intersect_rect == current_rect)
    {
        intersected = 1;
    }
    else
```

```
    {
        intersected = 0;
    }
    // Return the intersected flag.
    return intersected;
}
```

The `IntersectRect()` function used earlier makes a CRect object equal to the intersection of two existing rectangles, where the intersection is the largest rectangle contained in both the existing rectangles [1]. Here, this is used to determine whether a diagram item described by "current_rect" lies within and equivalently intersects the bounding "temp_tracker" rubber-band-enclosing rectangular region.

11.3.2 ADD THE `DetermineTrackerDeltaPosition()` FUNCTION

Add a public member function to the CDiagramEngDoc class with the following prototype: `int DetermineTrackerDeltaPosition(CWnd *pWnd, CPoint point, CPoint tracker_init, CPoint &delta_posn)` and edit the code as shown later. Notice how "delta_posn" is being passed by reference into this function: this is required since it denotes the change in the position of the center point of the "m_RectTracker" object and is used in the calling function `TrackMultipleItems()` to set the new position of the item to be moved.

```
int CDiagramEngDoc::DetermineTrackerDeltaPosition(CWnd *pWnd, CPoint
  point, CPoint tracker_init, CPoint &delta_posn)
{
    int item_tracked = 0;
    CPoint tracker_final;

    // Track the rectangle and determine its change in position.
    m_RectTracker.Track(pWnd, point, TRUE);    // 0 => item not tracked,
      1 => item was tracked
    tracker_final = m_RectTracker.m_rect.CenterPoint();
    delta_posn = tracker_final - tracker_init;

    // Set the item_tracked flag
    if((delta_posn.x == 0) && (delta_posn.y == 0))
    {
        item_tracked = 0;
    }
    else
    {
        item_tracked = 1;
    }

    // Return a flag indicating a tracking event
    return item_tracked;
}
```

11.4 ADD A FUNCTION FOR A KEY-DOWN EVENT TO CDiagramEngView

In order to track multiple items, the "T" keyboard character needs to be pressed resulting in the "m_iKeyFlagTrack" variable being set to one, and in the `TrackItem()` function, a check is made, i.e., "if(m_iKeyFlagTrack == 1)", to determine whether the right character has been used. Hence, a function needs to be added to process keyboard input, i.e., "on-key-down" events, and set the member variable, "m_iKeyFlagTrack", of the CDiagramEngDoc class. Add an event-handler function for the WM_KEYDOWN event message for the CDiagramEngView class with the prototype void CDiagramEngView::OnKeyDown(UINT nChar, UINT nRepCnt, UINT nFlags), and edit it as shown.

```
void CDiagramEngView::OnKeyDown(UINT nChar, UINT nRepCnt, UINT nFlags)
{
    // TODO: Add your message handler code here and/or call default

    // DiagramEng (start)
    int key_flag = 0;       // local int
    char lchar;             // local character
    lchar = char(nChar);    // typecast the nChar

    // Get a ptr to the doc
    CDiagramEngDoc *pDoc = GetDocument();

    // Check that the "T" character has been pressed
    if(lchar == 'T')
    {
        key_flag = 1;
        pDoc->SetKeyFlagTrack(key_flag); // set the m_iKeyFlagTrack in
            the CDiagramEngDoc class
    }

    // DiagramEng (end)

    CView::OnKeyDown(nChar, nRepCnt, nFlags);
}
```

11.5   ADD KEY-FLAG-BASED MEMBERS TO CDiagramEngDoc

The TrackItem() function of the CDiagramEngDoc class performs a check to determine whether the "m_iKeyFlagTrack" variable has been set equal to one before a call to the TrackMultipleItems() function can be made. Hence, add a private integer member variable, "m_iKeyFlagTrack", to the CDiagramEngDoc class and initialize this to zero in the CDiagramEngDoc constructor as shown.

```
CDiagramEngDoc::CDiagramEngDoc()
{
    // TODO: add one-time construction code here

    // DiagramEng (start)
    m_iKeyFlagTrack = 0;
    m_iRubberBandCreated = 0;
    m_dDeltaLength = 50.0;
    // DiagramEng (end)
}
```

Now that the "m_iKeyFlagTrack" variable has been added to the CDiagramEngDoc class, an accessor function is required to set its value. Hence, add a public accessor function to the CDiagramEngDoc class, with the prototype void CDiagramEngDoc::SetKeyFlagTrack(int key_flag), and edit it as shown.

```
void CDiagramEngDoc::SetKeyFlagTrack(int key_flag)
{
    // Set the member variable.
    m_iKeyFlagTrack = key_flag;
}
```

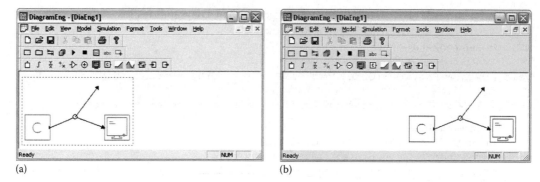

(a)   (b)

FIGURE 11.1 Moving a group of items: (a) block diagram items enclosed by a dotted rectangular rubber band and (b) diagram translated to the right using the mouse left-click–drag–release sequence.

Now, when the user runs the application, a rectangular rubber band region may be drawn from the initial point of the left-click event to the current point of the mouse cursor: when the user releases the left mouse button, a dotted rectangle appears, indicating the initial rubber band rectangular selection. Upon clicking within the rubber band region and moving the mouse cursor, the dotted rectangle then follows the mouse cursor. Diagram entities may then be selected and moved conveniently as a group. Figure 11.1a indicates two blocks, two connections, and a connection bend point, enclosed by a dotted rubber band region on the left side of the palette. The user may then click within the dotted-bordered region and move the enclosed items to a different location on the palette as shown in Figure 11.1b.

The developer will notice a conditional statement involving the flag-like variable, "manual_rect", in the function TrackMultipleItems() as shown in the following code excerpt (the ellipsis, "...", denotes omitted and unchanged code).

```
int CDiagramEngDoc::TrackMultipleItems(CPoint point, CWnd *pWnd)
{
    ...
    // Create a temporary rectangle indicating where the initial
      CRectTracker rectangle was.
    // This is done, since the temporary CRectTracker rectangle
      disappears upon fn exit.
    if(manual_rect)   // Manually create a red, dotted lined rectangle
    {
        CPen lpen(PS_DOT, 1, RGB(255,0,0));      // create a pen
        CPen *pOldPen = dc.SelectObject(&lpen); // create a copy
        dc.SetROP2(R2_NOTXORPEN);        // make the rectangle transparent
        dc.Rectangle(m_RectTracker.m_rect.TopLeft().x,
          m_RectTracker.m_rect.TopLeft().y, m_RectTracker.m_rect.
          BottomRight().x, m_RectTracker.m_rect.BottomRight().y);
          // create the rectangle using the m_RectTracker object coords.
        dc.SelectObject(pOldPen);        // reset the old pen
    }
    else  // Use the default black dotted lined rectangle
    {
        m_RectTracker.m_nStyle = CRectTracker::dottedLine;
        m_RectTracker.Draw(&dc);
    }
    ...
}
```

This simply allows the dotted rectangle to be drawn manually, or automatically, using the provided `Draw()` function. The manual method requires the developer to set up the four corner points of the rectangle object but does allow the developer to change the color of the rectangle* the default color is black. The statement `dc.SetROP2(R2_NOTXORPEN)` allows the enclosing rectangular region to be drawn transparently; otherwise, the circumscribed items would not be visible.

11.6 FLOW OF CONTROL IN THE `TrackMultipleItems()` FUNCTION

The developer will notice that the `TrackMultipleItems()` function is entered twice: (1) on the first occasion, a rubber band is created setting the "m_iRubberBandCreated" variable to one, and the function exits, and (2) on the second occasion, a check is made to determine whether the user left-clicks the mouse in the interior or exterior of the rubber band region. The "m_iKeyFlagTrack" variable is still set to one on initial exit of the `TrackMultipleItems()` function and is only set to zero after a subsequent left-click event, either within or outside of the rubber band region. Hence, the "m_iKeyFlagTrack" variable's purpose is to allow control in the `TrackItem()` function to progress to the `TrackMultipleItem()` call, since the complete multiple-item-tracking process requires two actions: creation of the rubber band and a check of the location of the subsequent left-click event.

Another important point is that the "tracker_flag" is initially set to one in the first conditional section of the `TrackMultipleItems()` function. This is required since `TrackItem()` will exit immediately after the `TrackMultipleItems()` call, and the returned nonzero value will cause the `OnLButtonDown()` function to exit also, without the possibility of unintentionally drawing a connection object on the palette while in the process of a multiple-item-tracking action that requires at least two entries into the `TrackMultipleItems()` function.

The developer will also notice that a CRectTracker, "temp_tracker", object is defined and assigned the value of the "m_RectTracker" object at the start of the third conditional section. This "temp_tracker" object is then used to determine the intersection of an item on the palette with the initial rubber band region circumscribing the group of objects to be moved. The "m_RectTracker" object cannot be used, since its coordinates will be updated on movement of the rubber band. The final "m_RectTracker" position is then evaluated in the `DetermineTrackerDeltaPosition()` function and is used to determine the change (δ) in position of the translated rubber band.

In addition to the three main conditional sections, i.e., to create the rubber band, to check whether the left-click event is outside of the rubber band region, and to move items accordingly if the left-click event is inside the rubber band region, there are three *for* loops in the conditional section concerning movement of the rubber band region: the first iterates through the list of blocks, the second iterates through the list of connections, and the third loop nested within the connection-based *for* loop iterates through the list of bend points that may exist on the current connection object.

Blocks may be moved by simply checking whether they intersect, i.e., lie inside the rubber band region, and updating their positions by the same amount, "delta_posn", that the rubber band was moved. Connection end points, i.e., head and tail points, may be moved in a similar manner. However, in the case of tail points, if the tail point's reference-from port (block port), or reference-from point (bend point) is NULL, as checked in the conditional clause, "`if( ( (*it_con)->GetRefFromPort() == NULL) && ( (*it_con)->GetRefFromPoint() == NULL) )`", only then is the tail point moved. This check is required since if the tail point is moved independently, i.e., not in conjunction with the block port or bend point from which it emanates, then this motion will break the connection to the block port or bend point: this is not desired. Similarly, in the case of head points, if the head point's reference-to port is NULL, as checked in the conditional clause, "`if( (*it_con)->GetRefToPort() == NULL)`", only then should the head point be moved. Again, since if it was not NULL, i.e., if the head point was connected to an input port, the independent head point movement would break the connection with the block port to which it

---

* The color of the rectangle is red, as may be observed when running the DiagramEng application.

should be connected. As a result, only head and tail points that are not connected to other diagram entities, i.e., bend points or ports, may be moved independently. Finally, in the section concerning only bend point movement, after a connection bend point is moved, any tail point connected to that bend point must be updated to the new bend point position, as implemented by the function call: "m_SystemModel.UpdateConnectionPointTailToBendPoint(&(*it_pt))".

11.7 ADD A TOOLBAR BUTTON TO ACTIVATE MULTIPLE ITEM TRACKING

At present, the tracking of multiple items requires the user to press the "T" key before enclosing the objects to be moved with a rubber band. This is processed in the OnKeyDown() function, and then the SetKeyFlagTrack() function is called to set the "m_iKeyFlagTrack" member variable of the CDiagramEngDoc class, required before the call to TrackMultipleItems() may be made from the TrackItem() function (shown previously).

A toolbar button was added earlier to the Common Operations toolbar (IDR_TB_COMMON_OPS) that is to have a similar purpose to the "T" key character in the OnKeyDown() function, resulting in the member variable, "m_iKeyFlagTrack", being set to one. Navigate to the IDR_TB_COMMON_OPS toolbar resource and make sure that the Track Multiple Items button is present with the settings shown in Table 11.1.

Now, a function needs to be added for the COMMAND event message for the Track Multiple Items button on the Common Operations toolbar. Invoke the ClassWizard and select CDiagramEngDoc as the class, since the event-handler to be added relates to setting the "m_iKeyFlagTrack" member variable through a call to SetKeyFlagTrack() of the CDiagramEngDoc class. Add a function for the COMMAND event message for the toolbar button with ID, ID_INIT_TRACK_MULTIPLE_ITEMS, as shown in Table 11.2. Edit the OnInitTrackMultipleItems() function as shown in the following, to call SetKeyFlagTrack(), which then sets the member variable, "m_iKeyFlagTrack".

```
void CDiagramEngDoc::OnInitTrackMultipleItems()
{
    // TODO: Add your command handler code here

    // DiagramEng (start)
    int key_flag = 1;              // 0 => can't call TrackMultipleItems(),
      1 => can call TrackMultipleItems.
```

TABLE 11.1
Common Operations Toolbar-Based Track Multiple Items Button
Object, Properties, Settings, and Icon

Object	Property	Setting	Icon
Track Multiple Items	ID	ID_INIT_TRACK_MULTIPLE_ITEMS	
	Prompts: status bar and tooltips	Initiate tracking of multiple items/nTrack Multiple Items	

TABLE 11.2
Common Operations Toolbar Button Settings: Object, ID, Class, and the Corresponding
Command Event-Handler Function

Object	ID	Class	COMMAND Event-Handler
Track multiple items	ID_INIT_TRACK_MULTIPLE_ITEMS	CDiagramEngDoc	OnInitTrackMultipleItems()

```
    // Set the m_iKeyFlagTrack member variable using SetKeyFlagTrack(1)
    SetKeyFlagTrack(key_flag);

    // DiagramEng (end)
}
```

Now, upon running the program, the Track Multiple Items button at the end of the Common Operations toolbar may be used for the initiation of the tracking of multiple items, rather than pressing the "T" key (this is somewhat easier). The tracking action ends automatically, either upon movement of the circumscribed items or upon clicking outside of the dotted rectangular region.

11.8 SUMMARY

The simultaneous movement of multiple items is achieved through the addition of a TrackMultipleItems() function to the CDiagramEngDoc class that makes use of a TrackRubberBand() function call upon a CRectTracker, "m_RectTracker", object. The TrackMultipleItems() function has three main conditional sections and is entered twice to perform the entire tracking action. The user can enclose the items to be moved with a rectangular rubber band, and then, upon left-clicking within the region, the enclosed items may be translated across the palette. In order to allow this function to work, additional methods and variables are introduced, including the DetermineCurrentAndIntersectRects() and DetermineTrackerDeltaPosition() functions, which determine the rectangular coordinates of an item on the palette and the change in position of the rubber band region, respectively. Finally, a keystroke ("T") or the Track Multiple Items toolbar button may be used to initiate the multiple-item-tracking operation.

REFERENCE

1. Microsoft Developer Network Library Visual Studio 6.0, Microsoft® Visual Studio™ 6.0 Development System, Microsoft Corporation, 1998.

12 Addition of a Tree View Control

12.1 INTRODUCTION

The current state of the DiagramEng application allows the user to draw a block diagram on the palette, including blocks, connections, and bend points. The user can insert the blocks by using the Block Library Dialog window to select multiple blocks or by clicking on the buttons of the Common Blocks toolbar (IDR_TB_COMMON_BLOCKS). Here, a Tree View control will be added to the application, initially as a dialog window with base class CDialog, and then this will be converted to a CDialogBar instance and docked to the application Main frame.

Adaptations are made here to the original instructions provided in an article made available by FunctionX, titled "TreeView on a dialog" [1], to clarify the addition of a Tree View control on a dialog window for an MDI application. In addition, provided here are instructions to dock the dialog window, upon which the Tree View control resides, to the left side of the application Main frame. The docking instructions follow closely the work of an article provided by Microsoft Support, titled "How to initialize child controls in a derived CDialogBar" [2], as explained in Section 12.3.

12.2 ADD A TREE VIEW CONTROL DIALOG WINDOW

A Tree View control is to be added to the graphical user interface (GUI) initially in a dialog window and involves the following general steps where specific details follow:

1. Insert a dialog window and add controls.
2. Attach a class to the dialog window.
3. Add functionality to invoke the Tree View dialog.
4. Attach a variable to the dialog window control.
5. Add the OnInitDialog() function to the CTreeDialog class.
6. Add icons to the Tree View control.
7. Add an event-handler function for Tree View node selection.

12.2.1 INSERT A DIALOG WINDOW AND ADD CONTROLS

Add a new dialog resource to contain the Tree View control to the project, with ID, IDD_TREE_DLG, and caption, TreeDialog. Both the maximize and minimize boxes should be selected for the Styles settings. Leave the OK and Cancel buttons on the dialog; these buttons will be removed later, but for now, they are necessary to close the application. Finally, add the controls provided in Table 12.1 and place them on the dialog window as shown in Figure 12.1; accept the default properties for the Tree Control but select the additional properties as indicated.

12.2.2 ATTACH A CLASS TO THE DIALOG WINDOW

A class is required to be attached to the dialog window resource, in order to present and retrieve information to and from the user, to invoke Tree View control–based functionality. Hence, select the IDD_TREE_DLG resource from the ResourceView tab on the Workspace pane to show the

TABLE 12.1
Dialog Window (IDD_TREE_DLG) Objects,
Properties, and Settings

Object	Property	Setting
Tree Control	ID	ID_TREE_DLG_TREE
	Has buttons	Checked
	Has lines	Checked
	Lines at root	Checked
Button	ID	IDOK
	Default button	Unchecked
	Caption	&OK
Button	ID	IDCANCEL
	Caption	&Cancel

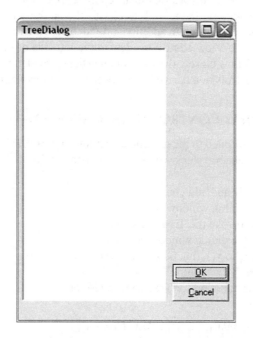

FIGURE 12.1   Tree Dialog window showing the controls as specified in Table 12.1.

corresponding dialog window in the editor area and right-click on the dialog box to invoke the ClassWizard. The Adding a Class message box appears; create a new class with name CTreeDialog and base class CDialog.

12.2.3 ADD FUNCTIONALITY TO INVOKE THE TREE VIEW DIALOG

The Common Operations toolbar currently has a button with ID, ID_EDIT_ADD_MULTI_BLOCKS, to invoke a block library listing in the form of a dialog window (IDD_BLOCKLIBDLG), represented by the folder icon (second from the left) on the toolbar (second from the top) shown in Figure 12.2. This button will now be used to invoke a Tree View–based block listing, still in the form of a dialog window (IDD_TREE_DLG). See Table 12.2 for the existing toolbar button setting.

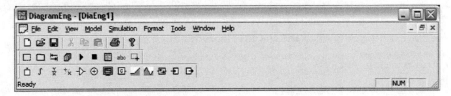

FIGURE 12.2 Common Operations toolbar (second from the top) showing the block library button represented by a closed folder icon (second from the left).

TABLE 12.2

Common Operations Toolbar Button Settings: Object, ID, Class, and the Corresponding Command Event-Handler Function

Object (Toolbar Button)	ID	Class	COMMAND Event-Handler
Add Multiple Blocks	ID_EDIT_ADD_MULTI_BLOCKS	CDiagramEngDoc	OnEditAddMultipleBlocks()

The developer will recall that the event-handler function to generate the Block Library Dialog window is CDiagramEngDoc::OnEditAddMultipleBlocks(). This function declares a CBlockLibDlg object, "oDlg", which allows the original check-box-based block-selection dialog window to be presented to the user as shown in Figure 12.3.

The OnEditAddMultipleBlocks() function is now modified, with the addition of an extra conditional statement "if(display_item == 2)", which declares a CTreeDialog object, "oDlg", which allows the Tree Dialog (IDD_TREE_DLG) added above, to display the Tree View control (ID_TREE_DLG_TREE).

Hence, edit the OnEditAddMultipleBlocks() function with the code shown in bold in the following. To compile and run the code, the header file "TreeDialog.h" needs to be included at the top of the "DiagramEngDoc.cpp" file since a CTreeDialog object is being implicitly constructed.

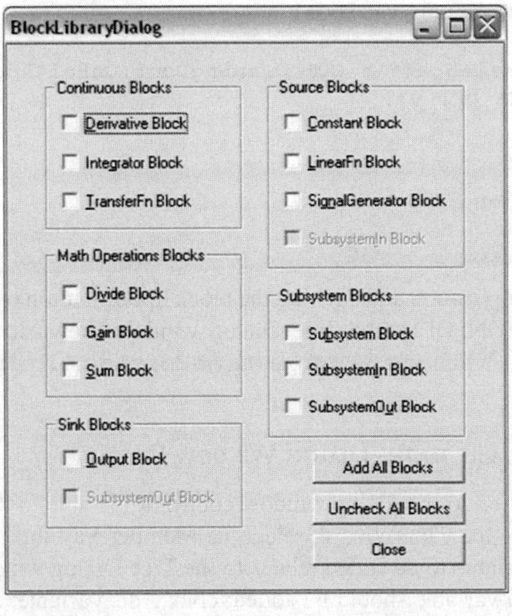

FIGURE 12.3 BlockLibraryDialog check-box-based dialog window allowing block selection.

```
void CDiagramEngDoc::OnEditAddMultipleBlocks()
{
    // TODO: Add your command handler code here

    // DiagramEng (start)

    // Local var declaration
    int display_item = 2; // used to display msg box or dlg wnd.

    // Display a msg.
    if(display_item == 0)
    {
        AfxMessageBox("\n CDiagramEngDoc::OnEditAddMultipleBlocks()n",
          MB_OK, 0);
    }
    else if(display_item == 1)
    {
        CBlockLibDlg oDlg; // create a dlg obj. of class CBlockLibDlg :
          public CDialog

        // Return val of DoModal() fn of ancestor class CDialog is
          checked to determine which btn was clicked.
        if(oDlg.DoModal() == IDOK)
        {
            //AfxMessageBox("\n CDiagramEngDoc::OnEditAddMultipleBlocks()
              n", MB_OK, 0);
        }
    }
    else if(display_item == 2)
    {
        CTreeDialog oDlg;  // create a dlg obj. of class CTreeDialog :
          public CDialog

        // Return val of DoModal() fn of ancestor class CDialog is
          checked to determine which btn was clicked.
        if(oDlg.DoModal() == IDOK)
        {
            AfxMessageBox("\n CDiagramEngDoc::OnEditAddMultipleBlocks()
              n", MB_OK, 0);
        }
    }

    // DiagramEng (end)
}
```

Now, upon running the application and clicking the block library button on the Common Operations toolbar (ID_TB_COMMON_OPS), the Tree Dialog window shown in Figure 12.1 will appear. Clicking OK then prints a simple message from the OnEditAddMultipleBlocks() function.

12.2.4 ATTACH A VARIABLE TO THE DIALOG WINDOW CONTROL

A variable is to be attached to the dialog window control to be able to display various Tree View properties. Hence, invoke the ClassWizard; select the Member Variables tab; choose CTreeDialog as the class, since the variable to be added relates to the Tree Dialog window control; select the ID of the control to which a variable should be added; click Add Variable; and specify the details as shown in Table 12.3.

TABLE 12.3

Dialog Window Control, Variable Name, Category, and Type for the IDD_TREE_DLG (Dialog Window) Resource

Control	Variable Name	Category	Type
ID_TREE_DLG_TREE	M_TreeCtrl	Control	CTreeCtrl

Notice how, upon using the ClassWizard to add the member variable, the DoDataExchange() function of the CTreeDialog class (as shown) is automatically updated with the DDX_Control() function call. The DDX_Control(), Dialog Data Exchange function, manages the data transfer between the dialog window control, i.e., the Tree Control (ID_TREE_DLG_TREE) and the variable attached to the control, i.e., the CTreeCtrl, "m_TreeCtrl", member variable of the CTreeDialog class. This variable is then used to present data to the user, e.g., through the use of the InsertItem() function to populate the branch names of the directory-structure-like Tree View.

```
void CTreeDialog::DoDataExchange(CDataExchange* pDX)
{
    CDialog::DoDataExchange(pDX);
    //{{AFX_DATA_MAP(CTreeDialog)
    DDX_Control(pDX, ID_TREE_DLG_TREE, m_TreeCtrl);
    //}}AFX_DATA_MAP
}
```

12.2.5 ADD THE OnInitDialog() FUNCTION TO THE CTreeDialog CLASS

An OnInitDialog() function needs to be added to the CTreeDialog class, as indicated in the following steps, in order to call the InitTreeControl() function to initialize the Tree View with the correct properties:

1. Invoke the ClassWizard, select the Message Maps tab, choose CTreeDialog as the class, and select CTreeDialog under the Object IDs section and WM_INITDIALOG as the message.
2. Add an initialization function named CTreeDialog::OnInitDialog(): the initialization cannot be done within the constructor, since the constructor can only handle variable initialization, not dialog function-call-based initialization.
3. Edit the CTreeDialog::OnInitDialog() function, as shown in the following, to call a specific InitTreeControl() function (in bold) wherein all the Tree View control initialization occurs.
4. Finally, add a public member function to the CTreeDialog class with the prototype void CTreeDialog::InitTreeControl(void), and edit it as shown.

```
BOOL CTreeDialog::OnInitDialog()
{
    CDialog::OnInitDialog();

    // TODO: Add extra initialization here

    // DiagramEng (start)

    // Specifically initialize the Tree control
    InitTreeControl();
```

```
    // DiagramEng (end)

    return TRUE; // return TRUE unless you set the focus to a control
                 // EXCEPTION: OCX Property Pages should return FALSE
}

void CTreeDialog::InitTreeControl()
{
    // DiagramEng (start)

    //AfxMessageBox("\n CTreeDialog::InitTreeControl()n", MB_OK, 0);

    // Tree label vars - Blocks level
    HTREEITEM hBlocks;
    HTREEITEM hContinuousBlocks;
    HTREEITEM hMathOperationsBlocks;
    HTREEITEM hSinkBlocks;
    HTREEITEM hSourceBlocks;
    HTREEITEM hSubsystemBlocks;

    // Tree label vars - ContinuousBlocks level
    HTREEITEM hDerivativeBlock;
    HTREEITEM hIntegratorBlock;
    HTREEITEM hTransferFnBlock;

    // Tree label vars - MathOperationsBlocks level
    HTREEITEM hDivideBlock;
    HTREEITEM hGainBlock;
    HTREEITEM hSumBlock;

    // Tree label vars - SinkBlocks level
    HTREEITEM hOutputBlock;
    //HTREEITEM hSubsystemOutBlock;  // defined under SubsystemBlocks

    // Tree label vars - SourceBlocks level
    HTREEITEM hConstantBlock;
    HTREEITEM hLinearFnBlock;
    HTREEITEM hSignalGeneratorBlock;
    //HTREEITEM hSubsystemInBlock;   // defined under SubsystemBlocks

    // Tree label vars - SubsystemBlocks level
    HTREEITEM hSubsystemBlock;
    HTREEITEM hSubsystemInBlock;
    HTREEITEM hSubsystemOutBlock;

    // Specification of vars - Blocks level
    hBlocks = m_TreeCtrl.InsertItem("DiagramEng Blocks", TVI_ROOT);
    hContinuousBlocks = m_TreeCtrl.InsertItem("ContinuousBlocks", hBlocks);
    hMathOperationsBlocks = m_TreeCtrl.InsertItem("MathOperationsBlocks",
      hBlocks);
    hSinkBlocks = m_TreeCtrl.InsertItem("SinkBlocks", hBlocks);
    hSourceBlocks = m_TreeCtrl.InsertItem("SourceBlocks", hBlocks);
    hSubsystemBlocks = m_TreeCtrl.InsertItem("SubsystemBlocks", hBlocks);

    // Specification of vars - ContinuousBlocks level
    //hContinuousBlocks = m_TreeCtrl.InsertItem("ContinuousBlocks",
      TVI_ROOT);
    hDerivativeBlock = m_TreeCtrl.InsertItem("DerivativeBlock",
      hContinuousBlocks);
    hIntegratorBlock = m_TreeCtrl.InsertItem("IntegratorBlock",
      hContinuousBlocks);
```

```
hTransferFnBlock = m_TreeCtrl.InsertItem("TransferFnBlock",
  hContinuousBlocks);

// Specification of vars - MathOperationsBlocks level
//hMathOperationsBlocks = m_TreeCtrl.InsertItem("MathOperationsBlocks",
  TVI_ROOT);
hDivideBlock = m_TreeCtrl.InsertItem("DivideBlock",
  hMathOperationsBlocks);
hGainBlock = m_TreeCtrl.InsertItem("GainBlock",
  hMathOperationsBlocks);
hSumBlock = m_TreeCtrl.InsertItem("SumBlock", hMathOperationsBlocks);

// Specification of vars - SinkBlocks level
//hSinkBlocks = m_TreeCtrl.InsertItem("SinkBlocks", TVI_ROOT);
hOutputBlock = m_TreeCtrl.InsertItem("OutputBlock", hSinkBlocks);
hSubsystemOutBlock = m_TreeCtrl.InsertItem("SubsystemOutBlock",
  hSinkBlocks);

// Specification of vars - SourceBlocks level
//hSourceBlocks = m_TreeCtrl.InsertItem("SourceBlocks", TVI_ROOT);
hConstantBlock = m_TreeCtrl.InsertItem("ConstantBlock",
  hSourceBlocks);
hLinearFnBlock = m_TreeCtrl.InsertItem("LinearFnBlock",
  hSourceBlocks);
hSignalGeneratorBlock = m_TreeCtrl.InsertItem("SignalGeneratorBlock",
  hSourceBlocks);
hSubsystemInBlock = m_TreeCtrl.InsertItem("SubsystemInBlock",
  hSourceBlocks);

// Specification of vars - SubsystemBlocks level
//hSubsystemBlocks = m_TreeCtrl.InsertItem("SubsystemBlocks",
  TVI_ROOT);
hSubsystemBlock = m_TreeCtrl.InsertItem("SubsystemBlock",
  hSubsystemBlocks);
hSubsystemInBlock = m_TreeCtrl.InsertItem("SubsystemInBlock",
  hSubsystemBlocks);
hSubsystemOutBlock = m_TreeCtrl.InsertItem("SubsystemOutBlock",
  hSubsystemBlocks);

  // DiagramEng (end)
}
```

Now, upon running the application and clicking the Add Multiple Blocks button on the Common Operations toolbar, the Tree Dialog window with the Tree View control showing the inserted directory structure, done using `InsertItem()` as specified in the `InitTreeControl()` function, is visible (Figure 12.4).

12.2.6 Add Icons to the Tree View Control

A CImageList object containing images may be used in conjunction with a Tree View control to place images next to the nodes of a Tree. The following instructions detail how node-associated images may be added to the Tree View control:

1. Select Resource from the Insert menu and choose Bitmap to add a bitmap resource.
2. Double click in the editor area to set the Bitmap properties as shown in Table 12.4: four icons, all with dimensions of 16 × 16 pixels, are provided for by using a total width of 64 pixels and a height of 16 pixels.

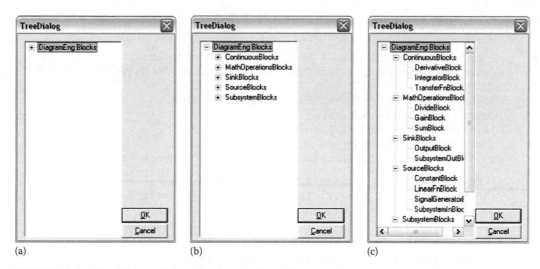

(a)   (b)   (c)

FIGURE 12.4   Tree Dialog window showing the Tree View control with its initial directory label values: (a) root DiagramEng Blocks directory, (b) block groups, and (c) specific available blocks.

TABLE 12.4

Bitmap Properties and Settings for the Four (Combined) Bitmap Images for the Tree View Control

Object	Property	Setting	Icon
Bitmap	ID File name: Width: Height: Colors:	IDB_BITMAP_TREE res\bitmap_t.bmp 64 16 16	

3. Draw four icons side by side in the editor area: (1) a closed folder, (2) a shaded folder, (3) an unchecked check box, and (4) a checked check box, as shown in Figure 12.5. Use the 16 × 16 pixel icons provided in the IDR_MAINFRAME toolbar resource as a drawing guide, being careful to stay within the 16 × 16 pixel limit for each icon.
4. Add a private member variable to the CTreeDialog class of type CImageList with name "m_TreeImageList".

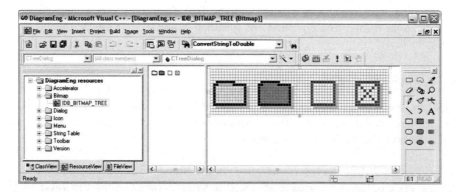

FIGURE 12.5   Sample icons for the node leaves of the Tree View control shown in the editor area: each icon is of size 16 × 16 pixels; hence, the total width of the bitmap property is 64 pixels (as shown in Table 12.4).

5. Complete the creation of the CImageList object by calling `Create()` on the object in the `InitTreeControl()` function, i.e., "`m_TreeImageList.Create(IDB_BITMAP_TREE, width, n_images, RGB(255, 255, 255))`", as shown in the following code.

6. Set the image list using the "normal" flag, TVSIL_NORMAL, which contains both the selected and unselected image icons for the Tree View control, i.e., "`m_TreeDialog. SetImageList(&m_TreeImageList, TVSIL_NORMAL)`".

7. Finally, insert the tree node identifiers including their associated images using the `InsertItem()` function as shown in the following code.

```
void CTreeDialog::InitTreeControl()
{
    // DiagramEng (start)
    int icon_flag = 1; // flag indicating whether tree has image icons
        associated with it (0) no, (1) yes.
    int i_selected;     // index of the selected image in the image list
    int i_unselected;   // index of the unselected image in the image list
    int n_images = 4;   // no. of images contained side-by-side in the
        bitmap resource.
    int width = 16;     // width (and height) of the square sub-image in
        the bitmap resource
    HTREEITEM hInsertAfter = TVI_LAST; // handle of item after which new
        item should be inserted.
    CString sMsg;           // main msg string
    UINT nType = MB_OK; // style of msg. box
    UINT nIDhelp = 0;   // help context ID for the msg.

    // Print a msg.
    sMsg.Format("\n CTreeDialog::InitTreeControl()nn");
    AfxMessageBox(sMsg, nType, nIDhelp);

    // Tree label vars - Blocks level
    HTREEITEM hBlocks;
    HTREEITEM hContinuousBlocks;
    HTREEITEM hMathOperationsBlocks;
    HTREEITEM hSinkBlocks;
    HTREEITEM hSourceBlocks;
    HTREEITEM hSubsystemBlocks;

    // Tree label vars - ContinuousBlocks level
    HTREEITEM hDerivativeBlock;
    HTREEITEM hIntegratorBlock;
    HTREEITEM hTransferFnBlock;

    // Tree label vars - MathOperationsBlocks level
    HTREEITEM hDivideBlock;
    HTREEITEM hGainBlock;
    HTREEITEM hSumBlock;

    // Tree label vars - SinkBlocks level
    HTREEITEM hOutputBlock;
    //HTREEITEM hSubsystemOutBlock; // defined under SubsystemBlocks

    // Tree label vars - SourceBlocks level
    HTREEITEM hConstantBlock;
    HTREEITEM hLinearFnBlock;
    HTREEITEM hSignalGeneratorBlock;
    //HTREEITEM hSubsystemInBlock;  // defined under SubsystemBlocks
```

```
// Tree label vars - SubsystemBlocks level
HTREEITEM hSubsystemBlock;
HTREEITEM hSubsystemInBlock;
HTREEITEM hSubsystemOutBlock;

// Display Tree with/without icons.
if(icon_flag == 0)
{
    // Specification of vars - Blocks level
    hBlocks = m_TreeCtrl.InsertItem("DiagramEng Blocks", TVI_ROOT);
    hContinuousBlocks = m_TreeCtrl.InsertItem("ContinuousBlocks",
      hBlocks);
    hMathOperationsBlocks = m_TreeCtrl.InsertItem("MathOperations
      Blocks", hBlocks);
    hSinkBlocks = m_TreeCtrl.InsertItem("SinkBlocks", hBlocks);
    hSourceBlocks = m_TreeCtrl.InsertItem("SourceBlocks", hBlocks);
    hSubsystemBlocks = m_TreeCtrl.InsertItem("SubsystemBlocks",
      hBlocks);

    // Specification of vars - ContinuousBlocks level
    //hContinuousBlocks = m_TreeCtrl.InsertItem("ContinuousBlocks",
      TVI_ROOT);
    hDerivativeBlock = m_TreeCtrl.InsertItem("DerivativeBlock",
      hContinuousBlocks);
    hIntegratorBlock = m_TreeCtrl.InsertItem("IntegratorBlock",
      hContinuousBlocks);
    hTransferFnBlock = m_TreeCtrl.InsertItem("TransferFnBlock",
      hContinuousBlocks);

    // Specification of vars - MathOperationsBlocks level
    //hMathOperationsBlocks = m_TreeCtrl.InsertItem("MathOperations
      Blocks", TVI_ROOT);
    hDivideBlock = m_TreeCtrl.InsertItem("DivideBlock",
      hMathOperationsBlocks);
    hGainBlock = m_TreeCtrl.InsertItem("GainBlock",
      hMathOperationsBlocks);
    hSumBlock = m_TreeCtrl.InsertItem("SumBlock",
      hMathOperationsBlocks);

    // Specification of vars - SinkBlocks level
    //hSinkBlocks = m_TreeCtrl.InsertItem("SinkBlocks", TVI_ROOT);
    hOutputBlock = m_TreeCtrl.InsertItem("OutputBlock", hSinkBlocks);
    hSubsystemOutBlock = m_TreeCtrl.InsertItem("SubsystemOutBlock",
      hSinkBlocks);

    // Specification of vars - SourceBlocks level
    //hSourceBlocks = m_TreeCtrl.InsertItem("SourceBlocks", TVI_ROOT);
    hConstantBlock = m_TreeCtrl.InsertItem("ConstantBlock",
      hSourceBlocks);
    hLinearFnBlock = m_TreeCtrl.InsertItem("LinearFnBlock",
      hSourceBlocks);
    vhSignalGeneratorBlock = m_TreeCtrl.InsertItem("SignalGenerator
      Block", hSourceBlocks);
    hSubsystemInBlock = m_TreeCtrl.InsertItem("SubsystemInBlock",
      hSourceBlocks);

    // Specification of vars - SubsystemBlocks level
    //hSubsystemBlocks = m_TreeCtrl.InsertItem("SubsystemBlocks",
      TVI_ROOT);
```

```
        hSubsystemBlock = m_TreeCtrl.InsertItem("SubsystemBlock",
          hSubsystemBlocks);
        hSubsystemInBlock = m_TreeCtrl.InsertItem("SubsystemInBlock",
          hSubsystemBlocks);
        hSubsystemOutBlock = m_TreeCtrl.InsertItem("SubsystemOutBlock",
          hSubsystemBlocks);
    }
    else
    {
        // -- Create the Image List
        m_TreeImageList.Create(IDB_BITMAP_TREE, width, n_images,
          RGB(255,255,255));

        // -- Set the Image List
        // TVSIL_NORMAL = sets the normal image list for unselected
        //   (image 1) and selected (image 2) node items.
        // TVSIL_STATE = sets the stage image list for Tree View items in
        //   a partic. user-defined state

        m_TreeCtrl.SetImageList(&m_TreeImageList, TVSIL_NORMAL);
        //m_TreeCtrl.SetImageList(&m_TreeImageList, TVSIL_STATE);

        // -- Specification of vars - Blocks level
        // Prototype: HTREEITEM InsertItem(UINT nMask, LPCTSTR
        //   lpszItem, int nImage, int nSelectedImage, UINT nState, UINT
        //   nStateMask, LPARAM lParam, HTREEITEM hParent, HTREEITEM
        //   hInsertAfter );

        // Choose which image to display for the parent node, based on
        //   whether the parent's child nodes are expanded
        i_unselected = 0;
        i_selected = 1;
        hBlocks = m_TreeCtrl.InsertItem("DiagramEng Blocks", i_unselected,
          i_selected, TVI_ROOT);
        //hBlocks = m_TreeCtrl.InsertItem(TVIF_STATE | TVIF_TEXT |
          TVIF_IMAGE, "DiagramEng Blocks", i_unselected, i_selected,
          TVIS_EXPANDED, TVIS_STATEIMAGEMASK, 0, TVI_ROOT,
          hInsertAfter);
        //hBlocks = m_TreeCtrl.InsertItem(TVIF_TEXT, "DiagramEng Blocks",
          i_unselected, i_selected, TVIS_EXPANDED, TVIS_STATEIMAGEMASK,
          0, TVI_ROOT, hInsertAfter);
        hContinuousBlocks = m_TreeCtrl.InsertItem("ContinuousBlocks",
          i_unselected, i_selected, hBlocks, hInsertAfter);
        hMathOperationsBlocks = m_TreeCtrl.InsertItem("MathOperationsBlocks",
          i_unselected, i_selected, hBlocks, hInsertAfter);
        hSinkBlocks = m_TreeCtrl.InsertItem("SinkBlocks", i_unselected,
          i_selected, hBlocks, hInsertAfter);
        hSourceBlocks = m_TreeCtrl.InsertItem("SourceBlocks",
          i_unselected, i_selected, hBlocks, hInsertAfter);
        hSubsystemBlocks = m_TreeCtrl.InsertItem("SubsystemBlocks",
          i_unselected, i_selected, hBlocks, hInsertAfter);

        // Specification of vars - ContinuousBlocks level
        i_unselected = 2;
        i_selected = 3;
        //hContinuousBlocks = m_TreeCtrl.InsertItem("ContinuousBlocks",
          TVI_ROOT);
        hDerivativeBlock = m_TreeCtrl.InsertItem("DerivativeBlock",
          i_unselected, i_selected, hContinuousBlocks, hInsertAfter);
```

```
        hIntegratorBlock = m_TreeCtrl.InsertItem("IntegratorBlock",
          i_unselected, i_selected, hContinuousBlocks, hInsertAfter);
        hTransferFnBlock = m_TreeCtrl.InsertItem("TransferFnBlock",
          i_unselected, i_selected, hContinuousBlocks, hInsertAfter);

        // Specification of vars - MathOperationsBlocks level
        //hMathOperationsBlocks = m_TreeCtrl.InsertItem("MathOperationsBl
          ocks", TVI_ROOT);
        hDivideBlock = m_TreeCtrl.InsertItem("DivideBlock", i_unselected,
          i_selected, hMathOperationsBlocks, hInsertAfter);
        hGainBlock = m_TreeCtrl.InsertItem("GainBlock", i_unselected,
          i_selected, hMathOperationsBlocks, hInsertAfter);
        hSumBlock = m_TreeCtrl.InsertItem("SumBlock", i_unselected,
          i_selected, hMathOperationsBlocks, hInsertAfter);

        // Specification of vars - SinkBlocks level
        //hSinkBlocks = m_TreeCtrl.InsertItem("SinkBlocks", TVI_ROOT);
        hOutputBlock = m_TreeCtrl.InsertItem("OutputBlock", i_unselected,
          i_selected, hSinkBlocks, hInsertAfter);
        hSubsystemOutBlock = m_TreeCtrl.InsertItem("SubsystemOutBlock",
          i_unselected, i_selected, hSinkBlocks, hInsertAfter);

        // Specification of vars - SourceBlocks level
        //hSourceBlocks = m_TreeCtrl.InsertItem("SourceBlocks", TVI_ROOT);
        hConstantBlock = m_TreeCtrl.InsertItem("ConstantBlock",
          i_unselected, i_selected, hSourceBlocks, hInsertAfter);
        hLinearFnBlock = m_TreeCtrl.InsertItem("LinearFnBlock",
          i_unselected, i_selected, hSourceBlocks, hInsertAfter);
        hSignalGeneratorBlock = m_TreeCtrl.InsertItem("SignalGenerator
          Block", i_unselected, i_selected, hSourceBlocks,
          hInsertAfter);
        hSubsystemInBlock = m_TreeCtrl.InsertItem("SubsystemInBlock",
          i_unselected, i_selected, hSourceBlocks);

        // Specification of vars - SubsystemBlocks level
        //hSubsystemBlocks = m_TreeCtrl.InsertItem("SubsystemBlocks",
          TVI_ROOT);
        hSubsystemBlock = m_TreeCtrl.InsertItem("SubsystemBlock",
          i_unselected, i_selected, hSubsystemBlocks, hInsertAfter);
        hSubsystemInBlock = m_TreeCtrl.InsertItem("SubsystemInBlock",
          i_unselected, i_selected, hSubsystemBlocks, hInsertAfter);
        hSubsystemOutBlock = m_TreeCtrl.InsertItem("SubsystemOutBlock",
          i_unselected, i_selected, hSubsystemBlocks, hInsertAfter);
    }

    // DiagramEng (end)
}
```

Now, upon running the code, the Tree View is visible, as shown in Figure 12.6, with the associated node images for the unselected and selected states as specified in the CImageList object "m_TreeImageList".

12.2.7   ADD AN EVENT-HANDLER FUNCTION FOR TREE VIEW NODE SELECTION

An event-handler function needs to be added for a double-click event on a particular node of the Tree View control, to invoke the correct block construction function, based on the CString,

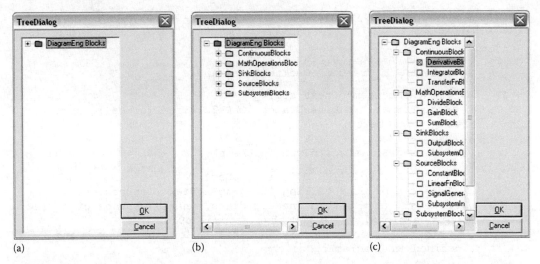

FIGURE 12.6 Tree Dialog window showing the Tree View control with images next to the directory labels: (a) root DiagramEng Blocks directory, (b) block groups, and (c) specific available blocks.

"item_text" value, and the block should appear on the palette as it does when using a toolbar button, or the Block Library Dialog window:

1. Select the ResourceView of the Workspace pane, choose the ID of the Tree Dialog, i.e., IDD_TREE_DLG, and right-click on the Tree View control to invoke the ClassWizard.
2. Select CTreeDialog as the class name, ID_TREE_DLG_TREE as the Object ID, and NM_DBLCLK as the message.
3. Add a function for the NM_DBLCLK message, named OnDblclkTreeDlgTree(), to the CTreeDialog class and edit it as shown in the following.

```
void CTreeDialog::OnDblclkTreeDlgTree(NMHDR* pNMHDR, LRESULT* pResult)
{
    // TODO: Add your control notification handler code here

    // DiagramEng (start)
    CDiagramEngDoc *pDoc = NULL; // declare pDoc to be a ptr to
      CDiagramEngDoc.
    CString item_text;          // text label of tree ctrl item
    CString sMsg;               // main msg string
    CString sMsg1;              // substring
    EBlockType e_block_type;    // enum block type defined in
      DiagramEngDoc.cpp
    HTREEITEM handle_1;         // tree ctrl. item handle
    HTREEITEM handle_2;         // tree ctrl. item handle
    UINT nType = MB_OK;         // style of msg. box
    UINT nIDhelp = 0;           // help context ID for the msg.

    // Print a msg.
    //sMsg.Format("\n CTreeDialog::OnDblclkTreeDlgTree(), code = %d,
      idFrom = %dn", pNMHDR->code, pNMHDR->idFrom);
    //AfxMessageBox(sMsg, nType, nIDhelp);

    // Get the selected tree ctrl item.
    handle_1 = m_TreeCtrl.GetSelectedItem();

    // Get the children nodes of the selected item.
    handle_2 = m_TreeCtrl.GetChildItem(handle_1);
```

```
// If the node has no children, then it's a leaf node.
if(handle_2 == NULL)
{
    // -- Get the item's text string
    item_text = m_TreeCtrl.GetItemText(handle_1);

    // Print the item's text string.
    //sMsg1.Format("\n CTreeDialog::OnDblclkTreeDlgTree(), name =
      %sn", item_text);
    //sMsg += sMsg1;
    //AfxMessageBox(sMsg, nType, nIDhelp);

    // -- GET A PTR TO THE DOC, i.e. pDoc.
    // This can be done calling CDiagramEngView::GetDocument().
    // However, from within the Dlg class, in the absence of a View
      obj., a global fn is rqd that returns pDoc.
    // This global fn header is declared in DiagramEngDoc.h and
      defined in DiagramEngDoc.cpp

    pDoc = GetDocumentGlobalFn();

    // -- SET THE BLOCK ENUMERATED TYPE based on the "item_text"
      CString value.

    // -- CONTINUOUS BLOCKS
    if(item_text == "DerivativeBlock")
    {
        e_block_type = eDerivativeBlock;
    }
    else if(item_text == "IntegratorBlock")
    {
        e_block_type = eIntegratorBlock;
    }
    else if(item_text == "TransferFnBlock")
    {
        e_block_type = eTransferFnBlock;
    }

    // -- MATH OPS BLOCKS
    else if(item_text == "DivideBlock")
    {
        e_block_type = eDivideBlock;
    }
    else if(item_text == "GainBlock")
    {
        e_block_type = eGainBlock;
    }
    else if(item_text == "SumBlock")
    {
        e_block_type = eSumBlock;
    }

    // -- SINK BLOCKS
    else if(item_text == "OutputBlock")
    {
        e_block_type = eOutputBlock;
    }

    // -- SOURCE BLOCKS
    else if(item_text == "ConstantBlock")
```

```
        {
            e_block_type = eConstBlock;
        }
        else if(item_text == "LinearFnBlock")
        {
            e_block_type = eLinearFnBlock;
        }
        else if(item_text == "SignalGeneratorBlock")
        {
            e_block_type = eSignalGenBlock;
        }
        // -- SUBSYSTEM BLOCKS
        else if(item_text == "SubsystemBlock")
        {
            e_block_type = eSubsysBlock;
        }
        else if(item_text == "SubsystemInBlock")
        {
            e_block_type = eSubsysInBlock;
        }
        else if(item_text == "SubsystemOutBlock")
        {
            e_block_type = eSubsysOutBlock;
        }// end if block type

        // -- CONSTRUCT BLOCK based on the enumerated type value.
        pDoc->ConstructBlock(e_block_type);

        // Print the final concatenated msg. using a msg. box.
        //AfxMessageBox(sMsg, nType, nIDhelp);
    }// end if leaf node

    // DiagramEng (end)

    *pResult = 0;
}
```

The OnDblclkTreeDlgTree() function makes use of the GetSelectedItem() function to retrieve the handle of the selected item at the point of the double-click event. This handle is used to obtain any child items it may have through the call to GetChildItem(). If there are child items, then the selected item is not a leaf, and if there are no child items, then the selected item is a leaf and further action should be taken. To identify which item is selected, the function GetItemText() is called to get the text item that was set using InsertItem() in the InitTreeControl() function. Then, based upon the CString, "item_text" value, the appropriate action may be taken, i.e., the enumerated type (EBlockType) "e_block_type" is set, in preparation for the call to ConstructBlock(e_block_type) following the conditional section.

However, as ConstructBlock() is called on the pointer-to-CDiagramEngDoc, "pDoc", and the EnumBlockType enumerated type is used, include the "DiagramEngDoc.h" header file at the top of the "TreeDialog.cpp" source file.

12.3   DOCKING OF THE TREE DIALOG WINDOW AS A TREE DIALOG BAR

The docking of the Tree Dialog window (IDD_TREE_DLG) needs to be performed manually, since the CTreeDialog class originally inherited from the CDialog base class, rather than the CDialogBar class. The following instructions present the necessary changes to allow the Tree Dialog window (IDD_TREE_DLG) with the Tree View control (ID_TREE_DLG_TREE) to be docked to the left side of the Main frame window as a dialog bar.

The instructions herein follow very closely the work of an article that was published by Microsoft Support, titled "How to initialize child controls in a derived CDialogBar" [2]. These instructions consist of nine steps to perform the conversion of a CDialog-based dialog control to a CControlBar-based control, intended for complex controls to be placed in a control bar rather than on a dialog window. Here, all nine steps are implemented for the current DiagramEng project. A summary of these steps is as follows:

1. Change the base class from CDialog to CDialogBar.
2. Change the constructor and DoDataExchange() methods.
3. Add a new declaration for the OnInitDialog() function with different parameters.
4. Alter the message map to invoke the OnInitDialog() function.
5. Add the implementation of the new OnInitDialog() function.
6. Alter the dialog box resource styles.
7. Add an instance of the CDialogBar to the CMainFrame class.
8. Invoke the Create() method for the new CDialogBar instance.
9. Add support for dynamic docking and resizing of the CDialogBar instance.

12.3.1   Step 1: Change the Base Class from **CDialog** to **CDialogBar**

1. Change the base class of the dialog control from CDialog to CDialogBar. That is, change the declaration "class CTreeDialog : public CDialog" to "class CTreeDialog : public CDialogBar", as shown in bold in the following.

```
// CTreeDialog dialog

//class CTreeDialog : public CDialog
class CTreeDialog : public CDialogBar // -- STEP 1: CONVERSION of CDialog
  to CDialogBar
{
// Construction
public:
    ...
```

2. In the message map section of the dialog-based source file, change "BEGIN_MESSAGE_MAP(CTreeDialog, CDialog)" to "BEGIN_MESSAGE_MAP(CTreeDialog, CDialogBar)", as shown in bold in the following.

```
//BEGIN_MESSAGE_MAP(CTreeDialog, CDialog)
BEGIN_MESSAGE_MAP(CTreeDialog, CDialogBar) // -- STEP 1: CONVERSION of
CDialog to CDialogBar
    //{{AFX_MSG_MAP(CTreeDialog)
    ON_NOTIFY(NM_DBLCLK, ID_TREE_DLG_TREE, OnDblclkTreeDlgTree)
    //}}AFX_MSG_MAP
END_MESSAGE_MAP()
```

12.3.2   Step 2: Change the Constructor and **DoDataExchange()** Methods

1. In the dialog header file, change the constructor declaration from the one that takes a pointer-to-CWnd and calls the base class constructor CDialog, to one that takes no arguments and does not call a base class constructor. That is, change "CTreeDialog(CWnd* pParent = NULL)" to "CTreeDialog()" as shown in bold in the following.

```
// CTreeDialog dialog

//class CTreeDialog : public CDialog
```

```
class CTreeDialog : public CDialogBar // -- STEP 1: CONVERSION of CDialog
  to CDialogBar
{
// Construction
public:
    void InitTreeControl(void);
    //CTreeDialog(CWnd* pParent = NULL); // standard constructor
    CTreeDialog(); // -- STEP 2: CONVERSION of CDialog to CDialogBar
    ...
```

2. In the dialog source file, make changes to the constructor definition to correspond to the changes made to the declaration in the header file (as shown earlier) to yield the following:

```
//CTreeDialog::CTreeDialog(CWnd* pParent /* =NULL*/)
// : CDialog(CTreeDialog::IDD, pParent)
CTreeDialog::CTreeDialog() // -- STEP 2: CONVERSION of CDialog to
  CDialogBar
{
    //{{AFX_DATA_INIT(CTreeDialog)
        // NOTE: the ClassWizard will add member initialization here
    //}}AFX_DATA_INIT
}
```

3. In the dialog source file, change the DoDataExchange() function by converting "CDialog::DoDataExchange(pDX)" to "CDialogBar::DoDataExchange(pDX)", as follows:

```
void CTreeDialog::DoDataExchange(CDataExchange* pDX)
{
    //CDialog::DoDataExchange(pDX);
    CDialogBar::DoDataExchange(pDX); // -- STEP 2: CONVERSION of CDialog
      to CDialogBar
    //{{AFX_DATA_MAP(CTreeDialog)
    DDX_Control(pDX, ID_TREE_DLG_TREE, m_TreeCtrl);
    //}}AFX_DATA_MAP
}
```

12.3.3 Step 3: Add a New Declaration for the OnInitDialog() Function with Different Parameters

The original OnInitDialog() function was the event-handler function associated with the WM_INITDIALOG event message. Now, a new OnInitDialog() function will be added and is associated with the ON_MESSAGE() function that takes the event message WM_INITDIALOG and the function name OnInitDialog as parameters:

1. Hence, comment out the existing "virtual BOOL OnInitDialog()" function declaration in the dialog class and replace it with "afx_msg LONG OnInitDialog(UINT wParam, LONG lParam)", resulting in the following code shown in bold.

```
//class CTreeDialog : public CDialog
class CTreeDialog : public CDialogBar // -- STEP 1: CONVERSION of CDialog
  to CDialogBar
{
// Construction
```

```
public:
    void InitTreeControl(void);
    //CTreeDialog(CWnd* pParent = NULL); // standard constructor
    CTreeDialog(); // -- STEP 2: CONVERSION of CDialog to CDialogBar

// Dialog Data
    //{{AFX_DATA(CTreeDialog)
    enum { IDD = IDD_TREE_DLG };
    CTreeCtrl m_TreeCtrl;
    //}}AFX_DATA

// Overrides
    // ClassWizard generated virtual function overrides
    //{{AFX_VIRTUAL(CTreeDialog)
    protected:
    virtual void DoDataExchange(CDataExchange* pDX); // DDX/DDV support
    //}}AFX_VIRTUAL

// Implementation
protected:

    // Generated message map functions
    //{{AFX_MSG(CTreeDialog)
    //virtual BOOL OnInitDialog();
    afx_msg LONG OnInitDialog(UINT wParam, LONG lParam); // -- STEP 3:
      CONVERSION of CDialog to CDialogBar
    afx_msg void OnDblclkTreeDlgTree(NMHDR* pNMHDR, LRESULT* pResult);
    //}}AFX_MSG
    DECLARE_MESSAGE_MAP()
private:
    CImageList m_TreeImageList;
};
```

2. Now, in the dialog-based source file, comment out the original OnInitDialog() function and replace it with an empty one with the new function prototype, as shown in bold in the following:

```
// -- STEP 3: CONVERSION of CDialog to CDialogBar
/*BOOL CTreeDialog::OnInitDialog()
{
    CDialog::OnInitDialog();

    // TODO: Add extra initialization here

    // DiagramEng (start)

    // Specifically initialize the Tree control
    InitTreeControl();

    // DiagramEng (end)

    return TRUE; // return TRUE unless you set the focus to a control
                 // EXCEPTION: OCX Property Pages should return FALSE
}*/

// -- STEP 3: CONVERSION of CDialog to CDialogBar
LONG CTreeDialog::OnInitDialog(UINT wParam, LONG lParam)
{
    // empty for now.
}
```

12.3.4 Step 4: Alter the Message Map to Invoke the OnInitDialog() Function

In the dialog-based source file, locate the BEGIN_MESSAGE_MAP section of the code, and alter the existing code, shown here,

```
//BEGIN_MESSAGE_MAP(CTreeDialog, CDialog)
BEGIN_MESSAGE_MAP(CTreeDialog, CDialogBar) // -- STEP 1: CONVERSION of
  CDialog to CDialogBar
    //{{AFX_MSG_MAP(CTreeDialog)
    ON_NOTIFY(NM_DBLCLK, ID_TREE_DLG_TREE, OnDblclkTreeDlgTree)
    //}}AFX_MSG_MAP
END_MESSAGE_MAP()
```

to the following modified version with the call ON_MESSAGE(WM_INITDIALOG, OnInitDialog) as follows:

```
//BEGIN_MESSAGE_MAP(CTreeDialog, CDialog)
BEGIN_MESSAGE_MAP(CTreeDialog, CDialogBar)  // -- STEP 1: CONVERSION of
CDialog to CDialogBar
    //{{AFX_MSG_MAP(CTreeDialog)
    ON_NOTIFY(NM_DBLCLK, ID_TREE_DLG_TREE, OnDblclkTreeDlgTree)
    //}}AFX_MSG_MAP
ON_MESSAGE(WM_INITDIALOG, OnInitDialog)    // -- STEP 4: CONVERSION of
CDialog to CDialogBar
END_MESSAGE_MAP()
```

12.3.5 Step 5: Add the Implementation of the New OnInitDialog() Function

In step 3 mentioned earlier, the original OnInitDialog() function was replaced with a new function stub. Now, complete the implementation of the new function by commenting out the lines "CDialog::OnInitDialog()" and "return TRUE" and add the new code as shown in the following.

```
// -- STEP 3: CONVERSION of CDialog to CDialogBar
LONG CTreeDialog::OnInitDialog(UINT wParam, LONG lParam)
{
    //CDialog::OnInitDialog();

    // TODO: Add extra initialization here

    // -- STEP 5: CONVERSION of CDialog to CDialogBar
    BOOL bRet = HandleInitDialog(wParam, lParam);
    if(!UpdateData(FALSE))
    {
        TRACE0("Warning: UpdateData failed during dialog init.n");
    }

    // DiagramEng (start)

    // Specifically initialize the Tree control
    InitTreeControl();

    // DiagramEng (end)

    return bRet;    // -- STEP 5: CONVERSION of CDialog to CDialogBar

    //return TRUE;    // return TRUE unless you set the focus to a control
                      // EXCEPTION: OCX Property Pages should return FALSE
}
```

Microsoft Support [2] indicates that "The CDialogBar class does not have a virtual `OnInitDialog()` function, and therefore calling one does not work. UpdateData is called to subclass or initialize any child controls." This is why `CDialog::OnInitDialog()` is commented out and `UpdateData()` is introduced.

Notice how the `InitTreeControl()` function is being called (after `HandleInitDialog()` and `UpdateData()`) from within the `OnInitDialog()` function: this function is specific to the actual Tree View control on the dialog window, wherein all Tree View control initialization takes place. This call was also made from within the original `OnInitDialog()` function: the initialization logic is unchanged here.

12.3.6   Step 6: Alter the Dialog Box Resource Styles

The dialog resource properties, i.e., the dialog window properties (styles), as opposed to the properties of a particular control on the dialog window, need to be updated as follows: (1) Style: Child, (2) Border: None, and (3) Visible: unchecked (blank box).

12.3.7   Step 7: Add an Instance of the **CDialogBar** to the **CMainFrame** Class

1. An instance of the transformed dialog needs to be added to the CMainFrame class, i.e., add a protected member variable of type CTreeDialog with name "m_TreeDlgBar" (see the code in bold in the following).
2. This requires the "TreeDialog.h" header file to be included (also shown in bold in the following) within the inclusion-guard-bound code, since a CTreeDialog object is being added to the CMainFrame class.

```
// -- STEP 7: CONVERSION of CDialog to CDialogBar
#include "TreeDialog.h" // rqd. since m_TreeDlgBar is of type CTreeDialog
  and is a member var. of CMainFrame

class CMainFrame : public CMDIFrameWnd
{
    DECLARE_DYNAMIC(CMainFrame)
public:
    CMainFrame();

// Attributes
public:

// Operations
public:

// Overrides
    // ClassWizard generated virtual function overrides
    //{{AFX_VIRTUAL(CMainFrame)
    virtual BOOL PreCreateWindow(CREATESTRUCT& cs);
    //}}AFX_VIRTUAL

// Implementation
public:
    virtual ~CMainFrame();
#ifdef _DEBUG
    virtual void AssertValid() const;
    virtual void Dump(CDumpContext& dc) const;
#endif

protected:  // control bar embedded members
    CStatusBar    m_wndStatusBar;
```

```
    CToolBar m_wndToolBar;
    CTreeDialog m_TreeDlgBar;    // -- STEP 7: CONVERSION of CDialog to
      CDialogBar

// Generated message map functions
protected:
    //{{AFX_MSG(CMainFrame)
    afx_msg int OnCreate(LPCREATESTRUCT lpCreateStruct);
        // NOTE - the ClassWizard will add and remove member functions
          here.
        // DO NOT EDIT what you see in these blocks of generated code!
    //}}AFX_MSG
    DECLARE_MESSAGE_MAP()
};
```

12.3.8 STEP 8: INVOKE THE Create() METHOD FOR THE NEW CDialogBar INSTANCE

The original dialog window has now been converted to a dialog bar and an instance is declared in the CMainFrame class. To complete the creation of this CTreeDialog instance as a dialog bar, the Create() function needs to be called on the member object from within CMainFrame::OnCreate(), i.e., "m_TreeDlgBar.Create(this, IDD_TREE_DLG, CBRS_LEFT, IDD_TREE_DLG)", as shown in the following. The first parameter is a pointer to the parent window upon which the dialog bar should be docked, the second parameter is the resource ID, the third parameter denotes the alignment style of the dialog bar, and the last parameter is the control ID of the dialog bar: here, the resource and control share the same ID.

Two examples of the OnCreate() function are provided in the following: (1) a simplified version, for clarity reasons, involving the provided toolbar (IDR_MAINFRAME) and status bar, and the new CDialogBar-based "m_TreeDlgBar" Tree View dialog bar (IDD_TREE_DLG) of a bare implementation, and (2) the more complicated current DiagramEng application version, including the provided toolbars, the Common Blocks (IDR_TB_COMMON_BLOCKS) and Common Operations (IDR_TB_COMMON_OPS) toolbars, and the new Tree View dialog bar (IDD_TREE_DLG). The code to be inserted at steps 8 and 9 is shown in boldface.

```
int CMainFrame::OnCreate(LPCREATESTRUCT lpCreateStruct)
{
    if (CMDIFrameWnd::OnCreate(lpCreateStruct) == -1)
        return -1;

    if (!m_wndToolBar.CreateEx(this, TBSTYLE_FLAT, WS_CHILD | WS_VISIBLE |
      CBRS_TOP
        | CBRS_GRIPPER | CBRS_TOOLTIPS | CBRS_FLYBY | CBRS_SIZE_DYNAMIC) ||
        !m_wndToolBar.LoadToolBar(IDR_MAINFRAME) )
    {
        TRACE0("Failed to create toolbarn");
        return -1; // fail to create
    }

    if (!m_wndStatusBar.Create(this) ||
        !m_wndStatusBar.SetIndicators(indicators,
          sizeof(indicators)/sizeof(UINT) ) )
    {
        TRACE0("Failed to create status barn");
        return -1;  // fail to create
    }

    // -- STEP 8: CONVERSION of CDialog to CDialogBar
    if(!m_TreeDlgBar.Create(this, IDD_TREE_DLG, CBRS_LEFT, IDD_TREE_DLG) )
```

```
    {
        TRACE0("Failed to create dialog barn");
        return -1;   // failed to create
    }
    // TODO: Delete these three lines if you don't want the toolbar to
    // be dockable
    m_wndToolBar.EnableDocking(CBRS_ALIGN_ANY);
    EnableDocking(CBRS_ALIGN_ANY);
    DockControlBar(&m_wndToolBar);

    // -- STEP 9: CONVERSION of CDialog to CDialogBar
    //m_TreeDlgBar.SetBarStyle(m_wndToolBar.GetBarStyle() | CBRS_TOOLTIPS |
      CBRS_FLYBY | CBRS_SIZE_DYNAMIC);
    //m_TreeDlgBar.EnableDocking(CBRS_ALIGN_ANY);
    //DockControlBar(&m_TreeDlgBar);

    return 0;
}
int CMainFrame::OnCreate(LPCREATESTRUCT lpCreateStruct)
{
    if (CMDIFrameWnd::OnCreate(lpCreateStruct) == -1)
        return -1;
    if (!m_wndToolBar.CreateEx(this, TBSTYLE_FLAT, WS_CHILD | WS_VISIBLE |
      CBRS_TOP
        | CBRS_GRIPPER | CBRS_TOOLTIPS | CBRS_FLYBY | CBRS_SIZE_DYNAMIC) ||
        !m_wndToolBar.LoadToolBar(IDR_MAINFRAME) )
    {
        TRACE0("Failed to create toolbarn");
        return -1;   // fail to create
    }

    // DiagramEng (start)

    // -- CREATE THE CommonOps TOOLBAR
    // NOTE: 'this' is the ptr to the parent frame wnd to which the
      toolbar will be attached.
    // CreateEx creates the toolbar
    // LoadToolBar loads the toolbar specified by the ID
    if(!m_wndTBCommonOps.CreateEx(this, TBSTYLE_FLAT, WS_CHILD |
      WS_VISIBLE | CBRS_TOP | CBRS_GRIPPER | CBRS_TOOLTIPS |
        CBRS_FLYBY | CBRS_SIZE_DYNAMIC) || !m_wndTBCommonOps.
          LoadToolBar(IDR_TB_COMMON_OPS) )
    {
        // Failed to create msg.
        TRACE0("Failed to create toolbarn");
        return -1;
    }
    // -- END CREATION OF CommonOps TOOLBAR

    // -- CREATE THE CommonBlocks TOOLBAR

    // NOTE: 'this' is the ptr to the parent frame wnd to which the
      toolbar will be attached.
    // CreateEx creates the toolbar
    // LoadToolBar loads the toolbar specified by the ID
    if(!m_wndTBCommonBlocks.CreateEx(this, TBSTYLE_FLAT, WS_CHILD |
      WS_VISIBLE | CBRS_TOP | CBRS_GRIPPER | CBRS_TOOLTIPS |
        CBRS_FLYBY | CBRS_SIZE_DYNAMIC) || !m_wndTBCommonBlocks.
          LoadToolBar(IDR_TB_COMMON_BLOCKS) )
```

```
{
    // Failed to create msg.
    TRACE0("Failed to create toolbarn");
    return -1;
}
// -- END CREATION OF CommonBlocks TOOLBAR

// DiagramEng (end)

if (!m_wndStatusBar.Create(this) ||
    !m_wndStatusBar.SetIndicators(indicators,
      sizeof(indicators)/sizeof(UINT)))
{
    TRACE0("Failed to create status barn");
    return -1;  // fail to create
}

// -- STEP 8: CONVERSION of CDialog to CDialogBar
if(!m_TreeDlgBar.Create(this, IDD_TREE_DLG, CBRS_LEFT, IDD_TREE_DLG))
{
    TRACE0("Failed to create dialog barn");
    return -1;  // failed to create
}

// TODO: Delete these three lines if you don't want the toolbar to
// be dockable
m_wndToolBar.EnableDocking(CBRS_ALIGN_ANY);

// DiagramEng (start)
// -- ENABLE DOCKING OF TOOLBARS
// Enable docking for the Common Ops toolbar (IDR_TB_COMMON_OPS)
// NOTE: enables the toolbar for docking with the frame wnd.
m_wndTBCommonOps.EnableDocking(CBRS_ALIGN_ANY);

// Enable docking for the Common Blocks toolbar (IDR_TB_COMMON_BLOCKS)
// NOTE: enables the toolbar for docking with the frame wnd.
m_wndTBCommonBlocks.EnableDocking(CBRS_ALIGN_ANY);

// DiagramEng (end)

EnableDocking(CBRS_ALIGN_ANY); // called for the frame wnd.
DockControlBar(&m_wndToolBar); // frame wnd fn passed & of toolbar var.
  physically docks the toolbar to the frame wnd.

// DiagramEng (start)
// -- DOCK TOOLBARS
// Dock the Common Ops toolbar.
DockControlBar(&m_wndTBCommonOps);

// Dock the Common Blocks toolbar.
DockControlBar(&m_wndTBCommonBlocks);

// DiagramEng (end)

// -- STEP 9: CONVERSION of CDialog to CDialogBar
//m_TreeDlgBar.SetBarStyle(m_wndToolBar.GetBarStyle() | CBRS_TOOLTIPS |
  CBRS_FLYBY | CBRS_SIZE_DYNAMIC);
//m_TreeDlgBar.EnableDocking(CBRS_ALIGN_ANY);
//DockControlBar(&m_TreeDlgBar);

return 0;
}
```

12.3.9 STEP 9: ADD SUPPORT FOR DYNAMIC DOCKING AND RESIZING OF THE CDialogBar INSTANCE

The bar style and dynamic docking of the CDialogBar may be set using SetBarStyle() and EnableDocking(), respectively, as shown in the following code. However, if permanent docking is desired, then these lines may be commented out. Note that this addition should be inserted at the end of the CMainFrame::OnCreate() function as shown earlier.

```
// -- STEP 9: CONVERSION of CDialog to CDialogBar
m_TreeDlgBar.SetBarStyle(m_wndToolBar.GetBarStyle() | CBRS_TOOLTIPS |
  CBRS_FLYBY | CBRS_SIZE_DYNAMIC);
m_TreeDlgBar.EnableDocking(CBRS_ALIGN_ANY);
DockControlBar(&m_TreeDlgBar);
```

12.4 RESETTING THE APPROPRIATE DIALOG

Finally, upon compiling the code, an error occurred in the OnEditAddMultipleBlocks() function, which was originally bound to the button-click event for the button (ID_EDIT_ADD_MULTI_BLOCKS) placed on the toolbar (IDR_TB_COMMON_OPS) resource. The error reads:

```
"... error C2039: 'DoModal' : is not a member of 'CTreeDialog' ..."
"... see declaration of 'CTreeDialog'".
```

The OnEditAddMultipleBlocks() function contains a CTreeDialog instance, "oDlg", and DoModal() is called upon the CDialog-based resource as shown in bold in the following "else if(display_item == 2)" conditional section.

```
void CDiagramEngDoc::OnEditAddMultipleBlocks()
{
    // TODO: Add your command handler code here

    // DiagramEng (start)

    // Local var declaration
    int display_item = 2;  // used to display msg box or dlg wnd.

    // Display a msg.
    if(display_item == 0)
    {
        AfxMessageBox("\n CDiagramEngDoc::OnEditAddMultipleBlocks()n",
          MB_OK, 0);
    }
    else if(display_item == 1)
    {
        CBlockLibDlg oDlg;    // create a dlg obj. of class CBlockLibDlg :
          public CDialog

        // Return val of DoModal() fn of ancestor class CDialog is
          checked to determine which btn was clicked.
        if(oDlg.DoModal() == IDOK)
        {
            //AfxMessageBox("\n CDiagramEngDoc::OnEditAddMultipleBlocks()
              n", MB_OK, 0);
        }
    }
    /*else if(display_item == 2)
```

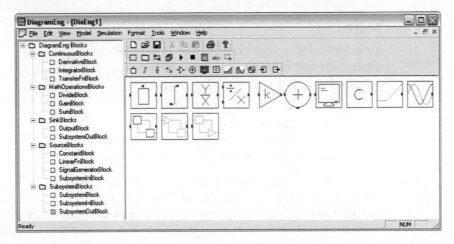

FIGURE 12.7 DiagramEng application showing the block library directory as a CDialogBar instance bound to the left side of the Main frame.

```
    {
        CTreeDialog oDlg;   // create a dlg obj. of class CTreeDialog :
        public CDialog

        // Return val of DoModal() fn of ancestor class CDialog is
          checked to determine which btn was clicked.
        if(oDlg.DoModal() == IDOK)
        {
            AfxMessageBox("\n CDiagramEngDoc::OnEditAddMultipleBlocks()
              n", MB_OK, 0);
        }
    }*/

    // DiagramEng (end)
}
```

However, since the CTreeDialog class has had its base class changed from CDialog to CDialogBar, and DoModal() is based upon CDialog and not CDialogBar, then calling DoModal() on the CDialogBar-based object results in an error. Hence, the contents of the conditional "else if(display_item == 2)" section should be commented out, as shown. The developer will recall that a CTreeDialog variable, "m_TreeDlgBar", was added to the CMainFrame class, and the CMainFrame::OnCreate() function completes the creation of what is now a CDialogBar-based resource.

In addition, the integer "display_item" should be set to 1, since the user may still want to use the BlockLibraryDialog (IDD_BLOCKLIBDLG) dialog-based block insertion method: the Tree View form of the block library is now provided by default, attached to the Main frame, as a CDialogBar instance.

Now, upon running the program, the block library appears as a CDialogBar object bound to the left side (given commenting out of the code included at step 9 mentioned earlier) of the Main frame. To tidy the appearance of this CDialogBar instance, the original OK and Cancel buttons were removed and the window resized to convenient proportions, as shown in Figure 12.7.

12.5 CONTROLLING THE TOOLBAR VISIBILITY

Finally, the mechanism to control the visibility of the Tree View–based CDialogBar object "m_TreeDlgBar" needs to be added to the View menu. Hence, add an entry named Block Directory beneath the Common Blocks toolbar entry on the View menu with the properties and settings shown in Table 12.5.

TABLE 12.5
View Menu Entry Object, ID, Caption, Prompts
(Status Bar and Tooltips), and Settings

Object	Property	Setting
Block Directory	ID	ID_VIEW_BLOCK_DIR
	Caption	&BlockDirectory
	Prompts	View block directory\nBlock Directory

Invoke the ClassWizard, choose CMainFrame as the class, select ID_VIEW_BLOCK_DIR as the object ID, and add an event-handler function for the COMMAND message, with prototype void CMainFrame::OnViewBlockDirectory(void); edit it as shown in the following.

```
void CMainFrame::OnViewBlockDirectory()
{
    // TODO: Add your command handler code here

    // DiagramEng (start)
    BOOL bShow;

    // Check state of block library toolbar
    bShow = ((m_TreeDlgBar.GetStyle() & WS_VISIBLE) != 0);

    // Switch state
    // NOTE: & of toolbar, bool show/hide toolbar, delay showing toolbar
      (FALSE => no delay)
    ShowControlBar(&m_TreeDlgBar, !bShow, FALSE);

    // Recalculate layout
    RecalcLayout();

    // DiagramEng (end)
}
```

Now, the user interface needs to be updated with a tick-like check mark next to the menu entry when the toolbar is visible. Hence, invoke the ClassWizard, choose CMainFrame as the class, and select ID_VIEW_BLOCK_DIR as the object ID. Select UPDATE_COMMAND_UI as the message and add an event-handler function named OnUpdateViewBlockDirectory(). Edit it as shown in the following.

```
void CMainFrame::OnUpdateViewBlockDirectory(CCmdUI* pCmdUI)
{
    // TODO: Add your command update UI handler code here

    // DiagramEng (start)

    // Check the status of the CDialogBar (m_TreeDlgBar)
    // NOTE: get style of toolbar and mask out for the WS_VISIBLE style
      flag.
    // If the flag is in the current toolbar style, then the toolbar is
      visible.
    // The SetCheck() allows checking and unchecking the toolbar MENU
      entry (in the View menu here).
    pCmdUI->SetCheck(((m_TreeDlgBar.GetStyle() & WS_VISIBLE) != 0));

    // DiagramEng (end)
}
```

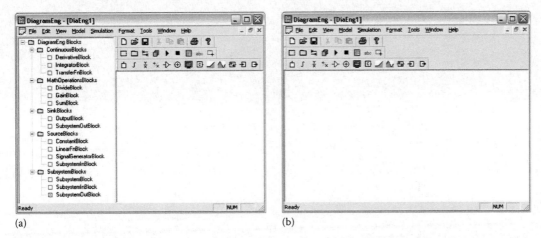

(a)   (b)

FIGURE 12.8 Block Directory entry under the View menu allows controlling the visibility of the block directory Tree View control: (a) viewing of the block directory and (b) hiding of the block directory.

Now, upon running the program, the user has the option of showing or hiding the block directory Tree View (CDialogBar) object as shown in Figure 12.8.

12.6 SUMMARY

A Tree Dialog resource is added to the project with class CTreeDialog and base class CDialog. A variable is attached to the dialog window control to be able to display Tree View properties. An `OnInitDialog()` function is added to the CTreeDialog class and this calls the `InitTreeControl()` function to initialize the Tree View control with the correct properties. Icons are added to the Tree View control and are displayed next to the leaves of the tree. An event-handler function `OnDblclkTreeDlgTree()` is added for the double-click event on a node of the Tree View control, which results in the correct block being constructed and positioned on the palette. The docking of the Tree Dialog window is performed manually, since the CTreeDialog class originally inherited from the CDialog base class, rather than the CDialogBar class. Nine steps, originally published by Microsoft Support [2], are followed to implement the docking of the Tree Dialog window to the Main frame. Finally, the visibility of the Tree View–based CDialogBar object is controlled by adding an entry to the View menu and event-handler functions to the CMainFrame class.

REFERENCES

1. TreeView on a dialog, http://www.functionx.com/visualc/treeview/tvdlg1.htm, FunctionX Inc., 1999.
2. How to initialize child controls in a derived CDialogBar, Microsoft Support, http://support.microsoft.com/kb/185672, Microsoft Corporation, 2006.

13 Review of Menu and Toolbar-Based Functionality
Part I

13.1 INTRODUCTION

The software development process thus far has resulted in building the main graphical user interface (GUI)-based functionality, allowing the user to construct a basic model diagram of the system to be simulated. However, various menu items and toolbar buttons have no working functionality but simply call an event-handler function that presents a message in a message box. A brief review of the developmental status is required to find out what functionality has and has not been implemented. The developer can then concentrate on the essential functionality required for the purpose of application demonstration, postponing nonessential items until later.

13.2 MENUS

The menus to be reviewed here are the Main frame–based menus (File, View, and Help) and the Child frame–based menus (File, Edit, View, Model, Simulation, Format, Tools, Window, and Help). All the menu items, their intended actions and developmental status, are listed in Tables 13.1 through 13.12.

13.2.1 MAIN FRAME–BASED MENUS

The Main frame–based menus are those found on the Main frame of the application window as shown in Figure 13.1. Tables 13.1 through 13.3 list all the menu items, where most of the functionality concerning the Main frame window is already provided in the MFC-based project. However, for the Open entry under the File menu to work properly, saving of the document contents is required before retrieval of all document-based information is possible. This saving, or serialization, will be added for the Child frame–based menu entries, File/Save and File/Save As, in Chapter 25 toward the end of the project. At that stage, the Open entry under the File menu for the Main frame–based window will chain up to that for the Child frame–based window.

13.2.2 CHILD FRAME–BASED MENUS

The Child frame–based menus are those found on the Child frame of the application window as indicated in Figure 13.2. Tables 13.4 through 13.12 list existing menu functionality and material to be implemented; the event-handler functions display a simple message using a message box, and "Incomplete" denotes further functionality is to be added.

13.2.3 CONTEXT MENU

The `Context menu` (IDR_CONTEXTMENU) is activated on a right-mouse-button-down event and currently has three entries as shown in Table 13.13. The `OnDeleteItem()` and `OnInsertBendPoint()` functions both work. However, the Set Properties menu entry has no event-handler function as yet to invoke a dialog window to set the properties of the selected object.

TABLE 13.1

Main Frame–Based File Menu Items, Intended Action, and Developmental Status

File	Action	Developmental Status
New	Creates a new document	Works
Open	Opens an existing document	Incomplete: to chain to Child frame–based action
Print Setup	Changes the printer and printing options	Works
Recent File	Views recent files	Incomplete: to chain to Child frame–based action
Exit	Quits the application	Works: no child document is present, so no prompting to save is necessary

TABLE 13.2

Main Frame–Based View Menu Items, Intended Action, and Developmental Status

View	Action	Developmental Status
Toolbar	Shows or hides the toolbar	Works
Status Bar	Shows or hides the status bar	Works

TABLE 13.3

Main Frame–Based Help Menu Item, Intended Action, and Developmental Status

Help	Action	Developmental Status
About DiagramEng	Displays program information, version number, and copyright	Works: as a dialog window

TABLE 13.4

Child Frame–Based File Menu Items, Intended Action, and Developmental Status

File	Action	Developmental Status
New	Creates a new document	Works
Open	Opens an existing document	Incomplete: opens a blank document
Close	Closes the active document	Incomplete: cannot save content
Save	Saves the active document	Incomplete: saves file but not content
Save As	Saves the active document with a new name	Incomplete: saves new file but not content
Print	Prints the active document	Incomplete: prints too small
Print Preview	Displays full pages	Incomplete: consistent with print
Print Setup	Changes the printer and printing options	Works
Recent File	Views recent files and prompts to open the document	Incomplete: no prior content saved on to-be-opened document
Exit	Quits the application and prompts to save documents	Incomplete: no content saved on document

TABLE 13.5

Child Frame–Based Edit Menu Items, Intended Action, and Developmental Status

Edit	Action	Developmental Status
Undo	Undoes the last action	Incomplete: not implemented
Cut	Cuts the selection and puts it on the Clipboard	Incomplete: not implemented
Copy	Copies the selection and puts it on the Clipboard	Incomplete: not implemented
Paste	Inserts Clipboard contents	Incomplete: not implemented
Delete	Deletes the selection	Incomplete: OnEditDelete()
Select All	Selects all content	Incomplete: OnEditSelectAll()
Add Multiple Blocks	Adds multiple blocks to the model	Works

TABLE 13.6

Child Frame–Based View Menu Items, Intended Action, and Developmental Status

View	Action	Developmental Status
Toolbar	Shows or hides the toolbar	Works
Status Bar	Shows or hides the status bar	Works
Common Ops. Toolbar	Shows or hides the Common Operations toolbar	Works
Common Blocks Toolbar	Shows or hides the Common Blocks toolbar	Works
Block Directory	Shows or hides the block directory	Works
Auto Fit Diagram	Automatically fits diagram to view	Incomplete: OnViewAutoFitDiagram()
Zoom In	Zooms in to detail	Incomplete: OnViewZoomIn()
Zoom Out	Zooms out of detail	Incomplete: OnViewZoomOut()

TABLE 13.7

Child Frame–Based Model Menu Items, Intended Action, and Developmental Status

Model	Action	Developmental Status
Build Model	Builds the active model	Incomplete: OnModelBuild()
Build Subsystem	Builds the selected model subsystem	Incomplete: OnModelBuildSubsys()

TABLE 13.8

Child Frame–Based Simulation Menu Items, Intended Action, and Developmental Status

Simulation	Action	Developmental Status
Start	Starts the simulation	Incomplete: OnSimStart()
Stop	Stops the simulation	Incomplete: OnSimStop()
Numerical Solver	Sets the numerical solver parameters	Incomplete: OnSimNumericalSolver()

TABLE 13.9

Child Frame–Based Format Menu Item, Intended Action, and Developmental Status

Format	Action	Developmental Status
Show Annotations	Shows diagram annotations	Incomplete: OnFormatShowAnnotations()

TABLE 13.10

Child Frame–Based Tools Menu Item, Intended Action, and Developmental Status

Tools	Action	Developmental Status
Diagnostic Info.	Presents diagnostic information	Incomplete: OnToolsDiagnosticInfo()

TABLE 13.11

Child Frame–Based Window Menu Items, Intended Action, and Developmental Status

Window	Action	Developmental Status
New Window	Opens another window for the active document	Works (provided)
Cascade	Arranges windows so they overlap	Works (provided)
Tile	Arranges windows as nonoverlapping tiles	Works (provided)
Arrange Icons	Arranges icons at the bottom of the window	Works (provided)
Close All Documents	Closes all documents	Incomplete: OnWndCloseAllDocs()
Name of child windows	Shows names of windows and activates the selected window	Works (provided)

TABLE 13.12

Child Frame–Based Help Menu Items, Intended Action, and Developmental Status

Help	Action	Developmental Status
About DiagramEng	Displays program information, version number and copyright	Works (dialog window)
Using DiagramEng	Displays information about using the DiagramEng application	Incomplete: OnHelpUsingDiagramEng()

FIGURE 13.1 Main frame window showing the menu items and limited toolbar functionality in the absence of a child (document) window.

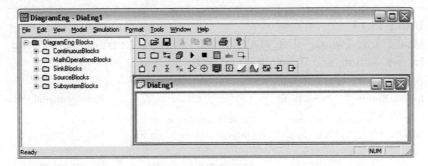

FIGURE 13.2 Child frame window showing the applicable menu items, toolbars, and an empty palette.

TABLE 13.13

Context Menu Items, Intended Action, and Developmental Status

Context	Action	Developmental Status
Delete Item	Deletes the selection	Works: OnDeleteItem()
Insert Bend Point	Inserts a bend point upon connection object	Works: OnInsertBendPoint()
Set Properties	Invokes a dialog window to set properties for the selection	No functionality at present

13.3 TOOLBARS

The existing toolbars are (1) the Main Frame toolbar (IDR_MAINFRAME), which presents general actions that may be found under the File, Edit, and Help menus; (2) the Common Operations toolbar (IDR_TB_COMMON_OPS), which provides common operations that may be found under the existing menus (see Figure 13.3); and (3) the Common Blocks toolbar (IDR_TB_COMMON_BLOCKS), which allows the user to easily add diagram blocks to the model. The Tables 13.14 through 13.16 list the functionality that should be associated with the existing toolbar buttons; this behavior is also available from the equivalent menu entries where appropriate.

13.3.1 MAIN FRAME TOOLBAR

The Main Frame toolbar buttons are shown in Table 13.14: the Cut, Copy, and Paste operations have not yet been implemented and the Print operation works but requires improvement (as indicated).

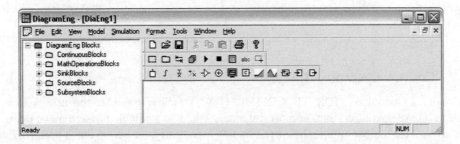

FIGURE 13.3 Three current toolbars of the DiagramEng application found directly beneath the Format menu: (1) Main Frame, (2) Common Operations, and (3) Common Blocks (top down).

TABLE 13.14

Main Frame Toolbar (IDR_MAINFRAME) Buttons, Corresponding Menu Entries, Action, and Developmental Status

Main Frame Toolbar Button	Corresponding Menu Item	Action	Developmental Status
New	File/New	Creates a new document	Works
Open	File/Open	Opens an existing document	Incomplete: opens a blank document
Save	File/Save	Saves the active document	Incomplete: saves file but not content
Cut	Edit/Cut	Cuts the selection and puts it on the Clipboard	Not implemented
Copy	Edit/Copy	Copies the selection and puts it on the Clipboard	Not implemented
Paste	Edit/Paste	Inserts Clipboard contents	Not implemented
Print	File/Print	Prints the active document	Prints too small
About	Help/About	Displays program information, version number, and copyright	Works (dialog window)

TABLE 13.15

Common Operations Toolbar (IDR_TB_COMMON_OPS) Buttons, Corresponding Menu Entries, Action, and Developmental Status

Common Operations Toolbar Button	Corresponding Menu Item	Action	Developmental Status
Select All	Edit/Select All	Selects the entire model	Incomplete: OnEditSelectAll()
Add Multiple Blocks	Edit/Add Multiple Blocks	Adds multiple blocks	Works: OnEditAddMultipleBlocks()
Auto Fit Diagram	View/Auto Fit Diagram	Automatically fits diagram to view	Incomplete: OnViewAutoFitDiagram()
Build Model	Model/Build	Builds the model	Incomplete: OnModelBuild()
Start Simulation	Simulation/Start	Starts the simulation	Incomplete: OnSimStart()
Stop Simulation	Simulation/Stop	Stops the simulation	Incomplete: OnSimStop()
Numerical Solver	Simulation/Numerical Solver	Sets the numerical solver parameters	Incomplete: OnSimNumericalSolver()
Show Annotations	Format/Show Annotations	Shows diagram annotations	Incomplete: OnFormatShowAnnotations()
Track Multiple Items	No corresponding menu item	Selects and moves multiple items	Works: TrackMultipleItems()

13.3.2 COMMON OPERATIONS TOOLBAR

The Common Operations (IDR_TB_COMMON_OPS) toolbar provides the user with a quick method to invoke operations that, in most instances, would be available through menu items. Table 13.15 indicates the toolbar button, the corresponding menu entry, the action that it performs, and the developmental status concerning its operability.

TABLE 13.16

Common Blocks Toolbar (IDR_TB_COMMON_BLOCKS) Buttons in the Order of Their Appearance on the Toolbar (from Left to Right), Block Type, Action, and Developmental Status

Common Blocks Toolbar Button	Block Type	Action	Developmental Status
Derivative Block	Continuous	Inserts Derivative Block	Works
Integrator Block	Continuous	Inserts Integrator Block	Works
TransferFn Block	Continuous	Inserts TransferFn Block	Works
Divide Block	Math Operations	Inserts Divide Block	Works
Gain Block	Math Operations	Inserts Gain Block	Works
Sum Block	Math Operations	Inserts Sum Block	Works
Output Block	Sink	Inserts Output Block	Works
Constant Block	Source	Inserts Constant Block	Works
LinearFn Block	Source	Inserts LinearFn Block	Works
Signal Generator Block	Source	Inserts SignalGenerator Block	Works
Subsystem Block	Subsystem	Inserts Subsystem Block	Works
SubsystemIn Block	Subsystem/Source	Inserts SubsystemIn Block	Works
SubsystemOut Block	Subsystem/Sink	Inserts SubsystemOut Block	Works

No menu item duplicates are available.

13.3.3 COMMON BLOCKS TOOLBAR

The Common Blocks toolbar (IDR_TB_COMMON_BLOCKS) buttons allow the user to efficiently add blocks to the diagram model: their actions and developmental status are listed in Table 13.16. No menu entries are provided for the block insertion operations since the use of menus is more cumbersome than buttons. Blocks may also be added using the block directory Tree View control (Figure 13.4a), which is a directory-based block listing, or a Block Library Dialog dialog window (Figure 13.4b).

13.4 FUNCTIONALITY TO BE ADDED

The listing of the aforementioned menu items and toolbar button–related event-handler functions clearly shows all the intended desired functionality and allows the engineer to determine the most important items that need to be further developed, in order that the software application can function in a basic form and can demonstrate the potential of the underlying concept toward possible future extension. Here, only the absolutely essential functionality is pursued to allow the user to perform model building, computation, and data serialization, where the remaining nonessential elements can be deferred until a later stage, with the intent to complete all the operations listed in the previous two sections. Tables 13.17 through 13.19 list the menu items that should be developed, their actions, and the desired results of the development: here, the Child frame–based menu items, Context menu–based items, and toolbar button–based functions require initial development, where the Main frame–based entries may chain up to the Child frame–based functionality as appropriate.

13.4.1 CHILD FRAME–BASED MENU ITEMS

The Child frame–based menu items that are essential are listed in Table 13.17. The File menu items, Open, Close, Save, Save As, and Exit, will all be implemented in Chapter 25 toward the end of the

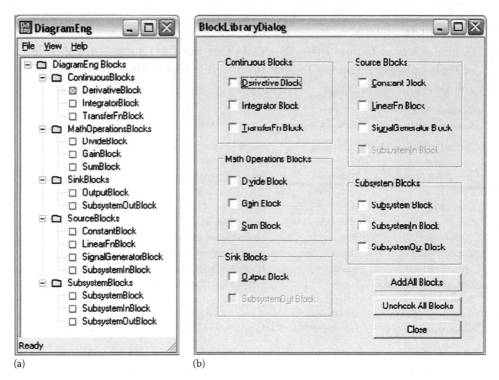

(a)   (b)

FIGURE 13.4   Block listing mechanisms: (a) Tree View control and (b) dialog window resource.

TABLE 13.17
Essential Development: Child Frame Menu Items, Actions, and Desired Developmental Results

Menu Item	Action	Developmental Result
File/Open	Opens a document	Opens a previously saved document with the content present
File/Close	Closes a document	Closes a document prompting to save if necessary
File/Save	Saves the active document	Saves the content of the model to a model file
File/Save As	Saves the active document with a new name	Saves the content of the model to a model file with a new name
File/Exit	Exits the application	Exits the application prompting to save if necessary
Edit/Delete	Deletes the selection	Links to the existing CDiagramEngDoc::OnDeleteItem() function
Model/Build Model	Builds the active model	Builds the model
Simulation/Start	Starts the simulation	Starts execution of the simulation
Simulation/Stop	Stops the simulation	Stops execution of the simulation
Simulation/Numerical Solver	Sets the numerical solver parameters	Generates a dialog window with which all system numerical solver parameters may be assigned
Window/Close All Documents	Closes all documents	Closes all documents sequentially prompting to save if necessary

TABLE 13.18

Essential Development: Context Menu Item, Its Intended Action, and Desired Developmental Result

Menu Item	Action	Developmental Result
Set Properties	Invokes a dialog window to set properties for the selection	Invokes a dialog window based on the location of the mouse pointer and sets properties for the selection

TABLE 13.19

Essential Development: Toolbars, Toolbar Buttons, Corresponding Menu Items, Actions, and Desired Developmental Results

Toolbar	Toolbar Button	Corresponding Menu Item	Action	Developmental Result
IDR_MAINFRAME	Open	File/Open	Opens a document	Opens a previously saved document
IDR_MAINFRAME	Save	File/Save	Saves the active document	Saves the document content to a file
IDR_TB_COMMON_OPS	Build Model	Model/Build	Builds the model	Builds the model
IDR_TB_COMMON_OPS	Start Simulation	Simulation/Start	Starts the simulation	Starts execution of the simulation
IDR_TB_COMMON_OPS	Stop Simulation	Simulation/Stop	Stops the simulation	Stops execution of the simulation
IDR_TB_COMMON_OPS	Numerical Solver	Simulation/ Numerical Solver	Configures the simulation parameters	Generates a dialog window to set numerical solver parameters

project, when all class data structures are established. The Delete entry under the Edit menu will be changed to Delete Grouped Items to delete multiple items requiring a special grouping selection rather than just one item at a time. Both a Delete Item and a Delete Grouped Items menu entry will eventually be placed on the Context menu, allowing the user multiple mechanisms to perform object deletion to complement the Edit menu entry. The Build Model entry under the Model menu will be implemented at the model validation stage of the project and is covered in Chapter 18. The Start and Stop entries under the Simulation menu will be implemented at the Signal Propagation stage of the project. However, the Numerical Solver item, used to generate a dialog window with which simulation parameters may be entered, will be completed in the next chapter. The Close All Documents item under the Window menu will close all Child frame–based documents and prompt the user to save if appropriate. This is related to data serialization and will be addressed in Chapter 25.

13.4.2 CONTEXT MENU ITEMS

The only Context menu item of those listed previously in Table 13.13 that requires development at present is the Set Properties entry, used to set the properties of blocks or invoke the Numerical Solver dialog window: this is completed in the next chapter. Other entries, e.g., Delete Grouped Items, will be added to the Context menu later in the project.

13.4.3 TOOLBAR BUTTON–BASED FUNCTIONALITY

The toolbar button event-handler functions also need to be developed and, in some cases, link up to the corresponding menu item event-handler functions. Table 13.19 lists the essential development for toolbar-based functionality, including the appropriate toolbar resource, toolbar button, corresponding menu item, action, and desired developmental result. The Open and Save buttons corresponding to the File menu entries of the same name will be addressed in Chapter 25. The Start Simulation and Stop Simulation entries will be implemented in the Signal Propagation stage of the project. The Numerical Solver dialog window is implemented in the following chapter.

The developer will notice that all of these toolbar button functions correspond to their menu item equivalents; hence, functionality need only be added to the event-handler function for the shared ID concerned, and both the menu item and toolbar button selection will yield the same functional result.

13.5   SUMMARY

A review is made of existing functionality to determine the essential items to be added to the project. The Main frame–based, Child frame–based, and Context menus are examined, and the important items to be added for the Main frame–based menu concern serialization and those of the Child frame–based menu involve serialization, model building, and simulation execution. The Context menu should be extended to facilitate context-based actions, e.g., the setting of item properties through the use of a dialog window and the deletion of individual or grouped items. The Main Frame, Common Blocks, and Common Operations toolbars are reviewed to guide further development, and the essential functionality concerns serialization, model building, simulation execution, and the setting of numerical solver properties. Extensions to the project, including GUI elements, model building and computation, and serialization, are individually documented in the relevant chapters that follow.

14 Context Menu Extension

14.1 INTRODUCTION

The Context menu is extended to allow the user to right-click on a diagram item, and based upon the location of the mouse cursor at the point of menu invocation, the appropriate context-specific functional operation occurs. A Numerical Solver dialog is added to the project that allows the user to set numerical solver properties that are used in model computation, and the dialog is invoked either through the use of the Numerical Solver entry of the Simulation menu, a Common Operations toolbar button, or quite easily via the Set Properties entry of the Context menu when the user right-clicks an empty portion of the palette. In addition, the Set Properties entry invokes functions to allow the user to set the properties of blocks and connections. A Delete Grouped Items entry is added to the Context and Edit menus, which allows the user to delete a selection of previously circumscribed items on the palette. The Context-menu-based approach allows for a more efficient usage of the DiagramEng application modeling features.

14.2 NUMERICAL SOLVER DIALOG WINDOW

A Numerical Solver dialog window is required to provide the user the means to set all the numerical solver parameter values, e.g., start and stop times, tolerance parameters, and the integration method, which are used in the numerical computation of the states of the underlying system model. Hence, there is to be a sharing of the parameter values of the class associated with the Numerical Solver dialog window, i.e., the to-be-added CNumericalSolverDialog class and that of the existing system model class, CSystemModel.

The developer will recall the previously introduced general procedure for adding a dialog window and transferring its values to its associated underlying class involving the following six logical steps:

1. Insert a new dialog window and add controls.
2. Attach a class to the dialog window.
3. Attach variables to the dialog window controls.
4. Add functionality to the dialog window buttons.
5. Add functionality to initialize variables.
6. Add a dialog window parameter input function to the underlying class.

Here, the Numerical Solver dialog is to be added to the project by implementing these six key steps, to allow the setting of the application's numerical solver properties.

14.2.1 INSERT A NEW DIALOG WINDOW AND ADD CONTROLS

Insert a new dialog resource; set the ID of the dialog to IDD_NUM_SOLVER_DLG and the caption to NumericalSolverDialog. Leave the OK and Cancel buttons on the dialog and add controls as shown in Table 14.1, placing them on the dialog window as shown in Figure 14.1.

TABLE 14.1

Numerical Solver Dialog Window Controls: Objects, Properties, and Settings

Object	Property	Setting
Group Box	ID	ID_NUM_SOLVER_DLG_GB_TIME
	Caption	Time Parameters
Static Text	ID	ID_NUM_SOLVER_DLG_TXT_TSTART
	Caption	Start Time:
Edit Box	ID	ID_NUM_SOLVER_DLG_TSTART
Static Text	ID	ID_NUM_SOLVER_DLG_TXT_TSTOP
	Caption	Stop Time:
Edit Box	ID	ID_NUM_SOLVER_DLG_TSTOP
Static Text	ID	ID_NUM_SOLVER_DLG_TXT_TSTEPSIZE
	Caption	Time Step Size:
Edit Box	ID	ID_NUM_SOLVER_DLG_TSTEPSIZE
Static Text	ID	ID_NUM_SOLVER_DLG_TXT_TSTEPTYPE
	Caption	Time Step Type:
Combo Box	ID	ID_NUM_SOLVER_DLG_CB_TSTEPTYPE
	Data	Fixed-step
		Variable-step
Group Box	ID	ID_NUM_SOLVER_DLG_GB_INTEGRATOR
	Caption	Integration Parameters
Static Text	ID	ID_NUM_SOLVER_DLG_TXT_INTEGRATOR
	Caption	Integration Method:
Combo Box	ID	ID_NUM_SOLVER_DLG_CB_INTEGRATOR
	Data	Euler (1st Order)
		Runge-Kutta (4th Order)
Static Text	ID	ID_NUM_SOLVER_DLG_TXT_ATOL
	Caption	Absolute Error Tolerance:
Edit Box	ID	ID_NUM_SOLVER_DLG_ATOL
Static Text	ID	ID_NUM_SOLVER_DLG_TXT_RTOL
	Caption	Relative Error Tolerance:
Edit Box	ID	ID_NUM_SOLVER_DLG_RTOL
Group Box	ID	ID_NUM_SOLVER_DLG_GB_WARNING
	Caption	Warning
Static Text	ID	ID_NUM_SOLVER_DLG_TXT_WARNING
	Caption	Warning Message:
Edit Box	ID	ID_NUM_SOLVER_DLG_WARNING
	Multiline	Checked
	Auto HScroll	Checked
	Auto VScroll	Checked
Button	ID	ID_NUM_SOLVER_DLG_BTN_OK
	Default button	Unchecked
	Caption	&OK
Button	ID	IDCANCEL
	Caption	&Cancel

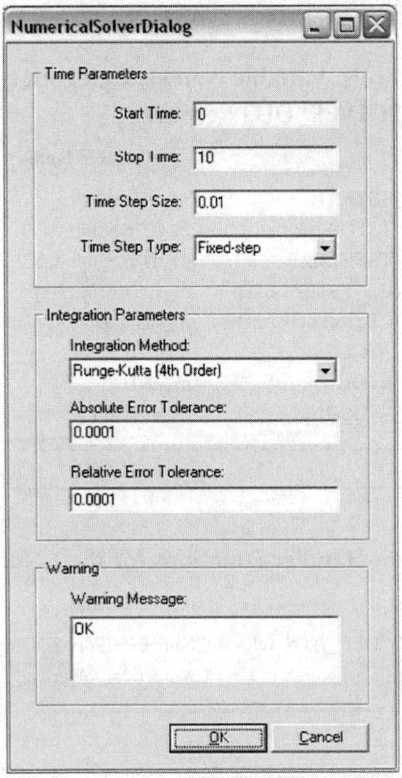

FIGURE 14.1   Numerical Solver dialog window showing the controls as specified in Table 14.1.

14.2.2   ATTACH A CLASS TO THE DIALOG WINDOW

Select the IDD_NUM_SOLVER_DLG resource from the ResourceView tab on the Workspace pane to show the corresponding dialog window in the editor area and right-click on the dialog box to invoke the ClassWizard. The Adding a Class message box appears: create a new class with name CNumericalSolverDialog and base class CDialog.

14.2.3   ATTACH VARIABLES TO THE DIALOG WINDOW CONTROLS

Invoke the ClassWizard, select the Member Variables tab, choose CNumericalSolverDialog as the class, since variables to be added relate to dialog window controls. Select the ID of the control to which a variable should be added, click Add Variable and specify the details as shown in Table 14.2.

Now add private member variables to the CSystemModel class of the same type and name as those in Table 14.2, since these variables will be updated with the values of those of the dialog class CNumericalSolverDialog: both classes share the same variable names for convenience. This step may require replacing existing placeholder variables in the CSystemModel class as appropriate.

14.2.4   ADD FUNCTIONALITY TO THE DIALOG WINDOW BUTTONS

The two buttons on the IDD_NUM_SOLVER_DLG dialog window are OK and Cancel. Add an event-handler function for the OK button, named `OnNumericalSolverDlgBtnOk()`, as shown in Table 14.3 and edit it as displayed. Leave the current event-handler function for the Cancel button as `OnCancel()`, since this already calls the `CDialog::OnCancel()` function so no new code is required.

TABLE 14.2

Dialog Window Controls, Variable Names, Categories, and Types for the IDD_NUM_SOLVER_DLG Resource

Control	Variable Name	Category	Type
ID_NUM_SOLVER_DLG_TSTART	m_dTimeStart	Value	double
ID_NUM_SOLVER_DLG_TSTOP	m_dTimeStop	Value	double
ID_NUM_SOLVER_DLG_TSTEPSIZE	m_dTimeStepSize	Value	double
ID_NUM_SOLVER_DLG_CB_TSTEPTYPE	m_strTimeStepType	Value	CString
ID_NUM_SOLVER_DLG_CB_INTEGRATOR	m_strIntegrationMethod	Value	CString
ID_NUM_SOLVER_DLG_ATOL	m_dATOL	Value	double
ID_NUM_SOLVER_DLG_RTOL	m_dRTOL	Value	double
ID_NUM_SOLVER_DLG_WARNING	m_strWarning	Value	CString

TABLE 14.3

Objects, IDs, Class and Event-Handler Functions for the CNumericalSolverDialog Class

Object	ID	Class	COMMAND Event-Handler
OK button	ID_NUM_SOLVER_DLG_BTN_OK	CNumericalSolverDialog	OnNumericalSolverDlgBtnOk()
Cancel button	IDCANCEL (default)	CNumericalSolverDialog	OnCancel()

```
void CNumericalSolverDialog::OnNumericalSolverDlgBtnOk()
{
    // TODO: Add your control notification handler code here
    // DiagramEng (start)

    //AfxMessageBox("\n CNumericalSolverDialog::OnNumericalSolverDlgBt
      nOk()\n", MB_OK, 0);

    // Update variable values with the Dlg Wnd control values
    UpdateData(TRUE);

    // Close the dialog wnd with OnOK()
    OnOK();

    // DiagramEng (end)
}
```

14.2.5   ADD FUNCTIONALITY TO INITIALIZE VARIABLES

The CNumericalSolverDialog class is that associated with the Numerical Solver dialog resource (IDD_NUM_SOLVER_DLG). However, this is simply a dialog window allowing the display and transfer of variable values to the underlying computational engine that resides in the CSystemModel class. Hence, initialization of the corresponding variables takes place in the CSystemModel class constructor as shown in the following code (the ellipsis ("…") denotes omitted but unchanged code), and then in the to-be-added dialog window parameter input function of the CSystemModel class, these values are transferred to the dialog window for viewing and alteration.

```
CSystemModel::CSystemModel(void)
{
    ...
    // Time parameters
```

```
    m_dTimeStart = 0.0;
    m_dTimeStop = 10.0;
    m_dTimeStepSize = 0.01;
    m_strTimeStepType = "Fixed-step";

    // Integration parameters
    m_dATOL = 0.0001;
    m_dRTOL = 0.0001;
    m_strIntegrationMethod = "Runge-Kutta (4th Order)";
    m_strWarning = "OK";
    …
}
```

14.2.6 ADD A DIALOG WINDOW PARAMETER INPUT FUNCTION TO THE UNDERLYING CLASS

To allow a transfer of the numerical-solver-related variables between the CSystemModel and CNumericalSolverDialog classes, a public member function is to be added to the CSystemModel class with the prototype void CSystemModel::DlgWndParameterInput(void): edit the latter as shown to obtain consistent numerical input.

The header file for the CNumericalSolverDialog class is required by the CSystemModel function, since an "oDlg" object of type CNumericalSolverDialog is used. Hence add #include "NumericalSolverDialog.h" at the top of the "SystemModel.cpp" source file.

```
void CSystemModel::DlgWndParameterInput()
{
    int input = 0;         // flag denoting correct input
    CString  sMsg;         // string to be displayed
    CString  sMsgTemp;     // temp string
    UINT nType = MB_OK;    // style of msg. box
    UINT nIDhelp = 0;      // help context ID for the msg.

    // Create a dialog object. of class CNumericalSolverDialog : public
      CDialog
    CNumericalSolverDialog oDlg;

    // Set the dialog class vars using the CSystemModel class vars
    oDlg.m_dTimeStart = m_dTimeStart;
    oDlg.m_dTimeStop = m_dTimeStop;
    oDlg.m_dTimeStepSize = m_dTimeStepSize;
    oDlg.m_strTimeStepType = m_strTimeStepType;
    oDlg.m_strIntegrationMethod = m_strIntegrationMethod;
    oDlg.m_dATOL = m_dATOL;
    oDlg.m_dRTOL = m_dRTOL;
    oDlg.m_strWarning = m_strWarning;

    // While not correct input
    while(input == 0)
    {
        // Return val of DoModal() fn of ancestor class CDialog is
          checked to determine which btn was clicked.
        if(oDlg.DoModal() == IDOK)
        {
            // Assign CNumericalSolverDialog variable values to
              CSystemModel variable values.
            m_dTimeStart = oDlg.m_dTimeStart;
            m_dTimeStop = oDlg.m_dTimeStop;
```

```
        m_dTimeStepSize = oDlg.m_dTimeStepSize;
        m_strTimeStepType = oDlg.m_strTimeStepType;
        m_strIntegrationMethod = oDlg.m_strIntegrationMethod;
        m_dATOL = oDlg.m_dATOL;
        m_dRTOL = oDlg.m_dRTOL;
        m_strWarning = oDlg.m_strWarning;

        // Print msg with variable value.
        //sMsg.Format("\n CSystemModel::DlgWndParameterInput(),
          m_strIntegrationMethod = %sn", m_strIntegrationMethod);
        //AfxMessageBox(sMsg, nType, nIDhelp);
    }

    // Check consistency of time-based paras.
    if((m_dTimeStart >= 0) && (m_dTimeStart < m_dTimeStop)
        && (m_dTimeStepSize > 0) && (m_dTimeStepSize <=
        (m_dTimeStop - m_dTimeStart)))
    {
        input = 1;
    }
    else
    {
        input = 0;
        // Print error msg.
        sMsg.Format("");            // reset the msg since within a
          while loop
        sMsgTemp.Format("\n CSystemModel::DlgWndParameterInput()\n\n");
        sMsg += sMsgTemp;
        sMsgTemp.Format(" Input error! Require the following: \n");
        sMsg += sMsgTemp;
        sMsgTemp.Format(" 0 <= t_init < t_final \n");
        sMsg += sMsgTemp;
        sMsgTemp.Format(" and \n");
        sMsg += sMsgTemp;
        sMsgTemp.Format(" 0 < delta_t <= (t_final - t_init) \n");
        sMsg += sMsgTemp;
        sMsgTemp.Format(" Please re-enter the correct time-based
          values.\n");
        sMsg += sMsgTemp;
        AfxMessageBox(sMsg, nType, nIDhelp);
    }
  } //end while
}
```

Initially an "oDlg" dialog object of type CNumericalSolverDialog is instantiated with the values of the CSystemModel class. Then, the *while* loop is executed to obtain correct user input through the dialog window: the time-based parameters must be consistent, i.e., the initial time, t_0, final time, t_f, and time-step size, δt, are subject to the conditions $0 \le t_0 < t_f$ and $0 < \delta t \le (t_f - t_0)$.

Note that upon compilation of the code, the following error occurred: "error C2065: 'IDD_NUM_SOLVER_DLG': undeclared identifier". To resolve this, add #include "Resource.h" at the top of the "NumericalSolverDialog.h" header file as shown in bold in the following.

```
#if !defined(AFX_NUMERICALSOLVERDIALOG_H__96D85E00_
  E756_467A_890C_76E3FF10F3E0__INCLUDED_)
#define AFX_NUMERICALSOLVERDIALOG_H__96D85E00_
  E756_467A_890C_76E3FF10F3E0__INCLUDED_
```

```
#if _MSC_VER > 1000
#pragma once
#endif // _MSC_VER > 1000

#include "Resource.h" // rqd. since resources are used to build the dlg. wnd.

// NumericalSolverDialog.h : header file

...

#endif // !defined(AFX_NUMERICALSOLVERDIALOG_H__96D85E00_
  E756_467A_890C_76E3FF10F3E0__INCLUDED_)
```

14.2.7 CALL THE DIALOG WINDOW PARAMETER INPUT FUNCTION

The Numerical Solver entry of the Simulation menu or the equivalent Common Operations toolbar button, both sharing the same ID, ID_SIM_NUM_SOLVER, may be used to invoke the Numerical Solver dialog window. At present the event-handler function OnSimNumericalSolver() associated with the shared ID, simply presents a message to the user, but no dialog window appears. Now, since the DlgWndParameterInput() function has been added to the CSystemModel class, this may be called using the CSystemModel object, "m_SystemModel", of the CDiagramEngDoc class, from within the CDiagramEngDoc::OnSimNumericalSolver() function, as shown in bold in the following.

```
void CDiagramEngDoc::OnSimNumericalSolver()
{
    // TODO: Add your command handler code here

    // DiagramEng (start)
    //AfxMessageBox("\n CDiagramEngDoc::OnSimNumericalSolver()\n", MB_OK, 0);

    // Transfer values bw CNumericalSolverDialog and CSystemModel
    m_SystemModel.DlgWndParameterInput();

    // DiagramEng (end)
}
```

Now if the developer builds and runs the DiagramEng application, the user is able to update the simulation parameters, through the Numerical Solver dialog, for the underlying model.

14.3 DELETING MULTIPLE GROUPED ITEMS

The Context menu Delete Item entry allows the user to delete a single item at a time, based on the location of the mouse pointer upon right-clicking the mouse button to invoke the menu: if the mouse pointer is on a block, connection bend point, or connection head point, then a block, bend point, or connection object will be deleted, respectively. However, to delete multiple items, a selection of items must first occur, followed by the delete-object action. The CRectTracker object may be used to enclose or group a selection of items within a bounding rectangle, or rubber band, then the appropriate entry on either the Edit or Context menus may be chosen to delete the circumscribed items: this menu entry may be called "Delete Grouped Items", indicating that a bounding rectangle should first be used to group the items prior to their deletion. The general steps to implement the deletion of multiple or grouped items are as follows and specific steps are given later:

1. Change the name of the Edit menu entry.
2. Add a Delete Grouped Items entry to the Context menu.
3. Add an event-handler function to delete grouped items.

14.3.1 Change the Name of the Edit Menu Entry

Invoke the ClassWizard, choose CDiagramEngDoc as the class name and ID_EDIT_DELETE as the object ID. Select COMMAND from the list of messages and then choose Delete Function to delete the association of the existing function with the COMMAND event message. In addition, manually remove the CDiagramEngDoc::OnEditDelete() function as indicated. Select the IDR_CHILDMENU resource and change the properties for the Delete entry, as shown in Table 14.4.

14.3.2 Add a Delete Grouped Items Entry to the Context Menu

Select the IDR_CONTEXTMENU resource and add a new menu entry to be used, for the deletion of a selection of grouped items, just below the Delete Item entry, with the properties shown in Table 14.5.

14.3.3 Add an Event-Handler Function to Delete Grouped Items

Now an event-handler function needs to be added for the new Delete Grouped Items entry on the Context menu. Invoke the ClassWizard, choose CDiagramEngDoc as the class and select ID_EDIT_DELETE_GROUPED_ITEMS as the object ID. Add an event-handler function named OnEditDeleteGrouperItems() for the COMMAND event message and edit it as follows.

```
void CDiagramEngDoc::OnEditDeleteGroupedItems()
{
    // TODO: Add your command handler code here
    int intersected = 0;
    int intersected_head = 0;
    int intersected_tail = 0;
    double blk_width;
    double delta = 0.25*m_dDeltaLength;
    CPoint bend_pt;
    CPoint blk_posn;
    CPoint head_pt;
    CPoint tail_pt;
    CRectTracker temp_tracker;
    list<CBlock*> &blk_list = GetSystemModel().GetBlockList();
    list<CBlock*>::iterator it_blk;
```

TABLE 14.4

Child Frame-Based Menu Item, ID, Caption, Prompts (Status Bar and Tooltips), and Settings

Menu Item	Property	Setting
Edit/Delete Grouped Items	ID	ID_EDIT_DELETE_GROUPED_ITEMS
	Caption	Delete &Grouped Items
	Prompts	Delete items enclosed by rectangle\nDelete Grouped Items

TABLE 14.5

Context Menu Item, ID, Caption, and Prompts (Status Bar and Tooltips)

Menu Item	ID	Caption	Prompts
Delete Grouped Items	ID_EDIT_DELETE_GROUPED_ITEMS	Delete &Grouped Items	Delete items enclosed by rectangle\nDelete Grouped Items

```
list<CConnection*>::iterator it_con;
list<CConnection*> &con_list = GetSystemModel().GetConnectionList();
list<CPoint>::iterator it_pt;

// -- IF A RUBBER BAND HAS BEEN CREATED
if(m_iRubberBandCreated == 1)
{
    // Create a temp tracker since m_RectTracker will have its coords
      updated when the rubber band is moved.
    temp_tracker = m_RectTracker;

    // -- ITERATE THROUGH BLOCKS
    it_blk = blk_list.begin();
    while(it_blk != blk_list.end())
    {
        // Get block properties
        blk_posn = (*it_blk)->GetBlockPosition();
        blk_width = (*it_blk)->GetBlockShape().GetBlockWidth();

        // Determine if item lies within rubber band
        intersected = DetermineCurrentAndIntersectRects
          (temp_tracker, blk_posn, (blk_width*0.5));
        if(intersected)
        {
            // Delete block
          delete *it_blk; // delete actual block pointed to by it_blk
          it_blk = blk_list.erase(it_blk); // delete element at
            offset it_blk in list (that held the block)
        }
        else // only increment the iterator if there were no
          intersection
        {
            it_blk++;
        }
    }// end for it_blk

    // -- ITERATE THROUGH ALL CONNECTIONS (of this model)
    it_con = con_list.begin();
    while(it_con != con_list.end())
    {
        // -- ITERATE THROUGH ALL BEND POINTS FOR THIS CONNECTION
        list<CPoint> &bend_pts_list = (*it_con)-
          >GetConnectionBendPointsList();

        it_pt = bend_pts_list.begin();
        while(it_pt != bend_pts_list.end())
        {
            // BEND POINT
            bend_pt = *it_pt;

            // Determine if item lies within rubber band
            intersected = DetermineCurrentAndIntersectRects
              (temp_tracker, bend_pt, delta);
            if(intersected)
            {
                // Unsnap any tail points connected to this bend
                  point prior to delete bend point
                DisconnectTailPointFromBendPoint(&(*it_pt));
                // pass address of the bend_pt
```

```
                 // Delete element at offset it_er in list
                   (that held the bend pt)
                 it_pt = bend_pts_list.erase(it_pt);
             }
             else
             {
                 it_pt++;
             }
         }// end for it_pt

         // -- DELETE WHOLE CONNECTION OJBJECT

         // -- Get Tail Point
         tail_pt = (*it_con)->GetConnectionPointTail();

         // Determine if item lies within rubber band
         intersected_tail = DetermineCurrentAndIntersectRects
           (temp_tracker, tail_pt, delta);

         // -- Get Head Point
         head_pt = (*it_con)->GetConnectionPointHead();

         // Determine if item lies within rubber band
         intersected_head = DetermineCurrentAndIntersectRects
           (temp_tracker, head_pt, delta);

         // -- Check if head or tail points circumscribed: if delete
           whole connection
         if(intersected_tail || intersected_head)
         {
             // Disconnect all tail points from all the bend points on
               this connection.
             DisconnectTailPointsFromBendPoints(*it_con);

             // Delete connection
             delete *it_con; // delete actual connection pointed to by
               it_con
             it_con = con_list.erase(it_con); // delete element at
               offset it_con in list (that held the connection)
         }
         else
         {
             it_con++;
         }
     }// end for it_con

     // Reset member vars.
     m_iRubberBandCreated = 0; // end the rubber band state
     SetKeyFlagTrack(0);       // reset the key-based track flag since
       tracking aborted

     // Set flags
     SetModifiedFlag(TRUE);    // set the doc. as having been modified
       to prompt user to save
     UpdateAllViews(NULL);     // indicate that sys. should redraw.

   }// end if m_iRubberBandCreated
}
```

The `CDiagramEngDoc::OnEditDeleteGroupedItems()` function allows the user to delete more than one item at a time through the use of a previously activated CRectTracker rectangular rubber band–like object: if the items to be deleted lie in the interior of the rectangular region, then they are deleted. This differs from the Delete Item entry on the Context menu (IDR_CONTEXT_MENU), which first checks that the location of the mouse pointer is on a (single) item to be deleted, prior to its deletion.

Initially the user must activate the tracking of multiple items by either pressing the "T" key, or the Track Multiple Items button (ID_INIT_TRACK_MULTI_ITEMS) on the Common Operations toolbar (IDR_TB_COMMON_OPS): this then sets the integer flag-like variable, "m_iKeyFlagTrack", via the `OnInitTrackMultipleItems()` function, indicating that a tracking rectangle will be drawn. Then, inside the `CDiagramEngDoc::TrackMultipleItems()` function, a CRectTracker "m_RectTracker" object is used to track a bounding rectangular rubber band, and after the rubber band is created, the integer member variable of the CDiagramEngDoc class, "m_iRubberBandCreated", is set to 1.

Upon selection of the Delete Grouped Items entry on the Context or Edit menus and subsequent entry into the `CDiagramEngDoc::OnEditDeleteGroupedItems()` function, a check is first made that a rubber band has been created: if so, then a group of items may be deleted simultaneously, if not, then no deletion action is taken. There are three *while*-loop conditional sections concerning blocks, connections, and connection bend points, and in each loop, a check is made to determine whether the item lies within, i.e., intersects, the bounding or grouping rectangular region.

Blocks are deleted by first deleting what is pointed to by the "it_blk" pointer, then erasing the element at offset "it_blk" in the block list. The "it_blk" pointer is then set to the value returned by the `erase()` function, i.e., the iterator of the next element in the list after the removed element [1]. This advances the "it_blk" iterator. If no block were erased, then the *else* section would be entered and the iterator would be explicitly incremented ("it_blk++"). A *while* loop rather than a *for* loop is required, since the size of the list is dynamic due to the ongoing deletion: a fixed size *for* loop iteration would go beyond the size of the list, if items were deleted from the list during the loop.

Connection bend points are deleted in a similar manner: a check is first made that the bend point lies within the bounding rectangle; if so, any connection tail points that may be connected to the bend point are disconnected with a call to `DisconnectTailPointFromBendPoint()`. Then, since an "it_pt" iterator points to a CPoint (bend point) object, it can be erased from the connection's bend points list ("m_lstBendPoints"). The return value of the `erase()` call, as described earlier, is an iterator to the next element, here a bend point, in the list after the one just removed.

Finally, a whole connection object may be removed by determining whether the head or the tail point of the connection lies within the bounding rectangle. If so, then any other (*secondary*) connection tail points that may be connected to the current (*primary*) connection's bend points, need to be disconnected through the call to `DisconnectTailPointsFromBendPoints()`. Thereafter, the "it_con" pointer is dereferenced to delete the connection object and then the element at offset, "it_con", is erased from the list.

The paired figures (Figure 14.2) indicate various before–after grouped deletion operations: (a) a selection of bend points where a tail point from another connection is attached and (b) deletion of bend points including the attached connection, leaving the main connection, (c) a selection of a block and a connection with other connections attached and (d) deletion of only the block and the main connection with a disconnection of the attached connections, (e) selection of a block and a connection that emanates from a bend point and (f) deletion of the block and connection leaving the main connection including its bend point, and finally (g) selection of a whole group of objects and (h) their complete deletion in one action.

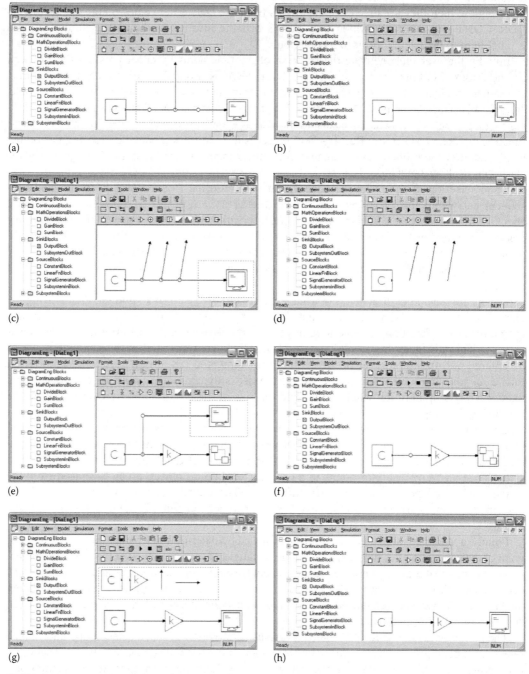

FIGURE 14.2 Paired before and after figures of selection and deletion operations, respectively: (a/b) deletion of bend points and an attached connection, (c/d) deletion of a block and a connection with a disconnection of tail points, (e/f) deletion of a block and connection emanating from a bend point, and (g/h) deletion of a group of objects.

14.4 SETTING OF ITEM PROPERTIES

The Context menu, activated by a right-mouse-button-down event, has a Set Properties entry that should be used to set the properties of the selected object, e.g., a block, by invoking a dialog window for user-defined parameter input. Table 14.6 indicates the current Context menu items and their properties.

Context menu-based functionality is to be added here for the Set Properties menu entry that is to invoke other item property–setting functions. Hence, invoke the ClassWizard and choose CDiagramEngDoc as the class and IDM_SET_ITEM_PROPERTIES as the object ID. Add an event-handler function for the COMMAND message, with name OnSetItemProperties() and edit it as follows.

```
void CDiagramEngDoc::OnSetItemProperties()
{
    // TODO: Add your command handler code here

    // DiagramEng (start)
    int item_clicked = 0;

    // Set properties for blocks
    item_clicked = DoubleLeftClickBlock(m_ptContextMenu);

    // Set properties for connections and connection bend points
    if(item_clicked == 0)
    {
        item_clicked = SetConnectionProperties(m_ptContextMenu);
    }

    // Set properties for the Numerical Solver
    if(item_clicked == 0)
    {
        OnSimNumericalSolver();
    }

    // DiagramEng (end)
}
```

The OnSetItemProperties() function first calls the DoubleLeftClickBlock() function passing in the point at which the Context menu was invoked, i.e., "m_ptContextMenu", a CDiagramEngDoc member variable. If the point resides on a block, then the particular block dialog window is presented for parameter input and the "item_clicked" flag is set to 1. If the "item_clicked" flag is zero, then a further test is made to determine whether a connection head point or bend point was clicked via a call to SetConnectionProperties() (see explanation in the following text),

TABLE 14.6
Context Menu Items, IDs, Captions, and Prompts

Menu Item	ID	Caption	Prompt
Delete Item	IDM_DELETE_ITEM	&Delete Item	Delete selected item\nDelete selected item
Delete Grouped Items	ID_EDIT_DELETE_GROUPED_ITEMS	Delete &Grouped Items	Delete items enclosed by rectangle\nDelete Grouped Items
Insert Bend Point	IDM_INSERT_BEND_POINT	&Insert Bend Point	Insert bend point\nInsert bend point
Set Properties	IDM_SET_ITEM_PROPERTIES	&Set Properties	Set item properties\nSet item properties

and if so, a simple message box appears (no dialog window parameter input has been built for connection objects as yet). Finally if no block or connection head or bend point was clicked, then the click point is deemed to have taken place on an empty part of the palette, and hence the numerical solver dialog window is presented via a call to OnSimNumericalSolver(), to allow user-defined parameter input.

Now add a new member function to the CDiagramEngDoc class, to be used to set the properties of Connection objects and their bend points, with the prototype, int CDiagramEngDoc:: SetConnectionProperties(CPoint m_ptContextMenu), and edit the function as follows.

```
int CDiagramEngDoc::SetConnectionProperties(CPoint point)
{
    int click_flag = 0; // (0) item not clicked, (1) item clicked
    double disc_r = 0.25*m_dDeltaLength; // disc of radius r
    double dist;    // dist bw mouse click pt and connection head pt. or
      bend pt.
    CPoint bend_pt;    // connection bend pt.
    CPoint head_pt;    // connection head pt.
    list<CConnection*>::iterator it_con;   // connection iterator
    list<CConnection*> con_list = GetSystemModel().GetConnectionList();
    list<CPoint>::iterator it_pt;

    // ITERATE THROUGH CONNECTION LIST

    for(it_con = con_list.begin(); it_con != con_list.end(); it_con++)
    {
        // CHECK IF CLICK ON CONNECTION HEAD POINT

        // Get head point of connection
        head_pt = (*it_con)->GetConnectionPointHead();

        // Determine Euclidean dist bw point and head pt
        dist = sqrt(pow(head_pt.x - point.x,2) +
          pow(head_pt.y - point.y,2));

        // If the head pt is clicked
        if(dist <= disc_r)
        {
            //AfxMessageBox("\n CDiagramEngDoc::SetConnectionProperties():
              connection\n", MB_OK, 0);
            click_flag = 1;
            break;
        }

        // CHECK IF CLICK ON CONNECTION BEND POINT

        // Get connection bend pts.
        list<CPoint> &bend_pts_list = (*it_con)-
          >GetConnectionBendPointsList();

        // Iterate through all bend pts. for this connection
        for(it_pt = bend_pts_list.begin(); it_pt != bend_pts_list.end();
          it_pt++)
        {
            bend_pt = *it_pt;

            // Determine Euclidean dist bw mouse point and connection
              bend pt.
            dist = sqrt(pow(bend_pt.x - point.x,2) +
              pow(bend_pt.y - point.y,2));
```

```
            // If the bend pt is clicked
            if(dist <= disc_r)
            {
                //AfxMessageBox("\n CDiagramEngDoc::SetConnectionProper
                  ties(): connection\n", MB_OK, 0);
                click_flag = 1;
                break;
            }
        }
    }

    return click_flag;
}
```

The SetConnectionProperties() function iterates through the system model's list of connections, first checking whether the connection head point was clicked: if so, a simple message is presented, the "click_flag" is set to 1 and the function returns. If not, the connection's bend points list is retrieved and a test is made to determine whether any of its bend points have been clicked; the action then proceeds as for a head point but with a different message. If neither a head point nor bend point was clicked, the function simply returns "click_flag = 0". At this stage in the project, no properties are actually set for the connection, but the structure may be used later when pursuing connection-centric signal propagation.

14.5 SUMMARY

The Context menu is extended with entries that invoke context-based functionality relevant to the point at which the menu is invoked. A Numerical Solver dialog window is added to the project, using six key steps, and works in conjunction with the CSystemModel class allowing the user to set model solver properties: the dialog may be invoked by the selection of a Simulation menu entry, a Common Operations toolbar button, or, most easily, through the Context menu. The deletion of grouped items is also implemented through the addition of a OnEditDeleteGroupedItems() function and requires the user to circumscribe the items with a CRectTracker object, and then upon right-clicking in the interior of the region and choosing Delete Grouped Items on the Context menu, the enclosed items are deleted. The Context menu is also extended to allow the setting of model diagram item properties using the OnSetItemProperties() function, which invokes the appropriate block dialog window or Numerical Solver dialog window.

REFERENCE

1. C++ Reference, http://en.cppreference.com/w/cpp

15 Setting Port Properties

15.1 INTRODUCTION

Block-based data is input by the user by double-clicking on a block or choosing Set Properties from the Context menu to invoke a block-specific dialog window. The underlying mechanism to invoke the correct block dialog window involves the `CDiagramEngView::OnLButtonDblClk()` function that calls the `CDiagramEngDoc::DoubleLeftClickBlock()` method, which then invokes the particular Block class' overriding `BlockDlgWndParameterInput()` function that creates the relevant dialog window and updates the Block class' variable values with those of its related Dialog class. For example, the CConstantBlock class' member variable values are updated with the CConstantBlockDialog class' values entered by the user through the Constant block dialog window.

Thus far, all the dialog-window-based entered data is saved to the particular CBlock-derived class' member variables. However, although the Divide block (CDivideBlock working with CDivideBlockDialog) accepts input for the number of multiplication and division inputs, and the Sum block (CSumBlock working with CSumBlockDialog) allows input for the number of addition and subtraction inputs, as shown by their dialog windows in Figure 15.1, the number and placement of input and output ports do not yet reflect the entered settings. Hence functionality is to be added herein, to set the numbers of ports to be consistent with those entered by the user.

15.2 SETTING DIVIDE BLOCK PORTS

The correct setting up of the Divide block ports involves additions and changes to the code, in particular resetting of input and output ports to be consistent with dialog-based user input, automatically calculating port position angles given the number of ports present and updating the `CDivideBlock::BlockDlgWndParameterInput()` function to call the port resetting methods.

15.2.1 RESET INPUT PORTS

To reassign the number of input ports and their properties, e.g., name, location, and arrow direction, a `ResetInputPorts()` function needs to be added to the CDivideBlock class, that compares the user input with the current port-based block state and makes the appropriate alterations. Hence, add a public member function to the CDivideBlock class with the prototype, `void CDivideBlock::ResetInputPorts(int n_mult_ports, int n_divide_ports)`, and edit the function as follows.

```
void CDivideBlock::ResetInputPorts(int n_mult_ports, int n_divide_ports)
{
    int i = 0;
    int cnt_mults = 0;     // no. of mult ports present in the vector
    int cnt_divides = 0;   // no. of divide ports present in the vector
    int connected = 0;     // flag indicating a connection "connected" to
      a port
    int delete_ports = 1;  // flag to control port deletion
    int n_inputs;          // total number of input ports for the Divide
      block.
    CString sMsg;          // string to be displayed
```

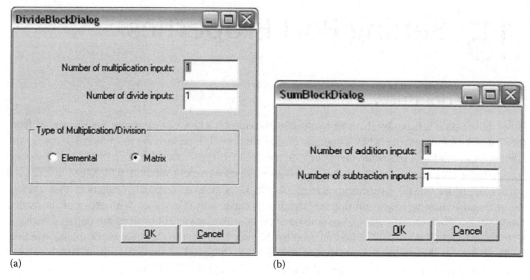

FIGURE 15.1   Dialog windows showing input port multiplicity settings: (a) Divide block and (b) Sum block.

```
UINT nType = MB_OK;    // style of msg. box
UINT nIDhelp = 0;      // help context ID for the msg.
list<CConnection*>::iterator it_con; // iterator for list of
  CConnection ptrs.
vector<CPort*>::iterator it_port;  // iterator for vector of CPort ptrs.

// Get connection list
CDiagramEngDoc *pDoc = GetDocumentGlobalFn();
list<CConnection*> &con_list = GetParentSystemModel()-
  >GetConnectionList();

// Get vec of input ports
vector<CPort*> &vec_input_ports = GetVectorOfInputPorts(); // vector
  of input ports

// -- ERASE INPUT PORTS FROM VEC THAT DO NOT HAVE CONNECTIONS ATTACHED
it_port = vec_input_ports.begin();
while(it_port != vec_input_ports.end())
{
    // Reset connectivity flag to "not connected"
    connected = 0;

    // Iterate through connection list
    for(it_con = con_list.begin(); it_con != con_list.end(); it_con++)
    {
        // If a connection is attached to this port
        if((*it_con)->GetRefToPort() == *it_port)
        {
            (*it_port)->SetPortArrowDirection(e_right_arrow);
            connected = 1;
        }
    }

    // If there are no connections to this port
    if(connected == 0)
    {
        // Delete the port
```

```
                delete *it_port;    // delete port pointed to by it_port
                it_port = vec_input_ports.erase(it_port); // delete element
                  at offset it_port and return the loc of the next item
        }
        else
        {
            it_port++;
        }
}// end while it_port

// -- GET THE NO. OF MULT AND DIVIDE PORTS (with connections
  attached) REMAINING IN THE DEPLETED LIST
for(it_port = vec_input_ports.begin(); it_port != vec_input_ports.
  end(); it_port++)
{
        if((*it_port)->GetPortName() == "*")
        {
            cnt_mults++;
        }
        if((*it_port)->GetPortName() == "/")
        {
            cnt_divides++;
        }
}

// Simple msg.
sMsg.Format("\n CDivideBlock::ResetInputPorts(), n_mult_ports = %d,
  cnt_mults = %d, n_divide_ports = %d, cnt_divides = %d\n",
  n_mult_ports, cnt_mults, n_divide_ports, cnt_divides);
//AfxMessageBox(sMsg, nType, nIDhelp);

// -- ADD OR DELETE THE DIFFERENCE IN THE NO. OF MULT PORTS
if(n_mult_ports > cnt_mults)
{
        for(i=0; i<(n_mult_ports - cnt_mults); i++)
        {
            CPort *p_input_port = new CPort(*this);
            p_input_port->SetPortName("*");           // "*" sign assoc.
              with mult input port
            p_input_port->SetPortArrowDirection(e_right_arrow);
              // input ports point to the right
            vec_input_ports.push_back(p_input_port); // add port to the
              end of the vector
        }
}
else if(n_mult_ports < cnt_mults)
{
        // -- DISCONNECT CONNECTIONS AND DELETE MULT PORTS
        it_port = vec_input_ports.begin();
        while((delete_ports == 1) && (it_port != vec_input_ports.
          end()))
        {
            if((*it_port)->GetPortName() == "*")
            {
                // Disconnect the connection object from the port
                pDoc->DisconnectEndPointFromPort(*it_port);

                // Delete port
```

```
        delete *it_port;   // delete actual port pointed to by
          it_port
        it_port = vec_input_ports.erase(it_port); // delete
          element at offset it_port in vec (that held the port)

        cnt_mults--;
    }
    else
    {
        it_port++;
    }

    if(n_mult_ports == cnt_mults)
    {
        delete_ports = 0;
    }
    }// end while
}

// -- ADD OR DELETE THE DIFFERENCE IN THE NO. OF DIVIDE PORTS
if(n_divide_ports > cnt_divides)
{
    for(i=0; i<(n_divide_ports - cnt_divides); i++)
    {
        CPort *p_input_port = new CPort(*this);
        p_input_port->SetPortName("/");   // "/" sign assoc. with
          divide input port

        p_input_port->SetPortArrowDirection(e_right_arrow);
          // input ports point to the right
        vec_input_ports.push_back(p_input_port); // add port to the
          end of the vector
    }
}
else if(n_divide_ports < cnt_divides)
{
    // -- DISCONNECT CONNECTIONS AND DELETE DIVIDE PORTS
    delete_ports = 1;
    it_port = vec_input_ports.begin();
    while((delete_ports == 1) && (it_port != vec_input_ports.end()))
    {
        if((*it_port)->GetPortName() == "/")
        {
            // Disconnect the connection object from the port
            pDoc->DisconnectEndPointFromPort(*it_port);

            // Delete port
            delete *it_port; // delete actual port pointed to by
              it_port
            it_port = vec_input_ports.erase(it_port);   // delete
              element at offset it_port in vec (that held the port)
            cnt_divides--;
        }
        else // only increment the iterator if there were no deletion
        {
            it_port++;
        }

        if(n_divide_ports == cnt_divides)
```

```
            {
                delete_ports = 0;
            }
        }// end while
    }

    // Simple msg.
    sMsg.Format("\n CDivideBlock::ResetInputPorts(), vec_input_ports.
      size() = %d\n", vec_input_ports.size());
    //AfxMessageBox(sMsg, nType, nIDhelp);

    // Calculate the port position angles to locate the ports on the left
      side of the Divide block.
    n_inputs = n_mult_ports + n_divide_ports;
    CalculatePortPositionAngles(n_inputs);

    // Set flags and redraw the doc
    pDoc->SetModifiedFlag(TRUE);   // set the doc. as having been modified
      to prompt user to save
    pDoc->UpdateAllViews(NULL);    // indicate that sys. should redraw.
}
```

In the first section of the ResetInputPorts() function, a check is made to determine whether any connections are attached to existing ports; if so, they are left connected, if not, then the port is deleted. This action results in either no ports being present on the block or only ports with connections attached. Thereafter a count is made to determine the number of remaining multiplication and division ports, "cnt_mults" and "cnt_divides", respectively.

The next two sections concern the addition or deletion of multiplication and division ports separately. If the current number of multiplication ports, "cnt_mults", is less than that entered by the user, "m_iNMultiplyInputs", or, equivalently, "n_mult_ports", then CPort objects are constructed and added to the vector of input ports, "vec_input_ports". If, however, less ports are desired than those present, then the connection object that is attached to the port should be disconnected, the port deleted, and the count, "cnt_mults", decremented until the correct number of ports remain.

A similar procedure takes place for the division ports: if the number desired is greater than that present, then more ports are added, if less, then connections are disconnected, ports deleted, and the count, "cnt_divides", decremented.

15.2.2 Calculate Port Position Angles

Toward the end of the ResetInputPorts() function a call to CalculatePortPosition Angles() is made to automatically calculate the angles used to define the location (CalculatePortPosition()) of the ports positioned at an equidistant spacing on the left side of the Divide block.

Consider the rectangular Divide block shown in Figure 15.2, with a local (x,y) coordinate system at its center; width, w; height, h; two ports, p_i and p_{i+1}, with equidistant spacing, $d = h/(n + 1)$, from the top and bottom of the block and from each other; and port (p_i) position angle $\theta_i = \pi - \alpha$, where $\alpha = \tan^{-1}(2b/w)$ and $b = h/2 - (i + 1)d$ is the y component of the port, where $i \in [0, n - 1]$ for n ports.

Add a public member function to the CDivideBlock class with the prototype void CDivideBlock:: CalculatePortPositionAngles(int n_inputs) and edit the function as follows.

```
void CDivideBlock::CalculatePortPositionAngles(int n_inputs)
{
    int i = 0;     // used to set the no. of distance increments (dist)
      from top of block
    double dist;   // dist from the top of the block
```

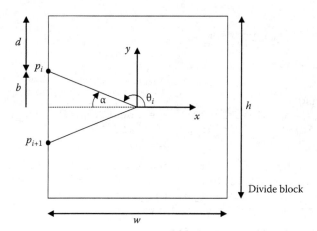

FIGURE 15.2   Divide block, of width, w, and height, h, showing two ports, p_i and p_{i+1}, where port p_i is located using a port position angle $\theta_i = \pi - \alpha$.

```
double b;              // dist from middle of block (local y=0) to port
  (up is > 0, down is < 0)
double height;         // height of block
double pi = PI;        // pi rounded.
double alpha;          // angle in radians
double theta;          // angle in radians
double width;          // width of block
CString sMsg;          // string to be displayed
UINT nType = MB_OK;    // style of msg. box
UINT nIDhelp = 0;      // help context ID for the msg.
vector<CPort*>::iterator it_port; // iterator for vector
  of CPort ptrs.

// Init paras
height = GetBlockShape().GetBlockHeight();
width = GetBlockShape().GetBlockWidth();
dist = height/(n_inputs + 1);

// Simple msg.
//sMsg.Format("\n CDivideBlock::CalculatePortPositionAngles(),
  height = %lf, width = %lf, dist = %lf\n", height, width, dist);
//AfxMessageBox(sMsg, nType, nIDhelp);

// Get vec of input ports
vector<CPort*> &vec_input_ports = GetVectorOfInputPorts();
  // vector of input ports

// Loop through the vector and set the port position angle
for(it_port = vec_input_ports.begin(); it_port != vec_input_ports.
  end(); it_port++)
{
    b = height/2 - (i+1)*dist;  // b = top of block - a multiple of
      dist
    alpha = atan(2.0*b/width);  // tan(theta) = b/(w/2) = opp./adj.
    theta = pi - alpha;         // theta w.r.t. block coord. sys.
    theta = theta*180.0/pi;     // convert from radians into degrees
    (*it_port)->SetPortPositionAngle(theta);  // set the port
      position angle
    (*it_port)->CalculatePortPosition(); // calculate port posn based
      on prev. angle.
```

```
        GetParentSystemModel()->UpdateConnectionPointHead(*it_port);
          // deref the iterator to get the ptr-to-CPort obj.
        i++;   // incr the multiplier of the no. of dists
    }
}
```

The developer will notice that in the *for* loop of the CalculatePortPositionAngles() function, the index, i, is used to multiply the inter-port distance spacing, d, to correctly set the vertical displacement, b, which is then used to determine α and then the port position angle, θ_i, of port p_i.

15.2.3 RESET OUTPUT PORTS

A function should also be added to reset the output port properties, i.e., the position angle, position, and port arrow direction. Currently there is no mechanism to change the number of output ports: there is only one per block, and hence the vector of output ports has size equal to 1. The port position angle of this one port should be set to $0°$ (SetPortPositionAngle(0.0)), such that it is positioned (CalculatePortPosition()) on the right side of the block. In addition, a message box warning should be placed in the ResetOutputPorts() function to warn the developer if there is more than one port. Hence, add a public member function to the CDivideBlock class with the prototype, void CDivideBlock::ResetOutputPorts(void), and edit the function as follows.

```
void CDivideBlock::ResetOutputPorts()
{
    int size;                         // size of vec of output ports
    CString sMsg;                     // main msg string
    UINT nType = MB_OK;               // style of msg. box
    UINT nIDhelp = 0;                 // help context ID for the msg.
    vector<CPort*>::iterator it_port; // iterator for vector of CPort ptrs.

    // Get the system model
    CDiagramEngDoc *pDoc = GetDocumentGlobalFn();  // get a ptr to
      the doc.

    // Get vec of output ports
    vector<CPort*> &vec_output_ports = GetVectorOfOutputPorts();
      // vector of input ports
    size = vec_output_ports.size();

    // Msg. box
    //sMsg.Format("\n CDivideBlock::ResetOutputPorts(): size = %d\n",
      size);
    //AfxMessageBox(sMsg, nType, nIDhelp);

    // Check size not greater than one, since only one output port per
      block
    if(size > 1)
    {
        sMsg.Format("\n CDivideBlock::ResetOutputPorts(): WARNING!
          size = %d != 1\n", size);
        AfxMessageBox(sMsg, nType, nIDhelp);
    }

    // Reset angle, posn, and arrow direc of output port(s)
    for(it_port = vec_output_ports.begin(); it_port != vec_output_ports.
      end(); it_port++)
```

```
    {
        (*it_port)->SetPortPositionAngle(0.0);
        (*it_port)->CalculatePortPosition();
        (*it_port)->SetPortArrowDirection(e_right_arrow);

        // Update any connection tail end point associated with the port.
        GetParentSystemModel()->UpdateConnectionPointTail(*it_port);
          // deref the iterator to get the ptr-to-CPort obj.
    }

    // Set flags and redraw the doc
    pDoc->SetModifiedFlag(TRUE); // set the doc. as having been modified
      to prompt user to save
    pDoc->UpdateAllViews(NULL);  // indicate that sys. should redraw.
}
```

Now the ResetInputPorts() and ResetOutputPorts() methods need to be called from within the CDivideBlock::BlockDlgWndParameterInput() function: hence amend the latter as shown in bold in the following.

```
void CDivideBlock::BlockDlgWndParameterInput()
{
    int  n_inputs = 0;   // number of input ports
    CString sMsg;        // string to be displayed
    CString sMsgTemp;    // temp string msg.
    UINT nType = MB_OK;  // style of msg. box
    UINT nIDhelp = 0;    // help context ID for the msg.

    // Create a dialog object. of class CDivideBlockDialog : public
      CDialog
    CDivideBlockDialog oDlg;

    // Set the dialog class vars using the block class vars
    oDlg.m_iMultType = m_iMultType;
    oDlg.m_iNDivideInputs = m_iNDivideInputs;
    oDlg.m_iNMultiplyInputs = m_iNMultiplyInputs;

    // While less than two input ports get user input
    while(n_inputs < 2)
    {
        // Return val of DoModal() fn of ancestor class CDialog is
          checked to determine which btn was clicked.
        if(oDlg.DoModal() == IDOK)
        {
            // Assign CDivideBlockDialog variable values to CDivideBlock
              variable values.
            m_iNDivideInputs = oDlg.m_iNDivideInputs;
            m_iNMultiplyInputs = oDlg.m_iNMultiplyInputs;
            m_iMultType = oDlg.m_iMultType;

            // Print msg with variable value.
            //sMsg.Format("\n CDivideBlock::BlockDlgWndParameterInput(),
              m_iMultType = %d\n", m_iMultType);
            //AfxMessageBox(sMsg, nType, nIDhelp);
        }

        // Check input for correctness and warn user if approp.
        n_inputs = m_iNDivideInputs + m_iNMultiplyInputs;

        if(n_inputs < 2)
```

```
        {
            sMsgTemp.Format("\n CDivideBlock::BlockDlgWndParameter
              Input()\n");
            sMsg += sMsgTemp;
            sMsgTemp.Format(" No. of input ports = %dn", n_inputs);
            sMsg += sMsgTemp;
            sMsgTemp.Format(" Two or more input ports are required!\n");
            sMsg += sMsgTemp;
            AfxMessageBox(sMsg, nType, nIDhelp);
            sMsg.Format("");    // reset the msg since within a while loop
        }
    }

    // Reset ports
    ResetInputPorts(m_iNMultiplyInputs, m_iNDivideInputs);
    ResetOutputPorts();
}
```

15.3   SETTING SUM BLOCK PORTS

A similar procedure to that of the Divide block should be followed for resetting the ports of the Sum block, i.e., input and output ports need to be reset given user input, port position angles need to be calculated, and the `CSumBlock::BlockDlgWndParameterInput()` method is to be updated to call the port resetting methods.

15.3.1   RESET INPUT PORTS

Add a public member function to the CSumBlock class to reset the input ports, with the prototype `void CSumBlock::ResetInputPorts(int n_add_ports, int n_subtract_ports)` and edit the function as follows.

```
void CSumBlock::ResetInputPorts(int n_add_ports, int n_subtract_ports)
{
    int i = 0;
    int cnt_adds = 0;         // no. of add ports present in the vector
    int cnt_subtracts = 0;    // no. of subtract ports present in the vector
    int connected = 0;        // flag indicating a connection "connected" to
      a port
    int delete_ports = 1;     // flag to control port deletion
    int n_inputs;             // total number of input ports for the Sum
      block.
    CString sMsg;             // string to be displayed
    UINT nType = MB_OK;       // style of msg. box
    UINT nIDhelp = 0;         // help context ID for the msg.
    list<CConnection*>::iterator it_con; // iterator for list of
      CConnection ptrs.
    vector<CPort*>::iterator it_port;    // iterator for vector of CPort
      ptrs.

    // Get connection list
    CDiagramEngDoc *pDoc = GetDocumentGlobalFn();
    list<CConnection*> &con_list = GetParentSystemModel()-
      >GetConnectionList();

    // Get vec of input ports
    vector<CPort*> &vec_input_ports = GetVectorOfInputPorts();
      // vector of input ports
```

```
// -- ERASE INPUT PORTS FROM VEC THAT DO NOT HAVE CONNECTIONS
   ATTACHED
it_port = vec_input_ports.begin();
while(it_port != vec_input_ports.end())
{
    // Reset connectivity flag to "not connected"
    connected = 0;

    // Iterate through connection list
    for(it_con = con_list.begin(); it_con != con_list.end(); it_con++)
    {
        // If a connection is attached to this port
        if((*it_con)->GetRefToPort() == *it_port)
        {
            (*it_port)->SetPortArrowDirection(e_right_arrow);
            connected = 1;
        }
    }

    // If there are no connections to this port
    if(connected == 0)
    {
        // Delete the port
        delete *it_port; // delete port pointed to by it_port
        it_port = vec_input_ports.erase(it_port); // delete element
          at offset it_port and return the loc of the next item
    }
    else
    {
        it_port++;
    }
}// end while it_port

// -- GET THE NO. OF ADD AND SUBTRACT PORTS (with connections
   attached) REMAINING IN THE DEPLETED LIST
for(it_port = vec_input_ports.begin(); it_port != vec_input_ports.
  end(); it_port++)
{
    if((*it_port)->GetPortName() == "+")
    {
        cnt_adds++;
    }
    if((*it_port)->GetPortName() == "-")
    {
        cnt_subtracts++;
    }
}

// Simple msg.
sMsg.Format("\n CSumBlock::ResetInputPorts(), n_add_ports = %d,
  cnt_adds = %d, n_subtract_ports = %d, cnt_subtracts = %d\n",
  n_add_ports, cnt_adds, n_subtract_ports, cnt_subtracts);
//AfxMessageBox(sMsg, nType, nIDhelp);

// -- ADD OR DELETE THE DIFFERENCE IN THE NO. OF ADD PORTS
if(n_add_ports > cnt_adds)
{
    for(i=0; i<(n_add_ports - cnt_adds); i++)
```

```
        {
            CPort *p_input_port = new CPort(*this);
            p_input_port->SetPortName("+");   // "*" sign assoc. with add
              input port
            vec_input_ports.push_back(p_input_port); // add port to the
              end of the vector
        }
    }
    else if(n_add_ports < cnt_adds)
    {
        // -- DISCONNECT CONNECTIONS AND DELETE ADD PORTS
        it_port = vec_input_ports.begin();
        while((delete_ports == 1) && (it_port != vec_input_ports.end()))
        {
            if((*it_port)->GetPortName() == "+")
            {
                // Disconnect the connection object from the port
                pDoc->DisconnectEndPointFromPort(*it_port);

                // Delete port
                delete *it_port; // delete actual port pointed to by
                  it_port
                it_port = vec_input_ports.erase(it_port);   // delete
                  element at offset it_port in vec (that held the port)

                cnt_adds--;
            }
            else
            {
                it_port++;
            }

            if(n_add_ports == cnt_adds)
            {
                delete_ports = 0;
            }
        }// end while
    }

    // -- ADD OR DELETE THE DIFFERENCE IN THE NO. OF SUBTRACT PORTS
    if(n_subtract_ports > cnt_subtracts)
    {
        for(i=0; i<(n_subtract_ports - cnt_subtracts); i++)
        {
            CPort *p_input_port = new CPort(*this);
            p_input_port->SetPortName("-");     // "-" sign assoc. with
              subtract input port
            vec_input_ports.push_back(p_input_port); // add port to the
              end of the vector
        }
    }
    else if(n_subtract_ports < cnt_subtracts)
    {
        // -- DISCONNECT CONNECTIONS AND DELETE SUBTRACT PORTS
        delete_ports = 1;
        it_port = vec_input_ports.begin();
        while((delete_ports == 1) && (it_port != vec_input_ports.end()))
```

```
    {
        if( (*it_port) ->GetPortName() == "-")
        {
            // Disconnect the connection object from the port
            pDoc->DisconnectEndPointFromPort(*it_port);

            // Delete port
            delete *it_port; // delete actual port pointed to by
              it_port
            it_port = vec_input_ports.erase(it_port); // delete
              element at offset it_port in vec (that held the port)

            cnt_subtracts--;
        }
        else // only increment the iterator if there were no deletion
        {
            it_port++;
        }

        if(n_subtract_ports == cnt_subtracts)
        {
            delete_ports = 0;
        }
    }// end while
}

// Simple msg.
sMsg.Format("\n CSumBlock::ResetInputPorts(), vec_input_ports.
  size() = %d\n", vec_input_ports.size());
//AfxMessageBox(sMsg, nType, nIDhelp);

// Calculate the port position angles to locate the ports on the left
  hemicircle of the Sum block.
n_inputs = n_add_ports + n_subtract_ports;
CalculatePortPositionAngles(n_inputs);

// Set flags and redraw the doc
pDoc->SetModifiedFlag(TRUE); // set the doc. as having been modified
  to prompt user to save
pDoc->UpdateAllViews (NULL); // indicate that sys. should redraw.
}
```

The ResetInputPorts() function for the Sum block works in a similar manner for the Divide block presented earlier. In the first section of the function, a check is made to determine whether any connections are attached to existing ports: if so, they are left connected, if not, the port is deleted. Thereafter, a count is made to determine the number of remaining addition and subtraction ports.

The next two sections concern the addition or deletion of ports. If the current number of ports is less than that entered by the user, then CPort objects are constructed and added to the appropriate port vector. If, however, less ports are desired than that present, then the connection that is attached to the port should be disconnected, the port deleted, and the port count decremented until the correct number remains.

15.3.2 Calculate Port Position Angles

The aforementioned ResetInputPorts() function makes a call to CalculatePortPosition Angles(), to automatically calculate the angles used to define the location of the ports, positioned at an equidistant angular arc spacing, on the left semicircle (standard left-to-right block layout) of the

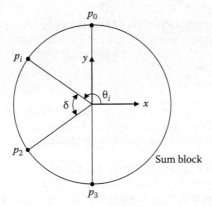

FIGURE 15.3 Sum block with port p_i, position angle $\theta_i = \pi/2 + i\delta$, and inter-port arc spacing $\delta = \pi/(n-1)$.

Sum block. Consider Figure 15.3 that shows a circular Sum block with a local (x,y) coordinate system at the center of the block; n ports, p_i, for $i \in [0, n-1]$ (here for simplicity $n = 4$), with equidistant angular arc spacing, $\delta = \pi/(n-1)$, from each other; and port (p_i) position angle, $\theta_i = \pi/2 + i\delta$, measured positively in the anticlockwise direction from the positive x axis.

Now add a public member function to the CSumBlock class with the prototype, `void CSumBlock::CalculatePortPositionAngles(int n_inputs)`, and edit the function as follows.

```
void CSumBlock::CalculatePortPositionAngles(int n_inputs)
{
    int i = 0;              // used to set the no. of arc spacing increments
    double arc_spacing;     // angular spacing bw. ports
    double eps = 10.0;      // angular epsilon
    double pi = PI;         // pi rounded.
    double theta;           // angle in radians
    CString sMsg;           // string to be displayed
    UINT nType = MB_OK;     // style of msg. box
    UINT nIDhelp = 0;       // help context ID for the msg.
    vector<CPort*>::iterator it_port; // iterator for vector
      of CPort ptrs.

    // Get vec of input ports
    vector<CPort*> &vec_input_ports = GetVectorOfInputPorts();
      // vector of input ports

    // -- CHECK THE NUMBER OF INPUT PORTS AND EITHER POSITION EXPLICITLY
       OR AUTOMATICALLY.

    // If no. of input ports <= 3, then place ports manually.
    if(n_inputs <= 3)
    {
        i = 1;
        for(it_port = vec_input_ports.begin(); it_port != vec_input_ports.
          end(); it_port++)
        {
            if(i == 1)
            {
                (*it_port)->SetPortArrowDirection(e_right_arrow);
                  // input ports point to the right
                (*it_port)->SetPortPositionAngle((i+1)*90);
            }
            else if(i == 2)
```

```cpp
        {
            (*it_port)->SetPortArrowDirection(e_up_arrow);
              // input ports point to the right
            (*it_port)->SetPortPositionAngle((i+1)*90);
        }
        else if(i == 3)
        {
            (*it_port)->SetPortArrowDirection(e_down_arrow);
              // input ports point to the right
            (*it_port)->SetPortPositionAngle(90);
        }
        (*it_port)->CalculatePortPosition();
        GetParentSystemModel()->UpdateConnectionPointHead(*it_port);
            // deref the iterator to get the ptr-to-CPort obj.

        i++;
    }// end for
}// end if

// If no. of input ports > 3, then place ports automatically.
if(n_inputs > 3)
{
    i = 0;
    arc_spacing = 180.0/(n_inputs - 1); // angular arc spacing bw
      ports within 180 semicircle.

    // Simple msg.
    sMsg.Format("\n CSumBlock::CalculatePortPositionAngles(),
      arc_spacing = %lf\n", arc_spacing);
    AfxMessageBox(sMsg, nType, nIDhelp);

    for(it_port = vec_input_ports.begin(); it_port != vec_input_ports.
      end(); it_port++)
    {
        // Get port position angle
        theta = 90.0 + i*arc_spacing;
        (*it_port)->SetPortPositionAngle(theta);
        (*it_port)->SetPortArrowDirection(e_right_arrow);

        // Manually set the arrow direction if close to the vertical
        if(fabs(theta - 90.0) < eps)
        {
            (*it_port)->SetPortArrowDirection(e_down_arrow);
        }
        if(fabs(theta - 270.0) < eps)
        {
            (*it_port)->SetPortArrowDirection(e_up_arrow);
        }

        // Calculate the new port position and snap any connections
          to port
        (*it_port)->CalculatePortPosition();
        GetParentSystemModel()->UpdateConnectionPointHead(*it_port);
          // deref the iterator to get the ptr-to-CPort obj.

        // Increment mult. of arc_spacing.
        i++;
    }// end for
}// end if
}
```

The developer will notice in the CalculatePortPositionAngles() function, for $n \le 3$, ports are placed explicitly on the left, bottom, and top of the block. However, for $n > 3$, the index $i \in [0, n-1]$ multiplies the arc spacing, δ, to determine the port position angle, $\theta_i = \pi/2 + i\delta$, of port, p_i.

15.3.3 RESET OUTPUT PORTS

A ResetOutputPorts() function needs to be added for the Sum block as it was for the Divide block. Hence, add a public member function to the CSumBlock class with the prototype, void CSumBlock::ResetOutputPorts(), and edit it as follows.

```
void CSumBlock::ResetOutputPorts()
{
    int size;                          // size of vec of output ports
    CString sMsg;                      // main msg string
    UINT nType = MB_OK;                // style of msg. box
    UINT nIDhelp = 0;                  // help context ID for the msg.
    vector<CPort*>::iterator it_port;  // iterator for vector
       of CPort ptrs.

    // Get the system model
    CDiagramEngDoc *pDoc = GetDocumentGlobalFn();  // get a ptr to the doc.

    // Get vec of output ports
    vector<CPort*> &vec_output_ports = GetVectorOfOutputPorts()
       // vector of input ports
    size = vec_output_ports.size();

    // Msg. box
    //sMsg.Format("\n CSumBlock::ResetOutputPorts(): size = %d\n", size);
    //AfxMessageBox(sMsg, nType, nIDhelp);

    // Check size not greater than one, since only one output port per block
    if(size > 1)
    {
        sMsg.Format("\n CSumBlock::ResetOutputPorts(): WARNING!
          size = %d != 1n", size);
        AfxMessageBox(sMsg, nType, nIDhelp);
    }

    // Reset angle, posn, and arrow direc of output port(s)
    for(it_port = vec_output_ports.begin(); it_port != vec_output_ports.
      end(); it_port++)
    {
        (*it_port)->SetPortPositionAngle(0.0);
        (*it_port)->CalculatePortPosition();
        (*it_port)->SetPortArrowDirection(e_right_arrow);

        // Update any connection tail end point associated with the port.
        GetParentSystemModel()->UpdateConnectionPointTail(*it_port);
          // deref the iterator to get the ptr-to-CPort obj.
    }

    // Set flags and redraw the doc
    pDoc->SetModifiedFlag(TRUE); // set the doc. as having been modified
      to prompt user to save
    pDoc->UpdateAllViews(NULL);  // indicate that sys. should redraw.
}
```

Now the ResetInputPorts() and ResetOutputPorts() methods need to be called from within the CSumBlock::BlockDlgWndParameterInput() function; hence, amend the latter as shown in bold in the following.

```cpp
void CSumBlock::BlockDlgWndParameterInput()
{
    int n_inputs = 0;     // number of input ports
    CString  sMsg;        // string to be displayed
    CString sMsgTemp;     // temp string msg.
    UINT nType = MB_OK;   // style of msg. box
    UINT nIDhelp = 0;     // help context ID for the msg.

    // Create a dialog object. of class CSumBlockDialog : public CDialog
    CSumBlockDialog oDlg;

    // Set the dialog class var using the block class var
    oDlg.m_iNAddInputs = m_iNAddInputs;
    oDlg.m_iNSubtractInputs = m_iNSubtractInputs;

    // While less than two input ports get user input
    while(n_inputs < 2)
    {
        // Return val of DoModal() fn of ancestor class CDialog is
          checked to determine which btn was clicked.
        if(oDlg.DoModal() == IDOK)
        {
            // Assign CSumBlockDialog variable values to CSumBlock
              variable values.
            m_iNAddInputs = oDlg.m_iNAddInputs;
            m_iNSubtractInputs = oDlg.m_iNSubtractInputs;

            // Print msg with variable value.
            //sMsg.Format("\n CSumBlock::BlockDlgWndParameterInput(),
              m_iNAddInputs = %d, m_iNSubractInputs = %d\n",
              m_iNAddInputs, m_iNSubtractInputs);
            //AfxMessageBox(sMsg, nType, nIDhelp);
        }

        // Check input for correctness and warn user if approp.
        n_inputs = m_iNAddInputs + m_iNSubtractInputs;

        if(n_inputs < 2)
        {
            sMsgTemp.Format("\n CSumBlock::BlockDlgWndParameterInput()\n");
            sMsg += sMsgTemp;
            sMsgTemp.Format(" No. of input ports = %d\n", n_inputs);
            sMsg += sMsgTemp;
            sMsgTemp.Format(" Two or more input ports are required!\n");
            sMsg += sMsgTemp;
            AfxMessageBox(sMsg, nType, nIDhelp);
            sMsg.Format("");   // reset the msg since within a while loop
        }
    }

    // Reset ports
    ResetInputPorts(m_iNAddInputs, m_iNSubtractInputs);
    ResetOutputPorts();
}
```

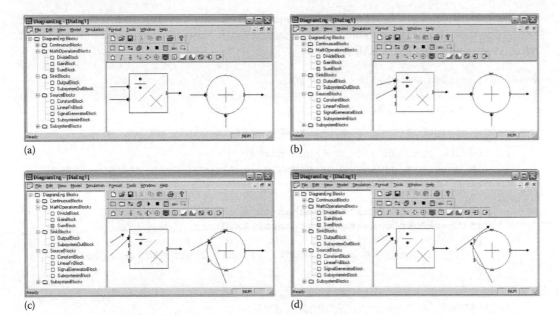

FIGURE 15.4 The Divide and Sum blocks: (a) their default number of ports with connections attached, (b) an increase in the number of ports preserving the connections, (c) an increase in the number of ports not preserving the connection order (zero multiplication ports and four division ports for the Divide block and four input ports for the Sum block), and (d) automatic detachment of all input port connections when switching completely from one port sign type to another.

Now upon running the program, a user-defined number of ports may be added to the Divide and Sum blocks, and connections may be attached to their ports, as shown in Figure 15.4. If more ports are desired, in addition to an existing connection, then they are added; if fewer ports are required, then ports are deleted and connections detached automatically.

The immediately recognizable problem with the current method of inputting multiplication, division, addition, and subtraction ports is that the user does not know the sign associated with the port and has limited control over where the ports should be located. Furthermore, there is an automatic reordering of the ports on the left face of the Divide block or on the left semicircle of the Sum block that places them from the top down, ordered in a sequential manner with multiplication ports preceding division ports (Divide block), and addition ports preceding subtraction ports (Sum block). These problems will be addressed later through the use of a Set Properties entry on the Context menu, which will allow the user to define the sign type and the port position angle, θ_i.

15.4 DRAWING PORTS DEPENDING ON CONNECTION STATUS

Presently, port icons represent block ports both when connections are attached and unattached: functionality is added here to only draw port icons when the connection object is unattached, but upon connection, the port icon disappears, signifying that the connection end point (head or tail) is properly connected. Later a port sign graphic will be added, indicating whether a multiplication, "×", division, "/", addition, "+", or subtraction, "−", input port was added.

The CBlock::DrawBlockPorts() function should be edited with a call to check whether a connection object is attached to a port: if so, then the port should not be drawn. Hence, edit the `DrawBlockPorts()` function with the conditional clause, "`if(CheckPortConnection(*it_port) == 0)`", prior to the call to `DrawPort()` for both the vector of input and output ports, as shown in bold in the following.

```
void CBlock::DrawBlockPorts(CDC *pDC)
{
    vector<CPort*>::iterator it_port; // vector iterator.

    //AfxMessageBox("\n CBlock::DrawBlockPorts()\n", MB_OK, 0);

    // Iterate through vec of input ports
    for(it_port = m_vecInputPorts.begin(); it_port != m_vecInputPorts.
      end(); it_port++)
    {
        // Draw port if not connected to a connection object
        if(CheckPortConnection(*it_port) == 0)
        {
            (*it_port)->DrawPort(pDC); // call CPort::DrawPort()
        }
    }

    // Iterate through vec of output ports
    for(it_port = m_vecOutputPorts.begin(); it_port != m_vecOutputPorts.
      end(); it_port++)
    {
        // Draw port if not connected to a connection object
        if(CheckPortConnection(*it_port) == 0)
        {
            (*it_port)->DrawPort(pDC); // call CPort::DrawPort()
        }
    }
}
```

Now add a public member function to the CBlock class taking a pointer-to-CPort argument, i.e., the address of the port, and returning an integer, identifying port connectivity: `int CBlock::CheckPortConnection(CPort *port)`. Edit the function as shown in the following, checking the reference-to-port, "m_pRefToPort", for an input port and the reference-from-port, "m_pRefFromPort", for an output port.

```
int CBlock::CheckPortConnection(CPort *port)
{
    // Input: ptr-to-CPort, i.e. the address of the port.
    list<CConnection*>::iterator it_con; // iterator for list of
      CConnection ptrs.

    // Get the connection list
    list<CConnection*> &con_list = GetParentSystemModel()-
      >GetConnectionList();

    // Iterate through the list of connections and check connectivity.
    for(it_con = con_list.begin(); it_con != con_list.end(); it_con++)
    {
        // Check whether a connection object is attached to the input
          port.
        if( (*it_con)->GetRefToPort() == port)
        {
            return 1;
        }
    }
```

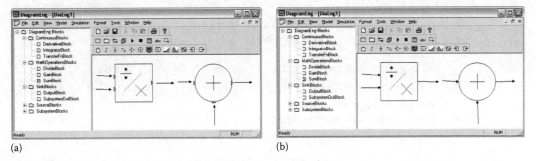

(a)   (b)

FIGURE 15.5 Port icons indicating connectivity of connection objects: (a) icons present, indicating no connections in the connected state, and (b) icons absent, indicating proper connection to ports.

```
        // Check whether a connection object is attached to the output
          port.
        if((*it_con)->GetRefFromPort() == port)
        {
            return 1;
        }
    }
    return 0;
}
```

Figure 15.5 indicates block input and output port icons prior to connection and their absence as a result of proper connection.

15.5 DRAWING PORT SIGNS

One of the problems with adding multiplication and division or addition and subtraction ports to the Divide and Sum blocks, respectively, is that the signs of the ports are not displayed. To make this port-based information clearer, a DrawPortSign() function call should be made from within the CBlock::DrawBlockPorts() method as shown in bold in the following.

```
void CBlock::DrawBlockPorts(CDC *pDC)
{
    vector<CPort*>::iterator it_port; // vector iterator.

    //AfxMessageBox("\n CBlock::DrawBlockPorts()\n", MB_OK, 0);

    // Iterate through vec of input ports
    for(it_port = m_vecInputPorts.begin(); it_port != m_vecInputPorts.
      end(); it_port++)
    {
        // Draw port if not connected to a connection object
        if(CheckPortConnection(*it_port) == 0)
        {
            (*it_port)->DrawPort(pDC); // call CPort::DrawPort()
        }

        // Draw port signs
        (*it_port)->DrawPortSign(pDC);
    }
    // Iterate through vec of output ports
    for(it_port = m_vecOutputPorts.begin(); it_port != m_vecOutputPorts.
      end(); it_port++)
```

```
    {
        // Draw port if not connected to a connection object
        if(CheckPortConnection(*it_port) == 0)
        {
            (*it_port)->DrawPort(pDC);   // call CPort::DrawPort()
        }

        // Draw port signs
        (*it_port)->DrawPortSign(pDC);
    }
}
```

Both the vector of input and output ports are iterated over, and DrawPortSign() is called upon the pointer-to-CPort object by dereferencing the "it_port" iterator. Now, add a public member function to the CPort class with the prototype void CPort::DrawPortSign(CDC *pDC) and edit the function as follows.

```
void CPort::DrawPortSign(CDC *pDC)
{
    int bounding_rect = 0; // bounding rectangle around the port sign
    int pen_color;         // local pen color
    int pen_width;         // local pen width
    double blk_width;      // block width
    double sign_width;     // sign squre ('block') width
    double scale = 0.85;   // scaling constant
    CPoint blk_posn;       // position of the block upon which the port
      and port sign reside
    CPoint pt[4];          // pt array holding pts to draw sign graphic
    CPoint sign_posn;      // position of the center of the box within
      which the sign is placed
    CString port_name;     // name of port, i.e. the sign to be placed
      next to the port
    // Get block and sign properties
    blk_width = m_rRefToBlock.GetBlockShape().GetBlockWidth();
    sign_width = 0.1*blk_width;

    // -- GET SIGN POSITION, i.e. center of square that holds the sign
      icon
    sign_posn = CalculatePortSignPosition(scale);

    // -- PREPARE PEN FOR DRAWING THE SIGN GRPHIC
    pen_color = RGB(0,0,0);  // White = RGB(255,255,255),
      Black = RGB(0,0,0)
    pen_width = 1;

    // Create the pen
    CPen lpen(PS_SOLID, pen_width, pen_color);

    // Select the pen as the drawing obj.
    // The value returned by SelectObject() is a ptr to the obj. being
      replaced, i.e. an old-pen-ptr.
    CPen *pOldPen = pDC->SelectObject(&lpen);

    // -- SET SIGN COORDS BASED UPON PORT NAME, I.E. PORT SIGN: '*', '/',
      '+', '-', or '_'
    port_name = GetPortName();

    if(port_name == "_")   // underscore not minus
```

```
    {
        // No sign to be drawn
        bounding_rect = 0;
    }
    else if(port_name == "*")
    {
        // Set coords of multiplication sign 'x'
        pt[0].x = sign_posn.x - 0.3*sign_width;
        pt[0].y = sign_posn.y - 0.3*sign_width;
        pt[1].x = sign_posn.x + 0.3*sign_width;
        pt[1].y = sign_posn.y + 0.3*sign_width;

        pt[2].x = pt[0].x;
        pt[2].y = pt[1].y;
        pt[3].x = pt[1].x;
        pt[3].y = pt[0].y;

        // Draw the sign
        pDC->MoveTo(pt[0]);
        pDC->LineTo(pt[1]);
        pDC->MoveTo(pt[2]);
        pDC->LineTo(pt[3]);

        // Redraw in reverse direction to make sign perfect.
        pDC->MoveTo(pt[1]);
        pDC->LineTo(pt[0]);
        pDC->MoveTo(pt[3]);
        pDC->LineTo(pt[2]);

        bounding_rect = 0;
    }
    else if(port_name == "/")
    {
        // Set coords of divide sign '/'
        pt[0].x = sign_posn.x - 0.3*sign_width;
        pt[0].y = sign_posn.y + 0.3*sign_width;
        pt[1].x = sign_posn.x + 0.3*sign_width;
        pt[1].y = sign_posn.y - 0.3*sign_width;

        // Draw the sign
        pDC->MoveTo(pt[0]);
        pDC->LineTo(pt[1]);

        // Redraw in reverse direction.
        pDC->MoveTo(pt[1]);
        pDC->LineTo(pt[0]);

        bounding_rect = 0;
    }
    else if(port_name == "+")
    {
        // Set coords of plus sign '+'
        pt[0].x = sign_posn.x;
        pt[0].y = sign_posn.y - 0.3*sign_width;
        pt[1].x = sign_posn.x;
        pt[1].y = sign_posn.y + 0.3*sign_width;

        pt[2].x = sign_posn.x - 0.3*sign_width;
        pt[2].y = sign_posn.y;
```

```
        pt[3].x = sign_posn.x + 0.3*sign_width;
        pt[3].y = sign_posn.y;

        // Draw the sign
        pDC->MoveTo(pt[0]);
        pDC->LineTo(pt[1]);
        pDC->MoveTo(pt[2]);
        pDC->LineTo(pt[3]);

        // Redraw in reverse direction
        pDC->MoveTo(pt[1]);
        pDC->LineTo(pt[0]);
        pDC->MoveTo(pt[3]);
        pDC->LineTo(pt[2]);

        bounding_rect = 0;
    }
    else if(port_name == "-")
    {
        // Set coords of minus sign '-'
        pt[0].x = sign_posn.x - 0.3*sign_width;
        pt[0].y = sign_posn.y;
        pt[1].x = sign_posn.x + 0.3*sign_width;
        pt[1].y = sign_posn.y;

        // Draw the sign
        pDC->MoveTo(pt[0]);
        pDC->LineTo(pt[1]);

        // Redraw in reverse direction
        pDC->MoveTo(pt[1]);
        pDC->LineTo(pt[0]);
        bounding_rect = 0;
    }

    // Draw a bounding rectangle
    if(bounding_rect)
    {
        // Set rectangle points
        pt[0].x = sign_posn.x - 0.3*sign_width;
        pt[0].y = sign_posn.y - 0.3*sign_width;
        pt[1].x = sign_posn.x + 0.3*sign_width;
        pt[1].y = sign_posn.y + 0.3*sign_width;

        pt[2].x = pt[0].x;
        pt[2].y = pt[1].y;
        pt[3].x = pt[1].x;
        pt[3].y = pt[0].y;

        // Draw bounding rectangle
        pDC->MoveTo(pt[0]);
        pDC->LineTo(pt[2]);
        pDC->LineTo(pt[1]);
        pDC->LineTo(pt[3]);
        pDC->LineTo(pt[0]);
    }

    // Reset the prev. pen
    pDC->SelectObject(pOldPen);
}
```

The DrawPortSign() function draws the correct sign type, "×", "/", "+", or "−", based on the CString member variable, "m_strPortName", denoting the name, or more specifically the identifier, of the input ports, "×", "/", "+", or "−", and output port, "_". Initially the block and sign parameters are set, then a call to CalculatePortSignPosition() is made to determine the correct position of the port sign. This function is very similar to CalculatePortPosition(), introduced in Chapter 4, but uses a scaling factor to place the sign associated with the port on the interior of the block toward the block center. The following changes should be made to implement the CalculatePortSignPosition() function:

1. Add a private CPoint member variable to the CPort class named "m_ptPortSignPosition".
2. Add a public member method to the CPort class with the prototype CPoint CPort::CalculatePortSignPosition(double scale).
3. Add a public member function to the CPort class to set the port sign position, with prototype void CPort::SetPortSignPosition(CPoint sign_posn).
4. Add a public constant member function to the CPort class to get the port sign position, with prototype, CPoint CPort::GetPortSignPosition(void) const.

Edit these functions as shown in the following.

```
CPoint CPort::CalculatePortSignPosition(double scale)
{
    int count;              // no. of times 360 divides into
      m_dPortPositionAngle.
    double c;               // length of ray from triangle CM to port posn
      on bndy of triangle.
    double d;               // opp. side length of a subtriangle with
      hypotenuse h, and adjacent side length width/2.
    double eps = 0.0087;    // epsilon value (radians) to allow setting of
      angle at 2*pi; (0.0087 radians = 0.5 degrees)
    double h;               // hypotenuse of a subtriangle with opp. side
      length d, and adjacent side length width/2.
    double height = m_rRefToBlock.GetBlockShape().GetBlockHeight();
    double pi = PI;
    double r;               // length of port sign posn vector.
    double theta;           // m_dPortPositionAngle converted to an angle
      in radians.
    double theta_crit;      // critical theta value used to determine
      sign_posn.x and sign_posn.y
    double width = m_rRefToBlock.GetBlockShape().GetBlockWidth();
    CPoint blk_posn = m_rRefToBlock.GetBlockPosition();
    CPoint sign_posn;
    EBlockDirection e_blk_direc = m_rRefToBlock.GetBlockShape().
      GetBlockDirection();
    EBlockShape e_blk_shape = m_rRefToBlock.GetBlockShape().
      GetBlockShapeType();

    CString sMsg;           // main msg string
    UINT nType = MB_OK;     // style of msg. box
    UINT nIDhelp = 0;       // help context ID for the msg.

    // Scale the width and height
    height = scale*height;
    width = scale*width;

    // Convert port position angle into domain [0,360]
    if(m_dPortPositionAngle > 360.00)
```

```
    {
        count = int(m_dPortPositionAngle/360.00);
        m_dPortPositionAngle = m_dPortPositionAngle - count*360.00;
    }
    if(m_dPortPositionAngle < 0.00)
    {
        count = int(fabs(m_dPortPositionAngle/360.00));
        m_dPortPositionAngle = m_dPortPositionAngle + (count + 1)*360.00;
    }

    // Convert port position angle from degrees into radians
    theta = m_dPortPositionAngle*pi/180.00;

    //sMsg.Format("\n CPort::CalculatePortSignPosition(),
    //  m_dPortPositionAngle = %lf, theta = %3.15lf, 2*pi+eps = %3.15lf\n",
    //  m_dPortPositionAngle, theta, 2*pi+eps);
    //AfxMessageBox(sMsg, nType, nIDhelp);

    // Switch upon shape
    switch(e_blk_shape)
    {
    case e_ellipse:

        sign_posn.x = blk_posn.x + 0.5*width*cos(theta);
        sign_posn.y = blk_posn.y - 0.5*width*sin(theta);
        break;

    case e_rectangle:   // rectangle caters for squares (width = height)
      and rectangles (width != height)

        theta_crit = atan(height/width);      // atan2(y,x) = arctangent
          of y/x

        if((theta >= 0) && (theta <= theta_crit))
        {
            r = width/(2*cos(theta));
            sign_posn.x = blk_posn.x + width*0.5;
            //sign_posn.y = blk_posn.y - r*sin(theta);
            sign_posn.y = m_ptPortPosition.y;
        }
        if((theta > theta_crit) && (theta < (pi - theta_crit)))
        {
            r = height/(2*sin(theta));
            //sign_posn.x = blk_posn.x + r*cos(theta);
            sign_posn.x = m_ptPortPosition.x;
            sign_posn.y = blk_posn.y - height*0.5;
        }
        if((theta >= (pi - theta_crit)) && (theta <= (pi + theta_crit)))
        {
            r = -width/(2*cos(theta));
            sign_posn.x = blk_posn.x - width*0.5;
            //sign_posn.y = blk_posn.y - r*sin(theta);
            sign_posn.y = m_ptPortPosition.y;
        }
        if((theta > (pi + theta_crit)) && (theta < (2*pi - theta_crit)))
        {
            r = -height/(2*sin(theta));
            //sign_posn.x = blk_posn.x + r*cos(theta);
```

```
            sign_posn.x = m_ptPortPosition.x;
            sign_posn.y = blk_posn.y + height*0.5;
    }
    if((theta >= (2*pi - theta_crit)) && (theta <= (2*pi + eps)))
    {
        r = width/(2*cos(theta));
        sign_posn.x = blk_posn.x + width*0.5;
        //sign_posn.y = blk_posn.y - r*sin(theta);
        sign_posn.y = m_ptPortPosition.y;
    }

    break;

case e_triangle:

    // Get lengths of subtriangle sides: hypotenuse h, opp. side
      length d., and base side length width/2.
    d = (width/2)*tan(pi/6);
    h = width/sqrt(3);

    if(e_blk_direc == e_right)         // triangle pointing to the
      right.
    {
        if((theta >= 0) && (theta < 2*pi/3))
        {
            c = h/(2*sin(5*pi/6 - theta)); // length of ray from CM
              to port sign posn near bndy of triangle.
            sign_posn.x = blk_posn.x + c*cos(theta);
            sign_posn.y = blk_posn.y - c*sin(theta);
        }
        if((theta >= 2*pi/3) && (theta <= 4*pi/3))
        {
            sign_posn.x = blk_posn.x - d;
            //sign_posn.y = blk_posn.y - d*tan(pi - theta);
            sign_posn.y = m_ptPortPosition.y;
        }
        if((theta > 4*pi/3) && (theta <= (2*pi + eps)))
        {
            c = h/(2*sin(theta - 7*pi/6));
            sign_posn.x = blk_posn.x + c*cos(theta);
            sign_posn.y = blk_posn.y - c*sin(theta);
        }
    }
    else if(e_blk_direc == e_left)  // triangle pointing to the left.
    {
        if((theta >= 0) && (theta <= pi/3))
        {
            sign_posn.x = blk_posn.x + d;
            //sign_posn.y = blk_posn.y - d*tan(theta);
            sign_posn.y = m_ptPortPosition.y;
        }
        if((theta > pi/3) && (theta <= pi))
        {
            c = h/(2*sin(theta - pi/6)); // length of ray from CM to
              port sign posn near bndy of triangle.
            sign_posn.x = blk_posn.x + c*cos(theta);
            sign_posn.y = blk_posn.y - c*sin(theta);
        }
```

```
            if( (theta > pi) && (theta < 5*pi/3) )
            {
                c = h/(2*sin(11*pi/6 - theta));
                sign_posn.x = blk_posn.x + c*cos(theta);
                sign_posn.y = blk_posn.y - c*sin(theta);
            }
            if( (theta >= 5*pi/3) && (theta <= (2*pi + eps)) )
            {
                sign_posn.x = blk_posn.x + d;
                //sign_posn.y = blk_posn.y + d*tan(2*pi - theta);
                sign_posn.y = m_ptPortPosition.y;
            }
        }
        else
        {
            // Print msg.
            //sMsg.Format("\n CPort::CalculatePortSignPosition()\n
              e_blk_direc for triangles should be e_left or e_right only!");
            //AfxMessageBox(sMsg, nType, nIDhelp);
        }

        break;

    default:
        // no code for now
        break;
    }// end switch

    // Set port sign position within CalculatePortSignPosition() to
      prevent an additional call.
    SetPortSignPosition(sign_posn);

    return sign_posn;
}


void CPort::SetPortSignPosition(CPoint sign_posn)
{
    m_ptPortSignPosition = sign_posn;
}


CPoint CPort::GetPortSignPosition() const
{
    return m_ptPortSignPosition;
}
```

The combination of the DrawPortSign() and CalculatePortSignPosition() func-
tions allows the port signs to be drawn by first setting the points of a CPoint array, and then using
MoveTo() and LineTo() passing the CPoint object as an argument. A bounding rectangle may
also be drawn around the sign if desired. A redrawing of the line segments used in the sign graphic
was done in both directions (as seen in the code) to obtain a completely symmetrical appearance.
This should not need to be performed but did resolve the unsymmetrical appearance problem that
occurred when only drawing lines in one direction.

Figure 15.6 shows the Divide and Sum blocks with port and port sign graphics: when a connection object is connected to a port, the port graphic disappears as desired, leaving the port sign visible
and indicating the type of mathematical operation to be conducted at the input port.

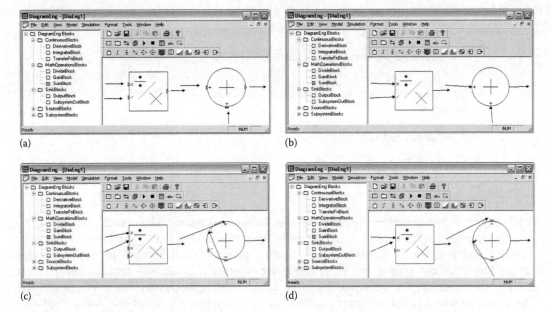

FIGURE 15.6 The port and port sign graphics: (a) default appearance, (b) connections attached resulting in the disappearance of the port icon, (c) more ports added, maintaining connectivity but automatically reorganizing the port layout, and (d) input ports reduced in number, resulting in automatic detachment of relevant connection objects and reorganization of the port layout.

15.6 PREPARATION FOR ADJUSTMENT OF PORT PROPERTIES

The setting of the number of ports or a particular sign type ("×", "/", "+", or "−") automatically sets their position, such that multiplication precedes division for the Divide block, and addition precedes subtraction for the Sum block, in the anticlockwise sense from the top left side of the block to the bottom. In addition, any ports with connections attached are also reordered upon changing the number of ports, such that they appear in the upper most positions. However, the user may want to manually adjust the port properties, i.e., the port position angle $\theta \in [0, 2\pi]$, port sign (consistent with block type), and port direction signified by a triangle pointing to the left, right, up, or down.

The Context menu has a Set Properties entry that upon selection calls the `OnSetItemProperties()` function of the CDiagramEngDoc class, which currently allows the user to set properties of a block or the system model's numerical solver. Augment this function to call the `SetBlockPortProperties()` method of the CDiagramEngDoc class as shown in bold in the following.

```
void CDiagramEngDoc::OnSetItemProperties()
{
    // TODO: Add your command handler code here

    // DiagramEng (start)
    int item_clicked = 0;

    // Set properties for blocks
    item_clicked = DoubleLeftClickBlock(m_ptContextMenu);

    // Set properties for block ports
    if(item_clicked == 0)
    {
        item_clicked = SetBlockPortProperties(m_ptContextMenu);
    }
```

```
    // Set properties for connections and connection bend points
    if(item_clicked == 0)
    {
        item_clicked = SetConnectionProperties(m_ptContextMenu);
    }

    // Set properties for the Numerical Solver
    if(item_clicked == 0)
    {
        OnSimNumericalSolver();
    }

    // DiagramEng (end)
}
```

Now add a public member function to the CDiagramEngDoc class with the prototype
int CDiagramEngDoc::SetBlockPortProperties(CPoint m_ptContextMenu)
and edit this function as shown in the following program. This is used to iterate through
all the blocks of the system model to determine whether a block was clicked, and if so, a
SetPortProperties() function should be called to alter the appropriate port's properties.
The developer will note that different conditions exist to determine whether the mouse pointer, at
the point of invoking the context menu, is upon the block: (1) for an ellipse block, the Euclidean
distance between the point and the center of the block is used (effectively a disc of radius r); (2)
for a rectangular block, the distances in the x and y directions are used; and (3) for the triangle
block, the Euclidean distance is compared with a disc of radius h, representing the hypotenuse of
a subtriangle within the equilateral triangle modeling the block (see Chapter 4 for further details).

```
int CDiagramEngDoc::SetBlockPortProperties(CPoint point)
{
    int click_flag = 0; // if port upon block clicked, flag = 1, else
        flag = 0.
    double blk_height;   // block height
    double blk_width;    // block width
    double dist;         // Euclidean dist bw mouse click and CM of block.
    double hyp;          // hypotenuse of subtriangle within equilateral
        triangle, used as a block-circumscribing disc radius
    CPoint blk_posn;     // block posn.
    EBlockShape e_blk_shape; // block shape = e_ellipse, e_rectangle,
        e_triangle.
    list<CBlock*>::iterator it_blk; // iterator

    // Get a copy of the blk_list in the system model
    list<CBlock*> &blk_list = GetSystemModel().GetBlockList();
        // MUST BE A REFERENCE!

    // Iterate through the list to find which block was selected.
    for(it_blk = blk_list.begin(); it_blk != blk_list.end(); it_blk++)
    {
        // Get block properties
        blk_posn = (*it_blk)->GetBlockPosition();
        blk_width = (*it_blk)->GetBlockShape().GetBlockWidth();
        blk_height = (*it_blk)->GetBlockShape().GetBlockHeight();
        e_blk_shape = (*it_blk)->GetBlockShape().GetBlockShapeType();

        if(e_blk_shape == e_ellipse)
        {
            // Get Euclidean distance between point and block
```

```
                    dist = sqrt(pow((blk_posn.x - point.x),2) +
                     pow((blk_posn.y - point.y),2));

                if(dist <= blk_width*0.5)
                {
                    //AfxMessageBox("\n CDiagramEngDoc::SetBlockPortPropert
                      ies()\n", MB_OK, 0);

                    // Set port properties for this partic. block. if so
                      port_click_flag = 1
                    click_flag = (*it_blk)->SetPortProperties(point);

                    break;
                }
            }
            else if(e_blk_shape == e_rectangle)
            {
                if((abs(point.x - blk_posn.x) <= blk_width*0.5)
                 && (abs(point.y - blk_posn.y) <= blk_height*0.5))
                {
                    //AfxMessageBox("\n CDiagramEngDoc::SetBlockPortPropert
                      ies()\n", MB_OK, 0);

                    // Set port properties for this partic. block. if so
                      port_click_flag = 1
                    click_flag = (*it_blk)->SetPortProperties(point);

                    break;
                }
            }
            else if(e_blk_shape == e_triangle)
            {
                // hypotenuse of subtriangle within equilateral triangle,
                  used as a block-circumscribing disc radius
                hyp = blk_width/sqrt(3);

                dist = sqrt(pow((blk_posn.x - point.x),2) +
                  pow((blk_posn.y - point.y),2));

                if(dist <= hyp)
                {
                    //AfxMessageBox("\n CDiagramEngDoc::SetBlockPortPropert
                      ies()\n", MB_OK, 0);

                    // Set port properties for this partic. block. if so
                      port_click_flag = 1
                    click_flag = (*it_blk)->SetPortProperties(point);

                break;
                }
            }
        }
    }

    // Return block click status
    return click_flag;
}
```

The `SetBlockProperties()` function calls the `SetPortProperties()` method upon a pointer-to-CBlock. Hence the `SetPortProperties()` method should be provided in the base CBlock class, and overridden in the CDivideBlock and CSumBlock classes, since the latter two classes have different port properties than those of other blocks. Hence, add a public virtual member function to the CBlock class with the prototype `virtual int CBlock::SetPortProperties(CPoint point)` and edit the base class version of this function as shown follows.

```
int CBlock::SetPortProperties(CPoint point)
{
    int port_flag = 0; // flag indicating whether port properties were
      changed
    int sign_flag = 0; // flag to toggle the approp. sign-based dlg wnd
      controls
    double blk_width;  // block width
    double sign_width; // port sign width
    CPoint sign_posn;  // port sign posn
    vector<CPort*>::iterator it_port; // vector iterator.
    CDiagramEngDoc *pDoc = GetDocumentGlobalFn();

    //AfxMessageBox("\n CBlock::SetPortProperties()\n", MB_OK, 0);

    // Port sign properties
    blk_width = GetBlockShape().GetBlockWidth();
    sign_width = 0.1*blk_width;

    // -- ITERATE THROUGH VEC OF INPUT PORTS
    for(it_port = m_vecInputPorts.begin(); it_port != m_vecInputPorts.
      end(); it_port++)
    {
        sign_posn = (*it_port)->GetPortSignPosition();

        // If the point is upon the current port sign
        if((abs(point.x - sign_posn.x) <= sign_width*0.5)
          && (abs(point.y - sign_posn.y) <= sign_width*0.5))
        {
            // Create the port properties dialog and populate the fields
            //CPortPropertiesDialog oDlg;
            CPortPropertiesDialog oDlg(sign_flag);
            oDlg.m_dPortPositionAngle = (*it_port)-
              >GetPortPositionAngle();
            oDlg.m_iPortArrowDirection = (*it_port)-
              >GetPortArrowDirection();

            // Set the port properties using dlg input.
            if(oDlg.DoModal() == IDOK)
            {
                (*it_port)->SetPortPositionAngle(oDlg.m_dPortPositionAngle);
                (*it_port)->CalculatePortPosition();
                (*it_port)->SetPortArrowDirection(EPortArrowDirection
                  (oDlg.m_iPortArrowDirection));

                // Update any connection head end point associated with
                  the port.
                m_pParentSystemModel->UpdateConnectionPointHead(*it_port);
                  // deref the iterator to get the ptr-to-CPort obj.
            }

            port_flag = 1;
            break;
        }
    }
}
```

```
    // -- ITERATE THROUGH VEC OF OUTPUT PORTS
    for(it_port = m_vecOutputPorts.begin(); it_port != m_vecOutputPorts.
      end(); it_port++)
    {
        sign_posn = (*it_port)->GetPortSignPosition();

        // If the point is upon the current port sign
        if((abs(point.x - sign_posn.x) <= sign_width*0.5) &&
          (abs(point.y - sign_posn.y) <= sign_width*0.5))
        {
            // Create the port properties dialog and populate the fields
            //CPortPropertiesDialog oDlg;
            CPortPropertiesDialog oDlg(sign_flag);
            oDlg.m_dPortPositionAngle = (*it_port)->GetPortPositionAngle();
            oDlg.m_iPortArrowDirection = (*it_port)-
              >GetPortArrowDirection();

            // Set the port properties using dlg input.
            if(oDlg.DoModal() == IDOK)
            {
                (*it_port)->SetPortPositionAngle
                  (oDlg.m_dPortPositionAngle);
                (*it_port)->CalculatePortPosition();
                (*it_port)->SetPortArrowDirection(EPortArrowDirection
                  (oDlg.m_iPortArrowDirection));

                // Update any connection tail end point associated with
                  the port.
                m_pParentSystemModel->UpdateConnectionPointTail(*it_port);
                  // deref the iterator to get the ptr-to-CPort obj.
            }

            port_flag = 1;
            break;
        }
    }

    // Mark the document as changed
    pDoc->SetModifiedFlag(TRUE); // prompt the user to save
    pDoc->UpdateAllViews(NULL);  // this fn calls OnDraw to redraw the
      system model.

    return port_flag;
}
```

The SetPortProperties() function iterates over the vector of input and output ports and checks whether the point at which the Context menu was invoked lies sufficiently close to a block port; if so, the to-be-added Port Properties dialog window is displayed, to allow the user to set specific port properties, e.g., the port position angle, the port arrow direction, and, if appropriate, the sign of the port.

15.7   DIALOG-BASED PORT PROPERTY SETTING

The SetPortProperties() function creates a dialog object, "oDlg", of type CPortPropertiesDialog and displays the current port values to the user and updates these values with any changes entered by the user through the Port Properties dialog window. The default implementation disables the controls for the port sign, i.e., addition, subtraction, multiplication, and division, since sign input is provided through the particular overriding Divide block and Sum block `SetPortProperties()` functions. The following general steps should be made in order to implement the desired dialog-based port property setting functionality; specific details are provided in the following sections.

1. Insert a dialog window and add controls.
2. Attach a class to the dialog window.
3. Attach variables to the dialog window controls.
4. Add functionality to the dialog window buttons.
5. Add overriding versions of the `SetPortProperties()` function.

15.7.1 INSERT A DIALOG WINDOW AND ADD CONTROLS

A new port properties dialog window is required to allow the user to set port properties, e.g., the port position angle, port direction, and port sign. Hence, insert a new dialog resource: set the ID of the dialog to IDD_PORT_PROPERTIES_DLG and the caption to PortPropertiesDialog. Leave the OK and Cancel buttons on the dialog.

Add controls provided in Table 15.1 and place them on the dialog window as shown in Figure 15.7, being careful to insert radio buttons in the order of their corresponding numerical value. That is, for the Arrow Direction controls, place the radio buttons on the palette in the order Left, Up, Right, and Down to match the numerical order of the declaration of the enumerated type: "enum EPortArrowDirection {e_left_arrow, e_up_arrow, e_right_arrow, e_down_arrow}". This order was chosen to be in the clockwise direction starting from the left.

15.7.2 ATTACH A CLASS TO THE DIALOG WINDOW

A class is to be attached to the dialog window to contain the variables associated with the dialog window controls. Hence, select the IDD_PORT_PROPERTIES_DLG resource from the ResourceView tab on the Workspace pane, to show the corresponding dialog window in the editor area, and right click on the dialog box to invoke the ClassWizard. The Adding a Class message box appears: create a new class with name, CPortPropertiesDialog and base class, CDialog.

15.7.3 ATTACH VARIABLES TO THE DIALOG WINDOW CONTROLS

Variables are to be attached to the dialog window controls where their values may be transferred to the associated CPort class. Invoke the ClassWizard, choose CPortPropertiesDialog as the class, since variables to be added relate to dialog window controls, and select the Member Variables tab. Select the ID of the control to which a variable should be added, click Add Variable, and specify the details as shown in Table 15.2.

The variables that are added here to the CPortPropertiesDialog class have their values transferred to the CPort class, and vice versa, as shown earlier in the `SetPortProperties()` function. Table 15.3 shows the CPortPropertiesDialog and corresponding CPort class member variables: two new variables could be added to the CPort class, e.g., "m_iPortSignMultiplication" and "m_iPortSignAddition", but since the "m_strPortName" variable is an indicator of sign type, and there is already a constant member function, `GetPortName()`, to retrieve the port name (sign), these two member variables and their associated accessor functions are unnecessary. Hence, they have been labeled accordingly and have not been added to the project.

The PortPropertiesDialog dialog window should initially have disabled sign-based controls: this will be overridden as appropriate in the derived versions of the `SetPortProperties()` function

TABLE 15.1

Port Properties Dialog Window Controls

Object	Property	Setting
Static Text	ID	ID_PORT_PROPS_DLG_TXT_ANGLE
	Caption	Position Angle:
Edit Box	ID	ID_PORT_PROPS_DLG_ANGLE
Group Box	ID	ID_PORT_PROPS_DLG_GB_DIREC
	Caption	Arrow Direction
Radio Button (0)	ID	ID_PORT_PROPS_DLG_RB_LEFT
	Group	Checked
	Caption	Left
Radio Button (1)	ID	ID_PORT_PROPS_DLG_RB_UP
	Group	Unchecked
	Caption	Up
Radio Button (2)	ID	ID_PORT_PROPS_DLG_RB_RIGHT
	Group	Unchecked
	Caption	Right
Radio Button (3)	ID	ID_PORT_PROPS_DLG_RB_DOWN
	Group	Unchecked
	Caption	Down
Group Box	ID	ID_PORT_PROPS_DLG_GB_SIGN
	Caption	Sign
Group Box	ID	ID_PORT_PROPS_DLG_GB_MULT
	Caption	Multiplication
Radio Button (0)	ID	ID_PORT_PROPS_DLG_RB_MULT
	Group	Checked
	Caption	Multiply
Radio Button (1)	ID	ID_PORT_PROPS_DLG_RB_DIVIDE
	Group	Unchecked
	Caption	Divide
Group Box	ID	ID_PORT_PROPS _DLG_GB_ADD
	Caption	Addition
Radio Button (0)	ID	ID_PORT_PROPS_DLG_RB_ADD
	Group	Checked
	Caption	Add
Radio Button (1)	ID	ID_PORT_PROPS_DLG_RB_SUBTRACT
	Group	Unchecked
	Caption	Subtract
Button	ID	ID_PORT_PROPS_DLG_BTN_OK
	Default button	Unchecked
	Caption	&OK
Button	ID	IDCANCEL
	Caption	&Cancel

for the CDivideBlock and CSumBlock classes. Hence, some additions and alterations need to be made to the CPortPropertiesDialog class:

1. A member variable should be added to the CPortPropertiesDialog class and used to switch on/off various dialog window controls.
2. The CPortPropertiesDialog constructor should be altered to allow object construction using an additional input argument.
3. An `OnInitDialog()` function should be added to the class to switch on/off the necessary controls.

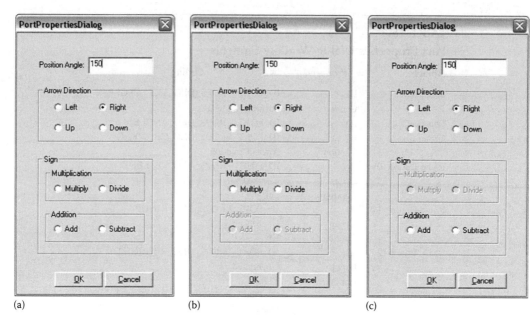

(a)　　　　　　　　　　(b)　　　　　　　　　　(c)

FIGURE 15.7　Port Properties dialog window showing the controls as specified in Table 15.1: (a) all controls enabled, (b) Addition controls disabled, and (c) Multiplication controls disabled.

TABLE 15.2

Dialog Window Controls, Variable Names, Categories, and Types for the IDD_PORT_PROPERTIES_DLG Resource

Control	Variable Name	Category	Type
ID_PORT_PROPS_DLG_ANGLE	m_dPortPositionAngle	Value	double
ID_PORT_PROPS_DLG_RB_LEFT	m_iPortArrowDirection	Value	int
ID_PORT_PROPS_DLG_RB_MULT	m_iPortSignMultiplication	Value	int
ID_PORT_PROPS_DLG_RB_ADD	m_iPortSignAddition	Value	int

TABLE 15.3

Corresponding Member Variables of the CPortPropertiesDialog and CPort Classes

Type	CPortPropertiesDialog Member Variables	CPort Member variables
double	m_dPortPositionAngle	m_dPortPositionAngle
int	m_iPortArrowDirection	m_ePortArrowDirec
int	m_iPortSignMultiplication	m_iPortSignMultiplication (unnecessary)
int	m_iPortSignAddition	m_iPortSignAddition (unnecessary)

Add a new private integer member variable to the CPortPropertiesDialog class with the name "m_iSignFlag", since this flag will be used to toggle the sign-based controls on the corresponding dialog window object (IDD_PORT_PROPERTIES_DLG).

Modify the existing `CPortPropertiesDialog()` constructor from the original to the one that follows, introducing an integer input argument in the function header and performing member variable initialization using this integer variable as shown.

```
CPortPropertiesDialog::CPortPropertiesDialog(CWnd* pParent /*=NULL*/)
    : CDialog(CPortPropertiesDialog::IDD, pParent)
{
    //{{AFX_DATA_INIT(CPortPropertiesDialog)
    m_dPortPositionAngle = 0.0;
    m_iPortSignMultiplication = -1;
    m_iPortSignAddition = -1;
    m_iPortArrowDirection = -1;
    //}}AFX_DATA_INIT
}
CPortPropertiesDialog::CPortPropertiesDialog(int sign_flag, CWnd* pParent
    /*=NULL*/)
    : CDialog(CPortPropertiesDialog::IDD, pParent)
{
    // Init.
    m_iSignFlag = sign_flag;

    //{{AFX_DATA_INIT(CPortPropertiesDialog)
    m_dPortPositionAngle = 0.0;
    m_iPortSignMultiplication = -1;
    m_iPortSignAddition = -1;
    m_iPortArrowDirection = -1;
    //}}AFX_DATA_INIT
}
```

Also alter the "PortPropertiesDialog.h" header file and change the original constructor function prototype to the new version with the integer flag-like variable "sign_flag" as follows.

```
//CPortPropertiesDialog(CWnd* pParent = NULL);      // original
  constructor
CPortPropertiesDialog(int sign_flag, CWnd* pParent = NULL);
  // new constructor with integer sign_flag
```

Now the OnInitDialog() function is to be added to the CPortPropertiesDialog class. Hence, invoke the ClassWizard, select the Message Maps tab, and choose CPortPropertiesDialog as the class and the object ID CPortPropertiesDialog. Add an initialization function for the WM_INITDIALOG message with name OnInitDialog(), and edit it as shown in the following to use the member variable, "m_iSignFlag", initialized in the constructor (earlier), to perform enabling and disabling of sign-based controls.

```
BOOL CPortPropertiesDialog::OnInitDialog()
{
    CDialog::OnInitDialog();

    // TODO: Add extra initialization here

    // DiagramEng (start)
    if(m_iSignFlag == 0)
    {
        // Disable all sign-based controls
        GetDlgItem(ID_PORT_PROPS_DLG_GB_SIGN)->EnableWindow(FALSE);
          // sign group box
        GetDlgItem(ID_PORT_PROPS_DLG_GB_MULT)->EnableWindow(FALSE);
          // mult/divide sign group box
        GetDlgItem(ID_PORT_PROPS_DLG_RB_MULT)->EnableWindow(FALSE);
          // mult sign radio button
```

```
        GetDlgItem(ID_PORT_PROPS_DLG_RB_DIVIDE)->EnableWindow(FALSE);
          // divide sign radio button
        GetDlgItem(ID_PORT_PROPS_DLG_GB_ADD)->EnableWindow(FALSE);
          // add/subtract sign group box
        GetDlgItem(ID_PORT_PROPS_DLG_RB_ADD)->EnableWindow(FALSE);
          // add sign radio button
        GetDlgItem(ID_PORT_PROPS_DLG_RB_SUBTRACT)->EnableWindow(FALSE);
          // subtract sign radio button
    }
    else if(m_iSignFlag == 1)
    {
        // Enable all Multiplication sign-based controls
        GetDlgItem(ID_PORT_PROPS_DLG_GB_SIGN)->EnableWindow(TRUE);
          // sign group box
        GetDlgItem(ID_PORT_PROPS_DLG_GB_MULT)->EnableWindow(TRUE);
          // mult/divide sign group box
        GetDlgItem(ID_PORT_PROPS_DLG_RB_MULT)->EnableWindow(TRUE);
          // mult sign radio button
        GetDlgItem(ID_PORT_PROPS_DLG_RB_DIVIDE)->EnableWindow(TRUE);
          // divide sign radio button
        GetDlgItem(ID_PORT_PROPS_DLG_GB_ADD)->EnableWindow(FALSE);
          // add/subtract sign group box
        GetDlgItem(ID_PORT_PROPS_DLG_RB_ADD)->EnableWindow(FALSE);
          // add sign radio button
        GetDlgItem(ID_PORT_PROPS_DLG_RB_SUBTRACT)->EnableWindow(FALSE);
          // subtract sign radio button
    }
    else if(m_iSignFlag == 2)
    {
        // Enable all Addition sign-based controls
        GetDlgItem(ID_PORT_PROPS_DLG_GB_SIGN)->EnableWindow(TRUE);
          // sign group box
        GetDlgItem(ID_PORT_PROPS_DLG_GB_MULT)->EnableWindow(FALSE);
          // mult/divide sign group box
        GetDlgItem(ID_PORT_PROPS_DLG_RB_MULT)->EnableWindow(FALSE);
          // mult sign radio button
        GetDlgItem(ID_PORT_PROPS_DLG_RB_DIVIDE)->EnableWindow(FALSE);
          // divide sign radio button
        GetDlgItem(ID_PORT_PROPS_DLG_GB_ADD)->EnableWindow(TRUE);
          // add/subtract sign group box
        GetDlgItem(ID_PORT_PROPS_DLG_RB_ADD)->EnableWindow(TRUE);
          // add sign radio button
        GetDlgItem(ID_PORT_PROPS_DLG_RB_SUBTRACT)->EnableWindow(TRUE);
          // subtract sign radio button
    }
    else if(m_iSignFlag == 3)
    {
        // Enable all sign-based controls
        GetDlgItem(ID_PORT_PROPS_DLG_GB_SIGN)->EnableWindow(TRUE);
          // sign group box
        GetDlgItem(ID_PORT_PROPS_DLG_GB_MULT)->EnableWindow(TRUE);
          // mult/divide sign group box
        GetDlgItem(ID_PORT_PROPS_DLG_RB_MULT)->EnableWindow(TRUE);
          // mult sign radio button
        GetDlgItem(ID_PORT_PROPS_DLG_RB_DIVIDE)->EnableWindow(TRUE);
          // divide sign radio button
```

```
        GetDlgItem(ID_PORT_PROPS_DLG_GB_ADD)->EnableWindow(TRUE);
          // add/subtract sign group box
        GetDlgItem(ID_PORT_PROPS_DLG_RB_ADD)->EnableWindow(TRUE);
          // add sign radio button
        GetDlgItem(ID_PORT_PROPS_DLG_RB_SUBTRACT)->EnableWindow(TRUE);
          // subtract sign radio button
    }

    // DiagramEng (end)
    return TRUE; // return TRUE unless you set the focus to a control
                 // EXCEPTION: OCX Property Pages should return FALSE
}
```

15.7.4 Add Functionality to the Dialog Window Buttons

The two buttons for the IDD_PORT_PROPERTIES_DLG dialog window are OK and Cancel. Add an event-handler function for the OK button named OnPortPropertiesDlgBtnOk() (see Table 15.4) and edit it as shown in the following program. Leave the current event-handler function for the Cancel button as OnCancel(), since this already calls the CDialog::OnCancel() function and no new code is required.

```
void CPortPropertiesDialog::OnPortPropertiesDlgBtnOk()
{
    // TODO: Add your control notification handler code here

    // DiagramEng (start)

    //AfxMessageBox("\n CPortPropertiesDialog::OnPortPropertiesDlgBtn
      Ok()\n", MB_OK, 0);

    // Update variable values with the Dlg Wnd control values
    UpdateData(TRUE);

    // Close the dialog wnd with OnOK()
    OnOK();

    // DiagramEng (end)
}
```

Upon compiling the program, the error message "error C2065: 'CPortPropertiesDialog' : undeclared identifier" is presented. To resolve this, add #include "PortPropertiesDialog.h" at the top of the "Block.cpp" source file. This is required since a CPortPropertiesDialog object is created in the CBlock::SetPortProperties() function.

15.7.5 Add Overriding Versions of the SetPortProperties() Function

The default CBlock base class version of the SetPortProperties() function is that shown earlier, where the integer "sign_flag" variable is set to zero to disable the Multiplication and Addition sign–based

---

TABLE 15.4

Objects, IDs, Class, and Event-Handler Functions for the CPortPropertiesDialog Class

Object	ID	Class	COMMAND Event-Handler
OK button	ID_PORT_PROPS_DLG_BTN_OK	CPortPropertiesDialog	OnPortPropertiesDlgBtnOk()
Cancel button	IDCANCEL (default)	CPortPropertiesDialog	OnCancel()

controls of the CPortPropertiesDialog, "oDlg", dialog window object. However, the Divide and Sum blocks must have Multiplication and Addition signs enabled, respectively. Hence, add overriding functions as follows and edit them as shown in the following program:

1. Add a public member function to the CDivideBlock class with the prototype: `int CDivide Block::SetPortProperties(CPoint point)`.
2. Add a public member function to the CSumBlock class with the prototype: `int CSum Block::SetPortProperties(CPoint point)`.

```
int CDivideBlock::SetPortProperties(CPoint point)
{
    int port_flag = 0;      // flag indicating whether port properties were
      changed
    int sign_flag = 1;      // flag to toggle the approp. sign-based dlg
      wnd controls
    double blk_width;       // block width
    double sign_width;      // port sign width
    CPoint sign_posn;       // port sign posn
    CString port_name;      // port name reflecting the sign type
    vector<CPort*>::iterator it_port; // vector iterator.
    vector<CPort*> &vec_of_input_ports = GetVectorOfInputPorts();
    vector<CPort*> &vec_of_output_ports = GetVectorOfOutputPorts();
    CDiagramEngDoc *pDoc = GetDocumentGlobalFn();

    //AfxMessageBox("\n CDivideBlock::SetPortProperties()\n", MB_OK, 0);

    // Port sign properties
    blk_width = GetBlockShape().GetBlockWidth();
    sign_width = 0.1*blk_width;

    // -- ITERATE THROUGH VEC OF INPUT PORTS
    for(it_port = vec_of_input_ports.begin(); it_port
      != vec_of_input_ports.end(); it_port++)
    {
        sign_posn = (*it_port)->GetPortSignPosition();

        // If the point is upon the current port sign
        if((abs(point.x - sign_posn.x) <= sign_width*0.5) &&
          (abs(point.y - sign_posn.y) <= sign_width*0.5))
        {
            // Create the port properties dialog and populate the fields
            //CPortPropertiesDialog oDlg;
            CPortPropertiesDialog oDlg(sign_flag);
            oDlg.m_dPortPositionAngle = (*it_port)-
              >GetPortPositionAngle();
            oDlg.m_iPortArrowDirection = (*it_port)-
              >GetPortArrowDirection();
            port_name = (*it_port)->GetPortName();

            if(port_name == "*")
            {
                oDlg.m_iPortSignMultiplication = 0;
            }
            else
            {
                oDlg.m_iPortSignMultiplication = 1;
            }
```

```
                // Set the port properties using dlg input.
                if(oDlg.DoModal() == IDOK)
                {
                    (*it_port)->SetPortPositionAngle
                      (oDlg.m_dPortPositionAngle);
                    (*it_port)->CalculatePortPosition();
                    (*it_port)->SetPortArrowDirection(EPortArrowDirection
                      (oDlg.m_iPortArrowDirection));

                    if(oDlg.m_iPortSignMultiplication == 0)
                    {
                        (*it_port)->SetPortName("*");
                    }
                    else
                    {
                        (*it_port)->SetPortName("/");
                    }
                    UpdateSignCount();

                    // Update any connection head end point associated with
                      the port.
                    GetParentSystemModel()->UpdateConnectionPointHead(*it_port);
                      // deref the iterator to get the ptr-to-CPort obj.
                }

            port_flag = 1;
            break;
        }
    }
}


// -- ITERATE THROUGH VEC OF OUTPUT PORTS
for(it_port = vec_of_output_ports.begin(); it_port
  != vec_of_output_ports.end(); it_port++)
{
    sign_posn = (*it_port)->GetPortSignPosition();

    // If the point is upon the current port sign
    if((abs(point.x - sign_posn.x) <= sign_width*0.5) &&
      (abs(point.y - sign_posn.y) <= sign_width*0.5))
    {
        // Create the port properties dialog and populate the fields
        //CPortPropertiesDialog oDlg;
        CPortPropertiesDialog oDlg(sign_flag);
        oDlg.m_dPortPositionAngle = (*it_port)-
          >GetPortPositionAngle();
        oDlg.m_iPortArrowDirection = (*it_port)-
          >GetPortArrowDirection();

        // DO NOT UPDATE PORT SIGN FOR OUTPUT PORT

        // Set the port properties using dlg input.
        if(oDlg.DoModal() == IDOK)
        {
            (*it_port)->SetPortPositionAngle
              (oDlg.m_dPortPositionAngle);
            (*it_port)->CalculatePortPosition();
            (*it_port)->SetPortArrowDirection(EPortArrowDirection
              (oDlg.m_iPortArrowDirection));
```

```
                    // DO NOT SET PORT SIGN FOR OUTPUT PORT SINCE THEY HAVE
                       NO SIGN ASSOCIATION

                    // Update any connection tail end point associated with
                       the port.
                    GetParentSystemModel()->UpdateConnectionPointT
                       ail(*it_port);   // deref the iterator to get the
                       ptr-to-CPort obj.
                }

                port_flag = 1;
                break;
            }
        }

        // Mark the document as changed
        pDoc->SetModifiedFlag(TRUE);   // prompt the user to save
        pDoc->UpdateAllViews(NULL);   // this fn calls OnDraw to redraw the
          system model.

        return port_flag;
}

int CSumBlock::SetPortProperties(CPoint point)
{
        int port_flag = 0;    // flag indicating whether port properties were
          changed
        int sign_flag = 2;    // flag to toggle the approp. sign-based dlg
          wnd controls
        double blk_width;     // block width
        double sign_width;    // port sign width
        CPoint sign_posn;     // port sign posn
        CString port_name;    // port name reflecting the sign type
        vector<CPort*>::iterator it_port; // vector iterator.
        vector<CPort*> &vec_of_input_ports = GetVectorOfInputPorts();
        vector<CPort*> &vec_of_output_ports = GetVectorOfOutputPorts();
        CDiagramEngDoc *pDoc = GetDocumentGlobalFn();

        //AfxMessageBox("\n CSumBlock::SetPortProperties()\n", MB_OK, 0);

        // Port sign properties
        blk_width = GetBlockShape().GetBlockWidth();
        sign_width = 0.1*blk_width;

        // -- ITERATE THROUGH VEC OF INPUT PORTS
        for(it_port = vec_of_input_ports.begin();
          it_port != vec_of_input_ports.end(); it_port++)
        {
            sign_posn = (*it_port)->GetPortSignPosition();

            // If the point is upon the current port sign
            if( (abs(point.x - sign_posn.x) <= sign_width*0.5) &&
              (abs(point.y - sign_posn.y) <= sign_width*0.5) )
            {
                // Create the port properties dialog and populate the fields
                //CPortPropertiesDialog oDlg;
                CPortPropertiesDialog oDlg(sign_flag);
                oDlg.m_dPortPositionAngle = (*it_port)-
                  >GetPortPositionAngle();
```

```
                oDlg.m_iPortArrowDirection =
                  (*it_port)->GetPortArrowDirection();
                port_name = (*it_port)->GetPortName();

                if(port_name == "+")
                {
                    oDlg.m_iPortSignAddition = 0;
                }
                else
                {
                    oDlg.m_iPortSignAddition = 1;
                }

                // Set the port properties using dlg input.
                if(oDlg.DoModal() == IDOK)
                {
                    (*it_port)->SetPortPositionAngle(oDlg.m_dPortPositionAngle);
                    (*it_port)->CalculatePortPosition();
                    (*it_port)->SetPortArrowDirection(EPortArrowDirection
                      (oDlg.m_iPortArrowDirection));

                    if(oDlg.m_iPortSignAddition == 0)
                    {
                        (*it_port)->SetPortName("+");
                    }
                    else
                    {
                        (*it_port)->SetPortName("-");
                    }
                    UpdateSignCount();

                    // Update any connection head end point associated with
                      the port.
                    GetParentSystemModel()->UpdateConnectionPointHead(*it_port);
                      // deref the iterator to get the ptr-to-CPort obj.
                }

                port_flag = 1;
                break;
            }
        }

// -- ITERATE THROUGH VEC OF OUTPUT PORTS
for(it_port = vec_of_output_ports.begin(); it_port
  != vec_of_output_ports.end(); it_port++)
{
    sign_posn = (*it_port)->GetPortSignPosition();

    // If the point is upon the current port sign
    if((abs(point.x - sign_posn.x) <= sign_width*0.5) &&
      (abs(point.y - sign_posn.y) <= sign_width*0.5))
    {
        // Create the port properties dialog and populate the fields
        //CPortPropertiesDialog oDlg;
        CPortPropertiesDialog oDlg(sign_flag);
        oDlg.m_dPortPositionAngle = (*it_port)-
          >GetPortPositionAngle();
        oDlg.m_iPortArrowDirection = (*it_port)-
          >GetPortArrowDirection();
```

```
        // DO NOT UPDATE PORT SIGN FOR OUTPUT PORT

        // Set the port properties using dlg input.
        if(oDlg.DoModal() == IDOK)
        {
            (*it_port)->SetPortPositionAngle(oDlg.m_dPortPositionAngle);
            (*it_port)->CalculatePortPosition();
            (*it_port)->SetPortArrowDirection(EPortArrowDirection
              (oDlg.m_iPortArrowDirection));
        }

        // DO NOT SET PORT SIGN FOR OUTPUT PORT SINCE THEY HAVE NO
          SIGN ASSOCIATION

        // Update any connection tail end point associated with the
          port.
        GetParentSystemModel()->UpdateConnectionPointTail(*it_port);
          // deref the iterator to get the ptr-to-CPort obj.

        port_flag = 1;
        break;
      }
    }

    // Mark the document as changed
    pDoc->SetModifiedFlag(TRUE);   // prompt the user to save
    pDoc->UpdateAllViews(NULL);    // this fn calls OnDraw to redraw the
      system model.

    return port_flag;
}
```

The developer will notice the call to UpdateSignCount() in both versions of the SetPortProperties() functions. This simply updates the sign count of the class concerned: "m_iNMultiplyInputs" and "m_iNDivideInputs" for the CDivideBlock class, and "m_iNAdds" and "m_iNSubtracts" for the CSumBlock class. Hence, add a public member function to both the CDivideBlock and CSumBlock classes with the following prototype void UpdateSignCount(void) and edit the functions as shown. These functions simply iterate through the vector of input ports and make a count of the sign type stored as the port name.

```
void CDivideBlock::UpdateSignCount()
{
    CString port_name;                 // port name, i.e. port sign
    vector<CPort*>::iterator it_port;  // vector iterator.

    // Get vector of input and output ports
    vector<CPort*> &vec_of_input_ports = GetVectorOfInputPorts();
    vector<CPort*> &vec_of_output_ports = GetVectorOfOutputPorts();

    // Reset member variables
    m_iNMultiplyInputs = 0;
    m_iNDivideInputs = 0;

    // -- ITERATE THROUGH INPUT PORTS
    for(it_port = vec_of_input_ports.begin(); it_port
      != vec_of_input_ports.end(); it_port++)
```

```
    {
        // Get port name, i.e. the port sign.
        port_name = (*it_port)->GetPortName();

        // Adjust the sign count
        if(port_name == "*")
        {
            m_iNMultiplyInputs++;
        }
        else if(port_name == "/")
        {
            m_iNDivideInputs++;
        }
    }

    // Do not iterate through output ports since they have no sign
    //   association!
}


void CSumBlock::UpdateSignCount()
{
    CString port_name;                      // port name, i.e. port sign
    vector<CPort*>::iterator it_port;  // vector iterator.

    // Get vector of input and output ports
    vector<CPort*> &vec_of_input_ports = GetVectorOfInputPorts();
    vector<CPort*> &vec_of_output_ports = GetVectorOfOutputPorts();

    // Reset member variables
    m_iNAddInputs = 0;
    m_iNSubtractInputs = 0;

    // -- ITERATE THROUGH INPUT PORTS
    for(it_port = vec_of_input_ports.begin(); it_port
      != vec_of_input_ports.end(); it_port++)
    {
        // Get port name, i.e. the port sign.
        port_name = (*it_port)->GetPortName();

        // Addjust the sign count
        if(port_name == "+")
        {
            m_iNAddInputs++;
        }
        else if(port_name == "-")
        {
            m_iNSubtractInputs++;
        }
    }

    // Do not iterate through output ports since they have no sign
    //   association!
}
```

Now upon running the program, the user may alter the port properties, e.g., the location, arrow direction and sign type, and then upon using the block dialog window to set block-based properties, the correct number of ports of a particular sign type is correctly reflected in the block dialog window, as shown in Figure 15.8.

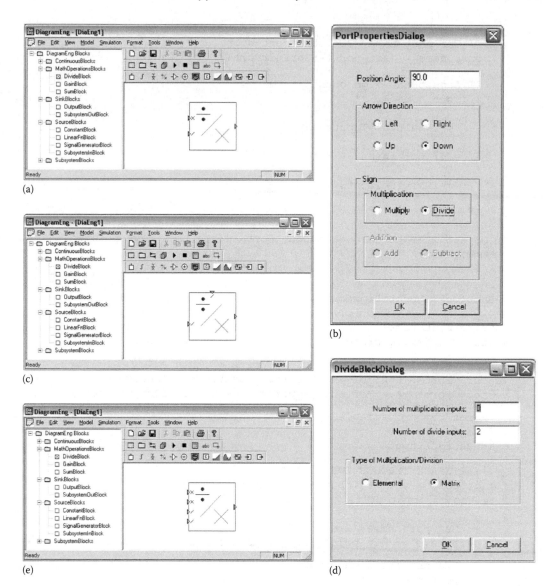

FIGURE 15.8 Setting of port properties: (a) Divide block in the default state; (b) changing of port position, direction, and sign using the port properties dialog window; (c) Divide block displaying updated port; (d) Divide block parameter input dialog window showing updated input count; and (e) automatic realignment of ports after using the block parameter input dialog window (here to increase the port count).

15.8 DELETING PORTS

The Delete Item entry on the Context menu allows the user to delete blocks, connection bend points and whole connection objects. However, the user should also be allowed to delete individual ports by clicking either on the port sign beside the port, or in the absence of a sign, beside the port in the interior of the block. Hence, add the code shown in bold to the existing OnDeleteItem() function of the CDiagramEngDoc class, placing the call to DeletePort() prior to that of DeleteConnection(), since connection head or tail points may be connected to ports, and inadvertent deletion of a connection object would have a greater undesirable affect than the deletion of a port.

```
void CDiagramEngDoc::OnDeleteItem()
{
    // TODO: Add your command handler code here

    // DiagramE3ng (start)
    int item_deleted = 0;

    // Delete a block
    item_deleted = DeleteBlock();
    if(item_deleted == 1)
    {
        return;
    }

    // Delete a block port
    item_deleted = DeletePort();
    if(item_deleted == 1)
    {
        return;
    }

    // Delete a connection bend point
    item_deleted = DeleteConnectionBendPoint();
    if(item_deleted == 1)
    {
        return;
    }

    // Delete a connection line
    item_deleted = DeleteConnection();
    if(item_deleted == 1)
    {
        return;
    }

    // DiagramEng (end)
}
```

Add a new public member function to the CDiagramEngDoc class with the prototype, int DeletePort(void), and edit the code as follows:

```
int CDiagramEngDoc::DeletePort()
{
    int port_flag = 0;                      // flag indicating whether port
      properties were changed
    double blk_width;                       // block width
    double sign_width;                      // port sign width
    CPoint point = m_ptContextMenu;         // point at which context menu
      was activated
    CPoint sign_posn;                       // sign position
    CString sMsg;                           // main msg string
    UINT nType = MB_OK;                     // style of msg. box
    UINT nIDhelp = 0;                       // help context ID for the msg.
    list<CBlock*>::iterator it_blk;         // block iterator
    list<CConnection*>::iterator it_con;    // connection iterator
    vector<CPort*>::iterator it_port;       // port iterator

    // Get connection list
    list<CConnection*> &con_list = GetSystemModel().GetConnectionList();
```

```
// Get a copy of the blk_list in the system model
list<CBlock*> &blk_list = GetSystemModel().GetBlockList();

// -- ITERATE THROUGH BLOCK LIST
for(it_blk = blk_list.begin(); it_blk != blk_list.end(); it_blk++)
{
    // Get block and sign properties
    blk_width = (*it_blk)->GetBlockShape().GetBlockWidth();
    sign_width = 0.1*blk_width;

    // Get vec of input ports
    vector<CPort*> &vec_input_ports =
      (*it_blk)->GetVectorOfInputPorts();

    // -- DELETE PORTS FROM BLOCKS WITH > 2 INPUT PORTS ONLY,
    //    i.e. SUM and DIVIDE blocks
    if(vec_input_ports.size() > 2)
    {
        // -- ITERATE THROUGH INPUT PORTS
        it_port = vec_input_ports.begin();
        while(it_port != vec_input_ports.end())
        {
            sign_posn = (*it_port)->GetPortSignPosition();

            // If the point is upon the current port sign
            if((abs(point.x - sign_posn.x) <= sign_width*0.5) &&
          (abs(point.y - sign_posn.y) <= sign_width*0.5))
            {
                // Iterate through connection list
                for(it_con = con_list.begin(); it_con != con_list.
                  end(); it_con++)
                {
                    // If a connection is attached to this port
                    if((*it_con)->GetRefToPort() == *it_port)
                    {
                        // Disconnect the connection object from
                          the port
                        DisconnectEndPointFromPort(*it_port);
                    }
                }

                // Delete port
                delete *it_port;  // delete actual port pointed to by
                  it_port
                it_port = vec_input_ports.erase(it_port);  // delete
                  element at offset it_port in vec (that held
                  the port)

                // Delete only one port per block then exit while loop
                port_flag = 1;
                break;
            }
            else
            {
                it_port++;
            }
        }
    }// end it_port
```

```
            // Check port_flag to exit it_blk loop
            if(port_flag == 1)
            {
                break;
            }

            // -- VECTOR OF OUTPUT PORTS
/*          vector<CPort*> &vec_output_ports =
              (*it_blk)->GetVectorOfOutputPorts();  // vector of output ports

            // Iterate through vec of input ports
            it_port = vec_output_ports.begin();
            while(it_port != vec_output_ports.end())
            {
                sign_posn = (*it_port)->GetPortSignPosition();

                // If the point is upon the current port sign
                if((abs(point.x - sign_posn.x) <= sign_width*0.5) &&
                  (abs(point.y - sign_posn.y) <= sign_width*0.5))
                {
                    // Iterate through connection list
                    for(it_con = con_list.begin(); it_con != con_list.end();
                      it_con++)
                    {
                        // If a connection is attached to this port
                        if((*it_con)->GetRefFromPort() == *it_port)
                        {
                            // Disconnect the connection object from the port
                            DisconnectEndPointFromPort(*it_port);
                        }
                    }

                    // Delete port
                    delete *it_port;  // delete actual port pointed to by
                      it_port
                    it_port = vec_output_ports.erase(it_port);  // delete
                      element at offset it_port in vec (that held the port)

                    // Delete only one port per block then exit while loop.
                    port_flag = 1;
                    break;
                }
                else
                {
                    it_port++;
                }
            }// end it_port
*/
            // Check port_flag to exit it_blk loop
            if(port_flag == 1)
            {
                break;
            }
        }// end it_blk

    return port_flag;
}
```

The `DeletePort()` function iterates through the block list and checks whether the point at which the Context menu is invoked is sufficiently close to an input port; if so, any connection that may be attached to the port is detached and the port deleted from the vector. The developer will notice that the section concerning the deletion of output ports is commented out (for now), since output ports should not be deleted from blocks that possess them. This can be changed, in future, by simply removing the comments as desired, if in fact required.

In addition, if a port is deleted from a Divide or Sum block, then the count of the multiplication and division, or addition and subtraction signs, must be updated prior to subsequent setting of block properties, via the Set Properties entry on the Context menu, in particular, programmatically through the `BlockDlgWndParameterInput()` functions. Hence, add the function call to `UpdateSignCount()` as shown in bold to the `BlockDlgWndParameterInput()` functions of the CDivideBlock and CSumBlock classes as shown in the following. This will result in the correct number of the relevant sign type being displayed in the block properties dialog window.

```
void CDivideBlock::BlockDlgWndParameterInput()
{
    int n_inputs = 0;          // number of input ports
    CString sMsg;              // string to be displayed
    CString sMsgTemp;          // temp string msg.
    UINT nType = MB_OK;        // style of msg. box
    UINT nIDhelp = 0;          // help context ID for the msg.

    // Create a dialog object. of class CDivideBlockDialog : public
      CDialog
    CDivideBlockDialog oDlg;

    // Update the sign count since a port may have been deleted
    UpdateSignCount();

    // Set the dialog class vars using the block class vars
    oDlg.m_iMultType = m_iMultType;
    oDlg.m_iNDivideInputs = m_iNDivideInputs;
    oDlg.m_iNMultiplyInputs = m_iNMultiplyInputs;

    // While less than two input ports get user input
    while(n_inputs < 2)
    {
        // Return val of DoModal() fn of ancestor class CDialog is
          checked to determine which btn was clicked.
        if(oDlg.DoModal() == IDOK)
        {
            // Assign CDivideBlockDialog variable values to CDivideBlock
              variable values.
            m_iNDivideInputs = oDlg.m_iNDivideInputs;
            m_iNMultiplyInputs = oDlg.m_iNMultiplyInputs;
            m_iMultType = oDlg.m_iMultType;

            // Print msg with variable value.
            //sMsg.Format("\n CDivideBlock::BlockDlgWndParameterInput(),
              m_iMultType = %d\n", m_iMultType);
            //AfxMessageBox(sMsg, nType, nIDhelp);
        }

        // Check input for correctness and warn user if approp.
        n_inputs = m_iNDivideInputs + m_iNMultiplyInputs;
```

```
        if(n_inputs < 2)
        {
            sMsgTemp.Format("\n CDivideBlock::BlockDlgWndParameter
              Input()\n");
            sMsg += sMsgTemp;
            sMsgTemp.Format(" No. of input ports = %d\n", n_inputs);
            sMsg += sMsgTemp;
            sMsgTemp.Format(" Two or more input ports are required!\n");
            sMsg += sMsgTemp;
            AfxMessageBox(sMsg, nType, nIDhelp);
            sMsg.Format("");     // reset the msg since within a
              while loop
        }
    }

    // Reset ports
    ResetInputPorts(m_iNMultiplyInputs, m_iNDivideInputs);
    ResetOutputPorts();
}

void CSumBlock::BlockDlgWndParameterInput()
{
    int n_inputs = 0;       // number of input ports
    CString sMsg;           // string to be displayed
    CString sMsgTemp;       // temp string msg.
    UINT nType = MB_OK;     // style of msg. box
    UINT nIDhelp = 0;       // help context ID for the msg.

    // Create a dialog object. of class CSumBlockDialog : public CDialog
    CSumBlockDialog oDlg;

    // Update the sign count since a port may have been deleted
    UpdateSignCount();

    // Set the dialog class var using the block class var
    oDlg.m_iNAddInputs = m_iNAddInputs;
    oDlg.m_iNSubtractInputs = m_iNSubtractInputs;

    // While less than two input ports get user input
    while(n_inputs < 2)
    {
        // Return val of DoModal() fn of ancestor class CDialog is
          checked to determine which btn was clicked.
        if(oDlg.DoModal() == IDOK)
        {
            // Assign CSumBlockDialog variable values to CSumBlock
              variable values.
            m_iNAddInputs = oDlg.m_iNAddInputs;
            m_iNSubtractInputs = oDlg.m_iNSubtractInputs;

            // Print msg with variable value.
            //sMsg.Format("\n CSumBlock::BlockDlgWndParameterInput(),
              m_iNAddInputs = %d, m_iNSubractInputs = %d\n",
              m_iNAddInputs, m_iNSubtractInputs);
            //AfxMessageBox(sMsg, nType, nIDhelp);
        }

        // Check input for correctness and warn user if approp.
        n_inputs = m_iNAddInputs + m_iNSubtractInputs;
```

```
        if(n_inputs < 2)
        {
            sMsgTemp.Format("\n CSumBlock::BlockDlgWndParameter
              Input()\n");
            sMsg += sMsgTemp;
            sMsgTemp.Format(" No. of input ports = %d\n", n_inputs);
            sMsg += sMsgTemp;
            sMsgTemp.Format(" Two or more input ports are required!\n");
            sMsg += sMsgTemp;
            AfxMessageBox(sMsg, nType, nIDhelp);
            sMsg.Format("");  // reset the msg since within a while loop
        }
    }
    // Reset ports
    ResetInputPorts(m_iNAddInputs, m_iNSubtractInputs);
    ResetOutputPorts();
}
```

Now upon running the program, the user may attach a connection to a port and then delete the port resulting in a detachment of the connection, as shown in Figure 15.9.

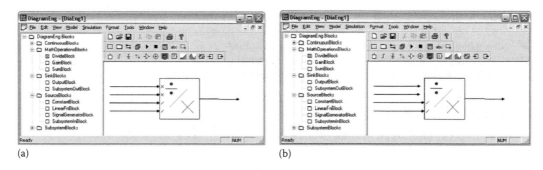

(a)   (b)

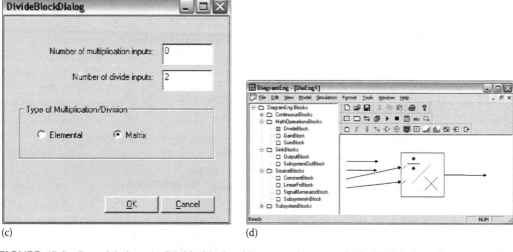

(c)   (d)

FIGURE 15.9 Port deletion: (a) Divide block with connections attached, (b) deletion of ports resulting in detachment of connections, (c) Divide block parameter input dialog showing updated input count, and (d) automatic realignment of ports after using the block parameter input dialog window.

15.9 SUMMARY

The setting of port properties involves the specification of the number of block ports and also their position, direction, and sign type, if appropriate. Functionality was added for the Divide and Sum blocks to allow the user to change the number of input ports of a particular sign type ("×", "/", "+", "−") and involved the functions ResetInputPorts(), ResetOutputPorts(), and CalculatePortPositionAngles(), where the resetting methods are called from the BlockDlgWndParameterInput() function. The drawing of block ports, depending on their connection status, was implemented using the CBlock methods: DrawBlockPorts() and CheckPortConnection(). The drawing of port signs, to be placed next to the ports for the Divide and Sum blocks, was performed using the CPort methods: DrawPortSign() and CalculatePortSignPosition().

The setting of specific port properties involved adding a SetBlockPortProperties() function to the CBlock class that calls the virtual CBlock::SetPortProperties() function to be overridden by the Divide and Sum block classes. A Port Properties dialog resource was added to the project and an instance of which created in the SetPortProperties() function to accept the user-specified port properties. In addition, the CPortPropertiesDialog() constructor was amended to include a flag-like variable used to initialize the Port Properties dialog controls. Finally, the deletion of ports was implemented by extension of the OnDeleteItem() function and the addition of the DeletePort() method, both of the CDiagramEngDoc class.

16 Key-Based Item Movement

16.1 INTRODUCTION

The drawing functionality of the DiagramEng application allows blocks to be connected by connection objects whose head and tail points are attached to block input and output ports, respectively. However, at present, fine-scale adjustment of the blocks and bend points to align the diagram as desired can only be performed using the mouse, which is cumbersome: no keyboard character input can assist the user. Hence, a new Context menu entry named Fine Movement is required that should allow the arrow keys, left, "←", right, "→", up, "↑", and down, "↓", to control incremental movement of a diagram entity, i.e., a block or connection bend point, one pixel at a time. The topics concerning the implementation of this functionality are as listed and specific details are presented in the sections that follow.

1. Add a Fine Move Item entry to the Context menu.
2. Add members to the CDiagramEngDoc class.
3. Edit the `CDiagramEngView::OnKeyDown()` function.
4. Add a `FineMoveItem()` function.
5. Add a `FineMoveBlock()` function.
6. Add a `FineMoveConnectionBendPoint()` function.
7. Fine movement process control flow.

16.2 ADD A FINE MOVE ITEM ENTRY TO THE CONTEXT MENU

A new entry is to be added to the Context menu to allow the fine movement of diagram entities. Hence, navigate to the Menu Designer and select the Context menu with the following ID: IDR_CONTEXT_MENU. Drag the blank entry at the bottom of the menu list, i.e., the entry below Set Properties, and place this in between Delete Grouped Items and Insert Bend Point (alphabetical order of first letter of menu entry). Add the menu entry shown in bold in Table 16.1, including the ID, caption, and prompts.

Now functionality is to be added for the new Fine Move Item entry to initialize the state of the interactive process. Hence, invoke the ClassWizard (ignore the Adding a Class dialog window and press cancel), choose the class name to be CDiagramEngDoc and select the Object ID to be IDM_FINE_MOVE_ITEM. Add an event-handler function for the COMMAND message, naming it `OnFineMoveItem()` and edit the code as shown in the following program to initialize a to-be-added flag-like member variable denoting the fine-movement state.

```
void CDiagramEngDoc::OnFineMoveItem()
{
    // TODO: Add your command handler code here

    // DiagramEng (start)

    // Set the member var. flag concerning fine movement
    m_iFineMoveFlag = 1;

    // DiagramEng (end)
}
```

TABLE 16.1

Context Menu Settings: IDs, Captions, and Prompts (Status Bar and Tooltips), and the New IDM_FINE_MOVE_ITEM Entry

ID	Caption	Prompts
IDM_DELETE_ITEM	&Delete Item	Delete selected item\nDelete selected item
ID_EDIT_DELETE_GROUPED_ITEMS	Delete &Grouped Items	Delete items enclosed by rectangle\nDelete grouped items
IDM_FINE_MOVE_ITEM	**&Fine Move Item**	**Fine movement of item\nFine movement of item**
IDM_INSERT_BEND_POINT	&Insert Bend Point	Insert bend point\nInsert bend point
IDM_SET_ITEM_PROPERTIES	&Set Properties	Set item properties\nSet item properties

16.3   ADD MEMBERS TO THE CDiagramEngDoc CLASS

The flag-like member variable, "m_iFineMoveFlag", set to "1", indicates that the fine movement of an item initiated by the selection of the Context menu entry, Fine Move Item, is currently in the active state. This allows the to-be-completed OnKeyDown() function of the CDiagramEngView class to correctly process keyboard input used for item movement.

Hence, add a private integer member variable named "m_iFineMoveFlag" to the CDiagramEngDoc class. Initialize this variable to "0" in the CDiagramEngDoc class constructor as shown in bold: "0" indicates that no fine movement action can occur; a number greater than "0" indicates that such an action can occur.

```
CDiagramEngDoc::CDiagramEngDoc()
{
    // TODO: add one-time construction code here

    // DiagramEng (start)
    m_iKeyFlagTrack = 0;
    m_iFineMoveFlag = 0;
    m_iRubberBandCreated = 0;
    m_dDeltaLength = 50.0;
    // DiagramEng (end)
}
```

Now accessor methods are required to set and retrieve the value of the member variable, "m_iFineMoveFlag". Hence, add two public member functions to the CDiagramEngDoc class with the following declarations and definitions.

1. void SetFineMoveFlag(int fine _ move _ flag)
2. int GetFineMoveFlag(void) const

```
void CDiagramEngDoc::SetFineMoveFlag(int fine_move_flag)
{
    // Set the member var.
    m_iFineMoveFlag = fine_move_flag;
}

int CDiagramEngDoc::GetFineMoveFlag() const
{
    // Return the member var.
    return m_iFineMoveFlag;
}
```

16.4   EDIT THE `CDiagramEngView::OnKeyDown()` FUNCTION

The user can perform incremental movement using the left, "←", right, "→", up, "↑", and down, "↓", arrow keys: the UINT numerical values for these keyboard characters are type cast ("lchar = char(nchar)") to the character values "37", "38", "39", and "40", respectively [1]. Hence, the `CDiagramEngView::OnKeyDown()` function should be augmented as shown in the following, to cater for this keyboard input.

```
void CDiagramEngView::OnKeyDown(UINT nChar, UINT nRepCnt, UINT nFlags)
{
    // TODO: Add your message handler code here and/or call default

    // DiagramEng (start)
    int key_flag = 0;           // local key flag
    char lchar;                 // local character
    lchar = char(nChar);        // typecast the nChar

    // Get a ptr to the doc
    CDiagramEngDoc *pDoc = GetDocument();

    // -- CHECK THAT THE "T" CHARACTER HAS BEEN PRESSED
    if(lchar == 'T')
    {
        key_flag = 1;
        pDoc->SetKeyFlagTrack(key_flag);       // set the m_iKeyFlagTrack
          in the CDiagramEngDoc class
    }

    // -- CHECK THAT THE FINE MOVE FLAG HAS BEEN SET INDICATING FINE
       MOVEMENT OF AN ITEM
    if(pDoc->GetFineMoveFlag() > 0)
    {
        // -- CHECK KEY PRESSED
        if(lchar == 37)                        // LEFT ARROW
        {
            key_flag = 37;
            pDoc->FineMoveItem(key_flag);      // move item left
        }
        else if(lchar == 38)                   // UP ARROW
        {
            key_flag = 38;
            pDoc->FineMoveItem(key_flag);      // move item up
        }
        else if(lchar == 39)                   // RIGHT ARROW
        {
            key_flag = 39;
            pDoc->FineMoveItem(key_flag);      // move item right
        }
        else if(lchar == 40)                   // DOWN ARROW
        {
            key_flag = 40;
            pDoc->FineMoveItem(key_flag);      // move item down
        }
        else                                   // NOT AN ARROW KEY
        {
            key_flag = 0;
```

```
        pDoc->SetFineMoveFlag(key_flag); // set move flag to zero to
          indicate no longer performing fine movement
      }
    }
    // DiagramEng (end)

    CView::OnKeyDown(nChar, nRepCnt, nFlags);
}
```

The OnKeyDown() function first checks that the member variable, "m_iFineMoveFlag", is greater than "0": if it is "0", then no fine movement action can occur, if greater than "0", then it can occur. Then a check is made to determine which key was pressed, and if an arrow key was pressed, then the FineMoveItem() function is called passing in the (integer) direction identifier in which motion should occur.

16.5   ADD A FineMoveItem() FUNCTION

The OnKeyDown() function calls the FineMoveItem() function passing an integer value indicating the direction of movement. Hence, add a public member function to the CDiagramEngDoc class with the prototype, void CDiagramEngDoc::FineMoveItem(int key_flag), and edit the function as follows.

```
void CDiagramEngDoc::FineMoveItem(int key_flag)
{
    int item_moved = 0;          // flag indicating entity movement

    // Check whether block was selected and moved
    item_moved = FineMoveBlock(key_flag);
    if(item_moved)
    {
        return;
    }

    // Check whether connection bend point was selected and moved
    item_moved = FineMoveConnectionBendPoint(key_flag);
    if(item_moved)
    {
        return;
    }

    // End fine movement action by switching m_iFineMoveFlag = 0
    if(item_moved == 0)
    {
        SetFineMoveFlag(item_moved);
    }
}
```

The FineMoveItem() function simply calls two item movement functions concerning blocks and connection bend points, passing in the direction in which they should be moved. However, if upon activation of the Context menu, the mouse pointer was not on a block or bend point, then these functions perform no item movement and return "0", and hence the fine movement action is ended in the final conditional section by setting the "m_iFineMoveFlag" variable to "0".

16.6   ADD A FineMoveBlock() FUNCTION

The FineMoveItem() method calls the FineMoveBlock() function to determine whether a block was selected upon right-clicking of the mouse when activating the Context menu and performs incremental movement in the appropriate direction as specified by the "key_flag" argument.

Hence, add a public member function to the CDiagramEngDoc class with the prototype, int CDiagramEngDoc::FineMoveBlock(int key_flag), and edit the function as follows.

```
int CDiagramEngDoc::FineMoveBlock(int key_flag)
{
    int delta_x = 1;                  // incr. in x direc.
    int delta_y = 1;                  // incr. in y direc.
    int move_flag = 0;                // flag indicating entity
      movement
    double dist;                      // Euclidean dist bw. block posn.
      and point posn.
    double width;                     // block width
    CPoint blk_posn;                  // block posn.
    CPoint point;                     // local point var.
    CString sMsg;                     // main msg string
    UINT nType = MB_OK;               // style of msg. box
    UINT nIDhelp = 0;                 // help context ID for the msg.
    list<CBlock*>::iterator it_blk;   // block iterator
    static CBlock *ptr_to_blk = NULL; // ptr-to-block to hold the
      chosen block's address.

    // Get the point at which the context menu was invoked
    point = m_ptContextMenu;          // init a local copy.

    // Print msg.
    //sMsg.Format("\n CDiagramEngDoc::FineMoveBlock(),
      point (x,y) = (%d,%d)\n", point.x, point.y);
    //AfxMessageBox(sMsg, nType, nIDhelp);

    // -- IF THIS IS THE FIRST ENTRY INTO THIS FN THEN RECORD THE ADDRESS
      OF THE SELECTED BLOCK (also move the block)
    if(GetFineMoveFlag() == 1)
    {
        // Get a copy of the blk_list in the system model
        list<CBlock*> &blk_list = GetSystemModel().GetBlockList();

        // -- ITERATE THROUGH THE BLOCK LIST
        for(it_blk = blk_list.begin(); it_blk != blk_list.end(); it_blk++)
        {
            move_flag = 0;
            blk_posn = (*it_blk)->GetBlockPosition();
            width = (*it_blk)->GetBlockShape().GetBlockWidth();
            dist = sqrt(pow((blk_posn.x - point.x),2) +
              pow((blk_posn.y - point.y),2));

            // -- IF USER CLICKED ON A BLOCK
            if(dist <= 0.5*width*0.5)
            {
                // -- FILTER THE KEY/DIRECTION (screen (0,0) top left
                  cnr., +ve x to right, +ve y downward
                if(key_flag == 37)    // LEFT ARROW
                {
                    // Update block posn.
                    blk_posn.x = blk_posn.x - delta_x;
                    (*it_blk)->SetBlockPosition(blk_posn);
                    ptr_to_blk = *it_blk; // record the address of the
                      block for subsequent movt.
```

```
                                move_flag = 1;
                    }
                    else if(key_flag == 38)     // UP ARROW
                    {
                        // Update block posn.
                        blk_posn.y = blk_posn.y - delta_y;
                        (*it_blk)->SetBlockPosition(blk_posn);
                        ptr_to_blk = *it_blk;  // record the address of the
                          block for subsequent movt.
                        move_flag = 1;
                    }
                    else if(key_flag == 39)     // RIGHT ARROW
                    {
                        // Update block posn.
                        blk_posn.x = blk_posn.x + delta_x;
                        (*it_blk)->SetBlockPosition(blk_posn);
                        ptr_to_blk = *it_blk;  // record the address of the
                          block for subsequent movt.
                        move_flag = 1;
                    }
                    else if(key_flag == 40)     // DOWN ARROW
                    {
                        // Update block posn.
                        blk_posn.y = blk_posn.y + delta_y;
                        (*it_blk)->SetBlockPosition(blk_posn);
                        ptr_to_blk = *it_blk;  // record the address of the
                          block for subsequent movt.
                        move_flag = 1;
                    }

                    if(move_flag == 1)
                    {
                        // Set flag
                        m_iFineMoveFlag = 2;

                        // Mark the document as changed
                        UpdateAllViews(NULL);  // this fn calls OnDraw to
                          redraw the system model.
                        SetModifiedFlag(TRUE); // prompt the user to save
                        break;                 // break out of for loop
                    }
            }// end if dist
        }// end it_blk
    }
    else if(m_iFineMoveFlag == 2)               // -- IF THIS IS NOT THE FIRST
      TIME INTO THE FN, THEN MOVE THE BLOCK USING IT'S ADDRESS
    {
        // -- FILTER THE KEY/DIRECTION (screen (0,0) top left cnr.,
          +ve x to right, +ve y downward
        if(key_flag == 37) // LEFT ARROW
        {
            // Update block posn.
            blk_posn = ptr_to_blk->GetBlockPosition();
            blk_posn.x = blk_posn.x - delta_x;
            ptr_to_blk->SetBlockPosition(blk_posn);
```

```
            move_flag = 1;
        }
        else if(key_flag == 38)              // UP ARROW
        {
            // Update block posn.
            blk_posn = ptr_to_blk->GetBlockPosition();
            blk_posn.y = blk_posn.y - delta_y;
            ptr_to_blk->SetBlockPosition(blk_posn);
            move_flag = 1;
        }
        else if(key_flag == 39)              // RIGHT ARROW
        {
            // Update block posn.
            blk_posn = ptr_to_blk->GetBlockPosition();
            blk_posn.x = blk_posn.x + delta_x;
            ptr_to_blk->SetBlockPosition(blk_posn);
            move_flag = 1;
        }
        else if(key_flag == 40)              // DOWN ARROW
        {
            // Update block posn.
            blk_posn = ptr_to_blk->GetBlockPosition();
            blk_posn.y = blk_posn.y + delta_y;
            ptr_to_blk->SetBlockPosition(blk_posn);
            move_flag = 1;
        }

        if(move_flag == 1)
        {
            // Mark the document as changed
            UpdateAllViews(NULL);              // this fn calls OnDraw to
              redraw the system model.
            SetModifiedFlag(TRUE);            // prompt the user to save
        }
    }

    return move_flag;
}
```

On the first entry to this function, "m_iFineMoveFlag" is equal to "1", and the block list is iterated over to determine which block was selected by the user upon activation of the Context menu. If a block was selected, i.e., the distance between the point of the right-click event and the block is less than or equal to one quarter of the block width, then movement action is processed according to the "key_flag" direction-specification variable, and the address of the block is statically stored ("static CBlock *ptr_to_blk = NULL" in combination with "ptr_to_blk = *it_blk";) for subsequent entry into the function. Prior to exiting the function the "m_iFineMoveFlag" variable is set to "2", indicating that subsequent movement concerns the stored block. Thereafter, key down events result in the second part of the conditional section, "else if(m_iFineMoveFlag == 2)", being executed, where the block to be moved is retrieved through the statically stored pointer-to-CBlock, "ptr_to_blk", variable and the new position updated.

If no block was selected, then the flag-like variable, "move_flag" is "0" and is returned to the FineMoveItem() function, which will then end the fine movement process by setting the member variable, "m_iFineMoveFlag", to "0".

16.7   ADD A `FineMoveConnectionBendPoint()` FUNCTION

The `FineMoveItem()` function also calls the `FineMoveConnectionBendPoint()` function to determine whether a connection bend point was selected. Hence, add a public member function to the CDiagramEngDoc class with the prototype, int CDiagramEngDoc::FineMoveConnection BendPoint(int key_flag), and edit the function as follows.

```
int CDiagramEngDoc::FineMoveConnectionBendPoint(int key_flag)
{
    int delta_x = 1;                        // incr. in x direc.
    int delta_y = 1;                        // incr. in y direc.
    int move_flag = 0;                      // flag indicating entity
      movement
    double disc_r = 0.25*m_dDeltaLength;    // disc of radius r about
      center of connection bend point.
    double dist;                            // Euclidean dist bw.
      connection bend point posn and point posn.
    CPoint bend_pt;                         // bend point posn.
    CPoint point;                           // local point var.
    CString sMsg;                           // main msg string
    UINT nType = MB_OK;                     // style of msg. box
    UINT nIDhelp = 0;                       // help context ID for the msg.
    list<CConnection*>::iterator it_con;    // connection iterator
    list<CPoint>::iterator it_pt;           // point iterator
    static CPoint *ptr_to_bend_pt = NULL;   // ptr-to-bend pt to hold the
      chosen bend point's address.

    // Get the system model
    CSystemModel &sys_model = GetSystemModel();

    // Get the point at which the context menu was invoked
    point = m_ptContextMenu;                // init a local copy.

    // Print msg.
    //sMsg.Format("\n CDiagramEngDoc::FineMoveConnectionBendPoint(),
      point (x,y) = (%d,%d)\n", point.x, point.y);
    //AfxMessageBox(sMsg, nType, nIDhelp);

    // -- IF THIS IS THE FIRST ENTRY INTO THIS FN THEN RECORD THE ADDRESS
      OF THE SELECTED BEND PT (also move the bend pt.)
    if(GetFineMoveFlag() == 1)
    {
        // Get a copy of the con_list in the system model
        list<CConnection*> con_list = sys_model.GetConnectionList();

        // -- ITERATE THROUGH THE BLOCK LIST
        for(it_con = con_list.begin(); it_con != con_list.end(); it_con++)
        {
            // Get the connection bend pts. list
            list<CPoint> &bend_pts_list = (*it_con)-
              >GetConnectionBendPointsList();

            // -- ITERATE THROUGH ALL BEND POINTS for this connection
            for(it_pt = bend_pts_list.begin(); it_pt != bend_pts_list.
              end(); it_pt++)
            {
                bend_pt = *it_pt;

                // Determine Euclidean dist bw mouse point and connection
                  bend pt.
```

```
            dist = sqrt(pow(bend_pt.x - point.x,2) +
              pow(bend_pt.y - point.y,2));


            // -- IF USER CLICKED ON A BEND POINT
            if(dist <= disc_r)
            {
                // -- FILTER THE KEY/DIRECTION (screen (0,0) top left
                  cnr., +ve x to right, +ve y downward
                if(key_flag == 37)        // LEFT ARROW
                {
                    // Update bend point posn.
                    bend_pt.x = bend_pt.x - delta_x;
                    *it_pt = bend_pt;
                    ptr_to_bend_pt = &(*it_pt); // record the address
                      of the bend pt for subsequent movt.
                     sys_model.UpdateConnectionPointTailToBendPoint
                      (&(*it_pt)); // update any tail pt connected
                      to bend pt.
                    move_flag = 1;
                }
                else if(key_flag == 38) // UP ARROW
                {
                    // Update bend point posn.
                    bend_pt.y = bend_pt.y - delta_y;
                    *it_pt = bend_pt;
                    ptr_to_bend_pt = &(*it_pt); // record the address
                      of the bend pt for subsequent movt.
                    sys_model.UpdateConnectionPointTailToBendPoint
                      (&(*it_pt)); // update any tail pt connected
                      to bend pt.
                    move_flag = 1;
                }
                else if(key_flag == 39) // RIGHT ARROW
                {
                    // Update bend point posn.
                    bend_pt.x = bend_pt.x + delta_x;
                    *it_pt = bend_pt;
                    ptr_to_bend_pt = &(*it_pt); // record the address
                      of the bend pt for subsequent movt.
                    sys_model.UpdateConnectionPointTailToBendPoint
                      (&(*it_pt));  // update any tail pt connected
                      to bend pt.
                    move_flag = 1;
                }
                else if(key_flag == 40)    // DOWN ARROW
                {
                    // Update bend point posn.
                    bend_pt.y = bend_pt.y + delta_y;
                    *it_pt = bend_pt;
                    ptr_to_bend_pt = &(*it_pt); // record the address
                      of the bend pt for subsequent movt.
                    sys_model.UpdateConnectionPointTailToBendPoint
                      (&(*it_pt));  // update any tail pt connected
                      to bend pt.
                    move_flag = 1;
                }
```

```
                    if(move_flag == 1)
                    {
                        // Set flag
                        m_iFineMoveFlag = 3;

                        // Mark the document as changed
                        UpdateAllViews(NULL);  // this fn calls OnDraw to
                          redraw the system model.
                        SetModifiedFlag(TRUE); // prompt the user to save
                        break;                 // break out of for loop
                    }
                }// end if dist
            }// end it_pt
        }// end it_con
}
else if(m_iFineMoveFlag == 3)              // -- IF THIS IS NOT THE
  FIRST TIME INTO THE FN, THEN MOVE THE BEND POINT USING IT'S
  ADDRESS
{
    // -- FILTER THE KEY/DIRECTION (screen (0,0) top left cnr.,
      +ve x to right, +ve y downward
    if(key_flag == 37)                     // LEFT ARROW
    {
        // Update CPoint bend point posn by dereferencing the ptr.
          (*ptr_to_bend_pt).x = (*ptr_to_bend_pt).x - delta_x;
        sys_model.UpdateConnectionPointTailToBendPoint(ptr_to_bend_pt);
          // update any tail pt connected to bend pt.
        move_flag = 1;
    }
    else if(key_flag == 38)                // UP ARROW
    {
        // Update CPoint bend point posn. by dereferencing the ptr.
          (*ptr_to_bend_pt).y = (*ptr_to_bend_pt).y - delta_y;
        sys_model.UpdateConnectionPointTailToBendPoint(ptr_to_bend_pt);
          // update any tail pt connected to bend pt.
        move_flag = 1;
    }
    else if(key_flag == 39)                // RIGHT ARROW
    {
        // Update CPoint bend point posn. by dereferencing the ptr.
        (*ptr_to_bend_pt).x = (*ptr_to_bend_pt).x + delta_x;
        sys_model.UpdateConnectionPointTailToBendPoint(ptr_to_bend_pt);
          // update any tail pt connected to bend pt.
        move_flag = 1;
    }
    else if(key_flag == 40)                // DOWN ARROW
    {
        // Update CPoint bend point posn. by dereferencing the ptr.
        (*ptr_to_bend_pt).y = (*ptr_to_bend_pt).y + delta_y;
        sys_model.UpdateConnectionPointTailToBendPoint(ptr_to_bend_pt);
          // update any tail pt connected to bend pt.
        move_flag = 1;
    }

    if(move_flag == 1)
    {
        // Mark the document as changed
```

```
                UpdateAllViews(NULL);                // this fn calls OnDraw to
                    redraw the system model.
            vSetModifiedFlag(TRUE);                  // prompt the user to save
            }
    }

    return move_flag;
}
```

The function `FineMoveConnectionBendPoint()` executes in a similar manner to `FineMoveBlock()`. On the first entry to the function, the member variable "m_iFineMoveFlag" is equal to "1" and the connection bend point is moved according to the direction specified by the variable "key_flag". In addition, the pointer-to-CPoint used to statically store the address of the bend point is assigned the address of the object that the "it_pt" list iterator is pointing to, i.e., "ptr_to_bend_pt = &(*it_pt)". After performing the initial movement, "m_iFineMoveFlag" is set to "3", indicating that upon the next key-down event, control flow should enter the second conditional section, "else if(m_iFineMoveFlag == 3)", and the position of the bend point, whose address was previously stored in the pointer-to-CPoint, "ptr_to_bend_pt", is updated in the appropriate direction. The developer will also notice that the function `UpdateConnectionPointTailToBendPoint()` is called to update any connection tail point that may be connected to the bend point being moved: this ensures that both the bend point and the connected tail point move together.

16.8   FINE MOVEMENT PROCESS CONTROL FLOW

The fine movement process control flow is as follows:

1. The Context menu is invoked and Fine Move Item is selected.
2. The `OnFineMovement()` function is called and "m_iFineMoveFlag" is set to "1".
3. A key-down action occurs and given that "m_iFineMoveFlag" is not "0", the `FineMoveItem()` function is called with the movement direction passed as an argument. If an arrow key was not selected, "m_iFineMoveFlag" is set to "0" and fine movement is terminated.
4. The `FineMoveItem()` function simply calls `FineMoveBlock()` and `FineMoveConnectionBendPoint()` sequentially: if an item was moved the function returns, if not, the fine movement action is terminated by setting "m_iFineMoveFlag" to "0".
5. `FineMoveBlock()` is entered repeatedly: initially "m_iFineMoveFlag" is "1" and the address of the selected block is stored statically and the block position is moved as appropriate. Then "m_iFineMoveFlag" is set to "2", indicating that upon subsequent entry, the stored block should simply be moved.
6. `FineMoveConnectionBendPoint()` is entered repeatedly: initially "m_iFineMoveFlag" is "1" and the address of the selected bend point is stored statically and the bend point position is moved as appropriate. Then "m_iFineMoveFlag" is set to "3", indicating that upon subsequent entry, the stored bend point should simply be moved.

The developer will notice that the indicator-like member variable, "m_iFineMoveFlag", has four different roles, as summarized in Table 16.2: (0) The fine movement action is terminated, (1) a block or bend point address is to be recorded, (2) a block is to be moved, or (3) a connection bend point is to be moved.

Hence, as a result of fine movement control of block and bend points, better diagrams may be drawn faster and with greater motion control. Figure 16.1 shows a typical control flow diagram representing: (a) a linear equation, e.g., $f(x) = kx + c$, and (b) a differential equation involving feedback, e.g., $\dot{x}(t) = f(t) + kx(t)$, where the drawn lines are perfectly horizontal or vertical.

TABLE 16.2

The Four Roles of the "m_iFineMoveFlag" Member Variable for Fine-Movement Action

"m_iFineMoveFlag"	Action
0	Fine movement action is terminated
1	Fine movement is initiated and a block or bend point address is to be recorded
2	Fine movement is in progress and recorded block is to be moved
3	Fine movement is in progress and recorded bend point is to be moved

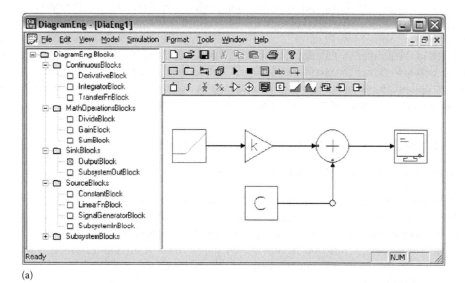

(a)

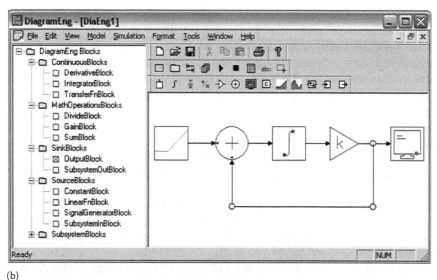

(b)

FIGURE 16.1 Control diagrams with perfectly horizontal and vertical control lines: (a) a linear equation model ($f(x) = kx + c$) and (b) a differential equation model ($\dot{x}(t) = f(t) + kx(t)$).

16.9 SUMMARY

The key-based pixel-by-pixel movement of diagram blocks and bend points is performed through the introduction of a Fine Move Item entry on the Context menu, which upon selection invokes the `OnFineMoveItem()` function that sets the value of a multiple-role, flag-like member variable, "m_iFineMoveFlag", used to process the fine-movement action. The `OnKeyDown()` function of the CDiagramEngView class is used to process keyboard input and calls the `FineMoveItem()` function of the CDiagramEngDoc class, which in turn calls `FineMoveBlock()` and `FineMoveConnectionBendPoint()`, to move blocks and bend points, respectively. Finally, the control flow of the fine movement process is presented in a listed sequence.

REFERENCE

1. Microsoft Developer Network Library Visual Studio 6.0, Microsoft® Visual Studio™ 6.0 Development System, Microsoft Corporation, 1998.

17 Reversing Block Direction

17.1 INTRODUCTION

Block diagrams can currently be drawn where the block direction, specified by the enumerated type, "EBlockDirection", is set to "e_right" by default, implying that the block points to the right. However, if the user wants to reverse the direction of a block, e.g., a Gain block to be used in a feedback rather than a feed-forward path, where the block points in the direction of the signal flow, then a "reverse block" option should be available to provide this change. The general steps concerning the implementation of this functionality are as listed where specific details are provided in the sections that follow.

1. Add a Reverse Block entry to the Context menu
2. Add a `ReverseBlockDirection()` function to the CBlock class
3. Add accessor methods to the CBlockShape class
4. Add accessor methods to the CPort class
5. Test the application

17.2 ADD A REVERSE BLOCK ENTRY TO THE CONTEXT MENU

Navigate to the Menu Designer and select the menu with ID: IDR_CONTEXT_MENU. Drag the blank entry at the bottom of the context menu list, i.e., the entry below Set Properties, and place this in between Insert Bend Point and Set Properties (alphabetical order of first letter of menu entry). Add the menu entry shown in bold in Table 17.1, including the ID, caption, and prompts.

Now an event-handler function needs to be attached to the new Context menu entry. Hence, invoke the ClassWizard (ignore the Adding a Class dialog window and press cancel), choose CDiagramEngDoc as the class, and select the Object ID to be IDM_REVERSE_BLOCK_DIREC. Add a function to the COMMAND message, naming it `OnReverseBlockDirection()` and edit it as follows.

```
void CDiagramEngDoc::OnReverseBlockDirection()
{
    // TODO: Add your command handler code here

    // DiagramEng (start)
    double dist;         // Euclidean dist bw. block posn and point posn.
    double width;        // block width
    CPoint blk_posn;     // block posn.
    CPoint point;        // local point var.
    CString sMsg;        // main msg string
    UINT nType = MB_OK;  // style of msg. box
    UINT nIDhelp = 0;    // help context ID for the msg.
    list<CBlock*>::iterator it_blk;   // iterator

    // Get the point at which the context menu was invoked
    point = m_ptContextMenu;           // init a local copy.
```

TABLE 17.1

Context Menu Settings: IDs, Captions, and Prompts (Status Bar and Tooltips), and the New IDM_REVERSE_BLOCK_DIREC Entry

ID	Caption	Prompts
IDM_DELETE_ITEM	&Delete Item	Delete selected item\nDelete selected item
ID_EDIT_DELETE_GROUPED_ITEMS	Delete &Grouped Items	Delete items enclosed by rectangle\nDelete grouped items
IDM_FINE_MOVE_ITEM	&Fine Move Item	Fine movement of item\nFine movement of item
IDM_INSERT_BEND_POINT	&Insert Bend Point	Insert bend point\nInsert bend point
IDM_REVERSE_BLOCK_DIREC	**&Reverse Block**	**Reverse block direction\nReverse block direction**
IDM_SET_ITEM_PROPERTIES	&Set Properties	Set item properties\nSet item properties

```
// Print msg.
//sMsg.Format("\n CDiagramEngDoc::OnReverseBlockDirection(), point
  (x,y) = (%d,%d)\n", point.x, point.y);
//AfxMessageBox(sMsg, nType, nIDhelp);

// Get a copy of the blk_list in the system model
list<CBlock*> &blk_list = GetSystemModel().GetBlockList();
  // MUST BE A REFERENCE!

// -- ITERATE THROUGH THE BLOCK LIST TO FIND SELECTED BLOCK
for(it_blk = blk_list.begin(); it_blk != blk_list.end(); it_blk++)
{
    blk_posn = (*it_blk)->GetBlockPosition();
    width = (*it_blk)->GetBlockShape().GetBlockWidth();
    dist = sqrt(pow((blk_posn.x - point.x),2) +
      pow((blk_posn.y - point.y),2));
    if(dist <= 0.5*width*0.5)
    {
        (*it_blk)->ReverseBlockDirection();   // reverse block and all
          its properties
        SetModifiedFlag(TRUE);                 // set the doc. as
          modified to prompt the user to save
        UpdateAllViews(NULL);                  // redraw the doc if
          block direction changed
        break;  // exit the for loop
    }
}// end it_blk

// DiagramEng (end)
}
```

The OnReverseBlockDirection() function iterates through the list of blocks and compares the position of the block with that of the point "m_ptContextMenu" at which the Context menu was invoked; if it is sufficiently close, then ReverseBlockDirection() is called to reverse the direction of the block.

17.3   ADD A `ReverseBlockDirection()` FUNCTION TO THE CBlock CLASS

The `OnReverseBlockDirection()` function calls `ReverseBlockDirection()` on the pointer-to-CBlock, since all the properties that need to be altered relate to a Block object and its member data. Hence, add a public member function to the CBlock class with the prototype void CBlock::ReverseBlockDirection(void) and edit it as follows.

```
void CBlock::ReverseBlockDirection()
{
    double theta;                        // port position angle in degrees
      (not radians)
    vector<CPort*>::iterator it_port;    // iterator for ptr-to-CPort
    EBlockDirection e_blk_direc;         // block direc. (of local coord
      sys x-axis)
    EPortArrowDirection e_port_direc;    // port direc, i.e. direc in which
      arrow points.

    // -- CHANGE THE BLOCK'S DIRECTION
    e_blk_direc = GetBlockShape().GetBlockDirection();

    if(e_blk_direc == e_left)
    {
        GetBlockShape().SetBlockDirection(e_right);
    }
    else if(e_blk_direc == e_right)
    {
        GetBlockShape().SetBlockDirection(e_left);
    }

    // -- CHANGE BLOCK PORT DIRECTIONS AND POSITIONS
    // Input ports
    for(it_port = m_vecInputPorts.begin(); it_port != m_vecInputPorts.
      end(); it_port++)
    {
        // Change port arrow direction
        e_port_direc = (*it_port)->GetPortArrowDirection();
        if(e_port_direc == e_left_arrow)
        {
            (*it_port)->SetPortArrowDirection(e_right_arrow);
        }
        else if(e_port_direc == e_right_arrow)
        {
            (*it_port)->SetPortArrowDirection(e_left_arrow);
        }

        // Change port position angle and recalculate position
        theta = (*it_port)->GetPortPositionAngle();
        theta = 180.0 - theta;
        (*it_port)->SetPortPositionAngle(theta);
        (*it_port)->CalculatePortPosition();

        // Update any connection head end point associated with the
          port.
        m_pParentSystemModel->UpdateConnectionPointHead(*it_port);
          // deref the iterator to get the ptr-to-CPort obj.
    }
```

```
    // Output ports
    for(it_port = m_vecOutputPorts.begin(); it_port != m_vecOutputPorts.
      end(); it_port++)
    {
        // Change port arrow direction
        e_port_direc = (*it_port)->GetPortArrowDirection();
        if(e_port_direc == e_left_arrow)
        {
            (*it_port)->SetPortArrowDirection(e_right_arrow);
        }
        else if(e_port_direc == e_right_arrow)
        {
            (*it_port)->SetPortArrowDirection(e_left_arrow);
        }

        // Change port position angle and recalculate position
        theta = (*it_port)->GetPortPositionAngle();
        theta = 180.0 - theta;
        (*it_port)->SetPortPositionAngle(theta);
        (*it_port)->CalculatePortPosition();

        // Update any connection tail end point associated with the port.
        m_pParentSystemModel->UpdateConnectionPointTail(*it_port);
          // deref the iterator to get the ptr-to-CPort obj.
    }
}
```

The ReverseBlockDirection() function initially sets the enumerated type variable, "m_eBlockDirection", of the CBlockShape class, to be the opposite of its current state; i.e., the states "e_left" and "e_right" are switched to "e_right" and "e_left", respectively. Then the vectors of input and output ports are iterated over and the port arrow directions reversed, the port position angles and locations set, and any attached connection end points are updated to their associated new port positions.

17.4   ADD ACCESSOR METHODS TO THE CBlockShape CLASS

The ReverseBlockDirection() function needs to get and set the block direction through the methods GetBlockDirection() and SetBlockDirection(), respectively. Hence, add these two accessor methods to the CBlockShape class with the prototypes listed and edit them as follows.

1. EBlockDirection CBlockShape::GetBlockDirection(void) const
2. void CBlockShape::SetBlockDirection(EBlockDirection e_blk_direc)

```
EBlockDirection CBlockShape::GetBlockDirection() const
{
    return m_eBlockDirection;
}

void CBlockShape::SetBlockDirection(EBlockDirection e_blk_direc)
{
    // Assign member variable.
    m_eBlockDirection = e_blk_direc;
}
```

17.5 ADD ACCESSOR METHODS TO THE CPort CLASS

The direction of the port arrows needs to be obtained and then modified using the `GetPortArrowDirection()` and `SetPortArrowDirection()` functions, respectively. Since these functions relate to CPort objects, they need to be added to the CPort class: their declarations and definitions are as follows.

1. `EPortArrowDirection CPort::GetPortArrowDirection(void) const`
2. `void CPort::SetPortArrowDirection(EPortArrowDirection e_port_direc)`

```
EPortArrowDirection CPort::GetPortArrowDirection() const
{
    return m_ePortArrowDirec;
}
void CPort::SetPortArrowDirection(EPortArrowDirection arrow_direc)
{
    m_ePortArrowDirec = arrow_direc;
}
```

17.6 TEST THE APPLICATION

Now the application may be built and run: the user can place blocks on the palette and attach connections to the ports and then reverse the block direction such that the connections remain attached to their corresponding ports, as shown in Figure 17.1. Then, upon using the Divide and Sum block dialog windows, DivideBlockDialog and SumBlockDialog, respectively, for parameter input, the ports are reset to their default right-facing directions.

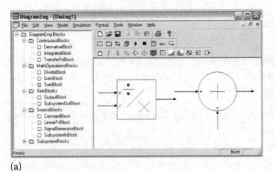

(a)

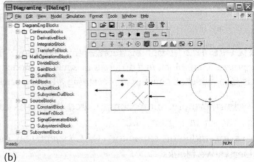

(b)

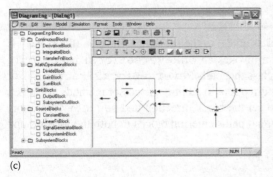

(c)

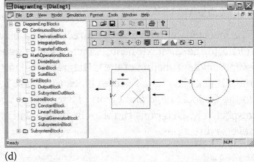

(d)

FIGURE 17.1 Reversing block direction: (a) connections attached in the feed-forward direction, (b) blocks reversed with connections attached to corresponding ports, (c) detachment of connections showing correct port arrow directions, and (d) default block-dialog-based port resetting.

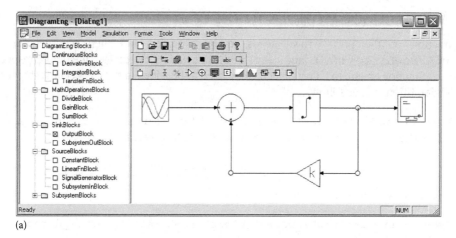

(a)

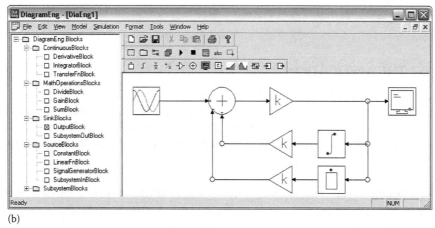

(b)

FIGURE 17.2 Diagrams representing equations modeling physical systems using block reversal: (a) a reversed Gain block in a differential equation model and (b) reversed Gain, Integrator, and Derivative blocks used to model an equation representing a RLC electrical circuit.

Furthermore, more complicated diagrams may be drawn using the reversed block directions, as shown in Figure 17.2: (a) a differential equation model using a reversed Gain block and (b) a resistor–inductor–capacitor (RLC) electrical circuit model using reversed Gain, Integrator, and Derivative blocks.

17.7 SUMMARY

The mechanism to reverse the direction of a block is added to the project. A Reverse Block entry is added to the Context menu, which upon selection invokes an `OnReverseBlockDirection()` event-handler function of the CDiagramEngDoc class that calls `ReverseBlockDirection()` of the CBlock class for a selected block to reverse its direction. In addition, accessor methods are added to the CBlockShape and CPort classes to get and set the block direction and port arrow direction, respectively. Diagrams can then be drawn with signal paths entering blocks in both the forward and reverse directions.

Part II

Model Computation and Data

INTRODUCTION

Part II consists of Chapters 18 through 25 and provides detailed instructions to implement diagram-based modeling and computation functionality. Model validation is explored to determine the type of diagram drawn, i.e., whether it contains feedback/algebraic loops: if a feedback loop is not present, then a non-feedback-based connection-centric signal propagation method is pursued, including block-based data operations to compute the model. However, if one or more feedback loops do exist, then a general Newton-method-based nonlinear equation solver is used to compute the system model, where the feedback or algebraic loops denote a set of simultaneous equations. Six key examples from the domains of mechanical engineering and nonlinear dynamics are explored and the graphical output presented may be used to confirm the underlying physics of the problems studied. In addition, serialization is implemented to allow the user to save and restore system model data and graphical output data for future use.

18 Model Validation

18.1 INTRODUCTION

A diagram model is a pictorial representation of a system of equations used to model a real-world system. The blocks represent source-signal generators, mathematical operations, subsystems, and computed output and are connected by connections that propagate signals, i.e., data values, from one block to the next. Mathematical operation blocks operate on input signal values, which then result in the generation of an output signal to be conveyed along the output connection to another block. In order to execute a model drawn on the palette, it first must be validated: this involves checking the model and its connectivity to allow the propagating of signals along connections linking the model blocks together.

18.2 VALIDATING A MODEL

Model validation involves performing checks to ensure that the model is structured properly, where any problems are highlighted to the user prior to an attempt to execute the model. The following validation actions are required:

1. Validation of model blocks—determines whether essential blocks have been placed on the palette to allow for proper model computation
2. Validation of block ports—identifies any disconnected ports that should either have connections attached or be deleted
3. Validation of connectivity—determines whether connection objects are connected to input and output ports or to connection bend points

To add the model validation functionality, edit the existing `CDiagramEngDoc::OnModelBuild()` function to call `ValidateModel()` upon the CSytemModel object, "m_SystemModel", as shown in the following.

```
void CDiagramEngDoc::OnModelBuild()
{
    // TODO: Add your command handler code here

    // DiagramEng (start)
    CString sMsg;      // string to be displayed
    UINT nType = MB_OK; // style of msg. box
    UINT nIDhelp = 0;  // help context ID for the msg.

    // Display a msg. box
    sMsg.Format("\n CDiagramEngDoc::OnModelBuild()\n\n");
    //AfxMessageBox(sMsg, nType, nIDhelp);

    // -- MODEL VALIDATION
    m_SystemModel.ValidateModel();

    // DiagramEng (end)
}
```

The `ValidateModel()` function should be added to the CSystemModel class, so too the functions that this member calls to perform all the necessary model validation. Hence, add the following functions to the CSystemModel class with the prototypes as indicated and edit the code as shown in the following sections.

1. void CSystemModel::ValidateModel(void)
2. int CSystemModel::ValidateModelBlocks(void)
3. int CSystemModel::ValidateModelBlockPorts(void)
4. int CSystemModel::ValidateModelConnections(void)

```cpp
void CSystemModel::ValidateModel()
{
    int i;
    int error1 = 0;           // error in model blocks: (0) no error,
      (1) error
    int error2 = 0;           // error in model ports: (0) no error,
      (1) error
    int error3 = 0;           // error in mode connections: (0) no error,
      (1) error
    int n_flashes = 3;       // no. of times red flashes after black
    int n_its;               // no. of loop iterations as a fn of n_flashes
    BOOL bkgd_erase = TRUE;  // specifies whether the background is to be
      erased
    CString sMsg;            // string to be displayed
    CString sMsgTemp;        // temp string
    DWORD nMilliSec = 200;   // 32 bit unsigned integer: no. of milliseconds
    UINT nType = MB_OK;      // style of msg. box
    UINT nIDhelp = 0;        // help context ID for the msg
    CDiagramEngDoc *pDoc = GetDocumentGlobalFn(); // declare pDoc to be a
      ptr to CDiagramEngDoc.

    // -- VALIDATE SYSTEM MODEL
    error1 = ValidateModelBlocks();
    error2 = ValidateModelBlockPorts();
    error3 = ValidateModelConnections();

    // -- INFORM USER OF END OF BUILD MODEL STAGE
    if((error1 == 1) || (error2 == 1) || (error3 == 1))
    {
        sMsgTemp.Format("\n WARNING!: Build model process ending. \n");
        sMsg += sMsgTemp;
        sMsgTemp.Format("\n Please take note of errors flashing in red. \n");
        sMsg += sMsgTemp;
        AfxMessageBox(sMsg, nType, nIDhelp);

        // -- FLASH MODEL BUILD ERRORS
        n_its = n_flashes*2 + 1;

        for(i=1; i<n_its; i++)
        {
            if(i%2 == 1)
            {
                SetModelStatusFlag(0); // results in ModelErrorPenColor()
                  leaving pen_color unchanged: black by default.
            }
            else if(i%2 == 0)
```

```
        {
            SetModelStatusFlag(1); // results in ModelErrorPenColor()
            setting pen_color to red.
        }
        // Get the position of the first view in the list of views
        //  for the current doc.
        POSITION posn = pDoc->GetFirstViewPosition();

        // Get a pointer to the view identified by posn.
        CView *pView = pDoc->GetNextView(posn);

        // Invalidate the entire client area of CWnd using the pView
        //  pointer-to-CView.
        pView->Invalidate(bkgd_erase);

        // Update the client by sending a WM_PAINT msg. if the update
        //  region is not empty.
        pView->UpdateWindow();

        // Suspend execution of the current thread for no. of
        //  milliseconds specified.
        Sleep(nMilliSec);

    }// end for
}
else
{
    sMsg.Format("\n No build errors. \n");
    AfxMessageBox(sMsg, nType, nIDhelp);
}
// -- CLEAR CONNECTIONS IN ERROR
m_lstConnectionError.clear(); // Note: if this is not cleared, then
  grouped item deletion will result in a crash.

// -- RESET MODEL STATUS AND REDRAW
SetModelStatusFlag(0);
pDoc->SetModifiedFlag(TRUE); // prompt the user to save
pDoc->UpdateAllViews(NULL);  // this fn calls OnDraw to redraw the
  system model.
}
```

The `ValidateModel()` function simply calls the other validation functions to check that model blocks, ports, and connections are in order. If the error values returned equal "0," then there are no validation errors in the system model, and the execution continues to the `SetModelStatusFlag()` call, which sets a model status flag to "0" indicating that no model errors need to be highlighted and that the validation stage is complete (see the following text for further details concerning the model status flag). If the model is in error, then this flag is set to "1" in `ValidateModelBlockPorts()` and `ValidateModelConnections()`, indicating that there are connectivity errors that are subsequently drawn in red (see `ModelErrorPenColor()` below).*

The purpose of the *for* loop in the `ValidateModel()` function is to repeatedly switch the model status flag on and off, resulting in a flashing of the errors from black to red on the screen, i.e., on the CView object. The pointer-to-CDiagramEngDoc, "pDoc", is used to get the position of the first View, and this position is used to get a pointer-to-CView, upon which `Invalidate()` and `UpdateWindow()` may be called, to redraw the system model via automatic invocation of the `DrawSystemModel()` function: this allows the View to be updated sufficiently fast such that the flashing effect may be observed.

---

* The developer will actually see the color changes when running the DiagramEng application: however, the red color in the figures is discernable as a lighter shade of grey than the black color.

Now the aforementioned model status-related members need to be added to the CSystemModel class. Hence, add a private integer member variable, named "m_iModelStatusFlag", to the CSystemModel class to record the status of the model and initialize this variable to "0" in the CSystemModel constructor as shown in bold in the following.

```
CSystemModel::CSystemModel(void)
{
    // Init.
    m_strModelName = "system_model";

    // Time parameters
    m_dTimeStart = 0.0;
    m_dTimeStop = 1.0;
    m_dTimeStepSize = 0.1;
    m_strTimeStepType = "Fixed-step";

    // Integration parameters
    m_dATOL = 0.0001;
    m_dRTOL = 0.0001;
    m_strIntegrationMethod = "Runge-Kutta (4th Order)";
    m_strWarning = "OK";
    m_iModelStatusFlag = 0;
}
```

Now add two accessor methods to retrieve and set the value of the "m_iModelStatusFlag" member variable with the declarations and definitions shown:

1. int CSystemModel::GetModelStatusFlag(void) const
2. void CSystemModel::SetModelStatusFlag(int model_status)

```
int CSystemModel::GetModelStatusFlag() const
{
    return m_iModelStatusFlag;
}
void CSystemModel::SetModelStatusFlag(int model_status)
{
    m_iModelStatusFlag = model_status;
}
```

18.2.1 VALIDATE MODEL BLOCKS

The first function called by ValidateModel() is ValidateModelBlocks() (shown in the following), which iterates through the block list to determine the number of source and sink blocks in the model: if there are none present, then a message is shown, and a Linear Function source block and a Output sink block are added automatically (see Figure 18.1). The user may not want the Linear Function block but prefer a Constant or Signal Generator source block: the block provided is just an example of a source block that should be added by the user to generate a source signal.

```
int CSystemModel::ValidateModelBlocks()
{
    int error = 0;          // error in model
    int n_source = 0;       // no. of model source blocks
    int n_output = 0;       // no. of model output blocks
    CString blk_name;       // blk name
    CString sMsg;           // string to be displayed
    CString sMsgTemp;       // temp msg.
```

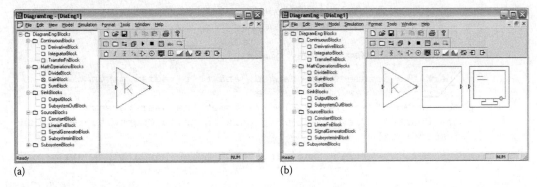

(a)   (b)

FIGURE 18.1   Validation of model blocks: (a) the original model without a source or sink block and (b) the automatic addition of a Linear Function source block and an Output sink block.

```
UINT nType = MB_OK;      // style of msg. box
UINT nIDhelp = 0;        // help context ID for the msg.
CDiagramEngDoc *pDoc = GetDocumentGlobalFn(); // declare pDoc to be a
  ptr to CDiagramEngDoc.
list<CBlock*>::iterator it_blk;

// Check the number of source blocks and output blocks in the
  model.
for(it_blk = m_lstBlock.begin(); it_blk != m_lstBlock.end();
  it_blk++)
{
    blk_name = (*it_blk)->GetBlockName();
    if((blk_name == "constant_block") || (blk_name ==
      "linear_fn_block") || (blk_name == "signal_generator_block"))
    {
        n_source++;
    }

    if(blk_name == "output_block")
    {
        n_output++;
    }
}

if((n_source == 0) || (n_output == 0))
{
    // Print msg with variable value.
    sMsgTemp.Format("\n WARNING!: Block error. \n");
    sMsg += sMsgTemp;

    if(n_source == 0)
    {
        sMsgTemp.Format("\n At least 1 Source block should be
          present: inserting automatically.");
        sMsg += sMsgTemp;
        pDoc->ConstructLinearFnBlock(); // automatically insert a
          LinearFn block (as an example)
    }
    if(n_output == 0)
    {
        sMsgTemp.Format("\n At least 1 Output block should be
          present: inserting automatically. \n");
        sMsg += sMsgTemp;
```

```
        pDoc->ConstructOutputBlock();    // automatically insert an
          Output block (as an example)
    }
    AfxMessageBox(sMsg, nType, nIDhelp); // msg. box

    // Mark the document as changed, and then redraw given the
      insertion of new blocks above.
    pDoc->SetModifiedFlag(TRUE); // prompt the user to save
    pDoc->UpdateAllViews(NULL); // this fn calls OnDraw to redraw the
      system model.
    error = 1;    // flag indicates that model has a block error
  }
  return error;

}
```

18.2.2 Validate Model Block Ports

The next function called by the `ValidateModel()` method is `ValidateModelBlockPorts()` as shown in the following. This function iterates through each block's vector of input and output ports and determines whether a connection is attached, and if not, a counter is incremented to record the total number of disconnected input and output ports, which is then displayed in a message to the user. In addition, the model status flag, "m_iModelStatusFlag", is set to "1," indicating that model validation is in progress and that an error occurred; in this case, a disconnected port was found.

```
int CSystemModel::ValidateModelBlockPorts()
{
    int error = 0;         // error in model
    int n_in_dc = 0;       // no. of disconnected inputs
    int n_out_dc = 0;      // no. of disconnected outputs
    int port_connected;    // port connection status (0) disconnected,
      (1) connected
    int print_msg = 1;     // print msg. flag
    CString sMsg;          // string to be displayed
    CString sMsgTemp;      // temp msg.
    UINT nType = MB_OK;    // style of msg. box
    UINT nIDhelp = 0;      // help context ID for the msg.
    list<CBlock*>::iterator it_blk;           // block iterator
    list<CConnection*>::iterator it_con;      // connection iterator
    vector<CPort*>::iterator it_port;         // port iterator
    CDiagramEngDoc *pDoc = GetDocumentGlobalFn(); // declare pDoc to be a
      ptr to CDiagramEngDoc.
    // -- ITERATE THROUGH BLOCK LIST
    for(it_blk = m_lstBlock.begin(); it_blk != m_lstBlock.end(); it_blk++)
    {
        // Get vecs of input and output ports
        vector<CPort*> vec_input_ports = (*it_blk)->GetVectorOfInputPorts();
        vector<CPort*> vec_output_ports = (*it_blk)->GetVectorOfOutputPorts();

        // -- CHECK CONNECTIVITY OF INPUT PORTS
        for(it_port = vec_input_ports.begin(); it_port !=
          vec_input_ports.end(); it_port++)
        {
            port_connected = 0;

            for(it_con = m_lstConnection.begin(); it_con
              != m_lstConnection.end(); it_con++)
```

```
            {
                if((*it_port) == (*it_con)->GetRefToPort())
                {
                    port_connected = 1;
                    break;
                }
            }
            if(port_connected == 0)
            {
                error = 1;       // flag indicates that model has a block
                  port error
                n_in_dc++;       // increment the no. of disconnected
                  inputs
            }
        }// end port

        // -- CHECK CONNECTIVITY OF OUTPUT PORTS
        for(it_port = vec_output_ports.begin(); it_port !=
          vec_output_ports.end(); it_port++)
        {
            port_connected = 0;

            for(it_con = m_lstConnection.begin(); it_con
              != m_lstConnection.end(); it_con++)
            {
                if((*it_port) == (*it_con)->GetRefFromPort())
                {
                    port_connected = 1;
                    break;
                }
            }
            if(port_connected == 0)
            {
                error = 1;       // flag indicates that model has a block
                  port error
                n_out_dc++;      // increment the no. of disconnected
                  outputs
            }
        }// end port
    }// end block

// -- SET THE MODEL STATUS FLAG AND REDRAW DOC
if(error == 1)
{
    SetModelStatusFlag(error);    // model status flag = 1, => a port
      disconnection error
    pDoc->SetModifiedFlag(TRUE); // prompt the user to save
    pDoc->UpdateAllViews(NULL);   // this fn calls OnDraw to redraw
      the system model.
}

// -- PRINT ERROR MSG.
if((error == 1) && (print_msg == 1))
{
    sMsgTemp.Format("\n WARNING!: Block port error.\n");
    sMsg += sMsgTemp;
    if(n_in_dc > 0)
```

```
        {
            sMsgTemp.Format("\n Total no. of disconnected input ports =
              %d. ", n_in_dc);
            sMsg += sMsgTemp;
        }
        if(n_out_dc > 0)
        {
            sMsgTemp.Format("\n Total no. of disconnected output ports =
              %d.", n_out_dc);
            sMsg += sMsgTemp;
        }
        AfxMessageBox(sMsg, nType, nIDhelp);
    }

    return error;
}
```

Finally, if there is a port that is not connected, i.e., if there is an error, then the `SetModifiedFlag()` and `UpdateAllViews()` functions should be called to redraw the model: this is required since the drawing of disconnected ports is done with a red pen color (`RGB(255,0,0)`) in the validation stage; otherwise, the pen color is black (`RGB(0,0,0)`).

To draw in the correct pen color at the model-validating stage, a new function is required that sets the pen color to red if the model is in error. Hence, add a public member function to the CSystemModel class with the prototype, `void CSystemModel::ModelErrorPenColor(int *pen_color)`, and edit it as shown in the following (note how the address of the "pen_color" variable should be passed into this function).

```
void CSystemModel::ModelErrorPenColor(int *pen_color)
{
    // Note: incoming argument &pen_color passed

    // If the model build resulted in an error
    if(m_iModelStatusFlag == 1)
    {
        *pen_color = RGB(255,0,0);   // White = RGB(255,255,255),
          Black = RGB(0,0,0)
    }
}
```

Now amend the existing `DrawPort()` function by calling the `ModelErrorPenColor()` method passing the address of the "pen_color" variable. If the model is in error at the model-validating stage, the returned color will be red (RGB(255,0,0)). The developer will notice that the call to `ModelErrorPenColor()` is made upon the pointer-to-CSystemModel object, "m_pParentSystemModel", which is the address of the parent system model to which the current block belongs. In addition, the block upon which the port resides may be obtained from the reference-to-CBlock variable, "m_rRefToBlock", a member of CPort. Hence, the call, "`m_rRefToBlock.GetParentSystemModel()->ModelErrorPenColor(&pen_color)`" may be made to set the correct pen color.

```
void CPort::DrawPort(CDC *pDC)
{
    int i;
    int brush_color;       // local brush color
    int model_status = 0;  // model status flag
    int pen_color;         // local pen color
    int pen_width;         // local pen width
```

```
int shift_left = 0;    // shift left arrow port graphic
int shift_up = 0;      // shift up arrow port graphic
int shift_right = 0;   // shift right arrow port graphic
int shift_down = 0;    // shift down arrow port graphic
double d;              // half the length of the longest port
  triangle side
double width;          // block width
CPoint pt_array[3];    // array of pts to draw the port graphic
CString sMsg;          // main msg string
UINT nType = MB_OK;    // style of msg. box
UINT nIDhelp = 0;      // help context ID for the msg.

// Msg. box
sMsg.Format("\n CPort::DrawPort(), m_ePortArrowDirec = %d\n",
  m_ePortArrowDirec);
//AfxMessageBox(sMsg, nType, nIDhelp);

// Get block width using the m_rRefToBlock
width = m_rRefToBlock.GetBlockShape().GetBlockWidth();
d = 0.05*width;  // d as a percentage of block width

// Switch on EPortArrowDirection m_ePortArrowDirec
switch(m_ePortArrowDirec)
{
case e_left_arrow:
    pt_array[0].x = m_ptPortPosition.x + 0.5*d;
    pt_array[0].y = m_ptPortPosition.y + d;
    pt_array[1].x = m_ptPortPosition.x - 0.5*d;
    pt_array[1].y = m_ptPortPosition.y;
    pt_array[2].x = pt_array[0].x;
    pt_array[2].y = m_ptPortPosition.y - d;

    // Shift pts as desired
    if(shift_left)
    {
        for(i=0;i<3;i++)
        {
            pt_array[i].x = pt_array[i].x - 0.5*d;
        }
    }
    break;

case e_up_arrow:
    pt_array[0].x = m_ptPortPosition.x - d;
    pt_array[0].y = m_ptPortPosition.y + 0.5*d;
    pt_array[1].x = m_ptPortPosition.x;
    pt_array[1].y = m_ptPortPosition.y - 0.5*d;
    pt_array[2].x = m_ptPortPosition.x + d;
    pt_array[2].y = pt_array[0].y;

    // Shift pts as desired
    if(shift_up)
    {
        for(i=0;i<3;i++)
        {
            pt_array[i].y = pt_array[i].y + 0.5*d;
        }
    }
    break;
```

```
case e_right_arrow:
    pt_array[0].x = m_ptPortPosition.x - 0.5*d;
    pt_array[0].y = m_ptPortPosition.y - d;
    pt_array[1].x = m_ptPortPosition.x + 0.5*d;
    pt_array[1].y = m_ptPortPosition.y;
    pt_array[2].x = pt_array[0].x;
    pt_array[2].y = m_ptPortPosition.y + d;

    // Shift pts as desired
    if(shift_right)
    {
        for(i=0;i<3;i++)
        {
            pt_array[i].x = pt_array[i].x + 0.5*d;
        }
    }
    break;
case e_down_arrow:
    pt_array[0].x = m_ptPortPosition.x + d;
    pt_array[0].y = m_ptPortPosition.y - 0.5*d;
    pt_array[1].x = m_ptPortPosition.x;
    pt_array[1].y = m_ptPortPosition.y + 0.5*d;
    pt_array[2].x = m_ptPortPosition.x - d;
    pt_array[2].y = pt_array[0].y;

    // Shift pts as desired
    if(shift_down)
    {
        for(i=0;i<3;i++)
        {
            pt_array[i].y = pt_array[i].y - 0.5*d;
        }
    }
    break;
default:
    // Use e_right_arrow case
    pt_array[0].x = m_ptPortPosition.x - 0.5*d;
    pt_array[0].y = m_ptPortPosition.y - d;
    pt_array[1].x = m_ptPortPosition.x + 0.5*d;
    pt_array[1].y = m_ptPortPosition.y;
    pt_array[2].x = m_ptPortPosition.x - 0.5*d;
    pt_array[2].y = m_ptPortPosition.y + d;

    // Shift pts as desired
    if(shift_right)
    {
        for(i=0;i<3;i++)
        {
            pt_array[i].x = pt_array[i].x + 0.5*d;
        }
    }
    break;
}// end switch

// -- FILL THE TRIANGULAR PORT POLYGON
// Create a brush
brush_color = RGB(200,200,200); // White = RGB(255,255,255),
  Black = RGB(0,0,0)
```

```
CBrush NewBrush(brush_color); // create a new brush using the
  brush_color
CBrush *pBrush;       // declare a ptr-to-CBrush (for resetting below)

// Select the new brush
pBrush = pDC->SelectObject(&NewBrush);

// Fill the polygon
pDC->Polygon(pt_array, 3);  // 3 vertices of triangle stored in
  pt_array enclose polygon region

// Reset the old brush
pDC->SelectObject(pBrush);

// -- DRAW THE BORDER OF THE TRIANGULAR PORT POLYGON
// Set a new pen color for the border only
pen_color = RGB(0,0,0);       // White = RGB(255,255,255),
  Black = RGB(0,0,0)
m_rRefToBlock.GetParentSystemModel()->ModelErrorPenColor(&pen_color);
  // change the pen color if model is in error
pen_width = 1;

// Create the pen
CPen lpen(PS_SOLID, pen_width, pen_color);

// Select the pen as the drawing obj.
// The value returned by SelectObject() is a ptr to the obj. being
  replaced, i.e. an old-pen-ptr.
CPen *pOldPen = pDC->SelectObject(&lpen);

// Draw the arrow/triangle (clockwise)
pDC->MoveTo(pt_array[0]);
pDC->LineTo(pt_array[1]);
pDC->LineTo(pt_array[2]);
pDC->LineTo(pt_array[0]);

// Reset the prev. pen
pDC->SelectObject(pOldPen);
}
```

Now upon running the program, if block ports are not connected by connections then these are displayed in red. The developer will be able to see this clearly on the screen: the ports of Figure 18.2(b) are slightly lighter in shade than those of Figure 18.2(a).

18.2.3 VALIDATE MODEL CONNECTIONS

The third call made from within ValidateModel() is ValidateModelConnections(): this function checks all connections in the model and indicates whether they are disconnected. A connection's head point should be connected to an input port and its tail point should be connected to either an output port or another connection's bend point. Hence, edit the ValidateModelConnections() function as shown in the following. (Note that there already exists a ValidateConnectivity() placeholder function in the CSystemModel class that exists from the Win32 Console Application stage: this is replaced here by the ValidateModelConnections() function.)

```
int CSystemModel::ValidateModelConnections()
{
    int error = 0;              // error in model
    int n_discon = 0;           // no. of disconnected connections
    int head_connected = 0;     // head connection status (0)
      disconnected, (1) connected
```

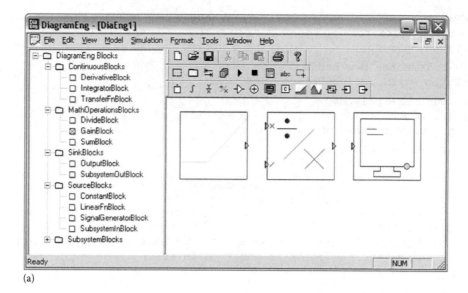

(a)

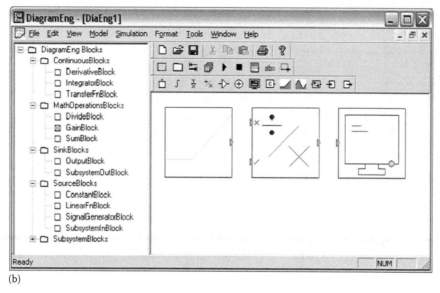

(b)

FIGURE 18.2 Validation of block ports: (a) disconnected blocks in the drawing stage prior to validating the model, and (b) upon validating the model, ports of disconnected blocks shown in a lighter shade (red, when running the program).

```
int print_msg = 1;            // print msg. flag
int tail_connected = 0;       // tail connection status
  (0) disconnected, (1) connected
CPoint tail_pt;               // connection tail point
CPort *from_port = NULL;      // port from which connection
  emanates
CPort *to_port = NULL;        // port to which connection is
  connected
CString sMsg;                 // string to be displayed
CString sMsgTemp;             // temp msg.
UINT nType = MB_OK;           // style of msg. box
UINT nIDhelp = 0;             // help context ID for the msg.
```

```
list<CBlock*>::iterator it_blk;          // block iterator
list<CConnection*>::iterator it_con;   // connection iterator
list<CConnection*>::iterator it_con2; // connection iterator of
  nested loop
list<CPoint>::iterator it_pt;            // point iterator
vector<CPort*>::iterator it_port;        // port iterator
CDiagramEngDoc *pDoc = GetDocumentGlobalFn(); // declare pDoc to be a
  ptr to CDiagramEngDoc.

// -- CLEAR CONNECTION LIST THAT RECORDS ERRORS, BUT DON'T DELETE
  WHAT THE CONTAINED POINTERS POINT AT.
m_lstConnectionError.clear();

// -- ITERATE THROUGH ALL CONNECTIONS
for(it_con = m_lstConnection.begin(); it_con != m_lstConnection.
  end(); it_con++)
{
    // Init. the connected state, for the current connection,
      to disconnected.
    head_connected = 0;
    tail_connected = 0;

    // Get connection reference from and to ports
    from_port = (*it_con)->GetRefFromPort();
    to_port = (*it_con)->GetRefToPort();

    // -- ITERATE THROUGH ALL BLOCKS
    for(it_blk = m_lstBlock.begin(); it_blk != m_lstBlock.end();
      it_blk++)
    {
        // Get vector of input and output ports
        vector<CPort*> vec_input_ports = (*it_blk)-
          >GetVectorOfInputPorts();
        vector<CPort*> vec_output_ports = (*it_blk)-
          >GetVectorOfOutputPorts();

        // -- ITERATE THROUGH VECTORS OF PORTS
        for(it_port = vec_input_ports.begin(); it_port
          != vec_input_ports.end(); it_port++)
        {
            if(to_port == (*it_port))
            {
                head_connected = 1;
                break;            // break from it_port
            }
        }// end it_port

        for(it_port = vec_output_ports.begin(); it_port
          != vec_output_ports.end(); it_port++)
        {
            if(from_port == (*it_port))
            {
                tail_connected = 1;
                break; // break from it_port
            }
        }// end it_port

        if((head_connected == 1) && (tail_connected == 1))
```

```
            {
                break; // break from it_blk
            }
        }// end it_blk

        // -- CHECK THAT THE CONNECTION TAIL POINT IS CONNECTED TO
          ANOTHER CONNECTION'S BEND POINT
        tail_pt = (*it_con)->GetConnectionPointTail();
          // current connection's tail point

        for(it_con2 = m_lstConnection.begin(); it_con2
          != m_lstConnection.end(); it_con2++)
        {
            // Other connection's bend points list
            list<CPoint> &bend_pts_list = (*it_con2)-
              >GetConnectionBendPointsList();

            for(it_pt = bend_pts_list.begin(); it_pt != bend_pts_list.
              end(); it_pt++)
            {
                if(tail_pt == *it_pt)  // if primary connection's tail
                  point is on another connection's bend point
                {
                    tail_connected = 1;
                    break;  // break from it_pt
                }
            }// end it_pt

            if(tail_connected == 1)
            {
                break;  // break from NESTED it_con2
            }
        }// end it_con (nested)

        // -- IF CONNECTION DISCONNECTED, ADD IT TO THE ERROR LIST
        if((head_connected == 0) || (tail_connected == 0))
        {
            // Set error flag, cnt, and record
            error = 1;
            n_discon++;
            m_lstConnectionError.push_back(*it_con);
        }
    }// end it_con

    // -- SET THE MODEL STATUS FLAG AND REDRAW DOC
    if(error == 1)
    {
        // Mark the document as changed, and then redraw.
        SetModelStatusFlag(1); // model status flag = 1, => a port
          disconnection error
        pDoc->SetModifiedFlag(TRUE); // prompt the user to save
        pDoc->UpdateAllViews(NULL);  // this fn calls OnDraw to redraw
          the system model.
    }

    // -- PRINT ERROR MSG.
    if((print_msg == 1) && (n_discon > 0))
    {
        sMsgTemp.Format("\n WARNING!: Connection error.\n");
```

```
        sMsg += sMsgTemp;
        sMsgTemp.Format("\n Total no. of disconnected connections = %d.",
          n_discon);
        sMsg += sMsgTemp;
        AfxMessageBox(sMsg, nType, nIDhelp);
    }

    return error;
}
```

The developer will notice that a list of "connections in error", i.e., "m_lstConnectionError", is used: this is a list of pointers-to-CConnection and records those connections that are currently in a disconnected state. Hence, add a private member variable to the CSystemModel class to record the disconnected connections of type, "list<CConnection*>" with name, "m_lstConnectionError". Add a public accessor function to the CSystemModel class to get the connection list by reference, with the prototype: list<CConnection*> &GetConnectionListError(void), and edit the function as shown in the following.

```
list<CConnection*> &CSystemModel::GetConnectionListError()
{
    // Return the connection list by reference
    return m_lstConnectionError;
}
```

The developer will also note that this error-recording connection list is cleared by the call "m_lstConnectionError.clear()", upon each entry to the function and also at the end of the model validating stage in the ValidateModel() function. This is necessary since, for each validation of the model, the list should only record disconnected connections. Note also that "delete *it_con" followed by "m_lstConnectionError.erase(it_con)" is not performed to clear the list since doing so would delete the actual connection objects of the system model. In addition, if clear() is not called at the end of the model validating stage, and if a previously disconnected connection were to be deleted from the model diagram by the user, then the "m_lstConnectionError" would hold a pointer to a Connection object that would no longer exist and the program would crash. Hence, the list, "m_lstConnectionError", must be promptly cleared at the end of the model validating stage.

Now, the disconnected connections, i.e., the "connections in error" recorded in the list "m_lstConnectionError", need to be drawn in red for easy identification by the user. Various changes need to be made to the program that affect existing functions and are introduced in the following sections.

18.3   CHANGES TO BE MADE TO DRAW IN THE CORRECT COLOR

The color that is used to draw connections was originally set in the particular drawing functions themselves, i.e., DrawConnection() and DrawArrowHead() using the familiar code shown in the following.

```
// Create the pen
CPen lpen(PS_SOLID, pen_width, pen_color);

// Select the pen as the drawing obj.
// The value returned by SelectObject() is a ptr to the obj. being
replaced, i.e. an old-pen-ptr.
CPen *pOldPen = pDC->SelectObject(&lpen);
```

Now, this setting up of the pen's attributes, i.e., the style, width, and color, should be performed in the DrawSystemModel() function, higher up in the function call tree, rather than in the various functions that are called by DrawSystemModel(). Then, depending upon what is to be drawn, e.g., a connected connection as opposed to a disconnected connection, the pen's attributes may be changed and the pointer-to-class-device-context, "pDC", will then reflect those changes. Hence, the following general changes need to be made, where specific details are provided in the sections that follow:

1. Modify the CSystemModel::DrawSystemModel() function to set up the correct pen.
2. Modify the CConnection::DrawConnection() function given the changes made in the DrawSystemModel() function.
3. Modify the CConnection::DrawArrowHead() function to extract the pen color from the pointer-to-CDC, "pDC".

18.3.1 MODIFY THE **CSystemModel::DrawSystemModel()** FUNCTION

Modify the CSystemModel::DrawSystemModel() function by introducing local variables and create the pen as shown in the following code, being sure to reset the previous pen at the end of the function. In addition, a new for loop is required to iterate over the "connections in error", i.e., the disconnected connections recorded in the list, "m_lstConnectionError". A second pen is created prior to this loop, with the value of "pen_color" to be that set in the ModelErrorPenColor() function, i.e., red, since this is the model validating stage and a connection error is being reported.

```
void CSystemModel::DrawSystemModel(CDC *pDC)
{
    // Iterates through the SystemModel lists drawing the stored
       entities.
    int pen_color = RGB(0,0,0); // White = RGB(255,255,255),
       Black = RGB(0,0,0)
    int pen_width = 1;          // thin = 1
    CString sMsg;               // main msg string
    UINT nType = MB_OK;         // style of msg. box
    UINT nIDhelp = 0;           // help context ID for the msg.

    // -- SET UP THE PEN AND pDC
    // Create the pen
    CPen lpen(PS_SOLID, pen_width, pen_color);

    // Select the pen as the drawing obj.
    // The value returned by SelectObject() is a ptr to the obj. being
       replaced, i.e. an old-pen-ptr.
    CPen *pOldPen = pDC->SelectObject(&lpen);

    // -- DRAW BLOCKS
    list<CBlock*>::iterator it_blk; // local iterator
    list<CBlock*> blk_list;         // local block list

    blk_list = GetBlockList();

    // Check size of block list
    //sMsg.Format("\n CSystemModel::DrawSystemModel(), size = %d\n",
       blk_list.size());
    //AfxMessageBox(sMsg, nType, nIDhelp);
```

```
    // Iterate through the list
    for(it_blk = blk_list.begin(); it_blk != blk_list.end(); it_blk++)
    {
        (*it_blk)->DrawBlock(pDC);   // DrawBlock() called on the
            ptr-to-CBlock
    }
    // -- DRAW CONNECTIONS
    list<CConnection*>::iterator it_con;   // local iterator
    list<CConnection*> con_list;           // local connection list
    list<CConnection*> con_list_e;         // local connection list in
        error (disconnected connections)

    con_list = GetConnectionList();
    con_list_e = GetConnectionListError();

    // Iterate through the connection list
    for(it_con = con_list.begin(); it_con != con_list.end(); it_con++)
    {
        (*it_con)->DrawConnection(pDC);
    }

    // Prepare the device context for the disconnected connections.
    ModelErrorPenColor(&pen_color);
    CPen lpen2(PS_SOLID, pen_width, pen_color);
    pDC->SelectObject(&lpen2);

    // Iterate through the connection list in error (i.e. disconnected
        connections)
    for(it_con = con_list_e.begin(); it_con != con_list_e.end(); it_con++)
    {
        (*it_con)->DrawConnection(pDC);
    }
    // -- RESET THE PREV. PEN
    pDC->SelectObject(pOldPen);
}
```

18.3.2 Modify the CConnection::DrawConnection() Function

Now that the DrawSystemModel() function sets up the pen and the pointer-to-CDC, "pDC", is being passed into the DrawConnection() function, then the redundant pen setup in the latter function may be removed, as shown in the following. This is substantially more elegant than before, and depending on what type of connection is to be drawn, i.e., connected or disconnected, it will appear in the correct color: black or red, respectively.

```
void CConnection::DrawConnection(CDC *pDC)
{
    double dDeltaLength;        // std default reference delta length
    double length;             // length of side of rectangle bounding
        ellipse
    CPoint bend_pt;            // temp pt. to hold bend pt.
    CPoint bottom_right;       // bottom right cnr. coord. of rectangle
        bounding ellipse
    CPoint final_pt = m_ptTail; // init as tail pt. in case there are no
        bend pts.
    CPoint top_left;           // top left cnr. coord. of rectangle
        bounding ellipse
    list<CPoint>::iterator it_pt;
```

```
// Set length
dDeltaLength = GetDocumentGlobalFn()->GetDeltaLength();
length = 0.2*dDeltaLength;

// Move to the tail pt.
pDC->MoveTo(m_ptTail);

// Iterate through the bend pts. drawing lines bw. them.
for(it_pt = m_lstBendPoints.begin(); it_pt != m_lstBendPoints.end();
  it_pt++)
{
    // Draw a line to the bend pt.
    pDC->LineTo(*it_pt);

    // Set the current bend pt. as the pt prior to the head_pt: used
      for DrawArrowHead().
    final_pt = *it_pt;
}

// Line to head pt.
pDC->LineTo(m_ptHead);

// Iterate through the bend pts. drawing ellipses at each pt.
for(it_pt = m_lstBendPoints.begin(); it_pt != m_lstBendPoints.end();
  it_pt++)
{
    // Draw an ellipse about the bend pt.
    bend_pt = *it_pt;
    top_left.x = (int)(bend_pt.x - length*0.5);
    top_left.y = (int)(bend_pt.y - length*0.5);
    bottom_right.x = (int)(bend_pt.x + length*0.5);
    bottom_right.y = (int)(bend_pt.y + length*0.5);
    pDC->Ellipse(top_left.x, top_left.y, bottom_right.x,
      bottom_right.y);
}

// Draw arrowhead
DrawArrowHead(pDC, final_pt, m_ptHead);
}
```

18.3.3 Modify the `CConnection::DrawArrowHead()` Function

The developer will notice the call to `DrawArrowHead()` at the end of the `DrawConnection()` function where the pointer-to-CDC, "pDC", is being passed in as an argument. This function is also reduced in size, since the device context's attributes are set up in the calling environment (`DrawSystemModel()`). The local variable "pen_width" is removed, so too the creation of a local pen. However, the pen color in `DrawArrowHead()` needs to be extracted from the "pDC" as follows:

```
// -- EXTRACT PEN COLOR FROM PEN
CPen *lpen = pDC->GetCurrentPen();
EXTLOGPEN elPen;
lpen->GetExtLogPen(&elPen);
pen_color = elPen.elpColor;
```

Firstly, the current pen is extracted using `GetCurrentPen()`, then an extended pen object of type EXTLOGPEN structure is declared and subsequently obtained through the call to `GetExtLogPen()` by passing its address [1]. Then the color is extracted from the extended pen's structural field.

As a result, the brush that is created can use the same color as that stored in the pointer-to-CDC, "pDC", and, hence, the lines that are drawn and the polygon that is filled are of uniform color. The modified and more elegant version of the DrawArrowHead() function is shown in the following. Note that only the previous brush needs to be reset since there is no selection (SelectObject()) of a new local pen in this function: only a retrieval of the current pen (GetCurrentPen()).

```cpp
void CConnection::DrawArrowHead(CDC *pDC, CPoint tail, CPoint head)
{
    int pen_color;            // pen color: White = RGB(255,255,255),
      Black = RBF(0,0,0)
    double d;                 // opp. side length of subtriangle with
      hypotenuse h and base side length length/2.
    double dDeltaLength;      // std ref delta length
    double h;                 // hypotenuse of subtriangle with opp. side
      length d and base side length length/2.
    double length;            // a fraction of a std ref delta length
    double length_u;          // length of vector u
    double length_v;          // length of vector v
    double theta;             // angle of ith body rotated positively
      clockwise w.r.t. the global screen coord sys. X axis.
    double u[2];        // one of two vectors used to determined angle
      theta
    double v[2];        // one of two vectors used to determined angle
      theta: the unit vector [1,0]
    CBrush *pBrush = NULL; // a ptr to brush
    CPoint A; // vertex in anticlock direc from pointing vertex B of
      arrowhead
    CPoint B; // vertex of arrowhead pointing in direc of arrow (m_ptHead)
    CPoint C; // vertex in clock direc from pointing vertex B of arrowhead
    CPoint vertices[3]; // vertices array to hold triangle vertices
    CString sMsg;       // main msg string
    UINT nType = MB_OK; // style of msg. box
    UINT nIDhelp = 0;   // help context ID for the msg.

    // Set length
    dDeltaLength = GetDocumentGlobalFn()->GetDeltaLength();
    length = 0.15*dDeltaLength;

    // Assign lengths to arrowhead (triangle) paras.
    d = 0.2887*length;
    h = 0.5773*length;

    // Print msg.
    sMsg.Format("\n CConnection::DrawArrowHead(), d = %lf, h = %lf\n", d, h);
    //AfxMessageBox(sMsg, nType, nIDhelp);

    // Length of vecs u and v
    v[0] = 1.0;               // x cmpt. of unit vector [1,0]
    v[1] = 0.0;               // y cmpt. of unit vector [1,0]
    u[0] = head.x - tail.x; // length in x direc of connection vector
    u[1] = head.y - tail.y; // length in y direc of connection vector

    length_u = sqrt(pow(u[0],2) + pow(u[1],2));
    length_v = sqrt(pow(v[0],2) + pow(v[1],2));

    // Angle between vecs u and v
    theta = acos((u[0]*v[0] + u[1]*v[1])/(length_u*length_v));
    if(u[1] < 0)
```

```
{
    theta = -theta;  // negate theta if y-cmpt of u < 0, since acos
       result is an element from [0,pi] radians ONLY (non-neg).
}
// Global position vecs of arrowhead triangle vertices
A.x = head.x + long(cos(theta)*(-(h+d)) - sin(theta)*(-length*0.5));
A.y = head.y + long(sin(theta)*(-(h+d)) + cos(theta)*(-length*0.5));

B.x = head.x;
B.y = head.y;

C.x = head.x + long(cos(theta)*(-(h+d)) - sin(theta)*(length*0.5));
C.y = head.y + long(sin(theta)*(-(h+d)) + cos(theta)*(length*0.5));
// -- EXTRACT PEN COLOR FROM PEN
CPen *lpen = pDC->GetCurrentPen();
EXTLOGPEN elPen;
lpen->GetExtLogPen(&elPen);
pen_color = elPen.elpColor;

// Draw arrowhead
pDC->MoveTo(A);
pDC->LineTo(B);
pDC->LineTo(C);
pDC->LineTo(A);
```

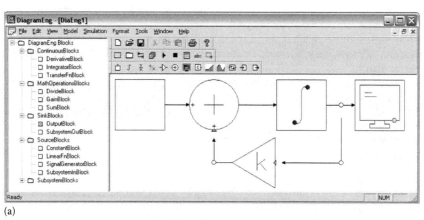

(a)

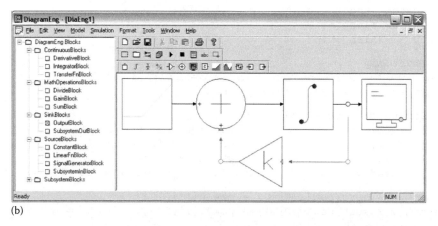

(b)

FIGURE 18.3 Validation of a model: (a) prior to validating the disconnected model and (b) upon validating the model showing disconnected block ports and connections in a lighter shade (red, when running the program), and connected connections in black.

```
    // Prepare for filling the polygon
    CBrush NewBrush(pen_color);    // create a new brush
    vertices[0] = A;
    vertices[1] = B;
    vertices[2] = C;

    // Select the new brush
    pBrush = pDC->SelectObject(&NewBrush);

    // Fill the polygon
    pDC->Polygon(vertices, 3);

    // Reset the prev. brush
    pDC->SelectObject(pBrush);
}
```

Now upon validating the system model, the disconnected block ports and connections are presented in red (when running the program) or in a lighter shade of gray as shown in Figure 18.3, but the connected connections are still in the black color. The View then flashes the errors in red several times before ending the validating stage.

18.4   UNIQUE PORT AND BEND POINT CONNECTION

At present, the user can insert connection objects on the palette and attach the end points, i.e., head and tail points, to input and output ports, respectively. However, there is no mechanism to prevent the user from attaching more than one connection end point to a port. Now, given the existing software structure, it is possible to make minor changes to the program to preserve the uniqueness of port-connection connectivity. One should note, however, that multiple connection tail points should be allowed to be connected to a single branch point, since multiple branches may be required to propagate signals in feed-forward and feedback paths simultaneously.

The CDiagramEngDoc::TrackConnectionEndPoint() function makes calls to three functions in an attempt to snap the connection end point to a port or bend point. The methods that need to be augmented here, to preserve the uniqueness of port-based connectivity, are (1) SnapConnectionHeadPointToPort(), which attaches a head point to a port and returns the address of the port (CPort*), and (2) SnapConnectionTailPointToPort(), which attaches a tail point to a port and returns the address of the port (CPort*).

18.4.1   AUGMENT THE SnapConnectionHeadPointToPort() FUNCTION

The original SnapConnectionHeadPointToPort() function is shown in the following, where the connection head point is passed as an argument and its position compared with that of the input port to which it is being attached: if it is sufficiently close, then its position is updated to be that of the port, and the address of the port, of type pointer-to-CPort, is returned. Then, in the TrackConnectionEndPoint() function, called as a result of moving a connection tail/head point to an output/input port, the CConnection class's reference-to-port member variable, "m_pRefToPort", is updated with the address of the port returned.

```
CPort* CDiagramEngDoc::SnapConnectionHeadPointToPort
  (CPoint &head_pt)
{
    // Passing in a point by reference, and returning a prt-to-CPort
      "m_pRefToPort".
    double disc_r = 0.1*m_dDeltaLength;
    double dist_to_port;
    CPoint port_posn;
    list<CBlock*>::iterator it_blk;
```

```
        list<CBlock*> blk_list = GetSystemModel().GetBlockList();
        vector<CPort*> vec_input_ports;
        vector<CPort*>::iterator it_port;

        // Iterate through block list
        for(it_blk = blk_list.begin(); it_blk != blk_list.end(); it_blk++)
        {
            vec_input_ports = (*it_blk)->GetVectorOfInputPorts();
            for(it_port = vec_input_ports.begin(); it_port
              != vec_input_ports.end(); it_port++)
            {
                port_posn = (*it_port)->GetPortPosition();
                dist_to_port = sqrt(pow(head_pt.x - port_posn.x,2) +
                  pow(head_pt.y - port_posn.y,2));

                if(dist_to_port <= disc_r)
                {
                    head_pt = port_posn;
                    return (*it_port);  // return CPort*, i.e. a to_port
                }
            }
        }

        // Return 0 if no "m_pRefToPort" returned earlier
        return 0;
}
```

The changes that need to be made here to the SnapConnectionHeadPointToPort() function involve checking whether the port to which the head point is intended to be attached is already connected to another connection object; if so, then an error message should inform the user that it is not possible to make the connection, and if not, then the original mechanism of updating the head point position and returning the address of the port should take effect. The modified version of the function with new code inserted in bold is shown in the following.

```
CPort* CDiagramEngDoc::SnapConnectionHeadPointToPort(CPoint &head_pt)
{
    // Passing in a point by reference, and returning a prt-to-CPort
      "m_pRefToPort".

    int port_connected = 0;
    double disc_r = 0.1*m_dDeltaLength;
    double dist_to_port;
    CPoint port_posn;
    CString sMsg;           // main msg string
    CString sMsgTemp;       // temp msg string
    UINT nType = MB_OK;     // style of msg. box
    UINT nIDhelp = 0;       // help context ID for the msg
    list<CBlock*>::iterator it_blk;
    list<CBlock*> blk_list = GetSystemModel().GetBlockList();
    vector<CPort*> vec_input_ports;
    vector<CPort*>::iterator it_port;

    // Iterate through block list
    for(it_blk = blk_list.begin(); it_blk != blk_list.end(); it_blk++)
    {
        vec_input_ports = (*it_blk)->GetVectorOfInputPorts();
```

```
          for(it_port = vec_input_ports.begin(); it_port
            != vec_input_ports.end(); it_port++)
          {
              port_posn = (*it_port)->GetPortPosition();
              dist_to_port = sqrt(pow(head_pt.x - port_posn.x,2) +
                pow(head_pt.y - port_posn.y,2));

              if(dist_to_port <= disc_r)
              {
                  // Check whether port is connected: (0) disconnected, (1)
                    connected
                  port_connected = (*it_blk)->CheckPortConnection(*it_port);
                  if(port_connected == 0) // if no connection to this port
                  {
                      head_pt = port_posn;
                      return (*it_port); // return CPort*, i.e. a to_port
                  }
                  else if(port_connected == 1)
                  {
                      // Error Msg.
                      sMsgTemp.Format("\n WARNING! Connection Failure.\n");
                      sMsg+=sMsgTemp;
                      sMsgTemp.Format("\n Existing connection attached to
                        this port.");
                      sMsg+=sMsgTemp;
                      sMsgTemp.Format("\n Please attach connection to an
                        alternative port.\n");
                      sMsg+=sMsgTemp;
                      AfxMessageBox(sMsg, nType, nIDhelp);
                  }
              }
          }
      }
  }

  // Return 0 if no "m_pRefToPort" returned earlier
  return 0;
}
```

Now upon running the code, the user may attach a connection to a port and attempt to connect another connection to the same port; as a result, an error message will be displayed indicating that an alternative port should be chosen (see Figure 18.4).

18.4.2 Augment the `SnapConnectionTailPointToPort()` Function

The changes that need to be made to the `SnapConnectionTailPointToPort()` function are very similar to those made to the `SnapConnectionHeadPointToPort()` function earlier. That is, if there already exists a tail point connected to an output port, then another tail point is not allowed to be connected to the same port. The original and modified versions of the former function are provided as follows, with the new code inserted shown in bold.

```
CPort* CDiagramEngDoc::SnapConnectionTailPointToPort(CPoint &tail_pt)
{
    // Passing in a point by reference, and returning a prt-to-CPort
      "m_pRefFromPort".
    double disc_r = 0.1*m_dDeltaLength;
    double dist_to_port;
```

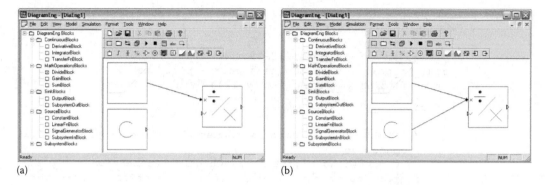

(a)   (b)

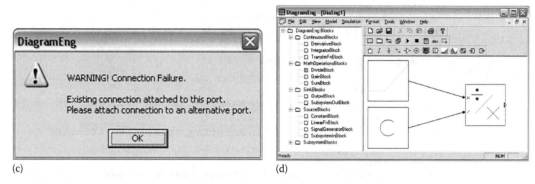

(c)   (d)

FIGURE 18.4   Preserving uniqueness of port-based connectivity: (a) a connection head point connected to a port, (b) an attempt to connect another head point to the same port, (c) the resulting error message, and (d) the selection of an alternative port.

```
CPoint port_posn;
list<CBlock*>::iterator it_blk;
list<CBlock*> blk_list = GetSystemModel().GetBlockList();
vector<CPort*> vec_output_ports;
vector<CPort*>::iterator it_port;

// Iterate through block list
for(it_blk = blk_list.begin(); it_blk != blk_list.end(); it_blk++)
{
    vec_output_ports = (*it_blk)->GetVectorOfOutputPorts();
    for(it_port = vec_output_ports.begin(); it_port
      != vec_output_ports.end(); it_port++)
    {
        port_posn = (*it_port)->GetPortPosition();
        dist_to_port = sqrt(pow(tail_pt.x - port_posn.x,2) +
          pow(tail_pt.y - port_posn.y,2));

        if(dist_to_port <= disc_r)
        {
            tail_pt = port_posn;
            return (*it_port);  // return CPort*, i.e. a from_port
        }
    }
}

// Return 0 if no "m_pRefFromPort" returned earlier
return 0;
}
```

```
CPort* CDiagramEngDoc::SnapConnectionTailPointToPort(CPoint &tail_pt)
{
// Passing in a point by reference, and returning a prt-to-CPort
   "m_pRefFromPort".
int port_connected;
double disc_r = 0.1*m_dDeltaLength;
double dist_to_port;
CPoint port_posn;
CString sMsg;          // main msg string
CString sMsgTemp;      // temp msg string
UINT nType = MB_OK;    // style of msg. box
UINT nIDhelp = 0;      // help context ID for the msg
list<CBlock*>::iterator it_blk;
list<CBlock*> blk_list = GetSystemModel().GetBlockList();
vector<CPort*> vec_output_ports;
vector<CPort*>::iterator it_port;

// Iterate through block list
for(it_blk = blk_list.begin(); it_blk != blk_list.end(); it_blk++)
{
    vec_output_ports = (*it_blk)->GetVectorOfOutputPorts();
    for(it_port = vec_output_ports.begin(); it_port
      != vec_output_ports.end(); it_port++)
    {
        port_posn = (*it_port)->GetPortPosition();
        dist_to_port = sqrt(pow(tail_pt.x - port_posn.x,2) +
          pow(tail_pt.y - port_posn.y,2));

        if(dist_to_port <= disc_r)
        {
            // Check whether port is connected: (0) disconnected,
              (1) connected
            port_connected = (*it_blk)->CheckPortConnection(*it_port);
            if(port_connected == 0) // if no connection to this port
            {
                tail_pt = port_posn;
                return (*it_port); // return CPort*, i.e. a from_port
            }
            else if(port_connected == 1)
            {
                // Error Msg.
                sMsgTemp.Format("\n WARNING! Connection Failure.\n");
                sMsg+=sMsgTemp;
                sMsgTemp.Format("\n Existing connection attached to
                  this port.");
                sMsg+=sMsgTemp;
                sMsgTemp.Format("\n Please attach connection to an
                  alternative port. \n");
                sMsg+=sMsgTemp;
                AfxMessageBox(sMsg, nType, nIDhelp);
            }
        }
    }
}

// Return 0 if no "m_pRefFromPort" returned earlier
return 0;
}
```

18.5 SUMMARY

The validating process is required before model computation in order to check that the model is correctly structured. A `ValidateModel()` function is used to call three entity-specific functions: (1) `ValidateModelBlocks()` checks that there exists at least one source and sink block in the model, (2) `ValidateModelBlockPorts()` checks the connection status of block ports and reports those that are disconnected, and (3) `ValidateModelConnections()` records any connections that are not fully connected to input and output ports or connection bend points. Changes are made to the program to draw model entities in the correct color, depending on the presence of model errors; the setting up of the pen's attributes is done higher in the call tree, in `CSystemModel::DrawSystemModel()`, rather than in the functions that are called from within this function, i.e., `DrawConnection()` and `DrawArrowHead()` of the CConnection class. Finally, the CDiagramEngDoc automatic connection functions, `SnapConnectionHeadPointToPort()` and `SnapConnectionTailPointToPort()` were modified with a call to `CBlock::CheckPortConnection()` to prevent the user from attaching more than one connection head or tail point to the same port.

REFERENCE

1. Microsoft Developer Network Library Visual Studio 6.0, Microsoft® Visual Studio™ 6.0 Development System, Microsoft Corporation, 1998.

19 Non-Feedback-Based Signal Propagation

19.1 INTRODUCTION

A feedback loop exists in a model when a connection emanating from a branch point is directed or fed back into the original direction of signal flow, reentering a prior block in the ordered sequence of block operations. An algebraic loop results when the output of a block operation is used as a part of the very same input to the block; e.g., output $y = u_1 + u_2$ involves the inputs u_1 and u_2, but input $u_2 = f(y)$. That is, the block output is a function of its input, as expected, yet that input is a function, although usually indirectly, of the same block's output. The feedback loop and algebraic loop are essentially equivalent in the context of using model diagrams to represent mathematical equations.

The material in this chapter introduces the mechanism for the detection of algebraic loops and for performing signal propagation for models not containing feedback loops, called non-feedback-based signal propagation or simply "direct signal propagation." However, before implementation instructions are given, a brief discussion of important concepts in the field of signals and systems is made here to refresh the reader of fundamentals that should be considered throughout signal propagation-related code development.

19.2 SIGNALS AND SYSTEMS

The engineer may have taken an undergraduate course in signals and systems if their interests were in electrical and electronic engineering and been exposed to fundamental concepts in signals and systems theory and their practical application. The material of Oppenheim et al. [1] is followed closely here, due to the clarity and completeness with which concepts are communicated, to provide a basic introduction to signals and systems that are relevant to the block-diagram-oriented software development. The interested reader should consult Refs. [1] and [2] and other relevant texts for more information.

19.2.1 CONTINUOUS-TIME AND DISCRETE-TIME SIGNALS

A signal is a method of conveying information, and this information is contained in a pattern of variations of some form [1]. For example, an electrical impulse down a wire or radio waves transmitted through a medium are signals containing information in a variational pattern. Signals in this area of work are represented by mathematical functions of at least one independent variable [1]. A continuous-time signal is one where the independent variable is continuous and is defined for a continuum of values of the independent variable [1]. A discrete-time signal is one where the independent variable is discrete and is defined for a discrete set of values of the independent variable [1]. In addition, digital processor-based systems use discrete-time sequences representing sampled versions of continuous-time signals [1].

19.2.2 CONTINUOUS-TIME AND DISCRETE-TIME SYSTEMS

A continuous-time system is a system in which continuous-time input signals are applied and result in continuous-time output signals [1]. A discrete-time system transforms discrete-time inputs into discrete-time outputs [1]. The reader should be aware that the blocks of the DiagramEng application being built in this work perform mathematical operations and may be used to model a continuous system, e.g., a differential equation representing a mass–spring–damper dynamical system. However, all operations are performed at finite time discretizations. For example, the Derivative block (to be introduced in Chapter 21) uses a finite difference calculation to determine the numerical derivative $f'(t)$ of a function $f(t)$ at time t, i.e.,

$$f'(t) \approx \frac{f(t) - f(t-h)}{h} \tag{19.1}$$

where the time-step size $h = \delta t$. Similarly, the Integrator block performs a finite difference calculation to determine the integral of a function at a certain time. For example, in the case of Euler integration, introduced in Chapter 21 when the integral of the function $f(t, y(t))$ over the interval $[t_0, t_1]$ is

$$\int_{t_0}^{t_1} f(t, y)\, dt \approx h f(t_0, y_0) \tag{19.2}$$

and results in the general finite difference formula

$$y(t_{n+1}) \approx y(t_n) + h f(t_n, y(t_n)) \tag{19.3}$$

which is Euler's method [3].

19.2.3　Memory-Based Systems and Memoryless Systems

A system that is memoryless is one whose output for each value of the independent variable at a given time is dependent on the input at only the same time [1]. For example, given an input $u(t)$ and an output $y(t)$, a memoryless system is one of the form

$$y(t) = f(t, u(t)) \tag{19.4}$$

A system with memory is one that is dependent on information stored at times other than the current time [1]. For example, the numerical derivative (19.1) stores information at the current and previous time points, and the numerical integral (19.3), introduced earlier, stores information at the previous time point that is used to determine the value at the current time point. Hence, the Derivative and Integral blocks are memory-based due to their storing of prior data or information.

19.2.4　Time Variant and Time Invariant Systems

Oppenheim introduces a time invariant system as one whose behavior and characteristics are fixed over time. That is, a system is time invariant if a time shift in the input signal results in an identical time shift in the output signal [1]. Let $u(t)$ and $y(t)$ denote the input and output of a system, respectively. If a time shift $t + \delta t$ is made to the input, changing the input from $u(t)$ to $u(t + \delta t)$, then the identical time shift in the output for the system to be time invariant is $y(t + \delta t)$. For example, if

$$y(t) = \sin(u(t)) \tag{19.5a}$$

then a time shift $t + \delta t$ in the input results in the identical time shift in the output, i.e.,

$$y(t + \delta t) = \sin(u(t + \delta t)) \tag{19.5b}$$

However, if

$$y(t) = tu(t) \tag{19.6}$$

since $y(t)$ is explicitly a function of time, i.e., the input $u(t)$ is premultiplied by time t, then it is not time invariant. The interested reader should consult Ref. [1] for further details.

19.2.5 LINEAR AND NONLINEAR SYSTEMS

A linear system is one for which the principle of superposition applies [2]. The principle of superposition indicates that if an input consists of the weighted sum of several signals, then the output is the superposition, i.e., the weighted sum, of the responses of the system to each of the signals [1]. In particular, the additivity property and the scaling or homogeneity property must both be satisfied [1]. The additivity property implies that, for a system with inputs $u_1(t)$ and $u_2(t)$ and corresponding responses $y_1(t)$ and $y_2(t)$, the response to the sum, $u_1(t) + u_2(t)$, is $y_1(t) + y_2(t)$ [1]. The homogeneity property indicates that the response to the input $au_1(t)$, where a is a complex constant, is $ay_1(t)$ [1]. Hence, combining the two conditions (for continuous time) implies that for a system to be linear, the input $au_1(t) + bu_2(t)$ results in the output $ay_1(t) + by_2(t)$, i.e., from [1],

$$au_1(t) + bu_2(t) \rightarrow ay_1(t) + by_2(t) \tag{19.7}$$

A similar argument holds for discrete-time systems.

19.2.6 STATE VARIABLES, STATE VECTORS, AND STATE SPACE

In the work that follows, the concept of state variables, state vectors, and state space will be encountered, in particular, when studying the state space equations in control engineering. Hence, a brief introduction is given here to clarify these terms and follows closely the work of Ogata [2].

The state of a dynamic system is the smallest set of variables such that the knowledge of these variables at $t = t_0$, where t_0 is the initial time point, together with knowledge of the input for $t \geq t_0$, completely determines the behavior of the system for any time $t \geq t_0$ [2].

The state variables of a dynamic system are the variables making up the smallest set of variables that determine the state of the dynamic system [2].

The state vector is a vector made up of the state variables needed to completely describe the behavior of a given system [2]. It is the vector that determines the system state $x(t)$ for $t \geq t_0$, once the state at $t = t_0$ is given and the input $u(t)$ for $t \geq t_0$ is specified [2].

The state space is the n-dimensional space for which x_i, $i \in [1, n]$, are the state variables [2] and where a point in which represents a system state [2]. The state space equations in control engineering are introduced in Chapter 22 when considering an order reduction of a second-order linear ordinary differential equation to two first-order linear differential equations for a mechanical dynamics example.

19.3 MODELS WITH ALGEBRAIC AND FEEDBACK LOOPS

Algebraic or feedback loops in a model represent the simultaneity of the underlying equations that the model diagram represents. If the system is linear, it may be cast in the form of a set of simultaneous linear equations, $Ax = b$, and be computed for the signal values, x. However, if the leading matrix, A, is ill-conditioned, or not invertible, attempted equation computation results in numerical problems.

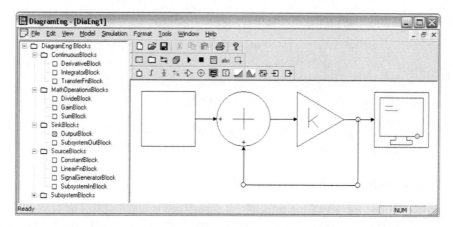

FIGURE 19.1 Model diagram with a simple feedback loop.

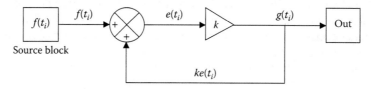

FIGURE 19.2 Simple model involving a feedback loop and Source, Sum, Gain, and Output blocks.

For example, consider the system modeled in Figure 19.1 with a simple feedback loop: the output of the Sum block is multiplied by a gain of k, and this is then fed back into the Sum block. Let the output of the Linear Function, Sum, and Gain blocks be $f(t)$, $e(t)$, and $g(t)$, respectively, as shown in Figure 19.2.

Hence, the system being modeled may be described as follows:

$$e(t) = f(t) + g(t) \qquad (19.8a)$$

$$g(t) = ke(t) \qquad (19.8b)$$

$$\Rightarrow \frac{g(t)}{f(t)} = \frac{k}{(1-k)}$$

System (19.8) may be written in matrix form, $\boldsymbol{Ax} = \boldsymbol{b}$, i.e.,

$$\begin{bmatrix} 1 & -1 \\ -k & 1 \end{bmatrix} \begin{bmatrix} e(t) \\ g(t) \end{bmatrix} = \begin{bmatrix} f(t) \\ 0 \end{bmatrix} \qquad (19.9)$$

where the leading matrix is $\boldsymbol{A}$, the output vector $\boldsymbol{x} = [e(t), g(t)]^T$, and the right-hand side vector $\boldsymbol{b} = [f(t), 0]^T$. The problem with this system lies with the gain constant k: if $k = 1$, then the rows of $\boldsymbol{A}$ are linearly dependent, and hence the inverse, $\boldsymbol{A}^{-1}$, does not exist. As a result, the numerical solution of (19.8) will be erroneous.

19.4 SIGNAL PROPAGATION

Signal propagation is the process of updating signal data (CSignal) associated with a parent connection (CConnection) object as a result of a block operation. Signal propagation may be direct (Figure 19.3a), where no feedback loops exist, or feedback-based (Figure 19.3b), where feedback loops exist.

In general, for a model involving no feedback loops, the signal flow is as follows: (1) the source block generates output signal data that are transmitted through its output port to the output connection, (2) the connection's signal data are transferred to the input port of the next block, (3) the block performs the appropriate operation on the data, and (4) the result of the operation forms the output signal, which is transmitted to the following block, and so on, until the Output sink block is reached, where the numerical result may be viewed in a graph by the user.

Figure 19.4 illustrates the passage of signal data through a simple model involving no feedback loops. Signals are initially generated by the source Signal Generator and Constant blocks. These are transmitted through their output ports to their output connections. The Signal Generator and Constant blocks' signals are then propagated to the Gain and Sum blocks, respectively. The Gain block performs its gain constant multiplication operation and sends the signal from its output port to its output connection, which is connected to the Sum block. The Sum block then checks whether its ports have valid input data signals provided by the input connections; if so, then the sum operation is performed, and the output is sent via the output port to the output connection, if not, then no sum operation can be performed and no output signal generated. The output signal is then propagated to the Output sink block where it may be viewed on a graph.

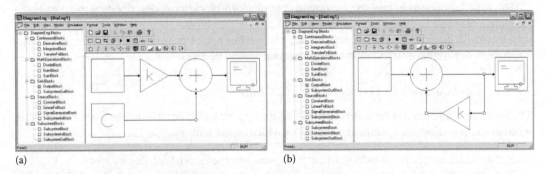

(a)   (b)

FIGURE 19.3 Model diagrams showing types of signal propagation: (a) direct signal propagation with no feedback loops and (b) a simple linear equation model involving a feedback loop.

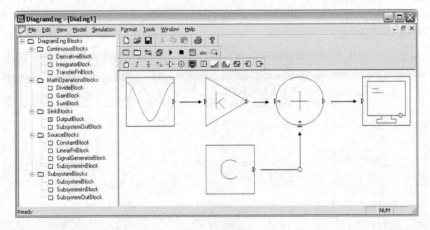

FIGURE 19.4 Direct signal propagation from the Signal Generator and Constant source blocks to an Output sink block involving two math operation blocks, Gain and Sum: the diagram is intentionally shown in its disconnected state where distinct ports and connections are clearly visible.

However, before a signal can be propagated in a direct manner, the connectivity of the model needs to be analyzed to detect the possible existence of feedback, equivalently algebraic, loops. If loops do not exist, then direct signal propagation can proceed; if they do, then an alternative method of equation computation is required, e.g., the computation of a set of simultaneous nonlinear equations (this is the subject of Chapters 22 and 23).

19.5　DETERMINATION OF FEEDBACK LOOPS

Consider the following diagram (Figure 19.5) showing a model with one source block, various mathematical operation blocks, two feedback loops, and two Output blocks.

Another general representation of the same model is shown in Figure 19.6 with blocks labeled A0 to J9, where the letters and numbers both represent the order in which the blocks were placed on the palette. Both letters and numbers are used to make the order of placement clear and to prevent confusion with the "0" and "1" values used to denote the state of connectivity.

The block-to-block connectivity matrix in the forward-direction sense, as represented by the direction of the existing arrows/arcs connecting the blocks, is shown in Table 19.1: "1" represents a forward connection, and an empty entry ("0" in the actual code) represents the lack of a forward connection.

Rows A0 and J9 are zero rows, indicating that there are no forward proceeding connections, and hence the blocks are Output blocks. Block E4 is a source block (as shown in Figure 19.6), as represented by a null column, and is the starting point for algorithmic loop detection. The various paths through the diagram and matrix ending at either a loop-repeated block or an Output block are shown in Table 19.2.

The code introduced in this section obtains the block-to-block tours described by the connectivity matrix that end in either loop-repeated blocks or Output blocks. If no feedback loop is found, then the direct signal propagation method may be used to perform signal computation, otherwise, an alternative simultaneous equation-based method should be used.

19.5.1　General Steps to Determine Feedback Loops

The individual functions to be added to the DiagramEng project to determine feedback or algebraic loops are as listed, where specific details are provided in the sections that follow:

1. `DetermineModelFeedbackLoops()`—determines model feedback loops
2. `SetRefFromPortOfConnectionFromBendPoint()`—sets a connection reference-from port
3. `AssignBlockConnectivityMatrixValues()`—assigns matrix values 1s and 0s
4. `DetermineLoopsFromConnectivityMatrix()`—determines loops from a connectivity matrix

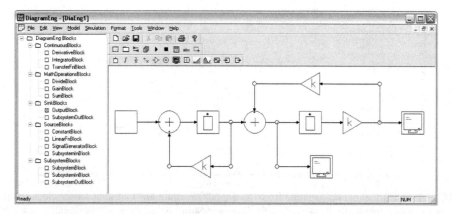

FIGURE 19.5　Model with two feedback loops.

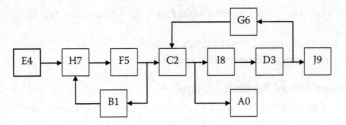

FIGURE 19.6 General representation of a model with two feedback loops, where the letters and numbers represent the order in which the blocks were placed on the palette.

TABLE 19.1

Block-to-Block Connectivity Matrix

	A0	B1	C2	D3	E4	F5	G6	H7	I8	J9
A0										
B1								1		
C2	1								1	
D3						1				1
E4								1		
F5		1	1							
G6			1							
H7						1				
I8			1							
J9										

Notes: A "1" indicates that a block on row $i \in [0,9]$ is connected to a block in column $j \in [0,9]$. Empty entries are considered to be "0".

TABLE 19.2

Tours through Block Diagram

Tours Ending at an Output Block	Tours Ending in a Loop-Repeated Block
$E \to H \to F \to C \to A$	$E \to H \to F \to B \to H$
$E \to H \to F \to C \to I \to D \to J$	$E \to H \to F \to C \to I \to D \to G \to C$

The functions that are required by and are related to the `DetermineLoopsFromConnectivity Matrix()` method are as follows:

1. `DetermineInitialNodeVector()`—determines the starting node vector
2. `BuildTour()`—builds a tour, ending at a loop-repeated block or an Output block
3. `FindCurrentTourPosition()`—finds the current position in the tour vector
4. `FindBranchNodes()`—finds blocks/nodes to which a connection is branched
5. `NumberOfOnesOnMatrixRow()`—finds the number of 1s on a matrix row
6. `CheckRepeatedEntries()`—checks a tour for repeated entries, denoting a feedback loop
7. `ResetTourVector()`—resets the tour vector after a tour has been found
8. `SaveTourVector()`—saves the tour vector after a tour has been found

Additional general purpose integer-based global functions to be added are as follows:

1. PrintMatrix()—prints integer matrix values
2. PrintVector()—prints integer vector values

19.5.1.1 Determine Model Feedback Loops

The current flow of control of the model validation process involves the following functions: OnModelBuild(), ValidateModel(), ValidateModelBlocks(), ValidateModelBlock Ports(), and ValidateModelConnections(). The checking of whether the model has feedback loops is also a part of the validation process, although the presence of a loop does not imply that the model is in error. Add a public member function to the CSystemModel class with the prototype, void CSystemModel::DetermineModelFeedbackLoops(void), and edit it as shown in the following.

```
void CSystemModel::DetermineModelFeedbackLoops()
{
    int i;                      // row index
    int j;                      // col index
    int ncols;                  // number of columns of block connectivity
       matrix
    int nrows;                  // number of rows of block connectivity matrix
    int **BlockConMatrix = NULL;// block connectivity matrix
    CPort *from_port = NULL;     // port from which a connection emanates
    CPort *to_port = NULL;       // port to which a connection is attached
    list<CBlock*>::iterator it_blk;
    list<CBlock*> &blk_list = GetBlockList();
    list<CConnection*>::iterator it_con;
    list<CPoint>::iterator it_pt;
    vector<CPort*>::iterator it_port;

    // Get the size of the block connectivity matrix
    nrows = blk_list.size();
    ncols = nrows;

    // MEMORY ALLOC
    BlockConMatrix = new int *[nrows];
    for(i=0; i<nrows; i++)
    {
        BlockConMatrix[i] = new int[ncols]; // allocate an array of ints,
            return & to BlockConMatrix[i]
    }

    // Init. block connectivity matrix
    for(i=0; i<nrows; i++)
    {
        for(j=0; j<ncols; j++)
        {
            BlockConMatrix[i][j] = 0;
        }
    }

    // Set reference from port of connections that are connected to bend
       points
    SetRefFromPortOfConnectionFromBendPoint();
```

```
    // CONSTRUCT BLOCK-TO-BLOCK CONNECTIVITY MATRIX
    // Iterate over all blocks
    for(it_blk = blk_list.begin(); it_blk != blk_list.end(); it_blk++)
    {
        vector<CPort*> &vec_of_output_ports = (*it_blk)-
          >GetVectorOfOutputPorts();

        // Iterate over output ports
        for(it_port = vec_of_output_ports.begin(); it_port
          != vec_of_output_ports.end(); it_port++)
        {
            // Iterate over all connections
            for(it_con = m_lstConnection.begin(); it_con != m_lstConnection.
              end(); it_con++)
            {
                // Get the reference from port of the current
                  connection
                from_port = (*it_con)->GetRefFromPort();

                // If the connection's from_port is the block's output
                  port,
                // i.e. if the connection is attached to the block
                  DIRECTLY, or INDIRECTLY via a bend pt.
                if(from_port == *it_port)
                {
                    // Get the input port to which the connection is
                      attached
                    to_port = (*it_con)->GetRefToPort();

                    // Get the reference to block of this port
                    CBlock &to_block = to_port->GetRefToBlock();

                    // Assign matrix values if from-block is connected to
                      to-block
                    AssignBlockConnectivityMatrixValues(*it_blk,
                      &to_block, BlockConMatrix);
                }
            }
        }
    }

    // Print the block connectivity matrix
    PrintMatrix(BlockConMatrix, nrows, ncols);

    // Before DetermineModelFeedbackLoops() was called, all ref-from-
      ports of connections attached to bend pts
    // were NULL, so now reset them to NULL, to leave the program state
      as it was previously.
    for(it_con = m_lstConnection.begin(); it_con != m_lstConnection.
      end(); it_con++)
    {
        if((*it_con)->GetRefFromPoint() != NULL)  // if connection
          attached to a bend POINT
        {
            (*it_con)->SetRefFromPort(NULL); // set its ref-from-port to
              NULL (since not attached to a block)
        }
    }
```

```
// Check the block connectivity matrix for feedback loops
DetermineLoopsFromConnectivityMatrix(BlockConMatrix, nrows, ncols);


// MEMORY DELETE
if(BlockConMatrix != NULL)
{
    for(i=0; i<nrows; i++)
    {
        delete [] BlockConMatrix[i];
    }
}
delete [] BlockConMatrix;

return;
}
```

The developer will notice the introduction of several functions here as indicated in the general steps listed earlier. However, not listed previously is GetRefToBlock(), which is called upon a "to_port" object of type pointer-to-CPort, to get a reference to the block upon which the port resides. Hence, add a public member function to the CPort class with the prototype, CBlock &GetRefToBlock(void), and edit it as follows.

```
CBlock &CPort::GetRefToBlock()
{
    return m_rRefToBlock;
}
```

Finally, make a call to DetermineModelFeedbackLoops() from within the ValidateModel() function. Changes to the latter are shown in bold; the rest of the function remains unchanged.

```
void CSystemModel::ValidateModel()
{
    ...
    // -- INFORM USER OF END OF BUILD MODEL STAGE
    if( (error1 == 1) || (error2 == 1) || (error3 == 1) )
    {
        ...
    }
    else
    {
        sMsg.Format("\n No build errors. \n");
        AfxMessageBox(sMsg, nType, nIDhelp);

        // Determine if the model has feedback loops, i.e. source-to-loop
          tours
        m_iNSourceLoopTours = 0;
        m_iNSourceOutputTours = 0;
        DetermineModelFeedbackLoops();

        if(m_iNSourceLoopTours > 0)
```

```
    {
        sMsg.Format("\n Note! The number of source-to-loop tours in
            the model is: %d. \n", m_iNSourceLoopTours);
        AfxMessageBox(sMsg, nType, nIDhelp);
    }
  }
  ...
}
```

The developer will notice the presence of two new member variables "m_iNSourceOutputTours" and "m_iNSourceLoopTours". These are used to record the number of tours from a source block that end in either an Output block or loop-repeated node (feedback loop), respectively, and these values are set in the `SaveTourVector()` function (see Section 19.5.2.8). Hence, add two new private integer member variables named "m_iNSourceOutputTours" and "m_iNSourceLoopTours" to the CSystemModel class, initializing them to 0 as shown in the `ValidateModel()` function previously.

The `DetermineModelFeedbackLoops()` function initially constructs a block connectivity matrix "BlockConMatrix" to be populated with values in a similar manner to that shown in Table 19.1. A call is made to set the reference-from ports of *secondary* connections not directly connected to a block, but rather emanating from a bend point of a *primary* connection, to share the same output port as the *primary* connection. A nested loop then iterates over the blocks, ports, and connections to determine the reference-from and reference-to ports of connection objects defining block-to-block connectivity. This connectivity is then recorded in the block connectivity matrix by the `AssignBlockConnectivityMatrixValues()` function. Thereafter, connections that emanate from bend points have their reference-from ports set to NULL, returning them to the state they were in prior to the function being called: this is the case since they are not physically attached to a port, but rather a bend point. Finally, the presence of feedback loops defined by the connectivity matrix needs to be determined using the `DetermineLoopsFromConnectivityMatrix()` function.

19.5.1.2 Set Reference-From Port of Connection Emanating from a Bend Point

The current program state only sets reference-from ports, of connection objects, to be that of the block port from which they directly emanate. However, if a *secondary* connection is attached to a bend point of a *primary* connection, then its reference-from port will be NULL. Hence the `SetRefFromPortOfConnectionFromBendPoint()` function sets the reference-from port of a *secondary* connection emanating from a bend point to be that of the *primary* connection to which it is attached. Add a public member function to the CSystemModel class with the prototype, void CSystemModel::SetRefFromPortOfConnectionFromBendPoint(void), and edit it as shown.

```
void CSystemModel::SetRefFromPortOfConnectionFromBendPoint()
{
    int ref_from_port_flag;  // flag indicating whether m_pRefFromPort
      was set
    CPort *from_port = NULL; // port from which primary connection
      emanates
    list<CPoint>::iterator it_pt;
    list<CConnection*>::iterator it_con;
    list<CConnection*>::iterator it_con_bend_pt;

    // Put connections emanating from bend points into a list
    list<CConnection*> connections_from_bend_pt_list;
    for(it_con = m_lstConnection.begin(); it_con != m_lstConnection.
      end(); it_con++)
```

```
{
    if((*it_con)->GetRefFromPoint() != NULL)  // if there is a ref-
      from POINT for this connection
    {
        connections_from_bend_pt_list.push_back(*it_con);
    }
}

// Set the reference-from-port for connections emanating from bend
  points.
it_con_bend_pt = connections_from_bend_pt_list.begin();
while(connections_from_bend_pt_list.size() > 0)
{
    // Init. ref_from_port_flag: (0) no m_pRefFromPort was set,
      (1) m_pRefFromPort was set.
    ref_from_port_flag = 0;

    // Iterate over PRIMARY connection list to find bend points with
      SECONDARY connections attached to them
    for(it_con = m_lstConnection.begin(); it_con != m_lstConnection.
      end(); it_con++)
    {
        list<CPoint> &bend_pts_list = (*it_con)-
          >GetConnectionBendPointsList(); // get the bend_pts_list

        // Iterate over bend points list of the current primary
          connection
        for(it_pt = bend_pts_list.begin(); it_pt != bend_pts_list.
          end(); it_pt++)
        {
            // Determine connectivity of a secondary connection's
              tail pt. to a primary connection's bend pt.
            if( ( (*it_con_bend_pt)->GetConnectionPointTail().x ==
              (*it_pt).x) && ( (*it_con_bend_pt)-
              >GetConnectionPointTail().y == (*it_pt).y) )
            {
                from_port = (*it_con)->GetRefFromPort(); // get the
                  primary connection's ref-from-port

                // A ref-from-port of a PRIMARY connection is NULL if
                  the primary connection is not directly
                // connected to a block port.
                // A ref-from-port of a TERTIARY connection is NULL
                  if it is connected to a bend pt. of a
                // SECONDARY connection that has not yet had its
                  m_pRefFromPort assigned (to be that of its
                // primary connection).
                if(from_port != NULL)
                {
                    // Set the m_pRefFromPort of the SECONDARY
                      connection that is attached to a PRIMARY
                    // connection's bend point, to be the same as the
                      PRIMARY connection's m_pRefFromPort.
                    (*it_con_bend_pt)->SetRefFromPort(from_port);

                    // Erase the connection from the
                      connections_from_bend_pt_list since its
                      m_pRefFromPort
```

```
                                      // has now been set to that of its PARENT
                                         (primary) connection.
                                      connections_from_bend_pt_list.erase(it_con_bend_pt);

                                      ref_from_port_flag = 1;   // m_pRefFromPort has
                                         now been set.

                                      break;      // break from it_pt (bend pts of
                                         primary connections)
                                }
                          }
                   }// end for it_pt

                   if(ref_from_port_flag == 1)
                   {
                          break;   // break from it_con (primary connections)
                   }
             }// end for it_con

             // If a ref-from-port was assigned to a secondary connection
                emanating from a bend pt., then this connection
             // was erased (as above), so set the starting pt. of iteration to
                the beginning of the now newly reduced list.
             if(ref_from_port_flag == 1)
             {
                   it_con_bend_pt = connections_from_bend_pt_list.begin();
             }
             else                // else increment the iterator of the
                connections_from_bend_pt_list.
             {
                   it_con_bend_pt++;
             }
       }// end while
}
```

Initially a list is formed, named "connections_from_bend_pt_list", of the *secondary* connections that emanate from other connection objects' bend points. The main *while* loop then iterates through this list, and when the "reference-from port" of a *secondary* connection is set, this connection is removed from the list, reducing its size.

The first *for* loop iterates through the list of connections in the model, and the second *for* loop iterates over the connection's bend points. The *if* clause then determines whether a *secondary* connection end point is attached to the bend point by comparing their Cartesian coordinates, and if connected, the "m_pRefFromPort" of the *primary* connection is obtained and assigned to that of the *secondary* connection. Once set, the *secondary* connection is removed from the list being searched, and the search then restarts from the beginning of the now newly reduced list.

The result of this is that, from the perspective of the calling environment, i.e., from DetermineModelFeedbackLoops(), the reference-from ports of all the connections are correctly set, and the block connectivity matrix can be properly constructed.

19.5.1.3 Assign Block Connectivity Matrix Values

The function DetermineModelFeedbackLoops() calls AssignBlockConnectivity MatrixValues() passing in the addresses of the "from_block" and "to_block": the former is the block from whose output port a connection exits, and the latter is the block to whose input port the connection enters. Add a public member function to the CSystemModel class with the prototype, void CSystemModel::AssignBlockConnectivity MatrixValues(CBlock *from_block, CBlock *to_block, int **BlockConMatrix), and edit it as shown.

```cpp
void CSystemModel::AssignBlockConnectivityMatrixValues(CBlock *from_block,
    CBlock *to_block, int **BlockConMatrix)
{
    int i = 0;          // row index: "from" block
    int j = 0;          // col index: "to" block
    list <CBlock*>::iterator it_blk;
    list<CBlock*> &blk_list = GetBlockList();

    // Obtain the row index, i.e. the "from" block
    for(it_blk = blk_list.begin(); it_blk != blk_list.end(); it_blk++)
    {
        if(from_block == (*it_blk))
        {
            break;
        }
        i++;    // increment the i-th "from" block row index
    }

    // Obtain the column index, i.e. the "to" block
    for(it_blk = blk_list.begin(); it_blk != blk_list.end(); it_blk++)
    {
        if(to_block == (*it_blk))
        {
            break;
        }
        j++;    // increment the j-th "to" block col index
    }

    // The connection from the "from" block to the "to" block is denoted
    //   by unity.
    BlockConMatrix[i][j] = 1;
}
```

The model's block list is iterated over, and if the "from_block" is the current block, then the loop is exited and the index used to denote the row of the block connectivity matrix. Similarly, if the "to_block" is the current block, then the index is used to denote the column of the matrix. A connection between the blocks is denoted by a "1," and "0" otherwise. The developer will notice that the numbers representing the model blocks are based on the order in which the blocks were added to the model's block list, i.e., the order in which they were placed on the palette by the user (later a reordering of blocks will be performed, but the logic to find the connectivity matrix is still applicable).

19.5.1.4 Determine Loops from Connectivity Matrix

The final function to be called from DetermineModelFeedbackLoops() is Determine LoopsFromConnectivityMatrix(), which calls DetermineInitialNodeVector(), to obtain the vector of starting source node(s), and BuildTour(), which finds tours in the connectivity matrix that end in loop-repeated block denoting a feedback loop, or at an Output block. Add a public member function to the CSystemModel class with the prototype, void CSystem

Model::DetermineLoopsFromConnectivityMatrix(int **A, int nrows, int ncols), and edit it as shown.

```cpp
void CSystemModel::DetermineLoopsFromConnectivityMatrix(int **A, int
  nrows, int ncols)
{
    int i;                      // index of i-th column of vector
    int n_nodes;                // number of initial nodes in node_vec,
      i.e., source nodes only, NOT ALL NODES.
    int source_flag;            // flag indicating the presence of source
      nodes
    int *node_vec = NULL;   // node vector that contains only the source
      node(s)
    int *tour_vec = NULL;   // vec that holds node-to-node tours, of size
      total number of nodes = ncols.
    CString sMsg;               // string to be displayed
    CString sMsgTemp;           // temp msg.
    UINT nType = MB_OK;       // style of msg. box
    UINT nIDhelp = 0;         // help context ID for the msg.

    // MEMORY ALLOC
    node_vec = new int[ncols]; // allocate enough space for all nodes,
      but only emplace source nodes.
    tour_vec = new int[ncols]; // allocate enough space for all nodes,
      since max tour length contains all nodes

    // Get the initial vector of source blocks/nodes
    source_flag = DetermineInitialNodeVector(A, nrows, ncols, node_vec,
      n_nodes);

    if(source_flag == -1)
    {
        sMsgTemp.Format("\n DetermineLoopsFromConnectivityMatrix(),
          node_vec error.\n");
        sMsg+=sMsgTemp;
        sMsgTemp.Format("\n No source nodes found: source_flag = %d\n",
          source_flag);
        sMsg+=sMsgTemp;
        AfxMessageBox(sMsg, nType, nIDhelp);
    }
    else if(source_flag == 0)
    {
        PrintVector(node_vec, ncols);
    }

    // Setup the initial tour vector by assigning unique initial negative
      values to the node entries
    // to the tour vector indicating no feasible tour found yet.
    for(i=0; i<ncols; i++)
    {
        tour_vec[i] = -(i+1);
    }
    PrintVector(tour_vec, ncols);

    // Construct node-arc tours
    if(source_flag == 0)
```

```
    {
        BuildTour(A, nrows, ncols, node_vec, n_nodes, tour_vec);
    }

    // MEMORY DELETE
    delete [] node_vec;
    delete [] tour_vec;
    return;
}
```

19.5.2 Determining Loops from the Connectivity Matrix

The functions that are required by and related to DetermineLoopsFromConnectivity Matrix(), as listed in the previous section, are now introduced to the project.

19.5.2.1 Determine Initial Node Vector

The initial node vector is the vector that contains the source nodes from which tours through the connectivity matrix begin. The DetermineInitialNodeVector() function takes as arguments the connectivity matrix; its dimensions; the node vector, "node_vec"; and the number of source nodes, "n_nodes". Add a public member function to the CSystemModel class with the prototype, int CSystemModel::DetermineInitialNodeVector(int **A, int nrows, int ncols, int *node_vec, int &n_nodes), and edit the function as shown in the following.

```
int CSystemModel::DetermineInitialNodeVector(int **A, int nrows, int
  ncols, int *node_vec, int &n_nodes)
{
    int i;
    int j;
    int offset = 0;       // node_vec offset
    int col_sum = 0;      // sum of col elements

    // A node on row i, is connected to a node on col j.
    // So if there is a col of zeros, then that col number represents a
      source node,
    // since no node is connected to it in the forward-direction sense.

    // Assign initial negative values
    for(i=0; i<ncols; i++)
    {
        node_vec[i] = -1;
    }

    // Iterate across the cols and down the rows
    for(j=0; j<ncols; j++)
    {
        col_sum = 0;
        for(i=0; i<nrows; i++)
        {
            col_sum = col_sum + A[i][j];  // col sum
        }
        if(col_sum == 0)
        {
            node_vec[offset] = j;  // place source node in node_vec
            offset++;
        }
    }
```

```
    // Assign the number of source nodes in the node_vec
    n_nodes = offset;

    // Return a flag indicating whether a row of zeros was found
    if(offset == 0)
    {
        return -1;      // error since no col of zeros, and hence no
            initial source node
    }
    else
    {
        return 0;       // a col of zeros was found, hence there exists a
            source node
    }
}
```

Initially the array "node_vec" is filled, by default, with "–1" values. Then the connectivity matrix is checked for null columns, which indicate that no block on row i is connected to the block represented by column j, in the forward-direction sense. Hence, the column number represents a source node. In total, a number of "n_nodes" are added to the node vector, "node_vec". Not all blocks can be source blocks: there must be at least one Output block in the model, in which case "n_nodes" is less than the total number of blocks represented by "nrows" and equivalently "ncols".

19.5.2.2 Build Tour

The final function called by `DetermineLoopsFromConnectivityMatrix()` is `BuildTour()`, which builds tours using the block connectivity matrix that end at an Output block, represented by a row of 0s, indicating no forward connection, or a feedback loop, where a block number appears twice in the tour vector. Add a public member function to the CSystemModel class with the prototype, `void CSystemModel::BuildTour(int **A, int nrows, int ncols, int *node_vec, int n_nodes, int *in_tour_vec)`, and edit it as shown in the following.

```
void CSystemModel::BuildTour(int **A, int nrows, int ncols,
  int *node_vec, int n_nodes, int *in_tour_vec)
{
    int i;
    int j;
    int posn;                   // posn of nodes in tour vector
    int n_branch_nodes;         // number of branch nodes present on a
      partic. row
    int node;                   // node number = row number = col number
    int tour_end = 0;           // flag identifying whether current tour
      has been found
    int *branch_node_vec = NULL; // vec of branch nodes to which current
      node can progress
    int *tour_vec = NULL;       // vec of nodes comprising the tour
    char t_string[20];          // time string
    time_t seconds;             // time var used to aid user when
      pressing return bw. iterations of for-node loop
    CString sMsg;               // string to be displayed
    CString sMsgTemp;           // temp msg.
    UINT nType = MB_OK;         // style of msg. box
    UINT nIDhelp = 0;           // help context ID for the msg.

    // -- MEMORY ALLOC
    tour_vec = new int[ncols];
```

```
// Copy the incoming tour vec into the local tour vec
for(j=0; j<ncols; j++)
{
    tour_vec[j] = in_tour_vec[j];
}

PrintVector(tour_vec, ncols);
PrintVector(node_vec, ncols);

// -- ITERATE OVER ONLY THE NODES IN THE NODE VECTOR FROM WHICH
   CONNECTIONS TO OTHER NODES ARE PREMISSABLE
for(node=0; node<n_nodes; node++)
{
    // Get the offset position in the tour vector into which the next
      node should be placed
    posn = FindCurrentTourPosition(in_tour_vec, ncols);

    // Get starting node, i.e. a node in the node vector (of source
      nodes or branch nodes)
    i = node_vec[node];
    tour_vec[posn] = i;
    tour_end = 0;
    PrintVector(tour_vec, ncols);

    // Check for repeated entries here, after the new node addition
      to the tour_vec: if there is a repeat, end tour.
    if(CheckRepeatedEntries(tour_vec, ncols) > 0)
    {
        tour_end = 1;
        SaveTourVector(tour_vec, ncols); // save tour_vec since tour
          has had an entry added but a loop exists
    }

    // -- WHILE TOUR NOT COMPLETE
    while(tour_end == 0)
    {
        // Get the offset position in the EVOLVING TOUR VECTOR into
          which the next node should be placed
        posn = FindCurrentTourPosition(tour_vec, ncols);

        if(posn >= ncols)  // if the posn is after the end of the
          array, then the tour vector is filled.
        {
            tour_end = 1;
            SaveTourVector(tour_vec, ncols); // save tour_vec since
              tour has ended due to no further connections
            break;         // break from while loop
        }

        // Find the number of connections i.e. branch nodes to the
          current node
        n_branch_nodes = NumberOfOnesOnMatrixRow(A, i, ncols);

        // If there are no 1's in the cols then there are no
          connecting nodes
        if(n_branch_nodes == 0)
        {
            tour_vec[posn] = -1;  // -1 indicates no fwd connection
              exists from the current node
            tour_end = 1;           // end tour
```

```
            SaveTourVector(tour_vec, ncols);  // save tour_vec since
              tour has ended due to no further connections
        }
        // If there is one 1, in the cols, then there is one
          connecting node
        else if(n_branch_nodes == 1)
        {
            for(j=0; j<ncols; j++)  // iterate over cols
            {
                if(A[i][j] == 1)    // if a col contains a 1, then,
                  node on row i, is connected to node in col j.
                {
                    tour_vec[posn] = j;  // new node traversed is
                      that in col j, connected to that in row i
                    i = j; // update row i with col j to continue to
                      the next connection
                    break;    // break from for loop
                }
            }

            PrintVector(tour_vec, ncols);
        }
        // If there is > one 1, in the cols, then there is > 1
          connecting node
        else if(n_branch_nodes > 1)
        {
            // MEMORY ALLOC
            branch_node_vec = new int[ncols];

            // Find all nodes that are connected/branched to the
              current node
            FindBranchNodes(A, i, ncols, branch_node_vec,
              n_branch_nodes);

            PrintVector(branch_node_vec, ncols);

            // RECURSIVELY CALL THE BuildTour() FUNCTION WITH THE NEW
              NODE VECTOR AND TOUR VECTOR
            BuildTour(A, nrows, ncols, branch_node_vec,
              n_branch_nodes, tour_vec);

            tour_end = 1;

            // MEMORY DELETE
            delete [] branch_node_vec;
        }

        // Check for repeated entries here, after the if-else-based
          node addition to the tour_vec.
        if(CheckRepeatedEntries(tour_vec, ncols) > 0)
        {
            tour_end = 1;
            SaveTourVector(tour_vec, ncols); // save tour_vec since
              tour has had an entry added but a loop exists
        }
        // Reset the tour_vec to be that of the incoming tour vector
        if(tour_end == 1)
```

```
            {
                ResetTourVector(tour_vec, in_tour_vec, ncols);
            }
        }// end while

        // Get the time of the end of this loop
        seconds = time(NULL);  // get seconds elapsed since 1-1-1970
        strftime(t_string, 20, "%H:%M:%S", localtime(&seconds));
           // get the local time as a string

        // Print msg. end of current node/block
        sMsgTemp.Format("\n BuildTour()\n");
        sMsg+=sMsgTemp;
        sMsgTemp.Format("\n End of for node = %d\n time: %s\n", node,
           t_string);
        sMsg+=sMsgTemp;
        AfxMessageBox(sMsg, nType, nIDhelp);

    }// end for

    // MEMORY DELETE
    delete [] tour_vec;

    return;
}
```

The workings of the `BuildTour()` function are somewhat difficult to understand since recursion is involved. Hence, the interested reader may like to experiment with the exploratory code provided in Appendix C, a Win32 Console Application titled NodeArcConnectivity that finds tours in a node-arc incidence matrix of 1s and 0s. The numerous output statements clarify the order of operations in the `BuildTour()` function and the manner in which it is recursively called.

At the start of the `BuildTour()` function mentioned earlier, the tour vector to be constructed is assigned the incoming tour, since the function is called recursively, and an incomplete tour needs to be initially copied before it can be worked upon further to be completed.

The main *for* loop iterates over the nodes/blocks in the node array/vector "node_vec": initially the "node_vec" contains all source nodes from which a tour may start, but during the tour building process, this "node_vec" contains the branch nodes, i.e., nodes that may be branched to, from a branch point. For the previous example, the initial node vector contains source block E4 followed by "−1" values for the remaining entries. However, three branches, and hence recursive calls, occur: (1) F5 branches to B1 and C2, (2) C2 branches to A0 and I8, and (3) D3 branches to G6 and J9. Hence, when iterating through the algorithm, these branch nodes will be used in the node vector.

At the start of the *for* loop, the current tour position, found using `FindCurrentTourPosition()`, is that of the first negative number in the incoming "tour_vec": initially the elements are initialized to be uniquely negative numbers, and node/blocks visited have uniquely nonnegative numbers. The node to be added to the tour is that in the "node_vec" for the current iteration. The `CheckRepeatedEntries()` function simply checks the tour for repeated numbers, signifying a feedback loop in the model: if there are repeated nodes, then a call is made to `SaveTourVector()` (discussed in the following).

The *while* loop iterates until a block-to-block tour is complete. Initially the current position in the evolving "tour_vec" at which a new entry should be placed is obtained (`FindCurrentTourPosition()`). Then three clauses of an *if-else* statement concerning the number of branch nodes, "n_branch_nodes", found by a call to `NumberOfOnesOnMatrixRow()` are tested: (1) if there are no branch nodes, then the tour ends at an Output block, and the tour may be saved using `SaveTourVector()`; (2) if there is just one branch node, then the tour progresses to that connected node; and (3) if there is more than one branch node, then the nodes are found using `FindBranchNodes()`, and the `BuildTour()` function is recursively called, passing in "branch_node_vec", to continue the search process.

At the end of the *while* loop, if a tour was found, the tour vector, "tour_vec", is set to be the (original) incoming tour vector, "in_tour_vec", since the sequence of nodes up to, but not beyond, the branch point needs to be reestablished for subsequent tours emanating from the branch point.

Finally, in the `SaveTourVector()` function, the number of tours that end at an Output block ("m_iNSourceOutputTours") or at a loop-repeated node ("m_iNSourceLoopTours") signifying a feedback loop is incremented.

The reader is encouraged to experiment with the aforementioned Win32 Console Application, NodeArcConnectivity, and view all the print statements indicating the progressive building of tours that exist in the sample model. In addition, the developer may like to use the debugger to step through the functions observing the changing program state (see Appendix D on how to use the debugger.).

19.5.2.3 Find Current Tour Position

The `FindCurrentTourPosition()` function simply iterates through the tour vector to find the first negative, non-node-filled entry, since originally all entries are uniquely negative numbers. The new, to-be-entered, nonnegative node/block number will then be placed at this location in the tour vector, "tour_vec". Hence, add a public member function to the CSystemModel class with the prototype, int `CSystemModel::FindCurrentTourPosition(int *tour_vec, int ncols)`, and edit it as shown.

```
int CSystemModel::FindCurrentTourPosition(int *tour_vec, int ncols)
{
    int i;

    // Iterate through the vector to find the first negative, non-node-
        filled, entry.
    for(i=0; i<ncols; i++)
    {
        if(tour_vec[i] < 0)
        {
            return i;
        }
    }

    // If no -ve value found then return the size of the array "ncols"
    return ncols;
}
```

19.5.2.4 Find Branch Nodes

The branch node vector is a vector of nodes to which signal flow may branch from the current node. That is, it is a vector of the column numbers representing blocks of the block connectivity matrix for which there exists a "1" on the current row. The example of a connectivity matrix provided earlier shows branching from C2, D3, and F5. Add a public member function to the CSystemModel class with the prototype, void `CSystemModel::FindBranchNodes(int **A, int i, int ncols, int *branch_node_vec, int &n_branch_nodes)`, and edit it as shown.

```
int CSystemModel::FindBranchNodes(int **A, int i, int ncols, int
   *branch_node_vec, int &n_branch_nodes)
{
    int j;        // col index
    int cnt = 0;  // branch_node_vec[] offset index

    // Negate the branch_node_vec
    for(j=0; j<ncols; j++)
```

```
    {
        branch_node_vec[j] = -1;
    }

    // Iterate over the cols of A for the current row (i), recording
      those with one's (1), indicating node connections.
    for(j=0; j<ncols; j++)
    {
        if(A[i][j] == 1)
        {
            branch_node_vec[cnt] = j;
            cnt++;
        }
    }
    n_branch_nodes = cnt; // update the number of connecting/branch nodes

    return 0;
}
```

19.5.2.5   Number of Ones on Matrix Row

The number of branch nodes, "n_branch_nodes", is first obtained in BuildTour() by a call to NumberOfOnesOnMatrixRow(), where the number of "1" entries on a particular row of the block connectivity matrix is returned: this specifies the number of branches from the block represented by the row number of the matrix. Hence, add a public member function to the CSystemModel class with the prototype, int CSystemModel::NumberOfOnesOnMatrixRow(int **A, int row, int ncols), and edit it as shown.

```
int CSystemModel::NumberOfOnesOnMatrixRow(int **A, int row, int ncols)
{
    int j;
    int n_ones = 0;

    // Count the number of ones on the partic. row.
    for(j=0; j<ncols; j++)
    {
        if(A[row][j] == 1)
        {
            n_ones++;
        }
    }

    return n_ones;
}
```

19.5.2.6   Check Repeated Entries

The BuildTour() function builds tours that may end either at an Output block or in a feedback loop, where a previous block recorded in the tour vector, "tour_vec", is revisited: this results in their being more than one occurrence of the block number in the vector. Hence, the CheckRepeatedEntries() function checks for repeated block numbers and returns the number of repeated entries in the vector. Add a public member function to the CSystemModel class with the prototype, int CSystemModel::CheckRepeatedEntries(int *tour_vec, int ncols), and edit it as shown.

```
int CSystemModel::CheckRepeatedEntries(int *tour_vec, int ncols)
{
    int i;
    int j;
    int n_repeats = 0;
```

```
    // Check tour vector for repeated entries (implying a loop)
    for(i=0; i<(ncols-1); i++)
    {
        for(j=(i+1); j<ncols; j++)
        {
            if(tour_vec[j] == tour_vec[i])
            {
                n_repeats++;
            }
        }
    }

    return n_repeats;
}
```

19.5.2.7 Reset Tour Vector

The ResetTourVector(), as described earlier, simply writes the values of the incoming tour vector, "in_tour_vec", into the current tour vector, "tour_vec", to reestablish the original tour vector up to a branch point, wherefrom different tours would result. Hence, add a public member function to the CSystemModel class with the prototype, void CSystemModel::ResetTourVector(int *tour_vec, int *in_tour_vec, int ncols), and edit it as shown.

```
void CSystemModel::ResetTourVector(int *tour_vec, int *in_tour_vec,
   int ncols)
{
    int j;

    // Reassign in_tour_vec to tour_vec
    for(j=0; j<ncols; j++)
    {
        tour_vec[j] = in_tour_vec[j];
    }
}
```

19.5.2.8 Save Tour Vector

At present, in the BuildTour() function, when a tour ends, either at an Output block or due to a feedback loop, a call to SaveTourVector() is made with the intention of saving the tour vector "tour_vec". However, at present, this is a placeholder function since a record of the tours is not required as yet, but rather only the number of tours that end at either an Output block ("m_iNSourceOutputTours") or a loop-repeated node (feedback loop) ("m_iNSourceLoopTours") needs to be recorded.

Hence, add a public member function to the CSystemModel class with the prototype: void CSystemModel::SaveTourVector(int *tour_vec, int ncols). Edit the function as shown in the following, noting that actual tour saving will be performed at a later stage in the project, but for now, only the manner in which the tour is ended is reported (either at an Output block or a feedback loop), the number of tours is incremented, and the "tour_vec" is printed using an integer form of the PrintVector() function.

```
void CSystemModel::SaveTourVector(int *tour_vec, int ncols)
{
    int n_repeats = 0;          // number of repeated entries
    //static int n_tours = 0;   // number of tours
```

```
    CString sMsg;          // string to be displayed
    CString sMsgTemp;      // temp msg.
    UINT nType = MB_OK;    // style of msg. box
    UINT nIDhelp = 0;      // help context ID for the msg.

    // Record the number of unique tours
    //n_tours++;

    // Check tour vector for repeated entries (implying a node-to-node
      loop)
    n_repeats = CheckRepeatedEntries(tour_vec, ncols);

    // Notify method of tour termination
    sMsgTemp.Format("\n SaveTourVector()\n");
    sMsg+=sMsgTemp;
    if(n_repeats == 0)
    {
        m_iNSourceOutputTours++;
        sMsgTemp.Format(" tour_vec that would be saved (output
          block):\n");
    }
    else if(n_repeats > 0)
    {
        m_iNSourceLoopTours++;    // record the number of source-to-loop
          tours
        sMsgTemp.Format(" tour_vec that would be saved (loop):\n");
    }
    sMsg+=sMsgTemp;
    AfxMessageBox(sMsg, nType, nIDhelp);

    PrintVector(tour_vec, ncols);

    return;
}
```

19.5.2.9 Print Integer Matrix

In the DetermineModelFeedbackLoops() function, there is a call to int PrintMatrix(int **M, int nrows, int ncols). This version differs to that introduced in the section concerning the conversion of strings to double values, whose prototype was int PrintMatrix(double **M, int nrows, int ncols).

Add a new global function prototype for the PrintMatrix() function to the "DiagramEngDoc.h" header file, beneath the existing double version as shown in bold, i.e., int PrintMatrix(int **M, int nrows, int ncols).

```
// Global Functions
CDiagramEngDoc* GetDocumentGlobalFn(void);
double **ConvertStringToDouble(CString string, int &nrows, int &ncols);
char *StripInputString(char *input_str);
int DetermineDataDimsByStrpbrk(char *in_str, int &nrows, int &ncols,
  int &max_row_length);
int DetermineDataDimsByStrtok(char *in_str, int &nrows, int &ncols,
  int &max_row_length);
double **ConvertStringMatrixToDoubleMatrix(char **str_matrix, int nrows,
  int ncols);
int PrintMatrix(double **M, int nrows, int ncols);
int PrintMatrix(int **M, int nrows, int ncols);
int PrintVector(double *v, int ncols);
```

Now add the new `PrintMatrix()` function to the "DiagramEngDoc.cpp" source file, beneath the existing global functions, and edit the code as shown in the following.

```
int PrintMatrix(int **M, int nrows, int ncols)
{
    int i;
    int j;
    CString sMsg;         // main msg string
    CString sMsgTemp;     // temp msg string
    UINT nType = MB_OK;   // style of msg. box
    UINT nIDhelp = 0;     // help context ID for the msg.

    // If the matrix is NULL then return.
    if(M == NULL)
    {
        return 1;
    }

    sMsgTemp.Format("\n PrintMatrix()\n");
    sMsg += sMsgTemp;

    // Print Matrix
    sMsgTemp.Format("\n");
    sMsg += sMsgTemp;

    for(i=0; i<nrows; i++)
    {
        for(j=0; j<ncols; j++)
        {
            sMsgTemp.Format(" %d", M[i][j]);  // standard double
                formatting
            sMsg += sMsgTemp;
        }
        sMsgTemp.Format("\n");
        sMsg += sMsgTemp;
    }
    sMsgTemp.Format("\n");
    sMsg += sMsgTemp;

    // Display msg. box
    AfxMessageBox(sMsg, nType, nIDhelp);

    return 0;
}
```

19.5.2.10 Print Integer Vector

There are numerous occurrences of calls to `int PrintVector(int *v, int ncols)` in the functions discussed earlier. This differs in its formal parameter list from the existing `int PrintVector(double *v, int ncols)` function that was introduced in the section concerning the conversion of strings to double values. Hence, add a new global function prototype for the `PrintVector()` function to the "DiagramEngDoc.h" header file, beneath the existing double version, as shown in bold, i.e., `int PrintVector(int *v, int ncols)`.

```
// Global Functions
CDiagramEngDoc* GetDocumentGlobalFn(void);
double **ConvertStringToDouble(CString string, int &nrows, int &ncols);
char *StripInputString(char *input_str);
```

```
int DetermineDataDimsByStrpbrk(char *in_str, int &nrows, int &ncols,
  int &max_row_length);
int DetermineDataDimsByStrtok(char *in_str, int &nrows, int &ncols,
  int &max_row_length);
double **ConvertStringMatrixToDoubleMatrix(char **str_matrix, int nrows,
  int ncols);
int PrintMatrix(double **M, int nrows, int ncols);
int PrintMatrix(int **M, int nrows, int ncols);
int PrintVector(double *v, int ncols);
int PrintVector(int *v, int ncols);
```

Now add the new integer version of `PrintVector()` to the "DiagramEngDoc.cpp" source file, beneath the existing double version, and edit the code as shown in the following.

```
int PrintVector(int *v, int ncols)
{
    int i;
    CString sMsg;          // main msg string
    CString sMsgTemp;      // temp msg string
    UINT nType = MB_OK;    // style of msg. box
    UINT nIDhelp = 0;      // help context ID for the msg.

    // If the vector is NULL then return.
    if(v == NULL)
    {
        return 1;
    }

    sMsgTemp.Format("\n PrintVector()\n");
    sMsg += sMsgTemp;

    // Print Vector
    sMsgTemp.Format("\n");
    sMsg += sMsgTemp;

    for(i=0; i<ncols; i++)
    {
        sMsgTemp.Format(" %d", v[i]);  // standard double formatting
        sMsg += sMsgTemp;
    }
    sMsgTemp.Format("\n");
    sMsg += sMsgTemp;

    // Display msg. box
    AfxMessageBox(sMsg, nType, nIDhelp);

    return 0;
}
```

19.5.2.11 Running the Application

Now, if the developer runs the program with, e.g., the model containing two feedback loops as shown in Figure 19.6, where the blocks are added to the model in the alphabetical and simultaneously numerical order specified, then the connectivity matrix will be correctly displayed, and the tour vectors printed to the screen in the form of message boxes. The number of feedback loops, "m_iNSourceLoopTours", is then correctly reported to be two. Four tours exist in total as shown in Table 19.2: two terminate at Output blocks and two terminate with repeated nodes in the tour vector, signifying a feedback loop.

19.6 SIGNAL-BASED CLASS STRUCTURE

At the time of writing the Win32 Console Application, ControlEng, the signal-based class structure involved a base class CSignal, and the derived classes: CDoubleSignal, CVectorSignal, and CMatrixSignal, to cater for double, vector, and matrix data objects, respectively. It is decided here that the CSignal class need not be inherited from, but rather can contain, double, vector, and matrix data and all the necessary methods to operate on that data. Hence, the CDoubleSignal, CVectorSignal, and CMatrixSignal code can now be deleted from the project, leaving the sole CSignal class containing the member variables and methods indicated in the revised class definition shown in the following. Some of these methods are simply placeholder functions and will be changed as required.

```
// Signal
class CSignal
{
public:
    CSignal(void);
    ~CSignal(void);

    // Accessor methods
    CString GetSignalName(void);
    void SetSignalData(double **matrix, int nrows, int ncols);
    void SetSignalName(CString name);
    void SetSignalValidity(int validity);

    private:
    int m_iNrows;             // no. of rows of signal matrix
    int m_iNcols;             // no. of cols of signal matrix
    int m_iValidity;          // signal data-based validity
    double **m_dSignalMatrix; // matrix signal value
    CString m_strSignalName;  // signal name
};
```

The developer will also note that the class member variables should be initialized as shown in the following class constructor CSignal(); the numerical variables are assigned to nullity, and the signal name is at present a generic placeholder name, "signal_name":

```
CSignal::CSignal(void)
{
    // Init.
    m_iNrows = 0;
    m_iNcols = 0;
    m_iValidity = 0;
    m_dSignalMatrix = NULL;
    m_strSignalName = "signal_name";
}
```

However, since a CSignal class has a matrix member variable, "m_dSignalMatrix", of dimension "m_iNrows" (number of rows) by "m_iNcols" (number of columns), which requires the allocation of memory to hold the connection-based signal data, the CSignal::~CSignal() destructor should deallocate this memory when called. Furthermore, when a connection object is deleted by the user, hence calling the CConnection::~CConnection() destructor, its contained CSignal object, "m_pSignal", should be destroyed through a call to the CSignal::~CSignal() destructor.

Hence, edit the `CConnection::~CConnection()` destructor function to delete the CSignal "m_pSignal" object upon connection-object deletion as shown.

```
CConnection::~CConnection(void)
{
    // Delete the connection-held signal data
    if(m_pSignal != NULL)
    {
        delete m_pSignal;
        m_pSignal = NULL;
    }
}
```

Edit the `CSignal::~CSignal()` destructor function as shown in the following to deallocate memory for the "m_dSignalMatrix" variable:

```
CSignal::~CSignal(void)
{
    int i;

    // MEMORY DELETE
    if(m_dSignalMatrix != NULL)
    {
        for(i=0; i<m_iNrows; i++)
        {
            delete [] m_dSignalMatrix[i];
        }
        delete [] m_dSignalMatrix;
        m_dSignalMatrix = NULL;
    }
}
```

Now if a connection object is deleted by the user and if it holds any CSignal data, this data will be deleted, preventing a memory leak.

19.7   ADDITIONS REQUIRED FOR DIRECT SIGNAL PROPAGATION

The determination of the presence of algebraic and feedback loops is necessary in order to choose the most appropriate form of signal propagation: if no loops exist, then a direct signal propagation method may be used; otherwise, if loops do exist, a simultaneous equation-based method is required to determine signal values.

19.7.1   ADDITION OF SIGNAL PROPAGATION CODE

The direct signal propagation method, described previously, may be initiated when the user selects Start from the application's Common Operations toolbar or from the Simulation menu. This will call the `CDiagramEngDoc::OnSimStart()` function, which currently takes no action. The following steps are required to augment the program to call and execute the appropriate signal propagation function:

1. Add code to the `CDiagramEngDoc::OnSimStart()` function.
2. Modify the `CSystemModel::ValidateModel()` function to return an error value.
3. Modify the `CDiagramEngDoc::OnModelBuild()` function to accept an error value.
4. Add a `CSystemModel::GetNFeedbackLoops()` function.

5. Add a `CSystemModel::SignalPropagationDirect()` function.
6. Add a `CSystemModel::DetermineNTimeSteps()` function.
7. Add a `CSignal::ResetSignalData()` function.
8. Add a `CSystemModel::SignalPropagationSystemOfEquations()` placeholder function.
9. Add a virtual `CBlock::OperateOnData()` function.

19.7.1.1 Add Code to the `CDiagramEngDoc::OnSimStart()` Function

The `CDiagramEngDoc::OnSimStart()` function simply presents a message to the user. Augment the function as shown in the following to call `ValidateModel()`, to determine model validity, and to check the returned error flag and number of feedback loops. Thereafter, based upon the flag values, the appropriate signal propagation method can be called: (1) `SignalPropagationDirect()` or (2) `SignalPropagationSystemOfEquations()`. Here, for now, both calls are commented out, since `SignalPropagationDirect()` makes use of the function `OperateOnData()`, which is to be added (later) for each derived CBlock class. The other signal propagation function `SignalPropagationSystemOfEquations()` is a placeholder function to be written later. (The signal propagation function calls may be uncommented after the functions have been added to the project.)

```
void CDiagramEngDoc::OnSimStart()
{
    // TODO: Add your command handler code here

    // DiagramEng (start)
    int error_flag = 0;    // flag indicating whether model is in error or
      has feedback loops
    CString sMsg;          // string to be displayed
    CString sMsgTemp;      // temp string msg.
    UINT nType = MB_OK;    // style of msg. box
    UINT nIDhelp = 0;      // help context ID for the msg.

    // Display a msg. box
    //sMsg.Format("\n CDiagramEngDoc::OnSimStart()\n\n");
    //AfxMessageBox(sMsg, nType, nIDhelp);

    // Validate model
    error_flag = m_SystemModel.ValidateModel();

    // Propagate signals
    if((error_flag == 0) && (m_SystemModel.GetNFeedbackLoops() == 0))
    {
        // m_SystemModel.SignalPropagationDirect();
    }
    else if((error_flag == 0) && (m_SystemModel.GetNFeedbackLoops() > 0))
    {
        // m_SystemModel.SignalPropagationSystemOfEquations();
    }
    else
    {
        sMsgTemp.Format("\n CDiagramEngDoc::OnSimStart() \n\n");
        sMsg+=sMsgTemp;
        sMsgTemp.Format(" Model is in error and simulation cannot
            start. \n");
        sMsg+=sMsgTemp;
        sMsgTemp.Format(" Please resolve model errors, before rebuilding/
            restarting. \n");
```

```
        sMsg+=sMsgTemp;
        AfxMessageBox(sMsg, nType, nIDhelp);
    }

    // DiagramEng (end)
}
```

19.7.1.2 Modify the `CSystemModel::ValidateModel()` Function

The ValidateModel() function calls ValidateModelBlocks(), ValidateModel
BlockPorts(), ValidateModelConnections(), and finally DetermineModelFeed
backLoops(). However, at this stage, diagnostic warnings are presented, and errors are flashed in
red, but no error flag is returned:

1. Change the prototype in the "SystemModel.h" header file to int CSystemModel::
   ValidateModel(void).
2. Modify the CSystemModel::ValidateModel() function as shown in bold in the following to return an error flag:

```
int CSystemModel::ValidateModel()
{
    int i;
    int error1 = 0;      // error in model blocks: (0) no error, (1) error
    int error2 = 0;      // error in model ports: (0) no error, (1) error
    int error3 = 0;      // error in mode connections: (0) no error,
      (1) error
    int error_flag = 0; // error flag returned if there are any build
      errors
    …
    if((error1 == 1) || (error2 == 1) || (error3 == 1))
    {
        error_flag = 1;
        …
    }
    …
    return error_flag;
}
```

19.7.1.3 Modify the `CDiagramEngDoc::OnModelBuild()` Function

The OnModelBuild() function currently calls ValidateModel(). However, since
ValidateModel() now returns an integer error flag value, indicating the presence of a model
error, modify the OnModelBuild() function as shown in bold in the following to accept this
returned value.

```
void CDiagramEngDoc::OnModelBuild()
{
    // TODO: Add your command handler code here

    // DiagramEng (start)
    int error_flag = 0;    // error flag for model validation
    CString sMsg;          // string to be displayed
    UINT nType = MB_OK;    // style of msg. box
    UINT nIDhelp = 0;      // help context ID for the msg.

    // Validate Model
    error_flag = m_SystemModel.ValidateModel();
```

```
// Display a msg. box
//sMsg.Format("\n CDiagramEngDoc::OnModelBuild() \n error_flag =
  %d \n\n", error_flag);
//AfxMessageBox(sMsg, nType, nIDhelp);

// DiagramEng (end)
}
```

19.7.1.4   Add a `CSystemModel::GetNFeedbackLoops()` Function

The `CDiagramEngDoc::OnSimStart()` function calls the appropriate signal propagation function based on conditions of the *if-else* statement: one condition concerns the "error_flag" value and the other, the number of feedback loops in the model. Hence, add a new public constant member function to the CSystemModel class with the prototype, `int CSystemModel::GetNFeedbackLoops(void) const`, and edit it as shown.

```
int CSystemModel::GetNFeedbackLoops() const
{
    // Return the number of source-to-loop tours in the model
    return m_iNSourceLoopTours;
}
```

19.7.1.5   Add a `CSystemModel::SignalPropagationDirect()` Function

The `CDiagramEngDoc::OnSimStart()` function calls the `CSystemModel::SignalPropagationDirect()` function if there are no errors or feedback loops. This function is a connection-signal centric function in that a block to which the connection is attached calls its `OperateOnData()` function (yet to be added) to operate on input signal data if there is an input signal, and generate output signal data to be passed along the connection to the next block. At this stage, the `ComputeModelSignals()` placeholder function from the Win32 Console Application, ControlEng, is now replaced with the `SignalPropagationDirect()` function.

Hence, add a new public member function to the CSystemModel class with the prototype: `void CSystemModel::SignalPropagationDirect(void)`. Edit the code as shown in the following to iterate over all time-steps of the simulation and the list of connections and to call the block's `OperateOnData()` function.

```
void CSystemModel::SignalPropagationDirect()
{
    int n_TimeSteps;                    // total no. of time steps for
      numerical integration
    int out_blk_state = 0;              // flag denoting output-block
      operation state
    int std_blk_state = 0;              // flag denoting standard-block
      operation state
    int t_cnt;                          // time counter
    clock_t tv1;                        // init time for execution time calc.
    clock_t tv2;                        // final time for execution time calc.
    double delta_t = m_dTimeStepSize;   // time step size of system model
      simulation
    double t;                           // i-th time point t_i = t
    double t_execution;                 // execution time
    double t_init = m_dTimeStart;       // time init of system model
      simulation
    CPort *ref_from_port = NULL;        // output port from which connection
      emanates
    CString sMsg;                       // string to be displayed
    CString sMsgTemp;                   // temp msg.
```

```
UINT nType = MB_OK;                    // style of msg. box
UINT nIDhelp = 0;                      // help context ID for the msg.
list<CBlock*>::iterator it_blk;        // iterator for list
  of CBlock ptrs.
list<CConnection*>::iterator it_con;  // iterator for list of
  CConnection ptrs.

// Get the actual connection list by reference
list<CConnection*> &con_list = GetConnectionList();
  // get the connection list

// SET REF-FROM-PORTS OF CONNECTIONS THAT EMANATE FROM BEND POINTS.
// These ref-from-ports are then RESET to NULL at the end of the fn
  (since they don't actually emanate from a PORT).
SetRefFromPortOfConnectionFromBendPoint();

// Get a copy of the connection list
list<CConnection*> con_list_copy = GetConnectionList();
  // get a copy of the connection list (NOT BY REFERENCE)

// -- MAIN ITERATION TIME LOOP
n_TimeSteps = DetermineNTimeSteps();  // no. of time steps

// -- EXECUTION TIME START
tv1 = clock();

// -- Loop for n_TimeSteps + 1, from t_0 = 0, UP TO AND INCLUDING the
  last time point t_n
for(t_cnt = 0; t_cnt <= n_TimeSteps; t_cnt++)
{
    t = t_init + t_cnt*delta_t;  // t cnt, i.e. i-th time point t_i,
      or simply t.

    sMsg.Format("");
    sMsgTemp.Format("\n SignalPropagationDirect(), t_cnt = %d,
      t = %lf", t_cnt, t);
    sMsg+=sMsgTemp;
    AfxMessageBox(sMsg, nType, nIDhelp);  // msg. box

    // -- ITERATE OVER CONNECTION LIST TO DETERMINE CONNECTION'S
      SIGNAL DATA
    while(con_list_copy.size() > 0)
    {
        for(it_con = con_list_copy.begin(); it_con != con_list_copy.
          end(); it_con++)
        {
            // Get port and then block
            ref_from_port = (*it_con)->GetRefFromPort();
              // output port of this connection
            CBlock &ref_to_block = ref_from_port->GetRefToBlock();
              // block of this (output) port

            // Perform block operation
            std_blk_state = ref_to_block.OperateOnData(t_cnt, t,
              delta_t);  // Overriding fn in CBlock derived classes

            // -- CHECK OPERATION
            if(std_blk_state == -1)  // OPERATIONAL ERROR: ABORT
              SIGNAL PROPAGATION
            {
                sMsg.Format("");
```

```
                    sMsgTemp.Format("\n SignalPropagationDirect()\n");
                    sMsg+=sMsgTemp;
                    sMsgTemp.Format("\n WARNING! Unsuccessful
                      (non-Output) block operation!\n");
                    sMsg+=sMsgTemp;
                    sMsgTemp.Format(" Aborting signal propagation!\n");
                    sMsg+=sMsgTemp;
                    AfxMessageBox(sMsg, nType, nIDhelp);  // msg. box
                    break;  // break from for loop
                }
            else if(std_blk_state == 0)  // NO SIGNAL DATA AVAILABLE
              FOR CURRENT CONNECTION, HENCE KEEP ITERATING
                {
                    // No action necessary: keep iterating until signal
                      data available upon connection
                }
            else if(std_blk_state == 1)  // DELETE LOCAL CONNECTION
              IF OPERATION SUCCESSFUL
                {
                    con_list_copy.erase(it_con);
                    break;  // break from for loop
                }
        }// end for

        if(std_blk_state == -1)
        {
            break;  // break from while loop
        }
    }// end while

    // -- EXECUTE ALL OUTPUT BLOCKS
    if(std_blk_state == 1)  // if all std block operations were
      successful
    {
        for(it_blk = m_lstBlock.begin(); it_blk != m_lstBlock.end();
          it_blk++)
        {
            if((*it_blk)->GetBlockName() == "output_block")
            {
                // Perform block operation
                out_blk_state = (*it_blk)->OperateOnData(t_cnt, t,
                  delta_t);

                if(out_blk_state == 0)  // Read/write error =>
                  out_blk_state = 0, NOT -1
                {
                    sMsg.Format("");
                    sMsgTemp.Format("\n SignalPropagationDirect()\n");
                    sMsg+=sMsgTemp;
                    sMsgTemp.Format("\n WARNING! Unsuccessful Output
                      block operation!\n");
                    sMsg+=sMsgTemp;
                    sMsgTemp.Format(" Output block unable to read
                      input signal!\n");
                    sMsg+=sMsgTemp;
                    sMsgTemp.Format(" Aborting signal propagation!\n");
                    sMsg+=sMsgTemp;
```

```
                        AfxMessageBox(sMsg, nType, nIDhelp);   // msg. box
                        break;
                    }
                }
            }// end it_blk
        }

        // -- RESET ALL CONNECTION-HELD SIGNAL DATA
        for(it_con = con_list.begin(); it_con != con_list.end();
          it_con++)
        {
            (*it_con)->GetSignal()->ResetSignalData();
        }

        // RE-OBTAIN A COPY OF THE CONNECTION LIST AT EACH TIME STEP
        // This copy of the connection list needs to be re-obtained since
          the previous copy was iterated over and
        // its elements erased after successful block operation
          (OperateOnData()).
        con_list_copy = GetConnectionList();

        // If a std block operation failed or if there was a read/write
          error for the output block, then break.
        if((std_blk_state == -1) || (out_blk_state == 0))
        {
            break;   // break from for loop
        }

    }// end (time)

    // -- EXECUTION TIME STOP
    tv2 = clock();
    t_execution = (double)(tv2 - tv1)/(double)CLOCKS_PER_SEC;

    // -- RESET ALL REF-FROM-PORTS OF CONNECTIONS EMANATING FROM BEND
      POINTS BACK TO NULL
    // Before SignalPropagationDirect() was called the ref-from-ports of
      connections emanating from bend points
    // were NULL. Now they need to be reset to NULL, to leave the program
      state as it was previously.

    for(it_con = con_list.begin(); it_con != con_list.end(); it_con++)
    {
        if((*it_con)->GetRefFromPoint() != NULL)   // if connection
          attached to a BEND POINT
        {
            (*it_con)->SetRefFromPort(NULL);   // set ref-from-port to
            NULL (since not attached to a block)
        }
    }

    // Msg. to user of end of simulation.
    sMsg.Format("");
    sMsgTemp.Format("\n End of SignalPropagationDirect() \n");
    sMsg+=sMsgTemp;
    sMsgTemp.Format("\n Execution time = %lf(s)\n", t_execution);
    sMsg+=sMsgTemp;
    AfxMessageBox(sMsg, nType, nIDhelp);

    return;
}
```

Initially the actual connection list is obtained by reference, and then the reference-from ports of connections emanating from bend points are set to be the same reference-from ports as their parent connections, via the call to `SetRefFromPortOfConnectionFromBendPoint()`. Then a copy of the connection list is obtained for the purpose of obtaining signal data (later).

At the start of the main iteration time-based loop, the total number of simulation time-steps, "n_TimeSteps", is determined through the call to `DetermineNTimeSteps()`, and then the simulation is iterated over for all time-steps using a "for(t_cnt)" loop, up to and including the last time-step: since "t_cnt" starts from 0, a total of "n_TimeSteps + 1" iterations actually occur. The *while* loop together with the contained "for(it_con)" loop iterates over a list of connections to allow the block from which the connection emanates, to generate signal data through the `OperateOnData()` function. This obtains the block's input signal data, performs a block operation, and then writes the output data to the output signal to be transmitted along the connection to the next block.

Output blocks, however, do not have output signals but rather only input signals, and hence they are iterated over separately, and `OperateOnData()` is called to determine the result to be displayed.

The `OperateOnData()` function is to be provided as a virtual function in the base CBlock class (later) and is to be overridden by all the CBlock-derived classes. The developer will notice that the returned value from `OperateOnData()` can be "−1," "0," or "1": "−1" indicates that an operational error occurred and signal propagation is terminated; "0" indicates that a read/write error occurred and that no signal was read from, or written to, a connection, so execution continues until signal data are available; and "1" indicates that the block operation was a success, the local connection is then deleted, and iteration continues over the remaining connections. The variables, "std_blk_state" (standard non-Output block state) and "out_blk_state" (Output block state), for non-Output and Output blocks, respectively, receive the returned result and are used to filter the course of action.

At the end of each time-step, `ResetSignalData()` is called on the pointer-to-CSignal object returned by `GetSignal()`, which itself is called upon the pointer-to-CConnection object, to reset each connection's CSignal-based data. In addition, a copy of the connection list needs to be re-obtained through a call to `GetConnectionList()`, since the previous copy was iterated over and its elements erased after successful block operation (`OperateOnData()`).

Finally, after the time-based iteration has finished ("for(t_cnt)"), all the reference-from ports of connections emanating from bend points need to be reset to NULL to leave the program in the state it was in, prior to the call to `SignalPropagationDirect()`: only after resetting the reference-from ports of these connections can the function return.

19.7.1.6 Add a `CSystemModel::DetermineNTimeSteps()` Function

The `SignalPropagationDirect()` function iterates over the total number of time-steps of the simulation. Hence a function is required that returns the total number of simulation time-steps. Add a public member function to the CSystemModel class with the prototype, int CSystemModel:: DetermineNTimeSteps(void), and edit it as shown.

```
int CSystemModel::DetermineNTimeSteps()
{
    int n_TimeSteps;                    // no. of integer time steps
    double delta_t = m_dTimeStepSize;   // time step size of system model
        simulation
    double t_init = m_dTimeStart;       // time init of system model
        simulation
    double t_final = m_dTimeStop;       // time final of system model
        simulation
    double t_final_revised;             // time final revised given
        integer no. of time steps
    CString sMsg;                       // string to be displayed
    CString sMsgTemp;                   // temp msg.
```

```
    UINT nType = MB_OK;          // style of msg. box
    UINT nIDhelp = 0;            // help context ID for the msg.

    // -- DETERMINE TIME BASED PARAMETERS
    if(t_final >= t_init)
    {
        n_TimeSteps = int((t_final - t_init)/delta_t);  // calculate no.
          of time steps
    }
    else
    {
        sMsgTemp.Format("\n CSystemModel::DetermineNTimeSteps() \n");
        sMsg+=sMsgTemp;
        sMsgTemp.Format(" WARNING! Time error!\n");
        sMsg+=sMsgTemp;
        sMsgTemp.Format("\n t_final should be greater than
          t_initial. \n");
        sMsg+=sMsgTemp;
        AfxMessageBox(sMsg, nType, nIDhelp);  // msg. box
        return 0;
    }

    // Recompute final time based on integer no. of time steps
    t_final_revised = t_init + n_TimeSteps*delta_t;

    sMsgTemp.Format("\n CSystemModel::DetermineNTimeSteps() \n");
    sMsg+=sMsgTemp;
    sMsgTemp.Format("\n t_init = %-10.3e, delta_t = %-10.3e,
      t_final_revised = %-10.3e, n_TimeSteps = %d\n", t_init, delta_t,
      t_final_revised, n_TimeSteps);
    sMsg+=sMsgTemp;
    AfxMessageBox(sMsg, nType, nIDhelp);  // msg. box

    return n_TimeSteps;
}
```

The total number of time-steps, "n_TimeSteps", is simply the difference between the final time, "m_dTimeStop", and initial time, "m_dTimeStart", divided by the simulation time-step size "m_dTimeStepSize". No class member variable is used to record this, since it can be evaluated by calling the `DetermineNTimeSteps()` function, and hence there is no need for a `GetNTimeSteps()` member function of the CSystemModel class (at least for now).

19.7.1.7   Add a `CSignal::ResetSignalData()` Function

Toward the end of the `SignalPropagationDirect()` function, just prior to the end of the time-based loop, the signal data associated with all connections need to be reset. Hence, add a public member function to the CSignal class with the prototype, `void CSignal::ResetSignalData(void)`, and edit it as shown.

```
void CSignal::ResetSignalData()
{
    int i;

    // MEMORY DELETE
    // Delete the arrays held at each of the entries of the column vector
    if(m_dSignalMatrix != NULL)
    {
        for(i=0; i<m_iNrows; i++)
```

```
        {
            delete [] m_dSignalMatrix[i];
        }
        delete [] m_dSignalMatrix;
    }

    // -- RESET VARS
    m_iNrows = 0;
    m_iNcols = 0;
    m_iValidity = 0;
    m_dSignalMatrix = NULL;

    return;
}
```

19.7.1.8 Add a `CSystemModel::SignalPropagationSystemOfEquations()` Function

The other signal propagation function is `SignalPropagationSystemOfEquations()` and is used for the computation of models with feedback loops. For now, this function is empty and will be pursued later in the project. Add a public member function to the CSystemModel class with the prototype, `void   CSystemModel::SignalPropagationSystemOfEquations(void)`, and edit it as follows.

```
void CSystemModel::SignalPropagationSystemOfEquations()
{
    // Material to be added later.
}
```

19.7.1.9 Add a Virtual `CBlock::OperateOnData()` Function

In order for `SignalPropagationDirect()` to work, the `OperateOnData()` function must be able to be called upon the reference-to-CBlock (CBlock) object. This requires that the `OperateOnData()` function be a virtual function of the base CBlock class, and all the derived CBlock classes, e.g., CConstantBlock, CDerivativeBlock, up to and including, CTransferFnBlock, provide their own overriding versions of the function. Then, based on the particular derived run-time CBlock type, the correct derived block's `OperateOnData()` function will be called.

This mechanism works in a similar manner to the virtual function `DrawBlock()` of the CBlock class. The `CSystemModel::DrawSystemModel()` function iterates through the block list, as shown in the following code excerpt, and calls `DrawBlock()` on the pointer-to-CBlock object, which results in the correct derived block's graphics being drawn within the primitive bounding block shape (ellipse, rectangle, or triangle).

```
void CSystemModel::DrawSystemModel(CDC *pDC)
{
    ...
    // Iterate through the list
    for(it_blk = blk_list.begin(); it_blk != blk_list.end(); it_blk++)
    {
        (*it_blk)->DrawBlock(pDC);   // DrawBlock() called on the ptr-to-
        CBlock
    }
    ...
}
```

Hence, add a virtual member function to the CBlock class with the prototype: virtual int CBlock::OperateOnData(int t_cnt, double t, double delta_t). Edit the code as shown in the following, where a message box is used to display the time-based parameters passed into the function, and for now, "valid" is set to "1", indicating a successful operation:

```
int CBlock::OperateOnData(int t_cnt, double t, double delta_t)
{
    // This fn has been made virtual and is to be overridden by all
      derived CBlock classes.

    int valid = 1;          // (-1) operational error, (0) read/write
      error, (1) no error
    CString sMsg;           // string to be displayed
    CString sMsgTemp;       // temp string msg.
    UINT nType = MB_OK;     // style of msg. box
    UINT nIDhelp = 0;       // help context ID for the msg.

    // Print msg.
    sMsgTemp.Format(" CBlock::OperateOnData(). \n\n");
    sMsg+=sMsgTemp;
    sMsgTemp.Format(" t_cnt = %d, t = %lf, delta_t = %lf. \n", t_cnt, t,
      delta_t);
    sMsg+=sMsgTemp;
    AfxMessageBox(sMsg, nType, nIDhelp);

    return valid;
}
```

19.8   PROPAGATING A SIMPLE DIRECT SIGNAL

Now that the initial functionality to call the appropriate signal propagation function has been introduced into the project, several more functions are required to test that the direct signal propagation method can actually work. This involves adding at least one source and sink block OperateOnData() function, e.g., for a Constant and an Output block, and the additional methods that these derived functions call to perform the correct operations on the signal data. A simple model involving just one Constant block connected directly to one Output block, with one connection object, (no feedback loop) can then be built, and a signal propagated directly from the Constant block to the Output block over the single connection, as shown in Figure 19.7.

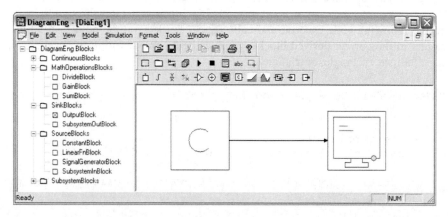

FIGURE 19.7   Simple model showing a Constant block linked directly to an Output block to test direct signal propagation.

19.8.1   IMPLEMENTATION OF SIMPLE SIGNAL PROPAGATION

The following steps are to be made to perform simple signal propagation, where specific details are provided in the ensuring sections.

1. Add a `CConstantBlock::OperateOnData()` function.
2. Add a `COutputBlock::OperateOnData()` function.
3. Add a `CBlock::WriteDataToOutputSignal()` function.
4. Add a `CBlock::ReadDataFromSingleInputSignal()` function.
5. Add accessor methods to get and set signal data and validity.

19.8.1.1   Add a `CConstantBlock::OperateOnData()` Function

A source Constant block can be added to a model to generate a constant signal value to be propagated through the output port along the connection linking it to the next block. Hence, add a public virtual member function to the CConstantBlock class, with prototype, `virtual int CConstantBlock:: OperateOnData(int t_cnt, double t, double delta_t)`, and edit it as shown to simply write data to its output signal.

```
int CConstantBlock::OperateOnData(int t_cnt, double t, double delta_t)
{
    int valid = 0;   // (-1) operational error, (0) read/write error,
       (1) no error

    // WRITE DATA TO OUTPUT SIGNAL
    valid = WriteDataToOutputSignal(m_dConstMatrix, m_iNrows, m_iNcols);

    return valid;
}
```

Here, the Constant block's `OperateOnData()` function calls `WriteDataToOutputSignal()` to write the constant data stored in "m_dConstMatrix" to the CConnection object's CSignal data, "m_dSignalMatrix", which is then passed "along the connection" to the next block: if the writing action is successful, "valid" is set to "1"; otherwise, it is set to "0."

19.8.1.2   Add a `COutputBlock::OperateOnData()` Function

A sink Output block can be added to a model to view the output, generated by other blocks, that it reads as an input signal passed along the connection attached to its input port. Add a public virtual member function to the COutputBlock class, with prototype `virtual int COutputBlock:: OperateOnData(int t_cnt, double t, double delta_t)`, and edit the function as shown in the following to read data from its input signal.

```
int COutputBlock::OperateOnData(int t_cnt, double t, double delta_t)
{
    int i;
    int j;
    int ncols;                    // no. of cols of input signal
    int nrows;                    // no. of rows of input signal
    int n_TimeSteps;              // total no. of time steps in simulation
    int valid = 0;                // (-1) operational error, (0) read/
       write error, (1) no error
    double **matrix_in = NULL;    // input signal
    CString sMsg;                 // string to be displayed
    CString sMsgTemp;             // temp msg.
    UINT nType = MB_OK;           // style of msg. box
    UINT nIDhelp = 0;             // help context ID for the msg.
```

```
// Get the no. of time steps
n_TimeSteps = GetParentSystemModel()->DetermineNTimeSteps();

// -- GET INPUT SIGNAL DATA
valid = ReadDataFromSingleInputSignal(matrix_in, &nrows, &ncols);
if(valid == 0)
{
    return valid;                  // Exit function since input invalid
}

// -- MEMORY NEW/DELETE
if(t_cnt == 0)
{
    // Delete m_dOutputMatrix if it already exists, i.e. non-NULL
    if(m_dOutputMatrix != NULL)
    {
        for(i=0; i<m_iNrows; i++)
        {
            delete [] m_dOutputMatrix[i];
        }
        delete [] m_dOutputMatrix;
    }

    // Allocate memory
    m_iNrows = nrows;
    m_iNcols = (n_TimeSteps + 1)*ncols;        // determine total no.
      of cols for data_record (t_cnt starts from 0)
    m_dOutputMatrix = new double *[m_iNrows];  // allocate an array
      of ptrs-to-double
    for(i=0; i<m_iNrows; i++)
    {
        m_dOutputMatrix[i] = new double[m_iNcols];
    }

    // Initialize matrix values to nullity.
    for(i=0; i<m_iNrows; i++)
    {
        for(j=0; j<m_iNcols; j++)
        {
            m_dOutputMatrix[i][j] = 0.0;
        }
    }
}

// -- ADD MATRIX INPUT SIGNAL DATA TO DATA RECORD
for(i=0; i<nrows; i++)
{
    for(j=0; j<ncols; j++)
    {
    m_dOutputMatrix[i][j + t_cnt*ncols] = matrix_in[i][j];
      // offset cols by t_cnt multiples of ncols
    }
}

// -- PLOT/PRINT INPUT SIGNAL AS SIMULATION OUTPUT
sMsgTemp.Format("\n COutputBlock::OperateOnData() \n");
sMsg+=sMsgTemp;
sMsgTemp.Format("\n t_cnt = %d, t = %lf\n", t_cnt, t);
//sMsgTemp.Format("\n t_cnt = %d, t = %10.5lf\n", t_cnt, t);
```

```
//sMsgTemp.Format("\n n_TimeSteps = %d, m_iNrows = %d\n",
  n_TimeSteps, m_iNrows);
sMsg+=sMsgTemp;
AfxMessageBox(sMsg, nType, nIDhelp); // msg. box

//PrintMatrix(matrix_in, nrows, ncols);
PrintMatrix(m_dOutputMatrix, m_iNrows, m_iNcols);

// -- MEMORY DELETE
// m_dOutputMatrix deleted above on t_cnt = 0, or in ~COutputBlock()
  destructor.

return valid;
}
```

This function initially calls `DetermineNTimeSteps()` to determine the total number of time-steps, "n_TimeSteps", of the simulation. This is required since the signal data stored using the variable, "m_dOutputMatrix", should have enough memory allocated to hold all output data signals passed to the Output block: in this case, "n_TimeSteps + 1" multiples of the incoming data structure's column-count (amount of columns) are required, since "t_cnt" starts from 0.

For example, consider a data matrix, "m_dOutputMatrix", of the following form:

$$M = \left[\begin{bmatrix} f_1(t_0) & f_2(t_0) \\ f_3(t_0) & f_4(t_0) \end{bmatrix} \begin{bmatrix} f_1(t_1) & f_2(t_1) \\ f_3(t_1) & f_4(t_1) \end{bmatrix}, \ldots, \begin{bmatrix} f_1(t_n) & f_2(t_n) \\ f_3(t_n) & f_4(t_n) \end{bmatrix} \right] \tag{19.10}$$

where $f_s(t)$, for $s \in \{1, \ldots, 4\}$ (four signals are used here for simplicity), are the individual signals stored in a 2×2 matrix, for each time point $t_i \in [t_0, t_n]$, for initial and final simulation time points, t_0 and t_n, respectively. The total number of time-steps is n, the total number of time points is $n + 1$, and the number of columns of each signal matrix generated at each time point is two; hence, the total columns of the entire matrix, "m_dOutputMatrix", equivalently, M, is $2(n + 1)$.

The data that are being passed as signals along the single connection object entering the Output block are read using a call to `ReadDataFromSingleInputSignal()`: if the data are invalid, i.e., are unavailable, the function returns; if not, the matrix input is stored in the member variable "m_dOutputMatrix" (after the "if(t_cnt == 0)" section).

If the data read in are valid, execution continues to the "if(t_cnt == 0)" section. On the first iteration, if "m_dOutputMatrix" is not NULL, i.e., if it holds data, then these data are deleted and new memory allocated to be of size "m_iNrows" by "m_iNcols". This is performed since between one rebuilding and execution of the entire block diagram model and another, the signal data size may have changed due to intervening user input, and hence the old model's output data structure needs to be renewed and reinitialized:

1. This `COutputBlock::OperateOnData()` function makes use of a variable, "m_dOutputMatrix"; hence add a private member variable of type "double**" named "m_dOutputMatrix" to the COutputBlock class.
2. Add two private integer variables named "m_iNrows" and "m_iNcols" to hold the size of this matrix.
3. Initialize these newly introduced variables in the class constructor as shown in bold.

```
COutputBlock::COutputBlock(CSystemModel *pParentSystemModel, CPoint
  blk_posn, EBlockShape e_blk_shape):
CBlock(pParentSystemModel, blk_posn, e_blk_shape)
{
    SetBlockName("output_block");
```

```
    // Set COutputBlock member var.
    m_iNrows = 0;
    m_iNcols = 0;
    m_iNotation = 0;
    m_iTimePtDisplay = 0;
    m_dOutputMatrix = NULL;

    // Create input port
    CPort *p_input_port = new CPort(*this);

    // Set the port name
    p_input_port->SetPortName("_"); // no sign assoc. with input port

    // Set the input port posn.
    p_input_port->SetPortPositionAngle(180.0);
    p_input_port->CalculatePortPosition();

    // Set the port ID
    p_input_port->SetPortArrowDirection(e_right_arrow);

    // Add the port to the vector of ports
    GetVectorOfInputPorts().push_back(p_input_port);
}
```

4. Add a public constant accessor method to return the data member with prototype, double
   **COutputBlock::GetOutputMatrix(void) const, and edit it as follows:

```
double** COutputBlock::GetOutputMatrix() const
{
    return m_dOutputMatrix;
}
```

5. Finally, if an Output block is deleted from the system model, then any allocated memory
   that would not be deallocated in the COutputBlock::OperateOnData() function
   itself should be freed in the COutputBlock destructor, as shown in the following.

```
COutputBlock::~COutputBlock(void)
{
    int i;

    // MEMORY DEALLOCATION

    // Delete the data matrix whose memory was allocated in
    //   COutputBlock::OperateOnData()
    if(m_dOutputMatrix != NULL)
    {
        for(i=0; i<m_iNrows; i++)
        {
            delete [] m_dOutputMatrix[i];
        }
        delete [] m_dOutputMatrix;
        m_dOutputMatrix = NULL;
    }

    // Reset member vars.
    m_iNrows = 0;
    m_iNcols = 0;
}
```

19.8.1.3 Add a `CBlock::WriteDataToOutputSignal()` Function

The `OperateOnData()` function of the CConstantBlock class writes the data that it generates to its output signal associated with its output connection through a call to `WriteDataToOutputSignal()`. This function will be used by the derived CBlock classes and hence should be a member of the CBlock class. Hence, add a public member function to the CBlock class with the prototype, `int CBlock::WriteDataToOutputSignal(double **matrix_out, int nrows, int ncols)`, and edit it as shown in the following to iterate over the vector of output ports and connections.

```
int CBlock::WriteDataToOutputSignal(double **matrix_out, int nrows,
  int ncols)
{
    int valid = 0;                             // (-1) operational error,
      (0) read/write error, (1) no error
    list<CConnection*>::iterator it_con;  // iterator for list of
      CConnection ptrs.
    vector<CPort*>::iterator it_port;       // iterator for vector of
      CPort ptrs.
    vector<CPort*> vector_of_output_ports = GetVectorOfOutputPorts();
      // vector of output ports

    // Get connection list
    list<CConnection*> &con_list = m_pParentSystemModel-
      >GetConnectionList();

    // -- WRITE OUTPUT DATA TO OUTPUT CONNECTION'S SIGNAL

    // Iterate over output ports
    for(it_port = vector_of_output_ports.begin(); it_port
      != vector_of_output_ports.end(); it_port++)
    {
        // Iterate over list of connections
        for(it_con = con_list.begin(); it_con != con_list.end();
          it_con++)
        {
            // If connection attached to output port: either directly or
              INDIRECTLY through a bend point
            if( (*it_con)->GetRefFromPort() == (*it_port) )
            {
                // Set signal properties for this connection
                valid = 1;
                (*it_con)->GetSignal()->SetSignalData(matrix_out, nrows,
                  ncols);
                (*it_con)->GetSignal()->SetSignalValidity(valid);

                // NOTE: "break" is not used here, after calling
                  SetSignalData(), since more than one Connection object
                // may share the same ref-from-port. For example, a
                  secondary connection emanating from a primary
                // connection's bend point, will share the same ref-from-
                  port as the primary connection, and hence
                // it too should have the same signal data matrix:
                  i.e. both connections share the same signal data.
            }
        }// end it_con
```

```
        if(valid)
        {
            break; // exit for it_port
        }
    }// end it_port

    return valid;
}
```

The `WriteDataToOutputSignal()` function first obtains the list of model connections through a call to `GetConnectionList()`, then, being a function of the CBlock class, iterates over the block's vector of output ports, and checks whether the connection object emanates from the block's output port through a call to `GetRefFromPort()`; if so, then the signal data and validity are set with calls to `SetSignalData()` and `SetSignalValidity()`, respectively. The developer will notice that a "`break()`" statement is not used directly after the signal data have been set. This is the case since more than one Connection object may share the same reference-from port. For example, a *secondary* connection emanating from a *primary* connection's bend point will share the same reference-from port as the *primary* connection, and hence it too should have the same signal data matrix: i.e., both connections share the same signal data (while the `SignalPropagationDirect()` function is in operation).

19.8.1.4   Add a `CBlock::ReadDataFromSingleInputSignal()` Function

The `OperateOnData()` function of the COutputBlock class reads the data from its input signal associated with its input connection through a call to `ReadDataFromSingleIntputSignal()`. This function will be used by the CBlock-derived classes and hence should be a member of the CBlock class. Hence, add a public member function to the CBlock class with the prototype, `int CBlock::ReadDataFromSingleInputSignal(double **&matrix_in, int *nrows_in, int *ncols_in)`, and edit it as shown in the following to iterate over the vector of input ports and connections, extracting the relevant CSignal data.

```
int CBlock::ReadDataFromSingleInputSignal(double **&matrix_in,
  int *nrows_in, int *ncols_in)
{
    // NOTE: The base address of the 2-dim array m_dSignalMatrix,
      obtained from GetSignalData() below,
    // is assigned to the var matrix_in (of the same double** type). But
      for the variable "matrix_in" in the calling
    // environment, i.e. the environment from which the current fn was
      called, to be assigned this address, it must be
    // passed by reference, resulting in the "matrix_in" variable in the
      current fn header, to be an alias (&) for the
    // var in the calling environment.
    //
    // Alternatively, using the call ReadDataFromSingleInputSignal
      (&matrix_in, &nrows, &ncols) from the calling environ,
    // would result in the prototype: ReadDataFromSingleInputSignal
      (double ***matrix_in, int *nrows_in, int *ncols_in).
    // That is, a triple-ptr-to-double would be required, in the same way
      a single ptr is used for nrows_in and ncols_in,
    // since the address of the 2-D array is being passed.

    int valid = 0;  // (-1) operational error, (0) read/write error,
      (1) no error
    list<CConnection*>::iterator it_con;  // iterator for list of
      CConnection ptrs.
```

```
vector<CPort*>::iterator it_port;  // iterator for vector of
  CPort ptrs.
vector<CPort*> vector_of_input_ports = GetVectorOfInputPorts();
  // vector of input ports

// Get connection list
list<CConnection*> &con_list = m_pParentSystemModel-
  >GetConnectionList();

// Iterate over ports
for(it_port = vector_of_input_ports.begin(); it_port
  != vector_of_input_ports.end(); it_port++)
{
    // Iterate over connections
    for(it_con = con_list.begin(); it_con != con_list.end();
      it_con++)
    {
        // Find connection attached to input port
        if((*it_con)->GetRefToPort() == (*it_port))
        {
            valid = (*it_con)->GetSignal()->GetSignalValidity();

            if(valid == 0)
            {
                return valid;
            }
            else
            {
                matrix_in = (*it_con)->GetSignal()-
                  >GetSignalData(nrows_in, ncols_in);  // nrows_in,
                  ncols_in are of type int*.
                break;  // only one input signal so exit "for it_con"
            }
        }
    }// end it_con

    if(valid)
    {
        break; // only one input port so exit "for it_port"
    }
}// end it_port

return valid;
}
```

The ReadDataFromSingleInputSignal() function of the CBlock class is used to get signal validity and data from a single input signal. The model's connection list is initially obtained, and then the vector of input ports and the connection list are iterated over to determine which connection is connected to the input port. Thereafter the signal validity and data are obtained through calls to GetSignalValidity() and GetSignalData(), respectively.

The developer will notice that the base address of the two-dimensional array "m_dSignalMatrix", obtained from GetSignalData(), is assigned to the variable "matrix_in" (of the same double** type). But for the variable "matrix_in" in the calling environment, i.e., the environment from which the current function was called, to be assigned this address, it must be passed by reference, resulting in the "matrix_in" variable in the current function header, to be an alias (&) for the variable in the calling environment.

An alternative approach would be to make a call to ReadDataFromSingleInputSignal (&matrix_in, &nrows, &ncols) in the calling environment, passing in the address of "matrix_in", but this would result in the function prototype: `ReadDataFromSingle InputSignal(double ***matrix_in, int *nrows_in, int *ncols_in)`. That is, a triple-pointer-to-double would be required in the same way a single-pointer is used for "nrows_in" and "ncols_in", since the address of a two-dimensional array is being passed. Accessing or writing to this variable would be performed as usual, by dereferencing, using a "*".

19.8.1.5 Add Accessor Methods to Get and Set Signal Data and Validity

The `WriteDataToOutputSignal()` and `ReadDataFromSingleInputSignal()` functions call the CSignal class accessor functions: `SetSignalData()`, `SetSignalValidity()`, `GetSignalData()`, and `GetSignalValidity()`. Hence these should be added to the CSignal class with the following declarations and definitions:

1. `double **CSignal::GetSignalData(int *nrows, int *ncols)`
2. `void CSignal::SetSignalData(double **matrix, int nrows, int ncols)`
3. `int CSignal::GetSignalValidity(void)`
4. `void CSignal::SetSignalValidity(int valid)`

The `GetSignalData()` function shown in the following simply assigns the incoming arguments, "nrows" and "ncols", and the values of the private member variables, "m_iNrows" and "m_iNcols", respectively, and returns the CSignal private member variable, "m_dSignalMatrix".

```
double** CSignal::GetSignalData(int *nrows, int *ncols)
{
    // Addresses of nrows and ncols are passed, hence deref. with a ptr.

    // Assign CSignal data values
    *nrows = m_iNrows;
    *ncols = m_iNcols;

    // Return member signal matrix data
    return m_dSignalMatrix;
}
```

The `SetSignalData()` function in the following initially deletes any existing signal data and then creates memory, using the "nrows" and "ncols" input dimensional arguments, for the private CSignal member variable, "m_dSignalMatrix", and assigns the incoming "matrix" data to "m_dSignalMatrix". The deletion of memory is required in case it was not deleted by a `ResetSignalData()` call elsewhere in the program flow. This may occur when a *secondary* connection object is attached indirectly to a block, and `ResetSignalData()` is called on the *primary* connection object directly attached to the block: the *primary* connection object's signal data would be reset, but the *secondary* connection object's data may not be. Hence, to prevent a possible memory leak, the member variable, "m_dSignalMatrix", is deleted if it is non-NULL upon entry into the function.

```
void CSignal::SetSignalData(double **matrix, int nrows, int ncols)
{
    int i;
    int j;

    // DELETE POSSIBLY EXISTING DATA
    // A resetting of signal data called upon a particular/single
      connection object
    // may not reset secondary connection object data. Hence, delete data
      here for any signal to be certain.
```

```
        if(m_dSignalMatrix != NULL)
        {
            for(i=0; i<m_iNrows; i++)
            {
                delete [] m_dSignalMatrix[i];
            }
            delete [] m_dSignalMatrix;
        }

        // Set member vars
        m_iNrows = nrows;
        m_iNcols = ncols;

        // -- MEMORY NEW
        // Allocate an array of ptrs-to-double and return the & to
          m_dSignalMatrix
        // Note: an array is of type ptr, hence an array of ptrs is of type
          ptr-ptr.
        m_dSignalMatrix = new double *[nrows];

        // Allocate an array of doubles for each of the entries (rows of the
          column vector) of m_dSignalMatrix,
        // and return the & to m_dSignalMatrix[i].
        // Note: an array is of type ptr, and its & is stored at location i
          in the array m_dSignalMatrix[]
        for(i=0; i<nrows; i++)
        {
            m_dSignalMatrix[i] = new double[ncols];  // allocate an array of
              doubles, return & to matrix[i]
        }

        // -- ASSIGN MATRIX VALUES TO THE SIGNAL
        for(i=0; i<nrows; i++)
        {
            for(j=0; j<ncols; j++)
            {
                m_dSignalMatrix[i][j] = matrix[i][j];
            }
        }

        return;
}
```

Finally, the accessor methods GetSignalValidity() and SetSignalValidity() return and assign a value to the private member variable, "m_iValidity", respectively, as shown in the following.

```
int CSignal::GetSignalValidity()
{
    return m_iValidity;
}

void CSignal::SetSignalValidity(int valid)
{
    // Assign integer validity
    m_iValidity = valid;
}
```

19.8.2 Running an Experiment

The simple model shown in Figure 19.7 may be constructed and parameters for it set using dialog windows as shown in Figure 19.8: the Constant block generates a constant column vector $c = [1\ 2\ 3]^T$, and the initial time, final time, and time-step size parameters are $t_0 = 0.0\,\text{s}$, $t_n = 10.0\,\text{s}$, and $\delta t = 1.0\,\text{s}$, respectively, resulting in a number of time-steps ("n_TimeSteps") equal to 10.

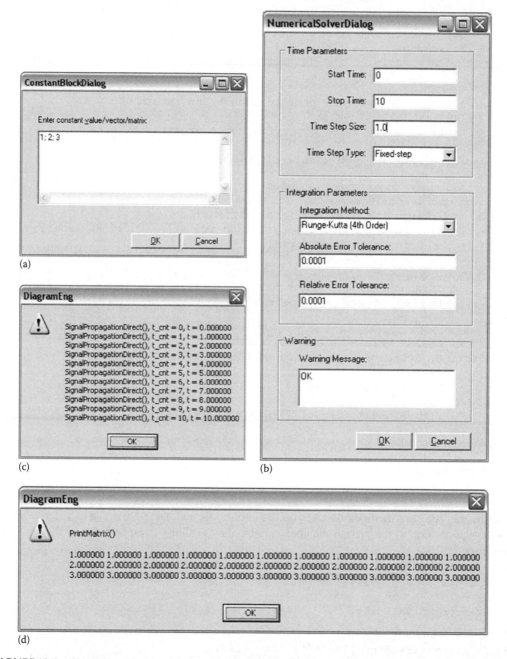

FIGURE 19.8 Simulation windows: (a) Constant block dialog window showing a column vector, (b) Numerical Solver dialog window showing input parameters, (c) output from the `SignalPropagationDirect()` method, and (d) output from the `COutputBlock::OperateOnData()` method, showing accumulated data from the Constant block for 10 time-steps with 11 data points.

The developer will notice that there are 11 columns of data printed in Figure 19.8d, yet there are only 10 time-steps ("n_TimeSteps") involved, where $t_0 = 0.0$ s. This is the case since in the `OperateOnData()` function of the COutputBlock, a total number of columns, "ncols_total", is set as "ncols_total = (n_TimeSteps + 1)*ncols;", where "ncols" is the number of columns of the signal data of the incoming connection; here, "ncols" is "1" since a single constant column vector (*c*) is being generated at each time-step. The extra column (+1) is present since "t_cnt" starts from "0" in `SignalPropagationDirect()`; hence there is one more data point than there are a number of time-steps. In brief, data for time points t_0 up to and including t_n are saved.

Now that a simple signal may be propagated from one block to another over one connection, as shown by the previous example, involving a Constant and an Output block, the `OperateOnData()` functions for the remaining CBlock-derived classes and additional functions to allow them to work need to be added to the project. Part III, after Chapter 21, explains the addition of the remaining block-based functions in order that correct signals may be propagated for all blocks through the model using the direct signal propagation method.

19.9 SUMMARY

Signal propagation can be performed once a model has been validated and is of essentially two different forms: (1) direct signal propagation, used where there are no feedback loops in a model, and (2) a simultaneous equation-based approach, used when feedback or algebraic loops exist. The key functions introduced to the project to determine the presence of feedback or algebraic loops are (1) `DetermineModelFeedbackLoops()`, to determine model feedback loops; (2) `SetRefFromPortOfConnectionFromBendPoint()`, to set a connection's reference-from port; (3) `AssignBlockConnectivityMatrixValues()`, to assign values in a matrix denoting block connectivity; and (4) `DetermineLoopsFromConnectivityMatrix()`, to determine feedback loops from the connectivity matrix. The key function required to determine the loops from the connectivity matrix is `BuildTour()`, which recursively builds tours using the block connectivity matrix that end at either an Output block or a repeated node, signifying a feedback loop. Various additions are made to allow direct signal propagation to work, including the `SignalPropagationDirect()` function in the CSystemModel class and the virtual `OperateOnData()` function in the CBlock class, to be overridden by the derived block classes, to perform block operations on input data, and to generate output signal data. Finally, the `ReadDataFromSingleInputSignal()` and `WriteDataToOutputSignal()` methods are added to the CBlock class to read and write signals on connection objects, using `CSignal::GetSignalData()` and `CSignal::SetSignalData()`, respectively.

REFERENCES

1. Oppenheim, A. V., Willsky, A. S., and Nawab, S. H., *Signals and Systems*, 2nd edn., Prentice Hall, Upper Saddle River, NJ, 1997.
2. Ogata, K., *Modern Control Engineering*, 4th edn., Prentice Hall, Upper Saddle River, NJ, 2002.
3. Shabana, A. A., *Computational Dynamics*, 2nd edn., John Wiley & Sons, New York, 2001.

20 Graph Drawing

20.1 INTRODUCTION

The Output block currently displays numerical data to the screen via a message box using an `AfxMessageBox()` function call. This mechanism is suitable only if specific numerical data values need to be verified, but typically, the user wants to see a graphical relation between the dependent variable, e.g., $f(t)$, $\mathbf{f}(t)$, or $\mathbf{F}(t)$, for scalar, vector, and matrix functions, respectively, and the independent variable t. That is, the output signal—a scalar, vector, or matrix value—is to be plotted with respect to time for all time points of the simulation. The following instructions indicate how graph-like drawing is added to the DiagramEng project to display the data of the Output block in a separate view window. The general steps to add this functionality are as listed while specific details are provided in the sections that follow:

1. Adding structure to display an empty view window
2. Supplementing existing classes to access Output block data
3. Plotting data as a text string
4. Plotting numerical data as a graph
5. Deleting an Output block and its view
6. Adding functionality to the Output block dialog window

20.2 ADDITION OF STRUCTURE TO DISPLAY AN EMPTY VIEW WINDOW

Various steps are required toward implementing functionality to draw a graph in a window associated with the Output block to display its contained accumulated simulation signal data. In an article titled "Multiple Document Interface Applications, Serialization and Multiple View Support" by Mahmood, the author mentions that when providing different view types to a document: (1) different pointers-to-CDocTemplate objects need to be declared in the CNameApp class, (2) pointers-to-CMultiDocTemplate objects need to be created in the `CNameApp::InitInstance()` function, and then (3) the pointers-to-CMultiDocTemplate are passed to the CMainFrame class to generate the different views (here Name denotes the application name and for the current project it is DiagramEng) [1].

The steps pursued here are (1) the addition of a Show Graph button with an event-handler function to the Output block dialog window, (2) the addition of a CDocTemplate object to the CDiagramEngApp class, (3) modification of the `InitInstance()` function to create a CMultiDocTemplate object, (4) addition of a new COutputBlockView class to support the drawing of graphical data within its view, (5) the addition of template-based functionality in the Show Graph function, and (6) the addition of the `OnInitialUpdate()` and `OnUpdate()` functions to the CDiagramEngView class.

20.2.1 ADD A SHOW GRAPH BUTTON TO THE OUTPUT BLOCK DIALOG

Select the IDD_OUTPUT_BLK_DLG dialog resource and add an additional Show Graph button control on the dialog (Figure 20.1) with the properties shown in Table 20.1.

Three buttons exist on the Output block dialog (IDD_OUTPUT_BLK_DLG) window as shown in Table 20.1. Add an event-handler function for the Show Graph button as shown in Table 20.2

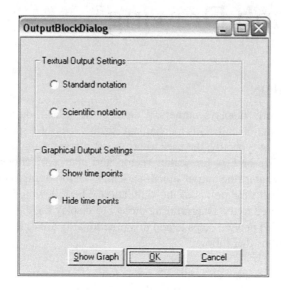

FIGURE 20.1   Output block dialog window showing the controls as specified in Table 20.1.

TABLE 20.1

Dialog Object, Properties, and Settings for the Output Block Dialog Window (IDD_OUTPUT_BLK_DLG)

Object	Property	Setting
Group box	ID	ID_OUTPUT_BLK_DLG_GPBOXNOT
	Caption	Textual Output Settings
Radio button	ID	ID_OUTPUT_BLK_DLG_RB_STDNOT
	Group	Checked
	Caption	Standard notation
Radio button	ID	ID_OUTPUT_BLK_DLG_RB_SCINOT
	Group	Unchecked
	Caption	Scientific notation
Group box	ID	ID_OUTPUT_BLK_DLG_GPBOXTPTS
	Caption	Graphical Output Settings
Radio button	ID	ID_OUTPUT_BLK_DLG_RB_TPTS
	Group	Checked
	Caption	Show time points
Radio button	ID	ID_OUTPUT_BLK_DLG_RB_NOTPTS
	Group	Unchecked
	Caption	Hide time points
Button	ID	ID_OUTPUT_BLK_DLG_BTN_OK
	Default button	Unchecked
	Caption	&OK
Button	ID	IDCANCEL
	Caption	&Cancel
Button	ID	ID_OUTPUT_BLK_DLG_BTN_SG
	Caption	&Show Graph

TABLE 20.2

Objects, IDs, Class, and Event-Handler Functions for the COutputBlockDialog Class

Object	ID	Class	COMMAND Event Handler
Show Graph button	ID_OUTPUT_BLK_DLG_BTN_SG	COutputBlockDialog	OnOutputBlkDlgBtnShowGraph()
OK button	ID_OUTPUT_BLK_DLG_BTN_OK	COutputBlockDialog	OnOutputBlkDlgBtnOk()
Cancel button	IDCANCEL (default)	COutputBlockDialog	OnCancel()

and edit the `OnOutputBlkDlgBtnShowGraph()` function as shown in the following with a simple message box call for now.

```
void COutputBlockDialog::OnOutputBlkDlgBtnShowGraph()
{
    // TODO: Add your control notification handler code here

    // DiagramEng (start)
    AfxMessageBox("\n COutputBlockDialog::OnOutputBlkDlgBtnShowGraph
      ()\n", MB_OK, 0);

    // VIEW CONSTRUCTION
    // To add later.

    // Close the dialog wnd with OnOK()
    OnOK();

    // DiagramEng (end)
}
```

The developer will notice the "view construction" section in the code given earlier. The construction of the Output block's graph-like view will be added after the supporting functionality is introduced to the project.

20.2.2 ADD A **CDocTemplate** OBJECT AND ACCESSOR FUNCTION TO THE **CDiagramEngApp** CLASS

A new view type is to be added to the CDiagramEngApp class, since the Output block needs to display its data as a graph to the user in a separate graph-containing view. Hence, add a private pointer-to-CDocTemplate variable to the CDiagramEngApp class with name: "m_pCOutputViewTemplate". Add a public accessor function to the CDiagramEngApp class with prototype, `CDocTemplate *CDiagramEngApp::GetCOutputViewTemplate()` const, and edit it as shown.

```
CDocTemplate *CDiagramEngApp::GetCOutputViewTemplate() const
{
    return m_pCOutputViewTemplate;
}
```

20.2.3 MODIFY **CDiagramEngApp::InitInstance()** TO CREATE A **CMultiDocTemplate** OBJECT

Now that the pointer-to-CDocTemplate object, "m_pCOutputViewTemplate", has been added to the CDiagramEngApp class, a new CMultiDocTemplate object may be created and the address returned to the member variable pointer: "m_pCOutputViewTemplate". Hence, edit the CDiagramEngApp::InitInstance() function with the code shown in bold in the following.

```
BOOL CDiagramEngApp::InitInstance()
{
    AfxEnableControlContainer();

    // Standard initialization
    // If you are not using these features and wish to reduce the size
    // of your final executable, you should remove from the following
    // the specific initialization routines you do not need.

#ifdef _AFXDLL
    Enable3dControls();        // Call this when using MFC in a shared DLL
#else
    Enable3dControlsStatic();  // Call this when linking to MFC statically
#endif

    // Change the registry key under which our settings are stored.
    // TODO: You should modify this string to be something appropriate
    // such as the name of your company or organization.
    SetRegistryKey(_T("Local AppWizard-Generated Applications"));

    LoadStdProfileSettings();  // Load standard INI file options
      (including MRU)

    // Register the application's document templates. Document templates
    // serve as the connection between documents, frame windows
      and views.

    CMultiDocTemplate* pDocTemplate;
    pDocTemplate = new CMultiDocTemplate(
        IDR_DIAGRATYPE,
        RUNTIME_CLASS(CDiagramEngDoc),
        RUNTIME_CLASS(CChildFrame), // custom MDI child frame
        RUNTIME_CLASS(CDiagramEngView));
    AddDocTemplate(pDocTemplate);

    // DiagramEng (start)

    // -- OUTPUT BLOCK VIEW TEMPLATE
    m_pCOutputViewTemplate = new CMultiDocTemplate(
        IDR_OUTPUTVIEW,                       // new menu resource
        RUNTIME_CLASS(CDiagramEngDoc),
        RUNTIME_CLASS(CChildFrame),           // custom MDI child frame
        // RUNTIME_CLASS(CDiagramEngView)); // old view type
        RUNTIME_CLASS(COutputBlockView));    // modifying the document
          template with the new view type (derived from CView)

    AddDocTemplate(m_pCOutputViewTemplate);

    // DiagramEng (end)

    // create main MDI Frame window
    CMainFrame* pMainFrame = new CMainFrame;
    if (!pMainFrame->LoadFrame(IDR_MAINFRAME))
        return FALSE;
    m_pMainWnd = pMainFrame;

    // Enable drag/drop open
    m_pMainWnd->DragAcceptFiles();
```

```
       // Enable DDE Execute open
       EnableShellOpen();
       RegisterShellFileTypes(TRUE);

       // Parse command line for standard shell commands, DDE, file open
       CCommandLineInfo cmdInfo;
       ParseCommandLine(cmdInfo);

       // Dispatch commands specified on the command line
       if (!ProcessShellCommand(cmdInfo))
           return FALSE;

       // The main window has been initialized, so show and update it.
       pMainFrame->ShowWindow(m_nCmdShow);

       pMainFrame->UpdateWindow();

       return TRUE;
}
```

The developer will have noticed that "IDR_OUTPUTVIEW" is used as the resource ID in the creation of a new CMultiDocTemplate object. This has not yet been created, but should be the same menu resource as the IDR_MAINFRAME. Hence, copy and paste the IDR_MAINFRAME menu resource in the Menu resource folder and rename it "IDR_OUTPUTVIEW"; the menus, File, View, and Help will then be available for the Output block view.

20.2.4   ADD A **COutputBlockView** CLASS TO SUPPORT DRAWING WITHIN ITS VIEW

The developer will have also noticed that in the CDiagramEngApp::InitInstance() function the final argument in the "new CMultiDocTemplate()" statement to create a pointer-to-CDocTemplate is "RUNTIME_CLASS(COutputBlockView)". This involves a new COutputBlockView class.

1. Hence, add a new MFC-type class to the project named, COutputBlockView, with base class CView.
2. Augment the class declaration with the code shown in bold in the following so that it is of a similar structure to the existing CDiagramEngView class (also derived from CView).
3. Add the inline definition of the GetDocument() function to the "OutputBlockView.h" header file beneath the class declaration as shown in bold in the following.
4. Since the definition of the GetDocument() function in the "OutputBlockView.h" header file returns a pointer-to-CDocument, the header file, "DiagramEngDoc.h", needs to be included at the top of the "OutputBlockView.h", also shown in bold.

```
#if !defined(AFX_OUTPUTBLOCKVIEW_H__251D1F63_48DA_42CF_A8C2_
  D74F7218BC88__INCLUDED_)
#define AFX_OUTPUTBLOCKVIEW_H__251D1F63_48DA_42CF_A8C2_D74F7218BC88__
  INCLUDED_

#if _MSC_VER > 1000
#pragma once
#endif // _MSC_VER > 1000
// OutputBlockView.h : header file
//
#include "DiagramEngDoc.h"   // rqd. since GetDocument() fn returns a
  CDiagramEngDoc-ptr
```

```
//////////////////////////////////////////////////////////////////////////
// COutputBlockView view

class COutputBlockView : public CView
{
protected:
    COutputBlockView(); // protected constructor used by dynamic creation
    DECLARE_DYNCREATE(COutputBlockView)

// Attributes
public:
    CDiagramEngDoc* GetDocument();  // Manually added (DiagramEng)

// Operations
public:

// Overrides
    // ClassWizard generated virtual function overrides
    //{{AFX_VIRTUAL(COutputBlockView)
    protected:
    virtual void OnDraw(CDC* pDC); // overridden to draw this view
    //}}AFX_VIRTUAL

// Implementation
protected:
    virtual ~COutputBlockView();
#ifdef _DEBUG
    virtual void AssertValid() const;
    virtual void Dump(CDumpContext& dc) const;
#endif

    // Generated message map functions
protected:
    //{{AFX_MSG(COutputBlockView)
        // NOTE - the ClassWizard will add and remove member functions
          here.
    //}}AFX_MSG
    DECLARE_MESSAGE_MAP()
};

// DiagramEng (start)
#ifndef _DEBUG // debug version in OutputBlockView.cpp
inline CDiagramEngDoc* COutputBlockView::GetDocument()
   { return (CDiagramEngDoc*)m_pDocument; }
#endif
// DiagramEng (end)
```

5. Add the definition (debug version) of the GetDocument() function to the "OutputBlockView.cpp" source file in the "COutputBlockView diagnostics" section, as shown in bold in the following.

```
//////////////////////////////////////////////////////////////////////////
// COutputBlockView diagnostics

#ifdef _DEBUG
void COutputBlockView::AssertValid() const
{
    CView::AssertValid();
}
```

```
void COutputBlockView::Dump(CDumpContext& dc) const
{
    CView::Dump(dc);
}
// DiagramEng (start)
CDiagramEngDoc* COutputBlockView::GetDocument()  // non-debug version is
  inline
{
    ASSERT(m_pDocument->IsKindOf(RUNTIME_CLASS(CDiagramEngDoc)));
    return (CDiagramEngDoc*)m_pDocument;
}
// DiagramEng (end)

#endif //_DEBUG
```

6. Now that the COutputBlockView class has been declared, the header file "OutputBlockView.h" needs to be included at the top of the "DiagramEng.cpp" source file (as shown in bold in the following) since a CDocTemplate object is created using the COutputBlockView class in the CDiagramEngApp::InitInstance() function.

```
// DiagramEng.cpp : Defines the class behaviors for the application.
//

#include "stdafx.h"
#include "DiagramEng.h"

#include "MainFrm.h"
#include "ChildFrm.h"
#include "DiagramEngDoc.h"
#include "DiagramEngView.h"
#include "OutputBlockView.h"  // rqd. since COutputBlockView is used in
  InitInstance()
```

The developer will notice that OnDraw() is provided in this new class since COutputBlockView inherits publicly from CView; code will be added for this later to draw graphs within the Output block's view window.

20.2.5 ADD TEMPLATE-BASED FUNCTIONALITY TO THE SHOW GRAPH EVENT-HANDLER FUNCTION

Functionality can now be added to the COutputBlockDialog::OnOutputBlkDlgBtn ShowGraph() function, associated with the Show Graph button on the Output block dialog (IDD_OUTPUT_BLK_DLG) window, to complete the displaying of the new view type (COutputBlockView derived from CView).

1. Edit COutputBlockDialog::OnOutputBlkDlgBtnShowGraph() as shown in the following.
2. Include the "MainFrm.h" header file at the top of the "OutputBlockDialog.cpp" file (as shown in bold), since a local variable of type pointer-to-CMainFrame is used.
3. In addition, "theApp" is used in OnOutputBlkDlgBtnShowGraph(), but it is declared in the "DiagramEng.cpp" source file; hence, the keyword "extern" is used to inform the compiler to look for it elsewhere (also shown in bold in the following).

```
// OutputBlockDialog.cpp : implementation file
//

#include "stdafx.h"
#include "DiagramEng.h"
```

```
#include "OutputBlockDialog.h"
#include "MainFrm.h"  // rqd. since a ptr-to-CMainFrame is used in
  OnOutputBlkDlgBtnShowGraph()

#ifdef _DEBUG
#define new DEBUG_NEW
#undef THIS_FILE
static char THIS_FILE[] = __FILE__;
#endif

// DiagramEng (start)
// theApp needs to be accessed from within the OutputBlockDialog.cpp
  file, although it's declared in the DiagramEng.cpp file.
// It is used in the fn OnOutputBlkDlgBtnShowGraph() below.
extern CDiagramEngApp theApp;
// DiagramEng (end)
//////////////////////////////////////////////////////////////////////
// COutputBlockDialog dialog

...

void COutputBlockDialog::OnOutputBlkDlgBtnShowGraph()
{
    // TODO: Add your control notification handler code here

    // DiagramEng (start)
    //AfxMessageBox("\n COutputBlockDialog::OnOutputBlkDlgBtnShowGraph
      ()\n", MB_OK, 0);

    // VIEW CONSTRUCTION
    CMainFrame *main_frame = (CMainFrame *)theApp.m_pMainWnd;
      // Get a pointer-to-CMainFrame.
    CMDIChildWnd *pActiveChild = main_frame->MDIGetActive();
      // Get a pointer to the active child window.

    if(pActiveChild != 0)
    {
        CDocument *pDocument = pActiveChild->GetActiveDocument();
          // Get a pointer to the active document.
        if(pDocument != 0)
        {
            CDiagramEngApp *pApp = (CDiagramEngApp *)AfxGetApp();
            CDocTemplate *pTemp = pApp->GetCOutputViewTemplate();
              // Get the document template for the new view.
            CFrameWnd *pFrame = pTemp->CreateNewFrame(pDocument,
              pActiveChild);  // Create a new frame.

            if(pFrame != 0)
            {
                pTemp->InitialUpdateFrame(pFrame, pDocument);
                  // Update the frame.
            }
        }
    }

    // Close the dialog wnd with OnOK()
    OnOK();

    // DiagramEng (end)
}
```

The method used in this function to construct the view was originally found in the aforementioned document by Mahmood [1]. The key steps are (1) a pointer-to-CMainFrame is obtained using "theApp", (2) a pointer to the active child window is retrieved using `MDIGetActive()` called upon "main_frame", (3) a pointer to the active document is obtained using `GetActiveDocument()` called upon "pActiveChild", (4) the document template is retrieved for the new view using `GetCOutputViewTemplate()`, (5) a new frame is created by calling `CreateNewFrame()` upon the document template, and (6) the frame is updated by calling `InitialUpdateFrame()` upon the document template [2].

20.2.6 ADD THE `OnInitialUpdate()` AND `OnUpdate()` FUNCTIONS TO THE **CDiagramEngView** CLASS

A Microsoft Developer Network (MSDN) Library Index topic states that `CView::OnInitialUpdate()`, associated with the CView class, "is called by the framework after the view is first attached to the document, but before the view is initially displayed" and "the default implementation calls the `OnUpdate()` member function" [2]. The `OnUpdate()` member function is "called by the framework after the view's document has been modified … and allows the view to update its display to reflect those modifications" [2]. Hence, to update the display after document modification, perform the following:

1. Invoke the Class Wizard selecting CDiagramEngView as the class.
2. Add a function for the OnInitialUpdate message named `OnInitialUpdate()`, and edit it as shown in the following.
3. Add a function for the OnUpdate message named `OnUpdate()`, and edit it as shown.

```
void CDiagramEngView::OnInitialUpdate()
{
    CView::OnInitialUpdate();

    // TODO: Add your specialized code here and/or call the base class

    // DiagramEng (start)
    InvalidateRect(NULL);  // Invalidates the client area, i.e. forces a
      redraw on the next WM_PAINT message.
    // DiagramEng (end)
}

void CDiagramEngView::OnUpdate(CView* pSender, LPARAM lHint, CObject*
  pHint)
{
    // TODO: Add your specialized code here and/or call the base class

    // DiagramEng (start)
    InvalidateRect(NULL);  // Invalidates the client area, i.e. forces a
      redraw on the next WM_PAINT message.
    // DiagramEng (end)
}
```

Now, upon running the application and clicking on the Show Graph button, an empty COutputBlockView window appears as shown in Figure 20.2 (right window).

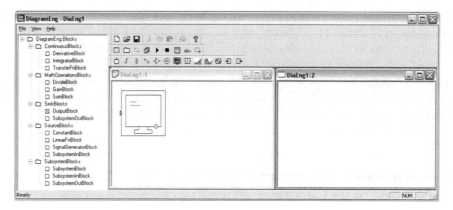

FIGURE 20.2   Output block (COutputBlock) (left) with its related empty view (COutputBlockView) (right).

20.3 SUPPLEMENTING EXISTING CLASSES TO ACCESS OUTPUT BLOCK DATA

To actually draw the data of the COutputBlock class, i.e., "m_dOutputMatrix", as a graph on the screen, the COutputBlockView::OnDraw() function needs to be completed. This OnDraw() member function of the COutputBlockView class will need to access the COutputBlock's data member variable, "m_dOutputMatrix", and extract the numerical data from it and plot it in the actual view. However, for the COutputBlockView class member functions to access the COutputBlock class data, various changes are required, as listed, where specific steps are provided in the sections that follow:

1. Add a member variable to the COutputBlockView class.
2. Modify the COutputBlock::BlockDlgWndParameterInput() function.
3. Add a member variable to the COutputBlockDialog class.
4. Modify the COutputBlockDialog constructor declaration and definition.
5. Add code to COutputBlockDialog::OnOutputBlkDlgBtnShowGraph().
6. Add accessor functions to the COutputBlockView class to get and set the block pointer.

20.3.1 ADD A MEMBER VARIABLE TO THE **COutputBlockView** CLASS

A reference-like member variable, i.e., a pointer to the Output block, the block upon which the BlockDlgWndParameterInput() function is called, is required in the COutputBlockView class, since the OnDraw() method needs to access the underlying COutputBlock class' numerical data: "m_dOutputMatrix". Hence, add a private member variable to the COutputBlockView class, of type, pointer-to-COutputBlock (COutputBlock*), named "m_pOutputBlk". Now the COutputBlockView class has a form of access to the COutputBlock class.

20.3.2 MODIFY **COutputBlock::BlockDlgWndParameterInput()**

The original COutputBlock::BlockDlgWndParameterInput() function constructed a COutputBlockDialog dialog object with no arguments; here, a dialog object is to be constructed using the "this" pointer, as shown in bold in the following. This is required since the "this" pointer points to the object upon which the current BlockDlgWndParameterInput() function is called, i.e., the Output block, and this will then be used (see the following) to set the COutputBlockDialog pointer-to-COutputBlock variable, "m_pOutputBlk".

```
void COutputBlock::BlockDlgWndParameterInput()
{
    CString sMsg;           // string to be displayed
    UINT nType = MB_OK;     // style of msg. box
    UINT nIDhelp = 0;       // help context ID for the msg.

    // Create a dialog object. of class COutputBlockDialog : public
      CDialog
    // COutputBlockDialog oDlg;
       COutputBlockDialog oDlg(this);

    // Set the dialog class vars using the block class vars
    oDlg.m_iNotation = m_iNotation;
    oDlg.m_iTimePtDisplay = m_iTimePtDisplay;

    // Return val of DoModal() fn of ancestor class CDialog is checked to
      determine which btn was clicked.
    if(oDlg.DoModal() == IDOK)
    {
        // Assign COutputBlockDialog variable values to COutputBlock
          variable values.
        m_iNotation = oDlg.m_iNotation;
        m_iTimePtDisplay = oDlg.m_iTimePtDisplay;

        // Print msg with variable value.
        sMsg.Format("\n COutputBlock::BlockDlgWndParameterInput(),
          m_iNotation = %d\n", m_iNotation);
        //AfxMessageBox(sMsg, nType, nIDhelp);
    }
}
```

20.3.3 ADD A MEMBER VARIABLE TO THE COutputBlockDialog CLASS

Now, a pointer-to-COutputBlock variable is required in the COutputBlockDialog class due to the revised method of constructing a COutputBlockDialog object using the "this" pointer. Hence, add a new private member variable to the COutputBlockDialog class of type COutputBlock* named "m_pOutputBlk". Since the dialog class requires knowledge of the COutputBlock class, include the "Block.h" header file at the top of the "OutputBlockDialog.h" header file as shown in bold in the following.

```
#if !defined(AFX_OUTPUTBLOCKDIALOG_H__5208CAE3_D388_416F_8FA9_
  F54111FEF27E__INCLUDED_)
#define AFX_OUTPUTBLOCKDIALOG_H__5208CAE3_D388_416F_8FA9_F54111FEF27E__
  INCLUDED_

#if _MSC_VER > 1000
#pragma once
#endif // _MSC_VER > 1000
// OutputBlockDialog.h : header file
//

#include "Block.h"  // rqd. since a ptr-to-COutputBlock is used in
  COutputBlockDialog

/////////////////////////////////////////////////////////////////////
// COutputBlockDialog dialog
...
```

20.3.4 Modify the COutputBlockDialog Constructor Declaration and Definition

The construction of a COutputBlockDialog "oDlg" object using the "this" pointer, as shown earlier in the COutputBlock::BlockDlgWndParameterInput() function, requires a change to be made to the COutputBlockDialog class constructor as shown in bold in the following (with the old version commented out). Notice how the "this" pointer points to the relevant block and is passed in as the pointer-to-COutputBlock, "ref_blk", argument; this is then used to set the pointer-to-COutputBlock member variable, "m_pOutputBlk", in the body of the constructor.

```
//COutputBlockDialog::COutputBlockDialog(CWnd* pParent /*=NULL*/)
//   : CDialog(COutputBlockDialog::IDD, pParent)
COutputBlockDialog::COutputBlockDialog(COutputBlock *ref_blk,
  CWnd* pParent /*=NULL*/)
    : CDialog(COutputBlockDialog::IDD, pParent)
{
    // DiagramEng (start)
    m_pOutputBlk = ref_blk;
    // DiagramEng (end)

    //{{AFX_DATA_INIT(COutputBlockDialog)
    m_iNotation = -1;
    //}}AFX_DATA_INIT
}
```

The declaration of the constructor in the "OutputBlockDialog.h" header file should also be amended to reflect the modified constructor definition in the "OutputBlockDialog.cpp" source file as shown in bold in the following:

```
/////////////////////////////////////////////////////////////////////////
// COutputBlockDialog dialog

class COutputBlockDialog : public CDialog
{
// Construction
public:
//   COutputBlockDialog(CWnd* pParent = NULL);  // standard constructor
    COutputBlockDialog(COutputBlock *ref_block, CWnd* pParent = NULL);
      // modified constructor
...
```

20.3.5 Add Code to COutputBlockDialog::OnOutput BlkDlgBtnShowGraph()

The COutputBlockDialog::OnOutputBlkDlgBtnShowGraph() function is called when the user clicks the Show Graph button residing on the Output block dialog window resource (IDD_OUTPUT_BLK_DLG). But because the COutputBlockView::OnDraw() function will be responsible for drawing the graph in the view window, the COutputBlockView class needs to know which Output block's data is to be drawn.

Hence, within the OnOutputBlkDlgBtnShowGraph() function, a pointer-to-COutputBlockView, "out_blk_view", is declared and upon which a member function is called (SetRefOutputBlock() to be added in the following) to set the pointer-to-COutputBlock member variable, "m_pOutputBlk" (introduced earlier) of the view class, as shown in bold in the following. The "m_pOutputBlk" variable used as an argument is that of the current COutputBlockDialog class. This should not be confused with the pointer of the same name in the COutputBlockView class.

```
void COutputBlockDialog::OnOutputBlkDlgBtnShowGraph()
{
    // TODO: Add your control notification handler code here

    // DiagramEng (start)
    int display_item = 0;    // flag to control msg box display
    CString sMsg;            // string to be displayed
    UINT nType = MB_OK;      // style of msg. box
    UINT nIDhelp = 0;        // help context ID for the msg.

    // Display a msg.
    if(display_item == 1)
    {
        sMsg.Format("\n COutputBlockDialog::OnOutputBlkDlgBtnShow
          Graph()\n\n");
        AfxMessageBox(sMsg, nType, nIDhelp);
    }

    // -- VIEW CONSTRUCTION

    CMainFrame *main_frame = (CMainFrame *) theApp.m_pMainWnd;
      // Get a pointer-to-CMainFrame.
    CMDIChildWnd *pActiveChild = main_frame->MDIGetActive();
      // Get a pointer to the active child window.

    if(pActiveChild != 0)
    {
        CDocument *pDocument = pActiveChild->GetActiveDocument();
          // Get a pointer to the active document.
        if(pDocument != 0)
        {
            CDiagramEngApp *pApp = (CDiagramEngApp *) AfxGetApp();
            CDocTemplate *pTemp;
            CFrameWnd *pFrame;
            pTemp = pApp->GetCOutputViewTemplate();  // Get the document
              template for the new view.
            pFrame = pTemp->CreateNewFrame(pDocument, pActiveChild);
              // Create a new frame.
            if(pFrame != 0)
            {
                pTemp->InitialUpdateFrame(pFrame, pDocument);
                  // Update the frame.
            }

            // Set the COutputBlockView ref-to-block
            COutputBlockView *out_blk_view = (COutputBlockView *)
              pFrame->GetActiveView();
            out_blk_view->SetRefOutputBlock(m_pOutputBlk);
        }
    }

    // Close the dialog wnd with OnOK()
    OnOK();

    // DiagramEng (end)
}
```

Now, since a pointer-to-COutputBlockView is used in the OnOutputBlkDlgBtnShowGraph() function, the "OutputBlockView.h" header file is required to be included at the top of the "OutputBlockDialog.cpp" source file as shown in bold in the following.

```
// OutputBlockDialog.cpp : implementation file
//

#include "stdafx.h"
#include "DiagramEng.h"
#include "OutputBlockDialog.h"
#include "MainFrm.h"            // rqd. since a ptr-to-CMainFrame is used
  in OnOutputBlkDlgBtnShowGraph()
#include "OutputBlockView.h"  // rqd. since a ptr-to-COutputBlockView is
  used in OnOutputBlkDlgBtnShowGraph()
...
```

20.3.6   ADD ACCESSOR FUNCTIONS TO THE **COutputBlockView** CLASS

In the previous step, the accessor function SetRefOutputBlock() was shown to be called upon a pointer-to-COutputBlockView ("out_blk_view"). Hence, add a public member method to the COutputBlockView class with the prototype, void COutputBlockView::SetRefOutputBlock (COutputBlock *ref_blk), and edit the code as follows.

```
void COutputBlockView::SetRefOutputBlock(COutputBlock *ref_blk)
{
    m_pOutputBlk = ref_blk;
}
```

In the development that follows, it will be necessary to obtain the pointer-to-COutputBlock, "m_pOutputBlk", of the COutputBlockView class. Hence, add a public member method to the COutputBlockView class with the prototype, COutputBlock *COutputBlockView::Get RefOutputBlock(void), and edit the code as shown.

```
COutputBlock* COutputBlockView::GetRefOutputBlock()
{
    return m_pOutputBlk;
}
```

The net effect of these changes allows the COutputBlock data member, "m_dOutputMatrix", to be accessed by the COutputBlockView::OnDraw() function via the pointer-to-COutput-Block variable, "m_pOutputBlk", set in a step-by-step manner by the aforementioned functions: BlockDlgWndParameterInput() of the COutputBlock class, the COutputBlockDialog() constructor, OnOutputBlkDlgBtnShowGraph() of the COutputBlockDialog class, and SetRefOutputBlock() of the COutputBlockView class.

20.4   PLOTTING DATA AS A TEXT STRING

Now that the pointer-to-COutputBlock variable "m_pOutputBlk" is available in the COutputBlockView class, the COutputBlockView::OnDraw() function can access the correct Output block's data, "m_dOutputMatrix", and print this graphically upon its view window. Initially, the OnDraw() function will be able to print numerical data as a string, and then it will be extended to plot the data as a graph.

The steps required toward plotting the Output block's numerical data, "m_dOutputMatrix", as a string on the view window are (1) the addition of a member function to the COutputBlock class to get the matrix dimensions and (2) the extension of the COutputBlockView::OnDraw() function to print text to the view.

20.4.1   ADD A **COutputBlock::GetDataDimensions()** FUNCTION

A member function is required to obtain the dimensions of the COuptutBlock data member "m_dOutputMatrix". Hence, add a public constant member function to the COutputBlock class with the prototype, void COutputBlock::GetDataDimensions(int &nrows, int &ncols) const, and edit it as shown.

```
void COutputBlock::GetDataDimensions(int &nrows, int &ncols) const
{
    // Assign nrows and ncols
    nrows = m_iNrows;
    ncols = m_iNcols;
}
```

20.4.2   EXTEND THE COutputBlockView::OnDraw() FUNCTION

Now that both the COuputBlock's data member ("m_dOutputMatrix") and dimensions ("m_iNrows" and "m_iNcols") may be retrieved, the COutputBlockView::OnDraw() function may be augmented to plot numerical data as text to the Output block's view window. Add code to the OnDraw() function as shown in the following. Note, however, that the OnDraw() function will be modified later and its current form is merely used to test primitive display functionality.

```
void COutputBlockView::OnDraw(CDC* pDC)
{
    CDocument* pDoc = GetDocument();
    // TODO: add draw code here
    // DiagramEng (start)
    int i;                          // row index
    int j;                          // col index
    int ncols;                      // no. of cols of m_dOutputMatrix
    int nrows;                      // no. of rows of m_dOutputMatrix
    int str_delta_x = 70;           // text space separation
    double **dOutputMatrix = NULL;  // local output matrix
    TEXTMETRIC tm;                  // text metric
    CPoint ptText(0,0);             // text posn
    CString string1;                // string to hold numerical data

    // -- Var init.
    pDC->GetTextMetrics(&tm);
    int nLineHeight = tm.tmHeight + tm.tmExternalLeading;

    // Get Output Matrix Data and Dimensions
    dOutputMatrix = m_pOutputBlk->GetOutputMatrix();
    m_pOutputBlk->GetDataDimensions(nrows, ncols);
    // PrintMatrix(dOutputMatrix, nrows, ncols);

    // -- Plot Data as Text
    for(i=0; i<nrows; i++) // row i
    {
        for(j=0; j<ncols; j++)     // col j
        {
            string1.Format(" %lf", dOutputMatrix[i][j]);
            pDC->TextOut(ptText.x, ptText.y, string1);
            ptText.x += str_delta_x;
        }
        ptText.x = 0;
        ptText.y += nLineHeight;
    }

    // DiagramEng (end)
}
```

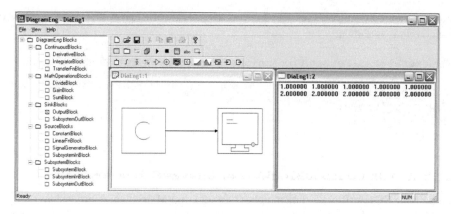

FIGURE 20.3 Simple model (left) involving a source constant vector whose data is output as text in the Output block's view window (right).

Now the code may be compiled and run, and a simple model involving a Constant and an Output block may be drawn as shown in Figure 20.3. A source constant vector $c = [1, 2]^T$ is generated for $t \in [0,5]$ with $\delta t = 1$, and the numerical data of "m_OutputMatrix" is output to the view window.

The developer will notice that the output matrix, "m_dOutputMatrix", is obtained by calling `GetOutputMatrix()` on the pointer-to-COutputBlock, "m_pOutputBlk", a member variable of the COutputBlockView class initialized in the `OnOutputBlkDlgBtnShowGraph()` function of the COutputBlockDialog class.

20.5 PLOTTING NUMERICAL DATA AS A GRAPH

The numerical data, "m_dOutputMatrix", can be retrieved via the pointer-to-COutputBlock, "m_pOutputBlk" and plotted as text on the COutputBlockView view window as shown in Figure 20.3, but now, the data need to be presented as a graphical plot in the form of a function $f(t)$ vs. t. The topics concerning the implementation of plotting data values are listed in the following text, while specific details are provided in the ensuing sections.

1. Modify the `OnDraw()` function in preparation for plotting graph curves.
2. Add a `DetermineMaxMinValues()` function to the COutputBlockView class.
3. Add a `DrawGraph()` function to the COutputBlockView class.
4. A drawing problem due to a change in active document status.
5. Add a `SelectGraphCurveColor()` function to the COutputBlockView class.
6. Add a `GetTimeParameters()` function to the CSystemModel class.

20.5.1 MODIFY `OnDraw()` IN PREPARATION FOR PLOTTING CURVES

The `OnDraw()` function is now revised in preparation for drawing graph curves on the output view window, where the new functions shown in the following code will be added as indicated in the ensuing instructions. Edit the `OnDraw()` function as shown.

```
void COutputBlockView::OnDraw(CDC* pDC)
{
    CDocument* pDoc = GetDocument();
    // TODO: add draw code here
    // DiagramEng (start)
    int ncols;                      // no. of cols of m_dOutputMatrix
    int nrows;                      // no. of rows of m_dOutputMatrix
```

```
int valid = 0;                // (-1) operational error, (1) no error
double min;                   // min data value
double max;                   // max data value
double **dOutputMatrix = NULL;// local output matrix
CString sMsg;                 // string to be displayed
LONG wnd_width;               // window width
LONG wnd_height;              // window height
RECT rect;                    // rectangle data structure (left, top,
  right, bottom)
UINT nType = MB_OK;           // style of msg. box
UINT nIDhelp = 0;             // help context ID for the msg.

// -- GET OUTPUT MATRIX DATA AND DIMENSIONS
if(m_pOutputBlk == NULL)
{
    return;  // no data to draw
}
dOutputMatrix = m_pOutputBlk->GetOutputMatrix();
m_pOutputBlk->GetDataDimensions(nrows, ncols);
//PrintMatrix(dOutputMatrix, nrows, ncols);

// -- DETERMINE MAX/MIN DATA VALS
valid = DetermineMaxMinValues(dOutputMatrix, nrows, ncols, max, min);
if(valid == 0)        // invalid data: hence nothing to graph
{
    //sMsg.Format("\n COutputBlockView::OnDraw(), no data to
      graph\n\n");
    //AfxMessageBox(sMsg, nType, nIDhelp);
    return;
}
//sMsg.Format("\n COutputBlockView::OnDraw(), min = %lf,
  max = %lf\n\\n", min, max);
//AfxMessageBox(sMsg, nType, nIDhelp);

// -- DETERMINE WINDOW DIMENSIONS
GetClientRect(&rect);
wnd_width = (rect.right - rect.left);    // rect.left = 0
wnd_height = (rect.bottom - rect.top);   // rect.top = 0
//sMsg.Format("\n COutputBlockView::OnDraw(), wnd_width = %d,
  wnd_height = %d\n\n", wnd_width, wnd_height);
//AfxMessageBox(sMsg, nType, nIDhelp);

// -- DRAW GRAPH
DrawGraph(pDC, wnd_width, wnd_height, dOutputMatrix, nrows, ncols,
  max, min);
// DiagramEng (end)
}
```

Initially the pointer-to-COutputBlock, "m_pOutputBlk", is checked to make sure it is not NULL, i.e., that there exists an Output block whose data is to be obtained and subsequently drawn. If there is no data, then the function returns; otherwise, the Output block's data "m_dOutputMatrix" and dimensions ("nrows" and "ncols") are retrieved. Then a call is made to DetermineMaxMinValues() to determine the maximum and minimum values of the data for the purpose of scaling the data in the view window.

To fit the output data on the graph-like view, the window dimensions are required; initially, the GetClientRect() function is called passing the address of a RECT (rectangle) data structure and then the width and height of the view window are obtained by accessing the structure's data members.

Finally, the `DrawGraph()` function is called to actually draw the signal data stored within the "m_dOutputMatrix" in the view window; the pointer-to-CDC, window dimensions, and data are passed as arguments.

20.5.2 ADD A `COutputBlockView::DetermineMaxMinValues()` FUNCTION

The maximum and minimum values of the Output block's data, "m_dOutputMatrix", need to be determined to scale the data values appropriately on the view window. Hence, add a public member function to the COutputBlockView class with the prototype, `int COutputBlockView::Deter mineMaxMinValues(double **matrix, int nrows, int ncols, double &max, double &min)`, and edit the code as shown.

```
int COutputBlockView::DetermineMaxMinValues(double **matrix, int nrows,
  int ncols, double &max, double &min)
{
    int i;
    int j;
    double dbl_max = 1.7976931348623157e+308;  // max floating point
      limit
    double dbl_min = 2.2250738585072014e-308;  // min floating point
      limit

    // Check that the matrix has values in it, if not, return
    if(matrix == NULL)
    {
        min = dbl_min;  // intentionally noticeably small
        max = dbl_max;  // intentionally noticeably large
        return 0;       // 0 denotes invalid op.
    }

    // Set max and min vals
    min = matrix[0][0];
    max = matrix[0][0];

    // Loop through data matrix and determine max min values.
    for(i=0; i<nrows; i++)
    {
        for(j=0; j<ncols; j++)
        {
            // Min
            if(matrix[i][j] < min)
            {
                min = matrix[i][j];
            }

            // Max
            if(matrix[i][j] > max)
            {
                max = matrix[i][j];
            }
        }
    }

    return 1;  // 1 denotes valid op.
}
```

The `DetermineMaxMinValues()` function first checks if the Output data matrix, "m_dOutputMatrix", exists, if not, the function sets "min" and "max" to noticeably extreme values and returns zero, denoting an invalid action. If there is valid data ("m_dOutputMatrix" is non-NULL), the function assigns the first matrix data element to the minimum and maximum values and then iterates through the matrix to find lower or higher values, updating the "min" and "max" values, respectively; the integer "1" is then returned, denoting a valid action.

20.5.3 ADD `DrawGraph()` TO THE **COutputBlockView** CLASS

Now that the Output block's data, "m_dOutputMatrix"; its dimensions, "nrows" and "ncols"; the maximum and minimum data values, "max" and "min"; and the window dimensions, "wnd_width" and "wnd_height", have been obtained, these may be passed into a graph drawing function to actually draw the signal data on the view window.

Hence, add a public member function to the COutputBlockView class with the prototype: void COutputBlockView::DrawGraph(CDC *pDC, LONG wnd_width, LONG wnd_height, double **dOutputMatrix, int nrows, int ncols, double max, double min). Edit the function as shown in the following to draw the bounding box rectangular region, the grid lines, the signal curves, e.g., $f(t)$ vs. t, and finally the graph labels. Include the "math.h" header file, i.e., add, #include <math.h>, at the top of the "OutputBlockView.cpp" source file, since the floating point absolute value function, fabs(), is used in DrawGraph().

```
void COutputBlockView::DrawGraph(CDC *pDC, LONG wnd_width, LONG
  wnd_height, double **dOutputMatrix, int nrows, int ncols, double f_max,
  double f_min)
{
    // Note: pDC is a ptr to the device context of "Class Device Context"
      (CDC)
    int i;
    int j;
    int border = 100;        // graph box border distance from wnd edga
    int box_width;           // width of bounding box
    int box_height;          // height of bounding box
    int col;                 // column no. of dOutputMatrix
    int color_cnt = 0;       // color counter to select curve color.
    int n_data_pts;          // no. of data points per graph
    int n_horiz_lines = 10;  // no. of horizontal lines of grid
    int n_signals_per_row;   // no. of signals per row of dOutputMatrix
    int n_TimeSteps;         // no. of simulation time steps
    int n_vertical_lines = 10; // no. of vertical lines of grid
    int pen_width = 1;       // pen width
    int pen_color = RGB(0,0,0); // red = RGB(255,0,0),
      green = RGB(0,255,0), blue = RGB(0,0,255), Black = RGB(0,0,0),
      White = (255,255,255)
    int sig;                 // signal no.
    double data_range;       // range of data values, i.e., max - min
    double delta_t;          // time step size
    double dot_radius = 3.0; // radius of graph curve dot
    double f;                // f = dOutputMatri[.][.], i.e. an element
      of the Output matrix
    double inter_pt_dist;    // distance bw. data points in x-direc.
    double t;                // time value
    double t_init;           // initial time
    double t_final;          // final time
    CPoint box_top_left;     // top left cnr. of graph-bounding box
    CPoint box_top_right;    // top right cnr. of graph-bounding box
    CPoint box_bottom_left;  // bottom left cnr. of graph-bounding box
```

```
CPoint box_bottom_right;      // bottom right cnr. of graph-bounding box
CPoint data_pt;               // data point
CPoint dot_bottom_right;      // graph curve dot bounding box coord
  (bottom right)
CPoint dot_top_left;          // graph curve dot bounding box coord
  (top left)
CPoint text_pt(0,0);          // text posn
CString sMsg;                 // string to be displayed
CString str_label;            // axes string label
UINT nType = MB_OK;           // style of msg. box
UINT nIDhelp = 0;             // help context ID for the msg.

// CREATE A PEN
pen_color = RGB(190, 190, 190);
CPen lpen(PS_SOLID, pen_width, pen_color);

// SET THE NEW PEN AS THE DRAWING OBJ.
CPen *pOldPen = pDC->SelectObject(&lpen);

// SET RECTANGLE POINTS
box_top_left.x = border;
box_top_left.y = border;
box_top_right.x = wnd_width - border;
box_top_right.y = border;
box_bottom_left.x = box_top_left.x;
box_bottom_left.y = wnd_height - border;
box_bottom_right.x = box_top_right.x;
box_bottom_right.y = box_bottom_left.y;

// DRAW RECTANGLE
pDC->MoveTo(box_top_left);
pDC->LineTo(box_top_right);
pDC->LineTo(box_bottom_right);
pDC->LineTo(box_bottom_left);
pDC->LineTo(box_top_left);

// DATA RANGE
data_range = fabs(f_max - f_min);

// NUMBER OF TIME STEPS AND DATA POINTS
CDiagramEngDoc *pDoc = GetDocument();
  // COutputBlockView::GetDocument()
n_TimeSteps = pDoc->GetSystemModel().DetermineNTimeSteps();
n_data_pts = n_TimeSteps + 1;

// BOUNDING BOX VARS
box_width = box_top_right.x - box_top_left.x;
box_height = box_bottom_left.y - box_top_left.y;
inter_pt_dist = (double)box_width/(double)n_TimeSteps;

// DRAW BOX VERTICAL GRID LINES
for(i=0; i<n_vertical_lines; i++)
{
    data_pt.x = box_bottom_left.x + i*((double)box_width/(double)
      n_vertical_lines);
    data_pt.y = box_bottom_left.y;
    pDC->MoveTo(data_pt);
    data_pt.y = box_top_left.y;
    pDC->LineTo(data_pt);
}
```

```
    // DRAW BOX HORIZONTAL GRID LINES
    for(i=0; i<n_horiz_lines; i++)
    {
        data_pt.x = box_top_left.x;
        data_pt.y = box_top_left.y + i*((double)box_height/(double)
          n_horiz_lines);
        pDC->MoveTo(data_pt);
        data_pt.x = box_top_right.x;
        pDC->LineTo(data_pt);
    }

    // NUMBER OF INDEP CURVES PER ROW OF DATA
    n_signals_per_row = ncols/n_data_pts;  // e.g. F(t) = [ [f_1_1,
      f_1_2], [f_2_1, f_2_2], … [f_n_1, f_n_2] ], n_signals_per_row = 2.

    // DRAW CURVES
    for(j=0; j<nrows; j++) // for each row of dOutputMatrix
    {
        for(sig=0; sig<n_signals_per_row; sig++)   // for one or more
          signals per row
        {
            // CREATE AND SELECT A NEW PEN
            pen_color = SelectGraphCurveColor(color_cnt);
            color_cnt++;

            // Create a pen
            CPen lnew_pen(PS_SOLID, pen_width, pen_color);

            // Set the new pen as the drawing obj.
            pDC->SelectObject(&lnew_pen);

            // FOR EACH DATA/TIME POINT OF A SIGNAL
            for(i=0; i<n_data_pts; i++)
            {
                data_pt.x = box_bottom_left.x + i*inter_pt_dist;
                  // x location of pt.
                col = sig + i*n_signals_per_row;  // col of dOutputMatrix
                f = dOutputMatrix[j][col];         // f(.) value stored in
                  dOutputMatrix
                data_pt.y = box_bottom_left.y - int((fabs(f - f_min)/
                  data_range)*box_height);  // y location of pt.

                //sMsg.Format("\n j= %d, sig = %d, i = %d, f = %lf,
                  data_pt.x = %d, data_pt.y = %d\n", j, sig, i, f,
                  data_pt.x, data_pt.y);
                //AfxMessageBox(sMsg, nType, nIDhelp);

                // Draw dot/circle about a pt
                dot_top_left.x = (int)(data_pt.x - dot_radius);
                dot_top_left.y = (int)(data_pt.y - dot_radius);
                dot_bottom_right.x = (int)(data_pt.x + dot_radius);
                dot_bottom_right.y = (int)(data_pt.y + dot_radius);
                pDC->Ellipse(dot_top_left.x, dot_top_left.y,
                  dot_bottom_right.x, dot_bottom_right.y);

                // Draw line connecting pts
                if(i == 0)
```

```
            {
                pDC->MoveTo(data_pt);
            }
            else
            {
                pDC->LineTo(data_pt);
            }
        }
    }
}

// X AXIS LABELS
pDoc->GetSystemModel().GetTimeParameters(t_init, t_final, delta_t);
for(i=0; i<=n_vertical_lines; i++)
{
    text_pt.x = box_bottom_left.x + i*((double)box_width/(double)
      n_vertical_lines) - 0.1*border;
    text_pt.y = box_bottom_left.y + 0.1*border;
    t = t_init + ((double)i/(double)
      n_vertical_lines)*(t_final - t_init);
    str_label.Format(" %lf", t);
    pDC->TextOut(text_pt.x, text_pt.y, str_label);
}
text_pt.x = box_bottom_left.x + 0.5*box_width;
text_pt.y = box_bottom_left.y + 0.475*border;
str_label.Format(" t (s)");
pDC->TextOut(text_pt.x, text_pt.y, str_label);

// Y AXIS LABELS
for(i=0; i<=n_horiz_lines; i++)
{
    text_pt.x = box_bottom_left.x - 0.75*border;
    text_pt.y = box_bottom_left.y - i*((double)box_height/(double)
      n_horiz_lines) - 0.075*border;

    f = f_min + ((double)i/(double)n_horiz_lines)*data_range;
    str_label.Format(" %lf", f);
    pDC->TextOut(text_pt.x, text_pt.y, str_label);
}
text_pt.x = box_bottom_left.x - 0.95*border;
text_pt.y = box_bottom_left.y - 0.475*box_height;
str_label.Format(" f(t)");
pDC->TextOut(text_pt.x, text_pt.y, str_label);

// Graph title
text_pt.x = box_bottom_left.x + 0.4*box_width;
text_pt.y = box_top_left.y - 0.5*border;
str_label.Format(" Plot of f(t) vs. t");
pDC->TextOut(text_pt.x, text_pt.y, str_label);

// RESET THE PREV. PEN
pDC->SelectObject(pOldPen);
}
```

Initially, a pen is created and selected and then the graph-bounding box rectangular coordinates are specified and the box drawn. A fixed number of horizontal and vertical lines are drawn evenly over the box.

Then the number of independent curves per row of numerical data is determined by dividing the total number of columns of "m_dOutputMatrix" by the number of time points at which signal output was generated. For example, if the matrix of output signals ("m_dOutputMatrix")

$$F(t) = \left[\begin{bmatrix} s_1(t_0) & s_2(t_0) \\ s_3(t_0) & s_4(t_0) \end{bmatrix}, \begin{bmatrix} s_1(t_1) & s_2(t_1) \\ s_3(t_1) & s_4(t_1) \end{bmatrix}, \ldots, \begin{bmatrix} s_1(t_n) & s_2(t_n) \\ s_3(t_n) & s_4(t_n) \end{bmatrix} \right] \tag{20.1}$$

where $s_i(t_k)$ are the components of the signal data for $i \in [1, S]$ and $k \in [0, n]$, where S denotes the total number of signals (four in this example) and n denotes the final time-point index of the simulation, then the number of signals per row (for this example) is $2(n + 1)/(n + 1) = 2$. Note that each signal submatrix is generated for each time point of the simulation.

A nested for loop is then entered to iterate over the rows of data ("for(j)"), the signals per row ("for(sig)"), and all time points for the particular signal ("for(i)"). The point on the graph to be drawn, denoted "data_pt", has its x and y components specified according to the current time point across the horizontal time-based domain and the fraction of the signal value of the total data range scaled within the box height, in the vertical domain, respectively. Curves are drawn in a unique color using the to-be-added SelectGraphCurveColors() function.

Finally, a call is made to GetTimeParameters() to obtain the initial (t_0) and final (t_n) simulation times and the time-step size (δt), and then the x and y axes text labels are placed on the graph beside the vertical and horizontal grid lines, respectively, using the function TextOut().

20.5.4 DRAWING PROBLEM DUE TO A CHANGE IN ACTIVE DOCUMENT STATUS

Note that in the DrawGraph() function mentioned earlier, the statement "CDiagramEngDoc *pDoc = GetDocument()" is made to get a pointer to the underlying document, i.e., a pointer-to-CDiagramEngDoc associated with the graph view. The GetDocument() function used is the inline definition of the function, i.e., COutputBlockView::GetDocument(), present in the "OutputBlockView.h" header file mentioned earlier (introduced when adding the COutputBlockView class to the project). If the global function, GetDocumentGlobalFn(), is used instead of the View class' version to get the active document, then the drawing would be correct if there were only one document. However, for multiple document interface (MDI) applications, if there were more than one document, each of which containing a system model with an output block for which there were a visible graph, then upon changing the "active" state of a document/window due to mouse movement by the user from one model to another, erroneous drawing would result. Hence, only the View class, COutputBlockView, version of GetDocument() and not the global definition, GetDocumentGlobalFn(), of the document retrieval function can be used.

The developer may experiment with this problem by creating a message box, using the following sample code, to display the address of the document being retrieved, both in the COutputBlockView::OnDraw() and COutputBlockView::DrawGraph() functions, where the GetDocument() and GetDocumentGlobalFn() functions are used in the former and latter, respectively. The addresses of the documents change upon changing the active window: this is a shock at first, but actually understandable, since the two versions of the document retrieval function behave differently! The GetDocument() function gets the document associated with the view, whereas the GetDocumentGlobalFn() function gets the active document!

```
CString sMsg;
sMsg.Format("\n OnDraw(): pDoc = %p\n", pDoc);
AfxMessageBox(sMsg, MB_OK, 0);

CString sMsg;
sMsg.Format("\n DrawGraph(): pDoc = %p\n", pDoc);
AfxMessageBox(sMsg, MB_OK, 0);
```

20.5.5 Add `SelectGraphCurveColor()` to the **COutputBlockView** Class

The user will have noticed the call to `SelectGraphCurveColor()` to set the color of the particular signal curve: this is done to differentiate between multiple signals on the same graph. Hence, add a public member function to the COutputBlockView class with the following prototype, `int COutpuBlockView::SelectGraphCurveColor(int k)`, and edit the code as shown.

```
int COutputBlockView::SelectGraphCurveColor(int k)
{
    int blue;                  // blue color cmpt.
    int green;                 // green color cmpt.
    int pen_color;             // red = RGB(255,0,0), green = RGB(0,255,0),
      blue = RGB(0,0,255), Black = RGB(0,0,0), White = (255,255,255)
    int random_no;            // integer random number generated
    int red;                   // red color cmpt.
    double uniformly_rand;    // uniformly random number

    // Switch upon integer
    switch(k)
    {
    case 0:
        // seed the random number generator with time value to get truly
          random numbers: done for the default case.
        srand((unsigned)time(NULL));

        pen_color = RGB(0,0,0);        // black
        break;
    case 1:
        pen_color = RGB(0,0,255);      // blue
        break;
    case 2:
        pen_color = RGB(255,0,0);      // red
        break;
    case 3:
        pen_color = RGB(0,255,0);      // green
        break;
    case 4:
        pen_color = RGB(148,0,211);    // dark violet
        break;
    case 5:
        pen_color = RGB(255,140,0);    // dark orange
        break;
    case 6:
        pen_color = RGB(139,69,19);    // dark saddle brown
        break;
    case 7:
        pen_color = RGB(255,20,147);   // deep pink
        break;
    case 8:
        pen_color = RGB(49,79,79);     // dark slate grey
        break;
    case 9:
        pen_color = RGB(119,136,153);  // light slate grey
        break;
```

```
     default:                              // assign a color at random
         random_no = rand();
         uniformly_rand = double(random_no)/double(RAND_MAX);
         red = int(uniformly_rand*255);

         random_no = rand();
         uniformly_rand = double(random_no)/double(RAND_MAX);
         green = int(uniformly_rand*255);

         random_no = rand();
         uniformly_rand = double(random_no)/double(RAND_MAX);
         blue = int(uniformly_rand*255);

         pen_color = RGB(red, green, blue);

         break;
     }// end switch

     return pen_color;
}
```

The *switch* statement is executed, where initially $k = 0$ and the random number generator is seeded in the event that more than 10 curve colors are required. The actual random number is generated using rand() and scaled uniformly to select a value between 0 and 255 in order to yield an appropriate pen color value (RGB(red, green, blue)). The first 10 colors are specifically set to be contrasting in nature.

20.5.6   ADD GetTimeParameters() TO THE CSystemModel CLASS

The user will have noticed the call to GetTimeParameters() made within DrawGraph(). Hence, add a public constant member function to the CSystemModel class with the prototype, void CSystemModel::GetTimeParameters(double &t_init, double &t_final, double &delta_t) const, and edit the code as follows.

```
void CSystemModel::GetTimeParameters(double &t_init, double &t_final,
  double &delta_t) const
{
   // Assign initial time (t0), final time (tn) and time step size
     (delta_t): note pass-by-reference
   t_init = m_dTimeStart;
   t_final = m_dTimeStop;
   delta_t = m_dTimeStepSize;
}
```

The CSystemModel time-based parameters—the initial time, t_0; final time, t_n; and time-step size, δt—are simply returned by reference.

Now upon running the DiagramEng application both the system model and its associated output view windows may be generated and viewed simultaneously (Figure 20.4): a sine curve signal is generated and three different gain constants are applied, resulting in three different output plots. In addition, unique graph curve colors are used to clearly differentiate between the curves in a view: this is visible when running the code but different shades of gray are visible in Figure 20.5.

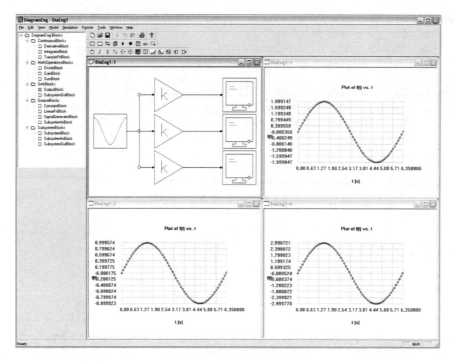

FIGURE 20.4   System model with three Output blocks and their associated views.

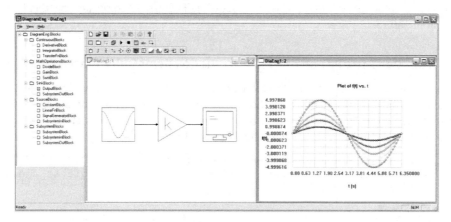

FIGURE 20.5   Simple system model with a gain vector applied to a source signal resulting in five curves of uniquely different colors (visible when running the code) or shades of gray (as displayed here in the text).

20.6   DELETING AN OUTPUT BLOCK AND ITS VIEW

Output blocks (COutputBlock) placed on the palette may be double-clicked to invoke the block dialog (COutputBlockDialog) window and the Show Graph button may be pressed to invoke the graph view window (COutputBlockView). However, now when an Output block is deleted, the pointer-to-COutputBlock, "m_pOutputBlk", of the COutputBlockView class should be assigned to NULL. Since in the COutputBlockView::OnDraw() function, "m_pOutputBlk" is used to get the Output block's data member, "m_dOutputMatrix", and if the Output block is deleted and hence it and its data no longer exist, then the data member should not be accessed: the conditional statement, "if(m_pOutputBlk == NULL)", in COutputBlockView::OnDraw(), prevents this access.

20.6.1 DELETE THE OUTPUT BLOCK VIEW

Deletion of blocks takes place through calls to either CDiagramEngDoc::DeleteBlock() or
CDiagramEngDoc::OnEditDeleteGroupedItems(). Now, add a public member method
to the CDiagramEngDoc class with the prototype, void CDiagramEngDoc::DeleteOutput
BlockView(CBlock *ptr_blk), and edit it as follows.

```
void CDiagramEngDoc::DeleteOutputBlockView(CBlock *ptr_blk)
{
    // Set the COutputBlockView ref-to-block to NULL
    POSITION posView = GetFirstViewPosition();
    while(posView)
    {
        CView *pView = GetNextView(posView);

        if( (pView != NULL) &&
          (pView->IsKindOf(RUNTIME_CLASS(COutputBlockView))))
        {
            if( ((COutputBlockView*)pView)->GetRefOutputBlock()
              == ptr_blk)
            {
                // Set the m_pOutputBlk of the COutputBlockView class to
                  NULL
                ((COutputBlockView*)pView)->SetRefOutputBlock(NULL);

                // Close the view wnd.
                pView->GetParent()->DestroyWindow();
            }
        }
    }
}
```

Include the "OutputBlockView.h" header file at the top of the "DiagramEngDoc.cpp" source
file as shown in bold in the following since a pointer-to-COutputBlockView is used in
DeleteOutputBlockView().

```
// DiagramEngDoc.cpp : implementation of the CDiagramEngDoc class
//

#include "stdafx.h"
#include "DiagramEng.h"
#include "DiagramEngDoc.h"
// DiagramEng (start)
#include <math.h>              // rqd. since OnDeleteItem() uses math fns.
#include "afxext.h"            // rqd. since TrackItem() uses a
  CRectTracker obj.
#include "BlockLibDlg.h"       // rqd. since OnEditAddMultipleBlocks() has
  a CBlockLibDlg obj.
//#include "TreeDialog.h"      // rqd. since OnEditAddMultipleBlocks() has
  a CTreeDialog obj.
#include "OutputBlockView.h"  // rqd. since DeleteOutputBlockView()
  declares a ptr-to-COutputBlockView
// DiagramEng (end)
...
```

The DeleteOutputBlockView() function deletes the view (COutputBlockView) associated with the Output block (COutputBlock) that is to be deleted in the calling environment by

CDiagramEngDoc::DeleteBlock() or CDiagramEngDoc::OnEditDeleteGrouped Items(). The pointer-to-CBlock is passed into the function and used to identify the correct block-related view to be deleted.

The call to GetFirstViewPosition() gets the first view in the list of views for the current document, i.e., for the instance of CDiagramEngDoc. GetNextView() is used to iterate through the list of views. The first conditional (*if*) statement checks to verify that the pointer-to-CView is not NULL and that it is a kind of COutputBlockView object. The second conditional (*if*) statement checks that the address of the block ("m_pOutputBlk") to which the view is associated is the same as that of the block, "ptr_blk", to be deleted, i.e., the correct Output block's view window will be destroyed. If so, the pointer-to-COutputBlock, "m_pOutputBlk", of the COutputBlockView class is set to NULL through a call to SetRefOutputBlock(NULL), preventing attempted access to nonexistent data, and the associated view window is destroyed using a call to DestroyWindow().

20.6.2 MODIFY CDiagramEngDoc::DeleteBlock()

Individual block deletion is performed by choosing Delete Item on the Context menu, whereupon OnDeleteItem() and then DeleteBlock() are sequentially called. Now, within the DeleteBlock() function, prior to block deletion, the DeleteOutputBlockView() function should be called to set its pointer-to-COutputBlock, "m_pOutputBlk", to NULL (as shown in the previous function) and close the view window. Hence, edit the function as shown in bold in the following.

```
int CDiagramEngDoc::DeleteBlock()
{
    int count = 0;        // counter
    int delete_blk = 0;   // blk deletion flag
    double dist;          // Euclidean dist bw. block posn and point posn.
    double width;         // block width
    CPoint blk_posn;      // block posn.
    CPoint point;         // local point var.
    CString sMsg;         // main msg string
    UINT nType = MB_OK;   // style of msg. box
    UINT nIDhelp = 0;     // help context ID for the msg.
    list<CBlock*>::iterator it_blk;        // iterator
    list<CBlock*>::iterator it_er = NULL; // element to erase

    // Get the point at which the context menu was invoked
    point = m_ptContextMenu;                // init a local copy.

    // Print msg.
    //sMsg.Format("\n CDiagramEngDoc::DeleteBlock(), point
      (x,y) = (%d,%d)\n", point.x, point.y);
    //AfxMessageBox(sMsg, nType, nIDhelp);

    // Get a copy of the blk_list in the system model
    list<CBlock*> &blk_list = GetSystemModel().GetBlockList();
      // MUST BE A REFERENCE!

    // Iterate through the list to find which item to delete.
    for(it_blk = blk_list.begin(); it_blk != blk_list.end(); it_blk++)
    {
        blk_posn = (*it_blk)->GetBlockPosition();
        width = (*it_blk)->GetBlockShape().GetBlockWidth();

        dist = sqrt(pow((blk_posn.x - point.x),2) +
          pow((blk_posn.y - point.y),2));
        if(dist <= 0.5*width*0.5)
```

```
            {
                //sMsg.Format("\n CDiagramEngDoc::DeleteBlock(),
                  blk(x,y) = (%d,%d), point(x,y) = (%d,%d)\n", blk_posn.x,
                  blk_posn.y, point.x, point.y);
                //AfxMessageBox(sMsg, nType, nIDhelp);

                // Record which block to erase
                delete_blk = 1;
                it_er = it_blk;
                break;
            }
        }

        // Delete the item in the list
        if(delete_blk == 1)
        {
            // Dereference block's ports (allowing previously connected
              connections to be reassigned to new ports)
            DisconnectEndPointsFromPorts(*it_er);

            // Delete Output Block View
            DeleteOutputBlockView(*it_er);

            // Delete block
            delete *it_er;          // delete actual block pointed to by it_er
            blk_list.erase(it_er);  // delete element at offset it_er in list
              (that held the block)

            count = m_SystemModel.GetBlockList().size();
            //sMsg.Format("\n CDiagramEngDoc::DeleteBlock(), size = %d\n",
              count);
            //AfxMessageBox(sMsg, nType, nIDhelp);
        }
        // Set as modified and redraw the doc.
        SetModifiedFlag(TRUE);      // set the doc. as having been modified to
          prompt user to save
        UpdateAllViews(NULL);       // indicate that sys. should redraw.

        // Return a flag indicating whether an item was deleted
        return delete_blk;
    }
```

20.6.3 MODIFY `CDiagramEngDoc::OnEditDeleteGroupedItems()`

A similar procedure is followed for the Delete Grouped Items entry on the Context menu. Edit the
CDiagramEngDoc::OnEditDeleteGroupedItems() function as shown in bold in the following; the rest of the function remains unchanged. Here, as stated earlier, the pointer-to-CBlock
is passed as an argument to the DeleteOutputBlockView() function to reset its pointer-to-
COutputBlock variable, "m_pOutputBlock" and close the window.

```
void CDiagramEngDoc::OnEditDeleteGroupedItems()
{
    // TODO: Add your command handler code here
    int intersected = 0;
    int intersected_head = 0;
    int intersected_tail = 0;
    double blk_width;
    double delta = 0.25*m_dDeltaLength;
```

```
CPoint bend_pt;
CPoint blk_posn;
CPoint head_pt;
CPoint tail_pt;
CRectTracker temp_tracker;
list<CBlock*> &blk_list = GetSystemModel().GetBlockList();
list<CBlock*>::iterator it_blk;
list<CConnection*>::iterator it_con;
list<CConnection*> &con_list = GetSystemModel().GetConnectionList();
list<CPoint>::iterator it_pt;

// -- IF A RUBBER BAND HAS BEEN CREATED
if(m_iRubberBandCreated == 1)
{
    // Create a temp tracker since m_RectTracker will have its coords
    //   updated when the rubber band is moved.
    temp_tracker = m_RectTracker;

    // -- ITERATE THROUGH BLOCKS
    it_blk = blk_list.begin();
    while(it_blk != blk_list.end())
    {
        // Get block properties
        blk_posn = (*it_blk)->GetBlockPosition();
        blk_width = (*it_blk)->GetBlockShape().GetBlockWidth();

        // Determine if item lies within rubber band
        intersected = DetermineCurrentAndIntersectRects
          (temp_tracker, blk_posn, (blk_width*0.5));
        if(intersected)
        {
            // Delete Output Block View
            DeleteOutputBlockView(* it_blk);

            // Delete block
            delete *it_blk; // delete actual block pointed to by
              it_blk
            it_blk = blk_list.erase(it_blk);  // delete element at
              offset it_blk in list (that held the block)
        }
        else // only increment the iterator if there were no
          intersection
        {
            it_blk++;
        }
    }// end for it_blk

    ...

}// end if m_iRubberBandCreated
}
```

20.7   ADDING FUNCTIONALITY TO THE OUTPUT BLOCK DIALOG WINDOW

Finally, to complete the graph-drawing process, functionality is to be added for the radio buttons on the Output block dialog window resource (IDD_OUTPUT_BLK_DLG); accessor functions are to be added to the COutputBlock class, and the COutputBlockView::DrawGraph() and COutputBlock::BlockDlgWndParameterInput() functions need to be amended.

20.7.1 ADD ACCESSOR FUNCTIONS TO THE **COutputBlock** CLASS

The radio button variables "m_iNotation" and "m_iTimePtDisplay" of the COutputBlock class need to be accessed from within the COutputBlockView::DrawGraph() function. Hence, add two public constant accessor methods to the COutputBlock class, with the following declarations and definitions.

1. int COutputBlock::GetNotation(void) const
2. int COutputBlock::GetTimePtDisplay(void) const

```
int COutputBlock::GetNotation() const
{
    return m_iNotation;
}

int COutputBlock::GetTimePtDisplay() const
{
    return m_iTimePtDisplay;
}
```

20.7.2 AMEND **COutputBlockView::DrawGraph()**

Now that the accessor functions are available in the COutputBlock class, these may be called upon the pointer-to-COutputBlock member variable, "m_pOutputBlk", of the COutputBlockView class, from within the COutputBlockView::DrawGraph() function. Hence, make the amendments shown in bold to the DrawGraph() function (the rest of the function remains unchanged from the previous code), such that (1) standard numerical notation (m_iNotation == 0) or scientific notation (m_iNotation == 1) may be displayed on the actual graph (in blue) and (2) time points may be displayed (m_iTimePtDisplay == 0) or not (m_iTimePtDisplay == 1) using a circular dot.

```
void COutputBlockView::DrawGraph(CDC *pDC, LONG wnd_width, LONG
  wnd_height, double **dOutputMatrix, int nrows, int ncols, double f_max,
  double f_min)
{
    // Note: pDC is a ptr to the device context of "Class Device Context"
      (CDC)
    int i;
    int j;
    ...
    int notation;// notation variable: (0) std notation,
      (1) sci notation.
    ...
    int time_pt_display;    // time point display variable: (0) show time
      points, (1) hide time points
    ...

    // DRAW CURVES
    time_pt_display = m_pOutputBlk->GetTimePtDisplay();  // get time
      point display value
    for(j=0; j<nrows; j++) // for each row of dOutputMatrix
    {
        for(sig=0; sig<n_signals_per_row; sig++)  // for one or more
          signals per row
```

```
    {
        ...
        // FOR EACH DATA/TIME POINT OF A SIGNAL
        for(i=0; i<n_data_pts; i++)
        {
            ...
            if(time_pt_display == 0)
            {
                pDC->Ellipse(dot_top_left.x, dot_top_left.y,
                  dot_bottom_right.x, dot_bottom_right.y);
            }
            ...
        }
    }
}

// X AXIS LABELS
notation = m_pOutputBlk->GetNotation();   // get notation type
pDoc->GetSystemModel().GetTimeParameters(t_init, t_final, delta_t);
  // get time parameters

for(i=0; i<=n_vertical_lines; i++)
{
    text_pt.x = box_bottom_left.x + i*((double)box_width/(double)
      n_vertical_lines) - 0.1*border;
    text_pt.y = box_bottom_left.y + 0.1*border;
    t = t_init + ((double)i/(double)n_vertical_lines)*(t_final - t_init);

    if(notation == 0)
    {
        str_label.Format(" %lf", t);
    }
    else
    {
        str_label.Format(" %-5.3e", t);
    }
    pDC->SetTextColor(RGB(0,0,255));
    pDC->TextOut(text_pt.x, text_pt.y, str_label);
}
text_pt.x = box_bottom_left.x + 0.5*box_width;
text_pt.y = box_bottom_left.y + 0.475*border;
str_label.Format(" t (s)");
pDC->SetTextColor(RGB(0,0,0));
pDC->TextOut(text_pt.x, text_pt.y, str_label);

// Y AXIS LABELS
for(i=0; i<=n_horiz_lines; i++)
{
    text_pt.x = box_bottom_left.x - 0.85*border;
    text_pt.y = box_bottom_left.y - i*((double)box_height/(double)
      n_horiz_lines) - 0.075*border;
    f = f_min + ((double)i/(double)n_horiz_lines)*data_range;

    if(notation == 0)
    {
        str_label.Format(" %lf", f);
    }
```

```
    else
    {
        str_label.Format(" %5.3e", f);
    }
    pDC->SetTextColor(RGB(0,0,255));
    pDC->TextOut(text_pt.x, text_pt.y, str_label);
}
text_pt.x = box_bottom_left.x - 0.95*border;
text_pt.y = box_bottom_left.y - 0.465*box_height;
str_label.Format(" f(t)");
pDC->SetTextColor(RGB(0,0,0));
pDC->TextOut(text_pt.x, text_pt.y, str_label);

// Graph title
text_pt.x = box_bottom_left.x + 0.4*box_width;
text_pt.y = box_top_left.y - 0.5*border;
str_label.Format(" Plot of f(t) vs. t");
pDC->TextOut(text_pt.x, text_pt.y, str_label);

// RESET THE PREV. PEN
pDC->SelectObject(pOldPen);
}
```

20.7.3 AMEND COutputBlock::BlockDlgWndParameterInput()

Finally, when the user has both the diagram model and the output graph windows visible, and then decides to switch between the radio button options (by double-clicking on the Output block to invoke the Output block dialog window and selecting the appropriate radio button followed by clicking the OK button), the desired graph properties should switch accordingly and immediately. To implement this updating of the graph window, amend the COutputBlock::BlockDlgWndParameterInput() function, as shown in bold in the following, to call SetModifiedFlag() and UpdateAllViews() upon the pointer-to-CDiagramEngDoc.

```
void COutputBlock::BlockDlgWndParameterInput()
{
    CString sMsg;              // string to be displayed
    UINT nType = MB_OK;       // style of msg. box
    UINT nIDhelp = 0;         // help context ID for the msg.

    // Create a dialog object. of class COutputBlockDialog : public
      CDialog
//  COutputBlockDialog oDlg;
    COutputBlockDialog oDlg(this);

    // Set the dialog class vars using the block class vars
    oDlg.m_iNotation = m_iNotation;
    oDlg.m_iTimePtDisplay = m_iTimePtDisplay;

    // Return val of DoModal() fn of ancestor class CDialog is checked to
      determine which btn was clicked.
    if(oDlg.DoModal() == IDOK)
    {
        // Assign COutputBlockDialog variable values to COutputBlock
          variable values.
        m_iNotation = oDlg.m_iNotation;
        m_iTimePtDisplay = oDlg.m_iTimePtDisplay;
```

```
        // Print msg with variable value.
        sMsg.Format("\n COutputBlock::BlockDlgWndParameterInput(),
          m_iNotation = %d\n", m_iNotation);
        //AfxMessageBox(sMsg, nType, nIDhelp);

        // Update the view, since changing the notation type changes the
          numbers on the graph.
        CDiagramEngDoc *pDoc = GetDocumentGlobalFn();
        pDoc->SetModifiedFlag(TRUE);  // set the doc. as having been
          modified to prompt user to save
        pDoc->UpdateAllViews(NULL);
    }
}
```

As a result, both standard and scientific notation may be used to display the numerical x and y axes values, and the user may switch between showing and hiding the time points, denoted as small circles, on the graph. For example, consider Figure 20.6 that shows the solution $y(t)$ of the differential equation

$$m\ddot{y}(t) + b\dot{y}(t) + ky(t) = u(t) \qquad (20.2)$$

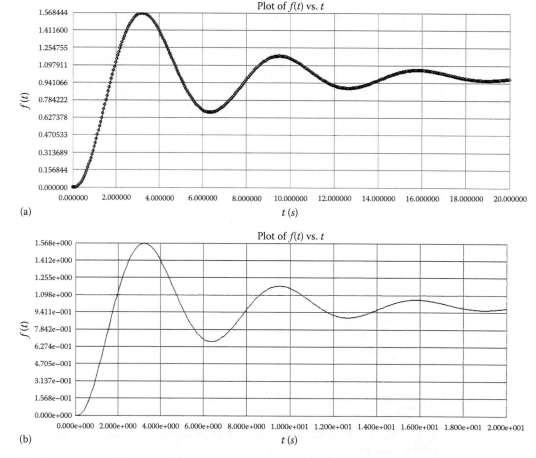

(a)

(b)

FIGURE 20.6 (a) Solution to (20.2) showing standard textual notation with circular time points. (b) Solution to (20.2) showing scientific textual notation without circular time points.

of an underdamped mass–spring–damper system, where m, b, k, $y(t)$, and $u(t)$ are the mass, damping constant, spring constant, output mass displacement from the equilibrium position, and external force input to the system (this will be treated in detail in a later chapter): Figure 20.6a shows the standard notation and circular time point display, and Figure 20.6b shows scientific notation without the circular time point display.

20.8 SUMMARY

To draw a graph of the Output block's data, six incremental steps were taken: (1) adding general structure to display an empty view window, (2) supplementing existing classes with methods and variables to access the output block's data, (3) plotting data as a text string in the view window, (4) plotting numerical data as graph curves in the view window, (5) deleting an Output block and its related view window, and (6) adding radio button functionality to the Output block's dialog window.

The first step, the addition of structure to display an empty view window, involved adding a CDocTemplate object to the application class, modifying the `InitInstance()` function to create a CMultiDocTemplate object, adding a new COutputBlockView class to support drawing within its view, adding template-based functionality to the Show Graph function, and adding the `OnInitialUpdate()` and `OnUpdate()` functions to the CDiagramEngView class.

The second step, supplementing existing classes to access Output block data, concerned addition of a pointer-to-COutputBlock variable in both the COutputBlockView and COutputBlockDialog classes, the construction of a COutputBlockDialog object using the "this" pointer to initialize the block-pointer variable, and the addition of code to the Show Graph function to set the COutputBlockView's block-pointer variable.

The third step simply showed that the numerical data, "m_dOutputMatrix", could be written as text on the Output block's view window through the `OnDraw()` function of the COutputBlockView class.

The fourth step showed how the numerical data could be drawn as graph curves on the view window and involved modifying the `OnDraw()` function, determining maximum and minimum data values, and adding the `DrawGraph()`, `SelectGraphCurveColor()`, and `GetTimeParameters()` functions to complete the drawing process. In addition, the difference in the usage of the `GetDocument()` function of the COutputBlockView class and the `GetDocumentGlobalFn()` that retrieves a pointer to the active document was explained.

The fifth step involved a `DeleteOutputBlockView()` function that resets the pointer-to-COutputBlock variable and closes the Output block view window prior to block deletion in the `DeleteBlock()` and `OnEditDeleteGroupedItems()` functions of the CDiagramEngDoc class.

Finally, the sixth step completed the graph-drawing process by indicating how functionality can be added for the radio buttons of the OutputBlockDialog dialog window to display numerical output with either default or scientific notation.

REFERENCES

1. Mahmood, A., Multiple document interface applications, serialization and multiple view support, Internal Article, CS440 MDI2, University of Bridgeport, Bridgeport, CT, http://www1bpt.bridgeport.edu/sed/fcourses/cs440/Lectures/ (accessed September 3, 2009).
2. MSDN, Microsoft Developer Network Library Visual Studio 6.0, Microsoft® Visual Studio™ 6.0 Development System, Microsoft Corporation, 1998.

21 Block Operations

21.1 INTRODUCTION

Chapter 19 introduced the idea of signal propagation and block-based data operation using a `SignalPropagationDirect()` function in the CSystemModel class and a virtual `OperateOnData()` function in the CBlock class, respectively. The CConstantBlock and COutputBlock versions of `OperateOnData()` were shown to work in a simple example involving a Constant and an Output block connected by a single connection object containing CSignal data. Here, various overriding `OperateOnData()` functions are added, including any subsidiary functions to allow them to work, to some of the remaining CBlock-derived classes, in particular, CDerivativeBlock, CDivideBlock, CGainBlock, CIntegratorBlock, CLinearFnBlock, CSignalGeneratorBlock, and CSumBlock. The implementation of the data operation functions of the subsystem-related and Transfer Function blocks will be postponed till later.

21.2 LINEAR FUNCTION BLOCK DATA OPERATION

The Linear Function block as pictured in Figure 21.1 is a Source block that, like the Signal Generator block, generates a scalar signal value at each time-step of the simulation. The dialog window input parameters for the Linear Function block are the initial and final times at which the signal is activated, t_{a0} and t_{af}, respectively, the initial value of the signal $f(t_{a0})$, and the derivative of the linear function, $f'(t)$, for $t \in [t_{a0}, t_{af}]$. Figure 21.2a shows an example of Linear Function block parameters: $t_{a0} = 2.0$s, $t_{af} = 8.0$s, $f(t_{a0}) = 0$, and $f'(t) = 1$, where the model simulation parameters are $t_0 = 0.0$s, $t_f = 10.0$s, and $\Delta t = 1.0$s. Hence, at simulation time point $t_2 = 2.0$s, the Linear Function will be activated and has a value $f(2) = 0.0$, then the value of $f(t)$ increases linearly up to time point $t_8 = 8.0$s, and thereafter $f(t) = 6.0$ until the end of the simulation, as shown by the generated numerical output in Figure 21.2b.

To generate a linear function-based signal, a block-based data operation function is required that converts dialog-based user input into a piecewise linear function. Hence, add a public virtual member function to the CLinearFnBlock class with the prototype: `virtual int CLinearFnBlock:: Operate OnData(int t_cnt, double t, double delta_t)`. Edit the function as shown to generate a scalar linear function value and to write it to its output connection's CSignal data member.

```
int CLinearFnBlock::OperateOnData(int t_cnt, double t, double delta_t)
{
    int i;
    int nrows = 1;                      // nrows of matrix Y
    int ncols = 1;                      // ncols of matrix Y
    int valid = 0;                      // (-1) operational error,
      (0) read/write error, (1) no error
    double c;                           // y intercept
    double m = m_dDerivative;           // gradient
    double t_init = m_dTimeInit;        // t_init
    double t_final = m_dTimeFinal;      // t_final
    double y;                           // y(t) = linear fn. val at time t.
    double y_init = m_dValueInit;       // y(t_init)
    double **Y_matrix = NULL;           // Y matrix to hold y(t) output value
```

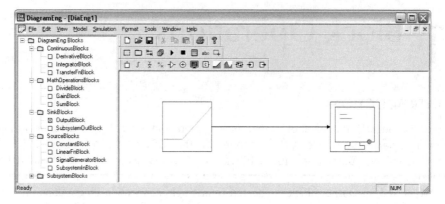

FIGURE 21.1   Linear Function block connected to an Output block in direct signal propagation.

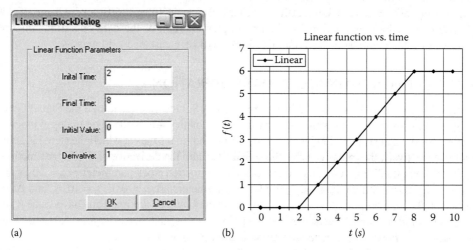

FIGURE 21.2   Linear Function block. (a) Parameter input dialog window showing the parameters, $t_{a0} = 2.0$ s, $t_{af} = 8.0$ s, $f(t_{a0}) = 0$, and $f'(t) = 1$ (with model simulation parameters $t_0 = 0.0$ s, $t_f = 10.0$ s, and $\delta t = 1.0$ s), and (b) corresponding graph.

```
// -- MEMORY NEW
Y_matrix = new double *[nrows];        // allocate an array of
  ptrs-to-double
for(i=0; i<nrows; i++)
{
    Y_matrix[i] = new double[ncols];   // allocate an array of doubles
}

// -- EVALUATE LINEAR FN SIGNAL
c = y_init - m*t_init;                 // y intercept "c" for the
  equ. of a line, y = mt + c

if(t < m_dTimeInit)                    // before linear fn starts
{
    y = y_init;
}
else if((t >= m_dTimeInit) && (t <= m_dTimeFinal)) // during linear fn
{
    y = m*t + c;
}
```

```
    else if(t > m_dTimeFinal)          // after linear fn ends
    {
        y = m*t_final + c;
    }

    Y_matrix[0][0] = y;                // assign linear fn signal to matrix

    // WRITE DATA TO OUTPUT SIGNAL
    valid = WriteDataToOutputSignal(Y_matrix, nrows, ncols);

    // -- MEMORY DELETE
    for(i=0; i<nrows; i++)
    {
    delete [] Y_matrix[i];             // delete the row arrays
    }
    delete [] Y_matrix;                // delete the array (column vector)
      holding the row arrays

    // Return connection signal status
    return valid;
}
```

The `OperateOnData()` function of the CLinearFnBlock class simply generates a scalar linear function value for each time ("t_cnt") it is called. Initially, memory is allocated as a two-dimensional array, since a matrix data structure is used in the call to `WriteDataToOutputSignal()`. Then, based upon the value of the time variable t, before the initial time point of signal activation $(t_0 \leq t < t_{a0})$, during the time domain of signal activation $(t_{a0} \leq t \leq t_{af})$, or after the final time point of signal activation $(t_{af} < t \leq t_f)$, the correct image value $f(t)$ is generated and written to the output connection's CSignal data member.

21.3   SIGNAL GENERATOR BLOCK DATA OPERATION

The Signal Generator block shown in Figure 21.3 is a Source block that generates a scalar signal value at each time-step of the simulation corresponding to one of the functions: sine, random, or square. The dialog window input parameters for the Signal Generator block are function type $f(t)$ (sine, random, or square), amplitude A, angular frequency $\omega = 2\pi/T$ (rad/s) (where T is the period), phase ϕ (rad), and the domain-based units, rad/s or Hz, as shown in Figure 21.4a. The sine and square waves are shown in Figure 21.4b; the random function simply generates a uniformly random number at each time-step.

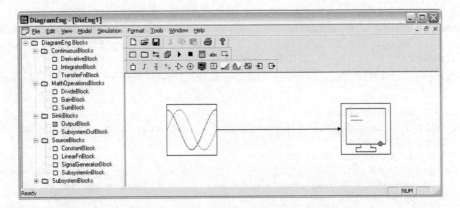

FIGURE 21.3   Simple model involving a Signal Generator and an Output block to test generated signals.

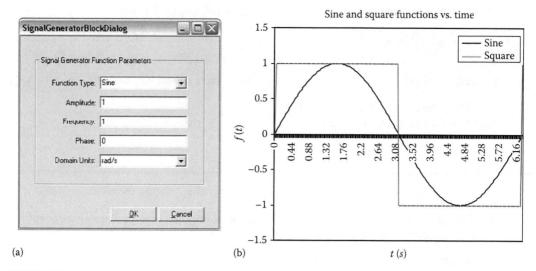

(a)   (b) t (s)

FIGURE 21.4   Signal Generator block. (a) Parameter input dialog window and (b) sine and square wave functions $f(t)$ vs. t.

Add a public virtual member function to the CSignalGeneratorBlock class with the prototype: virtual int CSignalGeneratorBlock::OperateOnData(int t_cnt, double t, double delta_t). Edit the function as shown in the following to generate one of three scalar function values per time-step and to write it to its output connection's CSignal data member.

```
int CSignalGeneratorBlock::OperateOnData(int t_cnt, double t,
double delta_t)
{
    int i;
    int nrows = 1;                          // nrows of matrix Y
    int ncols = 1;                          // ncols of matrix Y
    int valid = 0;                          // (-1) operational error,
      (0) read/write error, (1) no error
    int random_no;                          // integer random number
      generated
    static int rand_flag = 0;               // random no. generator seed
      flag
    double uniformly_rand;                  // random number converted
      to the unit interval
    double A = m_dAmplitude;                // amplitude
    double phase = m_dPhase;                // phase angle (rad)
    double omega = m_dFrequency;            // angular frequency (rad/s)
    double y;                               // y(t)
    double **Y_matrix = NULL;               // Y matrix to hold y(t)
      output value

    // -- MEMORY NEW
    Y_matrix = new double *[nrows];         // allocate an array of
      ptrs-to-double
    for(i=0; i<nrows; i++)
    {
        Y_matrix[i] = new double[ncols];    // allocate an array of
          doubles
    }
```

```
    // -- GENERATE SIGNAL
    if(m_strFnType == "Random")                 // uniformly random number [0,1]
    {
        if(rand_flag == 0)
        {
            srand((unsigned)time(NULL)); // seed the random number
                generator with time value to get truly random numbers
            rand_flag++;                        // seed once per simulation
        }
        random_no = rand();
        uniformly_rand = double(random_no)/double(RAND_MAX);
        y = uniformly_rand;
    }
    else if(m_strFnType == "Sine")          // sine wave
    {
        y = A*sin(omega*t + phase);
    }
    else if(m_strFnType == "Square")        // square wave based on sine wave
    {
        y = A*sin(omega*t + phase);         // use the sin wave to generate
          the square wave

        if(y > 0)
        {
            y = 1;
        }
        else if(y == 0)
        {
            y = 0;
        }
        else if(y < 0)
        {
            y = -1;
        }
    }


    Y_matrix[0][0] = y;                 // assign linear fn signal to matrix

    // WRITE DATA TO OUTPUT SIGNAL
    valid = WriteDataToOutputSignal(Y_matrix, nrows, ncols);

    // -- MEMORY DELETE
    for(i=0; i<nrows; i++)
    {
        delete [] Y_matrix[i];    // delete the row arrays
    }
    delete [] Y_matrix;                 // delete the array (column vector)
      holding the row arrays

    // Return connection signal status
    return valid;
}
```

The OperateOnData() function for the Signal Generator block is separated into three conditional sections to generate the random, sine, or square wave form. The random number generator is seeded once on the first call, and random numbers are generated and scaled to the unit interval to be uniformly random. The sine wave is of the usual form, $f(t) = A\sin(\omega t + \phi)$, and the square wave oscillates between +1 and −1 as shown.

21.4   GAIN BLOCK DATA OPERATION

The Gain block shown in Figure 21.5 is a mathematical operations block that allows signal values to be multiplied by the gain constant, in the form of a scalar, vector, or matrix value: the type of gain can be elemental (Elemental), a gain multiplying the input (Gain*Input), or an input multiplying the gain (Input*Gain), as shown in the parameter input dialog window (Figure 21.6). This block has a single input and a single output connection.

Add a public virtual member function to the CGainBlock class with the prototype: `virtual int CGainBlock::OperateOnData(int t_cnt, double t, double delta_t)`.

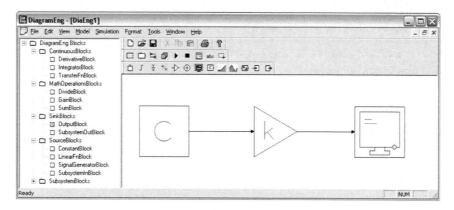

FIGURE 21.5   Simple direct signal propagation model involving a Constant, Gain, and an Output block.

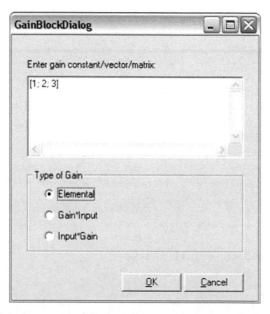

FIGURE 21.6   Gain block parameter input dialog window showing the gain (scalar, vector, or matrix) value and the type of gain: Elemental, Gain*Input, and Input*Gain.

Edit the function as shown in the following to perform the three forms of input-gain operations writing the result to the output connection's CSignal data member.

```
int CGainBlock::OperateOnData(int t_cnt, double t, double delta_t)
{
    int i;
    int j;
    int nrows_del = 0;          // no. of rows to delete of matrix_out
    int nrows_in = 0;           // nrows of input signal
    int ncols_in = 0;           // ncols of input signal
    int valid = 0;              // (-1) operational error,
      (0) read/write error, (1) no error
    double c;                   // input c as a scalar
    double k;                   // Gain k as a scalar
    double **matrix_in = NULL;  // matrix data of input signal
    double **matrix_out = NULL; // matrix data of output signal
    CString  sMsg;              // string to be displayed
    CString sMsgTemp;           // temp msg.
    UINT nType = MB_OK;         // style of msg. box
    UINT nIDhelp = 0;           // help context ID for the msg.


    // -- GET INPUT SIGNAL DATA
    valid = ReadDataFromSingleInputSignal(matrix_in, &nrows_in, &ncols_in);
    if(valid == 0)
    {
        return valid;           // Exit function since input invalid
    }
    else if(valid == 1)
    {
        valid = 0;              // Reset signal validity for output signal
    }
    // -- PERFORM GAIN OPERATION: GAIN = SCALAR
    if((m_iNrows == 1) && (m_iNcols == 1))
    {
        k = m_dGainMatrix[0][0];                // gain constant as a scalar

        // -- MEMORY NEW
        matrix_out = new double *[nrows_in]; // allocate an array of
          ptrs-to-double
        for(i=0; i<nrows_in; i++)
        {
            matrix_out[i] = new double[ncols_in]; // allocate an array of
              doubles
        }
        nrows_del = nrows_in;


        // OPERATE ON DATA
        for(i=0; i<nrows_in; i++)
        {
            for(j=0; j<ncols_in; j++)
            {
                matrix_out[i][j] = k*matrix_in[i][j];
            }
        }
```

```
        // WRITE DATA TO OUTPUT SIGNAL
        valid = WriteDataToOutputSignal(matrix_out, nrows_in, ncols_in);
}
// -- PERFORM GAIN OPERATION: INPUT = SCALAR
else if((nrows_in == 1) && (ncols_in == 1))
{
    c = matrix_in[0][0];                            // input as a scalar

    // -- MEMORY NEW
    matrix_out = new double *[m_iNrows];            // allocate an array
      of ptrs-to-double
    for(i=0; i<m_iNrows; i++)
    {
        matrix_out[i] = new double[m_iNcols];       // allocate an array
          of doubles
    }
    nrows_del = m_iNrows;

    // OPERATE ON DATA
    for(i=0; i<m_iNrows; i++)
    {
        for(j=0; j<m_iNcols; j++)
        {
            matrix_out[i][j] = c*m_dGainMatrix[i][j];
        }
    }


    // WRITE DATA TO OUTPUT SIGNAL
    valid = WriteDataToOutputSignal(matrix_out, m_iNrows, m_iNcols);
}
// -- PERFORM GAIN OPERATION: GAIN = NON-SCALAR
else if((m_iNrows > 1) || (m_iNcols > 1))
{
    if(m_iGainType == 0)        // ELEMENTAL OPERATION
    {
        if((m_iNrows == nrows_in) && (m_iNcols == ncols_in))
        {
            // -- MEMORY NEW
            matrix_out = new double *[m_iNrows];  // allocate an array
              of ptrs-to-double
            for(i=0;i<m_iNrows;i++)
            {
                matrix_out[i] = new double[m_iNcols];   // allocate an
                  array of doubles
            }
            nrows_del = m_iNrows;

            // ELEMENTAL OPERATION
            for(i=0; i<m_iNrows; i++)
            {
                for(j=0; j<m_iNcols; j++)
                {
                    matrix_out[i][j] = m_dGainMatrix[i]
                      [j]*matrix_in[i][j];
                }
            }
```

```
            // WRITE DATA TO OUTPUT SIGNAL
            valid = WriteDataToOutputSignal(matrix_out, m_iNrows,
             m_iNcols);
    }
    else if(((m_iNrows == 1) || (m_iNcols == 1)) &&
      (m_iNrows == ncols_in) && (m_iNcols == nrows_in))
    {
            // -- MEMORY NEW
            matrix_out = new double *[m_iNrows];           // allocate an
             array of ptrs-to-double
            for(i=0;i<m_iNrows;i++)
            {
                matrix_out[i] = new double[m_iNcols];    // allocate an
                  array of doubles
            }
            nrows_del = m_iNrows;

            // ELEMENTAL MULT
            for(i=0; i<m_iNrows; i++)
            {
                for(j=0; j<m_iNcols; j++)
                {
                    matrix_out[i][j] = m_dGainMatrix[i]
                      [j]*matrix_in[j][i];
                }
            }

            // WRITE DATA TO OUTPUT SIGNAL
            valid = WriteDataToOutputSignal(matrix_out, m_iNrows,
             m_iNcols);
    }
    else
    {
            valid = -1;            // operational error
    }
}
else if(m_iGainType == 1)      // Gain*Input OPERATION
{
            // Check dimensions
            if(m_iNcols == nrows_in)
            {
                // -- MEMORY NEW
                matrix_out = new double *[m_iNrows];           // allocate
                 an array of ptrs-to-double
                for(i=0;i<m_iNrows;i++)
                {
                    matrix_out[i] = new double[ncols_in];   // allocate
                      an array of doubles
                }
                nrows_del = m_iNrows;

                // Matrix mult: Gain*Input = Output
                MatrixMultiply(m_iNrows, m_iNcols, ncols_in,
                  m_dGainMatrix, matrix_in, matrix_out);

                // WRITE DATA TO OUTPUT SIGNAL
                valid = WriteDataToOutputSignal(matrix_out, m_iNrows,
                  ncols_in);
```

```
            }
            else
            {
               valid = -1;        // operational error
            }
      }
      else if(m_iGainType == 2)       // Input*Gain OPERATION
      {
          // Check dimensions
          if(ncols_in == m_iNrows)
          {
             // -- MEMORY NEW
             matrix_out = new double *[nrows_in];       // allocate an array
               of ptrs-to-double
             for(i=0;i<nrows_in;i++)
             {
                 matrix_out[i] = new double[m_iNcols]; // allocate an array
                   of doubles
             }
             nrows_del = nrows_in;
             // Matrix mult: Input*Gain = Output
             MatrixMultiply(nrows_in, ncols_in, m_iNcols, matrix_in,
               m_dGainMatrix, matrix_out);

             // WRITE DATA TO OUTPUT SIGNAL
             valid = WriteDataToOutputSignal(matrix_out, nrows_in,
               m_iNcols);
          }
          else
          {
             valid = -1;                // operational error
          }
      }
   }

   // -- Error msg concerning invalid signal or inconsistent data
     dimensions
   if(valid == 0)
   {
      sMsgTemp.Format("\n CGainBlock::OperateOnData()\n");
      sMsg+=sMsgTemp;
      sMsgTemp.Format("\n Error in writing data to output
        signal. \n");
      sMsg+=sMsgTemp;
      AfxMessageBox(sMsg, nType, nIDhelp);  // msg. box
   }
   else if(valid == -1)
   {
      sMsgTemp.Format("\n CGainBlock::OperateOnData()\n");
      sMsg+=sMsgTemp;
      sMsgTemp.Format("\n Error: inconsistent data dimensions, aborting
        operation. \n");
      sMsg+=sMsgTemp;
      AfxMessageBox(sMsg, nType, nIDhelp);  // msg. box
   }
```

```
    // -- MEMORY DELETE
    if(matrix_out != NULL)                              // only delete memory if it
      was in fact allocated
    {
        for(i=0; i<nrows_del; i++)
        {
            delete [] matrix_out[i];                    // delete the row arrays
        }
        delete [] matrix_out;                           // delete the array (column
          vector) holding the row arrays
    }

    return valid;
}
```

The CGainBlock's `OperateOnData()` function is separated into three main logical conditional sections: (1) the first concerns whether the gain value is a scalar, (2) the second considers whether the input value is a scalar, and (3) the third performs a nonscalar, i.e., matrix or vector, gain operation. The third section is itself decomposed into Elemental, Gain*Input, and Input*Gain operations: (1) the Elemental operation multiplies the elements of the gain matrix by the elements of the input matrix taking their dimensions into consideration, (2) the Gain*Input operation checks for consistent inner matrix dimensions and then performs matrix multiplication of the two data types, and (3) the Input*Gain operation is the reverse order of the previous, checking for correct inner dimensions and performing matrix multiplication. All forms of gain operation then write the output data to the output connection's CSignal data member using the call `WriteDataToOutputSignal()`.

The function returns a "valid" integer argument that may have three values: "–1" is returned if an attempt is made to perform a dimensionally inconsistent matrix operation, "0" is returned if the data cannot be read from an input signal or written to the output connection's CSignal object, and "1" is returned if the operation is successful and the output data are correctly written to the output connection's CSignal object. Prior to returning, the output matrix memory that was created to store the result of the gain operation is deleted.

The developer will notice that matrix multiplication is performed by the function `MatrixMultiply()`. Hence, add a new global function prototype, for the `MatrixMultiply()` function, to the "DiagramEngDoc.h" header file, where the existing global function prototypes are located, as shown in the following code excerpt: `void MatrixMultiply(int nrowsA, int ncolsA, int ncolsB, double **A, double **B, double **C)`.

```
// Global Functions
CDiagramEngDoc* GetDocumentGlobalFn(void);
double **ConvertStringToDouble(CString string, int &nrows, int &ncols);
char *StripInputString(char *input_str);
int DetermineDataDimsByStrpbrk(char *in_str, int &nrows, int &ncols, int
  &max_row_length);
int DetermineDataDimsByStrtok(char *in_str, int &nrows, int &ncols, int
  &max_row_length);
double **ConvertStringMatrixToDoubleMatrix(char **str_matrix, int nrows,
  int ncols);
void MatrixMultiply(int nrowsA, int ncolsA, int ncolsB, double **A,
  double **B, double **C);
int PrintMatrix(double **M, int nrows, int ncols);
int PrintMatrix(int **M, int nrows, int ncols);
int PrintVector(double *v, int ncols);
int PrintVector(int *v, int ncols);
```

Now add the `MatrixMultiply()` function to the "DiagramEngDoc.cpp" source file, beneath the matrix and vector printing functions, and edit the code as shown in the following.

```
void MatrixMultiply(int nrowsA, int ncolsA, int ncolsB, double **A,
   double **B, double **C)
{
    int i;
    int j;
    int k;

    // Matrix multiplication
    // A: nrowsA x ncolsA
    // B: nrowsB x ncolsB
    // C: nrowsA x ncolsB
    // C = A*B

    // Nullify C
    for(i=0; i<nrowsA; i++)
    {
        for(j=0; j<ncolsB; j++)
        {
            C[i][j] = 0.0;
        }
    }

    // Matrix multiplication
    for(k=0; k<ncolsB; k++)
    {
        for(i=0; i<nrowsA; i++)
        {
            for(j=0; j<ncolsA; j++)
            {
                C[i][k] = C[i][k] + A[i][j]*B[j][k];
                //printf(" C[%d][%d] = %lf\n", i, k, C[i][k]);
            }
        }
    }

    return;
}
```

The `MatrixMultiply()` function simply multiplies input matrices A and B to generate the result $C = AB$. A simple example model involving a Constant, Gain, and Output block is shown in Figure 21.5; the user may enter a constant value $C = \begin{bmatrix} 1 & 2 \\ 3 & 4 \end{bmatrix}$ and a gain value $k = [1, 2]^T$ and choose the Input*Gain, gain type, to test that the output $y = Ck = [5, 11]^T$.

21.5   SUM BLOCK DATA OPERATION

The Sum block as shown in Figure 21.7 is a mathematical operations block that adds or subtracts a minimum of two input signals and generates a single output signal. The user specifies the number of addition and subtraction inputs as shown in the parameter input dialog window (Figure 21.8) and may change the default port settings using the Port Properties dialog window if desired. The summation operation may be performed using scalar (c), vector (c), and matrix (C) data, provided the dimensions ("nrows" and "ncols") of the component signals being summed are the same.

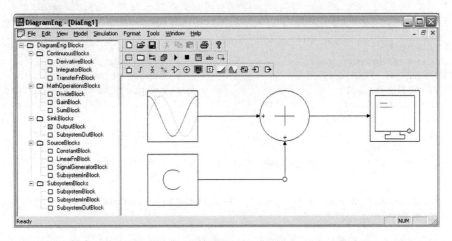

FIGURE 21.7   Scalar summation operation involving a Signal Generator block and a Constant block.

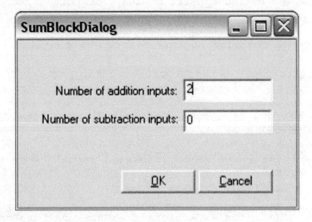

FIGURE 21.8   Sum block parameter input dialog window specifying the number of addition and subtraction inputs.

Add a public virtual member function to the CSumBlock class with the prototype: virtual int CSumBlock::OperateOnData(int t_cnt, double t, double delta_t). Edit the function as shown in the following to perform the addition and subtraction operations writing the result to the output connection's CSignal data member.

```
int CSumBlock::OperateOnData(int t_cnt, double t, double delta_t)
{
    int i;
    int j;
    int first_in = 1;            // first input data flag
    int nrows = 0;               // no. of rows of data
    int nrows_del;               // no. of rows to delete of matrix_out
    int ncols = 0;               // no. of cols of data
    int nrows_ref = 0;           // ref. no. of rows of data
    int ncols_ref = 0;           // ref. no. of cols of data
    int valid = 0;               // (-1) operational error,
      (0) read/write error, (1) no error
    double **matrix_in = NULL;   // input signal
    double **matrix_out = NULL;  // output signal
```

```
CString port_name;                    // port name for sum block:
  "+" or "-"
CString sMsg;                         // string to be displayed
CString sMsgTemp;                     // temp msg.
UINT nType = MB_OK;                   // style of msg. box
UINT nIDhelp = 0;                     // help context ID for the msg.
list<CConnection*>::iterator it_con;  // iterator for list of
  CConnection ptrs.
vector<CPort*>::iterator it_port;     // iterator for vector of
  CPort ptrs.
vector<CPort*> &vec_of_input_ports = GetVectorOfInputPorts();

// Get connection list
list<CConnection*> &con_list = GetParentSystemModel()
  ->GetConnectionList();

// -- ITERATE OVER ALL PORTS AND CHECK INPUT SIGNAL DATA
  DIMENSIONALITY
for(it_port = vec_of_input_ports.begin(); it_port != vec_of_input_ports.
  end(); it_port++)
{
    for(it_con = con_list.begin(); it_con != con_list.end(); it_con++)
    {
        if( (*it_con)->GetRefToPort() == *it_port)  // if the input
          port of this connection is the current port
        {
            valid = (*it_con)->GetSignal()->GetSignalValidity();
            if(valid == 0)
            {
               return valid;  // invalid signal hence return
            }
            else if(valid == 1)
            {
                (*it_con)->GetSignal()->GetSignalDataDimensions
                  (&nrows, &ncols);
                if(first_in)
                {
                   nrows_ref = nrows;
                   ncols_ref = ncols;
                   first_in = 0;
                }
                else
                {
                   if( (nrows != nrows_ref)  || (ncols != ncols_ref))
                   {
                       valid = -1;  // data dimensional inconsistency

                       // Error msg concerning invalid signal or
                         inconsistent data dimensions
                       sMsgTemp.Format("\n
                         CSumBlock::OperateOnData()\n");
                       sMsg+=sMsgTemp;
                       sMsgTemp.Format("\n Error! Inconsistent data
                         dimensions: aborting operation. \n");
                       sMsg+=sMsgTemp;
                       AfxMessageBox(sMsg, nType, nIDhelp);
                           // msg. box
```

```
                        return valid;
                    }
                }
            }
        }// end it_con
    }// end it_port


// -- MEMORY NEW
matrix_out = new double *[nrows];        // allocate an array of
  ptrs-to-double
for(i=0; i<nrows; i++)
{
    matrix_out[i] = new double[ncols];   // allocate an array
      of doubles
}
nrows_del = nrows;


// -- NULLIFY OUTPUT MATRIX
for(i=0; i<nrows; i++)
{
    for(j=0; j<ncols; j++)
    {
        matrix_out[i][j] = 0.0;
    }
}


// -- ITERATE OVER ALL PORTS AND PERFORM SUM OPERATION ON SIGNAL
  DATA
for(it_port = vec_of_input_ports.begin(); it_port != vec_of_input_ports.
  end(); it_port++)
{
    for(it_con = con_list.begin(); it_con != con_list.end();
      it_con++)
    {
        if((*it_con)->GetRefToPort() == *it_port)  // if the input
          port of this connection is the current port
        {
            matrix_in = (*it_con)->GetSignal()->GetSignalData
              (&nrows, &ncols);
            port_name = (*it_port)->GetPortName();


            // MATRIX OPERATION
            if(port_name == "+")
            {
                for(i=0; i<nrows; i++)
                {
                    for(j=0; j<ncols; j++)
                    {
                        matrix_out[i][j] = matrix_out[i][j]
                          + matrix_in[i][j];
                    }
                }
            }
            else if(port_name == "-")
```

```
        {
            for(i=0; i<nrows; i++)
            {
                for(j=0; j<ncols; j++)
                {
                    matrix_out[i][j] = matrix_out[i][j]
                      - matrix_in[i][j];
                }
            }
        }
    }// end it_con
}// end it_port


// WRITE DATA TO OUTPUT SIGNAL
valid = WriteDataToOutputSignal(matrix_out, nrows, ncols);

// Error msg.
if(valid == -1)
{
    sMsgTemp.Format("\n CSumBlock::OperateOnData()\n");
    sMsg+=sMsgTemp;
    sMsgTemp.Format("\n Error in data dimensionality. \n");
    sMsg+=sMsgTemp;
    AfxMessageBox(sMsg, nType, nIDhelp);  // msg. box
}


// -- MEMORY DELETE
for(i=0; i<nrows_del; i++)
{
    delete [] matrix_out[i];   // delete the row arrays
}
delete [] matrix_out;          // delete the array (column vector)
  holding the row arrays

return valid;
}
```

The `OperateOnData()` function of the CSumBlock is divided into two main sections. The first iterates over all the Sum block ports and determines whether the signal data dimensions of the connections attached to the ports are consistent through a call to `GetSignalDataDimensions()`; if the dimensions are inconsistent, an error message is printed and the function returns (valid = −1), and if the dimensions are consistent, then control flow progresses to the Sum operation section.

The Sum block iterates over all its ports, determines whether a connection is attached to the current port, and obtains the CSignal data and type of operation through the calls to `GetSignalData()` and `GetSignalName()`, respectively. Then a running sum is made by updating the output matrix with the new data, where the port sign, "port_name", indicates either the addition or subtraction operation. Finally, the output data are written to the output signal through a call to `WriteDataToOutputSignal()`.

The developer will have noticed that the signal dimensions are obtained through a call to `GetSignalDataDimensions()`. Hence, add a public member function to the CSignal class with the prototype: void `CSignal::GetSignalDataDimensions(int *nrows, int *ncols)`. Edit the function as shown in the following to simply write the value of the CSignal class member variables, "m_iNrows" and "m_iNcols", into the incoming arguments, "nrows" and "ncols", respectively.

```
void CSignal::GetSignalDataDimensions(int *nrows, int *ncols)
{
    // Addresses of nrows and ncols are passed, hence deref. with a ptr.

    // Assign CSignal data values
    *nrows = m_iNrows;
    *ncols = m_iNcols;

    return;
}
```

21.6   DERIVATIVE BLOCK DATA OPERATION

The Derivative block's OperateOnData() function performs either a three-point or a five-point derivative calculation $f'(t)$ given the input signal $f(t)$ at the current time point t and any required previous values $f(t - h)$ or $f(t - 2h)$, where $h = \Delta t$ is the time-step size of the simulation.

21.6.1   THREE-POINT DERIVATIVE

The three-point derivative of a function, as presented in Ref. [1], is

$$f'(t) \approx \frac{f(t+h) - f(t-h)}{2h} \tag{21.1}$$

However, to evaluate the derivative $f'(t)$ at the current time point t, the value of the function $f(t + h)$ at the next time point $t + h$ is required; this would not be available during the time-based simulation without performing an extrapolation, forward in time, of the function $f(t)$ being differentiated. Hence, to transform the expression of the derivative to one that involves known function values, a linear extrapolation is required. To perform a linear extrapolation, the two-point form of the equation of a line,

$$f(t^*) = f_0 + \frac{f_1 - f_0}{t_1 - t_0}(t^* - t_0) \tag{21.2}$$

may be used, where t^* is the time point at which $f(t)$ is to be extrapolated and $f_i = f(t_i)$ are values of the function at time points t_i for $i = 0, 1$ (in this case). If t^* is chosen to be $t_1 + h$ and $t_1 = t_0 + h$, hence $t_0 = t_1 - h$, and these quantities substituted into (21.2), then

$$f(t_1 + h) = 2f_1 - f_0$$

$$= 2f(t_1) - f(t_1 - h) \tag{21.3}$$

Now, from the definition of the three-point derivative (21.1), using $t = t_1$, one obtains

$$f'(t_1) \approx \frac{(f(t_1 + h) - f(t_1 - h))}{2h} \tag{21.4}$$

and substituting in expression (21.3) results in

$$f'(t_1) \approx (2f(t_1) - f(t_1 - h) - f(t_1 - h))\frac{1}{2h}$$

$$= \frac{f(t_1) - f(t_0)}{h} \tag{21.5}$$

That is, the formula for the derivative $f'(t_1)$ at the current time point t_1 now involves two known quantities: the current and previous values of the functions, $f(t_1)$ and $f(t_0)$, respectively, or more generally,

$$f'(t) \approx \frac{f(t) - f(t-h)}{h} \tag{21.6}$$

Hence, this form of the derivative should be used in place of the original three-point derivative (21.1) during the simulation for $t \geq t_1$.

21.6.2 FIVE-POINT DERIVATIVE

The five-point derivative of a function, as presented in Ref. [1], is

$$f'(t) \approx \frac{(-f(t+2h) + 8f(t+h) - 8f(t-h) + f(t-2h))}{12h} \tag{21.7}$$

However, as shown earlier, to compute this derivative, knowledge of two future values, $f(t + h)$ and $f(t + 2h)$, is required. A linear extrapolation may again be used to transform the expression of the derivative to involve only known values at the current time point t. Let $t_2 = t$, this implies that $t_0 = t - 2h$, $t_1 = t - h$, $t_3 = t + h$, and $t_4 = t + 2h$. Hence, to determine $f'(t_2)$, an estimation through extrapolation of $f(t)$ is required to obtain $f(t_3) = f(t + h)$ and $f(t_4) = f(t + 2h)$. Now, using the two-point form of the equation of a line (21.2),

$$f(t_3) = f(t_1) + \frac{f(t_2) - f(t_1)}{t_2 - t_1}(t_3 - t_1)$$

$$= 2f(t_2) - f(t_1) \tag{21.8}$$

and

$$f(t_4) = f(t_2) + \frac{f(t_3) - f(t_2)}{t_3 - t_2}(t_4 - t_2)$$

$$= 2f(t_3) - f(t_2) \tag{21.9}$$

Now, the five-point derivative (21.7) may be used to determine $f'(t_2)$ as follows:

$$f'(t_2) \approx (-f(t_4) + 8f(t_3) - 8f(t_1) + f(t_0))\frac{1}{12h} \tag{21.10}$$

and on substitution of the expressions for $f(t_3)$ and $f(t_4)$ given by (21.8) and (21.9), respectively, one obtains

$$f'(t_2) \approx \frac{(13f(t_2) - 14f(t_1) + f(t_0))}{12h} \tag{21.11}$$

That is, using extrapolation, the derivative $f'(t_2)$ at the current time point involves known function values: $f(t_2)$, $f(t_1)$, and $f(t_0)$ at the current and previous time points, or more generally,

$$f'(t) \approx \frac{(13f(t) - 14f(t-h) + f(t-2h))}{12h} \tag{21.12}$$

Hence, this form of the derivative should be used in place of the five-point derivative (21.7) during the simulation for $t \geq t_2$.

21.6.3 IMPLEMENTING THE OperateOnData() FUNCTION

To implement the CDerivativeBlock::OperateOnData() function, the following additions are required: (1) an OperateOnData() method, (2) a CalculateThreePointDerivative() function, (3) a CalculateFivePointDerivative() function, (4) class member variables, (5) a ResetBlockData() method, and (6) a ResetMemoryBasedBlockData() function.

21.6.3.1 Addition of an OperateOnData() Function

The OperateOnData() function for the CDerivativeBlock class calculates the numerical derivative of a function $f(t)$ to yield $f'(t)$ using either the three-point or five-point forms of the derivative. Add a public virtual member function to the CDerivativeBlock class with the prototype: virtual int CDerivativeBlock::OperateOnData(int t_cnt, double t, double delta_t). Edit the function as shown in the following, structuring the function to call either the three-point or five-point derivative functions and to write the derivative result to the output connection's CSignal data member.

```
int CDerivativeBlock::OperateOnData(int t_cnt, double t, double delta_t)
{
    int i;
    int j;
    int ncols_in = 0;              // ncols of input signal matrix
    int nrows_in = 0;              // nrows of input signal matrix
    int nsignals = 0;              // number of incoming signals
    int valid = 0;                 // (-1) operational error,
      (0) read/write error, (1) no error
    double f_dot = 0;              // f'(t), the derivative of f() at
      current time t
    double *f_at_t = NULL;         // f(t), the input signal vector to
      the block
    double **matrix_in = NULL;     // matrix data of input signals
    CString sMsg;                  // string to be displayed
    CString sMsgTemp;              // temp msg.
    UINT nType = MB_OK;            // style of msg. box
    UINT nIDhelp = 0;              // help context ID for the msg.

    // GET INPUT SIGNAL DATA
    valid = ReadDataFromSingleInputSignal(matrix_in, &nrows_in,
      &ncols_in);

    if(valid == 0)
    {
        return valid;     // exit function since input invalid
    }
    else if(valid == 1)
    {
        valid = 0;        // reset signal validity for output signal test
    }

    // CHECK IF INPUT SIGNAL IS NOT A SCALAR, ROW OR COLUMN VECTOR
    if((nrows_in > 1) && (ncols_in > 1))
    {
        sMsgTemp.Format("\n CDerivativeBlock::OperateOnData()\n");
```

```
        sMsg+=sMsgTemp;
        sMsgTemp.Format("\n WARNING: error in computing the numerical
          derivative!\n");
        sMsg+=sMsgTemp;
        sMsgTemp.Format(" Invalid input signal!\n");
        sMsg+=sMsgTemp;
        sMsgTemp.Format(" Input signal should be a scalar function, or a
          vector of scalar functions.\n");
        sMsg+=sMsgTemp;
        sMsgTemp.Format(" That is: signal = f(t), or signal = [f1(t),
          f2(t), …, fm(t)].\n");
        sMsg+=sMsgTemp;
        AfxMessageBox(sMsg, nType, nIDhelp);    // msg. box
        valid = -1;               // valid = -1 implies dimensionality error
        return valid;             // Exit function since input not a
          scalar fn of a scalar var, or a vector of scalar fns of
          scalar vars.
    }
    else
    {
        m_iNrows = nrows_in;    // record the no. of rows for memory
          deletion
    }

    //  SET TIME COUNT REF AND NO. OF TIMES THE FN IS CALLED AT THIS TIME
        POINT
    if(m_i_t_cnt_ref == t_cnt)
    {
        m_iNcallsPerTimeCnt++; // no. of calls per time-based iteration
          (t_cnt)
    }
    else
    {
        m_i_t_cnt_ref = t_cnt;
        m_iNcallsPerTimeCnt = 1;
    }

    //  WRITE DATA TO OUTPUT SIGNAL IF ALREADY DETERMINED ON A PREVIOUS CALL
    if(m_iNcallsPerTimeCnt > 1)
    {
        valid = WriteDataToOutputSignal(m_dMatrixOut, nrows_in, ncols_in);
        return valid;
    }

    //  GET THE NUMBER OF INCOMING SIGNALS
    if((nrows_in >= 1) && (ncols_in == 1))
    {
        nsignals = nrows_in;
    }
    else if((nrows_in == 1) && (ncols_in >= 1))
    {
        nsignals = ncols_in;
    }

    //  MEMORY ALLOC UPON EACH CALL TO THE FN
    f_at_t = new double[nsignals];    // memory alloc for double *f_at_t,
      i.e., f(t).
```

```
// MEMORY ALLOC OF VARS ONLY WHEN t = 0
if(t_cnt == 0)
{
    m_f_at_t_minus_h = new double[nsignals];     // memory alloc for
      double *m_f_at_t_minus_h member var (array): f(t-h).
    m_f_at_t_minus_2h = new double[nsignals];    // memory alloc for
      double *m_f_at_t_minus_2h member var (array): f(t-2h).
    m_dMatrixOut = new double *[nrows_in];        // allocate an array
      of ptrs-to-double
    for(i=0; i<nrows_in; i++)
    {
        m_dMatrixOut[i] = new double[ncols_in]; // allocate an array
          of doubles
    }
}

// ASSIGN INPUT SIGNAL MATRIX DATA TO f(t) VECTOR
if(nrows_in >= ncols_in)
{
    for(i=0; i<nsignals; i++)
    {
        f_at_t[i] = matrix_in[i][0];    // f(t) is current incoming
          signal at time t
    }
}
else if(ncols_in >= nrows_in)
{
    for(i=0; i<nsignals; i++)
    {
        f_at_t[i] = matrix_in[0][i];    // f(t) is current incoming
          signal at time t
    }
}

// -- THREE(3)-POINT DERIVATIVE
if((m_iDerivativeMethod == 0) && (t_cnt == 0))  // At time t_cnt = 0
{
    // No derivative can be determined
    for(i=0; i<nrows_in; i++)
    {
        for(j=0; j<ncols_in; j++)
        {
            m_dMatrixOut[i][j] = 0.0;
        }
    }

    // FOR EACH INCOMING SIGNAL STORED IN EACH ROW OF signal_vec
    for(i=0; i<nsignals; i++)
    {
        m_f_at_t_minus_h[i] = f_at_t[i];         // Set f(t-h) FOR THE
          NEXT ITERATION to be f(t) OF THE CURRENT ITERATION
    }
}
else if((m_iDerivativeMethod == 0) && (t_cnt >= 1))   // At time
  t_cnt >= 1
{
    // FOR EACH INCOMING SIGNAL STORED IN EACH ROW OF signal_vec
```

```
    for(i=0; i<nsignals; i++)
    {
        // Calculate 3-pt derivative using f(t), f(t-h) and delta_t
        f_dot = CalculateThreePointDerivative(m_f_at_t_minus_h[i],
          f_at_t[i], delta_t);

        // Assign f_dot = f'(t) to the output signal
        if(nrows_in >= ncols_in)
        {
            m_dMatrixOut[i][0] = f_dot;
        }
         else if(ncols_in >= nrows_in)
        {
            m_dMatrixOut[0][i] = f_dot;
        }

        // Set f(t-h) FOR THE NEXT ITERATION to be f(t) OF THE CURRENT
          ITERATION
        m_f_at_t_minus_h[i] = f_at_t[i];
    }
}


// -- FIVE(5)-POINT DERIVATIVE
if((m_iDerivativeMethod == 1) && (t_cnt < 2))    // At less than
  2 calls to the fn
{
    //  No derivative can be determined
    for(i=0; i<nrows_in; i++)
    {
        for(j=0; j<ncols_in; j++)
        {
            m_dMatrixOut[i][j] = 0.0;
        }
    }

    //  SET UP PREVIOUS VALUES f(t-2h) for t_cnt = 0, and f(t-h) for
        t_cnt = 1
    if(t_cnt == 0)
    {
        for(i=0; i<nsignals; i++)        // For each incoming signal
          stored in each row of signal_vec
        {
            m_f_at_t_minus_2h[i] = f_at_t[i]; // Set f(t-2h) FOR THE
              NEXT ITERATION to be f(t) OF THE CURRENT ITERATION
        }
    }
    else if(t_cnt == 1)
    {
        for(i=0; i<nsignals; i++)        // For each incoming signal
          stored in each row of signal_vec
        {
            m_f_at_t_minus_h[i] = f_at_t[i];      // Set f(t-h) FOR THE
              NEXT ITERATION to be f(t) OF THE CURRENT ITERATION
        }
    }
}
```

```
        else if( (m_iDerivativeMethod == 1) && (t_cnt >= 2))      // At time
          t_cnt >= 2
        {
            // FOR EACH INCOMING SIGNAL STORED IN EACH ROW OF signal_vec
            for(i=0; i<nsignals; i++)
            {
                // Calculate 5-pt derivative using f(t), f(t-h), f(t-2h) and
                  delta_t
                f_dot = CalculateFivePointDerivative(m_f_at_t_minus_2h[i],
                  m_f_at_t_minus_h[i], f_at_t[i], delta_t);

                // Assign f_dot = f'(t) to the output signal
                if(nrows_in >= ncols_in)
                {
                    m_dMatrixOut[i][0] = f_dot;
                }
                else if(ncols_in >= nrows_in)
                {
                    m_dMatrixOut[0][i] = f_dot;
                }

                // Set f(t-2h) and f(t-h) FOR THE NEXT ITERATION, to be f(t-h)
                  and f(t) OF THE CURRENT ITERATION, respectively.
                m_f_at_t_minus_2h[i] = m_f_at_t_minus_h[i];
                m_f_at_t_minus_h[i] = f_at_t[i];
            }
        }

        // WRITE DATA TO OUTPUT SIGNAL
        valid = WriteDataToOutputSignal(m_dMatrixOut, nrows_in, ncols_in);

        // MEMORY DELETE
        delete [] f_at_t;      // delete the incoming signal vector f(t)

        return valid;
}
```

The Derivative block's OperateOnData() function initially reads the single input signal "matrix_in" from the input connection and determines its size: "nrows_in" by "ncols_in". This signal is in fact $f(t)$, a row or column vector (at this stage of the development) containing scalar signals $f_i(t)$, for $i \in [1, n]$, where n is the number of signal components "nsignals". The input matrix, "matrix_in", is later assigned to the variable "f_at_t" representing $f(t)$. If the input matrix is of the right structure, i.e., if it is a row or a column vector (a scalar signal can be considered to be a one-element vector), then the member variable "m_iNrows", denoting the number of rows of the output matrix, is initialized; this size is required for memory deallocation purposes in ResetBlockData() (to be introduced).

After the data is checked that it conforms to a vector structure, a test is made to determine the number of times the OperateOnData() function is called for the current time point, "t_cnt". If the reference-like member variable, "m_i_t_cnt_ref", is equal to the current time point, "t_cnt", then the variable "m_iNcallsPerTimeCnt" is incremented; if not, then the time-count reference is updated and the variable recording the number of calls is reset to "1." This test is necessary since the Derivative block has memory, in that it records functional values at previous time points, i.e., $f(t - h)$ and $f(t - 2h)$; the output $f'(t)$ is a function of these previous values. If the block were called more than once (in between time-steps), as it will be in Chapter 23, and the input signal, $f(t)$, changed, then the internal memory of the block, i.e., the values $f(t - h)$ and $f(t - 2h)$, would not be those at previous time points, but rather at previous intermediary function-call occasions.

Hence, if the function OperateOnData() is called more than once per time-step, then the output to be generated, $f'(t)$ (recorded in "m_dMatrixOut"), is that already determined by the initial call to the function and the function returns.

However, if the call to `OperateOnData()` is the initial call at the current time point "t_cnt", then memory is allocated for the local variable "f_at_t" ($f(t)$) and for the class member variables "m_f_at_t_minus_h" ($f(t - h)$), "m_f_at_t_minus_2h" $f(t - 2h)$), and "m_dMatrixOut", which will ultimately hold $f'(t)$.

The three-point derivative section of the function initially records a zero value for $f'(t_0)$ since a value for the derivative is only available for $t \geq t_1$ as described in the discussion earlier. At $t = t_0$, $f(t_0)$ is the incoming signal vector as expected, but $f(t - h)$ is initialized to $f(t_0)$, i.e., $f(t - h) \leftarrow f(t_0)$ (where $\leftarrow$ denotes programmatic assignment), in preparation for the next time-step, when $t = t_1$, at which stage $f(t - h) = f(t_1 - h) = f(t_0)$, the current signal. For $t \geq t_1$, the `CalculateThreePointDerivative()` function is called passing in the values $f_i(t - h)$, $f_i(t)$, and Δt to yield $f_i'(t)$, given by expression (21.6), and these components form $f'(t)$, which is written to the output matrix, "m_dMatrixOut", a vector of output signals in matrix form. Again, in preparation for the next time-step, $f(t - h)$ is updated with $f(t)$, i.e., $f(t - h) \leftarrow f(t)$. See Figure 21.9 that shows the internal updating of the block's data structures at the first few time-steps (this concerns the five-point derivative calculation, but the same concept applies for the three-point derivative).

The five-point derivative section functions in a manner similar to the three-point derivative section, in that, at $t = t_0$, $f(t - 2h)$ is initialized to be the incoming signal, i.e., $f(t - 2h) \leftarrow f(t_0)$, and at $t = t_1$, $f(t - h)$ is similarly initialized, i.e., $f(t - h) \leftarrow f(t_1)$, such that, at $t = t_2$, the first derivative evaluation can occur through a call to `CalculateFivePointDerivative()` to yield the ith component $f_i'(t)$ given by (21.12) of $f'(t)$. Again, in preparation for the next time-step, $f(t - 2h)$ and $f(t - h)$ are updated with $f(t - h)$ and $f(t)$ of the current time-step, respectively, i.e., $f(t - 2h) \leftarrow f(t - h)$ and $f(t - h) \leftarrow f(t)$. In this regard, the Derivative block has time-based memory of the previous two input signals (at the previous two distinct time points). Figure 21.9 shows the updating of the internal data structures for the five-point derivative method.

Finally, after $f'(t)$ is written to the output signal using "m_dMatrixOut", memory allocated for the local variable, "f_at_t", representing $f(t)$, is deallocated.

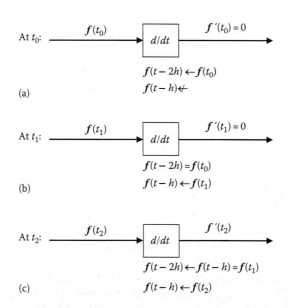

FIGURE 21.9 Numerical five-point derivative operation: (a) At t_0, both $f(t - 2h)$ and $f(t - h)$ are unknown; hence, $f'(t_0) = 0$. (b) At t_1, $f(t - 2h) = f(t_0)$ but $f(t - h)$ is unknown; hence, $f'(t_1) = 0$. (c) At t_2, $f(t - 2h) = f(t_0)$, $f(t - h) = f(t_1)$, and hence, $f'(t_2)$ is known.

21.6.3.2 Addition of the `CalculateThreePointDerivative()` Function

The `CalculateThreePointDerivative()` function simply returns $f'(t)$ given by (21.6). Add a public member function to the CDerivativeBlock class to compute the three-point derivative, with the prototype, double CDerivativeBlock::CalculateThreePointDerivative (double m_f_at_t_minus_h, double f_at_t, double delta_t), and edit it as shown to implement the derivative expression (21.6).

```
double CDerivativeBlock::CalculateThreePointDerivative(double
  m_f_at_t_minus_h, double f_at_t, double delta_t)
{
    // -- NUMERICAL 3-POINT DERIVATIVE
    // The 3-pt derivative of a fn f(t) is
    //          f'(t) = (f(t+h) - f(t-h))/2h
    //
    // However, f(t+h) = f(t + delta_t) is not available at time t, but
    //   may be obtained by linear extrapolation.
    //
    // Linear extrapolation: f(tk) = f0 + ((f1 - f0)/(t1 - t0))*(tk - t0)
    //
    // So, letting tk = t + h, f0 = f(t-h) and f1 = f(t), the
    //   extrapolated value f(tk) is
    //          f(t+h)  =f(t-h) + (f(t) - f(t-h))/(t - (t-h))*(t+h -(t-h))
    //                  = f(t-h) + 2(f(t) - f(t-h))
    //                  = 2f(t) - f(t-h)
    //
    // Now upon substituting the expression for f(t+h) into the
    //   definition of the derivative, one finds
    //          f'(t) = (f(t+h) - f(t-h))/2h
    //                = (2f(t) - f(t-h) - f(t-h))/2h
    //                = (f(t) - f(t-h))/h
    //
    // Hence, if linear extrapolation is used to determine f(t+h) in
    //   order to determine f'(t), then the formula
    // for f'(t) reduces to a fn involving known values, f(t) and f(t-h),
    //   at the current time point t.

    double f_dot_at_t;      // derivative f'(t) at time t.

    // 3-POINT DERIVATIVE
    f_dot_at_t = (f_at_t - m_f_at_t_minus_h)/delta_t;

    return f_dot_at_t;
}
```

21.6.3.3 Addition of the `CalculateFivePointDerivative()` Function

The `CalculateFivePointDerivative()` function simply returns the derivative value $f'(t)$ given by (21.12) involving the current and two previous functional evaluations. Add a public member function to the CDerivativeBlock class to compute the five-point derivative, with prototype, double CDerivativeBlock::CalculateFivePointDerivative(double m_f_at_t_minus_2h, double m_f_at_t_minus_h, double f_at_t, double delta_t), and edit it as shown to implement the derivative expression (21.12).

```
double CDerivativeBlock::CalculateFivePointDerivative(double
  m_f_at_t_minus_2h, double m_f_at_t_minus_h, double f_at_t, double delta_t)
```

```
{
    // -- NUMERICAL 5-POINT DERIVATIVE
    // The 5-pt derivative of a fn f(t) is
    //              f'(t) = (-f(t+2h) + 8f(t+h) - 8f(t-h) + f(t-2h))/12h
    //
    // However, f(t+h) and f(t+2h) are not available at time t, but may
      be obtained by linear extrapolation.
    //
    // Linear extrapolation: f(tk) = f0 + ((f1 - f0)/(t1 - t0))*(tk - t0)
    //
    // Let f(t-2h) = f0, f(t-h) = f1, f(t) = f2, f(t+h) = f3, and
      f(t+2h) = f4.
    // Then, RTF f(t+h) = f3 and f(t+2h) = f4, in order to use the
      expression for f'(t).
    //
    //              f3 = f1 + ((f2 - f1)/(t2 - t1))*(t3 - t1)
    //                 = 2f2 - f1
    // and
    //              f4 = f2 + ((f3 - f2)/(t3 - t2))*(t4 - t2)
    //                 = 2f3 - f2
    //
    // Now upon substituting the expressions for f(t+h) = f3 and f(t+2h)
      = f4 into the definition of the derivative f'(t),
    // one finds
    //              f'(t) = (-f(t+2h) + 8f(t+h) - 8f(t-h) + f(t-2h))/12h
    //                    = (-f4 + 8f3 - 8f1 + f0)/12h
    //                    = (-(2f3 - f2) + 8(2f2 - f1) - 8f1 + f0)/12h
    //                    = (13f2 - 14f1 + f0)/12h
    //                    = (13f(t) - 14f(t-h) + f(t-2h))/12h
    //
    // Hence, if linear extrapolation is used to determine f(t+h) and
      f(t+2h) in order to determine f'(t), then the formula
    // for f'(t) reduces to a fn involving known values, f(t), f(t-h) and
      f(t-2h), at the current time point t.

    double f_dot_at_t;      // derivative f'(t) at time t.

    // 5-POINT DERIVATIVE
    f_dot_at_t = (13*f_at_t - 14*m_f_at_t_minus_h + m_f_at_t_minus_2h)/
      (12*delta_t);

    return f_dot_at_t;
}
```

21.6.3.4 Addition of Class Member Variables and Their Initialization

The developer will have noticed the member variables that are used in the OperateOnData() function earlier. These need to be added to the CDerivativeBlock class and initialized in the constructor function:

1. Add a private integer variable, "m_iNcallsPerTimeCnt", to record the number of times a function is called per time point ("t_cnt") of the simulation.
2. Add a private integer variable, "m_i_t_cnt_ref", to keep track of the current time point of the simulation ("t_cnt").
3. Add a private variable, "m_f_at_t_minus_h", of type double*, to record $f(t - h)$.
4. Add a private variable, "m_f_at_t_minus_2h", of type double*, to record $f(t - 2h)$.

5. Add a private variable, "m_dMatrixOut", of type double**, to record the output signal (stored in a matrix).
6. Add a private integer variable, "m_iNrows", to record the number of rows of the signal matrix, "m_dMatrixOut"; this is used for memory deletion purposes.
7. In addition, the double variable "t_step_size_h" that exists in both the CDerivativeBlock and CIntegratorBlock classes can now be removed, as it is not used in either.
8. Finally, initialize these member variables as shown (in bold) in the CDerivativeBlock constructor; the rest of the constructor remains unchanged as denoted by the ellipsis, "…".

```
CDerivativeBlock::CDerivativeBlock(CSystemModel *pParentSystemModel,
  CPoint blk_posn, EBlockShape e_blk_shape):
CBlock(pParentSystemModel, blk_posn, e_blk_shape)
{
    ...
    // Set memory based vars.
    m_iNcallsPerTimeCnt = 0;   // no. of times the fn is called per t_cnt
      (time point)
    m_iNrows = 0;              // no. of rows of output matrix signal
    m_i_t_cnt_ref = 0;         // ref time cnt
    m_f_at_t_minus_2h = NULL;  // f(t-2h)
    m_f_at_t_minus_h = NULL;   // f(t-h)
    m_dMatrixOut = NULL;       // matrix output signal
}
```

21.6.3.5 Addition of a `ResetBlockData()` Function

At the end of each simulation, the memory that was allocated within the `OperateOnData()` function now needs to be deallocated and some of the member variables reset. This resetting of block-based data may need to be performed by other blocks, e.g., the Integrator block (to be added), which is also a memory-based block and will need its memory deallocated and variables reinitialized. Hence, a virtual `ResetBlockData()` function is required in the CBlock class and is to be overridden by CBlock-derived class implementations.

Add a public virtual member function to the CBlock class with the prototype, `virtual void CBlock::ResetBlockData(void)`, and edit it as shown to display a simple message.

```
void CBlock::ResetBlockData(void)
{
    // This fn has been made virtual and is to be overridden by all
      derived CBlock classes.

    //AfxMessageBox("\n CBlock::ResetBlockData() \n", MB_OK, 0);

    return;
}
```

Now add a public virtual member function to the CDerivativeBlock class with the prototype, `virtual void CDerivativeBlock::ResetBlockData(void)`, and edit it as shown to deallocate memory and reset member variables.

```
void CDerivativeBlock::ResetBlockData()
{
    int i;
```

```
    // Reinitialize member vars
    m_iNcallsPerTimeCnt = 0;            // no. of times the fn is called per
      t_cnt (time point)
    m_i_t_cnt_ref = 0;                  // ref time cnt

    // MEMORY DELETE
    if(m_dMatrixOut != NULL)
    {
        for(i=0; i<m_iNrows; i++)
        {
            delete [] m_dMatrixOut[i];// delete the row arrays
        }
        delete [] m_dMatrixOut;         // delete the array (column vector)
          holding the row arrays
        m_dMatrixOut = NULL;
    }

    if(m_f_at_t_minus_h != NULL)
    {
        delete [] m_f_at_t_minus_h;    // delete member var array f(t-h)
          holding all signal's f(t-h) values
        m_f_at_t_minus_h = NULL;
    }
    if(m_f_at_t_minus_2h != NULL)
    {
        delete [] m_f_at_t_minus_2h;   // delete member var array f(t-2h)
          holding all signal's f(t-2h) values
        m_f_at_t_minus_2h = NULL;
    }
}
```

The CDerivativeBlock::ResetBlockData() function is to be called at the end of each simulation (see Section 21.6.3.6), in which case all memory would be deleted and member variables reinitialized. For completeness, the ResetBlockData() function may also be called from the CDerivativeBlock::~CDerivativeBlock() destructor function as shown in the following. This is not explicitly necessary but placed here in case the code structure changes in future.

```
CDerivativeBlock::~CDerivativeBlock(void)
{
    // Reset block data
    ResetBlockData();       // reset: m_f_at_t_minus_h, m_f_at_t_minus_2h,
      m_dMatrixOut
}
```

21.6.3.6 Addition of a `ResetMemoryBasedBlockData()` Function

Now that the ResetBlockData() function for the CDerivativeBlock class is in place, it needs to be called from within a ResetMemoryBasedBlockData() function of the CSystemModel class, which in turn is called at the end of the SignalPropagationDirect() function.

Add a public member function to the CSystemModel class with the following prototype: void CSystemModel::ResetMemoryBasedBlockData(void). Edit the function as shown in the following to iterate through the block list and call the CBlock-derived ResetBlockData() function. Both the Derivative and Integrator blocks have internal memory that needs to be reset, and these blocks are explicitly identified.

```
void CSystemModel::ResetMemoryBasedBlockData()
{
    CString blk_name;        // block name
    list<CBlock*>::iterator it_blk;       // block iterator
    // Reset block data of those blocks that have memory, i.e. remember
      previous values
    for(it_blk = m_lstBlock.begin(); it_blk != m_lstBlock.end(); it_blk++)
    {
        blk_name = (*it_blk)->GetBlockName();

        if((blk_name == "derivative_block") || (blk_name == "integrator_
          block"))
        {
            (*it_blk)->ResetBlockData();
        }
    }
    return;
}
```

Finally, the `ResetMemoryBasedBlockData()` function needs to be called at the end of the `SignalPropagationDirect()` function, as shown in bold in the following (the rest of the function remains unchanged as denoted by the ellipsis "…").

```
void CSystemModel::SignalPropagationDirect()
{
    …
    // -- Loop for n_TimeSteps + 1, from t_0 = 0, UP TO AND INCLUDING the
      last time point t_n
    for(t_cnt = 0; t_cnt <= n_TimeSteps; t_cnt++)
    {
        …
    }// end (time)

    // -- RESET ALL BLOCKS THAT HAVE MEMORY, I.E. RETAIN PAST VALUES
    ResetMemoryBasedBlockData();

    // -- RESET ALL REF-FROM-PORTS OF CONNECTIONS EMANATING FROM BEND
      POINTS BACK TO NULL
    …
    return;
}
```

21.6.3.7   Testing the Derivative Block

A simple model involving direct signal propagation containing a Linear Function (Figure 21.10a) or a Signal Generator (Figure 21.10c) source block, connected to a Derivative and then an Output block, is shown in Figure 21.10. Either the three- or five-point derivative method may be selected using the block dialog parameter input window.

The Linear Function signal is defined as

$$f(t) = \begin{cases} 2.0, & t \in [0, 3)\,\mathrm{s} \\ t-1, & t \in [3, 8]\,\mathrm{s} \\ 7.0, & t \in (8, 10]\,\mathrm{s} \end{cases} \tag{21.13}$$

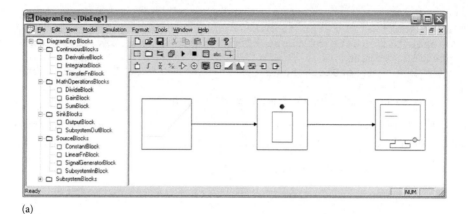

(a)

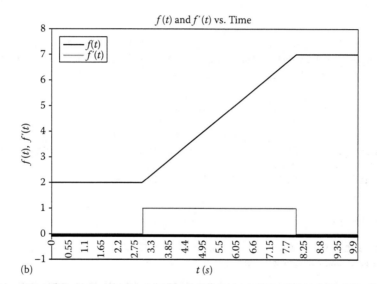

(b)

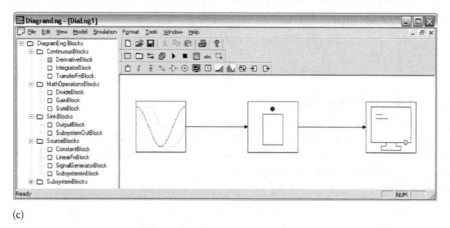

(c)

FIGURE 21.10   Simple Derivative block–based model: (a) a Linear Function block generating a linear signal, (b) the linear function $f(t)$ and its derivative $f'(t)$ (c) a Signal Generator block generating a sinusoidal function, and

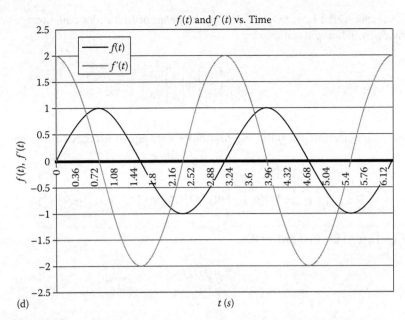

FIGURE 21.10 (continued)   (d) the sinusoidal function $f(t)$ and its derivative $f'(t)$.

and both the function $f(t)$ and its derivative $f'(t)$ are shown in Figure 21.10b. The Signal Generator block is used to generate a function $f(t) = A\sin(\omega t + \phi)$, where $A = 1$, $\omega = 2$, $\phi = 0$, and $t \in [0.0, 2\pi]$, and its derivative $f'(t) = \omega A\cos(\omega t + \phi)$ is evaluated numerically by the Derivative block, as shown in Figure 21.10d.

21.7   INTEGRATOR BLOCK DATA OPERATION

The OperateOnData() function of the CIntegratorBlock performs numerical integration of the incoming signal $\dot{y} = f(t, y)$ to yield the numerical state vector y. In the discussion that follows, the index n is used to denote the nth iteration.

21.7.1   INTEGRATION

Mathematical models of real-world systems are often written in the form of first-order ordinary differential equations (ODEs) through the use of order reduction by variable substitution. For example, consider Newton's second law of motion concerning a body of mass m acted upon by a spring–damper–actuator force, resulting in the equation

$$F = k(x - x_0) + c\dot{x} + f_a(x, \dot{x}, t)$$

$$= m\ddot{x} \tag{21.14}$$

where
  F is the total force
  k is the spring stiffness
  c is the damping coefficient
  $f_a(x, \dot{x}, t)$ is the actuator force
  x_0 is the undeformed length of the spring
  x is the body position
  $\dot{x}$ is the velocity
  $\ddot{x}$ is the acceleration
  t is the independent time variable

To reduce the second-order linear ODE (21.14) to a system of first-order equations, a variable substitution is made by defining a state vector

$$
\mathbf{y} = \begin{bmatrix} y_1 \\ y_2 \end{bmatrix} = \begin{bmatrix} x \\ \dot{x} \end{bmatrix}
\tag{21.15}
$$

and then upon differentiation, the following first-order state equations may be written

$$
\dot{\mathbf{y}} = \begin{bmatrix} \dot{y}_1 \\ \dot{y}_2 \end{bmatrix} = \begin{bmatrix} \dot{x} \\ \ddot{x} \end{bmatrix} = \begin{bmatrix} y_2 \\ F/m \end{bmatrix} = \begin{bmatrix} y_2 \\ m^{-1}(k(y_1 - y_{1,0}) + cy_2 + f_a(y_1, y_2, t)) \end{bmatrix}
\tag{21.16}
$$

where $y_{1,0} = x_0$. That is, the first-order ODE

$$
\dot{\mathbf{y}} = f(t, \mathbf{y})
\tag{21.17}
$$

results.

An analytic solution may not be readily available for the state space equations (21.17), and hence numerical methods must be used to compute a suitable solution, i.e., the state vector $\mathbf{y}$ representing the system being modeled. The following derivation of Euler's method used for numerical integration follows closely the work of Shabana [2].

The state space equations

$$
\dot{\mathbf{y}}(t) = \frac{d\mathbf{y}}{dt} = f(t, \mathbf{y})
\tag{21.18}
$$

with the initial condition, $\mathbf{y}(t = t_0) = \mathbf{y}_0$, may be integrated to obtain

$$
\int_{y_0}^{y_1} d\mathbf{y} = \int_{t_0}^{t_1} f(t, \mathbf{y}) dt
\tag{21.19}
$$

$$
\Rightarrow \mathbf{y}_1 - \mathbf{y}_0 = \int_{t_0}^{t_1} f(t, \mathbf{y}) dt
\tag{21.20}
$$

where the integral with respect to time may be approximated as

$$
\int_{t_0}^{t_1} f(t, \mathbf{y}) dt = hf(t_0, \mathbf{y}_0)
\tag{21.21}
$$

where the time-step size $h = t_1 - t_0 = \Delta t$, and upon substitution into (21.20), one obtains

$$
\mathbf{y}_1 = \mathbf{y}_0 + hf(t_0, \mathbf{y}_0)
\tag{21.22}
$$

This procedure may be repeated for consecutive values of t_n, $n = 0, 1, 2, \ldots$ to arrive at the general expression of Euler's method for the nth iteration

$$y_{n+1} = y_n + hf(t_n, y_n) \tag{21.23}$$

where the state vector $y_n = y(t = t_n)$.

21.7.2 TRUNCATION ERROR AND METHOD ORDER

The following discussion indicates the relationship between the truncation error and the order of a numerical method and follows closely the work of Fisher [3] and Fox et al. [4]. For the remainder of this section, let $y(t_{n+1})$ be the exact solution and y_{n+1} be its approximation through the use of a numerical method.

A recurrence relation is a numerical method that determines y_{n+1} from k previous values y_n, $y_{n-1}, \ldots, y_{n-k+1}$: if $k = 1$, then the method is a single-step method, and if $k > 1$, then it is a multistep method. Euler's method (21.23) determines y_{n+1} from only y_n (and of course t_n, h, and the definition of the derivative $\dot{y} = f(t_n, y_n)$), and hence it is a single-step method.

The local truncation error d_n for a vector system, or d_n for a scalar equation, is defined as the error made in one step of a numerical method, if the previous values were exact, and there were no roundoff error, i.e.,

$$d_n = y(t_{n+1}) - y_{n+1} \tag{21.24}$$

which is the difference between the actual and computed values of the function at t_{n+1}. The second term on the right-hand side of (21.24) is in fact

$$y_{n+1} = y(t_n) + hf(t_n, y(t_n)) \tag{21.25}$$

since the previous value $y(t_n)$ is assumed to be exact. Hence, for Euler's method,

$$d_n = y(t_{n+1}) - y_{n+1}$$
$$= y(t_{n+1}) - y(t_n) - hf(t_n, y(t_n)) \tag{21.26}$$

Now, if a Taylor series expansion of y is performed about t_n, given the existence of $\dot{y}$, $\ddot{y}$, $\partial f / \partial y$ and $\partial f / \partial t$ on (t_n, t_{n+1}), then

$$y(t_{n+1}) = y(t_n) + h\dot{y}(t_n) + O(h^2)$$
$$= y(t_n) + hf(t_n, y(t_n)) + O(h^2) \tag{21.27}$$

and substituting this in (21.26) yields

$$d_n = O(h^2) \tag{21.28}$$

as $h \to 0$.

The global truncation error e_n for a vector system, or e_n for a scalar equation, at t_n, is the difference between the actual $y(t_n)$ and computed y_n solutions disregarding roundoff error, i.e.,

$$e_n = y(t_n) - y_n \tag{21.29}$$

The accuracy of a numerical method is usually discussed in terms of its order that is expressed using the local truncation error d_n; if

$$d_n = O(h^{p+1}) \tag{21.30}$$

as $h \to 0$, then the numerical method is of order p. On comparison of (21.28) and (21.30), one will notice that Euler's method is of first order ($p = 1$).

21.7.3   HIGHER-ORDER METHODS

For real-world systems involving highly oscillatory dynamics modeled by, e.g., spring and damper forces, Shabana [2] indicates that the higher-order derivative terms involve higher powers of the system frequency, e.g., ω, and as ω increases, the error increases, since the error expression for Euler's method involves derivatives of second order and above, i.e., $\ddot{y} = f'(t, y)$. Hence, more accurate numerical integration schemes are used in practice, e.g., the fourth-order Runge–Kutta single-step scheme and the multistep predictor–corrector Adams' methods, where an explicit formula is used to predict the solution at t_{n+1}, and this predicted solution is substituted into a corrector formula to determine the corrected solution. This approach is used to control the size of the truncation error [2].

The single-step fourth-order Runge–Kutta method involves summation of terms evaluated using the current time t_n and vector y_n as follows:

$$y_{n+1} = y_n + \frac{h}{6}(k_1 + 2k_2 + 2k_3 + k_4) \tag{21.31}$$

where

$$k_1 = f(t_n, y_n)$$

$$k_2 = f\left(t_n + \frac{1}{2}h, y_n + \frac{1}{2}hk_1\right)$$

$$k_3 = f\left(t_n + \frac{1}{2}h, y_n + \frac{1}{2}hk_2\right)$$

$$k_4 = f(t_n + h, y_n + hk_3)$$

This method is only of fourth order if the fifth derivatives of y exist on the time interval in question, if not, then the method will be of lower order [4]. Clear examples of the first-order single-step Euler's scheme and the fourth-order single-step Runge–Kutta scheme may be found in Ref. [2].

21.7.4   IMPLEMENTING AN INTEGRATION FUNCTION

For the DiagramEng project, Euler's method is initially implemented to perform preliminary integration of models involving direct signal propagation. Consider the simple model shown in Figure 21.11, involving a Linear Function, Integrator, and an Output block. The function output

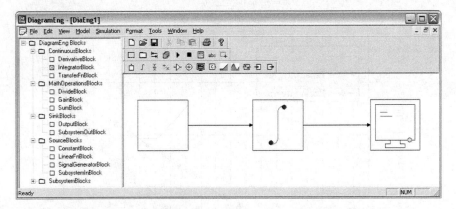

FIGURE 21.11 Simple model of direct integration (without a feedback loop) of a linear function involving a Linear Function, Integrator, and an Output block.

from the Linear Function block, which subsequently enters the Integrator block, for this example, is $f(t) = t$ and forms the right-hand side of the scalar state equation

$$\dot{y} = f(t, y) \tag{21.32}$$

(Vector systems may be constructed by multiplying scalar functions by the appropriate unit vector and summing them to form a first-order state vector (21.17).)

The scalar form of Euler's method

$$y_{n+1} = y_n + hf(t_n, y_n) \tag{21.33a}$$

or equivalently

$$y_n = y_{n-1} + hf(t_{n-1}, y_{n-1}) \tag{21.33b}$$

can be used to obtain approximate state values y_n where the corresponding exact values are $y(t_n) = t_n^2/2$, for $n = 0, 1, \ldots, N$, where N is the final time point of the simulation. Table 21.1 shows

TABLE 21.1

Numerical Integration of $\dot{y} = f(t, y) = t$ Using Euler's Method

n	t_n	$y_n = y_{n-1} + hf(t_{n-1}, y_{n-1})$	$y(t_n) = \dfrac{t_n^2}{2}$	$e_n = y(t_n) - y_n$
0	0	$y_0 = 0$	$y(0) = 0$	0
1	0.1	$y_1 = 0$	$y(0.1) = 0.005$	0.005
2	0.2	$y_2 = 0.01$	$y(0.2) = 0.02$	0.01
3	0.3	$y_3 = 0.03$	$y(0.3) = 0.045$	0.015
4	0.4	$y_4 = 0.06$	$y(0.4) = 0.08$	0.02
5	0.5	$y_5 = 0.10$	$y(0.5) = 0.125$	0.025
⋮	⋮	⋮	⋮	⋮
20	2.0	$y_{20} = 1.9$	$y(2.0) = 2.0$	0.10

y_n are the approximate values at iteration n, where $n \in [0, 20]$; $y(t_n)$ are the corresponding exact values; $e_n = y(t_n) - y_n$ are the global truncation error values; $y_0 = y(0) = 0$; $h = 0.1$ s.

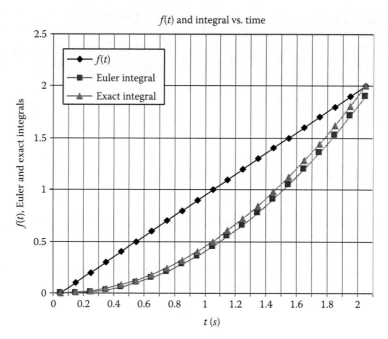

FIGURE 21.12   Linear function $f(t) = t$ and its exact $y(t_n)$ and numerical y_n integrals showing an increasing global truncation error e_n.

the results of the numerical integration: the iteration number $n \in [0, N]$, t_n is the time point that advances in constant time-steps $h = \Delta t = t_n - t_{n-1}$, and $e_n = y(t_n) - y_n$ is the global truncation error.

Figure 21.12 shows the graphs of the functions $\dot{y} = f(t, y) = t$, the approximate numerical integral values y_n, and the exact values $y(t_n)$ vs. time for $t \in [0, 2.0]$ with $h = 0.1s$, where the data correspond to that in the preceding table. The function $f(t, y)$ is linear, hence the integral is quadratic, and the global truncation error increases with time. For this example, after 20 iterations, $e_{20} = h$.

21.7.5   Implementing the `OperateOnData()` Function

To implement the `OperateOnData()` function for the CIntegratorBlock class, the following additions are required: (1) an `OperateOnData()` method, (2) an `EulerMethod()` function, (3) a `GetIntegrationMethod()` function, (4) class member variables, and (5) a `ResetBlockData()` method.

21.7.5.1   Addition of an `OperateOnData()` Function

The `OperateOnData()` function for the Integrator block performs the numerical integration of the incoming signal $\dot{y} = f(t, y)$ to yield the numerical state vector $y(t)$. Add a public virtual member function to the CIntegratorBlock class with the prototype: `virtual int CIntegratorBlock:: OperateOnData(int t_cnt, double t, double delta_t)`. Edit the function as shown in the following to call the Euler integration method and to write the integral result to the output connection's CSignal data member.

```
int CIntegratorBlock::OperateOnData(int t_cnt, double t, double delta_t)
{
    int i;
    int length_y;           // length of y vector
    int ncols;              // no. of cols of matrix_in
    int nrows;              // no. of rows of matrix_in
```

```
int valid = 0;              // (-1) operational error, (0) read/write
  error, (1) no error
double *y_at_t = NULL;      // y_i = y_i-1 + h*f(t_i-1, y_i-1)
double **matrix_in = NULL;  // input signal
CString sIntegrationMethod; // integration method
CString sMsg;               // string to be displayed
CString sMsgTemp;           // temp msg.
UINT nType = MB_OK;         // style of msg. box
UINT nIDhelp = 0;           // help context ID for the msg.

// -- GET SYS MODEL VAR
sIntegrationMethod = GetParentSystemModel()->GetIntegrationMethod();
  // get integration method from CSystemModel

// Inform user of default integration method
if(t_cnt == 0)
{
   if(sIntegrationMethod == "Runge-Kutta (4th Order)")
   {
      sMsgTemp.Format("\n CIntegratorBlock::OperateOnData() \n");
      sMsg += sMsgTemp;
      sMsgTemp.Format("\n No Runge-Kutta method specified as yet:
        defaulting to Euler method. \n");
      sMsg += sMsgTemp;
      AfxMessageBox(sMsg, nType, nIDhelp);
   }
}

// -- GET INPUT SIGNAL DATA
valid = ReadDataFromSingleInputSignal(matrix_in, &nrows, &ncols);
if(valid == 0)
{
   return valid;    // Exit function since input invalid
}
else if(valid == 1)
{
   valid = 0;
}

// -- CHECK SIZE OF MATRIX_IN
if((nrows > 1) && (ncols > 1))
{
   sMsgTemp.Format("\n CIntegratorBlock::OperateOnData()\n");
   sMsg+=sMsgTemp;
   sMsgTemp.Format(" Input signal is not a row or column vector, but
     a matrix.");
   sMsg+=sMsgTemp;
   sMsgTemp.Format(" Aborting integration operation.");
   sMsg+=sMsgTemp;
   AfxMessageBox(sMsg, nType, nIDhelp);    // msg. box

   valid = -1;   // dimensionality error
   return valid;
}

// -- DETERMINE CONSISTENCY OF LENGTHS OF Y AND Y_INIT_COND
if(nrows >= ncols)
```

```
{
   length_y = nrows;
}
else
{
   length_y = ncols;
}

// If incoming signal length not equal to length of init. cond.
 member variable vec, m_dICVector
if(length_y != m_iLength)
{
   sMsgTemp.Format("\n CIntegratorBlock::OperateOnData()\n");
   sMsg+=sMsgTemp;
   sMsgTemp.Format(" Input signal is not of same dimension as initial
     condition vector.");
   sMsg+=sMsgTemp;
   sMsgTemp.Format(" Aborting integration operation.");
   sMsg+=sMsgTemp;
   AfxMessageBox(sMsg, nType, nIDhelp);    // msg. box

   valid = -1;    // dimensionality error
   return valid;
}
else
{
   m_iNrowsOut = nrows;    // assign the no. of rows of the output
     matrix signal for memory deletion purposes
}

// SET TIME COUNT REF AND NO. OF TIMES THE FN IS CALLED AT THIS TIME
  POINT
if(m_i_t_cnt_ref == t_cnt)
{
   m_iNcallsPerTimeCnt++;
}
else
{
   m_i_t_cnt_ref = t_cnt;
   m_iNcallsPerTimeCnt = 1;
}

// WRITE DATA TO OUTPUT SIGNAL IF ALREADY DETERMINED ON A PREVIOUS
  CALL
if(m_iNcallsPerTimeCnt > 1)
{
   valid = WriteDataToOutputSignal(m_dMatrixOut, nrows, ncols);
   return valid;
}

// -- MEMORY NEW
y_at_t = new double[length_y];

if(t_cnt == 0)    // allocate memory for y_vec only a t_0
{
   m_y_at_t_minus_h = new double[length_y];
   m_y_dot_at_t_minus_h = new double[length_y];  // allocate an array
     of doubles
```

```
    m_dMatrixOut = new double *[nrows];          // allocate an array
      of ptrs-to-double to be same size as matrix_in
    for(i=0; i<nrows; i++)
    {
        m_dMatrixOut[i] = new double[ncols];     // allocate an array
          of doubles
    }
}

// -- ASSIGN IC VECTOR TO Y VECTOR INITIALLY (at t = 0)
if(t_cnt == 0)
{
    for(i=0; i<length_y; i++)
    {
        y_at_t[i] = m_dICVector[i];  // y_0 = y_init_cond = m_dICVector
    }
}


// -- PERFORM EULER INTEGRATION
// y_i+1 = y_i + delta_t*y_dot(t_i, y_i), and hence y must be static
  since it holds y_at_t_i and is updated to y_at_t_i+1, which
// then becomes y_at_t_i upon the next entry into the OperateOnData()
  fn, i.e. it must be "remembered" or remain
// persistent/static for the next iteration's evaluation. The vector
  y_dot is the incoming signal.

if(t_cnt > 0)
{
    // -- PERFORM CHOSEN NUMERICAL INTEGRATION
    if(sIntegrationMethod == "Euler (1st Order)")
    {
        EulerMethod(y_at_t, m_y_at_t_minus_h, m_y_dot_at_t_minus_h,
          delta_t, length_y);
    }
    else if(sIntegrationMethod == "Runge-Kutta (4th Order)")
    {
        // Default Euler method used in absence of Runge-Kutta method.
        EulerMethod(y_at_t, m_y_at_t_minus_h, m_y_dot_at_t_minus_h,
          delta_t, length_y);
    }
}

//sMsgTemp.Format("\n CIntegratorBlock::OperateOnData()\n");
//sMsg+=sMsgTemp;
//sMsgTemp.Format(" length_y = %d, y_at_t[0] = %lf,
  m_y_at_t_minus_h[0] = %lf, m_y_dot_at_t_minus_h[0] = %lf\n",
  length_y, y_at_t[0], m_y_at_t_minus_h[0], m_y_dot_at_t_minus_h[0]);
//sMsg+=sMsgTemp;
//AfxMessageBox(sMsg, nType, nIDhelp);    // msg. box

// -- ASSIGN MATRIX_IN TO Y_DOT: the incoming signal is y_dot = f(t,y).
if(nrows >= ncols)
{
    for(i=0; i<length_y; i++)
    {
        m_y_dot_at_t_minus_h[i] = matrix_in[i][0];
    }
```

```
    }
    else
    {
        for(i=0; i<length_y; i++)
        {
            m_y_dot_at_t_minus_h[i] = matrix_in[0][i];
        }
    }

    // -- UPDATE m_y_at_t_minus_h FOR NEXT ITERATION WITH y_at_t OF
    //    CURRENT ITERATION.
    for(i=0; i<length_y; i++)
    {
            m_y_at_t_minus_h[i] = y_at_t[i];
    }

    // -- WRITE DATA TO OUTPUT SIGNAL TO HAVE SAME DIMS AS INPUT SIGNAL
    if(nrows >= ncols)
    {
        for(i=0; i<length_y; i++)
        {
            m_dMatrixOut[i][0] = y_at_t[i];
        }
    }
    else
    {
        for(i=0; i<length_y; i++)
        {
            m_dMatrixOut[0][i] = y_at_t[i];
        }
    }
    valid = WriteDataToOutputSignal(m_dMatrixOut, nrows, ncols);
      // m_dMatrixOut is of same dim as matrix_in

    // -- MEMORY DELETE
    delete [] y_at_t;    // delete the y_dot array

    return valid;
}
```

The signal input and output of a block are considered to be generated at the current time value t_n, $n \in [0, N]$; e.g., for a Derivative block, if the input signal is $f(t_n)$, then the output signal is $f'(t_n)$. However, for the Integrator block, the expression to evaluate the numerical integral using, e.g., Euler's method (21.23), implies that the output signal y_{n+1}, at t_{n+1}, is at a time one time-step greater than the input signal, y_n, at t_n. In order that all model blocks behave in a consistent manner, Euler's method is still used, but in the following form:

$$y_n = y_{n-1} + hf(t_{n-1}, y_{n-1})$$
$$= y_{n-1} + h\dot{y}_{n-1} \tag{21.34}$$

i.e., the current value of y_n to be sent as an output signal at t_n is a function of the previous values y_{n-1} and $\dot{y}_{n-1}$; these must then be statically stored ("remembered") and updated appropriately. The developer will notice that the explicit time variable t_n is not actually used in the OperateOnData() function, since the input signal $\dot{y}_n$ $(= f(t_n, y_n))$ is already in numerical rather than analytic form and hence can be used directly.

Initially, the dimensions of the input signal are checked to make sure that it is in vector form, and then its length is determined and checked against the member variable, "m_iLength", the length of the initial condition vector. If the vector is of the correct structure, then the member variable, "m_iNrowsOut", used to record the number of rows of the output matrix signal is initialized; it is used for memory deallocation purposes in ResetBlockData() (to be introduced).

Thereafter a test is made to determine the number of times the OperateOnData() function is called for the current time point "t_cnt". This is the same check that was made for the Derivative block and is required since the Integrator block has memory, in that it records values at previous time points, i.e., $y(t - h)$ and $\dot{y}(t - h)$; the output $y(t)$ is a function of these previous values. If the block were called more than once (in between time-steps) and the input signal, $\dot{y}(t)$, changed, then the internal memory of the block, i.e., the values $y(t - h)$ and $\dot{y}(t - h)$, would not be those at previous time points, but rather at previous intermediary function-call occasions. Hence, if the function OperateOnData() is called more than once per time-step, then the output to be generated, $y(t)$ (recorded in "m_dMatrixOut"), is that already determined by the initial call to the function, and the function returns.

Then memory is allocated for $y_t \equiv y_n$, and initially at $t = 0$ for "m_dMatrixOut", $y_{t-h} \equiv y_{n-1}$ and $\dot{y}_{t-h} \equiv \dot{y}_{n-1}$, where the latter two variables hold ("remember") information generated at the previous time point $t - h \equiv t_{n-1}$.

Now for the first iteration, at $t_0 = 0$, $y(t_0) = y_0$, i.e., the output signal is the initial condition vector. The Euler integration recurrence method is skipped; $\dot{y}_{t-h}$ is set to be the current incoming signal, i.e., $\dot{y}_{t-h} \leftarrow \dot{y}_0$ (here the symbol $\leftarrow$ denotes programmatic assignment), and then y_{t-h} is assigned $y_t = y_0$, i.e., $y_{t-h} \leftarrow y_0$, in preparation for the next call of the OperateOnData() function. Then, the output data are written to the output signal, i.e., at $t_0 = 0$, $y(t_0) = y_0$. So the purpose of the first call to OperateOnData() is simply to prepare variables for numerical computation at the next iteration and to generate the initial condition vector y_0 as an output signal at t_0, as shown in Figure 21.13a.

For subsequent iterations, the numerical integration algorithm (here Euler's method) is called to determine y_t, given y_{t-h}, $\dot{y}_{t-h}$, and h. Then, after the output signal y_t has been determined,

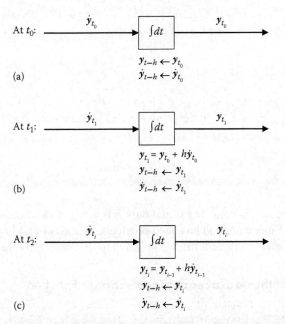

FIGURE 21.13 Numerical integration operation: (a) at t_0, the initial condition vector y_{t_0} is output and local variables updated; (b) at t_1, output y_{t_1} is determined using the previously stored variables according to Euler's method and the local variables updated again for the next iteration; and (c) in general, at t_i, output y_{t_i} is determined using previously stored values and the local variables are updated.

$\dot{y}_{t-h}$ is updated with the incoming signal $\dot{y}_t$ of the current iteration (t), i.e., $\dot{y}_{t-h} \leftarrow \dot{y}_t$, and y_{t-h} is updated with the current output signal y_t, i.e., $y_{t-h} \leftarrow y_t$, in preparation for the next call to the function, whereupon the previously recorded y_{t-h} and $\dot{y}_{t-h}$ values will be used to generate the next output signal, i.e., $y_t = y_{t-h} + h\dot{y}_{t-h}$, as shown in Figure 21.13b for t_1 and in general for t_i in Figure 21.13c.

That is, the signal y_t generated at time t makes use of the signals y_{t-h} and $\dot{y}_{t-h}$, i.e., the stored signal output and incoming input signal at the previous time-step, respectively. Hence, the current output y_t is not dependent on the current input $\dot{y}_t$, but $\dot{y}_t$ is required for storage purposes at the current time-step to be used at the next time-step.

Finally, the output signal, "m_dMatrixOut", is assigned y_t and written to the CConnection object's CSignal data member, and local memory is deleted.

21.7.5.2 Addition of the `EulerMethod()` Function

The `OperateOnData()` function makes use of the first-order Euler integration method as shown earlier. Add a public member function to the CIntegratorBlock class with the prototype: `int CIntegratorBlock::EulerMethod(double *y_at_t, double *m_y_at_t_minus_h, double *m_y_dot_at_t_minus_h, double delta_t, int length_y)`. Edit the code as shown in the following to perform one step of Euler's method (21.34).

```
int CIntegratorBlock::EulerMethod(double *y_at_t, double *m_y_at_t_minus_h,
  double *m_y_dot_at_t_minus_h, double delta_t, int length_y)
{
    int i;

    // Euler's Method: y_i = y_i-1 + h*y_dot_i-1
    for(i=0; i<length_y; i++)
    {
        y_at_t[i] = m_y_at_t_minus_h[i] + delta_t*m_y_dot_at_t_minus_h[i];
    }

    return 0;
}
```

Euler's method determines the state value y_t given the state value and its derivative at the previous time-step, y_{t-h} and $\dot{y}_{t-h}$ ($= f(t - h, y_{t-h})$), respectively, and the time-step size $h = \Delta t$, i.e.,

$$y_t = y_{t-h} + h\dot{y}_{t-h} \tag{21.35}$$

for $t \in [0, N]$. Only one step is being made and only y_t is being evaluated.

At this stage, only Euler's method has been provided; methods of higher order, e.g., the fourth-order Runge–Kutta method, will be written and added to the project in future.

21.7.5.3 Addition of the `GetIntegrationMethod()` Function

The developer will have noticed the call to `GetIntegrationMethod()` made upon the CSystemModel object, "m_SystemModel", in the `CIntegratorBlock::OperateOnData()` function mentioned earlier. Hence, add a public constant member method to the CSystemModel class with the prototype: `CString CSystemModel::GetIntegrationMethod(void) const`.

Edit the function as shown in the following to simply return the value of the CString variable, "m_strIntegration Method", of the CSystemModel class. The developer will notice that the numerical integration method–related variables are stored in the CSystemModel class rather than the CIntegratorBlock class; the latter holds the initial condition vector.

```
CString CSystemModel::GetIntegrationMethod() const
{
    return m_strIntegrationMethod;
}
```

21.7.5.4 Addition of Class Member Variables and Their Initialization

The developer will have noticed the member variables that are used in the OperateOnData() function mentioned earlier. These need to be added to the CIntegratorBlock class and initialized in the constructor function:

1. Add a private integer variable, "m_iNcallsPerTimeCnt", to record the number of times a function is called per time point ("t_cnt") of the simulation.
2. Add a private integer variable, "m_i_t_cnt_ref", to keep track of the current time point of the simulation ("t_cnt").
3. Add a private variable, "m_y_at_t_minus_h", of type double*, to record $y(t - h)$.
4. Add a private variable, "m_y_dot_at_t_minus_h", of type double*, to record $\dot{y}(t - h)$.
5. Add a private variable, "m_dMatrixOut", of type double**, to record the output signal (stored in a matrix).
6. Add a private integer variable, "m_iNrowsOut", to record the number of rows of the signal matrix, "m_dMatrixOut"; this is used for memory deletion purposes.
7. Finally, initialize these member variables as shown (in bold) in the CIntegratorBlock constructor; the rest of the constructor remains unchanged as denoted by the ellipsis, "...".

```
CIntegratorBlock::CIntegratorBlock(CSystemModel *pParentSystemModel,
  CPoint blk_posn, EBlockShape e_blk_shape):
CBlock(pParentSystemModel, blk_posn, e_blk_shape)
{
    ...
    // Set memory based vars.
    m_iNcallsPerTimeCnt = 0;        // no. of times the fn is called per
      t_cnt (time point)
    m_iNrowsOut = 0;                // no. of rows of output matrix signal
    m_i_t_cnt_ref = 0;             // ref time cnt
    m_dMatrixOut = NULL;           // output matrix signal
    m_y_at_t_minus_h = NULL;       // y(t-h)
    m_y_dot_at_t_minus_h = NULL;   // y_dot(t-h)
}
```

21.7.5.5 Addition of a ResetBlockData() Function

At the end of each simulation, the memory that was allocated within the OperateOnData() function now needs to be deallocated and some of the member variables reset. Hence, add a public virtual member function to the CIntegratorBlock class with the prototype, virtual void

CIntegratorBlock::ResetBlockData(void), and edit it as shown in the following to deallocate memory and reset member variables.

```
void CIntegratorBlock::ResetBlockData(void)
{
    int i;

    // Reinitialize member vars
    m_iNcallsPerTimeCnt = 0;        // no. of times the fn is called per
      t_cnt (time point)
    m_i_t_cnt_ref = 0;              // ref time cnt

    // MEMORY DELETE
    if(m_dMatrixOut != NULL)
    {
        for(i=0; i<m_iNrowsOut; i++)
        {
            delete [] m_dMatrixOut[i];     // delete the row arrays
        }
        delete [] m_dMatrixOut;            // delete the array
          (column vector) holding the row arrays
        m_dMatrixOut = NULL;
    }

    if(m_y_at_t_minus_h != NULL)
    {
        delete [] m_y_at_t_minus_h;        // delete member var array
          f(t-h) holding all signal's f(t-h) values

        m_y_at_t_minus_h = NULL;
    }
    if(m_y_dot_at_t_minus_h != NULL)
    {
        delete [] m_y_dot_at_t_minus_h;    // delete member var array
          f(t-2h) holding all signal's f(t-2h) values
        m_y_dot_at_t_minus_h = NULL;
    }
}
```

The CIntegratorBlock::ResetBlockData() function may be called from the CIntegratorBlock::~CIntegratorBlock() destructor function in a similar manner to that shown for the CDerivativeBlock, as follows. In addition, it is called from ResetMemoryBasedBlockData() of the CSystemModel class, shown earlier.

```
CIntegratorBlock::~CIntegratorBlock(void)
{
    // Delete the initial condition vector whose memory was allocated in
      ConvertStringToDoubleVector()
    if(m_dICVector != NULL)
    {
        delete [] m_dICVector;
        m_dICVector = NULL;
    }

    // Reset block data
    ResetBlockData();    // reset: m_y_at_t_minus_h, m_y_dot_at_t_minus_h,
      m_dMatrixOut
}
```

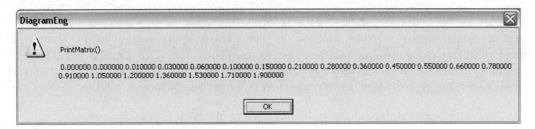

FIGURE 21.14 OutputBlock dialog window showing numerical state values y_t evaluated using Euler's method for $\dot{y} = f(t,y) = t$, $t \in [0, 2.0]$ s, $y_0 = 0$, and $h = 0.1$ s (cf. Table 21.1).

21.7.6 RUNNING AN EXPERIMENT

Figure 21.11 shows a simple model involving a Linear Function, an Integrator, and an Output block. The numerical properties of the simulation may be set using the block dialog windows, LinearFnBlockDialog, IntegratorBlockDialog, and NumericalSolverDialog, as follows: $\dot{y} = f(t,y) = t$, $t \in [0, 2.0]$ s, $y_0 = 0$, and $h = 0.1$ s. The output values are shown in the dialog window (Figure 21.14) and correspond to the output state values provided in Table 21.1.

21.8 DIVIDE BLOCK DATA OPERATION

The `OperateOnData()` function of the Divide block allows numerous signals to be operated upon using the multiplication and division operations in an elemental or a matrix-wise manner, as specified through the block dialog parameter input window. Successive multiplication or division operations are performed on the incoming signals attached to ports p_i, $i \in [1,P]$, where P is the total number of ports, ordered from the top of the block downward. Figure 21.15 shows a simple model of two Constant blocks connected to a Divide block, which is then connected to an Output block; the constant scalar (c), vector (c), or matrix (C) value of the Constant block attached to the upper port is first multiplied by unity and then divided by the value of the Constant block attached to the lower port (as specified by the multiply and divide signs).

In order to implement the multiplication and division operations of the Divide block, an `OperateOnData()` function and a `DivideMultiplyOperation()` function are to be added to the CDivideBlock class, where the latter calls the previously discussed MatrixMultiply() function. A new method to be added to the project, named GaussJordanEliminationFullPivoting(), is used to perform a matrix inversion (division operation) through Gauss–Jordan elimination using full pivoting, available from Press et al. [5] as `gaussj()`. The following steps indicate the process to add the necessary functionality to the project.

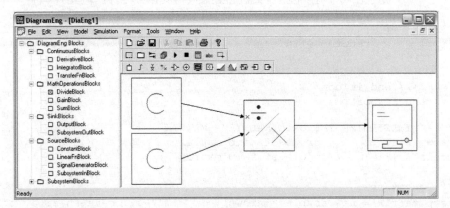

FIGURE 21.15 Two Constant blocks connected to a Divide block that is connected to an Output block; the constant value associated with the upper Constant block is divided by that associated with the lower Constant block.

21.8.1 IMPLEMENTING THE `OperateOnData()` FUNCTION

Add a public virtual member function to the CDivideBlock class with the prototype:
`virtual int CDivideBlock::OperateOnData(int t_cnt, double t, double delta_t)`. Edit the function as shown to call the `DivideMultiplyOperation()` function and write the resultant matrix to the output connection's CSignal data member if valid.

```cpp
int CDivideBlock::OperateOnData(int t_cnt, double t, double delta_t)
{
    int i;
    int ncols;           // no. of cols of temp matrix
    int nrows;           // no. of rows of temp matrix
    int ncols_R;         // no. of rows of Result
    int nrows_R;         // no. of cols of Result
    int port_cnt = 1;    // port counter
    int valid = 0;       // (-1) operational error, (0) read/write error,
      (1) no error
    double **matrix_in = NULL;   // input signal data
    double **Result = NULL;      // result of operation
    double **temp_matrix = NULL; // temp matrix which is written to
      output signal
    CString port_name;           // port name for divide block: "*" or "/"
    list<CConnection*>::iterator it_con; // iterator for list of
      CConnection ptrs.
    vector<CPort*>::iterator it_port;  // iterator for vector of CPort ptrs.
    vector<CPort*> &vec_of_input_ports = GetVectorOfInputPorts();

    // Get connection list
    list<CConnection*> &con_list = GetParentSystemModel()-
      >GetConnectionList();

    // -- ITERATE OVER ALL PORTS AND CHECK INPUT SIGNAL DATA VALIDITY
     for(it_port = vec_of_input_ports.begin(); it_port
      != vec_of_input_ports.end(); it_port++)
    {
     for(it_con = con_list.begin(); it_con != con_list.end(); it_con++)
     {
        if((*it_con)->GetRefToPort() == *it_port)    // if the input port
          of this connection is the current port
        {
            valid = (*it_con)->GetSignal()->GetSignalValidity();
            if(valid == 0)
            {
                return valid;
            }
        }
     }// end it_con
    }// end it_port

    // -- INITIALIZE THE ORIGINAL TEMP MATRIX
    nrows = 1;       // nrows of temp_matrix
    ncols = 1;       // ncols of temp_matrix

    // MEMORY NEW
    temp_matrix = new double *[nrows];       // allocate an array of
      ptrs-to-double
    for(i=0; i<nrows; i++)
```

```
    {
        temp_matrix[i] = new double[ncols];   // allocate an array of
          doubles
    }

    temp_matrix[0][0] = 1.0;                          // init 1x1 matrix to unity.

    // -- ITERATE OVER ALL PORTS AND PERFORM PAIRWISE OPERATIONS ON
      SIGNAL DATA
    for(it_port = vec_of_input_ports.begin(); it_port != vec_of_input_ports.
      end(); it_port++)
    {
        for(it_con = con_list.begin(); it_con != con_list.end(); it_con++)
        {
            if((*it_con)->GetRefToPort() == *it_port)  // if the input
              port of this connection is the current port
            {
                // NOTE: *it_con IS PASSED INTO DivideMultiplyOperation()
                  AND IS USED TO OBTAIN matrix_in, I.E.,
                // matrix_in = (*it_con)->GetSignalData(&nrows, &ncols);

                // Get the port name, i.e. the sign of the port
                  operation: "*" or "/".
                port_name = (*it_port)->GetPortName();

                Result = DivideMultiplyOperation(temp_matrix, nrows,
                  ncols, *it_con, port_name, nrows_R, ncols_R, valid);

                // MEMORY DELETE
                if(temp_matrix != NULL)
                {
                    for(i=0; i<nrows; i++)
                    {
                        delete [] temp_matrix[i]; // delete the row arrays
                    }
                    delete [] temp_matrix; // delete the array (column
                      vector) holding the row arrays
                }

                // ASSIGN RESULT TO TEMP_MATRIX (ASSIGNMENT OF A POINTER)
                temp_matrix = Result;

                // UPDATE nrows AND ncols USED IN DELETE OF temp_matrix
                  WHICH IS ASSIGNED Result
                nrows = nrows_R;
                ncols = ncols_R;
            }// end if it_con
        }// end it_con

        if(valid != 1)
        {
            break;     // Exit for it_port since DivideMultiplyOperation()
              is in error.
        }
        port_cnt++;
    }// end it_port

    // WRITE DATA TO OUTPUT SIGNAL (only if DivideMultiplyOperation()
      produces a valid result)
```

```
    if(valid == 1)
    {
        valid = WriteDataToOutputSignal(temp_matrix, nrows, ncols);
    }

    // -- MEMORY DELETE
    // DELETE temp_matrix, EQUIVALENTLY Result, SINCE temp_matrix WAS
      ASSIGNED Result AT THE LAST STEP (nrows = nrows_R),
    // AND Result's MEMORY WAS ALLOCATED WITHIN
      DivideMultiplyOperation().

    if(temp_matrix != NULL)
    {
        // MEMORY DELETE
        for(i=0; i<nrows; i++)
        {
            delete [] temp_matrix[i];   // delete the row arrays
        }
        delete [] temp_matrix;          // delete the array (column vector)
          holding the row array
    }

    return valid;
}
```

The `OperateOnData()` function of the Divide block first iterates over all its input ports and checks whether the signal data of the incoming connection objects are available (valid), if not, the function returns, if so, execution continues to perform pairwise operations on input data.

Consider a Divide block with two ports, p_1 and p_2, whose signs are multiply ($\times$) and divide (/), respectively, ordered from the top to the bottom of the left (input) side, admitting two connections whose signal data are P_1 and P_2, respectively (cf. Figure 21.15). On the first iteration of the pairwise operation loop, the "temp_matrix" is set equal to unity, the appropriate port name is obtained, in this case "multiply" ($\times$), and the `DivideMultiplyOperation()` function (introduced in Section 21.8.2) is called to perform the pairwise operation to produce the result ("Result")

$$R = 1P_1 \tag{21.36}$$

which is then assigned to the temporary matrix ("temp_matrix") in preparation for the next pairwise operation. On the second iteration, the result of the first iteration ("temp_matrix") is then the left argument of the ensuing operation, in this case divide (/), involving the second input signal argument P_2, i.e.,

$$R = \frac{1P_1}{P_2} = P_1 P_2^{-1} \tag{21.37}$$

where the repeated left-to-right operations correspond to a top-down order of port signs on the block itself.

In the to-be-added `DivideMultiplyOperation()` function, the left and right arguments forming the operation (op.), in A op. B, are denoted A and B, respectively. For the previous example, on the first iteration through the vector of input ports, $A = 1$ and $B = P_1$, and on the second iteration, $A = 1P_1$ and $B = P_2$, where the operations are multiply and divide, respectively.

After each call to the `DivideMultiplyOperation()` function, the temporary matrix "temp_matrix" has its memory deleted, and since memory is allocated for the result, "Result" (R), from within the `DivideMultiplyOperation()` function itself, the assignment of the (double) pointer, "temp_matrix = Result", is feasible, and its dimensions, "nrows_R" and "ncols_R", returned through the function's parameter list may be used in the deletion of "temp_matrix" on each following iteration, and finally before the function returns.

The "valid" variable passed back from the DivideMultiplyOperation() function can have the values "−1", "0", or "1", indicating an operational error, a signal data read/write error, or an operational success, respectively. If the divide/multiply operation is in error, then the operation is terminated and the value passed back to the calling environment, i.e., to SignalPropagationDirect(). However, if the operation is a success, then the final result is written to the output connection's CSignal data member.

21.8.2 Implementing the DivideMultiplyOperation() Function

Add a public member function to the CDivideBlock class with the prototype: double **CDivideBlock::DivideMultiplyOperation(double **A, int nrows_A, int ncols_A, CConnection *ptr_to_con, CString sign, int &nrows_R, int &ncols_R, int &valid). Notice that the dimensions of the resultant matrix and the "valid" integer indicator are passed by reference.

Now, as the prototype contains a pointer-to-CConnection, the CConnection class must be forward-declared just prior to the CDivideBlock class in the "Block.h" header file as shown in the following. In addition, the header file defining the CConnection class, i.e., "Signal.h", must be included; this is done (in previous work) at the top of the "SystemModel.h" header file.

```
// DivideBlock
class CConnection;    // predefining CConnection as it's rqd. by
CDivideBlock
class CDivideBlock : public CBlock
{
    ...
};
```

Finally, edit the code as shown in the following to filter through all the possible combinations of the input-argument dimensions, to perform either a multiplication or division operation, in an elemental or matrix-wise manner. Table 21.2 provides a summary of the dimension-filtering process and the

---

TABLE 21.2

Input-Argument Dimension-Filtering Process Used in the DivideMultiplyOperation() Function to Perform Multiplication and Division Operations

Case	Argument 1: a, a, A	Argument 2: b, b, B	Multiplication	Division
1	a	b	ab	a/b
2	a	$b(1 \times n)$	ab	a/b_i
3	a	$b(n \times 1)$	ab	a/b_i
4	$a(1 \times n)$	b	ba	a/b
5	$a(n \times 1)$	b	ab	a/b
6	a	B	aB	a/B_{ij}, aB^{-1}
7	A	b	bA	A/b
8	$a(1 \times n)$	$b(1 \times n)$	$a_i b_i$	a_i/b_i
9	$a(n \times 1)$	$b(n \times 1)$	$a_i b_i$	a_i/b_i
10	$a(1 \times n)$	$b(n \times 1)$	$a_i b_i$, ab	a_i/b_i
11	$a(n \times 1)$	$b(1 \times n)$	$a_i b_i$, ab	a_i/b_i
12	$A(n \times n)$	$B(n \times n)$	$A_{ij} B_{ij}$, AB	A_{ij}/B_{ij}, AB^{-1}
13	$A(n \times m)$	$B(m \times m)$	AB	AB^{-1}
14	$A(n \times m)$	$B(m \times p)$	AB	NA

Subscript notation denotes elemental operation and (here) $n \neq m \neq p$.

types of multiplication and division of the input arguments; notation without subscripts denotes standard matrix operation and that with subscripts indicates elemental operation.

```
double **CDivideBlock::DivideMultiplyOperation(double **A, int nrows_A,
int ncols_A, CConnection *ptr_to_con, CString sign, int &nrows_R, int
&ncols_R, int &valid)
{
    // Note: nrows_R, ncols_R and valid, are passed by reference for
      syntactically clean reasons.
    int i;
    int j;
    int ncols_B;              // no. of columns of matrix B
    int ncols_GJ_RHS = 1;     // no. of RHS vectors of the Gauss-Jordan
      elimination system.
    int nrows_B;              // no. of rows of matrix B
    double a;                 // scalar version of A
    double b;                 // scalar version of B
    double **B = NULL;        // matrix to which operator is applied w.r.t.
      matrix A
    double **B_inv = NULL;    // inverse of B to facilitate division
    double **GJ_RHS = NULL;   // Gauss-Jordan elimination system r.h.s.
    double **R = NULL;        // Result of the operation: A operator B.
    CString  sMsg;            // string to be displayed
    CString sMsgTemp;         // temp msg.
    UINT nType = MB_OK;       // style of msg. box
    UINT nIDhelp = 0;         // help context ID for the msg.

    // Get signal data and assign pointer to matrix B, but this is the
      actual signal data not a copy.
    B = ptr_to_con->GetSignal()->GetSignalData(&nrows_B, &ncols_B);

    // Assume operation will be valid unless explicitly assigned o/wise
      implying invalid
    // valid = (-3) dimensionality error, (-2) divide by zero error, (-1)
      singular matrix
    // THEN FINALLY: (-1) operational error, (0) read/write error, (1) no
      error
    valid = 1;


    // -- DIFFERENT CASES FOR VALUES A AND B -------------------
    //     Note: operations are performed as follows: R = A operator B.
    //
    //     The order of operations is performed in the order of the ports
      from top to bottom on the block.
    //     Initially, for the first operation, A = 1 (scalar) and B is the
      signal on the first connection,
    //     that enters the first port. After A op. B is performed, then
      the result R will re-enter as the new A,
    //     and the second connection's signal data will be B. Then A. op B
      is performed again.
    //     HENCE THE DEVELOPER MUST BE CLEAR ABOUT WHAT IN FACT IS THE
      CURRENT FORM OF A: scalar, vector or matrix!
    //
    //     "A" is the CURRENTLY-EVOLVED-TO DATA over the ports thus far,
      and STARTS AS UNITY (1) scalar on init. entry.
```

```
//    "B" is the SIGNAL DATA on the connection of the CURRENT PORT
  (top down) that forms the A op. B operation.
//
//    Example 1.
//    Let values on signals entering ports one and two be, v_1 = 2,
  and v_2 = [1, 2].
//    For a multiply operation on both ports, one has,
//    Entry 1: A = 1, B = v_1 = 2, R = A*B = 1*2 = 2,   (R is passed
  into A for the next iteration)
//    Entry 2: A = 2, B = v_2 = [1, 2], R = A*B = 2*[1, 2] = [2, 4],
  (R is then written to the output signal)
//
//    Example 2.
//    Let values on signals entering ports one and two be, v_1
  = [1, 2], and v_2 = [3, 4]
//    For an ELEMENTAL divide operation on BOTH ports, one has,
//    Entry 1: A = 1, B = v_1 = [1, 2], R = A/B = [1/1, 1/2],   (R is
  passed into A for the next iteration)
//    Entry 2: A = [1, 1/2], B = v_2 = [3, 4], R = A/B = [1/3, 1/8],
  (R is then written to the output signal)
// -----------------------------------------------------------------

// -- A AND B ARE BOTH SCALARS ------------------------------------
if((nrows_A == 1) && (ncols_A == 1) && (nrows_B == 1) && (ncols_B == 1))
{
    // MEMORY NEW
    nrows_R = 1;
    ncols_R = 1;
    R = new double *[nrows_R];  // allocate an array of ptrs-to-double
    for(i=0; i<nrows_R; i++)
    {
        R[i] = new double[ncols_R];  // allocate an array of doubles
    }

    a = A[0][0];
    b = B[0][0];

    if(sign == "*")
    {
        R[0][0] = a*b;
    }
    else if(sign == "/")
    {
        if(b != 0)
        {
            R[0][0] = a/b;
        }
        else
        {
            valid = -2;  // divide by zero error
        }
    }
}
// -- A IS A SCALAR AND B IS A VECTOR OR VICE VERSA ----------------
else if((nrows_A == 1) && (ncols_A == 1) && (nrows_B == 1) &&
  (ncols_B > 1))         // A = scalar, B = row vec
{
```

```
    // MEMORY NEW
    nrows_R = nrows_B;
    ncols_R = ncols_B;
    R = new double *[nrows_R];          // allocate an array of
      ptrs-to-double
    for(i=0; i<nrows_R; i++)
    {
        R[i] = new double[ncols_R]; // allocate an array of doubles
    }

    a = A[0][0];

    if(m_iMultType == 0)              // Elemental op.
    {
        if(sign == "*")
        {
          MatrixMultiply(nrows_A, ncols_A, ncols_B, A, B, R);
            // (1x1)*(1xn) = (1xn), A is a scalar
        }
        else if(sign == "/")
        {
            for(i=0; i<ncols_R; i++)
            {
                if(B[0][i] != 0)
                {
                   R[0][i] = a/B[0][i];
                }
                else
                {
                   valid = -2;      // divide by zero error
                   break;
                }
            }
        }
    }
    else if(m_iMultType == 1)       // Matrix op.
    {
        if(sign == "*")
        {
          MatrixMultiply(nrows_A, ncols_A, ncols_B, A, B, R);
            // (1x1)*(1xn) = (1xn)
        }
        else if(sign == "/")
        {
          valid = -3;      // dimensionality error (can't divide by
            a row vector)
        }
    }
}
else if((nrows_A == 1) && (ncols_A == 1) && (nrows_B > 1) && (ncols_B
  == 1))  // A = scalar, B = col vec
{
    // MEMORY NEW
    nrows_R = nrows_B;
    ncols_R = ncols_B;
    R = new double *[nrows_R];         // allocate an array of
      ptrs-to-double
```

```
            for(i=0; i<nrows_R; i++)
            {
                R[i] = new double[ncols_R]; // allocate an array of doubles
            }

            a = A[0][0];

            if(m_iMultType == 0)              // Elemental op.
            {
                if(sign == "*")
                {
                    MatrixMultiply(nrows_B, ncols_B, ncols_A, B, A, R);
                    // (nx1)*(1x1) = (nx1), A is a scalar
                }
                else if(sign == "/")
                {
                    for(i=0; i<nrows_R; i++)
                    {
                        if(B[i][0] != 0)
                        {
                            R[i][0] = a/B[i][0];
                        }
                        else
                        {
                            valid = -2;   // divide by zero error
                            break;
                        }
                    }
                }
            }
            else if(m_iMultType == 1)    // Matrix op.
            {
                if(sign == "*")
                {
                    MatrixMultiply(nrows_B, ncols_B, ncols_A, B, A, R);
                    // (nx1)*(1x1) = (nx1), A is a scalar
                }
                else if(sign == "/")
                {
                    valid = -3;   // dimensionality error (can't divide by a
                    col vector)
                }
            }
        }
        else if((nrows_A == 1) && (ncols_A > 1) && (nrows_B == 1) &&
          (ncols_B == 1))   // A = row vec, B = scalar
        {
            // MEMORY NEW
            nrows_R = nrows_A;
            ncols_R = ncols_A;
            R = new double *[nrows_R];       // allocate an array of
              ptrs-to-double
            for(i=0; i<nrows_R; i++)
            {
                R[i] = new double[ncols_R]; // allocate an array of doubles
            }
```

```
        b = B[0][0];

        // Elemental and Matrix operations are the same for: vector op.
          scalar (in that order)
        if(sign == "*")
        {
              MatrixMultiply(nrows_B, ncols_B, ncols_A, B, A, R);
                // (1x1)*(1xn) = (1xn), B is a scalar
        }
        else if(sign == "/")
        {
            for(i=0; i<ncols_R; i++)
            {
                if(b != 0)
                {
                   R[0][i] = A[0][i]/b;
                }
                else
                {
                   valid = -2; // divide by zero error
                   break;
                }
            }
        }
    }
    else if( (nrows_A > 1) && (ncols_A == 1) && (nrows_B == 1) &&
      (ncols_B == 1) )   // A = col vec, B = scalar
    {
        // MEMORY NEW
        nrows_R = nrows_A;
        ncols_R = ncols_A;
        R = new double *[nrows_R];       // allocate an array of
          ptrs-to-double
        for(i=0; i<nrows_R; i++)
        {
            R[i] = new double[ncols_R]; // allocate an array of doubles
        }
        b = B[0][0];

        // Elemental and Matrix operations are the same for: vector op.
                scalar (in that order)
        if(sign == "*")
        {
              MatrixMultiply(nrows_A, ncols_A, ncols_B, A, B, R);
                // (nx1)*(1x1) = (nx1), B is a scalar
        }
        else if(sign == "/")
        {
            for(i=0; i<nrows_R; i++)
            {
                if(b != 0)
                {
                   R[i][0] = A[i][0]/b;
                }
                else
                {
                      valid = -2;   // divide by zero error
```

```
                                    break;
                                }
                            }
                    }
            }
    // -- A IS A SCALAR AND B IS A MATRIX OR VICE VERSA ----------------
    else if((nrows_A == 1) && (ncols_A == 1) && (nrows_B > 1) && (ncols_B
        > 1))        // A = scalar, B = matrix
    {
            // MEMORY NEW
            nrows_R = nrows_B;
            ncols_R = ncols_B;
            R = new double *[nrows_R];        // allocate an array of
              ptrs-to-double
            for(i=0; i<nrows_R; i++)
            {
                R[i] = new double[ncols_R]; // allocate an array of doubles
            }

            a = A[0][0];

            if(m_iMultType == 0)     // Elemental op.
            {
                if(sign == "*")
                {
                    for(i=0; i<nrows_R; i++)
                    {
                        for(j=0; j<ncols_R; j++)
                        {
                            R[i][j] = a*B[i][j];
                        }
                    }
                }
                else if(sign == "/")
                {
                    for(i=0; i<nrows_R; i++)
                    {
                        for(j=0; j<ncols_R; j++)
                        {
                            if(B[i][j] != 0)
                            {
                                R[i][j] = a/B[i][j];
                            }
                            else
                            {
                                valid = -2;     // divide by zero error
                                break;
                            }
                        }
                        if(valid == -2)
                        {
                            break;
                        }
                    }
                }
            }
            else if(m_iMultType == 1)        // Matrix op.
```

```
        {
            if(sign == "*")
            {
                for(i=0; i<nrows_R; i++)
                {
                    for(j=0; j<ncols_R; j++)
                    {
                        R[i][j] = a*B[i][j];
                    }
                }
            }
            else if(sign == "/")
            {
                if(nrows_B == ncols_B)    // if B is a square matrix
                {
                    // MEMORY NEW
                    // Inverse matrix B_inv = B^-1
                    B_inv = new double *[nrows_B];      // allocate an
                      array of ptrs-to-double
                    for(i=0; i<nrows_B; i++)
                    {
                        B_inv[i] = new double[ncols_B];  // allocate an
                          array of doubles
                    }

                    // GAUSS-JORDAN ELIMINATION R.H.S. MATRIX (dummy
                      vector here since there is no equation soln rqd.)
                    GJ_RHS = new double *[nrows_B];  // allocate an array
                      of ptrs-to-double
                    for(i=0; i<nrows_B; i++)
                    {
                        GJ_RHS[i] = new double[ncols_GJ_RHS];  // allocate
                          an array of doubles
                    }

                    // Copy B into B_inv
                    for(i=0; i<nrows_B; i++)
                    {
                        for(j=0; j<ncols_B; j++)
                        {
                            B_inv[i][j] = B[i][j];
                        }
                    }
                }


                // -- GAUSS-JORDAN ELIMINATION WITH FULL PIVOTING
                // B_inv starts off as B (see above assig.), then is
                  overwritten with the inverse B^-1.
                // The r.h.s. matrix GJ_RHS is simply a dummy vector that
                  is not used.
                valid = GaussJordanEliminationFullPivoting(B_inv,
                  nrows_B, GJ_RHS, ncols_GJ_RHS);

                for(i=0; i<nrows_R; i++)
                {
                    for(j=0; j<ncols_R; j++)
```

```
                        {
                             R[i][j] = a*B_inv[i][j];    // a/B = a*B_inv
                        }
                    }

            // MEMORY DELETE
            for(i=0; i<nrows_B; i++)
            {
                delete [] B_inv[i];     // delete the row arrays
            }
            delete [] B_inv;            // delete the array (column
              vector) holding the row array

            for(i=0; i<nrows_B; i++)
            {
                delete [] GJ_RHS[i];    // delete the row arrays
            }
            delete [] GJ_RHS;           // delete the array (column
              vector) holding the row array
        }
        else
        {
            valid = -3;                 // dimensionality error
        }
        }
    }
}
else if((nrows_A > 1) && (ncols_A > 1) && (nrows_B == 1) &&
  (ncols_B == 1))    // A = matrix, B = scalar
{
        // MEMORY NEW
        nrows_R = nrows_A;
        ncols_R = ncols_A;
        R = new double *[nrows_R];      // allocate an array of
          ptrs-to-double
        for(i=0; i<nrows_R; i++)
        {
            R[i] = new double[ncols_R]; // allocate an array of
              doubles
        }
        b = B[0][0];

        // Elemental and matrix operations are the same for the order A
          op. B, where A is a matrix and B a scalar.
        if(sign == "*")
        {
            for(i=0; i<nrows_R; i++)
            {
                for(j=0; j<ncols_R; j++)
                {
                    R[i][j] = b*A[i][j];
                }
            }
        }
        else if(sign == "/")
        {
            if(b != 0)
```

```
            {
                for(i=0; i<nrows_R; i++)
                {
                    for(j=0; j<ncols_R; j++)
                    {
                        R[i][j] = A[i][j]/b;
                    }
                }
            }
        }
        else
        {
            valid = -2;        // divide by zero error
        }
    }
}


// -- A AND B ARE VECTORS -------------------------------------
else if((nrows_A == 1) && (ncols_A > 1) && (nrows_B == nrows_A) &&
  (ncols_B == ncols_A))      // A and B are row vecs of the same
  length
{
    // MEMORY NEW
    nrows_R = nrows_A;
    ncols_R = ncols_A;
    R = new double *[nrows_R]; // allocate an array of ptrs-to-double
    for(i=0; i<nrows_R; i++)
    {
        R[i] = new double[ncols_R];// allocate an array of doubles
    }

    if(m_iMultType == 0)     // Elemental op.
    {
        if(sign == "*")
        {
            for(i=0; i<ncols_R; i++)
            {
                R[0][i] = A[0][i]*B[0][i];
            }
        }
        else if(sign == "/")
        {
            for(i=0; i<ncols_R; i++)
            {
                if(B[0][i] != 0)
                {
                    R[0][i] = A[0][i]/B[0][i];
                }
                else
                {
                    valid = -2;     // divide by zero error
                    break;
                }
            }
        }
    }
    else if(m_iMultType == 1)     // Matrix op.
```

```
            {
                valid = -3;      // dimensionality error
            }
    }
    else if( (nrows_A > 1) && (ncols_A == 1) && (nrows_B == nrows_A) &&
      (ncols_B == ncols_A) ) // A and B are col vecs of the same length
    {
            // MEMORY NEW
            nrows_R = nrows_A;
            ncols_R = ncols_A;
            R = new double *[nrows_R]; // allocate an array of ptrs-to-double
            for(i=0; i<nrows_R; i++)
            {
                R[i] = new double[ncols_R]; // allocate an array of doubles
            }

            if(m_iMultType == 0)    // Elemental op.
            {
                if(sign == "*")
                {
                  for(i=0; i<nrows_R; i++)
                  {
                      R[i][0] = A[i][0]*B[i][0];
                  }
                }
                else if(sign == "/")
                {
                    for(i=0; i<nrows_R; i++)
                    {
                        if(B[i][0] != 0)
                        {
                            R[i][0] = A[i][0]/B[i][0];
                        }
                        else
                        {
                            valid = -2;     // divide by zero error
                            break;
                        }
                    }
                }
            }
            else if(m_iMultType == 1)     // Matrix op.
            {
                valid = -3;            // dimensionality error
            }
    }
    else if( (nrows_A == 1) && (ncols_A > 1) && (nrows_B == ncols_A) &&
      (ncols_B == nrows_A) )   // A = row vec, B = col vec, of same length
    {
        if(m_iMultType == 0)       // Elemental op.
        {
          // MEMORY NEW
          nrows_R = nrows_A;
          ncols_R = ncols_A;
          R = new double *[nrows_R];  // allocate an array of
            ptrs-to-double
          for(i=0; i<nrows_R; i++)
```

```
          {
            R[i] = new double[ncols_R]; // allocate an array of
              doubles
          }
          if(sign == "*")
          {
            for(i=0; i<ncols_R; i++)
            {
                R[0][i] = A[0][i]*B[i][0];
            }
          }
        else if(sign == "/")
        {
            for(i=0; i<ncols_R; i++)
            {
                if(B[i][0] != 0)
                {
                   R[0][i] = A[0][i]/B[i][0];
                }
                else
                {
                   valid = -2;    // divide by zero error
                   break;
                }
            }
        }
      }
    else if(m_iMultType == 1)    // Matrix op.
    {
        if(sign == "*")
        {
        // MEMORY NEW
         nrows_R = nrows_A;
         ncols_R = ncols_B;
         R = new double *[nrows_R];          // allocate an array of
          ptrs-to-double
         for(i=0; i<nrows_R; i++)
         {
            R[i] = new double[ncols_R];   // allocate an array of
              doubles
         }

        MatrixMultiply(nrows_A, ncols_A, ncols_B, A, B, R);
          // (1xn)*(nx1) = (1x1)
    }
    else if(sign == "/")
    {
        valid = -3;      // dimensionality error, B non-square
    }
    }
  }
  else if((nrows_A > 1) && (ncols_A == 1) && (nrows_B == ncols_A) &&
   (ncols_B == nrows_A))       // A = col vec, B = row vec, of same
   length
  {
      if(m_iMultType == 0)     // Elemental op.
```

```
        {
            // MEMORY NEW
            nrows_R = nrows_A;
            ncols_R = ncols_A;
            R = new double *[nrows_R];        // allocate an array of
             ptrs-to-double
            for(i=0; i<nrows_R; i++)
            {
                R[i] = new double[ncols_R]; // allocate an array of doubles
            }
            if(sign == "*")
            {
                for(i=0; i<nrows_R; i++)
                {
                    R[i][0] = A[i][0]*B[0][i];
                }
            }
            else if(sign == "/")
            {
                for(i=0; i<nrows_R; i++)
                {
                    if(B[0][i] != 0)
                    {
                        R[i][0] = A[i][0]/B[0][i];
                    }
                    else
                    {
                        valid = -2;   // divide by zero error
                        break;
                    }
                }
            }
        }
        else if(m_iMultType == 1)  // Matrix op.
        {
                if(sign == "*")
                {
            // MEMORY NEW
            nrows_R = nrows_A;
            ncols_R = ncols_B;
            R = new double *[nrows_R];          // allocate an array of
              ptrs-to-double
            for(i=0; i<nrows_R; i++)
            {
                R[i] = new double[ncols_R];     // allocate an array of
                  doubles
            }

            MatrixMultiply(nrows_A, ncols_A, ncols_B, A, B, R);
                // (nx1)*(1xn) = (nxn)
        }
        else if(sign == "/")
        {
            valid = -3;        // dimensionality error, B non-square
        }
    }
}
```

```
else if( (nrows_A == 1) && (ncols_A > 1) && (nrows_B == 1) &&
  (ncols_B != ncols_A) )        // row vecs not of same length
{
    valid = -3;    // dimensionality error
}
else if( (nrows_A > 1) && (ncols_A == 1) && (nrows_B != nrows_A) &&
  (ncols_B == 1) )  // col vecs not of same length
{
    valid = -3;    // dimensionality error
}
else if( (nrows_A == 1) && (ncols_A > 1) && (nrows_B != ncols_A) &&
  (ncols_B == 1) )  // length of row vec A and col vec B not equal
{
    valid = -3;    // dimensionality error
}
else if( (nrows_A > 1) && (ncols_A == 1) && (nrows_B == 1) &&
  (ncols_B != nrows_A) ) // length of col vec A and row vec B not equal
{
    valid = -3;    // dimensionality error
}


// -- A AND B ARE MATRICES -----------------------------------------
else if( (nrows_A == ncols_A) && (nrows_B == ncols_B) &&
  (ncols_A== nrows_B) )               // Square matrices of same dimensions
{
    // MEMORY NEW
    nrows_R = nrows_A;
    ncols_R = ncols_B;
    R = new double *[nrows_R]; // allocate an array of ptrs-to-double
    for(i=0; i<nrows_R; i++)
    {
        R[i] = new double[ncols_R]; // allocate an array of doubles
    }

    if(m_iMultType == 0)     // Elemental op.
    {
        if(sign == "*")
        {
            for(i=0; i<nrows_R; i++)
            {
                for(j=0; j<ncols_R; j++)
                {
                    R[i][j] = A[i][j]*B[i][j];
                }
            }
        }
        else if(sign == "/")
        {
            for(i=0; i<nrows_R; i++)
            {
                for(j=0; j<ncols_R; j++)
                {
                    if(B[i][j] != 0)
                    {
                        R[i][j] = A[i][j]/B[i][j];
                    }
```

```
                             else
                             {
                                  valid = -2; // divide by zero error
                                  break;
                             }
                        }
                        if(valid == -2)
                        {
                            break;
                        }
                   }
        }
    }
    else if(m_iMultType == 1)      // Matrix op.
    {
        if(sign == "*")
        {
            MatrixMultiply(nrows_A, ncols_A, ncols_B, A, B, R);
        }
        else if(sign == "/")
        {
                // MEMORY NEW
                B_inv = new double *[nrows_B];          // allocate an
                  array of ptrs-to-double
                for(i=0; i<nrows_B; i++)
                {
                    B_inv[i] = new double[ncols_B]; // allocate an array
                      of doubles
                }

                // GAUSS-JORDAN ELIMINATION R.H.S. MATRIX (dummy vector
                  here since there is no equation soln rqd.)
                GJ_RHS = new double *[nrows_B];    // allocate an array
                  of ptrs-to-double
                for(i=0; i<nrows_B; i++)
                {
                    GJ_RHS[i] = new double[ncols_GJ_RHS];    // allocate
                      an array of doubles
                }

                // Copy B into B_inv
                for(i=0; i<nrows_B; i++)
                {
                    for(j=0; j<ncols_B; j++)
                    {
                        B_inv[i][j] = B[i][j];
                    }
                }

                // -- GAUSS-JORDAN ELIMINATION WITH FULL PIVOTING
                // B_inv starts off as B (see above assig.), then is
                  overwritten with the inverse B^-1.
                // The r.h.s. matrix GJ_RHS is simply a dummy vector
                  that is not used.
                valid = GaussJordanEliminationFullPivoting(B_inv,
                  nrows_B, GJ_RHS, ncols_GJ_RHS);
```

```
                    MatrixMultiply(nrows_A, ncols_A, ncols_B, A, B_inv, R);

                    // MEMORY DELETE
                    for(i=0; i<nrows_B; i++)
                    {
                        delete [] B_inv[i];    // delete the row arrays
                    }
                    delete [] B_inv; // delete the array (column vector)
                      holding the row array

                    for(i=0; i<nrows_B; i++)
                    {
                        delete [] GJ_RHS[i];   // delete the row arrays
                    }
                    delete [] GJ_RHS;              // delete the array (column
                      vector) holding the row array
                }
            }
        }
        else if((nrows_A != ncols_A) && (ncols_A == nrows_B)
          && (nrows_B == ncols_B))    // A non-square, B square, inner dims
          equal, mult, divide, no element op.
        {
            // MEMORY NEW
            nrows_R = nrows_A;
            ncols_R = ncols_B;
            R = new double *[nrows_R]; // allocate an array of ptrs-to-double
            for(i=0; i<nrows_R; i++)
            {
                R[i] = new double[ncols_R];  // allocate an array of doubles
            }
            if(m_iMultType == 0)   // Elemental op.
            {
                valid = -3;   // dimensionality error
            }
            else if(m_iMultType == 1)    // Matrix op.
            {
                if(sign == "*")
                {
                    MatrixMultiply(nrows_A, ncols_A, ncols_B, A, B, R);
                }
                else if(sign == "/")    // B is square
                {
                    // MEMORY NEW
                    B_inv = new double *[nrows_B];   // allocate an array of
                      ptrs-to-double
                    for(i=0; i<nrows_B; i++)
                    {
                        B_inv[i] = new double[ncols_B]; // allocate an array
                          of doubles
                    }

                    // GAUSS-JORDAN ELIMINATION R.H.S. MATRIX (dummy vector
                      here since there is no equation soln rqd.)
                    GJ_RHS = new double *[nrows_B];  // allocate an array of
                      ptrs-to-double
```

```
                    for(i=0; i<nrows_B; i++)
                    {
                        GJ_RHS[i] = new double[ncols_GJ_RHS];   // allocate
                          an array of doubles
                    }

                    // Copy B into B_inv
                    for(i=0; i<nrows_B; i++)
                    {
                        for(j=0; j<ncols_B; j++)
                        {
                            B_inv[i][j] = B[i][j];
                        }
                    }

                    // -- GAUSS-JORDAN ELIMINATION WITH FULL PIVOTING
                    // B_inv starts off as B (see above assig.), then is
                      overwritten with the inverse B^-1.
                    // The r.h.s. matrix GJ_RHS is simply a dummy vector
                      that is not used.
                    valid = GaussJordanEliminationFullPivoting(B_inv,
                      nrows_B, GJ_RHS, ncols_GJ_RHS);

                    MatrixMultiply(nrows_A, ncols_A, ncols_B, A, B_inv, R);

                    // MEMORY DELETE
                    for(i=0; i<nrows_B; i++)
                    {
                        delete [] B_inv[i];   // delete the row arrays
                    }
                    delete [] B_inv;          // delete the array
                      (column vector) holding the row array

                    for(i=0; i<nrows_B; i++)
                    {
                        delete [] GJ_RHS[i];  // delete the row arrays
                    }
                    delete [] GJ_RHS;         // delete the array
                      (column vector) holding the row array
                }
            }
        }
        else if((ncols_A == nrows_B) && (nrows_B != ncols_B))  // Inner dims
          equal, B non-square (mult, no divide, no element op.)
        {
            // MEMORY NEW
            nrows_R = nrows_A;
            ncols_R = ncols_B;
            R = new double *[nrows_R];   // allocate an array of ptrs-to-double
            for(i=0; i<nrows_R; i++)
            {
                R[i] = new double[ncols_R];   // allocate an array of doubles
            }

            if(m_iMultType == 0)              // Elemental op.
            {
                valid = -3;                   // dimensionality error
            }
```

```
        else if(m_iMultType == 1) // Matrix op.
        {
            if(sign == "*")
            {
                MatrixMultiply(nrows_A, ncols_A, ncols_B, A, B, R);
            }
            else if(sign == "/")
            {
                valid = -3;   // dimensionality error
            }
        }
    }
    else if(ncols_A != nrows_B)     // Matrices can't be multiplied or
      divided or operated upon
    {
        valid = -3;   // dimensionality error
    }


    // -- ERROR MESSAGES
    if(valid == -1)
    {
        sMsgTemp.Format("\n WARNING: error in usage of Divide-Multiply
          block!\n");
        sMsg+=sMsgTemp;
        sMsgTemp.Format(" Check that the matrix to be inverted is not
          singular for division operation.\n");
        sMsg+=sMsgTemp;
        AfxMessageBox(sMsg, nType, nIDhelp);     // msg. box
    }
    else if(valid == -2)
    {
        sMsgTemp.Format("\n WARNING: error in usage of Divide-Multiply
          block!\n");
        sMsg+=sMsgTemp;
        sMsgTemp.Format(" Check that the denominator is not zero for
          division operation.\n");
        sMsg+=sMsgTemp;
        AfxMessageBox(sMsg, nType, nIDhelp);     // msg. box
    }
    else if(valid == -3)
    {
        sMsgTemp.Format("\n WARNING: error in usage of Divide-Multiply
          block!\n");
        sMsg+=sMsgTemp;
        sMsgTemp.Format("\n Check data dimensionality of all inputs
          arguments.\n");
        sMsg+=sMsgTemp;
        sMsgTemp.Format(" Check the type of multiplication/division
          selected: Elemental or Matrix.\n");
        sMsg+=sMsgTemp;
        sMsgTemp.Format(" Check the order of operations (top-down order
          of ports).\n");
        sMsg+=sMsgTemp;
        AfxMessageBox(sMsg, nType, nIDhelp);     // msg. box
    }
```

```
    // -- FINALLY SET VALID TO -1 IF VALID < 0
    if(valid < 0)
    {
        valid = -1;      // generalized block operational error
    }

    // -- MEMORY DELETE
    // Note! Memory for R is deleted in the calling environment
      CDivideBlock::OperateOnData,
    // after re-assignment to "temp_matrix". Hence it should not be
      deleted here.

    // Return result: R = A operator B
    return R;
}
```

The `DivideMultiplyOperation()` function is passed the left argument, A, of the operational sequence, A op. B, and a pointer-to-CConnection, from which it obtains the right argument, B, through a call to `GetSignal()` and then `GetSignalData()`. The divide/multiply operation is assumed to be valid, and hence "valid" is set to one: the other values that are used are "0", "–1", "–2", and "–3", which denote a read/write error, a general operational error including a singular matrix, a divide-by-zero error, and a dimensionality error, respectively. At the end of the function, if "valid" is less than zero, it is assigned the general operational error value, "–1".

Initially a test is made of the dimensions of the input arguments A and B, and the correct case, of those listed in Table 21.2, is executed. Each case, in general, involves the following flow of control: (1) memory is allocated for the resultant matrix R; (2) a test of an elemental (m_iMultType == 0) or a matrix (m_iMultType == 1) operation is made; and (3) the appropriate multiply ($\times$) or divide ($/$) operation is pursued through matrix multiplication, Gauss–Jordan elimination with full pivoting, or explicit mathematical operations. If one of the aforementioned errors results, then "valid" is set accordingly and the operation is aborted.

In the testing of the Divide block for operational consistency, the developer must be clear about what in fact is the current form of the input argument A, i.e., a scalar, vector, or matrix. It should be noted that A is the currently evolved-to data over the ports thus far (in a top-down sense) and starts as unity on initial entry into the `DivideMultiplyOperation()` function. The second argument B is the signal data of the connection of the current input port that forms the A op. B operation. The four test cases that were used to produce the resultant R are (1) "multiply-multiply" ($R = 1 \times A \times B$), (2) "multiply-divide" ($R = 1 \times A/B$), (3) "divide-multiply" ($R = (1/A) \times B$), and (4) "divide-divide" ($R = (1/A)/B$) (here $\times$ denotes generic multiplication, not cross-product), where operations are performed from left to right. For elemental operations, given that the dimensions of the arguments are the same, these cases become $R_{ij} = A_{ij}B_{ij}$, $R_{ij} = A_{ij}B_{ij}^{-1}$, $R_{ij} = A_{ij}^{-1}B_{ij}$, and $R_{ij} = A_{ij}^{-1}B_{ij}^{-1}$, respectively, for $i \in [1,m]$ and $j \in [1,n]$, where m and n are the equal number of rows and columns, respectively, of the input arguments for matrices. For vector operations, the length of the operands must be consistent. For matrix operations, given consistent dimensions, the cases are $R = AB$, $R = AB^{-1}$, $R = A^{-1}B$, and $R = A^{-1}B^{-1}$, respectively.

21.8.3 Implementing the `GaussJordanEliminationFullPivoting()` Function

The developer will have noticed the call to `GaussJordanEliminationFullPivoting()` to perform Gauss–Jordan elimination with full pivoting; this is used to obtain the inverse B^{-1} of a matrix B in an expression to determine the result $R = AB^{-1}$ of matrix A divided by matrix B. The code for this, shown in the following, is almost identical to that provided by Press et al. [5]. The only main alteration made to the code of Press et al. was to use an epsilon value to test for essentially zero values on the diagonal, i.e., if "$A_{kk} \in [-\varepsilon, \varepsilon]$" for $\varepsilon = 10^{-6}$, then the matrix is deemed to be singular; this was used in place of the original test for "$A_{kk} = 0$". Various other syntactic changes were made for ease of reading. The developer should consult the work of Press et al. [5] for the original version of the code.

Hence, add a new global function prototype, for the GaussJordanElimination FullPivoting() function, to the "DiagramEngDoc.h" header file, where the existing global function prototypes are located, as shown in the code excerpt in the following: void GaussJordan EliminationFullPivoting(double **A, int n, double **B, int m).

```
// Global Functions
CDiagramEngDoc* GetDocumentGlobalFn(void);
double **ConvertStringToDouble(CString string, int &nrows, int &ncols);
char *StripInputString(char *input_str);
int DetermineDataDimsByStrpbrk(char *in_str, int &nrows, int &ncols, int
  &max_row_length);
int DetermineDataDimsByStrtok(char *in_str, int &nrows, int &ncols, int
  &max_row_length);
int GaussJordanEliminationFullPivoting(double **A, int n, double **B,
  int m);
double **ConvertStringMatrixToDoubleMatrix(char **str_matrix, int nrows,
  int ncols);
void MatrixMultiply(int nrowsA, int ncolsA, int ncolsB, double **A,
  double **B, double **C);
int PrintMatrix(double **M, int nrows, int ncols);
int PrintMatrix(int **M, int nrows, int ncols);
int PrintVector(double *v, int ncols);
int PrintVector(int *v, int ncols);
```

Add the implementation of the GaussJordanEliminationFullPivoting() function to the "DiagramEngDoc.cpp" source file underneath the MatrixMultiply() function and edit the code as shown in the following.

```
int GaussJordanEliminationFullPivoting(double **A, int n, double **B,
  int m)
{
    // WARNING! THIS MATERIAL FOLLOWS CLOSELY THE WORK OF:
    // Numerical Recipes in C: The Art of Scientific Computing (2nd Ed.),
      sections 2.0 - 2.1.
    // by, W.H. Press, S.A. Teukolsky, W.T. Vetterling and B.P. Flannery.
    // Only minor syntactic changes are made here to the original,
      e.g. array indexing
    // (0 to n-1 is used here, rather than the original 1 to n).

    /* GaussJordanEliminationFullPivoting() solves the systems of
      equations represented by, e.g.,

      [A].[x_1, x_2, x_3, Y] = [b_1, b_2, b_3, I]

      where

      A.x_1 = b_1,
      A.x_2 = b_2,
      A.x_3 = b_3,

      and
      A.Y = I
  => Y = A^-1

      A:nxn = input matrix.
      This is overwritten with A^-1.
```

```
    B:nxm = input matrix containing the m r.h.s. vectors (of length n).
    This is overwritten with the corres. set of soln. vectors. That is,
    x_1 = A^-1.b_1,
    x_2 = A^-1.b_2,
    x_3 = A^-1.b_3.
*/


// Declaration
int i;
int icol;              // col index
int irow;              // row index
int j;
int k;
int u;
int v;
int valid = 1;         // validity of result: (-1) if singular,
  (1) if no error
int *index_c = NULL;   // col index used for pivoting
int *index_r = NULL;   // row index used for pivoting
int *ipiv = NULL;      // pivot index array
double big;
double dum;
double pivinv;
double eps = 1.0e-6;   // ALTERATION (BF): epsilon value to check for
  a "zero" on the diagonal

// MEMORY NEW
// Integer arrays used to manage the pivoting
index_c = new int[n];
index_r = new int[n];
ipiv = new int[n];

// Nullify the ipiv array
for(j=0; j<n; j++)
{
    ipiv[j] = 0;
}


// Main loop over the n columns to be reduced.
for(i=0; i<n; i++)
{
    big = 0.0;                                      // init big == 0.0

    // Outer loop of the search for a pivot element
    for(j=0; j<n; j++)
    {
        if(ipiv[j] != 1)                            // if the pivot array
          element != unity
        {
            for(k=0; k<n; k++)
            {
                if(ipiv[k] == 0)                    // if the pivot array
                  element == nullity
                {
                    if(fabs(A[j][k]) >= big)   // floating point
                      absolute value
```

```
                        {
                            big = fabs(A[j][k]);    // update big with the
                              double-type abs value of A[j][k]
                            irow = j;
                            icol = k;
                        }
                    }
                }// end for k
            }// end if ipiv[j]
        }// end for j

        ++(ipiv[icol]);

        // Now the pivot element is found, rows need to be interchanged,
          if rqd. to put the pivot element on the diag.
        // The cols are not physically interchanged, only relabelled:
        // index_c[i] the col of the ith pivot element is the ith col
          that is reduced
        // index_r[i] the row in which the pivot element was originally
          located.
        // If index_r[i] != index_c[i] there is an implied column
          interchange.
        // With this form of pivot management, the solutions x = A^-1.b
          which overwrite B, will end up in the correct order,
        // and the inverse matrix will be out of column alignment.

        if(irow != icol)
        {
            for(u=0; u<n; u++)
            {
                Swap(A[irow][u], A[icol][u]);
            }

            for(u=0; u<m; u++)
            {
                Swap(B[irow][u], B[icol][u]);
            }
        }

        // Pivot element indexing
        index_r[i] = irow;
        index_c[i] = icol;

        // Warn if there is a zero on the diag. implying a singular
          (non-invertible) matrix: was "if(A[icol][icol] == 0.0)"
        if((A[icol][icol] >= -eps) && (A[icol][icol] <= eps))
        {
            AfxMessageBox("\n GaussJordanEliminationFullPivoting():
              Singular Matrix \n", MB_OK, 0);
            valid = -1;  // operational error due to singular matrix
        }

        // Now the pivot row can be divided by the pivot element, located
          at irow and icol.
        pivinv = 1.0/A[icol][icol];
        A[icol][icol] = 1.0;
```

```
            for(u=0; u<n; u++)
            {
                A[icol][u] *= pivinv;
            }


            for(u=0; u<m; u++)
            {
                B[icol][u] *= pivinv;
            }


            // Now the rows are reduced, except for the pivot one.
            for(v=0; v<n; v++)
            {
                if(v != icol)
                {
                    dum = A[v][icol];
                    A[v][icol] = 0.0;


                    for(u=0; u<n; u++)
                    {
                        A[v][u] -= A[icol][u]*dum;
                    }


                    for(u=0; u<m; u++)
                    {
                        B[v][u] -= B[icol][u]*dum;
                    }
                }
            }
    }// end for i
    // The end of the main loop over columns of the reduction.


    // Realign the soln given the column interchanges. This is done by
      interchanging pairs of columns in the
    // reverse order to that in which the the permutation was built.
    for(u=(n-1); u>=0; u--)
    {
        if(index_r[u] != index_c[u])
        {
            for(k=0; k<n; k++)
            {
                Swap(A[k][index_r[u]], A[k][index_c[u]]);
            }
        }
    }


    // MEMORY DELETE
    delete [] index_c;
    delete [] index_r;
    delete [] ipiv;


    return valid;
}
```

The GaussJordanEliminationFullPivoting() function solves the simultaneous systems of equations

$$A[x_1, x_2, \ldots, x_m, Y] = [b_1, b_2, \ldots, b_m, I] \qquad (21.38)$$

where

    A is a $n \times n$ leading matrix

    x_i are the vectors of unknowns, for $i \in [1, m]$ of a total of m simultaneous systems, of the form

$$Ax_i = b_i \qquad (21.39)$$

$$\Rightarrow x_i = A^{-1}b_i \qquad (21.40)$$

with right-hand side vectors b_i. The system

$$AY = I \qquad (21.41)$$

$$\Rightarrow Y = A^{-1}I \qquad (21.42)$$

is used where Y holds the inverse, A^{-1}, of the leading matrix, A, at the end of system computation.

The function prototype, void GaussJordanEliminationFullPivoting(double **A, int n, double **B, int m), involves two matrices A and B that are passed into the function. On entry, A is the leading matrix and B an $n \times m$ matrix composed of the m right-hand side vectors b_i, and on return, A holds its own inverse A^{-1} (21.42) and B holds the m solution vectors x_i (21.40). If only the inverse of a matrix is desired and no solution x_i sought, then a "dummy" right-hand side vector can be used, as it is in the DivideMultiplyOperation() function when calling GaussJordanEliminationFullPivoting().

Appendix E contains a self-contained Win32 Console Application, titled MatrixInversion, that explores matrix inversion using the GaussJordanEliminationFullPivoting() function. The interested reader may like to experiment with this application first before implementing the GaussJordanEliminationFullPivoting() function in the DiagramEng application.

21.8.4 IMPLEMENTING THE Swap() FUNCTION

The developer will have noticed the call to Swap() in the previous function to swap two double-type elements. Hence, add a new global function prototype for the Swap() function to the "DiagramEngDoc.h" header file where the existing global function prototypes are located, as shown in the code excerpt in the following, i.e., void Swap(double &a, double &b).

```
// Global Functions
CDiagramEngDoc* GetDocumentGlobalFn(void);
double **ConvertStringToDouble(CString string, int &nrows, int &ncols);
char *StripInputString(char *input_str);
int DetermineDataDimsByStrpbrk(char *in_str, int &nrows, int &ncols, int
  &max_row_length);
int DetermineDataDimsByStrtok(char *in_str, int &nrows, int &ncols, int
  &max_row_length);
int GaussJordanEliminationFullPivoting(double **A, int n, double **B,
  int m);
```

```
double **ConvertStringMatrixToDoubleMatrix(char **str_matrix, int nrows,
  int ncols);
void MatrixMultiply(int nrowsA, int ncolsA, int ncolsB, double **A,
  double **B, double **C);
int PrintMatrix(double **M, int nrows, int ncols);
int PrintMatrix(int **M, int nrows, int ncols);
int PrintVector(double *v, int ncols);
int PrintVector(int *v, int ncols);
void Swap(double &a, double &b);
```

Add the implementation of the Swap() function to the "DiagramEngDoc.cpp" source file underneath the GaussJordanEliminationFullPivoting() function and edit the code as shown in the following.

```
void Swap(double &a, double &b)
{
    // NOTE: pass by reference uses syntactically clean pass-by-reference
      mechanism, i.e. without requiring
    // client of the fn to pass an address, which would then be reflected
      by a ptr-to-double in the arg. list.
    double temp;

    // Swap a and b
    temp = a;
    a = b;
    b = temp;
}
```

The Swap() function simply swaps the values stored in the variables a and b, where both arguments are references for those passed to the function. Alternatively, the addresses of the arguments may be passed and pointers used to access what is stored at the argument addresses.

21.9 REMAINING BLOCK OPERATION FUNCTIONS

The remaining blocks for which OperateOnData() methods should be provided are Subsystem, SubsystemIn, SubsystemOut, and Transfer Function. However, at the current stage of the project, these are not required and hence will be omitted here but added when necessary. Their basic form, with prototype, virtual int OperateOnData(int t_cnt, double t, double delta_t), should be consistent with the current functions; i.e., input/output signal data are to be read from and/or written to connections attached to input/output ports, where the block operation generates a general output signal value $f(t_i, s_i)$ at the current time point t_i given an input signal s_i for $i \in [0,n]$, where n is the final simulation iteration.

21.10 SUMMARY

The OperateOnData() functions for the Linear Function and Signal Generator (Source) blocks; the Divide, Gain, and Sum (Mathematical Operations) blocks; and the Derivative and Integrator (Continuous) blocks are added to the DiagramEng project. Parameters are set using the block dialog parameter input windows, and block operation is verified by inspecting the numerical data of the Output block. The Linear Function block generates a linear function value; the Signal Generator block generates a sine, random, or square wave signal; the Divide block filters input based on signal data dimensionality and performs elemental or matrix-wise division and multiplication operations; the Gain block performs elemental, gain-multiplied-by-input, or input-multiplied-by-gain operations; the Sum block adds or subtracts dimensionally consistent data; the Derivative block implements a three-point or five-point derivative $f'(t)$ expression using linear extrapolation; and finally, the Integrator block implements the single-step Euler method to determine state values y, given first-order ODE-based input $\dot{y} = \mathbf{f}(t, y)$.

REFERENCES

1. Scheid, F., *Schaum's Outline of Theory and Problems of Numerical Analysis*, 2nd edn., Schaum's Outline Series, McGraw-Hill, New York, 1988.
2. Shabana, A. A., *Computational Dynamics*, 2nd edn., John Wiley & Sons, New York, 2001.
3. Fisher, M. E., *Introductory Numerical Methods with the NAG Software Library*, The University of Western Australia, Perth, WA, 1989.
4. Fox, B., Jennings, L. S., and Zomaya, A. Y., *Constrained Dynamics Computations: Models and Case Studies*, World Scientific Series in Robotics & Intelligent Systems—Vol. 16, World Scientific, London, U.K., 2000.
5. Press, W. H., Teukolsky, S. A., Vetterling, W. T., and Flannery, B. P., *Numerical Recipes in C: The Art of Scientific Computing*, 2nd edn., Cambridge University Press, Cambridge, U.K., 2002.

22 Preparation for Feedback-Based Signal Propagation

22.1 INTRODUCTION

Direct signal propagation in the absence of a feedback loop was introduced in Chapter 19 and was implemented through the execution of the CSystemModel function `SignalPropagationDirect()`, which calls the CBlock function `OperateOnData()` for each block that generates output. This method of signal propagation was continued in Chapter 21, where further `OperateOnData()` functions were provided to result in simple signal output for the Constant, Linear Function, and Signal Generator (Source) blocks; the Divide, Gain, and Sum (Mathematical Operations) blocks; and the Derivative and Integrator (Continuous) blocks, where the Output (Sink) block displays the propagated signals as graphs in a View window.

However, the direct signal propagation approach is complicated by the presence of a feedback or algebraic loop, where as discussed earlier, the input of a block depends, usually indirectly, on its own output. In this case, a set of equations representing the block operations are to be constructed and computed simultaneously, either as a linear or a nonlinear system, depending on the type of block operations involved.

22.2 LINEAR SYSTEMS

Linear systems were introduced in Chapter 19 and are those to which the principle of superposition applies [1] and, in particular, satisfy the additivity property and scaling and homogeneity property [2]. Consider the simple linear system with Linear Function, Sum, Gain, and Output blocks shown in Figure 22.1: block functional operations are denoted $f_i(t)$, operating at the current time point $t \in [t_0, t_f]$ of the simulation, where t_0 and t_f are the initial and final time points, respectively; signal values are denoted x_i; and block numbers $i \in [0, n-1]$ are shown beneath the blocks for a total of n blocks.

The block equations for this model may be written as

$$x_0 = f_0(t)$$

$$x_1 = f_1(x_0, x_3) = x_0 + x_3$$

$$x_2 = f_2(x_1) = k_2 x_1 \tag{22.1}$$

$$x_3 = f_3(x_2) = k_3 x_2$$

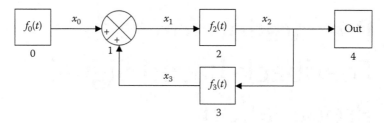

FIGURE 22.1 Simple linear system with Linear Function, Sum, Gain, and Output blocks: $f_i(t)$ and x_i denote the ith block operation and output signal, respectively, where block numbers appear beneath the blocks.

where k_2 and k_3 are the gain constants of blocks two and three, respectively, and the vector of output signals $x = [x_0, x_1, x_2, x_3]^T$: the Output block does not generate an output signal, i.e., x_4 does not exist and, hence, it does not appear in the block equations. The equivalent matrix–vector system is

$$
\begin{bmatrix}
1 & 0 & 0 & 0 \\
-1 & 1 & 0 & -1 \\
0 & -k_2 & 1 & 0 \\
0 & 0 & -k_3 & 1
\end{bmatrix}
\begin{bmatrix}
x_0 \\
x_1 \\
x_2 \\
x_3
\end{bmatrix}
=
\begin{bmatrix}
f_0(t) \\
0 \\
0 \\
0
\end{bmatrix}
\tag{22.2}
$$

i.e.,

$$
Ax = b \tag{22.3}
$$

$$
\Rightarrow x = A^{-1}b \tag{22.4}
$$

where
    A is the leading matrix
    b is the right-hand-side vector containing the Linear Function source signal $f_0(t)$

However, computation of this linear system, in particular, the existence of an inverse A^{-1}, is dependent on the numerical choice of the gain constants. In general, a model involving linear operations can be cast in the form of a linear system and computed with, e.g., the Gauss–Jordan elimination function with full pivoting, GaussJordanEliminationFullPivoting(), introduced for the Divide block operation in the previous chapter, for the block-output vector x. Note that a block diagram, e.g., Figure 22.1, represents a system of equations at any particular time instant and this system would then be computed for each time point $t \in [t_0, t_f]$ of the simulation.

22.3 NONLINEAR SYSTEMS

Nonlinear systems are those that do not satisfy the principle of superposition, in particular the properties of additivity and homogeneity [2]. The aforementioned model involves block operations $f_i(t)$ for source-signal-generating blocks and $f_i(x(t))$ for blocks with both input and output signals that are linear in the generalized output signal vector $x(t)$. However, if this is not guaranteed to be the case, then a linear system of the form $Ax = b$, shown earlier, cannot be constructed, and, hence, a nonlinear solution is required. In this case, the system of equations to be constructed is as follows:

$$
x_0 = f_0(t)
$$

$$x_1 = f_1(x_0, x_3)$$

$$x_2 = f_2(x_1) \tag{22.5}$$

$$x_3 = f_3(x_2)$$

i.e.,

$$\begin{bmatrix} x_0 \\ x_1 \\ x_2 \\ x_3 \end{bmatrix} - \begin{bmatrix} f_0(t) \\ f_1(\boldsymbol{x}) \\ f_2(\boldsymbol{x}) \\ f_3(\boldsymbol{x}) \end{bmatrix} = \boldsymbol{0} \tag{22.6}$$

or more generally

$$\boldsymbol{x}(t) - \boldsymbol{f}(\boldsymbol{x}(t)) = \boldsymbol{F}(\boldsymbol{x}(t)) = \boldsymbol{0} \tag{22.7}$$

where
   $\boldsymbol{x}(t) = [x_0(t), x_1(t), \ldots, x_{s-1}(t)]^T$ is the generalized output signal vector
   $\boldsymbol{f}(\boldsymbol{x}(t)) = [f_0(\boldsymbol{x}(t)), f_1(\boldsymbol{x}(t)), \ldots, f_{s-1}(\boldsymbol{x}(t))]^T$ is a vector of block-operation functions $f_i(\boldsymbol{x}(t))$ (here, for simplicity, scalar functions) for $i \in [0, s - 1]$ that is in general a function of the output signal vector $\boldsymbol{x}(t)$
   s is the number of blocks that produce output signals

The system vector $\boldsymbol{F}(\boldsymbol{x}(t))$ is the difference between the signal output vector $\boldsymbol{x}(t)$ and the block-operation function vector $\boldsymbol{f}(\boldsymbol{x}(t))$, which should be zero. The roots or zeros of this system are the vectors $\boldsymbol{x}_r(t)$ that satisfy (22.7) and form the output signal solution vector of this system at each time point of the simulation.

22.3.1 NEWTON'S METHOD

Consider a differentiable scalar function $f(x)$ (not to be confused with a block-operation function $f_i(\boldsymbol{x})$ as shown earlier) for which roots x_r are sought that satisfy the equation

$$f(x_r) = 0 \tag{22.8}$$

Newton's method, also called the Newton–Raphson method, as described by Fisher [3], is the process of making approximations x_{k+1}, which are the intersections, with the x axis, of the tangent line to the curve $y = f(x)$ at the point $(x_k, f(x_k))$, for $k = 0, 1, \ldots$. The equation of the tangent line at $(x_k, f(x_k))$ is

$$y = f(x_k) + (x - x_k)f'(x_k) \tag{22.9}$$

and since the point $(x_{k+1}, f(x_{k+1}))$ lies on the x axis, the earlier equation may be written as

$$0 = f(x_k) + (x_{k+1} - x_k)f'(x_k) \tag{22.10}$$

to yield an expression in terms of the function and its derivative for x_{k+1}, i.e., Newton's method,

$$x_{k+1} = x_k - \frac{f(x_k)}{f'(x_k)} \tag{22.11}$$

for $k = 0, 1, 2, \ldots$, given that $f'(x_k) \neq 0$ [3]. The convergence of Newton's method is dependent on the choice of the initial root x_0: if x_0 is too far away from the actual root x_r, then the method may not converge, or if the tangent lines to the curve result in an oscillation between consecutive values of x_k, then the method may enter an infinite cycle and not progress to the root.

Newton's method, as Fisher [3] indicates, may also be generalized to n dimensions. A linear approximation to $F(x)$, e.g., using a Taylor series expansion about x_k, is

$$F(x) \cong F(x_k) + J_F(x_k)(x - x_k) \tag{22.12}$$

where $J_F(x)$ is the Jacobian matrix of $F(x)$ at x, consisting of the first partial derivatives $\partial F_i / \partial x_j$ that are assumed to exist, where $i, j \in [1, n]$. In a similar manner to the scalar case, if at x_{k+1}, $F(x_{k+1}) = \underline{0}$, then Newton's method in n dimensions is

$$J_F(x_k)(x_{k+1} - x_k) = -F(x_k) \tag{22.13}$$

This is a linear system of the form $Aq = b$, where $A = J_F(x_k)$, $q = (x_{k+1} - x_k)$, and $b = -F(x_k)$, and consists of n equations in n unknowns and may be solved for $x_{k+1} = q + x_k$, since the initial value, a guess $x_k|_{k=0}$, is known and $q = A^{-1}b$.

22.3.2 Computing a Linear System with a Nonlinear Method

A linear system may be structured in the form of (22.3) and computed for the unknowns as in (22.4). However, a nonlinear system structured in the form of (22.7) is computed using an iterative method as presented by (22.11) and (22.13) for the scalar and vector cases, respectively. Here, an example is provided that shows if the system to be computed is linear and a general nonlinear iterative-based method is used, then the solution x, of $F(x) = \underline{0}$ (22.7), will converge in one Newton iteration.

Consider the model depicted in Figure 22.1 with the corresponding equation

$$\begin{bmatrix} x_0 \\ x_1 \\ x_2 \\ x_3 \end{bmatrix} - \begin{bmatrix} f_0(t) \\ f_1(x) \\ f_2(x) \\ f_3(x) \end{bmatrix} = \begin{bmatrix} x_0 \\ x_1 \\ x_2 \\ x_3 \end{bmatrix} - \begin{bmatrix} mt + c \\ x_0 + x_3 \\ k_2 x_1 \\ k_3 x_2 \end{bmatrix} = x - f(x) = F(x) = \underline{0} \tag{22.14}$$

where the function $f_0(t)$ is linear in time t with gradient m and $f_0(0) = c$ (the vector x is strictly a function of time, but for ease of comparison with the development mentioned earlier, t is omitted for Equations 22.14 through 22.16) and the Jacobian of the function $F(x)$ at $x = x_k$ is

$$J_F(x_k) = \begin{bmatrix} 1 & 0 & 0 & 0 \\ -1 & 1 & 0 & -1 \\ 0 & -k_2 & 1 & 0 \\ 0 & 0 & -k_3 & 1 \end{bmatrix}$$

The system

$$J_F(x_k)x_{k+1} = J_F(x_k)x_k - F(x_k)$$

$$= J_F(x_k)x_k - (x_k - f(x_k)) \tag{22.15}$$

may be written as

$$\begin{bmatrix} 1 & 0 & 0 & 0 \\ -1 & 1 & 0 & -1 \\ 0 & -k_2 & 1 & 0 \\ 0 & 0 & -k_3 & 1 \end{bmatrix} \begin{bmatrix} x_{0,k+1} \\ x_{1,k+1} \\ x_{2,k+1} \\ x_{3,k+1} \end{bmatrix} = \begin{bmatrix} 1 & 0 & 0 & 0 \\ -1 & 1 & 0 & -1 \\ 0 & -k_2 & 1 & 0 \\ 0 & 0 & -k_3 & 1 \end{bmatrix} \begin{bmatrix} x_{0,k} \\ x_{1,k} \\ x_{2,k} \\ x_{3,k} \end{bmatrix} - \begin{bmatrix} x_{0,k} \\ x_{1,k} \\ x_{2,k} \\ x_{3,k} \end{bmatrix} + \begin{bmatrix} f_0(t) \\ x_{0,k} + x_{3,k} \\ k_2 x_{1,k} \\ k_3 x_{2,k} \end{bmatrix} = \begin{bmatrix} f_0(t) \\ 0 \\ 0 \\ 0 \end{bmatrix}$$

$$\tag{22.16}$$

which is the same as (22.2), and, hence, regardless of the choice of x_k, the solution x_{k+1} of (22.14) is obtained in one Newton iteration. Note that here, the notation $x_{j,k}$ represents the jth component of the vector x at the kth iteration, for $j \in [0, s-1]$.

So for models that involve both linear and nonlinear functions, the most general approach to their computation is to structure them in the form

$$F(x(t)) = x(t) - f(x(t)) = \underline{0} \tag{22.17}$$

and to compute them using a nonlinear iterative scheme such as Newton's method or a similar globally convergent method.

22.4 MODEL ASSUMPTIONS

The system of equations represented by (22.17) is one that involves s-output-signal-producing functions $f_i(x(t))$ and s and unknowns $x_i(t)$ for $i \in [0, s-1]$ and is typically written in vector form. This suggests that the vector of unknowns $x(t)$ is composed of either component scalars or vectors, and the corresponding function $f(x(t))$ is composed of component scalar or vector functions, respectively. If the block operations are scalar or vector functions producing scalar or vector output signals, then a procedure for computing the vector-based equation (22.17) can be used. However, if this is not the case, then an alternative method should be pursued.

22.4.1 State-Space Equations

Consider the state-space approach to the modeling of a control system, resulting in the state and output equations in linear form:

$$\dot{x}(t) = A(t)x(t) + B(t)u(t) \tag{22.18a}$$

$$y(t) = C(t)x(t) + D(t)u(t) \tag{22.18b}$$

respectively, where $x(t)$, $u(t)$, and $y(t)$ are the state vector ($n \times 1$), control/input vector ($r \times 1$), and output vector ($m \times 1$), respectively, and $A(t)$, $B(t)$, $C(t)$, and $D(t)$ are the plant/state matrix ($n \times n$), control/input matrix ($n \times r$), output matrix ($m \times n$), and direct transmission matrix ($m \times r$), respectively [1,4]. If $\dot{x}(t)$ and $y(t)$ do not involve time explicitly, then Equation 22.18 involves matrices A, B, C, and D that are not functions of time and is then a time-invariant system [1]. The corresponding block diagram representation of the state and output equation (22.18) is shown in Figure 22.2.

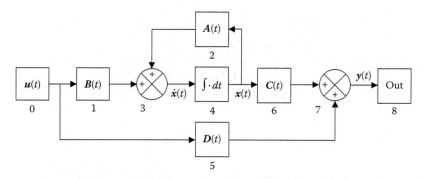

FIGURE 22.2 Block diagram representation of the state and output equations (22.18) where all block operations are vector functions and output signals are (column) vectors. (From Ogata, K., *Modern Control Engineering*, 4th edn., Prentice Hall, Upper Saddle River, NJ, 2002.)

The reader will notice that all input and output signals of the diagram entering or emanating from blocks are column vectors: $u(t)$ ($r \times 1$), $\dot{x}(t)$ ($n \times 1$), $x(t)$ ($n \times 1$), and $y(t)$ ($m \times 1$). The gain operations, through matrices $A(t)$, $B(t)$, $C(t)$, and $D(t)$, are all applied to their input vectors as shown in (22.18) and, hence, result in vector output. In this form, the system represented by (22.17) can be constructed as follows:

$$
F(q(t)) = q(t) - f(q(t)) =
\begin{bmatrix}
q_0(t) \\
q_1(t) \\
q_2(t) \\
q_3(t) \\
q_4(t) \\
q_5(t) \\
q_6(t) \\
q_7(t)
\end{bmatrix}
-
\begin{bmatrix}
u(t) \\
B(t)u(t) \\
A(t)x(t) \\
\dot{x}(t) \\
x(t) \\
D(t)u(t) \\
C(t)x(t) \\
y(t)
\end{bmatrix}
= \underline{0}
\tag{22.19}
$$

where $x(t)$ in (22.17) is replaced by the generalized output signal vector $q(t)$ to avoid confusion with the state vector $x(t)$ used in (22.18) and is composed of components $q_i(t)$, where the index i is that of a block that produces an output signal (here $i \in [0, 7]$, since block eight does not produce an output signal and, hence, is not part of the system of equations). This approach allows the system (22.18), cast as a set of $4n + 3m + r$ simultaneous equations (22.19), to be computed for the output signal vector $q(t)$ using Newton's method.

However, as far as the state equations are concerned, alternative methods exist for their computation. The time-invariant $(A, B \neq f(t))$ nonhomogeneous state equation is

$$
\dot{x}(t) = Ax(t) + Bu(t)
\tag{22.20}
$$

and Ogata [1] shows that the solution to this may be written as

$$
x(t) = e^{A(t-t_0)t}x(t_0) + \int_{t_0}^{t} e^{A(t-\tau)}Bu(\tau)d\tau
\tag{22.21}
$$

for an initial time t_0. The interested reader will appreciate the clarity with which Ogata presents his material, in particular, the consideration of the scalar case prior to the derivation of the aforementioned result (22.21). The scalar homogeneous equation considered is

$$\dot{x} = ax + bu \tag{22.22}$$

and its solution for an initial time $t_0 = 0$ is

$$x(t) = e^{at}x(0) + e^{at}\int_0^t e^{-a\tau}bu(\tau)d\tau \tag{22.23}$$

Once $x(t)$ is determined, the computation of the output equation (22.18b) may then proceed, since now both the state vector $x(t)$ and input vector $u(t)$ are known. In which case, casting the system in the form (22.19) and computing this using Newton's method would be unnecessary.

The reason why the Newton-method-based approach of iterative computation is introduced here is that a system of equations (represented by a block diagram) in general may not conform to a particular structure as is present in the linear nonhomogeneous state equation and output equation. Hence, a general method is required to compute the output signals $q(t)$ as a result of block operations $f(q(t))$ that may not necessarily be time invariant or even linear: the most general method would be one applicable to a non-memoryless, nonlinear, and time-variant dynamical system.

22.4.2 Resorting of the Block List

The block list, "m_lstBlock", is a list of pointers-to-CBlock (list<CBlock*> m_lstBlock) and is a private member variable of the CSystemModel class. The order of the blocks in this list is that in which they were placed on the palette by the user in the drawing of the block diagram. However, to construct the system (22.17), the reader will have noticed that the Output block is omitted from the system of equations, since it does not produce an output signal that needs to be computed. Hence, for ease of block management, a reordering of the block list can be performed that places the Constant, Linear Function, and Signal Generator (Source) blocks at the front of the list and the Output (Sink) block(s) (should there be more than one) at the back of the list. This will also help later with a block-operation-centric signal propagation method that should commence from the Source blocks to obtain preliminary signal data values, i.e., an initial guess $x_k|_{k=0}$ to be used in the iterative Newton method (22.13).

Hence, to reorder the block list, (1) add a public member function to the CSystemModel class with the prototype, void CSystemModel::OrderBlockList(void), and edit this function as shown in the following, and (2) add two private integer member variables to the CSystemModel class to hold the number of Source and Output blocks: "m_iNSourceBlocks" and "m_iNOutputBlocks", respectively.

```
void CSystemModel::OrderBlockList()
{
    int k;
    int chk_list = 0;       // flag to check blocks in block list
    CString blk_name;       // block name
    CString sMsg;           // string to be displayed
    CString sMsgTemp;       // temp string
    UINT nType = MB_OK;     // style of msg. box
    UINT nIDhelp = 0;       // help context ID for the msg
    list <CBlock *>::iterator it_blk;           // block list iterator
    list <CBlock *>::reverse_iterator it_blk_r; // reverse iterator
    list <CBlock *>::iterator it_tmp;           // temporary iterator
```

```
// Determine number of Source and Output blocks
m_iNSourceBlocks = 0;
m_iNOutputBlocks = 0;
for(it_blk = m_lstBlock.begin(); it_blk != m_lstBlock.end(); it_blk++)
{
   blk_name = (*it_blk)->GetBlockName();
   if((blk_name == "constant_block") || (blk_name == "linear_fn_block")
     || (blk_name == "signal_generator_block"))
   {
      m_iNSourceBlocks++;
   }

   if(blk_name == "output_block")
   {
      m_iNOutputBlocks++;
   }
}

// Place the Source blocks at the front of the list (retaining their
  original placement order)
for(k=0; k<m_iNSourceBlocks; k++)
{
   for(it_blk_r = m_lstBlock.rbegin(); it_blk_r != m_lstBlock.rend();
     it_blk_r++)
   {
      blk_name = (*it_blk_r)->GetBlockName();
      if((blk_name == "constant_block") || (blk_name ==
        "linear_fn_block") || (blk_name == "signal_generator_block"))
      {
         // Move element element at source posn, of the source list,
           to the front of the list (destination posn)
         // Argument order: destination position, list, source
           position
         it_tmp = it_blk_r.base();
         it_tmp--;
         m_lstBlock.splice(m_lstBlock.begin(), m_lstBlock, it_tmp);
         break;
      }
   }
}

// Check blocks
if(chk_list == 1)
{
   sMsgTemp.Format("\n CSystemModel::OrderBlockList(). \n");
   sMsg += sMsgTemp;
   for(it_blk = m_lstBlock.begin(); it_blk != m_lstBlock.end();
     it_blk++)
   {
      blk_name = (*it_blk)->GetBlockName();
      sMsgTemp.Format("%s \n", blk_name);
      sMsg += sMsgTemp;
   }
   AfxMessageBox(sMsg, nType, nIDhelp);
}

// Place the Output blocks at the back of the list (retaining their
  original placement order)
```

```
for(k=0; k<m_iNOutputBlocks; k++)
{
    for(it_blk = m_lstBlock.begin(); it_blk != m_lstBlock.end();
      it_blk++)
    {
        if( (*it_blk)->GetBlockName() == "output_block")
        {
            // Move element element at source posn, of the source list,
               to the end of the list (destination posn)
            // Argument order: destination position, list, source
               position
            it_tmp = it_blk;
            m_lstBlock.splice(m_lstBlock.end(), m_lstBlock, it_tmp);
            break;
        }
    }
}

// Check blocks
if(chk_list == 1)
{
    sMsgTemp.Format("\n CSystemModel::OrderBlockList(). \n");
    sMsg += sMsgTemp;
    for(it_blk = m_lstBlock.begin(); it_blk != m_lstBlock.end();
      it_blk++)
    {
        blk_name = (*it_blk)->GetBlockName();
        sMsgTemp.Format("%s \n", blk_name);
        sMsg += sMsgTemp;
    }
    AfxMessageBox(sMsg, nType, nIDhelp);
}
return;
}
```

Three main *for* loops are executed in the OrderBlockList() function. The first loop iterates through the block list and determines the number of Source and Output blocks and updates the class member variables appropriately. The second loop iterates over the number of Source blocks and searches the block list in reverse using a reverse iterator, once for each Source block, to locate the block and then place it at the beginning (begin()) of the list, using the overloaded version of the splice() function that takes three arguments: the destination position (the front of the list, begin()), the list (m_lstBlock), and the source position (it_blk) [5,6]. The function base() is called on the reverse iterator, since the splice() function takes an iterator argument rather than a reverse-iterator argument, and base() returns the base iterator, i.e., the element in the list next to the reverse iterator. However, the element is one position-offset less than it should be in the reverse direction, and, hence, "tmp--" is required for alignment purposes. The third loop iterates (forward) over the number of Output blocks and searches the block list, once for each Output block, to locate the block and then place it at the end (end()) of the list. Hence, after this process is complete, the Source and Output blocks are grouped at the front and back of the list, respectively, maintaining their order, and this may be verified using the list-checking conditional statements.

Reordering of the block list is only necessary prior to model execution or signal propagation when feedback loops exist, as will be shown later. However, for consistency reasons, i.e., having an ordered block list for both the direct signal propagation and feedback-loop-based signal propagation mechanisms, this reordering should take place at the model validation stage, i.e., within

`CSystemModel::ValidateModel()`. Hence, edit the `ValidateModel()` function as shown in bold to call the `OrderBlockList()` function prior to the calls to validate model entities.

```
int CSystemModel::ValidateModel()
{
    int i;
    ...
    // -- REORDER BLOCK LIST: Source, I/O, Output
    OrderBlockList();

    // -- VALIDATE SYSTEM MODEL
    error1 = ValidateModelBlocks();
    error2 = ValidateModelBlockPorts();
    error3 = ValidateModelConnections();
    ...
}
```

Now that the `OrderBlockList()` function is called prior to the `ValidateModelBlocks()` function, the variable values "m_iNSourceBlocks" and "m_iNOutputBlocks" are determined and can be used by other methods of the class, e.g., the `ValidateModelBlocks()` function. The developer can alter the workings of the `ValidateModelBlocks()` function given knowledge of the aforementioned values: alternatively, if the structure of `ValidateModelBlocks()` is left unchanged, work is simply duplicated in determining the number of Source and Output blocks locally.

22.4.3 SAVING TOUR VECTORS

The first stage of model validation is to order the block list and then to validate the model blocks, block ports, and connections: if there are no errors, control flow progresses through the functions `DetermineModelFeedbackLoops()`, `DetermineLoopsFromConnectivityMatrix()`, `BuildTour()`, and finally `SaveTourVector()` to record an integer vector of block numbers traversed when building the block-to-block tour. The two types of tours are (1) a Source-to-Output-block tour that starts at a Source block and ends at an Output block and (2) a Source-to-loop-repeated-block tour that starts at a Source block and ends at a repeated block forming a feedback loop. At present, the `SaveTourVector()` simply prints a message to the user indicating the tour that would be saved; now functionality is added to actually save the integer vectors containing block numbers of blocks forming the tours in the appropriate list.

1. Add two private member variables to the CSystemModel class to record the different types of tours: (1) list<int*> m_lstSourceOutputTour and (2) list<int*> m_lstSourceLoopTour.
2. Edit the `SaveTourVector()` function as shown in the following to add the integer array, representing the block-to-block tour, to the appropriate list.

```
void CSystemModel::SaveTourVector(int *tour_vec, int ncols)
{
    int i;
    int n_repeats = 0;          // number of repeated entries
    int *tour_vec_copy = NULL;  // copy of the incoming tour_vec
    CString sMsg;               // string to be displayed
    CString sMsgTemp;           // temp msg.
    UINT nType = MB_OK;         // style of msg. box
    UINT nIDhelp = 0;           // help context ID for the msg.
```

```
// MEMORY NEW
tour_vec_copy = new int[ncols];

// Copy the incoming tour_vec to the tour_vec_copy
// tour_vec is deleted in calling environment so can't be added to
   the list
// tour_vec_copy is deleted via a call to
   DeleteSourceOutputLoopLists()
for(i=0; i<ncols; i++)
{
    tour_vec_copy[i] = tour_vec[i];
}

// Check tour vector for repeated entries (implying a node-to-node
   loop)
n_repeats = CheckRepeatedEntries(tour_vec, ncols);

// Notify method of tour termination
sMsgTemp.Format("\n SaveTourVector()\n");
sMsg+=sMsgTemp;
if(n_repeats == 0)
{
    m_iNSourceOutputTours++;       // record number of source-to-output
       block tours
    sMsgTemp.Format("tour_vec saved (output block):\n");
    m_lstSourceOutputTour.push_back(tour_vec_copy);
}
else if(n_repeats > 0)
{
    m_iNSourceLoopTours++;          // record the number of source-to-
       loop-repeated block tours
    sMsgTemp.Format("tour_vec saved (loop):\n");
    m_lstSourceLoopTour.push_back(tour_vec_copy);
}
sMsg+=sMsgTemp;
AfxMessageBox(sMsg, nType, nIDhelp);

PrintVector(tour_vec, ncols);

return;
}
```

The developer will notice that a copy of the incoming "tour_vec" integer array is made, since in the calling environment, memory for "tour_vec" is allocated and deleted and, hence, can't be placed in the member variable lists to be stored persistently.

Now that the block-to-block tours are recorded as an array of integers and these arrays stored in the appropriate tour list, these lists need to have their contents deleted and then be subsequently cleared upon each new rebuilding of the block diagram model through ValidateModel(). Hence, the following steps are to be performed:

1. Add a public member function to the CSystemModel class with the prototype void CSystemModel::DeleteSourceOutputLoopLists().
2. Edit the function as shown in the following to iterate through the lists, delete the integer arrays, and finally clear the entire list.

```
void CSystemModel::DeleteSourceOutputLoopLists()
{
    list <int *>::iterator it_int;

    // Delete contents of m_lstSourceOutputTour
    for(it_int = m_lstSourceOutputTour.begin(); it_int
      != m_lstSourceOutputTour.end(); it_int++)
    {
      delete [] *it_int;
    }
    m_lstSourceOutputTour.clear();

    // Delete contents of m_lstSourceLoopTour
    for(it_int = m_lstSourceLoopTour.begin(); it_int
      != m_lstSourceLoopTour.end(); it_int++)
    {
      delete [] *it_int;
    }
    m_lstSourceLoopTour.clear();

    return;
}
```

3. Make a call to this function from within the `ValidateModel()` function, prior to the call to `DetermineModelFeedbackLoops()`, and in the `CSystemModel()` destructor, as shown in bold in the following.

```
int CSystemModel::ValidateModel()
{
    int i;
    ...
    // -- INFORM USER OF END OF BUILD MODEL STAGE
    if((error1 == 1) || (error2 == 1) || (error3 == 1))
    {
        ...
    }
    else
    {
        sMsgTemp.Format("\n CSystemModel::ValidateModel() \n");
        sMsg += sMsgTemp;
        sMsgTemp.Format("\n No build errors. \n");
        sMsg += sMsgTemp;
        AfxMessageBox(sMsg, nType, nIDhelp);

        // Delete any saved source-to-output or source-to-loop tour block
          lists
        DeleteSourceOutputLoopLists();

        // Determine if the model has feedback loops, i.e. source-to-loop
          tours
        m_iNSourceLoopTours = 0;
        m_iNSourceOutputTours = 0;
        DetermineModelFeedbackLoops();

        if(m_iNSourceLoopTours > 0)
        {
            sMsg.Format("\n Note! The number of source-to-loop tours in
              the model is: %d. \n", m_iNSourceLoopTours);
```

```
                AfxMessageBox(sMsg, nType, nIDhelp);
        }
    }
    ...
}

CSystemModel::~CSystemModel(void)
{
    // Delete block list
    DeleteBlockList();

    // Delete connection list
    DeleteConnectionList();

    // Delete source-to-output-block and source-to-loop-repeated-block
      lists
    DeleteSourceOutputLoopLists();
}
```

22.4.4 Get a Saved Tour Vector from a List

The lists "m_lstSourceOutputTour" and "m_lstSourceLoopTour" each contain integer tour vectors of tours that start at a Source block and end at an Output block or loop-repeated node, respectively. In the work that follows, signal propagation will need to be performed for these tours, and, hence, obtaining the right type of tour is necessary. Add a public member function to the CSystemModel class with the prototype, int *CSystemModel::GetTourVector(int tour_type, int i), and edit the code as shown in the following to obtain the right type and number of tour.

```
int *CSystemModel::GetTourVector(int tour_type, int i)
{
    int cnt;
    list <int *>::iterator it_int;

    // Get the right type of tour: (0) source-to-output tour,
      (1) source-to-loop tour
    if(tour_type == 0)
    {
        if((i >= 0) && (i < m_iNSourceOutputTours))
        {
            cnt = 0;
            for(it_int = m_lstSourceOutputTour.begin(); it_int
              != m_lstSourceOutputTour.end(); it_int++)
            {
                if(cnt == i)
                {
                    // Dereference the iterator to return the integer
                      array held in the tour list
                    return (*it_int);
                }
                cnt++;
            }
        }
    }
    else if(tour_type == 1)
    {
        if((i >= 0) && (i < m_iNSourceLoopTours))
```

```
        {
            cnt = 0;
            for(it_int = m_lstSourceLoopTour.begin(); it_int
              != m_lstSourceLoopTour.end(); it_int++)
            {
                if(cnt == i)
                {
                    // Dereference the iterator to return the integer
                      array held in the tour list
                    return (*it_int);
                }
                cnt++;
            }
        }
    }

    // Return a null pointer denoting an error regarding tour_type.
    return NULL;
}
```

The `GetTourVector()` function returns an array of integers denoting the block numbers that were traversed when forming either the Source-to-Output-block tour or the Source-to-loop-repeated-block tour, where the tours themselves are stored in their corresponding lists: "m_lstSourceOutputTour" and "m_lstSourceLoopTour", respectively. The "tour_type" argument denotes the type of tour ("0" and "1" denote a Source-to-Output-block and a Source-to-loop-repeated-block tour, respectively) and the offset integer "i" denotes the ith tour stored in the particular list. The iterator is dereferenced to access the integer array stored in the list. If a tour cannot be correctly found, then a NULL pointer is returned.

22.4.5 Building a Block List from an Integer Array

The Source-to-Output-block and Source-to-loop-repeated-block integer-based tours, stored in the "m_lstSourceOutputTour" and "m_lstSourceLoopTour", respectively, can be used to build a list of the actual blocks that the integers represent. This will become useful in the signal propagation stage, where various block sequences need to generate output signal values in order to obtain an initial guess x_0 for the iterative Newton method when computing the roots $x_r(t)$ of (22.17).

Add a public member function to the CSystemModel class with the prototype `void CSystemModel::ConvertIntegerTourToBlockList(int *tour_vec, list<CBlock*> &tour_blk_list)`. Edit the code as shown to extract blocks from the CSystemModel block list "m_lstBlock" and place them in the tour-based block list, "tour_blk_list": note also that the "tour_blk_list" argument is passed by reference.

```
void CSystemModel::ConvertIntegerTourToBlockList(int *tour_vec,
  list<CBlock*> &tour_blk_list)
{
    int i;
    int chk_list = 1;
    int cnt;
    int index_stop;
    int n_blks = m_lstBlock.size();
    CString blk_name;              // block name
    CString sMsg;                  // string to be displayed
    CString sMsgTemp;              // temp string
    UINT nType = MB_OK;            // style of msg. box
    UINT nIDhelp = 0;              // help context ID for the msg
    list <CBlock *>::iterator it_blk;
```

```
    // Clear the tour_blk_list of any pre-existing items
    tour_blk_list.clear();

    // Get the offset at which the tour ends
    // The tour ends at either:
    // 1) the first negative number or
    // 2) (n_blks - 1) if the tour length is equal to the number of
      blocks

    index_stop = n_blks - 1;  // default stopping index

    for(i=0; i<n_blks; i++)
    {
        if(tour_vec[i] < 0)
        {
            index_stop = i-1; // stopping index at one prior to the
              current negative number.
            break;
        }
    }

    // Iterate up to the offset at which the tour ends, i.e. iterate
      through the tour.
    for(i=0; i <= index_stop; i++)
    {
        // Traverse the block list and pick out the appropriately
          numbered blocks as recorded in the tour_vec.
        cnt = 0;
        for(it_blk= m_lstBlock.begin(); it_blk != m_lstBlock.end();
          it_blk++)
        {
            if(tour_vec[i] == cnt)
            {
                tour_blk_list.push_back(*it_blk);
                break;
            }
            cnt++;
        }
    }

    // Check blocks
    if(chk_list == 1)
    {
        sMsgTemp.Format("\n CSystemModel::ConvertIntegerTourToBlock
          List(). \n");
        sMsg += sMsgTemp;
        for(it_blk = tour_blk_list.begin(); it_blk != tour_blk_list.end();
          it_blk++)
        {
            blk_name = (*it_blk)->GetBlockName();
            sMsgTemp.Format("%s \n", blk_name);
            sMsg += sMsgTemp;
        }
        AfxMessageBox(sMsg, nType, nIDhelp);
    }

    return;
}
```

The ConvertIntegerTourToBlockList() function initially clears (clear()) the incoming list, "tour_blk_list", that may possibly hold the block-to-block tours from a previous call. Then the index offset at which the tour ends is determined. The default index setting is one less than the number of blocks: this is the case for a block-to-block tour that contains exactly the number of blocks in the original model's block list. However, if there are fewer blocks in the block-to-block tour than the total number of blocks in the model's block list, then the stopping index is that corresponding to the entry prior to a negative number in the integer "tour_vec" array: unique negative numbers fill the remaining elements in the integer "tour_vec" array after the nonnegative numbers denoting the actual blocks in the model's block list.

Thereafter, the block list of the CSystemModel class is iterated over, and the appropriate blocks that correspond numerically to the indices of the integer vector, "tour_vec", are extracted and added to the list, "tour_blk_list", recording the blocks of the particular block-to-block tour. Finally, a checking mechanism is in place for the developer to confirm correct block placement in the list.

22.5   DETERMINING INITIAL OUTPUT SIGNALS

The direct signal propagation method of SignalPropagationDirect(), introduced in Chapter 19, caters for block diagram models without feedback loops. However, when a feedback loop exists, then a simultaneous-equation-based computation of the structure given by (22.17) is required, as discussed earlier, which involves a vector of signal outputs $x(t)$ and a vector of functional block operations $f(x(t))$. The assumption that the ith output signal corresponding to block i must be a scalar $x_i(t)$ or vector $x_i(t)$ implies that the dimensions of the signals in a feedback loop involving any blocks except the Divide block may be determined by simple signal propagation. If the loop is formed by a Sum block, then due to the fact that all the Sum block input arguments must be of the same dimensions, preliminary signal values may be determined for all block-output signals. If the loop is formed by a Divide block, then it is difficult to determine the output signal dimensions, since they rely on the input signal dimensions, some of which may form the loop; hence, a mechanism is required to allow the user to explicitly set initial output signal values $x_i(t_0)$ or $x_i(t_0)$, in particular for the Divide block, but in general for any block that generates an output signal.

This section concerns preliminary signal propagation for models with a feedback loop involving a Sum block: the next section introduces the mechanism to allow the user to set initial output signal values such that preliminary signal values for loops containing a Divide block may be determined and which form the initial guess x_0 for the iterative Newton method (22.13).

22.5.1   CHECK SIGNAL VALIDITY

The user may enter block-output signal data directly, for each block, using the mechanism introduced in the following section, in which case there would be no need to perform a preliminary signal propagation to determine initial signal values automatically. Hence, a method to check that all signal data are valid is required. If so, then control flow would progress to constructing the system of equations (22.17), and if not, then preliminary signal propagation would be required to complete the initial guess, x_0, for the iterative Newton method (22.13).

Add a public member function to the CSystemModel class with the prototype int CSystemModel::CheckSystemSignalValidity(void). Edit the function as shown to iterate through the connection list and check that output signal data are valid.

```
int CSystemModel::CheckSystemSignalValidity()
{
    int valid = 1;
    list<CConnection*>::iterator it_con;

    // Iterate through all connections checking signal data
    for(it_con = m_lstConnection.begin(); it_con != m_lstConnection.end();
      it_con++)
```

```
   {
      valid = (*it_con)->GetSignal()->GetSignalValidity();
      if(valid == 0) // if invalid, return valid = 0
      {
         return valid;
      }
   }

   return valid;     // if valid, return valid = 1
}
```

The `CheckSystemSignalValidity()` function initially sets the "valid" variable to "1", indicating that all signals have valid output. Then the connection list, "m_lstConnection", is iterated over, and each connection's CSignal data are checked to determine its validity: if invalid, "valid" is set to "0" and the function returns, otherwise the function returns "valid" equal to "1".

Finally, this function should be called prior to the equation construction stage from within the `SignalPropagationSystemOfEquations()` function that was introduced to the project in Section 19.7.1.8 and is thus far empty. More details concerning this function are provided in Sections 22.7.1 and 22.8.2.

22.5.2 PRELIMINARY SIGNAL PROPAGATION FOR MODELS WITH FEEDBACK LOOPS

The system model signals are checked by `CheckSystemSignalValidity()` to determine whether they have valid data. If so, then a preliminary signal propagation is not required since all signals have preliminary values, but if not, then a preliminary signal propagation should be performed to obtain the initial signal values.

Add a public member function to the CSystemModel class with the prototype `int CSystemModel::PreliminarySignalPropagation(void)`. Edit the function as shown in the following to perform preliminary signal propagation for tours ending in an Output block and for those ending in a loop-repeated block.

```
int CSystemModel::PreliminarySignalPropagation()
{
   int i;
   int j;
   int valid = 0;                       // valid: (0) invalid, (1) valid
   int t_cnt = 0;                       // time count
   int tour_type;                       // (0) source-to-output,
      (1) source-to-loop
   int *tour_vec = NULL;                // tour_vec ptr-to-int to receive
      the tour_vec stored in a list
   double delta_t = m_dTimeStepSize;    // time step size delta_t = h.
   double t = 0.00;                     // current time point.
   double t_init = m_dTimeStart;        // time initial
   CString sMsg;                        // string to be displayed
   CString sMsgTemp;                    // temp msg.
   UINT nType = MB_OK;                  // style of msg. box
   UINT nIDhelp = 0;                    // help context ID for the msg.
   list<CBlock*> tour_blk_list;         // list of ptrs-to-block within a
      block tour
   list<CBlock*>::iterator it_blk;      // blk list iterator
   list<CBlock*>::iterator prev_blk;    // blk list iterator of the
      previous block in the list
```

```
//sMsgTemp.Format("\n PreliminarySignalPropagation()\n");
//sMsg += sMsgTemp;

// ITERATE THROUGH ALL SOURCE-TO-OUTPUT-BLOCK TOURS
tour_type = 0;
for(i=0; i<m_iNSourceOutputTours; i++)
{
    // Get the tour vector and convert it into a block list
    tour_vec = GetTourVector(tour_type, i);
    ConvertIntegerTourToBlockList(tour_vec, tour_blk_list);

    it_blk = tour_blk_list.begin();        // init. iterator to be at
      the start of the list

    // ITERATE THROUGH THE LIST A NUMBER OF TIMES = size - 1.
    for(j = 1; j < tour_blk_list.size(); j++)
    {
        valid = (*it_blk)->CheckBlockOutputSignalDataValidity();

        //sMsgTemp.Format("%d, %d, %s, valid = %d\n", tour_type, i,
          (*it_blk)->GetBlockName(), valid);
        //sMsg += sMsgTemp;

        if(!valid) // if there does not exist output signal data
        {
            if((*it_blk)->GetBlockName() == "sum_block") // skip sum
              blocks but transfer signals directly
            {
                prev_blk = it_blk;
                prev_blk--;
                TransferSignalDataToAnotherConnection(*prev_blk,
                  *it_blk);
                valid = 1;
            }
            else if((*it_blk)->GetBlockName() == "divide_block")
              // skip divide blocks since output signal data already
              provided by user
            {
                // Output signal data should already have been
                  entered by the user.
                valid = 0;
                sMsgTemp.Format("\n PreliminarySignalPropagation()\n");
                sMsg+=sMsgTemp;
                sMsgTemp.Format("\n WARNING! Divide block has
                  unspecified output signal!\n");
                sMsg+=sMsgTemp;
                sMsgTemp.Format("Please manually enter initial block
                  output signal data!\n");
                sMsg+=sMsgTemp;
                sMsgTemp.Format("Aborting signal propagation!\n");
                sMsg+=sMsgTemp;
                AfxMessageBox(sMsg, nType, nIDhelp); // msg. box
                return valid; // abort fn
            }
            else // Perform OperateOnData() to generate the output
              signal data
            {
                t = t_init + t_cnt*delta_t;
                valid = (*it_blk)->OperateOnData(t_cnt, t, delta_t);
```

```
                        if(valid <= 0)  // OPERATIONAL ERROR: ABORT SIGNAL
                          PROPAGATION
                        {
                            sMsgTemp.Format("\n PreliminarySignalPropagation()
                              \n");
                            sMsg+=sMsgTemp;
                            sMsgTemp.Format("\n WARNING! Unsuccessful
                              (non-Output) block operation!\n");
                            sMsg+=sMsgTemp;
                            sMsgTemp.Format("Aborting signal propagation!\n");
                            sMsg+=sMsgTemp;
                            AfxMessageBox(sMsg, nType, nIDhelp); // msg. box
                            valid = 0;
                            return valid; // abort fn
                        }
                    }
            }// end valid

            it_blk++;  // increment block list iterator at end of "for j"
              loop

        }// end j
    }// end i

    // ITERATE THROUGH ALL SOURCE-TO-LOOP-REPEATED-BLOCK TOURS
    tour_type = 1;
    for(i=0; i<m_iNSourceLoopTours; i++)
    {
        // Get the tour vector and convert it into a block list
        tour_vec = GetTourVector(tour_type, i);
        ConvertIntegerTourToBlockList(tour_vec, tour_blk_list);

        it_blk = tour_blk_list.begin();  // init. iterator to be at the
          start of the list

        // ITERATE THROUGH THE LIST A NUMBER OF TIMES = size - 1.
        for(j = 1; j < tour_blk_list.size(); j++)
        {
            valid = (*it_blk)->CheckBlockOutputSignalDataValidity();

            //sMsgTemp.Format("%d, %d, %s, valid = %d\n", tour_type, i,
              (*it_blk)->GetBlockName(), valid);
            //sMsg += sMsgTemp;

            if(!valid)  // if there does not exist output signal data
            {
                if((*it_blk)->GetBlockName() == "sum_block") // skip sum
                  blocks but transfer signals directly
                {
                    prev_blk = it_blk;
                    prev_blk-;
                    TransferSignalDataToAnotherConnection(*prev_blk,
                      *it_blk);
                    valid = 1;
                }
                else if((*it_blk)->GetBlockName() == "divide_block")
                  // skip divide blocks since output signal data already
                  provided by user
```

```
        {
            // Output signal data should already have been
              entered by the user.
            valid = 0;
            sMsgTemp.Format("\n PreliminarySignalPropagation()
              \n");
            sMsg+=sMsgTemp;
            sMsgTemp.Format("\n WARNING! Divide block has
              unspecified output signal!\n");
            sMsg+=sMsgTemp;
            sMsgTemp.Format("Please manually enter initial block
              output signal data!\n");
            sMsg+=sMsgTemp;
            sMsgTemp.Format("Aborting signal propagation!\n");
            sMsg+=sMsgTemp;
            AfxMessageBox(sMsg, nType, nIDhelp); // msg. box
            return valid; // abort fn
        }
        else  // Perform OperateOnData() to generate the output
          signal data
        {
            t = t_init + t_cnt*delta_t;
            valid = (*it_blk)->OperateOnData(t_cnt, t, delta_t);

            if(valid <= 0)  // OPERATIONAL ERROR: ABORT SIGNAL
              PROPAGATION
            {
                sMsgTemp.Format("\n PreliminarySignalPropagation()
                  \n");
                sMsg+=sMsgTemp;
                sMsgTemp.Format("\n WARNING! Unsuccessful (non-
                  Output) block operation!\n");
                sMsg+=sMsgTemp;
                sMsgTemp.Format("Aborting signal propagation!\n");
                sMsg+=sMsgTemp;
                AfxMessageBox(sMsg, nType, nIDhelp); // msg. box
                valid = 0;
                return valid;  // abort fn
            }
        }
    }// end valid

    it_blk++;  // increment block list iterator at end of "for j"
      loop

  }// end j
}// end i

// Check preliminary signal propagation
//AfxMessageBox(sMsg, nType, nIDhelp);

return valid;
}
```

The purpose of the `PreliminarySignalPropagation()` function is to automatically generate initial signal values $(x_i(t))$, from a Source block to either an Output block or a loop-repeated block, which collectively form the initial guess vector x_0 of (22.13), in preparation for computation of (22.17) by Newton iteration.

Two *for* loops are used: the first iterates through the list of Source-to-Output-block tours and the second iterates over the list of Source-to-loop-repeated-block tours, stored respectively, in "m_lstSourceOutputTour" and "m_lstSourceLoopTour". The integer tour array "tour_vec" is obtained via a call to `GetTourVector()`, and this is converted to a block list through a call to `ConvertIntegerTourToBlockList()`.

For each Source-to-Output-block tour or Source-to-loop-repeated-block tour, a *for* loop is executed to iterate $n - 1$ times, where n is the number of blocks in the list: this is done since a final Output block does not generate an output signal and a final loop-repeated block would already have been encountered earlier in the tour and its output signal data generated. Hence, the final block of a tour is not operated upon since the output data are not required. The block list iterator is incremented at the end of each *for* loop.

If the current block already has valid output-connection-based CSignal data, then no action is required to generate a signal, otherwise, three conditional clauses are processed: (1) if the current block is a Sum block, then output signal data from the previous block are simply transferred to the output signal data of the Sum block, since the dimensionality of the data would be unchanged; (2) if the block is a Divide block, then user-specified output signal data should already have been explicitly entered, and, hence, an error message is generated; and (3) for all other blocks, the `OperateOnData()` function is called and the validity of the operation assessed.

The developer will have noticed the call `CheckBlockOutputSignalDataValidity()` in the function mentioned earlier. The purpose of the `CheckBlockOutputSignalDataValidity()` function in the context of preliminary signal propagation (`PreliminarySignalPropagation()`) is to determine whether preliminary signal data already exist for an output-connection object of a particular block. If so, then the block's `OperateOnData()` function need not be executed and signal generation/propagation can progress to the next block in the block list, and if not, then `OperateOnData()` should be executed to generate output-connection-based CSignal data.

Hence, add a public member function to the CBlock class with prototype `int CBlock::CheckBlockOutputSignalDataValidity(void)`. Edit the function as shown to check output-connection-based CSignal member validity.

```
int CBlock::CheckBlockOutputSignalDataValidity()
{
    int valid = 0;                          // (0) invalid, (1) valid
    list<CConnection*>::iterator it_con; // iterator for list of
      CConnection ptrs.
    vector<CPort*>::iterator it_port;     // iterator for vector of CPort
      ptrs.
    vector<CPort*> vector_of_output_ports = GetVectorOfOutputPorts();
      // vector of output ports

    // Get connection list
    list<CConnection*> &con_list = m_pParentSystemModel-
      >GetConnectionList();

    // -- CHECK OUTPUT CONNECTION SIGNAL DATA VALIDITY

    // Iterate over output ports
    for(it_port = vector_of_output_ports.begin(); it_port
      != vector_of_output_ports.end(); it_port++)
    {
        // Iterate over list of connections
        for(it_con = con_list.begin(); it_con != con_list.end(); it_con++)
        {
            // If connection attached to output port: either directly or
            INDIRECTLY through a bend point
```

```
        if((*it_con)->GetRefFromPort() == (*it_port))
        {
            // Get signal properties for this connection
            valid = (*it_con)->GetSignal()->GetSignalValidity();

            if(valid == 0)
            {
                return valid;
            }
        }
    }// end it_con
}// end it_port

    return valid;
}
```

Two *for* loops exist in the previous code to iterate over the block's vector of output ports "vector_of_output_ports" and the model's connection list, stored locally in "con_list", and the conditional statement determines the correct output-connection object whose CSignal-based data validity is checked and its status ("valid") returned.

The other function to be added to the project that is called from within the PreliminarySignalPropagation() function provided earlier is TransferSignalData ToAnotherConnection(), which transfers signal data directly from one connection object to another, without the need to execute the intervening block's OperateOnData() function to generate the connection-based output CSignal data.

Add a public member function to the CSystemModel class with the prototype int CSystemModel::TransferSignalDataToAnotherConnection(CBlock *ptr_blk1, CBlock *ptr_blk2). Edit the function as shown in the following to transfer data from one block's connection object to another.

```
int CSystemModel::TransferSignalDataToAnotherConnection(CBlock *ptr_blk1,
  CBlock *ptr_blk2)
{
    int ncols;                          // ncols of matrix data
    int nrows;                          // nrows of matrix data
    int valid = 0;                      // validity of writing output
      data signal: (0) invalid, (1) valid
    double **matrix_data = NULL;        // matrix signal data
    list<CConnection*>::iterator it_con; // iterator for list of
      CConnection ptrs.
    vector<CPort*>::iterator it_port;   // iterator for vector of CPort
      ptrs.
    vector<CPort*> vec_output_ports_blk1 = ptr_blk1-
      >GetVectorOfOutputPorts();

    // Get the output matrix signal data of block 1
    for(it_port = vec_output_ports_blk1.begin(); it_port
      != vec_output_ports_blk1.end(); it_port++)
    {
        for(it_con = m_lstConnection.begin(); it_con != m_lstConnection.
          end(); it_con++)
        {
            if((*it_con)->GetRefFromPort() == (*it_port))  // the output
              connection from the output port
```

```
        {
            matrix_data = (*it_con)->GetSignal()-
              >GetSignalData(&nrows, &ncols);  // get signal data
              from output connection
            break;
        }
    }
}

// Transfer the output matrix signal data of block 1 to the output
  signal of block 2.
valid = ptr_blk2->WriteDataToOutputSignal(matrix_data, nrows, ncols);

return valid;
}
```

Two pointers-to-CBlock, "ptr_blk1" and "ptr_blk2", are passed into the aforementioned function, where the output-connection-based CSignal data of the first block, referred to by "ptr_blk1", are transferred to the output-connection object of the second block, referred to by "ptr_blk2". The iteration over the list of block ports and the model's list of connections is required to determine the output-connection object of the first block from which the output signal data may be retrieved. Thereafter, the output signal data are written directly to the output-connection-based CSignal data of the second block.

Usually, the two blocks referred to by "ptr_blk1" and "ptr_blk2" would be found in sequence, where the first is a non-Sum block and the second a Sum block, all of whose input signals may not be known, hence not allowing the OperateOnData() function to work properly. Hence, an initial "dummy" output signal can be copied across directly and forms the initial guess, $x_{i,k}|_{k=0}$, for the ith block, where $i \in [0, s - 1]$.

22.6 ADDING FUNCTIONALITY TO SET THE INITIAL OUTPUT SIGNAL

The previous section described how a preliminary signal propagation method may be used to automatically assign signal values to blocks of a model that involve a feedback loop, in particular, models that involve Sum blocks rather than Divide blocks. This is required, since an initial guess needs to be made of the signals $x_{i,k}|_{k=0}$, for the ith block, for $i \in [0, s - 1]$, where s is the number of blocks with output signals, which form the complete signal vector $x_k = [x_{0,k}^T, x_{1,k}^T, \dots, x_{s-1,k}^T]^T$ at the kth iteration, to start ($k = 0$) the iterative Newton method (22.13) to compute a system of the form (22.17).

However, if a Divide block forms the loop-repeated node in the Source-to-loop-repeated-block tour, then the dimensions of the Divide block's output signal is required in order to propagate the signal and must be entered by the user explicitly. In addition, if the user desires to provide an initial guess for any block-output signal $x_{i,k}|_{k=0}$, for $i \in [0, s - 1]$, then an interactive mechanism in the form of a Context menu linking up to a dialog window to allow user input is required.

22.6.1 ADDING A DIALOG WINDOW TO ALLOW USER INPUT

A dialog window with a simple edit box to enter numerical data, similar to that used for the Constant block, is to be added to allow the user to set initial output-connection-based CSignal data. The key steps to add a dialog window for user input to the project are as listed, while specific details are provided in the sections that follow.

1. Insert a dialog window and add controls.
2. Attach a class to the dialog window.
3. Attach variables to the dialog window controls.
4. Add functionality to the dialog window buttons.
5. Add functionality to initialize the dialog window variables.

TABLE 22.1
Output Signal Dialog Window Controls

Object	Property	Setting
Static Text	ID	ID_OUTPUT_SIG_DLG_TXT
	Caption	Enter initial output signal scalar or vector
Edit Box	ID	ID_OUTPUT_SIG_DLG_VALUE
	Multiline	Checked
	Horizontal scroll	Checked
	Vertical scroll	Checked
	Want return	Checked
Button	ID	ID_OUTPUT_SIG_DLG_BTN_OK
	Caption	&OK
Button	ID	IDCANCEL
	Caption	&Cancel

22.6.1.1 Insert a Dialog Window and Add Controls

Insert a new dialog resource: set the ID of the dialog to IDD_OUTPUT_SIG_DLG and the caption to OutputSignalDialog. Leave the OK and Cancel buttons on the dialog. Add controls as shown in Table 22.1 and place them on the dialog window as shown in Figure 22.3.

22.6.1.2 Attach a Class to the Dialog Window

Select the IDD_OUTPUT_SIG_DLG resource from the ResourceView tab on the Workspace pane to show the corresponding dialog window in the editor area. Right click on the dialog box to invoke the ClassWizard. The Adding a Class message box appears: create a new class named COutputSignalDialog with base class CDialog.

22.6.1.3 Attach Variables to the Dialog Window Controls

Open the ClassWizard and select the Member Variables tab. Choose the class name to be COutputSignalDialog, since variables to be added relate to dialog window controls. Select the ID of the control to which a variable should be added, click Add Variable, and specify the details as shown in Table 22.2. Add a private CString member variable to the CSignal class of the same name, "m_strOutputSignal", since this variable will be updated with the value of that of the dialog class and vice versa.

FIGURE 22.3 Output Signal Dialog window showing the controls as specified in Table 22.1.

TABLE 22.2

Dialog Window Controls, Variable Name, Category, and Type for the IDD_INIT_OUTPUT_SIG_DLG Dialog Resource

Control	Variable Name	Category	Type
ID_OUTPUT_SIG_DLG_VALUE	m_strOutputSignal	Value	CString

TABLE 22.3

Objects, IDs, Class, and Event-Handler Functions for the COutputSignalDialog Class

Object	ID	Class	COMMAND Event-Handler
OK button	ID_OUTPUT_SIGNAL_DLG_BTN_OK	COutputSignalDialog	OnOutputSignalDlgBtnOk()
Cancel button	IDCANCEL (default)	COutputSignalDialog	OnCancel()

22.6.1.4 Add Functionality to the Dialog Window Buttons

The two buttons for the IDD_OUTPUT_SIG_DLG dialog window are OK and Cancel. Add an event-handler function for the OK button as shown in Table 22.3. Leave the current event-handler function for the Cancel button as OnCancel(), since this already calls the CDialog::OnCancel() function so no new code is required. Edit the OnOutputSignalDlgBtnOk() function as shown in the following.

```
void COutputSignalDialog::OnOutputSignalDlgBtnOk()
{
    // TODO: Add your control notification handler code here

    // DiagramEng (start)

    //AfxMessageBox("\n COutputSignalDialog::OnOutputSignalDlgBtnOk()\n",
      MB_OK, 0);

    // Update variable values with the Dlg Wnd control values
    UpdateData(TRUE);

    // Close the dialog wnd with OnOK()
    OnOK();

    // DiagramEng (end)
}
```

22.6.1.5 Add Functionality to Initialize Variables

The variable "m_strOutputSignal" is a CString variable that contains the string entered by the user via the COutputSignalDialog dialog object and also reflects the current state of the output signal of the related CSignal class corresponding to the block's output-connection object.

1. Initialize this variable in the CSignal class' constructor as shown in bold in the following to be empty, since the initial signal is invalid.
2. The ConvertStringToDouble() function should not be called to convert the CString value to a double signal matrix, since the initial signal is invalid and of size zero, as indicated by the number of rows and columns of the signal data matrix, "m_iNrows" and "m_iNcols", respectively.

```
CSignal::CSignal(void)
{
    // Init.
    m_iNrows = 0;                       // no initial output signal data
      hence zero rows
    m_iNcols = 0;                       // no initial output signal data
      hence zero cols
    m_iValidity = 0;                    // initial invalid signal
    m_strSignalName = "signal_name";    // default place-holder name
    m_strOutputSignal = "";             // no initial output signal data
      hence empty string
    m_dSignalMatrix = NULL;             // no initial output signal data
      hence NULL matrix
}
```

3. Finally, the CSignal::ResetSignalData() function should be augmented with the line in bold, setting the "m_strOutputSignal" variable to an empty string, consistent with the values of the other variables.

```
void CSignal::ResetSignalData()
{
    int i;

    // MEMORY DELETE
    // Delete the arrays held at each of the entries of the column vector
    if(m_dSignalMatrix != NULL)
    {
        for(i=0; i<m_iNrows; i++)
        {
            delete [] m_dSignalMatrix[i];
        }
        delete [] m_dSignalMatrix;
    }

    // -- RESET VARS
    m_iNrows = 0;
    m_iNcols = 0;
    m_iValidity = 0;
    m_strOutputSignal = "";         // rqd as a result of introducing a
      COutputSignalDialog object into the project.
    m_dSignalMatrix = NULL;

    return;
}
```

22.6.2 Adding a Context Menu and Updating User Input

Now that a COutputSignalDialog dialog window has been constructed to allow the user to directly enter a signal value for the output-connection object of a block, a Context menu entry is required to invoke the dialog window and the relevant underlying mechanism should be put in place to update the user-specified signal data to the correct connection-based CSignal object. The general steps to implement this functionality are listed, while specific details are provided in the sections that follow.

1. Add a Context menu entry to set the initial output signal.
2. Add an event-handler function named OnSetOutputSignal().
3. Add an AssignOutputSignal() function to set the signal value.

TABLE 22.4

Context Menu Settings: IDs, Captions, and Prompts with the New IDM_SET_OUTPUT_SIGNAL Entry

ID	Caption	Prompts: Status Bar and Tooltips
IDM_DELETE_ITEM	&Delete Item	Delete selected item\nDelete selected item
ID_EDIT_DELETE_GROUPED_ITEMS	Delete &Grouped Items	Delete items enclosed by rectangle\nDelete grouped items
IDM_FINE_MOVE_ITEM	&Fine Move Item	Fine movement of item\nFine movement of item
IDM_INSERT_BEND_POINT	&Insert Bend Point	Insert bend point\nInsert bend point
IDM_REVERSE_BLOCK_DIREC	&Reverse Block	Reverse block direction\nReverse block direction
IDM_SET_OUTPUT_SIGNAL	**Set &Output Signal**	**Set block-output connection-based signal\nSet output signal**
IDM_SET_ITEM_PROPERTIES	&Set Properties	Set item properties\nSet item properties

22.6.2.1 Add a Context Menu Entry to Set the Initial Output Signal

Table 22.4 shows the current Context menu settings: the new menu item Set Output Signal to be added is shown in bold. Navigate to the Menu Designer and select the menu with ID: IDR_CONTEXT_MENU. Drag the blank entry at the bottom of the context menu list, i.e., the entry below Set Properties, and place this in between Reverse Block and Set Properties (alphabetical order). Add the menu entry listed in Table 22.4 in bold, with the ID, caption, and prompts.

22.6.2.2 Add an Event-Handler Function Named OnSetOutputSignal()

Attach functionality to the event message for the new entry: invoke the ClassWizard (ignore the Adding a Class dialog window and press cancel), choose the class name to be CDiagramEngDoc, and select the Object ID to be IDM_SET_OUTPUT_SIGNAL. Add a function to the Command message, naming it OnSetOutputSignal(), and edit the code as shown in the following.

```
void CDiagramEngDoc::OnSetOutputSignal()
{
    // TODO: Add your command handler code here
    // DiagramEng (start)
    double dist;        // Euclidean dist bw. block posn and point posn.
    double width;       // block width
    CPoint blk_posn;    // block posn.
    CPoint point;       // local point var.
    CString sMsg;       // main msg string
    UINT nType = MB_OK; // style of msg. box
    UINT nIDhelp = 0;   // help context ID for the msg.
    list<CBlock*>::iterator it_blk; // iterator

    // Get the point at which the context menu was invoked
    point = m_ptContextMenu; // init a local copy.

    // Print msg.
    //sMsg.Format("\n CDiagramEngDoc::OnSetOutputSignal(),
    //  point (x,y) = (%d,%d)\n", point.x, point.y);
    //AfxMessageBox(sMsg, nType, nIDhelp);
```

```
// Get a copy of the blk_list in the system model
list<CBlock*> &blk_list = GetSystemModel().GetBlockList();
  // MUST BE A REFERENCE!

// -- ITERATE THROUGH THE BLOCK LIST TO FIND SELECTED BLOCK
for(it_blk = blk_list.begin(); it_blk != blk_list.end(); it_blk++)
{
    blk_posn = (*it_blk)->GetBlockPosition();
    width = (*it_blk)->GetBlockShape().GetBlockWidth();
    dist = sqrt(pow((blk_posn.x - point.x),2) +
      pow((blk_posn.y - point.y),2));

    if(dist <= 0.5*width*0.5)
    {
        // Only allow setting of an output signal for the Divide block
        if((*it_blk)->GetBlockName() == "divide_block")
        {
            (*it_blk)->AssignBlockOutputSignal(); // assign output
              signal for current block
            break;                        // exit the for loop
        }
    }

}// end it_blk

// DiagramEng (end)
}
```

The selection of the Set Output Signal Context menu entry results in the OnSetOutputSignal() function being called. The purpose of this function is to determine the block whose output-connection-based CSignal data are to be set. A *for* loop iterates through the block list, and the conditional statements determine whether the mouse cursor position lies over a Divide block (at present, this function should be called only for the Divide block, but this may change in future); if so, the AssignBlockOutputSignal() function is called to specifically set the output connection's CSignal data.

22.6.2.3 Add an AssignBlockOutputSignal() Function to Set the Signal Value

The AssignBlockOutputSignal() function to be added to the CBlock base class is a function that works in a similar manner to the BlockDlgWndParameterInput() functions of the CBlock-derived block classes. That is, (1) a dialog object is instantiated (COutputSignalDialog), (2) the string value to appear in the dialog is assigned that of the associated underlying class (CSignal), (3) a while loop is entered to obtain user input via the dialog window, (4) the dialog window input is transferred to the underlying class, and (5) the (CSignal) string value is converted to a (CSignal) matrix value, i.e., the output signal matrix "m_dSignalMatrix". Although the function is designed primarily for the CDivideBlock, it is placed in the CBlock base class in case other blocks require it in future.

1. Add a public virtual member function to the CBlock class with the prototype virtual void CBlock::AssignBlockOutputSignal(void).
2. Edit the function as shown in the following to perform the five key data transfer steps earlier.
3. Include the header file, "OutputSignalDialog.h", towards the top of the "Block.cpp" source file, beneath the statement, include "TransferFnBlockDialog.h". This is required since a COutputSignalDialog dialog object is created within AssignBlockOutputSignal().

```
void CBlock::AssignBlockOutputSignal()
{
    int i;
    int attached = 0;                      // flag denoting the attachment
      of an output connection to a block output port
    int input = 0;                         // input: (0) incomplete,
      (1) complete
    int ncols;                             // no. of cols of data matrix
    int nrows;                             // no. of rows of data matrix
    int valid;                             // used to set signal validity
    double **matrix = NULL;                // data matrix
    CSignal *signal = NULL;                // local ptr-to-signal
    CString sMsg;                          // string msg. to be displayed
    CString sMsgTemp;                      // temp string msg.
    UINT nType = MB_OK;                    // style of msg. box
    UINT nIDhelp = 0;                      // help context ID for the msg.
    list<CConnection*>::iterator it_con; // iterator for list of
      CConnection ptrs.
    vector<CPort*>::iterator it_port;      // iterator for vector of
      CPort ptrs.
    vector<CPort*> vector_of_output_ports = GetVectorOfOutputPorts();
      // vector of output ports

    // Get connection list
    list<CConnection*> &con_list = m_pParentSystemModel-
      >GetConnectionList();

    // CHECK THAT THERE IS A CONNECTION ATTACHED TO THE OUTPUT PORT
    // Iterate over output ports
    for(it_port = vector_of_output_ports.begin(); it_port
      != vector_of_output_ports.end(); it_port++)
    {
        // Iterate over list of connections
        attached = 0;
        for(it_con = con_list.begin(); it_con != con_list.end();
          it_con++)
        {
            // If connection attached to output port: either directly or
              INDIRECTLY through a bend point
            if((*it_con)->GetRefFromPort() == (*it_port))
            {
                attached = 1;
                break;
            }
        }
        if(!attached)
        {
            sMsgTemp.Format("\n WARNING! Output signal assignment
              problem. \n");
            sMsg += sMsgTemp;
            sMsgTemp.Format("\n Output connection must be connected to
              block to set output signal. ");
            sMsg += sMsgTemp;
            sMsgTemp.Format("\n Aborting output signal assignment. \n");
            sMsg += sMsgTemp;
            AfxMessageBox(sMsg, nType, nIDhelp);
            sMsg.Format("");      // reset the msg since within a while loop
```

```
            return;
        }
}

// SET REF-FROM-PORTS OF CONNECTIONS THAT EMANATE FROM BEND POINTS.
// These ref-from-ports are then RESET to NULL at the end of the fn
//   (since they don't actually emanate from a PORT).
m_pParentSystemModel->SetRefFromPortOfConnectionFromBendPoint();

// Create a dlg obj. of class COutputSignalDialog : public CDialog
COutputSignalDialog oDlg;

// GET OUTPUT SIGNAL
// Iterate over output ports
for(it_port = vector_of_output_ports.begin(); it_port
  != vector_of_output_ports.end(); it_port++)
{
    // Iterate over list of connections
    for(it_con = con_list.begin(); it_con != con_list.end();
      it_con++)
    {
        // If connection attached to output port: either directly or
        //   INDIRECTLY through a bend point
        if((*it_con)->GetRefFromPort() == (*it_port))
        {
            // GET THE ptr-to-CSignal OBJECT OF THE OUTPUT CONNECTION.
            // Note: there could be more than one CConnection object
            //   with its CSignal data connected
            // to the current block's output port. But here the first
            //   CSignal object is retrieved,
            // since all CSignal data on CConnection objects
            //   associated with the current output port
            // will have identical data. Below, an update of all
            //   CConnection objects whose reference-from
            // port is the current output port will have their
            //   CSignal data updated individually.
            signal = (*it_con)->GetSignal();
            break;
        }
    }
}

// Set the COutputSignalDialog var using the CSignal var
oDlg.m_strOutputSignal = signal->GetOutputSignalString();

// WHILE NOT CORRECT INPUT
while(input == 0)
{
    // DISPLAY DIALOG TO USER USING DoModal() FN
    // Return val of DoModal() fn of ancestor class CDialog is
    //   checked to determine which btn was clicked.
    if(oDlg.DoModal() == IDOK)
    {
        // Assign COutputSignalDialog variable values to CSignal
        //   variable values.
        signal->SetOutputSignalString(oDlg.m_strOutputSignal);

        // Convert the input string into a double matrix and assign
        //   it below.
```

```
              matrix = ConvertStringToDouble(oDlg.m_strOutputSignal, nrows,
                ncols);
              //PrintMatrix(matrix, nrows, ncols);

              if(oDlg.m_strOutputSignal == "")    // Intentional setting of
                a NULL signal using an empty string
              {
                  signal->ResetSignalData();
                  input = 1;
              }
              else if(matrix == NULL)                // Unintentional
                setting of a NULL signal and hence re-enter string
              {
                  sMsgTemp.Format("\n WARNING!: Incorrect signal input. \n");
                  sMsg += sMsgTemp;
                  sMsgTemp.Format("\n Please enter consistent numerical
                    data. \n");
                  sMsg += sMsgTemp;
                  AfxMessageBox(sMsg, nType, nIDhelp);
                  sMsg.Format(""); // reset the msg since within a while
                    loop

                  input = 0;
              }
              else  // Non-NULL input
              {
                  // UPDATE ALL CONNECTION OBJECTS WHOSE REFERENCE-FROM
                    PORT IS THAT OF THE CURRENT BLOCK'S OUTPUT PORT
                  valid = WriteDataToOutputSignal(matrix, nrows, ncols);

                  // Matrix is non-NULL implying valid user input.
                  input = 1;

              }// end if-else
          }
      else // IDCANCEL is the only other return value from DoModal().
      {
          // Cancel signal data setting operation: no action to be
            taken (at present).
      }
  }

// -- RESET ALL REF-FROM-PORTS OF CONNECTIONS EMANATING FROM BEND
  POINTS BACK TO NULL
// Before AssignBlockOutputSignal() was called the ref-from-ports of
  connections emanating from bend points
// were NULL. Now they need to be reset to NULL, to leave the program
  state as it was previously.
for(it_con = con_list.begin(); it_con != con_list.end(); it_con++)
{
    if((*it_con)->GetRefFromPoint() != NULL)  // if connection
      attached to a BEND POINT
    {
        (*it_con)->SetRefFromPort(NULL);  // set ref-from-port to
          NULL (since not attached to a block)
    }
}
```

```
    // MEMORY DELETE
    if(matrix != NULL)
    {
        for(i=0; i<nrows; i++)
        {
            delete [] matrix[i];
        }
        delete [] matrix;
        matrix = NULL;
    }
}
```

Initially, the model's connection list is retrieved, and the vector of output ports and list of connections are iterated over to determine if all output ports (at this stage, there is only one output port per block) have connections attached. A CConnection object contains a CSignal object, and the absence of the former precludes the latter from being assigned or retrieved, and, hence, the function would return.

The developer will recall that more than one CConnection object may share the same "reference-from" port of a block: a *primary* connection may be directly attached to the output port, and a *secondary* connection may be connected to a *primary* connection through a connection bend point. Hence, the "reference-from" ports ("m_pRefFromPort") of connections that emanate from bend points are set to their parent connection's "from" port ("from_port"), such that when assigning an output signal of a particular block, all direct (*primary*) and indirect (*secondary*) connection objects have consistent signal data. At the end of the function, these *secondary* connection "reference-from" ports are then assigned to NULL to leave the program state unchanged, since *secondary* connection objects (attached to bend points) are not physically and directly attached to output ports.

A COutputSignalDialog object "oDlg" is then instantiated: but before the CSignal object's "m_strOutputSignal" CString variable can be assigned to the CString variable (of the same name) of the COutputSignalDialog dialog class, the correct signal object must be retrieved. Hence, nested *for* loops and a conditional statement determine the output-connection object and its associated signal data. Then the output signal CString member variable is obtained through a call to GetOutputSignalString() and assigned to the CString dialog object.

The *while* loop then iterates until valid user input is entered. The DoModal() function displays the dialog window to the user, and the returned value is checked to determine which button was clicked, using IDOK or IDCANCEL. If OK, the edit box string value is used to initialize the CSignal's CString member variable using the accessor function SetOutputSignalString(). The string variable is then converted into a two-dimensional double array through a call to ConvertStringToDouble(). The conditional section then processes three forms of input: (1) if the user enters an empty string, "", then the CSignal data of the connection object are reset; (2) if the matrix is NULL, then a prompt is issued to reenter signal data; and (3) if the resultant matrix is non-NULL, then it is used to set the output signal data via a call to WriteDataToOutputSignal(). The order of the three conditional statements is important here, since the empty string, "", results in a NULL matrix, where the desired intent is to reset the signal data.

The developer will have noticed the introduction of the two accessor functions GetOutputSignalString() and SetOutputSignalString() used to get and set the "m_strOutputSignal" CString member variable, respectively. Hence, the public member functions with the following declarations and definitions need to be added to the CSignal class:

1. CString CSignal::GetOutputSignalString(void)
2. void CSignal::SetOutputSignalString(CString string)

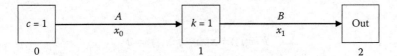

FIGURE 22.4 Simple Constant-Gain-Output model used to test signal assignment with direct signal propagation in the absence of a feedback loop: block numbers appear beneath the blocks.

```
CString CSignal::GetOutputSignalString(void)
{
    return m_strOutputSignal;
}

void CSignal::SetOutputSignalString(CString string)
{
    m_strOutputSignal = string;
}
```

The developer may now test the signal-assignment functionality on a model that does not involve a feedback loop. For example, consider Figure 22.4, involving a Constant block, generating a constant signal $c = 1$, a Gain block with gain constant $k = 1$, and an Output block used to display the resultant signals, for a simulation with $t_0 = 0$, $t_f = 10$, and $\delta t = 1.0$. The two connections joining the blocks are labeled A and B, and their corresponding signal values are $x_0(t)$ and $x_1(t)$, respectively.

Different results will be obtained depending on the order of placement of the connections A and B on the palette. If the user first places connection B and then connection A on the palette and interactively assigns, e.g., the output signal value, $x_0(t_0) = 5$, upon running the simulation, the first output value $y(t_0) = 5$. This is due to the `SignalPropagationDirect()` function being a connection-centric method, where the block associated with the output connection has its `OperateOnData()` function executed. So if the first connection is B, then the Gain block is executed prior to the Constant block. In this example, the output $y(t_0) = x_1(t_0) = kx_0(t_0) = 1 \times 5 = 5$. However, if the user first places connection A on the palette followed by connection B, then the first block to have its `OperateOnData()` function called is that associated with connection A, i.e., the Constant block, in which case, $x_0(t_0) = 1$ and the output $y(t_0) = x_1(t_0) = kx_0(t_0) = 1 \times 1 = 1$. In both cases, for $t > t_0$, $y(t) = 1$, since $x_0(t)$ would be the Constant-block-generated value $c = 1$ from the previous time-step and the initial user-entered signal value $x_0(t_0)$ would no longer be relevant (as expected).

This behavior is consistent and correct as far as the `SignalPropagationDirect()` method is concerned, since it is a connection-centric block execution procedure. For signal propagation involving feedback loops, the purpose of preliminary signal values is to allow the user to specify the output of a loop-repeated block, e.g., a Divide block, in the absence of knowing the exact values of its input arguments (as discussed later).

22.7 BUILDING THE SYSTEM OF EQUATIONS REPRESENTING THE BLOCK DIAGRAM

The previous sections introduced the programmatic mechanisms toward supporting the building of the vector-based system (22.17), repeated here for convenience in an extended form:

$$
F(x(t)) = \begin{bmatrix} F_0(x(t)) \\ F_1(x(t)) \\ \vdots \\ F_{s-1}(x(t)) \end{bmatrix} = \begin{bmatrix} x_0(t) \\ x_1(t) \\ \vdots \\ x_{s-1}(t) \end{bmatrix} - \begin{bmatrix} f_0(x(t)) \\ f_1(x(t)) \\ \vdots \\ f_{s-1}(x(t)) \end{bmatrix} = \begin{bmatrix} 0 \\ 0 \\ \vdots \\ 0 \end{bmatrix} \tag{22.24a}
$$

i.e.,

$$F(x(t)) = x(t) - f(x(t)) = \underline{0} \tag{22.24b}$$

which involves the block-output signal vectors $x_i(t)$ and block-operation functions, $f_i(x(t))$, for $i \in [0, s - 1]$, where s is the number of output-signal-generating blocks in the model diagram. Now the project code is to be extended to complete the previously introduced placeholder function `SignalPropagationSystemOfEquations()` and to call various functions introduced earlier to form the system (22.24) and then compute it using an iterative Newton method to determine the root or zero vector $x_r(t)$, i.e., the output signal vector solution that satisfies (22.24) for the model at the particular time-step $t \in [t_0, t_f]$ of the simulation.

22.7.1 ORDER OF OPERATIONS TO COMPUTE A MODEL WITH FEEDBACK LOOPS

Consider the model shown in Figure 22.5 that was introduced in Chapter 19. The block numbers are shown in an ordered manner, which would be provided by calling `OrderBlockList()`, with Source and Output blocks at the front and back of the block list, respectively. Blocks 1 and 3 may be either Sum or Divide blocks, as these are the only blocks that allow more than one input signal (at this stage). The output signals $x_i(t)$ for $i \in [0, s - 1]$, where $s = 8$ here, are all shown, for generality, to be vectors: the Constant, Linear Function, and Signal Generator (Source) blocks produce only scalar output signals, but in this development, a scalar signal may be considered to be a 1×1 vector. Output blocks, 8 and 9, do not generate output signals and, hence, do not need to be considered in equation construction.

The `SignalPropagationSystemOfEquations()` function needs to first combine all output signals $x_i(t)$, determined via preliminary signal propagation (`Preliminary SignalPropagation()`), into a system signal vector $x(t) = [x_0^T(t), x_1^T(t), \ldots, x_{s-1}^T(t)]^T$, and then pass this to the function `NewtonSolver()` (to be discussed later) in preparation for system computation. The `NewtonSolver()` function in turn calls a method that combines all respective functional block operations, $f_i(x(t))$, into the system function vector $f(x(t)) = [f_0(x(t))^T, f_1(x(t))^T, \ldots, f_{s-1}(x(t))^T]^T$, for $i \in [0, s - 1]$, and then forms the complete system equation vector, $F(x(t)) = x(t) - f(x(t))$. This system $(F(x(t)) = \underline{0})$ is then computed for the solution, or root vector $x_r(t)$, from which the component block-output signals $x_i(t)$ may then be extracted.

The `OnSimStart()` function of the CDiagramEngDoc class calls either the `Signal PropagationDirect()` or `SignalPropagationSystemOfEquations()` function for model diagrams in the absence or presence of feedback loops, respectively, as shown in bold in the following (where other functional details are omitted here for brevity).

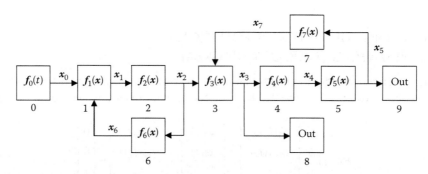

FIGURE 22.5 General representation of a model containing two feedback loops with block numbers (i), functional operations ($f_i(x(t))$), and output signals ($x_i(t)$) as shown (the variable t is omitted for brevity).

```
void CDiagramEngDoc::OnSimStart()
{
    ...
    // Validate model
    error_flag = m_SystemModel.ValidateModel();

    // Propagate signals
    if((error_flag == 0) && (m_SystemModel.GetNFeedbackLoops() == 0))
    {
        m_SystemModel.SignalPropagationDirect();
    }
    else if((error_flag == 0) && (m_SystemModel.GetNFeedbackLoops() > 0))
    {
        m_SystemModel.SignalPropagationSystemOfEquations();
    }
    ...
}
```

Now the SignalPropagationSystemOfEquations() function of the CSystemModel class is to be completed as shown in the following to perform the aforementioned building and computation of the system equations.

```
void CSystemModel::SignalPropagationSystemOfEquations()
{
    int n_TimeSteps;              // total no. of time steps for
      system computation/simulation
    int ncols;                    // total no. of cols of system
      equations vector x and fn vec f(x) (1 col)
    int nrows;                    // total no. of rows of system
      equations vector x and fn vec f(x)
    int t_cnt;                    // time counter
    int valid = 0;                // validity of function operation
      and of x_vec (x) or f_vec (f(x)) vector construction
    clock_t tv1;                  // init time for execution time
      calc.
    clock_t tv2;                  // final time for execution time
      calc.
    double delta_t = m_dTimeStepSize;// time step size of system model
      simulation
    double t;                     // i-th time point t_i = t
    double t_execution;           // execution time
    double t_init = m_dTimeStart; // time init of system model
      simulation
    double *x_vec = NULL;         // system equations vector x
    CString blk_name;             // block name
    CStringsMsg;                  // string to be displayed
    CString sMsgTemp;             // temp msg.
    UINT nType = MB_OK;           // style of msg. box
    UINT nIDhelp = 0;             // help context ID for the msg.
    list<CBlock*>::iterator it_blk;  // iterator for list of CBlock ptrs.
    list<CConnection*>::iterator it_con; // iterator for list of
      CConnection ptrs.

    // Get the actual connection list by reference
    list<CConnection*> &con_list = GetConnectionList(); // get the
      connection list
```

```
// SET REF-FROM PORTS OF CONNECTIONS THAT EMANATE FROM BEND POINTS.
// These ref-from-ports are then RESET to NULL at the end of the fn
   (since they don't actually emanate from a PORT).
SetRefFromPortOfConnectionFromBendPoint();

// PERFORM A PRELIMINARY SIGNAL PROPAGATION TO DETERMINE AN INITIAL
   GUESS OF SIGNAL DATA AND DIMENSIONS
// If the system model's connection-based signal data is not already
   set, then set/propagate preliminary signal values.
if(CheckSystemSignalValidity() != 1)
{
    valid = PreliminarySignalPropagation();
    // If PreliminarySignalPropagation() in error then reset ref-from
      ports and return.
    if(valid == 0)
    {
        // -- RESET ALL REF-FROM PORTS OF CONNECTIONS EMANATING FROM
           BEND POINTS BACK TO NULL
        // Before SignalPropagationSystemOfEquations() was called the
           ref-from-ports of connections emanating from bend points
        // were NULL. Now they need to be reset to NULL, to leave the
           program state as it was previously.
        for(it_con = con_list.begin(); it_con != con_list.end();
           it_con++)
        {
            if((*it_con)->GetRefFromPoint() != NULL) // if connection
               attached to a BEND POINT
            {
                (*it_con)->SetRefFromPort(NULL);      // set ref-from-
                   port to NULL (since not attached to a block)
            }
        }
        return; // abort since fn in error
    }
}

// DETERMINE TOTAL DATA DIMENSIONS FOR SIGNAL VECTOR x_vec (x) AND
   FUNCTION VECTOR f_vec (f(x))
valid = DetermineSystemEquationsDataDimensions(nrows, ncols);

// If dimensionality error reset ref-from ports and return.
if(valid == 0)
{
    // -- RESET ALL CONNECTION-HELD SIGNAL DATA TO NULL
    // Setting all connection-held signal data to null enforces
       PreliminarySignalPropagation() to be rerun to
    // generate new signal data after any alterations to the model by
       the user.
    for(it_con = con_list.begin(); it_con != con_list.end();
       it_con++)
    {
        (*it_con)->GetSignal()->ResetSignalData();
    }

    // -- RESET ALL REF-FROM-PORTS OF CONNECTIONS EMANATING FROM BEND
       POINTS BACK TO NULL
    // Before SignalPropagationSystemOfEquations() was called the
       ref-from-ports of connections emanating from bend points
```

```
            // were NULL. Now they need to be reset to NULL, to leave the
              program state as it was previously.
            for(it_con = con_list.begin(); it_con != con_list.end();
              it_con++)
            {
                if((*it_con)->GetRefFromPoint() != NULL) // if connection
                  attached to a BEND POINT
                {
                    (*it_con)->SetRefFromPort(NULL);      // set ref-from-port
                      to NULL (since not attached to a block)
                }
            }
            return;   // abort since fn in error
    }

    // MEMORY ALLOCATION
    x_vec = new double[nrows];  // memory alloc for system equations
      vector x = x_vec

    // -- MAIN ITERATION TIME LOOP
    n_TimeSteps = DetermineNTimeSteps();  // no. of time steps

    // -- EXECUTION TIME START
    tv1 = clock();
    // -- Loop for n_TimeSteps + 1, from t_0 = 0, UP TO AND INCLUDING the
      last time point t_n
    for(t_cnt = 0; t_cnt <= n_TimeSteps; t_cnt++)
    {
        t = t_init + t_cnt*delta_t;  // t cnt, i.e. i-th time point t_i,
          or simply t.

        //sMsg.Format(""); // clear the msg.
        //sMsgTemp.Format("\n SignalPropagationSystemOfEquations(),
          t_cnt = %d, t = %lf", t_cnt, t);
        //sMsg+=sMsgTemp;
        //AfxMessageBox(sMsg, nType, nIDhelp);

        // DETERMINE SYSTEM EQUATION VECTOR x_vec (x)
        // Retrieve the output signals and assemble into one large output
          signal vector x_vec (x) representing the system
        // x_vec = x = [x_0, x_1, …, x_s-1], where s = no. of blocks that
          generate output signals.
        valid = DetermineSystemEquationsSignalVector(x_vec);
        if(valid == 0)
        {
            break; // break from "for t_cnt"
        }

        // PERFORM NEWTON ITERATION TO DETERMINE THE VECTOR x_vec,
          i.e. x, THAT SATISFIES F(x) = x - f(x) = 0
        NewtonSolver(nrows, x_vec, t_cnt, t, delta_t);

        // Check the x_vec
        PrintVector(x_vec, nrows);

        // ASSIGN THE RESULTANT SIGNAL VECTOR x_vec TO THE BLOCK OUTPUT
          CONNECTION-BASED SIGNAL DATA DIRECTLY
        valid = AssignSystemEquationsSignalVector(x_vec);
```

```
        // -- EXECUTE ALL OUTPUT BLOCKS
        if(valid == 1)  // if all block output-connection-based signal
          data correctly assigned
        {
            for(it_blk = m_lstBlock.begin(); it_blk != m_lstBlock.end();
              it_blk++)
            {
                if((*it_blk)->GetBlockName() == "output_block")
                {
                    // Perform block operation
                    valid = (*it_blk)->OperateOnData(t_cnt, t, delta_t);

                    if(valid == 0)
                    {
                        sMsg.Format("");
                        sMsgTemp.Format("\n SignalPropagationSystemOf
                          Equations()\n");
                        sMsg+=sMsgTemp;
                        sMsgTemp.Format("\n WARNING! Unsuccessful Output
                          block operation!\n");
                        sMsg+=sMsgTemp;
                        sMsgTemp.Format(" Output block unable to read
                          input signal!\n");
                        sMsg+=sMsgTemp;
                        sMsgTemp.Format(" Aborting signal propagation!\n");
                        sMsg+=sMsgTemp;
                        AfxMessageBox(sMsg, nType, nIDhelp); // msg. box
                        break;
                    }
                }
            }
        }

        // If a signal data writing operation failed or if there was a
          read/write error for the output block, then break.
        if(valid == 0)
        {
            break; // break from "for t_cnt"
        }
}// end (time)

// -- EXECUTION TIME STOP
tv2 = clock();
t_execution = (double)(tv2 - tv1)/(double)CLOCKS_PER_SEC;

// -- RESET ALL BLOCKS THAT HAVE MEMORY, I.E. RETAIN PAST VALUES
ResetMemoryBasedBlockData();

// -- RESET ALL CONNECTION-HELD SIGNAL DATA
// Resetting the signal data at the end of each simulation, implies
  that when a new simulation is started,
// the preliminary signal data need to be regenerated using
  PreliminarySignalPropagation(), and are based upon
// the block dialog window parameter input data.
for(it_con = con_list.begin(); it_con != con_list.end(); it_con++)
{
    (*it_con)->GetSignal()->ResetSignalData();
}
```

```
//  --  RESET  ALL  REF-FROM  PORTS  OF  CONNECTIONS  EMANATING  FROM  BEND
    POINTS  BACK  TO  NULL
//  Before  SignalPropagationSystemOfEquations()  was  called  the  ref-
    from-ports  of  connections  emanating  from  bend  points
//  were  NULL.  Now  they  need  to  be  reset  to  NULL,  to  leave  the  program
    state  as  it  was  previously.
for(it_con  =  con_list.begin();  it_con  !=  con_list.end();  it_con++)
{
    if((*it_con)->GetRefFromPoint()  !=  NULL)  //  if  connection
      attached  to  a  BEND  POINT
    {
        (*it_con)->SetRefFromPort(NULL);         //  set  ref-from-port  to
            NULL  (since  not  attached  to  a  block)
    }
}

//  Msg.  to  user  of  end  of  simulation.
sMsg.Format("");
sMsgTemp.Format("\n  End  of  SignalPropagationSystemOfEquations()  \n");
sMsg+=sMsgTemp;
sMsgTemp.Format("\n  Execution  time  =  %lf(s)\n",  t_execution);
sMsg+=sMsgTemp;
AfxMessageBox(sMsg,  nType,  nIDhelp);

//  MEMORY  DELETE
delete  []  x_vec;
x_vec  =  NULL;

return;
}
```

22.7.1.1 Preliminary Signal Propagation

The first major step of the previous function is to determine whether the model has initial signal data, via a call to `CheckSystemSignalValidity()`. If so, then preliminary signal propagation (`PreliminarySignalPropagation()` as introduced earlier) may be skipped, and if not, then it should be performed to determine initial signal values $x_i(t)\big|_{t=t_0}$ for the ith block, for $i \in [0, s - 1]$, i.e., for all block-output-connection-based CSignal data. But before this can occur, the "reference-from" ports of *secondary* connections emanating from a *primary* connection's bend point need to be set to share the *primary* connection's "reference-from" port via a call to `SetRefFromPortOfConnectionFromBendPoint()`, since both connections share the same signal data. If there is an error in preliminary signal propagation, then the "reference-from" ports are reset to NULL to leave the program state unchanged on function exit.

22.7.1.2 Data Dimensions

The second step is the determination of the dimensions of the signal data via a call to the function `DetermineSystemEquationsDataDimensions()` (to be introduced) to check if the data conform to the column vector specification introduced earlier when discussing the state equations. If the data are not of vector form, then the connection-held CSignal data are reset using `ResetSignalData()`: this is done to ensure that `PreliminarySignalPropagation()` is called to recompute signal data dimensions upon rebuilding, after any changes to the model by the user. The number of rows of all the signal vectors $x_i(t)$, for $i \in [0, s - 1]$, is summed to yield the total number of system equations ("nrows"); this is then used to allocate memory for the three main system equation vectors, $x(t), f(x(t))$, and $F(x(t))$, present in (22.24).

22.7.1.3 Construction of System Signal Vector

The third step involves the actual iteration through the main time-based loop to compute the generalized signal vector $x(t) = [x_0^T(t), x_1^T(t), \ldots, x_{s-1}^T(t)]^T$, which is used in conjunction with the block-based functional operation vector, $f(x(t)) = [f_0(x(t))^T, f_1(x(t))^T, \ldots, f_{s-1}(x(t))^T]^T$, to form $F(x(t)) = x(t) - f(x(t))$, for iteration $t \in [t_0, t_f]$: the actual formation of $F(x(t))$ is performed in the function $\texttt{funcv()}$, to be introduced in the following chapter.

The developer should be aware of the difference in notation that is being used here to denote iterations: time-based iteration, denoted $t \in [t_0, t_f]$, concerns that of the system simulation, whereas Newton-method-based iteration, denoted $k = 0, 1, 2, \ldots$, concerns that of the iterative Newton method (22.13). The final root or zero of (22.24) is denoted x_{k+1} (equivalently $x_r(t)$), as in (22.11) for the scalar case or (22.13) for the vector case, for a suitable value of k to have allowed convergence of the Newton method. The result of the Newton method is then assigned to the system signal vector, i.e., $x(t) \leftarrow x_{k+1}$, where $\leftarrow$ denotes programmatic right-to-left assignment.

At $t = t_0$, the initial signal vector $x(t_0)$ is composed of signal data that are either explicitly entered by the user through the dialog-window-based mechanism introduced in Section 22.6 or in the absence of user input that is automatically generated using the preliminary signal propagation mechanism ($\texttt{PreliminarySignalPropagation()}$). This vector ($x(t)$) is returned by the $\texttt{DetermineSystemEquationsSignalVector()}$ function introduced in Section 22.7.2.2.

For $t \in [t_0, t_f]$, the signal vector $x(t)$ is that returned by the Newton-method-based solver and which is subsequently decomposed appropriately and assigned to the system's connection-based signals $x_i(t)$, for $i \in [0, s-1]$, through the call to $\texttt{AssignSystemEquationsSignalVector()}$ (discussed in Section 22.7.2.5). Hence, the signal vector $x(t)$ returned at the current iteration is in fact the vector returned by the function $\texttt{NewtonSolver()}$ at the previous iteration.

22.7.1.4 Construction of System Function Operation Vector

The second term to complete the system equations function vector, $F(x(t)) = x(t) - f(x(t))$, is the function operation vector, $f(x(t)) = [f_0(x(t))^T, f_1(x(t))^T, \ldots, f_{s-1}(x(t))^T]^T$, consisting of the component block-operation functions, $f_i(t)$, for $i \in [0, s-1]$. The function $\texttt{DetermineSystemEquationsFunction}$ $\texttt{OperationVector()}$ (introduced in Section 22.7.2.3), which determines $f(x(t))$, is not explicitly called from within $\texttt{SignalPropagationSystemOf Equations()}$ but rather from within the hierarchy of a Newton-method-based function called $\texttt{newt()}$ (to be introduced in the following chapter), which itself is called by $\texttt{NewtonSolver()}$ (introduced in Section 22.7.2.4 and completed in the following chapter).

22.7.1.5 Newton Solver

The system signal vector $x(t)$ is passed to the $\texttt{NewtonSolver()}$ function, wherein the Newton-method-based solver is called to obtain the system function vector $F(x(t)) = x(t) - f(x(t))$, composed of the system signal vector $x(t)$ and function operation vector $f(x(t))$. After the Newton iteration is complete, the root $x_r(t)$ of (22.24) is subsequently assigned to $x(t)$.

22.7.1.6 Signal Vector Assignment

The zero or root x_{k+1} of the Newton method, which is returned by the function $\texttt{NewtonSolver()}$, is passed to the $\texttt{AssignSystemEquationsSignalVector()}$ function (introduced in Section 22.7.2.5), which then decomposes it into its component signal vectors $x_i(t)$ and assigns these vector components to the appropriate connection-based CSignal data object.

22.7.1.7 Execution of Output Blocks

Execution of the $\texttt{OperateOnData()}$ function of all Output blocks is performed at the end of each time-step ("t_cnt"), i.e., for each $t \in [t_0, t_f]$, where the output signal data are presented in the form of a graph to the user.

22.7.1.8 Resetting of States

Before the function returns, the blocks with memory need to have allocated memory deallocated and some of their variables reset: this is performed via the call to `ResetMemoryBasedBlockData()` (introduced in the previous chapter). In addition, signal data need to be reset via a call to `ResetSignalData()`, since if a new simulation is started, the old (final) signal data should not be used as the initial signal values, but rather, new preliminary signals need to be generated based upon the block dialog window parameter values. Furthermore, the "reference-from" ports of potentially *secondary* connections emanating from a *primary* connection's bend point are set back to NULL (since they are not physically connected to a port) to leave the program state as it was prior to entry into the function. Finally, memory allocated for the vector $x(t)$ is deallocated.

22.7.2 ADDITIONAL FUNCTIONS REQUIRED TO COMPUTE A MODEL WITH FEEDBACK LOOPS

The developer will have noticed the requirement of the following functions in either the `SignalPropagationSystemOfEquations()` function or those related to the `Newton Solver()` function; these are now added to the project:

1. `DetermineSystemEquationsDataDimensions()`
2. `DetermineSystemEquationsSignalVector()`
3. `DetermineSystemEquationsFunctionOperationVector()`
4. `NetwonSolver()`
5. `AssignSystemEquationsSignalVector()`

22.7.2.1 Determining the System Equations Data Dimensions

The `DetermineSystemEquationsDataDimensions()` function is used to firstly check that all connection-based CSignal data $x_i(t)$, for $i \in [0, s-1]$, are column vectors and then to determine the (common) total number of rows of data for the system vectors: $x(t)$, $f(x(t))$, and $F(x(t))$ of (22.24). Hence, add a public member function to the CSystemModel class with the prototype `int CSystemModel::DetermineSystemEquationsDataDimensions(int &nrows_total, int &ncols_total)`. Edit the function as shown to check the dimensionality of signal data and to determine the dimensions of the system vectors.

```
int CSystemModel::DetermineSystemEquationsDataDimensions(int &nrows_total,
  int &ncols_total)
{
    int ncols = 0;                          // ncols of system equations
      vector x or fn f(x) (should be 1 col only)
    int nrows = 0;                          // nrows of system equations
      vector x or fn f(x)
    int valid = 0;                          // validity of data dimensions
    CStringsMsg;                            // string to be displayed
    CString sMsgTemp;                       // temp msg.
    UINT nType = MB_OK;                     // style of msg. box
    UINT nIDhelp = 0;                       // help context ID for the msg.
    list<CBlock*> equ_blk_list;             // block list of non-output
      blocks
    list<CBlock*>::iterator it_blk;         // iterator for list
      of CBlock ptrs.
    list<CConnection*>::iterator it_con;    // iterator for list of
      CConnection ptrs.
    vector<CPort*>::iterator it_port;       // iterator for vector of
      CPort ptrs.
```

```
// Get the system equations block list, i.e. all non-output blocks.
DetermineSystemEquationsBlockList(equ_blk_list);

// Initialize dimensions
nrows_total = 0;
ncols_total = 0;

// Iterate over the equations-based block list
for(it_blk = equ_blk_list.begin(); it_blk != equ_blk_list.end();
  it_blk++)
{
    // Iterate over the vector of output ports
    vector<CPort*> vector_of_output_ports = (*it_blk)-
      >GetVectorOfOutputPorts(); // vector of output ports

    for(it_port = vector_of_output_ports.begin(); it_port
      != vector_of_output_ports.end(); it_port++)
    {
        // Iterate over the list of connections
        for(it_con = m_lstConnection.begin(); it_con
          != m_lstConnection.end(); it_con++)
        {
            // If connection attached to output port: either directly
            //  or INDIRECTLY through a bend point
            if((*it_con)->GetRefFromPort() == (*it_port))
            {
                // Get signal data dimensions to make sure signal
                //  output is a column vector
                (*it_con)->GetSignal()->GetSignalDataDimensions
                  (&nrows, &ncols);

                if((nrows >= 1) && (ncols == 1))
                {
                    nrows_total += nrows;
                    ncols_total += ncols;

                    // There is only one signal vector for an
                    //  output-port-based-connection object.
                    // Although other connection objects share the
                    //  same ref-from-port, the signal (vector or
                    //  scalar)
                    // associated with these connections is the same.
                    //  Hence, break from the "for it_con" loop,
                    // as soon as the first output-port connection is
                    //  found and its signal data dimensions obtained.
                    valid = 1;
                    break;    // break from "for it_con"
                }
                else
                {
                    valid = 0;
                    sMsgTemp.Format("\n DetermineSystemEquationsData
                      Dimensions()\n");
                    sMsg+=sMsgTemp;
                    sMsgTemp.Format("\n WARNING! All signals should
                      be column vectors!\n");
                    sMsg+=sMsgTemp;
                    sMsgTemp.Format("Aborting function!\n");
```

```
                          sMsg+=sMsgTemp;
                          AfxMessageBox(sMsg, nType, nIDhelp); // msg. box
                          return valid;
                      }
                  }
          }// end it_con
          if(valid == 1)
          {
              break; // break from "for it_port"
          }
      }// end it_port
  }// end it_blk

  return valid;
}
```

The system equations (22.24), whose dimensionality is to be determined, concern only blocks that generate output signal data $x_i(t)$ for $i \in [0, s - 1]$. Hence, a revised equation-based block list, "equ_blk_list", for the purpose of equation construction, is required that contains only non-Output blocks: this list is obtained by the call to DetermineSystemEquationsBlockList() (introduced in the following). Thereafter, the list is iterated over and the output-connection-based CSignal data dimensions are checked and the total system vector dimensions, "nrows_total" and "ncols_total", are determined.

Add a public member function to the CSystemModel class with the prototype void CSystemModel::DetermineSystemEquationsBlockList(list<CBl ock*> &equ_blk_list). Edit the code as shown to extract non-Output blocks from the original block list "m_lstBlock".

```
void CSystemModel::DetermineSystemEquationsBlockList(list<CBlock*>
  &equ_blk_list)
{
    int chk_list = 0;             // flag to control msg.
    CString blk_name;             // block name
    CStringsMsg;                  // string to be displayed
    CString sMsgTemp;             // temp string
    UINT nType = MB_OK;           // style of msg. box
    UINT nIDhelp = 0;             // help context ID for the msg
    list<CBlock*>::iterator it_blk; // iterator for list of CBlock ptrs.

    // Iterate through the system model block list extracting only
      non-Output blocks
    for(it_blk = m_lstBlock.begin(); it_blk != m_lstBlock.end();
      it_blk++)
    {
        if((*it_blk)->GetBlockName() != "output_block")
        {
            equ_blk_list.push_back(*it_blk);
        }
    }

    // Check blocks
    if(chk_list == 1)
    {
        sMsgTemp.Format("\n CSystemModel::DetermineSystemEquationsBlock
          List(). \n");
```

```
        sMsg += sMsgTemp;
        for(it_blk = equ_blk_list.begin(); it_blk != equ_blk_list.end();
          it_blk++)
        {
            blk_name = (*it_blk)->GetBlockName();
            sMsgTemp.Format("%s \n", blk_name);
            sMsg += sMsgTemp;
        }
        AfxMessageBox(sMsg, nType, nIDhelp);
    }
}
```

22.7.2.2 Determining the System Equations Signal Vector

In order to build the system vector $F(x(t)) = x(t) - f(x(t))$, the generalized system signal vector $x(t) = [x_0^T(t), x_1^T(t), \ldots, x_{s-1}^T(t)]^T$ is required. This is obtained by extracting all connection-based CSignal data from block-output connections. Add a public member function to the CSystemModel class with the following prototype: int CSystemModel::DetermineSystemEquationsSignalVector (double *x_vec). Edit the function as shown to iterate over the equation-based block list and build the system signal vector out of the component signals.

```
int CSystemModel::DetermineSystemEquationsSignalVector(double *x_vec)
{
    int i;
    int cnt = 0;                        // counter used in the building
      of the x_vec
    int ncols = 0;                      // number of cols of data signal
    int nrows = 0;                      // number of rows of data signal
    int valid = 0;                      // validity of the connection-
      based signal data
    double **data_matrix = NULL;        // signal data matrix
    list<CBlock*> equ_blk_list;         // a list of ptrs to the Blocks
      used to form the simultaneous equations
    list<CBlock*>::iterator it_blk;     // iterator for list of
      CBlock ptrs.
    list<CConnection*>::iterator it_con; // iterator for list of
      CConnection ptrs.
    vector<CPort*>::iterator it_port;   // iterator for vector of
      CPort ptrs.

    // Get the list of blocks concerning the simultaneous equations
    DetermineSystemEquationsBlockList(equ_blk_list);

    // Get the actual connection list by reference
    list<CConnection*> &con_list = GetConnectionList();  // get the
      connection list

    // FOR ALL BLOCKS IN THE BLOCK LIST USED TO CONSTRUCT THE SYSTEM OF
      EQUATIONS (i.e. all non-Output blocks)
    for(it_blk = equ_blk_list.begin(); it_blk != equ_blk_list.end();
      it_blk++)
    {
        // GET THE EXISTING OUTPUT SIGNAL DATA
        vector<CPort*> vector_of_output_ports = (*it_blk)-
          >GetVectorOfOutputPorts(); // vector of output ports
```

```
for(it_port = vector_of_output_ports.begin(); it_port
  != vector_of_output_ports.end(); it_port++)
{
    // Iterate over list of connections
    for(it_con = con_list.begin(); it_con != con_list.end();
      it_con++)
    {
        // If connection attached to output port: either directly
          or INDIRECTLY through a bend point
        if((*it_con)->GetRefFromPort() == (*it_port))
        {
            // Check signal validity and get signal data
            valid = (*it_con)->GetSignal()->GetSignalValidity();
            if(valid == 0)
            {
                return valid;
            }
            else
            {
            // Get signal data dimensions to make sure signal
              output is a column vector
            (*it_con)->GetSignal()->GetSignalDataDimensions
              (&nrows, &ncols);

            if((nrows >= 1) && (ncols == 1))
            {
                // The signal data is that of the current
                  output connection
                data_matrix = (*it_con)->GetSignal()-
                  >GetSignalData(&nrows, &ncols);

                // Build up the total system signal vector
                  x_vec (x)
                // x_vec = x = [x_0, x_1, …, x_s], where s is
                  the no. of blocks generating output signals

                for(i=0; i<nrows; i++)
                {
                    x_vec[cnt] = data_matrix[i][0];
                    cnt++;
                }
            }
            else
            {
                valid = 0;
                return valid;
            }

            // Only one signal data matrix exists for the
              output connection although more than one
              connection
            // may emanate from the same output port due to
              ref-from port updating, in which case the
              signal
            // data is duplicated, and hence only one copy of
              the signal is required.
            break; // break from "for it_con"
        }
```

```
            }
        }// end it_con
        if(valid == 1)
        {
            break; // break from "for it_port"
        }
    }// end it_port
}// end it_blk

return valid;
}
```

Initially, the equation-based block list, "equ_blk_list", is obtained, then three *for* loops exist that iterate over the equation-based block list, the vector of output ports, and the list of system model connections to get the data dimensions of the output-connection-based CSignal data before extracting the actual signal data $x_i(t)$ and adding it to the system signal vector $x(t)$. A check of the signal validity and dimensionality is made to ensure that the signal data exist and are in fact a column vector. If an error in processing the data occurs, "valid" is set to "0" and the function returns.

The developer should be aware that only one signal data matrix exists for an output connection, although more than one connection may be associated with a single output port: e.g., a *secondary* connection attached to a *primary* connection's bend point shares the "reference-from" port of the *primary* connection. Hence, as soon as the *primary* or *secondary* connection's CSignal data are retrieved, the control flow breaks from the nested loops and continues to the next block in the list to retrieve the next signal $x_i(t)$.

22.7.2.3 Determining the System Equations Function Operation Vector

To complete the building of the system vector $F(x(t)) = x(t) - f(x(t))$, the system block-operation function vector $f(x(t)) = [f_0(x(t))^T, f_1(x(t))^T, ..., f_{s-1}(x(t))^T]^T$ is required. Add a public member function to the CSystemModel class with the following prototype: int CSystemModel::DetermineSystemEquationsFunctionOperationVector(int t_cnt, double t, double delta_t, double *x_vec, double *f_vec). Edit the function as shown to iterate over the equation-based block list and build the system function vector out of the block-operation-generated signals.

```
int CSystemModel::DetermineSystemEquationsFunctionOperationVector(int
  t_cnt, double t, double delta_t, double *x_vec, double *f_vec)
{
    int i;
    int cnt = 0;                        // counter used to build up f_vec
    int ncols = 0;                      // number of cols of data signal
    int nrows = 0;                      // number of rows of data signal
    int valid = 0;                      // validity of block operation
    double **data_matrix = NULL;        // signal data matrix
    CStringsMsg;                        // string to be displayed
    CString sMsgTemp;                   // temp msg.
    UINT nType = MB_OK;                 // style of msg. box
    UINT nIDhelp = 0;                   // help context ID for the msg.
    list<CBlock*> equ_blk_list;         // a list of ptrs to the Blocks
        used to form the simultaneous equations
    list<CBlock*>::iterator it_blk;     // iterator for list of CBlock
        ptrs.
    list<CConnection*>::iterator it_con;  // iterator for list of
        CConnection ptrs.
    vector<CPort*>::iterator it_port;   // iterator for vector of CPort
        ptrs.
```

```cpp
// Get the list of blocks concerning the simultaneous equations
DetermineSystemEquationsBlockList(equ_blk_list);

// Get the actual connection list by reference
list<CConnection*> &con_list = GetConnectionList();  // get the
  connection list

// FOR ALL BLOCKS IN THE BLOCK LIST USED TO CONSTRUCT THE SYSTEM OF
  EQUATIONS (i.e. all non-Output blocks)
for(it_blk = equ_blk_list.begin(); it_blk != equ_blk_list.end();
  it_blk++)
{
    // ASSIGN THE INCOMING SIGNAL VECTOR x (equivalently x_vec) TO
      THE BLOCK OUTPUT CONNECTION-BASED SIGNAL DATA DIRECTLY
    valid = AssignSystemEquationsSignalVector(x_vec);
    if(valid == 0)
    {
        sMsgTemp.Format("\n DetermineSystemEquationsFunctionOperation
          Vector()\n");
        sMsg+=sMsgTemp;
        sMsgTemp.Format("\n WARNING! Unsuccessful assignment of x to
          signal data!\n");
        sMsg+=sMsgTemp;
        AfxMessageBox(sMsg, nType, nIDhelp);
        return valid;
    }

    // EXECUTE THE BLOCK OPERATION FUNCTION OperateOnData() WHICH
      CALLS WriteDataToOutputSignal()
    valid = (*it_blk)->OperateOnData(t_cnt, t, delta_t);

    // If operational validity < 1 then operation in error and abort
      function vector f(x) determination
    if(valid < 1)
    {
        valid = 0;
        sMsgTemp.Format("\n DetermineSystemEquationsFunctionOperation
          Vector()\n");
        sMsg+=sMsgTemp;
        sMsgTemp.Format("\n WARNING! Unsuccessful (non-Output) block
          operation!\n");
        sMsg+=sMsgTemp;
        sMsgTemp.Format("Aborting f(x) vector construction!\n");
        sMsg+=sMsgTemp;
        AfxMessageBox(sMsg, nType, nIDhelp); // msg. box
        return valid;
    }

    // GET THE OUTPUT AS A RESULT OF THE BLOCK FUNCTIONAL OPERATION
    vector<CPort*> vector_of_output_ports = (*it_blk)-
      >GetVectorOfOutputPorts();  // vector of output ports

    for(it_port = vector_of_output_ports.begin(); it_port
      != vector_of_output_ports.end(); it_port++)
    {
        // Iterate over list of connections
        for(it_con = con_list.begin(); it_con != con_list.end();
          it_con++)
```

```
        {
            // If connection attached to output port: either directly
              or INDIRECTLY through a bend point
            if((*it_con)->GetRefFromPort() == (*it_port))
            {
                // Check signal validity and get signal data
                valid = (*it_con)->GetSignal()->GetSignalValidity();
                if(valid == 0)
                {
                    return valid;
                }
                else
                {
                    // Get signal data dimensions to make sure signal
                      output is a column vector
                    (*it_con)->GetSignal()->GetSignalDataDimensions
                      (&nrows, &ncols);

                    if((nrows >= 1) && (ncols == 1))
                    {
                        // The signal data is that generated by
                          OperateOnData() which called
                          WriteDataToOutputSignal()
                        data_matrix = (*it_con)->GetSignal()-
                          >GetSignalData(&nrows, &ncols);

                        // Build up the total functional operation
                          vector
                        for(i=0; i<nrows; i++)
                        {
                            f_vec[cnt] = data_matrix[i][0];
                            cnt++;
                        }
                    }
                    else
                    {
                        valid = 0;
                        return valid;
                    }

                    // Only one block operation concerning the output
                      connection
                    break; // break from "for it_con"
                }
            }
        }// end it_con
        if(valid == 1)
        {
            break; // break from "for it_port"
        }
    }// end it_port

}// end it_blk

return valid;
}
```

The functional operation vector is obtained by allowing each block to execute its `OperateOnData()` function given the input signal vector $x(t)$. The `OperateOnData()` function calls the `WriteDataToOutputSignal()` function to write the result of the individual block operation, $f_i(x(t))$, to the output connection's CSignal data member "m_pSignal". Thereafter, this result is obtained from the block's output connection via a call to `GetSignalData()` and emplaced in the system function vector $f(x(t))$.

The developer will notice the `AssignSystemEquationsSignalVector()` call being made for each iteration of the block list. This is done since the functional operation vector $f(x(t))$ is based on the input signal system vector $x(t)$. If the `AssignSystemEquationsSignalVector()` signal-assignment function were not called, then the individual block operations would change the connection-based CSignal data, which would subsequently be operated upon by other blocks (in the *for* loop), and the functional operations would then be made upon perturbed signal data rather than the original incoming vector $x(t)$. Hence, the input arguments to the blocks and upon which the block operates need to be reset with the original incoming vector $x(t)$.

22.7.2.4 Newton Method Iterative Solver

The `SignalPropagationSystemOfEquations()` function calls the `NewtonSolver()` function to obtain the root, x_{k+1}, which is assigned to $x(t)$ that satisfies $F(x(t)) = x(t) - f(x(t)) = \mathbf{0}$. The inner workings of the `NewtonSolver()` function simply prepare various arguments that are required by the globally convergent root-finding Newton-method-based solver, named "`newt()`", and its subsidiary functions, provided in Ref. [7]. For now, this is a placeholder function and will be completed, together with the aforementioned function `newt()`, in the following chapter. Hence, add a public member function to the CSystemModel class with the prototype, `int CSystemModel::NewtonSolver(int nrows, double *x_vec, int t_cnt, double t, double delta_t)`, and edit the function as shown.

```
int CSystemModel::NewtonSolver(int nrows, double *x_vec, int t_cnt,
  double t, double delta_t)
{
    int valid = 1;

    // Code to be added later.

    return valid;
}
```

22.7.2.5 Updating of the System Equations Signal Vector

Finally, after the Newton solver returns the vector $x(t)$ that satisfies $F(x(t)) = \mathbf{0}$, this signal vector needs to be decomposed into its constituent component signals, $x_i(t)$ for $i \in [0, s - 1]$, and assigned to the connection-based CSignal data members ("m_dSignalMatrix"). Add a public member function to the CSystemModel class with the following prototype: `int CSystemModel::AssignSystemEquationsSignalVector(double *x_vec)`. Edit the function as shown to iterate through the equation-based block list and write the signal data values to the appropriate connection-based CSignal data member.

```
int CSystemModel::AssignSystemEquationsSignalVector(double *x_vec)
{
    int i;
    int cnt = 0;                         // counter used to decompose system
      x_vec into cmpt vector signals x_0, x_1, …, x_s.
    int ncols = 0;                       // number of cols of data signal
    int nrows = 0;                       // number of rows of data signal
```

```
int valid = 0;                      // validity of operation
double **data_matrix = NULL;        // signal data matrix
list<CBlock*> equ_blk_list;         // a list of ptrs to the Blocks used
  to form the simultaneous equations
list<CBlock*>::iterator it_blk;  // iterator for list of CBlock ptrs.
list<CConnection*>::iterator it_con; // iterator for list of
  CConnection ptrs.
vector<CPort*>::iterator it_port; // iterator for vector of CPort ptrs.

// Get the list of blocks concerning the simultaneous equations
DetermineSystemEquationsBlockList(equ_blk_list);

// Get the actual connection list by reference
list<CConnection*> &con_list = GetConnectionList();  // get the
  connection list

// FOR ALL BLOCKS IN THE BLOCK LIST USED TO CONSTRUCT THE SYSTEM OF
  EQUATIONS (i.e. all non-Output blocks)
for(it_blk = equ_blk_list.begin(); it_blk != equ_blk_list.end();
  it_blk++)
{
    // Iterate over list of output ports
    vector<CPort*> vector_of_output_ports = (*it_blk)-
      >GetVectorOfOutputPorts(); // vector of output ports

    for(it_port = vector_of_output_ports.begin(); it_port
      != vector_of_output_ports.end(); it_port++)
    {
        // Iterate over list of connections
        for(it_con = con_list.begin(); it_con != con_list.end();
          it_con++)
        {
            // If connection attached to output port: either directly
            //   or INDIRECTLY through a bend point
            if((*it_con)->GetRefFromPort() == (*it_port))
            {
                // Get signal data dimensions to make sure signal
                //   output is a column vector
                (*it_con)->GetSignal()->GetSignalDataDimensions
                  (&nrows, &ncols);

                // GET THE EXISTING OUTPUT SIGNAL DATA
                if((nrows >= 1) && (ncols == 1))
                {
                    // MEMORY NEW
                    data_matrix = new double *[nrows];
                    for(i=0; i<nrows; i++)
                    {
                        data_matrix[i] = new double[ncols];
                    }

                    // BUILD UP THE COMPONENT VECTOR x_i from system
                    //   signal vector x_vec = x = [x_0, x_1, ..., x_s]
                    for(i=0; i<nrows; i++)
                    {
                        data_matrix[i][0] = x_vec[cnt];
                        cnt++;
                    }

                    // WRITE DATA TO THE OUTPUT SIGNAL
```

```
                        (*it_con)->GetSignal()->ResetSignalData();
                         // erase existing signal
                        valid = (*it_blk)->WriteDataToOutputSignal
                          (data_matrix, nrows, ncols);    // write new
                          signal data

                        // MEMORY DELETE
                        if(data_matrix != NULL)  // only delete memory if
                          it was in fact allocated
                        {
                            for(i=0; i<nrows; i++)
                            {
                                delete [] data_matrix[i]; // delete the
                                  row arrays
                            }
                            delete [] data_matrix; // delete the array
                              (column vector) holding the row arrays
                            data_matrix = NULL;
                        }

                        if(valid == 0)
                        {
                            return valid;
                        }
                    }
                    else
                    {
                        valid = 0;
                        return valid;
                    }
                    // Only one signal data matrix exists for the output
                      connection although more than one connection
                    // may emanate from the same output port due to
                      ref-port updating, in which case the signal data
                    // is duplicated for all relevant connections as
                      performed in WriteDataToOutputSignal().
                    break; // break from "for it_con"
                }
            }// end it_con
            if(valid == 1)
            {
                break; // break from "for it_port"
            }
        }// end it_port

    }// end it_blk

    return valid;
}
```

Initially, the equation-based block list that contains all blocks with output signals is obtained, and then for each block, the vector of output ports and the list of connections are iterated over to find the appropriate block-output-connection object. Then, a signal data dimensionality check is made, followed by a memory allocation of a matrix data structure in preparation for the ensuing assignment of the relevant rows of the vector $x(t)$ to the component connection-based CSignal vector $x_i(t)$. A call to ResetSignalData() is made to delete the existing connection-based CSignal data member prior to writing the new data to the output signal: this may not delete the data of possible *secondary* connections that share the same data, but in any case, memory is deleted in `SetSignalData()` to prevent a memory leak. The call, `WriteDataToOutputSignal()`, is used to make sure that all connection objects whose "reference-from" ports are that of the current block's output port have their signal data matrix ("m_dSignalMatrix") updated appropriately (a call to `SetSignalData()` is made). Thereafter, the local data matrix object has its memory deallocated.

22.7.3 TESTING THE CODE STRUCTURE

The functions introduced earlier may be checked for their correctness by running the application with a simple model containing at least one feedback loop. The user will observe the flow of control represented by the function-call tree in Table 22.5.

At this stage, signal data throughout the simulation, i.e., for $t \in [t_0, t_f]$, are that either initially set by the user or determined by `PreliminarySignalPropagation()`. If `PreliminarySignalPropagation()` is used, the initial signal data are assigned by executing either a block-based `OperateOnData()` function or the `TransferSignalDataToAnotherConnection()` operation. Upon execution of the functions in the time-based loop (those between "for(t_cnt)" and "end for(t_cnt)" in Table 22.5), the signal data are simply extracted from the connection objects using `DetermineSystemEquationsSignalVector()`; passed to `NewtonSolver()`, which at this stage does nothing; and then assigned back to the connection objects using `AssignSystemEquationsSignalVector()`; i.e., the signal data do not change, since no equation computation is being performed due to the nonexistence of the iterative Newton method in the project (at present). The computation of the signal values using the Newton-method-based iterative procedure is the subject of the next chapter.

The user may run the DiagramEng application and verify, through the use of the `PrintVector()` and `PrintMatrix()` functions (already in the previous code excerpts), that the vector $x(t)$, "x_vec" in the code, reflects the block-output signal data, either explicitly entered by the user or determined by preliminary signal propagation. For example, consider the diagram shown in Figure 22.5 involving two feedback loops through the junction nodes: blocks one and three. If nodes one and three are Divide blocks, then the user must explicitly set initial output signals $x_1(t_0)$ and $x_3(t_0)$. However, if these nodes are Sum blocks, then automatic signal data transfer is used to assign initial signal values in the absence of user input. At $t = t_0$, the initial signal vector after preliminary signal propagation is $x(t)\big|_{t_0} = [x_0^T(t_0), x_1^T(t_0), \dots, x_7^T(t_0)]^T$, and this remains constant throughout the time-based iteration due to the (at present) nonfunctioning `NewtonSolver()` method.

22.8   STOPPING A SIMULATION

The Newton-method-based solver, when implemented, will be able to compute systems of linear and nonlinear equations represented by a block diagram, modeling the system being studied. However, a mechanism is required to stop any simulation prematurely if desired by the user. The following implementation steps are required in order that the user be able to terminate a simulation essentially instantaneously:

1. Augment the `CSystemModel::SignalPropagationDirect()` method.
2. Augment the `CSystemModel::SignalPropagationSystemOfEquations()` method.
3. Add a `CheckStopButtonPressed()` method to the CSystemModel class.
4. Complete the `CDiagramEngDoc::OnSimStop()` event-handler function.

TABLE 22.5

Function-Call Tree Concerning a Model with at Least One Feedback Loop Beginning from `OnSimStart()`

Level 1	Level 2	Level 3	Level 4	Level 5
OnSimStart()				
	SignalPropagationSystemOfEquations()			
		GetConnectionList()		
		SetRefFromPortOfConnectionFromBendPoint()		
		CheckSystemSignalValidity()		
			GetSignalValidity()	
		PreliminarySignalPropagation()		
			GetTourVector()	
			ConvertIntegerTourToBlockList()	
			CheckBlockOutputSignalDataValidity()	
				GetSignalValidity()
			GetBlockName()	
			TransferSignalDataToAnotherConnection()	
				GetSignalData()
				WriteDataToOutputSignal()
			OperateOnData()	
		DetermineSystemEquationsDataDimensions()		
			DetermineSystemEquationsBlockList()	
			GetSignalDataDimensions()	
		DetermineNTimeSteps()		
		- - - for(t_cnt) - - -		
		DetermineSystemEquationsSignalVector()		
			DetermineSystemEquationsBlockList()	
			GetSignalValidity()	
			GetSignalDataDimensions()	
			GetSignalData()	
		ResetSignalData()		
		NewtonSolver()		
		AssignSystemEquationsSignalVector()		
			DetermineSystemEquationsBlockList()	
			GetSignalDataDimensions()	
			ResetSignalData()	
			WriteDataToOutputSignal()	
		OperateOnData()		
		- - - end for(t_cnt) - - -		
		ResetMemoryBasedBlockData()		
		ResetSignalData()		
		GetRefFromPoint()		
		SetRefFromPort()		

Important functions are shown, some of which are highlighted, and the code between the "for(t_cnt)" and "end for(t_cnt)" statements is contained in the time-based iterative loop.

22.8.1 AUGMENT THE **CSystemModel::SignalPropagationDirect()** METHOD

The CSystemModel::SignalPropagationDirect() method iterates from the initial time to the final simulation time in a main time-based loop. However, within the main loop, a check needs to be made at each time point to determine whether the user has pressed the Stop button on the Common Operations toolbar or selected the Stop entry of the Simulation menu, both sharing the same ID: ID_SIM_STOP. Hence, the SignalPropagationDirect() method is to be augmented as shown in bold in the following to call a to-be-added CheckStopButtonPressed() function: the ellipsis "..." denotes omitted but unchanged code.

```
void CSystemModel::SignalPropagationDirect()
{
    int n_TimeSteps;          // total no. of time steps for numerical
       integration
    int out_blk_state = 0;    // flag denoting output-block operation
       state
    int std_blk_state = 0;    // flag denoting standard-block operation
       state
    int t_cnt;                // time counter
    bool bStop = FALSE;       // stop simulation
    clock_t tv1;              // init time for execution time calc.
    clock_t tv2;              // final time for execution time calc.
    ...

    // -- MAIN ITERATION TIME LOOP
    n_TimeSteps = DetermineNTimeSteps();  // no. of time steps

    // -- EXECUTION TIME START
    tv1 = clock();

    // -- Loop for n_TimeSteps + 1, from t_0 = 0, UP TO AND INCLUDING the
       last time point t_n
    for(t_cnt = 0; t_cnt <= n_TimeSteps; t_cnt++)
    {
        t = t_init + t_cnt*delta_t;  // t cnt, i.e. i-th time point t_i,
           or simply t.
        ...
        // -- ITERATE OVER CONNECTION LIST TO DETERMINE CONNECTION'S
           SIGNAL DATA
        ...
        // -- EXECUTE ALL OUTPUT BLOCKS
        ...
        // -- RESET ALL CONNECTION-HELD SIGNAL DATA
        ...
        // RE-OBTAIN A COPY OF THE CONNECTION LIST AT EACH TIME STEP
        ...
        // If a std block operation failed or if there was a read/write
           error for the output block, then break.
        if((std_blk_state == -1) || (out_blk_state == 0))
        {
            break;  // break from for loop
        }

        // Check if stop button pressed
        bStop = CheckStopButtonPressed();
        if(bStop)
```

```
        {
            break;
        }
    }// end (time)
    ...
    return;
}
```

A Boolean variable is introduced, and if the `CheckStopButtonPressed()` function returns "true", then execution breaks out of the main time-based loop.

22.8.2 AUGMENT `CSystemModel::SignalPropagation` `SystemOfEquations()`

The `CSystemModel::SignalPropagationSystemOfEquations()` method introduced earlier also has a main time-based iterative loop within which the `NewtonSolver()` method is called. Augment the code as shown in bold in the following to call the `CheckStopButtonPressed()` function in a similar manner to the aforementioned `SignalPropagationDirect()` method.

```
void CSystemModel::SignalPropagationSystemOfEquations()
{
    int n_TimeSteps;              // total no. of time steps for system
      computation/simulation
    int ncols;                    // total no. of cols of system equations
      vector x and fn vec f(x) (1 col)
    int nrows;                    // total no. of rows of system equations
      vector x and fn vec f(x)
    int t_cnt;                    // time counter
    int valid = 0;                // validity of function operation and of
      x_vec (x) or f_vec (f(x)) vector construction
    bool bStop = FALSE;           // stop simulation
    clock_t tv1;                  // init time for execution time calc.
    clock_t tv2;                  // final time for execution time calc.
    ...
    // -- MAIN ITERATION TIME LOOP
    n_TimeSteps = DetermineNTimeSteps();  // no. of time steps

    // -- EXECUTION TIME START
    tv1 = clock();

    // -- Loop for n_TimeSteps + 1, from t_0 = 0, UP TO AND INCLUDING the
      last time point t_n
    for(t_cnt = 0; t_cnt <= n_TimeSteps; t_cnt++)
    {
        t = t_init + t_cnt*delta_t;  // t cnt, i.e. i-th time point t_i,
          or simply t.
        ...
        // DETERMINE SYSTEM EQUATION VECTOR x_vec (x)
        ...
        // PERFORM NEWTON ITERATION TO DETERMINE THE VECTOR x_vec,
          i.e. x, THAT SATISFIES F(x) = x - f(x) = 0
        ...
        // ASSIGN THE RESULTANT SIGNAL VECTOR x_vec TO THE BLOCK OUTPUT
          CONNECTION-BASED SIGNAL DATA DIRECTLY
```

```
    ...
    // -- EXECUTE ALL OUTPUT BLOCKS
    ...
    // If a signal data writing operation failed or if there was a
      read/write error for the output block, then break.
    if(valid == 0)
    {
        break;  // break from "for t_cnt"
    }

    // Check if stop button pressed
    bStop = CheckStopButtonPressed();
    if(bStop)
    {
        break;
    }
}// end (time)
...
return;
}
```

The `CheckStopButtonPressed()` method is called at the very end of the time-based loop as it is in the direct signal propagation method and breaks from the loop if the user selects either the Stop menu entry or toolbar button.

22.8.3   ADD A `CheckStopButtonPressed()` METHOD TO THE `C`SYSTEM`M`ODEL CLASS

In both the `SignalPropagationDirect()` and `SignalPropagationSystemOf Equations()` functions updated earlier, a call is made to `CheckStopButtonPressed()` of the same (CSystemModel) class and a Boolean value returned: "true" and "false" indicate whether the simulation is to be ended or not, respectively, through either the selection of the Stop entry under the Simulation menu or the Stop button of the Common Operations toolbar. Hence, add a public member function to the CSystemModel class with the prototype, `bool CSystemModel:: CheckStopButtonPressed(void)`, and edit it as shown.

```
bool CSystemModel::CheckStopButtonPressed()
{
    bool bStop = FALSE;             // btn pressed => bStop = true
    HWND hWnd = NULL;               // handle to window
    MSG msg;                        // MSG structure containing msg info
      from thread's msg queue
    UINT wMsgFilterMin = 0;         // first msg filter
    UINT wMsgFilterMax = 0;         // last msg filter
    UINT wRemovalMsg = PM_NOREMOVE; // removal flag: PM_REMOVE or PM_
      NOREMOVE
    CString sMsg;                   // AfxMessageBox() string

    // CHECK MESSAGES
    // PeekMessage() checks a thread msg queue for a msg and places the
      msg (if any) in msg structure [MSDN].
    while(::PeekMessage(&msg, hWnd, wMsgFilterMin, wMsgFilterMax,
      wRemovalMsg))
    {
        // PumpMessage() contains the thread's msg. loop.: called
          directly to force msgs to be processed
```

```
        AfxGetApp()->PumpMessage();

        // Filter WM_COMMAND event msg's only
        if(msg.message == WM_COMMAND)
        {
            WORD wNotifyCode = HIWORD(msg.wParam); // notification code:
              menu or toolbar = 0
            WORD wID = LOWORD(msg.wParam); // item, control, or
              accelerator identifier ID_SIM_STOP

            //sMsg.Format("message = %d, wNotifyCode = %d, wID = %d,
              ID_SIM_STOP = %d\n", msg.message, wNotifyCode, wID,
              ID_SIM_STOP);
            //AfxMessageBox(sMsg, MB_OK, 0);
            // If menu entry or toolbar button with ID, ID_SIM_STOP
              selected
            if(wID == ID_SIM_STOP)
            {
                //sMsg.Format("Stopping simulation … \n");
                //AfxMessageBox(sMsg, MB_OK, 0);

                bStop = TRUE;
            }
        }
    }
    return bStop;
}
```

Three key actions take place in the `CheckStopButtonPressed()` function: (1) checking of a thread message queue for a message using `PeekMessage()`, (2) forcing the processing of a message using `PumpMessage()`, and (3) filtering the message to determine whether the menu entry or toolbar button, both sharing the same ID, was selected.

The `PeekMessage()` function checks a thread message queue for a message and places the message (if any) in the specified structure [6]. The function takes five arguments: (1) a pointer to a message structure that receives message information (LPMSG), (2) a handle to the window whose messages are to be examined (HWND), (3) the value of the first message in the range of messages to be examined (UINT), (4) the value of the last message in the range of messages to be examined (UINT), and (5) a message removal flag (UINT) denoting how messages are to be handled [6].

The interested reader should consult Refs. [6,8,9] for further information concerning the `PeekMessage()` function and its arguments: all three references have been used here to explain function details. In the aforementioned code, the HWND argument is NULL, implying that both window and thread messages will be processed. The message filter arguments denote the range of message values being filtered: if both are set to zero, `PeekMessage()` returns all available messages and no range filtering is performed. The message removal flag is set to PM_NOREMOVE to indicate that messages are not to be removed from the queue after processing by the function. The return value of `PeekMessage()` is either nonzero or zero, denoting whether a message is available or unavailable for processing, respectively. Hence, while there are messages to be processed, the body of the loop is executed.

The first action that takes place within the loop is a call to `PumpMessage()`: this function contains the thread's message loop and calling it forces the messages to be processed [8]. For example, an event-handler function may be called to process a message. If this is not called, no processing takes place and the code halts.

The conditional section of the loop concerns the filtering of the message to determine whether the menu entry or toolbar button was selected. The first conditional clause determines whether the message is a command event message, denoted by WM_COMMAND: a command message is sent when the user selects a command item from a menu, when a control sends a notification message to its parent window, or when an accelerator keystroke is translated [6]. Here, the Simulation menu entry, Stop, will generate this message, but the Stop button on the Common Operations toolbar does not. This is treated in the following by the Stop button's event-handler function. The WM_COMMAND parameters are as follows: (1) a notification code (HIWORD(wParam)), (2) an item identifier (LOWORD(wParam)), and (3) a handle of the control ((HWND) lParam) (the interested reader should consult Ref. [6] for further details). The second conditional clause filters out the ID corresponding to the menu entry and toolbar button, i.e., ID_SIM_STOP. Finally, the function returns the Boolean value "TRUE", denoting whether the simulation was stopped.

22.8.4 Complete the `CDiagramEngDoc::OnSimStop()` Event-Handler Function

There is a slight problem concerning stopping the simulation. If the user runs a lengthy simulation, e.g., using `SignalPropagationDirect()`, and chooses Stop from the Simulation menu, the simulation stops as expected: but if the user clicks the Stop button on the Common Operations toolbar, only the `AfxMessagBox()` call, presenting the message box, is made but no WM_COMMAND message seems to have been generated and the simulation continues without stopping. In the preceding paragraph, it was stated that a command (WM_COMMAND) message is sent via a menu item, a control, or accelerator keystroke (see previous paragraph). Here, the `CDiagramEngDoc::OnSimStop()` event-handler function needs to be augmented as shown in the following to actually send a WM_COMMAND message.

```
void CDiagramEngDoc::OnSimStop()
{
    // TODO: Add your command handler code here

    // DiagramEng (start)
    HWND hWnd = NULL;               // handle to window whose window
      procedure is to receive the msg.
    LPARAM lParam = NULL;           // windows procedure based parameter
      with msg. specific info.
    UINT msg = WM_COMMAND;          // message
    WPARAM wParam = MAKEWPARAM(ID_SIM_STOP, BN_CLICKED); // make the para
      using ID and BN_CLICKED event

    //AfxMessageBox("\n CDiagramEngDoc::OnSimStop()\n", MB_OK, 0);

    // Post a message to be processed in CSystemModel::CheckStopButtonPre
      ssed()
    PostMessage(hWnd, msg, wParam, lParam);

    // DiagramEng (end)
}
```

The `PostMessage()` function places (posts) a message in the message queue associated with the thread that created the specified window and returns without waiting for the thread to process the message [8]. The parameters to the function are the following: (1) a handle to the window whose window procedure is to receive the message (HWND), (2) the message to be posted (UINT),

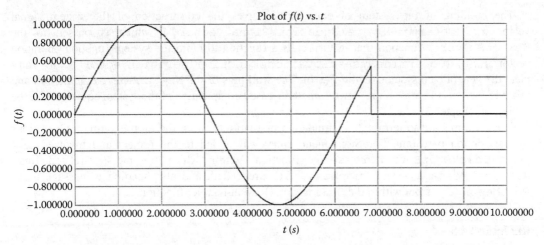

FIGURE 22.6 Simulation involving a Signal Generator block used to generate a sinusoidal signal for a 10 s interval that is prematurely terminated using the Stop button or menu entry.

(3) a window-procedure-based parameter with message-specific information (WPARAM), and (4) a window-procedure-based parameter with message-specific information (LPARAM) (see Refs. [6] and [8] for details). Here, the HWND argument is NULL, which makes the PostMessage() function behave like PostThreadMessage() with the (DWORD) "dwThreadId" parameter set to the identifier of the current thread [6]. The message, "msg", itself is WM_COMMAND. The WPARAM argument "wParam" is made from a combination of two WORD values, the shared ID of the button and menu entry, and BN_CLICKED, using the MAKEWPARAM macro, which concatenates the two values [6]. Finally, the LPARM argument, specifying additional message-based information is NULL.

Now, if the user runs a simulation using SignalPropagationDirect(), and later in the project, SignalPropagationSystemOfEquations(), either the Stop entry of the Simulation menu or the Stop button on the Common Operations toolbar may be used to prematurely terminate a simulation. For example, for a very simple model involving a Signal Generator and an Output block, the simulation may be started and then stopped prematurely: the graphical result shows the sinusoidal nature of the function prior to aborting the simulation, whereafter the function is its initialized zero value (Figure 22.6).

22.9 SUMMARY

The preparation for signal propagation in the context of a feedback loop involves the addition of member methods and variables to extend the existing project structure to be able to form, in general, a nonlinear system of equations, $F(x(t)) = x(t) - f(x(t)) = 0$, where $x(t)$ is the system signal vector, $f(x(t))$ is the system function operation vector, and $F(x(t))$ is the generalized system vector. The root or solution, $x_r(t)$, of this system is the vector of system signals at the current time-step, $t \in [t_0, t_f]$, forming the model output that may be displayed as a graph.

A discussion of linear and nonlinear systems is first made, including their computation using Newton's method. Model assumptions are then introduced and involve all block-generated output-connection-based signals, being column vectors. Preliminary signal propagation is used to generate initial signals for block-output connections by either performing an OperateOnData() operation or a signal data transfer (TransferSignalDataToAnotherConnection()) operation to obviate the need for block execution. Functionality is then added to allow user-defined setting of initial output signals using a Context menu and dialog window.

The building of the system of equations involves the construction of the system signal vector, $x(t)$ (DetermineSystemEquationsSignalVector()), which is passed to the NewtonSolver() function that in turn calls a function to build the system function operation vector, $f(x(t))$ (DetermineSystemEquationsFunctionOperationVector()), to complete the generalized system vector, $F(x(t))$. The workings of the NewtonSolver() method and related functions to perform the Newton-method-based computation of the system equations are the subject of Chapter 23.

Finally, a method to terminate a simulation prematurely using the Stop (Common Operations toolbar) button or (Simulation/Stop) menu entry was added to the project and involved calling a CheckStopButtonPressed() function, within which the message-related functions PeekMessage() and PumpMessage() are called, and also sending a message using PostMessage() from within the OnSimStop() event-handler function.

REFERENCES

1. Ogata, K., *Modern Control Engineering*, 4th edn., Prentice Hall, Upper Saddle River, NJ, 2002.
2. Oppenheim, A. V., Willsky, A. S., and Nawab, S. H., *Signals and Systems*, 2nd edn., Prentice Hall, Upper Saddle River, NJ, 1997.
3. Fisher, M. E., *Introductory Numerical Methods with the NAG Software Library*, The University of Western Australia, Perth, WA, 1989.
4. Nelson, R. C., *Flight Stability and Automatic Control*, 2nd edn., McGraw-Hill, Singapore, 1998.
5. C++ Reference, http://www.cppreference.com/wiki/
6. Microsoft Developer Network Library Visual Studio 6.0, Microsoft® Visual Studio™ 6.0 Development System, Microsoft Corporation, 1998.
7. Press, W. H., Teukolsky, S. A., Vetterling, W. T., and Flannery, B. P., *Numerical Recipes in C: The Art of Scientific Computing*, 2nd edn., Cambridge University Press, Cambridge, U.K., 2002.
8. "CWinThread::PumpMessage()", Microsoft Developer Network Library, http://msdn.microsoft.com/en-US/library/t1tkd768(v=VS.80).aspx, Microsoft Corporation, 2009, (accessed between 2008 and 2010).
9. "Using Messages and Message Queues", Microsoft Developer Network Library, http://msdn.microsoft.com/en-us/library/ms644928(v=VS.85).aspx#examining_queue, Microsoft Corporation, 2009, (accessed between 2008 and 2010).

23 Feedback-Based Signal Propagation

23.1 INTRODUCTION

The previous chapter concerned the addition of code in preparation for signal propagation in a feedback loop using Newton's method. This work is now extended, where all the Newton-method-based code is added, to allow the computation of a system of nonlinear equations of the form

$$F(x(t)) = x(t) - f(x(t)) = \mathbf{0} \tag{23.1}$$

for $t \in [t_0, t_f]$, where t_0 and t_f are the initial and final times of the simulation, respectively, and $x(t)$, $f(x(t))$, and $F(x(t))$ are the system signal vector, system block operational function vector, and generalized system vector, respectively. Newton's method is used to compute the solution vector, or root $x_r(t)$, that satisfies $F(x(t)) = \mathbf{0}$, and this may be decomposed into the component connection-based signals $x_i(t)$, for $i \in [0, s - 1]$, of the block diagram, where s is the total number of block output signals in the model (where there is only one output signal per block).

The main topics discussed herein involve (1) an initial brief exploration of the original Newton-method-based code of Press et al. [1], (2) a C++-oriented transformation of the Newton-method-based code, (3) the addition of the C++-oriented Newton-method-based code into the DiagramEng project to allow the iterative solution of (23.1) to obtain signal values for diagrams involving feedback loops, (4) a discussion of convergence of the Newton method, and (5) testing of the Newton-method-based code, when computing a model diagram involving at least one feedback loop, using six case studies.

23.2 NEWTON-METHOD-BASED SOLVER

A Newton-method-based solver presented by Press et al., in Chapter 9, Root Finding and Nonlinear Sets of Equations, of Refs. [1,2], is used to perform the computation of the (in general) nonlinear system (23.1). Initially the work of Press was transcribed into a Win32 Console Application to test its effectiveness on a small set of both linear and nonlinear, scalar and vector functions, but soon after, a different approach was pursued to improve the readability of the code and make it C++ oriented (see Section 23.3). This initial exploration involved the files: "Newton.cpp/.h" and "nrutil.cpp/.h" (not included here), which contained the Newton-method-specific code and general Numerical Recipes (NR) utility code, respectively. In addition, the functions `ludcmp()` and `lubksb()` of Section 2.3, LU Decomposition and Its Applications, of Press et al. [1,2] were used: the former performs a lower–upper (LU) decomposition of a matrix, and the latter solves a system of linear equations using the LU decomposition performing forward and backward substitution. The function call tree for the initial Win32

667

TABLE 23.1

Function Call Tree of the Newton-Method-Based Win32 Console Application Code Used to Test the Material Presented in Press et al.

Level 1	Level 2	Level 3	Level 4	Level 5	Level 6
main()					
	MyMathProblem()				
		newt()			
			fmin()		
				funcv()	
			fdjac()		
				funcv()	
			ludcmp()		
			lubksb()		
			lnsrch()		
				fmin()	
					funcv()
	PrintVector()				

Source: Press, W.H. et al., *Numerical Recipes in C: The Art of Scientific Computing*, 2nd edn., Cambridge University Press, Cambridge, U.K., 2002.

Console Application is presented in Table 23.1, and the initial function prototypes with brief descriptions of the functions are provided in Table 23.2.

Software developers familiar with the code of Press et al. (see the aforementioned function definitions in Ref. [1]) will notice that two global variables exist: "int nn" denotes the number of system equations and "float *fvec" is used for "communication purposes" between the functions that require values of $F(x)$, in particular, newt(), fmin(), and fdjac(). Steps may be taken to remove the global variables and pass these from one function to another, using extra function arguments. The steps to make the global "nn" variable local are as follows:

1. The global variable "nn" is first removed.
2. The statement "extern int nn" is removed from the "Newton.h" header file.
3. The assignment of "nn = n" is removed from the function newt().
4. The prototype "float fmin(float x[]);" is changed to "float fmin(float x[], int n);".
5. The function "fmin(float x[], int n)" is altered where "nn" is removed and replaced with "n".
6. The call to "fmin(x)" in newt() is changed to "fmin(x, n)".
7. The final argument of the lnsrch() function prototype is changed from "float (*func)(float [])" to "float (*func)(float [], int n)", due to fmin() having been changed.
8. The call to fmin() using "(*func)" in lnsrch() is changed from "*f = (*func)(x);" to "*f = (*func)(x, n);".

However, the global variable "fvec" still remained since the process of making it local would result in too many changes throughout the program making it difficult to read and understand. Hence, a different approach was required: an object-oriented-based transformation was selected, where "fvec" could be made a private member variable of a class (CNewtonMethod) and hence no longer be global.

TABLE 23.2

Original Function Prototypes and Brief Descriptions Used in the Newton-Method-Based Win32 Console Application (the Majority of These Prototypes and Descriptions May Be Found in Press et al.)

Function Prototypes and Descriptions

```
int main(int argc, char **argv);
// Calls MyMathProblem() to initiate the program.

int MyMathProblem(void);
// Sets up the initial vector x(t₀) and calls newt().
```
// Sets up the initial vector $x(t_0)$ and calls newt().

```
void fdjac(int n, float x[], float fvec[], float **df, void (*vecfunc)(int,
 float [], float []));
// Computes the forward finite difference approximation to the Jacobian.

float fmin(float x[]);
```
// Computes $F(x) \cdot F(x)/2$, a sum of squares of the function $F(x)$.

```
void funcv(int n, float x[], float f[]);
```
// Provides the user-supplied definition of the function $F(x)$.

```
void lnsrch(int n, float xold[], float fold, float g[], float p[], float x[],
 float *f, float stpmax, int *check, float (*func)(float []));
// A line search mechanism that finds a new point along a direction away from
 an old point for a sufficient decrease in the function "func".

void lubksb(float **a, int n, int *indx, float b[]);
// Solves a system of linear equations using the LU decomposition of a matrix
 performing forward and backward substitution.

void ludcmp(float **a, int n, int *indx, float *d);
// Performs a LU decomposition of a matrix.

void newt(float x[], int n, int *check, void(*vecfunc)(int, float[],
 float[]));
```
// Computes a root x, to a function $F(x) = \mathbf{0}$.

```
int PrintVector(float *v, int ncols);
// Prints a vector of floating point numbers.
```

Source: Press, W.H. et al., *Numerical Recipes in C: The Art of Scientific Computing*, 2nd edn., Cambridge University Press, Cambridge, U.K., 2002.

23.3 OBJECT-ORIENTED TRANSFORMATION OF THE NEWTON-METHOD-BASED SOLVER

A class-based approach was taken to remove the aforementioned global variable "fvec" and to transform the Newton-method-based code to be object oriented in preparation for its inclusion in the DiagramEng project. Function pointers that were used in the structured programming approach were removed and explicit function names used, as indicated in the code presented later, since their names are known prior to runtime (this makes reading the code somewhat easier). Memory allocation and deallocation, using the operators *new* and *delete*, and array indexing from "0" to "$n - 1$", rather than from "1" to "n", has been used throughout to conform to typical C/C++ programming style. In addition, the defined (#define) constants in the original code were replaced with constant integers and doubles where appropriate, and floating point arguments were changed to double type arguments throughout (this does improve the accuracy of the code and makes it less problematic to use).

Finally, the use of the system-provided `assert()` function, requiring the inclusion of the header file, "assert.h", was made in various locations to check that denominators are not equal to zero, thereby avoiding a possible divide-by-zero error. An additional manual version of this is also used to allow assertions in both the Debug and Release versions of the executable code.

23.3.1   HEADER FILE USED IN THE OBJECT-ORIENTED APPROACH

As a result of this transformation, the only header file used in the new object-oriented approach to the Newton-method-based problem is "Newton.h" and declares the CNewtonMethod class member functions and variables used. The only macros and functions required from the original "nrutil.h" file of Press et al. [1] are `FMAX()`, `SQR()`, and `nrerror()`, and these have been transferred to the "Newton.h" file; the rest of the utility functions are not used, and, hence, "nrutil.h" is no longer required. The developer will notice that functions that used to take function pointers as arguments have new prototypes with these arguments removed for convenience. The "Newton.h" header file with defined variables, the CNewtonMethod class, and additional functions, used in the revised object-oriented form of the Win32 Console Application, named NewtonSolver, is shown in the following.

```
// Newton.h

#ifndef NEWTON_H
    #define NEWTON_H

    // Defined Constructs
    #define AssertManual(expr) do{ if(!(expr)) {PrintAssertMsg
      (__FILE__, __LINE__); __asm{int 3}; } }while(0)

    // Constant Values
    const int PROBLEM_TYPE = 4;    // type of problem: 0, 1, 2, 3, 4

    // Constant Values Replacing Defined Vars in Numerical Recipes
    const int MAXITS = 200;        // max no. of iterations used in newt()
    const double ALF = 1.0e-4;     // used to ensure suff. decr in fn
      value, used in lnsrch()
    const double EPS = 1.0e-4;     // epsilon
    const double TINY = 1.0e-20;   // small value used in ludcmp()
    const double TOLF = 1.0e-4;    // sets the cgce criterion on fn vals,
      used in newt()
    const double TOLMIN = 1.0e-6; // sets the criterion for deciding
      whether spurious cgce to a min of fmin has occurred, used in newt()
    const double TOLX = 1.0e-7;    // cgce criterion on delta_x, used in
      lnsrch() and newt()
    const double STPMX = 100.0;    // scaled max step length allowed in
      line searched, used in newt()

    // Merging of nrutil.h code into the Newton.h file
    static double sqrarg;
    #define SQR(a) ((sqrarg = (a)) == 0.0 ? 0.0 : sqrarg*sqrarg)
    static double maxarg1, maxarg2;
    #define FMAX(a,b) (maxarg1 = (a), maxarg2 = (b), (maxarg1) >
      (maxarg2) ? (maxarg1) : (maxarg2))

    // Static vars
    static int prec = 15;

    // Main line fns
    int main(int argc, char **argv);
    int MyMathProblem(void);
```

```
    int AssertManualFn(bool expr, char *file_name, int line);
      // Assert coded manually as a fn.
    void PrintAssertMsg(char *file_name, int line);

    // Classes
    class CNewtonMethod
    {
    public:

        // Constr/Destr
        CNewtonMethod();
        ~CNewtonMethod();

        // Newton Method related fns
        //void fdjac(int n, float x[], float fvec[], float **df, void
          (*vecfunc)(int, float [], float []));
        void fdjac(int n, double *x, double *fvec, double **df);
        double fmin(double *x, int n);
        void funcv(int n, double *x, double *f);
        //void lnsrch(int n, float xold[], float fold, float g[], float
          p[], float x[], float *f, float stpmax, int *check, float
          (*func)(float [], int n));
        void lnsrch(int n, double *xold, double fold, double *g,
          double *p, double *x, double *f, double stpmax, int *check);
        void lubksb(double **a, int n, int *indx, double *b);
        void ludcmp(double **a, int n, int *indx, double *d);
        double** memory_dmatrix(int nrows, int ncols);
        void memory_delete_newt(int *indx, double *g, double *p,
          double *xold, double **fjac, int nrows);
        double* memory_dvector(int n);
        int* memory_ivector(int n);
        //void newt(float x[], int n, int *check, void(*vecfunc)(int,
          float[], float[]));
        void newt(double *x, int n, int *check);
        //void (CNewtonMethod::*nrfuncv)(int n, float v[], float f[]);
        void nrerror(char *error_text);

        // Printing fn
        int PrintVector(double *v, int ncols);

    private:
        double *fvec;
    };

#endif
```

The header file involves "const int" and "const double" statements, global functions, and the CNewtonMethod class declaration. The constant integer "PROBLEM_TYPE" denotes the type of problem being investigated (explained later). The constants "MAXITS" to "STPMAX" are used by newt()-related code, so too are the macros FMAX() and SQR(). The CNewtonMethod class involves the Newton-method-based code of Press et al. [1], i.e., fdjac(), fmin(), funcv(), lnsrch(), lubksb(), ludcmp(), and newt() (originally presented in Table 23.2). The function nrerror() is an error-handling method for newt()-related code. The memory management functions, memory_dmatrix(), memory_dvector(), and memory_ivector(), allocate memory for a double matrix, a double vector, and an integer vector, respectively, and memory_delete_newt() deallocates memory for newt()-related data structures. The developer will see in the "Newton.cpp" code later that the memory_delete_newt() function deletes not only the variables passed as arguments but also the class member variable, "fvec".

Finally, manually coded versions of assert() are provided in two forms: (1) as a function, AssertManualFn() and (2) as a macro, AssertManual(), where both of these functions call PrintAssertMsg() to print a message to the user via the screen and a log file. The assertion macro and function were provided by Jesse Pepper of Think Bottom Up [3].

23.3.2 SOURCE FILE USED IN THE OBJECT-ORIENTED APPROACH

The "Newton.cpp" source file containing definitions of all the aforementioned declared functions is provided in the following. The developer can create an experimental Win32 Console Application, titled, e.g., NewtonSolver, and add the header file, "Newton.h" and the source file, "Newton.cpp", to this project and run the five test cases using the (identifier-like) constant integer, "PROBLEM_TYPE" (with value "0" to "4"), in the "Newton.h" header file: a discussion of these cases is presented in the next section.

```
// Title:    Newton.cpp
// Purpose:  Performs computation of the system of nonlinear equations,
   F(x) = x - f(x) = 0.
//           That is, the solution, or root, or zero vector x that
   satisfies F(x) = 0, is returned.
// Source:   Numerical Recipes in C: The Art of Scientific Computing
   (2nd Ed.), sections 9.7, p. 383-389.
// Source:   Numerical Recipes in C++: The Art of Scientific Computing
   (2nd Ed.), sections 2.3 and 9.7.
// Refs.     See "Introductory Numerical Methods with the NAG Software
   Library" by Fisher. In particular
//           Chapter 4, Nonlinear Equations, p. 67-78.
//
//       FN CALL TREE:
//
//       main()
//           MyMathProblem()
//               newt()
//                   fmin()
//                       funcv()
//                   fdjac()
//                       funcv()
//                   ludcmp()
//                   lubksb()
//                   lnsrch()
//                       fmin()
//                           funcv()
//               PrintVector()

// Include files
#include <stdio.h>
#include <stdlib.h>
#include <iostream>
#include <iomanip>
#include <math.h>
#include "Newton.h"
#include "assert.h"     // used to make assertions
using namespace std;

// -- MAIN LINE FNS

int main(int argc, char **argv)
```

```
{
    cout << "\n main()\n";

    MyMathProblem();

    cout << endl;
    return 0;
}

// Driver function of the newt() method
int MyMathProblem()
{
    int n;
    int check;
    int problem_type = PROBLEM_TYPE;
    int valid = 1;
    double *x_vec = NULL;
    CNewtonMethod ProbObj;

    cout << "\n MyMathProblem()\n";

    // Init
    switch(problem_type)
    {
    case 0:
        n = 1;                      // size of system
        x_vec = new double[n];      // memory alloc
        // x_vec init
        x_vec[0] = 2;               // initial guess
        break;
    case 1:
        n = 2;                      // size of system
        x_vec = new double[n];      // memory alloc
        // x_vec init
        x_vec[0] = 5;               // initial guess
        x_vec[1] = 5;               // initial guess
        break;
    case 2:
        n = 4;                      // size of system
        x_vec = new double[n];      // memory alloc
        // x_vec init
        x_vec[0] = 5;               // initial guess
        x_vec[1] = 6;               // initial guess
        x_vec[2] = 7;               // initial guess
        x_vec[3] = 8;               // initial guess
        break;
    case 3:
        n = 2;                      // size of system
        x_vec = new double[n];      // memory alloc
        // x_vec init
        x_vec[0] = 10;              // initial guess
        x_vec[1] = 11;              // initial guess
        break;
    case 4:
        n = 2;                      // size of system
        x_vec = new double[n];      // memory alloc
        // x_vec init
        x_vec[0] = 1;               // initial guess
```

```
        x_vec[1] = 1;              // initial guess
        break;
    default:
        cout << "\n MyMathProblem(), incorrect problem_type value.\n";
        valid = 0;
        break;
    }

    if(valid != 0)
    {
        // Newton's Method to determine x that satisfied F(x) = 0.
        //ProbObj.newt(x_vec, n, &check, funcv);
        ProbObj.newt(x_vec, n, &check);

        cout << "\n MyMathProblem(), x_vec: \n";
        ProbObj.PrintVector(x_vec,n);
    }

    // FREE MEMORY
    if(x_vec != NULL)
    {
        delete [] x_vec;
        x_vec = NULL;
    }

    return valid;
}
// Assert coded manually as a fn.
int AssertManualFn(bool expr, char *file_name, int line)
{
    // Check truth of expr.
    if(!(expr))
    {
        // Print a msg to user
        PrintAssertMsg(file_name, line);

        // Native code generation for the fn.
        __asm{int 3};
    }

    return 0;
}
void PrintAssertMsg(char *file_name, int line)
{
    FILE *ofp = NULL;      // outfile pointer

    // Print msg. to user
    printf("\n PrintAssertMsg()\n Assertion failed:\n File = %s\n Line =
      %d.\n", file_name, line);

    // Open file for writing
    ofp = fopen("assert_log.txt", "w");

    // Warn if file could not be opened
    if(ofp == NULL)
    {
        cerr << "PrintAssertMsg(): WARNING! 'assert_log.txt' file could
          not be opened\n";
        cout << "\a";           // sound the alarm
    }
```

```
    else
    {
        fprintf(ofp, "Assertion failed, in file = %s, on line = %d.\n",
          file_name, line);  // write msg. to file
        fclose(ofp);              // close file
    }
}

// -- NEWTON METHOD FNS

// Constructor
CNewtonMethod::CNewtonMethod()
{
    cout << "\n CNewtonMethod()::CNewtonMethod()\n";

    // Init. class member pointer-to-double fvec
    fvec = NULL;
}

// Destructor
CNewtonMethod::~CNewtonMethod()
{
    cout << "\n CNewtonMethod::~CNewtonMethod()\n";

    // Delete pointer-to-double fvec if not already deleted in
      memory_delete_newt().
    if(fvec != NULL)
    {
        delete [] fvec;
        fvec = NULL;
    }
}

// User-defined function specifying mathematical function F(x) desired to
  be equal to zero and for which x is to be computed.
void CNewtonMethod::funcv(int n, double *x, double *f)
{
    int problem_type = PROBLEM_TYPE;
    // Init
    switch(problem_type)
    {
    case 0:               // scalar fn of a scalar var (nonlinear)
        f[0] = x[0]*x[0] - 1;
        break;
    case 1:               // vector fn of a vector var (linear
      and nonlinear)
        f[0] = x[0] + 2;
        f[1] = x[1]*x[1] - 1;
        break;
    case 2:               // vector fn of a vector var (linear)
        f[0] = x[0] - 1;
        f[1] = x[1] - x[0] - x[3];
        f[2] = x[2] - 2*x[1];
        f[3] = x[3] - 3*x[2];
        break;
    case 3:               // vector fn of a vector var (nonlinear)
        f[0] = x[0]*x[0] + x[1]*x[1] - 20;  // satisfied by x0 = 2,
          x1 = 4
```

```
        f[1] = 2*x[0]*x[1] - 16;                // satisfied by x0 = 2,
          x1 = 4
        break;
    case 4:                          // vector fn of a vector var (nonlinear)
        f[0] = x[0]*cos(x[1]) + 1;  // satisfied (approximately) by x0 =
          2.156, x1 = 4.230
        f[1] = (exp(x[0] - 2))*sin(x[1]*0.5) - 1;
          // satisfied (approximately) by x0 = 2.156, x1 = 4.230
        break;

    default:
        cout << "\n CNewtonMethod::funcv(), incorrect problem_type
          value.\n";
        break;
    }
}

// Newton Method: Numerical Recipes in C: Section 9.7
//void CNewtonMethod::newt(float x[], int n, int *check, void(*vecfunc)
  (int, float[], float[]))
void CNewtonMethod::newt(double *x, int n, int *check)
{
    int i;
    int its;
    int j;
    int *indx = NULL;
    double d;
    double den;
    double f;
    double fold;
    double stpmax;
    double sum;
    double temp;
    double test;
    double **fjac = NULL;
    double *g = NULL;
    double *p = NULL;
    double *xold = NULL;

    // MEMORY ALLOC
    indx = memory_ivector(n);
    g = memory_dvector(n);
    p = memory_dvector(n);
    xold = memory_dvector(n);
    fvec = memory_dvector(n);   // global var used (globally) in newt()
      and fmin(), and passed as an arg to fdjac() and funcv().
    fjac = memory_dmatrix(n,n);

    // define global variable
// nrfuncv = vecfunc;

    f = fmin(x, n);   // fvec is also computed by this call

    test = 0.0;       // test fo initial guess being a root. Use a more
      stringent test than simply TOLF.

    for(i=0; i<n; i++)
    {
        if(fabs(fvec[i]) > test)
```

```
          {
              test = fabs(fvec[i]);
          }
      }

      if(test < 0.01*TOLF)
      {
          *check = 0;
          memory_delete_newt(indx, g, p, xold, fjac, n);
          return;
      }

      for(sum=0.0, i=0; i<n; i++)
      {
          sum += SQR(x[i]);                // calculate stpmax for line searches
      }
      stpmax = STPMX*FMAX(sqrt(sum), (double)n);

      // Start of iteration loop
      for(its = 0; its < MAXITS; its++)
      {
//        fdjac(n, x, fvec, fjac, vecfunc);
          fdjac(n, x, fvec, fjac);

          for(i=0; i<n; i++)
          {
              for(sum=0.0, j=0; j<n; j++)
              {
                  sum += fjac[j][i]*fvec[j];
              }
              g[i] = sum;
          }

          for(i=0; i<n; i++)
          {
              xold[i] = x[i];          // store x
          }
          fold = f;  // store f

          for(i=0; i<n; i++)
          {
              p[i] = -fvec[i];         // rhs for linear equs
          }

          ludcmp(fjac, n, indx, &d);   // solve linear equs by LU decomp
          lubksb(fjac, n, indx, p);

          // lnsrch returns new x and f. It also calculates fvec at the new
          //  x when it calls fmin.
//        lnsrch(n, xold, fold, g, p, x, &f, stpmax, check, fmin);
          lnsrch(n, xold, fold, g, p, x, &f, stpmax, check);

          test = 0.0;                  // test for cgce on fn vals

          for(i=0; i<n; i++)
          {
              if(fabs(fvec[i]) > test)
              {
                  test = fabs(fvec[i]);
              }
          }
```

```
        if(test < TOLF)
        {
            *check = 0;
            memory_delete_newt(indx, g, p, xold, fjac, n);
            return;
        }

        // Check for gradient of f zero, i.e. spurious cgce.
        if(*check)
        {
            test = 0.0;
            den = FMAX(f, 0.5*n);
            for(i=0; i<n; i++)
            {
                temp = fabs(g[i])*FMAX(fabs(x[i]), 1.0)/den;
                if(temp > test)
                {
                    test = temp;
                }
            }
            *check = (test < TOLMIN ? 1 : 0);
            memory_delete_newt(indx, g, p, xold, fjac, n);
            return;
        }

        // Test for cgce on delta x
        test = 0.0;
        for(i=0; i<n; i++)
        {
            temp = (fabs(x[i] - xold[i]))/FMAX(fabs(x[i]), 1.0);
            if(temp > test)
            {
                test = temp;
            }
        }

        if(test < TOLX)
        {
            memory_delete_newt(indx, g, p, xold, fjac, n);
            return;
        }

    }// end "for its"

    nrerror("MAXITS exceeded in newt");
}

// Function Min: Numerical Recipes in C: Section 9.7
double CNewtonMethod::fmin(double *x, int n)
{
    int i;
    double sum;

// (CNewtonMethod::*nrfuncv)(n, x, fvec);
    funcv(n, x, fvec);

    for(sum = 0.0, i=0; i<n; i++)
    {
        sum += SQR(fvec[i]);
    }
```

```
        return 0.5*sum;
}

// Finite Difference Jacobian Method: Numerical Recipes in C: Section 9.7
//void CNewtonMethod::fdjac(int n, float x[], float fvec[], float **df,
  void (*vecfunc)(int, float [], float []))
void CNewtonMethod::fdjac(int n, double *x, double *fvec, double **df)
{
    int i;
    int j;
    double h;
    double temp;
    double *f = NULL;

    // MEMORY ALLOC
    f = memory_dvector(n);

    for(j=0; j<n; j++)
    {
        temp = x[j];
        h = EPS*fabs(temp);

        if(h == 0.0)
        {
            h = EPS;            // original NR code
            // h = (double)EPS; // BF altered
        }

        x[j] = temp + h;        // trick to reduce finite precision error
        h = x[j] - temp;

//      (*vecfunc)(n,x,f);
        funcv(n, x, f);

        x[j] = temp;

        for(i=0; i<n; i++)
        {
            df[i][j] = (f[i] - fvec[i])/h;  // forward difference formula
        }
    }// end for j

    // FREE MEMORY
    if(f != NULL)
    {
        delete [] f;
        f = NULL;
    }
}

// Line Search Method: Numerical Recipes in C: Section 9.7
//void CNewtonMethod::lnsrch(int n, float xold[], float fold, float g[],
  float p[], float x[], float *f, float stpmax, int *check, float (*func)
  (float [], int n))
void CNewtonMethod::lnsrch(int n, double *xold, double fold, double *g,
  double *p, double *x, double *f, double stpmax, int *check)
{
    int i;
    double a;
    double alam;
```

```
double alam2;
double alamin;
double b;
double disc;
double f2;
double rhs1;
double rhs2;
double slope;
double sum;
double temp;
double test;
double tmplam;

*check = 0;
for(sum=0.0, i=0; i<n; i++)
{
    sum += p[i]*p[i];
}

// Scale if attempted step is too big.
sum = sqrt(sum);
if(sum > stpmax)
{
    for(i=0; i<n; i++)
    {
        p[i] *= stpmax/sum;
    }
}

for(slope = 0.0, i=0; i<n; i++)
{
    slope += g[i]*p[i];
}

if(slope >= 0.0)
{
    nrerror("Roundoff problem in lnsrch().");
}

// Compute lambda min.
test = 0.0;
for(i=0; i<n; i++)
{
    temp = fabs(p[i])/FMAX(fabs(xold[i]), 1.0);

    if(temp > test)
    {
        test = temp;
    }
}

// Always try full Newton step first
// Assertion (BF altered)
assert(test != 0.0);
alamin = TOLX/test;
alam = 1.0;

// Start of iteration loop
for(;;)
```

```
        {
            for(i=0; i<n; i++)
            {
                x[i] = xold[i] + alam*p[i];
            }
//          *f = (*func)(x, n);
            *f = fmin(x, n);

            // Convergence on delta_x. For zero finding, the calling program
              should verify cgce.
            if(alam < alamin)
            {
                for(i=0; i<n; i++)
                {
                    x[i] = xold[i];
                }
                *check = 1;
                return;
            }
            else if(*f <= fold + ALF*alam*slope)    // Sufficient fn decrease.
            {
                return;
            }
            else  // Backtrack.
            {
                if(alam == 1.0)
                {
                    // Assertion (BF altered)
                    assert((*f - fold - slope) != 0.0);
                    tmplam = -slope/(2.0*(*f - fold - slope));
                }
                else
                {
                    // Assertion (BF altered)
                    assert(alam != 0.0);
                    assert(alam2 != 0.0);
                    assert((alam - alam2) != 0.0);

                    rhs1 = *f - fold - alam*slope;
                    rhs2 = f2 - fold - alam2*slope;
                    a = (rhs1/(alam*alam) - rhs2/(alam2*alam2))/
                      (alam - alam2);
                    b = (-alam2*rhs1/(alam*alam) + alam*rhs2/(alam2*alam2))/
                      (alam - alam2);
                    if(a == 0.0)
                    {
                        // Assertion (BF altered)
                        assert(b != 0.0);
                        tmplam = -slope/(2.0*b);
                    }
                    else
                    {
                        disc = b*b - 3.0*a*slope;
                        if(disc < 0.0)
                        {
                            tmplam = 0.5*alam;
                        }
```

```
                    else if(b <= 0.0)
                    {
                        // Assertion (BF altered)
                        assert(a != 0.0);
                        tmplam = (-b + sqrt(disc))/(3.0*a);
                    }
                    else
                    {
                        // Assertion (BF altered)
                        assert((b + sqrt(disc)) != 0.0);
                        tmplam = -slope/(b + sqrt(disc));
                    }
                }// end else

                if(tmplam > 0.5*alam)
                {
                    tmplam = 0.5*alam;  // lambda <= 0.5*lambda_1
                }

            }// end else

        }// end else

        alam2 = alam;
        f2 = *f;
        alam = FMAX(tmplam, 0.1*alam);  // lambda >= 0.1*lambda_1

    }// end for
}

// Lower Upper Decomposition with Back Substitution: Numerical Recipes
  in C: Section 2.3
void CNewtonMethod::lubksb(double **a, int n, int *indx, double *b)
{
    int i;
    int ii = 0;
    int ip;
    int j;
    double sum;

    for(i=0; i<n; i++)
    {
        ip = indx[i];
        sum = b[ip];
        b[ip] = b[i];

        if(ii != 0)
        {
            for(j=ii-1; j<i; j++)
            {
                sum -= a[i][j]*b[j];
            }
        }
        else if(sum != 0.0)
        {
            ii = i + 1;
        }
        b[i] = sum;
    }
```

```
    for(i=n-1; i>=0; i-)
    {
        sum = b[i];
        for(j=i+1; j<n; j++)
        {
            sum -= a[i][j]*b[j];
        }

        // Assertion (BF altered)
        assert(a[i][i] != 0.0);
        b[i] = sum/a[i][i];
    }
}

// Lower Upper Decomposition: Numerical Recipes in C: Section 2.3
void CNewtonMethod::ludcmp(double **a, int n, int *indx, double *d)
{
    int i;
    int imax;
    int j;
    int k;
    double big;
    double dum;
    double sum;
    double temp;
    double *vv = NULL;

    // Memory alloc
    vv = memory_dvector(n);

    *d = 1.0;
    for(i=0; i<n; i++)
    {
        big = 0.0;
        for(j=0; j<n; j++)
        {
            if((temp = fabs(a[i][j])) > big)
            {
                big = temp;
            }
        }
        if(big == 0.0)
        {
            nrerror("Singular matrix in routine ludcmp");
        }
        vv[i] = 1.0/big;
    }// end for i

    for(j=0; j<n; j++)
    {
        for(i=0; i<j; i++)
        {
            sum = a[i][j];
            for(k=0; k<i; k++)
            {
                sum -= a[i][k]*a[k][j];
            }
            a[i][j] = sum;
        }
```

```
        big = 0.0;
        for(i=j; i<n; i++)
        {
            sum = a[i][j];
            for(k=0; k<j; k++)
            {
                sum -= a[i][k]*a[k][j];
            }
            a[i][j] = sum;
            if((dum = vv[i]*fabs(sum)) >= big)
            {
                big = dum;
                imax = i;
            }
        }

        if(j != imax)
        {
            for(k=0; k<n; k++)
            {
                dum = a[imax][k];
                a[imax][k] = a[j][k];
                a[j][k] = dum;
            }
            *d = - (*d);
            vv[imax] = vv[j];
        }
        indx[j] = imax;

        if(a[j][j] == 0.0)
        {
            a[j][j] = TINY;             // original NR code
            //a[j][j] = (double)TINY;   // BF altered.
        }

        if(j != (n-1))
        {
            dum = 1.0/(a[j][j]);
            for(i=j+1; i<n; i++)
            {
                a[i][j] *= dum;
            }
        }
    }// end for j

    // Memory delete
    if(vv != NULL)
    {
        delete [] vv;
        vv = NULL;
    }
}

int CNewtonMethod::PrintVector(double *v, int ncols)
{
    cout << "CNewtonMethod::PrintVector()\n";

    int i;
```

```
    // Print Vector

    cout << endl;
    for(i=0; i<ncols; i++)
    {
        cout << "" << setprecision(prec) << v[i];
    }
    cout << "n\n";

    return 0;
}

double* CNewtonMethod::memory_dvector(int n)
{
    double *v = NULL;

    // Memory Alloc
    v = new double[n];

    // Check memory
    if(!v)
    {
        nrerror("memory_dvector(), memory allocation failure.");
    }

    return v;
}

int* CNewtonMethod::memory_ivector(int n)
{
    int *v = NULL;

    // Memory Alloc
    v = new int[n];

    // Check memory
    if(!v)
    {
        nrerror("int_vector(), memory allocation failure.");
    }

    return v;
}

double** CNewtonMethod::memory_dmatrix(int nrows, int ncols)
{
    int i;
    double **m = NULL;

    // Memory alloc of primary array
    // Allocate an array of ptrs-to-double and return the & to m
    // Note: an array is of type ptr, hence an array of ptrs is of type
    //   ptr-ptr.
    m = new double *[nrows];

    // Check new
    if(!m)
    {
        nrerror("memory_dmatrix(), memory allocation failure
            (array 1).");
    }
```

```
    // Memory alloc of secondary arrays
    // Allocate an array of doubles for each of the entries (rows of the
      column vector) of matrix, and return the & to m[i].
    // Note: an array is of type ptr, and its & is stored at location i
      in the array m[]
    for(i=0;i<nrows;i++)
    {
        m[i] = new double[ncols];  // allocate an array of doubles,
          return & to m[i]

        // Check new
        if(!m[i])
        {
            nrerror("memory_dmatrix(), memory allocation failure
              (array 2).");
        }
    }

    return m;
}

void CNewtonMethod::memory_delete_newt(int *indx, double *g, double *p,
  double *xold, double **fjac, int nrows)
{
    int i;

    // Memory Delete Vectors
    if(indx != NULL)
    {
        delete [] indx;
        indx = NULL;
    }
    if(g != NULL)
    {
        delete [] g;
        g = NULL;
    }
    if(p != NULL)
    {
        delete [] p;
        p = NULL;
    }
    if(xold != NULL)
    {
        delete [] xold;
        xold = NULL;
    }

    // WARNING! fvec is a class member variable: if it is declared
      locally in the fn header and fvec passed into the
    // memory_delete_newt() fn from the newt() calling environment, then
      the assignment fvec = NULL would not be
    // persistent outside of this fn as it would be a local statement.
    // Hence, fvec should not be passed into memory_delete_newt(), but
      rather simply deleted and reassigned to NULL
    // as it is a class member variable and memory_delete_newt() has
      access to it as a member fn.
    if(fvec != NULL)
```

```
    {
        delete [] fvec;
        fvec = NULL;
    }

    // Memory Delete Matrix
    if(fjac != NULL)
    {
        for(i=0; i<nrows; i++)
        {
            delete [] fjac[i];
        }
        delete [] fjac;
        fjac = NULL;
    }

    return;
}

void CNewtonMethod::nrerror(char *error_text)
{
    /* Numerical Recipes standard error handler */
    fprintf(stderr, "Numerical Recipes run-time error. …\n");
    fprintf(stderr, "%s\n", error_text);
    fprintf(stderr, "Now exiting to system. …\n");
    exit(1);
}
```

The developer will notice in the memory_delete_newt() function mentioned earlier that if the class member variable, "fvec", were to be passed into the function from the newt() calling environment, then it would assume a local declaration in the function header, and the assignment "fvec = NULL" would not be persistent outside the function in the class scope! The memory would be deleted, but the NULL assignment would not hold, and this would cause potential problems if the memory were attempted to be deleted more than once, e.g., in the CNewtonMethod class destructor! Hence, "fvec" should not be passed into memory_delete_newt(), but rather simply be deleted and reassigned to NULL: it is a class member variable and memory_delete_newt() has access to it as a member function.

23.3.3   Test Case Problems Computed Using Newton's Method

The reader will notice corresponding *switch* statements in the MyMathProblem() and CNewtonMethod::funcv() functions provided in the "Newton.cpp" file mentioned earlier that define the initial vector x and corresponding function $F(x)$, respectively, of the following five experimental cases.

23.3.3.1   Case 1
The first simple case (PROBLEM_TYPE = 0) is

$$F(x) = x^2 - 1 \tag{23.2}$$

and a solution or root, x_r, is desired to the equation $F(x) = \mathbf{0}$. Depending on an initial guess for x_0, two different solutions are possible: for $x_0 < 0$, $x_r = -1$ and for $x_0 > 0$, $x_r = 1$. The developer should be aware that when the vector "x" was of type float, at exactly $x_0 = 0$, the solver had difficulty in determining a solution and reported the detection of a singular matrix in the routine ludcmp() and terminated execution. However, after changing the type of "x" to double, for the initial guess $x_0 = 0$, the solution $x_r = 1$ was found.

23.3.3.2 Case 2

The second case (PROBLEM_TYPE = 1) involves the vector function of a vector variable

$$F(x) = \begin{bmatrix} F_0(x) \\ F_1(x) \end{bmatrix} = \begin{bmatrix} x_0 + 2 \\ x_1^2 - 1 \end{bmatrix} \tag{23.3}$$

The solution, x_r, to the equation $F(x) = \underline{0}$, differs for different initial values x_0, e.g., for $x_0 = [5, 5]^T$, $x_r = [-2, 1]^T$, and for $x_0 = [-5, -5]^T$, $x_r = [-2, -1]^T$.

23.3.3.3 Case 3

The third case (PROBLEM_TYPE = 2) involves the linear function represented by Equations 22.1 through 22.7 and Figure 22.1, i.e.,

$$F(x) = \begin{bmatrix} F_0(x) \\ F_1(x) \\ F_2(x) \\ F_3(x) \end{bmatrix} = \begin{bmatrix} x_0 - f_0 \\ x_1 - x_0 - x_3 \\ x_2 - k_2 x_1 \\ x_3 - k_3 x_2 \end{bmatrix} = \begin{bmatrix} x_0 - 1 \\ x_1 - x_0 - x_3 \\ x_2 - 2x_1 \\ x_3 - 3x_2 \end{bmatrix} \tag{23.4}$$

The reader will notice that a constant function $f_0 = 1$ and gain constants $k_2 = 2$ and $k_3 = 3$ are used. The solution or root of the equation $F(x) = \underline{0}$ is $x_r = [1, -0.2, -0.4, -1.2]^T$.

23.3.3.4 Case 4

The fourth case (PROBLEM_TYPE = 3) involves the nonlinear vector function

$$F(x) = \begin{bmatrix} F_0(x) \\ F_1(x) \end{bmatrix} = \begin{bmatrix} x_0^2 + x_1^2 - 20 \\ 2x_0 x_1 - 16 \end{bmatrix} \tag{23.5}$$

The solution to the equation $F(x) = \underline{0}$, for choices of x_0 in a (sufficiently large) neighborhood of the solution, is $x_r = [2, 4]^T$.

23.3.3.5 Case 5

The fifth case (PROBLEM_TYPE = 4) involves the nonlinear vector function provided by Fisher [4] (p. 77), i.e.,

$$F(x) = \begin{bmatrix} F_0(x) \\ F_1(x) \end{bmatrix} = \begin{bmatrix} x_0\cos(x_1 + 1) \\ e^{x_0 - 2}\sin(x_1 / 2) - 1 \end{bmatrix} \tag{23.6}$$

where the solution to the equation $F(x) = \underline{0}$ is, to three decimal places, $x_r = [2.156, 4.230]^T$.

23.4 ADDING THE NEWTON-METHOD-BASED SOLVER TO THE DiagramEng PROJECT

Now the object-oriented Newton-method-based code presented in the previous section needs to be added to the DiagramEng project, such that when feedback loops are detected in the model, the SignalPropagationSystemOfEquations() function is called and the NewtonSolver() function is then invoked to compute the system represented by (23.1), for each time-step of the simulation. The general steps involved to augment the DiagramEng project with the Newton-method-centric code are as listed, while specific details are provided in the sections that follow:

1. Addition of details to complete the NewtonSolver() function
2. Addition of the CNewtonMethod class with member declarations
3. Addition of the CNewtonMethod class member function definitions
4. Changes to be made to resolve exiting the program prematurely
5. Addition of the manual assertion functions to the project

23.4.1 Addition of Details to Complete the NewtonSolver() Function

Chapter 22 introduced the placeholder function CSystemModel::NewtonSolver() to be completed once the Newton-method-based code of Press et al. [1,2] was shown to work in an object-oriented manner as mentioned earlier.

1. The NewtonSolver() function may now be completed as shown in the following, to instantiate a CNewtonMethod object, upon which the function newt() is called to invoke the globally convergent Newton-method-based computational procedure.
2. Include the soon-to-be-added (see the following) "NewtonMethod.h" header file at the top of the "SystemModel.cpp" source file, i.e., add, #include "NewtonMethod.h", since the NewtonSolver() function instantiates a CNewtonMethod object.

```
int CSystemModel::NewtonSolver(int nrows, double *x_vec, int t_cnt,
  double t, double delta_t)
{
    int i;
    int check;
    int valid = 1;
    double *x = NULL;
    CNewtonMethod probObj(t_cnt, t, delta_t);  // a problem object upon
      which newt() is called

    // MEMORY ALLOC
    x = new double[nrows];
    if(!x)
    {
        valid = 0;
        return valid;
    }

    // Prepare x for newt() using x_vec
    for(i=0; i<nrows; i++)
    {
        x[i] = x_vec[i];
    }

    // Check input to newt()
    //probObj.PrintVector(x_vec, nrows);

    // CALL newt() TO OBTAIN THE VECTOR x THAT SATISFIES F(x) = x - f(x)
      (= 0).
    valid = probObj.newt(x, nrows, &check);

    if(valid != 1)   // if valid != 1 then newt() is in error
    {
        valid = 0;
        //probObj.PrintVector(x, nrows);
    }
```

```
// Prepare the solution vector x_vec from the vector x returned by
   newt() if newt() not in error.
if(valid == 1)
{
    for(i=0; i<nrows; i++)
    {
        x_vec[i] = x[i];
    }
}

// Check output from newt()
// probObj.PrintVector(x_vec, nrows);   // print the vector x_vec of
   type double

// MEMORY DELETE
if(x != NULL)
{
    delete [] x;
    x = NULL;
}

    return valid;
}
```

The call to newt() is made to obtain the vector $x(t)$, i.e., the root $x_r(t)$ that satisfies (23.1). Initially a CNewtonMethod object, "probObj", is instantiated, passing the time-based arguments, "t_cnt", "t", and "delta_t", as parameters: this is done since newt() indirectly calls funcv(), in which the generalized system function vector $F(x(t)) = x(t) - f(x(t))$ is formed, and this is composed of the block operational function vector $f(x(t))$, which itself is determined by invoking the block OperateOnData(int t, double t, double delta_t) methods, taking the three time-based arguments.

Thereafter memory for a local vector "x" is allocated, and the contents of the system vector, "x_vec", representing $x(t)$ in (23.1), are then written to "x" in preparation for the call to newt(). At $t = t_0$, the incoming vector, $x(t_0)$, is that determined by the function call to DetermineSystemEquationsSignalVector() made in the calling environment: SignalPropagationSystemOfEquations(). After the call to newt(), the solution vector or root $x_r(t)$ of (23.1), represented by "x", is written to $x(t)$, i.e., "x_vec", and this is then passed back to the calling environment (through the parameter list) and assigned to the component signal vectors using AssignSystemEquationsSignalVector() (within SignalPropagationSystemOfEquations()).

An aside: the developer should be aware that the vector "x" and the size of the system of equations, "nrows", are passed to newt(), wherein vectors have memory allocated from offset "0" to "nrows −1". In the original newt()-based code of Press et al. [1], array indices "1" to "n" are used, but in Ref. [2] and in the object-oriented transformation to C++-like code, array indices "0" to "$n − 1$" are used.

23.4.2 Addition of the CNewtonMethod Class with Member Declarations

The Newton-method-based member methods and variables need to be declared in the CNewtonMethod class. Hence, add a new generic class to the DiagramEng project with the name "CNewtonMethod": this results in a new source and header file, titled "NewtonMethod.cpp" and "NewtonMethod.h", respectively, being added to the project.

1. Edit the header file to have a similar structure to "Newton.h" introduced earlier, to result in the "NewtonMethod.h" header file shown in the following. Note that the manual assertion functions are added to the project later to the "DiagramEngDoc.cpp/.h" files and hence are omitted from the "NewtonMethod.cpp/.h" files.

2. Add three new private member variables to the CNewtonMethod class, as shown in bold in the following, to retain time-based information, i.e., an integer, "m_t_cnt", a double, "m_t" and a double, "m_delta_t". These are used to communicate the time-based parameter values from the CSystemModel-centric code to the CNewtonMethod-centric code (as described earlier).

3. Add a new public constructor function prototype to the CNewtonMethod class, i.e., CNewtonMethod::CNewtonMethod(int t_cnt, double t, double delta_t) taking three time-based arguments, as shown in bold in the following.

4. Add a new public function prototype to the CNewtonMethod class, i.e., int CNewtonMethod::CheckJacobian(double **fjac, int nrows, int ncols), as shown in bold in the following. This diagnostic function will be added to the project toward the end of the section.

```cpp
// NewtonMethod.h: interface for the CNewtonMethod class.
//
//////////////////////////////////////////////////////////////////////

#if !defined(AFX_NEWTONMETHOD_H__DC19AFC4_3263_4690_8914_B7F21D652DBD__
  INCLUDED_)
#define AFX_NEWTONMETHOD_H__DC19AFC4_3263_4690_8914_B7F21D652DBD__
  INCLUDED_

#if _MSC_VER > 1000
#pragma once
#endif // _MSC_VER > 1000

    // Constant Values Replacing Defined Vars in Numerical Recipes
    const int MAXITS = 200;         // max no. of iterations used in newt()
    const double ALF = 1.0e-4;      // used to ensure suff. decr in fn
      value, used in lnsrch()
    const double EPS = 1.0e-4;      // epsilon
    const double TINY = 1.0e-20;    // small value used in ludcmp()
    const double TOLF = 1.0e-4;     // sets the cgce criterion on fn vals,
      used in newt()
    const double TOLMIN = 1.0e-6;   // sets the criterion for deciding
      whether spurious cgce to a min of fmin has occured, used in newt()
    const double TOLX = 1.0e-7;     // cgce criterion on delta_x, used in
      lnsrch() and newt()
    const double STPMX = 100.0;     // scaled max step length allowed in
      line searched, used in newt()

    // Merging of nrutil.h code into the Newton.h file
    static double sqrarg;
    #define SQR(a) ((sqrarg = (a)) == 0.0 ? 0.0 : sqrarg*sqrarg)

    static double maxarg1, maxarg2;
    #define FMAX(a,b) (maxarg1 = (a), maxarg2 = (b), (maxarg1) >
      (maxarg2) ? (maxarg1) : (maxarg2))

    // Static vars
    static int prec = 15;

    // Classes
    class CNewtonMethod
```

```
{
public:
    // Constr/Destr
    CNewtonMethod();
    CNewtonMethod(int t_cnt, double t, double delta_t);
    virtual ~CNewtonMethod();

    // Newton Method related fns
    //void fdjac(int n, float x[], float fvec[], float **df, void
      (*vecfunc)(int, float [], float []));
    void fdjac(int n, double *x, double *fvec, double **df);
    double fmin(double *x, int n);
    void funcv(int n, double *x, double *f);
    //void lnsrch(int n, float xold[], float fold, float g[], float
      p[], float x[], float *f, float stpmax, int *check, float
      (*func)(float [], int n));
    void lnsrch(int n, double *xold, double fold, double *g, double
      *p, double *x, double *f, double stpmax, int *check);
    void lubksb(double **a, int n, int *indx, double *b);
    void ludcmp(double **a, int n, int *indx, double *d);
    double** memory_dmatrix(int nrows, int ncols);
    void memory_delete_newt(int *indx, double *g, double *p, double
      *xold, double **fjac, int nrows);
    double* memory_dvector(int n);
    int* memory_ivector(int n);
    //void newt(float x[], int n, int *check, void(*vecfunc)
      (int, float[], float[]));
    void newt(double *x, int n, int *check);
    //void (CNewtonMethod::*nrfuncv)(int n, float v[], float f[]);
    void nrerror(char *error_text);

    // Checking fns
    int CheckJacobian(double **fjac, int nrows, int ncols);

    // Printing fns
    int PrintVector(double *v, int ncols);

private:
    int m_t_cnt;        // time count
    double m_t;         // time value
    double m_delta_t;   // time step size delta_t
    double *fvec;
};

#endif // !defined(AFX_NEWTONMETHOD_H__DC19AFC4_3263_4690_8914_
  B7F21D652DBD__INCLUDED_)
```

23.4.3   ADDITION OF THE CNewtonMethod CLASS MEMBER FUNCTION DEFINITIONS

The "NewtonMethod.h" header file contains the declarations of the functions of the CNewtonMethod class, some of which are unchanged from the object-oriented implementation (shown earlier), i.e., fdjac(), fmin(), lnsrch(), lubksb(), ludcmp(), newt(), the memory management functions, and the destructor, ~CNewtonMethod(). The function funcv() that provides $F(x(t))$ given $x(t)$ is different, the three-argument construction function is new, and PrintVector() is modified.

1. Add (by copying and pasting) the implementations of the functions `fdjac()`, `fmin()`, `lnsrch()`, `lubksb()`, `ludcmp()`, `newt()`, the memory management functions, and the destructor, as shown earlier in "Newton.cpp" of the Win32 Console Application project, to the "NewtonMethod.cpp" source file of the DiagramEng project.
2. Include the "assert.h" header file at the top of the "NewtonMethod.cpp" source file, since the system-provided `assert()` function is introduced for the `newt()`-related code for diagnostic purposes; the manual implementations of assertions are introduced later.
3. Edit the new construction function as shown in the following to initialize the member variables "m_t_cnt", "m_t", "m_delta_t", and "fvec".

```
CNewtonMethod::CNewtonMethod(int t_cnt, double t, double delta_t)
{
    // Init time-based parameters
    m_t_cnt = t_cnt;
    m_t = t;
    m_delta_t = delta_t;

    // Init the fvec that is "communicated" by the fns within the class.
    fvec = NULL;
}
```

4. The `CNewtonMethod::funcv(int n, double *x, double *f)` function is called directly from `fmin()` and `fdjac()` as indicated by the function call tree shown in Table 23.1. Add the definition of the `CNewtonMethod::funcv()` function as shown in the following to the project, to return $F(x(t))$ given $x(t)$ where the corresponding variables, "f" and "x", are used, respectively.

```
void CNewtonMethod::funcv(int n, double *x, double *f)
{
    int i;
    int valid;
    double *F_vec = NULL;   // vector that receives F(x)
      of F(x) = x - f(x), when working with CSystemModel fns.
    double *f_vec = NULL;   // vector that receives f(x)
      of F(x) = x - f(x), when working with CSystemModel fns.
    double *x_vec = NULL;   // vector that receives x of F(x) = x - f(x),
      when working with CSystemModel fns.
    CString sMsg;           // string to be displayed
    CString sMsgTemp;       // temp msg.
    UINT nType = MB_OK;     // style of msg. box
    UINT nIDhelp = 0;       // help context ID for the msg.
    CDiagramEngDoc *pDoc = GetDocumentGlobalFn();

    // MEMORY ALLOC
    F_vec = memory_dvector(n);   // F_vec = F(x) = x - f(x) in the
      CSystemModel centric code, size = nrows
    f_vec = memory_dvector(n);   // f_vec = f(x), of F(x) = x - f(x),
      in the CSystemModel centric code, size = nrows
    x_vec = memory_dvector(n);   // x_vec = x, of F(x) = x - f(x),
      in the CSystemModel centric code, size = nrows

    // Assign incoming x vector of the CNewtonMethod centric code, to
      x_vec of the CSystemModel centric code.
    for(i=0; i<n; i++)
```

```
{
    x_vec[i] = x[i];
}

// DETERMINE SYSTEM EQUATION VECTOR f_vec (f(x) of CSystemModel
  centric code)
// Retrieve the functional operation values, given the initial output
  signal vector used by the block OperateOnData() fns.
// f_vec = f(x) = [f0(x), f1(x), …, fs-1(x)], where s = no. of blocks
  that generate output signals.
valid = pDoc->GetSystemModel().DetermineSystemEquationsFunctionOperation
  Vector(m_t_cnt, m_t, m_delta_t, x_vec, f_vec);
if(valid == 0)
{
    sMsgTemp.Format("\n CNewtonMethod::funcv()\n");
    sMsg+=sMsgTemp;
    sMsgTemp.Format("\n WARNING! Unsuccessful determination of
      f(x)!\n");
    sMsg+=sMsgTemp;
    AfxMessageBox(sMsg, nType, nIDhelp);
}

// BUILD F(x) = x - f(x) (= 0)
for(i=0; i<n; i++)
{
    F_vec[i] = x_vec[i] - f_vec[i];
}

// CONVERT F(x) of the CSystemModel centric code, to f(x) of the
  CNewtonSolver centric code
for(i=0; i<n; i++)
{
    f[i] = F_vec[i];
}

// Print vectors to check values
/*sMsgTemp.Format("\n Printing x_vec \n");
sMsg+=sMsgTemp;
AfxMessageBox(sMsg, nType, nIDhelp);
PrintVector(x_vec, n);

sMsgTemp.Format("\n Printing f_vec \n");
sMsg+=sMsgTemp;
AfxMessageBox(sMsg, nType, nIDhelp);
PrintVector(f_vec, n);

sMsgTemp.Format("\n Printing F_vec \n");
sMsg+=sMsgTemp;
AfxMessageBox(sMsg, nType, nIDhelp);
PrintVector(F_vec, n);
*/

// MEMORY DELETE
if(F_vec != NULL)
{
    delete [] F_vec;
    F_vec = NULL;
}
```

```
    if(f_vec != NULL)
    {
        delete [] f_vec;
        f_vec = NULL;
    }
    if(x_vec != NULL)
    {
        delete [] x_vec;
        x_vec = NULL;
    }
}
```

Initially memory is allocated, with the `memory_dvector()` function, for three vectors: the generalized system function vector, $F(x(t))$; the block operational function vector, $f(x(t))$; and the system signal vector, $x(t)$. The number of elements to be allocated (n) is the size of the system of equations (23.1). The incoming vector "x" is then assigned to "x_vec". The developer should be aware that the local variables "F_vec", "f_vec", and "x_vec" are concerned with CSystemModel-centric code, whereas the incoming arguments to `funcv()`, "x" and "f", are related to CNewtonMethod-centric code.

The next step is to determine the functional operation vector $f(x(t))$, which in conjunction with $x(t)$ can complete the generalized system function vector (23.1). In general, i.e., for an arbitrary time point, t, the functional operation vector $f(x(t))$ is composed of the output of the functional block operations $f_i(x(t))$, for $i \in [0, s-1]$, where the input arguments to the blocks and upon which the block operations are performed are the components $x_i(t)$ of the system signal vector, $x(t)$. The function vector, $f(x(t))$, is returned by the `DetermineSystemEquationsFunctionOperationVector()` function, which, being a member function of the CSystemModel class, is called upon the CSystemModel object via the pointer-to-CDiagramEngDoc, "pDoc".

Finally, the generalized system function vector $F(x(t)) = x(t) - f(x(t))$ is formed, represented by "F_vec" and written to the "f" variable to be returned to the calling environment, i.e., to the functions `fmin()` or `fdjac()` called from within the Newton-method-based solver `newt()` (see Table 23.1 for the function call tree). That is, given an input system signal vector $x(t)$, the output generalized system vector $F(x(t))$ is returned.

5. The function `fdjac()` makes use of the `fabs()` function, hence add, #include <math.h>, at the top of the "NewtonMethod.cpp" source file beneath the inclusion of the "NewtonMethod.h" header file.
6. The `funcv()` function shown earlier makes use of a pointer-to-CDiagramEngDoc, "pDoc"; hence, include "DiagramEngDoc.h" at the top of the "NewtonMethod.cpp" source file.
7. The double version of the `PrintVector()` function of the CNewtonMethod class needs to be altered to print the vector within an `AfxMessageBox()`, as shown in the following. This is identical to the double version of the `PrintVector()` function defined in the "DiagramEngDoc.cpp" file; it is added here to the CNewtonMethod class for completeness.

```
int CNewtonMethod::PrintVector(double *v, int ncols)
{
    int i;
    CString sMsg;          // main msg string
    CString sMsgTemp;      // temp msg string
    UINT nType = MB_OK;    // style of msg. box
    UINT nIDhelp = 0;      // help context ID for the msg.

    // If the vector is NULL then return.
    if(v == NULL)
```

```
    {
        return 1;
    }
    sMsgTemp.Format("\n PrintVector()\n");
    sMsg += sMsgTemp;

    // Print Vector
    sMsgTemp.Format("\n");
    sMsg += sMsgTemp;

    for(i=0; i<ncols; i++)
    {
        //sMsgTemp.Format("%-10.3e", v[i]); // left adjusted, total width
          10, 3 decimal places, exponential notation
        sMsgTemp.Format("%lf", v[i]);        // standard double formatting
          sMsg += sMsgTemp;
    }
    sMsgTemp.Format("\n");
    sMsg += sMsgTemp;

    // Display msg. box
    AfxMessageBox(sMsg, nType, nIDhelp);

    return 0;
}
```

Finally, the implementation of the `nrerror()` (`void nrerror(char *error_text)`) function taking a character array argument makes use of the `fprintf()` function to write a string to a file pointed to by the file pointer [5], in this case, "stderr". The developer can modify this function to write the error string in a message box, as shown in the following code.

```
void nrerror(char *error_text)
{
    //Numerical Recipes standard error handler
    CString sMsg;            // string to be displayed
    CString sMsgTemp;        // temp msg.
    UINT nType = MB_OK;      // style of msg. box
    UINT nIDhelp = 0;        // help context ID for the msg.

    // NR Impl.
    //fprintf(stderr, "Numerical Recipes run-time error …\n");
    //fprintf(stderr, "%s\n", error_text);
    //fprintf(stderr, "Now exiting to system.\n");

    // Message Box Impl.
    sMsgTemp.Format("Numerical Recipes run-time error …\n");
    sMsg+=sMsgTemp;
    sMsgTemp.Format("%s\n", error_text);
    sMsg+=sMsgTemp;
    sMsgTemp.Format("…now exiting to system…\n");
    sMsg+=sMsgTemp;
    AfxMessageBox(sMsg, nType, nIDhelp);

    // NR Impl. exit
    exit(1);
}
```

Now the code may be built with no build errors. However, there is a problem with the `nrerror()` function: a call to `exit()` is made whenever the `newt()`-based code experiences either memory

---

TABLE 23.3

CNewtonMethod Functions That Call `nrerror()` through Either Memory Allocation Failure or Numerical Error

Functions Calling `nrerror()` for Memory Allocation Failure	Functions Calling `nrerror()` for Numerical Error
`memory_dmatrix()`	`lnsrch()`
`memory_dvector()`	`ludcmp()`
`memory_ivector()`	`newt()`

---

allocation failure or numerical problems. The result of this is that the program, DiagramEng, is terminated and the user does not have a chance to modify the model diagram in an attempt to resolve any numerical anomalies. Hence, a mechanism should be in place to allow the Newton-method-based code to deallocate any allocated memory and return an error value to the calling environment (ultimately `SignalPropagationSystemOfEquations()`) to terminate model execution without terminating the DiagramEng application.

23.4.4 Changes to Be Made to Resolve Exiting the Program Prematurely

The functions that call `nrerror()` are listed in Table 23.3 and are separated into two groups: those that concern memory allocation failure, listed on the left, and those that involve numerical error, listed on the right.

At present all functions pass an error message in the form of a character array. However, an additional flag-like argument should be passed to indicate whether `exit()` should be called: for functions processing memory allocation failure, the call to `exit()` is required, but for functions that involve `newt()`-based numerical error, only an indicative message should be displayed and execution control should return to `SignalPropagationSystemOfEquations()` after the appropriate memory deallocation is preformed throughout the hierarchy of functions concerned. The changes to the program require modifying the following: (1) `nrerror()`, (2) `lnsrch()`, (3) `ludcmp()`, (4) `newt()`, (5) all `nrerror()` calls concerning memory allocation failure, and (6) relevant functions to process the integer value returned from `newt()`.

23.4.4.1 Modify `nrerror()`

The `nrerror()` function declaration needs to be altered to take a second integer argument. Hence, change the function prototype in the "NewtonMethod.h" header file to the following: `void CNewtonMethod::nrerror(char *error_text, int nr_status)`. Edit the `nrerror()` function as shown in bold in the following to process the "nr_status" argument and exit only if the value is "−1".

```
// DiagramEng altered (nr_status)
void CNewtonMethod::nrerror(char *error_text, int nr_status)
{
    // Numerical Recipes standard error handler
    CString sMsg;          // string to be displayed
    CString sMsgTemp;      // temp msg.
    UINT nType = MB_OK;    // style of msg. box
    UINT nIDhelp = 0;      // help context ID for the msg.

    // NR Impl.
    //fprintf(stderr, "Numerical Recipes run-time error …\n");
```

```
//fprintf(stderr, "%s\n", error_text);
//fprintf(stderr, "…now exiting to system…\n");

// DiagramEng-altered
// Start Message
sMsgTemp.Format("Numerical Recipes run-time error …\n\n");
sMsg+=sMsgTemp;
sMsgTemp.Format("%s\n", error_text);
sMsg+=sMsgTemp;

// Filter nr_status flag
// nr_status is the value indicating the nr method status:
//   -2 (numerical error), -1 (memory allocation error), 1 (no error)
if(nr_status == -2)  // Print message indicating a numerical error.
{
    AfxMessageBox(sMsg, nType, nIDhelp);
}
else if(nr_status == -1)  // Exit system only if there is a memory
  deallocation failure
{
    sMsgTemp.Format("Now exiting to system. \n");
    sMsg+=sMsgTemp;
    AfxMessageBox(sMsg, nType, nIDhelp);
    exit(1);
}
else
{
    // no action for now
}
}
```

23.4.4.2 Modify lnsrch()

The lnsrch() function may experience numerical problems when working with the newt()-based code. Modify the lnsrch() function prototype in the "NewtonMethod.h" header file as follows: int CNewtonMethod::lnsrch(int n, double *xold, double fold, double *g, double *p, double *x, double *f, double stpmax, int *check). Modify the lnsrch() function as shown in the following to either return "nr_status" with value "1" (no error) or call nrerror() with "nr_status" set to "–2", indicating that just the "error_text" message should be displayed without exiting to the system. Only relevant parts of the function have been changed, as shown in bold; the rest remains unchanged as indicated by the ellipsis, "…" (this convention denoting altered and unaltered code is used throughout the text).

```
// Line Search Method: Numerical Recipes in C: Section 9.7
//void CNewtonMethod::lnsrch(int n, float xold[], float fold, float g[],
  float p[], float x[], float *f, float stpmax, int *check, float (*func)
  (float [], int n))
int CNewtonMethod::lnsrch(int n, double *xold, double fold, double *g,
  double *p, double *x, double *f, double stpmax, int *check)
{
    int i;
    int nr_status = 1; // value indicating the nr method status:
      -2 (numerical error), -1 (memory allocation error), 1 (no error)
    …

    if(slope >= 0.0)
    {
        // DiagramEng-altered
```

```
        nr_status = -2;
        nrerror("Roundoff problem in lnsrch().", nr_status);
        return nr_status;
    }
    ...
    for(;;)
    {
        ...
        if(alam < alamin)
        {
            for(i=1; i<=n; i++)
            {
                x[i] = xold[i];
            }
            *check = 1;

            // DiagramEng-altered
            return nr_status;
        }
        else if(*f <= fold + ALF*alam*slope)    // Sufficient fn decrease.
        {
            // DiagramEng-altered
            return nr_status;
        }
        ...
    }// end for

    // DiagramEng-altered
    return nr_status;
}
```

23.4.4.3 Modify `ludcmp()`

The `ludcmp()` function, called by `newt()`, may experience numerical problems and hence generates an error message. However, as memory is allocated for the vector "vv", this should be deallocated prior to returning.

1. Modify the `ludcmp()` function prototype in the "NewtonMethod.h" header file as follows: int CNewtonMethod::ludcmp(double **a, int n, int *indx, double *d).
2. Edit the `ludcmp()` function as shown in bold in the following to either return "nr_status" with value "1" or call `nrerror()`, deallocate memory, and return "nr_status" with value "−2".

```
int CNewtonMethod::ludcmp(double **a, int n, int *indx, double *d)
{
    int i;
    ...
    int nr_status = 1; // value indicating the type of error:
      -2 (numerical error), -1 (memory allocation error), 1 (no error)
    ...
    for(i=0; i<n; i++)
    {
        ...
        if(big == 0.0)
        {
            // DiagramEng-altered
```

```
            nr_status = -2;
            nrerror("Singular matrix in routine ludcmp().", nr_status);
            if(vv != NULL)
            {
                delete [] vv;
                vv = NULL;
            }
            return nr_status;
        }
        vv[i] = 1.0/big;
    }// end for i

    for(j=0; j<n; j++)
    {
    ...
    }// end for j

    // Memory delete
    if(vv != NULL)
    {
        delete [] vv;
        vv = NULL;
    }

    // DiagramEng-altered
    return nr_status;
}
```

23.4.4.4 Modify newt()

The last function that calls nrerror() as a result of numerical problems is newt().

1. Modify the newt() function prototype in the "NewtonMethod.h" header file as follows: int CNewtonMethod::newt(double *x, int n, int *check).
2. Edit the newt() function, as shown in bold in the following, to return the value of "nr_status": nrerror() is called if "nr_status" is equal to "–2".

```
int CNewtonMethod::newt(double *x, int n, int *check)
{
    int i;
    ...
    int nr_status = 1; // value indicating the nr method status:
      -2 (numerical error), -1 (memory allocation error), 1 (no error)

    ...
    if(test < 0.01*TOLF)
    {
        *check = 0;
        memory_delete_newt(indx, g, p, xold, fjac, n);
        return nr_status;
    }

    ...
    // Start of iteration loop
    for(its = 0; its < MAXITS; its++)
    {
//      fdjac(n, x, fvec, fjac, vecfunc);
        fdjac(n, x, fvec, fjac);
```

```
    // -- DiagramEng-altered test of fjac
    nr_status = CheckJacobian(fjac, n, n);
    if(nr_status == -2)
    {
        nrerror("Numerical problem concerning fjac() detected in
          newt().", nr_status);
        memory_delete_newt(indx, g, p, xold, fjac, n);
        return nr_status;
    }
    ...
    // -- DiagramEng-altered
    nr_status = ludcmp(fjac, n, indx, &d);   // solve linear equs by
      LU decomp
    if(nr_status == -2)
    {
        nrerror("Numerical problem concerning ludcmp() detected in
          newt().", nr_status);
        memory_delete_newt(indx, g, p, xold, fjac, n);
        return nr_status;
    }

    lubksb(fjac, n, indx, p);

    // -- DiagramEng-altered
    nr_status = lnsrch(n, xold, fold, g, p, x, &f, stpmax, check);
    if(nr_status == -2)
    {
        nrerror("Numerical problem concerning lnsrch() detected in
          newt().", nr_status);
        memory_delete_newt(indx, g, p, xold, fjac, n);
        return nr_status;
    }
    ...
    if(test < TOLF)
    {
        *check = 0;
        memory_delete_newt(indx, g, p, xold, fjac, n);
        return nr_status;
    }

    // Check for gradient of f zero, i.e. spurious cgce.
    if(*check)
    {
        ...
        *check = (test < TOLMIN ? 1 : 0);
        memory_delete_newt(indx, g, p, xold, fjac, n);
        return nr_status;
    }
    ...
    if(test < TOLX)
    {
        memory_delete_newt(indx, g, p, xold, fjac, n);
        return nr_status;
    }
}// end "for its"
```

```
    // DiagramEng-altered
    nr_status = -2;
    nrerror("MAXITS exceeded in newt().", nr_status);
    memory_delete_newt(indx, g, p, xold, fjac, n);
    return nr_status;
}
```

The reader will have noticed a call to the diagnostic function CheckJacobian() (mentioned in Section 23.4.2): this is used to check whether the Jacobian matrix, "fjac", is singular, i.e., whether it contains a row of zeros. This test is actually made at the start of ludcmp() and is used in newt() to detect problems a little earlier.

1. Hence, edit the new public member function CheckJacobian() of the CNewtonMethod class, as shown in the following.
2. Also add a new public member function to the CNewtonMethod class to print the Jacobian matrix, with the prototype int CNewtonMethod::PrintMatrix(double **M, int nrows, int ncols), and edit it as shown in the following.

```
int CNewtonMethod::CheckJacobian(double **fjac, int nrows, int ncols)
{
    int i;
    int j;
    int nr_status = 1; // nr method status: -2 (numerical error),
      -1 (memory allocation error), 1 (no error)
    double big;
    double temp;

    // Check for zero row i.e. a singular Jacobian matrix
    for(i=0; i<nrows; i++)
    {
        big = 0.0;
        for(j=0; j<ncols; j++)
        {
            if(( temp = fabs(fjac[i][j]) ) > big)
            {
                big = temp;
            }
        }
        if(big == 0.0)
        {
            PrintMatrix(fjac,nrows,ncols);
            nr_status = -2;
            nrerror("CheckJacobian(): Jacobian fjac is singular.",
              nr_status);
            break;  // break from for loop since zero row is found
        }
    }

    return nr_status;
}

int CNewtonMethod::PrintMatrix(double **M, int nrows, int ncols)
{
    int i;
    int j;
    CString sMsg;        // main msg string
    CString sMsgTemp;    // temp msg string
```

```
    UINT nType = MB_OK;   // style of msg. box
    UINT nIDhelp = 0;     // help context ID for the msg.

    // If the matrix is NULL then return.
    if(M == NULL)
    {
        return 1;
    }

    sMsgTemp.Format("\n PrintMatrix()\n");
    sMsg += sMsgTemp;

    // Print Matrix
    sMsgTemp.Format("\n");
    sMsg += sMsgTemp;

    for(i=0; i<nrows; i++)
    {
        for(j=0; j<ncols; j++)
        {
            //sMsgTemp.Format("%-10.3e", M[i][j]); // left adjusted,
              total width 10, 3 decimal places, exponential notation
            sMsgTemp.Format("%lf", M[i][j]);  // standard double
              formatting
            sMsg += sMsgTemp;
        }
        sMsgTemp.Format("\n");
        sMsg += sMsgTemp;
    }
    sMsgTemp.Format("\n");
    sMsg += sMsgTemp;

    // Display msg. box
    AfxMessageBox(sMsg, nType, nIDhelp);

    return 0;
}
```

These changes to the CNewtonMethod functions allow for better error checking and a more informative termination of computation.

23.4.4.5 Modify All `nrerror()` Calls Concerning Memory Allocation Failure

Now all the functions (of the CNewtonMethod class) that call `nrerror()` due to a memory allocation failure, as listed in the left column of Table 23.3, i.e., `memory_dmatrix()`, `memory_dvector()`, and `memory_ivector()`, need to be modified to pass the "nr_status" value equal to "−1", indicating that the program should exit to the system. All of these calls are of the same form, i.e., `nrerror("string message", nr_status)`, equivalently, `nrerror("string message", −1)`. For example, the function, `memory_dvector()`, is modified as shown in bold in the following; the other functions may be augmented in a similar manner.

```
double* CNewtonMethod::memory_dvector(int n)
{
    double *v = NULL;

    // Memory Alloc
    v = new double[n];

    // Check memory
    if(!v)
```

```
    {
        //nrerror("memory_dvector(), memory allocation failure.");
        nrerror("memory_dvector(), memory allocation failure.", -1);
    }

    return v;
}
```

23.4.4.6   Modify Relevant Functions to Process the Integer Returned from `newt()`

Now the returned "nr_status" integer from `newt()` needs to be passed back to the `SignalPropagationSystemOfEquations()` function via the `NewtonSolver()` function. Hence, perform the following alterations.

1. Assign the result of the call to `newt()` to the variable, "valid", in `NewtonSolver()`, as shown in the following; if the `newt()` function evaluates successfully, then "nr_status" will be "1" and so too the variable "valid".

```
int CSystemModel::NewtonSolver(int nrows, double *x_vec, int t_cnt,
  double t, double delta_t)
{
    int i;
    int check;
    int valid = 1;

    ...

    valid = probObj.newt(x, nrows, &check);

    if(valid != 1)  // if valid != 1 then newt() is in error
    {
        valid = 0;
        probObj.PrintVector(x, nrows);
    }

    // Prepare the solution vector x_vec from the vector x returned by
      newt() if newt() not in error.
    if(valid == 1)
    {
        for(i=0; i<nrows; i++)
        {
            x_vec[i] = x[i];
        }
    }
    ...
    // MEMORY DELETE
    if(x != NULL)
    {
        delete [] x;
        x = NULL;
    }

    return valid;
}
```

2. Modify the `SignalPropagationSystemOfEquations()` function to process the integer value returned from `newt()` as shown in bold in the following.

```
void CSystemModel::SignalPropagationSystemOfEquations()
{
    ...
```

```
    // -- Loop for n_TimeSteps + 1, from t_0 = 0, UP TO AND INCLUDING the
      last time point t_n
    for(t_cnt = 0; t_cnt <= n_TimeSteps; t_cnt++)
    {
        …
        // PERFORM NEWTON ITERATION TO DETERMINE THE VECTOR x_vec,
          i.e. x, THAT SATISFIES F(x) = x - f(x) = 0
        valid = NewtonSolver(nrows, x_vec, t_cnt, t, delta_t);

        // If the NewtonSolver() function is in error, print a msg. and
          break from the time-based loop.
        if(valid == 0)
        {
            sMsg.Format("");
            sMsgTemp.Format("\n SignalPropagationSystemOfEquations()\n");
            sMsg+=sMsgTemp;
            sMsgTemp.Format("\n WARNING! Unsuccessful NewtonSolver()
              operation!\n");
            sMsg+=sMsgTemp;
            sMsgTemp.Format("Check all numerical values before restarting
              the simulation!\n");
            sMsg+=sMsgTemp;
            sMsgTemp.Format("Aborting simulation!\n");
            sMsg+=sMsgTemp;
            AfxMessageBox(sMsg, nType, nIDhelp);   // msg. box
            break; // break from "for t_cnt"
        }
        …
    }
    …
    return;
}
```

Now if the user experiences a memory allocation problem or a numerical problem in the newt()-based code, the code will either exit to the system (nr_status = −1) or abort the simulation (nr_status = −2), respectively. The user can experiment with numerical error detection by constructing a simple linear system with a feedback loop, as shown in Figure 23.1, and set the source function, $f_0(t) = 1$ (e.g., using a Linear Function block with $f_0(t) = t$, where $f(0) = 0$), and the gain constant, $k_2 = 1$, to make the system singular, i.e., the leading matrix of the system, $Ax = b$, is singular (as discussed in Chapter 19). The error reported reads as follows: "Numerical Recipes run-time error … Roundoff problem in lnsrch()." This is followed by error messages from functions higher up the hierarchy, i.e., in newt() and SignalPropagationSystemOfEquations().

23.4.5 Addition of the Manual Assertion Functions to the Project

The Win32 Console Application project involving the source and header files "Newton.cpp/.h" introduced manual implementations of the equivalent system-provided assert() function,

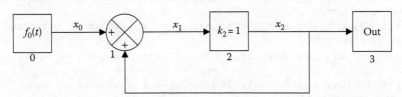

FIGURE 23.1 Simple linear system with a feedback loop that is singular if $f_0(t) = 1$ and $k_2 = 1$.

as a macro, `AssertManual()` and as a function, `AssertManualFn()`: this was done so that assertions can be made in both the Debug and Release configurations of the executable. Here, both manual assertions and the `PrintAssertMsg()` function are added to the DiagramEng project.

1. Add the `AssertManual()` macro at the top of the "DiagramEngDoc.h" header file, as shown in bold in the following code excerpt.
2. Add the following prototype at the global function definition section of the "DiagramEngDoc.h" header file, as shown in bold in the following: int `AssertManualFn(bool expr, char *file_name, int line)`.
3. Add the prototype of the printing function that works with the assertion functions, at the global function definition section of the "DiagramEngDoc.h" header file, as shown in bold in the following: void `PrintAssertMsg(char *file_name, int line)`.

```
// DiagramEngDoc.h : interface of the CDiagramEngDoc class
//
/////////////////////////////////////////////////////////////////////

#if !defined(AFX_DIAGRAMENGDOC_H__9DA8C218_5A85_4AB4_B77B_A9F8FF828990__
  INCLUDED_)
#define AFX_DIAGRAMENGDOC_H__9DA8C218_5A85_4AB4_B77B_A9F8FF828990__
  INCLUDED_
...
// User defined constructs
enum EBlockType{eChirpSignal, eConstBlock, eDerivativeBlock,
  eDivideBlock, eGainBlock, eIntegratorBlock, eLinearFnBlock,
                eOutputBlock, eSignalGenBlock, eSubsysBlock,
                  eSubsysInBlock, eSubsysOutBlock, eSumBlock,
                  eTransferFnBlock};

// AssertManual() - explicit version to work with Debug and Release
  versions of the exe.
#define AssertManual(expr) do{ if(!(expr)) {PrintAssertMsg(__FILE__,
  __LINE__); __asm{int 3}; } }while(0)
...
class CDiagramEngDoc : public CDocument
{
    ...
};

// -- GLOBAL FUNCTIONS
CDiagramEngDoc* GetDocumentGlobalFn(void);   // gets a ptr to the doc
int AssertManualFn(bool expr, char *file_name, int line);
double **ConvertStringMatrixToDoubleMatrix(char **str_matrix, int nrows,
  int ncols);
double **ConvertStringToDouble(CString string, int &nrows, int &ncols);
int DetermineDataDimsByStrpbrk(char *in_str, int &nrows, int &ncols,
  int &max_row_length);
int DetermineDataDimsByStrtok(char *in_str, int &nrows, int &ncols,
  int &max_row_length);
int GaussJordanEliminationFullPivoting(double **A, int n, double **B,
  int m);
void MatrixMultiply(int nrowsA, int ncolsA, int ncolsB, double **A,
  double **B, double **C);
void PrintAssertMsg(char *file_name, int line);
```

```
int PrintMatrix(double **M, int nrows, int ncols);
int PrintMatrix(int **M, int nrows, int ncols);
int PrintVector(double *v, int ncols);
int PrintVector(float *v, int ncols);
int PrintVector(int *v, int ncols);
char *StripInputString(char *input_str);
void Swap(double &a, double &b);

// DiagramEng (end)

/////////////////////////////////////////////////////////////////////

//{{AFX_INSER.T_LOCATION}}
// Microsoft Visual C++ will insert additional declarations immediately
  before the previous line.

#endif // !defined(AFX_DIAGRAMENGDOC_H__9DA8C218_5A85_4AB4_B77B_
  A9F8FF828990__INCLUDED_)
```

4. Finally, add the definitions for the `AssertManualFn()` and `PrintAssertMsg()` to the "DiagramEngDoc.cpp" source file, as shown in the following. The printing function has been modified from that presented in "Newton.cpp", such that output can be presented in a message box to the user.

```
int AssertManualFn(bool expr, char *file_name, int line)
{
    // Check truth of expr.
    if(!(expr))
    {
        // Print a msg to user
        PrintAssertMsg(file_name, line);

        // Native code generation for the fn.
        __asm{int 3};
    }
    return 0;
}

void PrintAssertMsg(char *file_name, int line)
{
    CString sMsg;            // main msg string
    FILE *ofp = NULL;        // outfile pointer
    UINT nType = MB_OK;      // style of msg. box
    UINT nIDhelp = 0;        // help context ID for the msg.

    // Print msg. to user
    sMsg.Format("\n PrintAssertMsg()\n Assertion failed:\n File = %s\n
      Line = %d.\n", file_name, line);
    AfxMessageBox(sMsg, nType, nIDhelp);

    // Open file for writing
    ofp = fopen("assert_log.txt", "w");

    // Warn if file could not be opened
    if(ofp == NULL)
    {
        sMsg.Format("");
        sMsg.Format("\n PrintAssertMsg(): WARNING! 'assert_log.txt' file
          could not be opened. \n");
```

```
            AfxMessageBox(sMsg, nType, nIDhelp);
    }
    else
    {
        fprintf(ofp, "Assertion failed, in file = %s, on line = %d.\n",
            file_name, line);   // write msg. to file
        fclose(ofp);            // close file
    }
}
```

Now the developer can place `AssertManual()` in the code, where the input argument is the expression whose validity is being questioned, for both the Debug and Release build configurations of the executable.

23.5   CONVERGENCE OF THE NEWTON METHOD USED TO COMPUTE MODELS WITH FEEDBACK LOOPS

The Newton-method-based solver `newt()` called from the `NewtonSolver()` function makes numerous calls to `funcv()`: directly via `fmin()` and `fdjac()`, and indirectly via `lnsrch()`. When `funcv()` is called via `fdjac()` and `lnsrch()`, the input argument "x", i.e., the signal vector $x(t)$, is intentionally perturbed, in an attempt to find the Jacobian matrix, and a new point $x(t)$ along a search direction that reduces the function value, respectively. For block $i \in [0, s - 1]$, whose output at the current time point, $x_i(t)$, is a function of the input at the current time point, $u_i(t)$, i.e., a block that is memoryless, a change to the signal value input will result in an immediate change in the block functional operation output. That is, for a system composed entirely of memoryless blocks, a change in the system signal vector $x(t)$ will result in a change in the system functional operation vector $f(x(t))$ at the current time point. This allows the Newton method to iteratively find a solution $x_r(t)$ to (23.1), i.e., the $x(t)$ that satisfies $F(x(t)) = x(t) - f(x(t)) = \mathbf{0}$.

However, if the blocks of the model involve a Derivative or an Integrator block, i.e., blocks with memory of values determined at previous time points, then changes in the system signal vector $x(t)$ at the current time point will not result in immediate changes in the block's functional operation output, $f_m(t)$, where m denotes the index of a block with memory, at the current time point, due to the inherent computational delay mechanism. Therefore, memory-based blocks cannot contribute to the convergence of the Newton-method-based code, `newt()`, in an effort to determine the solution vector $x_r(t)$ of (23.1).

The reader will recall in the section concerning the introduction of the `OperateOnData()` function for both the Derivative and Integrator blocks that a check is made to detect whether the function is called more than once per time-step, as shown by the following code excerpt, and if so, the stored value of the output signal, "m_dMatrixOut", is simply written to the output connection-based CSignal data member. That is, any change in the input signal in between time points will result in no change in the output signal, $f(x(t))$, for the current time point.

```
// SET TIME COUNT REF AND NO. OF TIMES THE FN IS CALLED AT THIS TIME
    POINT
if(m_i_t_cnt_ref == t_cnt)
{
    m_iNcallsPerTimeCnt++;  // no. of calls per time-based iteration
        (t_cnt)
}
else
```

```
{
    m_i_t_cnt_ref = t_cnt;
    m_iNcallsPerTimeCnt = 1;
}

// WRITE DATA TO OUTPUT SIGNAL IF ALREADY DETERMINED ON A PREVIOUS CALL
if(m_iNcallsPerTimeCnt > 1)
{
    valid = WriteDataToOutputSignal(m_dMatrixOut, nrows_in, ncols_in);
    return valid;
}
```

The Derivative block's `OperateOnData()` function takes input, $f(t)$, and generates the derivative output, $f'(t)$, using the internal ("remembered") data, $f(t - h)$ and $f(t - 2h)$ (for the five-point derivative calculation). Hence, any alteration or change in the input signal after the initial operation at the current time, t, would alter the internal data structures $f(t - h)$ and $f(t - 2h)$ through algorithmic updating, as shown in Figure 23.2: $f(t - 2h) \leftarrow f(t - h)$ and $f(t - h) \leftarrow f(t)$. Hence, the internal values would not in fact be those at the time points indicated, i.e., at $t - h$ and $t - 2h$, but rather at intermediary values. For this reason, the output signal, "m_dMatrixOut", determined on the first invocation of the `OperateOnData()` function, is returned for any intermediary calls made by `newt()`-based code.

The Integrator block's `OperateOnData()` function takes input, $\dot{y}(t) = f(y, t)$, and generates the integral output $y(t)$, using the internal data $y(t - h)$ and $\dot{y}(t - h)$, as shown in Figure 23.3, i.e., $y(t) = y(t - h) + h\dot{y}(t - h)$. In a similar manner to the Derivative block, any change in the input signal after the initial invocation of the `OperateOnData()` function at the current time, t, would alter the internal data $y(t - h)$ and $\dot{y}(t - h)$ through the algorithmic updating: $y(t - h) \leftarrow y(t)$ and $\dot{y}(t - h) \leftarrow \dot{y}(t)$. Hence, the internal values would not be those at the time specified, but at an intermediary time. Again, for this reason, the output signal, "m_dMatrixOut", determined on the first invocation of the `OperateOnData()` function, is returned for any intermediary calls made by `newt()`-based code.

Hence, memory-based blocks do not contribute to the convergence of the Newton-method-based code, since the output at a certain time point is fixed, regardless of a `newt()`-specified change in the block's input. The memoryless blocks do contribute to convergence, since their output at the current time point can change with a change in the input signal.

The mathematics student will recall that numerical integration schemes may be either explicit or implicit. Explicit schemes are those where the state of the system at the next time point, y_{n+1},

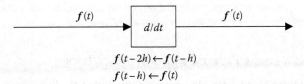

FIGURE 23.2 Algorithmic function of the Derivative block, for the five-point derivative calculation, updating the internal memory-based data structures.

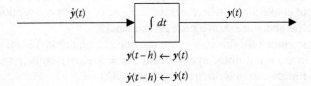

FIGURE 23.3 Algorithmic function of the Integrator block, using Euler's method, updating the internal memory-based data structures.

is a function of the states, y_n and y_{n-1}, at the current and previous times points, respectively. For example, the two-step midpoint method

$$y_{n+1} = y_{n-1} + 2hf(t_n, y_n) \qquad (23.7)$$

and Euler's method

$$y_{n+1} = y_n + hf(t_n, y_n) \qquad (23.8a)$$

(although this has been coded as

$$y_n = y_{n-1} + hf(t_{n-1}, y_{n-1}) \qquad (23.8b)$$

in the current project for reasons discussed earlier) are explicit schemes since $y_{n+1} = f(t_n, y_n, y_{n-1})$ [6]. Implicit schemes are those where the state of the system at the next time point, y_{n+1}, is a function of the states y_n and y_{n+1}, at the current and future time points, respectively. For example, the one-step trapezoidal method

$$y_{n+1} = y_n + \frac{h}{2}[f(t_n, y_n) + f(t_{n+1}, y_{n+1})] \qquad (23.9)$$

is an implicit scheme, since $y_{n+1} = f(t_n, t_{n+1}, y_n, y_{n+1})$ [6]. Hence, blocks with memory, i.e., those of "explicit" form, cannot contribute to the convergence of the Newton-based method, since their output is fixed at the current time point. However, blocks without memory, i.e., those of an "implicit" form, can contribute to convergence, since their output is variable at the current time point.

23.6 TESTING THE NEWTON-METHOD-BASED CODE FOR MODELS WITH FEEDBACK LOOPS

Now that all the necessary code in the "NewtonMethod.cpp/.h" files has been added to the DiagramEng project, a model with at least one feedback loop may be constructed, and then computed using the following programmatic control flow: `OnSimStart()` → `SignalPropagationSystemOfEquations()` → `NewtonSolver()` → `newt()`. Here, various linear and nonlinear test cases are presented to determine the accuracy of the Newton method implemented.

23.6.1 COMPUTING A LINEAR PROBLEM WITH A FEEDBACK LOOP

The previous chapter introduced a simple linear system with a feedback loop that involved Linear Function, Sum, Gain, and Output blocks, repeated here for convenience, where block functional operations are denoted $f_i(t)$, operating at the current time point $t \in [t_0, t_f]$, where t_0 and t_f denote the initial and final time points of the simulation, respectively, signals $x_i(t)$, for $i \in [0, s-1]$, are written above the block output connections, where s is the number of output connections (one per block) in the model, and block numbers are shown beneath the blocks.

The block-based equations for this model are provided in Equation 22.1 of the previous chapter and may be written in the usual linear system form, $Ax = b$. However, here the Newton method is used to compute the linear system written in the form (23.1), i.e.,

$$F(x(t)) = x(t) - f(x(t)) = \mathbf{0}$$

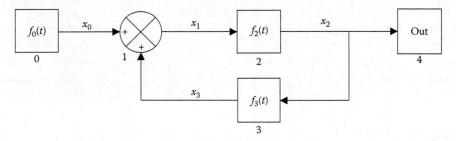

FIGURE 23.4 Simple linear system with a feedback loop: $f_i(t)$ and x_i denote the ith block operation and output signal, respectively, where block numbers appear beneath the blocks.

$$\Rightarrow \begin{bmatrix} F_0(\boldsymbol{x}(t)) \\ F_1(\boldsymbol{x}(t)) \\ F_2(\boldsymbol{x}(t)) \\ F_3(\boldsymbol{x}(t)) \end{bmatrix} = \begin{bmatrix} x_0(t) \\ x_1(t) \\ x_2(t) \\ x_3(t) \end{bmatrix} - \begin{bmatrix} f_0(t) \\ f_1(\boldsymbol{x}(t)) \\ f_2(\boldsymbol{x}(t)) \\ f_3(\boldsymbol{x}(t)) \end{bmatrix} = \begin{bmatrix} x_0(t) - f_0(t) \\ x_1(t) - x_0(t) - x_3(t) \\ x_2(t) - k_2 x_1(t) \\ x_3(t) - k_3 x_2(t) \end{bmatrix} = \underline{\boldsymbol{0}} \qquad (23.10)$$

where

k_2 and k_3 are the gain constants of blocks two and three, respectively

the vector of output signals at the current time point, t, is $\boldsymbol{x}(t) = [x_0(t), x_1(t), x_2(t), x_3(t)]^T$

The solution $\boldsymbol{x}_r(t)$ that satisfies (23.10) returned by the newt() function for $f_0(t) = 1$ and gain constants $k_2 = 2$ and $k_3 = 3$ is $\boldsymbol{x}_r(t) = [1, -0.2, -0.4, -1.2]^T$, as shown earlier in "Case 3" of Section 23.3.3. Throughout the simulation, i.e., for $t \in [t_0, t_f]$, the same solution vector $\boldsymbol{x}_r(t)$ will be generated, since the signal generated by block "0" is constant, i.e., $f_0(t) = 1$.

The user may experiment with different Source blocks and generate the corresponding output. For example, a Linear Function source signal block with initial value $f(t_0) = 0$, $f'(t) = 1$, $\delta t = 1.0\,\text{s}$, and initial and final times of signal activation, $t_{a0} = 0\,\text{s}$ and $t_{af} = 7\,\text{s}$, respectively, is used in place of block "0" in Figure 23.4, with gain constants $k_2 = 2$ and $k_3 = 3$. The corresponding output signal generated is that shown in Figure 23.5a. In addition, a Signal Generator block may be used in place of block "0" in Figure 23.4, with $f(t) = A \sin(\omega t + \phi)$, where $A = 1$, $\omega = 1\,\text{rad/s}$, $\phi = 0\,\text{rad}$, $t \in [0, 6.4]$, and $\delta t = 0.1\,\text{s}$. The corresponding output signal generated is that shown in Figure 23.5b.

23.6.2 COMPUTING AN ORDINARY DIFFERENTIAL EQUATION USING A FEEDBACK LOOP

Consider the simple first-order linear ordinary differential equation (ODE) presented in Ref. [7]:

$$\dot{y}(t) = -2y(t) + u(t) \qquad (23.11)$$

where y, t, and $u(t)$ are the dependent variable, independent variable, and source signal generation function, respectively. If the source signal is chosen to be $u(t) = 2t$, then the analytic solution to (23.11), determined using the "integrating factor" method and "integration by parts," is

$$y(t) = t - Ce^{-2t} - \frac{1}{2} \qquad (23.12)$$

where C is a constant. If the initial condition $y(0) = 0$ is chosen, then $C = -1/2$ and $y(t) \to t$ as $t \to \infty$. However, for different source functions $u(t)$, different solutions $y(t)$ will be obtained. This ODE can be modeled using a block diagram involving a feedback loop, as shown in Figure 23.6,

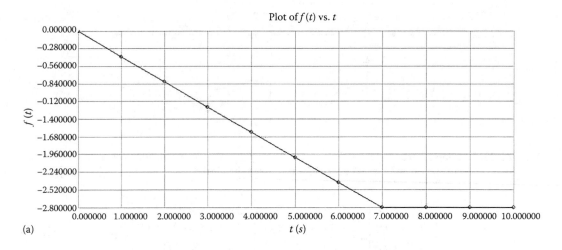

(a)

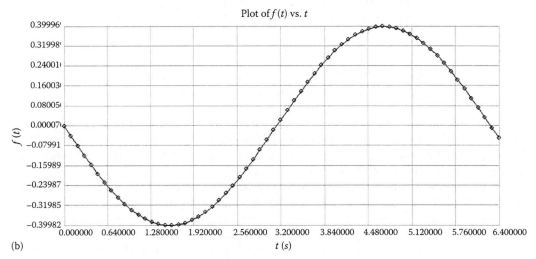

(b)

FIGURE 23.5   Output generated by computation of a linear system: (a) a Linear Function block is used as the source input signal, and (b) a Signal Generator block (sinusoidal function) is used as the source input signal.

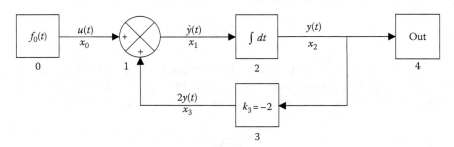

FIGURE 23.6   Block diagram model of the ODE $\dot{y}(t) = -2y(t) + u(t)$, with block numbers written below the blocks, and signals $x_i(t)$, for $i \in [0, s-1]$ written beneath the block output connections.

where block numbers are written below the blocks and signals $x_i(t)$, for $i \in [0, s - 1]$, are written beneath the block output connections.

The system of the form of (23.1) may be written as follows:

$$\begin{bmatrix} F_0(\boldsymbol{x}(t)) \\ F_1(\boldsymbol{x}(t)) \\ F_2(\boldsymbol{x}(t)) \\ F_3(\boldsymbol{x}(t)) \end{bmatrix} = \begin{bmatrix} x_0(t) \\ x_1(t) \\ x_2(t) \\ x_3(t) \end{bmatrix} - \begin{bmatrix} f_0(t) \\ f_1(\boldsymbol{x}(t)) \\ f_2(\boldsymbol{x}(t)) \\ f_3(\boldsymbol{x}(t)) \end{bmatrix} = \begin{bmatrix} x_0(t) - u(t) \\ x_1(t) - x_0(t) - x_3(t) \\ x_2(t) - \int x_1(t)dt \\ x_3(t) - k_3 x_2(t) \end{bmatrix} = \underline{\mathbf{0}} \qquad (23.13)$$

where the second equation $x_1(t) - x_0(t) - x_3(t) = 0$ represents the ODE (23.11) and the other equations complete the signal-function description. The solution vector $\boldsymbol{x}_r(t)$ to (23.13) may then be obtained from newt() for each time-step $t \in [t_0, t_f]$ of the simulation, where $x_2(t)$ represents the solution $y(t)$ given by (23.12). The developer may experiment with different signal generation functions $u(t)$, including constant, linear, and sinusoidal forms, and observe the resultant output of $y(t)$. For example, if the input signal $u(t) = 2t$ and $y(0) = 0$, then as described earlier, $y(t) \rightarrow t$ as $t \rightarrow \infty$, as shown in Figure 23.7a and b.

However, if $u(t) = c_1$, where c_1 is a constant, then the ODE

$$\dot{y}(t) = -2y(t) + c_1 \qquad (23.14)$$

may be solved analytically to yield

$$y(t) = \frac{c_1}{2} + (c_1 c_3 - c_2)e^{-2t} \qquad (23.15)$$

where c_2 and c_3 are constants of integration. As $t \rightarrow \infty$, $y(t) \rightarrow c_1/2$, as shown in Figure 23.8 where here $u(t) = c_1 = 1$.

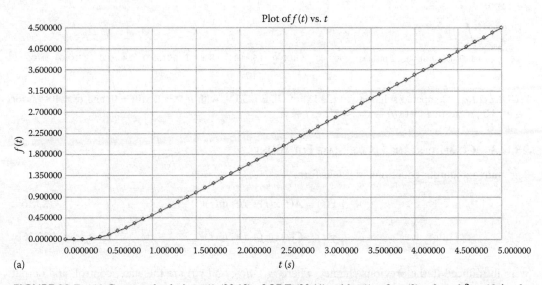

(a)

FIGURE 23.7   (a) Computed solution $y(t)$ (23.12) of ODE (23.11), with $u(t) = 2t$, $y(0) = 0$, and $\delta t = 10^{-1}$ s, for $t \in [0, 5.0]$.

(*continued*)

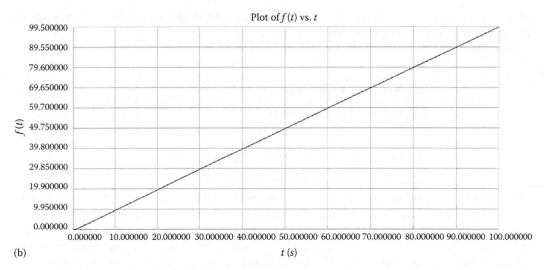

(b)

FIGURE 23.7 (continued)   (b) Computed solution $y(t)$ (23.12) of ODE (23.11), with $u(t) = 2t$, $y(0) = 0$, and $\delta t = 10^{-3}$ s, for $t \in [0, 100.0]$, showing that $y(t) \to t$ as $t \to \infty$.

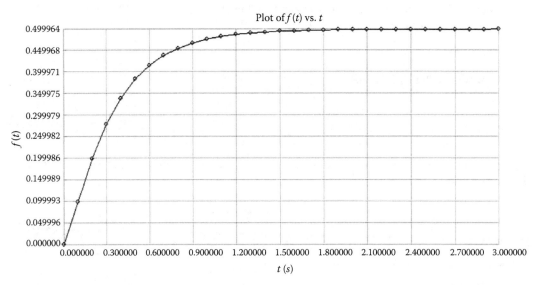

FIGURE 23.8   Computed solution $y(t)$ (23.15) of ODE (23.14), with $u(t) = 1$, $y(0) = 0$, and $\delta t = 10^{-1}$ s, for $t \in [0, 3.0]$, indicating that $y(t) \to c_1/2 = 1/2$ as $t \to \infty$.

23.6.3 COMPUTING THE LINEAR STATE EQUATIONS

The state and output equations in linear form

$$\dot{x}(t) = A(t)x(t) + B(t)u(t) \tag{23.16a}$$

$$y(t) = C(t)x(t) + D(t)u(t) \tag{23.16b}$$

were introduced in the previous chapter, where $x(t)$, $u(t)$, and $y(t)$ are the state, control, and output vectors, respectively, and $A(t)$, $B(t)$, $C(t)$, and $D(t)$ are the state, control, output, and direct transmission matrices, respectively [8]. The corresponding block diagram representation of the state and output equations (23.16) (repeated here for convenience) is shown in Figure 23.9.

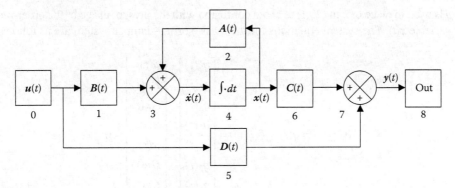

FIGURE 23.9 Block diagram representation of the state and output equations (23.16). (From Ogata, K., *Modern Control Engineering*, 4th edn., Prentice Hall, Upper Saddle River, NJ, 2002.)

23.6.3.1 Mechanical System

Ogata [8] introduces a simple second-order linear differential equation representing a mechanical mass–spring–damper system (Example 3-3 p. 73 [8])

$$m\ddot{y}(t) + b\dot{y}(t) + ky(t) = u(t) \tag{23.17}$$

where m, b, k, $y(t)$, and $u(t)$ are the mass, damping constant, spring constant, output mass displacement from the equilibrium position, and external force input to the system, respectively. An order reduction is used to reduce the second-order system to two first-order equations, where $x_1(t) = y(t)$ and $x_2(t) = \dot{y}(t)$, and results in the following system:

$$\begin{bmatrix} \dot{x}_1(t) \\ \dot{x}_2(t) \end{bmatrix} = \begin{bmatrix} 0 & 1 \\ -\dfrac{k}{m} & -\dfrac{b}{m} \end{bmatrix} \begin{bmatrix} x_1(t) \\ x_2(t) \end{bmatrix} + \begin{bmatrix} 0 \\ m^{-1} \end{bmatrix} u(t) \tag{23.18a}$$

$$y(t) = \begin{bmatrix} 1 & 0 \end{bmatrix} \begin{bmatrix} x_1(t) \\ x_2(t) \end{bmatrix} \tag{23.18b}$$

where (23.18a) is the state equation and (23.18b) the output equation, with [8]

$$A = \begin{bmatrix} 0 & 1 \\ -\dfrac{k}{m} & -\dfrac{b}{m} \end{bmatrix}, \quad B = \begin{bmatrix} 0 \\ m^{-1} \end{bmatrix}, \quad C = \begin{bmatrix} 1 & 0 \end{bmatrix} \quad \text{and} \quad D = 0$$

The control engineer will notice, for this example, that the state, control, output, and direct transmission matrices are not functions of time explicitly and hence the system (23.18) is a linear, time-invariant system.

The integration in the previous diagram concerns that of $\dot{x}(t)$ to yield $x(t)$, and since $x(t) = [y(t), \dot{y}(t)]^T$, then the initial condition for the Integrator block is $x(0) = [y(0), \dot{y}(0)]^T$; here $x(0) = [2, 0]^T$, i.e., the mass is initially at rest with displacement 2.0 m (the reader may like to review the mechanism of the Integrator block from a previous chapter concerning the initial condition required to start the integration process).

The system equations corresponding to the state and output equations that are to be computed by the Newton method were presented in the previous chapter (i.e., Equation 22.19), where the vector q is used in place of x in (23.1) to avoid confusion with the present usage of the order-reducing vector variable $x(t)$. The system equations for the mass–spring–damper system are as follows:

$$F(q(t)) = q(t) - f(q(t)) = \begin{bmatrix} q_0(t) \\ q_1(t) \\ q_2(t) \\ q_3(t) \\ q_4(t) \\ q_5(t) \\ q_6(t) \\ q_7(t) \end{bmatrix} - \begin{bmatrix} u(t) \\ Bu(t) \\ Ax(t) \\ \dot{x}(t) \\ x(t) \\ Du(t) \\ Cx(t) \\ y(t) \end{bmatrix} = \underline{0} \tag{23.19}$$

The engineer can draw Figure 23.9 using the DiagramEng application, as shown in Figure 23.10, and enter various selections of mechanical properties, m, b, and k and forcing functions $u(t)$, to generate different displacement outputs $y(t)$, to analyze the physical response behavior of the mass–spring–damper system.

The general analytic solution $y_g(t) \equiv y(t)$ to (23.17) is the sum of the homogeneous solution $y_h(t)$ and the particular solution $y_p(t)$, i.e.,

$$y_g(t) = y_h(t) + y_p(t) \tag{23.20}$$

The homogeneous solution is obtained by setting the right-hand side of (23.17) to zero as follows:

$$m\ddot{y}(t) + b\dot{y}(t) + ky(t) = 0 \tag{23.21a}$$

$$\Rightarrow \ddot{y}(t) + \frac{b}{m}\dot{y}(t) + \frac{k}{m}y(t) = 0 \tag{23.21b}$$

and letting $y(t) = e^{rt}$ results in the characteristic equation

$$r^2 + \frac{b}{m}r + \frac{k}{m} = 0 \tag{23.22a}$$

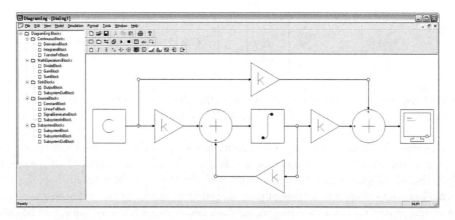

FIGURE 23.10   Block diagram model of the state and output equations (23.18) drawn with DiagramEng.

with roots

$$r_{1,2} = \frac{1}{2m}\left(-b \pm \sqrt{b^2 - 4km}\right) \tag{23.22b}$$

23.6.3.1.1 Underdamped Vibration ($b^2 - 4km < 0$)

If the discriminant $b^2 - 4km < 0$, then the motion of the mass–spring–damper system is said to be underdamped and the roots are complex, $r_{1,2} = \alpha \pm j\beta$, where $\alpha = -b/2m$, $\beta = (1/2m)\sqrt{4km - b^2}$, and $j = \sqrt{-1}$, and the homogeneous solution is

$$y_h(t) = e^{\alpha t}(C_1\cos(\beta t) + C_2\sin(\beta t)) \tag{23.23a}$$

which may also be written as

$$y_h(t) = C_3 e^{\alpha t}(\sin(\omega t) + C_4) \tag{23.23b}$$

where
  $\omega = \beta$ is the angular frequency
  C_i, for $i \in \{1, \ldots, 4\}$, are constants [9]

Values for the constants may be determined with knowledge of quantities b, k, m, $u(t)$ and the initial conditions $x(0)$. The mathematician will notice here that since $\alpha < 0$, $y_h(t) \to 0$ as $t \to \infty$, with a decaying oscillatory motion.

23.6.3.1.2 Critically Damped Vibration ($b^2 - 4km = 0$)

If the discriminant $b^2 - 4km = 0$, the motion of the system is said to be critically damped [9], and there exists a repeated root $r = -b/2m$, and the homogeneous solution is

$$y_h(t) = C_1 e^{-bt/2m} + C_2 t e^{-bt/2m} \tag{23.24}$$

Both exponents are negative, and, hence, $y_h(t) \to 0$ as $t \to \infty$, without oscillation.

23.6.3.1.3 Overdamped Vibration ($b^2 - 4km > 0$)

If the discriminant $b^2 - 4km > 0$, the motion of the system is said to be overdamped [9], and there exists two real roots as given by (23.22b) and the homogeneous solution

$$y_h(t) = C_1 e^{r_1 t} + C_2 e^{r_2 t} \tag{23.25}$$

Both roots are real but negative, and, hence, $y_h(t) \to 0$ as $t \to \infty$, without oscillation.

The particular solution of (23.17) may be found by the "Method of Undetermined Coefficients," and given initial conditions, the coefficients may be determined and a general solution found. For example, if $u(t) = 1$, a particular solution $y_p(t) = At + B$ may be sought, and upon substitution in (23.17), it is found that $A = 0$ and $B = 1/k$, to yield $y_p(t) = 1/k$. If, e.g., $u(t) = \sin(t)$, and the particular solution $y_p(t) = A\sin(t) + B\cos(t)$ is sought, then it may be shown that $A = (k - m)/((k - m)^2 + b^2)$ and $B = -b/((k - m)^2 + b^2)$. If $m = 1 = k$, then $A = 0$ and $B = -1/b$ and $y_p(t) = (-1/b)\cos(t)$.

Figure 23.11a through c illustrates the three different damping conditions where the homogeneous solutions ($y_h(t)$) are those provided by (23.23) through (23.25) and $y_p(t) = 1/k$ (given $u(t) = 1$) for the initial conditions $x(0) = [2, 0]^T$: (1) Figure 23.11a shows underdamped oscillatory vibration,

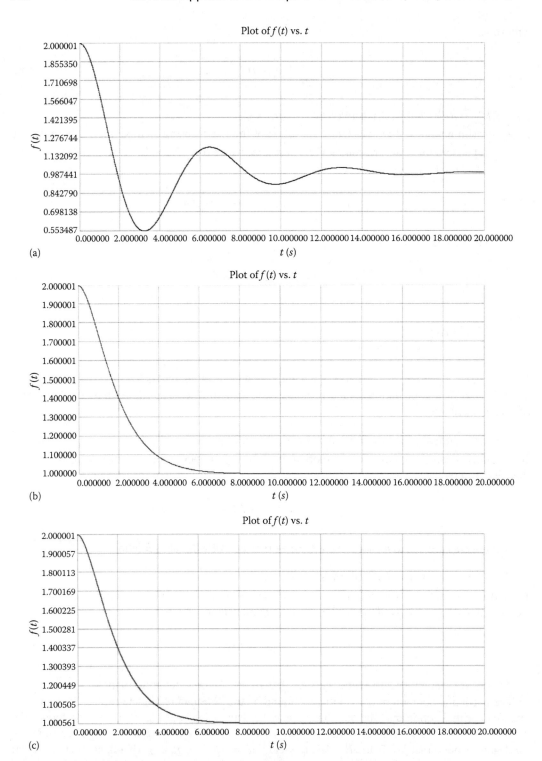

FIGURE 23.11   (a) Underdamped ($b^2 - 4km < 0$) oscillatory vibration, where $y_g(t) \to 1.0$ as $t \to \infty$, for $u(t) = 1$, $m = 1 = k$, $b = 0.5$, $\mathbf{x}(0) = [y(0), \dot{y}(0)]^T = [2, 0]^T$, and $\delta t = 10^{-3}$ s. (b) Critically damped ($b^2 - 4km = 0$) nonoscillatory vibration, where $y_g(t) \to 1.0$ as $t \to \infty$, for $u(t) = 1$, $m = 1 = k$, $b = 2$, $\mathbf{x}(0) = [y(0), \dot{y}(0)]^T = [2, 0]^T$, and $\delta t = 10^{-3}$ s. (c) Overdamped ($b^2 - 4km > 0$) nonoscillatory vibration, where $y_g(t) \to 1.0$ as $t \to \infty$, for $u(t) = 1$, $m = 1 = k$, $b = 3$, $\mathbf{x}(0) = [y(0), \dot{y}(0)]^T = [2, 0]^T$, and $\delta t = 10^{-3}$ s.

where $y_g(t) \to 1.0$ as $t \to \infty$, for $u(t) = 1$, $m = 1 = k$, and $b = 0.5$; (2) Figure 23.11b shows critically damped nonoscillatory vibration, where $y_g(t) \to 1.0$ as $t \to \infty$, for $u(t) = 1$, $m = 1 = k$, and $b = 2$; and (3) Figure 23.11c shows overdamped nonoscillatory vibration, where $y_g(t) \to 1.0$ as $t \to \infty$, for $u(t) = 1$, $m = 1 = k$, and $b = 3$.

23.6.3.1.4 Undamped Systems

The interested engineer may experiment with forced vibrations for an undamped system ($b = 0$) with external force $u(t) = F_0 \cos(\gamma t)$ in which case (23.17) may be written as

$$m\ddot{y}(t) + ky(t) = F_0 \cos(\gamma t) \tag{23.26}$$

and which has homogeneous solution

$$y_h(t) = C_1(\sin(\omega t) + C_2) \tag{23.27}$$

where $\omega = \sqrt{k/m}$. Sallas indicates that the nature of the vibration depends on the relationship between the applied frequency $f_a = \gamma/2\pi$ and the natural frequency of the system $f_s = \omega/2\pi$; if $\gamma \neq \omega$, the general solution

$$y_g(t) = C_1(\sin(\omega t) + C_2) + \frac{F_0/m}{\omega^2 - \gamma^2} \cos(\gamma t) \tag{23.28}$$

and the motion is bounded and may be periodic or aperiodic depending on the rationality of ω/γ, if $\gamma = \omega$,

$$y_g(t) = C_1(\sin(\omega t) + C_2) + \frac{F_0}{2\omega m} t \sin(\omega t) \tag{23.29}$$

the undamped system is said to be in resonance with aperiodic oscillatory motion and increasing amplitude of vibration [9].

23.6.3.1.5 Highly Oscillatory Motion

Systems whose state variable values and derivatives fluctuate in magnitude substantially with respect to time are considered to be stiff systems or systems with highly oscillatory dynamical behavior. The mass–spring–damper system (23.17) with $u(t) = A \sin(\omega t + \phi)$, $A = 0.5$, $\omega = 1$, $\phi = 0$, $m = 1$, $k = 10^3$, $b = 1$, and $x(0) = [y(0), \dot{y}(0)]^T = [2, 0]^T$ results in underdamped ($b^2 - 4km < 0$) oscillatory motion, that decays initially and then oscillates about $y(t) = 0$ with a small magnitude as $t \to \infty$, as shown in Figure 23.12.

It is interesting to note that the DiagramEng application can compute this oscillatory behavior provided that the time-step size δt is substantially small. In fact, Fox et al. [10] indicate that for the homogeneous case of (23.17), δt should be chosen according to the frequency of oscillation of the solution (23.23), i.e., $\omega \equiv \beta$. Here, δt should be smaller than the reciprocal of the frequency (provided also in Ref. [11]), i.e.,

$$\delta t < \omega^{-1} \equiv \beta^{-1} = \left((1/2m)\sqrt{4km - b^2}\right)^{-1} \tag{23.30}$$

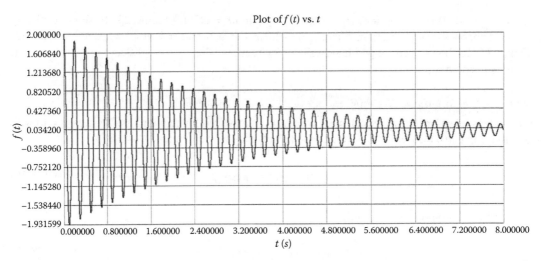

FIGURE 23.12 Underdamped $(b^2 - 4km < 0)$ highly oscillatory vibration, for $u(t) = 0.5 \sin(t)$, $m = 1$, $k = 10^3$, $b = 1$, $x(0) = [y(0), \dot{y}(0)]^T = [2, 0]^T$, and $\delta t = 10^{-4}$ s.

If b, k, and m are unity, then $\omega^{-1} \cong 1.15$ and $\delta t = 0.1$ s may be chosen; however, due to the numerical error incurred by Euler's method, a smaller δt should be selected. If $b = 1 = m$ and $k = 10^3$, then $\omega^{-1} \cong 0.03$ and $\delta t = 0.005$ s may be selected. If an oscillatory driving force is applied, then its frequency should also be considered, since as $t \to \infty$, $y_h(t) \to 0$, and $y_g(t) \to y_p(t)$. For the example provided earlier (Figure 23.12), $\delta t = 10^{-4}$ s, and the computation of the system with $\delta t > 10^{-4}$ s produced spurious results.

23.6.3.2 Electrical System

The mechanical system described earlier by (23.17) has an analogous electrical-circuit system representation, involving the sum of the voltages around a circuit loop involving a resistor R (ohm), inductor L (henry), and a capacitor C (farad), i.e,

$$V = V_R + V_L + V_C \tag{23.31a}$$

$$\Rightarrow iR + L\frac{di}{dt} + \frac{q}{C} = 0 \tag{23.31b}$$

where
    $i = dq/dt$ is the current
    $q(t)$ is the charge
    V_R, V_L, V_C, and V are the voltages of the resistor, inductor, capacitor, and the circuit loop, respectively [11]

If i is replaced with dq/dt in (23.31b), then the following second-order linear differential equation may be obtained:

$$\ddot{q}(t) + \frac{R}{L}\dot{q}(t) + \frac{1}{LC}q(t) = 0 \tag{23.32}$$

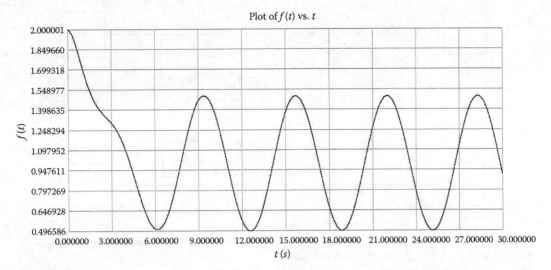

FIGURE 23.13 Underdamped ($R^2 - 4LC < 0$) oscillatory charge, where $q(t) \in [0.5, 1.5]$ as $t \to \infty$, for $u(t) = A\sin(t) + 1$, $A = 0.5$, $L = 1 = C$, $R = 1$, $x(0) = [q(0), \dot{q}(0)]^T = [2, 0]^T$, and $\delta t = 10^{-3}$ s.

where the mass m, spring constant k, and damping coefficient b of the mechanical system are equivalent to the inductance L, the inverse of the capacitance $1/C$, and the resistance R, respectively, as may be observed by comparison with (23.21). If $q(t) = e^{rt}$ is substituted in (23.32), then the following characteristic equation is obtained:

$$r^2 + \frac{R}{L}r + \frac{1}{LC} = 0 \tag{23.33a}$$

with roots

$$r_{1,2} = \frac{1}{2L}\left(-R \pm \sqrt{R^2 - \frac{4L}{C}}\right) \tag{23.33b}$$

The same analytic procedure as earlier may be followed to yield the underdamped ($R^2 - 4L/C < 0$), critically damped ($R^2 - 4L/C = 0$), and overdamped ($R^2 - 4L/C > 0$) cases, whose graphs will be of the same shape as those of the mechanical system if the initial conditions $x(0) = [q(0), \dot{q}(0)]^T = [Q, 0]^T$ are chosen, where $Q = 2$(F) is the initial charge, $i(0) = \dot{q}(0) = 0(\Omega)$ is the initial current, and an input voltage $u(t) = 1$ V is selected. In fact, if an alternating voltage source is supplied in conjunction with the unit voltage source, i.e., if $u(t) = A\sin(t) + 1$, where $A = 0.5$, then the charge and hence current will alternate about unity with amplitude A, as shown in Figure 23.13, since the homogeneous solution component would tend to zero.

23.6.4 Computing a Coupled Linear System

A coupled linear system is one that involves two or more input–output relationships that are interconnected usually by indirect feedback loops. Consider the following (simple demonstrative) coupled linear system:

$$x_2(t) = x_0(t) - \alpha x_3(t) \tag{23.34a}$$

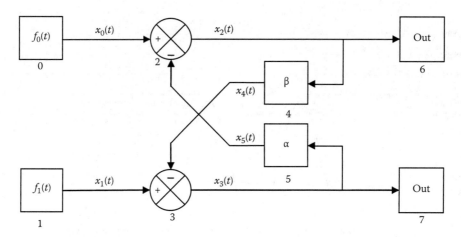

FIGURE 23.14 Coupled linear system (23.34) involving two input signals $x_0(t)$ and $x_1(t)$ and two output signals $x_2(t)$ and $x_3(t)$, where α and β are gain constants.

$$x_3(t) = x_1(t) - \beta x_2(t) \tag{23.34b}$$

where

$x_0(t)$ and $x_1(t)$ are independent input signals

$x_2(t)$ and $x_3(t)$ are the system output signals

α and β are gains applied to the output signals, as shown by the block diagram representation of Figure 23.14 (block numbers appear beneath the blocks)

The system may be structured in the form of (23.1), i.e.,

$$\begin{bmatrix} F_0(t) \\ F_1(t) \\ F_2(t) \\ F_3(t) \\ F_4(t) \\ F_5(t) \end{bmatrix} = \begin{bmatrix} x_0(t) \\ x_1(t) \\ x_2(t) \\ x_3(t) \\ x_4(t) \\ x_5(t) \end{bmatrix} - \begin{bmatrix} f_0(t) \\ f_1(t) \\ f_2(\boldsymbol{x}(t)) \\ f_3(\boldsymbol{x}(t)) \\ f_4(\boldsymbol{x}(t)) \\ f_5(\boldsymbol{x}(t)) \end{bmatrix} = \begin{bmatrix} x_0(t) - f_0(t) \\ x_1(t) - f_1(t) \\ x_2(t) - x_0(t) + \alpha x_5(t) \\ x_3(t) - x_1(t) + \beta x_4(t) \\ x_4(t) + \beta x_2(t) \\ x_5(t) + \alpha x_3(t) \end{bmatrix} = \boldsymbol{0} \tag{23.35}$$

and then computed using Newton's method. The mathematician will notice that the simultaneous coupled equations (23.34) may in fact be solved analytically in terms of the input signals, to yield

$$x_2(t) = \frac{x_0(t) - \alpha x_1(t)}{1 - \alpha \beta} \tag{23.36a}$$

and

$$x_3(t) = \frac{x_1(t) - \beta x_0(t)}{1 - \alpha \beta} \tag{23.36b}$$

where $\alpha \beta \neq 1$.

Experimentation with this system using the DiagramEng application will give the user insight into the nature of coupled systems, in particular the effect of the source signals and gain constants

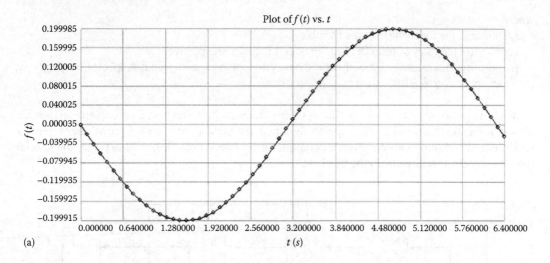

(a)

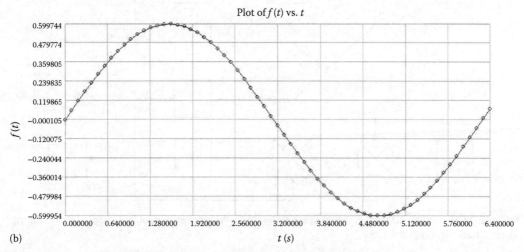

(b)

FIGURE 23.15 (a) Output $x_2(t)$ as a result of the coupling of source inputs $x_0(t) = \sin(t)$ and $x_1(t) = \sin(t)$. (b) Output $x_3(t)$ as a result of the coupling of source inputs $x_0(t) = \sin(t)$ and $x_1(t) = \sin(t)$.

on the different outputs. For example, if $x_0(t) = \sin(t)$, $x_1(t) = \sin(t)$, $\alpha = 2$, and $\beta = -2$, then the output signals $x_2(t)$ and $x_3(t)$, defined by (23.36), are those shown in Figure 23.15a and b, respectively, and are out of phase with differing magnitudes.

23.6.5 Computing the Lotka–Volterra Equations

A coupled nonlinear system differs from a coupled linear system in that the equations involved are nonlinear in the variables for which the system is to be computed. Consider the Lotka–Volterra system consisting of two coupled first-order nonlinear differential equations, describing the population dynamics of predator–prey interaction, presented in Ref. [12], where $x(t)$ and $y(t)$ are the populations of the prey and predator, respectively.

$$\frac{dx}{dt} = \alpha x - \beta xy \tag{23.37a}$$

$$\frac{dy}{dt} = -\gamma y + \delta xy \tag{23.37b}$$

where

t represents the independent time variable

α and γ are the rates of growth of the prey and predator, respectively

β and δ are the rates of competitive efficiency for the prey and predator species, respectively, where $\alpha, \beta, \gamma, \delta > 0$

A block diagram representation of this system (23.37) and its DiagramEng implementation are shown in Figures 23.16 and 23.17, respectively, where the input signals are the growth rates α and γ, which may be initially chosen given a condition of no interaction (β, $\delta = 0$) between the species (block numbers appear beneath the blocks).

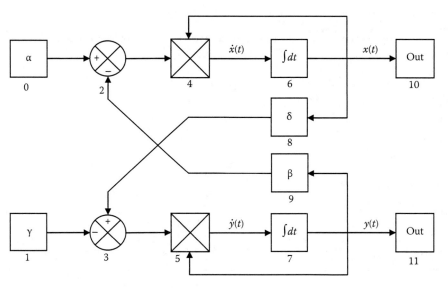

FIGURE 23.16   Block diagram representation of the Lotka–Volterra system of two coupled first-order nonlinear differential equations (23.37).

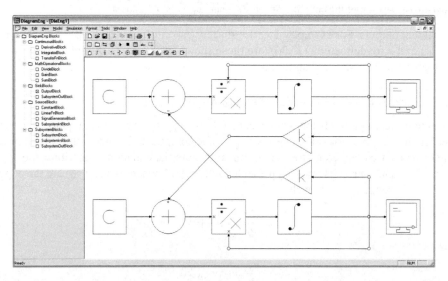

FIGURE 23.17   Block diagram representation of the Lotka–Volterra system made using DiagramEng.

In the case where β, $\delta = 0$, the equations of the populations are

$$\frac{dx}{dt} = \alpha x \Rightarrow x(t) = C_1 e^{\alpha t} \tag{23.38a}$$

$$\frac{dy}{dt} = -\gamma y \Rightarrow y(t) = C_2 e^{-\gamma t} \tag{23.38b}$$

where

C_1 and C_2 are constants

$x(t)$ and $y(t)$ are exponentially increasing and decreasing functions of time, for the prey and predator populations, respectively

The population of the prey in the absence of the predator increases and that of the predator decreases, as shown by Figure 23.18a and b, respectively.

Mathematicians familiar with the study of nonlinear dynamical systems and chaos, see, e.g., the texts of Kibble and Berkshire [12] and Strogatz [13], will recognize that the fixed points occur

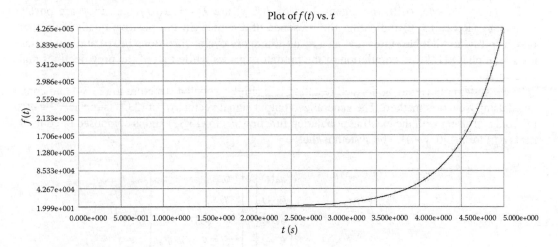

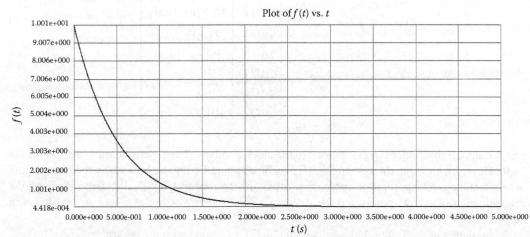

FIGURE 23.18 (a) Population of the prey, $x(t) = C_1 e^{\alpha t}$, in the absence of the predator: $x(0) = C_1 = 20$ and $\alpha = 2$. (b) The population of the predator, $y(t) = C_2 e^{\gamma t}$, in the absence of the prey: $y(0) = C_2 = 10$ and $\gamma = 2$.

when the populations are in equilibrium, i.e., when $\dot{x}(t) = 0$ and $\dot{y}(t) = 0$, resulting in two such points: $(x_0, y_0) = (0, 0)$ and $(x_1, y_1) = (\gamma/\delta, \alpha/\beta)$. The stability of these points may be determined by observing the eigenvalues of the Jacobian matrix of the system (23.37), i.e.,

$$J(x, y) = \begin{bmatrix} \dfrac{\partial \dot{x}}{\partial x} & \dfrac{\partial \dot{x}}{\partial y} \\ \dfrac{\partial \dot{y}}{\partial x} & \dfrac{\partial \dot{y}}{\partial y} \end{bmatrix} \tag{23.39a}$$

$$= \begin{bmatrix} \alpha - \beta y & -\beta x \\ \delta y & \delta x - \gamma \end{bmatrix} \tag{23.39b}$$

For $(x_0, y_0) = (0, 0)$, the eigenvalues of $J(x, y)$ are $\lambda_1 = \alpha$ and $\lambda_2 = -\gamma$, with corresponding eigenvectors $v_1 = [1, 0]^T$ (the unstable manifold, x axis) and $v_2 = [0, 1]^T$ (the stable manifold, y axis), respectively, and, hence, the critical point is a saddle point and the system is unstable, implying that the extinction of both species is unlikely.

For $(x_1, y_1) = (\gamma/\delta, \alpha/\beta)$, the eigenvalues of $J(x, y)$ are $\lambda_{1,2} = \pm i\sqrt{\alpha\gamma}$, i.e., they are purely imaginary ($\text{Re}(\lambda_{1,2}) = 0$) indicating the presence of a center (in the positive quadrant) rather than a spiral, and Kibble states that as a result, there are cyclic variations in $x(t)$ and $y(t)$ which are not in phase [12] (the population of the predators grows while that of the prey declines and vice versa).

Here, system (23.1) may be formed resulting in a similar coupled structure to (23.34) and computed using Newton's method. The generalized output signal vector $x(t)$ of (23.1) is replaced by $q(t)$ to avoid confusion with the existing population function $x(t)$ in (23.37) and is composed of components $q_i(t)$ for $i \in [0, s - 1]$. The system is thus

$$F(q(t)) = q(t) - f(q(t)) = \begin{bmatrix} q_0(t) \\ q_1(t) \\ q_2(t) \\ q_3(t) \\ q_4(t) \\ q_5(t) \\ q_6(t) \\ q_7(t) \\ q_8(t) \\ q_9(t) \end{bmatrix} - \begin{bmatrix} \alpha \\ \gamma \\ \alpha - \beta y(t) \\ -\gamma + \delta x(t) \\ (\alpha - \beta y(t))x(t) \\ (-\gamma + \delta x(t))y(t) \\ x(t) \\ y(t) \\ \delta x(t) \\ \beta y(t) \end{bmatrix} = \mathbf{0} \tag{23.40}$$

where output signal indices (i) correspond to the block numbers shown beneath the blocks in Figure 23.16. However, although the system (23.37) may be computed using the Newton method, one would expect that the more appropriate approach to study this nonlinear dynamical system is through the determination of critical points and the drawing of phase portraits in the x–y plane, as shown in Figure 23.20.

A simulation of the Lotka–Volterra system (23.37) was made with the parameters: $\alpha = 2$, $\gamma = 2$, $\beta = 1$, and $\delta = 0.5$, where the initial conditions of integration were $x(0) = 20$ and $y(0) = 10$, the initial output signals for the Divide blocks (which must be set since the Divide blocks are involved in

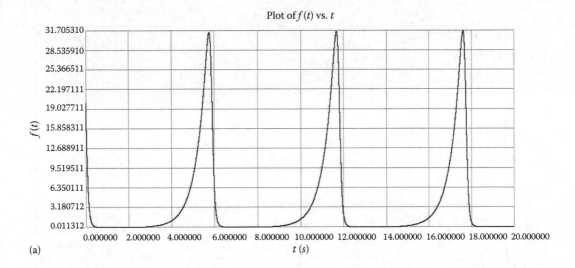

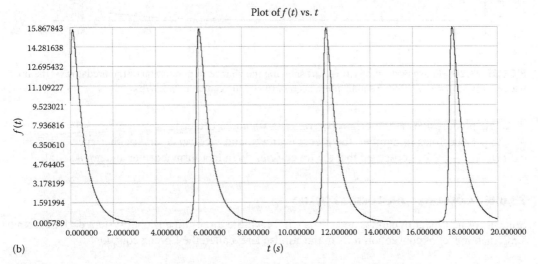

FIGURE 23.19 (a) Cyclic variations in the prey population for the Lotka–Volterra system (23.37) with parameters $\alpha = 2$, $\gamma = 2$, $\beta = 1$, and $\delta = 0.5$, where $x(0) = 20$ and $y(0) = 10$, and $\delta t = 10^{-4}$ s. (b) Cyclic variations in the predator population for the Lotka–Volterra system (23.37) with parameters $\alpha = 2$, $\gamma = 2$, $\beta = 1$, and $\delta = 0.5$, where $x(0) = 20$ and $y(0) = 10$, and $\delta t = 10^{-4}$ s.

two feedback loops) were $x_4(t_0) = -8$ and $x_5(t_0) = 8$, and a time-step size of $\delta t = 10^{-4}$ s was chosen. The cyclical variations in the populations of the prey and predators are shown in Figure 23.19a and b, respectively, where the population of the prey leads that of the predator, i.e., the variations are in fact not in phase.

The mathematician will notice that although the initial population sizes of the prey and predator are $x(0) = 20$ and $y(0) = 10$, respectively, as the system evolves, less than one of each species exists and then replicates to grow beyond their initial numbers. This is not biologically possible with the parameters chosen, but the results do indicate the presence of cyclic variations that are out of phase in the model. The interested researcher may like to experiment further with different parameters to produce biologically credible results, i.e., population sizes that do not fall below 2.

In addition, the phase portrait of the population of the predator vs. the prey, i.e., $y(t)$ vs. $x(t)$, may be generated, as shown in Figure 23.20, by saving the output data through the Output blocks and plotting the two population values against each other (in a third-party graphical application).

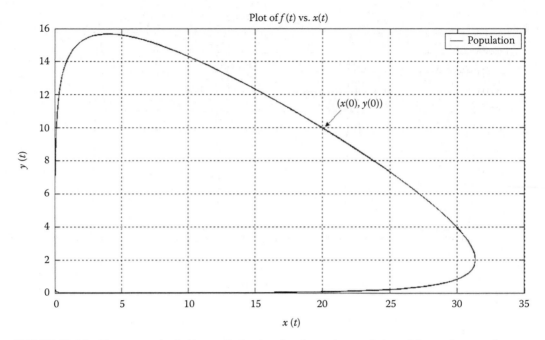

FIGURE 23.20   Phase portrait of $y(t)$ vs. $x(t)$ showing the change in population of the predator vs. the prey, where $(x(0), y(0)) = (20, 10)$: the saddle point is at $(0, 0)$ and the center at $(\gamma/\delta, \alpha/\beta)$.

A saddle point resides at the origin $(x_0, y_0) = (0, 0)$, and a center is present at $(x_1, y_1) = (\gamma/\delta, \alpha/\beta)$. As the prey declines in number, the predator grows, and vice versa, and neither species becomes extinct. As $t \to \infty$, it is observed that the trajectories do in fact form a center and not a spiral.

23.6.6   COMPUTING THE LORENZ EQUATIONS

Students of nonlinear dynamics and chaos will recall the three-dimensional system derived from a simplified model of convection rolls in the atmosphere, called the Lorenz equations,

$$\dot{x}(t) = \sigma(y(t) - x(t)) \tag{23.41a}$$

$$\dot{y}(t) = x(r - z(t)) - y(t) \tag{23.41b}$$

$$\dot{z}(t) = x(t)y(t) - bz(t) \tag{23.41c}$$

where
   $x(t)$, $y(t)$, and $z(t)$ are spatial coordinates that are functions of time t
   σ, r, and b are the Prandtl number, Rayleigh number, and a quantity related to the height of the fluid being modeled, respectively: $\sigma, r, b > 0$ [13]

For a thorough discussion of the Lorenz equations and the chaotic motion of the trajectories of the system that settle onto a set called a strange attractor, the interested reader should consult the work of Strogatz [13] (Chapter 9).

   The interest here in the Lorenz equations is to determine whether the DiagramEng application can generate the chaotic motion of the trajectories and reveal the complicated dynamics of this coupled nonlinear dynamical system. Figure 23.21 is the block diagram model of the Lorenz

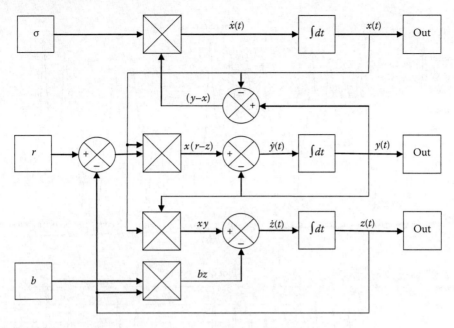

FIGURE 23.21 Block diagram model of the Lorenz equations (23.41).

equations (23.41) and shows the three Integrator blocks and numerous feedback paths: Figure 23.22 is the equivalent DiagramEng implementation of the model.

A simulation computing system (23.41) was conducted with the following parameter settings: $\sigma = 10$, $r = 28$, and $b = 8/3$. The initial conditions that appear often in the literature are $x(0) = 0$, $y(0) = 1$, and $z(0) = 1.05$. However, as a result, a simulation time of approximately $50\,\text{s}$ is required

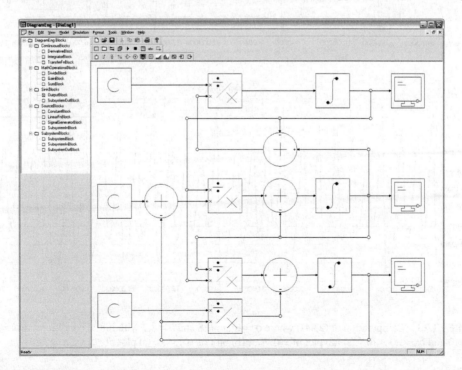

FIGURE 23.22 Block diagram model of the Lorenz equations made using DiagramEng, which is equivalent to Figure 23.21.

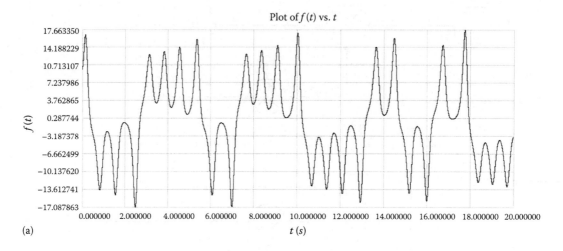

(a)

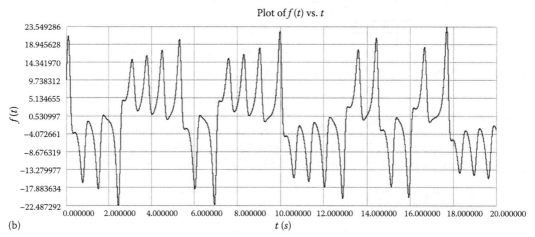

(b)

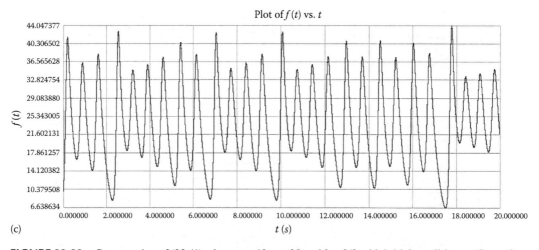

(c)

FIGURE 23.23   Computation of (23.41) where $\sigma = 10$, $r = 28$ and $b = 8/3$ with initial conditions, $x(0) = y(0) = z(0) = 10$ and $\delta t = 1.0 \times 10^{-6}$ (s): (a) plot of $x(t)$ vs. t, (b) plot of $y(t)$ vs. t, (c) plot of $z(t)$ vs. t.

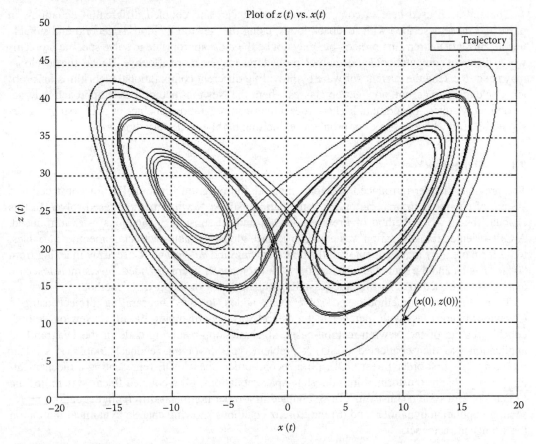

FIGURE 23.24 Phase portrait of $z(t)$ vs. $x(t)$ showing the chaotic motion on the strange attractor set, where $\sigma = 10$, $r = 28$, and $b = 8/3$ with initial conditions $x(0) = y(0) = z(0) = 10$.

to observe the aperiodic, irregular oscillation of the trajectories. Here, the initial conditions $x(0) = y(0) = z(0) = 10$ are chosen, to observe the erratic dynamics over a shorter time frame of 20 s. As there are Divide blocks that are the loop-repeated nodes in the model (see Chapters 19 and 22 concerning feedback loops in a model), the output signals for these blocks need to be set by the user: the initial values for the terms $\dot{x}(0)$, $x(r - z)$, xy, and bz were 0, 180, 100, and 26.6$\overline{6}$, respectively. The Euler integration scheme was used with a time-step size of $\delta t = 1.0 \times 10^{-6}$ s, but this is a problem due to its low order, and, hence, the solutions are not as accurate as those that may be determined by a fourth-order Runge–Kutta scheme.

The trajectories shown in Figure 23.23a through c were compared with those generated by MATLAB® and Simulink® for the same parameters and conditions stated earlier, including a relative error tolerance of 1.0×10^{-8}: in general the aperiodic oscillatory dynamics is present, but the results of the Euler scheme are not as accurate due to the accumulation of truncation and roundoff errors. It is interesting to note that with a slight change in parameter values and/or the initial conditions, or changes in spatial values due to accumulated numerical error, the resulting trajectories are substantially different. The interested reader may experiment with various initial conditions and parameter input and observe the significant changes in the computed trajectories for $x(t)$, $y(t)$, and $z(t)$. A higher-order numerical integration scheme, e.g., the fourth-order Runge–Kutta method, will be built into the DiagramEng software in future.

Figure 23.24 shows the phase portrait of the spatial coordinates $z(t)$ vs. $x(t)$ and reveals the chaotic motion on the strange attractor set, where $\sigma = 10$, $r = 28$, and $b = 8/3$, with initial conditions, $x(0) = 10$, $y(0) = 10$, and $z(0) = 10$.

The approach used here to compute linear, nonlinear, and coupled differential equations, in particular those described with feedback loops, using the Newton method, is general and suitable for the current DiagramEng project, but may not be the most appropriate to solve specific problems where different computational and analytic procedures may be more effective. Hence, the developer may need to extend the current software by providing different computational algorithms for problems belonging to certain application classes where the Newton-method-based approach may not be optimally suited. In addition, higher-order numerical integration schemes or stiff system solvers should be used where possible for problems exhibiting highly oscillatory dynamics.

23.7 SUMMARY

The previous chapter introduced Newton's method and program functionality for constructing a system of equations in preparation for computation using a Newton-method-based solver. In this chapter, the `newt()` method of Press et al. [1,2] and all subsidiary functions were introduced. A C++-oriented transformation was made, to replace global variables with class member variables, to perform memory management with the operators *new* and *delete*, and to use array indexing from "0" to "$n - 1$", and the source and header files "Newton.cpp/.h" were provided. Five simple test case examples were used to determine the feasibility and accuracy of the `newt()` method.

Then the Newton-method-based solver was added to the DiagramEng project using a CNewtonMethod class with member methods and variables involving the files "NewtonMethod.cpp/.h". Testing of the Newton-method-based algebraic-loop-resolving code in the DiagramEng application was then conducted using six problem types involving feedback loops: (1) a linear problem, (2) a first-order linear ODE, (3) a second-order linear ODE representing a mechanical/electrical problem transformed into the state-space equations, (4) a coupled linear system, (5) the Lotka–Volterra system consisting of two coupled first-order nonlinear differential equations representing population dynamics, and (6) the Lorenz equations showing chaotic dynamical motion on the strange attractor set.

REFERENCES

1. Press, W. H., Teukolsky, S. A., Vetterling, W. T., and Flannery, B. P., *Numerical Recipes in C: The Art of Scientific Computing*, 2nd edn., Cambridge University Press, Cambridge, U.K., 2002.
2. Press, W. H., Teukolsky, S. A., Vetterling, W. T., and Flannery, B. P., *Numerical Recipes in C++: The Art of Scientific Computing*, 2nd edn., Cambridge University Press, Cambridge, U.K., 2002.
3. Think Bottom Up Pty. Ltd., http://www.thinkbottomup.com.au/site/, (accessed in 2009).
4. Fisher, M. E., *Introductory Numerical Methods with the NAG Software Library*, The University of Western Australia, Perth, WA, 1989.
5. Kelley, A. and Pohl, I., *A Book On C: Programming in C*, 2nd edn., Benjamin Cummings, Redwood City, CA, 1990.
6. Shabana, A. A., *Computational Dynamics*, 2nd edn., John Wiley & Sons, New York, 2001.
7. *Simulink®* 6, *Using Simulink®*, MATLAB® & Simulink®, The MathWorks, Natick, MA, 2007.
8. Ogata, K., *Modern Control Engineering*, 4th edn., Prentice Hall, Upper Saddle River, NJ, 2002.
9. Salas, S. L. and Hille, E., *Calculus: One and Several Variables (Complex Variables, Differential Equations Supplement)*, 6th edn., John Wiley & Sons, New York, 1990.
10. Fox, B., Jennings, L. S., and Zomaya, A. Y., Numerical computation of differential-algebraic equations for non-linear dynamics of multibody systems involving contact forces, *ASME Journal of Mechanical Design*, 123(2), 272–281, 2001.
11. Sears, F. W., Zemansky, M. W., and Young, H. D., *University Physics*, 7th edn., Addison-Wesley, Reading MA, 1987.
12. Kibble, T. W. B. and Berkshire, F. H., *Classical Mechanics*, 5th edn., Imperial College Press, London, U.K., 2004.
13. Strogatz, S. H., *Nonlinear Dynamics and Chaos: With Applications to Physics, Biology, Chemistry, and Engineering*, Addison-Wesley, Reading MA, 1994.

24 Placing an Edit Box on a Toolbar

24.1 INTRODUCTION

Now that the `SignalPropagationDirect()` and `SignalPropagationSystemOfEqua` `tions()` functions have been shown to work consistently and predictably for a range of models, further additions and refinements may be made to the DiagramEng application to enhance its usefulness. The following instructions indicate how to place an Edit box control, of type CEdit, on a toolbar, which can be used to display the time value $t \in [t_0, t_f]$ (s) of the simulation and the execution time t_{exe} (s) required, where t_0 and t_f are the initial and final time points, respectively. The instructions presented in the ensuing sections follow the work of Chapman [1] (Chapter 12, pp. 257–270), where Chapman discusses the placement of a Combo box on a toolbar that accepts user input and displays selected output. Here, however, a read-only Edit box is introduced that simply displays time-based output, i.e., t and t_{exe}.

24.2 EDIT THE RESOURCE FILE

Edit the "DiagramEng.rc" resource file and place two separators at the end of the Common Operations toolbar (IDR_TB_COMMON_OPS) as shown in bold in the following code excerpt, using the Notepad editor (the ellipsis, "…", denotes omitted code for brevity). Chapman [1] indicates that the second separator acts as a placeholder for the control to be added at the end of the toolbar: here the Edit box.

```
//Microsoft Developer Studio generated resource script.
//
#include "resource.h"
...
IDR_TB_COMMON_OPS TOOLBAR DISCARDABLE 16, 15
BEGIN
    BUTTON      ID_EDIT_SELECTALL
    BUTTON      ID_EDIT_ADD_MULTI_BLOCKS
    BUTTON      ID_VIEW_AUTO_FIT_DIAGRAM
    BUTTON      ID_MODEL_BUILD
    BUTTON      ID_SIM_START
    BUTTON      ID_SIM_STOP
    BUTTON      ID_SIM_NUM_SOLVER
    BUTTON      ID_FORMAT_SHOW_NAMES
    BUTTON      ID_INIT_TRACK_MULTIPLE_ITEMS
    SEPARATOR
    SEPARATOR
END
...
/////////////////////////////////////////////////////////////////////////
#endif    // not APSTUDIO_INVOKED
```

24.3　CREATE THE TOOLBAR EDIT BOX

An Edit box control variable needs to be added to the CMainFrame class in order that an Edit box control can be added to the Common Operations toolbar.

1. Add a protected member variable to the CMainFrame class with the name "m_pctlEditBoxTime" of type pointer-to-CEdit (CEdit*).
2. Edit the CMainFrame::OnCreate() function as shown in bold to construct the Edit box and place it on the Common Operations toolbar (the rest of the function remains unchanged from Chapter 12).

```
int CMainFrame::OnCreate(LPCREATESTRUCT lpCreateStruct)
{
    ...

    // DiagramEng (start)

    // -- CREATE THE CommonOps TOOLBAR

    // NOTE: 'this' is the ptr to the parent frame wnd to which the
      toolbar will be attached.
    // CreateEx creates the toolbar
    // LoadToolBar loads the toolbar specified by the ID
    if(!m_wndTBCommonOps.CreateEx(this, TBSTYLE_FLAT, WS_CHILD |
      WS_VISIBLE | CBRS_TOP | CBRS_GRIPPER | CBRS_TOOLTIPS | CBRS_FLYBY |
      CBRS_SIZE_DYNAMIC) || !m_wndTBCommonOps.
      LoadToolBar(IDR_TB_COMMON_OPS))
    {
        // Failed to create msg.
        TRACE0("Failed to create toolbar\n");
        return -1;
    }

    // -- PLACING AN EDIT BOX ON THE CommonOps TOOLBAR
    // Properties of Edit box Control to be placed on CommonOps Toolbar
    int nEditBoxWidth = 200; // with of the Edit box control
    int nIndex = 10;         // index of button or separator whose info
      is to be set: btns (0-8), separator (9), separator placeholder (10)

    // Set Properties of Placeholder Separator for Edit box Control
    m_wndTBCommonOps.SetButtonInfo(nIndex, IDC_EB_COTB_TIME,
      TBBS_SEPARATOR, nEditBoxWidth);

    // Get the rectangle coords of the placeholder where the Edit box
      will be created.
    CRect rect;
    m_wndTBCommonOps.GetItemRect(nIndex, &rect);  // nIndex is index of
      button or separator whose rectangle cords are rqd.

    // Construct the CEdit object.
    m_pctlEditBoxTime = new CEdit;

    // Create the Edit box
    m_pctlEditBoxTime->Create(ES_LEFT|ES_READONLY|WS_BORDER|WS_
      CHILD|WS_VISIBLE, rect, &m_wndTBCommonOps, IDC_EB_COTB_TIME);
    // -- END OF PLACING AN EDIT BOX ON THE CommonOps TOOLBAR

    // -- END CREATION OF CommonOps TOOLBAR
```

TABLE 24.1

Properties of the Common Operations Toolbar Buttons

Entity Index	Entity (Button/Separator)	Entity ID	ID Value
0	Select All	ID_EDIT_SELECTALL	32773
1	Add Multiple Blocks	ID_EDIT_ADD_MULTI_BLOCKS	32839
2	Auto Fit Diagram	ID_VIEW_AUTO_FIT_DIAGRAM	32852
3	Build Model	ID_MODEL_BUILD	32783
4	Start Simulation	ID_SIM_START	32784
5	Stop Simulation	ID_SIM_STOP	32785
6	Numerical Solver	ID_SIM_NUM_SOLVER	32848
7	Show Annotations	ID_FORMAT_SHOW_ANNOTATIONS	32849
8	Track Multiple Items	ID_INIT_TRACK_MULTIPLE_ITEMS	32837
9	Separator	—	—
10	Separator (Placeholder)	To be: IDC_EB_COTB_TIME	

```
// -- CREATE THE CommonBlocks TOOLBAR
...
// -- END CREATION OF CommonBlocks TOOLBAR
...
return 0;
}
```

Initially the properties of the placeholder separator on the Common Operations toolbar need to be set to those of the to-be-created Edit box. Hence, the width is set to be the Edit box width, "nEditBoxWidth", and the index, "nIndex", is that of the button or separator (here the separator) whose information is to be set. Table 24.1 lists all the indices, names and IDs, of the entities on the Common Operations toolbar. The placeholder separator is used to position the Edit box, and its index is "10" as shown.

Then the SetButtonInfo() function is called passing in the index, "nIndex"; the ID of the Edit box control, "IDC_EB_COTB_TIME" (to be added); the type of control (a separator); and the width of the separator, i.e., the width of the Edit box to appear in this location.

3. A unique ID is to be used for the Edit box control: right click on the DiagramEng resources folder in the Resource View of the Workspace pane, select Resource Symbols, and add the new control ID, "IDC_EB_COTB_TIME", for the Edit box control residing on the Common Operations toolbar that will display the model's simulation and execution times, as shown in Figure 24.1. For example, choose the ID, 32700, since at present this is not in use, but check the "resource.h" header file to avoid a duplicate.

Then the rectangle coordinates of the placeholder, with index "nIndex", where the Edit box is to be created, are determined by the call to GetItemRect(). Thereafter the CEdit constructor is called to construct a CEdit object where the address returned by *new* is assigned to the pointer-to-CEdit, "m_pctlEditBoxTime". Finally, the Create() function is called upon the "m_pctlEditBoxTime" member variable, to create the Edit box. The first (compound) argument involves edit and window styles; the second is the control's size and position (rect); the third is the address of the control's parent window, i.e., the Common Operations toolbar; and the final argument is the ID of the Edit box control.

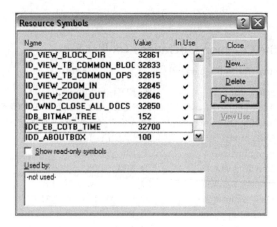

FIGURE 24.1   Resource Symbols showing the Edit box control ID, "IDC_EB_COTB_TIME".

24.4   UPDATE THE TOOLBAR EDIT BOX

The purpose of the Edit box control is to simply update the simulation and execution times to the user, but since the Edit box is specified to be a read-only control (ES_READONLY), it does not need to process user input since no user input is allowed. The following steps indicate how the Edit box may be updated.

1. A function in the Main frame class, CMainFrame, is to be called from the document class to update the Edit box. Hence, add a public member function to the CMainFrame class with the prototype void CMainFrame::UpdateEditBoxTimeOnCommonOps Toolbar(CString string), and edit the function as shown. The incoming argument is the simulation time (t) or execution time (t_{exe}) converted to a CString variable, originally generated by the signal propagation functions, SignalPropagationDirect() or SignalPropagationSystemOfEquations().

```
void CMainFrame::UpdateEditBoxTimeOnCommonOpsToolbar(CString string)
{
    CString str_empty = "";

    // Update the Edit box on the CommonOps Toolbar with the string
    // Note: SetWindowText() replaces all the text in the Edit control:
      the msg. used is WM_SETTEXT.
    // ReplaceSel() replaces the selected text: the msg. used is
      EM_REPLACESEL.
    m_pctlEditBoxTime->SetWindowText(str_empty);
      // CWnd::SetWindowText()
    m_pctlEditBoxTime->ReplaceSel(string, FALSE); // Replace the existing
      text with the new text
}
```

Here both SetWindowText() and ReplaceSel() are called upon the pointer-to-CEdit "m_pctlEditBoxSimTime": the former function replaces all the text in the Edit box with the empty string, in effect clearing the box, and the latter replaces the current selection with the incoming string, and the messages used are WM_SETTEXT and EM_REPLACESEL, respectively. If there is no current selection, as is the case here with the empty string in place, the replacement text is inserted at the current cursor location [2]. This combination of calls allows the Edit box to be refreshed immediately. If `SetWindowText()` is solely used where the argument is the incoming string, then the Edit box would not be refreshed fast enough to dynamically display the incrementing time values, t (s), during the simulation.

The reader will notice that `SetWindowText()` is a CWnd method, but because the Edit box control is of type CEdit, and CEdit derives from CWnd, then the function may be called on the CEdit control variable. The interested reader should consult the Microsoft Foundation Class Library Hierarchy Chart [2] to see the class structure.

2. Now the function in the document class needs to be added, to call the CMainFrame function to update the Edit box control. Hence, add a public member function to the CDiagramEngDoc class with the following prototype: `void CDiagramEngDoc::UpdateCommonOpsToolbar(CString string)`, and edit the function as shown.

```
void CDiagramEngDoc::UpdateCommonOpsToolbar(CString string)
{
    // Get the position of the first view
    POSITION pos = GetFirstViewPosition();
    if(pos != NULL)
    {
        // Get a ptr to the view in that position
        CView *pView = GetNextView(pos);
        if(pView)
        {
            // Get a ptr to the frame through the view
            CMainFrame *pFrame = (CMainFrame*)pView->GetTopLevelFrame();
            if(pFrame)
            {
                // Update the Edit box control on the CommonOps Toolbar
                //   through the frame
                pFrame->UpdateEditBoxTimeOnCommonOpsToolbar(string);
            }
        }
    }
}
```

This function gets the first view position, "pos"; the pointer to the view, "pView"; and then a pointer to the CMainFrame, "pFrame", upon which the previously introduced function, `UpdateEditBoxTimeOnCommonOpsToolbar()`, is called.

3. Since "pFrame" is of type pointer-to-CMainFrame, the "MainFrm.h" header file should be included at the top of the "DiagramEngDoc.cpp" source file, as indicated in bold.

```
// DiagramEngDoc.cpp : implementation of the CDiagramEngDoc class
//

#include "stdafx.h"
#include "DiagramEng.h"
#include "DiagramEngDoc.h"
// DiagramEng (start)
#include <math.h>            // rqd. since OnDeleteItem() uses math fns.
#include "afxext.h"          // rqd. since TrackItem() uses a
  CRectTracker obj.
#include "BlockLibDlg.h"     // rqd. since OnEditAddMultipleBlocks() has
  a CBlockLibDlg obj.
```

```
//#include "TreeDialog.h"    // rqd. since OnEditAddMultipleBlocks() has
  a CTreeDialog obj.
#include "OutputBlockView.h" // rqd. since DeleteOutputBlockView()
  declares a ptr-to-COutputBlockView
#include "MainFrm.h"         // rqd. since UpdateCommonOpsToolbar() uses
  a ptr-to-CMainFrame
// DiagramEng (end)
...
```

4. Now that the `CMainFrame::UpdateEditBoxTimeOnCommonOpsToolbar()` function can be called from within the `CDiagramEngDoc::UpdateCommonOps Toolbar()` function, the latter needs to be called from within the simulation functions `CSystemModel::SignalPropagationDirect()` and `CSystemModel:: SignalPropagationSystemOfEquations()`, to display the simulation and execution times to the user. Hence, edit these functions as shown in bold in the following, to first get a pointer-to-CDiagramEngDoc and then to call `UpdateCommonOpsToolbar()` upon the pointer, passing the CString simulation and execution time values: the ellipsis ("...") denotes omitted but unchanged code.

```
void CSystemModel::SignalPropagationDirect()
{
    int n_TimeSteps; // total no. of time steps for numerical integration
    ...
    list<CConnection*>::iterator it_con;  // iterator for list of
      CConnection ptrs.

    // Get a ptr-to-CDiagramEngDoc to call UpdateCommonOpsToolbar().
    CDiagramEngDoc *pDoc = GetDocumentGlobalFn();

    // Get the actual connection list by reference
    list<CConnection*> &con_list = GetConnectionList();  // get the
      connection list
    ...
    // -- Loop for n_TimeSteps + 1, from t_0 = 0, UP TO AND INCLUDING the
      last time point t_n
    for(t_cnt = 0; t_cnt <= n_TimeSteps; t_cnt++)
    {
        t = t_init + t_cnt*delta_t;  // t cnt, i.e. i-th time point t_i,
          or simply t.
        ...
        // Update the Edit box on the CommonOps toolbar with the
          simulation time value
        sMsg.Empty();
        sMsg.Format("t = %e/ %g (s)", t, m_dTimeStop);  // %g is the
          shorter of e-format or f-format
        pDoc->UpdateCommonOpsToolbar(sMsg);

        // Check if stop button pressed
        bStop = CheckStopButtonPressed();
        if(bStop)
        {
            break;
        }
    }// end (time)

    // -- EXECUTION TIME STOP
    tv2 = clock();
```

```
    t_execution = (double)(tv2 - tv1)/(double)CLOCKS_PER_SEC;
    sMsg.Empty();
    sMsg.Format("t_exe = %e (s)", t_execution);
    pDoc->UpdateCommonOpsToolbar(sMsg);

    // -- RESET ALL BLOCKS THAT HAVE MEMORY, I.E. RETAIN PAST VALUES
    ResetMemoryBasedBlockData();
    ...
    return;
}
void CSystemModel::SignalPropagationSystemOfEquations()
{
    int n_TimeSteps;  // total no. of time steps for system computation/
      simulation
    ...
    list<CConnection*>::iterator it_con;  // iterator for list of
      CConnection ptrs.

    // Get a ptr-to-CDiagramEngDoc to call UpdateCommonOpsToolbar().
    CDiagramEngDoc *pDoc = GetDocumentGlobalFn();

    // Get the actual connection list by reference
    list<CConnection*> &con_list = GetConnectionList();  // get the
      connection list
    ...
    // -- Loop for n_TimeSteps + 1, from t_0 = 0, UP TO AND INCLUDING the
      last time point t_n
    for(t_cnt = 0; t_cnt <= n_TimeSteps; t_cnt++)
    {
        t = t_init + t_cnt*delta_t;  // t cnt, i.e. i-th time point t_i,
          or simply t.
        ...
        // Update the Edit box on the CommonOps toolbar with the
          simulation time value
        sMsg.Empty();
        sMsg.Format("t = %e / %g (s)", t, m_dTimeStop);  // %g is the
          shorter of e-format or f-format
        pDoc->UpdateCommonOpsToolbar(sMsg);

        // Check if stop button pressed
        bStop = CheckStopButtonPressed();
        if(bStop)
        {
            break;
        }
    }// end (time)
    // -- EXECUTION TIME STOP
    tv2 = clock();
    t_execution = (double)(tv2 - tv1)/(double)CLOCKS_PER_SEC;
    sMsg.Empty();
    sMsg.Format("t_exe = %e (s)", t_execution);
    pDoc->UpdateCommonOpsToolbar(sMsg);

    // -- RESET ALL BLOCKS THAT HAVE MEMORY, I.E. RETAIN PAST VALUES
    ResetMemoryBasedBlockData();
    ...
    return;
}
```

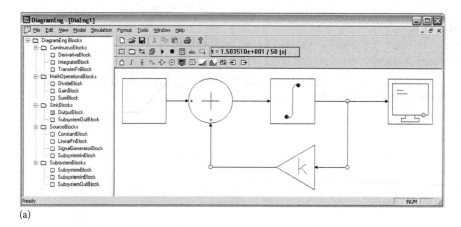

(a)

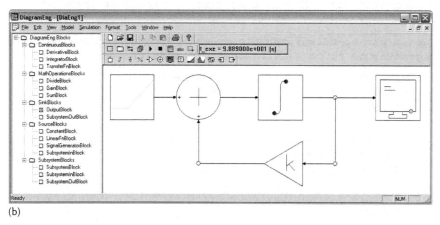

(b)

FIGURE 24.2 Display of time values in the Edit box control on the Common Operations toolbar: (a) model simulation time, t (s), (b) model execution time, t_{exe} (s).

The developer will notice that during the simulation, the current time point, t (s), is displayed in the Edit box (Figure 24.2a), and after the simulation, the execution time, t_{exe} (s), is displayed (Figure 24.2b), implicitly indicating the end of the experiment.

24.5 A MEMORY LEAK

However, there is a slight problem: if the developer performs a Debug-based build of the DiagramEng application and then runs it with the debugger, upon exiting the application, the following error message is generated in the Debug output window.

```
Detected memory leaks!
Dumping objects ->
C:BudFoxC++WorkDiagram Eng ProjectDiagramEng (13 signals newt C++)
  DiagramEngMainFrm.cpp(133) : {106} client block at 0x004929D0,
  subtype 0, 64 bytes long.
a CEdit object at $004929D0, 64 bytes long
Object dump complete.
```

The message indicates that there is a memory leak, in particular, that the CEdit object, which was created on line 133 of file "MainFrm.cpp", with the statement, "m_pctlEditBoxTime = new CEdit;", has not been deleted. Hence, delete the member variable "m_pcltEditBoxTime" of type pointer-to-CEdit in the CMainFrame class destructor as follows.

```
CMainFrame::~CMainFrame()
{
    // DiagramEng (start)
    if(m_pctlEditBoxTime != NULL)
    {
        delete m_pctlEditBoxTime;
        m_pctlEditBoxTime = NULL;
    }
    // DiagramEng (end)
}
```

Now the CMainFrame class constructor should be augmented to initialize the member variable to NULL to prevent erroneous deletion, as shown.

```
CMainFrame::CMainFrame()
{
    // TODO: add member initialization code here
    m_pctlEditBoxTime = NULL;
}
```

Now upon running the program using the debugger and then exiting normally, there is no memory leak reported in the Debug output window.

24.6   SUMMARY

The work of Chapman [1] originally discusses the placement of a Combo box on a toolbar, and here that development is adopted to place a read-only Edit box control on the Common Operations toolbar that allows the user to dynamically see the simulation time, t (s), of a running experiment and then the execution time, t_{exe} (s), at the end of the simulation. The resource file "DiagramEng.rc" is initially amended and two separators placed at the end of the Common Operations toolbar. Then a separator is set up using SetButtonInfo() in preparation for the creation of the Edit box control, using a pointer-to-CEdit variable "m_pctlEditBoxTime", and the functions GetItemRect() and Create(). The Edit box is updated through the CMainFrame function, UpdateEditBoxTimeOnCommonOpsToolbar(), which is called from the CDiagramEngDoc function, UpdateCommonOpsToolbar(), which in turn is called from the CSystemModel simulation functions, SignalPropagationDirect() and SignalPropagationSystemOfEquations(). Finally, a memory leak was detected using the debugger, and the CMainFrame class member variable, "m_pctlEditBoxTime", was initialized in the constructor and deleted in the destructor.

REFERENCES

1. Chapman, D., *Teach Yourself Visual C++ 6 in 21 Days*, Sams Publishing, Indianapolis, IN, 1998.
2. Microsoft Developer Network Library Visual Studio 6.0, Microsoft® Visual Studio™ 6.0 Development System, Microsoft Corporation, 1998.

25 Serialization

25.1 INTRODUCTION

"Serialization" and "deserialization" are the processes of storing and retrieving application data on and from the system drive in the form of a file, respectively [1]. This may be performed either by using the Document class `Serialize()` function in conjunction with the CArchive class or by writing a specialized (virtual void) `Serialize()` function for a particular user-defined class that performs the equivalent saving and restoring actions. In addition, two macros, DECLARE_SERIAL and IMPLEMENT_SERIAL, are used in the class declaration and definition, respectively [1]. The interested reader should consult the work of Chapman [1] for examples of the use of the `Serialize()` function, in particular, Chapter 10, Creating Single Document Interface Applications, and Chapter 13, Saving and Restoring Work—File Access.

Here, an alternative method is used to perform the equivalent serialization and deserialization actions, where data are written to and read from a file directly, using functions associated with the Open, Save, Save As, Close, and Exit entries under the File menu. All the system model data, including block-based, connection-based, and parameter-value-based data, are to be recorded such that upon opening a previously saved model, the entire model can be immediately restored and validated and the simulation rerun, to regenerate results identical to those obtained prior to serialization.

25.2 SYSTEM MODEL DATA STRUCTURE

The CDiagramEngDoc class contains a CSystemModel object, "m_SystemModel", and the CSystemModel class contains system model parameters and a list of block and connection pointers: "list<CBlock*> m_lstBlock" and "list<CConnection*> m_lstConnection". The base block class CBlock has member variables that include the block's name, position and shape, and two vectors of pointers-to-CPort: a vector of input ports, "vector<CPort*> m_vecInputPorts", and a vector of output ports, "vector<CPort*> m_vecOutputPorts". Each individual block has its own particular data members, some of which may be set using the block dialog parameter input window and parameter input function, `BlockDlgWndParameterInput()`.

The CConnection object that is used to connect all the blocks of a model has member data including a head point, "m_ptHead"; a tail point, "m_ptTail"; a reference-from point, "m_pRefFromPoint" (which could possibly be NULL); a reference-from port, "m_pRefFromPort"; a reference-to port, "m_pRefToPort"; a bend points list, "list<CPoint> m_lstBendPoints"; and a CSignal object, "m_pSignal". The signal data represent the numerical values generated during model computation, i.e., during the simulation, and are not saved to a file during the serialization process. However, output data displayed using the Output block at present cannot be saved; hence, functionality will be added to the Output Block Dialog window to allow the user to write output data directly to a file if desired (see instructions in Section 25.7). (The original placeholder functions `WriteOutputToFile()` and `WriteNthTimeStepToFile()` and `ReadInputFromFile()`, of the Win32 Console Application code, will be replaced with the Output block's file I/O methods.)

Saving and restoring of a system model's data in their entirety are hence involved processes that need to be performed in a structured and consistent manner to allow the correct writing to and reading from a file. These data are then used to reconstruct the system model and all its constituent components, i.e., the contained member objects of the main CSystemModel object, "m_SystemModel". The data in their most rudimentary form consist of character, integer, and double data types. Tables 25.1 through 25.19 present the data types, member variables, and brief descriptions of the data that are to be both written to and read from a model text ("*.txt") file: they are listed by data type for convenience. Variables that are of type CPoint in the DiagramEng project are written here in Cartesian component integer form. Some variables in Tables 25.1 through 25.19 are not explicitly saved for one or more reasons: (1) they are not set by the user through the dialog parameter input windows, (2) they have default static values used in object reconstruction, (3) they are determined dynamically, (4) they are the equivalent duplicates of existing member data in a different data type, (5) they represent contained objects whose explicit data are saved by the appropriate contained classes, or (6) they may be saved by alternative methods, e.g., the COutputBlock class will provide a special mechanism to save output data directly to a separate data file.

25.2.1   CSystemModel Data

The CSystemModel class includes numerical-method-based data, as shown in Table 25.1, and also the main-model-based lists: a list of pointers-to-CBlock, "list<CBlock*> m_lstBlock", and pointers-to-CConnection, "list<CConnection*> m_lstConnection". The integer data, and the lists themselves are not saved directly but rather are iterated over to access and write out the block-based and connection-based data.

25.2.2   CBlock Data

The base CBlock class contains data specific to all derived blocks that may be saved, as shown in Table 25.2. The vectors of pointers-to-CPort, "vector<CPort*> m_vecInputPorts" and "vector<CPort*> m_vecOutputPorts", are not saved directly but are iterated over to access the CPort-based data. The contained CBlockShape object "m_BlockShape" is also not saved directly but is accessed to extract block-related geometrical information. The pointer to the parent system model, "m_pParentSystemModel", does not need to be saved, and the pointer to a contained subsystem,

TABLE 25.1
CSystemModel Serialization Data: Data Type, Member Variable, and Description

Data Type	Member Variable	Description
int	m_iModelStatusFlag	Model status flag
int	m_iNOutputBlocks	No. of model output blocks
int	m_iNSourceBlocks	No. of model source blocks
int	m_iNSourceLoopTours	No. of source-to-loop-repeated-block tours
int	m_iNSourceOutputTours	No. of source-to-output-block tours
double	m_dATOL	Absolute error tolerance parameter
double	m_dRTOL	Relative error tolerance parameter
double	m_dTimeStart	Simulation start time
double	m_dTimeStepSize	Time-step size
double	m_dTimeStop	Simulation stop time
CString	m_strIntegrationMethod	Integration method: Euler, Runge–Kutta
CString	m_strModelName	Name of current system model
CString	m_strTimeStepType	Time-step type: fixed-step or variable-step
CString	m_strWarning	Diagnostic warning messages
list<int*>	m_lstSourceLoopTour	List of arrays of source-loop-block tours
list<int*>	m_lstSourceOutputTour	List of arrays of source-output-block tours
list<CBlock*>	m_lstBlock	List of blocks
list<CConnection*>	m_lstConnection	List of connections
list<CConnection*>	m_lstConnectionError	List of disconnected connections

TABLE 25.2

CBlock Serialization Data: Data Type, Member Variable, and Description

Data Type	Member Variable	Description
Int	m_ptBlockPosition.x	Block center of mass x-coordinate
Int	m_ptBlockPosition.y	Block center of mass y-coordinate
Int	m_iPenColor	Pen color used to draw blocks
int	m_iPenWidth	Pen width used to draw blocks
CBlockShape	m_BlockShape	Block-shape-contained member object
CString	m_strBlockName	Block name
CSystemModel*	m_pParentSystemModel	Pointer to the parent system model
CSystemModel*	m_pSubSystemModel	Pointer to a contained subsystem model
vector<CPort*>	m_vecInputPorts	Vector of block input ports
vector<CPort*>	m_vecOutputPorts	Vector of block output ports

"m_pSubSystemModel", is currently not in use since subsystem functionality has not been added to the project at this stage and is to be added later. The integer members "m_iPenColor" and "m_iPenWidth", used in the drawing of blocks, do not need to be serialized as these are internal data members and are not altered by the user. Only the block position "m_ptBlockPosition" and name "m_strBlockName" need to be saved.

25.2.3   CBlockShape Data

The CBlockShape object, "m_BlockShape", contained within the CBlock class, retains geometrical information concerning all block shapes, including their dimensions and enumerated-type-based data, as shown in Table 25.3.

25.2.4   CPort Data

The CBlock class has two vectors of pointers-to-CPort, i.e., a vector of input and output ports. Each CPort object has the data specified in Table 25.4, including the port position, name, and its direction. Most blocks have only a single input and output port, and typically default values can be used in their reconstruction. However, the Divide and Sum blocks may have a variable number of input ports with different signs. Hence, the relevant CPort class member data, including the port name "m_strPortName", port position angle "m_dPortPositionAngle" from which the port position may be calculated, and port arrow direction "m_ePortArrowDirec", need to be serialized. The member variable "m_rRefToBlock" of the CPort class is the only variable not required in serialization: it is used on CPort object construction and is a reference or alias for a derived CBlock object.

TABLE 25.3

CBlockShape Serialization Data: Data Type, Member Variable, and Description

Data Type	Member Variable	Description
double	m_dBlockHeight	Block height
double	m_dBlockWidth	Block width
EBlockDirection	m_eBlockDirection	Block direction: left, right, up, down
EBlockShape	m_eBlockShape	Block shape: ellipse, rectangle, triangle

TABLE 25.4

CPort Serialization Data: Data Type, Member Variable, and Description

Data Type	Member Variable	Description
int	m_ptPortPosition.x	Port position x-coordinate
int	m_ptPortPosition.y	Port position y-coordinate
int	m_ptPortSignPosition.x	Port sign position x-coordinate
int	m_ptPortSignPosition.y	Port sign position y-coordinate
double	m_dPortPositionAngle	Angle defining the location of the port
CBlock	&m_rRefToBlock	Reference to parent block
CString	m_strPortName	Port name that reflects the port sign
EPortArrowDirection	m_ePortArrowDirec	Port arrow direction: left, right, up, down

25.2.5   CConnection Data

The CSystemModel class has a list of pointers-to-CConnection which are used to connect blocks and hold bend/branch points to which other connections may be attached. The bend points are themselves stored in a list of CPoint objects, "m_lstBendPoints", and their x and y CPoint coordinates are saved. The reference-from port "m_pRefFromPort", reference-to port "m_pRefToPort", and reference-from point "m_pRefFromPoint", holding the addresses of their respective data types, are not required to be saved, since these values are assigned after snapping a connection end point to a port or bend point. The CSignal "m_pSignal" data, contained in the CConnection class, are the numerical data computed throughout the simulation and are not explicitly required to be written to or read from a file: the Output block will provide a mechanism to save any output data directly if the user desires. The integer and CPoint data that need to be written to and read from a file are shown in Table 25.5.

25.2.6   CSignal Data

The CSignal data held by a CConnection object are shown in Table 25.6 and include the data matrix, its size, and validity. The CSignal data may be recorded directly by the Output block but are otherwise not saved.

TABLE 25.5

CConnection Serialization Data: Data Type, Member Variable, and Description

Data Type	Member Variable	Description
int	m_ptHead.x	Head point x-coordinate
int	m_ptHead.y	Head point y-coordinate
int	m_ptTail.x	Tail point x-coordinate
int	m_ptTail.y	Tail point y-coordinate
CPoint*	m_pRefFromPoint	Point from which connection may be drawn
CPort*	m_pRefFromPort	Port from which connection emanates
CPort*	m_pRefToPort	Port to which connection is attached
CSignal*	m_pSignal	Signal object containing connection data
list<CPoint>	m_lstBendPoints	List of connection bend points

TABLE 25.6

CSignal Serialization Data: Data Type, Member Variable, and Description

Data Type	Member Variable	Description
int	m_iNcols	No. of columns of signal matrix
int	m_iNrows	No. of rows of signal matrix
int	m_iValidity	Signal-data-based validity
double**	m_dSignalMatrix	Matrix signal value
CString	m_strOutputSignal	Output signal as a CString
CString	m_strSignalName	Signal name

25.2.7 DERIVED-BLOCK CLASS DATA

All the CBlock-derived classes each have particular information in addition to that held by the aforementioned classes: CBlock, CBlockShape, and CPort.

25.2.7.1 CConstantBlock Data

The CConstantBlock class contains the constant value recorded in a matrix, "m_dConstMatrix", including its dimensions, "m_iNrows" and "m_iNcols". The CString variable "m_strConstValue" is not required for serialization purposes, since it represents the equivalent matrix data and can be reinitialized after reading in the double data followed by conversion of the double data to a CString (Table 25.7).

25.2.7.2 CDerivativeBlock Data

The CDerivativeBlock class contains data members used in the evaluation of the numerical derivative. The only variable that needs to be serialized is the derivative method, "m_iDerivativeMethod"; the remaining variables are used dynamically (Table 25.8).

25.2.7.3 CDivideBlock Data

The CDivideBlock class is used to perform division and multiplication of input signals; hence, the number of divide and multiply input ports, "m_iNDivideInputs" and "m_iNMultiplyInputs", respectively, are required and so too the multiplication type, "m_iMultType", denoting elemental or matrix multiplication (Table 25.9).

25.2.7.4 CGainBlock Data

The CGainBlock class is used to contain the gain matrix, "m_dGainMatrix"; its dimensions, "m_iNrows" and "m_iNcols"; and the gain type, "m_iGainType": elemental, gain-times-input, or input-times-gain. The CString variable has the same function as that in the CConstantBlock class

TABLE 25.7

CConstantBlock Serialization Data: Data Type, Member Variable, and Description

Data Type	Member Variable	Description
int	m_iNcols	No. of columns of constant matrix
int	m_iNrows	No. of rows of constant matrix
double**	m_dConstMatrix	Constant matrix
CString	m_strConstValue	CString constant matrix

TABLE 25.8
CDerivativeBlock Serialization Data: Data Type, Member Variable, and Description

Data Type	Member Variable	Description
int	m_i_t_cnt_ref	Reference time count
int	m_iDerivativeMethod	Derivative method: three-point, five-point
int	m_iNcallsPerTimeCnt	No. of times function called per time point
int	m_iNrows	No. of rows of incoming signal data
double*	m_f_at_t_minus_h	$f(t - h)$
double*	m_f_at_t_minus2h	$f(t - 2h)$
double**	m_dMatrixOut	Matrix data of output signal

TABLE 25.9
CDivideBlock Serialization Data: Data Type, Member Variable, and Description

Data Type	Member Variable	Description
int	m_iMultType	Multiplication type: elemental, matrix
int	m_iNDivideInputs	No. of division input ports
int	m_iNMultiplyInputs	No. of multiplication input ports

TABLE 25.10
CGainBlock Serialization Data: Data Type, Member Variable, and Description

Data Type	Member Variable	Description
int	m_iGainType	Gain type: elemental, gain × input, input × gain
int	m_iNcols	No. of columns of gain matrix
int	m_iNrows	No. of rows of gain matrix
double**	m_dGainMatrix	Gain matrix
CString	m_strGainValue	CString gain matrix

and records the gain matrix as a string for dialog window parameter input purposes and hence does not need to be serialized (Table 25.10).

25.2.7.5   CIntegrator Data

The CIntegratorBlock class holds member variables used to evaluate the numerical integral of an incoming signal. Most variables are used in the dynamic integral evaluation, but the initial condition vector, "m_dICVector", and its length, "m_iLength", are required for serialization purposes. The CString variable "m_strICVector" is the CString equivalent of the pointer-to-double "m_dICVector" and can be regenerated from double values and hence does not need to be saved (Table 25.11).

25.2.7.6   CLinearFnBlock Data

The CLinearFnBlock class retains data values concerning the generation of a linear function $f(t)$; with initial and final activation times, t_{a0} and t_{af}, respectively; an initial signal value $f(t_{a0})$; and derivative, $f'(t)$, for $t \in [t_{a0}, t_{af}]$. All member variable data need to be serialized (Table 25.12).

TABLE 25.11

CIntegratorBlock Serialization Data: Data Type, Member Variable, and Description

Data Type	Member Variable	Description
int	m_i_t_cnt_ref	Reference time count
int	m_iLength	Length of initial condition vector
int	m_iNcallsPerTimeCnt	No. of times function called per time point
int	m_iNcols	No. of columns of the initial condition vector
int	m_iNrows	No. of rows of the initial condition vector
int	m_iNrowsOut	No. of rows of output matrix data
double*	m_dICVector	Initial condition vector
double*	m_y_at_t_minus_h	$y(t - h)$
double*	m_y_dot_at_t_minus_h	$\dot{y}(t - h)$
double**	m_dMatrixOut	Matrix data of output signals
CString	m_strICVector	CString initial condition vector

TABLE 25.12

CLinearFnBlock Serialization Data: Data Type, Member Variable, and Description

Data Type	Member Variable	Description
double	m_dDerivative	Derivative of linear function
double	m_dTimeFinal	Final time of signal activation
double	m_dTimeInit	Initial time of signal activation
double	m_dValueInit	Initial value of signal

25.2.7.7 COutputBlock Data

The COutputBlock class will provide a mechanism for the user to save data directly via a dialog window button. Hence, the contained data matrix "m_dOutputMatrix" does not need to be serialized with the system model; only the block parameter options denoting notation "m_iNotation" and time point display "m_iTimePtDisplay" need to be saved (Table 25.13).

25.2.7.8 CSignalGeneratorBlock Data

The CSignalGeneratorBlock class retains information concerning the type of generated signal function, "m_strFnType"; its parameters, "m_dAmplitude", "m_dFrequency", and "m_dPhase"; and its units, "m_strUnits": all values need to be serialized (Table 25.14).

25.2.7.9 CSubsystemBlock Data

The CSubsystemBlock class at present simply holds the names of the input and output ports as CString arguments, "m_strInputPortName" and "m_strOutputPortName", respectively: both need to be serialized (Table 25.15).

25.2.7.10 CSubsystemInBlock Data

The CSubsystemInBlock class retains the CString name of the input port, "m_strInputPortName", which needs to be serialized (Table 25.16).

TABLE 25.13

COutputBlock Serialization Data: Data Type, Member Variable, and Description

Data Type	Member Variable	Description
int	m_iNcols	No. of columns of output matrix data
int	m_iNotation	Type of notation: standard, scientific
int	m_iNrows	No. of rows of output matrix data
int	m_iTimePtDisplay	Time point display: show, hide
double**	m_dOutputMatrix	Output matrix data

TABLE 25.14

CSignalGeneratorBlock Serialization Data: Data Type, Member Variable, and Description

Data Type	Member Variable	Description
double	m_dAmplitude	Amplitude of generated signal
double	m_dFrequency	Frequency of generated signal
double	m_dPhase	Phase of generated signal
CString	m_strFnType	Function type: random, sine, square
CString	m_strUnits	Units: Hz, rad/s

TABLE 25.15

CSubsystemBlock Serialization Data: Data Type, Member Variable, and Description

Data Type	Member Variable	Description
CString	m_strInputPortName	Input port name
CString	m_strOutputPortName	Output port name

TABLE 25.16

CSubsystemInBlock Serialization Data: Data Type, Member Variable, and Description

Data Type	Member Variable	Description
CString	m_strInputPortName	Input port name

25.2.7.11 CSubsystemOutBlock Data

The CSubsystemOutBlock class contains the CString name of the output port, "m_strOutputPortName", which needs to be serialized (Table 25.17).

25.2.7.12 CSumBlock Data

The CSumBlock class has only two private member variables that record the number of addition and subtraction input ports, "m_iNAddInputs" and "m_iNSubtractInputs", respectively: both integer variables need to be serialized (Table 25.18).

TABLE 25.17

CSubsystemOutBlock Serialization Data: Data Type, Member Variable, and Description

Data Type	Member Variable	Description
CString	m_strOutputPortName	Output port name

TABLE 25.18

CSumBlock Serialization Data: Data Type, Member Variable, and Description

Data Type	Member Variable	Description
int	m_iNAddInputs	No. of addition inputs
int	m_iNSubtractInputs	No. of subtraction inputs

TABLE 25.19

CTransferFnBlock Serialization Data: Data Type, Member Variable, and Description

Data Type	Member Variable	Description
int	m_iLengthDenom	Length of denominator coefficient vector
int	m_iLengthNumer	Length of numerator coefficient vector
double*	m_dDenomVector	Vector of denominator coefficients
double*	m_dNumerVector	Vector of numerator coefficients
CString	m_strDenomCoeffs	Denominator coefficients
CString	m_strNumerCoeffs	Numerator coefficients

25.2.7.13 CTransferFnBlock Data

The CTransferFnBlock class contains information about the numerator and denominator coefficient vectors used in a transfer function. The vectors "m_dNumerVector" and "m_dDenomVector" and their lengths "m_iLengthNumer" and "m_iLengthDenom" need to be serialized, but the CString equivalents of the vectors used for dialog window display purposes can be regenerated from their numerical counterparts and do not need to be serialized (Table 25.19).

25.3 EVENT-HANDLER FUNCTIONS FOR FILE INPUT/OUTPUT

The reading in and writing out of all the necessary data members of the classes listed earlier are initiated by choosing either the Open, Save, Save As, Close, or Exit options under the File menu of the DiagramEng application. The event-handler functions associated with these menu entries then create the familiar Open or Save As dialog window for opening or saving files, respectively.

25.3.1 CHILD FRAME–BASED EVENT-HANDLER FUNCTIONS

Five key event-handler functions need to be added to the CDiagramEngDoc and CDiagramEngApp classes for the Open, Save As, Save, Close, and Exit entries of the File menu: (1) Open opens an existing file, (2) Save As allows the user to save the document content in a user-specified file, (3) Save saves an existing file or prompts the user to provide a filename if one has not yet been provided, (4) Close checks whether the document content has been modified and prompts the user to save before closing the existing document, and (5) Exit closes existing documents and then exits the application. In addition, other functions are required to complete the serialization-based user interaction process and include saving all documents, opening recent files, closing all documents, and various utility accessor functions.

25.3.1.1 `CDiagramEngDoc::OnFileOpen()`

The `OnFileOpen()` function is required to initiate the opening of an existing file to restore a previously saved model diagram.

1. Add an event-handler function associated with the ID_FILE_OPEN object ID for the CDiagramEngDoc class with the prototype void CDiagramEngDoc::OnFileOpen (void).
2. Edit the function as shown to first check whether a model already exists and to prompt the user to erase it, generate a new document, or abort. If a new model is to be loaded, the file path is obtained and passed to the to-be-added ReadDiagramEngDataFromFile() function to read data from a file in order to restore a previously saved model.

```
void CDiagramEngDoc::OnFileOpen()
{
    // TODO: Add your command handler code here

    // DiagramEng (start)
    int btnSel;                             // button selection
    BOOL dlgType = TRUE;                    // TRUE => File Open dlg,
      FALSE => File Save dlg
    CString strDefExt = ".txt";             // default file extension
    CString strFileName = "model_data.txt"; // file name
    CString strFilter = "All Files (*.*)|*.*|Plain Text (*.txt)|*.txt||";
      // string pairs specifying filters for file list box
    CString sMsg;
    DWORD dwFlags = OFN_ENABLESIZING | OFN_HIDEREADONLY;
      // customization flags

    // Create a new document
    if((m_SystemModel.GetBlockList().size() != 0) || (m_SystemModel.
      GetConnectionList().size() != 0))
    {
        sMsg.Format(" A system model already exists. \n Do you want to
          erase it? \n");
        btnSel = AfxMessageBox(sMsg, MB_YESNOCANCEL, 0);

        if(btnSel == IDYES)
        {
            // Delete System Model Lists
            m_SystemModel.DeleteBlockList();
            m_SystemModel.DeleteConnectionList();
            m_SystemModel.DeleteSourceOutputLoopLists();

            // Set flags and redraw the doc
            SetModifiedFlag(TRUE);          // set the doc. as having
              been modified to prompt user to save
            UpdateAllViews(NULL);           // indicate that sys. should
              redraw.
        }
```

```
          else if(btnSel == IDNO)
          {
              // The application will create a new document and re-enter
                 the current CDiagramEngDoc::OnFileOpen() fn, i.e.:
              // CDiagramEngDoc::OnFileOpen(), (the current fn) calls
              // theApp.OnFileOpen(), (as shown in the code below),
                 i.e. CDiagramEngApp::OnFileOpen(), which calls
              // CDiagramEngDoc::OnFileOpenAccessor(), which chains to the
                 protected fn
              // CDiagramEngDoc::OnFileOpen(), i.e. the current function
                 but now with a NEW DOCUMENT in place.
              theApp.OnFileOpen();
              return;
          }
          else if(btnSel == IDCANCEL)
          {
              return;
          }
      }

      // Create a CFileDialog wnd
      CFileDialog dlgFile(dlgType, strDefExt, strFileName, dwFlags,
        strFilter, NULL);

      if(dlgFile.DoModal() == IDOK)
      {
          m_strFilePath = dlgFile.GetPathName();  // get the path name
            including file name and location
          SetTitle(m_strFilePath);                      // set the title of the
            document window

          // Read the model data from file
          if(ReadDiagramEngDataFromFile(m_strFilePath) == 0)  // read the
            model data from the file
          {
              theApp.AddToRecentFileList(m_strFilePath);  // if successful,
                add the file name to the recent file list.
          }
      }
      // DiagramEng (end)
}
```

The conditional section concerning whether an existing model resides on the current document is required to allow the user to either erase the existing model and hence load a new model on the current document, or leave the current model on the current document but generate a whole new document upon which a new model will be placed (Figure 25.1a). In the latter case, a call to OnFileOpen() is made upon the application object, "theApp": this function is described in Section 25.3.2, but the flow of control is pursued here to clarify the behavior of the file opening mechanism. CDiagramEngApp::OnFileOpen() calls CWinApp::OnFileNew() to create the new document, and then CDiagramEngDoc::OnFileOpen() is ultimately called upon the newly created document pointer. That is, the function mentioned earlier is in effect called a second time (indirect recursion), but now with the new document in place, upon which the user-selected model may be placed. The developer may comment out the line "theApp.OnFileOpen();", for now, and then uncomment it when the CDiagramEngApp::OnFileOpen() function is added to the project a little later.

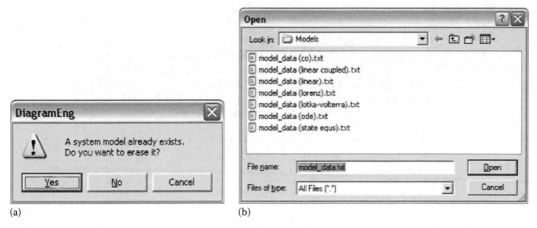

(a)   (b)

FIGURE 25.1   File opening process: (a) a message box providing the option to erase the existing model and (b) the CFileDialog Open dialog object created in the OnFileOpen() function.

Control flow then progresses to create a CFileDialog dialog window object used to present the File Open dialog as shown in Figure 25.1b: the dialog type is TRUE for the File Open rather than Save As dialog window, the default file extension is ".txt", the initial filename is "model_data.txt", the flag combination enables sizing and hides the read only check box, the string filter consists of string pairs to appear in the file list box, and the pointer to the dialog box's parent window is NULL [2].

The file path "m_strFilePath" is obtained using the function GetPathName() called upon the dialog object, and used to set the document window title using SetTitle(), and then passed to the ReadDiagramEngDataFromFile() function to be added in Section 25.5. If the read was successful, i.e., if ReadDiagramEngDataFromFile() returns "0" (no error), then the file is added to the application's recent file list via the call to AddToRecentFileList() (the reason for this will become clearer in the section concerning the OnFileRecentFileOpen() function). The member variable "m_strFilePath" is also used in the OnFileSave() function (see Section 25.3.1.4) and should be added to the document class.

1. Hence, add a CString private member variable to the CDiagramEngDoc class named "m_strFilePath".
2. Initialize this variable to an empty string in the CDiagramEngDoc constructor function as shown in bold.

```
CDiagramEngDoc::CDiagramEngDoc()
{
    // TODO: add one-time construction code here

    // DiagramEng (start)
    m_iKeyFlagTrack = 0;
    m_iFineMoveFlag = 0;
    m_iRubberBandCreated = 0;
    m_dDeltaLength = 50.0;
    m_strFilePath = "";
    // DiagramEng (end)
}
```

25.3.1.2 CDiagramEngDoc::ReadDiagramEngDataFromFile()

The CDiagramEngDoc::OnFileOpen() function calls the ReadDiagramEngDataFromFile()
method to open an existing document whose data are used to reconstruct a system model.

1. Add a public member function to the CDiagramEngDoc class with the prototype int
   CDiagramEngDoc::ReadDiagramEngDataFromFile(CString file_path).
2. Edit the function as shown to print out the file path and name: this function will be
   completed in the section concerning the reading of data from a file (later).

```
int CDiagramEngDoc::ReadDiagramEngDataFromFile(CString file_path)
{
    int file_flag = 0;          // (0) no error, (1) error
    CString sMsg;               // main msg string
    UINT nType = MB_OK;         // style of msg. box
    UINT nIDhelp = 0;           // help context ID for the msg.

    sMsg.Format("\n File path: %s\n", file_path);
    AfxMessageBox(sMsg, nType, nIDhelp);

    return file_flag;
}
```

25.3.1.3 CDiagramEngDoc::OnFileSaveAs()

The Save As option under the File menu allows the user to save a document in a particular user-
specified file.

1. Add an event-handler function associated with the ID_FILE_SAVE_AS object ID
   for the CDiagramEngDoc class with the prototype void CDiagramEngDoc::
   OnFileSaveAs(void).
2. Edit the function as shown to create the familiar Save As dialog window, obtaining the file
   path from the user input, setting the document window title using SetTitle(), and then
   calling the to-be-added WriteDiagramEngDataToFile() function, to save the model
   data to a file. The dialog type is set to FALSE, indicating that a Save As dialog window is
   to be presented, as shown in Figure 25.2.

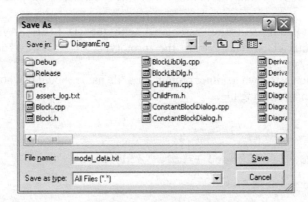

FIGURE 25.2 CFileDialog Save As dialog object created in the OnFileSaveAs() function.

```
void CDiagramEngDoc::OnFileSaveAs()
{
    // TODO: Add your command handler code here

    // DiagramEng (start)
    BOOL dlgType = FALSE;                          // TRUE => File Open dlg,
      FALSE => File Save dlg
    CString strDefExt = ".txt";                    // default file extension
    CString strFileName = "model_data.txt";    // file name
    CString strFilter = "All Files (*.*)|*.*|Plain Text (*.txt)|*.txt||";
      // string pairs specifying filters for file list box
    DWORD dwFlags = OFN_ENABLESIZING | OFN_HIDEREADONLY; // customization
      flags

    // Create a CFileDialog wnd
    CFileDialog dlgFile(dlgType, strDefExt, strFileName, dwFlags,
      strFilter, NULL);

    if(dlgFile.DoModal() == IDOK)
    {
        m_strFilePath = dlgFile.GetPathName();  // get the file path
          and name
        SetTitle(m_strFilePath);      // set the title of the current doc
        WriteDiagramEngDataToFile(m_strFilePath, 1);  // 1 implies
          overwrite warning will appear
    }
    // DiagramEng (end)
}
```

The member variable "m_strFilePath" is passed into the `WriteDiagramEngDataToFile()` function with a flag-like variable used for message display, here the number "1", indicating that if the file already exists, then a message is displayed to the user and provides the option to overwrite the existent file.

25.3.1.4 `CDiagramEngDoc::OnFileSave()`

The Save option allows the user to save a system model diagram: if the document content has changed (`IsModified()`) and has not yet been saved to a file (m_strFilePath == ""), then the Save As dialog should appear to obtain a file path from the user. If a file path already exists, then the document content is written directly (without prompting) to the file specified by the path "m_strFilePath".

1. Add an event-handler function associated with the ID_FILE_SAVE object ID for the CDiagramEngDoc class with the prototype void   CDiagramEngDoc:: OnFileSave(void).
2. Edit the function as shown to either prompt for a file name should one not already exist, or save directly to an existing file.

```
void CDiagramEngDoc::OnFileSave()
{
    // TODO: Add your command handler code here

    // DiagramEng (start)

    // Check whether document has been modified: non-zero => modified,
      zero => not modified
```

```
    if(IsModified())
    {
        // Check whether a file path already exists
        if(m_strFilePath == "")
        {
            OnFileSaveAs();
        }
        else
        {
            WriteDiagramEngDataToFile(m_strFilePath, 0);
        }
    }
    // DiagramEng (end)
}
```

The `WriteDiagramEngDataToFile()` function is called here with the flag-like variable set to "0", indicating that upon a file-save action, no diagnostic message is to appear to the user concerning file overwriting, since the intent of saving is to overwrite the contents of the existing file specified by the file path "m_strFilePath".

25.3.1.5 `CDiagramEngDoc::OnFileClose()`
The Close option under the File menu first checks that the current document has been modified using `IsModified()`; if so, a prompt appears asking the user if the changes to the document should be saved before possibly closing the document via `OnCloseDocument()`.

1. Add an event-handler function associated with the ID_FILE_CLOSE object ID for the CDiagramEngDoc class with the prototype int CDiagramEngDoc:: OnFileClose(void).
2. Edit the function as shown to prompt the user to save any changes made to the document before possibly closing the document.

```
int CDiagramEngDoc::OnFileClose()
{
    // TODO: Add your command handler code here

    // DiagramEng (start)
    int btnSel;          // button selection
    int cancel = 0;      // flag denoting cancellation of file-save action:
      (0) no cancel, (1) cancel

    // Check whether document has been modified: non-zero => modified,
      zero => not modified
    if(IsModified())
    {
        btnSel = AfxMessageBox("\n Do you want to save changes to the
          document? \n", MB_YESNOCANCEL, 0);

        if(btnSel == IDYES)          // save changes
        {
            OnFileSave();
        }
        else if(btnSel == IDNO)  // do not save changes
```

```
        {
            // no action to save
        }
        else if(btnSel == IDCANCEL)
        {
            cancel = 1;
            return cancel;
        }
    }

    // Close the document (regardless)
    OnCloseDocument();

    return cancel;
    // DiagramEng (end)
}
```

The developer will notice that if the document is modified, then a message box appears to allow the user to save the contents depending upon which button was selected: if "Yes", the OnFileSave() function is called and the document closed; if "No", the document is simply closed; and if "Cancel", then no action to save or close the document is taken, and the function returns "cancel" set to 1. This flag is required in the CDiagramEngApp::OnAppExit() function described as follows.

25.3.1.6 CDiagramEngApp::OnAppExit()

Exiting the application is currently performed by default via the CWinApp::OnAppExit() function located in the "Appui.cpp" source file. If the developer places a breakpoint in the CSystemModel destructor function and runs the program using the debugger and attempts to exit the application, the call stack may be observed and the CWinApp::OnAppExit() function found in the list of function calls. This default exiting mechanism will be over-ridden here by adding an event-handler function to the ID_APP_EXIT object ID for the CDiagramEngApp class such that active documents can be closed using the recently added OnFileClose() function and then the existing CWinApp::OnAppExit() function called to terminate the application.

1. Add an event-handler function associated with the ID_APP_EXIT object ID for the CDiagramEngApp class with the prototype void CDiagramEngApp::OnAppExit(void). The function will appear in the "DiagramEng.cpp" source file.
2. Edit the function as shown to first prompt the user to save document content, then get a pointer to the current document and check whether it is valid, i.e., that in fact a document exists, and if so, close the current document if appropriate and finally exit the application.

```
void CDiagramEngApp::OnAppExit()
{
    // TODO: Add your command handler code here

    // DiagramEng (start)
    int cancel = 0;                 // flag indicating whether exit should
      be cancelled: (0) do not cancel, (1) cancel
    CDiagramEngDoc *pDoc = NULL;  // pDoc used to call CDiagramEngDoc fns.

    // Save document contents
    cancel = SaveAllDocuments();
    if(cancel == 1)
```

```
{
    return;
}

// Get the first document
pDoc = GetDocumentGlobalFn(); // get a pointer-to-CDiagramEngDoc.

// While there are still valid documents
while(pDoc != NULL)
{
    if(pDoc != NULL)              // check that there is in fact a doc,
      i.e. the pDoc is not NULL
    {
        // The public OnFileCloseAccessor() is called since
          OnFileClose() is protected.
        cancel = pDoc->OnFileCloseAccessor();

        // If user cancels a file-save action in the OnFileClose()
          function then abort exit op.
        if(cancel == 1)
        {
            return;
        }
    }

    // Get the next document
    pDoc = GetDocumentGlobalFn(); // get a pointer-to-CDiagramEngDoc
      (the next doc).
}

CWinApp::OnAppExit();                      // call the existing MFC-provided
  OnAppExit() in "Appui.cpp".
// DiagramEng (end)
```

The call to the SaveAllDocuments() function is somewhat redundant since the OnFileClose() function already prompts the user to save and calls OnFileSave() for the document concerned. However, it is placed here since there was a problem in presenting the save-document-related AfxMessageBox() in OnFileClose() upon successively closing all documents in the application. The SaveAllDocuments() function is introduced in Section 25.3.1.7.

The *while* loop in the OnAppExit() function iterates through all open documents of the application, successively calling the OnFileCloseAccessor() function which chains up to the OnFileClose() function which may close the document using OnCloseDocument() if the user does not cancel the file-close operation: if the user does cancel the operation, the function returns without calling CWinApp::OnAppExit().

The engineer will notice that instead of calling OnFileClose() of the CDiagramEngDoc class directly, the function OnFileCloseAccessor() is called: this is due to OnFileClose() being a protected member method of the CDiagramEngDoc class, and hence to gain access to or interface with it, a public member method should be added to the CDiagramEngDoc class which calls the protected OnFileClose() function.

1. Hence, add a public member function to the CDiagramEngDoc class with the prototype int CDiagramEngDoc::OnFileCloseAccessor(void).
2. Edit the function as shown to simply call the protected OnFileClose() member function and return the value of the "cancel" variable to the calling environment, i.e., to CDiagramEngApp::OnAppExit().

```
int CDiagramEngDoc::OnFileCloseAccessor()
{
    int cancel = 0;
    // Public interfacing fn for the protected OnFileClose() fn.

    // Call the OnFileClose() event-handler fn.
    cancel = OnFileClose();

    return cancel;
}
```

Now upon exiting the application (without cancellation), the call sequence is as follows: OnAppExit() → SaveAllDocuments() → OnFileCloseAccessor() → OnFileClose() → OnFileSave(), which may be followed by OnFileSaveAs() if a file name has not yet been provided, → OnCloseDocument(), and finally → CWinApp::OnAppExit().

25.3.1.7 CDiagramEngApp::SaveAllDocuments()

The SaveAllDocuments() function in the CDiagramEngApp class iterates through all documents of the application, prompting the user to save if the document concerned had been modified.

1. Add a public member function to the CDiagramEngApp class with the following prototype: int CDiagramEngApp::SaveAllDocuments(void).
2. Edit the function as shown to iterate through all the documents of the application and prompt the user to save if necessary.

```
int CDiagramEngApp::SaveAllDocuments()
{
    int btnSel = -1;
    int cancel = 0;
    CString sMsg;
    CString sPathName;

    // Get the first doc template in the app
    POSITION pos = GetFirstDocTemplatePosition();

    // Iterate through all docs
    while(pos)
    {
        // Get the first CDocTemplate obj.
        CDocTemplate *pTemplate = GetNextDocTemplate(pos);

        // Get the string describing the doc
        CString sDocName;
        pTemplate->GetDocString(sDocName, CDocTemplate::docName);

        // If the doc is a DiagramEng "DiaEng" doc
        if(sDocName == _T("DiaEng"))
        {
            // Get the posn of the first doc in the list of docs
            //  associated with this template
            POSITION posDoc = pTemplate->GetFirstDocPosition();

            // While there is a first doc or a subsequent doc
```

```
        // If there is a first doc, then posDoc is not NULL: o/wise
         if there is no next doc, then posDoc = NULL.
        while(posDoc)
        {
            // Get a pointer to the doc
            CDiagramEngDoc* pDoc = (CDiagramEngDoc*)pTemplate-
              >GetNextDoc(posDoc);

            if(pDoc != NULL)
            {
                // Check whether document has been modified: non-zero
                 => modified, zero => not modified
                if(pDoc->IsModified())
                {
                    // Make the view active and flash it
                    POSITION pos_view = pDoc->GetFirstViewPosition();
                    if(pos_view != NULL)
                    {
                        CDiagramEngView* pFirstView =
                          (CDiagramEngView*)pDoc-
                          >GetNextView(pos_view);         // first view
                        CFrameWnd *pFrameWnd = pFirstView-
                          >GetParentFrame();              // get parent
                          frame
                        pFrameWnd->BringWindowToTop(); // bring
                          window to top
                        pFrameWnd->FlashWindow(TRUE);   // flash
                          window once
                    }

                    // Get path/file name
                    sPathName = pDoc->GetFilePath();
                    if(sPathName != "")
                    {
                        sMsg.Format("\n Do you want to save changes
                          to the document:\n %s? \n", sPathName);
                    }
                    else
                    {
                        sMsg.Format("\n Do you want to save changes
                          to the document? \n");
                    }

                    // Display msg. box and process btn selection
                    btnSel = AfxMessageBox(sMsg, MB_YESNOCANCEL, 0);

                    if(btnSel == IDYES)                 // save changes
                    {
                        pDoc->OnFileSaveAccessor();   // chain to
                          OnFileSave()
                    }
                    else if(btnSel == IDNO)             // do not save
                      changes
                    {
                        pDoc->SetModifiedFlag(FALSE); // set as
                          unmodified
                    }
```

```
                    else if(btnSel == IDCANCEL)         // do not save
                      changes
                    {
                        cancel = 1;
                        return cancel;
                    }
                }
            }
        }// end while(posDoc)

    }// end if(sDocName)

}// end while(pos)

return cancel;
}
```

The function works as follows: (1) the first document template position in the application is obtained via a call to GetFirstDocTemplatePosition(); (2) the position is used to get the first document template by a call to GetNextDocTemplate(); (3) the string describing the application is obtained using GetDocString(); (4) if the document is a DiagramEng ("DiaEng") document, the first document position is obtained via a call to GetFirstDocPosition() upon the pointer-to-CDocTemplate; (5) then a pointer to the document, i.e., "pDoc", of type pointer-to-CDiagramEngDoc, is obtained by a call to GetNextDoc(); (6) if the document is valid and has been modified, then the first view position is obtained by calling GetFirstViewPosition() and is used to get a pointer to the first view via the call to GetNextView(); (7) then using this pointer-to-CView, a pointer to the frame window is obtained by calling GetParentFrame(), and this pointer is used to bring the window to the top (BringWindowToTop()) and flash the window (FlashWindow()); (8) thereafter, a message box is displayed, prompting the user to save the document's contents (Figure 25.3); and finally, (9) if saving is desired, the OnFileSaveAccessor()

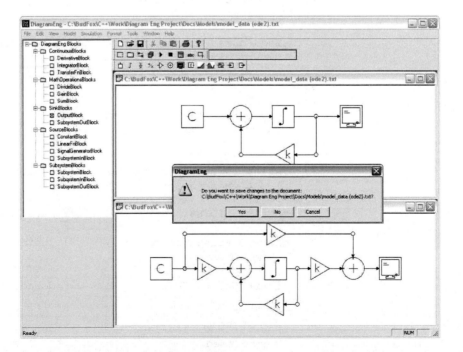

FIGURE 25.3 Message box displaying the prompt to save the stated file ("m_strFilePath").

function is called to chain to the `OnFileSave()` function to save the document. For more information on the functions called earlier, the reader should consult the Index field under the Help menu of MSDN Library Visual Studio 6.0 [2].

The developer will have noticed the call to `OnFileSaveAccessor()` rather than a direct call to `OnFileSave()`: this is necessary since the `OnFileSave()` function has protected access and cannot be called upon the document pointer "pDoc".

1. Add a public member function to the CDiagramEngDoc class with the following prototype: `void CDiagramEngDoc::OnFileSaveAccessor(void)`.
2. Edit the function as shown to simply chain up to the `OnFileSave()` protected member function.

```
void CDiagramEngDoc::OnFileSaveAccessor()
{
    OnFileSave();
}
```

Another call made in the `SaveAllDocuments()` function was that to obtain the file path using `GetFilePath()`.

1. Add a public member function to the CDiagramEngDoc class with the prototype `const CString &GetFilePath(void)`.
2. Edit the function as shown to simply return the member variable "m_strFilePath".

```
const CString& CDiagramEngDoc::GetFilePath()
{
    return m_strFilePath;
}
```

25.3.1.8 `CDiagramEngApp::OnFileRecentFileOpen`

The Recent File entry under the File menu is used to open the most recently used (MRU) files by the application, as shown by the highlighted entry in Figure 25.4, to open, e.g., the ordinary differential equation (ODE) model.

The file names that appear in this list are added by the `AddToRecentFileList()` function of the CWinApp class (as shown at the end of the `OnFileOpen()` function mentioned earlier). At present, when the user selects a recently used file, a document is opened with the correct

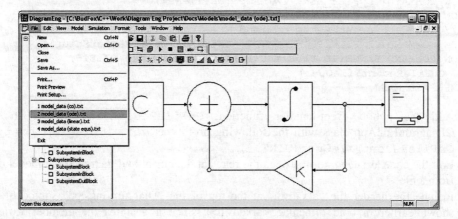

FIGURE 25.4 Four MRU files displayed under the File menu with the ODE model highlighted.

file name, but no model diagram content is present. Hence, the default command event-handler, OnOpenRecentFile(), of the CWinApp class, which calls the OpenDocumentFile() function, is to be overridden here. The following instructions have been derived from a document found at Microsoft Support [3], titled "How to add command handlers for MRU menu items in MFC applications," but they are altered here to suit the DiagramEng implementation.

1. Add an ON_COMMAND_RANGE macro in the message map section at the top of the "DiagramEng.cpp" source file that associates the to-be-provided event-handler function OnFileRecentFileOpen(), for the range of IDs, ID_FILE_MRU_FILE1 to ID_FILE_MRU_FILE16, as shown in bold in the following code excerpt.

```
// DiagramEng.cpp : Defines the class behaviors for the application.
//

#include "stdafx.h"
#include "DiagramEng.h"

#include "MainFrm.h"
#include "ChildFrm.h"
#include "DiagramEngDoc.h"
#include "DiagramEngView.h"
#include "OutputBlockView.h"  // rqd. since COutputBlockView is used in
  InitInstance()
#include <afxadv.h> // rqd. for CRecentFileList m_pRecentFileList, in
  OnFileRecentFileOpen()

#ifdef _DEBUG
#define new DEBUG_NEW
#undef THIS_FILE
static char THIS_FILE[] = __FILE__;
#endif

BEGIN_MESSAGE_MAP(CDiagramEngApp, CWinApp)
    //{{AFX_MSG_MAP(CDiagramEngApp)
    ON_COMMAND(ID_APP_ABOUT, OnAppAbout)
    ON_COMMAND(ID_APP_EXIT, OnAppExit)
    ON_COMMAND(ID_FILE_OPEN, OnFileOpen)
    ON_COMMAND(ID_WND_CLOSE_ALL_DOCS, OnWndCloseAllDocs)
    //}}AFX_MSG_MAP
    // Standard file based document commands
    ON_COMMAND(ID_FILE_NEW, CWinApp::OnFileNew)
    ON_COMMAND(ID_FILE_OPEN, CWinApp::OnFileOpen)
    // Standard print setup command
    ON_COMMAND(ID_FILE_PRINT_SETUP, CWinApp::OnFilePrintSetup)
    ON_COMMAND_RANGE(ID_FILE_MRU_FILE1, ID_FILE_MRU_FILE16,
      OnFileRecentFileOpen)
END_MESSAGE_MAP()
```

2. Add the public event-handler function, OnFileRecentFileOpen(), to the CDiagramEngApp class with the following prototype: void CDiagramEngApp:: OnFileRecentFileOpen(UINT i).
3. Edit the code as shown to first open the relevant document and then read the model data from a file.
4. Include the header file "afxadv.h" at the top of the "DiagramEng.cpp" source file as shown earlier in bold (#include <afxadv.h>), since it declares the member variable "m_pRecentFileList" of type CRecentFileList.

```
void CDiagramEngApp::OnFileRecentFileOpen(UINT i)
{
    int btnSel;                                 // button selection
    int nIndex = i - ID_FILE_MRU_FILE1;         // index of recent file
    CString strFileName;                        // file name and path
    CString sMsg;                               // msg
    CDiagramEngDoc *pDoc = GetDocumentGlobalFn();

    // ASSERTIONS
    ASSERT_VALID(this);
    ASSERT(m_pRecentFileList != NULL);
    ASSERT(i >= ID_FILE_MRU_FILE1);
    ASSERT(i < ID_FILE_MRU_FILE1 + (UINT)m_pRecentFileList->GetSize());
    ASSERT((*m_pRecentFileList)[nIndex].GetLength() != 0);

    // IF NO DOC, CREATE A DOC
    if(pDoc == NULL)
    {
        OnFileNew();
        pDoc = GetDocumentGlobalFn();
    }

    // CHECK pDoc
    if(pDoc == NULL)
    {
        return;
    }

    // CHECK FOR THE EXISTENCE OF A MODEL ON THE DOC: GET THE SYSTEM
      MODEL BY REFERENCE!
    CSystemModel &system_model = pDoc->GetSystemModel();
    if((system_model.GetBlockList().size() != 0) || (system_model.
      GetConnectionList().size() != 0))
    {
        sMsg.Format(" A system model already exists. \n Do you want to
          erase it? \n");
        btnSel = AfxMessageBox(sMsg, MB_YESNOCANCEL, 0);

        if(btnSel == IDYES)
        {
            // Delete System Model Lists
            system_model.DeleteBlockList();
            system_model.DeleteConnectionList();
            system_model.DeleteSourceOutputLoopLists();

            // Set flags and redraw the doc
            pDoc->SetModifiedFlag(TRUE);    // set the doc. as having been
              modified to prompt user to save
            pDoc->UpdateAllViews(NULL);     // indicate that sys. should
              redraw.
        }
        else if(btnSel == IDNO)
        {
            OnFileNew();                     // Create a new document
            pDoc = GetDocumentGlobalFn();   // Get a ptr to the new
              document in preparation for reading data from file
            if(pDoc == NULL)
```

```
                    {
                        return;
                    }
                }
                else if(btnSel == IDCANCEL)
                {
                    return;
                }
            }

            // GET THE FILE NAME/PATH
            strFileName = (LPCTSTR)(*m_pRecentFileList)[nIndex];
            pDoc->SetFilePath(strFileName);
            pDoc->SetTitle(strFileName);

            // IF UNABLE TO READ DATA FROM FILE, THEN REMOVE THE RECENT FILE LIST
            //   ENTRY: (0) NO ERROR, (1) ERROR
            if(pDoc->ReadDiagramEngDataFromFile(strFileName) == 1)
            {
                m_pRecentFileList->Remove(nIndex);
            }

            // MSGs
            //strMsg.Format(" CDiagramEngApp::OnFileRecentFileOpen()\n Open file
            //   (%d) '%s'.\n", ((nIndex) + 1), strFileName);
            //AfxMessageBox(strMsg);
}
```

The OnFileRecentFileOpen() function first performs various assertions concerning the recent file list–related variables. Then, if an underlying document does not exist (if(pDoc == NULL)), a new document is created (OnFileNew()) and the pointer "pDoc" checked again. If a system model is already existent, then the user is prompted to delete the model before a new one is loaded, as was the case in the CDiagramEngDoc::OnFileOpen() function. If the user chooses to not delete the existent model, a new document is created to hold the new model. The appropriate file name, "strFileName", is then obtained based on the recent file list "nIndex" argument, and this is passed to the ReadDiagramEngDataFromFile() function to load the model data onto the document as a diagram model. For example, Figure 25.5 shows two models presented on two separate documents. The return value from ReadDiagramEngDataFromFile() may be "0" or "1", indicating a file-read success or failure, respectively; in the event of a failure, then the file is removed (Remove()) from the recent file list.

The developer will have noticed the call to SetFilePath() to set the document class CString member variable "m_strFilePath", containing the file path and name of the document retaining the system model. This is required since in the OnFileSave() function, if the file path is not provided, the OnFileSaveAs() function is called to prompt the user to save the file explicitly, rather than simply saving the existing file without prompting.

1. Add a public member function to the CDiagramEngDoc class with the following prototype: void CDiagramEngDoc::SetFilePath(CString path).
2. Edit the function as shown to set the member variable "m_strFilePath" with the incoming argument.

```
void CDiagramEngDoc::SetFilePath(CString path)
{
    // Set file path including the file name
    m_strFilePath = path;
}
```

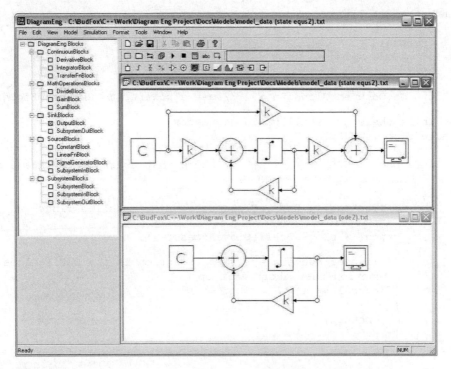

FIGURE 25.5 Two different model diagrams drawn on two separate documents: the upper diagram represents the state equations and the lower diagram a simple first-order linear ODE.

25.3.1.9 `CDiagramEngDoc::OnWndCloseAllDocs()`

The Close All Documents entry (ID_WND_CLOSE_ALL_DOCS) under the Window menu for the Child frame currently calls the event-handler function `OnWndCloseAllDocs()` of the CDiagramEngDoc class. However, now that the `CDiagramEngApp::OnAppExit()` method works by iterating through the existing documents of the application, the same structure can be used for the `OnWndCloseAllDocs()` function.

1. Delete the `OnWndCloseAllDocs()` event-handler function of the CDiagramEngDoc class associated with the ID, ID_WND_CLOSE_ALL_DOCS.
2. Add a new event-handler function to the CDiagramEngApp class for the same ID, i.e., ID_WND_CLOSE_ALL_DOCS, with the prototype `void CDiagramEngApp:: OnWndCloseAllDocs(void)`.
3. Edit the function as shown to operate in a similar manner to the `OnAppExit()` method.

```
void CDiagramEngApp::OnWndCloseAllDocs()
{
    // TODO: Add your command handler code here

    // DiagramEng (start)
    int cancel = 0;                    // flag indicating whether exit should
      be cancelled: (0) do not cancel, (1) cancel
    CDiagramEngDoc *pDoc = NULL;    // pDoc used to call
      CDiagramEngDoc fns.

    // Save document contents
    cancel = SaveAllDocuments();
```

```
    if(cancel == 1)
    {
        return;
    }

    // Get the first document
    pDoc = GetDocumentGlobalFn();   // get a pointer-to-CDiagramEngDoc.

    // While there are still valid documents
    while(pDoc != NULL)
    {
        if(pDoc != NULL)             // check that there is in fact a doc,
          i.e. the pDoc is not NULL
        {
            // The public OnFileCloseAccessor() is called since
              OnFileClose() is protected.
            cancel = pDoc->OnFileCloseAccessor();

            // If user cancels a file-save action in the OnFileClose()
              function then abort exit op.
            if(cancel == 1)
            {
                return;
            }
        }

        // Get the next document
        pDoc = GetDocumentGlobalFn();   // get a pointer-to-CDiagramEngDoc
          (the next doc).
    }

    // DiagramEng (end)
}
```

The `OnWndCloseAllDocs()` function is essentially the same as the `OnAppExit()` function, invoking `SaveAllDocuments()` before iterating through the documents calling `OnFileCloseAccessor()` introduced earlier, but differs by not calling `CWinApp::OnAppExit()` prior to returning. The `OnFileCloseAccessor()` function is simply the public accessor function of the CDiagramEngDoc class which calls the protected method, `OnFileClose()`, discussed earlier.

25.3.2 Main Frame–Based Event-Handler Functions

The Child frame–based serialization related functions included the CDiagramEngDoc class member methods, `OnFileOpen()`, `OnFileSaveAs()`, `OnFileSave()`, `OnFileSaveAccessor()`, `OnFileClose()`, and `OnFileCloseAccessor()`, and the CDiagramEngApp methods, `OnAppExit()`, `OnFileOpen()`, `OnFileRecentFileOpen()`, `OnWndCloseAllDocs()`, and `SaveAllDocuments()`. The Main frame–based serialization functions, typically of the CMainFrame class, are associated with the Open and Recent File entries under the File menu as shown in Table 25.20. An event-handler function needs to be added for the ID, ID_FILE_OPEN: the `OnFileRecentFileOpen()` function has already been added to the CDiagramEngApp class. However, although the event-handler function for the ID_FILE_OPEN ID can be added to the CMainFrame class, it is easier to add it to the CDiagramEngApp class since the application-based functions can be called directly without requiring to be called upon the application object, "theApp", for which there may be restricted access!

TABLE 25.20

File Menu Entry ID, Class, and Command Event-Handler Function

Object	ID	Class	Command Event-Handler
File/Open	ID_FILE_OPEN	CDiagramEngApp	OnFileOpen()
File/Recent File	ID_FILE_MRU_FILE1–16	CDiagramEngApp	OnFileRecentFileOpen()

25.3.2.1 `CDiagramEngApp::OnFileOpen()`

The Open entry under the File menu of the Main frame is to first open a new document and then chain up to the `OnFileOpen()` function of the CDiagramEngDoc class discussed earlier.

1. Add an event-handler function for the ID, ID_FILE_OPEN, of the CDiagramEngApp class with the prototype `void CDiagramEngApp::OnFileOpen(void)`.
2. Edit the function as shown to first call `OnFileNew()` of the CDiagramEngApp class and then to ultimately call `OnFileOpen()` of the CDiagramEngDoc class via the accessor function `OnFileOpenAccessor()`.

```
void CDiagramEngApp::OnFileOpen()
{
    // TODO: Add your command handler code here

    // DiagramEng (start)

    // Create a new document onto which a diagram may be drawn/loaded
    OnFileNew();

    // Call the OnFileOpen() fn of the CDiagramEngDoc class, i.e. the
      Child Frame fn.
    CDiagramEngDoc *pDoc = GetDocumentGlobalFn();
    pDoc->OnFileOpenAccessor();

    // DiagramEng (end)
}
```

The developer will notice the call to the accessor function `OnFileOpenAccessor()`: this is required since `OnFileOpen()` of the CDiagramEngDoc class is a protected method, and hence an interfacing function is required.

1. Add a public member method to the CDiagramEngDoc class with the prototype `void CDiagramEngDoc::OnFileOpenAccessor(void)`.
2. Edit the function as shown to simply call the protected `OnFileOpen()` function of the same class.

```
void CDiagramEngDoc::OnFileOpenAccessor()
{
    OnFileOpen();
}
```

Now, upon building and then running the DiagramEng application and selecting Open from the Main frame–based menu in the absence of an existing document, a new document is first created (`OnFileNew()`), and the familiar CFileDialog File Open dialog is presented (`OnFileOpen()`) as shown (Figure 25.6).

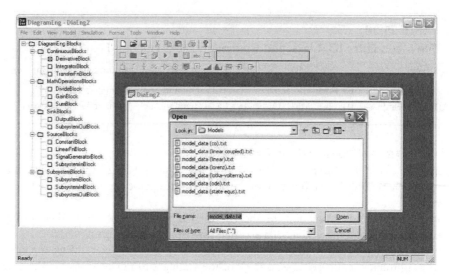

FIGURE 25.6 File Open dialog window generated via the Open entry under the File menu of the Main frame window after the creation of a new document (shown in the background as "DiaEng2").

25.4 WRITING DATA MEMBERS TO A FILE

The file-save action of the OnFileSave() and OnFileSaveAs() functions results in a call to the WriteDiagramEngDataToFile() function to write the application data to a file, including the system model data, the derived-block class, block shape and port data, and finally the connection data. Here, the following functions are introduced: WriteDiagramEngDataToFile(), WriteSystemModelDataToFile(), WriteBlock DataToFile(), WriteBlockShapeDataToFile(), WritePortDataToFile(), and WriteConnectionDataToFile().

25.4.1 WRITING CDiagramEngDoc DATA TO A FILE

The file-save action of the OnFileSave() and OnFileSaveAs() functions results in a call to the WriteDiagramEngDataToFile() function to write the application data to a file.

1. Add a public member function to the CDiagramEngDoc class with the prototype void CDiagramEngDoc::WriteDiagramEngDataToFile(CString file_ path, int display).
2. Edit the function as shown to open the file in output mode, to check its status, and to pass the ofstream object "fout" by reference to the soon-to-be-added WriteSystemModelDataToFile() function.

```
void CDiagramEngDoc::WriteDiagramEngDataToFile(CString file_path, int
  display)
{
    int btnSel = IDYES;     // button selection: default file output
      stream opening of file
    int set_prec = 1;       // precision setting flag: (0) unset, (1) set.
    ifstream fin;           // infile stream
    ofstream fout;          // outfile stream
    CString sCaption;       // message box caption
```

```
CString sMsg;              // main msg string
CString sMsgTemp;          // temp msg string
CWnd l_wnd;                // local CWnd
UINT nType = MB_OK;        // style of msg. box
UINT nIDhelp = 0;          // help context ID for the msg.

//sMsg.Format("\n CDiagramEngDoc::WriteDiagramEngDataToFile()\n");
//AfxMessageBox(sMsg, nType, nIDhelp);

// Check to see if file exists
fin.open(file_path, ios::in);          // open file in input mode
if(!fin)
{
    fout.open(file_path, ios::out);  // open file in output mode
}
else
{
    // Question user about overwriting existing file
    sMsgTemp.Format("%s already exists. \n", file_path);
    sMsg += sMsgTemp;
    sMsgTemp.Format("Do you want to replace it?\n");
    sMsg += sMsgTemp;
    sCaption = "DiagramEng - Overwrite";
    nType = MB_YESNO | MB_ICONEXCLAMATION;

    if(display)
    {
        btnSel = l_wnd.MessageBox(sMsg, sCaption, nType);
    }

    // Check button selection
    if(btnSel == IDYES)
    {
        fout.open(file_path, ios::out);  // open file in output mode
    }
    else if(btnSel == IDNO)
    {
        sMsg.Format("");
        sMsg.Format("\n Aborting writing model data to file. \n");
        nType = MB_OK | MB_ICONSTOP;
        //AfxMessageBox(sMsg, nType, nIDhelp);

        fin.close();
        fin.clear();
        return;
    }
}
fin.close();
fin.clear();

// Check if file open
if(!fout)        // if(!false) then execute
{
    sMsg.Format("");
    sMsgTemp.Format("\n CDiagramEngDoc::WriteDiagramEngDataToFile
        ()\n");
    sMsg += sMsgTemp;
    sMsgTemp.Format("\n Unable to open file: %s\n", file_path);
```

```
        sMsg += sMsgTemp;
        sMsgTemp.Format("Aborting file i/o.\n");
        sMsg += sMsgTemp;
        nType = MB_OK | MB_ICONSTOP;
        AfxMessageBox(sMsg, nType, nIDhelp);

        // Close the outfile stream and clear fail flag
        fout.close();
        fout.clear();  // clears fail flag setting from previous file io.
        return;
    }

    // SET PRECISION FOR OUTPUT FILE STREAM
    // Note: a double has an approx precision of 15 signif. digits and a
    //   range of 10^-308 to 10^+308.
    if(set_prec)
    {
        fout.setf(ios::scientific, ios::floatfield); // floatfield
            format: scientific (ios::scientific), fixed (ios::fixed)
        fout.precision(FILE_IO_PRECISION);              // file i/o precision
    }

    // Call the CSystemModel fn to start the writing of data to a file.
    GetSystemModel().WriteSystemModelDataToFile(fout);

    // Document has been saved
    SetModifiedFlag(FALSE);

    // Close the outfile stream and clear fail flag
    fout.close();
    fout.clear();  // clears fail flag setting from previous file i/o.
}
```

The developer will notice that if the output file already exists and the (incoming) "display" variable is nonzero, a MessageBox() call is made to inform the user and determine whether the existing file should be overwritten, as shown in Figure 25.7: if so, the WriteSystemModelDataToFile() function is called, and if not, the function simply returns. The "display" variable is "0" or "1" if the calling function is OnFileSave() or OnFileSaveAs(), respectively.

In addition, prior to the WriteSystemModelDataToFile() call being made, the precision of the output stream is set using setf() and precision(): the former has the "floatfield" format set to "scientific" rather than "fixed", and the precision is set using the constant integer "FILE_IO_PRECISION". Hence, add a constant integer to the "Block.h" header file, as shown in bold in the following code excerpt, defining the precision to be 20; the ellipsis, "...", denotes omitted code for brevity.

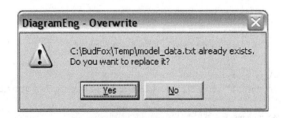

FIGURE 25.7   MessageBox dialog window used to check the overwriting of an existing file.

```
// Title:  Block.h

#ifndef BLOCK_H
    #define BLOCK_H        // inclusion guard

    #include <vector>      // rqd. for vector (below)
    using namespace std;

    // User defined consts/vars.
    const int FILE_IO_PRECISION = 20;  // precision specifying no. of
      digits after dec pt. (15 signif. digits for a double)
    const double PI = 3.14159265359;   // pi in radians (rounded)
    ...
#endif
```

Kelley and Pohl indicate that a double, d, has an approximate precision of 15 significant figures and an approximate range of $10^{-308} - 10^{+308}$, and then clarify by example that the statement $d = 123.45123451234512345$ will result in d being assigned a value stored approximately as $d = 0.123451234512345 \times 10^{+3}$ [4]. Hence, the precision of 20 significant digits set earlier is actually more than required: any extra digits present will be zeros.

The reason why a double involves only approximately 15 significant figures is because the double data type is represented by a 64-bit, base 2 number, according to the IEEE Standard for Floating-Point Arithmetic (IEEE 754-2008) [5]: 1 bit is used to denote the sign, 11 bits to denote the exponent, and the remaining 52 bits to denote the fraction or significand (the total precision is in fact 53 bits). Salas and Hille [6] indicate that the log of a value x to the base p is

$$\log_p x = \frac{\ln x}{\ln p} \tag{25.1}$$

where

$$\ln x = \log_e x \tag{25.2}$$

is the natural logarithm and is defined as

$$L(x) = \int_0^x \frac{dt}{t}, \quad x > 0 \tag{25.3}$$

Hence, $\log_{10} 2^{53} \cong 15.95$, i.e., 53 binary digits (bits) of precision is equivalent to approximately 15 decimal digits.

25.4.2 WRITING CSystemModel DATA TO A FILE

The `CDiagramEngDoc::WriteDiagramEngDataToFile()` function calls the `WriteSystemModelDataToFile()` function of the CSystemModel class, via the CSystemModel object, "m_SystemModel", as shown in the earlier code.

1. Hence, add a public member function to the CSystemModel class with the prototype `void CSystemModel::WriteSystemModelDataToFile(ofstream &fout)`, and edit it as shown.
2. This requires including the "fstream.h" (#include <fstream>) header file at the top of the "SystemModel.cpp" file just beneath the inclusion of the "stdafx.h" header file.

```
void CSystemModel::WriteSystemModelDataToFile(ofstream &fout)
{
    char strVar[L_FILE_IO_STR];           // local string var
    list<CBlock*>::iterator it_blk;       // blk list iterator
    list<CConnection*>::iterator it_con;  // iterator for list of
      CConnection ptrs.

    //AfxMessageBox("\n CSystemModel::WriteSystemModelDataToFile()\n",
      MB_OK, 0);

    // Write member data to file.
    strcpy(strVar, m_strModelName);
    fout << strVar << endl;

    fout << m_dATOL << endl;
    fout << m_dRTOL << endl;
    fout << m_dTimeStart << endl;
    fout << m_dTimeStepSize << endl;
    fout << m_dTimeStop << endl;

    strcpy(strVar, m_strIntegrationMethod);
    fout << strVar << endl;

    strcpy(strVar, m_strTimeStepType);
    fout << strVar << endl;

    strcpy(strVar, m_strWarning);
    fout << strVar << endl;

    // Iterate through the block list calling WriteBlockDataToFile()
    for(it_blk = m_lstBlock.begin(); it_blk != m_lstBlock.end();
      it_blk++)
    {
        (*it_blk)->WriteBlockDataToFile(fout);
    }

    // Iterate through the connection list calling
      WriteConnectionDataToFile()
    for(it_con = m_lstConnection.begin(); it_con != m_lstConnection.
      end(); it_con++)
    {
        (*it_con)->WriteConnectionDataToFile(fout);
    }
}
```

The `WriteSystemModelDataToFile()` function simply writes the values of the CSystemModel variables directly to the output file and iterates over the block and connection lists calling the `WriteBlockDataToFile()` and `WriteConnectionDataToFile()` functions, respectively. The reader will have noticed that the ofstream object "fout" with the operator "<<" cannot write CString data directly to a file but rather only character arrays; hence, the CString member variables are converted to character arrays using `strcpy()`, prior to being written to a file.

3. The developer will have recognized that the length of the character arrays is defined by "L_FILE_IO_STR"; hence, add this as a constant integer to the "Block.h" header file as shown in bold in the following code excerpt.

```
// Title:      Block.h
#ifndef BLOCK_H
    #define BLOCK_H                      // inclusion guard

    #include <vector>                    // rqd. for vector (below)
    using namespace std;

    // User defined consts/vars.
    const int FILE_IO_PRECISION = 20;    // precision specifying no. of
      digits after dec pt. (15 signif. digits for a double)
    const int L_FILE_IO_STR = 100;       // length of string used in
      file i/o
    const double PI = 3.14159265359;     // pi in radians (rounded)
    ...
#endif
```

25.4.3 Writing CBlock Data to a File

The WriteSystemModelDataToFile() function shown earlier calls the WriteBlockDataToFile() function upon the pointer-to-CBlock object when iterating over the block list. Then, based upon the run-time derived-block type, the correct derived block's WriteBlockDataToFile() function will be called.

1. Hence, add a public virtual member function to the CBlock class with the prototype virtual void CBlock::WriteBlockDataToFile(ofstream &fout).
2. Edit the function as shown to write CBlock-specific member data to a file and to call the contained CBlockShape object's WriteBlockShapeDataToFile() function and the CPort object's WritePortDataToFile() method.
3. Finally, include the "fstream.h" header file (#include <fstream>) at the top of the "Block. cpp" source file, just beneath the inclusion of the "stdafx.h" header file.

```
void CBlock::WriteBlockDataToFile(ofstream &fout)
{
    char strBlockName[L_FILE_IO_STR];  // local string reflecting
      m_strBlockName
    vector<CPort*>::iterator it_port;  // iterator for vector of
      CPort ptrs.

    //AfxMessageBox("\n CBlock::WriteBlockDataToFile()\n", MB_OK, 0);

    // Write CBlock member data to file.
    strcpy(strBlockName, m_strBlockName);
    fout << strBlockName << endl;
    fout << m_ptBlockPosition.x << "" << m_ptBlockPosition.y << endl;
    fout << m_vecInputPorts.size() << "" << m_vecOutputPorts.size()
      << endl;

    // Write CBlockShape member data to file
    m_BlockShape.WriteBlockShapeDataToFile(fout);

    // Write CPort member data to file
    // Input ports
    for(it_port = m_vecInputPorts.begin(); it_port != m_vecInputPorts.end();
      it_port++)
```

```
        {
            (*it_port)->WritePortDataToFile(fout);
        }

        // Output ports
        for(it_port = m_vecOutputPorts.begin(); it_port != m_vecOutputPorts.end();
          it_port++)
        {
            (*it_port)->WritePortDataToFile(fout);
        }
}
```

25.4.4 WRITING **CBlockShape** DATA TO A FILE

The `WriteBlockDataToFile()` function of the base CBlock class calls the `WriteBlockShape DataToFile()` function via the contained "m_BlockShape" member object.

1. Add a public member function to the CBlockShape class with the prototype void `CBlockShape::WriteBlockShapeDataToFile(ofstream &fout)`.
2. Edit the function as shown to simply write the CBlockShape member data to a file.

```
void CBlockShape::WriteBlockShapeDataToFile(ofstream &fout)
{
    //AfxMessageBox("\n CBlockShape::WriteBlockShapeDataToFile()\n",
      MB_OK, 0);

    // Write CBlockShape member data to file.
    fout << m_dBlockWidth << "" << m_dBlockHeight << endl;
    fout << m_eBlockShape << endl;
    fout << m_eBlockDirection << endl;
}
```

25.4.5 WRITING **CPort** DATA TO A FILE

The `CBlock::WriteBlockDataToFile()` function iterates over the vector of input and output ports calling the `CPort::WritePortDataToFile()` function on the pointer-to-CPort object. This delegation of file input/output responsibility allows the CPort class to write the relevant port-based data to a file.

1. Add a public member function to the CPort class with the prototype void `CPort::WritePortDataToFile(ofstream &fout)`.
2. Edit the function as shown to write the relevant port member data to a file.

```
void CPort::WritePortDataToFile(ofstream &fout)
{
    char strPortName[L_FILE_IO_STR];  // char array reflecting
      m_strPortName

    //AfxMessageBox("\n CPort::WritePortDataToFile()\n", MB_OK, 0);

    // Write CPort member data to file
    strcpy(strPortName, GetPortName());
    fout << GetPortPositionAngle() << "" << strPortName << endl;
    fout << m_ePortArrowDirec << endl;
}
```

25.4.6 WRITING DERIVED-BLOCK CLASS DATA TO A FILE

All the CBlock-derived classes each have their own implementation of the virtual WriteBlockDataToFile() function which writes their member data to the output file stream object "fout".

25.4.6.1 CConstantBlock::WriteBlockDataToFile()

The CConstantBlock class' data members to be written to a file are those shown in Table 25.7, i.e., the number of rows, "m_iNrows", and columns, "m_iNcols", of data and the data matrix, "m_dConstMatrix", itself.

1. Add a public virtual member function to the CConstantBlock class with the prototype virtual void CConstantBlock::WriteBlockDataToFile(ofstream &fout).
2. Edit the function as shown to write the Constant-block-specific member data to a file after first calling the base CBlock class' WriteBlockDataToFile() method.

```
void CConstantBlock::WriteBlockDataToFile(ofstream &fout)
{
    int i;
    int j;

    //AfxMessageBox("\n CConstantBlock::WriteBlockDataToFile()\n", MB_OK, 0);

    // Write CBlock member data to file
    CBlock::WriteBlockDataToFile(fout);

    // Write CConstantBlock member data to file.
    fout << m_iNrows << endl;
    fout << m_iNcols << endl;

    for(i=0; i<m_iNrows; i++)
    {
        for(j=0; j<m_iNcols; j++)
        {
            fout << m_dConstMatrix[i][j] << "";
        }
        fout << endl;
    }
}
```

25.4.6.2 CDerivativeBlock::WriteBlockDataTofile()

The CDerivativeBlock class only needs to write the derivative method, "m_iDerivativeMethod", to a file.

1. Add a public virtual member function to the CDerivativeBlock class with the prototype virtual void CDerivativeBlock::WriteBlockDataToFile(ofstream &fout).
2. Edit the function as shown to call the base CBlock class' WriteBlockDataToFile() method and then to write the CDerivativeBlock member data to a file.

```
void CDerivativeBlock::WriteBlockDataToFile(ofstream &fout)
{
    //AfxMessageBox("\n CDerivativeBlock::WriteBlockDataToFile()\n",
      MB_OK, 0);

    // Write CBlock member data to file
    CBlock::WriteBlockDataToFile(fout);

    // Write CDerivativeBlock member data to file.
    fout << m_iDerivativeMethod << endl;
}
```

25.4.6.3 CDivideBlock::WriteBlockDataToFile()

The Divide block has member variables that record the number of multiplication and division input ports, denoted by "m_iNDivideInputs" and "m_iNMultiplyInputs", respectively. The type of multiplication or division recorded in "m_iMultType" may be elemental- or matrix-based. Hence, all three data members need to be recorded. The port name reflects the port sign, equivalently the mathematical operator, which is already handled by the CPort::WritePortDataToFile() function.

1. Add a public virtual member function to the CDivideBlock class with the prototype virtual void CDivideBlock::WriteBlockDataToFile(ofstream &fout).
2. Edit the function as shown to first call the base CBlock class' WriteBlockDataToFile() method and then to write the CDivideBlock member data to a file.

```
void CDivideBlock::WriteBlockDataToFile(ofstream &fout)
{
    //AfxMessageBox("\n CDivideBlock::WriteBlockDataToFile()\n",
      MB_OK, 0);

    // Write CBlock member data to file
    CBlock::WriteBlockDataToFile(fout);

    // Write CDivideBlock member data to file.
    fout << m_iNDivideInputs << endl;
    fout << m_iNMultiplyInputs << endl;
    fout << m_iMultType << endl;
}
```

25.4.6.4 CGainBlock::WriteBlockDataToFile()

The CGainBlock class' data members to be written to a file are shown in Table 25.10, i.e., the number of rows, "m_iNrows", and columns, "m_iNcols", of data and the data matrix, "m_dConstMatrix", itself as well as the type of gain, "m_iGainType", i.e., the order of the gain operation.

1. Add a public virtual member function to the CGainBlock class with the prototype virtual void CGainBlock::WriteBlockDataToFile(ofstream &fout).
2. Edit the function as shown to call the base CBlock class WriteBlockDataToFile() function before writing the CGainBlock member data to a file.

```
void CGainBlock::WriteBlockDataToFile(ofstream &fout)
{
    int i;
    int j;

    //AfxMessageBox("\n CGainBlock::WriteBlockDataToFile()\n",
      MB_OK, 0);

    // Write CBlock member data to file
    CBlock::WriteBlockDataToFile(fout);

    // Write CGainBlock member data to file.
    fout << m_iGainType << endl;
    fout << m_iNrows << endl;
    fout << m_iNcols << endl;
```

```
    for(i=0; i<m_iNrows; i++)
    {
        for(j=0; j<m_iNcols; j++)
        {
            fout << m_dGainMatrix[i][j] << "";
        }
        fout << endl;
    }
}
```

25.4.6.5 `CIntegratorBlock::WriteBlockDataToFile()`

The CIntegratorBlock class' member data are shown in Table 25.11, where only the initial condition vector, "m_dICVector", and its length, "m_iLength", need to be written to a file.

1. Add a public virtual member function to the CIntegratorBlock class with the prototype `virtual void CIntegratorBlock::WriteBlockDataToFile(ofstream &fout)`.
2. Edit the function as shown to call the base CBlock class `WriteBlockDataToFile()` function before writing the CIntegratorBlock data to a file.

```
void CIntegratorBlock::WriteBlockDataToFile(ofstream &fout)
{
    int i;

    //AfxMessageBox("\n CIntegratorBlock::WriteBlockDataToFile()\n",
      MB_OK, 0);

    // Write CBlock member data to file
    CBlock::WriteBlockDataToFile(fout);

    // Write CIntegratorBlock member data to file.
    fout << m_iLength << endl;

    for(i=0; i<m_iLength; i++)
    {
        fout << m_dICVector[i] << "";
    }
    fout << endl;
}
```

25.4.6.6 `CLinearFnBlock::WriteBlockDataToFile()`

The CLinearFnBlock's member data are shown in Table 25.12 and involve four double-type member variables defining the linear function source signal.

1. Add a public virtual member function to the CLinearFnBlock class with the prototype `virtual void CLinearFnBlock::WriteBlockDataToFile (ofstream &fout)`.
2. Edit the function as shown to call the base CBlock class' `WriteBlockDataToFile()` method and to write the CLinearFnBlock data to a file.

```
void CLinearFnBlock::WriteBlockDataToFile(ofstream &fout)
{
    //AfxMessageBox("\n CLinearFnBlock::WriteBlockDataToFile()\n",
      MB_OK, 0);

    // Write CBlock member data to file
    CBlock::WriteBlockDataToFile(fout);
```

```
    // Write CLinearFnBlock member data to file.
    fout << m_dDerivative << endl;
    fout << m_dTimeInit << endl;
    fout << m_dTimeFinal << endl;
    fout << m_dValueInit << endl;
}
```

25.4.6.7 COutputBlock::WriteBlockDataToFile()

The COutputBlock class will have a mechanism added that will allow the user to save numerical data separately to a file. For the purpose of restoring a saved model, only the type of notation, "m_iNotation", and time point display, "m_iTimePtDisplay", options, as shown in Table 25.13, need to be saved.

1. Add a public virtual member function to the COutputBlock class with the prototype virtual void COutputBlock::WriteBlockDataToFile(ofstream &fout).
2. Edit the function as shown to call the base CBlock class' WriteBlockDataToFile() method and to write the COutputBlock output graph options to a file.

```
void COutputBlock::WriteBlockDataToFile(ofstream &fout)
{
    //AfxMessageBox("\n COutputBlock::WriteBlockDataToFile()\n",
      MB_OK, 0);

    // Write CBlock member data to file
    CBlock::WriteBlockDataToFile(fout);

    // Write COutputBlock member data to file.
    fout << m_iNotation << endl;
    fout << m_iTimePtDisplay << endl;
}
```

25.4.6.8 CSignalGeneratorBlock::WriteBlockDataToFile()

The CSignalGeneratorBlock class' member data to be written to a file are shown in Table 25.14: the CString data first need to be converted to character arrays prior to using "fout".

1. Add a public virtual member function to the CSignalGeneratorBlock class with the prototype virtual void CSignalGeneratorBlock::WriteBlockDataToFile (ofstream &fout).
2. Edit the function as shown to call the base CBlock class' WriteBlockDataToFile() method and to write all CSignalGeneratorBlock member data to a file.

```
void CSignalGeneratorBlock::WriteBlockDataToFile(ofstream &fout)
{
    char strData[L_FILE_IO_STR]; // char array reflecting member CString
      data

    //AfxMessageBox("\n CSignalGeneratorBlock::WriteBlockDataToFile()\n",
      MB_OK, 0);

    // Write CBlock member data to file
    CBlock::WriteBlockDataToFile(fout);

    // Write CSignalGeneratorBlock member data to file
    fout << m_dAmplitude << endl;
```

```
    fout << m_dFrequency << endl;
    fout << m_dPhase << endl;

    strcpy(strData, m_strFnType);
    fout << strData << endl;

    strcpy(strData, m_strUnits);
    fout << strData << endl;
}
```

25.4.6.9 `CSubsystemBlock::WriteBlockDataToFile()`

The CSubsystemBlock class' member data at present consist of only the input and output port names, "m_strInputPortName" and "m_strOutputPortName", respectively, as shown in Table 25.15.

1. Add a public virtual member function to the CSubsystemBlock class with the prototype `virtual void CSubsystemBlock::WriteBlockDataToFile(ofstream &fout)`.
2. Edit the function as shown to call the base CBlock class' `WriteBlockDataToFile()` method and to write the two CSubsystemBlock data members to a file by first using `strcpy()`.

```
void CSubsystemBlock::WriteBlockDataToFile(ofstream &fout)
{
    char strPortName[L_FILE_IO_STR];  // char array reflecting the input
      and output port names

    //AfxMessageBox("\n CSubsystemBlock::WriteBlockDataToFile()\n",
      MB_OK, 0);

    // Write CBlock member data to file
    CBlock::WriteBlockDataToFile(fout);

    // Write CSubsystemBlock member data to file
    strcpy(strPortName, m_strInputPortName);
    fout << strPortName << endl;

    strcpy(strPortName, m_strOutputPortName);
    fout << strPortName << endl;

}
```

25.4.6.10 `CSubsystemInBlock::WriteBlockDataToFile()`

The CSubsystemInBlock class' member data consist of only the input port name, "m_strInputPortName", which is to be written to a file.

1. Add a public virtual member function to the CSubsystemInBlock class with the prototype `virtual void CSubsystemInBlock::WriteBlockDataToFile(ofstream &fout)`.
2. Edit the function as shown to call the base CBlock class' `WriteBlockDataToFile()` method and to write the CSubsystemInBlock member data to a file.

```
void CSubsystemInBlock::WriteBlockDataToFile(ofstream &fout)
{
    char strPortName[L_FILE_IO_STR];  // char array reflecting the input
      port name

    //AfxMessageBox("\n CSubsystemInBlock::WriteBlockDataToFile()\n",
      MB_OK, 0);
```

```
    // Write CBlock member data to file
    CBlock::WriteBlockDataToFile(fout);

    // Write CSubsystemInBlock member data to file
    strcpy(strPortName, m_strInputPortName);
    fout << strPortName << endl;
}
```

25.4.6.11   CSubsystemOutBlock::WriteBlockDataToFile()

The CSubsystemOutBlock class' member data consist of only the output port name, "m_strOutputPortName", which is to be written to a file.

1. Add a public virtual member function to the CSubsystemOutBlock class with the prototype virtual void CSubsystemOutBlock::WriteBlockDataToFile(ofstream &fout).
2. Edit the function as shown to call the base CBlock class' WriteBlockDataToFile() method and to write the CSubsystemOutBlock member data to a file.

```
void CSubsystemOutBlock::WriteBlockDataToFile(ofstream &fout)
{
    char strPortName[L_FILE_IO_STR];   // char array reflecting the output
      port name

    //AfxMessageBox("\n CSubsystemOutBlock::WriteBlockDataToFile()\n",
      MB_OK, 0);

    // Write CBlock member data to file
    CBlock::WriteBlockDataToFile(fout);

    // Write CSubsystemOutBlock member data to file
    strcpy(strPortName, m_strOutputPortName);
    fout << strPortName << endl;
}
```

25.4.6.12   CSumBlock::WriteBlockDataToFile()

The CSumBlock's member data are shown in Table 25.18 and consist of the number of addition and subtraction inputs, "m_iNAddInputs" and "m_iNSubtractInputs", respectively, that are to be written to a file.

1. Add a public virtual member function to the CSumBlock class with the prototype virtual void CSumBlock::WriteBlockDataToFile(ofstream &fout).
2. Edit the function as shown to call the base CBlock class' WriteBlockDataToFile() method and to write the CSumBlock integer member data to a file.

```
void CSumBlock::WriteBlockDataToFile(ofstream &fout)
{
    //AfxMessageBox("\n CSumBlock::WriteBlockDataToFile()\n", MB_OK, 0);

    // Write CBlock member data to file
    CBlock::WriteBlockDataToFile(fout);

    // Write CSumBlock member data to file
    fout << m_iNAddInputs << endl;
    fout << m_iNSubtractInputs << endl;
}
```

25.4.6.13 `CTransferFnBlock::WriteBlockDataToFile()`

The CTransferFnBlock's member data are shown in Table 25.19: only the numerator and denominator vectors, "m_dNumerVector" and "m_iDenomVector", and their lengths, "m_iLengthNumer" and "m_iLengthDenom", need to be written to a file.

1. Add a public virtual member function to the CTransferFnBlock class with the prototype virtual `void CTransferFnBlock::WriteBlockDataToFile(ofstream &fout)`.
2. Edit the function as shown to call the base CBlock class' `WriteBlockDataToFile()` method and to write the CTransferFnBlock integer and double data to a file.

```
void CTransferFnBlock::WriteBlockDataToFile(ofstream &fout)
{
    int i;

    //AfxMessageBox("\n CTransferFnBlock::WriteBlockDataToFile()\n",
      MB_OK, 0);

    // Write CBlock member data to file
    CBlock::WriteBlockDataToFile(fout);

    // Write CTransferFnBlock member data to file
    fout << m_iLengthNumer << endl;
    fout << m_iLengthDenom << endl;

    for(i=0; i<m_iLengthNumer; i++)
    {
        fout << m_dNumerVector[i] << "";
    }
    fout << endl;

    for(i=0; i<m_iLengthDenom; i++)
    {
        fout << m_dDenomVector[i] << "";
    }
    fout << endl;
}
```

25.4.7 Writing CConnection Data to a File

The `CSystemModel::WriteSystemModelDataToFile()` function iterates through both the list of blocks and connections and calls `WriteBlockDataToFile()` and `WriteConnectionDataToFile()`, respectively.

1. Add a public member function to the CConnection class with the prototype `void CConnection::WriteConnectionDataToFile(ofstream &fout)`.
2. Edit the function as shown to write CConnection member data to a file, including the head and tail points, "m_ptHead" and "m_ptTail", respectively, and to iterate over the list of bend points, "m_lstBendPoints", writing out the *x* and *y* coordinates of each point.
3. Finally, include the "fstream.h" header file (#include <fstream>) at the top of the "Signal. cpp" source file just beneath the inclusion of the "stdafx.h" header file.

```
void CConnection::WriteConnectionDataToFile(ofstream &fout)
{
    char strName[L_FILE_IO_STR];    // name of connection
    list<CPoint>::iterator it_pt;   // bend points list iterator
```

```
//AfxMessageBox("\n CConnection::WriteConnectionDataToFile()\n",
  MB_OK, 0);

// Write CConnection member data to file.
strcpy(strName, "connection");
fout << strName << endl;
fout << m_ptHead.x << "" << m_ptHead.y << endl;
fout << m_ptTail.x << "" << m_ptTail.y << endl;
fout << m_lstBendPoints.size() << endl;

for(it_pt = m_lstBendPoints.begin(); it_pt != m_lstBendPoints.end();
  it_pt++)
{
    fout << (*it_pt).x << "" << (*it_pt).y << endl;
}
}
```

25.4.8 EXAMPLE OF FILE OUTPUT

Consider the first-order linear ordinary differential equation (ODE)

$$\dot{y}(t) = -2y(t) + u(t) \tag{25.4}$$

introduced in Chapter 23, where y, t, and $u(t)$ are the dependent variable, independent variable, and source signal generation function, respectively. The model diagram, repeated here for convenience, is shown in Figure 25.8, and the equivalent DiagramEng model diagram is shown in Figure 25.9.

The content of the output data file "model_data.txt" is shown in the left column of Table 25.21: the right column provides a brief description of each line of the file which is not present in the

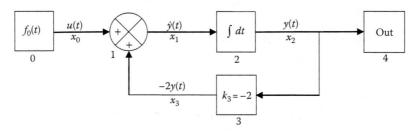

FIGURE 25.8 Block diagram model of the ODE $\dot{y}(t) = -2y(t) + u(t)$, with block numbers written below the blocks, and signals $x_i(t)$, for $i \in [0, s-1]$ written beneath the block output connections, where s is the number of blocks with output signals.

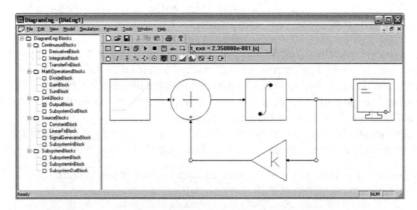

FIGURE 25.9 Block diagram model of the ODE (25.4) drawn with DiagramEng.

TABLE 25.21

**The Content of the Output Data File "model_data.txt"
and a Brief Description of Each Line of Output**

Content of Output File	Description of Content
system_model	m_strModelName
0.0001	m_dATOL
0.0001	m_dRTOL
0	m_dTimeStart
0.01	m_dTimeStepSize
5	m_dTimeStop
Euler (1st Order)	m_strIntegrationMethod
Fixed-step	m_strTimeStepType
OK	m_strWarning
linear_fn_block	m_strBlockName
71 86	m_ptBlockPosition.x, m_ptBlockPosition.y
0 1	no. of input ports, no. of output ports
100 100	m_dBlockWidth, m_dBlockHeight
1	m_eBlockShape (e_rectangle)
1	m_eBlockDirection (e_right)
0 _	m_dPortPositionAngle, m_strPortName (no sign)
2	m_ePortArrowDirec (e_right_arrow)
2	m_dDerivative
0	m_dTimeInit
10	m_dTimeFinal
0	m_dValueInit
sum_block	m_strBlockName
219 86	m_ptBlockPosition.x, m_ptBlockPosition.y
2 1	no. of input ports, no. of output ports
100 100	m_dBlockWidth, m_dBlockHeight
0	m_eBlockShape (e_ellipse)
1	m_eBlockDirection (e_right)
180 +	m_dPortPositionAngle, m_strPortName (addition)
2	m_ePortArrowDirec (e_right_arrow)
270 +	m_dPortPositionAngle, m_strPortName (addition)
1	m_ePortArrowDirec (e_up_arrow)
0 _	m_dPortPositionAngle, m_strPortName (no sign)
2	m_ePortArrowDirec (e_right_arrow)
2	m_iNAddInputs
0	m_iNSubtractInputs
integrator_block	m_strBlockName
403 86	m_ptBlockPosition.x, m_ptBlockPosition.y
1 1	no. of input ports, no. of output ports
100 100	m_dBlockWidth, m_dBlockHeight
1	m_eBlockShape (e_rectangle)
1	m_eBlockDirection (e_right)
180 _	m_dPortPositionAngle, m_strPortName (no sign)
2	m_ePortArrowDirec (e_right_arrow)
0 _	m_dPortPositionAngle, m_strPortName (no sign)
2	m_ePortArrowDirec (e_right_arrow)
1	m_iLength
0	m_dICVector

(continued)

TABLE 25.21 (continued)
The Content of the Output Data File "model_data.txt"
and a Brief Description of Each Line of Output

Content of Output File	Description of Content
gain_block	m_strBlockName
425 233	m_ptBlockPosition.x, m_ptBlockPosition.y
1 1	no. of input ports, no. of output ports
100 100	m_dBlockWidth, m_dBlockHeight
2	m_eBlockShape (e_triangle)
0	m_eBlockDirection (e_left)
0 _	m_dPortPositionAngle, m_strPortName (no sign)
0	m_ePortArrowDirec (e_left_arrow)
180 _	m_dPortPositionAngle, m_strPortName (no sign)
0	m_ePortArrowDirec (e_left_arrow)
1	m_iGainType (gain-times-input)
1	m_iNrows
1	m_iNcols
-2	m_dGainMatrix
output_block	m_strBlockName
668 86	m_ptBlockPosition.x, m_ptBlockPosition.y
1 0	no. of input ports, no. of output ports
100 100	m_dBlockWidth, m_dBlockHeight
1	m_eBlockShape (e_rectangle)
1	m_eBlockDirection (e_right)
180 _	m_dPortPositionAngle, m_strPortName (no sign)
2	m_ePortArrowDirec (e_right_arrow)
0	m_iNotation (standard notation)
0	m_iTimePtDisplay (show time points)
connection	connection identifier (connection 0)
169 86	m_ptHead.x, m_ptHead.y
121 86	m_ptTail.x, m_ptTail.y
0	no. of bend points
connection	connection identifier (connection 1)
353 86	m_ptHead.x, m_ptHead.y
269 86	m_ptTail.x, m_ptTail.y
0	no. of bend points
connection	connection identifier (connection 2)
618 86	m_ptHead.x, m_ptHead.y
453 86	m_ptTail.x, m_ptTail.y
1	no. of bend points
527 86	*bend_point.x, bend_point.y*
connection	connection identifier (connection 3)
453 233	m_ptHead.x, m_ptHead.y
527 86	*m_ptTail.x, m_ptTail.y*
1	no. of bend points
527 233	bend_point.x, bend_point.y
connection	connection identifier (connection 4)
219 136	m_ptHead.x, m_ptHead.y
367 233	m_ptTail.x, m_ptTail.y
1	no. of bend points
219 233	bend_point.x, bend_point.y

actual text file. The reader will notice that as the connection entering the Gain block is attached to the bend point of the connection emanating from the Integrator block, its tail point coordinates are the same as the bend point coordinates (the description concerned is shown in italics). In addition, the numerical values have been generated, for ease of viewing here, using "set_prec" assigned to "0" in the function WriteDiagramEngDataToFile(): this can be reset to "1" for scientific notation as desired.

25.5 READING DATA MEMBERS FROM A FILE

The CDiagramEngDoc OnFileOpen() function introduced earlier calls the ReadDiagramEngDataFromFile() member method, where the CSystemModel function ReadSystemModelDataFromFile() is now called upon the system model object, as shown in bold in the following. The ifstream object, "fin", is then passed into all data-reading functions in a similar manner to the passage of the ofstream object, "fout", in the data-writing functions of the previous section.

```
int CDiagramEngDoc::ReadDiagramEngDataFromFile(CString file_path)
{
    int file_flag = 0;     // (0) no error, (1) error
    ifstream fin;          // infile stream
    CString sMsg;          // main msg string
    CString sMsgTemp;      // temp msg string
    UINT nType = MB_OK;    // style of msg. box
    UINT nIDhelp = 0;      // help context ID for the msg.

    //sMsg.Format("\n CDiagramEngDoc::ReadDiagramEngDataFromFile()\n");
    //AfxMessageBox(sMsg, nType, nIDhelp);

    // Open file for reading
    fin.open(file_path, ios::in); // open the infile stream, in mode

    if(!fin)                       // if(!false) then execute
    {
        sMsg.Format("");
        sMsgTemp.Format("\n CDiagramEngDoc::ReadDiagramEngDataFromFile
          ()\n");
        sMsg += sMsgTemp;
        sMsgTemp.Format("\n Unable to open file: %s\n", file_path);
        sMsg += sMsgTemp;
        sMsgTemp.Format("Aborting file i/o.\n");
        sMsg += sMsgTemp;
        AfxMessageBox(sMsg, nType, nIDhelp);

        fin.close();
        fin.clear();

        file_flag = 1;     // error
        return file_flag;
    }

    // Call the CSystemModel fn to start the reading of data from a file.
    GetSystemModel().ReadSystemModelDataFromFile(fin);

    // Snap connection end points to port or bend point
    SnapConnectionEndPointsAfterInitialConstruction();
```

```
// Redraw original diagram and mark as saved
UpdateAllViews(NULL);  // this fn calls OnDraw to redraw the system
  model.
SetModifiedFlag(TRUE);

// Close the infile stream and clear fail flag
fin.close();
fin.clear();        // clears fail flag setting from previous file i/o.

return file_flag;
}
```

The developer will have noticed that after the `ReadSystemModelDataFromFile()` function is called, the `SnapConnectionEndPointsAfterInitialConstruction()` is called to snap any model connection end points to either an input/output port or a bend point residing on another connection object. Thereafter, the `UpdateAllViews()` function is called to invoke the `OnDraw()` method to draw the newly loaded model. The `SetModifiedFlag()` function is called with the argument set to FALSE since as the model has just been loaded, then there is no need to mark the document as having been changed. Finally, the input file stream is closed and its flags reset.

25.5.1 READING CSystemModel DATA FROM A FILE

A `ReadSystemModelDataFromFile()` function needs to be added to the CSystemModel class to read data from a file and to set up the CSystemModel object, "m_SystemModel". In addition, all the block and connection data in the file need to be read and the relevant objects constructed to complete the model.

1. Add a public member function to the CSystemModel class with the prototype
   `void CSystemModel::ReadSystemModelDataFromFile(ifstream &fin)`.
2. Edit the function as shown, to iterate through the whole data file in a while loop and filter out string name identifiers to construct the relevant model objects.

```
void CSystemModel::ReadSystemModelDataFromFile(ifstream &fin)
{
    int cnt = 0;                        // counter to discern correctness of
      first line of file
    int error_cnt = 0;                 // counter to discern an inf. loop
    int max_cnt = 10000;               // max cnt for error detection
    char strLine[L_FILE_IO_STR];       // current line as a character array
    char strVar[L_FILE_IO_STR];        // character array var to work with
      "fin >>"
    CString sMsg;                      // msg string
    CString sMsgTemp;                  // temp msg string
    streampos stream_posn;             // position in the stream

    //AfxMessageBox("\n CSystemModel::ReadSystemModelDataFromFile()\n",
      MB_OK, 0);

    // READ THROUGH CONTENTS OF FILE
    while(!fin.eof())
    {
        // Get current stream posn
        stream_posn = fin.tellg();

        // Get current line (NOTE: getline() did not work as expected
          here and returned an empty line)
        fin >> strLine;
```

```
    // Now go back to the start of the line, such that the first data
     element can be read in.
    fin.seekg(stream_posn);

    // IF NOT EMPTY STR, THEN CONTINUE
    // If the comparison of "strLine" with the empty string equals
     zero, then "strLine" is the empty string.
    // If the comparison of "strLine" with the empty string != zero,
     then "strLine" is not the empty string.
    if(strcmp(strLine, "") != 0)
    {
        // SYSTEM MODEL
        // Check that this is a model_data.txt file with
         "system_model" as the first line

        // If first readable line is not "system_model" then abort
         file i/o
        if((strcmp(strLine, "system_model") != 0) && (cnt == 0))
        {
            sMsg.Format("");
            sMsgTemp.Format("\n CSystemModel::ReadSystemModelDataFrom
             File() \n");
            sMsg += sMsgTemp;
            sMsgTemp.Format("File incorrectly formatted.\n");
            sMsg += sMsgTemp;
            sMsgTemp.Format("Aborting file i/o.\n");
            sMsg += sMsgTemp;
            AfxMessageBox(sMsg, MB_OK | MB_ICONSTOP, 0);
            return;
        }
        cnt++;

        // If strLine is "system_model" then read in the data
        if(strcmp(strLine, "system_model") == 0)
        {
            fin >> strVar;
            m_strModelName = strVar;
            fin >> m_dATOL;
            fin >> m_dRTOL;
            fin >> m_dTimeStart;
            fin >> m_dTimeStepSize;
            fin >> m_dTimeStop;

            // Integration method
            while(fin.getline(strVar, L_FILE_IO_STR, '\n'))
            {
                // If string not empty then assume string on line is
                 correct
                if(strcmp(strVar, "") != 0)
                {
                    m_strIntegrationMethod = strVar;
                    break;
                }
            }

            // Time-step type
            while(fin.getline(strVar, L_FILE_IO_STR, '\n'))
```

```
        {
            // If string not empty then assume string on line is
              correct
            if(strcmp(strVar, "") != 0)
            {
                m_strTimeStepType = strVar;
                break;
            }
        }

        // Warning msg.
        while(fin.getline(strVar, L_FILE_IO_STR, '\n'))
        {
            // If string not empty then assume string on line is
              correct
            if(strcmp(strVar, "") != 0)
            {
                m_strWarning = strVar;
                break;
            }
        }
    }// end system model

    // CONNECTION
    if(strcmp(strLine, "connection") == 0)
    {
        CConnection *pCon = new CConnection(CPoint(0,0),
          CPoint(100,100));                        // pass in dummy
          connection head and tail pts.
        pCon->ReadConnectionDataFromFile(fin);  // read and
          assign the connections member data
        m_lstConnection.push_back(pCon);         // add the
          connection to the connection list
    }

    // CONSTANT BLOCK
    if(strcmp(strLine, "constant_block") == 0)
    {
        CBlock *p_block = new CConstantBlock(this,
          CPoint(100,100), e_rectangle);       // pass in
          &system_model, a dummy block posn and shape
        p_block->ReadBlockDataFromFile(fin);  // read and assign
          the block member data
        m_lstBlock.push_back(p_block);          // add the block to
          the block list
    }

    // DERIVATIVE BLOCK
    if(strcmp(strLine, "derivative_block") == 0)
    {
        CBlock *p_block = new CDerivativeBlock(this,
          CPoint(100,100), e_rectangle);
        p_block->ReadBlockDataFromFile(fin);
        m_lstBlock.push_back(p_block);
    }

    // DIVIDE BLOCK
    if(strcmp(strLine, "divide_block") == 0)
```

```
{
    CBlock *p_block = new CDivideBlock(this, CPoint(100,100),
      e_rectangle);
    p_block->ReadBlockDataFromFile(fin);
    m_lstBlock.push_back(p_block);
}

// GAIN BLOCK
if(strcmp(strLine, "gain_block") == 0)
{
    CBlock *p_block = new CGainBlock(this, CPoint(100,100),
      e_triangle);
    p_block->ReadBlockDataFromFile(fin);
    m_lstBlock.push_back(p_block);
}

// INTEGRATOR BLOCK
if(strcmp(strLine, "integrator_block") == 0)
{
    CBlock *p_block = new CIntegratorBlock(this,
      CPoint(100,100), e_rectangle);
    p_block->ReadBlockDataFromFile(fin);
    m_lstBlock.push_back(p_block);
}

// LINEAR FN BLOCK
if(strcmp(strLine, "linear_fn_block") == 0)
{
    CBlock *p_block = new CLinearFnBlock(this, CPoint(100,100),
      e_rectangle);
    p_block->ReadBlockDataFromFile(fin);
    m_lstBlock.push_back(p_block);
}

// OUTPUT BLOCK
if(strcmp(strLine, "output_block") == 0)
{
    CBlock *p_block = new COutputBlock(this, CPoint(100,100),
      e_rectangle);
    p_block->ReadBlockDataFromFile(fin);
    m_lstBlock.push_back(p_block);
}

// SIGNAL GENERATOR BLOCK
if(strcmp(strLine, "signal_generator_block") == 0)
{
    CBlock *p_block = new CSignalGeneratorBlock(this,
      CPoint(100,100), e_rectangle);
    p_block->ReadBlockDataFromFile(fin);
    m_lstBlock.push_back(p_block);
}

// SUBSYSTEM BLOCK
if(strcmp(strLine, "subsystem_block") == 0)
{
    CBlock *p_block = new CSubsystemBlock(this,
      CPoint(100,100), e_rectangle);
    p_block->ReadBlockDataFromFile(fin);
```

```
                m_lstBlock.push_back(p_block);
            }

            // SUBSYSTEM IN BLOCK
            if(strcmp(strLine, "subsystem_in_block") == 0)
            {
                CBlock *p_block = new CSubsystemInBlock(this,
                   CPoint(100,100), e_rectangle);
                p_block->ReadBlockDataFromFile(fin);
                m_lstBlock.push_back(p_block);
            }

            // SUBSYSTEM OUT BLOCK
            if(strcmp(strLine, "subsystem_out_block") == 0)
            {
                CBlock *p_block = new CSubsystemOutBlock(this,
                   CPoint(100,100), e_rectangle);
                p_block->ReadBlockDataFromFile(fin);
                m_lstBlock.push_back(p_block);
            }

            // SUM BLOCK
            if(strcmp(strLine, "sum_block") == 0)
            {
                CBlock *p_block = new CSumBlock(this, CPoint(100,100),
                   e_ellipse);
                p_block->ReadBlockDataFromFile(fin);
                m_lstBlock.push_back(p_block);
            }

            // TRANSFER FN BLOCK
            if(strcmp(strLine, "transfer_fn_block") == 0)
            {
                CBlock *p_block = new CTransferFnBlock(this,
                   CPoint(100,100), e_rectangle);
                p_block->ReadBlockDataFromFile(fin);
                m_lstBlock.push_back(p_block);
            }

        }// end strcmp()

        // CHECK FOR FILE READ ERROR I.E. AN INF. LOOP
        error_cnt++;

        if(error_cnt > max_cnt)
        {
            sMsg.Format("");
            sMsgTemp.Format("\n CSystemModel::ReadSystemModelDataFrom
              File() \n");
            sMsg += sMsgTemp;
            sMsgTemp.Format("File incorrectly formatted.\n");
            sMsg += sMsgTemp;
            sMsgTemp.Format("Aborting file i/o.\n");
            sMsg += sMsgTemp;
            AfxMessageBox(sMsg, MB_OK | MB_ICONSTOP, 0);
            return;
        }

    }// end while
}
```

The ReadSystemModelDataFromFile() function reads the system model data file in a *while* loop until the input file stream reaches the end of the file ("fin.eof()") or an error condition occurs ("error_cnt > max_cnt"). Initially the current position of the pointer in the stream is obtained by a call to tellg(), then the first line of the file is read into the local variable character array, "strLine", and then the stream pointer is reset to the beginning of the line, since the line contains information that needs to be processed later.

The first conditional statement "if(strcmp(strLine, "") != 0)" checks whether the first line is empty, and if not, "strLine" is filtered using a string comparison by the nested conditional statements to detect whether a system model, connection, or a derived-block object is to have its data read. The first item in the model data file is in fact a system model object (see WriteSystemModelDataToFile() for the writing sequence); hence, data are read into the member variables through the input file stream "fin". The getline() function calls, within the *while* statements, are used to get a complete line of data that is stored in the character array "strVar". This is necessary since if the array is empty, then the next line of data is to be retrieved; if the array is found by comparison to not be empty, then it is assumed to hold the value of a CSystemModel member variable to which it is subsequently assigned. If the first line of data does not begin with "system_model", then the file is assumed to be of the incorrect format and the function returns.

After the CSystemModel member variables have been assigned, control flow returns to the top of the *while* loop for the next line of data to be obtained, which is the identifier of the type of object that needs to be reconstructed: either a CConnection or a derived CBlock object. The constructor function is called for each object, and then the ReadConnectionDataFromFile() or ReadBlockDataFromFile() functions are called upon the pointer-to-CConnection or pointer-to-CBlock objects, respectively. Finally, the constructed object with the correct member data is added to the appropriate list.

The following sections detail all the file-reading functions to be added to the project, i.e., the public virtual function CBlock::ReadBlockDataFromFile(), CBlockShape:: ReadBlockShapeDataFromFile(), CConnection::ReadConnectionDataFrom File(), CPort::ReadPortDataFromFile(), and all the overriding derived-block ReadBlockDataFromFile() functions that facilitate a polymorphic file-reading behavior: the correct derived-block function is called based on the derived run-time type of the pointer-to-CBlock, "p_block".

25.5.2 Reading CConnection Data from a File

The first object that is constructed in the function mentioned earlier is the system model "m_SystemModel", and the next conditional filter-like statement concerns CConnection objects. A new CConnection object is constructed with a default (dummy) length, and then ReadConnectionDataFromFile() is called upon the pointer-to-CConnection object, "pCon", before it is added to the connection list.

1. Add a public member function to the CConnection class with the prototype
   void CConnection::ReadConnectionDataFromFile(ifstream &fin).
2. Edit the function as shown to read in the CConnection data and assign it to the class member variables.

```
void CConnection::ReadConnectionDataFromFile(ifstream &fin)
{
    int i;
    int n_bend_pts;              // no. of bend points
    char strVar[L_FILE_IO_STR];  // character array var to work with
      "fin >>"
    CPoint point;                // bend point
```

```
//AfxMessageBox("\n CConnection::ReadConnectionDataFromFile()\n",
  MB_OK, 0);

// Read CConnection member data from file
fin >> strVar;                 // connection string ID
fin >> m_ptHead.x;
fin >> m_ptHead.y;
fin >> m_ptTail.x;
fin >> m_ptTail.y;
fin >> n_bend_pts;

for(i=0; i<n_bend_pts; i++)
{
    fin >> point.x >> point.y;
    m_lstBendPoints.push_back(point);
}
}
```

25.5.3   READING CBlock DATA FROM A FILE

The ReadBlockDataFromFile() function in the base CBlock class is used to read in the basic block data for each block. Hence, a virtual function is required, which is to be overridden by all the derived-block classes with a method of the same name.

1. Add a public virtual member function to the CBlock class with the following prototype:
   virtual void CBlock::ReadBlockDataFromFile(ifstream &fin).
2. Edit the function as shown to read in the block data in the same order as it was written out by the WriteBlockDataToFile() function given in the previous section, and to call the CBlockShape and CPort data-reading functions.

```
void CBlock::ReadBlockDataFromFile(ifstream &fin)
{
    int i;
    int n_extra_ports;              // no. of extra input ports than
      the constructed amount
    int n_input_ports;             // no. of input ports
    int n_output_ports;            // no. of output ports
    char strBlockName[L_FILE_IO_STR]; // local string reflecting
      m_strBlockName
    CPort *p_port = NULL;          // pointer-to-CPort
    vector<CPort*>::iterator it_port; // iterator for vector of CPort ptrs.

    //AfxMessageBox("\n CBlock::ReadBlockDataFromFile()\n", MB_OK, 0);

    // READ CBlock MEMBER DATA FROM FILE
    fin >> strBlockName;
    m_strBlockName = strBlockName;
    fin >> m_ptBlockPosition.x >> m_ptBlockPosition.y;
    fin >> n_input_ports >> n_output_ports;

    // READ CBlockShape MEMBER DATA FROM FILE
    m_BlockShape.ReadBlockShapeDataFromFile(fin);

    // READ CPort MEMBER DATA FROM FILE
    // Add more ports to block if necessary: the CSumBlock and
      CDivideBlock could have more ports than the constructed amount
    n_extra_ports = n_input_ports - m_vecInputPorts.size();
```

```
        if(n_extra_ports > 0)
        {
            for(i=0; i<n_extra_ports; i++)
            {
                p_port = new CPort(*this);
                m_vecInputPorts.push_back(p_port);
            }
        }

        // Input ports
        for(it_port = m_vecInputPorts.begin(); it_port != m_vecInputPorts.end();
          it_port++)
        {
            (*it_port)->ReadPortDataFromFile(fin);
        }

        // Output ports
        for(it_port = m_vecOutputPorts.begin(); it_port != m_vecOutputPorts.end();
          it_port++)
        {
            (*it_port)->ReadPortDataFromFile(fin);
        }
}
```

The derived-block constructors set a default number of input and output ports for each block type, e.g., the Derivative block has one input and one output port. However, the Sum and Divide blocks have a user-defined number of input ports that could exceed the default setting. Hence, if the number of input ports being read in from a file is larger than the default value, extra ports are constructed and added to the vector of input ports, before their data are read using ReadPortDataFromFile().

25.5.4   Reading CBlockShape Data from a File

The base CBlock's ReadBlockDataFromFile() function shown earlier calls the CBlockShape's ReadBlockShapeDataFromFile() function upon the CBlockShape object, "m_BlockShape".

1. Add a public member function to the CBlockShape class with the following prototype:
   void CBlockShape::ReadBlockShapeDataFromFile(ifstream &fin).
2. Edit the function as shown to read in the block shape data in the same order it was written out by the WriteBlockShapeDataToFile() function.

```
void CBlockShape::ReadBlockShapeDataFromFile(ifstream &fin)
{
    int l_e_block_shape;        // local EBlockShape
    int l_e_block_direction;    // local EBlockDirection

    //AfxMessageBox("\n CBlockShape::ReadBlockShapeDataFromFile()\n",
      MB_OK, 0);

    // Read CBlockShape member data from file
    fin >> m_dBlockWidth >> m_dBlockHeight;

    fin >> l_e_block_shape;
    m_eBlockShape = static_cast<EBlockShape>(l_e_block_shape);

    fin >> l_e_block_direction;
    m_eBlockDirection = static_cast<EBlockDirection>(l_e_block_
      direction);
}
```

25.5.5   READING **CPort** DATA FROM A FILE

The CBlock's `ReadBlockDataFromFile()` function reconstructs the vector of input and output ports based on information read from a file. The CPort object properties are then set via a call to `ReadPortDataFromFile()` for all the input and output ports in the same order in which their properties were written to a file.

1. Add a public member function to the CPort class with the following proto-type: `void CPort::ReadPortDataFromFile(ifstream &fin)`.
2. Edit the function as shown to read in the CPort data in the same order it was written out by the `WritePortDataToFile()` function.

```
void CPort::ReadPortDataFromFile(ifstream &fin)
{
    int l_e_port_arrow_direc;        // local port arrow direction
    char strPortName[L_FILE_IO_STR]; // char array reflecting
      m_strPortName

    //AfxMessageBox("\n CPort::ReadPortDataFromFile()\n", MB_OK, 0);

    // Read CPort member data from file
    fin >> m_dPortPositionAngle >> strPortName;
    m_strPortName = strPortName;

    fin >> l_e_port_arrow_direc;
    m_ePortArrowDirec = static_cast<EPortArrowDirection>
      (l_e_port_arrow_direc);

    // Calculate the port position based on the m_dPortPositionAngle
      (already having been set)
    CalculatePortPosition();
}
```

The reader will notice the call to `CalculatePortPosition()` to calculate the port position from the port position angle member variable, "m_dPortPositionAngle": this calculates the port's position and stores it in the member variable, "m_ptPortPosition".

25.5.6   READING DERIVED-BLOCK CLASS DATA FROM A FILE

All the CBlock-derived classes each have their own implementation of the virtual `ReadBlockDataFromFile()` function, to read in the class member data from the ifstream object, "fin".

25.5.6.1   `CConstantBlock::ReadBlockDataFromFile()`

The CConstantBlock's `ReadBlockDataFromFile()` function is called upon the pointer-to-CBlock after a new CConstantBlock is created in the CSystemModel's `ReadSystemModelDataFromFile()` function as shown earlier.

1. Add a public virtual member function to the CConstantBlock class with the following prototype: `virtual void CConstantBlock::ReadBlockDataFromFile(ifstream &fin)`.
2. Edit the function as shown to read in the base CBlock class' member data before reading in the CConstantBlock data members.

```
void CConstantBlock::ReadBlockDataFromFile(ifstream &fin)
{
    int i;
    int j;

    //AfxMessageBox("\n CConstantBlock::ReadBlockDataFromFile()\n",
      MB_OK, 0);

    // MEMORY DELETE - delete data matrix whose memory was allocated in
      CConstantBlock::CConstantBlock()
    if(m_dConstMatrix != NULL)
    {
        for(i=0; i<m_iNrows; i++)
        {
            delete [] m_dConstMatrix[i];
        }
        delete [] m_dConstMatrix;
    }

    // Reset member vars.
    m_dConstMatrix = NULL;
    m_iNrows = 0;
    m_iNcols = 0;

    // Read CBlock member data from file
    CBlock::ReadBlockDataFromFile(fin);

    // Read CConstantBlock member data from file
    fin >> m_iNrows;
    fin >> m_iNcols;

    // MEMORY NEW - allocate memory to hold data being read in from a
      file
    m_dConstMatrix = new double *[m_iNrows];
    for(i=0; i<m_iNrows; i++)
    {
        m_dConstMatrix[i] = new double[m_iNcols];  // allocate an array
          of doubles, return & to matrix[i] }
    }

    // Read in the constant matrix
    for(i=0; i<m_iNrows; i++)
    {
        for(j=0; j<m_iNcols; j++)
        {
            fin >> m_dConstMatrix[i][j];
        }
    }

    // Assign the member string using the double data
    ConvertDoubleMatrixToString(m_strConstValue, m_dConstMatrix,
      m_iNrows, m_iNcols);
}
```

The initial construction of a CConstantBlock object in the CSystemModel's ReadSystem ModelDataFromFile() function results in a default construction which initializes the CConstantBlock's member variables. However, as the data being read from a file may be of arbitrary size, the initial constant matrix, "m_dConstMatrix", needs its existing memory deallocated and new memory allocated of the appropriate size.

In addition, there is a call to the `ConvertDoubleMatrixToString()` global function to initialize the CString member variable, "m_strConstValue", using the double matrix.

3. Add a global function prototype to the "DiagramEngDoc.h" header file at the "Global Functions" section, of the form `int ConvertDoubleMatrixToString(CString &str, double **matrix, int nrows, int ncols)`.
4. Edit the function in the "DiagramEngDoc.cpp" source file as shown to convert the double matrix data to the equivalent string form.

```
int ConvertDoubleMatrixToString(CString &str, double **matrix, int nrows,
   int ncols)
{
    int i;
    int j;
    CString strTemp;

    //AfxMessageBox("\n ConvertDoubleMatrixToString()\n", MB_OK, 0);

    // Convert double matrix to CString form

    // Init the incoming string
    str.Format("");

    // Matrix content
    for(i=0; i<nrows; i++)
    {
        for(j=0; j<ncols; j++)
        {
            strTemp.Format("%.10lf", matrix[i][j]);   // convert to
              10 decimal places
            str += strTemp;
        }

        // NOTE: NO '/n' CHARACTER IS PERMITTED HERE, ONLY THE ";" END OF
          LINE, DEMARCATION.
        if(i < (nrows - 1))
        {
            strTemp.Format(";");
            str += strTemp;
        }
    }

    return 0;
}
```

25.5.6.2 `CDerivativeBlock::ReadBlockDataFromFile()`

A CDerivativeBlock is constructed in a similar manner to the CConstantBlock in the `ReadSystemModelDataFromFile()` function, and its data are read from a file using the `ReadBlockDataFromFile()` function.

1. Add a public virtual member function to the CDerivativeBlock class with the following prototype: `virtual void CDerivativeBlock::ReadBlockDataFromFile (ifstream &fin)`.
2. Edit the function as shown to first call the base CBlock class' `ReadBlockDataFromFile()` function and then read in all the CDerivativeBlock data members.

```
void CDerivativeBlock::ReadBlockDataFromFile(ifstream &fin)
{
    //AfxMessageBox("\n CDerivativeBlock::ReadBlockDataFromFile()\n",
      MB_OK, 0);

    // Read CBlock member data from file
    CBlock::ReadBlockDataFromFile(fin);

    // Read CDerivativeBlock member data to file.
    fin >> m_iDerivativeMethod;
}
```

25.5.6.3 CDivideBlock::ReadBlockDataFromFile()

The CDivideBlock object is constructed and has ReadBlockDataFromFile() called upon it in a similar manner to the previous blocks.

1. Add a public virtual member function to the CDivideBlock class with the following prototype: virtual void CDivideBlock::ReadBlockDataFromFile (ifstream &fin).
2. Edit the function as shown to call the CBlock class' file-reading function and then to read in all the CDivideBlock data members.

```
void CDivideBlock::ReadBlockDataFromFile(ifstream &fin)
{
    //AfxMessageBox("\n CDivideBlock::ReadBlockDataFromFile()\n",
      MB_OK, 0);

    // Read CBlock member data from file
    CBlock::ReadBlockDataFromFile(fin);

    // Read CDivideBlock member data from file.
    fin >> m_iNDivideInputs;
    fin >> m_iNMultiplyInputs;
    fin >> m_iMultType;
}
```

The developer can experiment with setting more than the two default input ports, to test that the CBlock::ReadBlockDataFromFile() function does in fact add as many ports as specified in the data file.

25.5.6.4 CGainBlock::ReadBlockDataFromFile()

The ReadBlockDataFromFile() for the Gain block is similar in its structure to that of the CConstantBlock, since user input is allowed to set the gain constant "m_strGainValue", equivalently "m_dGainMatrix".

1. Add a public virtual member function to the CGainBlock class with the following prototype: virtual void CGainBlock::ReadBlockDataFromFile (ifstream &fin).
2. Edit the function as shown to delete any existing memory as a result of block construction, to call the base class ReadBlockDataFromFile() function, then read in all the CGainBlock data members, and finally initialize "m_strGainValue" using the double data and the call to ConvertDoubleMatrixToString().

```
void CGainBlock::ReadBlockDataFromFile(ifstream &fin)
{
    int i;
    int j;

    //AfxMessageBox("\n CGainBlock::ReadBlockDataFromFile()\n", MB_OK, 0);

    // MEMORY DELETE - delete data matrix whose memory was allocated in
      CGainBlock::CGainBlock()
    if(m_dGainMatrix != NULL)
    {
        for(i=0; i<m_iNrows; i++)
        {
            delete [] m_dGainMatrix[i];
        }
        delete [] m_dGainMatrix;
    }

    // Reset member vars.
    m_dGainMatrix = NULL;
    m_iNrows = 0;
    m_iNcols = 0;

    // Read CBlock member data from file
    CBlock::ReadBlockDataFromFile(fin);

    // Read CGainBlock member data from file.
    fin >> m_iGainType;
    fin >> m_iNrows;
    fin >> m_iNcols;

    // MEMORY NEW - allocate memory to hold data being read in from a
      file
    m_dGainMatrix = new double *[m_iNrows];
    for(i=0; i<m_iNrows; i++)
    {
        m_dGainMatrix[i] = new double[m_iNcols];  // allocate an array of
          doubles, return & to matrix[i] }
    }

    // Read in the gain matrix
    for(i=0; i<m_iNrows; i++)
    {
        for(j=0; j<m_iNcols; j++)
        {
            fin >> m_dGainMatrix[i][j];
        }
    }

    // Assign the member string using the double data
    ConvertDoubleMatrixToString(m_strGainValue, m_dGainMatrix, m_iNrows,
      m_iNcols);
}
```

25.5.6.5 CIntegratorBlock::ReadBlockDataFromFile()

The data to be read in for the CIntegratorBlock class consist of the length of the initial condition vector, "m_iLength", and the double vector itself, "m_dICVector". The CIntegratorBlock constructor converts a default string into a double vector, allocating memory for it in the process.

Hence, memory needs to be first deallocated and then the size of the vector read in and new memory allocated, in a similar manner to that required for the Constant and Gain blocks.

1. Add a public virtual member function to the CIntegratorBlock class with the following prototype: `virtual void CIntegratorBlock::ReadBlockDataFromFile (ifstream &fin)`.
2. Edit the function as shown to delete any existing memory, read in the vector length, allocate new memory, read in the vector values, and finally initialize the "m_strICVector" using the double data and the call to `ConvertDoubleVectorToString()`.

```
void CIntegratorBlock::ReadBlockDataFromFile(ifstream &fin)
{
    int i;

    //AfxMessageBox("\n CIntegratorBlock::ReadBlockDataFromFile()\n",
      MB_OK, 0);

    // MEMORY DELETE
    if(m_dICVector != NULL)
    {
        delete [] m_dICVector;
    }

    // Reset member vars
    m_dICVector = NULL;
    m_iLength = 0;

    // Read CBlock member data from file
    CBlock::ReadBlockDataFromFile(fin);

    // Read CIntegratorBlock member data from file
    fin >> m_iLength;

    // MEMORY NEW
    m_dICVector = new double[m_iLength];

    // Read in the initial condition vector
    for(i=0; i<m_iLength; i++)
    {
        fin >> m_dICVector[i];
    }

    // Assign the member string using the double data
    ConvertDoubleVectorToString(m_strICVector, m_dICVector, m_iLength);
}
```

The developer will have noticed the call to a new function, `ConvertDoubleVector ToString()`: this is similar in operation to the matrix conversion function introduced earlier.

3. Add a global function prototype to the "DiagramEngDoc.h" header file at the "Global Functions" section, of the form `int ConvertDoubleVectorToString(CString &str, double *vec, int length)`.
4. Edit the function in the "DiagramEngDoc.cpp" source file as shown to convert the double vector data to the equivalent string form.

```
int ConvertDoubleVectorToString(CString &str, double *vec, int length)
{
    int i;
    CString strTemp;

    //AfxMessageBox("\n ConvertDoubleVectorToString()\n", MB_OK, 0);

    // Convert double vector to CString form

    // Init the incoming string
    str.Format("");

    // Vector content
    for(i=0; i<length; i++)
    {
        strTemp.Format("%.10lf", vec[i]); // convert to 10 decimal places
        str += strTemp;
    }

    return 0;
}
```

25.5.6.6 `CLinearFnBlock::ReadBlockDataFromFile()`

The CLinearFnBlock simply writes and reads four double-type variables to and from a file, as shown in Table 25.12: there are no vector or matrix member objects and the constructor does not explicitly allocate any memory.

1. Add a public virtual member function to the CLinearFnBlock class with the prototype `virtual void CLinearFnBlock::ReadBlockDataFromFile(ifstream &fin)`.
2. Edit the function as shown to call the base CBlock class file-reading function and then to read in its own class member data.

```
void CLinearFnBlock::ReadBlockDataFromFile(ifstream &fin)
{
    //AfxMessageBox("\n CLinearFnBlock::ReadBlockDataFromFile()\n",
      MB_OK, 0);

    // Read CBlock member data from file
    CBlock::ReadBlockDataFromFile(fin);

    // Read CLinearFnBlock member data from file.
    fin >> m_dDerivative;
    fin >> m_dTimeInit;
    fin >> m_dTimeFinal;
    fin >> m_dValueInit;
}
```

25.5.6.7 `COutputBlock::ReadBlockDataFromFile()`

The COutputBlock writes and reads two integer variables to and from a file. The constructor function initializes the member matrix variable "m_dOutputMatrix" to NULL but does not allocate any memory.

1. Add a public virtual member function to the COutputBlock class with the prototype `virtual void COutputBlock::ReadBlockDataFromFile(ifstream &fin)`.
2. Edit the function as shown to call the base CBlock class' `ReadBlockDataFromFile()` function and then to read in the COutputBlock class integer data.

```
void COutputBlock::ReadBlockDataFromFile(ifstream &fin)
{
    //AfxMessageBox("\n COutputBlock::ReadBlockDataFromFile()\n",
      MB_OK, 0);

    // Read CBlock member data from file
    CBlock::ReadBlockDataFromFile(fin);

    // Read COutputBlock member data from file.
    fin >> m_iNotation;
    fin >> m_iTimePtDisplay;
}
```

25.5.6.8 CSignalGeneratorBlock::ReadBlockDataFromFile()

The CSignalGeneratorBlock class has double and CString member data types. The double data can simply be read in directly from a file, but the CString data need to be read into character arrays using the getline() function to capture all words on a particular line separated with spaces.

1. Add a public virtual member function to the CSignalGeneratorBlock class with the prototype virtual void CSignalGeneratorBlock::ReadBlockDataFromFile (ifstream &fin).
2. Edit the function as shown to call the base CBlock class' ReadBlockDataFromFile() function and then to read in the CSignalGeneratorBlock class data using getline() within a while loop.

```
void CSignalGeneratorBlock::ReadBlockDataFromFile(ifstream &fin)
{
    char strVar[L_FILE_IO_STR];    // character array var to work with
      "fin >>"

    //AfxMessageBox("\n CSignalGeneratorBlock::ReadBlockDataFromFile()\n",
      MB_OK, 0);

    // Read CBlock member data from file
    CBlock::ReadBlockDataFromFile(fin);

    // Read CSignalGeneratorBlock member data from file
    fin >> m_dAmplitude;
    fin >> m_dFrequency;
    fin >> m_dPhase;

    // Note: geline() is used here since the string may consist of blank
      spaces.
    // Fn type
    while(fin.getline(strVar, L_FILE_IO_STR, '\n'))
    {
        // If strVar not an empty string then assume the string is the
          complete identifier on the line
        if(strcmp(strVar, "") != 0)
        {
            m_strFnType = strVar;
            break;
        }
    }

    // Units
    while(fin.getline(strVar, L_FILE_IO_STR, 'n'))
```

```
    {
        // If strVar not an empty string then assume the string is the
          complete identifier on the line
        if(strcmp(strVar, "") != 0)
        {
            m_strUnits = strVar;
            break;
        }
    }
}
```

25.5.6.9 `CSubsystemBlock::ReadBlockDataFromFile()`

The CSubsystemBlock at present simply has two CString member variables that are to be read in from a file: "m_strInputPortName" and "m_strOutputPortName".

1. Add a public virtual member function to the CSubsystemBlock class with the prototype `virtual void CSubsystemBlock::ReadBlockDataFromFile(ifstream &fin)`.
2. Edit the function as shown to call the base CBlock class' reading operation and then to read in the CSubsystemBlock class CString data using `getline()`.

```
void CSubsystemBlock::ReadBlockDataFromFile(ifstream &fin)
{
    char strVar[L_FILE_IO_STR]; // character array var to work with "fin >>"

    //AfxMessageBox("\n CSubsystemBlock::ReadBlockDataFromFile()\n",
      MB_OK, 0);

    // Read CBlock member data from file
    CBlock::ReadBlockDataFromFile(fin);

    // Read CSubsystemBlock member data from file
    // Note: geline() is used here since the name the user enters may
      consist of blank spaces.

    // Input port name
    while(fin.getline(strVar, L_FILE_IO_STR, '\n'))
    {
        // If strVar not an empty string then assume the string is the
          complete name on the line
        if(strcmp(strVar, "") != 0)
        {
            m_strInputPortName = strVar;
            break;
        }
    }

    // Output port name
    while(fin.getline(strVar, L_FILE_IO_STR, '\n'))
    {
        // If strVar not an empty string then assume the string is the
          complete name on the line
        if(strcmp(strVar, "") != 0)
        {
            m_strOutputPortName = strVar;
            break;
        }
    }
}
```

The developer will notice that getline() is used in the reading of the name variables: this is required since the default names and those that the user chooses may have spaces, e.g., "input port name" rather than "input_port_name". Hence, the whole line is read in and stored in the local character array "strVar", and if it is nonempty, it is assigned to the CString member variable.

25.5.6.10 `CSubsystemInBlock::ReadBlockDataFromFile()`

The CSubsystemInBlock's file I/O is similar to that of the CSubsystemBlock where only one CString member variable is present: "m_strInputPortName".

1. Add a public virtual member function to the CSubsystemInBlock class with the prototype virtual void CSubsystemInBlock::ReadBlockDataFromFile(ifstream &fin).
2. Edit the function as shown to call the base class file-reading function and then read in the member variable using getline().

```
void CSubsystemInBlock::ReadBlockDataFromFile(ifstream &fin)
{
    char strVar[L_FILE_IO_STR];  // character array var to work with
      "fin >>"

    //AfxMessageBox("\n CSubsystemInBlock::ReadBlockDataFromFile()\n",
      MB_OK, 0);

    // Read CBlock member data from file
    CBlock::ReadBlockDataFromFile(fin);

    // Input port name
    while(fin.getline(strVar, L_FILE_IO_STR, '\n'))
    {
        // If strVar not an empty string then assume the string is the
          complete name on the line
        if(strcmp(strVar, "") != 0)
        {
            m_strInputPortName = strVar;
            break;
        }
    }
}
```

25.5.6.11 `CSubsystemOutBlock::ReadBlockDataFromFile()`

The CSubsystemOutBlock's file I/O is similar to that of the CSubsystemInBlock where only one CString member variable is present: "m_strOutputPortName".

1. Add a public virtual member function to the CSubsystemOutBlock class with the prototype virtual void CSubsystemOutBlock::ReadBlockDataFromFile (ifstream &fin).
2. Edit the function as shown in a similar manner to the previous function.

```
void CSubsystemOutBlock::ReadBlockDataFromFile(ifstream &fin)
{
    char strVar[L_FILE_IO_STR];  // character array var to work with
      "fin >>"

    //AfxMessageBox("\n CSubsystemOutBlock::ReadBlockDataFromFile()\n",
      MB_OK, 0);
```

```
    // Read CBlock member data from file
    CBlock::ReadBlockDataFromFile(fin);

    // Input port name
    while(fin.getline(strVar, L_FILE_IO_STR, '\n'))
    {
        // If strVar not an empty string then assume the string is the
          complete name on the line
        if(strcmp(strVar, "") != 0)
        {
            m_strOutputPortName = strVar;
            break;
        }
    }
}
```

25.5.6.12 `CSumBlock::ReadBlockDataFromFile()`

The CSumBlock class has two integer member variables, "m_iNAddInputs" and "m_iNSubtractInputs", denoting the number of addition and subtraction input ports on the Sum block, respectively. There are two default input ports set up in the constructor, but the user may change the number of input ports in a similar manner to that when working with the Divide block. Hence, the `CBlock::ReadBlockDataFromFile()` function adds any additional ports as specified in the data file and the CPort function then sets the appropriate port values.

1. Add a public virtual member function to the CSumBlock class with the prototype `virtual void CSumBlock::ReadBlockDataFromFile(ifstream &fin)`.
2. Edit the function as shown to read in the number of addition and subtraction ports.

```
void CSumBlock::ReadBlockDataFromFile(ifstream &fin)
{
    //AfxMessageBox("\n CSumBlock::ReadBlockDataFromFile()\n", MB_OK, 0);

    // Read CBlock member data from file
    CBlock::ReadBlockDataFromFile(fin);

    // Read CSumBlock member data from file
    fin >> m_iNAddInputs;
    fin >> m_iNSubtractInputs;
}
```

25.5.6.13 `CTransferFnBlock::ReadBlockDataFromFile()`

The CTransferFnBlock member data consist of two double arrays and their integer lengths. The constructor function, called from within `CSystemModel::ReadSystemModelDataFromFile()`, uses default string values to initialize the double arrays, allocating memory for them in the process. This memory needs to be deallocated in the CTransferFnBlock's `ReadBlockDataFromFile()` function, and new memory allocated, corresponding to the array lengths read from the file. Finally, the double data are converted to the equivalent representative string form for use in the `BlockDlgWndParameterInput()` function.

1. Add a public virtual member function to the CTransferFnBlock class with the prototype `virtual void  CTransferFnBlock::ReadBlockDataFromFile(ifstream &fin)`.
2. Edit the function as shown to deallocate memory, read member data, allocate new memory, and initialize the CString variables.

```
void CTransferFnBlock::ReadBlockDataFromFile(ifstream &fin)
{
    int i;

    //AfxMessageBox("\n CTransferFnBlock::ReadBlockDataFromFile()\n",
      MB_OK, 0);

    // MEMORY DELETE
    if(m_dNumerVector != NULL)
    {
        delete [] m_dNumerVector;
    }

    if(m_dDenomVector != NULL)
    {
        delete [] m_dDenomVector;
    }

    // Reset member vars
    m_dNumerVector = NULL;
    m_dDenomVector = NULL;
    m_iLengthNumer = 0;
    m_iLengthDenom = 0;

    // Read CBlock member data from file
    CBlock::ReadBlockDataFromFile(fin);

    // Read CTransferfnBlock member data from file
    fin >> m_iLengthNumer;
    fin >> m_iLengthDenom;

    // MEMORY NEW
    m_dNumerVector = new double[m_iLengthNumer];
    m_dDenomVector = new double[m_iLengthDenom];

    // Read in the coefficient vectors
    for(i=0; i<m_iLengthNumer; i++)
    {
        fin >> m_dNumerVector[i];
    }
    for(i=0; i<m_iLengthDenom; i++)
    {
        fin >> m_dDenomVector[i];
    }

    // Assign the member string using the double data
    ConvertDoubleVectorToString(m_strNumerCoeffs, m_dNumerVector,
      m_iLengthNumer);
    ConvertDoubleVectorToString(m_strDenomCoeffs, m_dDenomVector,
      m_iLengthDenom);
}
```

25.6 SAVING THE INITIAL OUTPUT SIGNAL FOR THE DIVIDE BLOCK

At present, for model diagrams involving feedback loops where the loop-repeated or junction node is a Divide block, the initial output signal must be set by the user via the COutputSignalDialog dialog window object. This is activated by right-clicking on the Divide block and selecting "Set Output Signal" from the Context menu, which then calls CDiagramEngDoc::OnSetOuputSignal()

followed by `CBlock::AssignBlockOutputSignal()`. This initial output signal set by the user has not yet been retained after the simulation as a class member variable, nor has it been serialized.

The `AssignBlockOutputSignal()` function was initially placed in the base CBlock class as a virtual function such that its functionality would be available to all derived-block objects. However, the CDivideBlock class should remember the initial output signal entered by the user, in the form of a combination of class member variables, and this information needs to be serialized such that upon starting a new simulation from a previously recorded model, the initial output signal of a Divide block should appear in the COutputSignalDialog-based dialog window. The following steps are required to add this functionality to the DiagramEng project:

1. Add member variables to the CDivideBlock class.
2. Amend the CDivideBlock class constructor and destructor functions.
3. Add the overriding `AssignBlockOutputSignal()` function to the CDivideBlock class.
4. Amend the CDivideBlock class serialization functions.
5. Amend the `PreliminarySignalPropagation()` function.

25.6.1 ADD MEMBER VARIABLES TO THE **CDivideBlock** CLASS

Four new private member variables need to be added to the CDivideBlock class to record the initial output signal for the Divide block as follows:

1. Add two private integer member variables to the CDivideBlock class to record the number of rows and columns of the initial output signal matrix, i.e., "m_iNrowsInitSignal" and "m_iNcolsInitSignal", respectively.
2. Add a private variable, "m_dInitSignalMatrix", of type "double**" to the CDivideBlock class to record the initial output signal as a matrix.
3. Finally, add a private CString variable, "m_strInitSignal", to the CDivideBlock class to record the CString equivalent of the double matrix for dialog window display purposes.

25.6.2 AMEND THE **CDivideBlock** CONSTRUCTOR AND DESTRUCTOR FUNCTIONS

Now that four new private member variables have been added to the CDivideBlock class, they need to be initialized in the class constructor as shown in bold in the following code.

```
CDivideBlock::CDivideBlock(CSystemModel *pParentSystemModel, CPoint
  blk_posn, EBlockShape e_blk_shape):
CBlock(pParentSystemModel, blk_posn, e_blk_shape)
{
    SetBlockName("divide_block");

    // Set the Divide block member vars
    m_iNMultiplyInputs = 1;
    m_iNDivideInputs = 1;
    m_iMultType = 1;

    // Set the initial signal member vars for a Divide block forming a
      loop-repeated node.
    m_iNrowsInitSignal = 0;
    m_iNcolsInitSignal = 0;
    m_dInitSignal = NULL;
    m_strInitSignal = "";

    // Create input and output ports
    ...
}
```

The class destructor, empty thus far in the project, should be amended as shown in bold in the following to delete any allocated memory that was used to hold the initial output signal, "m_dInitSignal".

```
CDivideBlock::~CDivideBlock(void)
{
    int i;

    // MEMORY DELETE
    // Delete the initial signal matrix whose memory was allocated in
      AssignBlockOutputSignal()
    if(m_dInitSignal != NULL)
    {
        for(i=0; i<m_iNrowsInitSignal; i++)
        {
            delete [] m_dInitSignal[i];
        }
        delete [] m_dInitSignal;
        m_dInitSignal = NULL;
    }
}
```

25.6.3 ADD THE OVERRIDING `AssignBlockOutputSignal()` FUNCTION TO THE **CDivideBlock** CLASS

The original base CBlock class' `AssignBlockOutputSignal()` method is designed to provide a general mechanism for all blocks to be able to assign an initial output signal value to their output connection object. Here the CDivideBlock class provides a specialization of this general function such that the Divide block's initial output signal can be serialized.

1. Add a public virtual member function to the CDivideBlock class with the following prototype: `virtual void CDivideBlock::AssignBlockOutputSignal(void)`.
2. Edit the function as shown to perform a similar general operation to the base class version, but to also add specific functionality to allow the CDivideBlock class to remember the initial output signal entered by the user through the dialog window.

```
void CDivideBlock::AssignBlockOutputSignal()
{
    int i;
    int attached = 0;         // flag denoting the attachment of an output
      connection to a block output port
    int input = 0;            // input: (0) incomplete, (1) complete
    int valid;                // used to set signal validity
    CSignal *signal = NULL;   // local ptr-to-signal
    CString sMsg;             // string msg. to be displayed
    CString sMsgTemp;         // temp string msg.
    UINT nType = MB_OK;       // style of msg. box
    UINT nIDhelp = 0;         // help context ID for the msg.
    list<CConnection*>::iterator it_con;  // iterator for list of
      CConnection ptrs.
    vector<CPort*>::iterator it_port;     // iterator for vector of CPort
      ptrs.
    vector<CPort*> vector_of_output_ports = GetVectorOfOutputPorts();
      // vector of output ports
```

```
// Get connection list
CDiagramEngDoc *pDoc = GetDocumentGlobalFn();
list<CConnection*> &con_list = GetParentSystemModel()-
  >GetConnectionList();

// CHECK THAT THERE IS A CONNECTION ATTACHED TO THE OUTPUT PORT
// Iterate over output ports
for(it_port = vector_of_output_ports.begin(); it_port
  != vector_of_output_ports.end(); it_port++)
{
    // Iterate over list of connections
    attached = 0;
    for(it_con = con_list.begin(); it_con != con_list.end();
      it_con++)
    {
        // If connection attached to output port: either directly or
          INDIRECTLY through a bend point
        if((*it_con)->GetRefFromPort() == (*it_port))
        {
            attached = 1;
            break;
        }
    }
    if(!attached)
    {
        sMsgTemp.Format("\n WARNING! Output signal assignment
          problem. \n");
        sMsg += sMsgTemp;
        sMsgTemp.Format("\n Output connection must be connected to
          block to set output signal.");
        sMsg += sMsgTemp;
        sMsgTemp.Format("\n Aborting output signal assignment. \n");
        sMsg += sMsgTemp;
        AfxMessageBox(sMsg, nType, nIDhelp);
        sMsg.Format("");      // reset the msg since within a
          while loop
        return;
    }
}

// SET REF-FROM-PORTS OF CONNECTIONS THAT EMANATE FROM BEND POINTS.
// These ref-from-ports are then RESET to NULL at the end of the fn
  (since they don't actually emanate from a PORT).
GetParentSystemModel()->SetRefFromPortOfConnectionFromBendPoint();

// MEMORY DELETE
if(m_dInitSignal != NULL)
{
    for(i=0; i<m_iNrowsInitSignal; i++)
    {
        delete [] m_dInitSignal[i];
    }
    delete [] m_dInitSignal;

    m_dInitSignal = NULL;
    m_iNrowsInitSignal = 0;
```

```
          m_iNcolsInitSignal = 0;
          // NOTE: m_strInitSignal is not set to empty, since its value is
              used to setup the new matrix m_dInitSignal
      }

      // GET OUTPUT SIGNAL
      // Iterate over output ports
      for(it_port = vector_of_output_ports.begin(); it_port !=
        vector_of_output_ports.end(); it_port++)
      {
          // Iterate over list of connections
          for(it_con = con_list.begin(); it_con != con_list.end(); it_con++)
          {
              // If connection attached to output port: either directly or
                INDIRECTLY through a bend point
              if((*it_con)->GetRefFromPort() == (*it_port))
              {
                  // GET THE ptr-to-CSignal OBJECT OF THE OUTPUT
                    CONNECTION.
                  // Note: there could be more than one CConnection object
                    with its CSignal data connected
                  // to the current block's output port. But here the first
                    CSignal object is retrieved,
                  // since all CSignal data on CConnection objects
                    associated with the current output port
                  // will have identical data. Below, an update of all
                    CConnection objects whose reference-from
                  // port is the current output port will have their
                    CSignal data updated individually.
                  signal = (*it_con)->GetSignal();
                  break;
              }
          }
      }

      // Create a dlg obj. of class COutputSignalDialog : public CDialog
      COutputSignalDialog oDlg;

      // Set the COutputSignalDialog var using the CDivideBlock var
      oDlg.m_strOutputSignal = m_strInitSignal;

      // WHILE NOT CORRECT INPUT
      while(input == 0)
      {
          // DISPLAY DIALOG TO USER USING DoModal() FN
          // Return val of DoModal() fn of ancestor class CDialog is
            checked to determine which btn was clicked.
          if(oDlg.DoModal() == IDOK)
          {
              // Assign COutputSignalDialog variable values to CDivideBlock
                variable values.
              m_strInitSignal = oDlg.m_strOutputSignal;

              // Convert the input string into a double matrix and assign
                it below.
              m_dInitSignal = ConvertStringToDouble(m_strInitSignal,
                m_iNrowsInitSignal, m_iNcolsInitSignal);
              //PrintMatrix(matrix, nrows, ncols);
```

```
    if(oDlg.m_strOutputSignal == "")  // Intentional setting of a
      NULL signal using an empty string
    {
        signal->ResetSignalData();
        m_iNrowsInitSignal = 0;
        m_iNcolsInitSignal = 0;
        // m_dInitSignal will already be NULL as returned from
          ConvertStringToDouble() if string is empty.
        input = 1;
    }
    else if(m_dInitSignal == NULL)  // Unintentional setting of a
      NULL signal and hence re-enter string
    {
        sMsgTemp.Format("\n WARNING!: Incorrect signal input. \n");
        sMsg += sMsgTemp;
        sMsgTemp.Format("\n Please enter consistent numerical
          data. \n");
        sMsg += sMsgTemp;
        AfxMessageBox(sMsg, nType, nIDhelp);
        sMsg.Format("");  // reset the msg since within a while
          loop

        input = 0;
    }
    else                      // Non-NULL input
    {
        // UPDATE ALL CONNECTION OBJECTS WHOSE REFERENCE-FROM
          PORT IS THAT OF THE CURRENT BLOCK'S OUTPUT PORT
        valid = WriteDataToOutputSignal(m_dInitSignal,
          m_iNrowsInitSignal, m_iNcolsInitSignal);

        // Matrix is non-NULL implying valid user input.
        input = 1;

    }// end if-else

    // Set the doc as having been modified to prompt to save.
    pDoc->SetModifiedFlag(TRUE);
}
else // IDCANCEL is the only other return value from DoModal().
{
    // Cancel signal data setting operation: no action to be
      taken (at present).
    input = 1;
}
}

// -- RESET ALL REF-FROM-PORTS OF CONNECTIONS EMANATING FROM BEND
  POINTS BACK TO NULL
// Before AssignBlockOutputSignal() was called the ref-from-ports of
  connections emanating from bend points
// were NULL. Now they need to be reset to NULL, to leave the program
  state as it was previously.
for(it_con = con_list.begin(); it_con != con_list.end(); it_con++)
{
    if((*it_con)->GetRefFromPoint() != NULL)  // if connection
      attached to a BEND POINT
```

```
            {
                (*it_con)->SetRefFromPort(NULL); // set ref-from-port to
                NULL (since not attached to a block)
            }
        }

    // MEMORY DELETE
    // m_dInitSignal is deleted upon entry into this fn and then in the
    CDivideBlock destructor.
}
```

The differences between the CDivideBlock and CBlock versions of the AssignBlockOutputSignal() are shown earlier in bold. The main feature is that the CSignal object is not used to retrieve or set the output signal string, but rather the CDivideBlock member variable, "m_strInitSignal", is used directly. In addition, memory deletion of "m_dInitSignal" is performed on entry to the function, and the string "m_strInitSignal", obtained from file input or via the dialog window, is then converted from a string to the double matrix, "m_dInitSignal".

25.6.4 AMEND THE CDivideBlock CLASS SERIALIZATION FUNCTIONS

The WriteBlockDataToFile() and ReadBlockDataFromFile() serialization functions need to be amended to write and read the new initial-signal member data to and from a file, respectively. Augment the WriteBlockDataToFile() function as shown in bold in the following, to write the dimensions "m_iNrowsInitSignal" and "m_iNcolsInitSignal" and data matrix "m_dInitSignal" to a file.

```
void CDivideBlock::WriteBlockDataToFile(ofstream &fout)
{
    int i;
    int j;

    //AfxMessageBox("\n CDivideBlock::WriteBlockDataToFile()\n",
      MB_OK, 0);

    // Write CBlock member data to file
    CBlock::WriteBlockDataToFile(fout);

    // Write CDivideBlock member data to file.
    fout << m_iNDivideInputs << endl;
    fout << m_iNMultiplyInputs << endl;
    fout << m_iMultType << endl;

    // Write CDivideBlock initial signal data to file (only numerical not
      CString)
    fout << m_iNrowsInitSignal << endl;
    fout << m_iNcolsInitSignal << endl;
    for(i=0; i<m_iNrowsInitSignal; i++)
    {
        for(j=0; j<m_iNcolsInitSignal; j++)
        {
            fout << m_dInitSignal[i][j] << "";
        }
        fout << endl;
    }
}
```

Augment the `ReadBlockDataFromFile()` function as shown in bold in the following, to read the dimensions of the data matrix, allocate new memory, read in the data, and then convert the double data to the string variable "m_strInitSignal" for COutputSignalDialog-based dialog window input purposes.

```
void CDivideBlock::ReadBlockDataFromFile(ifstream &fin)
{
    int i;
    int j;

    //AfxMessageBox("\n CDivideBlock::ReadBlockDataFromFile()\n",
      MB_OK, 0);

    // Read CBlock member data from file
    CBlock::ReadBlockDataFromFile(fin);

    // Read CDivideBlock member data from file.
    fin >> m_iNDivideInputs;
    fin >> m_iNMultiplyInputs;
    fin >> m_iMultType;

    // Read CDivideBlock initial signal data from file (only numerical
      not CString)
    fin >> m_iNrowsInitSignal;
    fin >> m_iNcolsInitSignal;

    // MEMORY NEW - Allocate memory to hold data being read in from a
      file
    m_dInitSignal = new double *[m_iNrowsInitSignal];
    for(i=0; i<m_iNrowsInitSignal; i++)
    {
        m_dInitSignal[i] = new double[m_iNcolsInitSignal];  // allocate
          an array of doubles, return & to matrix[i] }
    }

    // Read in the signal matrix
    for(i=0; i<m_iNrowsInitSignal; i++)
    {
        for(j=0; j<m_iNcolsInitSignal; j++)
        {
            fin >> m_dInitSignal[i][j];
        }
    }

    // Assign the member string using the double data
    ConvertDoubleMatrixToString(m_strInitSignal, m_dInitSignal,
      m_iNrowsInitSignal, m_iNcolsInitSignal);
}
```

25.6.5 Amend the `PreliminarySignalPropagation()` Function

The `PreliminarySignalPropagation()` function at present checks whether a Divide block is the loop-repeated node in a feedback loop, and if so, prompts the user to enter an initial output signal via the COutputSignalDialog dialog window. Now that the CDivideBlock data may be read directly from a file, any valid initial signal data can be written directly to the output connection's CSignal object using the `WriteDataToOutputSignal()` of the CBlock class, without using the dialog window. An accessor method is to be added to the CDivideBlock class, and then the PreliminarySignalPropagation() function needs to be amended.

1. Add a public member function to the CDivideBlock class with the prototype double **GetInitialSignalMatrix(int &nrows, int &ncols).
2. Edit the function as shown to assign the initial signal matrix ("m_dInitSignal") dimensions and to return its base address.

```
double** CDivideBlock::GetInitialSignalMatrix(int &nrows, int &ncols)
{
    // Assign the member variables
    nrows = m_iNrowsInitSignal;
    ncols = m_iNcolsInitSignal;

    // Return the signal matrix, regardless of whether it is NULL or not.
    return m_dInitSignal;
}
```

The PreliminarySignalPropagation() function is now to be amended as shown in bold in the following: first, the CDivideBlock's "m_dInitSignal" matrix and its dimensions are retrieved, and then, this signal is written directly to the output connection's CSignal member using WriteDataToOutputSignal().

```
int CSystemModel::PreliminarySignalPropagation()
{
    int i;
    int j;
    int ncols;                 // ncols of matrix
    int nrows;                 // nrows of matrix
    ...
    double **matrix = NULL;    // matrix returned from
      GetInitialSignalMatrix()
    ...

    // ITERATE THROUGH ALL SOURCE-TO-OUTPUT-BLOCK TOURS
    tour_type = 0;
    for(i=0; i<m_iNSourceOutputTours; i++)
    {
        ...

        // ITERATE THROUGH THE LIST A NUMBER OF TIMES = size - 1.
        for(j = 1; j < tour_blk_list.size(); j++)
        {
            ...
            if(!valid)  // if there does not exist output signal data
            {
                if((*it_blk)->GetBlockName() == "sum_block")  // skip sum
                  blocks but transfer signals directly
                {
                    ...
                }
                else if((*it_blk)->GetBlockName() == "divide_block")
                  // skip divide blocks since output signal data already
                  provided by user
                {
                    // CHECK IF THERE IS AN INITIAL SIGNAL AVAIL IN THE
                      CDivideBlock CLASS AND WRITE IT DIRECTLY
```

```
            matrix = ((CDivideBlock*)(*it_blk))->GetInitialSigna
              lMatrix(nrows, ncols);
            if((matrix != NULL) && (nrows > 0) && (ncols > 0))
            {
                valid = ((CDivideBlock*)(*it_blk))->WriteDataTo
                  OutputSignal(matrix, nrows, ncols);
            }

            // IF SIGNAL INVALID THEN ENTER VIA DLG WND
            if(valid == 0)
            {
                valid = 0;
                sMsgTemp.Format("\n PreliminarySignalPropagation
                  ()\n");
                sMsg+=sMsgTemp;
                sMsgTemp.Format("\n WARNING! Divide block has
                  unspecified output signal!\n");
                sMsg+=sMsgTemp;
                sMsgTemp.Format("Please manually enter initial
                  block output signal data!\n");
                sMsg+=sMsgTemp;
                sMsgTemp.Format("Aborting signal
                  propagation!\n");
                sMsg+=sMsgTemp;
                AfxMessageBox(sMsg, nType, nIDhelp); // msg. box
                return valid;  // abort fn
            }
        }
        else    // Perform OperateOnData() to generate the output
          signal data
        {
            ...
        }
    }// end valid

    it_blk++;  // increment block list iterator at end of "for j"
      loop

    }// end j
}// end i

// ITERATE THROUGH ALL SOURCE-TO-LOOP-REPEATED-BLOCK TOURS
tour_type = 1;
for(i=0; i<m_iNSourceLoopTours; i++)
{
    ...
    // ITERATE THROUGH THE LIST A NUMBER OF TIMES = size - 1.
    for(j = 1; j < tour_blk_list.size(); j++)
    {
        ...
        if(!valid)   // if there does not exist output signal data
        {
            if((*it_blk)->GetBlockName() == "sum_block")  // skip sum
              blocks but transfer signals directly
            {
                ...
            }
```

```
                    else if((*it_blk)->GetBlockName() == "divide_block")
                      // skip divide blocks since output signal data already
                      provided by user
                    {
                        // CHECK IF THERE IS AN INITIAL SIGNAL AVAIL IN THE
                          CDivideBlock CLASS AND WRITE IT DIRECTLY
                        matrix = ((CDivideBlock*)(*it_blk))->GetInitialSignal
                          Matrix(nrows, ncols);
                        if((matrix != NULL) && (nrows > 0) && (ncols > 0))
                        {
                            valid = ((CDivideBlock*)(*it_blk))->WriteDataTo
                              OutputSignal(matrix, nrows, ncols);
                        }

                        // IF SIGNAL INVALID THEN ENTER VIA DLG WND
                        if(valid == 0)
                        {
                            sMsgTemp.Format("\n PreliminarySignalPropagation
                              ()\n");
                            sMsg+=sMsgTemp;
                            sMsgTemp.Format("\n WARNING! Divide block has
                              unspecified output signal!\n");
                            sMsg+=sMsgTemp;
                            sMsgTemp.Format("Please manually enter initial
                              block output signal data!\n");
                            sMsg+=sMsgTemp;
                            sMsgTemp.Format("Aborting signal
                              propagation!\n");
                            sMsg+=sMsgTemp;
                            AfxMessageBox(sMsg, nType, nIDhelp);
                              // msg. box
                            return valid;     // abort fn
                        }
                    }
                    else     // Perform OperateOnData() to generate the output
                      signal data
                    {
                        ...
                    }
                }// end valid

            it_blk++;   // increment block list iterator at end of
              "for j" loop

        }// end j
    }// end i
    ...
    return valid;
}
```

The developer will notice the type cast "(CDivideBlock*)(*it_blk)" used to cast what was a pointer-to-CBlock "*it_blk" to now a pointer-to-CDivideBlock, prior to calling the GetInitialSignalMatrix() function (introduced earlier). This is necessary as the function GetInitialSignalMatrix() belongs to the CDivideBlock class and not the CBlock class and is only called for a Divide block, the name of which was filtered via a call to GetBlockName().

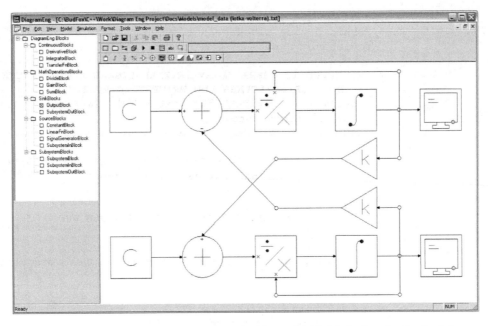

FIGURE 25.10   Lotka–Volterra predator–prey model with two Divide blocks forming feedback loops.

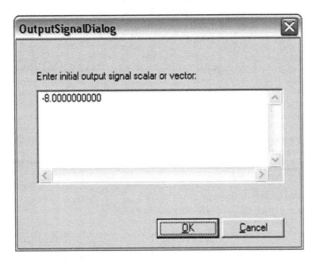

FIGURE 25.11   OutputSignalDialog dialog window used to set the initial output signal of a Divide block forming a feedback loop.

Now the code may be recompiled and rerun. If the user builds a model, where the Divide block is the junction node in a feedback loop (Figure 25.10), then its initial output signal, "m_dInitSignal", entered via the dialog window (Figure 25.11), is recorded upon saving the model. Then, after reloading the model, the correct output signal value will automatically be present in the COutputSignalDialog dialog window and written to the output connection's CSignal data member. That is, the user need not reenter the initial signal value after reloading a model if it was saved to the model data file.

25.7   ADDING DATA-WRITING FUNCTIONALITY TO THE OUTPUT BLOCK

The current Output Block Dialog window is shown in Figure 25.12a and includes textual and graphical output settings and has three buttons: Show Graph, OK, and Cancel. A new button, named Save Data, is to be added, as shown in Figure 25.12b, that upon clicking will create a CFileDialog object allowing the user to enter a file name to which the COutputBlock numerical data, "m_dOutputMatrix", may be written with respect to time, in a similar manner to its display as a graph.

The following steps indicate how a new button and its associated functionality are added for the Output Block Dialog resource and include (1) adding a new button and (2) adding an event-handler function to create a Save As dialog window to initiate the writing of data to a file.

25.7.1   Add a Save Data Button to the Output Block Dialog Resource

Select the IDD_OUTPUT_BLK_DLG_BTN_SD dialog resource from the ResourceView of the Workspace pane and add an additional Save Data button control on the dialog (Figure 25.12b) with the properties shown in Table 25.22: existing controls are shown shaded in gray.

25.7.2   Add an Event-Handler Function for the Save Data Button

Add an event-handler function for the ID_OUTPUT_BLK_DLG_BTN_SD object ID associated with the Save Data button to the COutputBlockDialog class with the prototype void COutputBlockDialog::OnOutputBlkDlgBtnSaveData(), as shown in Table 25.23.

Edit the COutputBlockDialog::OnOutputBlkDlgBtnSaveData() function as shown to create a CFileDialog dialog window object prompting the user for a file name to initiate the saving of the numerical data and then to set up an output file stream object, "fout". As an output file stream object "fout" is being used, the "fstream.h" header file needs to be included at the top of the "COutputBlockDialog.cpp" file just below the #include "stdafx.h" statement, i.e., add, #include <fstream>.

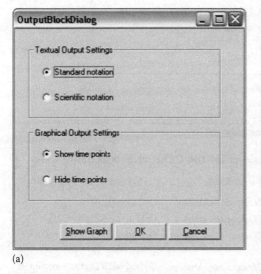
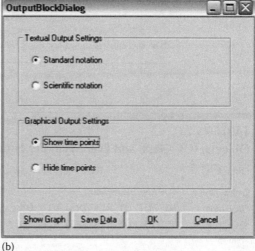

(a)   (b)

FIGURE 25.12 OutputBlockDialog dialog window used to set properties to display signals on a graph: (a) its current form and (b) with the intended Save Data button.

TABLE 25.22

Dialog Object, Properties, and Settings for the OutputBlockDialog Dialog Window (IDD_OUTPUT_BLK_DLG)

Object	Property	Setting
Group Box	ID	ID_OUTPUT_BLK_DLG_GPBOXNOT
	Caption	Textual Output Settings
Radio Button	ID	ID_OUTPUT_BLK_DLG_RB_STDNOT
	Group	Checked
	Caption	Standard notation
Radio Button	ID	ID_OUTPUT_BLK_DLG_RB_SCINOT
	Group	Unchecked
	Caption	Scientific notation
Group Box	ID	ID_OUTPUT_BLK_DLG_GPBOXTPTS
	Caption	Graphical Output Settings
Radio Button	ID	ID_OUTPUT_BLK_DLG_RB_TPTS
	Group	Checked
	Caption	Show time points
Radio Button	ID	ID_OUTPUT_BLK_DLG_RB_NOTPTS
	Group	Unchecked
	Caption	Hide time points
Button	ID	ID_OUTPUT_BLK_DLG_BTN_OK
	Default button	Unchecked
	Caption	&OK
Button	ID	IDCANCEL
	Caption	&Cancel
Button	ID	ID_OUTPUT_BLK_DLG_BTN_SG
	Caption	&Show Graph
Button	ID	ID_OUTPUT_BLK_DLG_BTN_SD
	Caption	Save &Data

The new entry is shown last (Save Data button).

TABLE 25.23

Objects, IDs, Class, and Event-Handler Functions for the COutputBlockDialog Class

Object	ID	Class	Command Event-Handler
Cancel button	IDCANCEL (default)	COutputBlockDialog	OnCancel()
OK button	ID_OUTPUT_BLK_DLG_BTN_OK	COutputBlockDialog	OnOutputBlkDlgBtnOk()
Save Data button	ID_OUTPUT_BLK_DLG_BTN_SD	COutputBlockDialog	OnOutputBlkDlgBtnSaveData()
Show Graph button	ID_OUTPUT_BLK_DLG_BTN_SG	COutputBlockDialog	OnOutputBlkDlgBtnShowGraph()

```
void COutputBlockDialog::OnOutputBlkDlgBtnSaveData()
{
    // TODO: Add your control notification handler code here

    // DiagramEng (start)
    int btnSel;             // button selection
    ifstream fin;           // infile stream
    ofstream fout;          // outfile stream
    BOOL dlgType = FALSE;   // TRUE => File Open dlg, FALSE => File
      Save dlg
    CString sCaption = "DiagramEng - Overwrite";   // message box caption
    CString strDefExt = ".txt";                    // default file
      extension
    CString strFileName = "output_data.txt";       // file name
    CString strFilePath;                           // local file path var
    CString strFilter = "All Files (*.*)|*.*|Plain Text (*.txt)|*.txt||";
      // string pairs specifying filters for file list box
    CString sMsg;           // main msg string
    CString sMsgTemp;       // temp msg string
    CWnd l_wnd;             // local CWnd
    DWORD dwFlags = OFN_ENABLESIZING | OFN_HIDEREADONLY; // customization
      flags
    UINT nType = MB_OK;     // style of msg. box
    UINT nIDhelp = 0;       // help context ID for the msg.

    //sMsg.Format("\n COutputBlockDialog::OnOutputBlkDlgBtnSaveData()\n");
    //AfxMessageBox(sMsg, nType, nIDhelp);

    // CREATE A CFileDialog DIALOG WND
    CFileDialog dlgFile(dlgType, strDefExt, strFileName, dwFlags,
      strFilter, NULL);

    // CHECK BUTTON SELECTION
    if(dlgFile.DoModal() == IDOK)
    {
        strFilePath = dlgFile.GetPathName();

        // CHECK TO SEE IF FILE EXISTS
        fin.open(strFilePath, ios::in);          // open file in input mode
        if(!fin)
        {
            fout.open(strFilePath, ios::out);  // open file in output
              mode
        }
        else
        {
            // Question user about overwriting existing file
            sMsgTemp.Format("%s already exists. \n", strFilePath);
            sMsg += sMsgTemp;
            sMsgTemp.Format("Do you want to replace it?\n");
            sMsg += sMsgTemp;
            nType = MB_YESNO | MB_ICONEXCLAMATION;

            btnSel = l_wnd.MessageBox(sMsg, sCaption, nType);

            // Check button selection
            if(btnSel == IDYES)
```

```
            {
                fout.open(strFilePath, ios::out);    // open file in
                  output mode
            }
            else if(btnSel == IDNO)
            {
                sMsg.Format("");
                sMsg.Format("\n Aborting writing model data to file. \n");
                nType = MB_OK | MB_ICONSTOP;
                //AfxMessageBox(sMsg, nType, nIDhelp);

                fin.close();
                fin.clear();
                return;
            }
        }
        fin.close();
        fin.clear();

        // CHECK IF FILE OPEN
        if(!fout)               // if(!false) then execute
        {
            sMsg.Format("");
            sMsgTemp.Format("\n COutputBlockDialog::OnOutputBlkDlgBtnSave
              Data()\n");
            sMsg += sMsgTemp;
            sMsgTemp.Format("\n Unable to open file: %s\n", strFilePath);
            sMsg += sMsgTemp;
            sMsgTemp.Format("Aborting file i/o.\n");
            sMsg += sMsgTemp;
            nType = MB_OK | MB_ICONSTOP;
            AfxMessageBox(sMsg, nType, nIDhelp);

            // Close the outfile stream and clear fail flag
            fout.close();
            fout.clear();    // clears fail flag setting from previous
              file io.
            return;
        }

        // CALL THE COutputBlock FN TO WRITE THE NUMERICAL DATA TO A FILE
        m_pOutputBlk->WriteNumericalOutputDataToFile(fout);
    }

    // Close the outfile stream and clear fail flag
    fout.close();
    fout.clear();                  // clears fail flag setting from previous
      file i/o.

    // DiagramEng (end)
}
```

The OnOutputBlkDlgBtnSaveData() method is similar to the conjunction of the OnFileSaveAs() and WriteDiagramEngDataToFile() methods of the CDiagramEngDoc class. The developer will notice that a call is made to WriteNumericalOuputDataToFile(), to write the numerical data to an output file using the reference-like pointer-to-CBlock variable, "m_pOutputBlk", of the COutputBlock class, passing the output file stream object, "fout", as an argument.

Hence, add a public member function to the COutputBlock class with the prototype void COutputBlock::WriteNumericalOutputDataToFile(ofstream &fout). Edit the function as shown to iterate through the data matrix "m_dOutputMatrix" and print the data to a file in columns.

```cpp
void COutputBlock::WriteNumericalOutputDataToFile(ofstream &fout)
{
    int j;
    int col;                    // column no.
    int n_data_pts;             // no. of data points per signal
    int n_signals_per_row;      // no. of signals per row of
      m_dOutputMatrix
    int n_TimeSteps;            // no. of simulation time steps
    int sig;                    // signal no.
    int t_cnt;                  // time-based counter
    double delta_t;             // time step size of simulation
    double t;                   // time pt
    double t_final;             // final simulation time
    double t_init;              // initial simulation time
    CString sMsg;               // main msg string
    CString sMsgTemp;           // temp msg string
    UINT nType = MB_OK;         // style of msg. box
    UINT nIDhelp = 0;           // help context ID for the msg.

    //sMsg.Format("\n COutputBlock::WriteNumericalOutputDataToFile()\n");
    //AfxMessageBox(sMsg, nType, nIDhelp);

    // GET TIME DATA
    GetParentSystemModel()->GetTimeParameters(t_init, t_final, delta_t);
      // passing time parameters by reference
    n_TimeSteps = GetParentSystemModel()->DetermineNTimeSteps();
    n_data_pts = n_TimeSteps + 1;

    // NUMBER OF INDEP CURVES PER ROW OF DATA
    // e.g. F(t) = [ [f1(t0), f2(t0)], [f1(t1), f2(t1)], …, [f1(tn),
      f2(tn)] ], n_signals_per_row = 2: f1(t) and f2(t)
    n_signals_per_row = m_iNcols/n_data_pts;

    // FOR EACH DATA/TIME POINT OF A SIGNAL
    for(t_cnt=0; t_cnt<n_data_pts; t_cnt++)
    {
        t = t_init + t_cnt*delta_t;         // time value is a multiple of
          the time step size

        fout << t << "t";                   // first column of output is
          time

        // FOR EACH ROW OF m_dOutputMatrix EQUIVALENTLY EACH ROW OF THE
          SUBMATRIX WITHIN m_dOutputMatrix
        for(j=0; j<m_iNrows; j++)
        {
            // FOR EACH SIGNAL ON A ROW
            for(sig=0; sig<n_signals_per_row; sig++)  // for one or more
              signals per row
            {
                col = sig + t_cnt*n_signals_per_row;  // colum no. of
                  m_dOutputMatrix extracting correct signal's data
```

```
        fout << m_dOutputMatrix[j][col] << "t";   // all signals
           printed out on one row for current time point

      //sMsg.Format("\n t_cnt = %d, j = %d, sig = %d, col = %d,
         f = %lf\n", t_cnt, j, sig, col, m_dOutputMatrix[j][col]);
      //AfxMessageBox(sMsg, nType, nIDhelp);
    }
  }
    fout << endl;     // new line for each time point
  }
}
```

Consider a data matrix, "m_dOutputMatrix", of the following form:

$$
M = \left[\begin{bmatrix} f_1(t_0) & f_2(t_0) \\ f_3(t_0) & f_4(t_0) \end{bmatrix} \begin{bmatrix} f_1(t_1) & f_2(t_1) \\ f_3(t_1) & f_4(t_1) \end{bmatrix}, \dots, \begin{bmatrix} f_1(t_n) & f_2(t_n) \\ f_3(t_n) & f_4(t_n) \end{bmatrix} \right]
\tag{25.5}
$$

where, $f_s(t)$, for $s \in \{1, \dots, 4\}$ (four signals are used here for simplicity), are the individual signals being recorded for each time point $t_i \in [t_0, t_n]$, for initial and final simulation time points, t_0 and t_n, respectively. The `WriteNumericalOutputDataToFile()` function first determines the time-based data, t_0, t_n; the time-step size, δt; and the number of data points, equivalently, the number of submatrices within the data matrix M. Then, for each time point t_i, represented by "t_cnt", the rows ("m_iNrows") of the matrix and the number of signals per row ("n_signals_per_row") are both iterated over, and the particular signal value located at column, "col", is extracted and written to a file. The effect of this nested iteration is to write a data file where each row of data in the output file corresponds to all signal output for a particular time point t_i and is hence of the following form:

$$
\begin{aligned}
&t_0, f_1(t_0), f_2(t_0), f_3(t_0), f_4(t_0) \\
&t_1, f_1(t_1), f_2(t_1), f_3(t_1), f_4(t_1) \\
&\quad\vdots \\
&t_n, f_1(t_n), f_2(t_n), f_3(t_n), f_4(t_n)
\end{aligned}
\tag{25.6}
$$

If there are no data in the output matrix, "m_dOutputMatrix", then the number of rows and the number of columns, "m_iNrows" and "m_iNcols", respectively, are zero, and only the time points corresponding to the system model simulation parameters will be written to the output file with the default name "output_data.txt".

25.8   SUMMARY

The serialization process involves writing and reading data to and from a file using output (ofstream) and input (ifstream) file stream objects, respectively, supported by the file stream header file "fstream.h". Initially, the DiagramEng project data structure was revised to determine the member data to be written to and read from a file. The classes involved were CSystemModel, CBlock, CBlockShape, CPort, CConnection, and the derived CBlock-based classes. The CSignal member data were not serialized since they are determined dynamically during a simulation.

Event-handler functions were added for the Main frame– and Child frame–based windows to the CDiagramEngApp and CDiagramEngDoc classes to initiate the serialization process. The CDiagramEngDoc functions added include OnFileOpen(), OnFileSaveAs(), OnFileSave(), and `OnFileClose()`. The CDiagramEngApp functions added include `OnFileOpen()`, `OnFileRecentFileOpen()`, `OnWndCloseAllDocs()`, `SaveAllDocuments()`, and `OnAppExit()`.

The `OnFileSave()` and `OnFileSaveAs()` functions call the `CDiagramEngDoc::WriteDiagramEngDataToFile()` method, which in turn invokes the `CSystemModel::WriteSystemModelDataToFile()` method, which iterates through the list of blocks and connections calling `WriteBlockDataToFile()` and `WriteConnectionDataToFile()`, respectively. The `CBlock::WriteBlockDataToFile()` function calls `CBlockShape::WriteBlockShapeDataToFile()` and `CPort::WritePortDataToFile()`: all the derived-block classes call the base CBlock class data-writing method before writing their own data to the file. An example data file was provided for a simple first-order linear differential equation system model.

The reading of data from a file is the reverse operation of writing to a file and is initiated by the `OnFileOpen()` function which calls `CDiagramEngDoc::ReadDiagramEngDataFromFile()`, followed by `CSystemModel::ReadSystemModelDataFromFile()`, wherein conditional statements filter through the input file to determine the appropriate objects to construct and then initialize with the file data. Other data-reading functions include `CConnection::ReadConnectionDataFromFile()`, `CBlock::ReadBlockDataFromFile()`, `CBlockShape::ReadBlockShapeDataFromFile()`, `CPort::ReadPortDataFromFile()`, and the CBlock-based derived classes' file-reading functions.

The initial output signal of a Divide block, which forms the loop-repeated node in a feedback loop, was then serialized by introducing member variables to the CDivideBlock class, amending the class constructor and destructor, adding an overriding `AssignBlockOutputSignal()` function, changing the CDivideBlock serialization functions, and modifying the `PreliminarySignalPropagation()` method of the CSystemModel class.

Finally, numerical-result-like data-writing functionality was augmented to the COutputBlock class through the addition of a new Save Data button to the Output Block Dialog resource—the associated button-based event-handler function `OnOutputBlkDlgBtnSaveData()`—and a `COutputBlock::WriteNumericalOutputDataToFile()` member method, to write numerical data to a user-specified output file.

REFERENCES

1. Chapman, D., *SAMS Teach Yourself Visual C++ 6 in 21 Days*, Sams Publishing, Indianapolis, IN, 1998.
2. Microsoft Developer Network Library Visual Studio 6.0, Microsoft® Visual Studio™ 6.0 Development System, Microsoft Corporation, 1998.
3. Microsoft Support, How to add command handlers for MRU menu items in MFC applications, Microsoft Corporation, 2009. http://support.microsoft.com/kb/243751
4. Kelley, A. and Pohl, I., *A Book On C: Programming in C*, 2nd edn., Benjamin Cummings, Redwood City, CA, 1990.
5. IEEE Standard for Floating-Point Arithmetic (IEEE 754-2008), IEEE, 2008.
6. Salas, S. L. and Hille, E., *Calculus: One and Several Variables (Complex Variables, Differential Equations Supplement)*, 6th edn., John Wiley & Sons, New York, 1990.

Part III

Refinement

INTRODUCTION

Part III, consisting of Chapters 26 through 34, starts by reviewing the existing menu and toolbar-based functionality in the project to determine the remaining features that need to be added to allow the user to perform efficient modeling and simulation activities. Printing and print previewing is facilitated by adding key functionality to set the number of pages to be printed, to prepare the device context, set mapping modes, and to perform a transformation between the window and viewport rectangles. Modifications are then made to implement a scrolling view to permit the user to draw large diagrams: conversions are required between device points and logical points to accommodate for the change in position of the view. Automatic fitting of the viewport scale to the physical window, zooming in and out, and resetting the default diagram geometry are also implemented. The Edit menu is extended with the Undo, Redo, Cut, Copy, and Paste actions, which, through the use of a clipboard object and the relevant copy constructors and assignment operators, allow the user to efficiently edit a model diagram. Annotations are then introduced to add explanative detail to a model diagram and involve attributes, including the font, that are specified using a dialog window. The Tools menu is augmented with a diagnostic information entry that upon selection displays process physical and virtual memory usage information. The Help menu is completed with a Using DiagramEng entry that invokes a process to display instructions to the user about the usage of the application. Finally, a concluding section summarizes the developmental process and presents suggestions for improving the software application.

26 Review of Menu and Toolbar-Based Functionality
Part II

26.1 INTRODUCTION

The previous chapters provided instructions to add functionality to the DiagramEng project for the Main frame and Child frame window-based menu items, the Context menu, and the Main frame, Common Operations, and Common Blocks toolbars. A consolidation was made in Chapter 13 to assess the most important features to be developed at that stage. The current chapter reviews the remaining menu and toolbar-based functionality to be added, specifically for the Child frame–based menus, since the Main frame–based operations work as desired.

26.2 FUNCTIONALITY TO BE ADDED

Figure 26.1 shows an instance of the application with a diagram model on a child window and the Child frame menus: File, Edit, View, Model, Simulation, Format, Tools, Window, and Help. Table 26.1 shows each of the menus with their corresponding entries for which functionality is to be added: the Simulation and Window menus do not require any additional functionality and are left blank.

The File menu presents the Print and Print Preview entries that already have MFC-provided functional support in the form of the `OnPreparePrinting()`, `OnBeginPrinting()`, and `OnEndPrinting()` functions added to the CDiagramEngView class by the MFC AppWizard on the creation of the DiagramEng application. Extensions to these functions and additional overriding methods need to be added to complete the printing and print previewing processes.

The Edit menu has entries, Undo, Cut, Copy, Paste, and Select All: the first four of which are associated with the identifiers, ID_EDIT_UNDO, ID_EDIT_CUT, ID_EDIT_COPY, and ID_EDIT_PASTE, respectively. However, no event-handler functionality has been associated with these IDs: in addition, a Redo entry with ID, ID_EDIT_REDO, will also be added. The Select All entry has an event-handler function, `OnEditSelectAll()`, of the CDiagramEngDoc class, but currently takes no action.

The View menu currently has three items to be developed: Auto Fit Diagram, Zoom In, and Zoom Out, with event-handler functions, `OnViewAutoFitDiagram()`, `OnViewZoomIn()`, and `OnViewZoomOut()`, respectively, belonging to the CDiagramEngView class. However, no working functionality is currently present. In addition, a Reset Diagram entry will be added later to reset a model diagram to its original size and location.

The Model menu requires functionality to be added to the CDiagramEngDoc event-handler function, `OnModelBuildSubsystem()`, associated with the Build Subsystem entry. At present, the user cannot create a working subsystem in a model diagram and hence the addition of working details will be postponed till later.

The Format menu has a Show Annotations entry associated with its event-handler function, `OnFormatShowAnnotations()`, of the CDiagramEngDoc class. The intent is to provide a mechanism by which the software user can annotate a diagram with user-specified names to appear next to diagram entities and to toggle their display.

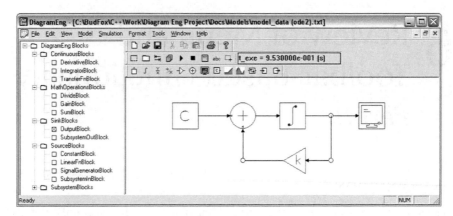

FIGURE 26.1   DiagramEng MDI application with Child frame–based menus visible.

TABLE 26.1

Key Child Frame Menus and Their Corresponding Entries for Which Functionality Is to Be Added

File	Edit	View	Model	Simulation	Format	Tools	Window	Help
Print	Undo	Auto Fit Diagram	Build Subsystem		Show Annotations	Diagnostic Info.		Using DiagramEng
Print Preview	Cut	Zoom In						
	Copy	Zoom Out						
	Paste							
	Select All							

The Simulation and Window menus do not require further development (blank).

The Tools menu has a Diagnostic Info. entry to which the event-handler function of the CDiagramEngDoc class, `OnToolsDiagnosticInfo()`, is attached. The function will ultimately activate a dialog window that will provide useful information to the user concerning memory usage information for the system and main application process.

Finally, the Help menu has an entry titled Using DiagramEng with the associated event-handler function, `OnHelpUsingDiagramEng()`, of the CDiagramEngDoc class, that is to generate a Portable Document Format (PDF) document named, "UsingDiagramEng.pdf", providing instructions and examples on how to use the DiagramEng software application for modeling and simulation.

In each of the following chapters, a menu and its entries will be discussed and functionality added to the project, to allow the user to easily interact in a predictable manner with the application, to print, edit, view, simulate, and format model diagrams.

26.3   SUMMARY

A brief review is made of the remaining Child frame–based menu functionality that is to be added to the DiagramEng project to allow the user to perform efficient modeling and simulation. The key menus, for which details are to be added in the following chapters, are: File, Edit, View, Model, Format, Tools, and Help.

27 Printing and Print Preview

27.1 INTRODUCTION

The previous chapter reviewed the remaining functionality to be added for the Child frame window-based menu items for the DiagramEng project. The File menu entries, Print and Print Preview, and the functions `OnPreparePrinting()`, `OnBeginPrinting()`, and `OnEndPrinting()` are provided by the MFC AppWizard on the creation of the DiagramEng application since support was chosen for printing and print preview. However, to get printing and print preview to work properly and consistently, such that the model diagram drawn in print is the same size as that on screen and paginated correctly upon output, additional details and overriding methods need to be added to the CDiagramEngView class.

The developer is enthusiastically encouraged to read Chapter 6 "Printing and Print Preview" of *Using Visual C++ 6* by Gregory [1] and Chapter 4 "Basic Event Handling, Mapping Modes, and a Scrolling View" and Chapter 19 "Printing and Print Preview" of *Programming Visual C++* by Kruglinski et al. [2].

Gregory [1] provides a very clear introduction to the Printing and Print Preview processes with an example that draws rectangles on the screen upon mouse-button-click events. Scaling, Printing Multiple Pages, Setting the Origin, and MFC and Printing are the four sections presented that cover the responsibilities of the developer to make the Printing and Print Preview processes work properly. The key functions to be added by the developer to the CView-derived class, as Gregory presents them, are `OnDraw()`, `OnBeginPrinting()`, and `OnPrepareDC()`. `OnDraw()` is used to draw on the screen, print to the printer, and draw the print preview; `OnBeginPrinting()` is used to set the maximum number of pages to be printed (`SetMaxPage()`); and `OnPrepareDC()` is used to set the viewport origin (`SetViewportOrg()`), such that the correct page appears in print preview and on printing. In addition, MSDN Library for Visual Studio 6.0 [3] presents a flowchart diagram (see Figure 27.1), indicating the order of the MFC-based printing process function calls in the Printing Loop: `OnPrint()` invokes the `OnDraw()` method and `OnPrint()` and `OnPrepareDC()` are called for each page to be printed. The dashed arrows and lines (added by the authors here) represent inherent and suggested function calls, respectively. In addition, the MSDN Library for Visual Studio 6.0 [3] provides the brief descriptions presented in Table 27.1, for the functions shown in Figure 27.1.

Kruglinski et al. [2] also discuss the Printing and Print Preview processes and provide examples concerning printing text and graphics on the screen. The interested reader should consult exercise 19B for an example of using the `OnPrint()` function to augment the printable output with headers and footers. In Chapter 4 of Ref. [2], a section titled "Mapping Modes" discusses the common mapping modes used to provide a coordinate conversion from the logical coordinate system to the device coordinate system. In particular, the MM_TEXT, MM_ISOTROPIC, and MM_ANISOTROPIC modes are explained in detail. The software developer will appreciate the discussion on scaling between the logical and device coordinate systems; this is also addressed in the instructions that follow.

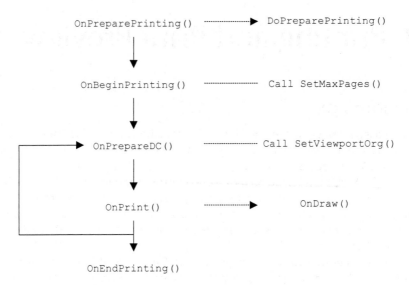

FIGURE 27.1 The MFC-based Printing process calling CView-derived member functions (with annotations to the right). (From Microsoft Developer Network Library Visual Studio 6.0, Microsoft® Visual Studio™ 6.0 Development System, Microsoft Corporation, 1998.)

TABLE 27.1

Descriptions of the Functions Used in the Printing Loop

Function	Description
OnPreparePrinting()	Override to enable printing and print preview and call DoPreparePrinting() passing the CPrintInfo *pInfo parameter
DoPreparePrinting()	Called to invoke the Print dialog box and to create a printer device context
OnBeginPrinting()	Override to allocate GDI resources, e.g., pens and fonts specifically needed for printing. SetMaxPage() may also be called from here
OnPrepareDC()	Override to adjust the attributes of the device context. SetViewportOrg() may also be called from here
OnPrint()	Called by the framework to print or preview a page of the document. The default implementation calls the OnDraw() member function
OnDraw()	Called by the framework to perform screen display, printing, and print preview, and passes a different device context in each case
OnEndPrinting()	Override to free any GDI resources that may have been allocated in OnBeginPrinting()

Source: Microsoft Developer Network Library Visual Studio 6.0, Microsoft® Visual Studio™ 6.0 Development System, Microsoft Corporation, 1998.

27.2   ADDITIONS TO THE DiagramEng PROJECT

The current state of the DiagramEng application allows the user to perform printing and print previewing of diagrams drawn on the palette, but at a substantially reduced scale. This is the case since the screen device has 96 pixels/in., whereas the printer device has 600 dots/in.; hence, the diagram becomes compressed due to the comparatively higher resolution of the printer to that of the screen. To correct this, the work of Gregory [1] and Kruglinski et al. [2] is used to define a mapping mode to scale/enlarge the diagram prior to printing or print preview and to add functionality to three key print/print preview-centric functions: `OnBeginPrinting()`, `OnPrepareDC()`, and `OnDraw()`. In addition, a new function, `DetermineDiagramCoordinateExtrema()`, is added here to obtain the extreme x and y Cartesian coordinates of points of the drawn model, which are then used to set the maximum page number (`SetMaxPage()`) for printing purposes. The following sections cover all material to implement the correct printing and print preview functionality: (1) Mapping Modes, (2) `OnBeginPrinting()`, (3) `OnPrepareDC()`, and (4) Augmenting `OnDraw()`.

27.3 MAPPING MODES

The mapping mode, according to Ref. [3], defines the unit of measure used to transform page-space units into device-space units and also defines the orientation of the device's x and y axes. The mapping mode of the specified device context is set using the `SetMapMode()` function. Two coordinate systems are often used in the discussion of the transformation of document-related information to the device context: the logical coordinate system may be thought of as that of the document and the device coordinate system as that of the device context, e.g., the screen or printer. The various mapping modes that may be used are shown in Table 27.2, where one logical unit is transformed into the stated device scale.

For example, the default mapping mode is MM_TEXT and maps one unit to one device pixel. So if a rectangle of 200 logical units square is to be drawn, it would appear as 200 device pixels square on the screen. Further, if there are 96 pixels/in. on screen, then a 200 device pixels square would appear as a 2.08 in. square on screen. If the MM_LOENGLISH mapping mode is selected, then one unit is mapped to 0.01 in. So if a 200 logical units square is desired, this would appear as a 2 in. square on screen.

The DiagramEng application makes use of many MFC-provided functions, in particular for drawing diagram entities on the screen, e.g., those used to draw lines/connections and rectangles/ blocks, and the default MM_TEXT mapping mode is consistent with the inherent drawing functionality and uses x and y axes that increase to the right and downward, respectively. However, for printing and print preview, since the printer device has a higher resolution than that of the screen, an alternative user-defined mapping mode is required to set both the scale of the transformation and the positive directions of the x and y coordinates. Here, the MM_ISOTROPIC mapping mode is used since it is the only mapping mode that allows the developer to preserve the directions of positive increase of the coordinate system consistent with the inherent MFC functions already in use; all that needs to be added is the scale of the transformation of the diagram before printing.

TABLE 27.2

Mapping Modes to Transform Page-Space Units into Device-Space Units [3]

Mapping Mode	Details
MM_ANISOTROPIC	Unit: application-specified. (x, y) axes increase is application-specified
MM_HIENGLISH	Unit: 0.001 inch. (x, y) axes increase (right, up)
MM_HIMETRIC	Unit: 0.01 millimetre. (x, y) axes increase (right, up)
MM_ISOTROPIC	Unit: application-specified. (x, y) axes increase is application-specified
MM_LOENGLISH	Unit: 0.01 inch. (x, y) axes increase (right, up)
MM_LOMETRIC	Unit: 0.1 millimetre. (x, y) axes increase (right, up)
MM_TEXT	Unit: device pixel. (x, y) axes increase (right, down)
MM_TWIPS	Unit: 1/1400 inch. (x, y) axes increase (right, up)

Source: Microsoft Developer Network Library Visual Studio 6.0, Microsoft® Visual Studio™ 6.0 Development System, Microsoft Corporation, 1998.

27.3.1 COORDINATE AXES

The positive directions of the coordinate axes are set using a combination of a window (CRect) rectangle and a viewport (CRect) rectangle, and the functions SetWindowExt(), SetWindowOrg(), SetViewportExt(), and SetViewportOrg() for these rectangles called upon the printing device context. The MSDN Library Help topics [3] indicate that the window along with the device-context viewport defines how the Graphics Device Interface (GDI) maps points in the logical coordinate system to points in the device coordinate system, i.e., how logical coordinates are converted into device coordinates. SetWindowExt() sets the x and y extents of the window associated with the device context, SetWindowOrg() sets the window origin of the device context, SetViewportExt() sets the x and y extents of the viewport of the device context, and SetViewportOrg() sets the viewport origin of the device context [3].

The window-specific code shown in the following will be added to the CDiagramEngView::OnDraw() function discussed later and shows how the window rectangle is set up to have top left and bottom right corner coordinates, $(x_1, y_1) = (0, 0)$ and $(x_2, y_2) = (1000, 1000)$, respectively.

```
// Window Rectangle
int iWndRect_x1 = 0;                    // x1 coord of window rectangle
int iWndRect_y1 = 0;                    // y1 coord of window rectangle
int iWndRect_x2 = 1000;                 // x2 coord of window rectangle
int iWndRect_y2 = 1000;                 // y2 coord of window rectangle

CRect WndRect(iWndRect_x1, iWndRect_y1, iWndRect_x2, iWndRect_y2);
  // (x1, y1, x2, y2)
pDC->SetWindowExt(WndRect.Size());      // set extent of Window rect
pDC->SetWindowOrg(WndRect.TopLeft()); // set origin of Window rect
```

The viewport-specific code, also to be added to OnDraw(), shows how the viewport rectangle is set up; in this case, the x and y extents of the viewport are scaled up from the window extents to enlarge the diagram for printing and print preview purposes only (scaling is discussed in Section 27.3.2). For simple drawing to the screen, i.e., when not printing (IsPrinting() returns FALSE), no scaling needs to be performed.

```
// Viewport Rectangle
int iVptRectExt_x;                      // x extent of viewport
int iVptRectExt_y;                      // y extent of viewport
double scale = 1.0;                     // scale of the transformation

CRect client;                           // client rect
GetClientRect(&client);                 // get client rect
iVptRectExt_x = int(scale*(iWndRect_x2 - iWndRect_x1));  // x extent of
  viewport
iVptRectExt_y = int(scale*(iWndRect_y2 - iWndRect_y1));  // y extent of
  viewport
pDC->SetViewportExt(iVptRectExt_x, iVptRectExt_y);       // set extent of
  viewport
pDC->SetViewportOrg(client.TopLeft()) // set origin of viewport
```

The developer should keep in mind in which quadrant a drawing should be placed. If, e.g., a diagram is drawn in the positive quadrant in the logical coordinate system, where x increases to the right and y increases downward, then the statement CRect WndRect(0, 0, 1000, 1000) (where the arguments in order specify the left, top, right, and bottom positions of the CRect object) with SetWindowExt(1000, 1000) would allow the drawing to appear on screen exactly as it does in the logical coordinate system. If, however, CRect WndRect(–500, 500, 500, –500) and

SetWindowExt(1000, -1000) were used, then the drawing would still appear in the positive quadrant, but this quadrant would be the upper left corner of the display, i.e., the *y* axis would appear flipped vertically about the *x* axis and would increase upward. The developer should experiment with various values to gain insight into the way the transformation is made.

27.3.2 SCALE OF TRANSFORMATION

The scale of the transformation between the window rectangle and the viewport rectangle, i.e., between the logical and device coordinate systems, is determined by the difference in magnitude between the resolution of the screen and the printing device, i.e., the printer. The GetDeviceCaps() function called upon the pointer-to-class-device-context (CDC *pDC) allows the device capacity to be determined: if displaying on the screen, then the call to GetDeviceCaps(LOGPIXELSX) retrieves the number of pixels per logical inch along the display width [3]; if printing, the same call retrieves the number of pixels per logical inch of the printer device. For example, for the screen device, the call may return 96 pixels/in.; however, for the printer, 600 dots/in. may likely be returned. Hence, the scale, *s*, of the transformation is determined as follows:

$$s = \frac{x_p}{x_s} \tag{27.1}$$

where x_p and x_s are the number of pixels per logical inch along the device width for the printer and screen, respectively. The code excerpt shown in the following makes the assumption that $x_s = 96$ pixels and that the scaling only occurs upon printing, where the call to IsPrinting() returns TRUE.

```
int iLogPixelsXPrinter;     // number of dots per logical inch of the
   printer device
int iLogPixelsXScreen;      // number of pixels per logical inch of the
   screen device
double scale;               // scale of the transformation bw. the screen
   and printer

// If printing, adjust scale, otherwise, if drawing leave at 1.0.
if(pDC->IsPrinting())
{
    iLogPixelsXPrinter = pDC->GetDeviceCaps(LOGPIXELSX); // no. of dots
       per logical inch of printer device
    iLogPixelsXScreen = 96;   // default no. of pixels per logical inch of
       the screen device
    scale = double(iLogPixelsXPrinter)/double(iLogPixelsXScreen); // scale
       ratio
}
else
{
    scale = 1.0;
}
```

Other arguments may also be passed to the GetDeviceCaps() function to retrieve information about the capacity of the device; a selection is shown in Table 27.3.

If the developer runs an application and uses the debugger or a message box to display the returned value of GetDeviceCaps(), called upon a pointer-to-CDC (CDC *pDC), using the arguments provided in Table 27.3, then depending on whether the application is printing (IsPrinting() = TRUE) or simply drawing in the absence of printing (IsPrinting() = FALSE),

TABLE 27.3

A Selection of Arguments for `GetDeviceCaps()` to Obtain Information about the Capacity of the Device

Argument	Description
HORZRES	Width of the display in pixels
VERTRES	Height of the display in pixels
HORZSIZE	Width of the physical display in millimeters (mm)
VERTSIZE	Height of the physical display in millimeters (mm)
LOGPIXELSX	Number of pixels per logical inch along the display width
LOGPIXELSY	Number of pixels per logical inch along the display height

Source: Microsoft Developer Network Library Visual Studio 6.0, Microsoft® Visual Studio™ 6.0 Development System, Microsoft Corporation, 1998.

TABLE 27.4

Sample Returned Values When Calling `GetDeviceCaps()` with a Selection of Arguments, When Printing (`IsPrinting()` = TRUE) or Drawing without Printing (`IsPrinting()` = FALSE)

Argument	IsPrinting() = TRUE, Printer Device	IsPrinting() = FALSE, Screen Device
HORZRES	4760 pixels	1280 pixels
VERTRES	6779 pixels	1024 pixels
HORZSIZE	202 mm	375 mm
VERTSIZE	287 mm	300 mm
LOGPIXELSX	600 pixels/in.	96 pixels/in.
LOGPIXELSY	600 pixels/in.	96 pixels/in.

different values will be returned corresponding to the device context being passed, as shown in Table 27.4; when `IsPrinting()` is TRUE or FALSE, the printer device context or screen device context is used, respectively. These values can then be used for scaling and setting the viewport origin (`SetViewportOrg()`) such that upon printing, the correct diagram scale is used and page is printed.

27.4 AUGMENTING THE CDiagramEngView `OnBeginPrinting()` FUNCTION

The `OnBeginPrinting()` function may be used to set the maximum number of pages to be printed once the printing device is known. This involves determining the page height, h (mm), of the printer device using the VERTSIZE argument in the `GetDeviceCaps()` function call upon printing and the extreme (x_e, y_e) coordinates of the drawing that appears on the client window converted into the common millimeter measurement, and dividing the latter by the former, i.e., y_e/h. If the diagram drawn on the screen is wider than the screen width, then the page width, w (mm), of the printer device should also be obtained using the HORZSIZE argument in the call to `GetDeviceCaps()`; the number of pages in width is then x_e/w. However, since integer arguments are being used, an extra page is to be added for both the vertical and horizontal ranges. Hence, the total number of pages, n, to be printed is then

$$n = \left(\frac{x_e}{w} + 1\right)\left(\frac{y_e}{h} + 1\right) \tag{27.2}$$

Currently, the `OnBeginPrinting()` function appears as shown in the following in the CDiagramEngView class, with the arguments "pDC" and "pInfo" commented out to prevent compilation warnings due to their absence of use: "pDC" is a pointer to the current device context (CDC), and "pInfo" is a pointer to a CPrintInfo object that stores information about a print or print-preview job and is created each time the Print or Print Preview command is chosen and destroyed when the command is completed [3].

```
void CDiagramEngView::OnBeginPrinting(CDC* /*pDC*/, CPrintInfo*
  /*pInfo*/)
{
    // TODO: add extra initialization before printing
}
```

The `OnBeginPrinting()` function can now be augmented to set the maximum number of pages to be printed via a call to `SetMaxPage()` upon the "pInfo" pointer-to-CPrintInfo as shown.

```
void CDiagramEngView::OnBeginPrinting(CDC* pDC, CPrintInfo* pInfo)
{
    // TODO: add extra initialization before printing

    // DiagramEng (start)
    int numPages;              // no. of pages
    int pageHeight;            // page height of printer device (mm)
    int pageWidth;             // page width of printer device (mm)
    double max_x;              // extreme x posn (mm)
    double max_y;              // extreme y posn (mm)
    CPoint ptMax;              // pseudo extreme point on diagram (extreme
      coords may be from diff. elements)
    CDiagramEngDoc *pDoc = GetDocument();

    // Get page width and height
    pageHeight = pDC->GetDeviceCaps(VERTSIZE);   // height of page in mm
    pageWidth = pDC->GetDeviceCaps(HORZSIZE);    // width of page in mm

    // Get extreme coords from diagram entities and convert to mm. (96
      pixels = 1 inch = 25.4 mm)
    ptMax = pDoc->GetSystemModel().DetermineDiagramCoordinateExtrema();
    max_x = 25.4*double(ptMax.x)/96.0;
    max_y = 25.4*double(ptMax.y)/96.0;

    // Calculate no. of pages
    m_iNpagesWide = int(max_x/pageWidth) + 1;
    m_iNpagesHigh = int(max_y/pageHeight) + 1;
    numPages = m_iNpagesWide*m_iNpagesHigh;

    // Set max page
    pInfo->SetMaxPage(numPages);
    // DiagramEng (end)
}
```

Initially the page width and height in millimeters are obtained via the calls to `GetDeviceCaps()` with the arguments HORZSIZE and VERTSIZE, respectively, made on the "pDC" pointer-to-CDC, in this case, the printing device. Then a call is made to `DetermineDiagramCoordinateExtrema()` to retrieve the most extreme positive (x_e, y_e) coordinates of diagram entities, i.e., blocks, connection head or tail points, and connection bend points. The extreme coordinates are then converted into the common millimeter measurement, given 96 pixels/in. for the screen device, and the number of pages horizontally ("m_iNpagesWide") and vertically ("m_iNpagesHigh") are determined and used to set the total number of pages ("m_numPages") (*n* in (27.2)) to be printed via the call to SetMaxPage().

The developer will have noticed the introduction of two new member variables to record the number of pages horizontally and vertically; these are used later in the OnPrepareDC() function to set the viewport origin such that the correct page may be previewed or printed. Hence, add two new private integer member variables to the CDiagramEngView class with names "m_iNpagesWide" and "m_iNpagesHigh" to record the number of pages to be printed horizontally and vertically, respectively.

The new function to determine the coordinate extrema is added to the project as follows.

1. Add a public member function to the CSystemModel class with the prototype: CPoint CSystemModel::DetermineDiagramCoordinateExtrema(void).
2. Edit the function as shown to iterate through the list of blocks, connections, and connection bend points to determine the diagram object CPoint coordinate extrema.

```
CPoint CSystemModel::DetermineDiagramCoordinateExtrema(void)
{
    int pt_rad = 5;      // radius of a bend point (assume fixed and small)
    double blk_height;   // block width
    double blk_width;    // block height
    CPoint ptBend;       // bend point
    CPoint ptBlkPosn;    // block position
    CPoint ptHead;       // connection head point
    CPoint ptMax;        // pseudo extreme point (extreme coords may be
      from diff. elements)
    CPoint ptTail;       // connection tail point
    CPoint ptTemp;       // temporary point
    list<CBlock*>::iterator it_blk;        // block iterator
    list<CConnection*>::iterator it_con;   // connection iterator
    list<CPoint>::iterator it_pt;          // bend points iterator

    // Init extreme point to the origin.
    ptMax.x = 0;
    ptMax.y = 0;

    // ITERATE THROUGH BLOCK LIST
    for(it_blk = m_lstBlock.begin(); it_blk != m_lstBlock.end(); it_blk++)
    {
        ptBlkPosn = (*it_blk)->GetBlockPosition();
        blk_height = (*it_blk)->GetBlockShape().GetBlockHeight();
        blk_width = (*it_blk)->GetBlockShape().GetBlockWidth();
        ptTemp.x = ptBlkPosn.x + int(0.5*blk_width);
        ptTemp.y = ptBlkPosn.y + int(0.5*blk_height);

        if(ptTemp.x > ptMax.x)
        {
            ptMax.x = ptTemp.x;
        }
        if(ptTemp.y > ptMax.y)
        {
            ptMax.y = ptTemp.y;
        }
    }
```

```
    // ITERATE THROUGH ALL CONNECTIONS
    for(it_con = m_lstConnection.begin(); it_con != m_lstConnection.
      end(); it_con++)
    {
        // Compare head point
        ptHead = (*it_con)->GetConnectionPointHead();

        if(ptHead.x > ptMax.x)
        {
            ptMax.x = ptHead.x;
        }
        if(ptHead.y > ptMax.y)
        {
            ptMax.y = ptHead.y;
        }

        // Compare tail point
        ptTail = (*it_con)->GetConnectionPointTail();

        if(ptTail.x > ptMax.x)
        {
            ptMax.x = ptTail.x;
        }
        if(ptTail.y > ptMax.y)
        {
            ptMax.y = ptTail.y;
        }

        // Compare connection's bend points
        list<CPoint> &lstBendPoints = (*it_con)-
          >GetConnectionBendPointsList();

        for(it_pt = lstBendPoints.begin(); it_pt != lstBendPoints.end();
          it_pt++)
        {
            // Ellipse surrounds the bend point with radius r (pt_rad).
            ptTemp.x = (*it_pt).x + pt_rad;
            ptTemp.y = (*it_pt).y + pt_rad;

            if(ptTemp.x > ptMax.x)
            {
                ptMax.x = ptTemp.x;
            }
            if(ptTemp.y > ptMax.y)
            {
                ptMax.y = ptTemp.y;
            }
        }
    }

    return ptMax;
}
```

The function simply iterates through the list of blocks, connections, and connection bend points, retrieving their (x, y) coordinate locations, making a comparison with the current extremum coordinates (x_e, y_e), "ptMax.x" and "ptMax.y", and updating them appropriately. For blocks, the block width and height are added to the block position denoting the extreme point of the block and a comparison made. For connection bend points, a distance equal to the radius of the bend point's ellipse is added to the bend point coordinates and a comparison made. Thereafter, the pseudo extreme point (CPoint), "ptMax", is updated and returned. The extreme point is described as being "pseudo" extreme since the x_e and y_e components defining the point may be updated independently from different diagram entities. For example, given two diagram entities' coordinates (x_1, y_1) and (x_2, y_2), if $x_1 > x_2$ and $y_2 > y_1$, then the pseudo extreme point, "ptMax", has coordinates $(x_e, y_e) = (x_1, y_2)$.

27.5   AUGMENTING THE CDiagramEngView `OnPrepareDC()` FUNCTION

The purpose of the `OnPrepareDC()` function is to allow the developer to (1) adjust attributes of the device context as needed for the specified page, e.g., setting of the mapping mode, (2) perform print-time pagination, and (3) send escape codes to the printer on a page-by-page basis [3]. Here, the first two actions will be taken: setting of the mapping mode and performing print-time pagination. The `OnPrepareDC()` function needs to be overridden and added to the CDiagramEngView class by the developer and edited as follows:

1. Invoke the ClassWizard and choose the Message Maps tab.
2. Select CDiagramEngView as both the Class Name and as the Object ID.
3. Select `OnPrepareDC()` in the Messages box and click Add Function to add the function.
4. Edit the function as shown to first chain up to the CView base class version of the function, `CView::OnPrepareDC()`, passing the "pDC" and "pInfo" arguments of type CDC* and CPrintInfo*, respectively, and then to perform the relevant printing-related actions.

```
void CDiagramEngView::OnPrepareDC(CDC* pDC, CPrintInfo* pInfo)
{
    // TODO: Add your specialized code here and/or call the base class

    // DiagramEng (start)
    CView::OnPrepareDC(pDC, pInfo); // call base class version first

    if(pDC->IsPrinting())
    {
        int i;                      // row index
        int j;                      // col index
        int originX;                // x-coord of viewport origin
        int originY;                // y-coord of viewport origin
        int page_no;                // page number calculated
        int pageHeight;             // page height in dots
        int pageWidth;              // page width in dots
        int val = 0;                // loop-breaking value

        // SET MAPPING MODE
        pDC->SetMapMode(MM_ISOTROPIC);

        // PAGE DIMS IN DOTS
        pageHeight = pDC->GetDeviceCaps(VERTRES);
        pageWidth = pDC->GetDeviceCaps(HORZRES);

        // LOOP THROUGH ROWS AND COLS OF PAGES AND DETERMINE ORIGIN
          COORDS
        for(j=0; j<m_iNpagesWide; j++)
        {
            for(i=0; i<m_iNpagesHigh; i++)
```

```
        {
            page_no = j*m_iNpagesHigh + i + 1; // add 1, since
             m_nCurPage is an element of [1,n] (starts from 1).

            // Compare current and calculated pages
            if(pInfo->m_nCurPage == page_no)
            {
                originX = pageWidth*j; // column multiples of
                  pageWidth
                originY = pageHeight*i; // row multiples of pageHeight
                val = -1;
                break;                        // break from i loop
            }
        }
        if(val == -1)
        {
            break;                        // break from j loop
        }
    }

    // SET VIEWPORT ORIGIN
    // Think: "Pull origin left and up by originX and originY,
      respectively,
    // leaving the appropriate portion of the document on the current
      printing page".
    pDC->SetViewportOrg(-originX,-originY);
  }

  // DiagramEng (end)
}
```

Initially, the base class version of the OnPrepareDC() function, CView::OnPrepareDC(), is called and allows the base class implementation to execute first. This is important when a view class is derived from CScrollView, which will be done in the following chapter.

As an aside, "CScrollView overrides OnPrepareDC() and in it calls CDC::SetMapMode() to set the mapping mode and CDC::SetViewportOrg() to translate the viewport origin an amount that equals the horizontal and vertical scroll positions" [4]. Hence, if CScrollView::OnPrepareDC() were called after the IsPrinting() section, then the mapping mode and viewport origin would not be correctly set for printing and print previewing purposes when in the context of a scrolling view.

Then, within the printing section (IsPrinting()), the mapping mode is set to MM_ISOTROPIC, and then the page width and height are obtained via calls to GetDeviceCaps() passing the HORZRES and VERTRES arguments to get the number of pixels, effectively printer dots, horizontally and vertically, respectively. Thereafter, the viewport origin coordinates are determined based on the current page being printed, ("m_nCurPage"), the page width ("pageWidth") and height ("pageHeight"), and the number of pages high ("m_iNpagesHigh") and wide ("m_iNpagesWide") required to present the diagram for printing or print preview. Finally, the viewport origin is set via a call to SetViewportOrg() such that the correct page will appear at print-time (IsPrinting() = TRUE). Figure 27.2 shows a sample diagrammatic representation of the algorithm in OnPrepareDC() used to determine the viewport origin for multiple page printing, where "m_iNpagesWide" and "m_iNpagesHigh" are four and three, respectively, and the loop indices and page numbers are shown.

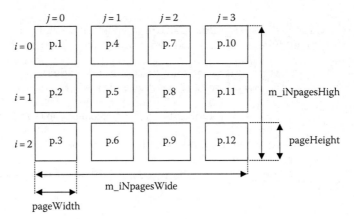

FIGURE 27.2 A sample diagrammatic representation of the algorithm used to set the viewport origin for a multiple page print or print preview instance, with "m_iNpagesWide" and "m_iNpagesHigh" set to 4 and 3, respectively.

27.6   AUGMENTING THE CDiagramEngView OnDraw() FUNCTION

The OnDraw() function of the CDiagramEngView class is shown in the following to take a pointer-to-CDC (CDC *pDC) and call DrawSystemModel() of the CSystemModel class; in its current form, no provision is made as to whether drawing is being performed for the screen, the printer, or print preview, and hence, no scaling of the diagram model is present.

```
void CDiagramEngView::OnDraw(CDC* pDC)
{
    CDiagramEngDoc* pDoc = GetDocument();
    ASSERT_VALID(pDoc);
    // TODO: add draw code for native data here

    // DiagramEng (start)

    pDoc->GetSystemModel().DrawSystemModel(pDC);

    // DiagramEng (end)
}
```

The OnDraw() function should be augmented as shown in the following to first set the window dimensions, followed by a scaling of the window dimensions to create an enlarged viewport in preparation for printing and print preview. The setting of the window and viewport extents and origins, to affect the transformation, is discussed in Section 27.3.1, and the scaling used based upon the different resolutions of the screen and printer is explained in Section 27.3.2.

```
void CDiagramEngView::OnDraw(CDC* pDC)
{
    CDiagramEngDoc* pDoc = GetDocument();
    ASSERT_VALID(pDoc);
    // TODO: add draw code for native data here

    // DiagramEng (start)
```

```
    // IF PRINTING THEN SCALE THE DIAGRAM
    if(pDC->IsPrinting())
    {
        int iLogPixelsXPrinter;   // number of dots per logical inch of
          the printer device
        int iLogPixelsXScreen;    // number of pixels per logical inch of
          the screen device
        int iWndRect_x1 = 0;      // x1 coord of window rectangle
        int iWndRect_y1 = 0;      // y1 coord of window rectangle
        int iWndRect_x2 = 1000;   // x2 coord of window rectangle
        int iWndRect_y2 = 1000;   // y2 coord of window rectangle
        int iVptRectExt_x;        // x extent of viewport
        int iVptRectExt_y;        // y extent of viewport
        double scale = 1.0;       // scale of the transformation bw. the
          screen and printer (default: 1.0)

        // Set mapping mode (set in OnPrepareDC())
        // pDC->SetMapMode(MM_ISOTROPIC);

        // Scale
        iLogPixelsXPrinter = pDC->GetDeviceCaps(LOGPIXELSX);
          // no. of dots per logical inch of printer device
        iLogPixelsXScreen = 96; // default no. of pixels per logical inch
          of the screen device
        scale = double(iLogPixelsXPrinter)/double(iLogPixelsXScreen);
          // scale ratio

        // Window Rectangle
        CRect WndRect(iWndRect_x1, iWndRect_y1, iWndRect_x2, iWndRect_y2);
          // (x1, y1, x2, y2)
        pDC->SetWindowExt(WndRect.Size()); // set extent of Window rect
        pDC->SetWindowOrg(WndRect.TopLeft()); // set origin of Window rect

        // Viewport Rectangle
        CRect client;             // client rect
        GetClientRect(&client);   // get client rect
        iVptRectExt_x = int(scale*(iWndRect_x2 - iWndRect_x1));
          // x extent of viewport
        iVptRectExt_y = int(scale*(iWndRect_y2 - iWndRect_y1));
          // y extent of viewport
        pDC->SetViewportExt(iVptRectExt_x, iVptRectExt_y);
          // set extent of viewport
        //pDC->SetViewportOrg(client.TopLeft()); // viewport origin set
          in OnPrepareDC()
    }
    // DRAW SYSTEM MODEL
    pDoc->GetSystemModel().DrawSystemModel(pDC);

    // DiagramEng (end)
}
```

The developer will notice that SetMapMode() and SetViewportOrg() are not called in
OnDraw() since they are already called upon printing (IsPrinting()) in OnPrepareDC().

Finally, the user may draw a diagram model that occupies large a screen area, and upon printing and print preview, the whole diagram is presented on numerous pages of output as shown in
Figure 27.3.

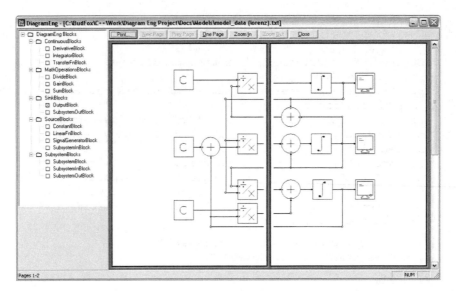

FIGURE 27.3   The Lorenz equation model diagram requiring two pages for printing and print preview: "m_iNpagesHigh" and "m_iNpagesWide" are 1 and 2, respectively.

27.7   SUMMARY

The Printing and Print Preview processes, the action of which is identified via a call to IsPrinting(), typically involve the CView-derived functions: OnPreparePrinting(), DoPreparePrinting(), OnBeginPrinting(), OnPrepareDC(), OnPrint(), OnDraw(), and OnEndPrinting(), where OnPrepareDC() and OnPrint() are iteratively called for each page to be printed. A mapping mode defines the transformation from page-space units into device-space units and the axis orientations. The window and viewport rectangles with the extent- and origin-setting functions, SetWindowExt(), SetWindowOrg(), SetViewportExt(), and SetViewportOrg(), define the mapping from the window to the viewport. In addition, a scaling may be used in the transformation and is typically based upon the ratio of the screen and printer device capacities obtained using the GetDeviceCaps() function passing the appropriate argument.

The three key methods to which functionality is added are OnBeginPrinting(), OnPrepareDC(), and OnDraw(). OnBeginPrinting() is used to set the maximum number of pages to be printed via a call to SetMaxPage(); OnPrepareDC() prepares the device context, sets the mapping mode via SetMapMode(), and sets the viewport origin using a call to SetViewportOrg(); and, finally, OnDraw() performs the appropriate transformation including scaling between the window and the viewport rectangles, before drawing the model diagram.

REFERENCES

1. Gregory, K., *Using Visual C++ 6: Special Edition*, Que Publishing, Indianapolis, IN, 1998.
2. Kruglinski, D. J., Wingo, S., and Shepherd, G., *Programming Visual C++*, 5th edn., Microsoft Press, Redmond, WA, 1998.
3. Microsoft Developer Network Library Visual Studio 6.0, Microsoft® Visual Studio™ 6.0 Development System, Microsoft Corporation, 1998.
4. Brinkster, ScrollViews, http://aclacl.brinkster.net//MFC//ch10b.htm, (accessed June 30, 2010).

28 Implementing a Scroll View

28.1 INTRODUCTION

The previous chapter demonstrated how a diagram that encompasses a large viewing area may be aptly printed on multiple pages. This was achieved using a transformation-defining mapping mode and the setting of the extents of the window and viewport rectangles using scaling and the inbuilt convenience of scroll bars in Print Preview mode. However, when not in Printing or Print Preview mode, no vertical or horizontal scroll bars are present on the main CView-derived (model-drawing) window, and hence, the user is limited in the amount of space available to draw a model diagram. Hence, changes need to be made to the DiagramEng project to convert the existing CView-based code to a CScrollView-based implementation.

The CView-based functionality supported at present allows the software user to draw model diagrams that typically consist of blocks, connections, and connection bend points in a CView-derived view window. Connections may be drawn by clicking the left mouse button, moving the mouse, and releasing the button. Diagram entities may be moved by left-clicking an item and dragging it to a different location, or grouping a selection of items explicitly and moving them simultaneously, through the use of a CRectTracker object. In addition, the user may double-left-click a block to set its properties or right-click an entity to invoke a Context menu to perform deletion, insertion, movement, orientation, and property-setting actions.

The CDiagramEngView class was originally derived from the CView class, using the AppWizard upon application construction, as may be seen in the "DiagramEngView.h" header file, i.e., "class CDiagramEngView : public CView". The instructions here detail the changes that need to be made to the declarations and definitions of various functions to convert them from CView-derived methods to CScrollView-derived methods. However, in converting the main CView-based view window to a CScrollView-based scrolling view, the CPoint, "point", arguments used in mouse-button-click-related user interaction sequences, e.g., that in `CDiagramEngView::OnLButtonDown(UINT nFlags, CPoint point)`, need to be converted from the device coordinate system to the logical coordinate system for consistent underlying document-related action due to a scroll-based shift of the logical coordinate system with respect to the device coordinate system. In addition, CScrollView-related characteristics need to be set up in the `CDiagramEngView::OnInitialUpdate()` function. Finally, the tracking of individual and multiple items needs to be altered to cater for the new scrolling view. The following instruction is divided into seven sections: (1) coordinate systems, (2) conversion from CView to CScrollView, (3) device point to logical point coordinate conversions, (4) tracking of multiple items, (5) limiting diagram entity placement, (6) fitting the logical view to the physical view, and (7) zooming in and out of the view.

28.2 COORDINATE SYSTEMS

The developer should be aware that "many Windows functions take logical units as parameters" and "Windows translates these units to physical device units based on the mapping mode of the device, window origin, window extents, viewport origin, and viewport extents" [1]. The logical coordinate system is that of the current mapping mode, and the device coordinate system is that used by a graphics device to create images. Further, "the default mapping mode for a device context is the MM_TEXT mode," and "the point (0, 0) is the origin of the logical and physical coordinate systems

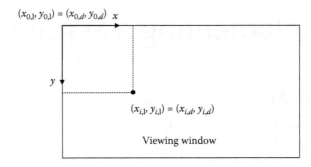

FIGURE 28.1   Coincident logical $(x_{i,1}, y_{i,1})$ and device $(x_{i,d}, y_{i,d})$ coordinate systems using a CView-derived view, with no scroll bars and the default MM_TEXT mapping mode ($i \in [0, n-1]$).

in this mode," with "a one-to-one mapping ratio of logical to physical device units" [1], where the horizontal (x) and vertical (y) axes increase to the right and downward, respectively.

The DiagramEng application, up until now, has used a CView-derived class, CDiagramEngView, and a view window through which user interaction may take place. Without scroll bars and no change in the window and viewport origins and extents, using the default MM_TEXT mapping mode, the device coordinates $(x_{i,d}, y_{i,d})$ and logical coordinates $(x_{i,1}, y_{i,1})$ are coincident, and no conversion needs to be made of the CPoint, "point", object (x_i, y_i) between the device and logical coordinate systems (Figure 28.1), for $i \in [0, n-1]$, where n is the number of coordinates, or points, being transformed, and the subscripts d and l refer to device and logical points, respectively. However, with scroll bars, due to a moving view, the CPoint, "point", object of the device coordinate system is different to that of the logical coordinate system, and a conversion is necessary from the device point to logical point coordinates (DPtoLP()) and in certain situations from the logical point to device point coordinates (LPtoDP()).

Figure 28.2 shows the effect of scrolling on the transformation between the device and logical coordinate systems using the default MM_TEXT mapping mode without a change in the window and viewport origins and extents; as the user scrolls down and across, the effective logical coordinate system is offset from the device by the amount scrolled in both the x and y directions, Δx and Δy, respectively. That is, the ith logical coordinate is related to the device coordinate as follows: $(x_{i,1}, y_{i,1}) = (x_{i,d} + \Delta x, y_{i,d} + \Delta y)$ for $i \in [0, n-1]$.

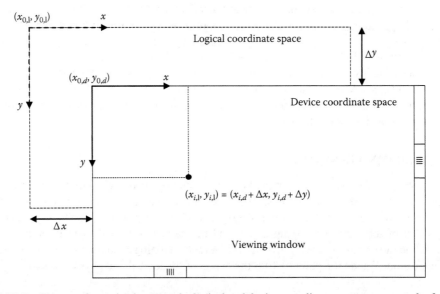

FIGURE 28.2   The transformation between the logical and device coordinate systems as a result of scrolling in the horizontal and vertical directions using the default MM_TEXT mapping mode.

In fact, the (constant) function, `CScrollView::GetScrollPosition()`, "returns the horizontal and vertical positions, in logical coordinates, of the scroll boxes as a CPoint object," and "this coordinate pair $(\Delta x, \Delta y)$ corresponds to the location in the document to which the upper-left corner of the view has been scrolled" [2]. If device rather than logical units is desired, then the function `CScrollView::GetDeviceScrollPosition()` should be called.

28.3 CONVERSION FROM CView TO CScrollView

To make the conversion from the existing CView-based code to the desired CScrollView-based form, the following changes need to be made: (1) CView should be replaced by CScrollView in two locations in the "DiagramEngView.h" header file, (2) CView should be replaced by CScrollView in numerous locations in the "DiagramEngView.cpp" source file, and (3) scrolling characteristics need to be set up in the `CDiagramEngView::OnInitalUpdate()` function.

28.3.1 CHANGES TO "DiagramEngView.h"

The "DiagramEngView.h" header file, with the CDiagramEngView class declaration, needs to be changed as indicated in bold in the following, i.e., the base class is now CScrollView and the `OnUpdate()` prototype is changed; the ellipsis "..." denotes omitted unchanged code.

```
// DiagramEngView.h : interface of the CDiagramEngView class
//
/////////////////////////////////////////////////////////////////////

#if !defined(AFX_DIAGRAMENGVIEW_H__F56802D6_1338_49D5_8641_978B85C9
  9CF4__INCLUDED_)
#define AFX_DIAGRAMENGVIEW_H__F56802D6_1338_49D5_8641_978B85C99CF4__
  INCLUDED_

#if _MSC_VER > 1000
#pragma once
#endif // _MSC_VER > 1000

//class CDiagramEngView : public CView
class CDiagramEngView : public CScrollView    // DiagramEng: CView changed
  to CScrollView
{
    ...
// Overrides
    ...
    virtual void OnUpdate(CScrollView* pSender, LPARAM lHint, CObject*
      pHint);  // DiagramEng: CView changed to CScrollView
    ...
};
...
//#endif // !defined(AFX_DIAGRAMENGVIEW_H__F56802D6_1338_49D5_8641_978B85
  C99CF4__INCLUDED_)
```

28.3.2 CHANGES TO "DiagramEngView.cpp"

The changes to the "DiagramEngView.cpp" source file involve changes to the IMPLEMENT_DYNCREATE macro, the message map section, and the following CDiagramEngView functions (listed in alphabetical order): `AssertValid()`, `Dump()`, `OnInitialUpdate()`, `OnKeyDown()`, `OnLButtonDblClk()`, `OnLButtonDown()`, `OnLButtonUp()`, `OnMouseMove()`, `OnPrepareDC()`, `OnUpdate()`, and `PreCreateWindow()`.

The IMPLEMENT_DYNCREATE macro is changed as shown in bold in the following, where CView is replaced by CScrollView:

```
IMPLEMENT_DYNCREATE(CDiagramEngView, CScrollView)  // DiagramEng: CView
  changed to CScrollView
```

The message map section is altered as shown in bold below, where CView is replaced by CScrollView.

```
BEGIN_MESSAGE_MAP(CDiagramEngView, CScrollView)      // DiagramEng: CView
  changed to CScrollView
    //{{AFX_MSG_MAP(CDiagramEngView)
    ON_COMMAND(ID_VIEW_ZOOM_IN, OnViewZoomIn)
    ON_COMMAND(ID_VIEW_ZOOM_OUT, OnViewZoomOut)
    ON_COMMAND(ID_VIEW_AUTO_FIT_DIAGRAM, OnViewAutoFitDiagram)
    ON_WM_LBUTTONDOWN()
    ON_WM_MOUSEMOVE()
    ON_WM_LBUTTONUP()
    ON_WM_CONTEXTMENU()
    ON_WM_LBUTTONDBLCLK()
    ON_WM_KEYDOWN()
    //}}AFX_MSG_MAP
    // Standard printing commands
    ON_COMMAND(ID_FILE_PRINT, CScrollView::OnFilePrint)
      // DiagramEng: CView changed to CScrollView
    ON_COMMAND(ID_FILE_PRINT_DIRECT, CScrollView::OnFilePrint)
      // DiagramEng: CView changed to CScrollView
    ON_COMMAND(ID_FILE_PRINT_PREVIEW, CScrollView::OnFilePrintPreview)
      // DiagramEng: CView changed to CScrollView
END_MESSAGE_MAP()
```

The aforementioned functions are now changed in the same manner, where CView is replaced by CScrollView, as shown in bold in the following:

```
void CDiagramEngView::AssertValid() const
{
    CScrollView::AssertValid();      // DiagramEng: CView changed to
      CScrollView
}

void CDiagramEngView::Dump(CDumpContext& dc) const
{
    CScrollView::Dump(dc);           // DiagramEng: CView changed to
      CScrollView
}

void CDiagramEngView::OnInitialUpdate()
{
    CScrollView::OnInitialUpdate(); // DiagramEng: CView changed to
      CScrollView

    // TODO: Add your specialized code here and/or call the base class

    // DiagramEng (start)
    InvalidateRect(NULL);            // Invalidates the client area,
      i.e. forces a redraw on the next WM_PAINT message.
```

```
    // DiagramEng (end)
}

void CDiagramEngView::OnKeyDown(UINT nChar, UINT nRepCnt, UINT nFlags)
{
    // TODO: Add your message handler code here and/or call default

    // DiagramEng (start)
    …
    // DiagramEng (end)

    CScrollView::OnKeyDown(nChar, nRepCnt, nFlags);  // DiagramEng: CView
        changed to CScrollView
}

void CDiagramEngView::OnLButtonDblClk(UINT nFlags, CPoint point)
{
    // TODO: Add your message handler code here and/or call default

    // DiagramEng (start)
    …
    // DiagramEng (end)

    CScrollView::OnLButtonDblClk(nFlags, point);    // DiagramEng: CView
        changed to CScrollView
}

void CDiagramEngView::OnLButtonDown(UINT nFlags, CPoint point)
{
    // TODO: Add your message handler code here and/or call default

    // DiagramEng (start)
    …
    // DiagramEng (end)

    CScrollView::OnLButtonDown(nFlags, point);      // DiagramEng: CView
        changed to CScrollView
}

void CDiagramEngView::OnLButtonUp(UINT nFlags, CPoint point)
{
    // TODO: Add your message handler code here and/or call default

    // DiagramEng (start)
    …
    // DiagramEng (end)

    CScrollView::OnLButtonUp(nFlags, point);        // DiagramEng: CView
        changed to CScrollView
}

void CDiagramEngView::OnMouseMove(UINT nFlags, CPoint point)
{
    // TODO: Add your message handler code here and/or call default

    // DiagramEng (start)
    …
    // DiagramEng (end)

    CScrollView::OnMouseMove(nFlags, point);        // DiagramEng: CView
        changed to CScrollView
}
```

```
void CDiagramEngView::OnPrepareDC(CDC* pDC, CPrintInfo* pInfo)
{
    // TODO: Add your specialized code here and/or call the base class

    // DiagramEng (start)
    CScrollView::OnPrepareDC(pDC, pInfo);   // call base class version
      first, CView changed to CScrollView

    if(pDC->IsPrinting())
    {
        ...
    }

    // DiagramEng (end)
}
```

The reader will recall from Chapter 27 that the call to `CView::OnPrepareDC()` (now `CScrollView::OnPrepareDC()` as shown earlier in `CDiagramEngView::OnPrepareDC()`) was made prior to the conditional section concerning printing (`IsPrinting()`). This is necessary since "CScrollView overrides `OnPrepareDC()` and in it calls `CDC::SetMapMode()` to set the mapping mode and `CDC::SetViewportOrg()` to translate the viewport origin an amount that equals the horizontal and vertical scroll positions" [3]. In addition, "when `CScrollView::OnPrepareDC()` returns, the device context's mapping mode is set to the mapping mode specified when `SetScrollSizes()` is called" [4]; `SetScrollSizes()` is called in `CDiagramEngView::OnInitialUpdate()` introduced in the following, defining the mapping mode and the size of the scroll view. Thus, `CScrollView::OnPrepareDC()` should be called prior to the conditional printing section, as shown earlier, for the correct mapping mode and viewport origin to take effect for printing and print previewing purposes.

```
void CDiagramEngView::OnUpdate(CScrollView* pSender, LPARAM lHint,
  CObject* pHint)                    // DiagramEng: CView changed to CScrollView
{
    // TODO: Add your specialized code here and/or call the base class

    // DiagramEng (start)
    InvalidateRect(NULL);   // Invalidates the client area, i.e. forces a
      redraw on the next WM_PAINT message.
    // DiagramEng (end)
}

BOOL CDiagramEngView::PreCreateWindow(CREATESTRUCT& cs)
{
    // TODO: Modify the Window class or styles here by modifying
    // the CREATESTRUCT cs

    return CScrollView::PreCreateWindow(cs);   // DiagramEng: CView
      changed to CScrollView
}
```

In addition, the developer should be aware that no changes from CView to CScrollView need to be made to the functions: `CDiagramEngDoc::DeleteOutputBlockView()`, `CDiagramEngDoc::UpdateCommonOpsToolbar()`, and `CSystemModel::ValidateModel()`. This is the case since within all three functions, a call to `GetNextView()` is made to obtain a pointer-to-CView, "pView", and because CScrollView is derived from CView, i.e., as it is a kind of CView, then this pointer ("pView") is of the right base type and suffices for the view-based action taken in these functions.

28.3.3 CHANGES TO `CDiagramEngView::OnInitialUpdate()`

Finally, in the `CDiagramEngView::OnInitialUpdate()` function, scrolling characteristics need to be set up by a call to `SetScrollSizes()` for initial document display and for when the document size changes. Four arguments may be specified where the first two are required and the others optional: (1) the integer mapping mode (here the default MM_TEXT is used); (2) the CSize, "sizeTotal", variable setting the horizontal ("sizeTotal.cx") and vertical ("sizeTotal.cy") extents of the view, where the sizes are in logical units; (3) the CSize "sizePage" variable used to set the horizontal ("sizePage.cx") and vertical ("sizePage.cy") amounts to scroll in each direction upon clicking a scroll bar shaft; and (4) the CSize "sizeLine" variable used to set the horizontal ("sizeLine.cx") and vertical ("sizeLine.cy") amounts to scroll in each direction upon clicking a scroll bar arrow [2]. The additions to the function are shown in bold in the following.

```
void CDiagramEngView::OnInitialUpdate()
{
    //CView::OnInitialUpdate();
    CScrollView::OnInitialUpdate();  // DiagramEng: CView changed to
      CScrollView

    // TODO: Add your specialized code here and/or call the base class

    // DiagramEng (start)
    // CScrollView specific setup
    CSize sizeTotal;        // total size of scroll view: cx and cy are
      horiz and vert extents, sizes are in logical units
    sizeTotal.cx = 5000;  // horizontal extent of the scroll view
    sizeTotal.cy = 5000;  // vertical extent of the scroll view

    SetScrollSizes(MM_TEXT, sizeTotal); // set scrolling characteristics,
      for initial document display or size changes

    InvalidateRect(NULL); // Invalidates the client area, i.e. forces a
      redraw on the next WM_PAINT message.
    // DiagramEng (end)
}
```

Now the software user may load or draw a diagram on the palette, as shown in Figure 28.3, and use the scroll bars to pan horizontally and vertically. However, interaction with the diagram entities is inconsistent after scrolling of the diagram since no point conversions have yet been made to align the device and logical coordinates coherently.

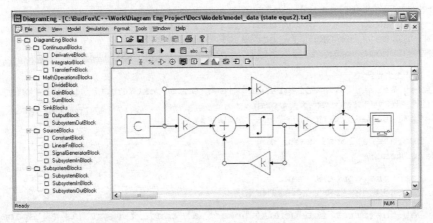

FIGURE 28.3 The placement of scroll bars on the view window allowing the user to pan horizontally and vertically.

28.4   DEVICE POINT TO LOGICAL POINT COORDINATE CONVERSIONS

Now that the CScrollView-based view structure is in place, the conversion from device points to logical points (DPtoLP()) and from logical points to device points (LPtoDP()) needs to be made where necessary in the functions that process user interaction. The functions that need to be altered are (in alphabetical order) the CDiagramEngView functions, OnContextMenu(), OnLButtonDblClk(), OnLButtonDown(), OnLButtonUp(), and OnMouseMove(); and the CDiagramEngDoc functions, TrackBlock(), TrackConnectionBendPoint(), and TrackConnectionEndPoint(). Later, changes will be made to the TrackMultipleItems() and DetermineTrackerDeltaPosition() functions of the CDiagramEngDoc class, where the CRectTracker ("m_RectTracker") object is used in DPtoLP() conversion.

28.4.1   AMENDING THE **CDiagramEngView-Based** FUNCTIONS

The CDiagramEngView functions that need to be altered are OnContextMenu(), OnLButtonDblClk(), OnLButtonDown(), OnLButtonUp(), and OnMouseMove(). All require similar changes, i.e., the creation of a device context of type CClientDC, the preparation of the device context by calling OnPrepareDC(), and finally the conversion from device units to logical units, using DPtoLP().

28.4.1.1   `CDiagramEngView::OnContextMenu()`

The changes that need to be made to the OnContextMenu() function are shown in bold in the following. A device context, "dc", of type CClientDC is required in order to call the DPtoLP() conversion function to convert the CPoint, "ptClient", variable from device coordinates to logical coordinates. The conversion is required, as illustrated in Section 28.2, since if the user scrolls the view, then the appropriate logical coordinate $(x_{i,l}, y_{i,l})$ needs to be obtained using the device coordinate $(x_{i,d}, y_{i,d})$ and the amount scrolled in the horizontal (Δx) and vertical (Δy) directions, i.e., $(x_{i,l}, y_{i,l}) = (x_{i,d} + \Delta x, y_{i,d} + \Delta y)$, where, here, the ith point is that at which the right-mouse-button-down event invokes the Context menu.

```
void CDiagramEngView::OnContextMenu(CWnd* pWnd, CPoint point)
{
    // TODO: Add your message handler code here

    // DiagramEng (start)
    CPoint ptClient;      // used to store the converted screen pt coords
      to the client coord sys.
    CString sMsg;         // main msg string
    UINT nType = MB_OK;   // style of msg. box
    UINT nIDhelp = 0;     // help context ID for the msg.

    // Print msg.
    //sMsg.Format("\n CDiagramEngView::OnContextMenu(), point (x,y) =
      (%d,%d)\n", point.x, point.y);
    //AfxMessageBox(sMsg, nType, nIDhelp);

    // Declare a local menu obj.
    CMenu menu;

    // Load the context menu
    menu.LoadMenu(IDR_CONTEXTMENU);

    // Get the first sub-menu (the actual context menu has a 'space' to
      diff. it from std. menus).
    CMenu *pContextMenu = menu.GetSubMenu(0);
```

```
    // Display the context menu for the user
    pContextMenu->TrackPopupMenu(TPM_LEFTALIGN + TPM_RIGHTBUTTON +
        TPM_TOPALIGN, point.x, point.y, this, NULL);

    // Set the m_ptContextMenu var in the doc class first converting the
        Screen coord to the Client coord
    ptClient = point;              // make a copy of the screen coord
    ScreenToClient(&ptClient);     // overwrite the screen coord with the
        client coord

    // CScrollView-related change
    CClientDC dc(this);            // create a device context using the
        pointer-to-CWnd "this"
    OnPrepareDC(&dc);              // prepare the device context
    dc.DPtoLP(&ptClient);          // use the dc to convert the ptClient
        from device to logical units

    GetDocument()->SetContextMenuPoint(ptClient);  // set the client
        coord in the CDiagramEngDoc class.

    // DiagramEng (end)
}
```

An implicit call to the CClientDC constructor is made, passing the "this" pointer, of type pointer-to-CWnd, as an argument to construct a device context, "dc", object that "accesses the client area of the CWnd pointed to by pWnd" [2]. The MSDN Library resource documents indicate that the OnPrepareDC() function is invoked before OnDraw() is called for screen display and before OnPrint() is called for each page during printing or print preview [2]. Furthermore, the MSDN Library resource documents state that the default implementation takes no action for screen display, but the function is overridden in derived classes, e.g., CScrollView, to adjust attributes of the device context [2]. Here, given that the CDiagramEngView class is now derived from the CScrollView base class, the OnPrepareDC() function is called to set up the device context, then the device point to logical point conversion function, DPtoLP(), is called upon the "dc" object, where the address of the client CPoint coordinate, "ptClient", is passed as an argument and the point ultimately used to set the document class's copy of the Context menu point, "m_ptContextMenu", via a call to SetContextMenuPoint().

28.4.1.2 CDiagramEngView::OnLButtonDblClk()

The changes to the OnLButtonDblClk() function are shown in bold in the following: initially a device context object is created using the "this" pointer of type pointer-to-CWnd, the attributes of the device context are set up via the call to OnPrepareDC(), and finally the CPoint "point" object is converted from device units to logical units using the call to DPtoLP() prior to calling the DoubleLeftClickBlock() function of the CDiagramEngDoc class, used to check whether a model block is double clicked.

```
void CDiagramEngView::OnLButtonDblClk(UINT nFlags, CPoint point)
{
    // TODO: Add your message handler code here and/or call default

    // DiagramEng (start)
    int dbl_click_flag = 0;

    // CScrollView-related change
    CClientDC dc(this);   // create a device context using the pointer-to-
        CWnd "this"
    OnPrepareDC(&dc);     // prepare the device context
    dc.DPtoLP(&point);    // use the dc to convert point from device to
        logical units
```

```
      // Assume that a block is being double-clicked: if so
        dbl_click_flag = 1, if not, dlb_click_flag = 0.
      dbl_click_flag = GetDocument()->DoubleLeftClickBlock(point);

      // DiagramEng (end)

      //CView::OnLButtonDblClk(nFlags, point);
      CScrollView::OnLButtonDblClk(nFlags, point);   // DiagramEng: CView
        changed to CScrollView
}
```

28.4.1.3 CDiagramEngView::OnLButtonDown()

The OnLButtonDown() function is invoked when the user presses the left mouse button,
where the arguments, "nFlags" and "point", represent a combination of virtual key flags and
the CPoint, "point", coordinate location of the cursor. The TrackItem() function performs its
own local processing of the "point" object and is discussed later; if no object is being tracked
(tracker_flag == 0), then the familiar CScrollView-related modifications are made as shown in
bold in the following. The device context is created using the "this" pointer, the device context
attributes are set up, and then the "point" object is converted from device units to logical units
to correctly record the points, "m_ptPrevPos" and "m_ptOrigin", used for both drawing and
constructing a connection object.

```
void CDiagramEngView::OnLButtonDown(UINT nFlags, CPoint point)
{
      // TODO: Add your message handler code here and/or call default

      // DiagramEng (start)
      int tracker_flag;     // 0 => no tracker and hence a connector,
        1 => tracker and hence no connector

      //AfxMessageBox("\n CDiagramEngView::OnLButtondown()\n", MB_OK, 0);

      // Assume an item is being tracked: if so tracker_flag = 1, if not:
        tracker_flag = 0.
      tracker_flag = GetDocument()->TrackItem(point, this);   // this is a
        ptr-to-CWnd, i.e. CWnd *pWnd.

      // If nothing was tracked, i.e. tracker_flag = 0, then record points
        to draw and construct a connector.
      if(tracker_flag == 0)
      {
          // CScrollView-related change
          CClientDC dc(this);     // create a device context using the
            pointer-to-CWnd "this"
          OnPrepareDC(&dc);       // prepare the device context
          dc.DPtoLP(&point);      // use the dc to convert point from device
            to logical units

          // Capture the mouse so no other apps. can get it.
          SetCapture();

          // Save the pt that the cursor is at, upon left-btn-down,
            i.e. init member var with incoming CPoint var.
          m_ptPrevPos = point;    // Init the prev. pt, to be used in
            OnMouseMove(), to the current point
          m_ptOrigin = point;     // Init the origin of the ensuing line, to
            be drawn in OnMouseMove(), to be the starting pt.
      }
```

```
    // DiagramEng (end)

    //CView::OnLButtonDown(nFlags, point);
    CScrollView::OnLButtonDown(nFlags, point); // DiagramEng: CView
      changed to CScrollView
}
```

28.4.1.4 CDiagramEngView::OnLButtonUp()

The OnLButtonUp() function is invoked upon releasing the left mouse button, whereupon the CPoint, "point", object is used to define the end point of a connection object if no model entity tracking is being performed (cf. OnLButtonDown()). The CScrollView-related changes are shown in bold in the following, where the three familiar steps are taken, i.e., the device context is constructed, and its attributes are defined and then used to convert the "point" object from device to logical units.

```
void CDiagramEngView::OnLButtonUp(UINT nFlags, CPoint point)
{
    // TODO: Add your message handler code here and/or call default

    // DiagramEng (start)
    int valid = 0;              // validity of connection object (length)

    // CScrollView-related change
    CClientDC dc(this);         // create a device context using the
      pointer-to-CWnd "this"
    OnPrepareDC(&dc);           // prepare the device context
    dc.DPtoLP(&point);          // use the dc to convert point from device
      to logical units

    // Check to see if mouse has been captured
    if(GetCapture() == this) // if what has been captured is the obj.
      that the "this" ptr. is pointing to.
    {
        // Add the connection to the connection list
        valid = GetDocument()->GetSystemModel().AddConnection(m_ptOrigin,
          point);

        if(valid)
        {
            // Attempt snapping of connection end points to ports or bend
              points
            GetDocument()->SnapConnectionEndPointsAfterInitialConstruct
              ion();
        }

        // Make the document redraw itself using either Invalidate(TRUE)
          or UpdateAllViews(NULL)
        //Invalidate(TRUE);
        GetDocument()->UpdateAllViews(NULL);

        // Release the capture so other apps. can have access to the
          mouse.
        ReleaseCapture();
    }

    // DiagramEng (end)

    //CView::OnLButtonUp(nFlags, point);
    CScrollView::OnLButtonUp(nFlags, point);  // DiagramEng: CView
      changed to CScrollView
}
```

28.4.1.5 `CDiagramEngView::OnMouseMove()`

The final CDiagramEngView-based function to be altered is `OnMouseMove()`, which is used to draw a connection object ("con_obj2") from the starting point, "m_ptOrigin", to the current cursor point, "point", and reverse the drawing color, effectively overwriting the previous connection ("con_obj1"), defined by the starting and ending points, "m_ptOrigin" and "m_ptPrevPos", respectively. Similar modifications made to the previous functions, concerning the device context, need to be performed here, with the addition of a new local CPoint variable, "ptLogical", recording the CPoint, "point", coordinates converted from device to logical units; this is required since the original "point" argument is finally used in the framework-provided call to the base class function `CScrollView::OnMouseMove()` before the function returns. The changes required are shown in bold in the following.

```
void CDiagramEngView::OnMouseMove(UINT nFlags, CPoint point)
{
    // TODO: Add your message handler code here and/or call default

    // DiagramEng (start)

    // Check to see if the left mouse btn. is down
    if((nFlags & MK_LBUTTON) == MK_LBUTTON)
    {
        // Check to see if mouse is captured
        if(GetCapture() == this)          // If what has been captured is
          the obj. upon which the present fn is called.
        {
            // CScrollView-related change
            CClientDC dc(this);           // create a device context using
              the pointer-to-CWnd "this"
            CPoint ptLogical = point;  // local point to record the point
              in logical units
            OnPrepareDC(&dc);             // prepare the device context
            dc.DPtoLP(&ptLogical);        // use the dc to convert ptLogical
              from device to logical units

            // Reverse the pixel color from the original pt to the
              prev pt.
            // SetROP2() sets the current foreground mix mode.
            dc.SetROP2(R2_NOT);           // R2_NOT => pixel is the inverse
              of the screen color

            // Declare a CConnection obj in order to call
              DrawConnection()
            CConnection con_obj1(m_ptOrigin, m_ptPrevPos);
            con_obj1.DrawConnection(&dc);

            // Declare a CConnection obj in order to call
              DrawConnection()
            // Draw the current stretch of line (but don't save it until
              OnLButtonUp().
            //CConnection con_obj2(m_ptOrigin, point);
            CConnection con_obj2(m_ptOrigin, ptLogical); // CScrollView-
              related change: point changed to ptLogical
            con_obj2.DrawConnection(&dc);

            // Save the current pt (point) as the prev. pt (m_ptPrevPos)
              of the CView class.
            //m_ptPrevPos = point;
```

```
            m_ptPrevPos = ptLogical;   // CScrollView-related change:
               point changed to ptLogical
         }
      }

   // DiagramEng (end)

   //CView::OnMouseMove(nFlags, point);
   CScrollView::OnMouseMove(nFlags, point);   // DiagramEng: CView
      changed to CScrollView
}
```

28.4.2 AMENDING THE **CDiagramEngDoc-Based** FUNCTIONS

The CDiagramEngDoc functions that need to be modified, given the introduction of the CScrollView base class for CDiagramEngView, are TrackBlock(), TrackConnectionBendPoint(), and TrackConnectionEndPoint(). All three functions require similar changes to those made in the CDiagramEngView-based functions shown earlier, i.e., the creation of a CClientDC device context, the call to OnPrepareDC() to prepare the device context, and the use of the conversion functions DPtoLP() and/or LPtoDP(). The remaining CDiagramEngDoc functions, TrackMultipleItems() and DetermineTrackerDeltaPosition(), are considered in the following section.

28.4.2.1 `CDiagramEngDoc::TrackBlock()`

The CDiagramEngDoc::TrackBlock() function shown in the following is initially called from within the TrackItem() function of the same class to determine whether a block is being independently tracked/moved. The main *for* loop iterates over the list of blocks, and the conditional statement determines whether the block has been clicked; if so, the CRectTracker object, "m_RectTracker", is set up (SetRect()), the mouse cursor position is tracked (Track()), and the final block position is set (CenterPoint() and SetBlockPosition()).

However, due to the presence of the CScrollView base class, a conversion needs to be made between the screen device coordinates and the underlying document logical coordinates. Initially a local CPoint object, "ptLogical", is declared and initialized to that of the CPoint, "point", object. Then the device context "dc" is initially constructed using the pointer-to-CWnd, "pWnd". However, to call OnPrepareDC() from within the CDiagramEngDoc-based function, the pointer-to-CWnd, "pWnd", is first cast to a pointer-to-CScrollView, and then the device context attributes are set. Thereafter, the cursor point is converted from device units to logical units in order to determine the Euclidean distance between the cursor point ("ptLogical") and the block position ("blk_posn").

If the block is clicked, the CRectTracker, "m_RectTracker", object's top-left ("top_left") and bottom-right ("bottom_right") coordinates need to be set based upon the logical-units-based block position. Since the "m_RectTracker" concerns the screen device coordinates, then the "top_left" and "bottom_right" coordinates need to be converted from the underlying logical coordinates to device coordinates using LPtoDP(). Finally, after the block has been moved, the block position, "blk_posn", determined via CenterPoint() and hence in device units needs to be converted from device units to logical units using DPtoLP().

```
int CDiagramEngDoc::TrackBlock(CPoint point, CWnd *pWnd)
{
    int delta;                 // integer increment
    int tracker_flag = 0;
    double blk_width;
    double dist;
    CPoint bottom_right;
    CPoint top_left;
```

```
CPoint blk_posn;
list<CBlock*>::iterator it_blk;
list<CBlock*> blk_list = GetSystemModel().GetBlockList();

// CScrollView-related change
CPoint ptLogical = point;  // local point to record the point in
  logical units
CClientDC dc(pWnd);          // create a device context using the
  pointer-to-CWnd pWnd
((CScrollView *)pWnd)->OnPrepareDC(&dc);  // prepare the device
  context casting pWnd to ptr-to-CScrollView
dc.DPtoLP(&ptLogical);       // use the dc to convert ptLogical from
  device to logical units

// Iterate through block list
for(it_blk = blk_list.begin(); it_blk != blk_list.end(); it_blk++)
{
    blk_posn = (*it_blk)->GetBlockPosition();
    blk_width = (*it_blk)->GetBlockShape().GetBlockWidth();
    // dist = sqrt(pow(blk_posn.x - point.x,2)
    //   + pow(blk_posn.y - point.y,2));
    dist = sqrt(pow(blk_posn.x - ptLogical.x,2)
      + pow(blk_posn.y - ptLogical.y,2));
      // CScrollView-related change using ptLogical

    // If the block is clicked
    if(dist <= 0.5*blk_width*0.5)
    {
        delta = (int)(blk_width*0.5);
        top_left.x = blk_posn.x - delta;
        top_left.y = blk_posn.y - delta;
        bottom_right.x = blk_posn.x + delta;
        bottom_right.y = blk_posn.y + delta;

        // CScrollView-related change
        dc.LPtoDP(&top_left);        // convert logical pt based on
          logical block position to device pt
        dc.LPtoDP(&bottom_right);  // convert logical pt based on
          logical block position to device pt

        // Set the rect tracker's position
        m_RectTracker.m_rect.SetRect(top_left.x, top_left.y,
          bottom_right.x, bottom_right.y);

        // Track the mouse's position till left mouse button up
        tracker_flag = m_RectTracker.Track(pWnd, point, TRUE);
          // 0 => item not tracked, 1 => item was tracked

        // Get the new tracker position and update the new block
          position with the tracker position
        blk_posn = m_RectTracker.m_rect.CenterPoint();

        dc.DPtoLP(&blk_posn);        // CScrollView-related change:
          convert device units to logical units

        (*it_blk)->SetBlockPosition(blk_posn);

        // Set flags
        SetModifiedFlag(TRUE);       // set the doc. as having been
          modified to prompt user to save
```

```
                UpdateAllViews(NULL);   // indicate that sys. should redraw.
                break;
            }
        }

    // Return flag indicating if an item was tracked: 0 => not tracked,
       1 => tracked.
    return tracker_flag;
}
```

28.4.2.2 `CDiagramEngDoc::TrackConnectionBendPoint()`

The changes to be made to the `TrackConnectionBendPoint()` function, shown in bold in the following, are very similar to those made for the `TrackBlock()` function earlier, i.e., (1) a local CPoint object to record a logical point is initialized, (2) the device context is constructed, (3) the attributes of the device context are set, (4) the cursor point in device units is converted to logical units (`DPtoLP()`), (5) the Euclidean distance between the logical point ("ptLogical") and a connection bend point ("bend_pt") is determined, (6) the "m_RectTracker" bounding coordinates, "top_left" and "bottom_right", determined using the logical bend point position, are converted from logical units to device units, and, finally, (7) after the bend point is moved, the bend point position (`CenterPoint()`) is converted from device units back to the underlying document-based logical units.

```
int CDiagramEngDoc::TrackConnectionBendPoint(CPoint point, CWnd *pWnd)
{
    int delta = (int)(0.25*m_dDeltaLength);   // integer increment
    int tracker_flag = 0;
    double disc_r = 0.1*m_dDeltaLength;
    double dist;
    CPoint bend_pt;
    CPoint bottom_right;
    CPoint top_left;
    list<CConnection*>::iterator it_con;
    list<CConnection*> con_list = GetSystemModel().GetConnectionList();
    list<CPoint>::iterator it_pt;

    // CScrollView-related change
    CPoint ptLogical = point;   // local point to record the point in
      logical units
    CClientDC dc(pWnd);              // create a device context using the
      pointer-to-CWnd pWnd.
    ((CScrollView*)pWnd)->OnPrepareDC(&dc);   // prepare the device
      context casting pWnd to ptr-to-CScrollView
    dc.DPtoLP(&ptLogical);         // use the dc to convert ptLogical from
      device to logical units

    // Iterate through connection list
    for(it_con = con_list.begin(); it_con != con_list.end(); it_con++)
    {
        // Get connection bend pts.
        list<CPoint> &bend_pts_list = (*it_con)-
          >GetConnectionBendPointsList();

        // Iterate through all bend pts. for this connection
        for(it_pt = bend_pts_list.begin(); it_pt != bend_pts_list.end();
          it_pt++)
        {
            bend_pt = *it_pt;
```

```
        // Determine Euclidean dist bw mouse point and connection
          bend pt.
        // dist = sqrt(pow(bend_pt.x - point.x,2) +
          pow(bend_pt.y - point.y,2));
        dist = sqrt(pow(bend_pt.x - ptLogical.x,2) +
          pow(bend_pt.y - ptLogical.y,2));
          // CScrollView-related change using ptLogical

        // If the bend pt is clicked
        if(dist <= disc_r)
        {
            // Assign rectangle setting values
            top_left.x = bend_pt.x - delta;
            top_left.y = bend_pt.y - delta;
            bottom_right.x = bend_pt.x + delta;
            bottom_right.y = bend_pt.y + delta;

            // CScrollView-related change
            dc.LPtoDP(&top_left);        // convert logical pt based on
              logical block position to device pt
            dc.LPtoDP(&bottom_right);  // convert logical pt based on
              logical block position to device pt

            // Set the rect tracker's position
            m_RectTracker.m_rect.SetRect(top_left.x, top_left.y,
              bottom_right.x, bottom_right.y);

            // Track the mouse's position till left mouse button up
            tracker_flag = m_RectTracker.Track(pWnd, point, TRUE);
              // 0 => item not tracked, 1 => item was tracked

            // Get the new tracker position and update the connection
              bend pt position with the tracker position
            *it_pt = m_RectTracker.m_rect.CenterPoint();

            dc.DPtoLP(&(*it_pt));        // CScrollView-related change
              convert device units to logical units

            // Update any connection's tail point if it was connected
              to this bend point
            m_SystemModel.UpdateConnectionPointTailToBendPoint
              (&(*it_pt));

            // Set flags
            SetModifiedFlag(TRUE);  // set the doc. as having been
              modified to prompt user to save
            UpdateAllViews(NULL);   // indicate that sys. should
              redraw.
            break;

        }// end if dist
    }// end for it_pt
}// end for it_con

    return tracker_flag;
}
```

28.4.2.3 CDiagramEngDoc::TrackConnectionEndPoint()

The changes to be made to the TrackConnectionEndPoint() function are essentially the same as those made for the TrackConnectionBendPoint() function, except both head and tail points need to be considered; the seven changes made earlier are implemented in the appropriate locations as shown in bold in the following.

```
int CDiagramEngDoc::TrackConnectionEndPoint(CPoint point, CWnd *pWnd)
{
    int delta = (int)(0.25*m_dDeltaLength);  // integer increment
    int tracker_flag = 0;
    double disc_r = 0.1*m_dDeltaLength;
    double dist_to_tail;
    double dist_to_head;
    CPoint bottom_right;
    CPoint *from_point = NULL;
    CPoint head_pt;
    CPoint tail_pt;
    CPoint top_left;
    CPort *from_port = NULL;
    CPort *to_port = NULL;
    list<CConnection*>::iterator it_con;
    list<CConnection*> con_list = GetSystemModel().GetConnectionList();

    // CScrollView-related change
    CPoint ptLogical = point;  // local point to record the point in
      logical units
    CClientDC dc(pWnd);             // create a device context using the
      pointer-to-CWnd pWnd.
    ((CScrollView*)pWnd)->OnPrepareDC(&dc);  // prepare the device
      context casting pWnd to ptr-to-CScrollView
    dc.DPtoLP(&ptLogical);          // use the dc to convert ptLogical from
      device to logical units

    // Iterate through connection list
    for(it_con = con_list.begin(); it_con != con_list.end(); it_con++)
    {
        // Get tail and head points of connection
        tail_pt = (*it_con)->GetConnectionPointTail();
        head_pt = (*it_con)->GetConnectionPointHead();

        // Determine Euclidean dist bw point and tail and head pts
        // dist_to_tail = sqrt(pow(tail_pt.x - point.x,2) +
          pow(tail_pt.y - point.y,2));
        // dist_to_head = sqrt(pow(head_pt.x - point.x,2) +
          pow(head_pt.y - point.y,2));

        // CScrollView-related change
        dist_to_tail = sqrt(pow(tail_pt.x - ptLogical.x,2) +
          pow(tail_pt.y - ptLogical.y,2));
        dist_to_head = sqrt(pow(head_pt.x - ptLogical.x,2) +
          pow(head_pt.y - ptLogical.y,2));

        // If the tail pt is clicked
        if(dist_to_tail <= disc_r)
        {
            top_left.x = tail_pt.x - delta;
            top_left.y = tail_pt.y - delta;
            bottom_right.x = tail_pt.x + delta;
            bottom_right.y = tail_pt.y + delta;
```

```
// CScrollView-related change
dc.LPtoDP(&top_left);        // convert logical pt based on
  logical block position to device pt
dc.LPtoDP(&bottom_right);   // convert logical pt based on
  logical block position to device pt

// Set the rect tracker's position
m_RectTracker.m_rect.SetRect(top_left.x, top_left.y,
  bottom_right.x, bottom_right.y);

// Track the mouse's position till left mouse button up
tracker_flag = m_RectTracker.Track(pWnd, point, TRUE);
  // 0 => item not tracked, 1 => item was tracked

// Get the new tracker position and update the new connection
  end pt position with the tracker position
tail_pt = m_RectTracker.m_rect.CenterPoint();

dc.DPtoLP(&tail_pt);  // CScrollView-related change convert
  device units to logical units

// Check to snap connector to port
if((*it_con)->GetRefFromPort() == NULL)  // If not already a
  ref_from port
{
    from_port = SnapConnectionTailPointToPort(tail_pt);
      // tail_pt passed by ref. and may be updated.
    if(from_port != NULL)
    {
        (*it_con)->SetRefFromPort(from_port);
    }
}
else     // If already a ref-from-port, then the intention on
  moving the end pt. is to break the assoc. with the port.
{
    (*it_con)->SetRefFromPort(NULL);
}
(*it_con)->SetConnectionPointTail(tail_pt);

// Check to snap connector to bend point
if((*it_con)->GetRefFromPoint() == NULL)  // If not already a
  ref_from point
{
    from_point = SnapConnectionTailPointToBendPoint(tail_pt);
      // tail_pt passed by ref. and may be updated.
    if(from_point != NULL)
    {
        (*it_con)->SetRefFromPoint(from_point);
    }
}
else     // If already a ref-from-point, then the intention on
  moving the end pt. is to break the assoc. with the point.
{
    (*it_con)->SetRefFromPoint(NULL);
}
(*it_con)->SetConnectionPointTail(tail_pt);
```

```
            // Set flags
            SetModifiedFlag(TRUE);      // set the doc. as having been
              modified to prompt user to save
            UpdateAllViews(NULL);       // indicate that sys. should redraw.
            break;
    }

    // If the head pt is clicked
    if(dist_to_head <= disc_r)
    {
        top_left.x = head_pt.x - delta;
        top_left.y = head_pt.y - delta;
        bottom_right.x = head_pt.x + delta;
        bottom_right.y = head_pt.y + delta;

        // CScrollView-related change
        dc.LPtoDP(&top_left);        // convert logical pt based on
          logical block position to device pt
        dc.LPtoDP(&bottom_right); // convert logical pt based on
          logical block position to device pt

        // Set the rect tracker's position
        m_RectTracker.m_rect.SetRect(top_left.x, top_left.y,
          bottom_right.x, bottom_right.y);

        // Track the mouse's position till left mouse button up
        tracker_flag = m_RectTracker.Track(pWnd, point, TRUE);
          // 0 => item not tracked, 1 => item was tracked

        // Get the new tracker position and update the new connection
          end pt position with the tracker position
        head_pt = m_RectTracker.m_rect.CenterPoint();

        dc.DPtoLP(&head_pt);   // CScrollView-related change convert
          device units to logical units

        // Check to snap connector to port
        if((*it_con)->GetRefToPort() == NULL)  // If not already a
          ref_to port
        {
            to_port = SnapConnectionHeadPointToPort(head_pt);
              // head_pt passed by ref. and may be updated.
            if(to_port != NULL)
            {
                (*it_con)->SetRefToPort(to_port);
            }
        }
        else  // If already a ref-to-port, then the intention on
          moving the end pt. is to break the assoc. with the port.
        {
            (*it_con)->SetRefToPort(NULL);
        }
        (*it_con)->SetConnectionPointHead(head_pt);

        // Set flags
        SetModifiedFlag(TRUE);  // set the doc. as having been
          modified to prompt user to save
```

```
                UpdateAllViews(NULL);     // indicate that sys. should redraw.
                break;
        }

    }// end for

    // Return flag indicating if an item was tracked: 0 => not tracked,
      1 => tracked.
    return tracker_flag;
}
```

28.5   TRACKING OF MULTIPLE ITEMS

The tracking of multiple items is initiated from the CDiagramEngDoc::TrackItem() function wherein a call is made to CDiagramEngDoc::TrackMultipleItems(), passing in the mouse cursor CPoint, "point", and the pointer-to-CWnd, "pWnd", objects. Prior to making the necessary CScrollView-related changes, the reader should review the operation of the TrackMultipleItems() function, first presented in Chapter 11 in particular Section 11.6; a brief explanation is provided here for convenience.

The TrackMultipleItems() function allows the creation of a rubber band to enclose a region of items on the palette, and then the enclosed items may be selected by left-clicking the interior of the bounded region (rubber band), and all contained items may be moved, i.e., translated, to a new location. The function has three main conditional clauses: (1) if a rubber band has not been created, then it is to be (initially) created, (2) if a rubber band has been created but a left-click event subsequently occurs outside the rubber band region, then the region containing items cannot be moved, so no movement action is taken, and (3) if a rubber band has been created and a left-click event subsequently occurs inside the rubber band region, then the region containing items can be translated to a new location, and the positions of the contained items are updated accordingly. The complete action of the TrackMultipleItems() function requires two entries into the function: creation of the rubber band and a check of the location of the subsequent left-click event. In addition, DetermineCurrentAndIntersectRects() determines whether a diagram entity lies within the rubber band region, and DetermineTrackerDeltaPosition() determines the change in position (translation) of the rubber band region through the initial and final positions of the center point of the "m_RectTracker" object.

The changes to be made to the TrackMultipleItems() function to allow it to work properly in the context of the scroll view are shown in bold in the following and involve (1) creating a logical CPoint object, (2) converting the tracker's position from device to logical coordinates for manual drawing of the tracking rectangle, (3) using the logical point, "ptLogical", in conditional tests, and (4) calling DetermineTrackerDeltaPosition() with the logical point to determine the change in position of the tracking rectangle.

```
int CDiagramEngDoc::TrackMultipleItems(CPoint point, CWnd *pWnd)
{
    int intersected = 0;
    int item_tracked = 0;
    int manual_rect = 1;
    int tracker_flag = 0;
    double blk_width;
    double delta = 0.25*m_dDeltaLength;
    static CPoint tracker_init;  // require tracker_init for else clause
      on re-entry of OnLButtonDown
    CPoint bend_pt;
    CPoint blk_posn;
    CPoint delta_posn;
```

```
CPoint head_pt;
CPoint tail_pt;
CRectTracker temp_tracker;
list<CBlock*> &blk_list = GetSystemModel().GetBlockList();
list<CBlock*>::iterator it_blk;
list<CConnection*>::iterator it_con;
list<CConnection*> &con_list = GetSystemModel().GetConnectionList();
list<CPoint>::iterator it_pt;
CClientDC dc(pWnd);

// CScrollView-related change
CPoint ptLogical;        // logical point given change in scroll
  position.
((CScrollView*)pWnd)->OnPrepareDC(&dc);   // prepare the dc given the
  usage of the CScrollView base class
ptLogical = point;        // make a copy of the device point
dc.DPtoLP(&ptLogical);   // change point from device to logical coords

// -- IF A RUBBER BAND HAS NOT BEEN CREATED, THEN CREATE IT.
if(m_iRubberBandCreated == 0)
{
    // Create a rubber band
    m_RectTracker.TrackRubberBand(pWnd, point, TRUE);
    m_RectTracker.m_rect.NormalizeRect();
    dc.DPtoLP(&m_RectTracker.m_rect);  // CScrollView-related change:
      change to logical coords
    tracker_init = m_RectTracker.m_rect.CenterPoint();

    // Create a temporary rectangle indicating where the initial
      CRectTracker rectangle was.
    // This is done, since the temporary CRectTracker rectangle
      disappears upon fn exit.
    if(manual_rect)     // Manually create a red, dotted lined
      rectangle
    {
        CPen lpen(PS_DOT, 1, RGB(255,0,0));        // create a pen
        CPen *pOldPen = dc.SelectObject(&lpen);  // create a copy
        dc.SetROP2(R2_NOTXORPEN);   // make the rectangle transparent
        dc.Rectangle(m_RectTracker.m_rect.TopLeft().x,
          m_RectTracker.m_rect.TopLeft().y, m_RectTracker.m_rect.
          BottomRight().x, m_RectTracker.m_rect.BottomRight().y);
        // create the rectangle using the m_RectTracker object
        coords.

        dc.SelectObject(pOldPen);     // reset the old pen
    }
    else          // Use the default black dotted lined rectangle
    {
        m_RectTracker.m_nStyle = CRectTracker::dottedLine;
        m_RectTracker.Draw(&dc);
    }

    // Set flags.
    m_iRubberBandCreated = 1;  // rubber band state is active
    tracker_flag = 1;          // tracking of multiple items has
      commenced
    return tracker_flag;
}
```

```
// -- IF A RUBBER BAND HAS BEEN CREATED, BUT LEFT-CLICK OUTSIDE OF
   ENCLOSING REGION, THEN END TRACK ACTION.
// CScrollView-related change: use the logical point "ptLogical"
   rather than the device point "point"
//else if((m_RectTracker.HitTest(point) == CRectTracker::hitNothing)
   && (m_iRubberBandCreated == 1))
else if((m_RectTracker.HitTest(ptLogical) ==
   CRectTracker::hitNothing) && (m_iRubberBandCreated == 1))
{
    m_iRubberBandCreated = 0;    // end the rubber band state
    SetKeyFlagTrack(0);          // reset the key-based track flag
      since tracking aborted
    tracker_flag = 0;            // tracking did not occur
    return tracker_flag;
}
// -- IF A RUBBER BAND HAS BEEN CREATED, AND LEFT-CLICK INSIDE
   ENCLOSING REGION, THEN POSSIBLY MOVE ITEMS.
// CScrollView-related change: use the logical point "ptLogical"
   rather than the device point "point"
//else if((m_RectTracker.HitTest(point) != CRectTracker::hitNothing)
   && (m_iRubberBandCreated == 1))
else if((m_RectTracker.HitTest(ptLogical) !=
   CRectTracker::hitNothing) && (m_iRubberBandCreated == 1))
{
    // Create a temp tracker since m_RectTracker will have its coords
      updated when the rubber band is moved.
    temp_tracker = m_RectTracker;

    // -- ITERATE THROUGH BLOCKS
    for(it_blk = blk_list.begin(); it_blk != blk_list.end();
      it_blk++)
    {
        // BLOCK
        blk_posn = (*it_blk)->GetBlockPosition();
        blk_width = (*it_blk)->GetBlockShape().GetBlockWidth();

        // Determine if item lies within rubber band
        intersected = DetermineCurrentAndIntersectRects
          (temp_tracker, blk_posn, (blk_width*0.5));
        if(intersected)
        {
            if(item_tracked == 0)
            {
                // Determine the tracker's change in position
                // CScrollView-related change: use the logical point
                  "ptLogical" rather than the device point "point"
                //item_tracked = DetermineTrackerDeltaPosition
                  (pWnd, point, tracker_init, delta_posn);
                item_tracked = DetermineTrackerDeltaPosition
                  (pWnd, ptLogical, tracker_init, delta_posn);
            }

            // Update the block posn.
            (*it_blk)->SetBlockPosition(blk_posn + delta_posn);

            // Set flags
            SetModifiedFlag(TRUE);  // set the doc. as having been
              modified to prompt user to save
```

```
                    UpdateAllViews (NULL);  // indicate that sys. should
                      redraw.
                }
        }// end for it_blk

        // -- ITERATE THROUGH ALL CONNECTIONS (of this model)
        for(it_con = con_list.begin(); it_con != con_list.end();
          it_con++)
        {
            // TAIL POINT
            tail_pt = (*it_con)->GetConnectionPointTail();

            // Determine if item lies within rubber band
            intersected = DetermineCurrentAndIntersectRects
              (temp_tracker, tail_pt, delta);
            if(intersected)
            {
                if(item_tracked == 0)
                {
                    // Determine the tracker's change in position
                    // CScrollView-related change: use the logical point
                      "ptLogical" rather than the device point "point"
                    //item_tracked = DetermineTrackerDeltaPosition
                      (pWnd, point, tracker_init, delta_posn);
                    item_tracked = DetermineTrackerDeltaPosition
                      (pWnd, ptLogical, tracker_init, delta_posn);
                }

                // Check if the TAIL POINT is NOT CONNECTED to a PORT or
                  a BEND POINT: if so move it.
                if( ( (*it_con)->GetRefFromPort() == NULL) &&
                  ( (*it_con)->GetRefFromPoint() == NULL) )
                {
                    // Update tail pt. posn.
                    (*it_con)->SetConnectionPointTail
                      (tail_pt + delta_posn);

                    // Set flags
                    SetModifiedFlag(TRUE);  // set the doc. as having
                      been modified to prompt user to save
                    UpdateAllViews(NULL);   // indicate that sys. should
                      redraw.
                }
            }

            // HEAD POINT
            head_pt = (*it_con)->GetConnectionPointHead();

            // Determine if item lies within rubber band
            intersected = DetermineCurrentAndIntersectRects
              (temp_tracker, head_pt, delta);
            if(intersected)
            {
                if(item_tracked == 0)
                {
                    // Determine the tracker's change in position
                    // CScrollView-related change: use the logical point
                      "ptLogical" rather than the device point "point"
```

```
        //item_tracked = DetermineTrackerDeltaPosition
          (pWnd, point, tracker_init, delta_posn);
        item_tracked = DetermineTrackerDeltaPosition
          (pWnd, ptLogical, tracker_init, delta_posn);
    }


    // Check if the HEAD POINT is NOT CONNECTED to a PORT: if
      so move it.
    if((*it_con)->GetRefToPort() == NULL)
    {
        // Update head pt. posn.
        (*it_con)->SetConnectionPointHead(head_pt +
          delta_posn);

        // Set flags
        SetModifiedFlag(TRUE);  // set the doc. as having
          been modified to prompt user to save
        UpdateAllViews(NULL);   // indicate that sys. should
          redraw.
    }
}


// -- ITERATE THROUGH ALL BEND POINTS FOR THIS CONNECTION

list<CPoint> &bend_pts_list = (*it_con)-
  >GetConnectionBendPointsList();

for(it_pt = bend_pts_list.begin(); it_pt != bend_pts_list.
  end(); it_pt++)
{
    // BEND POINT
    bend_pt = *it_pt;

    // Determine if item lies within rubber band
    intersected = DetermineCurrentAndIntersectRects
      (temp_tracker, bend_pt, delta);
    if(intersected)
    {
        if(item_tracked == 0)
        {
            // Determine the tracker's change in position
            // CScrollView-related change: use the logical
              point "ptLogical" rather than the device point
              "point"
            //item_tracked = DetermineTrackerDeltaPosition
              (pWnd, point, tracker_init, delta_posn);
            item_tracked = DetermineTrackerDeltaPosition
              (pWnd, ptLogical, tracker_init, delta_posn);
        }

        // Update the connection bend pt posn.
        *it_pt = *it_pt + delta_posn;

        // Update any connection's tail point if it was
          connected to this bend point
        m_SystemModel.UpdateConnectionPointTailToBendPoint
          (&(*it_pt));
```

```
                        // Set flags
                        SetModifiedFlag(TRUE); // set the doc. as having been
                          modified to prompt user to save
                        UpdateAllViews(NULL);  // indicate that sys. should
                          redraw.
                }
            }// end for it_pt
        }// end for it_con

        // Set flags
        m_iRubberBandCreated = 0;   // end the rubber band state
        SetKeyFlagTrack(0);         // reset the key-based track flag
          since tracking aborted

        if(item_tracked == 0)       // if no item was tracked
        {
            tracker_flag = 0;
            return tracker_flag;
        }
        else                        // if an item was tracked
        {
            tracker_flag = 1;
            return tracker_flag;
        }
    }

    // Return the tracker_flag
    return tracker_flag;
}
```

The developer will notice the four calls to DetermineTrackerDeltaPosition() in the TrackMultipleItems() function earlier to determine the change in position of the CRectTracker object, "m_RectTracker", used to reposition blocks and connection-based head, tail, and bend points. Similar alterations to those given earlier need to be made to the DetermineTrackerDeltaPosition() function as shown in the following. Now that a CScrollView base class is used, a call to DPtoLP() with the address of "m_RectTracker.m_rect" as the argument is required to cater for any scrolling. Then the logical CPoint coordinates of the initial and final positions of the tracker object, "tracker_init" and "tracker_final", respectively, are used to determine the change in the tracker's position, "delta_posn" (δx, δy) (passed by reference).

```
int CDiagramEngDoc::DetermineTrackerDeltaPosition(CWnd *pWnd, CPoint
  point, CPoint tracker_init, CPoint &delta_posn)
{
    int item_tracked = 0;
    CPoint tracker_final;

    // CScrollView-related change: create a dc, then prepare it for
      subsequent DPtoLP() usage.
    CClientDC dc(pWnd);
    ((CScrollView*)pWnd)->OnPrepareDC(&dc);

    // Track the rectangle and determine its change in position.
    m_RectTracker.Track(pWnd, point, TRUE); // 0 => item not tracked,
      1 => item was tracked

    // CScrollView-related change: convert device point to logical point
    dc.DPtoLP(&m_RectTracker.m_rect);
```

```
    tracker_final = m_RectTracker.m_rect.CenterPoint();

    delta_posn = tracker_final - tracker_init;

    // Set the item_tracked flag
    if((delta_posn.x == 0) && (delta_posn.y == 0))
    {
        item_tracked = 0;
    }
    else
    {
        item_tracked = 1;
    }

    // Return a flag indicating a tracking event
    return item_tracked;
}
```

28.6 LIMITING DIAGRAM ENTITY PLACEMENT

The presence of scroll bars allows the user to access more room on the palette to draw model diagrams. However, there is an interactivity problem: if the user selects a diagram entity and moves it wildly upward or to the left, such that it is no longer visible on the screen due to its CPoint position x and y coordinate components being made negative, usage of the scroll bars cannot redisplay the invisible items. Hence, a mechanism is required to set negative coordinate components of diagram entities to be zero. Alterations are to be made to the CSystemModel::AddConnection() function, and a new function, named CSystemModel::NullifyNegativeCoordinates(), is to be added to the project.

Edit the AddConnection() function as shown in bold in the following to nullify the negative CPoint coordinate components; the ellipsis denotes omitted, unchanged code.

```
int CSystemModel::AddConnection(CPoint ptFrom, CPoint ptTo)
{
    int valid = 0;  // validity of connection: (0) not long enough,
      (1) long enough
    ...

    // Set min length
    dDeltaLength = GetDocumentGlobalFn()->GetDeltaLength();
    min_length = 0.5*dDeltaLength;

    // CScrollView-related change: nullify negative coordinate components
    if(ptTo.x < 0)
    {
        ptTo.x = 0;
    }
    if(ptTo.y < 0)
        ptTo.y = 0;
    }

    // Check to make sure that connection is greater than the rqd. min.
      connection length.
    con_length = sqrt(pow((ptFrom.x - ptTo.x),2) +
      pow((ptFrom.y - ptTo.y),2));
    if(con_length < min_length)
```

```
    {
        …
    }
    else
    {
        …
    }

    return valid;
}
```

The movement of diagram entity items is initiated in the `CDiagramEngDoc::TrackItem()` function; hence, the function to check for negative diagram entity coordinate components should be invoked here as shown in bold.

```
int CDiagramEngDoc::TrackItem(CPoint point, CWnd *pWnd)
{
    int tracker_flag = 0;

    // Track block
    tracker_flag = TrackBlock(point, pWnd);
    if(tracker_flag != 0)
    {
        GetSystemModel().NullifyNegativeCoordinates();
          // CScrollView-related change
        return tracker_flag;  // return since an item was tracked
    }

    // Track connection end point
    tracker_flag = TrackConnectionEndPoint(point, pWnd);
    if(tracker_flag != 0)
    {
        GetSystemModel().NullifyNegativeCoordinates();
          // CScrollView-related change
        return tracker_flag;  // return since an item was tracked
    }

    // Track connection bend point
    tracker_flag = TrackConnectionBendPoint(point, pWnd);
    if(tracker_flag != 0)
    {
        GetSystemModel().NullifyNegativeCoordinates();
          // CScrollView-related change
        return tracker_flag;   // return since an item was tracked
    }

    // Track multiple items
    if(m_iKeyFlagTrack == 1)
    {
        tracker_flag = TrackMultipleItems(point, pWnd);

        if(tracker_flag !=0)
        {
            GetSystemModel().NullifyNegativeCoordinates();
              // CScrollView-related change
            return tracker_flag;  // return since an item was tracked
        }
    }
```

```
    else
    {
        tracker_flag = 0;
    }

    // Return flag indicating if an item was tracked: 0 => not tracked,
      1 => tracked.
    return tracker_flag;
}
```

Finally, add a new public member function to the CSystemModel class with the prototype, int CSystemModel::NullifyNegativeCoordinates(void), and edit the function as shown. The NullifyNegativeCoordinates() function simply iterates through the list of blocks and connection head, tail, and bend points and assigns any negative coordinate components to zero.

```
int CSystemModel::NullifyNegativeCoordinates(void)
{
    CPoint ptBlk;                          // block position
    CPoint ptCon;                          // connection-based point
      location
    list<CBlock*>::iterator it_blk;        // block iterator
    list<CConnection*>::iterator it_con;   // connection iterator
    list<CPoint>::iterator it_pt;          // point iterator

    // CHECK BLOCK COORDINATES
    for(it_blk = m_lstBlock.begin(); it_blk != m_lstBlock.end();
      it_blk++)
    {
        ptBlk = (*it_blk)->GetBlockPosition();
        if(ptBlk.x < 0)
        {
            ptBlk.x = 0;
        }
        if(ptBlk.y < 0)
        {
            ptBlk.y = 0;
        }
        (*it_blk)->SetBlockPosition(ptBlk);
    }

    // CHECK CONNECTION COORDINATES
    for(it_con = m_lstConnection.begin(); it_con != m_lstConnection.
      end(); it_con++)
    {
        // HEAD POINT
        ptCon = (*it_con)->GetConnectionPointHead();
        if(ptCon.x < 0)
        {
            ptCon.x = 0;
        }
        if(ptCon.y < 0)
        {
            ptCon.y = 0;
        }
        (*it_con)->SetConnectionPointHead(ptCon);
```

```
        // TAIL POINT
        ptCon = (*it_con)->GetConnectionPointTail();
        if(ptCon.x < 0)
        {
            ptCon.x = 0;
        }
        if(ptCon.y < 0)
        {
            ptCon.y = 0;
        }
        (*it_con)->SetConnectionPointTail(ptCon);

        // BEND POINTS
        list<CPoint> &bend_pts_list = (*it_con)-
          >GetConnectionBendPointsList();

        for(it_pt = bend_pts_list.begin(); it_pt != bend_pts_list.end();
          it_pt++)
        {
            if((*it_pt).x < 0)
            {
                (*it_pt).x = 0;
            }

            if((*it_pt).y < 0)
            {
                (*it_pt).y = 0;
            }
        }
    }

    return 0;
}
```

Figure 28.4 shows the result of trying to drag blocks and connections off the palette in the negative coordinate directions; the relevant components are reset to zero. Note that block position coordinates locate the center of the block.

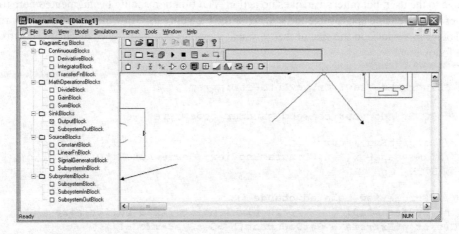

FIGURE 28.4 Diagram blocks and connections whose relevant coordinates are nullified as a result of an attempted placement in the negative *x* and *y* directions.

TABLE 28.1
Menu Entry Object, ID, Caption, Prompts, and Settings

Object	Property	Setting
View/Auto Fit Diagram	ID	ID_VIEW_AUTO_FIT_DIAGRAM
	Caption	Auto Fit &Diagram
	Prompts: status bar and tooltips	Auto fit diagram to viewnAuto Fit Diagram
View/Zoom In	ID	ID_VIEW_ZOOM_IN
	Caption	Zoom &In
	Prompts: status bar and tooltips	Zoom in to detail\nZoom In
View/Zoom Out	ID	ID_VIEW_ZOOM_OUT
	Caption	Zoom &Out
	Prompts: status bar and tooltips	Zoom out of detail\nZoom Out

28.7 FITTING THE LOGICAL VIEW TO THE PHYSICAL VIEW

The View menu has three diagram-scaling-related entries, as shown in Table 28.1, Auto Fit Diagram, Zoom In, and Zoom Out; the Auto Fit Diagram functionality may also be invoked by selecting the corresponding button on the Common Operations toolbar.

Now that the scroll bars are in place, the user may draw a large diagram (in logical coordinates) on the palette that extends beyond the physical view, i.e., the viewing window, such that only a portion of the diagram may be visible at any one time on the screen. To set the viewport size to the window size, i.e., to view the whole diagram in the physical view, the CScrollView:: SetScaleToFitSize(SIZE sizeTotal) function may be called, where the SIZE, "size-Total", argument represents the horizontal ("sizeTotal.cx") and vertical ("sizeTotal.cy") sizes to which the (logical-coordinate-based) view is to be scaled [2]. The developer will recall that in the previous chapter, the function CSystemModel::DetermineDiagramCoordinateExtrema() returns as a CPoint argument, the extreme logical coordinates (x, y) of the model diagram; this CPoint value should be used to scale the viewport, effectively allowing the whole diagram to fit to the viewing window. After scaling, the user may choose to revert to the original drawing scale by selecting the View menu entry, Auto Fit Diagram, again, whereupon SetScrollSizes() is to be called to reinstate the scrolling view.

Currently, the CDiagramEngView::OnViewAutoFitDiagram() function displays a simple message to the user, but otherwise takes no action. The function should be augmented here to allow the user to both enable and disable the scaling of the viewport size (in which the logical-coordinate-based diagram resides) to the size of the (physical viewing) window; the changes are shown in bold in the following.

```
void CDiagramEngView::OnViewAutoFitDiagram()
{
    // TODO: Add your command handler code here

    // DiagramEng (start)
    //AfxMessageBox("\n CDiagramEngView::OnViewAutoFitDiagram()\n",
      MB_OK, 0);

    // CScrollView-related change
    int buffer = 20;        // 20 pixel point fixed buffer size
    CPoint ptExtreme = GetDocument()->GetSystemModel().
      DetermineDiagramCoordinateExtrema();  // get extreme coords
    SIZE szExtreme;         // extreme size
```

```
        // Assign scale size using extreme point
        szExtreme.cx = ptExtreme.x + buffer;        // extreme horizontal size
        szExtreme.cy = ptExtreme.y + buffer;        // extreme vertical size

        // If the integer flag, to enable/disable setting of viewport scale
          to fit view window, modulus two, is zero, then scale to fit
        if(m_iAutoFitFlag%2 == 0)                   // FIT VIEWPORT SCALE
          TO WND
        {
            SetScaleToFitSize(szExtreme);           // set the viewport scale
              to fit the physical view window
        }
        else                                        // UNFIT VIEWPORT BY
          SETTING SCROLL SIZES
        {
            CSize sizeTotal;                        // total size of scroll
              view: cx and cy are horiz and vert extents (logical units)
            sizeTotal.cx = 5000;                    // horizontal extent of the
              scroll view
            sizeTotal.cy = 5000;                    // vertical extent of the
              scroll view
            SetScrollSizes(MM_TEXT, sizeTotal);     // call to adjust scrolling
              characteristics, for initial document display or size changes
        }
        m_iAutoFitFlag++;                           // increment flag such that
          subsequent call results in correct operation

    // DiagramEng (end)
}
```

The developer will notice the introduction of the member variable, "m_iAutoFitFlag", which is required to toggle between fitting the diagram to the view window and resetting the scroll view. In addition, the member variable is used to update the user interface, i.e., the View menu itself, with a tick-like check mark (✓), indicating that the Auto Fit Diagram option has been selected. Hence, add a private integer member variable to the CDiagramEngView class, named "m_iAutoFitFlag", and initialize it in the CDiagramEngView constructor to zero. The first time the user selects Auto Fit Diagram from the View menu, the member variable, "m_iAutoFitFlag", has value zero, and the viewport scale is fit to the physical viewing window. The subsequent call has the effect of reinstating the scroll view through the call to SetScrollSizes().

To implement the check mark feature, perform the following.

1. Add an event-handler function to the CDiagramEngView class for the UPDATE_COMMAND_UI event message associated with the ID_VIEW_AUTO_FIT_DIAGRAM menu entry.
2. Edit the code as shown in the following to set the check mark next to the View menu entry denoting whether auto scaling is in effect.

```
void CDiagramEngView::OnUpdateViewAutoFitDiagram(CCmdUI* pCmdUI)
{
    // TODO: Add your command update UI handler code here

    // DiagramEng (start)
    UINT nID = ID_VIEW_AUTO_FIT_DIAGRAM;            // menu entry ID
```

```
    // Get the correct menu item
    CMenu *pMenu = AfxGetApp()->GetMainWnd()->GetMenu();   // get the main
      wnd menu
    //CMenu *pSubMenu = pMenu->GetSubMenu(2);   // get submenu: (0) File,
      (1) Edit, (2) View. Actually unnec.

    // If the integer flag, to enable/disable setting of viewport scale
      to fit view window, modulus two, is zero, then uncheck menu item
    if (m_iAutoFitFlag%2 == 0)
    {
        //pSubMenu->CheckMenuItem(nID, MF_UNCHECKED | MF_BYCOMMAND);
          // inconsistent behaviour when using the maximize button
        pMenu->CheckMenuItem(nID, MF_UNCHECKED | MF_BYCOMMAND);
    }
    else
    {
        //pSubMenu->CheckMenuItem(nID, MF_CHECKED | MF_BYCOMMAND);
          // inconsistent behaviour when using the maximize button
        pMenu->CheckMenuItem(nID, MF_CHECKED | MF_BYCOMMAND);
    }

    // DiagramEng (end)
}
```

The purpose of the function is to toggle the check mark reflecting the view-based toggling of the OnViewAutoFitDiagram() function; if the SetScaleToFitSize() function is called in the latter, then upon exiting the function, the "m_iAutoFitFlag" modulus two will not have value zero, and hence, the Auto Fit Diagram entry under the View menu will have a check mark beside it ($1\%2 \neq 0$).

To actually place a check mark next to the menu item, first, the address of the main menu, "pMenu", is retrieved via the pointer-to-CWinThread, "m_pMainWnd", obtained through GetMainWnd(), then a call to CheckMenuItem() is made upon the menu pointer, where the first argument, "nID", is the ID of the View menu entry, i.e., ID_VIEW_AUTO_FIT_DIAGRAM, and the second argument is a combination of flags: MF_CHECKED or MF_UNCHECKED with MF_BYCOMMAND or MF_BYPOSITION [2].

An aside: initially a pointer to the main menu was retrieved, and then the address of the submenu, "pSubMenu", was obtained via a call to GetSubMenu(2), where the argument refers to the submenu with index two, i.e., the View menu (File (0), Edit (1), and View (2)). However, there appeared to be a problem when calling CheckMenuItem() upon the submenu pointer. If the user creates a drawing in a child document that is not maximized to fit the main window, then upon selecting and deselecting the Auto Fit Diagram entry, the check mark would correctly appear and disappear, respectively, next to the View menu entry. However, if the child document is maximized to fit the parent window, then the state of the menu item is persistently that prior to maximizing the window regardless of whether the Auto Fit Diagram state is toggled. This is inconsistent, as indicated in the comments in the code earlier, and hence, the main menu pointer, "pMenu", rather than the submenu pointer, "pSubMenu", was used to call CheckMenuItem() instead.

Figure 28.5 shows the before and after states of fitting a diagram to the window extents: (a) the state equation diagram that is larger than the window size with scroll bars visible and (b) the same diagram scaled to fit the window whereupon the scroll bars automatically disappear.

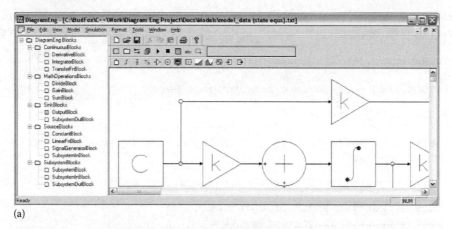

(a)

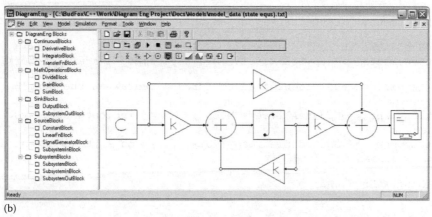

(b)

FIGURE 28.5 Scaling of the linear state equation diagram: (a) unscaled view requiring a greater window size and (b) scaled view to automatically fit the current window.

28.8 ZOOMING IN AND OUT OF THE VIEW

The OnViewAutoFitDiagram() function of the CDiagramEngView class allows the user to automatically zoom the diagram either in or out using SetScaleToFitSize(), such that the viewport size fits the window size and, in the process, removes the scroll bars. However, the user may want more control over the zooming process to increase or decrease the size of the underlying diagram entities. This may be accomplished by either (1) setting mapping modes and viewport and window origins and extents or (2) performing a manual scaling of the underlying model objects, e.g., blocks and connections, through the use of additional member functions. The general steps taken to perform the manual scaling of the model diagram are as listed, where specific details follow:

1. Addition of detail to the CDiagramEngView zooming functions
2. Addition of a ScaleSystemModel() function to the CSystemModel class

28.8.1 ADDITION OF DETAIL TO THE **CDiagramEngView** ZOOMING FUNCTIONS

Table 28.1 (Section 28.7) shows the objects, properties, and settings for the View menu, where the corresponding event hander functions for the zooming actions are OnViewZoomIn() and OnViewZoomOut() of the CDiagramEngView class. Code is to be added to these functions to set a scale factor variable, "scale_factor", whose value and reciprocal are used by the zoom in and zoom out functions, respectively, to scale the system model's underlying diagram entity coordinates.

```
void CDiagramEngView::OnViewZoomIn()
{
    // TODO: Add your command handler code here

    // DiagramEng (start)
    double length;                    // used to scale m_dDeltaLength
    double scale_factor = 1.1;   // scale factor: inverse of that used in
      OnViewZoomOut()

    //AfxMessageBox("\n CDiagramEngView::OnViewZoomIn()\n", MB_OK, 0);

    // Scale m_dDeltaLength of CDiagramEngDoc
    length = GetDocument()->GetDeltaLength();
    length = length*scale_factor;
    GetDocument()->SetDeltaLength(length);

    // Scale the current diagram
    GetDocument()->GetSystemModel().ScaleSystemModel(scale_factor);

    // Invalidate the client area to force a redraw on the next WM_PAINT
      message.
    GetDocument()->UpdateAllViews(NULL);      // indicate that sys. should
      redraw.
    GetDocument()->SetModifiedFlag(TRUE);      // mark the document as
      having been modified

    // DiagramEng (end)
}

void CDiagramEngView::OnViewZoomOut()
{
    // TODO: Add your command handler code here

    // DiagramEng (start)
    double length;                      // used to scale m_dDeltaLength
    double scale_factor = 1/1.1;   // scale factor: inverse of that used
      in OnViewZoomIn()

    //AfxMessageBox("\n CDiagramEngView::OnViewZoomOut()\n", MB_OK, 0);

    // Scale m_dDeltaLength of CDiagramEngDoc
    length = GetDocument()->GetDeltaLength();
    length = length*scale_factor;
    GetDocument()->SetDeltaLength(length);

    // Scale the current diagram
    GetDocument()->GetSystemModel().ScaleSystemModel(scale_factor);

    // Invalidate the client area to force a redraw on the next WM_PAINT
      message.
    GetDocument()->UpdateAllViews(NULL);      // indicate that sys.
      should redraw.
    GetDocument()->SetModifiedFlag(TRUE);      // mark the document as
      having been modified

    // DiagramEng (end)
}
```

The developer will notice that the scale factor, "scale_factor", is first set and then used to scale the "m_dDeltaLength" variable of the CDiagramEngDoc class prior to being passed to the ScaleSystemModel() function of the CSystemModel class. Hence, add a public member function to the CDiagramEngDoc class with the following prototype, void CDiagramEngDoc:: SetDeltaLength(double length), and edit it as shown.

```
void CDiagramEngDoc::SetDeltaLength(double length)
{
    m_dDeltaLength = length;
}
```

28.8.2   ADDITION OF A `ScaleSystemModel()` FUNCTION TO THE CSystemModel CLASS

A call is made to scale the system model in the OnViewZoomIn() and OnViewZoomOut() functions shown earlier. Hence, add a public member function to the CSystemModel class with the following prototype, void CSystemModel::ScaleSystemModel(double scale_factor), and edit it as follows.

```
void CSystemModel::ScaleSystemModel(double scale_factor)
{
    double height;                        // block height
    double width;                         // block width
    CPoint ptBend;                        // connection-based bend point
    CPoint ptBlk;                         // block position
    CPoint ptHead;                        // head point
    CPoint ptTail;                        // tail point
    list<CBlock*>::iterator it_blk;       // block iterator
    list<CConnection*>::iterator it_con;  // connection iterator
    list<CPoint>::iterator it_pt;         // bend point iterator

    // Note: order of operations is important to ensure that items remain
      connected.
    // Connection end points if attached should remain attached.
    // Block ports should scale correctly with block scaling.

    // SCALE CONNECTION-RELATED VARS
    for(it_con = m_lstConnection.begin(); it_con != m_lstConnection.
      end(); it_con++)
    {
        // Bend points
        list<CPoint> &lstBendPts = (*it_con)-
          >GetConnectionBendPointsList();
        for(it_pt = lstBendPts.begin(); it_pt != lstBendPts.end();
          it_pt++)
        {
            ptBend = (*it_pt);
            ptBend.x = scale_factor*ptBend.x;
            ptBend.y = scale_factor*ptBend.y;
            (*it_pt) = ptBend;
            UpdateConnectionPointTailToBendPoint(&(*it_pt));
              // update any tail pt connected to bend pt.
        }

        // Head point - scale if head point not connected to an input
          port
        ptHead = (*it_con)->GetConnectionPointHead();
```

```
            if((*it_con)->GetRefToPort() == NULL)
            {
                ptHead.x = scale_factor*ptHead.x;
                ptHead.y = scale_factor*ptHead.y;
                (*it_con)->SetConnectionPointHead(ptHead);
            }

            // Tail point - scale if tail point not connected to an output
              port or bend point
            ptTail = (*it_con)->GetConnectionPointTail();
            if(((*it_con)->GetRefFromPort() == NULL) && ((*it_con)-
              >GetRefFromPoint() == NULL))
            {
                ptTail.x = scale_factor*ptTail.x;
                ptTail.y = scale_factor*ptTail.y;
                (*it_con)->SetConnectionPointTail(ptTail);
            }
        }

    // SCALE BLOCK-RELATED VARS
    for(it_blk = m_lstBlock.begin(); it_blk != m_lstBlock.end();
      it_blk++)
    {
        // Block width
        width = (*it_blk)->GetBlockShape().GetBlockWidth();
        width = scale_factor*width;
        (*it_blk)->GetBlockShape().SetBlockWidth(width);

        // Block height
        height = (*it_blk)->GetBlockShape().GetBlockHeight();
        height = scale_factor*height;
        (*it_blk)->GetBlockShape().SetBlockHeight(height);

        // Block posn
        ptBlk = (*it_blk)->GetBlockPosition();
        ptBlk.x = scale_factor*ptBlk.x;
        ptBlk.y = scale_factor*ptBlk.y;
        (*it_blk)->SetBlockPosition(ptBlk);
    }
}
```

The ScaleSystemModel() function simply iterates through the list of connections and blocks and scales the relevant variables. For connections, the list of bend points, "m_lstBendPts", is retrieved, and the bend points scaled before any connected tail points are updated (UpdateConnectionPointTailToBendPoint()) so as to remain connected. If the head point is not connected to a block input port (GetRefToPort()), then it is scaled, and if the tail point is not connected to a block output port (GetRefFromPort()) or does not emanate from a bend point (GetRefFromPoint()), then it too is scaled. For blocks, first the block width and height are scaled followed by the block position. Now upon zooming in or out of a view, the diagram increases and decreases in size, respectively, as shown in Figure 28.6.

28.8.3 RESETTING THE DEFAULT MODEL GEOMETRY

Finally, to restore the default size of "m_dDeltaLength" to that specified in the CDiagramEngDoc constructor and to rescale the entire model diagram accordingly, a new public member function is to

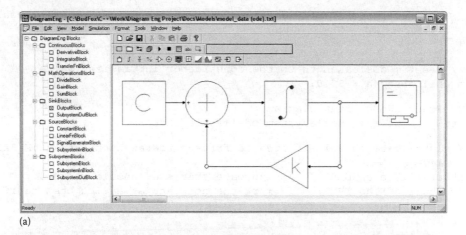

(a)

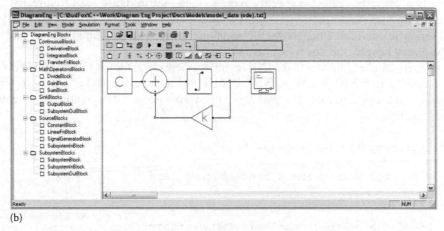

(b)

FIGURE 28.6 Zooming in and out of a diagram representing an ordinary differential equation: (a) zooming in increases the diagram size and (b) zooming out decreases the diagram size.

be added to the CDiagramEngDoc class with the following prototype: void CDiagramEngDoc:: ResetDefaultGeometry(void). Edit the function as shown to determine the scale factor given the default value (50.0) and current value of "m_dDeltaLength" and call ScaleSystemModel() to reset all diagram entity components.

```
void CDiagramEngDoc::ResetDefaultGeometry()
{
    double scale_factor;

    // Divide the original Constructor initialized value by the current
     value of m_dDeltaLength
    if(m_dDeltaLength != 0)
    {
        scale_factor = 50.0/m_dDeltaLength;  // 50.0 is the default value
         of m_dDeltaLength
    }
    else
    {
        scale_factor = 1.0;
```

```
    AfxMessageBox("\n CDiagramEngDoc::ResetDefaultGeometry(): scaling
        error.\n", MB_OK, 0);
}

// Reset m_dDeltaLength to the constructor initialized value
m_dDeltaLength = 50.0;

// Scale the current diagram
GetSystemModel().ScaleSystemModel(scale_factor);

// Invalidate the client area to force a redraw on the next WM_PAINT
    message.
UpdateAllViews(NULL);    // indicate that sys. should redraw.
SetModifiedFlag(TRUE);    // mark the document as having been modified
}
```

This function may be called explicitly via a View menu entry and indirectly via the `CDiagramEngDoc::OnFileSave()` and `CDiagramEngDoc::OnFileSaveAs()` functions prior to serialization. Table 28.2 shows the additional entry and its properties and settings that should be placed beneath the Zoom Out item on the View menu.

Add an event-handler function to the CDiagramEngView class, for the COMMAND event message associated with the ID_VIEW_RESET_DIAGRAM menu entry, and edit it as shown in the following to call `ResetDefaultGeometry()` upon a pointer-to-CDiagramEngDoc returned by `GetDocument()`.

```
void CDiagramEngView::OnViewResetDiagram()
{
    // TODO: Add your command handler code here

    // DiagramEng (start)

    // Reset the default model diagram geometry
    GetDocument()->ResetDefaultGeometry();

    // DiagramEng (end)
}
```

The developer should be warned, however, that since CPoint arguments involve integer coordinate values and numerous zooming in and out action scale diagram entities using a double type scale factor, there will inevitably be a loss of accuracy, and the original diagram geometry may not be able to be perfectly recovered through a resetting operation.

In addition, prior to any serialization, the diagram can be rescaled to its default "m_dDeltaLength"-based geometry. This is done such that upon restoring a previously saved diagram and adding new diagram entities to it, all blocks and connections on the palette will have default uniform size. Hence, augment the `OnFileSave()` and `OnFileSaveAs()`

TABLE 28.2

Menu Entry Object, ID, Caption, Prompts, and Settings

Object	Property	Setting
View/Reset Diagram	ID	ID_VIEW_RESET_DIAGRAM
	Caption	R&eset Diagram
	Prompts: status bar and tooltips	Reset diagram to default scale\nReset Diagram

functions of the CDiagramEngDoc class as shown in bold in the following to call ResetDefaultGeometry() prior to serialization.

```cpp
void CDiagramEngDoc::OnFileSave()
{
    // TODO: Add your command handler code here

    // DiagramEng (start)

    // Check whether document has been modified: non-zero => modified,
      zero => not modified
    if(IsModified())
    {
        // Reset default geometry as a result of zooming in/out
        ResetDefaultGeometry();

        // Check whether a file path already exists
        if(m_strFilePath == "")
        {
            OnFileSaveAs();
        }
        else
        {
            WriteDiagramEngDataToFile(m_strFilePath, 0);   // 0 implies
              overwrite warning will not appear
        }
    }
    // DiagramEng (end)
}

void CDiagramEngDoc::OnFileSaveAs()
{
    // TODO: Add your command handler code here

    // DiagramEng (start)
    BOOL dlgType = FALSE;  // TRUE => File Open dlg, FALSE => File
      Save dlg
    CString strDefExt = ".txt";   // default file extension
    CString strFileName = "model_data.txt";    // file name
    CString strFilter = "All Files (*.*)|*.*|Plain Text (*.txt)|*.txt||";
      // string pairs specifying filters for file list box
    DWORD dwFlags = OFN_ENABLESIZING | OFN_HIDEREADONLY;
      // customization flags

    // Create a CFileDialog wnd
    CFileDialog dlgFile(dlgType, strDefExt, strFileName, dwFlags,
      strFilter, NULL);

    if(dlgFile.DoModal() == IDOK)
    {
        // Reset default geometry as a result of zooming in/out
        ResetDefaultGeometry();
        m_strFilePath = dlgFile.GetPathName();  // get the file path
          and name
        SetTitle(m_strFilePath); // set the title of the current doc
        WriteDiagramEngDataToFile(m_strFilePath, 1); // 1 implies
          overwrite warning will appear
    }
    // DiagramEng (end)
}
```

The reason why the scaled diagram using the zooming functions is not serialized is that the View menu entries concern, primarily, viewing of a model and not the editing of its underlying data attributes.

28.9 SUMMARY

The implementation of a scroll view requires deriving the original CView-based CDiagramEngView class from CScrollView and changing CDiagramEngView- and CDiagramEngDoc-based functions; the `CDiagramEngView::OnInitalUpdate()` function, wherein a call to `CScrollView::SetScrollSizes()` is made, is used to set scrolling characteristics.

However, since a scroll view is in place, a conversion is required to be made between device points and logical points `DPtoLP()` and vice versa, `LPtoDP()`, and the points are related as follows, $(x_{i,l}, y_{i,l}) = (x_{i,d} + \Delta x, y_{i,d} + \Delta y)$, where the change in scroll position, $(\Delta x, \Delta y)$, may be obtained using `CScrollView::GetScrollPosition()`. The functions that required explicit point conversions are the CDiagramEngView-based methods, `OnContextMenu()`, `OnLButtonDblClk()`, `OnLButtonDown()`, `OnLButtonUp()`, and `OnMouseMove()`; and the CDiagramEngDoc-based methods, `TrackBlock()`, `TrackConnectionBendPoint()`, `TrackConnectionEndPoint()`, `TrackMultipleItems()`, and `DetermineTracker DeltaPosition()`. As a result of the scroll-view-based changes, the user could place blocks off the palette, and hence, a `CSystemModel::NullifyNegativeCoordinates()` function was introduced to reset negative coordinate values to zero.

The automatic fitting of the viewport scale to the physical window is performed using the `CScrollView::SetScaleToFitSize()` function, and a member variable, "m_iAutoFitFlag", was introduced to toggle between the original and the scaled views and set a check mark (`CheckMenuItem()`) next to the "Auto Fit Diagram" View menu entry.

Zooming in and out of a view displaying the model diagram was performed using the CDiagramEngView event-handler functions `OnViewZoomIn()` and `OnViewZoomOut()`, and the `CSystemModel::ScaleSystemModel()` function used to scale the underlying diagram entities' geometry, including that of blocks, connection head, tail, and bend points, and the CDiagramEngDoc member variable, "m_dDeltaLength".

Finally, to complete the View menu, a Reset Diagram entry and its `OnViewResetDiagram()` event-handler function were added to call the `ResetDefaultGeometry()` method of the CDiagramEngDoc class to allow the user to reset the default diagram geometry; this function is also called by the `OnFileSave()` and `OnFileSaveAs()` methods of the same class prior to serialization.

REFERENCES

1. Microsoft Support, Logical and Physical Coordinate Relationship, http://support.microsoft.com/kb/74044, (accessed July 31, 2010).
2. Microsoft Developer Network Library Visual Studio 6.0, Microsoft® Visual Studio™ 6.0 Development System, Microsoft Corporation, 1998.
3. Brinkster, Scroll Views, http://aclacl.brinkster.net/MFC/ch10b.htm, (accessed July 31, 2010).
4. Prosise, J., Programming Windows 95 with MFC, Part VIII: Printing and print previewing, *Microsoft Systems Journal*, 11(4), 39–58, April, 1996.

29 Edit Menu

29.1 INTRODUCTION

The Edit menu currently has the entries, Undo, Cut, Copy, Paste, Delete Grouped Items, Select All, and Add Multiple Blocks, as shown in Table 29.1: functionality exists for Delete Grouped Items and Add Multiple Blocks, but is absent for the remaining items. Here, all event-handler functions and related class member methods will be added for the Edit menu to allow the user to easily and efficiently perform the most common editing actions typically available in Windows-based applications. The CDiagramEngDoc-based event-handler functions, `OnEditUndo()`, `OnEditCut()`, `OnEditCopy()`, and `OnEditPaste()`, listed in Table 29.1, are intended, but do not currently exist in the project, and `OnEditSelectAll()` exists but currently has no working functionality.

29.2 SELECTION OF ALL CONTENT

To perform an editing action, the CRectTracker object, "m_RectTracker", is to be used to first circumscribe the item, before subsequently invoking an event-handler function to change the data-structure state of the system model. Currently the user can click the Track Multiple Items button on the Common Operations toolbar and then use the cursor to draw a red dotted rectangle about the items to be acted upon. A similar action is to be taken to select all document-based content, where a tracking rectangle is automatically set up based on the extreme coordinate points of diagram entities on the palette, without the user needing to manually circumscribe items using the mouse. The changes to be made to the project to allow complete automatic selection of diagram items using a CRectTracker object are as listed where specific details follow:

1. Add a select-all-related member variable to the CDiagramEngDoc class.
2. Complete the `CDiagramEngDoc::OnEditSelectAll()` function.
3. Add a function to the CSystemModel class to get the diagram coordinate minima.
4. Add a resetting mechanism to cancel the select-all operation.

29.2.1 ADD A SELECT-ALL-RELATED MEMBER VARIABLE TO THE CDiagramEngDoc CLASS

The select-all state, to be denoted by an integer member variable, is to be activated upon entry in the `CDiagramEngDoc::OnEditSelectAll()` function and reset in either `OnInitTrackMultipleItems()` of the same class, or `CDiagramEngView::OnL ButtonDown()`. Hence, add a private integer member variable to the CDiagramEngDoc class with the name, "m_iSelectAll". Initialize this variable to zero in the CDiagramEngDoc constructor function as shown in bold in the following.

```
CDiagramEngDoc::CDiagramEngDoc()
{
    // TODO: add one-time construction code here

    // DiagramEng (start)
```

TABLE 29.1

Menu Entry Objects, IDs, Captions, Prompts, Settings, and Event-Handler Functions

Object	Property	Setting	Event-Handler Function
Edit/Undo	ID	ID_EDIT_UNDO	OnEditUndo()
	Caption	&Undo\tCtrl+Z	
	Prompts	Undo the last action\nUndo	
Edit/Cut	ID	ID_EDIT_CUT	OnEditCut()
	Caption	Cu&t\tCtrl+X	
	Prompts	Cut the selection and put it on the Clipboard\nCut	
Edit/Copy	ID	ID_EDIT_COPY	OnEditCopy()
	Caption	&Copy\tCtrl+C	
	Prompts	Copy the selection and put it on the Clipboard\nCopy	
Edit/Paste	ID	ID_EDIT_PASTE	OnEditPaste()
	Caption	&Paste\tCtrl+V	
	Prompts	Insert Clipboard contents\nPaste	
Edit/Delete Grouped Items	ID	ID_EDIT_DELETE	OnEditDeleteDeleteGroupedItems()
	Caption	&Delete	
	Prompts	Delete the selection\nDelete	
Edit/Select All	ID	ID_EDIT_SELECTALL	OnEditSelectAll()
	Caption	Select &All	
	Prompts	Selection of all content\nSelect All	
Edit/Add Multiple Blocks	ID	ID_EDIT_ADD_MULTI_BLOCKS	OnEditAddMultipleBlocks()
	Caption	Add &Multiple Blocks	
	Prompts	Add multiple blocks\nAdd Multiple Blocks	

```
    m_iKeyFlagTrack = 0;
    m_iFineMoveFlag = 0;
    m_iRubberBandCreated = 0;
    m_iSelectAll = 0;
    m_dDeltaLength = 50.0;
    m_strFilePath = "";
    // DiagramEng (end)
}
```

29.2.2 COMPLETE THE `CDiagramEngDoc::OnEditSelectAll()` FUNCTION

The purpose of the `CDiagramEngDoc::OnEditSelectAll()` function is to automatically set up the CRectTracker object, "m_RectTracker", without the user needing to do so explicitly with the mouse. Hence, add the detail to the `OnEditSelectAll()` member function, as shown, to do the following: (1) get a pointer to the view, "pView", associated with the document, (2) use "pView" to create a device context, (3) cast the pointer-to-CView to a pointer-to-CScrollView to prepare the device context (`OnPrepareDC()`), (4) determine the diagram coordinate minima and extrema, (5) set up the CRectTracker object, "m_RectTracker", and (6) manually draw a rectangle circumscribing the selected content.

```
void CDiagramEngDoc::OnEditSelectAll()
{
    // TODO: Add your command handler code here

    // DiagramEng (start)
    int buffer = 20;          // 20 point buffer
    CPoint ptExtrema;         // extreme coordinates of diagram entities
      of system model
    CPoint ptMinima;          // minimum coordinates of diagram entities
      of system model

    //AfxMessageBox("\n CDiagramEngDoc::OnEditSelectAll()\n", MB_OK, 0);

    // Get the position of the first view in the list of views for the
      current doc.
    POSITION posn = GetFirstViewPosition();

    // Get a pointer to the view identified by posn.
    CView *pView = GetNextView(posn);         // CView is derived from
      CWnd, so pView can be used with the rect tracker

    // Create a device context using CView *pView where CView is derived
      from CWnd
    CClientDC dc(pView);

    // CScrollView-related impl.
    ((CScrollView*)pView)->OnPrepareDC(&dc); // prepare device context
      casting pView to ptr-to-CScrollView

    // Determine Diagram Coordinate Minima and Extrema and creating a
      bounding box
    ptMinima = m_SystemModel.DetermineDiagramCoordinateMinima();
      // pseudo minima
    ptExtrema = m_SystemModel.DetermineDiagramCoordinateExtrema();
      // pseudo maxima
    ptMinima.x -= buffer;
    ptMinima.y -= buffer;
    ptExtrema.x += buffer;
    ptExtrema.y += buffer;

    // -- IF A TRACKER NOT BEEN CREATED, THEN CREATE IT.
    if(m_iRubberBandCreated == 0)
    {

        // Set up the CRectTracker "m_RectTracker" object directly
        m_RectTracker.m_rect.SetRect(ptMinima, ptExtrema);

        // Manually create a dotted lined rectangle circumscribing all
          diagram entities
        CPen lpen(PS_DOT, 1, RGB(50,50,50));      // create a pen:
          RGB(0,0,0) black
        CPen *pOldPen = dc.SelectObject(&lpen);  // create a copy
        dc.SetROP2(R2_NOTXORPEN);                 // make the rectangle
          transparent
        dc.Rectangle(m_RectTracker.m_rect.TopLeft().x, m_RectTracker.
          m_rect.TopLeft().y, m_RectTracker.m_rect.BottomRight().x,
          m_RectTracker.m_rect.BottomRight().y);// create the rectangle
          using the m_RectTracker object coords.
        dc.SelectObject(pOldPen);                 // reset the old pen
```

```
      // Set flags.
      m_iRubberBandCreated = 1;                    // rubber band state is
         active
      m_iSelectAll = 1;                            // select all state is active
   }

   // DiagramEng (end)
}
```

The developer will notice that usually to construct a device context object of type `CClientDC()` that a pointer-to-CWnd is required. However, as `OnEditSelectAll()` is a CDiagramEngDoc member method, the "this" pointer, e.g., cannot be used to set up the device context as it could be in a CDiagramEngView member function. Hence, a pointer-to-CView is obtained, and because CView is derived from CWnd and thus a type of CWnd, it may be used to construct the device context. Then on preparing the device context using `OnPrepareDC()`, the pointer-to-CView needs to be cast as a pointer-to-CScrollView, since CDiagramEngView is now derived from CScrollView (see Chapter 28).

29.2.3   ADD A FUNCTION TO THE **CSystemModel** CLASS
TO GET THE DIAGRAM COORDINATE MINIMA

The developer will have noticed the call to the CSystemModel function `DetermineDiagramCoordinateExtrema()`, introduced in Chapter 27, to determine the CPoint coordinate extrema of diagram entities on the palette. Now a similar function is to be introduced to determine the CPoint coordinate minima. Hence, add a public member function to the CSystemModel class with the following prototype, `CPoint CSystemModel::Determine DiagramCoordinateMinima(void)`, and edit as shown.

```
CPoint CSystemModel::DetermineDiagramCoordinateMinima()
{
   int pt_rad = 5;                         // radius of a bend point
      (assume fixed and small)
   int int_max = 2147483647;               // INT_MAX = 2147483647.
   double blk_height;                      // block width
   double blk_width;                       // block height
   CPoint ptBend;                          // bend point
   CPoint ptBlkPosn;                       // block position
   CPoint ptHead;                          // connection head point
   CPoint ptMin;                           // pseudo minimum point
      (minimum coords may be from diff. elements)
   CPoint ptTail;                          // connection tail point
   CPoint ptTemp;                          // temporary point
   list<CBlock*>::iterator it_blk;         // block iterator
   list<CConnection*>::iterator it_con;    // connection iterator
   list<CPoint>::iterator it_pt;           // bend points iterator

   // Init minimum point to INT_MAX
   ptMin.x = int_max;
   ptMin.y = int_max;

   // ITERATE THROUGH BLOCK LIST
   for(it_blk = m_lstBlock.begin(); it_blk != m_lstBlock.end(); it_blk++)
   {
      ptBlkPosn = (*it_blk)->GetBlockPosition();
      blk_height = (*it_blk)->GetBlockShape().GetBlockHeight();
```

```
    blk_width = (*it_blk)->GetBlockShape().GetBlockWidth();
    ptTemp.x = ptBlkPosn.x - int(0.5*blk_width);
    ptTemp.y = ptBlkPosn.y - int(0.5*blk_height);

    if(ptTemp.x < ptMin.x)
    {
        ptMin.x = ptTemp.x;
    }
    if(ptTemp.y < ptMin.y)
    {
        ptMin.y = ptTemp.y;
    }
}

// ITERATE THROUGH ALL CONNECTIONS
for(it_con = m_lstConnection.begin(); it_con != m_lstConnection.
  end(); it_con++)
{
    // Compare head point
    ptHead = (*it_con)->GetConnectionPointHead();

    if(ptHead.x < ptMin.x)
    {
        ptMin.x = ptHead.x;
    }
    if(ptHead.y < ptMin.y)
    {
        ptMin.y = ptHead.y;
    }

    // Compare tail point
    ptTail = (*it_con)->GetConnectionPointTail();

    if(ptTail.x < ptMin.x)
    {
        ptMin.x = ptTail.x;
    }

    if(ptTail.y < ptMin.y)
    {
        ptMin.y = ptTail.y;
    }

    // Compare connection's bend points
    list<CPoint> &lstBendPoints = (*it_con)-
      >GetConnectionBendPointsList();
    for(it_pt = lstBendPoints.begin(); it_pt != lstBendPoints.end();
      it_pt++)
    {

        // Ellipse surrounds the bend point with radius r (pt_rad).
        ptTemp.x = (*it_pt).x - pt_rad;
        ptTemp.y = (*it_pt).y - pt_rad;

        if(ptTemp.x < ptMin.x)
        {
            ptMin.x = ptTemp.x;
        }
```

```
            if(ptTemp.y < ptMin.y)
            {
                ptMin.y = ptTemp.y;
            }
        }
    }

    return ptMin;
}
```

The function iterates through the list of blocks, connections, and connection-based bend points; determines the minimum coordinates; and returns the coordinate minima as a CPoint object: in this regard, the actual CPoint object is a pseudominimum point, since its individual coordinate components may come from two different diagram entities (as is the case with the DetermineDiagramCoordinateExtrema() function).

29.2.4 ADD A RESETTING MECHANISM TO CANCEL THE SELECT-ALL OPERATION

The user, after selecting all diagram-based content, needs a way to abort or reset the action: this is done by a ResetSelectAll() function that is to be called from either the CDiagramEngView:: OnLButtonDown() or CDiagramEngDoc::OnInitTrackMultipleItems() functions. Hence, add a public member function to the CDiagramEngDoc class with the following prototype, int CDiagramEngDoc::ResetSelectAll(void), and edit it as shown.

```
int CDiagramEngDoc::ResetSelectAll()
{
    int buffer = 20;        // 20 point buffer
    CPoint ptExtrema;       // extreme coordinates of diagram entities of
        system model
    CPoint ptMinima;        // minimum coordinates of diagram entities of
        system model

    //AfxMessageBox("\n CDiagramEngDoc::ResetSelectAll()\n", MB_OK, 0);

    // Reset flags
    if(m_iSelectAll == 1)
    {
        m_iRubberBandCreated = 0;
        m_iSelectAll = 0;
    }

    // Get the position of the first view in the list of views for the
        current doc.
    POSITION posn = GetFirstViewPosition();

    // Get a pointer to the view identified by posn.
    CView *pView = GetNextView(posn);    // CView is derived from CWnd, so
        pView can be used with the rect tracker

    // Create a device context using CView *pView where CView is derived
        from CWnd
    CClientDC dc(pView);
```

```
    // CScrollView-related impl.
    ((CScrollView*)pView)->OnPrepareDC(&dc);    // prepare device context
      casting pView to ptr-to-CScrollView

    // Determine Diagram Coordinate Minima and Extrema and creating a
      bounding box
    ptMinima = m_SystemModel.DetermineDiagramCoordinateMinima();
      // pseudo minima
    ptExtrema = m_SystemModel.DetermineDiagramCoordinateExtrema();
      // pseudo maxima
    ptMinima.x -= buffer;
    ptMinima.y -= buffer;
    ptExtrema.x += buffer;
    ptExtrema.y += buffer;

    // Manually create a white-line rectangle to overdraw a possibly
      existing rectangle
    CPen lpen(PS_DOT, 1, RGB(255,255,255));      // create a pen: RGB(0,0,0)
      black
    CPen *pOldPen = dc.SelectObject(&lpen);      // create a copy
    dc.SetROP2(R2_NOTXORPEN);                     // make the rectangle
      transparent
    dc.Rectangle(ptMinima.x, ptMinima.y, ptExtrema.x, ptExtrema.y);
      // create the rectangle
    dc.SelectObject(pOldPen);                    // reset the old pen

    // Invalidate the client area to force a redraw on the next WM_PAINT
      message.
    UpdateAllViews(NULL);    // indicate that sys. should redraw.
    SetModifiedFlag(TRUE);   // mark the document as having been modified
    return 0;
}
```

In the CDiagramEngDoc::OnEditSelectAll() function introduced earlier, the member variables, "m_iSelectAll" and "m_iRubberBandCreated", were both set to one. Hence, upon resetting the select-all state, these variables need to be reset to zero. In addition, the rectangle drawn earlier now needs to be overdrawn in white and then UpdateAllViews() called to invalidate the client area to force a redraw on the next WM_PAINT message.

The CDiagramEngDoc::ResetSelectAll() function now needs to be called under two circumstances to reset the select-all state: (1) if the user left-clicks the mouse button and (2) if the Track Multiple Items button on the Common Operations toolbar is clicked.

Edit the CDigramEngView::OnLButtonDown() function as shown in bold, to first get the status of the select-all action, recorded in "m_iSelectAll", via a call to GetSelectAllFlag(), and if the select-all mechanism is active, then it should be deactivated or equivalently reset.

```
void CDiagramEngView::OnLButtonDown(UINT nFlags, CPoint point)
{
    // TODO: Add your message handler code here and/or call default

    // DiagramEng (start)

    int tracker_flag;        // 0 => no tracker and hence a connector, 1 =>
      tracker and hence no connector
```

```
//AfxMessageBox("\n CDiagramEngView::OnLButtondown()\n", MB_OK, 0);

// Assume an item is being tracked: if so tracker_flag = 1, if not:
  tracker_flag = 0.
tracker_flag = GetDocument()->TrackItem(point, this);   // this is a
  ptr-to-CWnd, i.e. CWnd *pWnd.

// Reset Select-All Action
if(GetDocument()->GetSelectAllFlag() == 1)
{
  GetDocument()->ResetSelectAll();
}

// If nothing was tracked, i.e. tracker_flag = 0, then record points
  to draw and construct a connector.
if(tracker_flag == 0)
{
    // CScrollView-related change
    CClientDC dc(this); // create a device context using the pointer-
      to-CWnd "this"
    OnPrepareDC(&dc);   // prepare the device context
    dc.DPtoLP(&point);  // use the dc to convert the point from device
      to logical units

    // Capture the mouse so no other apps. can get it.
    SetCapture();

    // Save the pt that the cursor is at, upon left-btn-down,
      i.e. init member var with incoming CPoint var.
      m_ptPrevPos = point;    // Init the prev. pt, to be used in
        OnMouseMove(), to the current point
      m_ptOrigin = point;     // Init the origin of the ensuing line,
        to be drawn in OnMouseMove(), to be the starting pt.
}

// DiagramEng (end)

//CView::OnLButtonDown(nFlags, point);
CScrollView::OnLButtonDown(nFlags, point); // DiagramEng: CView
  changed to CScrollView
}
```

The developer will have noticed that the member variable "m_iSelectAll" is returned using the accessor function GetSelectAllFlag(). Hence, add a public constant member function to the CDiagramEngDoc class with the following prototype, int   CDiagramEngDoc::GetSelectAllFlag(void)   const, and edit the function as shown to return the member variable:

```
int CDiagramEngDoc::GetSelectAllFlag() const
{
    return m_iSelectAll;
}
```

Finally, given that the CRectTracker object, "m_RectTracker", may be set up in both the CDiagramEngDoc functions, OnEditSelectAll() and TrackMultipleItems(), to avoid a conflict in the context of its use, upon clicking the Track Multiple Items button on the Common

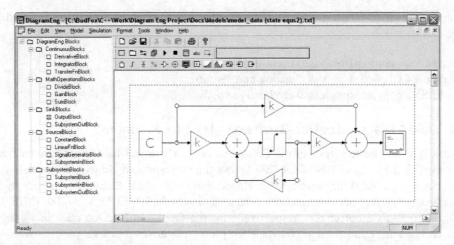

FIGURE 29.1 Selecting the complete diagram automatically, as shown by the gray rectangle, by choosing Select All from the Edit menu.

Operations toolbar, the state of the select-all action (if active) needs to be reset. Hence, add the code shown in bold to the `CDiagramEngDoc::OnInitTrackMultipleItems()` function, to turn off the select-all state prior to performing any diagram entity movement subsequently done via `CDiagramEngDoc::TrackItem()`.

```
void CDiagramEngDoc::OnInitTrackMultipleItems()
{
    // TODO: Add your command handler code here

    // DiagramEng (start)
    int key_flag = 1;      // 0 => can't call TrackMultipleItems(),
      1 => can call TrackMultipleItems.

    // Reset select-all action
    ResetSelectAll();

    // Set the m_iKeyFlagTrack member variable using SetKeyFlagTrack(1)
    SetKeyFlagTrack(key_flag);

    // DiagramEng (end)
}
```

Now if the user runs the application and chooses Select All from the Edit menu, the entire diagram is selected as shown in Figure 29.1. If the user performs a left-button-down event or selects the Track Multiple Items button, then the select-all state is deactivated.

29.3 CUT, COPY, AND PASTE

The cut, copy, and paste operations allow the user to edit a system model diagram through the use of a clipboard object that has a list of blocks and connections to store selected diagram entities. In order to copy blocks and connections, copy constructors and the related accessor methods need to be added to the project for the following classes (in alphabetical order): CBlock, CBlockShape, CConnection, and CPort, and all the derived CBlock-based classes. In addition, the CDiagramEngDoc-based event-handler functions, `OnEditCut()`, `OnEditCopy()`, and `OnEditPaste()`, need to be associated with their corresponding object IDs to perform editing operations. The general steps to add the edit-based functionality to the project are as listed, where specific details follow:

1. Add CDiagramEngDoc-based event-handler functions.
2. Add the CClipboard class declaration and definition.
3. Add class copy constructors and related methods.

29.3.1   ADD CDiagramEngDoc-BASED EVENT-HANDLER FUNCTIONS

The Cut, Copy, and Paste entries of the Edit menu currently do not have event-handler functions associated with their object IDs: Table 29.1 shows the corresponding object, properties, settings, and functions to be added for these actions. Hence, add the OnEditCut(), OnEditCopy(), and OnEditPaste() event-handler functions corresponding to the ID_EDIT_CUT, ID_EDIT_COPY, and ID_EDIT_PASTE object IDs, respectively, for the CDiagramEngDoc class using the Class Wizard, and edit these functions as shown. Their prototypes are as follows.

1. void CDiagramEngDoc::OnEditCut(void)
2. void CDiagramEngDoc::OnEditCopy(void)
3. void CDiagramEngDoc::OnEditPaste(void)

```
void CDiagramEngDoc::OnEditCut()
{
    // TODO: Add your command handler code here
    // DiagramEng (start)
    int intersected = 0;
    int intersected_head = 0;
    int intersected_tail = 0;
    double blk_width;
    double delta = 0.25*m_dDeltaLength;
    //CBlock *pBlock = NULL;
    //CConnection *pCon = NULL;
    CPoint blk_posn;
    CPoint head_pt;
    CPoint tail_pt;
    CRectTracker temp_tracker;
    list<CBlock*> &blk_list = m_SystemModel.GetBlockList();
    //list<CBlock*> &blk_list_cb = m_Clipboard.GetBlockList();
    list<CBlock*>::iterator it_blk;
    list<CConnection*> &con_list = m_SystemModel.GetConnectionList();
    //list<CConnection*> &con_list_cb = m_Clipboard.GetConnectionList();
    list<CConnection*>::iterator it_con;

    // -- IF A RUBBER BAND HAS BEEN CREATED
    if(m_iRubberBandCreated == 1)
    {
        // Create a temp tracker since m_RectTracker will have its coords
        //   updated when the rubber band is moved.
        temp_tracker = m_RectTracker;

        // -- ITERATE THROUGH BLOCKS
        it_blk = blk_list.begin();
        while(it_blk != blk_list.end())
        {
            // Get block properties
            blk_posn = (*it_blk)->GetBlockPosition();
            blk_width = (*it_blk)->GetBlockShape().GetBlockWidth();
```

```
            // Determine if item lies within rubber band
            intersected = DetermineCurrentAndIntersectRects
              (temp_tracker, blk_posn, (blk_width*0.5));
            if(intersected)
            {
                // COPY BLOCK TO CLIPBOARD BLOCK LIST
                //pBlock = (*it_blk)->CopyBlockData();
                //blk_list_cb.push_back(pBlock);

                // Delete Output Block View
                DeleteOutputBlockView(*it_blk);

                // Delete block
                delete *it_blk;     // delete block pointed to by it_blk
                it_blk = blk_list.erase(it_blk); // delete element at
                  offset it_blk in list (that held the block)
            }
            else    // only increment the iterator if there were no
              intersection
            {
                it_blk++;
            }
        }// end for it_blk

        // -- ITERATE THROUGH ALL CONNECTIONS (of this model)
        it_con = con_list.begin();
        while(it_con != con_list.end())
        {
            // -- CHECK HEAD OR TAIL POINT SELECTED (denoting connection
              selection)

            // -- Get Tail Point
            tail_pt = (*it_con)->GetConnectionPointTail();

            // Determine if item lies within rubber band
            intersected_tail = DetermineCurrentAndIntersectRects
              (temp_tracker, tail_pt, delta);

            // -- Get Head Point
            head_pt = (*it_con)->GetConnectionPointHead();

            // Determine if item lies within rubber band
            intersected_head = DetermineCurrentAndIntersectRects
              (temp_tracker, head_pt, delta);

            // -- Check if head or tail points circumscribed
            if(intersected_tail || intersected_head)
            {
                // COPY CONNECTION TO CLIPBOARD CONNECTION LIST
                //pCon = new CConnection(**it_con);
                //con_list_cb.push_back(pCon);

                // Disconnect all tail points from all the bend points on
                  this connection.
                DisconnectTailPointsFromBendPoints(*it_con);
                // Delete connection
                delete *it_con;     // delete actual connection pointed to
                  by it_con
```

```
            it_con = con_list.erase(it_con); // delete element at
              offset it_con in list (that held the connection)
        }
        else
        {
            it_con++;
        }
    }// end for it_con

    // Reset member vars.
    m_iRubberBandCreated = 0;  // end the rubber band state
    SetKeyFlagTrack(0);        // reset the key-based track flag since
      tracking aborted

    // Set flags
    SetModifiedFlag(TRUE);     // set the doc. as having been modified
      to prompt user to save
    UpdateAllViews(NULL);      // indicate that sys. should redraw.

  }// end if m_iRubberBandCreated

  // DiagramEng (end)
}
```

The CDiagramEngDoc::OnEditCut() method functions in a similar manner to the OnEditDeleteGroupedItems() function of the same class: the list of blocks and connections are iterated over, and if they lie within the tracking rectangle (DetermineCurrentAndIntersectRects()), they may be cut from the system model and copied to a to-be-added clipboard. The lines commented out (shown in bold) will be uncommented later once the clipboard and copy constructor functionality is added to the project.

The CopyBlockData() function is called on the pointer-to-CBlock, "pBlock", and based on the derived runtime type of the pointer, the correct CBlock-derived class version of this method will be called to initiate block copy construction (added later).

The connections are also copy-constructed by calling the CConnection copy constructor within the connection-based for loop. The connection-based iterator, "it_con", is dereferenced twice: once to gain access to the pointer-to-CConnection and then a second time to access the CConnection object which is then used in CConnection copy construction (added later).

```
void CDiagramEngDoc::OnEditCopy()
{
    // TODO: Add your command handler code here
    // DiagramEng (start)
    int intersected = 0;
    int intersected_head = 0;
    int intersected_tail = 0;
    double blk_width;
    double delta = 0.25*m_dDeltaLength;
    //CBlock *pBlock = NULL;
    //CConnection *pCon = NULL;
    CPoint blk_posn;
    CPoint head_pt;
    CPoint tail_pt;
    CRectTracker temp_tracker;
    list<CBlock*> &blk_list = m_SystemModel.GetBlockList();
    //list<CBlock*> &blk_list_cb = m_Clipboard.GetBlockList();
```

```
list<CBlock*>::iterator it_blk;
list<CConnection*> &con_list = m_SystemModel.GetConnectionList();
//list<CConnection*> &con_list_cb = m_Clipboard.GetConnectionList();
list<CConnection*>::iterator it_con;

// -- IF A RUBBER BAND HAS BEEN CREATED
if(m_iRubberBandCreated == 1)
{
   // Create a temp tracker since m_RectTracker will have its coords
     updated when the rubber band is moved.
   temp_tracker = m_RectTracker;

   // -- ITERATE THROUGH BLOCKS
   for(it_blk = blk_list.begin(); it_blk != blk_list.end(); it_blk++)
   {
       // Get block properties
       blk_posn = (*it_blk)->GetBlockPosition();
       blk_width = (*it_blk)->GetBlockShape().GetBlockWidth();

       // Determine if item lies within rubber band
       intersected = DetermineCurrentAndIntersectRects
         (temp_tracker, blk_posn, (blk_width*0.5));
       if(intersected)
       {
          //COPY BLOCK TO CLIPBOARD BLOCK LIST
          //pBlock = (*it_blk)->CopyBlockData();
          //blk_list_cb.push_back(pBlock);

       }
   }// end for it_blk

   // -- ITERATE THROUGH ALL CONNECTIONS (of this model)
   for(it_con = con_list.begin(); it_con != con_list.end(); it_con++)
   {
       // -- CHECK HEAD OR TAIL POINT SELECTED (denoting connection
         selection)

       // -- Get Tail Point
       tail_pt = (*it_con)->GetConnectionPointTail();

       // Determine if item lies within rubber band
       intersected_tail = DetermineCurrentAndIntersectRects
         (temp_tracker, tail_pt, delta);

       // -- Get Head Point
       head_pt = (*it_con)->GetConnectionPointHead();

       // Determine if item lies within rubber band
       intersected_head = DetermineCurrentAndIntersectRects
         (temp_tracker, head_pt, delta);

       // -- Check if head or tail points circumscribed
       if(intersected_tail || intersected_head)
       {
          // COPY CONNECTION TO CLIPBOARD CONNECTION LIST
          // pCon = new CConnection(**it_con);
          // con_list_cb.push_back(pCon);
       }
   }// end for it_con
```

```
        // Reset member vars.
        m_iRubberBandCreated = 0;  // end the rubber band state
        SetKeyFlagTrack(0);         // reset the key-based track flag since
        tracking aborted

        // Set flags
        SetModifiedFlag(TRUE);      // set the doc. as having been modified
        to prompt user to save
        UpdateAllViews (NULL);      // indicate that sys. should redraw.

    }// end if m_iRubberBandCreated

    // DiagramEng (end)
}
```

The CDiagramEngDoc::OnEditCopy() function is similar in structure to OnEditCut() with the exception of deleting any system-model-based entities, i.e., blocks or connections. In addition, the developer will notice that only whole connections and not individual connection-based bend points may be cut or copied: this is the case since a bend point is associated with a connection object and is not treated as a separate entity.

```
void CDiagramEngDoc::OnEditPaste()
{
    // TODO: Add your command handler code here
    // DiagramEng (start)
    list<CBlock*> &blk_list = m_SystemModel.GetBlockList();
    //list<CBlock*> &blk_list_cb = m_Clipboard.GetBlockList();
    list<CBlock*>::iterator it_blk;
    list<CConnection*> &con_list = m_SystemModel.GetConnectionList();
    //list<CConnection*> &con_list_cb = m_Clipboard.
      GetConnectionList();
    list<CConnection*>::iterator it_con;

    // Add clipboard block list contents to end of system model block
      list
    // merge() merges the arg list into the list upon which merge() is
      called leaving, the arg list empty.
    //blk_list.merge(blk_list_cb);

    // Add clipboard connection list contents to end of system model
      connection list
    // merge() merges the arg list into the list upon which merge() is
      called, leaving the arg list empty.
    //con_list.merge(con_list_cb);

    // Snap connection end points to port or bend point
    SnapConnectionEndPointsAfterInitialConstruction();

    // Set flags
    SetModifiedFlag(TRUE);          // set the doc. as having been modified
      to prompt user to save
    UpdateAllViews (NULL);          // indicate that sys. should redraw.

    // DiagramEng (end)
}
```

The CDiagramEngDoc::OnEditPaste() function gets the block list, "blk_list_cb", and connection list, "con_list_cb", from the clipboard object, "m_Clipboard" (to be added later), and merges these lists with the corresponding system-model-based lists, "blk_list and "con_list", respectively.

The "merge" operation for the lists used earlier merges the list argument with "*this", i.e., the object upon which merge is called, and empties the argument list [1]: i.e., the clipboard lists are merged with the system model lists and the former lists emptied. After the merge is complete, the function `SnapConnectionEndPointsAfterInitialConstruction()` is called, since in the copy construction procedure (to be added), the CConnection-based pointer members, "m_pRefFromPort", "m_pRefToPort", and "m_pRefFromPoint", are intentionally set to NULL (see the following text), and hence, these need to be set after the underlying block and connection lists have been established. These pointers are set to NULL for two reasons: (1) if a copy (using Edit/Copy) of a connection is being made and the connection is attached to a bend point or a port, then the copy cannot refer to the same port in the diagram from which it was copy-constructed, and (2) if a connection is being cut (using Edit/Cut) and an associated bend point or port is not selected (using the tracking rectangle) in the cut operation, then the pointers should not refer to any port or point but rather be NULL.

29.3.2   ADD THE CClipboard CLASS DECLARATION AND DEFINITION

The `OnEditCut()`, `OnEditCopy()`, and `OnEditPaste()` functions provided earlier all make use of a clipboard object, "m_Clipboard", of type CClipboard, to store the edited selection, i.e., blocks and connections, in the form of lists. Hence, a new class is to be added to the DiagramEng project and can be done so by right-clicking the uppermost node named "DiagramEng Classes" in the ClassView tab of the Workspace pane of the IDE. The class declaration shown in the "Clipboard.h" header file has a constructor, destructor, list deletion functions, accessor methods, and two member variables: a list of pointers-to-CBlock, "list<CBlock*> m_lstBlock", and a list of pointers-to-CConnection, "list<CConnection*> m_lstConnection".

```
// Clipboard.h: interface for the CClipboard class.
//
//////////////////////////////////////////////////////////////////////
#if !defined(AFX_CLIPBOARD_H__5210B53D_33D5_4DB0_8E84_E3E7727EE65B__INCLUDED_)
#define AFX_CLIPBOARD_H__5210B53D_33D5_4DB0_8E84_E3E7727EE65B__INCLUDED_

#if _MSC_VER > 1000
#pragma once
#endif // _MSC_VER > 1000

class CClipboard
{
public:
    // Constr./Destr.
    CClipboard();
    virtual ~CClipboard();

    // General Fns.
    void DeleteBlockList(void);
    void DeleteConnectionList(void);

    // Accessor Fns.
    list<CBlock*> &GetBlockList(void);
    list<CConnection*> &GetConnectionList(void);

private:
    list<CBlock*> m_lstBlock;              // list of ptrs-to-CBlock
    list<CConnection*> m_lstConnection; // list of ptrs-to-CConnection
};

#endif // !defined(AFX_CLIPBOARD_H__5210B53D_33D5_4DB0_8E84_
  E3E7727EE65B__INCLUDED_)
```

The class member methods may be added either through the Workspace pane or manually, as shown in the "Clipboard.cpp" source file. The developer will need to include both the "Block.h" and "Signal.h" header files for CBlock and CConnection class declarations, respectively, as shown.

```cpp
// Clipboard.cpp: implementation of the CClipboard class.
//
//////////////////////////////////////////////////////////////////////

#include "stdafx.h"
#include "DiagramEng.h"
#include "Block.h"        // rqd. for CBlock objs.
#include "Signal.h"       // rqd. for CConnection objs.
#include "Clipboard.h"

#ifdef _DEBUG
#undef THIS_FILE
static char THIS_FILE[]=__FILE__;
#define new DEBUG_NEW
#endif

//////////////////////////////////////////////////////////////////////
// Construction/Destruction
//////////////////////////////////////////////////////////////////////

CClipboard::CClipboard()
{
    // Do nothing for now
}

CClipboard::~CClipboard()
{
    // Delete block list
    DeleteBlockList();

    // Delete connection list
    DeleteConnectionList();
}

list<CBlock*> &CClipboard::GetBlockList()
{
    return m_lstBlock;
}

list<CConnection*> &CClipboard::GetConnectionList()
{
    // Return the connection list by reference
    return m_lstConnection;
}

void CClipboard::DeleteBlockList()
{
    list<CBlock*>::iterator it_blk;

    // Delete block list
    for(it_blk = m_lstBlock.begin(); it_blk != m_lstBlock.end();
      it_blk++)
```

```
    {
        delete (*it_blk);  // delete what it_blk is pointing to:
            i.e. deref the it_blk ptr and delete the ptr-to-CBlock.
    }
    m_lstBlock.clear();
}
void CClipboard::DeleteConnectionList()
{
    list<CConnection*>::iterator it_con;

    // Delete connection list
    for(it_con = m_lstConnection.begin(); it_con != m_lstConnection.
      end(); it_con++)
    {
        delete (*it_con);  // delete what it_conn is pointing to:
            i.e. deref the it_conn ptr and delete the ptr-to-CConnection.
    }
    m_lstConnection.clear();
}
```

The class constructor function does nothing at present but may be added to later. The class destructor deletes the block and connection lists using DeleteBlockList() and DeleteConnectionList(), respectively: these functions both iterate through their respective member lists, dereferencing the list iterator and deleting the pointer, implicitly calling the appropriate class destructors to destroy their objects. Thereafter, the lists are cleared using clear(). The accessor functions GetBlockList() and GetConnectionList() simply return, by reference, the member lists, "m_lstBlock" and "m_lstConnection", respectively. The behavior of the accessor functions and list deletion methods is identical to those used for the CSystemModel class.

Finally, add the new CClipboard object named, "m_Clipboard", to the CDiagramEngDoc class declaration. No special construction is required for this object in the CDiagramEngDoc class constructor, and hence, the latter need not be changed. In addition, the "Clipboard.h" header file should be included at the top of the "DiagramEngDoc.h" header file, since the CDiagramEngDoc class contains the CClipboard object, "m_Clipboard".

29.3.3 ADD CLASS COPY CONSTRUCTORS AND RELATED METHODS

The CDiagramEngDoc functions OnEditCut() and OnEditCopy() shown earlier both initiate the block copying procedure using a function named CopyBlockData() that is called upon a pointer-to-CBlock, "pBlock": this is the case since the blocks that need to be copied are all derived from the base CBlock class and a virtual method is required such that the correct copy constructor can be invoked based upon the derived runtime type of the CBlock pointer. The CConnection class has no derived classes, and hence, the copy constructor for connection objects may be called directly.

29.3.3.1 CBlock Copy Constructor

The base CBlock class methods to be added to the project to allow general block copy construction are CopyBlockData() and the new CBlock copy constructor. Hence, add a virtual function to the CBlock class with the following prototype, virtual CBlock *CBlock::CopyBlockData(void), and edit it as shown.

```
CBlock *CBlock::CopyBlockData()
{
    return NULL;     // derived block class will return newly constructed
    blocks
}
```

The developer will notice that this virtual base CBlock class version of the `CopyBlockData()` function returns a NULL pointer: the derived block class implementations will return a pointer-to-CBlock, i.e., the address of a new block object constructed using the appropriate derived block class copy constructor. But since only derived blocks represent complete blocks, the base `CBlock::CopyBlockData()` method should return a NULL pointer.

The base CBlock class copy constructor may be added with prototype, `CBlock::CBlock(constCBlock &blk)`, as shown, to invoke the CBlockShape copy constructor through initialization and then extract the variable values from the reference-to-constant-CBlock variable, "blk", and assign these to the underlying member variables of the block under construction.

```
CBlock::CBlock(const CBlock &blk):
m_BlockShape(blk.m_BlockShape)    // call the contained object's copy
  constructor
{
    m_iPenColor = blk.GetPenColor();
    m_iPenWidth = blk.GetPenWidth();
    m_pParentSystemModel = blk.GetParentSystemModel();
    m_pSubSystemModel = blk.GetSubSystemModel();
    m_ptBlockPosition = blk.GetBlockPosition();
    m_strBlockName = blk.GetBlockName();
}
```

The developer will have noticed the call to get a pointer to a possibly contained subsystem model, "m_pSubSystemModel". Hence add a public member function to the CBlock class with the following prototype, `CSystemModel *CBlock::GetSubSystemModel(void) const`, and edit the function as shown:

```
CSystemModel *CBlock::GetSubSystemModel() const
{
    return m_pSubSystemModel;
}
```

The accessor functions used in the CBlock copy constructor provided earlier are all constant member functions: this is consistent with the incoming argument "blk" being a reference-to-a-constant-CBlock object.

In the work that follows, the derived block classes are required to make a copy of the vectors of input and/or output ports. At present, the functions `GetVectorOfInputPorts()` and `GetVectorOfOutputPorts()` return, as a reference-to-vector<CPort*>, the underlying members "m_vecInputPorts" and "m_vecOutputPorts", respectively. This is useful if the underlying members are to be acted upon, or changed, in which case these accessor functions should not be constant. However, for the purpose of derived (CBlock) type copy construction and the need for constructor arguments to be constant, two new member functions need to be introduced to the CBlock class that return the base address of these vectors: i.e., a pointer-to-a-constant-vector<CPort*> is returned. Hence, add two constant public member functions to the CBlock class with the following prototypes, and edit the functions as shown.

1. `const vector<CPort*> *CBlock::GetVectorOfOutputPortsCopy(void) const`
2. `const vector<CPort*> *CBlock::GetVectorOfInputPortsCopy(void) const`

```
const vector<CPort*> *CBlock::GetVectorOfOutputPortsCopy() const
{
    // For the fn to be const, a ptr-to-const type (vector<CPort*>) is
      returned.
    return &m_vecOutputPorts;
}
```

```
const vector<CPort*> *CBlock::GetVectorOfInputPortsCopy() const
{
    // For the fn to be const, a ptr-to-const type (vector<CPort*>) is
      returned.
    return &m_vecInputPorts;
}
```

The keyword "const" is required for the function itself and also the pointer being returned, since to satisfy the constant state, what is being pointed to (as a result of using the "address of" (&) operator), i.e., the vector of CPort pointers (vector<CPort*>), must also be constant.

29.3.3.2 CBlockShape Copy Constructor

The CBlock class has a contained CBlockShape object named, "m_BlockShape", as may be seen in the CBlock declaration in the "Block.h" header file. In the CBlock copy constructor provided earlier, the copy constructor of the CBlockShape class is called passing in the "m_BlockShape" member to be used in the ensuing initialization. Hence, add a copy constructor to the CBlockShape class with the prototype, CBlockShape(const CBlockShape &bs), and edit it as shown:

```
CBlockShape::CBlockShape(const CBlockShape &bs)
{
    m_eBlockDirection = bs.GetBlockDirection();
    m_eBlockShape = bs.GetBlockShapeType();
    m_dBlockWidth = bs.GetBlockWidth();
    m_dBlockHeight = bs.GetBlockHeight();
}
```

The four constant accessor methods are called upon the incoming argument "bs" to initialize the underlying CBlockShape object.

29.3.3.3 CPort Copy Constructor

Each block has two vectors of pointers-to-CPort: one for input ports, "m_vecInputPorts", and the other for output ports, "m_vecOutputPorts". In the derived block class methods, these vectors of pointers-to-CPort objects are iterated over, and new ports may be constructed based upon two arguments: the port object and also the block upon which the port resides. This is required, since in the construction of a new port, the reference-to-CBlock member variable, "m_rRefToBlock", needs to be initialized. Hence, add a copy constructor to the CPort class with the following prototype, CPort::CPort(const CPort &port, CBlock &blk), and edit the function as shown.

```
CPort::CPort(const CPort &port, CBlock &blk):
m_rRefToBlock(blk)
{
    m_ePortArrowDirec = port.GetPortArrowDirection();
    m_dPortPositionAngle = port.GetPortPositionAngle();
    m_ptPortPosition = port.GetPortPosition();
    m_ptPortSignPosition = port.GetPortSignPosition();
    m_strPortName = port.GetPortName();
}
```

The developer should be aware that the reference-to-CBlock, "blk", is not constant, since the member variable, "m_rRefToBlock", being initialized with "blk" is itself not a constant reference-to-CBlock. However, all the CPort accessor methods are constant.

29.3.3.4 CConnection Copy Constructor

The CConnection class is not derived from a superclass nor are subclasses derived from it: however, it does contain a pointer-to-CSignal, "m_pSignal", which records the signal data value that is passed from one block to another. As this is a transient object, its initialization is not required, although it must still be constructed. Here, a copy constructor is to be provided for the CConnection class with prototype, CConnection::CConnection(const CConnection &con), and edited as shown.

```
CConnection::CConnection(const CConnection &con)
{
    // NOTE - The copying action does not copy the pointer references.
    // Hence, SnapConnectionEndPointsAfterInitialConstruction() must be
      called to initialize the pointers (later).

    m_lstBendPoints = con.GetConnectionBendPointsListCopy();  // get a
      copy of the bend pts list (by val, not by ref.)
    m_ptHead = con.GetConnectionPointHead();   // pt to which connection
      is drawn
    m_ptTail = con.GetConnectionPointTail();   // pt from which connection
      is drawn
    m_pRefFromPoint = NULL;                     // not connected to a bend
      point initially
    m_pRefFromPort = NULL;                      // from-port ref.
    m_pRefToPort = NULL;                        // to-port ref.
    m_pSignal = new CSignal;                    // contained ptr-to-CSignal
      (no data)
}
```

The developer will notice that in order to preserve the constant nature of the incoming "con" argument, the connection-based bend points list, "m_lstBendPoints", must be retrieved by value rather than by reference. Previously, the GetConnectionBendPointsList() function was used to return a reference-to-list<CPoint>: here, however, a copy of the list should be returned (by value). Hence, add a constant public member function to the CConnection class with the following prototype, list<CPoint> CConnection::GetConnectionBendPointsListCopy() const, and edit the function as shown, to return a copy of the member list.

```
list<CPoint> CConnection::GetConnectionBendPointsListCopy() const
{
    // Return A COPY OF the connection's bend points list (i.e. not by
      reference)
    return m_lstBendPoints;
}
```

29.3.3.5 CConstantBlock Copy Constructor

All the CBlock-based derived block classes require copy constructors, where the input argument is a reference to a CBlock object. Hence, add a copy constructor to the CConstantBlock class with the following prototype, CConstantBlock::CConstantBlock(const CConstantBlock &blk),

and edit it as shown. Note the call to the base CBlock class copy constructor in the initialization list (shown in bold): this allows the base member variables to be constructed prior to construction of the derived member variables.

```
CConstantBlock::CConstantBlock(const CConstantBlock &blk):
CBlock(blk)
{
    m_strConstValue = blk.GetStringConstValue();
    m_dConstMatrix = ConvertStringToDouble(m_strConstValue, m_iNrows,
      m_iNcols);

    // Port Construction
    const vector<CPort*> *p_vec_output_ports = blk.
      GetVectorOfOutputPortsCopy();
    vector<CPort*>::const_iterator it_port;   // const iterator for const
      vector of CPort ptrs.

    for(it_port = (*p_vec_output_ports).begin(); it_port
      != (*p_vec_output_ports).end(); it_port++)
    {
        // Deref it_port to get ptr-to-CPort and then deref the
          ptr-to-CPort to get CPort.
        CPort *p_output_port = new CPort(**it_port, *this); // CPort copy
          constructor
        GetVectorOfOutputPorts().push_back(p_output_port);   // add the
          new port
    }
}
```

The developer will have noticed the call to a new method named, GetStringConstValue(): this function returns the CString, "m_strConstValue", member which retains the CString equivalent of the double constant matrix, "m_dConstMatrix". The double constant matrix and its dimensions are then reconstructed based upon the CString member through the call to ConvertStringToDouble(). Hence, add a new constant public member function to the CConstantBlock class with the prototype, CString CConstantBlock::GetStringConstValue(void) const, and edit it as shown.

```
CString CConstantBlock::GetStringConstValue() const
{
    return m_strConstValue;
}
```

In addition, for the input argument to the CConstantBlock copy constructor to be a reference to a constant CBlock, the CBlock::GetVectorOfOutputPortsCopy() function, introduced earlier, is called to return a pointer to a constant vector of pointers-to-CPort (const vector<CPort*> *).

Furthermore, when iterating through the vector, the iterator, "it_port", must be a constant iterator, "const_iterator", to be consistent with the const vector of pointers-to-CPort. To start the *for* loop, the pointer, "p_vec_output_ports", is dereferenced to access the first element of the vector, i.e., (*p_vec_output_ports).begin(). In the body of the loop, when the CPort copy constructor is called, the iterator is dereferenced twice (**it_port): once to gain access to the CPort-pointer and a second time to dereference the CPort-pointer to gain access to the CPort object itself. This object is then passed as an argument to the constructor, where upon entry in the latter, is a reference to a constant CPort object (as shown in Section 29.3.3.3).

Finally, to invoke the copy constructor, the virtual method, `CopyBlockData()`, is to be overridden in the derived CConstantBlock class. Hence, add a new public virtual member function to the CConstantBlock class with the prototype, `virtual CBlock *CConstantBlock::CopyBlockData(void)`, and edit it as shown.

```
CBlock *CConstantBlock::CopyBlockData(void)
{
    //AfxMessageBox("\n CConstantBlock::CopyBlockData()\n", MB_OK, 0);

    // Create a new CConstantBlock
    CBlock *pBlock = new CConstantBlock(*this);

    return pBlock;
}
```

29.3.3.5.1 Testing the Cut, Copy, and Paste Operations

Now that the copy constructors are in place for the CBlock, CBlockShape, CConnection, CConstantBlock, and CPort classes, the lines commented out in bold in the `OnEditCut()`, `OnEditCopy()`, and `OnEditPaste()` functions introduced earlier may now be uncommented and the application tested, to see if a connection object and a constant block may be edited. Figure 29.2 shows (a) a selection of items, including a Constant block and connections attached to bend points and an output port, and (b) the pasted items after the original selection was moved to the right after copying initiated, to make room for the ensuing paste. Upon moving the items, all connection end points remain connected to their respective bend points or block output port since the function `SnapConnectionEndPointsAfterInitialConstruction()` is called in `CDiagramEngDoc::OnEditPaste()`.

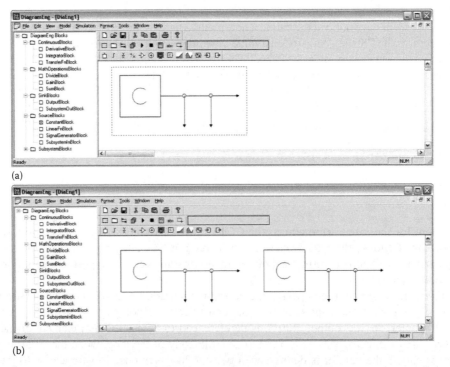

FIGURE 29.2 A copy and paste action of CConstantBlock and CConnection objects: (a) a selection of items to be edited and (b) items pasted after moving the original selection to the right.

29.3.3.6   CDerivativeBlock Copy Constructor

The CDerivativeBlock copy constructor is of a similar structure to that of the CConstantBlock in that a CBlock reference is passed as a parameter and the CBlock base class constructor is initially called. Add a public member function to the CDerivativeBlock class with the following prototype, CDerivativeBlock::CDerivativeBlock(const CDerivativeBlock &blk), and edit the function as shown.

```
CDerivativeBlock::CDerivativeBlock(const CDerivativeBlock &blk):
CBlock(blk)
{
    m_iDerivativeMethod = blk.GetDerivativeMethod(); // derivative method

    // Dynamical variables reset for each new simulation
    m_iNcallsPerTimeCnt = 0;          // no. of times the fn is called per
      t_cnt (time point)
    m_iNrows = 0;                     // no. of rows of output matrix signal
    m_i_t_cnt_ref = 0;                // ref time cnt
    m_f_at_t_minus_h = NULL;          // f(t-h)
    m_f_at_t_minus_2h = NULL;         // f(t-2h)
    m_dMatrixOut = NULL;              // matrix output signal

    // Port Construction
    const vector<CPort*> *p_vec_input_ports = blk.
      GetVectorOfInputPortsCopy();
    const vector<CPort*> *p_vec_output_ports = blk.
      GetVectorOfOutputPortsCopy();
    vector<CPort*>::const_iterator it_port;     // const iterator for
      const vector of CPort ptrs.

    for(it_port = (*p_vec_input_ports).begin(); it_port
      != (*p_vec_input_ports).end(); it_port++)
    {
        // Deref it_port to get ptr-to-CPort and then deref the
          ptr-to-CPort to get CPort.
        CPort *p_input_port = new CPort(**it_port, *this);  // CPort copy
          constructor
        GetVectorOfInputPorts().push_back(p_input_port);    // add the
          new port
    }

    for(it_port = (*p_vec_output_ports).begin(); it_port
      != (*p_vec_output_ports).end(); it_port++)
    {
        // Deref it_port to get ptr-to-CPort and then deref the
          ptr-to-CPort to get CPort.
        CPort *p_output_port = new CPort(**it_port, *this); // CPort copy
          constructor
        GetVectorOfOutputPorts().push_back(p_output_port);  // add the
          new port
    }
}
```

The developer will notice that in the constructor, the derivative method is obtained by an accessor function. Hence, add a public constant member function to the CDerivativeBlock class with the following prototype, `int CDerivativeBlock::GetDerivativeMethod(void) const`, and edit it as shown.

```
int CDerivativeBlock::GetDerivativeMethod() const
{
    return m_iDerivativeMethod;
}
```

Finally, the overriding public virtual `CopyBlockData()` function needs to be added to the CDerivativeBlock class. The prototype is `virtual CBlock *CDerivativeBlock::CopyBlockData(void)`, and the function should be edited as shown.

```
CBlock* CDerivativeBlock::CopyBlockData()
{
    // Create a new CDerivativeBlock
    CBlock *pBlock = new CDerivativeBlock(*this);

    return pBlock;
}
```

29.3.3.7   CDivideBlock Copy Constructor

Add the public CDivideBlock copy constructor function to the CDivideBlock class, with prototype, `CDivideBlock::CDivideBlock(const CDivideBlock &blk)`, and edit it as shown.

```
CDivideBlock::CDivideBlock(const CDivideBlock &blk):
CBlock(blk)
{
    m_iNMultiplyInputs = blk.GetNMultiplyInputs();
    m_iNDivideInputs = blk.GetNDivideInputs();
    m_iMultType = blk.GetMultType();
    m_strInitSignal = blk.GetStringInitialSignal();
    m_dInitSignal = ConvertStringToDouble(m_strInitSignal,
      m_iNrowsInitSignal, m_iNcolsInitSignal);

    // Port Construction
    const vector<CPort*> *p_vec_input_ports = blk.
      GetVectorOfInputPortsCopy();
    const vector<CPort*> *p_vec_output_ports = blk.
      GetVectorOfOutputPortsCopy();
    vector<CPort*>::const_iterator it_port;    // const iterator for
      const vector of CPort ptrs.

    for(it_port = (*p_vec_input_ports).begin(); it_port
      != (*p_vec_input_ports).end(); it_port++)
    {
        // Deref it_port to get ptr-to-CPort and then deref the
          ptr-to-CPort to get CPort.
        CPort *p_input_port = new CPort(**it_port, *this);  // CPort copy
          constructor
        GetVectorOfInputPorts().push_back(p_input_port);    // add the
          new port
    }

    for(it_port = (*p_vec_output_ports).begin(); it_port
      != (*p_vec_output_ports).end(); it_port++)
```

```
    {
        // Deref it_port to get ptr-to-CPort and then deref the
        ptr-to-CPort to get CPort.
        CPort *p_output_port = new CPort(**it_port, *this); // CPort copy
        constructor
        GetVectorOfOutputPorts().push_back(p_output_port);  // add the
        new port
    }
}
```

Four constant accessor functions, with the prototypes given, need to be added to the CDivideBlock class to retrieve the member variables: edit these functions as shown.

1. int CDivideBlock::GetNMultiplyInputs(void) const
2. int CDivideBlock::GetNDivideInputs(void) const
3. int CDivideBlock::GetMultType(void) const
4. CString CDivideBlock::GetStringInitialSignal(void) const

```
int CDivideBlock::GetNMultiplyInputs() const
{
    return m_iNMultiplyInputs;
}

int CDivideBlock::GetNDivideInputs() const
{
    return m_iNDivideInputs;
}

int CDivideBlock::GetMultType() const
{
    return m_iMultType;
}

CString CDivideBlock::GetStringInitialSignal() const
{
    return m_strInitSignal;
}
```

Finally, the public virtual CopyBlockData() method with the prototype, virtual CBlock *CDivideBlock::CopyBlockData(void), may be added as shown.

```
CBlock* CDivideBlock::CopyBlockData()
{
    // Create a new CDivideBlock
    CBlock *pBlock = new CDivideBlock(*this);

    return pBlock;
}
```

29.3.3.8 CGainBlock Copy Constructor

Add the public CGainBlock copy constructor function to the CGainBlock class, with prototype, CGainBlock::CGainBlock(const CGainBlock &blk), and edit it as shown.

```
CGainBlock::CGainBlock(const CGainBlock &blk):
CBlock(blk)
{
    m_iGainType = blk.GetGainType();
    m_strGainValue = blk.GetStringGainValue();
    m_dGainMatrix = ConvertStringToDouble(m_strGainValue, m_iNrows, m_iNcols);
```

```
    // Port Construction
    const vector<CPort*> *p_vec_input_ports = blk.
      GetVectorOfInputPortsCopy();
    const vector<CPort*> *p_vec_output_ports = blk.
      GetVectorOfOutputPortsCopy();
    vector<CPort*>::const_iterator it_port;    // const iterator for
      const vector of CPort ptrs.

    for(it_port = (*p_vec_input_ports).begin(); it_port
      != (*p_vec_input_ports).end(); it_port++)
    {
        // Deref it_port to get ptr-to-CPort and then deref the ptr-to-
          CPort to get CPort.
        CPort *p_input_port = new CPort(**it_port, *this);   // CPort copy
          constructor
        GetVectorOfInputPorts().push_back(p_input_port);     // add the
          new port
    }

    for(it_port = (*p_vec_output_ports).begin(); it_port
      != (*p_vec_output_ports).end(); it_port++)
    {
        // Deref it_port to get ptr-to-CPort and then deref the
          ptr-to-CPort to get CPort.
        CPort *p_output_port = new CPort(**it_port, *this); // CPort copy
          constructor
        GetVectorOfOutputPorts().push_back(p_output_port);  // add the
          new port
    }
}
```

The developer will have noticed the introduction of two accessor functions to retrieve the gain type, "m_iGainType", and CString gain value, "m_strGainValue", which is then converted into a double matrix. Hence, add the following public constant member functions, and edit them as shown.

1. int CGainBlock::GetGainType() const
2. CString CGainBlock::GetStringGainValue() const

```
int CGainBlock::GetGainType() const
{
    return m_iGainType;
}

CString CGainBlock::GetStringGainValue() const
{
    return m_strGainValue;
}
```

Finally, the public virtual CopyBlockData() method with the prototype, virtual CBlock *CGainBlock::CopyBlockData(void), may be added as shown:

```
CBlock* CGainBlock::CopyBlockData()
{
    // Create a new CGainBlock
    CBlock *pBlock = new CGainBlock(*this);

    return pBlock;
}
```

29.3.3.9   CIntegratorBlock Copy Constructor

Add the public CIntegratorBlock copy constructor function to the CIntegratorBlock class, with prototype, CIntegratorBlock::CIntegratorBlock(const CIntegratorBlock &blk), and edit it as shown.

```
CIntegratorBlock::CIntegratorBlock(const CIntegratorBlock &blk):
CBlock(blk)
{
    m_strICVector = blk.GetStringICVector();
    m_dICVector = ConvertStringToDoubleVector(m_strICVector, m_iNrows,
      m_iNcols);
    m_iLength = blk.GetLengthICVector();

    // Dynamical variables reset for each new simulation
    m_iNcallsPerTimeCnt = 0;       // no. of times the fn is called per
      t_cnt (time point)
    m_iNrowsOut = 0;               // no. of rows of output matrix signal
    m_i_t_cnt_ref = 0;             // ref time cnt
    m_dMatrixOut = NULL;           // output matrix signal
    m_y_at_t_minus_h = NULL;       // y(t-h)
    m_y_dot_at_t_minus_h = NULL;   // y_dot(t-h)

    // Port Construction
    const vector<CPort*> *p_vec_input_ports = blk.
      GetVectorOfInputPortsCopy();
    const vector<CPort*> *p_vec_output_ports = blk.
      GetVectorOfOutputPortsCopy();
    vector<CPort*>::const_iterator it_port;    // const iterator for
      const vector of CPort ptrs.

    for(it_port = (*p_vec_input_ports).begin(); it_port
      != (*p_vec_input_ports).end(); it_port++)
    {
        // Deref it_port to get ptr-to-CPort and then deref the
          ptr-to-CPort to get CPort.
        CPort *p_input_port = new CPort(**it_port, *this);  // CPort copy
          constructor
        GetVectorOfInputPorts().push_back(p_input_port);    // add the
          new port
    }

    for(it_port = (*p_vec_output_ports).begin(); it_port
      != (*p_vec_output_ports).end(); it_port++)
    {
        // Deref it_port to get ptr-to-CPort and then deref the
          ptr-to-CPort to get CPort.
        CPort *p_output_port = new CPort(**it_port, *this); // CPort copy
          constructor
        GetVectorOfOutputPorts().push_back(p_output_port);  // add the
          new port
    }
}
```

The developer will have noticed the introduction of two new public constant accessor functions to return the initial condition vector as a CString, "m_strICVector" and the length of the corresponding double vector, "m_iLength". Hence, add the public constant member functions, with the provided prototypes, and edit them as shown.

1. `CString CIntegratorBlock::GetStringICVector(void) const`
2. `int CIntegratorBlock::GetLengthICVector(void) const`

```
CString CIntegratorBlock::GetStringICVector() const
{
    return m_strICVector;
}

int CIntegratorBlock::GetLengthICVector() const
{
    return m_iLength;
}
```

Finally, the public `virtual CopyBlockData()` method with the prototype, `virtual CBlock *CIntegratorBlock::CopyBlockData(void)`, may be added as shown:

```
CBlock* CIntegratorBlock::CopyBlockData()
{
    // Create a new CIntegratorBlock
    CBlock *pBlock = new CIntegratorBlock(*this);

    return pBlock;
}
```

29.3.3.10   CLinearFnBlock Copy Constructor

Add the public CLinearFnBlock copy constructor function to the CLinearFnBlock class, with prototype, `CLinearFnBlock::CLinearFnBlock(const CLinearFnBlock &blk)`, and edit it as shown.

```
CLinearFnBlock::CLinearFnBlock(const CLinearFnBlock &blk):
CBlock(blk)
{
    m_dTimeInit = blk.GetTimeInitial();
    m_dTimeFinal = blk.GetTimeFinal();
    m_dValueInit = blk.GetValueInitial();
    m_dDerivative = blk.GetDerivative();

    // Port Construction
    const vector<CPort*> *p_vec_output_ports = blk.
      GetVectorOfOutputPortsCopy();
    vector<CPort*>::const_iterator it_port;     // const iterator for
      const vector of CPort ptrs.

    for(it_port = (*p_vec_output_ports).begin(); it_port
      != (*p_vec_output_ports).end(); it_port++)
    {
        // Deref it_port to get ptr-to-CPort and then deref the
          ptr-to-CPort to get CPort.
        CPort *p_output_port = new CPort(**it_port, *this); // CPort copy
          constructor
        GetVectorOfOutputPorts().push_back(p_output_port);  // add the
          new port
    }
}
```

The developer will have noticed the introduction of four new public constant member functions to access private member data. Hence, add these accessor functions with the declarations and definitions provided as follows.

1. `double CLinearFnBlock::GetTimeInitial(void) const`
2. `double CLinearFnBlock::GetTimeFinal(void) const`
3. `double CLinearFnBlock::GetValueInitial(void) const`
4. `double CLinearFnBlock::GetDerivative(void) const`

```
double CLinearFnBlock::GetTimeInitial() const
{
    return m_dTimeInit;
}

double CLinearFnBlock::GetTimeFinal() const
{
    return m_dTimeFinal;
}

double CLinearFnBlock::GetValueInitial() const
{
    return m_dValueInit;
}

double CLinearFnBlock::GetDerivative() const
{
    return m_dDerivative;
}
```

Finally, the public `virtual CopyBlockData()` method with the prototype, `virtual CBlock *CLinearFnBlock::CopyBlockData(void)`, may be added as shown:

```
CBlock* CDivideBlock::CopyBlockData()
{
    // Create a new CDivideBlock
    CBlock *pBlock = new CDivideBlock(*this);

    return pBlock;
}
```

29.3.3.11 COutputBlock Copy Constructor

Add the public COutputBlock copy constructor function to the COutputBlock class, with prototype, `COutputBlock::COutputBlock(const COutputBlock &blk)`, and edit it as shown.

```
COutputBlock::COutputBlock(const COutputBlock &blk):
CBlock(blk)
{
    int i;
    int j;
    double **matrix = NULL;

    m_iNotation = blk.GetNotation();
    m_iTimePtDisplay = blk.GetTimePtDisplay();
```

```
blk.GetDataDimensions(m_iNrows, m_iNcols);
matrix = blk.GetOutputMatrix();

// MEMORY NEW
m_dOutputMatrix = new double *[m_iNrows];
for(i=0; i<m_iNrows; i++)
{
    m_dOutputMatrix[i] = new double[m_iNcols];
}

// Assign initial signal values
for(i=0; i<m_iNrows; i++)
{
    for(j=0; j<m_iNcols; j++)
    {
        m_dOutputMatrix[i][j] = matrix[i][j];
    }
}

// Port Construction
const vector<CPort*> *p_vec_input_ports = blk.
  GetVectorOfInputPortsCopy();
vector<CPort*>::const_iterator it_port;    // const iterator for const
  vector of CPort ptrs.

for(it_port = (*p_vec_input_ports).begin(); it_port
  != (*p_vec_input_ports).end(); it_port++)
{
    // Deref it_port to get ptr-to-CPort and then deref the
      ptr-to-CPort to get CPort.
    CPort *p_input_port = new CPort(**it_port, *this);  // CPort copy
      constructor
    GetVectorOfInputPorts().push_back(p_input_port);    // add the
      new port
}
}
```

The developer will notice the four public constant accessor methods that were introduced in the project at an earlier developmental stage. The constant nature of the GetOutputMatrix() function implies that the pointer being returned, i.e., "m_dOutputMatrix" (of the incoming argument "blk"), is constant, although the data pointed to by the pointer may change. After the data and their dimensions are retrieved, new memory is allocated and the data values assigned to the underlying member variable, "m_dOutputMatrix".

Finally, the public virtual CopyBlockData() method with the prototype, virtual CBlock *COutputBlock::CopyBlockData(void), may be added as shown.

```
CBlock* COutputBlock::CopyBlockData()
{
    // Create a new COutputBlock
    CBlock *pBlock = new COutputBlock(*this);

    return pBlock;
}
```

29.3.3.12 CSignalGeneratorBlock Copy Constructor

Add the public CSignalGeneratorBlock copy constructor function to the CSignalGeneratorBlock class, with prototype, `CSignalGeneratorBlock::CSignalGeneratorBlock(const CSignalGeneratorBlock &blk)`, and edit it as shown.

```
CSignalGeneratorBlock::CSignalGeneratorBlock(const CSignalGeneratorBlock &blk):
CBlock(blk)
{
    m_dAmplitude = blk.GetAmplitude();
    m_dFrequency = blk.GetFrequency();
    m_dPhase = blk.GetPhase();
    m_strFnType = blk.GetFnType();
    m_strUnits = blk.GetUnits();

    // Port Construction
    const vector<CPort*> *p_vec_output_ports = blk.
      GetVectorOfOutputPortsCopy();
    vector<CPort*>::const_iterator it_port;        // const iterator for
      const vector of CPort ptrs.

    for(it_port = (*p_vec_output_ports).begin(); it_port
      != (*p_vec_output_ports).end(); it_port++)
    {
        // Deref it_port to get ptr-to-CPort and then deref the
          ptr-to-CPort to get CPort.
        CPort *p_output_port = new CPort(**it_port, *this); // CPort copy
          constructor
        GetVectorOfOutputPorts().push_back(p_output_port);  // add the
          new port
    }
}
```

The developer will have noticed the introduction of five new public constant member functions to access the private member data of the CSignalGeneratorBlock class. Hence, add the accessor methods with the declarations and definitions provided as follows.

1. `double CSignalGeneratorBlock::GetAmplitude() const`
2. `double CSignalGeneratorBlock::GetFrequency() const`
3. `double CSignalGeneratorBlock::GetPhase() const`
4. `CString CSignalGeneratorBlock::GetFnType() const`
5. `CString CSignalGeneratorBlock::GetUnits() const`

```
double CSignalGeneratorBlock::GetAmplitude() const
{
    return m_dAmplitude;
}

double CSignalGeneratorBlock::GetFrequency() const
{
    return m_dFrequency;
}

double CSignalGeneratorBlock::GetPhase() const
{
    return m_dPhase;
}
```

```
CString CSignalGeneratorBlock::GetFnType() const
{
    return m_strFnType
}

CString CSignalGeneratorBlock::GetUnits() const
{
    return m_strUnits;
}
```

Finally, the public `virtual CopyBlockData()` method with the prototype, `virtual CBlock *CSignalGeneratorBlock::CopyBlockData(void)`, may be added as shown.

```
CBlock* CSignalGeneratorBlock::CopyBlockData()
{
    // Create a new CSignalGeneratorBlock
    CBlock *pBlock = new CSignalGeneratorBlock(*this);

    return pBlock;
}
```

29.3.3.13 CSubsystemBlock Copy Constructor

Add the public CSubsystemBlock copy constructor function to the CSubsystemBlock class, with prototype, `CSubsystemBlock::CSubsystemBlock(const CSubsystemBlock &blk)`, and edit it as shown.

```
CSubsystemBlock::CSubsystemBlock(const CSubsystemBlock &blk):
CBlock(blk)
{
    m_strInputPortName = blk.GetInputPortName();
    m_strOutputPortName = blk.GetOutputPortName();

    // Port Construction
    const vector<CPort*> *p_vec_input_ports = blk.
      GetVectorOfInputPortsCopy();
    const vector<CPort*> *p_vec_output_ports = blk.
      GetVectorOfOutputPortsCopy();
    vector<CPort*>::const_iterator it_port;    // const iterator for
      const vector of CPort ptrs.

    for(it_port = (*p_vec_input_ports).begin(); it_port
      != (*p_vec_input_ports).end(); it_port++)
    {
        // Deref it_port to get ptr-to-CPort and then deref the
          ptr-to-CPort to get CPort.
        CPort *p_input_port = new CPort(**it_port, *this);  // CPort copy
          constructor
        GetVectorOfInputPorts().push_back(p_input_port);    // add the
          new port
    }

    for(it_port = (*p_vec_output_ports).begin(); it_port
      != (*p_vec_output_ports).end(); it_port++)
    {
        // Deref it_port to get ptr-to-CPort and then deref the
          ptr-to-CPort to get CPort.
```

```
            CPort *p_output_port = new CPort(**it_port, *this); // CPort copy
                constructor
            GetVectorOfOutputPorts().push_back(p_output_port);   // add the
                new port
    }
}
```

The developer will have noticed the two new public constant methods to retrieve the CString member variables. Hence, add the accessor methods with the declarations and definitions provided as follows.

1. CString CSubsystemBlock::GetInputPortName(void) const
2. CString CSubsystemBlock::GetOutputPortName(void) const

```
CString CSubsystemBlock::GetInputPortName() const
{
    return m_strInputPortName;
}

CString CSubsystemBlock::GetOutputPortName() const
{
    return m_strOutputPortName;
}
```

Finally, the public virtual CopyBlockData() method with the prototype, virtual CBlock *CSubsystemBlock::CopyBlockData(void), may be added as shown:

```
CBlock* CSubsystemBlock::CopyBlockData()
{
    // Create a new CSubsystemBlock
    CBlock *pBlock = new CSubsystemBlock(*this);

    return pBlock;
}
```

29.3.3.14   CSubsystemInBlock Copy Constructor

Add the public CSubsystemInBlock copy constructor function to the CSubsystemInBlock class, with prototype, CSubsystemInBlock::CSubsystemInBlock(const CSubsystemInBlock &blk), and edit it as shown.

```
CSubsystemInBlock::CSubsystemInBlock(const CSubsystemInBlock &blk):
CBlock(blk)
{
    m_strInputPortName = blk.GetInputPortName();

    // Port Construction

    const vector<CPort*> *p_vec_output_ports = blk.
      GetVectorOfOutputPortsCopy();
    vector<CPort*>::const_iterator it_port;    // const iterator for
      const vector of CPort ptrs.

    for(it_port = (*p_vec_output_ports).begin(); it_port
      != (*p_vec_output_ports).end(); it_port++)
```

```
    {
        // Deref it_port to get ptr-to-CPort and then deref the
          ptr-to-CPort to get CPort.
        CPort *p_output_port = new CPort(**it_port, *this); // CPort copy
          constructor
        GetVectorOfOutputPorts().push_back(p_output_port);  // add the
          new port
    }
}
```

The developer will have noticed the accessor method to retrieve the input port name. Hence, add a public constant accessor method to the CSubsystemInBlock class with the following prototype, `CString CSubsystemInBlock::GetInputPortName() const`, and edit the function as shown.

```
CString CSubsystemInBlock::GetInputPortName() const
{
    return m_strInputPortName;
}
```

Finally, the public virtual `CopyBlockData()` method with the prototype, `virtual CBlock *CSubsystemInBlock::CopyBlockData(void)`, may be added as shown:

```
CBlock* CSubsystemInBlock::CopyBlockData()
{
    // Create a new CSubsystemInBlock
    CBlock *pBlock = new CSubsystemInBlock(*this);

    return pBlock;
}
```

29.3.3.15 CSubsystemOutBlock Copy Constructor

Add the public CSubsystemOutBlock copy constructor function to the CSubsystemOutBlock class, with prototype, `CSubsystemOutBlock::CSubsystemOutBlock(const CSubsystemOutBlock &blk)`, and edit it as shown.

```
CSubsystemOutBlock::CSubsystemOutBlock(const CSubsystemOutBlock &blk):
CBlock(blk)
{
    m_strOutputPortName = blk.GetOutputPortName();

    // Port Construction
    const vector<CPort*> *p_vec_input_ports = blk.
      GetVectorOfInputPortsCopy();

    vector<CPort*>::const_iterator it_port;    // const iterator for
      const vector of CPort ptrs.

    for(it_port = (*p_vec_input_ports).begin(); it_port
      != (*p_vec_input_ports).end(); it_port++)
    {
        // Deref it_port to get ptr-to-CPort and then deref the
          ptr-to-CPort to get CPort.
        CPort *p_input_port = new CPort(**it_port, *this);  // CPort copy
          constructor
        GetVectorOfInputPorts().push_back(p_input_port);    // add the
          new port
    }
}
```

The developer will have noticed the accessor method to retrieve the output port name. Hence, add a public constant accessor method to the CSubsystemOutBlock class with the following prototype, CString CSubsystemOutBlock::GetOutputPortName() const, and edit the function as shown.

```
CString CSubsystemOutBlock::GetOutputPortName() const
{
    return m_strOutputPortName;
}
```

Finally, the public virtual CopyBlockData() method with the prototype, virtual CBlock *CSubsystemOutBlock::CopyBlockData(void), may be added as shown.

```
CBlock* CSubsystemOutBlock::CopyBlockData()
{
    // Create a new CSubsystemOutBlock
    CBlock *pBlock = new CSubsystemOutBlock(*this);

    return pBlock;
}
```

29.3.3.16   CSumBlock Copy Constructor

Add the public CSumBlock copy constructor function to the CSumBlock class, with prototype, CSumBlock::CSumBlock(const CSumBlock &blk), and edit it as shown.

```
CSumBlock::CSumBlock(const CSumBlock &blk):
CBlock(blk)
{
    m_iNAddInputs = blk.GetNAddInputs();
    m_iNSubtractInputs = blk.GetNSubtractInputs();

    // Port Construction
    const vector<CPort*> *p_vec_input_ports = blk.
      GetVectorOfInputPortsCopy();
    const vector<CPort*> *p_vec_output_ports = blk.
      GetVectorOfOutputPortsCopy();
    vector<CPort*>::const_iterator it_port;    // const iterator for
      const vector of CPort ptrs.

    for(it_port = (*p_vec_input_ports).begin(); it_port
      != (*p_vec_input_ports).end(); it_port++)
    {
        // Deref it_port to get ptr-to-CPort and then deref the
          ptr-to-CPort to get CPort.
        CPort *p_input_port = new CPort(**it_port, *this);  // CPort copy
          constructor
        GetVectorOfInputPorts().push_back(p_input_port);    // add the
          new port
    }
```

```
    for(it_port = (*p_vec_output_ports).begin(); it_port
      != (*p_vec_output_ports).end(); it_port++)
    {
        // Deref it_port to get ptr-to-CPort and then deref the
          ptr-to-CPort to get CPort.
        CPort *p_output_port = new CPort(**it_port, *this); // CPort copy
          constructor
        GetVectorOfOutputPorts().push_back(p_output_port);  // add the
          new port
    }
}
```

The developer will have noticed the introduction of two public constant accessor methods to retrieve the number of addition and subtraction inputs. Hence, add the accessor methods with the declarations and definitions provided as follows.

1. int CSumBlock::GetNAddInputs(void) const
2. int CSumBlock::GetNSubtractInputs(void) const

```
int CSumBlock::GetNAddInputs() const
{
    return m_iNAddInputs;
}

int CSumBlock::GetNSubtractInputs() const
{
    return m_iNSubtractInputs;
}
```

Finally, the public virtual CopyBlockData() method with the prototype, virtual CBlock *CSumBlock::CopyBlockData(void), may be added as shown.

```
CBlock* CSumBlock::CopyBlockData()
{
    // Create a new CSumBlock
    CBlock *pBlock = new CSumBlock(*this);

    return pBlock;
}
```

29.3.3.17 CTransferFnBlock Copy Constructor

Add the public CTransferFnBlock copy constructor function to the CTransferFnBlock class, with prototype, CTransferFnBlock::CTransferFnBlock(const CTransferFnBlock &blk), and edit it as shown.

```
CTransferFnBlock::CTransferFnBlock(const CTransferFnBlock &blk):
CBlock(blk)
{
    m_strNumerCoeffs = blk.GetStringNumerCoeffs();
    m_strDenomCoeffs = blk.GetStringDenomCoeffs();
    m_dNumerVector = ConvertStringToDoubleVector(m_strNumerCoeffs,
      m_iLengthNumer);
    m_dDenomVector = ConvertStringToDoubleVector(m_strDenomCoeffs,
      m_iLengthDenom);
```

```
    // Port Construction
    const vector<CPort*> *p_vec_input_ports = blk.
      GetVectorOfInputPortsCopy();
    const vector<CPort*> *p_vec_output_ports = blk.
      GetVectorOfOutputPortsCopy();
    vector<CPort*>::const_iterator it_port;    // const iterator for
      const vector of CPort ptrs.

    for(it_port = (*p_vec_input_ports).begin(); it_port
      != (*p_vec_input_ports).end(); it_port++)
    {
        // Deref it_port to get ptr-to-CPort and then deref the
          ptr-to-CPort to get CPort.
        CPort *p_input_port = new CPort(**it_port, *this);  // CPort copy
          constructor
        GetVectorOfInputPorts().push_back(p_input_port);    // add the
          new port
    }

    for(it_port = (*p_vec_output_ports).begin(); it_port
      != (*p_vec_output_ports).end(); it_port++)
    {
        // Deref it_port to get ptr-to-CPort and then deref the
          ptr-to-CPort to get CPort.
        CPort *p_output_port = new CPort(**it_port, *this); // CPort copy
          constructor
        GetVectorOfOutputPorts().push_back(p_output_port);  // add the
          new port
    }
}
```

The developer will have noticed the two public constant accessor methods to retrieve the numerator and denominator coefficients as CString arguments, i.e., "m_strNumerCoeffs" and "m_strDenomCoeffs". Hence, add the accessor methods with the declarations and definitions provided as follows.

1. CString CTransferFnBlock::GetStringNumerCoeffs(void) const
2. CString CTransferFnBlock::GetStringDenomCoeffs(void) const

```
CString CTransferFnBlock::GetStringNumerCoeffs() const
{
    return m_strNumerCoeffs;
}

CString CTransferFnBlock::GetStringDenomCoeffs() const
{
    return m_strDenomCoeffs;
}
```

Finally, the public virtual CopyBlockData() method with the prototype, virtual CBlock *CTransferFnBlock::CopyBlockData(void), may be added as shown:

```
CBlock* CTransferFnBlock::CopyBlockData()
{
    // Create a new CTransferFnBlock
    CBlock *pBlock = new CTransferFnBlock(*this);

    return pBlock;
}
```

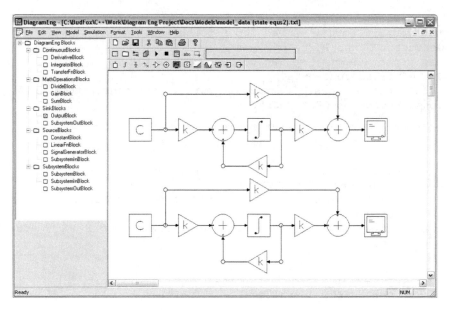

FIGURE 29.3   A copy and paste operation of a block diagram model of the state and output equations resulting in two identical models on the same document.

29.3.4 Testing the Cut, Copy, and Paste Operations for a Complete Model

Now that all copy constructors, constant accessor methods, and virtual `CopyBlockData()` functions of the CBlock-derived classes have been added, the Cut, Copy, and Paste operations may be
tested for a complete system model. Figure 29.3 shows a block diagram model of the state and output
equations introduced in Chapters 22 and 23 for modeling second-order linear ordinary differential
equations: the whole diagram may be selected and copied onto the same document to result in two
identical diagrams.

29.4 UNDOING AND REDOING EDITING ACTIONS

The remaining functionality to be added to the Edit menu is the undoing (Edit/Undo) and redoing
(Edit/Redo) of editing actions typically invoked using the key combinations "Ctrl+Z" and "Ctrl+Y",
respectively. The serialization covered in Chapter 25 concerned the CSystemModel class and its
contained or associated classes: CBlock, CBlockShape, CConnection, CPort, and the CBlock-
derived block classes. The CDiagramEngApp, CDiagramEngDoc, and CDiagramEngView classes
did not need to be serialized, and the CSignal class represents transient data determined in the
course of a simulation and was also not required to have its member data saved. However, to save
the system model state each time an editing action occurs, the entire system model is to be recorded
and stored in a list, and, depending on whether the action is to undo or redo a step, the list index
identifier is decremented or incremented, respectively, and the appropriate saved model restored.

Consider, e.g., the following schematic diagram shown in Figure 29.4, representing steps in the
evolving editing of a system model. The system models are numbered starting from zero. Figure
29.4a shows four successive steps in editing and saving a model where each model is saved in a list
of system models: the horizontal row of model diagrams represents the list. System model zero is
intentionally empty, signifying the start of the editing process; system model one consists of just
one rectangle block; system model two consists of a rectangle block and a connection object; and
system model three consists of a rectangle block, a connection, and an ellipse block. If the user saves
the model content after each editing action, then undoing an action would simply allow the user to

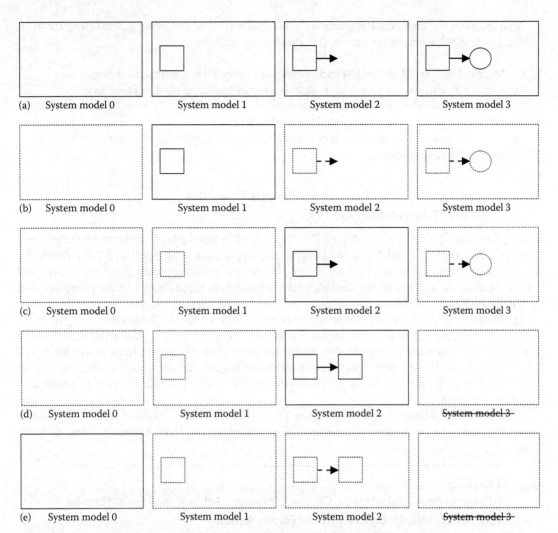

FIGURE 29.4 (a) An evolving editing and successive saving of system models that form a list of system models (0–3): system model zero is intentionally empty, denoting the start of the editing procedure. (b) Undoing two steps, making system model one in vogue: the other models remain in the list and are shown with a dashed outline. (c) Redoing one step, making system model two in vogue: the other models remain in the list and are shown with a dashed outline. (d) Undoing one step reverting to system model one, followed by adding another connection and block and saving the changes into the next available position in the list (system model two): the following models are erased from the list (struck out). (e) Undoing two steps, making the empty system model zero, in vogue: models one and two still remain in the list and are shown with dashed outlines.

backtrack to a previous model state (Figure 29.4b), and redoing an action would advance the user to the next saved state (Figure 29.4c): this is the case if no further editing and saving is performed, but rather simply undoing or redoing a previous action. However, if the user backtracks, or undoes successive actions to arrive at, e.g., system model one, and then makes a change to the diagram followed by a saving of the content (Figure 29.4d), then the remaining system models in the list are erased, and the newly saved diagram stored at the next available position in the list: i.e., system model one is edited and saved as the new system model two. Subsequent undoing would take the user back, e.g., to system model zero (Figure 29.4e). Then, the user would not be able to undo prior to system model zero, nor redo beyond system model two, as expected, since no models exist or are accessible beyond the bounds of the list.

To implement the Undo and Redo actions of the Edit menu, the following general steps are to be taken, where specific details are provided in the ensuing sections:

1. Add the Undo and Redo event-handler functions to the CDiagramEngDoc class.
2. Add functionality to save system models to a list to the CDiagramEngDoc class.
3. Add a copy constructor to the CSystemModel class.
4. Add an assignment operator to the CSystemModel class.
5. Add functionality to update the user interface to the CDiagramEngView class.
6. Testing the editing actions.

29.4.1 ADD THE UNDO AND REDO EVENT-HANDLER FUNCTIONS TO THE **CDiagramEngDoc** CLASS

Table 29.1 shows the menu entry objects, IDs, captions, prompts, settings, and event-handler functions that are currently available in the DiagramEng application. The Edit/Undo entry should be accompanied by the associated Edit/Redo entry to redo the previously undone action. Hence, add the new Edit/Redo menu entry beneath the existing Edit/Undo menu entry with the properties and settings shown in Table 29.2.

Incidentally, to allow the key combination specified next to the Edit/Redo menu entry in Table 29.2, the Accelerator key settings need to be set as follows: (1) navigate to the Accelerator menu under the DiagramEng resources menu in the Resources pane, (2) double-click IDR_MAINFRAME, (3) right-click the ID title and select New Accelerator to generate the dialog window shown in Figure 29.5, and (4) enter ID_EDIT_REDO as the ID, "Y" as the key, "Ctrl" as the modifier, and VirtKey as the type.

Now the event-handler functions associated with the menu entry IDs need to be added to the project (using the ClassWizard), to perform the undoing and redoing editing actions. Both of

---

TABLE 29.2

Edit Menu Entry Objects, IDs, Captions, Prompts, Settings, and Event-Handler Functions for the Undo/Redo Paired Editing Action

Object	Property	Setting	Event-Handler Function
Edit/Undo	ID	ID_EDIT_UNDO	OnEditUndo()
	Caption	&Undo\tCtrl+Z	
	Prompts	Undo the last action\nUndo	
Edit/Redo	ID	ID_EDIT_REDO	OnEditRedo()
	Caption	&Redo\tCtrl+Y	
	Prompts	Redo the previously undone action\nRedo	

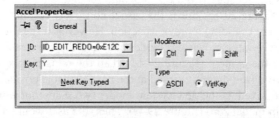

FIGURE 29.5 Accelerator key properties for the ID, ID_EDIT_REDO, corresponding to the Edit/Redo menu entry.

these functions are to be added to the CDiagramEngDoc class, since this class has as a member variable, a CSystemModel "m_SystemModel" object, and will also contain a list of pointers-to-CSystemModel, i.e., "list<CSystemModel*> m_lstSystemModel", that will record the various saved changes to the evolving editing of a system model. Hence, add the OnEditUndo() event-handler function to the CDiagramEngDoc class for the ID_EDIT_UNDO object ID, and edit it as shown.

```cpp
void CDiagramEngDoc::OnEditUndo()
{
    // TODO: Add your command handler code here
    // DiagramEng (start)
    int i;
    CSystemModel *pSystemModel = NULL;
    list<CSystemModel*>::iterator it_sm;

    // Check index denoting position in list
    if(m_iIndexSystemModel == 0)
    {
        m_iEditUndoFlag = 0;      // menu disable flag set to disabled
        return;
    }
    else
    {
        m_iIndexSystemModel--;    // decrement index to get previous item
          in list

        // Adjust undo flag
        if(m_iIndexSystemModel == 0)
        {
            m_iEditUndoFlag = 0;  // menu disable flag set to disabled
        }
        else
        {
            m_iEditUndoFlag = 1;  // menu disable flag set to enabled
        }

        // Adjust redo flag
        m_iEditRedoFlag = 1;
    }

    // GET A SAVED SYSTEM MODEL FROM THE LIST OF PTRS-TO-CSystemModel
    it_sm = m_lstSystemModel.begin();
    for(i=0; i<m_iNSystemModels; i++)
    {
        if(i == m_iIndexSystemModel)
        {
            pSystemModel = *it_sm;
            break;
        }
        else
        {
            it_sm++;
        }
    }

    // ASSIGN SYSTEM MODEL IN LIST TO STANDALONE SYSTEM MODEL USING
      ASSIGNMENT OPERATOR
```

```
    // m_SystemModel = *pSystemModel; is equivalent to, m_SystemModel.
      operator=(*pSystemModel);
    m_SystemModel.operator=(*pSystemModel);

    // Snap connection end points
    SnapConnectionEndPointsAfterInitialConstruction();

    // Update All Views
    UpdateAllViews(NULL);

    // DiagramEng (end)
}
```

The developer will notice that in the CDiagramEngDoc::OnEditUndo() function provided
earlier, an integer index-like variable, "m_iIndexSystemModel", is used to denote the position in the list of system models, "m_lstSystemModel", of the model in vogue, which is then
extracted from the list and assigned to the existent, "m_SystemModel" object that may be subsequently edited. The assignment is performed using an assignment operator (to be added later).
The maximum number of items in the list is fixed and is denoted by "m_iNSystemModels". In
addition, the integer flag-like variables, "m_iEditUndoFlag" and "m_iEditRedoFlag", are used
to enable or disable the Undo and Redo entries on the Edit menu, respectively: e.g., when the
undoing action reaches the beginning of the system model list, the Undo action will be disabled,
or otherwise it is enabled; similarly, when the redoing action reaches the end of the system
model list, the Redo action will be disabled, or otherwise it is enabled. The updating of the user
interface is actually performed by the OnUpdateEditUndo() function to be added to the
CDiagramEngView class later.

In addition, the SnapConnectionEndPointsAfterInitialConstruction() function
needs to be called, to set the "m_pRefFromPoint", "m_pRefFromPort", and "m_RefToPort" of the
CConnection objects concerned, directly after the "m_SystemModel" object is assigned the member data of the model stored in the list.

Hence, the developer should add the following private member variables to the CDiagramEngDoc
class: four integer variables, "m_iIndexSystemModel", "m_iNSystemModels", "m_iEditRedoFlag",
and "m_iEditUndoFlag", and one list of pointers-to-CSystemModel, "list<CSystemModel*>
m_lstSystemModel" (initialization is performed in the constructor later).

Now, add the OnEditRedo() event-handler function to the CDiagramEngDoc class for the
ID_EDIT_REDO object ID using the ClassWizard, and edit it as shown.

```
void CDiagramEngDoc::OnEditRedo()
{
    // TODO: Add your command handler code here
    // DiagramEng (start)
    int i;
    int size;
    CSystemModel *pSystemModel = NULL;
    list<CSystemModel*>::iterator it_sm;

    // Check index denoting position in list
    size = m_lstSystemModel.size();
    if((size == 0) || (m_iIndexSystemModel == (size - 1)))
    {
        m_iEditRedoFlag = 0;       // menu disable flag set to disabled
        return;
    }
    else
```

```
    {
        m_iIndexSystemModel++;    // increment index to get next item in
         list

        // Adjust redo flag
        if(m_iIndexSystemModel == (m_lstSystemModel.size() - 1))
        {
            m_iEditRedoFlag = 0;  // menu disable flag set to disabled
        }
        else
        {
            m_iEditRedoFlag = 1;  // menu disable flag set to enabled
        }

        // Adjust undo flag
        m_iEditUndoFlag = 1;
    }

    // GET A SAVED SYSTEM MODEL FROM THE LIST OF PTRS-TO-CSystemModel
    it_sm = m_lstSystemModel.begin();
    for(i=0; i<m_iNSystemModels; i++)
    {
        if(i == m_iIndexSystemModel)
        {
            pSystemModel = *it_sm;
            break;
        }
        else
        {
            it_sm++;
        }
    }

    // ASSIGN SYSTEM MODEL IN LIST TO STANDALONE SYSTEM MODEL USING
      ASSIGNMENT OPERATOR
    // m_SystemModel = *pSystemModel; is equivalent to, m_SystemModel.
      operator=(*pSystemModel);
    m_SystemModel.operator=(*pSystemModel);

    // Snap connection end points
    SnapConnectionEndPointsAfterInitialConstruction();

    // Update All Views
    UpdateAllViews(NULL);

    // DiagramEng (end)
}
```

The CDiagramEngDoc::OnEditRedo() function performs a similar action to the associated Undo action, but increments rather than decrements the index variable "m_iIndexSystemModel" and sets the integer flag-like variable, "m_iEditRedoFlag", to zero when at the end of the list and one otherwise and adjusts the "m_iEditUndoFlag" accordingly.

Initialize all the introduced integer variables in the CDiagramEngDoc constructor as shown in bold. The maximum number of system models, "m_iNSystemModels", to be stored in the system model list, can be increased as desired.

```
CDiagramEngDoc::CDiagramEngDoc()
{
    // TODO: add one-time construction code here

    // DiagramEng (start)
    m_iEditRedoFlag = 0;
    m_iEditUndoFlag = 0;
    m_iFineMoveFlag = 0;
    m_iIndexSystemModel = 0;
    m_iKeyFlagTrack = 0;
    m_iNSystemModels = 10;
    m_iRubberBandCreated = 0;
    m_iSelectAll = 0;
    m_dDeltaLength = 50.0;
    m_strFilePath = "";
    // DiagramEng (end)
}
```

Later, the CDiagramEngView class will need to access the "m_iEditUndoFlag" and "m_iEditRedoFlag" variables to update the user interface: hence, add two public constant accessor functions with the following prototypes to the CDiagramEngDoc class, and edit them as shown:

1. int CDiagramEngDoc::GetEditUndoFlag(void) const
2. int CDiagramEngDoc::GetEditRedoFlag(void) const

```
int CDiagramEngDoc::GetEditUndoFlag() const
{
    return m_iEditUndoFlag;
}

int CDiagramEngDoc::GetEditRedoFlag() const
{
    return m_iEditRedoFlag;
}
```

Finally, now that a list of pointers-to-CSystemModel, "m_lstSystemModel", has been introduced to the CDiagramEngDoc class, upon closing a document this list needs to be deleted. Hence, add a public member function to the CDiagramEngDoc class with the prototype, void CDiagramEngDoc::DeleteSystemModelList(void), and edit the function as shown:

```
void CDiagramEngDoc::DeleteSystemModelList()
{
    list<CSystemModel*>::iterator it_sm;

    // Delete system model list
    for(it_sm = m_lstSystemModel.begin(); it_sm != m_lstSystemModel.
      end(); it_sm++)
    {
        delete (*it_sm);   // delete what it_sm is pointing to:
          i.e. deref the it_sm ptr and delete the ptr-to-CSystemModel.
    }
    m_lstSystemModel.clear();
}
```

The system model list-deletion function now needs to be called from the CDiagramEngDoc destructor as shown in bold in the following.

```
CDiagramEngDoc::~CDiagramEngDoc()
{
    // Delete the list of pointers-to-CSystemModel "m_lstSystemModel"
    DeleteSystemModelList();
}
```

29.4.2 Add Functionality to Save System Models to a List to the CDiagramEngDoc Class

Throughout the software development project, whenever a user-defined change was made to the underlying document-based data, including changes to the CSystemModel object "m_SystemModel", the CDocument::SetModifiedFlag() function was called with the Boolean argument, "bModified", set to "TRUE": if no changes were made, then the argument was, on occasion, set to "FALSE". However, now that the undoing and redoing editing actions require successive system models to be stored in a list ("m_lstSystemModel"), a call to a function to do so is required from within the SetModifiedFlag() function. Hence, a new virtual function is to be added to the CDiagramEngDoc class to override the base CDocument class version and to chain to the base class method and initiate the saving of a system model to a list. Add a function to the CDiagramEngDoc class with the following prototype, virtual void CDiagramEngDoc:: SetModifiedFlag(BOOL bModified), and edit it as shown.

```
void CDiagramEngDoc::SetModifiedFlag(BOOL bModified)
{
    // Chain to base class version
    CDocument::SetModifiedFlag(bModified);

    // Check whether saving to a list is rqd.
    if(bModified == TRUE)
    {
        SaveSystemModelToList(); // explicitly save the current system
          model to a list
    }
    else
    {
        // No need to save system model to list
    }
}
```

Initially the base CDocument::SetModifiedFlag() function is called, and then, depending on the state of the Boolean flag-like variable, "bModified", the address of the current system model ("&m_SystemModel") is saved to a list of system models ("m_lstSystemModel") through a call to the function SaveSystemModelToList(). Hence, add a public member function to the CDiagramEngDoc class with the following prototype, void CDiagramEngDoc:: SaveSystemModelToList(void), and edit the function as shown.

```
void CDiagramEngDoc::SaveSystemModelToList()
{
    int i;
    int lst_size;
    list<CSystemModel*>::iterator it_sm;
    list<CSystemModel*>::iterator it_sm_erase_start;
```

```
CSystemModel *pSystemModel = NULL;

// Place an empty model in the list to begin with representing an
  empty palette
if(m_iIndexSystemModel == 0)
{
    // Copy constructor called to construct a copy of a system model
    pSystemModel = new CSystemModel(m_SystemModel);

    pSystemModel->DeleteBlockList();
    pSystemModel->DeleteConnectionList();
    pSystemModel->DeleteSourceOutputLoopLists();

    m_lstSystemModel.push_back(pSystemModel);
}

// Determine start point for erase
it_sm_erase_start = m_lstSystemModel.end();      // initialize iterator
  to the end of the array
it_sm = m_lstSystemModel.begin();                // initialize iterator
  to the beginning of the array
for(i=0; i<m_iNSystemModels; i++)
{
    if(i == (m_iIndexSystemModel + 1))
    {
        it_sm_erase_start = it_sm;
        break;
    }
    else
    {
        it_sm++;
    }
}

// Delete unwanted elements and then erase the portion of the list
for(it_sm = it_sm_erase_start; it_sm != m_lstSystemModel.end();
  it_sm++)
{
    delete (*it_sm);   // delete the ptr-to-CSystemModel pointed to
  by it_sm
}
m_lstSystemModel.erase(it_sm_erase_start, m_lstSystemModel.end());

// Create a new system model using the class member m_SystemModel and
  the copy constructor
pSystemModel = new CSystemModel(m_SystemModel);

// Put address of the newly created system model at the back of
  m_lstSystemModel
m_lstSystemModel.push_back(pSystemModel);

// If list too big delete the first element and take it off the list
lst_size = m_lstSystemModel.size();
if(lst_size > m_iNSystemModels)
{
    it_sm = m_lstSystemModel.begin();
    delete (*it_sm);   // delete the ptr-to-CSystemModel pointed to
      by it_sm
    m_lstSystemModel.pop_front();
}
```

```
    // Adjust index
    lst_size = m_lstSystemModel.size();
    m_iIndexSystemModel = lst_size - 1;

    // Adjust Undo/Redo flags
    if(m_iIndexSystemModel == 0)  // if at the beginning of the list
    {
        m_iEditUndoFlag = 0;        // can't undo
    }
    else
    {
        m_iEditUndoFlag = 1;        // can undo
    }
    m_iEditRedoFlag = 0;    // at the end of the list so can't redo
}
```

Initially ("m_iIndexSystemModel == 0"), a blank system model (Figure 29.4a system model zero) is to be placed in the list of system models, "m_lstSystemModel", since this allows the user to undo editing actions until an empty palette occurs, implicitly signifying the start of the editing procedure. If this were not the case, the user could only revert back to the original, nonempty model, which would not feel intuitive. The copy constructor is used to make a copy of the existing model, and then list deletion functions are called to empty the model.

Then, as explained using Figure 29.4, if a model is being saved (Figure 29.4d), all items in the list following that specified by the index, "m_iIndexSystemModel", are erased, where the address of the new model is to be placed at the new end of the list. The iterator "it_sm" is incremented to determine the starting position of the erase action, which is performed using the list function erase(). However, prior to erasing list elements, *delete* is called to invoke the destructor to delete the system model, the pointer to which is accessed by dereferencing the "it_sm" iterator.

The CSystemModel copy constructor is then used to make a copy of the current system model and saves its address, denoted by "pSystemModel", in the list of system models, "m_lstSystem-Model". A check is then made to determine whether the list size is greater than the maximum allowed, "m_iNSystemModels": if so, then the element at the front of the list is deleted, using *delete* and then removed using pop _ front(). If *delete* is not called to destroy the system model object, then a memory leak would occur. The interested reader may choose to experiment with this and run a debug-build configuration of the application using the debugger, and upon exiting the application, the leaks will be displayed in the Debug output window of the IDE.

Finally, the integer index, "m_iIndexSystemModel", is incremented and denotes the position of the last system model in the list, and the Edit/Undo and Edit/Redo flag-like variables are set.

29.4.3 ADD A COPY CONSTRUCTOR TO THE **CSystemModel** CLASS

The developer will have noticed in the CDiagramEngDoc::SaveSystemModelToList() function provided earlier that a copy of the current system model, "m_SystemModel", is made and its address stored in "pSystemModel" prior to being placed in the list, "m_lstSystemModel". Hence, a copy constructor is required to be added to the CSystemModel class with the following prototype, CSystemModel::CSystemModel(const CSystemModel &sm), and edited as follows.

```
CSystemModel::CSystemModel(const CSystemModel &sm)
{
    int i = 0;
    int ncols = 0;
    int *tour_vec_copy = NULL;
    CBlock *pBlock = NULL;
    CConnection *pCon = NULL;
```

```
list<CBlock*>::const_iterator it_blk;
list<CConnection*>::const_iterator it_con;
list<int*>::const_iterator it_tr;

// INTEGER DATA
m_iModelStatusFlag = sm.GetModelStatusFlag();
m_iNOutputBlocks = sm.GetNOutputBlocks();
m_iNSourceBlocks = sm.GetNSourceBlocks();
m_iNSourceLoopTours = sm.GetNSourceLoopTours();
m_iNSourceOutputTours = sm.GetNSourceOutputTours();

// DOUBLE DATA
m_dATOL = sm.GetATOL();
m_dRTOL = sm.GetRTOL();
m_dTimeStart = sm.GetTimeStart();
m_dTimeStepSize = sm.GetTimeStepSize();
m_dTimeStop = sm.GetTimeStop();

// CString DATA
m_strIntegrationMethod = sm.GetIntegrationMethod();
m_strModelName = sm.GetModelName();
m_strTimeStepType = sm.GetTimeStepType();
m_strWarning = sm.GetWarning();

// LIST DATA
// Copy Block List
const list<CBlock*> *plstBlock = sm.GetBlockListCopy();

for(it_blk = (*plstBlock).begin(); it_blk != (*plstBlock).end();
  it_blk++)
{
    pBlock = (*it_blk)->CopyBlockData();
    m_lstBlock.push_back(pBlock);
}

// Copy Connection List
const list<CConnection*> *plstConnection =
  sm.GetConnectionListCopy();

for(it_con = (*plstConnection).begin(); it_con != (*plstConnection).
  end(); it_con++)
{
    pCon = new CConnection(**it_con);
    m_lstConnection.push_back(pCon);
}

// Copy Source Loop Tour List
const list<int*> *plstSLT = sm.GetSourceLoopTourListCopy();

for(it_tr = (*plstSLT).begin(); it_tr != (*plstSLT).end(); it_tr++)
{
    ncols = sizeof(*it_tr)/sizeof(int);    // get size of array
    tour_vec_copy = new int[ncols]; // allocate memory
    for(i=0; i<ncols; i++)
    {
        tour_vec_copy[i] = (*it_tr)[i];
    }
    m_lstSourceLoopTour.push_back(tour_vec_copy);
}
```

```
    // Copy Source Output Tour List
    const list<int*> *plstSOT = sm.GetSourceOutputTourListCopy();

    for(it_tr = (*plstSOT).begin(); it_tr != (*plstSOT).end(); it_tr++)
    {
        ncols = sizeof(*it_tr)/sizeof(int);    // get size of array
        tour_vec_copy = new int[ncols];        // allocate memory
        for(i=0; i<ncols; i++)
        {
            tour_vec_copy[i] = (*it_tr)[i];
        }
        m_lstSourceOutputTour.push_back(tour_vec_copy);
    }
}
```

Initially, local variables are declared, and then the copying of member data from the incoming object, "sm", to the object being constructed is performed. The assignment of integer, double, and CString data involves public constant accessor functions as shown. The copying of the list-based data is somewhat more involved and includes lists of pointers-to-CBlock, pointers-to-CConnection, and pointers-to-int (integer arrays).

The block list is obtained by the constant accessor function GetBlockListCopy(), which returns the address of the member list, "m_lstBlock", as a pointer-to-a-constant list of pointers-to-CBlock, i.e., "const list<CBlock*> *plstBlock". This list is iterated over, and the derived runtime type of the CBlock pointer is used to invoke the correct CopyBlockData() function (introduced earlier in the project), to copy the block's data, and the address of the new block is assigned to the pointer, "pBlock", which is then placed in the block list.

The copying of the connection list works in a similar fashion: the constant accessor function GetConnectionListCopy() returns the address of the connection list, and this is assigned to the pointer-to-a-constant list of pointers-to-CConnection, i.e., "const list<CConnection*> *plstConnection". Thereafter, the list is iterated over, and the iterator dereferenced, once to get the pointer-to-CConnection and then a second time to get the CConnection object, which is then passed to the CConnection copy constructor and the address of the new object placed in the list, "m_lstConnection".

The source-to-loop-block and source-to-output-block node-to-node tours, determined at the model validation stage, are recorded in integer arrays, and these arrays are then stored in the lists "m_lstSourceLoopTour" and "m_lstSourceOutputTour", respectively. The constant accessor functions, GetSourceLoopTourListCopy() and GetSourceOutputTourListCopy(), are used to return the addresses of the relevant lists as a pointer-to-a-constant list of pointers-to-int, i.e., "const list<int*> *plst", or equivalently a pointer-to-a-constant list of integer arrays.

Hence, the following public constant accessor methods, with the declarations and definitions provided, are to be added to the CSystemModel class. The developer will recall that some of the functions used in the copy constructor were introduced in the project at an earlier developmental stage; hence, only new functions are provided here.

1. int CSystemModel::GetNOutputBlocks(void) const
2. int CSystemModel::GetNSourceBlocks(void) const
3. int CSystemModel::GetNSourceLoopTours(void) const
4. int CSystemModel::GetNSourceOutputTours(void) const
5. double CSystemModel::GetATOL(void) const
6. double CSystemModel::GetRTOL(void) const
7. double CSystemModel::GetTimeStart(void) const
8. double CSystemModel::GetTimeStepSize(void) const
9. double CSystemModel::GetTimeStop(void) const
10. CString CSystemModel::GetTimeStepType(void) const

11. CString CSystemModel::GetWarning(void) const
12. const list<CBlock*> *CSystemModel::GetBlockListCopy(void) const
13. const list<CConnection*> *CSystemModel::GetConnectionListCopy(void) const
14. const list<int*> *CSystemModel::GetSourceLoopTourListCopy(void) const
15. const list<int*> *CSystemModel::GetSourceOutputTourListCopy(void) const

```cpp
int CSystemModel::GetNOutputBlocks() const
{
    return m_iNOutputBlocks;
}

int CSystemModel::GetNSourceBlocks() const
{
    return m_iNSourceBlocks;
}

int CSystemModel::GetNSourceLoopTours() const
{
    return m_iNSourceLoopTours;
}

int CSystemModel::GetNSourceOutputTours() const
{
    return m_iNSourceOutputTours;
}

double CSystemModel::GetATOL() const
{
    return m_dATOL;
}

double CSystemModel::GetRTOL() const
{
    return m_dRTOL;
}

double CSystemModel::GetTimeStart() const
{
    return m_dTimeStart;
}

double CSystemModel::GetTimeStepSize() const
{
    return m_dTimeStepSize;
}

double CSystemModel::GetTimeStop() const
{
    return m_dTimeStop;
}

CString CSystemModel::GetTimeStepType() const
{
    return m_strTimeStepType;
}
```

```
CString CSystemModel::GetWarning() const
{
    return m_strWarning;
}

const list<CBlock*> *CSystemModel::GetBlockListCopy() const
{
    // For the fn. to be const, a pointer-to-const type is returned.
    return &m_lstBlock;
}

const list<CConnection*> *CSystemModel::GetConnectionListCopy() const
{
    // For the fn. to be const, a pointer-to-const type is returned.
    return &m_lstConnection;
}

const list<int*> *CSystemModel::GetSourceLoopTourListCopy() const
{
    // For the fn. to be const, a pointer-to-const type is returned.
    return &m_lstSourceLoopTour;
}

const list<int*> *CSystemModel::GetSourceOutputTourListCopy() const
{
    // For the fn. to be const, a pointer-to-const type is returned.
    return &m_lstSourceOutputTour;
}
```

29.4.4   ADD AN ASSIGNMENT OPERATOR TO THE **CSystemModel** CLASS

The developer will also have noticed that in the OnEditUndo() and OnEditRedo() functions of the CDiagramEngDoc class, the appropriate system model, whose address is stored in the list "m_lstSystemModel", is assigned to the standalone "m_SystemModel" object (of the CDiagramEngDoc class). This is done by overriding the assignment operator, operator = (), for the CSystemModel class. In fact, the statement, "m_SystemModel=*pSystemModel;", is equivalent to the more explicit statement, "m_SystemModel.operator=(*pSystemModel);", where the latter shows the use of the membership operator (".") being used to call the member function (operator = ()) upon the underlying system model object ("m_SystemModel"), passing the object as an argument ("*pSystemModel"). This form is used here as a reminder that the operator = () function has been overridden in the CSystemModel class.

Hence, add a new public member function to the CSystemModel class with the following prototype, CSystemModel &CSystemModel::operator=(const CSystemModel &sm), and edit the function as shown. The developer should add the prototype manually to the actual class declaration to ensure that the class has the overriding version.

```
CSystemModel &CSystemModel::operator=(const CSystemModel &sm)
{
    int i = 0;
    int ncols = 0;
    int *tour_vec_copy = NULL;
    CBlock *pBlock = NULL;
    CConnection *pCon = NULL;
    list<CBlock*>::const_iterator it_blk;
    list<CConnection*>::const_iterator it_con;
    list<int*>::const_iterator it_tr;
```

```
// CHECK FOR SELF-ASSIGNMENT
if(this == &sm)          // if the address of the current object,
  "this", is the address of the incoming obj.
{
    return *this;        // deref the "this" pointer to return the obj.
}

// DELETE SYSTEM MODEL LISTS
DeleteBlockList();                  // Delete block list
DeleteConnectionList();             // Delete connection list
DeleteSourceOutputLoopLists();      // Delete source-to-output-block
  and source-to-loop-repeated-block lists

// INTEGER DATA
m_iModelStatusFlag = sm.GetModelStatusFlag();
m_iNOutputBlocks = sm.GetNOutputBlocks();
m_iNSourceBlocks = sm.GetNSourceBlocks();
m_iNSourceLoopTours = sm.GetNSourceLoopTours();
m_iNSourceOutputTours = sm.GetNSourceOutputTours();

// DOUBLE DATA
m_dATOL = sm.GetATOL();
m_dRTOL = sm.GetRTOL();
m_dTimeStart = sm.GetTimeStart();
m_dTimeStepSize = sm.GetTimeStepSize();
m_dTimeStop = sm.GetTimeStop();

// CString DATA
m_strIntegrationMethod = sm.GetIntegrationMethod();
m_strModelName = sm.GetModelName();
m_strTimeStepType = sm.GetTimeStepType();
m_strWarning = sm.GetWarning();

// LIST DATA
// Copy Block List
const list<CBlock*> *plstBlock = sm.GetBlockListCopy();

for(it_blk = (*plstBlock).begin(); it_blk != (*plstBlock).end();
  it_blk++)
{
    pBlock = (*it_blk)->CopyBlockData();   // calls the appropriate
      copy constructor and returns a ptr-to-CBlock
    m_lstBlock.push_back(pBlock);
}

// Copy Connection List
const list<CConnection*> *plstConnection =
  sm.GetConnectionListCopy();

for(it_con = (*plstConnection).begin(); it_con != (*plstConnection).
  end(); it_con++)
{
    pCon = new CConnection(**it_con);       // deref the iterator and
      then the ptr-to-CConnection to pass the CConnection obj.
    m_lstConnection.push_back(pCon);
}
```

```
    // Copy Source Loop Tour List
    const list<int*> *plstSLT = sm.GetSourceLoopTourListCopy();

    for(it_tr = (*plstSLT).begin(); it_tr != (*plstSLT).end(); it_tr++)
    {
        ncols = sizeof(*it_tr)/sizeof(int);      // get size of array
        tour_vec_copy = new int[ncols];          // allocate memory
        for(i=0; i<ncols; i++)
        {
            tour_vec_copy[i] = (*it_tr)[i];
        }
        m_lstSourceLoopTour.push_back(tour_vec_copy);
    }

    // Copy Source Output Tour List
    const list<int*> *plstSOT = sm.GetSourceOutputTourListCopy();

    for(it_tr = (*plstSOT).begin(); it_tr != (*plstSOT).end(); it_tr++)
    {
        ncols = sizeof(*it_tr)/sizeof(int);      // get size of array
        tour_vec_copy = new int[ncols];          // allocate memory
        for(i=0; i<ncols; i++)
        {
            tour_vec_copy[i] = (*it_tr)[i];
        }
        m_lstSourceOutputTour.push_back(tour_vec_copy);
    }

    // RETURN THE CURRENT OBJECT
    return *this;    // deref the "this" pointer to return the underlying
       obj.
}
```

Initially, the overriding assignment operator function checks for self-assignment, by comparing the address of the object upon which the function is called, stored in "this", with the address of the incoming argument, "sm", and if so, returns the object upon which the function is called by dereferencing the "this" pointer. If self-assignment is not being attempted, the rest of the function body is executed: first the contained system model lists are deleted, including the list of pointers-to-CBlock, list of pointers-to-CConnection, and lists of integer arrays, and then the assignment of the incoming object's data members is made to the underlying object upon which the function is called. The member assignment part of the function is identical to that of the copy constructor introduced earlier.

29.4.5 Add Functionality to Update the User Interface to the CDiagramEngView Class

The software user may select the Undo or Redo entries under the Edit menu to undo and redo editing actions, respectively, as discussed. However, as presented in Figure 29.4, if the user undoes successive editing actions to arrive at the front of the list (Figure 29.4e), or redoes actions to move to the end of the list (Figure 29.4d), the Undo and Redo menu entries should be presented in a disabled state, respectively, and enabled otherwise. To update the user interface with enabled or disabled Edit menu entries, two functions need to be added for the UPDATE_COMMAND_UI event messages for the corresponding menu entry IDs:

1. Add an event-handler function, to the CDiagramEngView class, for the UPDATE_COMMAND_UI event message associated with the ID, ID_EDIT_UNDO, for the Undo menu entry, and edit it as shown.
2. Add an event-handler function, to the CDiagramEngView class, for the UPDATE_COMMAND_UI event message associated with the ID, ID_EDIT_REDO, for the Redo menu entry, and edit it as shown.

```cpp
void CDiagramEngView::OnUpdateEditUndo(CCmdUI* pCmdUI)
{
    // TODO: Add your command update UI handler code here
    // DiagramEng (start)
    UINT nID = ID_EDIT_UNDO;        // menu entry ID

    // Get the correct menu item
    //CMenu *pMenu = AfxGetApp()->GetMainWnd()->GetMenu();  // get the
      main wnd menu

    // If integer flag indicating whether undo is possible is: (0)
      disable menu entry, (1) enable menu entry
    if(GetDocument()->GetEditUndoFlag() == 0)
    {
        //pMenu->CheckMenuItem(nID, MF_UNCHECKED | MF_BYCOMMAND);
        //pMenu->EnableMenuItem(nID, MF_GRAYED | MF_BYCOMMAND);
        pCmdUI->Enable(FALSE);
    }
    else
    {
        //pMenu->CheckMenuItem(nID, MF_CHECKED | MF_BYCOMMAND);
        //pMenu->EnableMenuItem(nID, MF_ENABLED | MF_BYCOMMAND);
        pCmdUI->Enable(TRUE);
    }

    // DiagramEng (end)
}
```

The OnUpdateEditUndo() function gets the state of the CDiagramEngDoc member variable, "m_iEditUndoFlag", retrieved by a call to GetEditUndoFlag() upon the document pointer, and then uses the pointer-to-class-Command-User-Interface, "pCCmdUI", to call Enable() with the appropriate Boolean argument: FALSE and TRUE imply disabling and enabling, respectively [2]. Alternatively, a pointer to the main menu may be obtained and EnableMenuItem() called, passing the menu item ID and a flag combination.*

```cpp
void CDiagramEngView::OnUpdateEditRedo(CCmdUI* pCmdUI)
{
    // TODO: Add your command update UI handler code here
    // DiagramEng (start)
    UINT nID = ID_EDIT_REDO;        // menu entry ID

    // Get the correct menu item
    // CMenu *pMenu = AfxGetApp()->GetMainWnd()->GetMenu(); // get the
      main wnd menu
```

---

* Although CheckMenuItem() did work using "pMenu", Enable() was called using (class Command-User-Interface) pointer, "pCmdUI".

```
    // If integer flag indicating whether redo is possible is: (0)
      disable menu entry, (1) enable menu entry
    if(GetDocument()->GetEditRedoFlag() == 0)
    {
        //pMenu->CheckMenuItem(nID, MF_UNCHECKED | MF_BYCOMMAND);
        //pMenu->EnableMenuItem(nID, MF_GRAYED | MF_BYCOMMAND);
        pCmdUI->Enable(FALSE);
    }
    else
    {
        //pMenu->CheckMenuItem(nID, MF_CHECKED | MF_BYCOMMAND);
        //pMenu->EnableMenuItem(nID, MF_ENABLED | MF_BYCOMMAND);
        pCmdUI->Enable(TRUE);
    }

    // DiagramEng (end)
}
```

The `OnUpdateEditRedo()` method works in a similar manner to the `OnUpdateEditUndo()` function: the "m_iEditRedoFlag" value is obtained and used in conjunction with `Enable()` called upon the (class Command-User-Interface) pointer, "pCmdUI", to enable or disable the menu entry.

29.4.6 Testing the Editing Actions

Now that functionality has been added to the CDiagramEngDoc, CDiagramEngView, and CSystemModel classes, the user may experiment with successively editing a system model (Figure 29.6) and then perform undoing and redoing actions followed by additional editing, to determine whether the behavior, similar to that described for Figure 29.4, is consistent.

Figure 29.7 shows a model diagram representing an ordinary differential equation: if the user selects the diagram with the tracking device (Figure 29.7a) and moves it to another location on the palette (Figure 29.7b) and then successively presses Ctrl+Z to undo the movement action (Figure 29.7c through j), the diagram is relocated back to its original position (Figure 29.7a and j), element-by-element, as shown.

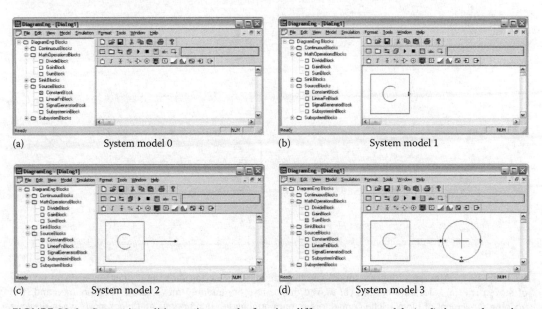

(a)   System model 0

(b)   System model 1

(c)   System model 2

(d)   System model 3

FIGURE 29.6 Successive editing actions made, forming different system models (a–d) that can be undone and redone, corresponding to Figure 29.4a.

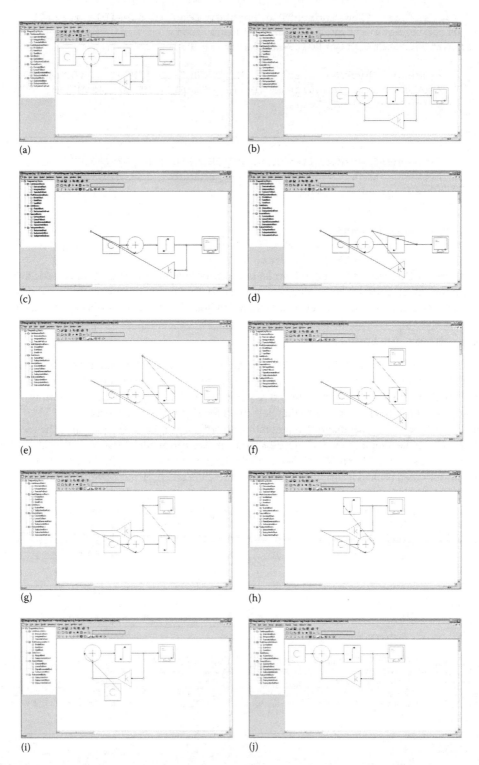

(a)

(b)

(c)

(d)

(e)

(f)

(g)

(h)

(i)

(j)

FIGURE 29.7 Moving a diagram model and then undoing the action showing element-by-element reversal of movement: (a) selected diagram, (b) moved diagram, (c–e) undoing movement of bend points, and (f–j) undoing movement of blocks. The connectors remain attached to bend points and block ports when they are moved in the undoing action (as expected).

29.5 SUMMARY

The Edit menu allows the software user to perform the following operations: Undo, Redo, Cut, Copy, Paste, Delete Grouped Items, Select All, and Add Multiple Blocks. The selection of all diagram model content involves adding the OnEditSelectAll() method to the CDiagramEngDoc class, in which the DetermineDiagramCoordinateExtrema() and DetermineDiagramCoordinateMinima() methods of the CSystemModel class are called to determine diagram-based extreme pseudo-CPoint values. The ResetSelectAll() method of the CDiagramEngDoc class is called by either CDiagramEngView::OnLButtonDown() or CDiagramEngDoc::OnInitTrackMultipleItems() to cancel the Select-All action.

The Cut, Copy, and Paste operations are implemented using the OnEditCut(), OnEditCopy(), and OnEditPaste() event-handler functions of the CDiagramEngDoc class, where in the first two methods, copies of diagram entities are made, and within the latter, block (list<CBlock*>) and connection (list<CConnection*>) lists of a CClipboard object, "m_Clipboard", residing in the CDiagramEngDoc class, are merged with the underlying system model.

The copying of blocks is initiated through the use of a virtual CBlock function, CopyBlock Data(), that, depending on the derived runtime type of the block concerned, the correct block copy constructor is called. The copying of CConnection objects is done directly using the class copy constructor. Copy constructors are added for the main DiagramEng classes, CBlock, CBlockShape, CConnection, CPort, and the CBlock-derived block classes, and are in general of the form, CTypeName::CTypeName(const CTypeName &obj), where "CTypeName" and "obj" refer to the user-defined type and object, respectively, and member initialization should occur for a base class if appropriate.

The undoing (Edit/Undo) and redoing (Edit/Redo) of editing actions, initiated from the OnEditUndo() and OnEditRedo() event-handler functions of the CDiagramEngDoc class, involve creating a list of system model pointers ("list<CSystemModel*> m_lstSystemModel") and saving or retrieving the addresses of system models to and from the list. The storing of models is performed by overriding the virtual CDocument::SetModifiedFlag() function, which chains to the base class version and also calls the SaveSystemModelToList() method, which uses a CSystemModel copy constructor to copy models, the addresses of which are added to the list. An assignment operator of the form, CTypeName &CTypeName::operator = (const CTypeName &obj), is also added to the CSystemModel class and is used in the undoing and redoing functions, where the address retrieved from the system model list, "m_lstSystemModel", is dereferenced to access the system model, which is then assigned to the system model member object, "m_SystemModel" (of CDiagramEngDoc). Finally, the CDiagramEngView user interface update functions, OnUpdateEditUndo() and OnUpdateEditRedo(), are used to both enable and disable their corresponding Edit menu items depending on the value of the list index, "m_iIndexSystemModel".

REFERENCES

1. C++ Reference, http://www.cppreference.com/wiki/, (accessed 2010).
2. Microsoft Developer Network Library Visual Studio 6.0, Microsoft® Visual Studio™ 6.0 Development System, Microsoft Corporation, 1998.

30 Annotations

30.1 INTRODUCTION

At the current stage in the project development, a user can draw a model diagram on the palette consisting of blocks and adjoining connections, where the block graphics indicate the type of block being used. However, it is difficult to discern what the underlying diagram represents without annotations describing, e.g., the independent and dependent variables, signal forms, mathematical expressions, feedback loops, and the inclusion of general notes to add clarifying detail to the system being modeled. Hence, annotations are required and these should be made, in their most general form, at the system model level, rather than be associated with specific diagram entities, e.g., blocks or connections. Annotation objects stored in the CSystemModel class may also make for easier data management, since then, changes need to be made to the CSystemModel class methods rather than numerous other diagram-entity classes, e.g., the CConnection and CBlock-based classes.

New classes, member methods, and variables need to be added to the project to allow the user to enter information describing the model. A CAnnotation class working in conjunction with a CAnnotationDialog class, to allow description-centric user input through the use of a dialog window, appears to be appropriate, and the CSystemModel class could then contain a list of pointers-to-CAnnotation, i.e., "list<CAnnotation*> m_lstAnnotation", to hold all the annotation instances for the model. The topics that need to be addressed, which will ultimately involve making various changes or additions to existing code, are listed as follows, where specific details are provided in the ensuing sections:

1. Add a CAnnotation Class to the Project.
2. Add an Annotation Dialog Window to the Project.
3. Add an Annotation to a System Model.
4. Delete Annotations.
5. Move Annotations.
6. View Menu–Based Actions.
7. Format Menu–Based Actions.
8. Edit Menu–Based Actions.
9. Serialize of the CAnnotation Class.

30.2 ADD A CAnnotation CLASS TO THE PROJECT

An annotation is essentially a string describing a system model entity and in its most basic form includes the attributes string content, font, style, size, color, and location. Hence, add a new generic class to the project by right-clicking on "DiagramEng classes" in the ClassView tab of the Workspace pane and choose New Class. Add the private member variables shown in the class declaration in the following that will represent an annotation instance, i.e., the integer variable, "m_iSize", the CPoint variable, "m_ptPosition" and the CString variables, "m_strAnnotation", "m_strColor", "m_strFont", and "m_strStyle". In addition, add the public accessor methods whose declarations and definitions are listed as follows.

```
 1. int CAnnotation::GetSize(void) const
 2. void CAnnotation::SetSize(int size)
 3. CPoint CAnnotation::GetPosition(void) const
 4. void CAnnotation::SetPosition(CPoint point)
 5. CString CAnnotation::GetStringAnnotation(void) const
 6. void CAnnotation::SetStringAnnotation(CString an)
 7. CString CAnnotation::GetColor(void) const
 8. void CAnnotation::SetColor(CString color)
 9. CString CAnnotation::GetStringFont(void) const
10. void CAnnotation::SetStringFont(CString font)
11. CString CAnnotation::GetStyle(void) const
12. void CAnnotation::SetStyle(CString style)
```

```
// Annotation.h: interface for the CAnnotation class.
//
//////////////////////////////////////////////////////////////////////

#if !defined(AFX_ANNOTATION_H__83108C7E_DAD7_45E3_BB3E_2711F6679D78__
INCLUDED_)
#define AFX_ANNOTATION_H__83108C7E_DAD7_45E3_BB3E_2711F6679D78__INCLUDED_

#if _MSC_VER > 1000
#pragma once
#endif // _MSC_VER > 1000

class CAnnotation
{

public:
    void SetStyle(CString style);
    CString GetStyle(void) const;
    void SetStringFont(CString font);
    CString GetStringFont(void) const;
    void SetColor(CString color);
    CString GetColor(void) const;
    void SetStringAnnotation(CString an);
    CString GetStringAnnotation(void) const;
    void SetPosition(CPoint point);
    CPoint GetPosition(void) const;
    void SetSize(int size);
    int GetSize(void) const;
    CAnnotation();
    virtual ~CAnnotation();

private:
    int m_iSize;
    CPoint m_ptPosition;
    CString m_strAnnotation;
    CString m_strColor;
    CString m_strFont;
    CString m_strStyle;
};
```

```
#endif // !defined(AFX_ANNOTATION_H__83108C7E_DAD7_45E3_
  BB3E_2711F6679D78__INCLUDED_)
```

The accessor methods may be edited as follows, where the retrieval ("get") methods are constant (const) functions since they do not modify the underlying object.

```
int CAnnotation::GetSize() const
{
    return m_iSize;
}

void CAnnotation::SetSize(int size)
{
    m_iSize = size;
}

CPoint CAnnotation::GetPosition() const
{
    return m_ptPosition;
}

void CAnnotation::SetPosition(CPoint point)
{
    m_ptPosition = point;
}

CString CAnnotation::GetStringAnnotation() const
{
    return m_strAnnotation;
}

void CAnnotation::SetStringAnnotation(CString an)
{
    m_strAnnotation = an;
}

CString CAnnotation::GetColor() const
{
    return m_strColor;
}

void CAnnotation::SetColor(CString color)
{
    m_strColor = color;
}

CString CAnnotation::GetStringFont() const
{
    return m_strFont;
}

void CAnnotation::SetStringFont(CString font)
{
    m_strFont = font;
}

CString CAnnotation::GetStyle() const
{
    return m_strStyle;
}
```

```
void CAnnotation::SetStyle(CString style)
{
    m_strStyle = style;
}
```

Finally, the member variables may be initialized with default values as shown in the class constructor. The class destructor takes no action at present as indicated by the comment.

```
CAnnotation::CAnnotation()
{
    // Member init.
    m_iSize = 10;                                   // default size
    m_ptPosition = CPoint(0,0);                     // origin location
    m_strAnnotation = "Enter annotation here";      // initial string
    m_strColor = "red";                             // color
    m_strFont = "Arial";                            // font
    m_strStyle = "Regular";                         // style
}

CAnnotation::~CAnnotation()
{
    // Do nothing for now.
}
```

30.3 ADD AN ANNOTATION DIALOG WINDOW TO THE PROJECT

To add an annotation to the model diagram, the user will need to right-click on the palette at the location of the desired annotation and select Format Annotation from the Context menu; if no annotation currently resides at the point of the right-click or equivalently the right-mouse-button-down event, then a new annotation is to be added. If an annotation does exist, then it is to be formatted according to the formatting fields of an annotation-supporting dialog window, which includes the input fields: annotation string, font, style, size, and color.

30.3.1 ADD THE FORMAT ANNOTATION ENTRY TO THE CONTEXT MENU

Table 30.1 shows the available entries of the Context menu, with the new "Format Annotation" item shown in bold; add this new item with the stated ID, caption, and prompts.

TABLE 30.1

Context Menu Settings: IDs, Captions, and Prompts, and the New Format Annotation Entry

ID	Caption	Prompt: Status Bar and Tooltips
IDM_DELETE_ITEM	&Delete Item	Delete selected item\nDelete selected item
ID_EDIT_DELETE_GROUPED_ITEMS	Delete &Grouped Items	Delete items enclosed by rectangle\nDelete grouped items
IDM_FINE_MOVE_ITEM	&Fine Move Item	Fine movement of item\nFine movement of item
IDM_FORMAT_ANNOTATION	**Format &Annotation**	**Format annotation\nFormat annotation**
IDM_INSERT_BEND_POINT	&Insert Bend Point	Insert bend point\nInsert bend point
IDM_REVERSE_BLOCK_DIREC	&Reverse Block	Reverse block direction\nReverse block direction
IDM_SET_OUTPUT_SIGNAL	Set &Output Signal	Set block output connection-based signal\nSet Output Signal
IDM_SET_ITEM_PROPERTIES	&Set Properties	Set item properties\nSet item properties

---

An event-handler function needs to be added for the new Context menu entry to allow the user to either format an existing annotation or create a new one. Hence, invoke the ClassWizard, select the class name to be CDiagramEngDoc, select the Object ID to be IDM_FORMAT_ANNOTATION, and add a function to the Command message, naming it OnFormatAnnotation(); edit it as shown.

```
void CDiagramEngDoc::OnFormatAnnotation()
{
    // TODO: Add your command handler code here
    // DiagramEng (start)
    int annotation_found = 0;              // flag indicating whether
       annotation found
    bool flag = FALSE;                     // flag indicating whether "OK"
       or "Cancel" was selected in FormatAnnotation()
    double dist;                           // Euclidean dist bw. annotation
       posn and point posn.
    double length = 0.25*m_dDeltaLength;   // reference length
    CPoint annotation_posn;                // annotation posn.
    CPoint point;                          // local point var.
    CString sMsg;                          // main msg string
    list<CAnnotation*>::iterator it_an;    // iterator

    // Get the point at which the context menu was invoked
    point = m_ptContextMenu;  // init a local copy.

    // Print msg.
    //sMsg.Format("\n CDiagramEngDoc::OnFormatAnnotation(), point (x,y)
       = (%d,%d)\n", point.x, point.y);
    //AfxMessageBox(sMsg, MB_OK, 0);

    // Get a copy of the annotation list in the CSystemModel class
    list<CAnnotation*> &annotation_list = GetSystemModel();
       GetAnnotationList();

    // ITERATE THROUGH THE ANNOTATION LIST TO FIND SELECTED ANNOTATION
    for(it_an = annotation_list.begin(); it_an != annotation_list.
       end(); it_an++)
    {
        annotation_posn = (*it_an)->GetPosition();
        dist = sqrt(pow((annotation_posn.x - point.x),2)+
          pow((annotation_posn.y - point.y),2));

        if(dist <= length)
        {
            flag = (*it_an)->FormatAnnotation(point);   // format the
              annotation
            if(flag == TRUE)     // if the annotation was changed
            {
                SetModifiedFlag(TRUE);   // set the doc. as modified to
                  prompt the user to save
                UpdateAllViews(NULL);    // redraw the doc since annotation
                  has changed
            }
            annotation_found = 1;        // an annotation was found for
              formatting
            break;   // exit the for loop
        }
    }
}
```

```
    // CREATE A NEW ANNOTATION AT THE POINT AT WHICH THE CONTEXT MENU WAS
      INVOKED
    if(annotation_found == 0)
    {
        // Create an annotation object
        CAnnotation *pAn = new CAnnotation();    // default constructor
          for CAnnotation object
        flag = pAn->FormatAnnotation(point);     // format the annotation

        // If the "OK" rather than "Cancel" button was clicked, then add
          the annotation.
        if(flag == TRUE)
        {
            annotation_list.push_back(pAn);      // add the new annotation
              to the actual list (passed by ref.)
            SetModifiedFlag(TRUE);               // set the doc. as
              modified to prompt the user to save
            UpdateAllViews(NULL);                // redraw the doc since
              annotation has been added
        }
        else
        {
            delete pAn;            // delete the recently created annotation
        }
    }

    // DiagramEng (end)
}
```

The code given earlier uses a pointer-to-CAnnotation, hence including the "Annotation.h" header file at the top of the "DiagramEngDoc.cpp" source file. In addition, the developer will have noticed the call to FormatAnnotation() in two locations in the function given earlier; if the user clicks upon an existing annotation, then it is formatted, and if not, a new annotation is created at the point, "point" (equivalently "m_ptContextMenu"), and then the formatting function called upon the CAnnotation pointer, "pAn". However, if in the FormatAnnotation() function the Cancel button is selected, then for the existing annotation, the formatting action is aborted, and for the newly created annotation through the use of the *new* operator, the annotation is deleted (*delete*) and not added to the annotation list.

Now, add a new public member function to the CAnnotation class with the prototype, bool CAnnotation::FormatAnnotation(CPoint point), and edit it as shown to return a Boolean value indicating whether the OK or Cancel buttons were clicked on the to-be-added annotation formatting dialog window.

```
bool CAnnotation::FormatAnnotation(CPoint point)
{
    char strSize[20];     // local string with enough space to hold
      integer printed as a string
    // Create a dlg obj. of class CAnnotationDialog : public CDialog
    CAnnotationDialog oDlg;

    // Set the dialog class vars using the CAnnotation class vars
    sprintf(strSize, "%d", m_iSize);            // convert integer "m_iSize"
      to string
    oDlg.m_strSize = strSize;                   // size
    oDlg.m_strAnnotation = m_strAnnotation;     // annotation
```

```
    oDlg.m_strColor = m_strColor;           // color
    oDlg.m_strFont = m_strFont;             // font
    oDlg.m_strStyle = m_strStyle;           // style

    // Return val of DoModal() fn of ancestor class CDialog is checked to
      determine which btn was clicked.
    if(oDlg.DoModal() == IDOK)
    {
        // Assign CAnnotationDialog variable values to CAnnotation
          variable values.
        m_iSize = atoi(oDlg.m_strSize);        // convert the string
          to an int
        m_ptPosition = point;                  // position
        m_strAnnotation = oDlg.m_strAnnotation; // annotation
        m_strColor = oDlg.m_strColor;          // color
        m_strFont = oDlg.m_strFont;            // font
        m_strStyle = oDlg.m_strStyle;          // style
        //CreateAnnotationFont(m_fAnnotationFont); // create the font
        return TRUE;      // "OK" has been clicked
    }
    else
    {
        return FALSE;     // "Cancel" has been clicked
    }
}
```

The `FormatAnnotation()` function first initializes the dialog object's member variables with those of the associated CAnnotation class. The first instance of the dialog object will have the initial values set in the CAnnotation constructor; however, on subsequent invocation, the variable values will reflect the current state of the CAnnotation class. If the OK button is selected, then the dialog control values are updated to the CAnnotation class variables; if the Cancel button is selected, then the updating of the variables does not occur and the Boolean flag FALSE is returned to abort the editing action. The `CreateAnnotationFont()` call in the function given earlier, where the member variable, "m_fAnnotationFont", is actually passed by reference, will be added later and is commented out for now. The dialog object is added in the following section.

In addition, a CSystemModel function to retrieve the list of annotations is required. Hence, add a private member variable of type list<CAnnotation*> with name "m_lstAnnotation" to the CSystemModel class. This will require including the "Annotation.h" header file at the top of the "SystemModel.h" header file. Finally, add a (nonconstant) public member function to the CSystemModel class with the prototype, list<CAnnotation*> &CSystemModel:: GetAnnotationList(void), and edit it as shown to return the actual member list, "m_lstAnnotation", by reference.

```
list<CAnnotation*> &CSystemModel::GetAnnotationList(void)
{
    // Return the actual annotation list by reference (non constant fn).
    return m_lstAnnotation;
}
```

But now that operator *new* is used in CDiagramEngDoc::OnFormatAnnotation() to allocate memory for a CAnnotation object, the address of which is stored in the pointer-to-CAnnotation "pAn" and this pointer added to the list of annotations, "m_lstAnnotation", upon destroying a CSystemModel object, the list must be deleted to prevent memory leaks. Hence, add a public member function to the CSystemModel class with the prototype, void CSystemModel::Delete AnnotationList(void), and edit it as shown.

```
void CSystemModel::DeleteAnnotationList()
{
    list<CAnnotation*>::iterator it_an;

    // Delete annotation list
    for(it_an = m_lstAnnotation.begin(); it_an != m_lstAnnotation.
      end(); it_an++)
    {
        delete (*it_an);            // delete what it_an is pointing
          to: i.e. deref the it_an ptr and delete the ptr-to-CAnnotation
    }
    m_lstAnnotation.clear();
}
```

Finally, call the DeleteAnnotationList() method from the CSystemModel destructor as shown in bold in the following, to ensure memory is deleted, thus preventing a memory leak.

```
CSystemModel::~CSystemModel(void)
{
    // Delete block list
    DeleteBlockList();

    // Delete connection list
    DeleteConnectionList();

    // Delete source-to-output-block and source-to-loop-repeated-block
      lists
    DeleteSourceOutputLoopLists();

    // Delete annotation list
    DeleteAnnotationList();
}
```

30.3.2 Add the New Dialog Window and Associated Functionality

In the CAnnotation::FormatAnnotation() function given earlier, a dialog object, "oDlg", of type CAnnotationDialog is created and used to obtain user input and transfer these data to the underlying CAnnotation class. The general procedure for adding a dialog window for the CAnnotation class is separated into five specific steps:

1. Insert a new dialog window and add all necessary controls.
2. Attach a class to the dialog window.
3. Attach variables to the dialog window controls.
4. Attach functionality to display a font list.
5. Add functionality to the dialog window buttons.

30.3.2.1 Insert a New Dialog Window and Add All Necessary Controls

To insert a new dialog window, go to the ResourceView tab of the Workspace pane and right-click on Dialog and insert a new dialog. A new dialog will appear in the Dialog directory. Rename it, by right-clicking on the dialog window itself to activate the Dialog Properties window, and change the ID to reflect the nature of the dialog window, e.g., IDD_ANNOTATION_DLG, for annotation-related dialog-based user input: use the caption "AnnotationDialog". Leave the OK and Cancel buttons on the dialog. Add the controls shown in Table 30.2 and place them on the dialog window as shown in Figure 30.1.

TABLE 30.2

Annotation Dialog Window Control Objects, Properties, and Settings

Object	Property	Settings
Group Box	ID	ID_ANNOTATION_DLG_GB
	Caption	Annotation Settings
Static Text	ID	ID_ANNOTATION_DLG_TXT_AN
	Caption	&Annotation:
	Extended Styles	Right aligned text
Edit Box	ID	ID_ANNOTATION_DLG_EB_AN
	Multiline	Checked
	Horizontal scroll	Checked
	Vertical scroll	Checked
	Want return	Checked
Static Text	ID	ID_ANNOTATION_DLG_TXT_FONT
	Caption	&Font:
	Extended Styles	Right aligned text
Combo Box	ID	ID_ANNOTATION_DLG_CB_FONT
	Data	(Leave empty.[a])
	Sort	Checked
Static Text	ID	ID_ANNOTATION_DLG_TXT_STYLE
	Caption	&Style:
	Extended Styles	Right aligned text
Combo Box	ID	ID_ANNOTATION_DLG_CB_STYLE
	Data	Regular
	Sort	Italic
		Bold
		Bold Italic
		Unchecked
Static Text	ID	ID_ANNOTATION_DLG_TXT_SIZE
	Caption	Si&ze:
	Right aligned text	Checked
Combo Box	ID	ID_ANNOTATION_DLG_CB_SIZE
	Data	8; 9; 10; 11; 12; 14; 16; 18; 20; 22; 24; 26; 28; 36; 48; 72[b]
	Sort	Unchecked
Static Text	ID	ID_ANNOTATION_DLG_TXT_COLOR
	Caption	Co&lor:
	Right aligned text	Checked
Combo Box	ID	ID_ANNOTATION_DLG_CB_COLOR
	Data	Red
	Sort	Green
		Blue
		Black
		Unchecked
Button	ID	ID_ANNOTATION_DLG_BTN_OK
	Default button	Unchecked
	Caption	&OK
Button	ID	IDCANCEL
	Caption	&Cancel

[a] Font list to be added by functions.

[b] The semicolons used here should be replaced with new lines when setting up the combo box.

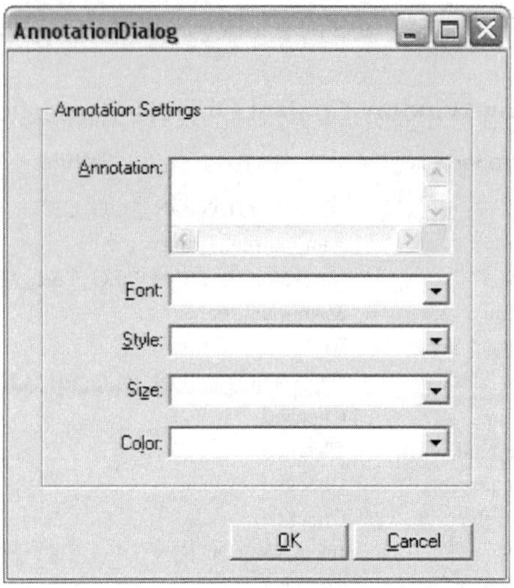

FIGURE 30.1   AnnotationDialog dialog window showing the controls as specified in Table 30.2.

Add maximize and minimize buttons and scroll bars to the dialog if desired. Specify the control tab order by choosing Layout and Tab Order. Finally, to check for duplicate mnemonics, right-click on the dialog window and select "Check Mnemonics".

30.3.2.2   Attach a Class to the Dialog Window
Now that a dialog resource has been added to the project, a class is to be attached to it so that it can operate with the CAnnotation class (added earlier), through, e.g., the `FormatAnnotation()` function given earlier. Select the IDD_ANNOTATION_DLG resource from the ResourceView tab on the Workspace pane, to show the corresponding dialog window in the editor area. Right-click on the dialog box to invoke the ClassWizard. A message box appears with the following content: "IDD_ANNOTATION_DLG is a new resource. Since it is a dialog resource you probably want to create a new class for it. You can also select an existing class." Create a new class with the name CAnnotationDialog, with base class CDialog.

30.3.2.3   Attach Variables to the Dialog Window Controls
The new AnnotationDialog dialog window has controls to which variables need to be attached so that the user selections can be stored in the CAnnotationDialog class and ultimately transferred to the associated CAnnotation class via the `FormatAnnotation()` function. To attach variables to the controls, open the ClassWizard and select the Member Variables tab, select the class name to be CAnnotationDialog, since variables to be added relate to dialog window controls, select the ID of the control to which a variable should be added, click Add Variable, and specify the details as shown in Table 30.3.

The developer will recognize the CAnnotationDialog member variables, "m_strAnnotation", "m_strColor", "m_strFont", "m_strSize", and "m_strStyle", from the function, CAnnotation:: `FormatAnnotation()`, introduced earlier, whose values are assigned to the corresponding member variables of the CAnnotation class through the use of the CAnnotationDialog, "oDlg", object.

Now that the CAnnotationDialog class is declared and defined in "AnnotationDialog.h" and "AnnotationDialog.cpp", respectively, the header file may be included at the top of the "Annotation.cpp" source file, since the `FormatAnnotation()` function makes use of a CAnnotationDialog, "oDlg", object.

TABLE 30.3

Dialog Window Control Objects, Variable Name, Category, and Type, for the IDD_ANNOTATION_DLG Dialog Resource

Control Object	Variable Name	Category	Type
ID_ANNOTATION_DLG_CB_COLOR	m_strColor	Value	CString
ID_ANNOTATION_DLG_CB_FONT	m_ctlFontList	Control	CComboBox
	m_strFont	Value	CString
ID_ANNOTATION_DLG_CB_SIZE	m_strSize	Value	CString
ID_ANNOTATION_DLG_CB_STYLE	m_strStyle	Value	CString
ID_ANNOTATION_DLG_EB_AN	m_strAnnotation	Value	CString

Note that two variables are added for the control with ID ID_ANNOTATION_DLG_CB_FONT, i.e., "m_cltFontList" and "m_strFont".

30.3.2.4 Attach Functionality to Display a Font List

At present, when the user runs the application, the data in the combo boxes may be viewed for the Style, Size, and Color fields, but not the Font field. Functionality is to be added to display a list of fonts in the Font combo box and involves the following steps:

1. Add a `EnumFontFamProc()` function declaration to the "AnnotationDialog.h" header file.
2. Add the `EnumFontFamProc()` function definition to the "AnnotationDialog.cpp" source file.
3. Add a `GenerateFonts()` function to the CAnnotationDialog class.
4. Create the font.

Steps similar to those listed earlier were originally presented in Chapter 7, "Working with Text and Fonts," of Ref. [1] and are implemented here with slight modifications to suit the current AnnotationDialog dialog window. The interested reader may like to read the explanations describing the functionality underling the font-listing code and experiment with the material in Ref. [1] before implementing the following steps, in order to have a more complete understanding of code function and behavior.

30.3.2.4.1 Add the `EnumFontFamProc()` Function Declaration "AnnotationDialog.h"

The `EnumFontFamiliesEx()` function is used to request a list of the available fonts on the system and takes, as an argument, the function name, EnumFontFamProc, which is an application-defined callback function that receives data describing the available system fonts [2]. The `EnumFontFamiliesEx()` function is called from within `GenerateFonts()` in the following.

Hence, add the declaration for the callback function to the "AnnotationDialog.h" header file, with the following prototype, int CALLBACK EnumFontFamProc(LPENUMLOGFONT lpelf, LPNEWTEXTMETRIC lpntm, DWORD nFontType, long lParam), as shown in bold in the following code. (See Ref. [1] for further details.)

```
#if !defined(AFX_ANNOTATIONDIALOG_H__26315A8C_66F3_40D8_A1F7_
  D63C5FC40863__INCLUDED_)
#define AFX_ANNOTATIONDIALOG_H__26315A8C_66F3_40D8_A1F7_D63C5FC40863__
  INCLUDED_

#if _MSC_VER > 1000
#pragma once
#endif // _MSC_VER > 1000
// AnnotationDialog.h : header file
//
```

```
// DiagramEng (start)
// Callback fn to get the list of fonts
int CALLBACK EnumFontFamProc(LPENUMLOGFONT lpelf, LPNEWTEXTMETRIC lpntm,
DWORD nFontType, long lParam);
// DiagramEng (end)

/////////////////////////////////////////////////////////////////////////
// CAnnotationDialog dialog

class CAnnotationDialog : public CDialog
{
// Construction
public:
    CAnnotationDialog(CWnd* pParent = NULL);   // standard constructor

// Dialog Data
    //{{AFX_DATA(CAnnotationDialog)
    enum { IDD = IDD_ANNOTATION_DLG };
    CComboBox  m_ctlFontList;
    CString    m_strAnnotation;
    CString    m_strFont;
    CString    m_strStyle;
    CString    m_strSize;
    CString    m_strColor;
    //}}AFX_DATA


// Overrides
    // ClassWizard generated virtual function overrides
    //{{AFX_VIRTUAL(CAnnotationDialog)
    protected:
    virtual void DoDataExchange(CDataExchange* pDX); // DDX/DDV support
    //}}AFX_VIRTUAL

// Implementation
protected:

    // Generated message map functions
    //{{AFX_MSG(CAnnotationDialog)
        // NOTE: the ClassWizard will add member functions here
    //}}AFX_MSG
    DECLARE_MESSAGE_MAP()
};

//{{AFX_INSERT_LOCATION}}
// Microsoft Visual C++ will insert additional declarations immediately
  before the previous line.

#endif // !defined(AFX_ANNOTATIONDIALOG_H__26315A8C_66F3_40D8_A1F7_
  D63C5FC40863__INCLUDED_)
```

30.3.2.4.2   Add the EnumFontFamProc() *Function Definition to "AnnotationDialog.cpp"*

Add the EnumFontFamProc() function definition manually to the "AnnotationDialog.cpp" source file as shown. This function gets the font list and adds it to the combo box on the AnnotationDialog window; a pointer-to-CAnnotationDialog is declared and used to access the

combo box control, "m_ctlFontList", in which the font name string is added (AddString())
(see Ref. [1] for further details).

```
// DiagramEng (start)
// Callback fn to get the list of fonts
int CALLBACK EnumFontFamProc(LPENUMLOGFONT lpelf, LPNEWTEXTMETRIC lpntm,
  DWORD nFontType, long lParam)
{
    // Create a pointer to the dlg wnd.
    CAnnotationDialog *pWnd = (CAnnotationDialog*)lParam;

    // Add the font name to the list box
    pWnd->m_ctlFontList.AddString(lpelf->elfLogFont.lfFaceName);

    return 1;
}
// DiagramEng (end)
```

30.3.2.4.3 Add a GenerateFonts() Function to the CAnnotationDialog Class

The callback function given earlier is used to add fonts to the list of fonts in the combo box, but
this function needs to be called using the EnumFontFamiliesEx() function from within a function of the CAnnotationDialog (dialog) class. Hence, add a new private member function to the
CAnnotationDialog class with the prototype, void CAnnotationDialog::GenerateFonts
(void), and edit the function as shown.

```
void CAnnotationDialog::GenerateFonts()
{
        int cnt;
        int nFonts;
        CString sNameCurrent;
        CString sNamePrevious = "";
        LOGFONT lf;

        // Init. struct
        lf.lfCharSet = DEFAULT_CHARSET;
        strcpy(lf.lfFaceName, "");

        // Clear combo box
        m_ctlFontList.ResetContent();

        // Device Context
        CClientDC dc(this);

        // Enumerate
        ::EnumFontFamiliesEx((HDC) dc, &lf, (FONTENUMPROC)
          EnumFontFamProc, (LPARAM)this, 0);

        // Get Font Count
        nFonts = m_ctlFontList.GetCount();

        // Loop in reverse searching for and deleting duplicate entries
        for(cnt = nFonts; cnt > 0; cnt--)
        {
                // Current Font
```

```
            m_ctlFontList.GetLBText((cnt - 1), sNameCurrent);
             // numbering from 0 to cnt - 1

            // Check Duplicate
            if(sNameCurrent == sNamePrevious)
            {
                    m_ctlFontList.DeleteString((cnt - 1));
                     // delete font
            }

            // Update Font
            sNamePrevious = sNameCurrent;
        }
}
```

The GenerateFonts function calls the EnumFontFamiliesEx() function with the function pointer argument, EnumFontFamProc, to obtain a list of the available system fonts. The loop iterates from the end of the font list and deletes any duplicate entries (as indicated in Ref. [1]).

Now, the GenerateFonts function needs to be called from a dialog initialization function since it cannot be called from within CAnnotation::FormatAnnotation(). Hence, invoke the ClassWizard, choose the Message Maps tab with class name CAnnotationDialog and add an event-handler function for the WM_INITDIALOG message, and edit the code as shown in bold.

```
BOOL CAnnotationDialog::OnInitDialog()
{
    CDialog::OnInitDialog();

    // TODO: Add extra initialization here

    // DiagramEng (start)
    // Initialization that must be performed here and that cannot be done
      in CAnnotation::FormatAnnotation()

    // Generate the fonts for the "m_ctlFontList" dialog control
    GenerateFonts();
    UpdateData(FALSE); // FALSE => var values updated to dlg wnd controls

    // DiagramEng (end)

    return TRUE; // return TRUE unless you set the focus to a control
                 // EXCEPTION: OCX Property Pages should return FALSE
}
```

The private GenerateFonts() function is called to generate the fonts in the combo box control, represented by the variable, "m_ctlFontList", and then the underlying class variable values are updated to the dialog window controls using UpdateData(FALSE) as reflected in Figure 30.2.

30.3.2.4.4 Create the Font

Now to create the font, a private CFont variable and a public CreateAnnotationFont() function need to be added to the CAnnotation class. Hence, add a private CFont variable named "m_fAnnotationFont" and a public constant member function with the prototype, void CAnnotation::CreateAnnotationFont(CFont &fAnnotationFont) const,

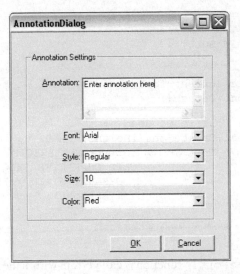

FIGURE 30.2 AnnotationDialog dialog window used to set up the annotation, showing the default variable settings.

to the CAnnotation class and edit it as shown. The idea concerning the introduction of the private CFont variable and `CreateAnnotationFont()` method follows the work of Chapman [1].

```cpp
void CAnnotation::CreateAnnotationFont(CFont &fAnnotationFont) const
{
    int iHeight = 0;            // height of display area
    int iItalic = 0;           // italic font: (0) regular, (1) italic
    int iWeight = FW_REGULAR;  // weight corres. to style

    // Check if a font has been selected
    if(m_strFont != "")
    {
        // Size
        iHeight = m_iSize;

        // Style
        if(m_strStyle == "Regular")
        {
            iItalic = 0;
            iWeight = FW_REGULAR;
        }
        else if(m_strStyle == "Italic")
        {
            iItalic = 1;
            iWeight = FW_REGULAR;
        }
        else if(m_strStyle == "Bold")
        {
            iItalic = 0;
            iWeight = FW_BOLD;
        }
        else if(m_strStyle == "Bold Italic")
```

```
{
   iItalic = 1;
   iWeight = FW_BOLD;
}

// Release the current font
fAnnotationFont.Detach();

// Create the font to be used
fAnnotationFont.CreateFont(iHeight, 0, 0, 0, iWeight, iItalic,
   0, 0, DEFAULT_CHARSET, OUT_CHARACTER_PRECIS,
                        CLIP_CHARACTER_PRECIS, DEFAULT_QUALITY,
                        DEFAULT_PITCH | FF_DONTCARE,
                        m_strFont);

}
}
```

The `CreateAnnotationFont()` function is called from within the `FormatAnnotation()` function, where the member variable "m_fAnnotationFont" is passed in by reference as the argument, assuming the local identity "fAnnotationFont". The properties of the to-be-created font are set, then the existing font is detached (`Detach()`) before a new font is created (`CreateFont()`), resulting in the variable in the calling environment (typically "m_fAnnotationFont") being updated.

Now that the `CreateAnnotationFont()` method has been added to the CAnnotation class, the call to the latter in the `FormatAnnotation()` function may be uncommented. To confirm the status of the annotation settings, an event-handler function is to be added to the BN_CLICKED event message for the OK dialog button, to be added in the following section.

Finally, to gain access to the CFont variable, add a public member function to the CAnnotation class with the prototype, `CFont &CAnnotation::GetAnnotationFont(void)`, and edit it as shown to return the member variable by reference.

```
CFont &CAnnotation::GetAnnotationFont()
{
   return m_fAnnotationFont;
}
```

30.3.2.5 Add Functionality to the Dialog Window Buttons

The two buttons on the IDD_ANNOTATION_DLG dialog window are OK and Cancel, and their event-handler functions are shown in Table 30.4. Add the `OnAnnotationDlgBtnOk()` event-handler function for the BN_CLICKED event message for the OK button with ID, ID_ANNOTATION_DLG_BTN_OK, and edit it as shown. The `OnCancel()` function is the default function for the Cancel button with ID, IDCANCEL; this can be left unchanged.

TABLE 30.4

Objects, IDs, Class, and Event-Handler Functions for the CAnnotationDialog Class

Object	ID	Class	COMMAND Event-Handler
OK button	ID_ANNOTATION_DLG_BTN_OK	CAnnotationDialog	OnAnnotationDlgBtnOk()
Cancel button	IDCANCEL[a]	CAnnotationDialog	OnCancel()

[a] IDCANCEL is the default ID for the Cancel button.

```
void CAnnotationDialog::OnAnnotationDlgBtnOk()
{
    // TODO: Add your control notification handler code here
    // DiagramEng (start)

    // Check the value of all member vars
    UpdateData(TRUE);  // TRUE => dlg wnd control vals updated to vars.

    // Check validity of font size arg.
    int size = atoi(m_strSize);

    if((size >= 1) && (size <= 1638))
    {
        // Print a CString msg.
        CString sMsg;
        CString sMsgTemp;

        sMsgTemp.Format(" CAnnotationDialog::OnAnnotationDlgBtnOk()\t \n\n");
        sMsg += sMsgTemp;
        sMsgTemp.Format(" m_strAnnotation\t = %s\n m_strFont\t = %s\n
          m_strStyle\t = %s\n m_strSize\t = %s\n m_strColor\t = %s\n",
                m_strAnnotation, m_strFont, m_strStyle, m_strSize,
                    m_strColor);
        sMsg += sMsgTemp;
        AfxMessageBox(sMsg, MB_OK, 0);

        // Chain to base class version of the fn.
        CDialog::OnOK();
    }
    else
    {
        AfxMessageBox("\n The font size should be in the interval
          [1, 1638]. \n", MB_OK, 0);
        return;
    }

    // DiagramEng (end)
}
```

(In the event that an "undeclared dialog identifier" message appears upon compilation, the "Resource.h" header file should be included at the top of the "AnnotationDialog.h" header file. However, this was not necessary here.)

Now, upon running the application, the dialog window control values are updated to the underlying variables using UpdateData(TRUE), and a message box is displayed (Figure 30.3), showing the values of the relevant variables used to set the font properties; the AfxMessageBox() call

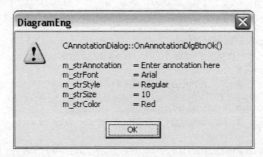

FIGURE 30.3 Message box generated from within the CAnnotationDialog::OnAnnotationDlg BtnOk() function displaying the values of the underlying CAnnotationDialog (dialog) class member variables.

confirming the font settings may be commented out once the function works as expected. Finally, if the user enters the correct input, the base class version of the function, CDialog::OnOK(), is called to close the dialog window; otherwise, the user is prompted to change the input.

If the user invokes the Context menu from a particular point on the palette and formats an annotation, and then subsequently clicks on the palette at exactly the same location, then the recently formatted annotation's values will appear in the invoked dialog window, verifying the correct behavior of the CDiagramEngDoc::OnFormatAnnotation() function; if the user clicks on a different location, then a new annotation object is created and added to the list of annotations.

30.4 ADD AN ANNOTATION TO A SYSTEM MODEL

Now that a CAnnotation object has been created and its address stored in the list of annotations, (list<CAnnotation*>) "m_lstAnnotation" in the CSystemModel class, it needs to be displayed on the screen at the location specified by the CPoint member variable, "m_ptPosition". Currently, the DrawSystemModel() function of the CSystemModel class iterates through the list of blocks and connections, calling DrawBlock() and DrawConnection(), respectively, to draw blocks and connection objects on the palette. The DrawSystemModel() function can now be augmented to iterate through the list of annotation objects, "m_lstAnnotation", and call DrawAnnotation() upon the CAnnotation pointers, passing in the pointer-to-CDC argument, "pDC", as shown in bold in the following.

```
void CSystemModel::DrawSystemModel(CDC *pDC)
{
    int pen_color = RGB(0,0,0);            // White = RGB(255,255,255),
       Black = RGB(0,0,0)
    int pen_width = 1;                     // thin = 1
    CString sMsg;                          // main msg string
    UINT nType = MB_OK;                    // style of msg. box
    UINT nIDhelp = 0;                      // help context ID for the msg.
    list<CAnnotation*>::iterator it_an;    // m_lstAnnotation iterator
    list<CBlock*>::iterator it_blk;        // m_lstBlock iterator
    list<CConnection*>::iterator it_con;   // m_lstConnection iterator

    // Iterate through the SystemModel lists drawing the stored entities.

    // -- SET UP THE PEN AND pDC -----
    // Create the pen

    CPen lpen(PS_SOLID, pen_width, pen_color);

    // Select the pen as the drawing obj.
    // The value returned by SelectObject() is a ptr to the obj. being
       replaced, i.e. an old-pen-ptr.
    CPen *pOldPen = pDC->SelectObject(&lpen);

    // -- DRAW BLOCKS ----------------
    list<CBlock*> blk_list = GetBlockList();   // local block list

    // Check size of block list
    //sMsg.Format("\n CSystemModel::DrawSystemModel(), size = %d\n",
       blk_list.size());
    //AfxMessageBox(sMsg, nType, nIDhelp);

    // Iterate through the block list
    for(it_blk = blk_list.begin(); it_blk != blk_list.end(); it_blk++)
    {
        (*it_blk)->DrawBlock(pDC);           // DrawBlock() called on the
           ptr-to-CBlock
    }
```

```
        // -- DRAW CONNECTIONS -----------
        list<CConnection*> con_list = GetConnectionList(); // local
          connection list
        list<CConnection*> con_list_e = GetConnectionListError();  // local
          connection list in error (disconnected connections)

        // Iterate through the connection list
        for(it_con = con_list.begin(); it_con != con_list.end(); it_con++)
        {
            (*it_con)->DrawConnection(pDC);
        }

        // Prepare the device context for the disconnected connections.
        ModelErrorPenColor(&pen_color);
        CPen lpen2(PS_SOLID, pen_width, pen_color);
        pDC->SelectObject(&lpen2);

        // Iterate through the connection list in error (i.e. disconnected
          connections)
        for(it_con = con_list_e.begin(); it_con != con_list_e.end();
          it_con++)
        {
            (*it_con)->DrawConnection(pDC);
        }

        // -- DRAW ANNOTATIONS -----------
        // Iterate through the annotation list
        for(it_an = m_lstAnnotation.begin(); it_an != m_lstAnnotation.end();
          it_an++)
        {
            (*it_an)->DrawAnnotation(pDC);
        }

        // -- RESET THE PREV. PEN --------
        pDC->SelectObject(pOldPen);
}
```

The DrawAnnotation() function called earlier now needs to be added to the CAnnotation class to actually present each annotation in the list on the screen. Hence, add a public member function to the CAnnotation class with the prototype, void CAnnotation::DrawAnnotation(CDC *pDC), and edit the function as shown.

```
void CAnnotation::DrawAnnotation(CDC *pDC)
{
    // Select the new font
    CFont *pOldFont = pDC->SelectObject(&m_fAnnotationFont);

    // Set the color
    if(m_strColor == "Red")
    {
        pDC->SetTextColor(RGB(255,0,0));
    }
    else if(m_strColor == "Green")
    {
        pDC->SetTextColor(RGB(0,255,0));
    }
    else if(m_strColor == "Blue")
```

```
{
    pDC->SetTextColor(RGB(0,0,255));
}
else
{
    pDC->SetTextColor(RGB(0,0,0));   // m_strColor == "Black"
        or otherwise.
}

// Display the annotation in the current font
pDC->TextOut(m_ptPosition.x, m_ptPosition.y, m_strAnnotation);

// Record the size of the text
m_sOutputTextSize = pDC->GetOutputTextExtent(m_strAnnotation);

// Reset the old font
pDC->SelectObject(pOldFont);
}
```

The new font, "m_fAnnotationFont", is used in the call to SelectObject() to select the object into the device context [2]. The annotation color is then set using the member variable, "m_strColor" and SetTextColor(). The annotation, "m_strAnnotation", is then displayed using TextOut() and positioned at the point, "m_ptPosition", on the screen. Then the size of the output text output is recorded in the CSize member variable, "m_sOutputTextSize" (to be used later). Finally, the old font, "pOldFont", is reselected into the device context. Now, when the user runs the application, the annotation details entered through the dialog window may be viewed on the screen, as shown in Figure 30.4.

The diagram represents the linear state equations used to model a second-order linear differential equation representing a mechanical mass–spring–damper system (Example 3-3, p. 73 of Ref. [3])

$$m\ddot{y}(t) + b\dot{y}(t) + ky(t) = u(t) \tag{30.1}$$

where m, b, k, $y(t)$, and $u(t)$ are the mass, damping constant, spring constant, output mass displacement from the equilibrium position, and external force input to the system, respectively.

The state and output equations in linear form are

$$\dot{x}(t) = A(t)x(t) + B(t)u(t) \tag{30.2a}$$

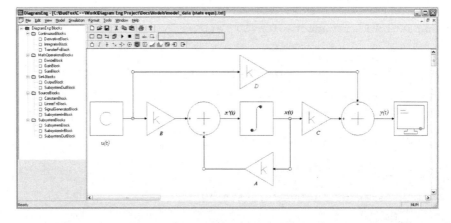

FIGURE 30.4   The state and output equations model diagram augmented with mathematical annotations.

$$y(t) = C(t)x(t) + D(t)u(t) \qquad (30.2b)$$

where

x(t), u(t), and y(t) are the state, control, and output vectors, respectively

A(t), B(t), C(t), and D(t) are the state, control, output, and direct transmission matrices, respectively [3]

The user will have noticed the new CSize member variable, "m_sOutputTextSize", used in the DrawAnnotation() function given earlier. Hence, add this new private CSize member variable to the CAnnotation class. In addition, add a public constant accessor function to the CAnnotation class with prototype, CSize CAnnotation::GetOutputTextSize(void) const, and edit it as shown to return the member variable.

```
CSize CAnnotation::GetOutputTextSize() const
{
    return m_sOutputTextSize;
}
```

30.5   DELETING ANNOTATIONS

Now that annotations exist on the model diagram, the user should be able to delete them using the Context menu in a similar manner to the deletion of blocks, connections, connection-based bend points, and block-based ports. Hence, edit the CDiagramEngDoc::OnDeleteItem() function as shown in bold in the following to call the DeleteAnnotation() function.

```
void CDiagramEngDoc::OnDeleteItem()
{
    // TODO: Add your command handler code here

    // DiagramEng (start)
    int item_deleted = 0;

    // Delete a block
    item_deleted = DeleteBlock();
    if(item_deleted == 1)
    {
        return;
    }

    // Delete a block port
    item_deleted = DeletePort();
    if(item_deleted == 1)
    {
        return;
    }

    // Delete a connection bend point
    item_deleted = DeleteConnectionBendPoint();
    if(item_deleted == 1)
    {
        return;
    }

    // Delete a connection line
    item_deleted = DeleteConnection();
    if(item_deleted == 1)
    {
        return;
    }
```

```
    // Delete an annotation
    item_deleted = DeleteAnnotation();
    if(item_deleted == 1)
    {
        return;
    }

    // DiagramEng (end)
}
```

Now add the DeleteAnnotation() function to the CDiagramEngDoc class with the proto-type, int CDiagramEngDoc::DeleteAnnotation(void), and edit the function as shown to iterate through the list of annotations, "m_lstAnnotation", and delete the appropriate proximal annotation.

```
int CDiagramEngDoc::DeleteAnnotation()
{
    int     delete_an = 0;                   // annotation deletion flag
    double dist;      // Euclidean dist bw. annotation posn and point posn.
    double length = 0.25*m_dDeltaLength; // reference length
    CPoint an_posn;                          // annotation posn.
    CPoint point;                            // local point var.
    list<CAnnotation*>::iterator it_an;          // iterator
    list<CAnnotation*>::iterator it_er = NULL;   // element to erase

    // Get the point at which the context menu was invoked
    point = m_ptContextMenu;  // init a local copy.

    // Get a copy of the annotation list in the system model
    list<CAnnotation*> &annotation_list = GetSystemModel().
      GetAnnotationList(); // MUST BE A REFERENCE!

    // Iterate through the list to find which item to delete.
    for(it_an = annotation_list.begin(); it_an != annotation_list.end();
      it_an++)
    {
        an_posn = (*it_an)->GetPosition();

        dist = sqrt(pow((an_posn.x - point.x),2) + pow((an_posn.y
          - point.y),2));
        if(dist <= length)
        {
            // Record which annotation to erase
            delete_an = 1;
            it_er = it_an;
            break;
        }
    }

    // Delete the item in the list
    if(delete_an == 1)
    {
        // Delete annotation
        delete *it_er;  // delete actual annotation pointed to by it_er
        annotation_list.erase(it_er); // delete element at offset it_er
          in list (that held the annotation)
```

```
        // Set as modified and redraw the doc.
        SetModifiedFlag(TRUE);   // set the doc. as having been modified
          to prompt user to save
        UpdateAllViews(NULL);    // indicate that sys. should redraw.
    }

    // Return a flag indicating whether an item was deleted
    return delete_an;
}
```

The DeleteAnnotation() function behaves in a similar manner to the DeleteBlock() function; the list of annotations is iterated over and if the position of the annotation is within a disk or radius "length" (as named in the code given earlier), then the iterator is recorded ("it_er = it_an") and used to delete the CAnnotation pointer in the underlying list, "m_lstAnnotation".

Now that an individual annotation may be deleted, a group of annotations needs to be deleted via selection of the Delete Grouped Items entry on the Context menu. Hence, edit the CDiagramEngDoc::OnEditDeleteGroupedItems() function as shown in bold in the following; the ellipsis, "…", denotes omitted but unchanged code.

```
void CDiagramEngDoc::OnEditDeleteGroupedItems()
{
    // TODO: Add your command handler code here
    int intersected = 0;
    int intersected_head = 0;
    int intersected_tail = 0;
    double blk_width;
    double delta = 0.25*m_dDeltaLength;
    CPoint an_posn;
    CPoint bend_pt;
    CPoint blk_posn;
    CPoint head_pt;
    CPoint tail_pt;
    CRectTracker temp_tracker;
    list<CAnnotation*> &annotation_list = GetSystemModel().
      GetAnnotationList();
    list<CAnnotation*>::iterator it_an;
    list<CBlock*> &blk_list = GetSystemModel().GetBlockList();
    list<CBlock*>::iterator it_blk;
    list<CConnection*>::iterator it_con;
    list<CConnection*> &con_list = GetSystemModel().GetConnectionList();
    list<CPoint>::iterator it_pt;

    // -- IF A RUBBER BAND HAS BEEN CREATED
    if(m_iRubberBandCreated == 1)
    {
        // Create a temp tracker since m_RectTracker will have its coords
          updated when the rubber band is moved.
        temp_tracker = m_RectTracker;

        // -- ITERATE THROUGH BLOCKS
        …

        // -- ITERATE THROUGH ALL CONNECTIONS (of this model)
        …

        // -- ITERATE THROUGH ANNOTATIONS
        it_an = annotation_list.begin();
```

```
while(it_an != annotation_list.end())
{
    // Get annotation position
    an_posn = (*it_an)->GetPosition();

    // Determine if item lies within rubber band
    intersected = DetermineCurrentAndIntersectRects(temp_tracker,
      an_posn, delta);
    if(intersected)
    {
        // Delete annotation
        delete *it_an;    // delete actual annotation pointed to
          by it_an
        it_an = annotation_list.erase(it_an);  // delete element
          at offset it_an in list
    }
    else // only increment the iterator if there were no
      intersection
    {
        it_an++;
    }

}// end for it_an

// Reset member vars.
m_iRubberBandCreated = 0;   // end the rubber band state
SetKeyFlagTrack(0);         // reset the key-based track flag
  since tracking aborted

// Set flags
SetModifiedFlag(TRUE);      // set the doc. as having been
  modified to prompt user to save
UpdateAllViews (NULL);      // indicate that sys. should redraw.

}// end if m_iRubberBandCreated
}
```

The annotation deletion is very similar to block deletion; the position of the annotation is obtained and used to determine whether the annotation lies within the bounding rubber-band rectangular region, and if so, the annotation is deleted.

30.6 MOVING ANNOTATIONS

The movement of blocks may be performed by three different methods: (1) by selecting the block using a left-mouse-button-down action and dragging it to the desired location, (2) by right-clicking the block to invoke the Context menu and selecting Fine Move Item to subsequently move the item using the arrow keys, or (3) by circumscribing the block with the rubber band ("m_RectTracker") and clicking within the region and dragging the enclosed items to another location. The movement of annotations must also be performed in the same manner.

30.6.1 FINE MOVEMENT OF AN ANNOTATION

The flow of control for the existing keyboard-based fine movement of a diagram entities involves the following key functions: (1) CDiagramEngDoc::OnFineMoveItem(), (2) CDiagramEngView:: OnKeyDown(), (3) CDiagramEngDoc::FineMoveItem(), and (4) the CDiagram EngDoc functions, FineMoveBlock() or FineMoveConnectionBendPoint(), for movement of blocks and connection bend points, respectively. Code needs to be added to the

CDiagramEngDoc::FineMoveItem() function as shown in bold in the following to call the FineMoveAnnotation() function added later.

```
void CDiagramEngDoc::FineMoveItem(int key_flag)
{
    int item_moved = 0;   // flag indicating entity movement

    // Check whether block was selected and moved
    item_moved = FineMoveBlock(key_flag);
    if(item_moved)
    {
        return;
    }

    // Check whether connection bend point was selected and moved
    item_moved = FineMoveConnectionBendPoint(key_flag);
    if(item_moved)
    {
        return;
    }

    // Check whether annotation was selected and moved
    item_moved = FineMoveAnnotation(key_flag);
    if(item_moved)
    {
        return;
    }

    // End fine movement action by switching m_iFineMoveFlag = 0
    if(item_moved == 0)
    {
        SetFineMoveFlag(item_moved);
    }
}
```

Add a public member function to the CDiagramEngDoc class with the following prototype, int CDiagramEngDoc::FineMoveAnnotation(int key_flag), and edit it as shown to process the initial and subsequent entries into the function and move the annotation according to the key pressed.

```
int CDiagramEngDoc::FineMoveAnnotation(int key_flag)
{
    int delta_x = 1;                        // incr. in x direc.
    int delta_y = 1;                        // incr. in y direc.
    int move_flag = 0;                      // flag indicating entity movement
    double dist;     // Euclidean dist bw. annotation posn and point posn.
    double length = 0.25*m_dDeltaLength;  // reference length
    CPoint an_posn;                         // annotation posn.
    CPoint point;                           // local point var.
    list<CAnnotation*>::iterator it_an;     // annotation iterator
    static CAnnotation *pAn = NULL;         // ptr-to-annotation to hold
      the chosen annotation's address.

    // Get the point at which the context menu was invoked
    point = m_ptContextMenu;                // init a local copy.

    // -- IF THIS IS THE FIRST ENTRY INTO THIS FN THEN RECORD THE ADDRESS
      OF THE SELECTED ANNOTATION
```

```cpp
if(GetFineMoveFlag() == 1)
{
    // Get a copy of the annotation_list in the system model
    list<CAnnotation*> &annotation_list = GetSystemModel().
      GetAnnotationList();

    // -- ITERATE THROUGH THE ANNOTATION LIST
    for(it_an = annotation_list.begin(); it_an != annotation_list.end();
      it_an++)
    {
        move_flag = 0;
        an_posn = (*it_an)->GetPosition();
        dist = sqrt(pow((an_posn.x - point.x),2) +
          pow((an_posn.y - point.y),2));

        // -- IF USER CLICKED ON AN ANNOTATION
        if(dist <= length)
        {
            // -- FILTER THE KEY/DIRECTION (screen (0,0) top left
            //    cnr., +ve x to right, +ve y downward
            if(key_flag == 37)          // LEFT ARROW
            {
                // Update annotation posn.
                an_posn.x = an_posn.x - delta_x;
                (*it_an)->SetPosition(an_posn);
                pAn = *it_an; // record address of annotation for
                  subsequent movt.
                move_flag = 1;
            }
            else if(key_flag == 38)  // UP ARROW
            {
                // Update annotation posn.
                an_posn.y = an_posn.y - delta_y;
                (*it_an)->SetPosition(an_posn);
                pAn = *it_an;    // record address of annotation for
                  subsequent movt.
                move_flag = 1;
            }
            else if(key_flag == 39)    // RIGHT ARROW
            {
                // Update annotation posn.
                an_posn.x = an_posn.x + delta_x;
                (*it_an)->SetPosition(an_posn);
                pAn = *it_an;    // record address of annotation for
                  subsequent movt.
                move_flag = 1;
            }
            else if(key_flag == 40)    // DOWN ARROW
            {
                // Update annotation posn.
                an_posn.y = an_posn.y + delta_y;
                (*it_an)->SetPosition(an_posn);
                pAn = *it_an;              // record address of
                  annotation for subsequent movt.
                move_flag = 1;
            }
```

```
                    if(move_flag == 1)
                    {
                        // Set flag
                        m_iFineMoveFlag = 4;

                        // Mark the document as changed
                        UpdateAllViews(NULL);    // this fn calls OnDraw to
                          redraw the system model.
                        SetModifiedFlag(TRUE);   // prompt the user to save
                        break;                   // break out of for loop
                    }
                }// end if dist
            }// end it_blk
    }
    else if(m_iFineMoveFlag == 4) // -- IF THIS IS NOT THE FIRST TIME
      INTO THE FN, THEN MOVE THE ANNOTATION USING IT'S ADDRESS
    {
        // -- FILTER THE KEY/DIRECTION (screen (0,0) top left cnr.,
          +ve x to right, +ve y downward
        if(key_flag == 37)    // LEFT ARROW
        {
            // Update annotation posn.
            an_posn = pAn->GetPosition();
            an_posn.x = an_posn.x - delta_x;
            pAn->SetPosition(an_posn);
            move_flag = 1;
        }
        else if(key_flag == 38)  // UP ARROW
        {
            // Update annotation posn.
            an_posn = pAn->GetPosition();
            an_posn.y = an_posn.y - delta_y;
            pAn->SetPosition(an_posn);
            move_flag = 1;
        }
        else if(key_flag == 39)  // RIGHT ARROW
        {
            // Update annotation posn.
            an_posn = pAn->GetPosition();
            an_posn.x = an_posn.x + delta_x;
            pAn->SetPosition(an_posn);
            move_flag = 1;
        }
        else if(key_flag == 40)   // DOWN ARROW
        {
            // Update annotation posn.
            an_posn = pAn->GetPosition();
            an_posn.y = an_posn.y + delta_y;
            pAn->SetPosition(an_posn);
            move_flag = 1;
        }

        if(move_flag == 1)
        {
            // Mark the document as changed
```

```
            UpdateAllViews(NULL);   // this fn calls OnDraw to redraw the
              system model.
            SetModifiedFlag(TRUE); // prompt the user to save
        }
    }

    return move_flag;
}
```

The developer will notice that FineMoveAnnotation() is of the same structure as FineMoveBlock() and FineMoveConnectionBendPoint(). However, the integer flag-like variable, "m_iFineMoveFlag", is set to four in the code given earlier, to indicate that an annotation is being moved; in FineMoveBlock(), this variable is set to two, and in FineMoveConnectionBendPoint(), it is set to three, denoting the (consistent) independent movement of blocks and bend points respectively.

30.6.2 DIRECT MOVEMENT OF AN ANNOTATION

The software user needs to also be able to left-click an annotation and move it directly, in the same way a block can be selected and moved via a left-button-down action. The flow of control for the direct movement of a block involves the following function calls: (1) CDiagramEngView::OnLButton Down(), (2) CDiagramEngDoc::TrackItem(), and (3) CDiagramEngDoc::TrackBlock(), wherein the latter, the CRectTracker object, "m_RectTracker", is used to update the block position. Here, the CDiagramEngDoc::TrackItem() function should be augmented as shown in bold in the following to call the CDiagramEngDoc::TrackAnnotation() function to be added next.

```
int CDiagramEngDoc::TrackItem(CPoint point, CWnd *pWnd)
{
    int tracker_flag = 0;

    // Track block
    tracker_flag = TrackBlock(point, pWnd);

    if(tracker_flag != 0)
    {
        GetSystemModel().NullifyNegativeCoordinates();
          // CScrollView-related change
        return tracker_flag;    // return since an item was tracked
    }

    // Track connection end point
    tracker_flag = TrackConnectionEndPoint(point, pWnd);
    if(tracker_flag != 0)
    {
        GetSystemModel().NullifyNegativeCoordinates();
          // CScrollView-related change
        return tracker_flag;    // return since an item was tracked
    }

    // Track connection bend point
    tracker_flag = TrackConnectionBendPoint(point, pWnd);
    if(tracker_flag != 0)
```

```
    {
        GetSystemModel().NullifyNegativeCoordinates();
          // CScrollView-related change
        return tracker_flag;  // return since an item was tracked
    }

    // Track annotation
    tracker_flag = TrackAnnotation(point, pWnd);
    if(tracker_flag != 0)
    {
        GetSystemModel().NullifyNegativeCoordinates();
          // CScrollView-related change
        return tracker_flag;  // return since an item was tracked
    }
    // Track multiple items
    if(m_iKeyFlagTrack == 1)
    {
        tracker_flag = TrackMultipleItems(point, pWnd);

        if(tracker_flag !=0)
        {
            GetSystemModel().NullifyNegativeCoordinates();
              // CScrollView-related change
            return tracker_flag;     // return since an item was tracked
        }
    }
    else
    {
        tracker_flag = 0;
    }

    // Return flag indicating if an item was tracked: 0 => not tracked,
      1 => tracked.
    return tracker_flag;
    }
```

The code given earlier calls the `TrackAnnotation()` function passing in the (CPoint) point at which the left-button-down event occurred. Hence, add a public member function to the CDiagramEngDoc class with the prototype, `int CDiagramEngDoc::TrackAnnotation (CPoint point, CWnd *pWnd)`, and edit the code as shown.

```
int CDiagramEngDoc::TrackAnnotation(CPoint point, CWnd *pWnd)
{
    int tracker_flag = 0;
    double dist;                          // Euclidean distance
    double length = 0.25*m_dDeltaLength;  // reference length
    CPoint an_posn;                       // annotation position
    CSize an_size;                        // annotation output text size
    CPoint bottom_right;
    CPoint top_left;
    list<CAnnotation*>::iterator it_an;
    list<CAnnotation*> &annotation_list = GetSystemModel().
      GetAnnotationList();

    // CScrollView-related change
    CPoint ptLogical = point;  // local point to record the point in
      logical units
```

```
CClientDC dc(pWnd);              // create a device context using the
  pointer-to-CWnd pWnd.
((CScrollView*)pWnd)->OnPrepareDC(&dc);    // prepare the device
  context casting pWnd to ptr-to-CScrollView
dc.DPtoLP(&ptLogical);          // use the dc to convert ptLogical from
  device to logical units

// Iterate through annotation list
for(it_an = annotation_list.begin(); it_an != annotation_list.end();
  it_an++)
{
    an_posn = (*it_an)->GetPosition();
    //dist = sqrt(pow(an_posn.x - point.x,2) +
      pow(an_posn.y - point.y,2));
    dist = sqrt(pow(an_posn.x - ptLogical.x,2) +
      pow(an_posn.y - ptLogical.y,2));
      // CScrollView-related change using ptLogical

    // If annotation is clicked
    if(dist <= length)
    {
        an_size = (*it_an)->GetSize();  // annotation font size
        top_left.x = an_posn.x;          // an_posn is not the center
          of the tracking rectangle but top left
        top_left.y = an_posn.y;
        an_size = (*it_an)->GetOutputTextSize();   // size of
          annotation output text
        bottom_right.x = an_posn.x + an_size.cx;
        bottom_right.y = an_posn.y + an_size.cy;

        // CScrollView-related change
        dc.LPtoDP(&top_left);            // convert logical pt based on
          logical annotation posn to device pt
        dc.LPtoDP(&bottom_right);        // convert logical pt based
          on logical annotation posn to device pt

        // Set the rect tracker's position
        m_RectTracker.m_rect.SetRect(top_left.x, top_left.y,
          bottom_right.x, bottom_right.y);

        // Track the mouse's position till left mouse button up
        tracker_flag = m_RectTracker.Track(pWnd, point, TRUE);
          // 0 => item not tracked, 1 => item was tracked

        // Get new tracker position and update new annotation
          position with tracker position
        // Since tracking rectangle was sized from annotation
          position downward, use top left cnr. not center point.
        //an_posn = m_RectTracker.m_rect.CenterPoint();  // center
          point of rectangle
        an_posn = m_RectTracker.m_rect.TopLeft();        // top left
          cnr of rectangle

        dc.DPtoLP(&an_posn);            // CScrollView-related change:
          convert device units to logical units

        (*it_an)->SetPosition(an_posn);

        // Set flags
        SetModifiedFlag(TRUE);          // set the doc. as having been
          modified to prompt user to save
```

```
                UpdateAllViews(NULL); // indicate that sys. should redraw.
                break;
        }
    }

    // Return flag indicating if an item was tracked: 0 => not tracked, 1
      => tracked.
    return tracker_flag;
}
```

The developer will notice the similarities between TrackAnnotation() shown above and TrackBlock() introduced earlier in the project. For blocks, the tracking rectangle is precisely the outline of the block, and the final position of the block is the center point (CenterPoint()) of the tracking rectangle. For annotations, the top left corner of the tracking rectangle demarks the annotation position, and the rectangle is set up such that it outlines the output text, the size of which, "m_sOutputTextSize", is retrieved by the call to GetOutputTextSize(). After movement, the annotation position is thus the top left corner of the tracking rectangle, i.e., "an_posn = m_RectTracker.m_rect.TopLeft()".

Finally, in the TrackItem() method given earlier, after the TrackAnnotation() function call, NullifyNegativeCoordinates() is invoked to nullify any coordinate values that may have been negated through a tracking motion beyond the left or top edge of the document window. Hence, edit the NullifyNegativeCoordinates() function as shown in bold in the following; the ellipsis denotes omitted, unchanged code.

```
int CSystemModel::NullifyNegativeCoordinates()
{
    CPoint ptAn;        // annotation position
    CPoint ptBlk;       // block position
    CPoint ptCon;       // connection-based point location
    list<CAnnotation*>::iterator it_an;      // annotation iterator
    list<CBlock*>::iterator it_blk;          // block iterator
    list<CConnection*>::iterator it_con;    // connection iterator
    list<CPoint>::iterator it_pt; // point iterator

    // CHECK BLOCK COORDINATES
    ...

    // CHECK CONNECTION COORDINATES
    ...

    // CHECK ANNOTATION COORDINATES
    for(it_an = m_lstAnnotation.begin(); it_an != m_lstAnnotation.end();
      it_an++)
    {
        ptAn = (*it_an)->GetPosition();
        if(ptAn.x < 0)
        {
            ptAn.x = 0;
        }
        if(ptAn.y < 0)
        {
            ptAn.y = 0;
        }
        (*it_an)->SetPosition(ptAn);
    }

    return 0;
}
```

30.6.3 MULTIPLE ANNOTATION MOVEMENT

Multiple diagram entities may be moved simultaneously by first circumscribing them with a tracking rectangle and then clicking inside the rectangle followed by movement to an alternative location. The flow of control for the tracking of multiple items involves the following function calls: (1) CDiagramEngView::OnLButtonDown(), (2) CDiagramEngDoc::TrackItem(), and (3) CDiagramEngDoc::TrackMultipleItems(). The TrackMultipleItems() function may be augmented as shown in bold in the following, to iterate through the annotation list and update the annotation positions; the ellipsis ("…") denotes omitted, unchanged code.

```cpp
int CDiagramEngDoc::TrackMultipleItems(CPoint point, CWnd *pWnd)
{
    int intersected = 0;
    int item_tracked = 0;
    int manual_rect = 1;
    int tracker_flag = 0;
    double blk_width;
    double delta = 0.25*m_dDeltaLength;
    static CPoint tracker_init;   // require tracker_init for else clause
      on re-entry of OnLButtonDown
    CPoint an_posn;
    CPoint bend_pt;
    CPoint blk_posn;
    CPoint delta_posn;
    CPoint head_pt;
    CPoint tail_pt;
    CRectTracker temp_tracker;
    list<CAnnotation*> &annotation_list = GetSystemModel().
      GetAnnotationList();
    list<CAnnotation*>::iterator it_an;
    list<CBlock*> &blk_list = GetSystemModel().GetBlockList();
    list<CBlock*>::iterator it_blk;
    list<CConnection*>::iterator it_con;
    list<CConnection*> &con_list = GetSystemModel().GetConnectionList();
    list<CPoint>::iterator it_pt;
    CClientDC dc(pWnd);

    // CScrollView-related change
    …

    // -- IF A RUBBER BAND HAS NOT BEEN CREATED, THEN CREATE IT.
    if(m_iRubberBandCreated == 0)
    {
        …
    }
    // -- IF A RUBBER BAND HAS BEEN CREATED, BUT LEFT-CLICK OUTSIDE OF
    //    ENCLOSING REGION, THEN END TRACK ACTION.
    // CScrollView-related change: use the logical point "ptLogical"
    //   rather than the device point "point"
    //else if((m_RectTracker.HitTest(point) == CRectTracker::hitNothing)
      && (m_iRubberBandCreated == 1))
    else if((m_RectTracker.HitTest(ptLogical) ==
      CRectTracker::hitNothing) && (m_iRubberBandCreated == 1))
    {
        …
    }
```

```
    // -- IF A RUBBER BAND HAS BEEN CREATED, AND LEFT-CLICK INSIDE
      ENCLOSING REGION, THEN POSSIBLY MOVE ITEMS.
    // CScrollView-related change: use the logical point "ptLogical"
      rather than the device point "point"
    //else if((m_RectTracker.HitTest(point) != CRectTracker::hitNothing)
      && (m_iRubberBandCreated == 1))
    else if((m_RectTracker.HitTest(ptLogical)
      != CRectTracker::hitNothing) && (m_iRubberBandCreated == 1))
    {
        // Create a temp tracker since m_RectTracker will have its coords
          updated when the rubber band is moved.
        temp_tracker = m_RectTracker;

        // -- ITERATE THROUGH BLOCKS
        for(it_blk = blk_list.begin(); it_blk != blk_list.end();
          it_blk++)
        {
            …
        }// end for it_blk

        // -- ITERATE THROUGH ALL CONNECTIONS (of this model)
        for(it_con = con_list.begin(); it_con != con_list.end();
          it_con++)
        {
            …
        }// end for it_con

        // -- ITERATE THROUGH ANNOTATIONS
        for(it_an = annotation_list.begin(); it_an != annotation_list.
          end(); it_an++)
        {
            // ANNOTATION
            an_posn = (*it_an)->GetPosition();

            // Determine if item lies within rubber band
            intersected = DetermineCurrentAndIntersectRects
              (temp_tracker, an_posn, delta);
            if(intersected)
            {
                if(item_tracked == 0)
                {
                    // Determine the tracker's change in position
                    // CScrollView-related change: use the logical point
                      "ptLogical" rather than the device point "point"
                    //item_tracked = DetermineTrackerDeltaPosition
                      (pWnd, point, tracker_init, delta_posn);
                    item_tracked = DetermineTrackerDeltaPosition
                      (pWnd, ptLogical, tracker_init, delta_posn);
                }

                // Update annotation posn.
                (*it_an)->SetPosition(an_posn + delta_posn);

                // Set flags
                SetModifiedFlag(TRUE);  // set the doc. as having been
                  modified to prompt user to save
```

```
            UpdateAllViews (NULL);  // indicate that sys. should
                redraw.
        }
    }// end for it_an

    // Set flags
    ...
}

// Return the tracker_flag
return tracker_flag;
}
```

The developer will notice the similarities between the tracking of multiple blocks and annotations. The annotation position is first obtained and used to check whether the annotation lies within the bound tracking rectangle; if so, the annotation position is updated by the change in position of the tracking rectangle.

30.7 VIEW MENU–BASED ACTIONS

At present, annotations may be added to a system model and formatted to allow changes to their content ("m_strAnnotation"), font ("m_strFont"), style ("m_strStyle"), size ("m_iSize"), and color ("m_strColor"), and these changes are reflected in the underlying CFont variable "m_fAnnotationFont". However, the View menu functionality now needs to be augmented to work on annotation instances, changing their position and size and involves the entry-invoked actions: Auto Fit Diagram, Zoom In, Zoom Out, and Reset Diagram.

30.7.1 AUGMENTING AUTO FIT DIAGRAM

The CDiagramEngView::OnAutoFitDiagram() function, called upon selection of the Auto Fit Diagram entry of the View menu, invokes the CSystemModel method DetermineDiagramCoordinateExtrema() to determine the pseudo extreme point on a model diagram; the list of blocks, connections, and connection-based bend points are iterated over and the maximum coordinate components recorded. This function is now augmented to also iterate over the list of annotations, "m_lstAnnotation", and determine the extreme points of the annotation string, "m_strAnnotation", using the text extents, obtained by calling GetOutputTextSize(). Edit the function as shown in bold in the following; the ellipsis ("…") denotes omitted but unchanged code.

```
CPoint CSystemModel::DetermineDiagramCoordinateExtrema(void)
{
    int pt_rad = 5;                          // radius of a bend point
        (assume fixed and small)
    double blk_height;                       // block width
    double blk_width;                        // block height
    CPoint ptAnPosn;                         // annotation position
    CPoint ptBend;                           // bend point
    CPoint ptBlkPosn;                        // block position
    CPoint ptHead;                           // connection head point
    CPoint ptMax;                            // pseudo extreme point
        (extreme coords may be from diff. elements)
    CPoint ptTail;                           // connection tail point
    CPoint ptTemp;                           // temporary point
    CSize an_text_size;                      // annotation text size
    list<CAnnotation*>::iterator it_an;      // annotation iterator
    list<CBlock*>::iterator it_blk;          // block iterator
```

```
    list<CConnection*>::iterator it_con;    // connection iterator
    list<CPoint>::iterator it_pt;           // bend points iterator

    // Init extreme point to the origin.
    ptMax.x = 0;
    ptMax.y = 0;

    // ITERATE THROUGH BLOCK LIST
    ...

    // ITERATE THROUGH ALL CONNECTIONS
    ...

    // ITERATE THROUGH ANNOTATION LIST
    for(it_an = m_lstAnnotation.begin(); it_an != m_lstAnnotation.end();
      it_an++)
    {
        // Dimensions
        ptAnPosn = (*it_an)->GetPosition();
        an_text_size = (*it_an)->GetOutputTextSize();

        // Annotation string extreme point coords
        ptTemp.x = ptAnPosn.x + an_text_size.cx;
        ptTemp.y = ptAnPosn.y + an_text_size.cy;

        if(ptTemp.x > ptMax.x)
        {
                ptMax.x = ptTemp.x;
        }

        if(ptTemp.y > ptMax.y)
        {
            ptMax.y = ptTemp.y;
        }
    }

    return ptMax;
}
```

Later in the development, the CSystemModel::DetermineDiagramCoordinateMinima()
method will be used to obtain diagram-entity coordinate minima, to be returned as a pseudo minimum CPoint argument. Hence, augment the function as shown in bold in the following in a similar
manner to that shown earlier.

```
CPoint CSystemModel::DetermineDiagramCoordinateMinima()
{
    int pt_rad = 5;                          // radius of a bend point
      (assume fixed and small)
    int int_max = 2147483647;                // INT_MAX = 2147483647.
    double blk_height;                       // block width
    double blk_width;                        // block height
    CPoint ptAnPosn;                         // annotation position
    CPoint ptBend;                           // bend point
    CPoint ptBlkPosn;                        // block position
    CPoint ptHead;                           // connection head point
    CPoint ptMin;                            // pseudo minimum point
      (minimum coords may be from diff. elements)
    CPoint ptTail;                           // connection tail point
    CPoint ptTemp;                           // temporary point
    list<CAnnotation*>::iterator it_an;      // annotation iterator
```

```
list<CBlock*>::iterator it_blk;          // block iterator
list<CConnection*>::iterator it_con;     // connection iterator
list<CPoint>::iterator it_pt;            // bend points iterator

// Init minimum point to INT_MAX
ptMin.x = int_max;
ptMin.y = int_max;

// ITERATE THROUGH BLOCK LIST
...

// ITERATE THROUGH ALL CONNECTIONS
...

// ITERATE THROUGH ANNOTATION LIST
for(it_an = m_lstAnnotation.begin(); it_an != m_lstAnnotation.end();
  it_an++)
{
    // Dimensions
    ptAnPosn = (*it_an)->GetPosition();
    ptTemp = ptAnPosn;       // upper left corner is min pt and also
      annotation posn

    if(ptTemp.x < ptMin.x)
    {
        ptMin.x = ptTemp.x;
    }
    if(ptTemp.y < ptMin.y)
    {
        ptMin.y = ptTemp.y;
    }
}

return ptMin;
}
```

To check that the text size, recorded in "m_sOutputTextSize", is in fact correct, the user may place annotations on a diagram and choose the Select All button to select all diagram content, as shown in Figure 30.5. The `CDiagramEngDoc::OnEditSelect All()` function calls both the `DetermineDiagramCoordinateMinima()` and

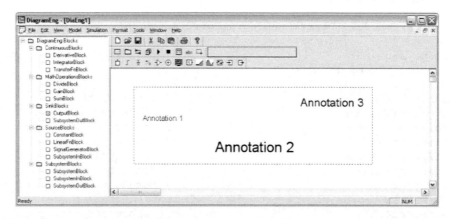

FIGURE 30.5 Selection of all diagram content, indicating the pseudo extreme points and hence the text sizes are correct.

`DetermineDiagramCoordinateExtrema()` methods to determine the pseudo extreme points, here based on the size of the annotation text, and places a bounding rectangle (including a buffer region) around all diagram entities.

30.7.2 ZOOMING IN AND OUT OF A DIAGRAM

The View menu entries Zoom In and Zoom Out chain to the CDiagramEngView functions `OnViewZoomIn()` and `OnViewZoomOut()`, respectively, to increase or decrease a local "scale_factor", scaling variable, followed by a call to `CSystemModel::ScaleSystemModel()`. The `ScaleSystemModel()` function scales connection related variables, i.e., the head, tail, and bend points, and block related variables, i.e., the block width, height, and position; this function is augmented as shown in bold in the following, to scale the annotation position and size (the ellipsis ("…") denotes omitted but unchanged code from Chapter 28).

```
void CSystemModel::ScaleSystemModel(double scale_factor)
{
    int size;                              // annotation size
    double height;                         // block height
    double width;                          // block width
    CPoint ptAn;                           // annotation position
    CPoint ptBend;                         // connection-based bend point
    CPoint ptBlk;                          // block position
    CPoint ptHead;                         // head point
    CPoint ptTail;                         // tail point
    list<CAnnotation*>::iterator it_an;    // annotation iterator
    list<CBlock*>::iterator it_blk;        // block iterator
    list<CConnection*>::iterator it_con;   // connection iterator
    list<CPoint>::iterator it_pt;          // bend point iterator

    // Note: order of operations is important to ensure that items remain
       connected.
    // Connection end points if attached should remain attached.
    // Block ports should scale correctly with block scaling.

    // SCALE CONNECTION-RELATED VARS
    ...

    // SCALE BLOCK-RELATED VARS
    ...

    // SCALE ANNOTATION-RELATED VARS
    for(it_an = m_lstAnnotation.begin(); it_an != m_lstAnnotation.end();
      it_an++)
    {
        // Annotation size
        size = (*it_an)->GetSize();
        size = scale_factor*size;
        (*it_an)->SetSize(size);
        (*it_an)->CreateAnnotationFont((*it_an)->GetAnnotationFont());

        // Annotation position
        ptAn = (*it_an)->GetPosition();
        ptAn.x = scale_factor*ptAn.x;
        ptAn.y = scale_factor*ptAn.y;
        (*it_an)->SetPosition(ptAn);
    }
}
```

The developer will notice that after the size is set, `CreateAnnotationFont()` is called, passing by reference, the member variable, "m_fAnnotationFont", as the argument, such that a new font can be created.

30.7.3 Resetting Initial Diagram Geometry

The user may reset the size of an enlarged or reduced diagram model by selecting the Reset Diagram entry of the View menu; this invokes the event-handler function `CDiag ramEngView::OnViewResetDiagram()` which calls the CDiagramEngDoc method `ResetDefaultGeometry()` wherein the scale factor, to rescale the diagram to its original size, is determined using the current value of "m_dDeltaLength" and passed to `ScaleSystemModel()`.

 The developer will notice that the `OnViewZoomIn()`, `OnViewZoomOut()`, and `ResetDefaultGeometry()` methods all use a scale factor, "scale_factor", of type double, and this is used in the `ScaleSystemModel()` function to scale CPoint (x, y) variables with integer type components, in particular, the block position; the connection object-based head, tail, and bend points; and the recently added annotation position, "m_ptPosition", and size, "m_iSize". There is a slight problem: when the rescaling is performed, the exact position and size are not recovered due to the rounding involved when using a double scaling factor applied to integer arguments. To solve this problem, member variables may be added to the classes concerned to record the initial values of the integer members concerned, and these may be used to reset the initial diagram geometry. Alternatively, no action could be taken, since all diagram entities would be acted upon with the same scale factor and hence any pixel-level discrepancy would be equal across all CPoint arguments. However, the original size of the annotation, "m_iSize", may not be recovered exactly. The interested reader may like to improve the code to prevent this subtle scaling problem.

30.8 FORMAT MENU–BASED ACTIONS

The Format menu currently has one entry in it named Show Annotations, with ID, ID_FORMAT_SHOW_ANNOTATIONS, and corresponding CDiagramEngDoc-based command event-handler function, `CDiagramEngDoc::OnFormatShowAnnotations()`. The purpose of the `OnFormatShowAnnotations()` function is to allow the user to toggle between the showing and hiding of annotations, to reduce diagram clutter, and this is accomplished by setting an integer flag-like variable in the CSystemModel class which controls annotation display.

30.8.1 Augment Document–Based Classes

Additions are required to the CDiagramEngDoc and CSystemModel classes. Add a private integer member variable to the CSystemModel class with the name "m_iDrawAnnotationFlag"; initialize the variable to the default value "1" in the CSystemModel class constructor, since the "1" and "0" states indicate the showing and hiding of annotations, respectively.

 Add a public constant member function to the CSystemModel class with the prototype, `int CSystemModel::GetDrawAnnotationFlag(void) const`, and edit it as shown to retrieve the member variable.

```
int CSystemModel::GetDrawAnnotationFlag() const
{
    return m_iDrawAnnotationFlag;
}
```

Add the accompanying accessor method with the prototype, void CSystemModel::
SetDrawAnnotationFlag(int draw), and edit it as shown.

```
CSystemModel::SetDrawAnnotationFlag(int draw)
{
    m_iDrawAnnotationFlag = draw;
}
```

Now that the member variable and the associated accessor methods have been introduced to the
CSystemModel class, edit the CSystemModel::DrawSystemModel() function as shown
in bold in the following to draw annotations if applicable (the ellipsis ("...") denotes omitted,
unchanged code).

```
void CSystemModel::DrawSystemModel(CDC *pDC)
{
    int pen_color = RGB(0,0,0);          // White = RGB(255,255,255),
      Black = RGB(0,0,0)
    int pen_width = 1;                   // thin = 1
    CString sMsg;                        // main msg string
    UINT nType = MB_OK;                  // style of msg. box
    UINT nIDhelp = 0;                    // help context ID for the msg.
    list<CAnnotation*>::iterator it_an;  // m_lstAnnotation iterator
    list<CBlock*>::iterator it_blk;      // m_lstBlock iterator
    list<CConnection*>::iterator it_con; // m_lstConnection iterator

    // Iterate through the SystemModel lists drawing the stored entities.

    // -- SET UP THE PEN AND pDC ----------
    ...

    // -- DRAW BLOCKS --------------------
    ...

    // -- DRAW CONNECTIONS ---------------
    ...

    // -- DRAW ANNOTATIONS ---------------
    // Iterate through the annotation list
    if(m_iDrawAnnotationFlag == 1)
    {
        for(it_an = m_lstAnnotation.begin(); it_an != m_lstAnnotation.
          end(); it_an++)
        {
            (*it_an)->DrawAnnotation(pDC);
        }
    }

    // -- RESET THE PREV. PEN ------------
    pDC->SelectObject(pOldPen);
}
```

Finally, both the CSystemModel copy constructor and assignment operator need to be augmented
given the introduction of the new integer member variable, "m_iDrawAnnotationFlag". Hence,
make the additions to the CSystemModel::CSytemModel(const CSystemModel &sm)

copy constructor as shown in bold in the following; the rest of the function remains unchanged, as indicated by the ellipsis ("...").

```
CSystemModel::CSystemModel(const CSystemModel &sm)
{
    int i = 0;
    int ncols = 0;
    int *tour_vec_copy = NULL;
    CAnnotation *pAn = NULL;
    CBlock *pBlock = NULL;
    CConnection *pCon = NULL;
    list<CAnnotation*>::const_iterator it_an;
    list<CBlock*>::const_iterator it_blk;
    list<CConnection*>::const_iterator it_con;
    list<int*>::const_iterator it_tr;

    // INTEGER DATA
    m_iDrawAnnotationFlag = sm.GetDrawAnnotationFlag();
    m_iModelStatusFlag = sm.GetModelStatusFlag();
...
}
```

The assignment operator, CSystemModel::operator = (const CSystemModel &sm), may be edited in a similar manner as shown in bold in the following.

```
CSystemModel &CSystemModel::operator=(const CSystemModel &sm)
{
    int i = 0;
    int ncols = 0;
    int *tour_vec_copy = NULL;
    CAnnotation *pAn = NULL;
    CBlock *pBlock = NULL;
    CConnection *pCon = NULL;
    list<CAnnotation*>::const_iterator it_an;
    list<CBlock*>::const_iterator it_blk;
    list<CConnection*>::const_iterator it_con;
    list<int*>::const_iterator it_tr;

    // CHECK FOR SELF-ASSIGNMENT
    if(this == &sm)        // if the address of the current object, "this",
      is the address of the incoming obj.
    {
        return *this;    // deref the "this" pointer to return the obj.
    }

    // DELETE SYSTEM MODEL LISTS
    ...

    // INTEGER DATA
    m_iDrawAnnotationFlag = sm.GetDrawAnnotationFlag();
    m_iModelStatusFlag = sm.GetModelStatusFlag();
    ...

    // RETURN THE CURRENT OBJECT
    return *this;  // deref the "this" pointer to return the underlying obj.
}
```

Now edit the existing CDiagramEngDoc::OnFormatShowAnnotations() function as shown to toggle the annotation-display state.

```
void CDiagramEngDoc::OnFormatShowAnnotations()
{
    // TODO: Add your command handler code here

    // DiagramEng (start)
    CSystemModel &system_model = GetSystemModel();

    int list_size = system_model.GetAnnotationList().size();

    //AfxMessageBox("\n CDiagramEngDoc::OnFormatShowAnnotations()\n",
      MB_OK, 0);

    if((list_size > 0) && (system_model.GetDrawAnnotationFlag() == 0))
    {
        system_model.SetDrawAnnotationFlag(1);     // toggle the
          annotation-drawing state
        SetModifiedFlag(TRUE);                        // set the doc. as
          having been modified to prompt user to save
        UpdateAllViews(NULL);       // indicate that sys. should redraw.
    }
    else if((list_size > 0) && (system_model.GetDrawAnnotationFlag() == 1))
    {
        system_model.SetDrawAnnotationFlag(0);     // toggle the
          annotation-drawing state
        SetModifiedFlag(TRUE);                        // set the doc. as
          having been modified to prompt user to save
        UpdateAllViews(NULL);       // indicate that sys. should redraw.
    }

    // DiagramEng (end)
}
```

30.8.2 UPDATING THE USER INTERFACE

The user can select Show Annotations from the Format menu if annotations exist in the system model, and the menu entry should be updated with a check mark (✓) next to it when displaying annotations; otherwise, the entry should be unchecked. If there are no annotations in the model, then the Format menu entry should be disabled. To implement the updating of the user interface, perform the following.

1. Add an event-handler function, to the CDiagramEngView class, for the UPDATE_ COMMAND_UI event message associated with the ID_FORMAT_SHOW_ ANNOTATIONS menu entry, with the name OnUpdateFormatShowAnnotations().
2. Edit the code as shown to set the check mark next to the Format menu entry denoting whether annotation display is in effect.

```
void CDiagramEngView::OnUpdateFormatShowAnnotations(CCmdUI* pCmdUI)
{
    // TODO: Add your command update UI handler code here

    // DiagramEng (start)
    int draw_an = GetDocument()->GetSystemModel().
      GetDrawAnnotationFlag();     // show annotation state
```

```
    int list_size = GetDocument()->GetSystemModel().GetAnnotationList().
      size();     // annotation list size
    UINT nID = ID_FORMAT_SHOW_ANNOTATIONS;                      // menu entry ID

    // Get the correct menu item
    CMenu *pMenu = AfxGetApp()->GetMainWnd()->GetMenu(); // get the main
      wnd menu

    // Check Annotation List Size
    if(list_size == 0)
    {
        pCmdUI->Enable(FALSE);
        pMenu->CheckMenuItem(nID, MF_UNCHECKED | MF_BYCOMMAND);
        return;
    }
    else if(list_size > 0)
    {
        pCmdUI->Enable(TRUE);
    }

    // Check Display State
    if(draw_an == 1)
    {
        pMenu->CheckMenuItem(nID, MF_CHECKED | MF_BYCOMMAND);
    }
    else if(draw_an == 0)
    {
        pMenu->CheckMenuItem(nID, MF_UNCHECKED | MF_BYCOMMAND);
    }

    // DiagramEng (end)
}
```

The CSystemModel "m_iDrawAnnotationFlag" variable is set in the CDiagramEngDoc::
OnFormatShowAnnotations() method and is used to set or unset the check mark
(CheckMenuItem()) of the Format menu entry from within the CDiagramEngView::OnUpdate
FormatShowAnnotations() function.

The enabling and disabling are done using the pointer-to-CCmdUI, "pCmdUI", and a
call to Enable() with the appropriate Boolean argument; FALSE and TRUE imply disabling and enabling of the entry, respectively [2]. To place a check mark next to the menu
item, first the address of the main menu, "pMenu", is retrieved via the pointer-to-CWinThread,
"m_pMainWnd", obtained through GetMainWnd(), and then a call to CheckMenuItem() is
made upon the menu pointer, where the first argument, "nID", is the ID of the Format menu entry,
i.e., ID_FORMAT_SHOW_ANNOTATIONS, and the second argument is a combination of flags:
MF_CHECKED or MF_UNCHECKED with MF_BYCOMMAND or MF_BYPOSITION [2].

30.9   EDIT MENU–BASED ACTIONS

Chapter 29 presented implementation details for the Cut, Copy, Paste, Undo, and Redo editing
actions, which required the existence of a CClipboard object, "m_Clipboard", and a list of system models, "list<CSystemModel*> m_lstSystemModel", in the CDiagramEngDoc class. In order
to cut and copy diagram entities, copy constructors were required for the main classes, and to
undo and redo actions, the system models were retrieved from and stored in the system model
list through the use of a CSystemModel copy constructor and an assignment operator. Now that

CAnnotation objects are stored in a list of annotations, "m_lstAnnotation", a copy constructor should be provided to allow the editing actions to work in a similar manner to those for the other diagram-entity classes.

30.9.1 CUT, COPY, AND PASTE ACTIONS INVOLVING ANNOTATIONS

The event-handler function `CDiagramEngDoc::OnEditCut()`, for the Cut entry of the Edit menu currently iterates through the list of blocks and connection objects and checks whether the relevant diagram entity lies within the rubber band selection region; if so, a copy constructor is called to copy the entity and place it into the corresponding CClipboard-based list before deleting the entity from the list in the CSystemModel class, and if not, no action is taken. The `OnEditCopy()` method functions in a similar manner, with the exception of deleting the underlying CSystemModel-based diagram entity from the relevant list. The `OnEditPaste()` function simply merges the CClipboard-based lists with the underlying CSystemModel-based lists. To extend the cut, copy, and paste functionality for CAnnotation instances, the following additions are required:

1. Add a copy constructor and relevant methods to the CAnnotation class.
2. Add CAnnotation specific variables and methods to the CClipboard class.
3. Augment the `OnEditCut()`, `OnEditCopy()`, and `OnEditPaste()` functions.

30.9.1.1 Add a Copy Constructor and Relevant Methods to the CAnnotation Class

A (public) copy constructor is to be added to the CAnnotation class with the prototype, `CAnnotation::CAnnotation(const CAnnotation &an)`, and edited as shown. The CAnnotation class is not derived from a base class and hence does not need to call a base class constructor through member initialization.

```
CAnnotation::CAnnotation(const CAnnotation &an)
{
    // Copy incoming argument values to object under construction

    m_sOutputTextSize = an.GetOutputTextSize();
    an.CreateAnnotationFont(m_fAnnotationFont);     // pass underlying
      member var by ref to create new font
    m_iSize = an.GetSize();
    m_ptPosition = an.GetPosition();
    m_strAnnotation = an.GetStringAnnotation();
    m_strColor = an.GetColor();
    m_strFont = an.GetStringFont();
    m_strStyle = an.GetStyle();
}
```

The developer will notice that `CAnnotation::CreateAnnotationFont()` is called upon the incoming reference-to-a-constant-CAnnotation object, "an", where the member variable, "m_fAnnotationFont", of the to-be-constructed object is passed as an argument by reference. This is acceptable since the `CreateAnnotationFont()` function is constant and hence does not alter the object upon which it is called: here, "an".

An alternative way to construct a copy of the font was attempted and involved declaring a LOGFONT structure "LogFont" and then performing the following calls.

```
an.GetAnnotationFontCopy().GetLogFont(&LogFont);
m_fAnnotationFont.CreateFontIndirect(&LogFont);
```

However, this does not work, since although the constant `GetAnnotationFontCopy()` function may be of the form shown, the `GetLogFont()` function is in fact nonconstant, and hence, the constant nature of the copy constructor would not be upheld.

```
const CFont &CAnnotation::GetAnnotationFontCopy() const
{
    return m_fAnnotationFont;
}
```

As a result of this dilemma, the constant `CreateAnnotationFont()` function must be called passing the member variable as an argument, by reference (tricky)!

30.9.1.2 Add CAnnotation Specific Variables and Methods to the CClipboard Class

The `OnEditCut()` and `OnEditCopy()` methods both copy selected diagram entities to the appropriate lists of the CClipboard class; the `OnEditPaste()` method then merges these lists with the corresponding lists in the CSystemModel class. Hence, add a private member variable, named "m_lstAnnotation", to the CClipboard class, with the type, list<CAnnotation*>. Add a public accessor function with prototype, `list<CAnnotation*> &GetAnnotationList(void)`, to retrieve the list by reference and edit it as shown. This will require including the "Annotation.h" header file at the top of the "Clipboard.cpp" source file.

```
list<CAnnotation*> &CClipboard::GetAnnotationList()
{
    return m_lstAnnotation;
}
```

Now the CClipboard class destructor should be augmented to delete the list of CAnnotation pointers, "m_lstAnnotation", as shown in bold in the following.

```
CClipboard::~CClipboard()
{
    // Delete annotation list
    DeleteAnnotationList();

    // Delete block list
    DeleteBlockList();

    // Delete connection list
    DeleteConnectionList();
}
```

Finally, add a public member function to the CClipboard class with the prototype, `void CClipboard::DeleteAnnotationList(void)`, and edit it as shown to first delete (*delete*) the pointers-to-CAnnotation in the list and then clear (`clear()`) the list.

```
void CClipboard::DeleteAnnotationList()
{
    list<CAnnotation*>::iterator it_an;

    // Delete annotation list
```

```
      for(it_an = m_lstAnnotation.begin(); it_an != m_lstAnnotation.end();
        it_an++)
      {
          delete (*it_an);     // delete what it_an is pointing to:
            i.e. deref the it_an ptr and delete the ptr-to-CAnnotation.
      }
      m_lstAnnotation.clear();
}
```

30.9.1.3 Augment the `OnEditCut()`, `OnEditCopy()`, and `OnEditPaste()` Functions

Now the cut, copy, and paste functions need to be augmented to iterate through the list of CAnnotation pointers, "m_lstAnnotation", and perform copy construction and merging operations. Edit the CDiagramEngDoc::OnEditCut() function as shown in bold in the following (the ellipsis ("…") denotes omitted and unchanged code for brevity).

```
void CDiagramEngDoc::OnEditCut()
{
    // TODO: Add your command handler code here
    // DiagramEng (start)
    int intersected = 0;
    int intersected_head = 0;
    int intersected_tail = 0;
    double blk_width;
    double delta = 0.25*m_dDeltaLength;
    CAnnotation *pAn = NULL;
    CBlock *pBlock = NULL;
    CConnection *pCon = NULL;
    CPoint an_posn;
    CPoint blk_posn;
    CPoint head_pt;
    CPoint tail_pt;
    CRectTracker temp_tracker;
    list<CAnnotation*> &an_list = m_SystemModel.GetAnnotationList();
    list<CAnnotation*> &an_list_cb = m_Clipboard.GetAnnotationList();
    list<CAnnotation*>::iterator it_an;
    list<CBlock*> &blk_list = m_SystemModel.GetBlockList();
    list<CBlock*> &blk_list_cb = m_Clipboard.GetBlockList();
    list<CBlock*>::iterator it_blk;
    list<CConnection*> &con_list = m_SystemModel.GetConnectionList();
    list<CConnection*> &con_list_cb = m_Clipboard.GetConnectionList();
    list<CConnection*>::iterator it_con;

    // -- IF A RUBBER BAND HAS BEEN CREATED
    if(m_iRubberBandCreated == 1)
    {
        ...

        // -- ITERATE THROUGH BLOCKS
        ...

        // -- ITERATE THROUGH ALL CONNECTIONS (of this model)
        ...

        // -- ITERATE THROUGH ANNOTATIONS
        it_an = an_list.begin();
        while(it_an != an_list.end())
```

```
    {
        // Get annotation properties
        an_posn = (*it_an)->GetPosition();

        // Determine if item lies within rubber band
        intersected = DetermineCurrentAndIntersectRects(temp_tracker,
          an_posn, delta);
        if(intersected)
        {
            // COPY ANNOTATION TO CLIPBOARD BLOCK LIST
            pAn = new CAnnotation(**it_an);
            an_list_cb.push_back(pAn);

            // Delete annotation
            delete *it_an;   // delete annotation pointed to by it_an
            it_an = an_list.erase(it_an);   // delete element at
              offset it_an in list (that held the annotation)
        }
        else // only increment the iterator if there were
          no intersection
        {
            it_an++;
        }
    }// end for it_an

    // Reset member vars.
    m_iRubberBandCreated = 0;   // end the rubber band state
    SetKeyFlagTrack(0);         // reset the key-based track flag
      since tracking aborted

    // Set flags
    SetModifiedFlag(TRUE);   // set the doc. as having been modified
      to prompt user to save
    UpdateAllViews(NULL);    // indicate that sys. should redraw.

    }// end if m_iRubberBandCreated

    // DiagramEng (end)
}
```

Initially the CSystemModel and CClipboard annotation lists, "an_list" and "an_list_cb", respectively, are retrieved, and then the CSystemModel list is iterated over and new CAnnotation objects created; the "it_an" iterator is dereferenced once to obtain the pointer-to-CAnnotation, and then again, to access the object, which is used by the copy constructor to create a new CAnnotation instance. Thereafter, the pointer is added to the CClipboard-based list, "an_list_cb", and the annotation deleted and erased from the CSystemModel-based list, "an_list" or, equivalently, "m_lstAnnotation"; the deletion is necessary for the cut operation.

Edit the CDiagramEngDoc::OnEditCopy() function in a similar manner to the OnEditCut() function presented earlier, as shown in bold in the following; here, no deletion or erasing is performed on the CSystemModel-based annotation list, "an_list" or, equivalently, "m_lstAnnotation", and hence, a *for* rather than a *while* loop is used to iterate over the list.

```
void CDiagramEngDoc::OnEditCopy()
{
    // TODO: Add your command handler code here
    // DiagramEng (start)
    int intersected = 0;
```

```
        int intersected_head = 0;
        int intersected_tail = 0;
        double blk_width;
        double delta = 0.25*m_dDeltaLength;
        CAnnotation *pAn = NULL;
        CBlock *pBlock = NULL;
        CConnection *pCon = NULL;
        CPoint an_posn;
        CPoint blk_posn;
        CPoint head_pt;
        CPoint tail_pt;
        CRectTracker temp_tracker;
        list<CAnnotation*> &an_list = m_SystemModel.GetAnnotationList();
        list<CAnnotation*> &an_list_cb = m_Clipboard.GetAnnotationList();
        list<CAnnotation*>::iterator it_an;
        list<CBlock*> &blk_list = m_SystemModel.GetBlockList();
        list<CBlock*> &blk_list_cb = m_Clipboard.GetBlockList();
        list<CBlock*>::iterator it_blk;
        list<CConnection*> &con_list = m_SystemModel.GetConnectionList();
        list<CConnection*> &con_list_cb = m_Clipboard.GetConnectionList();
        list<CConnection*>::iterator it_con;


        // -- IF A RUBBER BAND HAS BEEN CREATED
        if(m_iRubberBandCreated == 1)
        {
            …


            // -- ITERATE THROUGH BLOCKS
            …

            // -- ITERATE THROUGH ALL CONNECTIONS (of this model)
            …

            // -- ITERATE THROUGH ANNOTATIONS
            for(it_an = an_list.begin(); it_an != an_list.end(); it_an++)
            {
                // Get annotation properties
                an_posn = (*it_an)->GetPosition();

                // Determine if item lies within rubber band
                intersected = DetermineCurrentAndIntersectRects(temp_tracker,
                  an_posn, delta);
                if(intersected)
                {
                    // COPY ANNOTATION TO CLIPBOARD BLOCK LIST
                    pAn = new CAnnotation(**it_an);
                    an_list_cb.push_back(pAn);
                }
            }// end for it_an


        // Reset member vars.
        m_iRubberBandCreated = 0;        // end the rubber band state
        SetKeyFlagTrack(0);             // reset the key-based track flag
          since tracking aborted
```

```
        // Set flags
        SetModifiedFlag(TRUE);          // set the doc. as having been
          modified to prompt user to save
        UpdateAllViews (NULL);          // indicate that sys. should redraw.

    }// end if m_iRubberBandCreated

    // DiagramEng (end)
}
```

Finally, the CDiagramEngDoc::OnEditPaste() function may be augmented as shown in bold in the following to merge (merge()) the annotation list of the CClipboard class, "an_list_cb", with the annotation list of the CSystemModel class, "an_list", or equivalently, "m_lstAnnotation", where the former list is emptied by the merge() operation (as discussed in the preceding chapter).

```
void CDiagramEngDoc::OnEditPaste()
{
    // TODO: Add your command handler code here
    // DiagramEng (start)
    list<CAnnotation*> &an_list = m_SystemModel.GetAnnotationList();
    list<CAnnotation*> &an_list_cb = m_Clipboard.GetAnnotationList();
    list<CAnnotation*>::iterator it_an;
    list<CBlock*> &blk_list = m_SystemModel.GetBlockList();
    list<CBlock*> &blk_list_cb = m_Clipboard.GetBlockList();
    list<CBlock*>::iterator it_blk;
    list<CConnection*> &con_list = m_SystemModel.GetConnectionList();
    list<CConnection*> &con_list_cb = m_Clipboard.GetConnectionList();
    list<CConnection*>::iterator it_con;

    // Add clipboard block list contents to end of system model block
      list
    // merge() merges the arg list into the list upon which merge() is
      called leaving, the arg list empty.
    blk_list.merge(blk_list_cb);

    // Add clipboard connection list contents to end of system model
      connection list
    // merge() merges the arg list into the list upon which merge() is
      called, leaving the arg list empty.
    con_list.merge(con_list_cb);

    // Snap connection end points to port or bend point
    SnapConnectionEndPointsAfterInitialConstruction();

    // Add clipboard annotation list contents to end of system model
      annotation list
    // merge() merges the arg list into the list upon which merge() is
      called leaving, the arg list empty.
    an_list.merge(an_list_cb);

    // Set flags
    SetModifiedFlag(TRUE);     // set the doc. as having been modified to
      prompt user to save
    UpdateAllViews (NULL);     // indicate that sys. should redraw.

    // DiagramEng (end)
}
```

30.9.2 Undo and Redo of Editing Actions Involving Annotations

The Undo and Redo entries of the Edit menu allow the user to undo and redo system model based editing actions, and assign a system model stored in the system model list, "m_lstSystemModel", to the (in vogue) system model object, "m_SystemModel", through the use of the CSystemModel assignment operator, CSystemModel::operator=(). However, to initially place the system models into the list, the CDiagramEngDoc::SaveSystemModelToList() function is called, wherein the copy constructor, CSystemModel::CSystemModel(const CSystemModel &sm), is invoked to make a copy of the current system model before its address is added to the list. Now, given the introduction of a list of annotations, "m_lstAnnotation", to the CSystemModel class, changes need to be made to the following methods:

1. CDiagramEngDoc::SaveSystemModelToList()
2. CSystemModel::CSystemModel(const CSystemModel &sm)
3. CSystemModel::operator=(const CSystemModel &sm)

30.9.2.1 Augment the Model Saving Function

The purpose of the CSystemModel::SaveSystemModelToList() function is to initially save an empty system model in the list of system models, "m_lstSystemModel", and, thereafter, save the current (in vogue) system model, "m_SystemModel", to the list, through the use of the CSystemModel copy constructor. Hence, augment the SaveSystemModelToList() function as shown in bold in the following, to delete the list of annotation objects required for the generation of an initial empty model. Only one line of additional code is required; unchanged and omitted code is denoted by an ellipsis ("…").

```
void CDiagramEngDoc::SaveSystemModelToList()
{
    int i;
    int lst_size;
    list<CSystemModel*>::iterator it_sm;
    list<CSystemModel*>::iterator it_sm_erase_start;
    CSystemModel *pSystemModel = NULL;

    // Place an empty model in the list to begin with, representing an
      empty palette
    if(m_iIndexSystemModel == 0)
    {
        // Copy constructor called to construct a copy of a system model
        pSystemModel = new CSystemModel(m_SystemModel);

        pSystemModel->DeleteBlockList();
        pSystemModel->DeleteConnectionList();
        pSystemModel->DeleteSourceOutputLoopLists();
        pSystemModel->DeleteAnnotationList();

        m_lstSystemModel.push_back(pSystemModel);
    }

    // Determine start point for erase
    ...

    // Delete unwanted elements and then erase the portion of the list
    ...
```

```
    // Create a new system model using the class member m_SystemModel and
      the copy constructor
    pSystemModel = new CSystemModel(m_SystemModel);

    // Put address of the newly created system model at the back of
      m_lstSystemModel
    m_lstSystemModel.push_back(pSystemModel);

    // If list too big delete the first element and take it off the list
    …

    // Adjust index
    …

    // Adjust Undo/Redo flags
    …
}
```

30.9.2.2   Augment the CSystemModel Copy Constructor

The CSystemModel copy constructor is used in `SaveSystemModelToList()` to make a copy of the current (in vogue) system model, "m_SystemModel", and return its address, of type pointer-to-CSystemModel, to be stored in the list, "m_lstSystemModel". Hence, augment the CSystemModel copy constructor as shown in bold in the following with CAnnotation-specific details (the ellipsis ("…") denotes unchanged, omitted code).

```
CSystemModel::CSystemModel(const CSystemModel &sm)
{
    int i = 0;
    int ncols = 0;
    int *tour_vec_copy = NULL;
    CAnnotation *pAn = NULL;
    CBlock *pBlock = NULL;
    CConnection *pCon = NULL;
    list<CAnnotation*>::const_iterator it_an;
    list<CBlock*>::const_iterator it_blk;
    list<CConnection*>::const_iterator it_con;
    list<int*>::const_iterator it_tr;

    // INTEGER DATA
    …

    // DOUBLE DATA
    …

    // CString DATA
    …

    // LIST DATA
    // Copy Block List
    …

    // Copy Connection List
    …

    // Copy Source Loop Tour List
    …

    // Copy Source Output Tour List
    …

    // Copy Annotation List
```

```
    const list<CAnnotation*> *plstAnnotation =
      sm.GetAnnotationListCopy();

    for(it_an = (*plstAnnotation).begin(); it_an != (*plstAnnotation).
      end(); it_an++)
    {
        pAn = new CAnnotation(**it_an);
        m_lstAnnotation.push_back(pAn);
    }
}
```

The developer will have noticed the call to GetAnnotationListCopy() in the copy constructor given earlier; this accessor function obtains the address of the annotation list which is then assigned to the pointer-to-a-constant list of CAnnotation pointers, i.e., "const list<CAnnotation*> *plstAnnotation". Hence, add a public member function to the CSystemModel class with the prototype, const list<CAnnotation*> *CSystemModel::GetAnnotationListCopy() const, and edit it as shown.

```
const list<CAnnotation*> *CSystemModel::GetAnnotationListCopy() const
{
    // For the fn. to be const, a pointer-to-const type is returned.
    return &m_lstAnnotation;
}
```

The function is necessarily constant, in order to satisfy the constant nature of the incoming "sm" argument to the copy constructor, and hence the address of the annotation list returned, "&m_lstAnnotation" must also be constant, as reflected by the accessor method's return type: "const list<CAnnotation*> *".

The retrieved annotation list is iterated over and new CAnnotation objects created using the CAnnotation copy constructor; the iterator, "it_an", is dereferenced once to access the pointer-to-CAnnotation, and then a second time to access the CAnnotation object, which is ultimately passed as a reference-to-a-constant-CAnnotation object to the copy constructor. The address of the new annotation object, stored in "pAn", is then added to the member list, "m_lstAnnotation", of the CSystemModel object under construction.

30.9.2.3 Augment the CSystemModel Assignment Operator

The CSystemModel assignment operator, CSystemModel::operator=(), is used in both the CDiagramEngDoc editing functions, OnEditUndo() and OnEditRedo(), to assign a system model in the list, "m_lstSystemModel", to the current (in vogue) model, "m_SystemModel", i.e., "m_SystemModel.operator=(*pSystemModel)", where "pSystemModel" is the address of a system model in the list. The assignment operator should be augmented in a similar manner to the copy constructor, as shown in bold in the following.

```
CSystemModel &CSystemModel::operator=(const CSystemModel &sm)
{
    int i = 0;
    int ncols = 0;
    int *tour_vec_copy = NULL;
    CAnnotation *pAn = NULL;
    CBlock *pBlock = NULL;
    CConnection *pCon = NULL;
    list<CAnnotation*>::const_iterator it_an;
    list<CBlock*>::const_iterator it_blk;
    list<CConnection*>::const_iterator it_con;
    list<int*>::const_iterator it_tr;
```

```
// CHECK FOR SELF-ASSIGNMENT
if(this == &sm)        // if the address of the current object,
  "this", is the address of the incoming obj.
{
    return *this;      // deref the "this" pointer to return the obj.
}


// DELETE SYSTEM MODEL LISTS
DeleteBlockList();                      // Delete block list
DeleteConnectionList();                 // Delete connection list
DeleteSourceOutputLoopLists();          // Delete source-to-output-block
  and source-to-loop-repeated-block lists
DeleteAnnotationList();                 // Delete annotation list

// INTEGER DATA
...

// DOUBLE DATA
...

// CString DATA
...

// LIST DATA
...

// Copy Annotation List
const list<CAnnotation*> *plstAnnotation =
  sm.GetAnnotationListCopy();

for(it_an = (*plstAnnotation).begin(); it_an != (*plstAnnotation).
  end(); it_an++)
{
    pAn = new CAnnotation(**it_an);
    m_lstAnnotation.push_back(pAn);
}

// RETURN THE CURRENT OBJECT
return *this;  // deref the "this" pointer to return the underlying obj.
}
```

The developer will notice that first the underlying annotation list is deleted through the call to
DeleteAnnotationList(). Then, the annotation list of the incoming system model object,
"sm", is retrieved and iterated over, and new CAnnotation objects created and added to the underlying system model object's annotation list, "m_lstAnnotation".

30.10   SERIALIZATION OF THE CAnnotation CLASS

An earlier chapter discussed the serialization (saving) and deserialization (restoring) required by
the DiagramEng application and concerned the CSystemModel class and its contained classes,
including CBlock, CBlockShape, CConnection, CPort, and the derived CBlock classes. The main
DiagramEng classes CDiagramEngApp, CDiagramEngDoc, and CDiagramEngView, and the
transient connection-based CSignal data did not need to be serialized. However, now that the

TABLE 30.5

CAnnotation Serialization Data: Data Type, Member Variable, and Description

Data Type	Member Variable	Description
int	m_iSize	Size of text
int	m_ptPosition.x	Annotation position x-coordinate
int	m_ptPosition.y	Annotation position y-coordinate
int	m_sOutputTextSize.cx	Width of output text
int	m_sOutputTextSize.cy	Height of output text
CFont	m_fAnnotationFont	Annotation font
CString	m_strAnnotation	Annotation string identifier
CString	m_strColor	Color: Red, Green, Blue, Black
CString	m_strFont	Font string identifier
CString	m_strStyle	Style: Regular, Italic, Bold, Bold Italic

CAnnotation class has been added to the project and a list of annotations, "m_lstAnnotation", is stored in the CSystemModel class, the serialization-centric code needs to be augmented in various locations. The implementation topics are as follows:

1. CAnnotation class serialization
2. CSystemModel class serialization
3. Augmenting the file open methods

30.10.1   CAnnotation Class Serialization

The CAnnotation class has eight member variables, some of which need to be serialized as shown in Table 30.5; the CFont, "m_fAnnotationFont", variable does not need to be serialized since it may be reconstructed from the other variables via a call to the CreateAnnotationFont() function, where the member variable is passed as an argument by reference. The CPoint and CSize variables, "m_ptPosition" and "m_sOutputTextSize", respectively, are saved and restored using their (x, y) or (cx, cy) component integer data as shown.

30.10.1.1   CAnnotation::WriteAnnotationDataToFile()

The responsibility of the CAnnotation::WriteAnnotationDataToFile() method is to write the serialization data to the output file stream, "ofstream", object (denoted "fout" in the following); this works in a similar way to existing data-writing functions by first writing the identifier, "annotation", followed by the member variable values.

1. Add a public member function to the CAnnotation class with the prototype, void CAnnotation::WriteAnnotationDataToFile(ofstream &fout), and edit it as shown.

```
void CAnnotation::WriteAnnotationDataToFile(ofstream &fout)
{
    char strVar[L_FILE_IO_STR];    // char array used with fout

    // Write CAnnotation member data to file.
    strcpy(strVar, "annotation");
    fout << strVar << endl;
```

```
        fout << m_ptPosition.x << " " << m_ptPosition.y << endl;
        fout << m_sOutputTextSize.cx << " " << m_sOutputTextSize.cy << endl;
        fout << m_iSize << endl;

        strcpy(strVar, m_strAnnotation);
        fout << strVar << endl;

        strcpy(strVar, m_strColor);
        fout << strVar << endl;

        strcpy(strVar, m_strFont);
        fout << strVar << endl;

        strcpy(strVar, m_strStyle);
        fout << strVar << endl;
}
```

The developer will notice the use of the character array, "strVar"; this is required since the ofstream object, "fout", with the operator "<<" is not designed to write out CString data, but rather a character array.

2. Include the file-stream header file, "fstream.h", (#include <fstream>) prior to the class declaration in the "Annotation.h" header file since it declares an "ofstream" object, "fout".
3. In addition, add "using namespace std" beneath the included header file to cater for the "ofstream" identifier as shown in bold in the header file in the following.
4. Finally, include the "Block.h" header file at the top of the "Annotation.cpp" source file since the length of a string used in file input/output, L_FILE_IO_STR, is defined in this file.

```
// Annotation.h: interface for the CAnnotation class.
//
//////////////////////////////////////////////////////////////////////

#if !defined(AFX_ANNOTATION_H__DE65EA5D_AEE5_456C_97DD_9BEA04E3ACE2__
  INCLUDED_)
#define AFX_ANNOTATION_H__DE65EA5D_AEE5_456C_97DD_9BEA04E3ACE2__INCLUDED_

#if _MSC_VER > 1000
#pragma once
#endif // _MSC_VER > 1000

#include <fstream>      // rqd. for serialization
using namespace std;    // rqd. for ofstream

class CAnnotation
{
    void WriteAnnotationDataToFile(ofstream &fout);
    ...
};

#endif // !defined(AFX_ANNOTATION_H__DE65EA5D_
  AEE5_456C_97DD_9BEA04E3ACE2__INCLUDED_)
```

30.10.1.2 CAnnotation::ReadAnnotationDataFromFile()

The annotation data may be read from a model-data file through the use of a data-reading function and an input file stream, "ifstream", object (denoted "fin" in the following). Hence, add a public

member function to the CAnnotation class with the prototype, void CAnnotation::Read
AnnotationDataFromFile(ifstream &fin), and edit it as shown. The reading and writing
actions are required to be in the same order for consistency.

```
void CAnnotation::ReadAnnotationDataFromFile(ifstream &fin)
{
    char strVar[L_FILE_IO_STR];     // char array used with fin

    // Read CAnnotation member data from file
    fin >> strVar;      // connection string ID
    fin >> m_ptPosition.x;
    fin >> m_ptPosition.y;
    fin >> m_sOutputTextSize.cx;
    fin >> m_sOutputTextSize.cy;
    fin >> m_iSize;

    // Annotation string
    while(fin.getline(strVar, L_FILE_IO_STR, '\n'))
    {
        // If string not empty then assume string on line is correct
        if(strcmp(strVar, "") != 0)
        {
            m_strAnnotation = strVar;
            break;
        }
    }

    // Annotation color
    while(fin.getline(strVar, L_FILE_IO_STR, '\n'))
    {
        // If string not empty then assume string on line is correct
        if(strcmp(strVar, "") != 0)
        {
            m_strColor = strVar;
            break;
        }
    }

    // Font string
    while(fin.getline(strVar, L_FILE_IO_STR, '\n'))
    {
        // If string not empty then assume string on line
          is correct
        if(strcmp(strVar, "") != 0)
        {
            m_strFont = strVar;
            break;
        }
    }

    // Style string
    while(fin.getline(strVar, L_FILE_IO_STR, '\n'))
    {
        // If string not empty then assume string on line is
          correct
```

```
        if(strcmp(strVar, "") != 0)
        {
            m_strStyle = strVar;
            break;
        }
    }

    // Create the annotation font m_fAnnotationFont
    CreateAnnotationFont(m_fAnnotationFont);
}
```

The developer will notice the call to `CreateAnnotationFont()` after the CAnnotation data have been read in from a file. This is required since the CFont member variable, "m_fAnnotationFont", is not serialized, but needs to be created using the other member variables (see the definition of the `CAnnotation::CreateAnnotationFont()` method provided in Section 30.3.2.4).

30.10.2 CSystemModel Class Serialization

The CSystemModel data considered for serialization were presented in an earlier chapter, where only double and CString type data were needed to be serialized, as indicated (in regular style) in Table 30.6. Although a CAnnotation class has been added to the project and the CSystemModel class has a list of annotation objects, "m_lstAnnotation", and a variable, "m_iDrawAnnotationFlag", to control their display, these new items (shown in italics) do not need to be serialized.

The CSystemModel serialization functions `WriteSystemModelDataToFile()` and `ReadSystemModelDataFromFile()` now need to be augmented to cater for the list of

TABLE 30.6
CSystemModel Serialization Data: Data Type, Member Variable, and Description

Data Type	Member Variable	Description
int	*m_iDrawAnnotationFlag*	*Draw annotation flag*
int	m_iModelStatusFlag	Model status flag
int	m_iNOutputBlocks	No. of model output blocks
int	m_iNSourceBlocks	No. of model source blocks
int	m_iNSourceLoopTours	No. of source-to-loop-repeated-block tours
int	m_iNSourceOutputTours	No. of source-to-output-block tours
double	m_dATOL	Absolute error tolerance parameter
double	m_dRTOL	Relative error tolerance parameter
double	m_dTimeStart	Simulation start time
double	m_dTimeStepSize	Time-step size
double	m_dTimeStop	Simulation stop time
CString	m_strIntegrationMethod	Integration method: Euler, Runge–Kutta
CString	m_strModelName	Name of current system model
CString	m_strTimeStepType	Time-step type: fixed-step or variable-step
CString	m_strWarning	Diagnostic warning messages
list<int*>	m_lstSourceLoopTour	List of arrays of source-loop-block tours
list<int*>	m_lstSourceOutputTour	List of arrays of source-output-block tours
list<CAnnotation>*	*m_lstAnnotation*	*List of annotations*
list<CBlock*>	m_lstBlock	List of blocks
list<CConnection*>	m_lstConnection	List of connections
list<CConnection*>	m_lstConnectionError	List of disconnected connections

Unshaded entries are to be serialized.

CAnnotation objects, "m_lstAnnotation". The data-writing function simply iterates through the list of annotations and calls the CAnnotation::WriteAnnotationDataToFile() method upon the pointer-to-CAnnotation, as shown in bold in the following.

```
void CSystemModel::WriteSystemModelDataToFile(ofstream &fout)
{
    char strVar[L_FILE_IO_STR];            // local string var
    list<CAnnotation*>::iterator it_an;    // annotation list iterator
    list<CBlock*>::iterator it_blk;        // blk list iterator
    list<CConnection*>::iterator it_con;   // connection list iterator

    //AfxMessageBox("\n CSystemModel::WriteSystemModelDataToFile()\n",
      MB_OK, 0);

    // Write member data to file.
    strcpy(strVar, m_strModelName);
    fout << strVar << endl;

    fout << m_dATOL << endl;
    fout << m_dRTOL << endl;
    fout << m_dTimeStart << endl;
    fout << m_dTimeStepSize << endl;
    fout << m_dTimeStop << endl;

    strcpy(strVar, m_strIntegrationMethod);
    fout << strVar << endl;

    strcpy(strVar, m_strTimeStepType);
    fout << strVar << endl;

    strcpy(strVar, m_strWarning);
    fout << strVar << endl;

    // Iterate through the block list calling WriteBlockDataToFile()
    for(it_blk = m_lstBlock.begin(); it_blk != m_lstBlock.end(); it_blk++)
    {
        (*it_blk)->WriteBlockDataToFile(fout);
    }

    // Iterate through the connection list calling
      WriteConnectionDataToFile()
    for(it_con = m_lstConnection.begin(); it_con != m_lstConnection.
      end(); it_con++)
    {
        (*it_con)->WriteConnectionDataToFile(fout);
    }

    // Iterate through the annotation list calling
      WriteAnnotationDataToFile()
    for(it_an = m_lstAnnotation.begin(); it_an != m_lstAnnotation.end();
      it_an++)
    {
        (*it_an)->WriteAnnotationDataToFile(fout);
    }
}
```

The data-reading method, ReadSystemModelDataFromFile(), uses a *while* loop to iterate through the contents of the input data file, reading each line until the end of the file. A string comparison, using strcmp(), is made to filter the identifier denoting the type of object to be reconstructed and whose data are to be read in from a file. Here, the function is augmented as shown in bold in the following to filter a CAnnotation object, using the string identifier, "annotation"; thereafter, a new CAnnotation object is constructed and its data read using the ReadAnnotationDataFromFile() method (the ellipsis ("...") denotes omitted and unchanged code).

```
void CSystemModel::ReadSystemModelDataFromFile(ifstream &fin)
{
    int cnt = 0;                    // counter to discern correctness of
      first line of file
    int error_cnt = 0;             // counter to discern an inf. loop
    int max_cnt = 10000;           // max cnt for error detection
    char strLine[L_FILE_IO_STR];   // current line as a character array
    char strVar[L_FILE_IO_STR];    // character array var to work with
      "fin >>"
    CString sMsg;                   // msg string
    CString sMsgTemp;               // temp msg string
    streampos stream_posn;          // position in the stream

        //AfxMessageBox("n CSystemModel::ReadSystemModelDataFromFile()\n",
          MB_OK, 0);

    // READ THROUGH CONTENTS OF FILE
    while(!fin.eof())
    {
        // Get current stream posn
        stream_posn = fin.tellg();

        // Get current line (NOTE: getline() did not work as expected
          here and returned an empty line)
        fin >> strLine;

        // Now go back to the start of the line, such that the first data
          element can be read in.
        fin.seekg(stream_posn);

        // IF NOT EMPTY STR, THEN CONTINUE
        // If the comparison of "strLine" with the empty string equals
          zero, then "strLine" is the empty string.
        // If the comparison of "strLine" with the empty string != zero,
          then "strLine" is not the empty string.
        if(strcmp(strLine, "") != 0)
        {
            // SYSTEM MODEL
            // Check that this is a model_data.txt file with
              "system_model" as the first line
              ...

            // If strLine is "system_model" then read in the data
            if(strcmp(strLine, "system_model") == 0)
            {
                ...
            }// end system model

            // ANNOTATION
            if(strcmp(strLine, "annotation") == 0)
            {
                CAnnotation *pAn = new CAnnotation();
                pAn->ReadAnnotationDataFromFile(fin);     // read and
                  assign annotation member data
```

```
              m_lstAnnotation.push_back(pAn);      // add annotation to
                annotation list
          }

          // CONNECTION
          ...

          // CONSTANT BLOCK
          ...

      }// end strcmp()
      // CHECK FOR FILE READ ERROR I.E. AN INF. LOOP
      ...

  }// end while
}
```

The developer will recognize that as the model data file, e.g., "model_data.txt", uses identifiers denoting objects to be reconstructed, e.g., "system_model", "connection", etc., and whose data are subsequently read, no change needs to be made to old model files that were saved with a previous version of the code. If, upon reading an old file, the recently introduced identifier reflecting a new class instance is not detected, then the corresponding object is simply not constructed. However, if the identifier is present, as it may be in the event that a new class instance is used, here e.g., a CAnnotation object, then the newly introduced filter, e.g., "if(strcmp(strLine, "annotation") == 0)", will detect the object to be reconstructed.

30.10.3 AUGMENTING THE FILE OPEN METHODS

The methods used to initiate the opening of an existing file are CDiagramEngDoc::OnFileOpen() and CDiagramEngApp::OnFileRecentFileOpen(). If a system model already exists on the palette at the time of an attempt to open an existing file, a message is presented to the user to determine whether the intention is to overwrite the model; if not, the function returns, but if so, then the current model on the palette is to have its member lists erased. Now that the CSystemModel class contains a list of annotations, "m_lstAnnotation", its contents need to be erased in both file-opening functions as shown in bold in the code in the following (the ellipsis ("…") denotes omitted and unchanged code).

```
void CDiagramEngDoc::OnFileOpen()
{
    // TODO: Add your command handler code here
    // DiagramEng (start)
    int btnSel;     // button selection
    ...

    // Create a new document
    if((m_SystemModel.GetBlockList().size() != 0) || (m_SystemModel.
      GetConnectionList().size() != 0) || (m_SystemModel.
      GetAnnotationList().size() != 0))
    {
        sMsg.Format(" A system model already exists. \n Do you want to
          erase it? \n");
        btnSel = AfxMessageBox(sMsg, MB_YESNOCANCEL, 0);

        if(btnSel == IDYES)
        {
            // Delete System Model Lists
            m_SystemModel.DeleteBlockList();
            m_SystemModel.DeleteConnectionList();
```

```
                    m_SystemModel.DeleteSourceOutputLoopLists();
                    m_SystemModel.DeleteAnnotationList();
                    ...
                }
                else if(btnSel == IDNO)
                {
                    ...
                }
                else if(btnSel == IDCANCEL)
                {
                    return
                }
            }
            ...
            // DiagramEng (end)
        }

        void CDiagramEngApp::OnFileRecentFileOpen(UINT i)
        {
            int btnSel;      // button selection
            ...

            // CHECK FOR THE EXISTENCE OF A MODEL ON THE DOC: GET THE SYSTEM
              MODEL BY REFERENCE!
            CSystemModel &system_model = pDoc->GetSystemModel();
            if((system_model.GetBlockList().size() != 0) || (system_model.
              GetConnectionList().size() != 0) || (system_model.
              GetAnnotationList().size() != 0))
            {
                sMsg.Format(" A system model already exists. \n Do you want to
                  erase it? \n");
                btnSel = AfxMessageBox(sMsg, MB_YESNOCANCEL, 0);

                if(btnSel == IDYES)
                {
                    // Delete System Model Lists
                    system_model.DeleteBlockList();
                    system_model.DeleteConnectionList();
                    system_model.DeleteSourceOutputLoopLists();
                    system_model.DeleteAnnotationList();

                    // Set flags and redraw the doc
                    pDoc->SetModifiedFlag(TRUE);     // set the doc. as having
                      been modified to prompt user to save
                    pDoc->UpdateAllViews(NULL);      // indicate that sys. should
                      redraw.
                }
                else if(btnSel == IDNO)     // Create a new document for the model
                {
                    ...
                }
                else if(btnSel == IDCANCEL)
                {
                    return;
                }
            }
            ...
        }
```

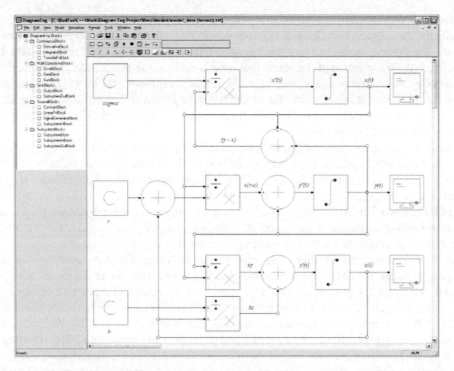

FIGURE 30.6 The diagrammatic representation of the Lorenz equations showing mathematical annotations.

The developer will notice that the only modification in both functions are to extend a conditional check and call DeleteAnnotationList() on the CSystemModel object, "m_SystemModel"; otherwise, the functions remain unchanged.

Now the user can save and restore a model diagram with annotation information describing model entities, as shown in the diagrammatic representation of the Lorenz equations, in Figure 30.6. The system of equations, representing a simplified model of convection rolls in the atmosphere, repeated for convenience here is

$$\dot{x}(t) = \sigma(y(t) - x(t)) \tag{30.3a}$$

$$\dot{y}(t) = x(r - z(t)) - y(t) \tag{30.3b}$$

$$\dot{z}(t) = x(t)y(t) - bz(t) \tag{30.3c}$$

where
  $x(t)$, $y(t)$, and $z(t)$ are spatial coordinates that are functions of time t
  σ, r, and b are the Prandtl number, Rayleigh number, and a quantity related to the height of the fluid being modeled, respectively: $\sigma, r, b > 0$ [4]

30.11 SUMMARY

The introduction of annotations to the DiagramEng project required the addition of two new classes that work together in the FormatAnnotation() function: CAnnotation, which manages the annotation object variables and methods, and CAnnotationDialog, used to present a dialog window and obtain user-specified annotation settings.

Functionality was added to the project to generate a font list, through a `GenerateFonts()` method that calls the `EnumFontFamiliesEx()` function to request a list of the available system fonts, where the `EnumFontFamProc()` callback function, passed as an argument, receives data describing the fonts [2]. The creation of the actual font is performed in the `CreateAnnotationFont()` method of the CAnnotation class, where, typically, the class member variable, "m_fAnnotationFont", is passed as an argument by reference; the function is called from within `FormatAnnotation()`, the CAnnotation copy constructor, the `ReadAnnotationDataFromFile()` function and the `ScaleSystemModel()` method.

Annotations are drawn via the `DrawSystemModel()` and `DrawAnnotation()` functions, where the latter calls `TextOut()` to display the text on the screen: `GetOutputTextExtent()` is also called to get the width and height of the annotation. Annotations are deleted through a call to `OnDeleteItem()` followed by `DeleteAnnotation()`, or by invoking `OnEditDeleteGroupedItems()`. The movement of annotations is performed by one of three mechanisms: (1) `FineMoveItem()` and `FineMoveAnnotation()`, (2) `TrackItem()` and `TrackAnnotation()`, or (3) `TrackMultipleItems()`.

The View menu functionality was augmented to cater for the existence of annotations and included the Auto Fit Diagram, Zoom In/Out, and Reset Diagram actions. The Auto Fit Diagram action uses the `DetermineDiagramCoordinateExtrema()` and `DetermineDiagramCoordinateMinima()` functions, which where both extended to include retrieval of the extreme points of annotations. The Zoom In/Out actions involved extending the `ScaleSystemModel()` function to rescale and reposition the annotation. The resetting of the initial diagram geometry involves calling the `ScaleSystemModel()` function.

The Format menu was extended through the use of the `OnFormatShowAnnotations()` and `OnUpdateFormatShowAnnotations()` functions to allow the user to show or hide diagram annotations, and changes were made to the `DrawSystemModel()` method, the CSystemModel copy constructor, and the assignment operator.

The Edit menu–based actions, Cut, Copy, and Paste, required the introduction of a CAnnotation copy constructor and augmenting the CDiagramEngDoc, `OnEditCut()`, `OnEditCopy()`, and `OnEditPaste()` methods to work with the list of annotations, "m_lstAnnotation". The Undo and Redo actions required changes to the `SaveSystemModelToList()` function and the CSystemModel copy constructor and the assignment operator.

The serialization of the CAnnotation class data involved the introduction of the `ReadAnnotationDataFromFile()` and `WriteAnnotationDataToFile()` member functions, wherein the former the `CreateAnnotationFont()` function is called to create the annotation font from member variable values. The CSystemModel reading and writing methods were also augmented to cater for annotations. Finally, the file open methods, `CDiagramEngDoc::OnFileOpen()` and `CDiagramEngApp::OnFileRecentFileOpen()`, where altered to call `DeleteAnnotationList()` in the event that the user chooses to overwrite an existing model.

REFERENCES

1. Chapman, D., *Teach Yourself Visual C++ 6 in 21 Days*, SAMS Publishing, Indianapolis, IN, 1998.
2. Microsoft Developer Network Library Visual Studio 6.0, Microsoft® Visual Studio™ 6.0 Development System, Microsoft Corporation, 1998.
3. Ogata, K., *Modern Control Engineering*, 4th edn., Prentice Hall, Upper Saddle River, NJ, 2002.
4. Strogatz, S. H., *Nonlinear Dynamics and Chaos: With Applications to Physics, Biology, Chemistry, and Engineering*, Addison-Wesley, Reading MA, 1994.

31 Tools Menu

31.1 INTRODUCTION

At present, the user can perform basic modeling and simulation activities for time-based linear and nonlinear dynamical systems represented by differential equations that may be numerically integrated to yield generalized coordinates and their time derivatives for insightful time periods. However, it is important for the user to know more detail about the system and process memory usage, e.g., the working set size and pagefile usage.

31.2 TOOLS MENU IMPLEMENTATION: DIAGNOSTIC INFORMATION

The Diagnostic Info entry under the Tools menu will be used to display information about the state of physical and virtual memory and memory statistics for the current application process. A dialog window displaying this information will be created from within the existing event-handler function, named, `CDiagramEngDoc::OnToolsDiagnosticInfo()`. The two key structures used to obtain memory information are PROCESS_MEMORY_COUNTERS and MEMORYSTATUS: the former contains the memory statistics for a process and the latter contains information about the current state of both physical and virtual memory [1].

31.2.1 PRESENTATION SPACE APPLICATION PROGRAMMING INTERFACE

To present memory statistics for a process, the PROCESS_MEMORY_COUNTERS structure, declared in the Presentation Space Application Programming Interface (PSAPI) header file, "psapi.h", is required and so too the "psapi.lib" library and "psapi.dll" dynamic-link library that defines the `GetProcessMemoryInfo()` function used to obtain information about memory usage of a particular process. However, for Visual C++ 6.0 [2], the "psapi.h", "psapi.lib", and "psapi.dll" files are not automatically available and need to be obtained and added to the project as follows:

1. Download the "psapi.h", "psapi.dll", and "psapi.lib" files from an appropriate website.
2. Add all three files to the DiagramEng directory containing all project files.
3. Include the "psapi.h" header file (#include "psapi.h") at the top of the "DiagramEngDoc. cpp" source file, in which the `CDiagramEngDoc::OnToolsDiagnosticInfo()` function is defined.
4. Add the "psapi.lib" module to the project by selecting Project then Settings, choose the Link tab, and in the "Object/library modules" Edit box, add "psapi.lib" to the end of the list of libraries, as shown in Figure 31.1. This must also be done for the Win32 Release configuration of the application.

In addition, the "windows.h" header file is required for various type and function definitions used for memory-information-based functions. Hence, include "windows.h" (#include <windows.h>) at the top of the "DiagramEngDoc.cpp" source file prior to the inclusion of the "psapi.h" header file.

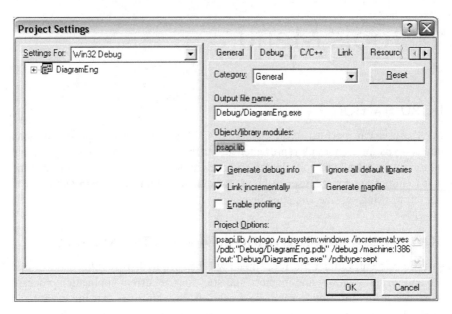

FIGURE 31.1   Project Settings dialog window showing the inclusion of the (highlighted) "psapi.lib" module.

31.2.2   STRUCTURES, FUNCTIONS, AND FIELDS REQUIRED FOR MEMORY-RELATED INFORMATION

The PROCESS_MEMORY_COUNTERS structure, used to obtain memory statistics for a process, that may be viewed via the Help index of the Visual Studio development environment [1] is shown in the following, where all members except "cb" and "PageFaultCount" represent sizes in bytes. All fields except "cb" will be used to display information to the user about memory statistics for an application process: "cb" simply holds the size of the actual structure in bytes.

```
typedef struct _PROCESS_MEMORY_COUNTERS {
    DWORD cb;
    DWORD PageFaultCount;
    DWORD PeakWorkingSetSize;
    DWORD WorkingSetSize;
    DWORD QuotaPeakPagedPoolUsage;
    DWORD QuotaPagedPoolUsage;
    DWORD QuotaPeakNonPagedPoolUsage;
    DWORD QuotaNonPagedPoolUsage;
    DWORD PagefileUsage;
    DWORD PeakPagefileUsage;
} PROCESS_MEMORY_COUNTERS;
```

The function GetCurrentProcess() will be used to get a pseudo handle to the current process, which is then passed to GetProcessMemoryInfo() to obtain information about memory usage of the specified process, which is recorded in the PROCESS_MEMORY_COUNTERS structure [1]. The idea for this work follows that presented in an article by Microsoft Corp. [3].

The MEMORYSTATUS structure, available from Ref. [1] shown in the following, is used to display information about the state of physical and virtual memory. The "dwLength" field will not be used on the dialog window as it is the size of the structure itself: the memory load, "dwMemoryLoad", is a percentage value, and the remaining values denote amounts in bytes.

```
typedef struct_MEMORYSTATUS {    // mst
    DWORD dwLength;              // sizeof(MEMORYSTATUS)
    DWORD dwMemoryLoad;         // percent of memory in use
    DWORD dwTotalPhys;          // bytes of physical memory
    DWORD dwAvailPhys;          // free physical memory bytes
    DWORD dwTotalPageFile;      // bytes of paging file
    DWORD dwAvailPageFile;      // free bytes of paging file
    DWORD dwTotalVirtual;       // user bytes of address space
    DWORD dwAvailVirtual;       // free user bytes
} MEMORYSTATUS, *LPMEMORYSTATUS;
```

The function `GlobalMemoryStatus()` obtains information about the computer system's current usage of both physical and virtual memory and stores this information in the MEMORYSTATUS structure [1].

31.2.3   ADD A DIALOG WINDOW TO DISPLAY DIAGNOSTIC MEMORY-RELATED INFORMATION

To add a dialog window to display diagnostic memory-related information to the user, six key steps used at various stages of the development need to be taken as follows:

1. Insert a new dialog window and add all necessary controls.
2. Attach a class to the dialog window.
3. Attach variables to the dialog window controls.
4. Add functionality to the dialog window buttons.
5. Add functionality to initialize variables.
6. Create the dialog window.

31.2.3.1   Insert a New Dialog Window and Add All Necessary Controls

Insert a new dialog resource and set the ID of the dialog to IDD_DIAGNOSTIC_INFO_DLG and the caption to DiagnosticInformationDialog. Leave the OK and Cancel buttons on the dialog. Add controls as shown in Table 31.1 and place them on the dialog window as shown in Figure 31.2: the developer will notice that static text strings are right-justified, and borders have been placed around the empty strings to contain the memory-related information.

31.2.3.2   Attach a Class to the Dialog Window

Select the IDD_DIAGNOSTIC_INFO_DLG resource from the ResourceView tab on the Workspace pane to show the corresponding dialog window in the editor area. Right-click on the dialog box to invoke the ClassWizard. The "Adding a Class" message box appears with the message: "IDD_DIAGNOSTIC_INFO_DLG is a new resource. Since it is a dialog resource you probably want to create a new class for it. You can also select an existing class." Create a new class with the name, CDiagnosticInfoDialog derived from the base class CDialog.

31.2.3.3   Attach Variables to the Dialog Window Controls

Open the ClassWizard, select the Member Variables tab, and select the class name to be CDiagnosticInfoDialog, since variables to be added relate to dialog window controls. Select the ID of the control to which a variable should be added, click Add Variable, and specify the details as shown in Table 31.2.

31.2.3.4   Add Functionality to the Dialog Window Buttons

The two buttons for the IDD_DIAGNOSTIC_INFO_DLG dialog window are "OK" and "Cancel". As no user input is to be processed by the dialog window, event-handler functions need not be added.

TABLE 31.1

DiagnosticInformationDialog Dialog Window Controls:
Objects, Properties, and Settings

Object	Property	Setting
Group Box	ID	ID_DIAGNOSTIC_INFO_DLG_GB_PROCMEM
	Caption	Process Memory Data (Kilobytes)
Static Text	ID	ID_DIAGNOSTIC_INFO_DLG_STXT_PFC
	Caption	Page Fault Count:
Static Text	ID	ID_DIAGNOSTIC_INFO_DLG_TXT_PFC
	Caption	Empty string
Static Text	ID	ID_DIAGNOSTIC_INFO_DLG_STXT_PWSS
	Caption	Peak Working Set Size:
Static Text	ID	ID_DIAGNOSTIC_INFO_DLG_TXT_PWSS
	Caption	Empty string
Static Text	ID	ID_DIAGNOSTIC_INFO_DLG_STXT_WSS
	Caption	Working Set Size:
Static Text	ID	ID_DIAGNOSTIC_INFO_DLG_TXT_WSS
	Caption	Empty string
Static Text	ID	ID_DIAGNOSTIC_INFO_DLG_STXT_QPPPU
	Caption	Quota Peak Paged Pool Usage:
Static Text	ID	ID_DIAGNOSTIC_INFO_DLG_TXT_QPPPU
	Caption	Empty string
Static Text	ID	ID_DIAGNOSTIC_INFO_DLG_STXT_QPPU
	Caption	Quota Paged Pool Usage:
Static Text	ID	ID_DIAGNOSTIC_INFO_DLG_TXT_QPPU
	Caption	Empty string
Static Text	ID	ID_DIAGNOSTIC_INFO_DLG_STXT_QPNPPU
	Caption	Quota Peak Non Paged Pool Usage:
Static Text	ID	ID_DIAGNOSTIC_INFO_DLG_TXT_QPNPPU
	Caption	Empty string
Static Text	ID	ID_DIAGNOSTIC_INFO_DLG_STXT_QNPPU
	Caption	Quota Non Paged Pool Usage:
Static Text	ID	ID_DIAGNOSTIC_INFO_DLG_TXT_QNPPU
	Caption	Empty string
Static Text	ID	ID_DIAGNOSTIC_INFO_DLG_STXT_PFU
	Caption	Pagefile Usage:
Static Text	ID	ID_DIAGNOSTIC_INFO_DLG_TXT_PFU
	Caption	Empty string
Static Text	ID	ID_DIAGNOSTIC_INFO_DLG_STXT_PPFU
	Caption	Peak Pagefile Usage:
Static Text	ID	ID_DIAGNOSTIC_INFO_DLG_TXT_PPFU
	Caption	Empty string
Static Text	ID	ID_DIAGNOSTIC_INFO_DLG_STXT_PMUP
	Caption	Physical Memory Used by Process:
Static Text	ID	ID_DIAGNOSTIC_INFO_DLG_TXT_PMUP
	Caption	Empty string
Group Box	ID	ID_DIAGNOSTIC_INFO_DLG_GB_SYSMEM
	Caption	System Memory Data (Kilobytes)
Static Text	ID	ID_DIAGNOSTIC_INFO_DLG_STXT_ML
	Caption	Memory Load:

TABLE 31.1 (continued)
DiagnosticInformationDialog Dialog Window Controls:
Objects, Properties, and Settings

Object	Property	Setting
Static Text	ID	ID_DIAGNOSTIC_INFO_DLG_TXT_ML
	Caption	Empty string
Static Text	ID	ID_DIAGNOSTIC_INFO_DLG_STXT_TPM
	Caption	Total Physical Memory:
Static Text	ID	ID_DIAGNOSTIC_INFO_DLG_TXT_TPM
	Caption	Empty string
Static Text	ID	ID_DIAGNOSTIC_INFO_DLG_STXT_APM
	Caption	Available Physical Memory:
Static Text	ID	ID_DIAGNOSTIC_INFO_DLG_TXT_APM
	Caption	Empty string
Static Text	ID	ID_DIAGNOSTIC_INFO_DLG_STXT_TPFM
	Caption	Total Pagefile Memory:
Static Text	ID	ID_DIAGNOSTIC_INFO_DLG_TXT_TPFM
	Caption	Empty string
Static Text	ID	ID_DIAGNOSTIC_INFO_DLG_STXT_APFM
	Caption	Available Pagefile Memory:
Static Text	ID	ID_DIAGNOSTIC_INFO_DLG_TXT_APFM
	Caption	Empty string
Static Text	ID	ID_DIAGNOSTIC_INFO_DLG_STXT_TVMU
	Caption	Total Virtual Memory (User):
Static Text	ID	ID_DIAGNOSTIC_INFO_DLG_TXT_TVMU
	Caption	Empty string
Static Text	ID	ID_DIAGNOSTIC_INFO_DLG_STXT_AVMU
	Caption	Available Virtual Memory (User):
Static Text	ID	ID_DIAGNOSTIC_INFO_DLG_TXT_AVMU
	Caption	Empty string
Static Text	ID	ID_DIAGNOSTIC_INFO_DLG_STXT_TVM
	Caption	Total Virtual Memory:
Static Text	ID	ID_DIAGNOSTIC_INFO_DLG_TXT_TVM
	Caption	Empty string
Static Text	ID	ID_DIAGNOSTIC_INFO_DLG_STXT_VMU
	Caption	Virtual Memory Used:
Static Text	ID	ID_DIAGNOSTIC_INFO_DLG_TXT_VMU
	Caption	Empty string
Static Text	ID	ID_DIAGNOSTIC_INFO_DLG_STXT_PMU
	Caption	Physical Memory Used:
Static Text	ID	ID_DIAGNOSTIC_INFO_DLG_TXT_PMU
	Caption	Empty string
Button	ID	IDOK
	Default button	Unchecked
	Caption	&OK
Button	ID	IDCANCEL
	Caption	&Cancel

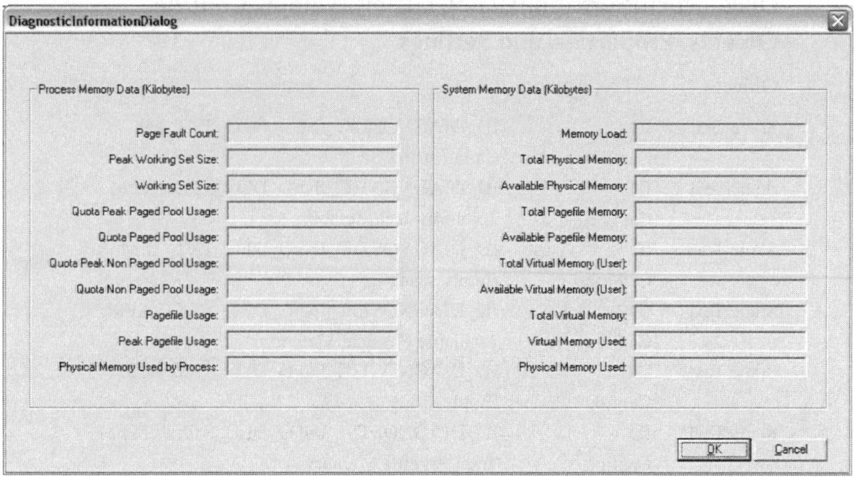

FIGURE 31.2   DiagnosticInformationDialog dialog window showing the controls as specified in Table 31.1.

TABLE 31.2

Dialog Window Controls, Variable Names, Categories, and Types, for the IDD_DIAGNOSTIC_INFO_DLG (Dialog Window) Resource

Control	Variable Name	Category	Type
ID_DIAGNOSTIC_INFO_DLG_TXT_PFC	m_strPageFaultCount	Value	CString
ID_DIAGNOSTIC_INFO_DLG_TXT_PWSS	m_strPeakWorkingSetSize	Value	CString
ID_DIAGNOSTIC_INFO_DLG_TXT_WSS	m_strWorkingSetSize	Value	CString
ID_DIAGNOSTIC_INFO_DLG_TXT_QPPPU	m_strQuotaPeakPagedPoolUsage	Value	CString
ID_DIAGNOSTIC_INFO_DLG_TXT_QPPU	m_strQuotaPagedPoolUsage	Value	CString
ID_DIAGNOSTIC_INFO_DLG_TXT_QPNPPU	m_strQuotaPeakNonPagedPoolUsage	Value	CString
ID_DIAGNOSTIC_INFO_DLG_TXT_QNPPU	m_strQuotaNonPagedPoolUsage	Value	CString
ID_DIAGNOSTIC_INFO_DLG_TXT_PFU	m_strPagefileUsage	Value	CString
ID_DIAGNOSTIC_INFO_DLG_TXT_PPFU	m_strPeakPagefileUsage	Value	CString
ID_DIAGNOSTIC_INFO_DLG_TXT_PMUP	m_strPhysicalMemoryUsedProcess	Value	CString
ID_DIAGNOSTIC_INFO_DLG_TXT_ML	m_strMemoryLoad	Value	CString
ID_DIAGNOSTIC_INFO_DLG_TXT_TPM	m_strTotalyPhysicalMemory	Value	CString
ID_DIAGNOSTIC_INFO_DLG_TXT_APM	m_strAvailPhysicalMemory	Value	CString
ID_DIAGNOSTIC_INFO_DLG_TXT_TPFM	m_strTotalPagefileMemory	Value	CString
ID_DIAGNOSTIC_INFO_DLG_TXT_APFM	m_strAvailPagefileMemory	Value	CString
ID_DIAGNOSTIC_INFO_DLG_TXT_TVMU	m_strTotalVirtualMemoryUser	Value	CString
ID_DIAGNOSTIC_INFO_DLG_TXT_AVMU	m_strAvailVirtualMemoryUser	Value	CString
ID_DIAGNOSTIC_INFO_DLG_TXT_TVM	m_strTotalVirtualMemory	Value	CString
ID_DIAGNOSTIC_INFO_DLG_TXT_VMU	m_strVirtualMemoryUsed	Value	CString
ID_DIAGNOSTIC_INFO_DLG_TXT_PMU	m_strPhysicalMemoryUsed	Value	CString

The order of variables is the same as in Table 31.1.

TABLE 31.3

Objects, IDs, Class, and Event-Handler Functions for the CDiagnosticInfoDialog Class

Object	ID	Class	COMMAND Event Handler
OK button	IDOK (default)	CDiagnosticInfoDialog	OnOK()
Cancel button	IDCANCEL (default)	CDiagnosticInfoDialog	OnCancel()

However, if the developer desires functions for potential future use, then `OnOK()` and `OnCancel()` may be added as shown in Table 31.3, and within which the base class functions `CDialog::OnOK()` and `CDialog::OnCancel()` are called, respectively.

31.2.3.5   Add Functionality to Initialize Variables

At present, the constructor for the CDiagnosticInfoDialog class associated with the DiagnosticInformationDialog dialog window resource uses a data-type mapping (_T(" ")) that converts the following character or string to its Unicode counterpart [1]. The setting of the actual variable values is performed within the `CDiagramEngDoc::OnToolsDiagnosticInfo()` function via calls to the process- and memory-related functions: `GetCurrentProcess()`, `GetProcessMemoryInfo()`, and `GlobalMemoryStatus()`. Hence, for now, the `CDiagnosticInfoDialog()` constructor may be left as it stands.

31.2.3.6   Create the Dialog Window

Finally, to display the DiagnosticInformationDialog dialog window, an instance of the CDiagnosticInfoDialog class "oDlg" needs to be constructed from within the `OnToolsDiagnosticInfo()` function of the CDiagramEngDoc class. This will require including the "DiagnosticInfoDialog.h" header file at the top of the "DiagramEngDoc.cpp" source file. However, prior to dialog window display, the `GetCurrentProcess()` function is called to get a pseudo handle to the current process, and this is passed along with the address of the PROCESS_MEMORY_COUNTERS structure, "pmc", into the `GetProcessMemoryInfo()` function to obtain the memory statistics for the current application process. Thereafter, the `GlobalMemoryStatus()` function is called passing in the address of the MEMORYSTATUS structure, "msMemStatus", to yield the system's physical and virtual memory details.

```
void CDiagramEngDoc::OnToolsDiagnosticInfo()
{
    // TODO: Add your command handler code here

    // DiagramEng (start)
    int bik = 1024;                 // no. of bytes in 1 kilobyte
    char strVar[50];                // string var used in sprintf() statements
    CString sMsg = "";              // msg string
    CString sMsgTemp = "";          // temp msg string
    DWORD physMemUsed;              // physical memory used
    DWORD virtualMemUsed;           // virtual memory used
    HANDLE hProcess;                // handle to the process
    PROCESS_MEMORY_COUNTERS pmc;    // structure containing memory
        statistics for a process
    MEMORYSTATUS msMemStatus;       // structure containing info about
        current state of physical and virtual memory

    // AfxMessageBox("\n CDiagramEngDoc::OnToolsDiagnosticInfo()\n",
        MB_OK, 0);
```

```cpp
// Create a dlg obj. of class CDiagnosticInfoDialog :
  public CDialog
CDiagnosticInfoDialog oDlg;

// GET PROCESS MEMORY INFO //////////////////////
hProcess = GetCurrentProcess();

if(GetProcessMemoryInfo(hProcess, &pmc, sizeof(pmc)))
{
    // Page Fault Count
    sprintf(strVar, "%d", pmc.PageFaultCount);
    oDlg.m_strPageFaultCount = strVar;

    // Peak Working Set Size
    sprintf(strVar, "%d", pmc.PeakWorkingSetSize/bik);
    oDlg.m_strPeakWorkingSetSize = strVar;

    // Working Set Size
    sprintf(strVar, "%d", pmc.WorkingSetSize/bik);
    oDlg.m_strWorkingSetSize = strVar;

    // Quota Peak Paged Pool Usage
    sprintf(strVar, "%d", pmc.QuotaPeakPagedPoolUsage/bik);
    oDlg.m_strQuotaPeakPagedPoolUsage = strVar;

    // Quota Paged Pool Usage
    sprintf(strVar, "%d", pmc.QuotaPagedPoolUsage/bik);
    oDlg.m_strQuotaPagedPoolUsage = strVar;

    // Quota Peak Non Paged Pool Usage
    sprintf(strVar, "%d", pmc.QuotaPeakNonPagedPoolUsage/bik);
    oDlg.m_strQuotaPeakNonPagedPoolUsage = strVar;

    // Quota Non Paged Pool Usage
    sprintf(strVar, "%d", pmc.QuotaNonPagedPoolUsage/bik);
    oDlg.m_strQuotaNonPagedPoolUsage = strVar;

    // Pagefile Usage
    sprintf(strVar, "%d", pmc.PagefileUsage/bik);
    oDlg.m_strPagefileUsage = strVar;

    // Peak Pagefile Usage
    sprintf(strVar, "%d", pmc.PeakPagefileUsage/bik);
    oDlg.m_strPeakPagefileUsage = strVar;

    // Physical Memory Used by Process
    sprintf(strVar, "%d", pmc.WorkingSetSize/bik);
    oDlg.m_strPhysicalMemoryUsedProcess = strVar;
}
else
{
    sMsgTemp.Format("\n CDiagramEngDoc::OnToolsDiagnosticInfo() \n");
    sMsg += sMsgTemp;
    sMsgTemp.Format("\n GetProcessMemoryInfo() failed: %d. \n",
      GetLastError());
    sMsg += sMsgTemp;
    AfxMessageBox(sMsg, MB_OK, 0);
}

// MEMORY STATUS ////////////////////////////////
```

```
    // GlobalMemoryStatus() obtains info about computer system's current
      usage of physical and virtual memory
    GlobalMemoryStatus(&msMemStatus);   // no return value to check.

    // Memory Load
    sprintf(strVar, "%d%%", msMemStatus.dwMemoryLoad);
    oDlg.m_strMemoryLoad = strVar;

    // Total Physical Memory
    sprintf(strVar, "%d", msMemStatus.dwTotalPhys/bik);
    oDlg.m_strTotalPhysicalMemory = strVar;

    // Available Physical Memory
    sprintf(strVar, "%d", msMemStatus.dwAvailPhys/bik);
    oDlg.m_strAvailPhysicalMemory = strVar;

    // Total Pagefile Memory
    sprintf(strVar, "%d", msMemStatus.dwTotalPageFile/bik);
    oDlg.m_strTotalPagefileMemory = strVar;

    // Available Pagefile Memory
    sprintf(strVar, "%d", msMemStatus.dwAvailPageFile/bik);
    oDlg.m_strAvailPagefileMemory = strVar;

    // Total Virtual Memory (User)
    sprintf(strVar, "%d", msMemStatus.dwTotalVirtual/bik);
    oDlg.m_strTotalVirtualMemoryUser = strVar;

    // Available Virtual Memory (User)
    sprintf(strVar, "%d", msMemStatus.dwAvailVirtual/bik);
    oDlg.m_strAvailVirtualMemoryUser = strVar;

    // Total Virtual Memory
    sprintf(strVar, "%d", msMemStatus.dwTotalPageFile/bik);
    oDlg.m_strTotalVirtualMemory = strVar;

    // Virtual Memory Used
    virtualMemUsed = msMemStatus.dwTotalPageFile - msMemStatus.
      dwAvailPageFile;
    sprintf(strVar, "%d", virtualMemUsed/bik);
    oDlg.m_strVirtualMemoryUsed = strVar;

    // Physical Memory Used
    physMemUsed = msMemStatus.dwTotalPhys - msMemStatus.dwAvailPhys;
    sprintf(strVar, "%d", physMemUsed/bik);
    oDlg.m_strPhysicalMemoryUsed = strVar;

    // DISPLAY DLG WND /////////////////////////////
    // Return val of DoModal() fn of ancestor class CDialog is checked to
      determine which btn was clicked.
    if(oDlg.DoModal() == IDOK)
    {
        // No action to be taken at present
    }
    else
    {
        // No action to be taken at present
    }

    // DiagramEng (end)
}
```

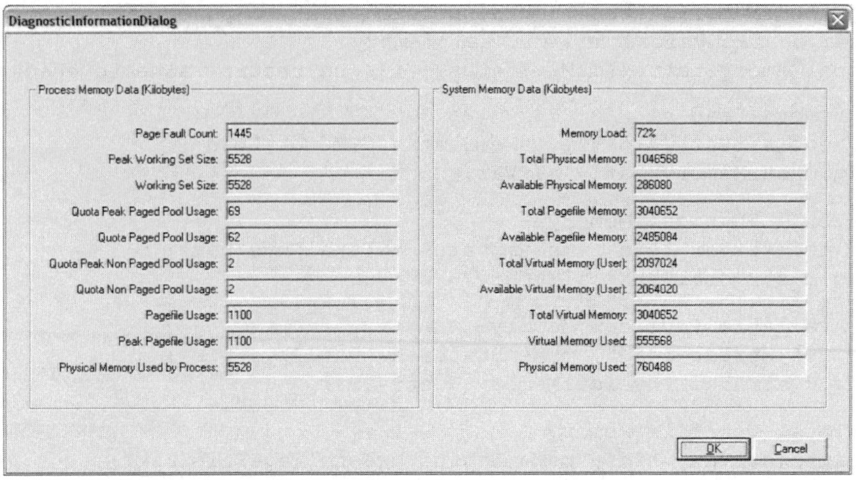

FIGURE 31.3 Process memory statistics and system physical and virtual memory details: memory is quoted in kilobytes.

The interested reader should consult an article titled "How to determine CPU and memory consumption from inside a process?" published on Stackoverflow [4] for details concerning process-based CPU and memory usage: some ideas presented here follow this work. Of note, are the following details: (1) the physical memory used by a process is in fact the "working set size" ("pmc.WorkingSetSize"), (2) the total virtual memory is the total pagefile size ("msMemStatus. dwTotalPageFile"), (3) the virtual memory used is the difference between the total pagefile and available pagefile sizes ("virtualMemUsed = msMemStatus.dwTotalPageFile-msMemStatus. dwAvailPageFile"), and (4) the physical memory used is the difference between the total physical memory and the available physical memory ("physMemUsed = msMemStatus.dwTotalPhys - msMemStatus.dwAvailPhys") [4].

Finally, upon running the DiagramEng application and choosing Diagnostic Info under the Tools menu, the memory statistics for the current application process, and the system physical and virtual memory details, are displayed as shown in Figure 31.3. The interested developer may compare the memory statistics presented in the dialog window with those of Task Manager or an equivalent application that presents information about applications and processes and common performance measures.

The reader will notice that all memory-based values are presented in kilobytes (KB) for convenience: if a field has the value "0", this indicates that less that 1 KB is in use rather than 0 bytes in total. The page fault count is a DWORD value, which is a 32-bit unsigned integer or the address of a segment and its associated offset [1]: here, it can be considered to be an integer value. The memory load is a DWORD value that represents the percentage value of memory use.

Further to the earlier discussion, from Figure 31.3, the memory-conscious developer will notice that the "working set size" and the "physical memory used by the process" are the same value (they share the same variable, "pmc.WorkingSetSize"). In addition, the "total virtual memory" is the same as the "total pagefile memory" ("msMemStatus.dwTotalPageFile"): both of these fields are displayed for clarity and convenience.

31.3 SUMMARY

The Diagnostic Information entry under the Tools menu invokes the `CDiagramEngDoc::` `OnToolsDiagnosticInfo()` method within which two structures are used to store memory usage information: (1) PROCESS_MEMORY_COUNTERS contains memory statistics for a process and (2) MEMORYSTATUS retains information about the current state of the system physical and virtual memory. The `GetCurrentProcess()` and `GetProcessMemoryInfo()` functions are used to retrieve the process-based memory, and the `GlobalMemoryStatus()` function is used to determine the system-based memory. The PSAPI header file and library module is required to be added to the project for Visual C++ 6 [2].

A DiagnosticInformationDialog dialog window was added to the project and the CDiagnosticInfoDialog class attached to the dialog. An instance of the class is created in the `OnToolsDiagnosticInfo()` function and used to display the process and system memory usage information: the "working set size" is the physical memory used by a process.

REFERENCES

1. Microsoft Developer Network Library Visual Studio 6.0, Microsoft® Visual Studio™ 6.0 Development System, Microsoft Corporation, 1998.
2. Microsoft Visual C++® 6.0, Microsoft® Visual Studio™ 6.0 Development System, Professional Edition, Microsoft Corporation, 1998.
3. Microsoft Developer Network, Collecting memory usage information for a process (Windows), http://msdn.microsoft.com/en-us/library/ms682050(VS.85).aspx, 2008.
4. Stackoverflow, How to determine CPU and memory consumption from inside a process?, http://stackoverflow.com/questions/63166/how-to-determine-cpu-and-memory-consumption-from-inside-a-process, (accessed August 2010).

32 Help Menu

32.1 INTRODUCTION

The Child frame–based Help menu has two entries, About DiagramEng and Using DiagramEng: the former displays a dialog window with program, version number, and copyright information, and the latter needs to present the instructions on how to use the DiagramEng application to the user, complete with a discussion of all menu and toolbar-based functionality and typical real-world engineering examples. The instructions should be presented as a Portable Document Format (PDF) document and hence would require the user to have Adobe Reader [1] installed on the client machine. The particular sections of the Using DiagramEng topics are Introduction, Menus, Toolbars, Examples, Output, and Non-functional items. Finally, the Using DiagramEng instructions are presented to the user by calling `CreateProcess()` to create a process invoking the Adobe "Acrobat.exe" executable and opening the PDF document.

32.2 USING DiagramEng

The Using DiagramEng document provides the user with a brief overview of the DiagramEng application including an introduction to its purpose and the particular features that allow an engineer to perform modeling and simulation activities. Examples are provided that show how linear and nonlinear differential equations may be represented diagrammatically and then computed to generate output data that may be saved to a file. Appendix F presents the "Using DiagramEng" document that is converted to a PDF file and is ultimately displayed using `CreateProcess()` (see Section 32.3). The content of the document is as follows.

A description of the DiagramEng application is presented in Section F.1 and briefly explains its purpose. Section F.2 presents the Main frame–based menus, Child frame–based menus, and the Context menu and lists all their entries and associated functions. Section F.3 displays the Main frame–based toolbar and Child frame–based, Common Operations, and Common Blocks toolbars and lists all their buttons and functionality. Section F.4 provides two common examples in engineering modeling and computation: (1) a second-order linear ordinary differential equation converted into the state-space equations using order reduction and (2) a system of coupled differential equations representing a nonlinear dynamical system. Section F.5 demonstrates how output data of a specified format may be saved using the Output block dialog window and briefly mentions the model data file used to save and restore a system model. Section F.6 lists the nonfunctional items that may be completed in a future extension of the project. Finally, a summary and the references used conclude the document.

32.3 CREATING THE USING DiagramEng DOCUMENT

The Using DiagramEng document can be saved as a PDF document with the name, "UsingDiagramEng.pdf" and placed in the same directory as the "DiagramEng.exe" executable file: no blank spaces should be used in the name to make it easier to invoke the "Acrobat.exe" [1] executable, where the file name, appended to its directory location, is used as the execution parameter. To display the PDF document, the `CreateProcess()` function needs to be called from within the `CDiagramEngDoc::OnHelpUsingDiagramEng()` function.

32.3.1 `CreateProcess()` Function

The function prototype for the process creation function is presented here with a brief explanation of the arguments that follows closely the material presented in Ref. [2] (the interested reader should consult Ref. [2] for further details).

```
BOOL CreateProcess(
    LPCTSTR lpApplicationName,                 // pointer to name of
        executable module
    LPTSTR lpCommandLine,                       // pointer to command
        line string
    LPSECURITY_ATTRIBUTES lpProcessAttributes,  // process security
        attributes
    LPSECURITY_ATTRIBUTES lpThreadAttributes,   // thread security
        attributes
    BOOL bInheritedHandles,                     // handle inheritance
        flag
    DWORD dwCreationFlags,                      // creation flags
    LPVOID lpEnvironment,                       // pointer to new
        environment block
    LPCTSTR lpCurrentDirectory,                 // pointer to current
        directory name
    LPSTARTUPINFO lpStartupInfo,                // pointer to STARTUPINFO
    LPPROCESS_INFORMATION lpProcessInformation  // pointer to
        PROCESS_INFORMATION
);
```

The application name pointer, "lpApplicationName", is set to NULL, since the command line argument, "lpCommandLine", is a concatenation of the executable name "Acrobat.exe", the directory path denoting the location of the "UsingDiagramEng.pdf" and the PDF file (parameter) itself. The pointer-to-LPSECURITY_ATTRIBUTES-type arguments, "lpProcessAttributes" and "lpThreadAttributes", are both NULL, indicating that the returned handle cannot be inherited by child processes. The handle inheritance flag, "bInheritedHandles", is set to FALSE, implying that the new process does not inherit handles from the calling process. The DWORD, "dwCreatingFlags", argument specifies flags that control the priority class and the creation of the process: here, this is set to zero, indicating no creation flags are used. The "lpEnvironment" argument is a pointer to an environment block for the new process: here, it is NULL, specifying that the new process uses the environment of the calling process. The "lpCurrentDirectory" argument is a pointer to a string specifying the drive and directory for the child process: NULL implies that the new process is created with the same drive and directory as the calling process. The STARTUPINFO structure, "lpStartupInfo", is used to specify the appearance of the main window for the new process: in the following code, the address of the structure-type variable is passed as an argument. The PROCESS_INFORMATION structure, "lpProcessInformation", is used to receive identification information about the new process: the address of this structure-type variable is passed as an argument as shown in the following.

32.3.2 `OnHelpUsingDiagramEng()` Function

The structure of the `OnHelpUsingDiagramEng()` function in the following, and the manner in which the `CreateProcess()` function is called, follows an article titled "Creating Processes" found on the Microsoft Developer Network website [3]. The main tasks of the function are as follows: (1) set up the arguments for the `CreateProcess()` function, (2) call `CreateProcess()`, (3) wait for the process if appropriate using `WaitForSingleObject()`, and (4) close the handles of the newly created process by calling `CloseHandle()`.

```
void CDiagramEngDoc::OnHelpUsingDiagramEng()
{
    // TODO: Add your command handler code here

    // DiagramEng (start)
    int lenBuffer = 0;                  // length of buffer to get dir name
    char *appName = NULL;               // app name (not used since cmd
      line used instead)
    char cmdLine[1024] = "Acrobat.exe ";   // cmd line, starting with the
      app name
    char dirPath[1024] = "";            // dir path
    char dirPathExe[1024] = "";         // dir path including exe file name
    CString sMsg = "";                  // msg string
    CString sMsgTemp = "";              // temp msg string
    DWORD retval = 0;                   // return val of
      GetCurrentDirectory()
    PROCESS_INFORMATION pi;             // PROCESS_INFORMATION structure
    STARTUPINFO si;                     // STARTUPINFO structure

    //AfxMessageBox("\n CDiagramEngDoc::OnHelpUsingDiagramEng()\n",
      MB_OK, 0);

    // GET CURRENT DIR (DiagramEng.exe) /////////
    lenBuffer = sizeof(dirPathExe)/sizeof(char);
    retval = GetModuleFileName(AfxGetInstanceHandle(), dirPathExe,
      lenBuffer);

    if(retval == 0)                     // handle error
    {
        sMsgTemp.Format("\n CDiagramEngDoc::OnHelpUsingDiagramEng() \n");
        sMsg += sMsgTemp;
        sMsgTemp.Format("\n GetModuleFileName() failed: %d \n",
          GetLastError());
        sMsg += sMsgTemp;
        AfxMessageBox(sMsg, MB_OK, 0);
    }
    else
    {
        // Truncate dir path since it includes "\DiagramEng.exe":
          i.e. remove last 15 chars.
        strncpy(dirPath, dirPathExe, (retval - strlen("\\DiagramEng.exe")));

        sMsg.Format("\n %s has %d chars not including the null char. \n",
          dirPathExe, retval);
        //AfxMessageBox(sMsg, MB_OK, 0);
    }

    // CONSTRUCT THE CMD LINE ///////////////////
    // WARNING!
    // If there are spaces in the dir path then quotes must surround the
      path.
    // E.g., "C:\BudFox\C++\Work\Diagram Eng Project\DiagramEng
      (19 finalize)\DiagramEng\UsingDiagramEng.pdf"
    // If there are no spaces in the dir path, then quotes need not
      surround the path.
    // E.g., C:\BudFox\Temp\UsingDiagramEng.pdf
    // Hence, place quotes around the dir path to be safe.
    // An explicit example without spaces in the dir path is:
```

```
// char cmdLine[1024] = "Acrobat.exe C:\\BudFox\\Temp\\
UsingDiagramEng.pdf"
// The surrounding quotes are necessary here purely to init the char
array as a string.
// The escape char, \, is used, as in, \\, to allow a, \, to be
present in the string.

// Concatenate the cmd line
// Acrobat.exe + "C:\BudFox\C++\Work\Diagram Eng Project\DiagramEng +
\UsingDiagramEng.pdf"
strcat(cmdLine, "\"");  // cmdLine = Acrobat.exe "
strcat(cmdLine, dirPath);     // cmdLine = Acrobat.exe "dir path
strcat(cmdLine, "\\UsingDiagramEng.pdf\"");      // cmdLine =
Acrobat.exe "dir path\UsingDiagramEng.pdf"
//AfxMessageBox(cmdLine, MB_OK, 0);

// FILL BLOCKS OF MEMORY WITH ZEROS /////////
ZeroMemory(&si, sizeof(si));
si.cb = sizeof(si);
ZeroMemory(&pi, sizeof(pi));

// CREATE THE PROCESS ////////////////////////
if(!CreateProcess(appName, cmdLine, NULL, NULL, FALSE, 0, NULL, NULL,
&si, &pi))
{
    sMsg = "";
    sMsgTemp.Format("\n\n Failed to open the \"UsingDiagramEng.pdf\"
      document. \n");
    sMsg += sMsgTemp;
    sMsgTemp.Format("\n Check the following to resolve this problem:
      \n\n");
    sMsg += sMsgTemp;
    sMsgTemp.Format(" 1) The \"UsingDiagramEng.pdf\" document is in
      the same directory as \"DiagramEng.exe\". \n");
    sMsg += sMsgTemp;
    sMsgTemp.Format(" 2) The location of \"Acrobat.exe\" is specified
      in the Path variable. \n");
    sMsg +=sMsgTemp;
    sMsgTemp.Format("\n To set the Path variable on Windows, perform
      the following steps: \n\n");
    sMsg += sMsgTemp;
    sMsgTemp.Format(" 1) Left click Start, right click My Computer
      and select Properties. \n");
    sMsg += sMsgTemp;
    sMsgTemp.Format(" 2) In the System Properties dialog window
      select the Advanced tab and click Environment Variables. \n");
    sMsg += sMsgTemp;
    sMsgTemp.Format(" 3) In the System Variables group box scroll
      down and highlight the Path variable. \n");
    sMsg += sMsgTemp;
    sMsgTemp.Format(" 4) Click the Edit button to edit the path,
      typing in the new path: click OK to save the setting. \n");
    sMsg += sMsgTemp;
    sMsgTemp.Format(" 5) Restart the DiagramEng application. \n");
    sMsg += sMsgTemp;
    AfxMessageBox(sMsg, MB_OK, 0);
}
```

```
    // Wait until child process exists
    WaitForSingleObject(pi.hProcess, 0);      // wait for 0 milliseconds
      not INFINITE

    // CLOSE THE NEWLY OPENED PROCESS AND THREAD HANDLES
    if(!CloseHandle(pi.hProcess))                 // close handle of the newly
      created process
    {
        sMsg = "";
        sMsgTemp.Format("\n CDiagramEngDoc::OnHelpUsingDiagramEng() \n");
        sMsg += sMsgTemp;
        sMsgTemp.Format("\n CloseHandle(pi.hProcess) failed: %d \n",
          GetLastError());
        sMsg += sMsgTemp;
        AfxMessageBox(sMsg, MB_OK, 0);
    }

    if(!CloseHandle(pi.hThread))                  // close handle of the
      primary thread of the newly created process
    {
        sMsg = "";
        sMsgTemp.Format("\n CDiagramEngDoc::OnHelpUsingDiagramEng() \n");
        sMsg += sMsgTemp;
        sMsgTemp.Format("\n CloseHandle(pi.hThread) failed: %d \n",
          GetLastError());
        sMsg += sMsgTemp;
        AfxMessageBox(sMsg, MB_OK, 0);
    }

    // DiagramEng (end)
}
```

The command line argument, "cmdLine", is a character array that holds the complete statement to invoke an executable file (here, "Acrobat.exe"), whose location is specified in the Path environment variable, where the parameter to the executable (here, "UsingDiagramEng.pdf") is appended to the directory path denoting its location. The help file, "UsingDiagramEng.pdf", is to reside in the same location as the "DiagramEng.exe" executable file; hence, the GetModuleFileName() function may be called to determine the "full path and filename for the executable file containing the specified module" [2]. The arguments to the latter are (1) the handle to the module whose executable filename is being sought, which is returned by AfxGetInstanceHandle(), (2) a string pointer to contain the path of the executable ("DiagramEng.exe"), including its name, and (3) the length of the character array buffer to hold the path, here, "dirPathExe". However, since "DiagramEng.exe" is part of the path contained by "dirPathExe", the characters "DiagramEng. exe" need to be removed when specifying the directory path for the PDF document: this is done using strncpy().

Thereafter, to complete the command line, the individual strings are concatenated. However, if the directory path does not contain white space, then there is no need to place quotes around it, but if it does, then the quotes are necessary. The string construction is performed as follows: (1) the initial characters are "Acrobat.exe " (note the white space following "exe"), (2) "Acrobat. exe" is then adjoined to an open quote, ", required for the directory path containing white spaces, (3) "Acrobat.exe", is then adjoined to the directory path, e.g., C:\Name\C++\Work\Diagram Eng Project\DiagramEng, and (4) finally the PDF file is appended to the directory path, to result, e.g., in the string:

Acrobat.exe "C:\Name\C++\WorkDiagram Eng Project\DiagramEng\UsingDiagramEng.pdf"

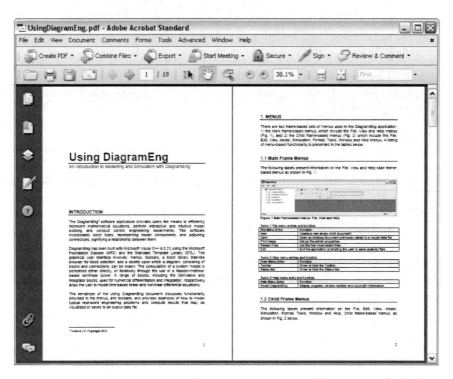

FIGURE 32.1   The "UsingDiagramEng.pdf" document displayed when selecting Using DiagramEng from the Help menu.

The ZeroMemory() function is called to fill a block of memory with zeros [2], and this should be done after the declaration of the structures, "si" and "pi", to make sure that known (nonspurious) values reside in the structures.

Thereafter, the CreateProcess() function is called with the arguments discussed earlier: if the Boolean return value is FALSE, then an error message is displayed informing the user to check the location of the "UsingDiagramEng.pdf" help file and to make sure that the Path environment variable for the "Acrobat.exe" executable is set correctly, with instructions on how to do so.

The WaitForSingleObject() function call is used to check the state of the specified object: if the state is nonsignaled, the calling thread enters an efficient wait state [2]. Here, no waiting is really required, and hence, the DWORD, "dwMilliseconds", argument is set to 0. The call is included here should this need to change in the future.

Finally, CloseHandle() is called to close the open handle of the newly created process ("pi. hProcess") and the primary thread of the newly created process ("pi.hThread"). This should be done once the object is no longer required. MSDN indicated that "CloseHandle() invalidates the specified object handle, decrements the object's handle count, and performs object retention checks" [2].

Now upon running the DiagramEng application and choosing Using DiagramEng from the Help menu, the PDF document appears as shown in Figure 32.1.

32.4   SUMMARY

The selection of the Using DiagramEng entry under the Help menu invokes the CDiagramEngDoc::OnHelpUsingDiagramEng() method that calls CreateProcess() to execute the "Acrobat.exe" application with the "UsingDiagramEng.pdf" file as a parameter. The directory path of the file is determined through the use of GetModuleFileName(), and this is concatenated with the "Acrobat.exe" executable and the target file name "UsingDiagramEng.pdf" to form the command line argument.

The topics covered in the Help document, "UsingDiagramEng.pdf", as presented in Appendix F include (1) the Main frame–based menu, Child frame–based menu, and Context menu; (2) the Main frame–based toolbar and the Child frame–based Common Operations and Common Blocks toolbars; (3) two real-world engineering examples concerning the modeling and computation of ordinary differential equations and nonlinear dynamical systems; (4) forms of output data including numerical simulation data ("output_data.txt") and system model data ("model_data.txt"); and (5) nonfunctional elements that will be completed in the next version of the software.

REFERENCES

1. Adobe: http://www.adobe.com/products/acrobat/
2. Microsoft Developer Network Library Visual Studio 6.0, Microsoft® Visual Studio™ 6.0 Development System, Microsoft Corporation, 1998.
3. Microsoft Developer Network, Creating processes, http://msdn.microsoft.com/en-us/library/ms682512(VS.85).aspx, (accessed September, 2010).

33 Finalizing the Project

33.1 INTRODUCTION

The purpose of the development of the DiagramEng demonstration software application is to build a foundation upon which extensions can be made to allow the efficient modeling and simulation of mathematical and control-engineering-based problems. Most of the necessary key modules have been implemented. However, some features are not present in this first version of the software and include the implementation of the Subsystem, Subsystem In, Subsystem Out, and Transfer Function blocks and development of the fourth-order Runge–Kutta numerical integration and variable-order schemes with the associated tolerance parameter-based error-checking features, as shown in Table 33.1. The nonfunctional elements need to be either disabled or automatically invoke alternative default behavior.

33.2 PREVENTING USAGE OF NONFUNCTIONAL BLOCKS

At present, the Subsystem, Subsystem In, Subsystem Out, and Transfer Function blocks have no working `OperateOnData()` methods; hence, they should not be present at the signal propagation or equivalently the model computation stage. The flow of control for model validation involves the user selecting either the Build Model item under the Model menu or the Start Simulation button on the Common Operations toolbar, which invoke the `CDiagramEngDoc` methods `OnModelBuild()` and `OnSimStart()`, respectively, both of which call the `CSystemModel::ValidateModel()` function. Model validation involves validating model blocks, block ports, and connections, which is performed by the CSystemModel functions `ValidateModelBlocks()`, `ValidateModelBlockPorts()`, and `ValidateModelConnections()`, respectively.

Currently, the `ValidateModelBlocks()` function iterates through the block list to determine the presence of at least one source and output block in the model and adds any missing blocks if required. This function should now be extended to screen out the four aforementioned blocks for which no block operation (`OperateOnData()`) is being performed. Hence, augment the `CSystemModel::ValidateModelBlocks()` function as shown in bold in the following to detect and delete the relevant blocks, presenting an informative message to the user: the ellipsis "..." denotes omitted but unchanged code from previous work.

```
int CSystemModel::ValidateModelBlocks()
{
    int error = 0;          // error in model
    int n_source = 0;       // no. of model source blocks
    int n_output = 0;       // no. of model output blocks
    int screen_out = 0;     // flag to screen out non-functional blocks
    CString blk_name;       // blk name
    CString sMsg;           // string to be displayed
    CString sMsgTemp;       // temp msg.
    UINT nType = MB_OK;     // style of msg. box
    UINT nIDhelp = 0;       // help context ID for the msg.
```

TABLE 33.1

Incomplete Application Items: Blocks, Menu Entries, and Dialog Window Fields

Item	Status
Blocks	Subsystem, Subsystem In, Subsystem Out, and Transfer Function blocks currently do not perform data operations.
Model Menu	The Build Subsystem entry does not function as subsystem blocks are not implemented.
Numerical Solver	The absolute and relative error tolerance parameters are not currently used, the Time-step Type is "Fixed-step" and the Integration Method is "Euler (1st Order)."

```
CDiagramEngDoc *pDoc = GetDocumentGlobalFn(); // declare pDoc to be a
  ptr to CDiagramEngDoc.
list<CBlock*>::iterator it_blk;

// CHECK THE NO. OF SOURCE BLOCKS AND OUTPUT BLOCKS IN THE MODEL
for(it_blk = m_lstBlock.begin(); it_blk != m_lstBlock.end(); it_blk++)
{
    ...
}

if((n_source == 0) || (n_output == 0))
{
    ...
}

// DELETE BLOCKS FOR WHICH FUNCTIONALITY DOES NOT EXIST
it_blk = m_lstBlock.begin();
while(it_blk != m_lstBlock.end())
{
    // Get block name to screen out relevant non-functional blocks
    blk_name = (*it_blk)->GetBlockName();

    if((blk_name == "subsystem_block") || (blk_name ==
      "subsystem_in_block") || (blk_name == "subsystem_out_block")
      || (blk_name == "transfer_fn_block"))
    {
        // Print message on first occurrence only.
        if(screen_out == 0)
        {
            sMsg.Format("");
            sMsgTemp.Format("\n CSystemModel::ValidateModelBlocks() \n");
            sMsg += sMsgTemp;
            sMsgTemp.Format("\n Deleting non-functional blocks. \n");
            sMsg += sMsgTemp;
            AfxMessageBox(sMsg, nType, nIDhelp);
            screen_out = 1;
        }

        // Delete block
        delete *it_blk; // delete actual block pointed to by it_blk
        it_blk = m_lstBlock.erase(it_blk);  // delete element at
          offset it_blk in list (that held the block)
    }
```

```
        else // only increment the iterator if there were no deletion
        {
            it_blk++;
        }
    }

    return error;
}
```

Now upon running the application and placing any of the nonfunctional blocks on the palette, these are removed at the model validation stage accompanied by a message to the user. Alternatively, the developer can disable the Common Blocks toolbar buttons corresponding to the nonfunctional blocks, by invoking the Class Wizard, selecting the CDiagramEngDoc class and the appropriate toolbar button ID, and then deleting the event-handler function associated with the Command message.

33.3　PREVENTING THE BUILDING OF SUBSYSTEMS

The Child frame–based Model menu allows the user to build a model or subsystem using the Build Model and Build Subsystem entries, respectively. At present, as subsystem functionality has not been added to the project, selecting the Build Subsystem entry should invoke a message box indicating the developmental status to the user. Hence, edit the CDiagramEngDoc::OnModelBuild Subsystem() function as shown with the appropriate message.

```
void CDiagramEngDoc::OnModelBuildSubsystem()
{
    // TODO: Add your command handler code here

    // DiagramEng (start)
    CString sMsg;
    CString sMsgTemp;

    sMsgTemp.Format("\n CDiagramEngDoc::OnModelBuildSubsystem() \n");
    sMsg += sMsgTemp;
    sMsgTemp.Format("\n At present there is no subsystem building
        functionality. \n");
    sMsg += sMsgTemp;
    AfxMessageBox(sMsg, MB_OK, 0);

    // DiagramEng (end)
}
```

Alternatively, the developer can invoke the Class Wizard and select CDiagramEngDoc as the class and ID_MODEL_BUILD_SUBSYSTEM as the ID, and delete the event-handler function, CDiagramEngDoc::OnModelBuildSubsystem(), associated with the Command event message.

33.4　DISABLING NONFUNCTIONAL ITEMS

The NumericalSolverDialog dialog window has the fields shown in Figure 33.1a. However, at this stage of the development, various fields are either not used or result in default functionality being invoked. The fields that are not used, i.e., the absolute and relative error tolerance parameter edit boxes, are to be disabled as shown in Figure 33.1b: this is done by choosing the Disable option on the General tab pane of the Edit Properties dialog window for the edit box control. The Time-step Type (Fixed-step or Variable-step) and Integration Method (Euler [1st Order] or Runge–Kutta

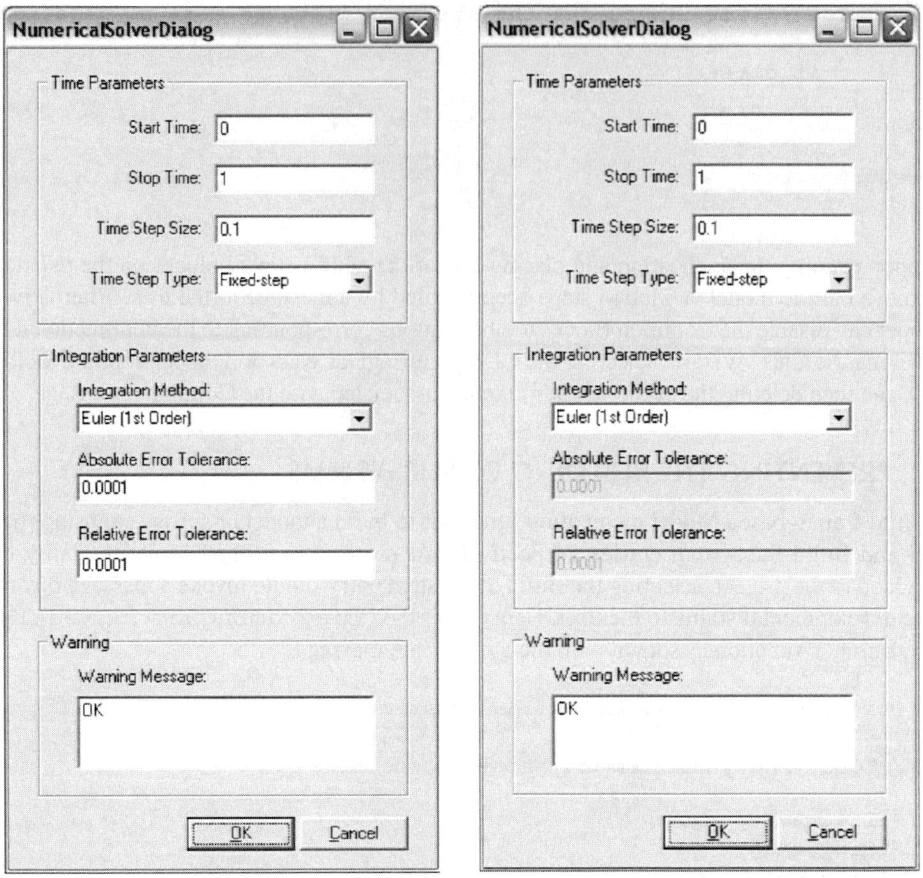

FIGURE 33.1   The NumericalSolverDialog dialog window: (a) all fields enabled and (b) fields not used shown disabled.

[4th Order]) fields show their default settings that are used regardless of the user selection. The developer will recall that in the `CIntegratorBlock::OperateOnData()` function, a check is made of the choice of the integration method and a message displayed informing the user of the default fixed-step Euler integration scheme being used.

33.5   PREPARING THE SOURCE AND EXECUTABLE FILES

Now that all software application elements have been completed, the code may be tested for memory leaks and then prepared for source and executable file distribution. At various times in the project, particularly after using the *new* and *delete* operators to allocate and deallocate memory, the topic of "memory leakage" was raised. Memory leaks are actually reported in the Debug output window of the integrated development environment (IDE) after performing a Debug-build of the software and then running the application with the debugger.

33.5.1   MEMORY LEAK DETECTION

To perform a Debug-build of the application, do the following: (1) select Set Active Configurations under the Build menu of the IDE, (2) choose DiagramEng—Win32 Debug as the project configuration, and (3) choose Rebuild All under the Build menu to rebuild the entire application. To run the Debug-build configuration of the application, select Start Debug under the Build menu and choose

Go (F5). After using the application to perform modeling and simulation activities and then exiting, the output in the Debug output window may be checked for the presence of memory leaks. Usually, a message appears giving the developer an indication as to the type of leak that is present: leaks commonly arise by not matching a *delete* operation to a corresponding *new* operation where the two may not be of the same code locality, i.e., they may be present in different functions and the intended control path was not executed. For more information about detecting memory leaks involving the creation of a CMemoryState object and using the `Checkpoint()` member function, the interested reader should consult the Detecting Memory Leaks topic available under the Help menu of the Visual C++ IDE [1]. For information on the usage of the IDE-based Debugging tool, the reader should consult Appendix D.

33.5.2 RELEASE VERSION OF THE SOFTWARE

Finally to prepare the software for release, the developer should do the following: (1) select Set Active Configurations under the Build menu of the IDE, (2) choose DiagramEng—Win32 Release as the project configuration, and (3) choose Rebuild All under the Build menu to rebuild the entire application. If there is a link error when performing a Release-build rather than a Debug-build configuration of the application, then any libraries that were required for the Debug-build form should be included for the Release-build form. For example, select Settings under the Project menu of the IDE to yield the following Project Settings dialog window (Figure 33.2).

In the "Object/library modules" edit box, the "psapi.lib" library module is included for the Win32 Release configuration of the application, as it was for the Win32 Debug configuration. The developer will recall that this was required earlier in the project to obtain process memory utilization statistics for the Diagnostic Info. entry under the Tools menu (Chapter 31).

Finally, the "DiagramEng.exe" executable file together with the "UsingDiagramEng.pdf" help file should be placed in the same "Executable" directory when porting the application (for reasons discussed when adding functionality for the Help menu (Chapter 32)). In addition, any sample model files ("model_data (…).txt") can also be placed in a "Data" directory to be loaded by the DiagramEng application. A sample directory structure to port the Release configuration of the DiagramEng software application is shown in Table 33.2.

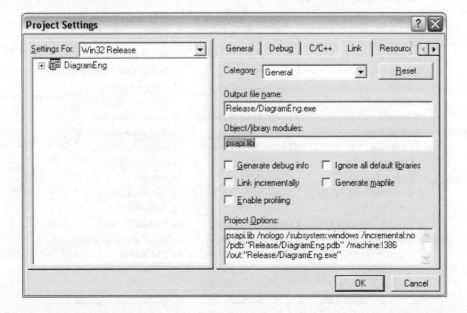

FIGURE 33.2 Project Settings dialog window showing the inclusion of the (highlighted) "psapi.lib" module.

TABLE 33.2

**Sample Directory Structure Showing Files
for Porting the Release Version of DiagramEng**

Directory	Subdirectory	Files
DiagramEng	Executable	"DiagramEng.exe"
		"UsingDiagramEng.pdf"
	Data	"model_data (lotka-volterra).txt"
		"model_data (state equs).txt"

33.5.3 SOURCE CODE

The source code of the DiagramEng software application is to be made available so that other developers may extend the current functionality to suit their domain requirements. Table 33.3 presents an alphabetically ordered listing of the classes under the "DiagramEng classes" folder of the ClassView pane of the IDE, including the Globals folder denoting global functions and variables.

The source code to be made available to the developer community involves the entire DiagramEng project and sample data files and should be structured as shown in Table 33.4: the file extensions denote the types of files present.

The developer choosing to modify or extend the code will require at least the Microsoft Visual Studio 6.0 Development System (IDE) [2] (or later editions) running on a personal computer with a Windows-based operating system, e.g., Microsoft Windows XP. The amount of RAM required depends on the number of Output blocks and the size of their contained data structure, which is itself determined by the total simulation time and the size of the finite time intervals δt s used in time-based system modeling. A system with a 2.0 GHz processor and 1.0 GB of RAM should be

TABLE 33.3

DiagramEng Class Listing

Classes	Classes Continued	Classes Continued
CAboutDlg	CDivideBlock	CSignal
CAnnotation	CDivideBlockDialog	CSignalGeneratorBlock
CAnnotationDialog	CGainBlock	CSignalGeneratorBlockDialog
CBlock	CGainBlockDialog	CSubsystemBlock
CBlockLibDlg	CIntegratorBlock	CSubsystemBlockDialog
CBlockShape	CIntegratorBlockDialog	CSubsystemInBlock
CChildFrame	CLinearFnBlock	CSubsystemInBlockDialog
CClipboard	CLinearFnBlockDialog	CSubsystemOutBlock
CConnection	CMainFrame	CSubsystemOutBlockDialog
CConstantBlock	CNewtonMethod	CSumBlock
CConstantBlockDialog	CNumericalSolverDialog	CSumBlockDialog
CDerivativeBlock	COutputBlock	CSystemModel
CDerivativeBlockDialog	COutputBlockDialog	CTransferFnBlock
CDiagnosticInfoDialog	COutputBlockView	CTransferFnBlockDialog
CDiagramEngApp	COutputSignalDialog	CTreeDialog
CDiagramEngDoc	CPort	Globals
CDiagramEngView	CPortPropertiesDialog	

TABLE 33.4

Sample Directory Structure for the DiagramEng Source Code Showing File Extensions

Directory	Subdirectory	File Extensions
DiagramEng		aps, clw, cpp, dll, dsp, dsw, h, lib, ncb, opt, pdf, plg, rc, reg, txt
	Data	txt
	Debug	bsc, exe, idb, ilk, obj, pch, pdb, pdf, res, sbr
	Release	bsc, exe, idb, obj, pch, pdf, res, sbr
	res	bmp, ico, rc2

TABLE 33.5

Properties of the Computer System, Operating System, and Software Used to Develop the DiagramEng Application

Computer System	Operating System	Software
Intel® Core™ 2 Duo CPU	Microsoft Windows XP	Microsoft Visual C++® 6.0
E4400 @ 2.00 GHz	Professional	Microsoft Visual Studio 6.0
2.00 GHz, 1.00 GB of RAM	Version 2002	Professional Edition
Physical Address Extension	Service Pack 2	MSDN Library Visual Studio 6.0

sufficient to run exploratory simulations for which the DiagramEng application was designed. The DiagramEng application was developed on a computer system and using an operating system and software with the properties listed in Table 33.5.

33.6 SUMMARY

The finalizing of the DiagramEng project involves the prevention of usage or disabling of nonfunctional elements, e.g., blocks, menu items, and dialog window fields, or providing alternative default behavior. The preparation of the source and executable files involves a check for memory leaks using a Debug-build configuration of the application and the running of the debugger and observing the messages in the Debug output window. Alternatively, a CMemoryState object can be created and the Checkpoint() member function used for memory leak detection. Any required modules need to be included using the "Object/library modules" edit box of the Link pane of the Project Setting dialog window. Finally, sample directory structures are provided to organize the application files.

REFERENCES

1. Microsoft Developer Network Library Visual Studio 6.0, Microsoft® Visual Studio™ 6.0 Development System, Microsoft Corporation, 1998.
2. Microsoft Visual C++® 6.0, Microsoft® Visual Studio™ 6.0 Development System, Professional Edition, Microsoft Corporation, 1998.

34 Conclusion

34.1 INTRODUCTION

At the beginning of the text, the contents of the project were presented, which included an introduction that described the developmental details of all the chapters in the book separated into three main parts: User Interaction, Model Computation and Data, and Refinement. In addition, at the end of each chapter, a summary was provided that reviewed the specific design and implementation details, including various classes and methods that were added to build functionality into the DiagramEng project. Here, a brief review is made of the development process, summarizing the implementation steps and providing suggestions for improving the software for future extension.

34.2 PROJECT REVIEW

The development of the DiagramEng, block-diagram-based engineering software prototype, involved many implementation steps that led the developer through design, graphical user interface (GUI) development, model computation, serialization, and the addition of features common in Windows-based environments to allow for user-friendly operation of the application.

34.2.1 USER INTERACTION

The software development process started with an object-oriented analysis and design phase that involved the requirements, use case narratives, and conversations, to identify the user actions and system responsibilities, toward generating candidate, responsibilities, and collaborators (CRC) cards to capture the candidate classes and the initial software object model.

The development of the GUI included the setting up of menus, toolbars, dialog windows, and event-handler functions in preparation for future functionality to be added to the project. A global function was introduced that allows a pointer to a document associated with the active view to be obtained from outside the CView-based CDiagramEngView class.

The construction of CBlock-derived blocks was performed, and these were drawn using a virtual function that, based upon the derived runtime type of the object, resulted in the appropriate specific graphical details being presented. The construction and setup of block ports then followed where a port positioning angle was used to place the port on a side face of its parent block.

A connection object, represented by the CConnection class, contains CSignal member data which are transferred from one block to the next in the course of computation. The drawing of connections including head, tail, and bend points was performed using mouse-based event-handler functions and upon construction were added to the CSystemModel-based connection list.

The movement of block, connection end points, and bend points is performed through the use of a CRectTracker object which allows the user to attach connection head and tail points to input and output ports, respectively, and attach a *secondary* connection's tail point to a *primary* connection's bend point to form a branch or feedback loop in the model diagram. The insertion and deletion of bend points and the deletion of connection objects were facilitated through functions associated with the relevant entries on the Context menu.

Block dialog window resources were introduced to the project to allow the user to specify various block properties and involved six key steps: (1) insertion of a dialog window resource and its controls, (2) creation of a class for the dialog, (3) attachment of variables to the dialog controls, (4) attachment of functionality to the dialog buttons, (5) initialization of class member variables, and (6) the addition of a parameter input function to create an instance of the appropriate block dialog window. These six steps were used repeatedly throughout the project when a dialog resource was added and data required to be updated its associated underlying class. A conversion of string input to double data was also required for various dialog resources since the application operates on numerical data that are initially entered by the user as a string.

The moving of multiple items was implemented through a sequence of actions that involved the construction of a CRectTracker object used to circumscribe diagram entities within a rectangular rubber-band-like region: initially the region is defined, and then upon selecting the interior of the region, the entities may be moved with the mouse.

A Tree View control was added to the project by creating a dialog resource, attaching a class to the dialog, attaching a variable to the dialog to display Tree View items, performing initialization, and inserting icons to be displayed for the Tree View leaves. The Tree dialog window was then docked to the Main frame manually, since the CTreeDialog class is inherited from the CDialog base class, rather than the CDialogBar class.

The Context menu was extended to allow the setting of the properties of the numerical solver, blocks and ports, where the appropriate dialog window was invoked based upon the (contextual) location of the point at which the right-mouse-button-down event occurred. In addition, the deletion of blocks and ports via the Context menu was implemented. The drawing of ports and port signs was added and the port icons conditionally displayed, depending on the attachment of a connection.

Finally, key-based item movement and the reversing of block direction allows the user to present a diagram with horizontal and vertical connections and feed-forward and feedback control paths such that typical control-engineering-like diagrams may be drawn, the computation of which is pursued in the following section.

34.2.2 MODEL COMPUTATION AND DATA

The final stage of the User Interaction development phase involved the drawing of diagrams with feedback loops. However, the developmental work concerning the computation of models was separated into two procedures: a direct signal propagation approach and a Newton-method-based technique to compute models in the absence and presence of feedback loops, respectively.

The validating of a model involved checking for the presence of model blocks and the connectivity of ports and connections. A node–arc connectivity matrix representing the model diagram was then used to determine block-to-block tours that ended at an Output block or a repeated block, the latter signifying the presence of a feedback loop. Then a connection-centric non-feedback-based signal propagation technique was implemented for models without feedback loops and involved execution of block-based data operation functions to generate connection-based signal data to be propagated from a source node through to an Output block.

The visualization of the generated output using a graph-drawing window was implemented through six steps: (1) structure was added to display an empty view window associated with the output block, (2) methods and variables were added to existing classes to access the output block's numerical data, (3) textual data were plotted in the view window, (4) numerical data were plotted as graphical curves in the view window, (5) button-based functionality was added to implement data display options, and (6) an output block and its view window were deleted.

Block operations were then added for the Derivative and Integrator (Continuous) blocks; the Divide, Gain, and Sum (Math Operations) blocks; the Output (Sink) block; and the Constant, Linear Function, and Signal Generator (Source) blocks. These block-based operations were shown to work using the conceptually simple direct signal propagation method.

A model diagram possessing a feedback loop was computed using Newton's method that involved the construction of, in general, a system of nonlinear equations of the form, $F(x(t)) = x(t) - f(x(t)) = \mathbf{0}$, where $F(x(t))$ is the generalized system vector, $x(t)$ is the generalized output signal vector, and $f(x(t))$ is the generalized block operation function vector, and a solution or root, $x_r(t)$, to the system is sought, which is a vector of system signals at the current time-step. Examples of real-world problems were then computed and involved linear and nonlinear differential equations from the domains of mechanical engineering and nonlinear dynamics.

An Edit box was placed on the Common Operations toolbar to display both the simulation time during a running experiment and the total execution time at the end of the simulation: the updating of the time values is initiated from the two main signal propagation functions.

The final development activity of the Model Computation and Data phase involved serialization, i.e., the writing and reading of class member data, to and from a file, respectively. Event-handler functions were added for the Main frame and Child frame based window menus to initiate the serialization process, where all system-model-based data and contained class data are recorded. In addition, the initial output signal of a Divide block and the recorded data of an Output block were also serialized.

34.2.3 REFINEMENT

The Refinement phase of the project involved adding typical features found in Windows-based applications that make for a more intuitive, consistent, and complete modeling and simulation user experience. Printing and print previewing functionality was implemented by adding code to three key CView-based methods: `OnBeginPrinting()`, to set the maximum number of pages to be printed, `OnPrepareDC()`, to prepare the device context and set mapping modes, and `OnDraw()`, to perform a transformation and scaling between the window and viewport rectangles before drawing the model diagram.

The implementation of a scrolling view was required since a model diagram may take up more than the physical viewing area. The original CView-based class was then derived from CScrollView, and numerous changes were required throughout the code to convert between device points and logical points, given changes in the scroll position. Functionality to automatically fit the viewport scale to the physical window, to zoom in and out of a view, and to reset the original diagram geometry was also added.

The Edit menu was then augmented with the typical entries found in Windows-based applications, i.e., Undo, Redo, Cut, Copy, Paste, and Select All. A clipboard object was used to make copies of blocks and connections of a system model through the relevant class copy constructors. The Undo and Redo actions involved creating a list of system model pointers to record the addresses of system models. A copy constructor was introduced to make a copy of the system model, "m_SystemModel", of the CDiagramEngDoc class, to be stored in the list, and an assignment operator used to assign a stored list-based system model to the member object, "m_SystemModel".

Functionality was then added to allow the user to annotate a model diagram through the use of an annotation class and a dialog window to set key member attributes: a list of the available system fonts is displayed and the font created based on user-selected properties. The annotations are stored in the system model class, and hence, editing and serialization actions were augmented to cater for the new data structure.

The Tools menu was then completed with a diagnostic information entry used to display process, physical and virtual memory usage information. The Help menu was finalized with a Using DiagramEng entry that upon selection invokes a process to display application instructions to the user. Finally, the project was completed by providing default settings for certain controls, disabling of nonfunctional items, checking for memory leaks using a Debug-build configuration of the application, and organizing the source and executable code.

34.3   IMPROVEMENTS

At the design stage of the project, not all implementation complexities can be fully appreciated, and as the development progressed, various problems arose suggesting an improvement could be made in project structure and software function. The following ideas indicate how the software can be improved.

34.3.1   OBJECT-ORIENTED ANALYSIS AND DESIGN

The Document-View architecture of a multiple document interface (MDI) application involves the key classes CWinApp, CMDIFrameWnd, CMDIChildWnd, CDocument, and CView [1], which, for the DiagramEng application, correspond to the classes CDiagramEngApp, CMainFrame, CChildFrame, CDiagramEngDoc, and CDiagramEngView, respectively. The CDocument-derived class, CDiagram EngDoc, then contained an instance of the CSystemModel retaining all the data of the system model.

34.3.1.1   Class Hierarchy

Chapter 3 presents a class hierarchical diagram showing the association relationships (generalization and composition), between the classes of the project. It is clear from the diagram that the base CBlock class is inherited from by the derived classes, but only CBlock-derived objects are actually instantiated: not the base class object. In addition, numerous functions are made virtual in the CBlock base class, to be overridden by the derived block classes, i.e., `AssignBlockOutputSignal()`, `BlockDlgWndParameterInput()`, `CopyBlockData()`, `DrawBlock()`, `OperateOnData()`, `ReadBlockDataFromFile()`, `ResetBlockData()`, `SetPortProperties()`, and `Write BlockDataToFile()`. The CBlock class should really have been made an abstract data type (ADT) with various pure virtual functions that necessarily must be overridden by the derived block classes. A clearer CBlock interface would make for a more orderly extension of the hierarchy by future developers.

In addition, the CDiagramEngDoc class has as a member variable a CSystemModel object, "m_SystemModel". This, in hindsight, could have been a pointer-to-CSystemModel, since the pointer can offer more flexibility and passing the address of the system model would be more efficient.

Furthermore, the developer will have noticed in Chapters 1 and 3 that the class association relationships involved pointers, such that the connectivity between related classes can be known to their actual object instances. For example, the CSystemModel class contains a list of pointers-to-CBlock, recording the addresses of the blocks in the model. The CBlock class has two association-related pointers-to-CSystemModel: "m_pParentSystemModel" and "m_pSubSystemModel", which record the addresses of the system model to which the block belongs and the contained subsystem model (if present), respectively. In addition, the CBlock class contains vectors of pointers-to-CPort, and the CPort class has a reference to the block (CBlock&) upon which it resides, i.e., "m_rRefToBlock", which is initialized upon CPort object construction.

The developer should think carefully about how and when the association relationships can be made visible or known to the objects concerned. If this is not done at the design stage, then significant changes may have to be made to the code after coding commences. For example, to place the pointer-to-CSystemModel, "m_pParentSystemModel", in the CBlock class at a later stage in the project would involve the following changes:

1. Addition of the CBlock private member variable, "m_pParentSystemModel"
2. Addition of the accessor function, `GetSystemModel()`, to retrieve the variable
3. Modification of CBlock-derived class constructors, e.g., `CConstantBlock()`
4. Modification of the CBlock base class constructor to initialize the new variable
5. Modification of all `CDiagramEngDoc::ConstructNameBlock()`* functions
6. Modification of all CBlock-related code that may have used `GetDocumentGlobalFn()` to indirectly get the system model, to simply retrieve it using `GetSystemModel()`, since it would be visible at CBlock class scope

---

* *Name* in `ConstructNameBlock()` denotes the name of the block to be constructed.

The developer can see from the previous list that the method of object construction with the new pointer variable is naturally more complicated and the changes to existing code would be numerous and possibly problematic at a time after the design stage. However, a carefully designed class hierarchy before coding commences will end up saving more development time than that used to make the necessary modifications to implement a structural change at a later stage in the project.

34.3.1.2 Retrieving the Address of the Document

The CView-derived class, CDiagramEngView, can retrieve the address of the CDocument-derived class, CDiagramEngDoc, using the `CView::GetDocument()` member method. However, when outside of the CView-derived class, access to the document was made through the global function, `GetDocumentGlobalFn()`: the code for this function and an accompanying explanation was introduced in Chapter 2. The key feature is that the function returns the address of the active document associated with the active child window. If the function returned the first document in the list of documents, but not the active document, then when switching between different views, containing, e.g., different models, the wrong document would be returned.

In addition, the developer will recall from Section 20.5.4 that the Output block's data can be presented in the form of a graph, using the `DrawGraph()` function of the CView-derived class, COutputBlockView. The `GetDocument()` function of the COutputBlockView class is called to obtain the correct system-model-based data to be displayed, i.e., that associated with the Output block. If the `GetDocumentGlobalFn()` were to be called instead and there were more than one document, then the data to be displayed would be that of the active document, not the document associated with the Output block's viewing/graphing window, and changing the active document status would result in erroneous graphical output.

Hence, the developer should be very careful when using a function to retrieve the address of the document: calling `GetDocument()` from within the CView-derived class should suffice, but when outside of the CView-derived class, care must be taken to get the appropriate (active but not first) document. In the DiagramEng project, the call to `GetDocumentGlobalFn()` is made numerous times: sometimes this is unavoidable, but if pointers are used to access classes higher up in the hierarchy, then accessing data need not occur from the top (CDiagramEngDoc) down, but rather from the bottom up (e.g., CBlock), without relying on a global function (see point six in Section 34.3.1.1).

34.3.2 Addition of Classes

Chapter 3 shows how the Win32 Console Application, ControlEng, is merged with the Visual C++ DiagramEng application. Although the ControlEng application has a purpose, in that it represents the initial class hierarchy organizing the user-defined types, this structure does not need to be ported into the DiagramEng application directly. It would be better to simply add classes manually to the DiagramEng application, when required, thus automatically generating individual source and header files for each class, containing the definitions and declarations, respectively. This would result in better code locality and file-based organizational structure for developers choosing to extend the software.

34.3.3 Unnecessary Features

The Block Library Dialog window (IDD_BLOCKLIBDLG) was initially used to add multiple blocks to the model simultaneously. However, the Common Blocks toolbar with buttons representing all the blocks of the application, and then later the Tree View control, allow the user to add blocks to the system model very easily: in fact the toolbar-based approach is the most efficient. Hence, the Block Library Dialog resource and potentially the Tree View control could possibly be omitted from the development. The Tree View control could be used for a different function given the existence of the

Common Blocks toolbar, e.g., it could be used to choose the type of connection objects used to link blocks together: straight lines, spline curves, or a connection with integrated bend points.

In addition, certain controls are not operational, others result in default functionality, and four blocks currently do not have working OperateOnData() functions. These nonfunctional items could be deleted, disabled, or completed with at least a functional purpose (time permitting). Various enumerated type values are also redundant and could possibly be removed, e.g., EBlockDirection has two fields, "e_up" and "e_down", which are currently not in use but could possibly be used at a later stage.

34.3.4 NAMING CONVENTION

Initially when the project started, a naming convention was used, but as more complexity was added, it became apparent that a more rigorous and consistent approach was desired. The naming convention shown in Table 34.1 may be of benefit to the developer when organizing a large number of variables: class member variables should be preceded with "m_", and local variables should be similarly named but without the "m_" prefix.

If, however, in particular circumstances, a variable is somewhat long, e.g., "m_y_dot_at_t_minus_h", representing $\dot{y}_{t-h}$, then the type may be discernible from the context, and its explicit indication omitted due to potential confusion: e.g., "m_dy_dot_at_t_minus_h", could be mistakenly interpreted as the derivative, $d\dot{y}_{t-h}$, rather than a double-typed value. Furthermore, if code is being ported from another source, as it was with the Newton method solver of Press et al. [2], then for clarity with respect to the original source, some variable names should be left unchanged and placed in a special class to contain them, e.g., the "fvec" double vector located in the CNewtonMethod class.

34.3.5 MEMBER VARIABLES AND CONSTANT ACCESSOR METHODS

Member variables were added to classes throughout the development and accessor methods used to retrieve and set their values. The retrieval methods should be made constant as they should not

---

TABLE 34.1

Naming Convention for Class Member Variables for Common Types and an Example of Its Use

Type	Convention	Example Used
Boolean	m_b	m_bChkBoxConstBlock
Control	m_ctl	m_ctlFontList
CPoint	m_pt	m_ptPosition
CString	m_str	m_strConstValue
Double	m_d	m_dConstMatrix
Enumerated	m_e	m_eBlockDirection
Float[a]	m_f	m_fValue
Integer	m_i	m_iNrows
List	m_lst	m_lstBlock
Object or instance	m_o or m_	m_SystemModel
Pointer	m_p	m_pParentSystemModel
Reference	m_r	m_rRefToBlock
Vector	m_vec	m_vecInputPorts
Window	m_wnd	m_wndToolBar

[a] Values of type float were changed to be of type double for greater computational accuracy.

---

modify the variable value: where this may not be true is when the underlying object is retrieved by reference with the intention to modify its value. In some cases, the suffix "Copy" can be added to the function name to explicitly indicate that a copy is being retrieved: however, the function prototype should suffice. In addition, accessor methods should be added at the time when the member variable itself is being added to a class. The constant nature of member functions can make it easier to write copy constructors, since the latter is declared to be constant and hence any methods that it calls should also be constant.

34.3.6 PROGRAM STATE

On various occasions during the project when implementing functions involving connections and ports, the "reference-from" ("m_pRefFromPort") ports of two different CConnection objects may be shared: a *primary* connection may be directly attached to a block output port, and a *secondary* connection may be attached to a *primary* connection through a bend point and, hence, have its "reference-from" port set to that of the *primary* connection. This is done, since when assigning an output signal of a particular block, all direct (*primary*) and indirect (*secondary*) connection objects must have consistent signal data. Then, at the end of the relevant function, these *secondary* connection "reference-from" ports are assigned to NULL, to leave the program state unchanged, since *secondary* connection objects (attached to bend points) are not physically and directly attached to output ports.

This process of assigning an address to the "m_pRefFromPort" variable at the beginning of a function and then reassigning it to NULL after data have been written to the output connection is somewhat laborious. The WriteDataToOutputSignal() function iterates over the vector of output ports and connections, and checks whether the address held in the "m_pRefFromPort" variable of a connection object is that of the output port; if so, data are written to the *primary* connection and any associated *secondary* connections.

The data writing function (WriteDataToOutputSignal()) should simply write data to a *primary* connection object attached to the block's output port and then leave the responsibility of propagating the signal data to the *primary* connection object. For example, the *primary* connection could simply iterate through its list of bend points, and if a *secondary* connection is attached, then it would share the same data. In this way, the program state need not be switched upon entry to and then exit from a function.

34.3.7 GENERIC CONTAINERS

The conversion of string input to double data that was required when processing user input entered through a dialog window for various blocks relied on typical C functions without exploring the power of C++. Koenig and Moo [3] explore string-based operations and indicate that a "string is a special kind of container … and supports some container operations." They then present an example of string manipulation involving string-based operations and a vector to store substrings. This approach of using C++ containers and iterators is more mature than that used in the DiagramEng project. The developer is encouraged to read Chapter 5, "Using Sequential Containers and Analyzing Strings," of Ref. [3], for more information about containers, iterators, and the <cctype> header file, which provides functions to operate on character data.

34.3.8 BASE CLASS SELECTION

At the initial stage of the project, the MFC AppWizard [4] was used to build the application shell, and on stage six, the developer can choose the type of base class for the project's view class: CView was chosen as the CDiagramEngView base class. However, later in the development, CScrollView was required to implement a scrolling view, and manual changes had to be made to make the conversion from the original CView class. In hindsight, using the CView class to begin with may actually have been the right choice, since then the complexity of dealing with device and logical point conversion and accommodating for the change in scroll position would not be a concern. Hence, the developer needs to make a decision between introducing possibly unwanted complexity earlier in the project, but having the convenience of the appropriate base class, or making a conversion later in the project to the appropriate base class, after initial functionality is shown to work.

34.3.9 Serialization

The serialization of class member variables should be performed in a structured manner such that the addition of more classes to the project as it evolves should not affect the existing data reading and writing functions of other classes. This allows serialization to be performed at a relatively early stage in the project, for class member data that need to be saved and then later restored to perform various activities that would take too long to manually reinstate. For example, the Lorenz system in diagrammatic form is time consuming to redraw, and if software testing is to be conducted at the end of each developmental stage, then being able to save and restore this diagram would be more convenient. However, in general, serialization should be left till a later stage in the development after the class structure is more stable or complete.

34.3.10 Activity Organization

A project of significant complexity to be completed in a short duration requires many people to work together in a well-organized manner. Hence, the separation of software development activities needs to be carefully planned with all contributing members present when making organizational decisions. The object-oriented analysis and design stage should involve all members since thorough planning and careful consideration about the relationships between classes needs to be made before coding commences. The building of the basic GUI, e.g., menus, toolbars, Tree Views, dialog windows, and preliminary event-handler functions, can be performed separately from, e.g., the mathematical modeling and computational activities that may be introduced as functional operations at a later stage. However, often programmers working together on the same problem can achieve more than working separately, yet concurrently, on different problems. In addition, preliminary Win32 Console Application projects may be used to explore features that are difficult to implement, where the resulting code is transferred to the main application after it is shown to work as expected.

The three stages of development pursued for the DiagramEng project were User Interaction, Model Computation and Data, and Refinement. The first phase, User Interaction, involved GUI-specific development that could be separated from the more mathematical work of the Model Computation and Data stage, e.g., the implementation of the block operation functions, the connection-centric signal propagation, and the Newton-method-based equation computation. The Refinement stage was performed last as it was not central to the purpose of the demonstration prototype and represented activities to make the software more consistent with Windows-based applications. Figure 34.1 shows a possible Gantt chart that orders software development activities, denoted by the chapter numbers and titles used in the text, with respect to time: the developer will notice that the suggested order of some of the tasks is changed from that taken in the actual project and those occupying the same column can be performed concurrently. This is not a unique order, and the development team should work together to find the most suitable sequence of activities to minimize any restructuring of the class hierarchy or unnecessarily revisiting earlier actions.

Project Activity	Time Period													
	1	2	3	4	5	6	7	8	9	10	11	12	13	14
Object Oriented Analysis & Design	1													
Initial Graphical User Interface		2												
Placing an Edit Box on a Toolbar		24												
Constructing Blocks			3											
Constructing Block Ports				4										
Constructing Connections				5										
Automatic Block Placement				7										
Connection-Based Bend Points					8									
Block Dialog Windows					9									
Conversion of String Input to Double Data					10									
Addition of a Tree View Control					12									
Moving Blocks & Connections						6								
Moving Multiple Items							11							
Key-Based Item Movement							16							
Block Operations							21							
Context Menu Extension								14						
Setting Port Properties								15						
Reversing Block Direction								17						
Model Validation								18						
Non-Feedback-Based Signal Propagation									19					
Graph Drawing									20					
Preparation for Feedback-Based Signal Propagation										22				
Printing & Print Preview										27				
Implementing a Scroll View										28				
Feedback-Based Signal Propagation											23			
Annotations											30			
Tools Menu											31			
Edit Menu												29		
Serialization													25	
Help Menu														32
Finalizing the Project														33

FIGURE 34.1   A possible Gantt chart showing the order and concurrency of software development activities.

34.4   SUMMARY

A review of the DiagramEng software prototype development project was made that summarized all the development activities of the three main phases: User Interaction, Model Computation and Data, and Refinement. Suggested improvements included: (1) a more thorough object-oriented analysis and design stage employing ADTs and hierarchy-navigating pointers used to retrieve the correct document address, (2) the usage of a common development environment and adding classes carefully observing code locality, (3) the disabling of incomplete features, (4) a rigorous naming convention, (5) the usage of constant functions where possible, (6) consideration of program state, (7) observing the power of generic containers, (8) careful selection of base classes, (9) serialization to be performed toward the end of the project, and, finally, (10) organizing the project carefully to perform activities concurrently whenever possible.

REFERENCES

1. Chapman, D., *Teach Yourself Visual C++ 6 in 21 Days*, Sams Publishing, Indianapolis, IN, 1998.
2. Press, W. H., Teukolsky, S. A., Vetterling, W. T., and Flannery, B. P., *Numerical Recipes in C: The Art of Scientific Computing*, 2nd edn., Cambridge University Press, Cambridge, MA, 2002.
3. Koenig, A. and Moo, B. E., *Accelerated C++: Practical Programming by Example*, Addison-Wesley, Boston, MA, 2009.
4. Microsoft Developer Network Library Visual Studio 6.0, Microsoft® Visual Studio™ 6.0 Development System, Microsoft Corporation, 1998.

Appendix A: ControlEng: Win32 Console Application

A.1 INTRODUCTION

Chapter 1 introduced a preliminary class structure for a Win32 Console Application project, titled ControlEng. Table A.1 lists the header files and the contained classes in the order of their appearance. The actual source (*.cpp) and header (*.h) files are provided in alphabetical order in the following (header files are shown first). The application was developed using the Microsoft Visual C++® 6.0, Microsoft® Visual Studio™ 6.0 Development System (integrated development environment [IDE]) [1].

The developer can port this code in an application titled, e.g., ControlEng, denoting "control engineering," and compile and run the executable to see simple constructor and destructor statements being displayed in an output console window as shown in Figure A.1. The developer will notice that objects of the following types are constructed (listed in the order of their construction): CSystemModel, CBlockShape, CBlock, CPort, CConnection, and CSignal.

A.2 SOURCE CODE

The header and source files for the ControlEng Win32 Console Application are provided in the following; the "Title" identifier placed in a comment denotes the name of the file.

A.2.1 HEADER FILES

The header files listed are "Block.h", "ControlEng.h", "Signal.h", and "SystemModel.h". The developer will notice that the CBlock destructor is made virtual since the design indicates that the CBlock is a base class, and any pointers to CBlock that are to be used in the project actually refer to the CBlock-derived concrete objects. Hence, upon deletion of a pointer-to-CBlock, the virtual destructor will guarantee that the CBlock-derived block's destructor is invoked.

```
// Title:   Block.h

#ifndef BLOCK_H
    #define BLOCK_H     // inclusion guard

    // User defined consts/vars.

    // User defined types
    enum EBlockShape {e_elipse, e_rectangle, e_triangle};  // block
      shapes
    enum EDirection {e_left, e_right, e_up, e_down}; // block direction
      (triangle specific)
    enum EIntegrationMethod {e_Euler, e_RungeKutta}; // integration
      schemes, (Euler) 1st and (RK) 4th order
    enum EMultAction {e_element_wise, e_mat_x_input, e_input_x_mat,
      e_divide}; // multiplication action, form and order
    enum EOutputDataFormat {e_dep_var, e_dep_and_indep_var}; // form of
      output: dependent and independent vars
```

TABLE A.1

Win32 Console Application Header Files and Contained Classes in Order of Appearance in the Actual Header Files

Block.h	ControlEng.h	Signal.h	SystemModel.h
CBlockShape	No class definition	CSignal	CSystemModel
CPort		CDoubleSignal	
CBlock		CMatrixSignal	
CConstantBlock		CVectorSignal	
CDerivativeBlock		CConnection	
CDivideBlock			
CGainBlock			
CIntegratorBlock			
CLinearFnBlock			
COutputBlock			
CSignalGeneratorBlock			
CSubsystemBlock			
CSubsystemInBlock			
CSubsystemOutBlock			
CSumBlock			
CTransferFnBlock			

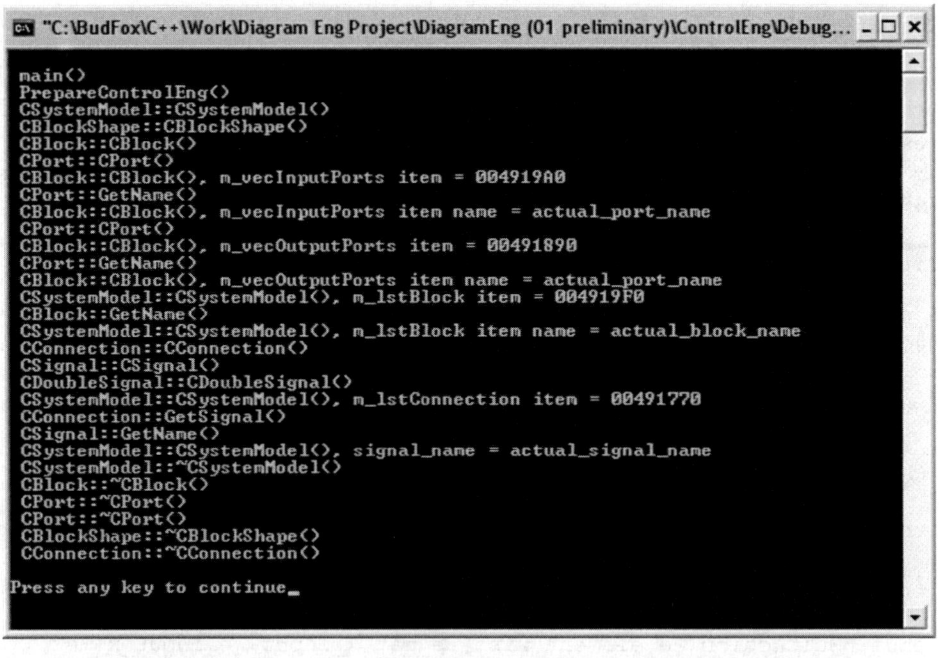

```
"C:\BudFox\C++\Work\Diagram Eng Project\DiagramEng (01 preliminary)\ControlEng\Debug...

main()
PrepareControlEng()
CSystemModel::CSystemModel()
CBlockShape::CBlockShape()
CBlock::CBlock()
CPort::CPort()
CBlock::CBlock(), m_vecInputPorts item = 004919A0
CPort::GetName()
CBlock::CBlock(), m_vecInputPorts item name = actual_port_name
CPort::CPort()
CBlock::CBlock(), m_vecOutputPorts item = 00491890
CPort::GetName()
CBlock::CBlock(), m_vecOutputPorts item name = actual_port_name
CSystemModel::CSystemModel(), m_lstBlock item = 004919F0
CBlock::GetName()
CSystemModel::CSystemModel(), m_lstBlock item name = actual_block_name
CConnection::CConnection()
CSignal::CSignal()
CDoubleSignal::CDoubleSignal()
CSystemModel::CSystemModel(), m_lstConnection item = 00491770
CConnection::GetSignal()
CSignal::GetName()
CSystemModel::CSystemModel(), signal_name = actual_signal_name
CSystemModel::~CSystemModel()
CBlock::~CBlock()
CPort::~CPort()
CPort::~CPort()
CBlockShape::~CBlockShape()
CConnection::~CConnection()

Press any key to continue_
```

FIGURE A.1 Console-based output concerning basic object construction and destruction for the Win32 Console Application, ControlEng.

```
enum EPortID {e_left_arrow, e_up_arrow, e_right_arrow, e_down_arrow};
  // left '<', up '^', right '>', and, down 'v'
enum ESignalForm {e_sine, e_cosine, e_square, e_sawtooth, e_random};
  // form of signal/wave
enum EUnits {e_m, e_s, e_kg, e_radians, e_hertz, e_radians_per_sec};
  // units

// BlockShape
class CBlockShape
{
public:
    CBlockShape(void);
    ~CBlockShape(void);

private:
    double geometry[3];    // square (l,w,thick), circle (r,d,thick),
      triangle (l,direc,thick)
    EBlockShape m_eBlockShape;
};

// Port
class CBlock;    // predefining CBlock as it's rqd. by CPort,
  additionally CBlock rqes. CPort
class CPort
{
public:
    CPort(CBlock &block_ref);
    ~CPort(void);

    // Accessor methods
    char *GetName(void);

private:
    char *port_name;              // name of either input or output port
    double port_position[2];    // ordered pair denoting (x,y)
      location of port w.r.t. block CofM
    CBlock &m_rRefToBlock;       // reference to its parent/own block
      upon which the port resides
    EPortID e_port_id;           // '>' arrow pts away/towards block
      center for output/input (left, up, right, down)
};

// Block
class CSystemModel; // predefining CSystemModel as it's rqd. by
  CBlock, additionally CSystemModel rqes. CBlock
class CBlock
{
public:
    CBlock(void);
    ~CBlock(void);

    // Accessor methods
    char* GetName(void);

private:
    char *block_name;            // block name
    double block_position[2];    // ordered pair denoting (x,y)
      location of CofM of block
```

```
    CBlockShape m_BlockShape;              // member obj of type
      CBlockShape
    vector<CPort*> m_vecInputPorts;        // vector of ptrs to CPort
    vector<CPort*> m_vecOutputPorts;       // vector of ptrs to CPort
    CSystemModel *m_pParentSystemModel;    // ptr to parent system model
    CSystemModel *m_pSubSystemModel;       // ptr = NULL => no
      contained system/sub model, ptr != NULL => system model
};

// ConstantBlock
class CConstantBlock : public CBlock
{
public:
    CConstantBlock(void);
    ~CConstantBlock(void);

private:
    double scalar_const;
    double *vector_const;
    double **matrix_const;
};

// DerivativeBlock
class CDerivativeBlock : public CBlock
{
public:
    CDerivativeBlock(void);
    ~CDerivativeBlock(void);

private:
    int derivative_method;    // 3-pt method, 5-pt method
    double t_step_size_h;     // time step size 'h' used in the defn
      of the numerical derivative
};

// DivideBlock
class CDivideBlock : public CBlock
{
public:
    CDivideBlock(void);
    ~CDivideBlock(void);

private:
    int m_iNMultiplyInputs;
    int m_iNDivideInputs;
    EMultAction e_mult_action;    // if divide used for a matrix,
      then matrix inverse is rqd.
};

// GainBlock
class CGainBlock : public CBlock
{
public:
    CGainBlock(void);
    ~CGainBlock(void);

private:
    double scalar_gain;
    double *vector_gain;
```

```cpp
    double **matrix_gain;
    EMultAction e_mult_action;
};

// IntegratorBlock
class CIntegratorBlock : public CBlock
{
public:
    CIntegratorBlock(void);
    ~CIntegratorBlock(void);

private:
    double t_step_size_h;     // time step size "h"
    double *ic_vector;        // initial condition vector
    EIntegrationMethod e_integration_method;
};

// LinearFnBlock
class CLinearFnBlock : public CBlock
{
public:
    CLinearFnBlock(void);
    ~CLinearFnBlock(void);

private:
    double fn_derivative;      // slope of linear fn or "curve"
    double signal_init_val;    // init val of signal (at time t0)
    double t_signal_start;     // start time of signal
};

// OutputBlock
class COutputBlock : public CBlock
{
public:
    COutputBlock(void);
    ~COutputBlock(void);

private:
    char *file_name;
    double t_start;
    double t_stop;
    EOutputDataFormat e_data_format;
};

// SignalGeneratorBlock
class CSignalGeneratorBlock : public CBlock
{
public:
    CSignalGeneratorBlock(void);
    ~CSignalGeneratorBlock(void);

private:      // externally generated signal is being ignored
  for now.
    double amplitude;
    double frequency;
    EUnits e_units;
    ESignalForm e_signal_form;
};
```

```cpp
// SubsystemBlock
class CSubsystemBlock : public CBlock
{
public:
    CSubsystemBlock(void);
    ~CSubsystemBlock(void);

private:
    int port_number_label_1;    // number to appear as the port label
    int port_number_label_2;    // number to appear as the port label
    char *port_signal_label_1;  // signal identifier (name) to appear
      as the port label
    char *port_signal_label_2;  // signal identifier (name) to appear
      as the port label
};

// SubsystemInBlock
class CSubsystemInBlock : public CBlock
{
public:
    CSubsystemInBlock(void);
    ~CSubsystemInBlock(void);

private:
    int port_number_label;      // number to appear as the port label
    char *port_signal_label;    // signal identifier (name) to appear
      as the port label
};

// SubsystemOutBlock
class CSubsystemOutBlock : public CBlock
{
public:
    CSubsystemOutBlock(void);
    ~CSubsystemOutBlock(void);

private:
    int port_number_label;      // number to appear as the port label
    char *port_signal_label;    // signal identifier (name) to appear
      as the port label
};

// SumBlock
class CSumBlock : public CBlock
{
public:
    CSumBlock(void);
    ~CSumBlock(void);

private:
    int no_of_plus_inputs;
    int no_of_minus_inputs;
};

// TransferFnBlock
class CTransferFnBlock : public CBlock
{
public:
    CTransferFnBlock(void);
    ~CTransferFnBlock(void);
```

```
    private:
        double *numerator_coeffs_vec;      // vector of numerator coeffs
        double *denominator_coeffs_vec;    // vector of denominator
          coeffs
    };

#endif

// eof
```

// Title: ControlEng.h

```
#ifndef CONTROL_ENG_H
    #define CONTROL_ENG_H     // inclusion guard

    // User defined consts/vars.

    // User defined types

    // Main line fn prototypes
    int main(int argc, char **argv);
    int PrepareControlEng(void);

#endif

// eof
```

// Title: Signal.h

```
#include "Block.h"

#ifndef SIGNAL_H
    #define SIGNAL_H     // inclusion guard

    // User defined types

    // Signal
    class CSignal
    {
    public:
        CSignal(void);     // creates a Signal obj. based on the datatype
          of the evolved (due to block ops.) signal
        ~CSignal(void);

        // Accessor methods
        char *GetName(void);

    private:
        char *signal_name;    // name of the current Signal
    };

    // DoubleSignal
    class CDoubleSignal : public CSignal
    {
    public:

        CDoubleSignal(void);
        ~CDoubleSignal(void);

    private:
        double var;    // each signal will have some numerical val
    };
```

```
    // MatrixSignal
    class CMatrixSignal : public CSignal
    {
    public:
        CMatrixSignal(void);
        ~CMatrixSignal(void);

    private:
        int nrows;
        int ncols;
        double **matrix_signal;     // matrix of signal vals
    };

    // VectorSignal
    class CVectorSignal : public CSignal
    {
    public:
        CVectorSignal(void);
        ~CVectorSignal(void);

    private:
        int length;
        double *vector_signal;     // vector of signal vals
    };

    // Connection
    class CConnection
    {
    public:
        CConnection(void);
        ~CConnection(void);

        // Accessor methods
        CSignal *GetSignal(void);     // gets the private member var
          signal of type ptr-to-CSignal

    private:
        double start_pt[2];     // start pt. (x,y) ordered pair
        double end_pt[2];       // end pt. (x,y) ordered pair
        CPort *m_pRefFromPort;  // singular, since 1 connection has only
          1 from-port (ptr used since block ports not know at this stage)
        CPort *m_pRefToPort;    // singular, since 1 connection has only 1
          to-port (ptr used since block ports not know at this stage)
        CSignal *m_pSignal;     // singular, since 1 signal (like a
          current) travels down 1 connection (like a wire)
    };

#endif

// eof

// Title:    SystemModel.h

#include "Block.h"
#include "Signal.h"

#ifndef SYSTEM_MODEL_H
    #define SYSTEM_MODEL_H     // inclusion guard
```

```
    // User defined consts/vars.

    // User defined types

    // SystemModel
    class CSystemModel
    {
    public:
        CSystemModel(void);
        ~CSystemModel(void);
        ComputeModelSignals();     // computes all Signals across all
           Connections according to math ops.
        char *GetName(void);       // gets model name
        ReadInputFromFile();       // reads: time, states
        WriteOutputToFile();       // writes: time, states, output, final
           states
        WriteNthTimeStepToFile(); // writes: every n-th time step to file
        ValidateConnectivity();    // validates Blocks are connected by
           Connections, warns of alg. loops

    private:
        char *model_name;                      // name of the current
           SystemModel
        double t_start;                        // simulation start time
        double t_stop;                         // simulation stop time
        list<CBlock*> m_lstBlock;              // list of ptrs to the
           Blocks of the current SystemModel
        list<CConnection*> m_lstConnection;   // list of ptrs to the
           Connections of the current SystemModel
    };

#endif

// eof
```

A.2.2 SOURCE FILES

The source files listed in the following are "Block.cpp", "ControlEng.cpp", "Signal.cpp", and "SystemModel.cpp". The "ControlEng.cpp" source file simply instantiates a CSystemModel object, and the other files provide the constructor and destructor definitions.

```
// Title:     Block.cpp
// Purpose:   Contains all Block related code.

#include <iostream>
#include <string.h>
#include <vector>
#include <list>
using namespace std;
#include "Block.h"
#include "SystemModel.h"     // rqd. since Block() destr potentially
deletes a ptr-to-CSystemModel (m_pSubSystemModel)

// CBlockShape

CBlockShape::CBlockShape(void)
{
    cout << "CBlockShape::CBlockShape()\n";
```

```cpp
    // Init
    int     i;
    double    d = 1.0;
    m_eBlockShape = e_rectangle;

    for(i=0; i<3; i++)
    {
        geometry[i] = d;    // add temp elements to the array
    }
}

CBlockShape::~CBlockShape(void)
{
    cout << "CBlockShape::~CBlockShape()\n";
}


// CPort

CPort::CPort(CBlock &block_ref):
m_rRefToBlock(block_ref)    // must init the m_rRefToBlock rather than
assign on CPort obj. creation
{
    cout << "CPort::CPort()\n";

    // Init
    port_name = new char[32];                  // allocate space for port_name
    strcpy(port_name, "actual_port_name");  // copy actual port name into
      the var port_name

    port_position[0] = 1.0;
    port_position[1] = 0.0;
    e_port_id = e_right_arrow;
}

CPort::~CPort(void)
{
    cout << "CPort::~CPort()\n";
}

char *CPort::GetName(void)
{
    cout << "CPort::GetName()\n";

    return port_name;
}

// CBlock

CBlock::CBlock(void)
{
    cout << "CBlock::CBlock()\n";

    // Init
    block_name = new char[32];
    strcpy(block_name, "actual_block_name");
    block_position[0] = 1.0;
    block_position[1] = 1.0;
```

```
    // -- Vector of input ptrs-to-CPort
    CPort *p_port_in = new CPort(*this);
    vector<CPort*>::iterator it_in;                 // generate an iterator
      for vec-of-ptrs-to-CPort

    it_in = m_vecInputPorts.begin();                // start of the vec
    m_vecInputPorts.insert(it_in, p_port_in);   // insert a new
      ptr-to-CPort in the vector

    for(it_in = m_vecInputPorts.begin(); it_in < m_vecInputPorts.end();
      it_in++)
    {
        cout << "CBlock::CBlock(), m_vecInputPorts item =" << *it_in <<
          endl; // deref the iterator to get the ptr-to-CPort
        cout << "CBlock::CBlock(), m_vecInputPorts item name ="
          << (*it_in)->GetName() << endl; // deref the iterator to get
          the ptr-to-CPort and call GetName()
    }

    // -- Vector of output ptrs-to-CPort
    CPort *p_port_out = new CPort(*this);
    vector<CPort*>::iterator it_out;    // generate an iterator for
      vec-of-ptrs-to-CPort

    it_out = m_vecOutputPorts.begin();              // start of the vec
    m_vecOutputPorts.insert(it_out, p_port_out);    // insert a new
      ptr-to-CPort in the vector

    for(it_out = m_vecOutputPorts.begin(); it_out < m_vecOutputPorts.
      end(); it_out++)
    {
        cout << "CBlock::CBlock(), m_vecOutputPorts item =" << *it_out
          << endl; // deref the iterator to get the ptr-to-CPort
        cout << "CBlock::CBlock(), m_vecOutputPorts item name =" <<
          (*it_out)->GetName() << endl; // deref the iterator to get the
          ptr-to-CPort and call GetName()
    }

    m_pSubSystemModel = NULL;    // ptr to a possibly CONTAINED SUB
      MODEL: ptr = NULL => no contained system model, ptr = !NULL =>
      system model
}

CBlock::~CBlock(void)

{
    cout << "CBlock::~CBlock()\n";

    // MEMORY DELETE

    if(block_name != NULL)
    {
        delete [] block_name;
    }

    vector<CPort*>::iterator it_in;    // generate an iterator for
      vec-of-ptrs-to-CPort
    vector<CPort*>::iterator it_out;    // generate an iterator for
      vec-of-ptrs-to-CPort
```

```
    for(it_in = m_vecInputPorts.begin(); it_in < m_vecInputPorts.end();
      it_in++)
    {
        delete (*it_in);    // delete what it_in is pointing to:
            i.e. deref the it_in ptr and delete the ptr-to-CPort.
    }
    // vector is then destroyed automatically by vector destructor
    for(it_out = m_vecOutputPorts.begin(); it_out < m_vecOutputPorts.
      end(); it_out++)
    {
        delete (*it_out);    // delete what it_out is pointing to:
            i.e. deref the it_out ptr and delete the ptr-to-CPort.
    }
    // vector is then destroyed automatically by vector destructor

    if(m_pSubSystemModel != NULL)
    {
        delete m_pSubSystemModel;
        m_pSubSystemModel = NULL;
    }
}

char *CBlock::GetName(void)

{
    cout << "CBlock::GetName()\n";

    return block_name;
}

// CConstantBlock

CConstantBlock::CConstantBlock(void)
{
    cout << "CConstantBlock::CConstantBlock()\n";
}

CConstantBlock::~CConstantBlock(void)
{
    cout << "CConstantBlock::~CConstantBlock()\n";
}

// CDerivativeBlock

CDerivativeBlock::CDerivativeBlock(void)
{
    cout << "CDerivativeBlock::CDerivativeBlock()\n";
}

CDerivativeBlock::~CDerivativeBlock(void)
{
    cout << "CDerivativeBlock::~CDerivativeBlock()\n";
}

// CDivideBlock

CDivideBlock::CDivideBlock(void)
{
    cout << "CDivideBlock::CDivideBlock()\n";
}
```

```cpp
CDivideBlock::~CDivideBlock(void)
{
    cout << "CDivideBlock::~CDivideBlock()\n";
}

// CGainBlock

CGainBlock::CGainBlock(void)
{
    cout << "CGainBlock::CGainBlock()\n";
}

CGainBlock::~CGainBlock(void)
{
    cout << "CGainBlock::~CGainBlock()\n";
}

// CIntegratorBlock

CIntegratorBlock::CIntegratorBlock(void)
{
    cout << "CIntegratorBlock::CIntegratorBlock()\n";
}

CIntegratorBlock::~CIntegratorBlock(void)
{
    cout << "CIntegratorBlock::~CIntegratorBlock()\n";
}

// CLinearFnBlock

CLinearFnBlock::CLinearFnBlock(void)
{
    cout << "CLinearFnBlock::CLinearFnBlock()\n";
}

CLinearFnBlock::~CLinearFnBlock(void)
{
    cout << "CLinearFnBlock::~CLinearFnBlock()\n";
}

// COutputBlock

COutputBlock::COutputBlock(void)
{
    cout << "COutputBlock::COutputBlock()\n";
}

COutputBlock::~COutputBlock(void)
{
    cout << "COutputBlock::~COutputBlock()\n";
}

// CSignalGeneratorBlock

CSignalGeneratorBlock::CSignalGeneratorBlock(void)
{
    cout << "CSignalGeneratorBlock::CSignalGeneratorBlock()\n";
}
```

```
CSignalGeneratorBlock::~CSignalGeneratorBlock(void)
{
    cout << "CSignalGeneratorBlock::~CSignalGeneratorBlock()\n";
}

// CSubsystemBlock

CSubsystemBlock::CSubsystemBlock(void)
{
    cout << "CSubsystemBlock::CSubsystemBlock()\n";
}

CSubsystemBlock::~CSubsystemBlock(void)
{
    cout << "CSubsystemBlock::~CSubsystemBlock()\n";
}

// CSubsystemInBlock

CSubsystemInBlock::CSubsystemInBlock(void)
{
    cout << "CSubsystemInBlock::CSubsystemInBlock()\n";
}

CSubsystemInBlock::~CSubsystemInBlock(void)
{
    cout << "CSubsystemInBlock::~CSubsystemInBlock()\n";
}

// CSubsystemOutBlock

CSubsystemOutBlock::CSubsystemOutBlock(void)
{
    cout << "CSubsystemOutBlock::CSubsystemOutBlock()\n";
}

CSubsystemOutBlock::~CSubsystemOutBlock(void)
{
    cout << "CSubsystemOutBlock::~CSubsystemOutBlock()\n";
}

// CSumBlock

CSumBlock::CSumBlock(void)
{
    cout << "CSumBlock::CSumBlock()\n";
}

CSumBlock::~CSumBlock(void)
{
    cout << "CSumBlock::~CSumBlock()\n";
}

// CTransferFnBlock

CTransferFnBlock::CTransferFnBlock(void)
{
    cout << "CTransferFnBlock::CTransferFnBlock()\n";
}
```

```
CTransferFnBlock::~CTransferFnBlock(void)
{
    cout << "CTransferFnBlock::~CTransferFnBlock()\n";
}

// eof
```

// Title: ControlEng.cpp
```
// Purpose:  Contains all ControlEng related code: main line of project.

#include <iostream>
#include <string.h>
#include <vector>
#include <list>
using namespace std;
#include "ControlEng.h"
#include "SystemModel.h"

int main(int argc, char **argv)
{
    // input: arg count int, and an array of ptrs-to-char, a 2-dim array
      of chars

    cout << "\n main()\n";

    PrepareControlEng();

    cout << endl;

    return 0;
}

int PrepareControlEng(void)
{
    cout << "PrepareControlEng()\n";

    CSystemModel system_model;

    return 0;
}

// eof
```

// Title: Signal.cpp
```
// Purpose:    Contains all Signal related code.

#include <iostream>
#include <string.h>
#include <vector>
#include <list>
using namespace std;
#include "Signal.h"

// CSignal

CSignal::CSignal(void)
{
    cout << "CSignal::CSignal()\n";

    signal_name = new char[32];     // allocate space for signal_name
    strcpy(signal_name, "actual_signal_name");    // copy actual signal
      name into the var signal_name
}
```

```
CSignal::~CSignal(void)
{
    cout << "CSignal::~CSignal()\n";
}


char *CSignal::GetName(void)
{
    cout << "CSignal::GetName()\n";

    return signal_name;
}

// CDoubleSignal

CDoubleSignal::CDoubleSignal(void)
{
    cout << "CDoubleSignal::CDoubleSignal()\n";

    var = 0.0;     // init double signal to zero.
}


CDoubleSignal::~CDoubleSignal(void)
{
    cout << "CDoubleSignal::~CDoubleSignal()\n";
}

// CMatrixSignal

CMatrixSignal::CMatrixSignal(void)
{
    cout << "CMatrixSignal::CMatrixSignal()\n";

    nrows = 0;
    ncols = 0;
    matrix_signal = NULL;    // init matrix_signal ptr to NULL (allocate
      memory for this elsewhere)
}

CMatrixSignal::~CMatrixSignal(void)
{
    cout << "CMatrixSignal::~CMatrixSignal()\n";
}

// CVectorSignal

CVectorSignal::CVectorSignal(void)
{
    cout << "CVectorSignal::CVectorSignal()\n";

    length = 0;
    vector_signal = NULL;    // init vector_signal ptr to NULL (allocate
      memory for this elsewhere)
}

CVectorSignal::~CVectorSignal(void)
{
    cout << "CVectorSignal::~CVectorSignal()\n";
}
```

```cpp
// CConnection

CConnection::CConnection(void)

{
    cout << "CConnection::CConnection()\n";

    start_pt[0] = 0.0;                    // start pt. (x,y) ordered pair: x cmpt.
    start_pt[1] = 0.0;                    // start pt. (x,y) ordered pair: y_cmpt.
    end_pt[0] = 1.0;                      // end pt. (x,y) ordered pair: x_cmpt.
    end_pt[1] = 1.0;                      // end pt. (x,y) ordered pair: y_cmpt.
    m_pRefFromPort = NULL;                // from-port ref.
    m_pRefToPort = NULL;                  // to-port ref.
    m_pSignal = new CDoubleSignal;        // contained ptr-to-CSignal init.
      to NULL.
}

CConnection::~CConnection(void)
{
    cout << "CConnection::~CConnection()\n";
}

CSignal *CConnection::GetSignal(void)
{
    cout << "CConnection::GetSignal()\n";

    return m_pSignal;      // return private member var signal of type
      ptr-to-CSignal
}

// eof

// Title:        SystemModel.cpp
// Purpose:      Contains all SystemModel related code.

#include <iostream>
#include <string.h>
#include <vector>
#include <list>
using namespace std;
#include "SystemModel.h"

// CSystemModel

CSystemModel::CSystemModel(void)
{
    cout << "CSystemModel::CSystemModel()\n";

    model_name = new char[32];            // alloc mem for model_name
    strcpy(model_name, "model_name");     // temp model name
    t_start = 0.0;                        // sim start time
    t_stop = 10.0;                        // sim stop time

    // -- Block list

    CBlock *p_block1 = new CBlock;        // new returns & of mem. loc. to
      hold a CBlock obj.

    list<CBlock*>::iterator it_blk;       // iterator for list of CBlock-ptrs

    m_lstBlock.push_front(p_block1);      // insert a new element at the
      beginning of the list (a ptr-to-CBlock)
```

```cpp
    for(it_blk = m_lstBlock.begin(); it_blk != m_lstBlock.end(); it_blk++)
    {
        cout << "CSystemModel::CSystemModel(), m_lstBlock item =" <<
          *it_blk << endl;    // deref the iterator to get the
          ptr-to-CBlock
        cout << "CSystemModel::CSystemModel(), m_lstBlock item name =" <<
          (*it_blk)->GetName() << endl;
    }

    // -- Connection list
    CConnection *p_conn = new CConnection;    // new returns & of mem.
      loc. to hold a CConnection obj.
    list<CConnection*>::iterator it_conn;    // iterator for list of
      CConnection-ptrs

    m_lstConnection.push_front(p_conn);        // insert a new element at
      the beginning of the list (a ptr-to-CConnection)

    for(it_conn = m_lstConnection.begin(); it_conn != m_lstConnection.
      end(); it_conn++)
    {
        cout << "CSystemModel::CSystemModel(), m_lstConnection item =" <<
          *it_conn << endl; // deref the iterator to get the ptr-to-
          CConnection
        cout << "CSystemModel::CSystemModel(), signal_name =" <<
          (*it_conn)->GetSignal()->GetName() << endl;
    }
}

CSystemModel::~CSystemModel(void)
{
    cout << "CSystemModel::~CSystemModel()\n";

    // Delete mem
    list<CBlock*>::iterator it_blk;
    list<CConnection*>::iterator it_conn;

    for(it_blk = m_lstBlock.begin(); it_blk != m_lstBlock.end(); it_blk++)
    {
        delete (*it_blk);     // delete what it_blk is pointing to:
          i.e. deref the it_blk ptr and delete the ptr-to-CBlock.
    }
    // list destr. automatically destroys the list

    for(it_conn = m_lstConnection.begin(); it_conn != m_lstConnection.
      end(); it_conn++)
    {
        delete (*it_conn);     // delete what it_conn is pointing to:
          i.e. deref the it_conn ptr and delete the ptr-to-CConnection.
    }
    // list destr. automatically destroys the list
}

char *CSystemModel::GetName(void)
{
    cout << "CSystemModel::GetName()\n";

    return model_name;
}

// eof
```

A.3 SUMMARY

A preliminary Win32 Console Application, named ControlEng, is used to implement the initial class hierarchical association relationships of Chapter 1 and shows basic construction and destruction of objects of the following key user-defined types: CSystemModel, CBlockShape, CBlock, CPort, CConnection, and CSignal.

REFERENCE

1. Microsoft Visual C++® 6.0, Microsoft® Visual Studio™ 6.0 Development System, Professional Edition, Microsoft Corporation, 1998.

Appendix B: Constructing Connections: An Exploration

B.1 INTRODUCTION

An exploration is made into the construction and drawing of connection lines with arrowheads attached that indicate the direction in which they are oriented. These connections are then used in the main DiagramEng project to connect blocks using their input and output ports, where the direction of the connection, specified by the arrowhead, indicates the direction of signal flow, i.e., data transfer, from one block to another.

The work here follows closely the material presented in Chapter 10 of Ref. [1] that introduces the drawing of lines and saving them into a document object. Here, the Day10 project, pp. 202–213, of Ref. [1] is revisited in the form of a separate exercise named Exp10, and alterations are made to reflect, in part, the DiagramEng structure and to facilitate the actual implementation of connections in the DiagramEng project, covered in Chapter 5.

B.2 DRAWING BASIC CONNECTIONS

The general steps to implement the drawing of connection objects on a palette are listed in the following, where specific details are presented in the sections that follow:

1. Build the application shell
2. Add a new CConnection class
3. Add a function to add the connection to the list
4. Add a function to get the connection list
5. Add an `OnLButtonDown()` function
6. Add an `OnMouseMove()` function
7. Add an `OnLButtonUp()` function
8. Draw connections
9. Build and run the application

B.2.1 BUILD THE APPLICATION SHELL

Create a new AppWizard project named Exp10 to experiment with the material presented in Day10 of Ref. [1]: (1) choose Single Document on step 1, (2) use default values for step 2, (3) deselect support for ActiveX Controls on step 3, (4) choose the default values on step 4, but enter "dvp" as the three-letter file extension, (5) use the default values on step 5, and (6) on step 6, choose CView as the base class upon which the project view class will be based [1]. After building the application shell, the classes present are CAboutDlg, CExp10App, CExp10Doc, CExp10View, and CMainFrame.

B.2.2　ADD A NEW **CConnection** CLASS

A new class, CConnection, is required in the project to manage the connection objects. Hence, add a new class to the project, select Generic Class for the class type and CConnection for the class name, and leave the "Base class(es)" box empty since the class is not derived from a base class:

1. Add two private CPoint member variables to the CConnection class with the names "m_ptFrom" and "m_ptTo", representing the tail and head points of the connection, respectively.
2. Add a new public constructor to the CConnection class with the prototype, CConnection::CConnection(CPoint ptFrom, CPoint ptTo), and edit the function as shown in the following to initialize the member variables.

```
CConnection::CConnection(CPoint ptFrom, CPoint ptTo)
{
    // Init of member vars.
    m_ptFrom = ptFrom;
    m_ptTo = ptTo;
}
```

B.2.3　ADD A FUNCTION TO ADD THE CONNECTION TO THE LIST

The CConnection object should be added to a list of connection objects for convenient storage; a member variable and method are required. Hence, add a private member variable of type list<CConnection*> with name "m_lstConnection" to the CExp10Doc class. The warning "Template declarations or definitions cannot be added" is presented. Hence, add a private integer "m_lstConnection" to the CExp10Doc class and then change it manually to "list<CConnection*> m_lstConnection", and make the changes to the function prototype in both the source, "Exp10Doc.cpp", and header, "Exp10Doc.h", files.

Add a public member function to the CExp10Doc class to add the CConnection object to the list of connections, "m_lstConnection", with the prototype, void CExp10Doc::AddConnection(CPoint ptFrom, CPoint ptTo), and edit the function as follows.

```
void CExp10Doc::AddConnection(CPoint ptFrom, CPoint ptTo)
{
    CString sMsg;          // main msg string
    UINT nType = MB_OK;    // style of msg. box
    UINT nIDhelp = 0;      // help context ID for the msg.

    // Print msg.
    sMsg.Format("\n CExp10Doc::AddConnection(), from (%d,%d)
      to (%d,%d)\n", ptFrom.x, ptFrom.y, ptTo.x, ptTo.y);
    // AfxMessageBox(sMsg, nType, nIDhelp);

    // Create a new CConnection obj.
    CConnection *pCon = new CConnection(ptFrom, ptTo);

    // Add the new connection to the connection list
    m_lstConnection.push_back(pCon);

    // Mark the document as being modified
    SetModifiedFlag();
}
```

B.2.4   ADD A FUNCTION TO GET THE CONNECTION LIST

The connection list needs to be obtained from the CDocument-derived CExpl0Doc class in order that it can be manipulated, i.e., in order for individual connections to be added to it or deleted from it. Hence, add a public member function to the CExpl0Doc class with prototype, list<CConnection*> &CExpl0Doc::GetConnectionList(void), and edit the code as shown in the following to return the connection list, "m_lstConnection", by reference. Again, the warning "Template declarations or definitions cannot be added" is presented. Hence, use an "int &" return type and then manually alter the function prototype declaration in the header file, "Expl0Doc.h", and the definition in the source file, "Expl0Doc.cpp".

```
list<CConnection*> &CExpl0Doc::GetConnectionList()
{
    return m_lstConnection;
}
```

B.2.5   ADD AN `OnLButtonDown()` FUNCTION

The user can draw a connection on the palette by clicking the left mouse button and moving the mouse pointer and then releasing the left button. Hence, these events should have functions associated with them. To add functionality to the left-button-down event, invoke the ClassWizard, choose CExpl0View as the class, WM_LBUTTONDOWN as the event message, and add the event-handler function with the prototype: CExpl0View::OnLButtonDown(UINT nFlags, CPoint point). Edit the function as shown in the following.

```
void CExpl0View::OnLButtonDown(UINT nFlags, CPoint point)
{
    // TODO: Add your message handler code here and/or call default
    // DiagramEng (start)
    // Capture the mouse so no other apps. can get it.
    SetCapture();

    // Save the pt that the cursor is at, upon left-btn-down, i.e. init
       member var with incoming CPoint var.
    m_ptPrevPos = point;   // Init the prev. pt, to be used in
       OnMouseMove(), to the current point
    m_ptOrigin = point;    // Init origin of ensuing line, to be drawn in
       OnMouseMove(), to be the starting pt.

    // DiagramEng (end)
    CView::OnLButtonDown(nFlags, point);
}
```

The developer will notice that this function uses the member variables "m_ptPrevPos" and "m_ptOrigin" to record the previous and origin points to be used in the following OnMouseMove() and OnLButtonUp() methods. Hence, add these two private CPoint member variables to the CExpl0View class.

B.2.6   ADD AN `OnMouseMove()` FUNCTION

Functionality is now added to the mouse movement event that takes place after the left-button-down event. Invoke the ClassWizard, select CExpl0View as the class, and add an event-handler function with the prototype, `void CExp10View::OnMouseMove(UINT nFlags, CPoint point)`, for the WM_MOUSEMOVE event message, and edit the function as shown in the following.

```
void CExp10View::OnMouseMove(UINT nFlags, CPoint point)
{
    // TODO: Add your message handler code here and/or call default

    // DiagramEng (start)

    // Check to see if the left mouse btn. is down
    if((nFlags & MK_LBUTTON) == MK_LBUTTON)
    {
        // Check to see if mouse is captured
        if(GetCapture() == this)  // If what has been captured is the obj.
          upon which the present fn is called.
        {
            // Get the device context
            CClientDC dc(this);

            // Reverse the pixel color from the original pt to the prev pt.
            // SetROP2() sets the current foreground mix mode.
            dc.SetROP2(R2_NOT);    // R2_NOT => pixel is the inverse of the
              screen color
            dc.MoveTo(m_ptOrigin);
            dc.LineTo(m_ptPrevPos);

            // Draw the current stretch of line (but don't save it until
              OnLButtonUp().
            dc.MoveTo(m_ptOrigin);
            dc.LineTo(point);

            // Save the current pt (point) as the prev. pt (m_ptPrevPos)
              of the CView class.
            m_ptPrevPos = point;
        }
    }

    // DiagramEng (end)

    CView::OnMouseMove(nFlags, point);
}
```

The `OnMouseMove()` function draws a line from the origin point, "m_ptOrigin", to the mouse cursor point, "point"; this is achieved using `MoveTo(m_ptOrigin)` followed by `LineTo(point)`. However, firstly the previous line drawn needs to be erased; otherwise it would remain on the screen: this is performed by reversing the color, using `SetROP2(R2_NOT)` and overdrawing the previous line using `MoveTo(m_ptOrigin)` followed by `LineTo(m_ptPrevPos)`. Finally, the current mouse cursor point, "point", is assigned to "m_ptPrevPos", to make a record of what will become the previous point, to be subsequently used when overdrawing the line on the next entry into the `OnMouseMove()` function.

B.2.7 ADD AN `OnLButtonUp()` FUNCTION

The left-button-up event signifies the end of the connection-drawing process, at which time the drawn connection should be added to the list of connections. Hence, invoke the ClassWizard and choose CExp10View as the class, select WM_LBUTTONUP as the event message, and add an event handler function with the prototype, void CExp10View::OnLButtonUp(UINT nFlags, CPoint point). Edit the function as shown in the following.

```
void CExp10View::OnLButtonUp(UINT nFlags, CPoint point)
{
    // TODO: Add your message handler code here and/or call default

    // DiagramEng (start)

    // Check to see mouse has been captured
    if(GetCapture() == this) // if what has been captured is the obj.
      that the "this" ptr. is pointing to.
    {
        // Add the connection to the connection list
        GetDocument()->AddConnection(m_ptOrigin, point);

        // Release the capture so other apps. can have access to the
          mouse.
        ReleaseCapture();
    }

    // DiagramEng (end)

    CView::OnLButtonUp(nFlags, point);
}
```

The developer will notice that the AddConnection() function is called upon the pointer-to-CExp10Doc, retrieved by the call to GetDocument() of the CExp10View class. The AddConnection() function creates the connection using the CConnection constructor taking two CPoint arguments and adds it to the list of connections, "m_lstConnection", as shown earlier.

B.2.8 Draw Connections

The CView-based CExp10View class has an OnDraw() function that is called by the framework to render an image of the document [2]. Hence, augment the CExp10View::OnDraw() function with a call to draw the connections of the diagram, as shown in the following code.

```
void CExp10View::OnDraw(CDC* pDC)
{
    CExp10Doc* pDoc = GetDocument();
    ASSERT_VALID(pDoc);
    // TODO: add draw code for native data here

    // DiagramEng (start)
    pDoc->DrawConnections(pDC);
    // DiagramEng (end)
}
```

The call to DrawConnections() (note the plural) is used to draw the connections stored in the connection list, "m_lstConnection", residing in the CExp10Doc class. Hence, add a public member function to the CExp10Doc class with the prototype void CExp10Doc::DrawConnections(CDC *pDC) and edit it as follows. Note how the list of connections is iterated over and DrawConnection() is called on the pointer-to-CConnection object.

```
void CExp10Doc::DrawConnections(CDC *pDC)
{
    // DiagramEng (start)

    CString sMsg;                              // main msg string
    UINT nType = MB_OK;                        // style of msg. box
    UINT nIDhelp = 0;                          // help context ID for the msg.
    list<CConnection*>::iterator it_con;       // local iterator
    list<CConnection*> con_list;               // local connection list

    // -- Print msg.
    sMsg.Format("\n CExp10Doc::DrawConnections()\n");
    // AfxMessageBox(sMsg, nType, nIDhelp);

    // Get the connection list
    con_list = GetConnectionList();

    // Iterate through the list
    for(it_con = con_list.begin(); it_con != con_list.end(); it_con++)
    {
        (*it_con)->DrawConnection(pDC);   // DrawConnection() called on the
            ptr-to-CConnection
    }

    // DiagramEng (end)
}
```

Now the actual function to draw the connection object from the starting point, "m_ptFrom", to the ending point, "m_ptTo", is required. Hence, add a public member function to draw a single connection, with the prototype, void CConnection::DrawConnection(CDC *pDC), and edit the function as shown in the following to use the MoveTo() and LineTo() functions of the Device Context class (CDC).

```
void CConnection::DrawConnection(CDC *pDC)
{
    int pen_color = RGB(0,0,0);   // White = RGB(255,255,255),
      Black = RGB(0,0,0).
    int pen_width = 1;            // pen width

    // Create the pen
    CPen lpen(PS_SOLID, pen_width, pen_color);

    // Select the pen as the drawing obj.
    // The value returned by SelectObject() is a ptr to the obj. being
      replaced, i.e. an old-pen-ptr.
    CPen *pOldPen = pDC->SelectObject(&lpen);

    // Draw connection line
    pDC->MoveTo(m_ptFrom);
    pDC->LineTo(m_ptTo);

    // Reset the prev. pen
    pDC->SelectObject(pOldPen);
}
```

B.2.9   BUILD AND RUN THE APPLICATION

Now that the relevant connection construction and drawing functionality has been added to the project, it may be built and run. However, on doing so, a compilation error concerning "<list>" occurred. The developer will notice that the list of connections, or more specifically, a list of pointers-to-CConnection, i.e., "list<CConnection*> m_lstConnection", is a member of the CExp10Doc class. Hence, make the following additions:

1. Add #include "Connection.h" to the files "Exp10Doc.cpp" and "Exp10Doc.h".
2. Add #include <list> to the "Exp10Doc.cpp" source file and "Exp10Doc.h" header file, within the inclusion guard contained code (shown in the following).
3. Insert using namespace std after the #include <list> statements in the source file, "Exp10Doc.cpp", and in the header file, "Exp10Doc.h", within the inclusion guard contained code.

```
// Exp10Doc.h : interface of the CExp10Doc class
//
/////////////////////////////////////////////////////////////////////

#if !defined(AFX_EXP10DOC_H__B651D73A_C544_43B2_80B7_8149922FC9AC__
  INCLUDED_)
#define AFX_EXP10DOC_H__B651D73A_C544_43B2_80B7_8149922FC9AC__INCLUDED_

// DiagramEng (start)
#include "Connection.h"
#include <list>
using namespace std;
// DiagramEng (end)
...
#endif // !defined(AFX_EXP10DOC_H__B651D73A_C544_43B2_80B7_8149922FC9AC__
  INCLUDED_)
```

Individual lines may be added to the diagram as indicated in Figure B.1. Each line is drawn from the origin point, "m_ptOrigin", upon a left-mouse-button-down event, to the final point, "point", upon the left-mouse-button-up event. On moving the mouse, the line is simply redrawn to the position of the mouse cursor, "point". The connection line is added to the connection list, "m_lstConnection", upon the left-mouse-button-up event.

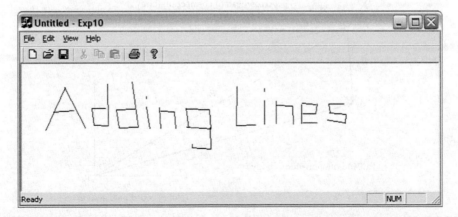

FIGURE B.1   Lines are drawn on the palette using left-button-down, mouse-move, and left-button-up events.

B.3   EXTENSIONS TO THE PROJECT

Extensions are now made to the current Exp10 project in preparation for drawing connections in the DiagramEng project. Initially the geometry of an arrowhead is considered prior to drawing it on screen, and then a mechanism to dynamically draw a connection to a moving mouse cursor is added.

B.3.1   ADD ARROWHEADS TO CONNECTION LINES

An arrowhead is added to a connection line in preparation for the indication of the direction of "signal flow" from the following points: (1) "m_ptOrigin" to "point" (as in `CExp10View::OnLButtonUp()`), (2) equivalently from "ptFrom" to "ptTo" (as in `CExp10Doc::AddConnection()`), or (3) equivalently from "m_ptFrom" to "m_ptTo" (as in `CConnection::CConnection()`).

To draw an arrowhead, the vertices of the triangle representing the arrowhead must be determined. Care must be taken to structure the derivation of expressions denoting the vertex position with respect to the screen coordinate system. Figure B.2 indicates the screen coordinate system (X, Y) and the arrowhead-based local body coordinate system (x_i, y_i) for the ith connection. The user will notice, however, that the following diagram has intentionally been turned upside down since the screen coordinate system is usually positive from the top down, and from left to right. This has been done purely for ease-of-mathematical-derivation reasons; the relative directions of the coordinate systems are consistent.

The position vector, $\boldsymbol{r}_{p_i}$, of point p_i, representing a triangle vertex, i.e., A_i, B_i, and C_i, in Figure B.2, residing on the ith connection arrowhead, is given by

$$\boldsymbol{r}_{p_i} = \boldsymbol{R}_i + \boldsymbol{G}(\theta_i)\bar{\boldsymbol{u}}_{p_i} \tag{B.1}$$

where

$\boldsymbol{R}_i$ is the position vector locating the center of mass of body i, i.e., vertex B
$\bar{\boldsymbol{u}}_{p_i}$ is the local position vector of point p_i (here, vertices A_i, B_i, and C_i) with respect to the origin (vertex B_i) of the local coordinate system (x_i, y_i) of connection i
$\boldsymbol{G}(\theta_i)$ is the rotation matrix specifying body rotation, by an angle θ_i, in the clockwise sense about the z axis oriented positively downward (into the page), i.e.,

$$\boldsymbol{G}(\theta_i) = \begin{bmatrix} \cos(\theta_i) & -\sin(\theta_i) \\ \sin(\theta_i) & \cos(\theta_i) \end{bmatrix} \tag{B.2}$$

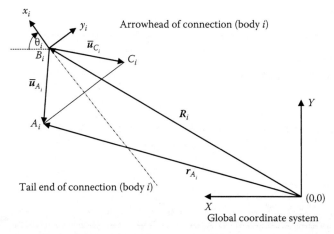

FIGURE B.2   Global screen coordinate system (X, Y) and local body coordinate system (x_i, y_i) of the arrowhead of the ith connection, indicating the positive clockwise direction of rotation (θ_i).

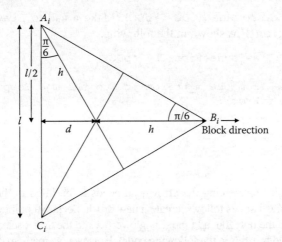

FIGURE B.3 A triangle block representing the arrowhead of the ith connection of side length l, where h is the hypotenuse of a subtriangle, with opposite side length d and base length $l/2$.

This general geometrical method to denote the position vector of a point on a rotating body follows the work of Shabana [3].

Consider Figure B.3, showing an arrowhead represented by an equilateral triangle, with base length l that is composed of subtriangles with a hypotenuse h and opposite side length d, such that the bisector of a side of the equilateral triangle is of length $h + d$. This geometry is used here to determine the global position vectors of the vertices A_i, B_i, and C_i of the equilateral arrowhead triangle on the head-end of a connection.

The global position vectors of the vertices for the ith connection's arrowhead are

$$r_{A_i} = \begin{bmatrix} r_{A_i,x} \\ r_{A_i,y} \end{bmatrix} = \begin{bmatrix} R_{i,x} \\ R_{i,y} \end{bmatrix} + \begin{bmatrix} \cos(\theta_i) & -\sin(\theta_i) \\ \sin(\theta_i) & \cos(\theta_i) \end{bmatrix} \begin{bmatrix} -(h+d) \\ -1/2 \end{bmatrix} \tag{B.3}$$

$$r_{B_i} = \begin{bmatrix} r_{B_i,x} \\ r_{B_i,y} \end{bmatrix} = \begin{bmatrix} R_{i,x} \\ R_{i,y} \end{bmatrix} \tag{B.4}$$

and

$$r_{C_i} = \begin{bmatrix} r_{C_i,x} \\ r_{C_i,y} \end{bmatrix} = \begin{bmatrix} R_{i,x} \\ R_{i,y} \end{bmatrix} + \begin{bmatrix} \cos(\theta_i) & -\sin(\theta_i) \\ \sin(\theta_i) & \cos(\theta_i) \end{bmatrix} \begin{bmatrix} -(h+d) \\ 1/2 \end{bmatrix} \tag{B.5}$$

where $R_i = [R_{i,x}, R_{i,y}]^T = [\text{m\_ptTo.x}, \text{m\_ptTo.y}]^T$ is the position vector of the end point of the connection at which the arrowhead is to be drawn, and $\bar{u}_{B_i} = [0,0]^T$ since the center of mass is considered to be located at point B_i (for simplicity).

B.3.2 Add the **DrawArrowHead()** Function

The `CExp10View::OnDraw()` function calls `CExp10Doc::DrawConnections()`, and this function then calls `CConnection::DrawConnection()`. However, here an arrowhead is to be drawn from within the `CConnection::DrawConnection()` function. Hence, add a public member function to the CConnection class with the prototype, void

`CConnection::DrawArrowHead(CDC *pDC)`. Make a call to `DrawArrowHead()` from within `DrawConnection()` as shown in the following.

```
void CConnection::DrawConnection(CDC *pDC)
{
    // Draw a line from the m_ptFrom pt. to the m_ptTo pt.
    pDC->MoveTo(m_ptFrom);
    pDC->LineTo(m_ptTo);

    // Draw arrow head
    DrawArrowHead(pDC);
}
```

Now the polygon triangle representing the arrowhead needs to be filled in the `DrawArrowHead()` function. The steps involved are as follows: create a new brush, declare a pointer-to-CBrush, declare an array of points that form the polygon, add the triangle vertices to the array, select the new brush, fill the polygon, and reset the old brush (see the following code). However, as mathematical functions, i.e., sin() and cos(), are used, the math header file, "math.h", should be included, i.e., #include <math.h>, at the top of the source file, "Connection.cpp". Edit the `DrawArrowHead()` function as shown.

```
void CConnection::DrawArrowHead(CDC *pDC)
{
    int pen_color = RGB(0,0,0);   // pen color: White = RGB(255,255,255),
      Black = RBF(0,0,0)
    int pen_width = 1;            // pen width
    double d;                     // opp. side length of subtriangle with
      hypotenuse h and base side length length/2.
    double dDeltaLength = 50;     // std ref delta length
    double h;                     // hypotenuse of subtriangle with opp.
      side length d and base side length length/2.
    double length;          // a fraction of dDeltaLength
    double length_u;        // length of vector u
    double length_v;        // length of vector v
    double theta;           // angle of ith body rotated positively
      clockwise w.r.t. the global screen coord sys. X axis.
    double u[2];    // one of two vectors used to determined angle theta
    double v[2];    // one of two vectors used to determined angle theta:
      the unit vector [1,0]
    CBrush *pBrush = NULL; // a ptr to brush
    CPoint A;               // vertex in anticlock direc from pointing
      vertex B of arrowhead
    CPoint B;               // vertex of arrowhead pointing in direc of
      arrow (m_ptTo)
    CPoint C;               // vertex in clock direc from pointing vertex
      B of arrowhead
    CPoint vertices[3];     // vertices array to hold triangle vertices
    CString sMsg;           // main msg string
    UINT nType = MB_OK;     // style of msg. box
    UINT nIDhelp = 0;       // help context ID for the msg.

    // Assign lengths to arrowhead (triangle) paras.
    length = 0.5*dDeltaLength;
    d = 0.2887*length;
    h = 0.5773*length;

    // Print msg.
    sMsg.Format("\n CConnection::DrawArrowHead(), d = %lf, h = %lf\n", d, h);
    // AfxMessageBox(sMsg, nType, nIDhelp);
```

```
// Length of vecs u and v
v[0] = 1.0;                         // x cmpt. of unit vector [1,0]
v[1] = 0.0;                         // y cmpt. of unit vector [1,0]
u[0] = m_ptTo.x - m_ptFrom.x;       // length in x direc of connection
    vector
u[1] = m_ptTo.y - m_ptFrom.y;       // length in y direc of connection
    vector

length_u = sqrt(pow(u[0],2) + pow(u[1],2));
length_v = sqrt(pow(v[0],2) + pow(v[1],2));

// Angle between vecs u and v
theta = acos((u[0]*v[0] + u[1]*v[1])/(length_u*length_v));
if(u[1] < 0)
{
    theta = -theta;       // negate theta if y-cmpt of u < 0, since acos
        result is an element from [0,pi] radians ONLY (non-neg).
}

// Global position vecs of arrowhead triangle vertices
A.x = m_ptTo.x + long(cos(theta)*(-(h+d)) - sin(theta)*(-length*0.5));
A.y = m_ptTo.y + long(sin(theta)*(-(h+d)) + cos(theta)*(-length*0.5));
B.x = m_ptTo.x;
B.y = m_ptTo.y;
C.x = m_ptTo.x + long(cos(theta)*(-(h+d)) - sin(theta)*(length*0.5));
C.y = m_ptTo.y + long(sin(theta)*(-(h+d)) + cos(theta)*(length*0.5));

// Create the pen
CPen lpen(PS_SOLID, pen_width, pen_color);

// Select the pen as the drawing obj.
// The value returned by SelectObject() is a ptr to the obj. being
  replaced, i.e. an old-pen-ptr.
CPen *pOldPen = pDC->SelectObject(&lpen);

// Draw arrowhead
pDC->MoveTo(A);
pDC->LineTo(B);
pDC->LineTo(C);
pDC->LineTo(A);

// Prepare for filling the polygon
CBrush NewBrush(RGB(0,0,0)); // create a new brush

vertices[0] = A;
vertices[1] = B;
vertices[2] = C;

// Select the new brush
pBrush = pDC->SelectObject(&NewBrush);

// Fill the polygon
pDC->Polygon(vertices, 3);

// Reset the prev. pen and brush
pDC->SelectObject(pOldPen);
pDC->SelectObject(pBrush);
}
```

The developer will notice that the previous code simply implements the mathematical derivation provided earlier. This geometrical method of determining the arrowhead vertices to draw the arrowhead is required in order that the direction of the connection be accurately represented.

B.3.3 ADD CODE TO ALLOW DYNAMIC DRAWING ON MOUSE MOVEMENT

Currently upon moving the mouse, the `CExp10View::OnMouseMove(UINT nFlags, CPoint point)` function is called. The limited explicit drawing within `OnMouseMove()` simply draws a line from "m_ptOrigin" to "point", but there are two problems:

1. The arrowheads are not drawn on `OnLButtonUp()`.
2. The arrowheads are not drawn during mouse movement events, i.e., on `OnMouseMove()`.

To solve these problems, only small changes need to be made to the existing code, without the need for elaborate global functions, where class code would otherwise be extracted away from a class, or the obtaining of document pointers followed by cumbersome invocation. The steps to solve these problems are as follows:

1. `OnLButtonUp()` should be edited with the code Invalidate(TRUE) to make the document redraw itself.
2. `OnMouseMove()` should be edited to declare local objects of class CConnection, and `DrawConnection()` should be called on those objects, i.e., comment out the existing explicit drawing mechanism and make the calls as shown in the following.

```
void CExp10View::OnMouseMove(UINT nFlags, CPoint point)
{
    // TODO: Add your message handler code here and/or call default

    // DiagramEng (start)

    // Check to see if the left mouse btn. is down
    if((nFlags & MK_LBUTTON) == MK_LBUTTON)
    {
        // Check to see if mouse is captured
        if(GetCapture() == this) // If what has been captured is the obj.
          upon which the present fn is called.
```

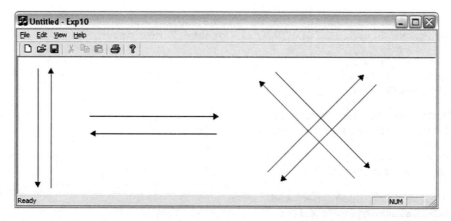

FIGURE B.4   Connection objects may be drawn on the palette, with the arrowhead indicating the intended direction.

```
        {
            // Get the device context
            CClientDC dc(this);

            // Reverse the pixel color from the original pt to the prev pt.
            // SetROP2() sets the current foreground mix mode.
            dc.SetROP2(R2_NOT);     // R2_NOT => pixel is the inverse of the
              screen color

            // Declare a CConnection obj in order to call DrawConnection()
            CConnection con_obj1(m_ptOrigin, m_ptPrevPos);
            con_obj1.DrawConnection(&dc);
            // dc.MoveTo(m_ptOrigin);
            // dc.LineTo(m_ptPrevPos);

            // Declare a CConnection obj in order to call DrawConnection()
            // Draw the current stretch of line (but don't save it until
              OnLButtonUp().
            CConnection con_obj2(m_ptOrigin, point);
            con_obj2.DrawConnection(&dc);
            // dc.MoveTo(m_ptOrigin);
            // dc.LineTo(point);

            // Save the current pt (point) as the prev. pt (m_ptPrevPos)
              of the CView class.
            m_ptPrevPos = point;
        }
    }

    // DiagramEng (end)

    CView::OnMouseMove(nFlags, point);
}
```

Finally, upon building and running the Exp10 application, connection objects with arrowheads attached may be drawn vertically, horizontally, and at various angles, as shown in Figure B.4.

B.4   SUMMARY

An exploration was made, based upon material found in Ref. [1], to draw connection objects with arrowheads attached, indicating their direction. A CConnection class was added to define a connection, and a list of pointers-to-CConnection, "m_lstConnection", was added to the Document class to store the connections. Event-handler functions were added to the CView-derived class to set the points of the connection (OnLButtonDown()), to explicitly draw the connection (OnMouseMove()), and to add the connection to the list (OnLButtonUp()). The more general drawing of connections is initiated from the CView-derived class' OnDraw() method, which calls DrawConnections(), to iterate over the list of connections, calling DrawConnection(). Extensions to the project involved a mathematical discussion of the geometry of an arrowhead, drawing of arrowheads on the end of connections and dynamically drawing a connection with an arrowhead to the mouse cursor point.

REFERENCES

1. Chapman, D., *Teach Yourself Visual C++ 6 in 21 Days*, Sams Publishing, Indianapolis, IN, 1998.
2. Microsoft Developer Network Library Visual Studio 6.0, Microsoft® Visual Studio™ 6.0 Development System, Microsoft Corporation, 1998.
3. Shabana, A. A., *Computational Dynamics*, 2nd edn., John Wiley & Sons, New York, 2001.

Appendix C: NodeArcConnectivity: Win32 Console Application

C.1 INTRODUCTION

The presence of an algebraic or equivalently a feedback loop in a model diagram needs to be detected to determine the appropriate method of model computation; if a loop does not exist, then a direct signal propagation method is used, and if a loop does exist, then a simultaneous equation-based approach is made. A node-arc binary matrix is used to denote the block-to-block connectivity of a model diagram, and this matrix is analyzed to determine the various tours that may be made through the diagram that start at a source block and end at either an Output block or loop-repeated block, signifying the presence of an algebraic loop.

A Win32 Console Application, titled NodeArcConnectivity, is presented here to allow the developer to explore the flow of control of the tour-building process, performed by a function named `BuildTour()`. Print statements clearly show the evolution of the process, and the interested developer should step through the application with a debugger to pursue the flow of control and observe the change in program state indicated in the Variables and Watch windows.

C.2 EXAMPLE PROBLEM

Consider Figure C.1, showing a model diagram, referred to as "Example 3" in the code, with one source block, E4; various intermediate blocks, B1, C2, D3, F5, G6, H7, and I8; two feedback loops; and two Output blocks, A0 and J9. The letters and numbers represent the order in which the blocks were placed on the palette. Both letters and numbers are used to make the order of placement clear and to prevent confusion with the "0" and "1" values used to denote the state of connectivity in the binary matrix.

The block-to-block connectivity matrix in the forward-direction sense, as represented by the direction of the existing arrows/arcs connecting the blocks, is shown in Table C.1: a "1" represents a forward connection, and an empty entry ("0" in the actual code) represents the lack of a forward connection.

Rows A0 and J9 are zero rows, indicating that there are no forward proceeding connections, and hence, the blocks are Output blocks. Block E4 is a source block as represented by a null column and is the starting point for algorithmic loop detection. The various paths through the diagram and matrix ending at either an Output block or a loop-repeated block are shown in Table C.2.

The developer can choose "Example 3" by setting "EXAMPLE" to "3" in the header file, "NodeArcCon.h", presented in the next section. Then upon building and running the code, the tours presented in Table C.2 will be generated in the output statements.

C.3 NodeArcConnectivity APPLICATION

The NodeArcConnectivity Win32 Console Application consists of two files: a header and a source file named "NodeArcCon.h" and "NodeArcCon.cpp", which contain function declarations and definitions, respectively.

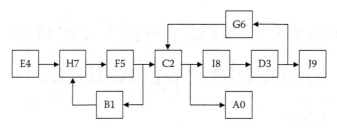

FIGURE C.1 General representation of a model with two feedback loops, where the letters and numbers represent the order in which the blocks were placed on the palette.

TABLE C.1

Block-to-Block Connectivity Matrix

	A0	B1	C2	D3	E4	F5	G6	H7	I8	J9
A0										
B1								1		
C2	1								1	
D3							1			1
E4								1		
F5		1	1							
G6			1							
H7						1				
I8			1							
J9										

A "1" indicates that a block on row $i \in [0,9]$ is connected to a block in column $j \in [0,9]$. Empty entries are considered to be "0".

TABLE C.2

Tours through Block Diagram

Tours Ending at an Output Block	Tours Ending in a Loop-Repeated Block
$E \to H \to F \to C \to A$	$E \to H \to F \to B \to H$
$E \to H \to F \to C \to I \to D \to J$	$E \to H \to F \to C \to I \to D \to G \to C$

C.3.1 HEADER FILE

The "NodeArcCon.h" header file is presented in the following and contains node-arc tour-building functions, matrix and vector setup functions, and simple integer printing functions used to display the evolving state of the tour-building process.

```
// NodeArcCon.h

#ifndef NODE_ARC_CON_H
    #define NODE_ARC_CON_H

    // Static vars
    const int EXAMPLE = 3;    // example type used for setting up problem

    // Main line fns
    int main(int argc, char **argv);
    int NodeArcConnectivity(void);
```

```
        // Node-Arc tour building fns
        int BuildTour(int **A_mat, int nrows, int ncols, int *node_vec, int
          n_nodes, int *tour_vec);
        int CheckRepeatedEntries(int *tour, int ncols);
        int FindBranchNodes(int **A, int i, int ncols, int *branch_node_vec,
          int &n_branch_nodes);
        int FindCurrentTourPosition(int *tour_vec, int ncols);
        int NumberOfOnes(int **A, int row, int ncols);


        // Setup vectors and matrices fns
        void ResetTourVector(int *tour_vec, int *in_tour_vec, int ncols);
        int SetProblemDimensions(int &nrows, int &ncols);
        int SetupConnectivityMatrix(int **matrix, int nrows, int ncols);
        int DetermineInitialNodeVector(int **A, int nrows, int ncols, int
          *node_vec, int &n_nodes);
        int SetupInitialTourVector(int *tour_vec, int ncols);
        void SaveTourVector(int *tour_vec, int ncols);


        // Printing fns
        int PrintMatrix(int **M, int nrows, int ncols);
        int PrintVector(int *v, int ncols);

#endif

// eof
```

C.3.2 SOURCE FILE

The following "NodeArcCon.cpp" source file contains the definitions of the functions declared in the header file earlier. The NodeArcConnectivity() function calls five main functions to determine the node-to-node tours represented by a node-arc connectivity matrix: (1) SetProblemDimensions() sets the numbers of rows and columns of the node-arc connectivity matrix based on a problem-defining constant integer value ("EXAMPLE = 3"), (2) SetupConnectivityMatrix() sets up the connectivity matrix consisting of ones and zeros denoting node-to-node connectivity, (3) DetermineInitialNodeVector() constructs the initial node vector containing the source nodes of a model diagram, (4) SetupInitialTourVector() places "−1" values in the tour vector that is to contain the positive numbers of the nodes of a tour, and (5) BuildTour() recursively builds all the possible tours through a node-arc connectivity matrix that either end at an output node or a loop-repeated node, signifying a feedback loop. The timing functions, time() and strftime(), found in the work of Kelley and Pohl [1], were used in the program to denote the end of the "for(node)" loop, for ease of identification purposes, in the BuildTour() function.

An explanation of the functions (in alphabetical order), BuildTour(), CheckRepeated Entries(), DetermineInitialNodeVector(), FindBranchNodes(), FindCurrent TourPosition(), NumberOfOnes(),* ResetTourVector(), and SaveTourVector(), is made in Chapter 19 upon their introduction into the DiagramEng application and is not repeated here; the code presented in the following is self-contained and may be run as an independent and easier-to-understand application. The remaining functions, SetProblemDimensions(),

---

* NumberOfOnes() of the NodeArcConnectivity application is equivalent to NumberOfOnesOnMatrixRow() of the DiagramEng application.

SetupConnectivityMatrix(), and SetupInitialTourVector(), are used to set up the problem being investigated.

```cpp
// Title:    NodeArcCon.cpp
// Purpose:  Experiments with node-arc connectivity matrices and
   recording node tours.

#include <stdio.h>
#include <stdlib.h>
#include <iostream>
#include <math.h>
#include <time.h>

#include "NodeArcCon.h"
using namespace std;

int main(int argc, char **argv)
{

    cout << "\n main()\n";

    NodeArcConnectivity();

    cout << endl;
    return 0;
}


int NodeArcConnectivity(void)
{
    int i;
    int n_nodes;    // number of initial nodes in node_vec, i.e., source
      nodes only, NOT ALL NODES.
    int ncols;      // number of cols of node-arc matrix (number of nodes)
    int nrows;      // number of rows of node-arc matrix (number of nodes)
    int *node_vec = NULL;    // node vector that contains only the source
      node(s)
    int *tour_vec = NULL;    // vec that holds node-to-node tours, of
      size total number of nodes = ncols.
    int **A = NULL;          // nod-arc matrix

    cout << "\n NodeArcConnectivity()\n";

    // Get the number of rows and cols for the partic. example type.
    SetProblemDimensions(nrows, ncols);

    // MEMORY ALLOC
    node_vec = new int[ncols];    // allocate enough space for all nodes,
      but only emplace source nodes.
    tour_vec = new int[ncols];    // allocate enough space for all nodes,
      since max tour length contains all nodes
    A = new int *[nrows];
    for(i=0; i<nrows; i++)
    {
        A[i] = new int[ncols];    // allocate an array of doubles, return
          & to matrix[i]
    }
```

```
        // Setup data structures
        SetupConnectivityMatrix(A, nrows, ncols);
        PrintMatrix(A, nrows, ncols);

        DetermineInitialNodeVector(A, nrows, ncols, node_vec, n_nodes);
        PrintVector(node_vec, ncols);

        SetupInitialTourVector(tour_vec, ncols);
        PrintVector(tour_vec, ncols);

        // Construct node-arc tours
        BuildTour(A, nrows, ncols, node_vec, n_nodes, tour_vec);

        // MEMORY DELETE
        delete [] node_vec;
        delete [] tour_vec;
        if(A != NULL)
        {
            for(i=0; i<nrows; i++)
            {
            delete [] A[i];
            }
            delete [] A;
        }


        return 0;
}

int SetProblemDimensions(int &nrows, int &ncols)
{
        int example = EXAMPLE;

        switch(example)
        {
        case 0:    // Example 0: feedback case with multiple paths
            nrows = 5;
            ncols = nrows;
            break;
        case 1:    // Example 1: feed forward case with multiple paths
            nrows = 6;
            ncols = nrows;
            break;
        case 2:    // Example 2: feedback case with multiple source nodes
            nrows = 7;
            ncols = nrows;
            break;
        case 3:    // Example 3: feedback case with multiple feedback loops
            nrows = 10;
            ncols = nrows;
            break;
        case 4:    // Example 4: feed forward case with only two blocks
            nrows = 2;
            ncols = nrows;
            break;
        case 5:    // Example 5: simple feedback loop without intervening
          block
```

```
            nrows = 4;
            ncols = nrows;
            break;
        case 6:     // Example 6: simple feedback loop with and without
          intervening block
            nrows = 5;
            ncols = nrows;
            break;
        default:
            printf("\n SetProblemDimensions(), select a feasible example
              number.\n");
            break;
        }


        return 0;
}

int SetupConnectivityMatrix(int **matrix, int nrows, int ncols)
{
        int i;
        int j;
        int example = EXAMPLE;     // example type

        cout << "\n SetupConnectivityMatrix()\n";

        // Nullify matrix
        for(i=0; i<nrows; i++)
        {
            for(j=0; j<ncols; j++)
            {
                matrix[i][j] = 0;
            }
        }

        // Assign one's (1) indicating node in row i, connected to node in col j.
        // The node numbers are represented by the row and column numbers.
        // A node is attached to itself, but for simplicity the diag elements
          are zero not one.

        switch(example)
        {
        case 0:     // Example 0: feedback case with multiple paths
            matrix[0][4] = 1;
            matrix[2][4] = 1;
            matrix[3][1] = 1;
            matrix[3][2] = 1;
            matrix[4][3] = 1;
            break;
        case 1:     // Example 1: feed forward case with multiple paths
            matrix[0][5] = 1;
            matrix[1][3] = 1;
            matrix[2][5] = 1;
            matrix[4][0] = 1;
            matrix[4][2] = 1;
            matrix[4][5] = 1;
            matrix[5][1] = 1;
            break;
```

```
    case 2:    // Example 2: feedback case with multiple source nodes
        matrix[0][6] = 1;
        matrix[1][3] = 1;
        matrix[3][0] = 1;
        matrix[4][6] = 1;
        matrix[5][3] = 1;
        matrix[6][2] = 1;
        matrix[6][3] = 1;
        break;
    case 3:    // Example 3: feedback case with multiple feedback loops
        matrix[1][7] = 1;
        matrix[2][0] = 1;
        matrix[2][8] = 1;
        matrix[3][6] = 1;
        matrix[3][9] = 1;
        matrix[4][7] = 1;
        matrix[5][1] = 1;
        matrix[5][2] = 1;
        matrix[6][2] = 1;
        matrix[7][5] = 1;
        matrix[8][3] = 1;
        break;
    case 4:    // Example 4: feed forward case with only two blocks
        matrix[0][1] = 1;
        break;
    case 5:    // Example 5: simple feedback loop without intervening block
        matrix[0][2] = 1;
        matrix[0][3] = 1;
        matrix[1][3] = 1;
        matrix[3][0] = 1;
        break;
    case 6:    // Example 6: simple feedback loop with and without
      intervening block
        matrix[0][2] = 1;
        matrix[0][3] = 1;
        matrix[0][4] = 1;
        matrix[1][3] = 1;
        matrix[3][0] = 1;
        matrix[4][3] = 1;
        break;
    default:
        printf("\n SetupConnectivityMatrix(), select a feasible example
            number.\n");
        break;
    }

    return 0;
}


int DetermineInitialNodeVector(int **A, int nrows, int ncols, int
  *node_vec, int &n_nodes)
{
    int i;
    int j;
    int offset = 0;      // node_vec offset
    int col_sum = 0;     // sum of col elements
```

```
        printf("\n DetermineInitialNodeVector()\n");

    // A node on row i, is connected to a node on col j.
    // So if there is a col of zeros, then that col number represents a
      source node,
    // since no node is connected to it in the forward-direction sense.

    // Assign initial negative values
    for(i=0; i<ncols; i++)
    {
        node_vec[i] = -1;
    }

    // Iterate across the cols and down the rows
    for(j=0; j<ncols; j++)
    {
        col_sum = 0;
        for(i=0; i<nrows; i++)
        {
            col_sum = col_sum + A[i][j];      // col sum

        }
        if(col_sum == 0)
        {
            node_vec[offset] = j;     // place source node in node_vec
            offset++;
        }
    }

    // Assign the number of source nodes in the node_vec
    n_nodes = offset;

    // Return a flag indicating whether a row of zeros was found
    if(offset == 0)
    {
        return -1;     // error since no col of zeros, and hence no
          initial source node
    }
    else
    {
        return 0;     // a col of zeros was found, hence there exists a
          source node
    }
}

int SetupInitialTourVector(int *tour_vec, int ncols)
{
    int i;

    printf("\n SetupInitialTourVector()\n");

    // Assign unique initial negative values to the node entries of the
      tour vec indicating no tour
    for(i=0; i<ncols; i++)
    {
        tour_vec[i] = -(i+1);
    }

    return 0;
}
```

```
int BuildTour(int **A, int nrows, int ncols, int *node_vec, int n_nodes,
  int *in_tour_vec)
{
    int i;
    int j;
    int posn;              // posn of nodes in tour vector
    int n_branch_nodes;    // number of branch nodes present on a partic. row
    int node;              // node number = row number = col number
    int tour_end = 0;      // flag identifying whether current tour has
      been found
    int *branch_node_vec = NULL;  // vec of branch nodes to which current
      node can progress
    int *tour_vec = NULL;         // vec of nodes comprising the tour
    time_t seconds;               // time var used to aid user when
      pressing return bw. iterations of for-node loop
    char t_string[20];            // time string

    cout <<"\n - BuildTour()\n";

    // -- MEMORY ALLOC
    tour_vec = new int[ncols];

    // Copy the incoming tour vec into the local tour vec
    for(j=0; j<ncols; j++)
    {
        tour_vec[j] = in_tour_vec[j];
    }

    printf("\n tour_vec:\n");
    PrintVector(tour_vec, ncols);

    printf("\n node_vec:\n");
    PrintVector(node_vec, ncols);

    // -- ITERATE OVER ONLY THE NODES IN THE NODE VECTOR FROM WHICH
    //    CONNECTIONS TO OTHER NODES ARE PREMISSABLE
    for(node=0; node<n_nodes; node++)
    {
        // Get the offset position in the tour vector into which the next
        //   node should be placed
        posn = FindCurrentTourPosition(in_tour_vec, ncols);
        printf("\n For node = %d < %d, posn = %d\n", node, n_nodes, posn);

        // Get starting node, i.e. a node in the node vector (of source
        //   nodes or branch nodes)
        i = node_vec[node];
        tour_vec[posn] = i;
        tour_end = 0;

        printf("\n Prior to while(), tour_end = %d, i = node_vec[%d] = %d,
          tour_vec:\n", tour_end, node, i);
        PrintVector(tour_vec, ncols);

        // Check for repeated entries here, after the new node addition
        //   to the tour_vec: if there is a repeat, end tour.
        if(CheckRepeatedEntries(tour_vec, ncols) > 0)
        {
            tour_end = 1;
```

```
        printf("\n repeated entries, tour_end = %d\n", tour_end);

        SaveTourVector(tour_vec, ncols);    // save tour_vec since
          tour has had an entry added but a loop exists
}


// -- WHILE TOUR NOT COMPLETE
while(tour_end == 0)
{
    // Get the offset position in the EVOLVING TOUR VECTOR into
      which the next node should be placed
    posn = FindCurrentTourPosition(tour_vec, ncols);
    printf("\n Inside while, before if, posn = %d, ncols = %d\n",
      posn, ncols);

    if(posn >= ncols)     // if the posn is after the end of the
      array, then the tour vector is filled.
    {
        tour_end = 1;
        SaveTourVector(tour_vec, ncols);    // save tour_vec
          since tour has ended due to no further connections
        break;     // break from while loop
    }

        // Find the number of connections i.e. branch nodes to
          the current node
    n_branch_nodes = NumberOfOnes(A, i, ncols);

    // If there are no 1's in the cols then there are no
      connecting nodes
    if(n_branch_nodes == 0)
    {
        printf("\n n_branch_nodes = %d\n", n_branch_nodes);

        tour_vec[posn] = -1;    // -1 indicates no fwd connection
          exists from the current node
        tour_end = 1;               // end tour
        SaveTourVector(tour_vec, ncols);    // save tour_vec
          since tour has ended due to no further connections
    }
    // If there is one 1, in the cols, then there is one
      connecting node
    else if(n_branch_nodes == 1)
    {
        printf("\n n_branch_nodes = %d\n", n_branch_nodes);

        for(j=0; j<ncols; j++)     // iterate over cols
        {
            if(A[i][j] == 1)     // if a col contains a 1, then,
              node on row i, is connected to node in col j.
            {
                tour_vec[posn] = j;    // new node traversed is
                  that in col j, connected to that in row i
                i = j;     // update row i with col j to continue
                  to the next connection
```

```
                        break;      // break from for loop
                }
        }

        printf("\n tour_vec:\n");
        PrintVector(tour_vec, ncols);
}
// If there is > one 1, in the cols, then there is > 1
  connecting node
else if(n_branch_nodes > 1)
{
        // MEMORY ALLOC
        branch_node_vec = new int[ncols];

        // Find all nodes that are connected/branched to the
          current node
        FindBranchNodes(A, i, ncols, branch_node_vec,
          n_branch_nodes);

        printf("\n n_branch_nodes = %d, branch_node_vec:\n",
          n_branch_nodes);
        PrintVector(branch_node_vec, ncols);

        // RECURSIVELY CALL THE BuildTour() FUNCTION WITH THE NEW
          NODE VECTOR AND TOUR VECTOR
        BuildTour(A, nrows, ncols, branch_node_vec, n_branch_nodes,
          tour_vec);

        printf("\n After recursive BuildTour() call\n");

        tour_end = 1;

        // MEMORY DELETE
        delete [] branch_node_vec;
}

// Check for repeated entries here, after the if-else-based
  node addition to the tour_vec.
if(CheckRepeatedEntries(tour_vec, ncols) > 0)
{
        tour_end = 1;
        printf("\n repeated entries, tour_end = %d\n", tour_end);

        SaveTourVector(tour_vec, ncols);     // save tour_vec
          since tour has had an entry added but a loop exists
}

// Reset the tour_vec to be that of the incoming tour vector
if(tour_end == 1)
{
        ResetTourVector(tour_vec, in_tour_vec, ncols);
}
}// end while

// Get the time of the end of this loop
seconds = time(NULL);     // get seconds elapsed since 1-1-1970
strftime(t_string, 20, "%H:%M:%S", localtime(&seconds));
  // get the local time as a string
printf("\n ----- End of for node = %d \t\t\t time: %s\n", node,
  t_string);
//printf("\n time: %s\n", t_string);
```

```
            //printf("\n Press return to continue … \t\t\t\t time: %s\n",
              t_string);
            printf("\n Press return to continue … \n");
            getchar();

    }// end for

    // MEMORY DELETE
    delete [] tour_vec;

    return 0;
}

int FindCurrentTourPosition(int *tour_vec, int ncols)
{
    int i;

    //printf("\n FindCurrentTourPosition()\n");

    // Iterate through the vector to find the first negative,
      non-node-filled, entry.
    for(i=0; i<ncols; i++)
    {
    if(tour_vec[i] < 0)
        {
            return i;
        }
    }

    // If no -ve value found then return the size of the array "ncols"
    return ncols;
}

int FindBranchNodes(int **A, int i, int ncols, int *branch_node_vec, int
  &n_branch_nodes)
{
    int j;      // col index
    int cnt = 0;     // branch_node_vec[] offset index

    //printf("\n FindBranchNodes()\n");

    // Negate the branch_node_vec
    for(j=0; j<ncols; j++)
    {
        branch_node_vec[j] = -1;
    }

    // Iterate over the cols of A for the current row (i), recording
      those with one's (1), indicating node connections.
    for(j=0; j<ncols; j++)
    {
        if(A[i][j] == 1)
        {
            branch_node_vec[cnt] = j;
            cnt++;
        }
    }
    n_branch_nodes = cnt;    // update the number of connecting/branch
      nodes
```

```
        return 0;
}

int NumberOfOnes(int **A, int row, int ncols)
{
        int j;
        int n_ones = 0;

        //printf("\n NumberOfOnes()\n");

        // Count the number of ones on the partic. row.
        for(j=0; j<ncols; j++)
        {
                if(A[row][j] == 1)
                {
                        n_ones++;
                }
        }

        //printf("\n n_ones = %d\n", n_ones);

        return n_ones;
}

int CheckRepeatedEntries(int *tour, int ncols)
{
        int i;
        int j;
        int n_repeats = 0;

        //printf("\n CheckRepeatedEntries()\n");
        // Check tour vector for repeated entries (implying a loop)
        for(i=0; i<(ncols-1); i++)
        {
                for(j=(i+1); j<ncols; j++)
                {
                        if(tour[j] == tour[i])
                        {
                                n_repeats++;
                        }
                }
        }

        //printf("\n n_repeats = %d\n", n_repeats);

        return n_repeats;
}

void ResetTourVector(int *tour_vec, int *in_tour_vec, int ncols)
{
        int j;

        // Reassign in_tour_vec to tour_vec
        for(j=0; j<ncols; j++)
        {
                tour_vec[j] = in_tour_vec[j];
        }
}
```

```cpp
void SaveTourVector(int *tour_vec, int ncols)
{
    int n_repeats = 0;          // number of repeated entries
    static int n_loops = 0;     // number of tours with feedback loops
    static int n_tours = 0;     // number of tours

    printf("\n -> SaveTourVector(),");

    // WARNING! This fn should save all tours, but doesn't here since
      nothing is done with them.
    // This could be performed in the following ways:
    // 1) Run NodeArcConnectivity() to determine the exact n_tours, then
      allocate enough memory, the rerun to obtain the tours.
    // 2) Run NodeArcConnectivity() and simply add each tour to a growing
      static int 2-D array that is large enough.

    // Record the number of unique tours
    n_tours++;

    printf(" n_tours = %d,", n_tours);

    //printf("\n CheckRepeatedEntries()\n");

    // Check tour vector for repeated entries (implying a node-to-node
      loop)
    n_repeats = CheckRepeatedEntries(tour_vec, ncols);

    // Notify method of tour termination
    if(n_repeats == 0)
    {
        printf(" tour_vec that would be saved (output block):\n");
    }
    else if(n_repeats > 0)
    {
        n_loops++;      // record the number of tours with feedback loops
        printf(" tour_vec that would be saved (loop)\n");
    }

    PrintVector(tour_vec, ncols);

    return;
}

// -- PRINTING FNS

int PrintMatrix(int **M, int nrows, int ncols)
{
    int i;
    int j;

    cout << "\n PrintMatrix()\n";

    // If the matrix is NULL then return.
    if(M == NULL)
    {
        return 1;
    }

    // Print Matrix
    cout << endl;
```

```
    for(i=0; i<nrows; i++)
    {
        for(j=0; j<ncols; j++)
        {
            printf(" %d", M[i][j]);
        }
        cout << endl;
    }
    cout << endl;

    return 0;
}

int PrintVector(int *v, int ncols)
{
    int i;

    //cout << "\n PrintVector()\n";

    // If the vector is NULL then return.
    if(v == NULL)
    {
        return 1;
    }

    // Print Vector
    printf("\n");
    for(i=0; i<ncols; i++)
    {
        printf(" %d", v[i]);
    }
    printf("\n\n");

    return 0;
}

//eof
```

C.4 SUMMARY

A Win32 Console Application titled NodeArcConnectivity, with header and source files, "NodeArcCon.h" and "NodeArcCon.cpp", respectively, is presented that computes the block-to-block tours through a node-arc graph representing a block diagram. The main `BuildTour()` function is called recursively to determine all possible tours in a graph, from the starting source node, through branching nodes, and finally to Output nodes or loop-repeated nodes, where a repeated node signifies a feedback or algebraic loop in the block diagram.

REFERENCE

1. Kelley, A. and Pohl, I., *A Book On C: Programming in C*, 2nd edn., Benjamin Cummings, Redwood City, CA, 1990.

Appendix D: Debugging: An Introduction

D.1 INTRODUCTION

Debugging is the process of interactively examining the flow of control and the changing state of a program during execution to gain insight into the cause and effect behavior of logical and computational expressions, with an aim to rectify erroneous actions or unintended side effects. Usually, when a program does not work as intended, the developer may have an idea as to what is wrong, but may not know where to start examining the code. Sometimes print statements or message boxes (AfxMessageBox()) are used to provide some sort of information about the program state, but these are cumbersome to use and may not provide the amount of information required to solve a problem effectively going to the specific line of code that is of concern. The efficient use of a debugging tool, e.g., that provided with the Microsoft Visual C++® 6.0 Visual Studio™ 6.0 Development System (integrated development environment [IDE])* [1], allows the developer to quickly and easily find the cause of an error and spend valuable time solving a problem rather than waste time feeling helpless and not know where to begin. The current appendix firstly briefly introduces the features of the debugger provided with the Microsoft Visual C++® 6.0 IDE [1] and then shows how the debugger is used in the context of an easy-to-understand dialog-based application built specifically to examine program state, flow of control, errors, and memory leaks.

D.2 MICROSOFT VISUAL C++® 6.0 IDE DEBUGGER

The Microsoft Visual C++ 6.0 IDE has the following visible menu entries when editing a project: File, Edit, View, Insert, Project, Build, Tools, Window, and Help. However, debugging features may be found distributed over various menus and include (1) Breakpoints under the Edit menu; (2) Debug Windows under the View menu, with subfields Watch, Call Stack, Memory, Variables, Registers, and Disassembly; and (3) Start Debug under the Build menu, with subfields Go, Step Into, Run to Cursor, and Attach to Process. The Build menu actually disappears after debugging is initiated (Build/Start Debug/Go†) and is replaced with the Debug menu with the following entries: Go, Restart, Stop Debugging, Break, Apply Code Changes, Step Into, Step Over, Step Out, Run to Cursor, Step Into Specific Function, Exceptions, Threads, Modules, Show Next Statement, and Quick Watch. Explanations for all these features may be found by selecting the Index entry under the Help menu of the IDE and then searching the listed topics of the MSDN Library Visual Studio 6.0 [2] by keyword. Brief explanations of these features are provided for convenience in Table D.1 and follow closely the definitions provided in the library resource [2].

The developer may start the debugger by selecting Build/Start Debug, followed by Go (F5), and then upon selecting the Debug menu, the underlying entries may be observed as shown in Figure D.1. Alternatively, selecting Tools/Customize, followed by selection of the Debug toolbar in the Toolbars list box, presents the Debug toolbar shown to the right of the Build Minibar in Figure D.1. (The DebugEx application, the subject of Figure D.1, will actually be set up in the next section and used to explore the various debugging features.)

---

* Microsoft Visual C++® 6.0 Visual Studio™ 6.0 Development System is abbreviated here as Microsoft Visual C++® 6.0 IDE.
† The notation "/" used herein denotes menu and menu entry association, e.g., "menu/menu entry".

TABLE D.1

Brief Definitions of Menu Entry–Invoked Debugging-Related Actions

Menu Entry and Key Combination	Explanation
Edit/Breakpoints (Alt + F9)	Displays the Breakpoints dialog to set Location, Data, and Message-related information
View/Debug Windows/Watch (Alt + 3)	Displays the Watch window used to view variable values or expressions
View/Debug Windows/Call Stack (Alt + 7)	Displays the Call Stack window showing a list of active procedures or stack frames for the executing thread
View/Debug Windows/Memory (Alt + 6)	Displays the Memory window to view memory contents at or to specify an expression for a memory location
View/Debug Windows/Variables (Alt + 4)	Displays the variable properties in the current context using three tabbed panes: Auto, Locals, and This
View/Debug Windows/Registers (Alt + 5)	Displays the contents of the CPU registers, flags, and floating-point stack
View/Debug Windows/Disassembly (Alt + 8)	Displays disassembled code with source-code annotations and symbols in the Disassembly window
Build/Start Debug/Go (F5)	Executes code from the current statement until a breakpoint, pause for user input, or the end of the program
Build/Start Debug/Step Into (F11)	Single-steps through program instructions entering invoked functions
Build/Start Debug/Run to Cursor (Ctrl + F10)	Executes the program up to the line containing the insertion point, equivalent to a temporary breakpoint
Build/Start Debug/Attach to Process …	Attaches the debugger to an active running process that is running outside of Visual Studio
Debug/Go (F5)	Executes code from the current statement until a breakpoint, pause for user input, or the end of the program
Debug/Restart (Ctrl + Shift + F5)	Terminates a debugging session, rebuilds and then reruns the application from the start
Debug/Stop Debugging (Shift + F5)	Terminates a debugging session and returns to a normal editing session
Debug/Break	Temporarily stops execution of all processes in a debugging session
Debug/Apply Code Changes (Alt + F10)	Applies code changes while the program is being debugged using the Edit and Continue feature
Debug/Step Into (F11)	Single-steps through program instructions entering invoked functions
Debug/Step Over (F10)	Single-steps through program instructions executing a function call without stepping through it
Debug/Step Out (Shift + F11)	Executes the remaining lines of a function in which the execution point lies
Debug/Run to Cursor (Ctrl + F10)	Executes the program up to the line containing the insertion point, equivalent to a temporary breakpoint
Debug/Step Into Specific Function	Single-steps through program instructions and enters the specified function call
Debug/Exceptions …	Displays the Exceptions dialog to specify how the debugger is to handle program exceptions
Debug/Threads …	Displays the Threads dialog to suspend, resume, or set focus to program threads
Debug/Modules …	Displays the Modules dialog to view the module, its address, path, and loading order
Debug/Show Next Statement (Alt + Num*)	Shows the next statement in the program code or in the Disassembly window if code is unavailable
Debug/Quick Watch … (Shift + F9)	Displays the Quick Watch window in which expressions and variable values are examined

Source: Microsoft Developer Network Library Visual Studio 6.0, Microsoft® Visual Studio™ 6.0 Development System, Microsoft Corporation, 1998.

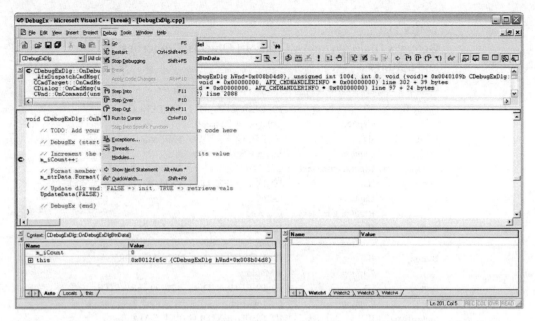

FIGURE D.1 The Debug menu entries visible after starting the debugger and the Debug toolbar shown to the right of the Build Minibar.

D.3 APPLICATION TO EXPLORE THE DEBUGGER

To experiment with the aforementioned available debugging features, a simple dialog-based application will now be built with an interface allowing the user to intentionally select buttons that invoke functions that create typical scenarios to be explored with the debugger. For example, the user will modify class member data, intentionally overwrite the end of an array to generate a crash, and not free memory using the *delete* operator that was originally allocated using the *new* operator. The steps involved to create the dialog-based application are listed, where specific details follow:

1. Create a dialog-based application with MFC support.
2. Attach variables to the dialog controls.
3. Attach functionality to the dialog buttons.

D.3.1 CREATE A DIALOG-BASED APPLICATION WITH MFC SUPPORT

The dialog-based application to be built will present a simple dialog window with various buttons on it which upon selection invoke event-handler functions. Hence, create an MFC AppWizard (exe) project with the name DebugEx. On step one of the AppWizard, select "Dialog based" as the type of application to be created. Deselect support for ActiveX controls on step two since they are not required for the current application. Leave the default settings on step three, and select Finish on step four to complete the application shell.

The developer will notice that upon right-clicking the top border of the dialog and selecting properties, the ID of the dialog window is IDD_DEBUGEX_DIALOG and the caption DebugEx: these may be left unchanged. Add controls to the dialog with the properties shown in Table D.2 and organize their layout as shown in Figure D.2.

D.3.2 ATTACH VARIABLES TO THE DIALOG CONTROLS

There are three static text fields beneath the buttons on the DebugEx dialog that will be used to display class member data to the user that reflects the state of the application. Hence, invoke the

TABLE D.2

DebugEx Dialog Window Controls: Objects, Properties, and Settings

Object	Property	Setting
Group Box	ID	ID_DEBUGEX_DLG_GB_DEBUG
	Caption	Debugging Concepts
Static Text	ID	ID_DEBUGEX_DLG_TXT_MSG
	Caption	Select Button:
	Right aligned text	Checked
Static Text	ID	ID_DEBUGEX_DLG_TXT_OUTPUT
	Caption	Output:
	Right aligned text	Checked
Button	ID	ID_DEBUGEX_DLG_BTN_DATA
	Caption	&Data
Button	ID	ID_DEBUGEX_DLG_BTN_MEMORY
	Caption	&Memory
Button	ID	ID_DEBUGEX_DLG_BTN_OVERWRITE
	Caption	O&verwrite
Static Text	ID	ID_DEBUGEX_DLG_TXT_DATA
	Caption	Empty string
	Border	Checked
	Center vertically	Checked
Static Text	ID	ID_DEBUGEX_DLG_TXT_MEMORY
	Caption	Empty string
	Border	Checked
	Center vertically	Checked
Static Text	ID	ID_DEBUGEX_DLG_TXT_OVERWRITE
	Caption	Empty string
	Border	Checked
	Center vertically	Checked
Button	ID	IDOK
	Default button	Checked
	Caption	&OK
Button	ID	IDCANCEL
	Caption	&Cancel

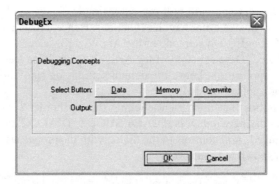

FIGURE D.2   The DebugEx dialog window with controls specified in Table D.2.

TABLE D.3

Dialog Window Controls, Variable Names, Categories, and Types for the Dialog (IDD_DEBUGEX_DLG) Resource

Control	Variable Name	Category	Type
ID_DEBUGEX_DLG_TXT_DATA	m_strData	Value	CString
ID_DEBUGEX_DLG_TXT_MEMORY	m_strMemory	Value	CString
ID_DEBUGEX_DLG_TXT_OVERWRITE	m_strOverwrite	Value	CString

ClassWizard, select the Member Variables tab and CDebugExDlg as the class, and add the three member variables for the dialog controls as specified in Table D.3.

In addition, add three private integer member variables to the CDebugExDlg class, named "m_iCount", "m_iDelete", and "m_iSize", denoting the number of times the Data button is pressed, the number of times memory is deleted, and the size of an array, respectively; these will be used with the CString values to display output data to the user. Initialize all member variable values in the CDebugExDlg::OnInitDialog() function as shown in bold in the following. The ellipsis, "...", denotes code automatically added by the AppWizard and is not of concern here.

```
BOOL CDebugExDlg::OnInitDialog()
{
    CDialog::OnInitDialog();
    ...

    // TODO: Add extra initialization here

    // DebugEx (start) /////////////////////////

    // INITIALIZE MEMBER VARS
    m_iCount = 0;       // button press count
    m_strData.Format("%d", m_iCount);

    m_iDelete = 1;      // memory deletion count
    m_strMemory.Format("%d", m_iDelete);

    m_iSize = 10;       // size of array
    m_strOverwrite.Format("%d", m_iSize);

    // UPDATE DLG WND: FALSE => init, TRUE => retrieve vals
    UpdateData(FALSE);

    // DebugEx (end) /////////////////////////////

    return TRUE; // return TRUE unless you set the focus to a control
}
```

D.3.3 Attach Functionality to the Dialog Buttons

There are five buttons on the DebugEx dialog window that upon selection will invoke an associated event-handler function to either explore a debugging concept or close the dialog window. Add event-handler functions for the buttons as shown in Table D.4 by invoking the ClassWizard and selecting CDebugExDlg as the class, choosing the appropriate button object ID, and then adding a function for the BN_CLICKED (button clicked) event. Leave the current event handlers for the OK and Cancel buttons, as shown in the following, since these call CDialog::OnOK() and CDialog::OnCancel(), respectively, and close the dialog; hence, no new code is required.

TABLE D.4

Objects, IDs, Class, and Event-Handler Functions for the CDebugExDlg Class

Object	ID	Class	COMMAND Event Handler
Data button	ID_DEBUGEX_DLG_BTN_DATA	CDebugExDlg	OnDebugExDlgBtnData()
Memory button	ID_DEBUGEX_DLG_BTN_MEMORY	CDebugExDlg	OnDebugExDlgBtnMemory()
Overwrite button	ID_DEBUGEX_DLG_BTN_OVERWRITE	CDebugExDlg	OnDebugExDlgBtnOverwrite()
OK button	IDOK	CDebugExDlg	OnOK()
Cancel button	IDCANCEL	CDebugExDlg	OnCancel()

```
void CDebugExDlg::OnCancel()
{
    // TODO: Add extra cleanup here

    CDialog::OnCancel();
}

void CDebugExDlg::OnOK()
{
    // TODO: Add extra validation here

    CDialog::OnOK();
}
```

D.3.3.1   Data Button Functionality

The Data button on the dialog window has a bordered text box beneath it that is to display the value of a counter-like variable that is incremented every time the user selects the button. Edit the CDebugExDlg::OnDebugExDlgBtnData() function as shown in the following to simply increment the value of the "m_iCount" variable and display its value using "m_strData" in the bordered text box.

```
void CDebugExDlg::OnDebugExDlgBtnData()
{
    // TODO: Add your control notification handler code here

    // DebugEx (start)

    // Increment the member variable and display its value
    m_iCount++;

    // Format member var
    m_strData.Format("%d", m_iCount);

    // Update dlg wnd: FALSE => init, TRUE => retrieve vals
    UpdateData(FALSE);

    // DebugEx (end)
}
```

Now when running the application, the initial dialog window appears as shown in Figure D.3a, and upon successively clicking the Data button, the integer variable is incremented as shown in Figure D.3b.

D.3.3.2   Memory Button Functionality

The Memory button, when clicked, invokes the CDebugExDlg::OnDebugExDlgBtnMemory() function, within which memory is allocated with operator *new*, but then is either (1) not deleted,

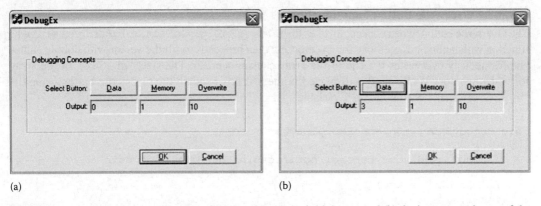

(a)   (b)

FIGURE D.3   The DebugEx dialog window showing (a) the initial state and (b) the incremented state of the "m_iCount" variable, displayed using the "m_strData" variable.

generating a memory leak ("m_iDelete = 0"); (2) deleted once using operator *delete* ("m_iDelete = 1"); or (3) deleted, erroneously, twice, causing a crash ("m_iDelete = 2"). Edit the CDebugExDlg::OnDebugExDlgBtnMemory() method as shown in the following with the three memory deletion options.

```
void CDebugExDlg::OnDebugExDlgBtnMemory()
{
    // TODO: Add your control notification handler code here

    // DebugEx (start)
    double *v = NULL;     // vector

    // Msg
    AfxMessageBox("\n CDebugExDlg::OnDebugExDlgBtnMemory() \n", MB_OK, 0);

    // MEMORY NEW
    v = new double[m_iSize];
    // MEMORY DELETE
    if(m_iDelete == 0)
    {
        // No deletion, causing a memory leak.
    }
    else if(m_iDelete == 1)
    {
        // Delete once
        delete [] v;
    }
    else if(m_iDelete == 2)
    {
        // Delete twice, erroneously, causing a crash.
        delete [] v;
        delete [] v;
    }

    // DebugEx (end)
}
```

The text box beneath the Memory button displays the value of the integer member variable, "m_iDelete", denoting the number of times memory is deleted, using the CString variable, "m_strMemory".

D.3.3.3 Overwrite Button Functionality

The Overwrite button, when clicked, invokes the CDebugExDlg::OnDebugDlgBtnOverwrite()
function which allocates memory for a vector and then proceeds to fill the vector with double values
but erroneously overwrites the end of the array causing a crash. The size, "m_iSize", of the array
for which memory is allocated is displayed in the text box beneath the Overwrite button using the
"m_strOverwrite" CString member variable.

```
void CDebugExDlg::OnDebugExDlgBtnOverwrite()
{
    // TODO: Add your control notification handler code here

    // DebugEx (start)
    int i;
    double *v = NULL;

    // Msg
    AfxMessageBox("\n CDebugExDlg::OnDebugExDlgBtnOverwrite()\n",
      MB_OK, 0);

    // MEMORY NEW
    v = new double[m_iSize];

    // Overwrite end of array
    for(i=0; i<(m_iSize+10); i++)
    //for(i=0; i<m_iSize; i++)
    {
        v[i] = i;
    }

    PrintVector(v, m_iSize);

    // MEMORY DELETE
    delete [] v;

    // DebugEx (end)
}
```

In addition, there is a PrintVector() function that has been used earlier, if execution reaches it,
to print the contents of the vector. Hence, add a public member function to the CDebugExDlg class
with the prototype, void CDebugExDlg::PrintVector(double *v, int n), and edit it
as shown in the following to print the pointer-to-double argument, equivalently the array of double
values, in a message box (AfxMessageBox()).

```
void CDebugExDlg::PrintVector(double *v, int n)
{
    // DebugEx (start)
    int i;
    CString sMsg;
    CString sMsgTemp;

    // Format output
    sMsgTemp.Format("\n\n CDebugExDlg::PrintVector() \n\n");
    sMsg += sMsgTemp;
    sMsgTemp.Format(" vector = [");
    sMsg += sMsgTemp;
```

```
for(i=0; i<n; i++)
{
    sMsgTemp.Format(" %lf", v[i]);
    sMsg += sMsgTemp;
}
sMsgTemp.Format("] \n\n");
sMsg += sMsgTemp;

// Display vector
AfxMessageBox(sMsg, MB_OK, 0);

// DebugEx (end)
}
```

D.4   USING THE DEBUGGER

Now that the DebugEx dialog application has been constructed, it can be experimented with to cause erroneous program behavior and the debugger used to identify the offending line(s) of code. The features of the debugger to be explored are (1) Breakpoints, (2) Variables and Watch Windows, (3) Call Stack Window, (4) Edit and Continue, and (5) Memory Leak detection.

D.4.1   BREAKPOINTS

A breakpoint is a line-based location in the code where execution pauses allowing the developer to make the next debugging action, e.g., step over or into a function. To set a breakpoint, the user can place the cursor on the line of code of interest and then press the Insert/Remove breakpoint button (hand icon) on the Build MiniBar, where the breakpoint is denoted by the (red) dot, as shown in Figure D.4a, or select Edit/Breakpoints which invokes the dialog shown in Figure D.4b. (The developer will notice that here the Debug toolbar has been removed for convenience; this is done to save space when displaying the screen output.)

D.4.2   VARIABLES AND WATCH WINDOWS

Now with the breakpoint set, the user can click Go (F5) to run the program with the debugger; this then invokes the dialog window (Figure D.3a) waiting for user input. If the user then clicks the Data button in an attempt to increment the class member variable, "m_iCount", from "0" to "1", execution pauses at line 203 upon which the "m_iCount++" increment operation is to take place, as shown by the (yellow) arrow in Figure D.5a. The developer can then type the variable name of interest, e.g., "m_iCount", in the Name field of the Watch window shown in the bottom right corner of the screen and will observe that the variable at this stage is "0" (prior to being incremented), as may be confirmed in the Variables window in the bottom left corner of the screen.

If the user then presses Go (F5) again (executing line 203), the DebugEx dialog window reappears, showing that the "m_iCount" variable was incremented to value "1" as is visible in the text box beneath the Data button in Figure D.5b.

Clicking the Data button again and hence invoking the event-handler function, CDebugExDlg::OnDebugExDlgBtnData(), results in the program pausing at the location of the breakpoint a second time, as shown in Figure D.5c. The developer will notice that "m_iCount" now has value "1", prior to being incremented, as shown in both the Variables and Watch windows; the red color (observable on the screen) denotes that the value of the variable has changed (from "0" to "1").

The developer will notice the "this" pointer highlighted in the list of variables in the Variables window shown in Figure D.5d. The "this" pointer is a variable that holds the address of the object upon which a function is called, in this case, a CDebugExDlg object. In the list, the member variables of the CDebugExDlg class may be seen, in particular, "m_iCount" and "m_strData", as well as the other dialog-related variables, "m_iDelete", "m_strMemory", "m_iSize", and "m_strOverwrite", and that the base class of CDebugExDlg is CDialog.

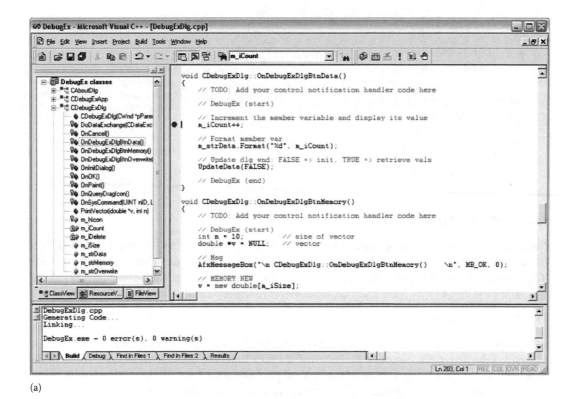

(a)

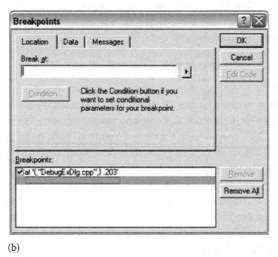

(b)

FIGURE D.4   (a) A breakpoint set on line 203 of "DebugExDlg.cpp", where "m_iCount" changes. (b) The Breakpoints dialog window showing an existing breakpoint on line 203 of "DebugExDlg.cpp".

To gain information quickly about a variable, the mouse cursor may be placed over the variable of interest, and the DataTips window displays its value. In addition, if the user right-clicks the mouse upon a variable or expression, thereby invoking the Context menu, and chooses Quick Watch, the Quick Watch dialog window appears showing the name and value of the variable or expression, as shown in Figure D.5e.

If the user clicks Go (F5) again, the DebugEx dialog window will reappear showing the newly incremented value of "m_iCount" equal to "2". Clicking OK or Cancel will end program execution.

D.4.3 CALL STACK WINDOW

The Call Stack window is displayed in the upper part of the screen in Figure D.5a, c, and d and shows the flow of control that led to the current (uppermost) function being called. The developer may like to edit the `CDebugExDlg::OnDebugExDlgBtnOverwrite()` function as shown in bold in the following to intentionally overwrite the end of the "v" double-typed vector/array of length "m_iSize":

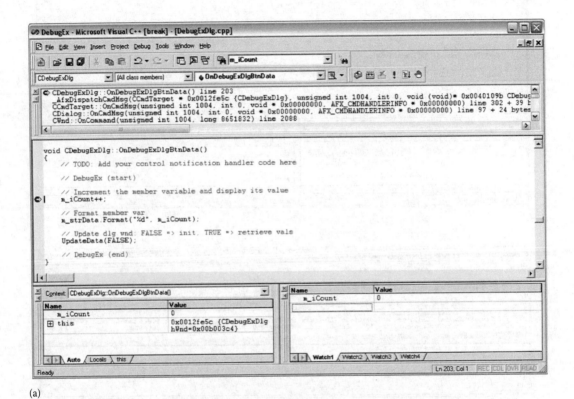

(a)

(b)

FIGURE D.5 (a) Program execution pausing at the breakpoint: "m_iCount" is "0" in both the Variables window (left) and Watch window (right). (b) The DebugEx dialog window showing the updated value of "m_iCount" after being incremented from "0" to "1".

(continued)

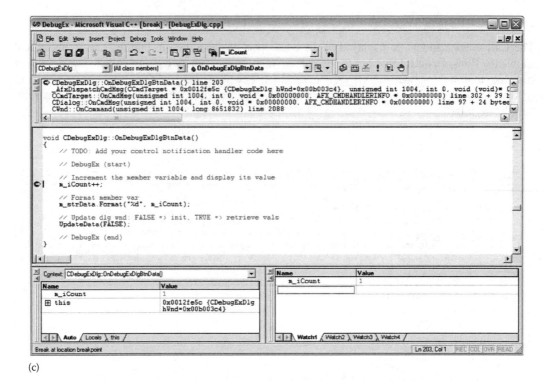

(c)

(d)

FIGURE D.5 (continued) (c) Program execution pausing at the breakpoint: "m_iCount" is "1". (d) The "this" pointer holding the address of the current object with all CDebugExDlg integer and CString member variables visible.

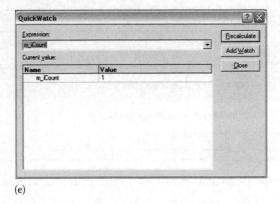

(e)

FIGURE D.5 (continued)   (e) The QuickWatch dialog window showing the name and value of the "m_iCount" variable of interest.

```
void CDebugExDlg::OnDebugExDlgBtnOverwrite()
{
    // TODO: Add your control notification handler code here

    // DebugEx (start)
    int i;
    double *v = NULL;

    // Msg
    AfxMessageBox("\n CDebugExDlg::OnDebugExDlgBtnOverwrite()\n", MB_OK, 0);

    // MEMORY NEW
    v = new double[m_iSize];

    // Overwrite end of array
    for(i=0; i<(m_iSize+10); i++)
    //for(i=0; i<m_iSize; i++)
    {
        v[i] = i;
    }

    PrintVector(v, m_iSize);

    // MEMORY DELETE
    delete [] v;

    // DebugEx (end)
}
```

Upon rebuilding and then rerunning the DebugEx application, the familiar dialog (Figure D.3a) appears, and then clicking the Overwrite button results in the previous function being called. In fact, the PrintVector() function is also called to print out the contents of the vector, but soon after, the following message is displayed: "DAMAGE: after Normal block (#80) at 0x004211A0" (Figure D.6).

If the developer chooses not to insert a breakpoint, but rather run the code again, but this time in the debugger, and then click the Retry button (Figure D.6) to debug the application, then the call stack in Figure D.7 may be observed; clicking on the recognizable CDebugExDlg:: OnDebugExDlgBtnOverwrite() function takes the developer to the line at which the problem is detected (but not necessarily caused) indicating that there is a problem with the "v" data structure.

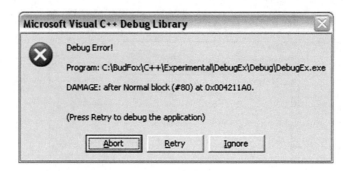

FIGURE D.6 Error message displayed when running the erroneous code, where the address "0x004211A0" is of concern.

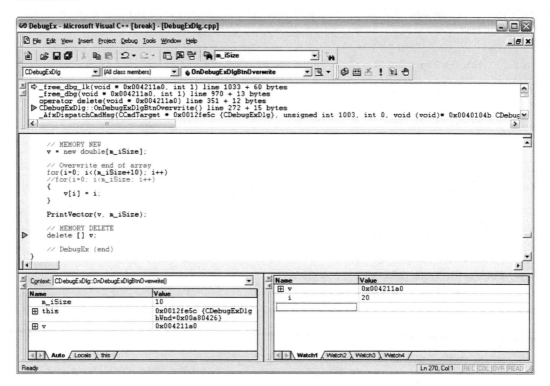

FIGURE D.7 Selection of the `CDebugExDlg::OnDebugExDlgBtnOverwrite()` function in the Call Stack window taking the user to the line at which the problem is detected.

Incidentally, the address of "v", "0x004211a0", highlighted in the Variables and Watch windows, is that displayed in the previous error dialog (Figure D.6).

Now, knowing there is a problem with the "v" vector, the developer may place a breakpoint on the line where memory is allocated and then step over (F10) consecutive lines of code, checking the number of loop iterations versus the size of the array. Figure D.8 indicates the problem; after consecutive steps, the loop counter "i" has value "10", as shown in both the Variables and Watch windows, but the size of the array, "m_iSize", is "10"; hence, the loop has incremented past the last element of the array, "v[9]". Here, the problem is obvious, but in more complicated code, the value of the index used to specify the array offset may be evaluated using an expression that, under certain circumstances, may be outside the bounds of the array.

However, if the developer were impatient and did not want to iterate through the entire loop, but rather skip to the line after the closing brace, then the mouse cursor may be placed on this line, and

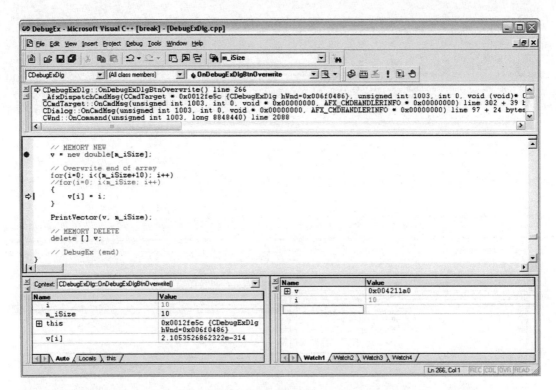

FIGURE D.8 Consecutive stepping over (F10) lines of code revealing the array offset problem.

"Run to Cursor" (Ctrl + F10) selected (from the Debug menu), where the cursor would represent a temporary breakpoint. The (yellow)* arrow indicates the line at which execution has paused, as shown in Figure D.9, and the values of "m_iSize" and "i", i.e., the size of the array and the final loop index value, respectively, may be checked for consistency. Here, it is clear that the loop has overwritten the bounds of the array since in the Watch window, "i" is "20", yet "m_iSize" in the Variables window is "10".

The developer could also check the CDebugExDlg::PrintVector() function to make sure that the vector "v" were not being altered erroneously. In Figure D.9, the (yellow) arrow denoting the current line to be executed contains the call to PrintVector(), and stepping into (F11) the member method would place the arrow on the first line of the invoked function. There, the user could either step through the function using step over (F10) or, upon realizing that the code does not change the contents of the "v" array, could step out (Shift + F11) of the function, causing the rest of the function to execute resulting in the PrintVector()-based AfxMessageBox() being displayed, then returning the user to the next executable line following the function call in the calling environment, i.e., in CDebugExDlg::OnDebugExDlgBtnOverwrite(), at the "delete [] v;" statement.

D.4.4 EDIT AND CONTINUE

The CDebugExDlg::OnDebugExDlgBtnOverwrite() function mentioned earlier has the obvious error, "for(i=0; i<(m_iSize+10); i++)", which the developer may recognize while iterating through the loop. The developer can in fact change this line, e.g., when "i=5", during the debugging process and replace it with the following, "for(i=0; i<m_iSize; i++)", and continue stepping over lines of code; the changes made are updated to the code without requiring the developer to rebuild the application, which may be time consuming. This feature is called "Edit and Continue", and Gregory [3] indicates that simple alterations may be made, but the code must be rebuilt after

---

* The colors placed in brackets in Appendix D are those observable when using the debugger and a color monitor, and serve to clarify the items being referred to.

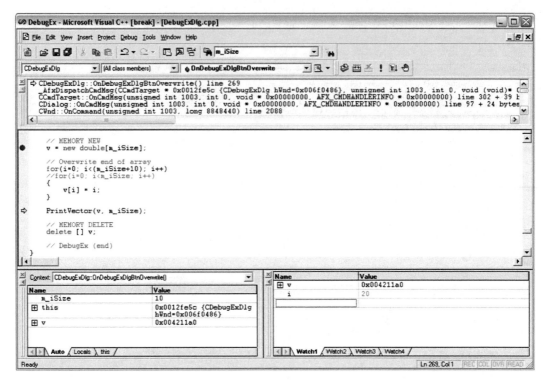

FIGURE D.9   Placing the mouse cursor beneath the loop and selecting "Run to Cursor" (Ctrl + F10) to obtain the values of "m_iSize" and "i" at the end of the loop, revealing the offset error.

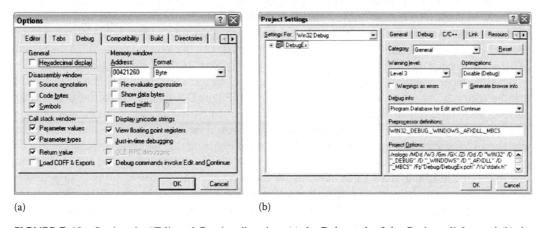

(a)   (b)

FIGURE D.10   Setting the "Edit and Continue" option: (a) the Debug tab of the Options dialog and (b) the C/C++ tab of the Project Settings dialog, with relevant fields selected.

changes to any of the following: (1) a header file, (2) a C++ class definition, (3) a function prototype, or (4) a global function or static member function.

To make sure that the "Edit and Continue" option is enabled, Gregory [3] indicates that the user should choose Tools/Options, followed by the Debug tab, and then select the lower right check box named "Debug commands invoke Edit and Continue", as shown in Figure D.10a. Then, upon choosing Project/Settings, followed by the C/C++ tab, the "Debug info" item should have the "Program Database for Edit and Continue" selected as shown in Figure D.10b.

Figure D.11a shows a breakpoint set on the line of the *for* loop, "for(i=0; i<(m_iSize+10); i++)", where the current iteration index "i" has value "5". However, at this point, the developer may realize

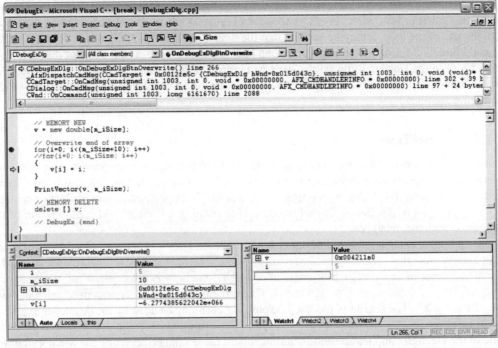

(a)

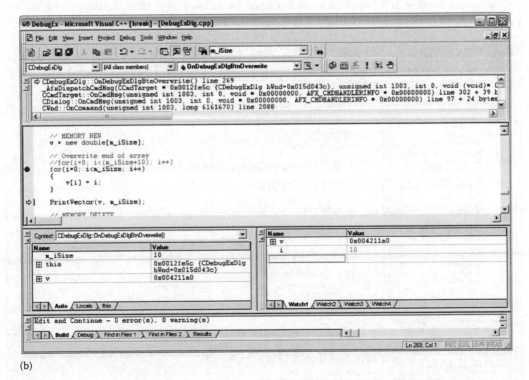

(b)

FIGURE D.11 (a) A breakpoint set on the line of an erroneous *for* loop where the iteration index "i" is "5". (b) The code edited and debugging continued: the breakpoint is updated to the new *for* loop statement where the correct upper bound prevents overwriting the end of the array.

the mistake in the code and comment out the erroneous line and in its place, use the alternative loop condition, "for(i=0; i<m_iSize; i++)", as shown in Figure D.11b, and continue stepping over code until the end of the loop. It may be verified that the final value of "i" is "10", which does not satisfy the condition, "i<m_iSize", and hence, the loop ends without overwriting the end of the array, "v". In addition, in the (lower) Build output pane in Figure D.11b, the developer will notice the "Edit and Continue – 0 error(s), 0 warning(s)" statement, indicating that editing has been performed and debugging continued.

D.4.5 MEMORY LEAKS

A memory leak occurs when memory is allocated on the heap (e.g., using operator *new*) but is not deleted (e.g., using operator *delete*), or if memory that has already been deallocated is mistakenly used [2]. The DebugEx dialog-based application has MFC support, and memory leaks are automatically dumped in the Debug Output window after running a Debug-build configuration of the application with the debugger.

The DebugEx application has a Memory button (Figure D.2) which upon selection invokes the event-handler function CDebugExDlg::OnDebugExDlgBtnMemory() presented earlier that has three courses of action after memory is allocated: (1) memory is not deleted ("m_iDelete = 0"), (2) memory is deleted once ("m_iDelete = 1"), and (3) memory is erroneously deleted twice ("m_iDelete = 2"). The setting of the "m_iDelete" variable may be done by the developer explicitly in CDebugExDlg::OnInitDialog() to explore these three cases. If the user performs a Debug-build of the DebugEx application and then runs it with the debugger, selecting the Memory button, with "m_iDelete = 0", then upon exiting the application, the memory leaks are reported in the Debug Output window. If the user then selects one of the dumped objects, as highlighted (in blue) in Figure D.12, the (blue) arrow in the editor area points to the object for which memory was not freed.

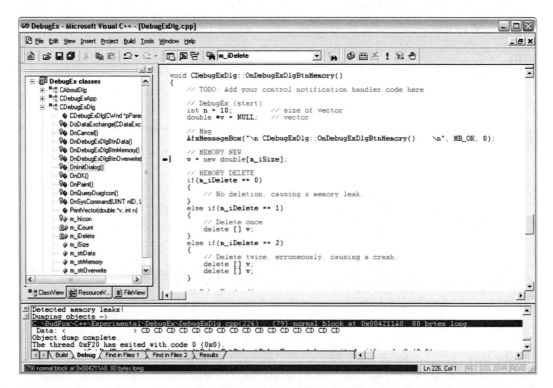

FIGURE D.12 Memory leaks reported in the Debug Output window of the IDE, and upon selection, the (blue) arrow indicates the offending variable in the editor area.

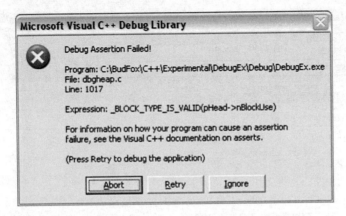

FIGURE D.13   Debug Assertion Failed message concerning memory on the heap.

The developer can prevent the leak by setting "m_iDelete = 1", in which case no memory leaks are present or reported.

If the developer sets "m_iDelete = 2" to experiment with the erroneous double deletion of memory and runs the code with the debugger, then the Debug Assertion Failed error message presented in the dialog window (Figure D.13) indicates a problem with memory on the heap.

If the developer clicks Retry to debug the DebugEx application, the following screen is presented (Figure D.14a), and the Call Stack window shows the flow of control that led to the crash. In particular, the function CDebugExDlg::OnDebugExDlgBtnMemory() calls operator delete, and

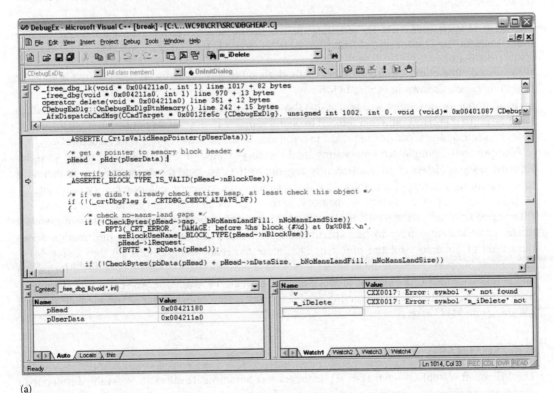

(a)

FIGURE D.14   (a) The line of code showing the assertion failure after the user clicks Retry on the Microsoft Visual C++ Debug Library dialog box (Figure D.13).

(continued)

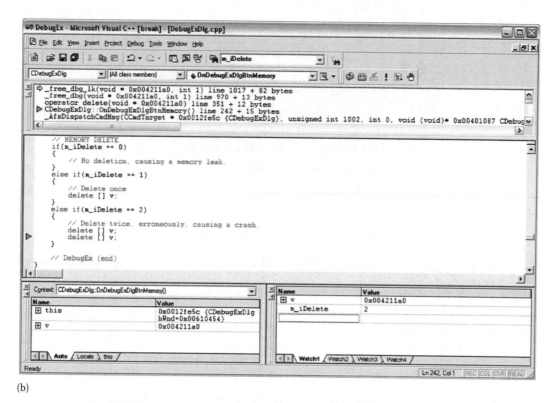

(b)

FIGURE D.14 (continued)   (b) The offending line indicated by the (green) arrow as a result of double-clicking the `CDebugExDlg::OnDebugExDlgBtnMemory()` function in the Call Stack window.

if the user double-clicks on this member method, then the (green) arrow appears on the line of the offending code as shown in Figure D.14b.

In addition, the developer will notice that the address of the vector "v" displayed in the Variables window is "0x004211a0" and that the call to operator *delete* in the call stack uses an input argument with the same address, confirming that the erroneous deletion involves this data structure.

The previous example presents a simplified memory-related problem that is clear and straightforward to solve. However, in practice, this may not be the case, and the developer may in fact have to search for the address of the object that is the subject of a memory leak or memory overwrite.

Other tools exist to detect a memory leak, e.g., using CMemoryState objects and the `Checkpoint()` and `Difference()` methods to determine the difference in the state of memory usage, and these may have to be experimented with to obtain more specific information about the nature of a memory-related problem. The interested reader should look up the "Using MFC Debugging Support" topic in the MSDN Library Visual Studio 6.0 [2], which contains information on the following: MFC debugging support, diagnostic features, using the ASSERT_VALID macro, tracking memory allocations, detecting memory leaks, using object dumps, and viewing the call stack after an MFC assert.

D.5   SUMMARY

The Microsoft Visual C++ 6.0 IDE [1] debugger has numerous features to assist the developer in debugging applications, including the setting of breakpoints; viewing of output in the Variables, Watch, and Quick Watch windows; viewing the call stack in the Call Stack window; and incrementally exploring code using the Step Into, Step Over, Step Out, and Run to Cursor options on the Debug menu.

A simple dialog-based application with MFC support was built to explore various scenarios invoked through event-handler functions attached to the buttons on the dialog, i.e., changing class member data, overwriting the end of an array, and allocation and deallocation of memory. The application was then used to explore five key debugging features: (1) the setting of breakpoints, (2) the monitoring of variable values and expressions using the Variables and Watch windows, (3) the examination of the flow of control using the Call Stack window, (4) the use of Edit and Continue to make changes to a program while in the process of debugging without rebuilding, and (5) the detection and resolution of memory leaks by observing output automatically presented in the Debug Output window when running a Debug-build configuration of the application with the debugger.

REFERENCES

1. Microsoft Visual C++® 6.0, Microsoft® Visual Studio™ 6.0 Development System, Professional Edition, Microsoft Corporation, 1998.
2. Microsoft Developer Network Library Visual Studio 6.0, Microsoft® Visual Studio™ 6.0 Development System, Microsoft Corporation, 1998.
3. Gregory, K., *Using Visual C++ 6: Special Edition*, Que Publishing, Indianapolis, IN, 1998.

Appendix E: MatrixInversion: Win32 Console Application

E.1 INTRODUCTION

Two common tasks often encountered in computational linear algebra are the computation of sets of linear equations and the determination of the inverse of a square matrix. The Win32 Console Application titled MatrixInversion, presented here, is used to compute the inverse A^{-1} of a matrix A and the solution vector x of a system, $Ax = b$. The work of Press et al. [1] is closely followed, where the "Gauss–Jordan elimination with full pivoting" method is used. The only main alteration made to the code of Press et al. was to use an epsilon value to test for essentially zero values on the diagonal, i.e., if "$A_{kk} \in [-\varepsilon, \varepsilon]$" for $\varepsilon = 10^{-6}$, then the matrix is deemed to be singular: this was used in place of the original test for "$A_{kk} = 0$". Various other syntactic changes were made for ease of reading. The developer should consult the work of Press et al. [1] for the original version of the code.

E.2 GAUSS–JORDAN ELIMINATION WITH FULL PIVOTING

The GaussJordanEliminationFullPivoting() function presented in the following source file "MatrixInverse.cpp" and which follows very closely the function, gaussj(), of Press et al. [1] solves the simultaneous systems of equations:

$$A[x_1, x_2, \ldots, x_m, Y] = [b_1, b_2, \ldots, b_m, I] \tag{E.1}$$

where
A is a $n \times n$ leading matrix
x_i are the vectors of unknowns, for $i \in [1, m]$ of a total of m simultaneous systems, of the form

$$Ax_i = b_i \tag{E.2}$$

$$\Rightarrow x_i = A^{-1}b_i \tag{E.3}$$

with right-hand-side vectors b_i. The system

$$AY = I \tag{E.4}$$

$$\Rightarrow Y = A^{-1}I \tag{E.5}$$

is used where Y holds the inverse A^{-1} of the leading matrix A at the end of system computation.

The function prototype used, i.e., void GaussJordanEliminationFullPivoting (double **A, int n, double **B, int m), involves two matrices, A and B, that are passed into the function: on entry A is the leading matrix and B an $n \times m$ matrix composed of the m right-hand-side vectors b_i, and on return, A holds its own inverse A^{-1} (E.5) and B holds the *m* solution vectors x_i (E.3). If only the inverse of a matrix is desired and no solution x_i sought, then a "dummy" right-hand-side vector can be used, as it is in the functions presented in the following that actually call GaussJordanEliminationFullPivoting().

E.3 MATRIX INVERSION APPLICATION

The MatrixInversion Win32 Console Application consists of two files: a header and a source file named "MatrixInverse.h" and "MatrixInverse.cpp", which contain function declarations and definitions, respectively.

E.3.1 HEADER FILE

The "MatrixInverse.h" header file is presented in the following and declares the key functions involved in determining the inverse of a matrix and checking the accuracy of the result.

```
// MatrixInverse.h

#ifndef MATRIX_INVERSE_H
    #define MATRIX_INVERSE_H

    // -- defined vars

    #define NROWS 4
    #define NCOLS 6

    // -- static vars
    static int prec = 15;
    // static int nrows = 4;          // NOTE: can't use static ints for
      array dimensions.
    // static int ncols = 5;

    // Main line fns
    int main(int argc, char **argv);
    int PrepareMatrixInversion(void);
    int PrepareMatrixInversionLargeSystem(void);
    int PrepareMatrixMult(void);
    int PrepareSwap(void);

    // Matrix-based functions
    void GaussJordanEliminationFullPivoting(double **A, int n, double
      **B, int m);
    void MatrixMult(int nrowsA, int ncolsA, int ncolsB, double **A,
      double **B, double **C);
    double MatrixNorm(int nrows, int ncols, double **M);
    int SetupMatrix(void);

    // Misc. fns
    void Swap(double &a, double &b);

    // Print fns
    int PrintMatrix(double **M, int nrows, int ncols);
    int PrintVector(double *v, int ncols);

    // -- classes
    // none yet.
#endif

// eof
```

E.3.2   SOURCE FILE

The following "MatrixInverse.cpp" source file contains the definitions of the functions declared in the earlier header file. SetupMatrix() is used to set up a matrix and test the PrintMatrix() and PrintVector() functions. PrepareMatrixMult() prepares three matrices, *A*, *B*, and *C*, and then calls the matrix multiplication function MatrixMult() to determine *C = AB*. The PrepareSwap() function simply tests the invocation of the Swap() method that is used by the GaussJordanEliminationFullPivoting() function. The two matrix inversion preparation functions PrepareMatrixInversion() and PrepareMatrixInversionLargeSystem() simply set up the matrices to be inverted through calls to GaussJordanEliminationFullPivoting(): the former concerns a small system and the latter a larger system. The MatrixNorm() function is then called to test the accuracy of computed solutions, i.e., A^{-1} and x_i of (E.3).

```cpp
// Title: MatrixInverse.cpp
// Purpose: Performs matrix inversion using Gauss-Jordan elimination with
//   full pivoting.
// Source: Numerical Recipes in C: The Art of Scientific Computing
//   (2nd Ed.), sections 2.0 - 2.1.

#include <iostream>
#include <iomanip>
#include <math.h>
#include <time.h>
#include "MatrixInverse.h"
using namespace std;

int main(int argc, char **argv)
{
    cout << "\n main()\n";

    SetupMatrix();          // dynamic hence more variable/general
    PrepareMatrixMult();
    PrepareSwap();
    PrepareMatrixInversion();
    PrepareMatrixInversionLargeSystem();

    cout << endl;
    return 0;
}

int SetupMatrix(void)
{
    cout << " SetupMatrix()\n";

    int i;
    int j;
    int cnt = 0;
    int nrows = NROWS;
    int ncols = NCOLS;
    double *vector = NULL;       // vector is a ptr to double.
    double **matrix = NULL;      // matrix

    // MEMORY NEW
    // Allocate an array of doubles, and return the & to vector: hence
    //   vector is of type ptr.
    vector = new double[ncols];
```

```cpp
    // Allocate an array of ptrs-to-double and return the & to matrix
    // Note: an array is of type ptr, hence an array of ptrs is of type
      ptr-ptr.
    matrix = new double *[nrows];

    // Allocate an array of doubles for each of the entries (rows of the
      column vector) of matrix,
    // and return the & to matrix[i].
    // Note: an array is of type ptr, and its & is stored at location i
      in the array matrix[]
    for(i=0;i<nrows;i++)
    {
        matrix[i] = new double[ncols];        // allocate an array of
          doubles, return & to matrix[i]
    }


    // SETUP MATRIX
    cout << endl;
    for(i=0;i<nrows;i++)
    {
        for(j=0;j<ncols;j++)
        {
            matrix[i][j] = cnt;
            cnt++;
        }
    }

    PrintMatrix(matrix, nrows, ncols);

    // SETUP VECTOR
    for(i=0;i<ncols;i++)
    {
        vector[i] = i+3;
    }

    PrintVector(vector, ncols);

    // MEMORY DELETE
    delete [] vector;

    for(i=0;i<nrows;i++)
    {
        delete [] matrix[i];
    }
    delete [] matrix;

    return 0;
}

int PrepareMatrixMult()
{
    int i;
    int j;
    int cnt = 0;
    int nrowsA = 2;
    int ncolsA = 3;
    int nrowsB = ncolsA;
    int ncolsB = 4;
```

```
int nrowsC = nrowsA;
int ncolsC = ncolsB;
double **A = NULL;
double **B = NULL;
double **C = NULL;

cout << "\n PrepareMatrixMult()\n";

// MEMORY ALLOC
A = new double *[nrowsA];       // allocate an array of ptrs-to-double
for(i=0;i<nrowsA;i++)
{
    A[i] = new double[ncolsA]; // allocate an array of doubles,
        return & to matrix[i]
}

B = new double *[nrowsB];       // allocate an array of ptrs-to-double
for(i=0;i<nrowsB;i++)
{
    B[i] = new double[ncolsB]; // allocate an array of doubles,
        return & to matrix[i]
}

C = new double *[nrowsC];       // allocate an array of ptrs-to-double
for(i=0;i<nrowsC;i++)
{
    C[i] = new double[ncolsC]; // allocate an array of doubles,
        return & to matrix[i]
}

// SETUP MATRICES
for(i=0; i<nrowsA; i++)
{
    for(j=0; j<ncolsA; j++)
    {
        cnt++;
        A[i][j] = cnt;
    }
}

cnt = -1;
for(i=0; i<nrowsB; i++)
{
    for(j=0; j<ncolsB; j++)
    {
        cnt++;
        B[i][j] = cnt;
    }
}

// Matrix mult
MatrixMult(nrowsA, ncolsA, ncolsB, A, B, C);

PrintMatrix(A, nrowsA, ncolsA);
PrintMatrix(B, nrowsB, ncolsB);
PrintMatrix(C, nrowsC, ncolsC);

// -- FREM MEM
// Delete A
```

```cpp
    for(i=0;i<nrowsA;i++)
    {
        delete [] A[i];
    }
    delete [] A;

    // Delete B
    for(i=0;i<nrowsB;i++)
    {
        delete [] B[i];
    }
    delete [] B;

    // Delete C
    for(i=0;i<nrowsC;i++)
    {
        delete [] C[i];
    }
    delete [] C;

    return 0;
}

void MatrixMult(int nrowsA, int ncolsA, int ncolsB, double **A,
  double **B, double **C)
{
    int i;
    int j;
    int k;

    // Matrix multiplication
    // A: nrowsA x ncolsA
    // B: nrowsB x ncolsB
    // C: nrowsA x ncolsB
    // C = A*B

    cout << "\n MatrixMult()\n\n";

    // Nullify C
    for(i=0; i<nrowsA; i++)
    {
        for(j=0; j<ncolsB; j++)
        {
            C[i][j] = 0.0;
        }
    }

    // Matrix multiplication
    for(k=0; k<ncolsB; k++)
    {
        for(i=0; i<nrowsA; i++)
        {
            for(j=0; j<ncolsA; j++)
            {
                C[i][k] = C[i][k] + A[i][j]*B[j][k];
                //printf(" C[%d][%d] = %lf\n", i, k, C[i][k]);
            }
        }
    }
```

```
        return;
}

int PrepareSwap(void)
{
        double a = 1;
        double b = 2;

        cout << "\n PrepareSwap()\n";
        cout << " a = " << a << " b = " << b << endl;

        Swap(a,b);

        cout << " a = " << a << " b = " << b << endl;

        return 0;
}

void Swap(double &a, double &b)
{
        // NOTE: pass by reference uses syntactically clean pass-by-reference
           mechanism, i.e. without requiring
        // client of the fn to pass an address, which would then be reflected
           by a ptr-to-double in the arg. list.
        double temp;

        // Swap a and b
        temp = a;
        a = b;
        b = temp;
}

int PrepareMatrixInversion(void)
{
        int i;
        int j;
        int nrowsA = 3;
        int ncolsA = 3;
        int nrowsB = 3;
        int ncolsB = 1;
        double norm;                   // matrix Euclidean norm of matrix difference
        double sum = 0.0;              // sum of squares of error
        double **A = NULL;             // leading matrix in A.x = b
        double **A_copy = NULL;        // copy of leading matrix in A.x = b
        double **B = NULL;             // r.h.s. vector in A.x = b
        double **B_copy = NULL;        // copy of r.h.s. vector in A.x = b
        double **C = NULL;             // matrix used to check that A.A^-1 = I
        double **D = NULL;             // matrix used to check that A.A^-1.b = b
        double **E = NULL;             // Error matrix = B_copy - D. Here D =
           A.A^-1.b

        cout << "\n PrepareMatrixInversion()\n";

        // MEMORY ALLOC
        A = new double *[nrowsA];           // allocate an array of ptrs-to-double
        for(i=0;i<nrowsA;i++)
        {
             A[i] = new double[ncolsA]; // allocate an array of doubles,
                return & to matrix[i]
        }
```

```
A_copy = new double *[nrowsA]; // allocate an array of ptrs-to-double
for(i=0;i<nrowsA;i++)
{
    A_copy[i] = new double[ncolsA];    // allocate an array of
      doubles, return & to matrix[i]
}

B = new double *[nrowsB];      // allocate an array of ptrs-to-double
for(i=0;i<nrowsB;i++)
{
    B[i] = new double[ncolsB]; // allocate an array of doubles,
      return & to matrix[i]
}

B_copy = new double *[nrowsB]; // allocate an array of ptrs-to-double
for(i=0;i<nrowsB;i++)
{
    B_copy[i] = new double[ncolsB];    // allocate an array of
      doubles, return & to matrix[i]
}

C = new double *[nrowsA];      // allocate an array of ptrs-to-double
for(i=0;i<nrowsA;i++)
{
    C[i] = new double[ncolsA];    // allocate an array of doubles,
      return & to matrix[i]
}

D = new double *[nrowsB];      // allocate an array of ptrs-to-double
for(i=0;i<nrowsB;i++)
{
    D[i] = new double[ncolsB];       // allocate an array of doubles,
      return & to matrix[i]
}

E = new double *[nrowsB];      // allocate an array of ptrs-to-double
for(i=0;i<nrowsB;i++)
{
    E[i] = new double[ncolsB];        // allocate an array of
      doubles, return & to matrix[i]
}

// Setup A and B
A[0][0] = 1.0;
A[1][0] = 2.0;
A[2][0] = 1.0;
A[0][1] = 2.0;
A[1][1] = 5.0;
A[2][1] = 0.0;
A[0][2] = 3.0;
A[1][2] = 3.0;
A[2][2] = 8.0;

B[0][0] = 1.0;
B[1][0] = 1.0;
B[2][0] = 1.0;
```

```
    // Make a copy of A
    for(i=0; i<nrowsA; i++)
    {
        for(j=0; j<ncolsA; j++)
        {
            A_copy[i][j] = A[i][j];
        }
    }

    // Make a copy of B
    for(i=0; i<nrowsB; i++)
    {
        for(j=0; j<ncolsB; j++)
        {
            B_copy[i][j] = B[i][j];
        }
    }

    // Print A and B

    cout << "\n A:\n";
    PrintMatrix(A, nrowsA, ncolsA);

    cout << "\n B:\n";
    PrintMatrix(B, nrowsB, ncolsB);

    // -- COMPUTE THE INVERSE AND THE SOLN VECTOR
    GaussJordanEliminationFullPivoting(A, nrowsA, B, ncolsB);

    // Print A^-1 and the soln vec. x = A^-1.b
    cout << "\n A^-1:\n";
    PrintMatrix(A, nrowsA, ncolsA);

    cout << "\n x = A^-1.B\n";
    PrintMatrix(B, nrowsB, ncolsB);

    // -- COMPUTE THE ERRORS IN THE MATRIX AND R.H.S. VECTOR

    // Check the inversion: A.A^-1
    MatrixMult(nrowsA, ncolsA, ncolsA, A_copy, A, C);        // A.A^-1 = C

    cout << "\n I = A.A^-1\n";
    PrintMatrix(C, nrowsA, ncolsA);

    // Check the soln vector: x = A^-1.b => b = A.A^-1.b
    MatrixMult(nrowsA, ncolsA, ncolsB, A_copy, B, D);       // A.A^-1.b = b

    cout << "\n b = A.A^-1.b\n";
    PrintMatrix(D, nrowsB, ncolsB);

    // Determine the differences bw. the original B and the recovered B,
    //   i.e. A.A^-1.b = D
    for(i=0; i<nrowsB; i++)
    {
        for(j=0; j<ncolsB; j++)
        {
            E[i][j] = B_copy[i][j] - D[i][j];
        }
    }
```

```cpp
// Check the matrix norm of the difference bw. original and recovered
  B matrices
norm = MatrixNorm(nrowsB, ncolsB, E);
//printf("\n norm = %7.4lf\n", norm);

// MEMORY DELETE
// Delete A
for(i=0;i<nrowsA;i++)
{
    delete [] A[i];
}
delete [] A;

// Delete A_copy
for(i=0;i<nrowsA;i++)
{
    delete [] A_copy[i];
}
delete [] A_copy;

// Delete B
for(i=0;i<nrowsB;i++)
{
    delete [] B[i];
}

delete [] B;

// Delete B_copy
for(i=0;i<nrowsB;i++)
{
    delete [] B_copy[i];
}

delete [] B_copy;

// Delete C
for(i=0;i<nrowsA;i++)
{
    delete [] C[i];
}
delete [] C;

// Delete D
for(i=0;i<nrowsB;i++)
{
    delete [] D[i];
}
delete [] D;

// Delete E
for(i=0;i<nrowsB;i++)
{
    delete [] E[i];
}
delete [] E;

return 0;
}
```

```
int PrepareMatrixInversionLargeSystem(void)
{
    int i;
    int j;
    int nrowsA = 100;
    int ncolsA = 100;
    int nrowsB = 100;
    int ncolsB = 1;
    double max = 0.0;
    double min = 0.0;
    double norm;              // matrix Euclidean norm of matrix difference
    double random_no;         // random no.
    double sum = 0.0;         // sum of squares of error
    double uniformly_rand;    // uniformly random no.
    double **A = NULL;        // leading matrix in A.x = b
    double **A_copy = NULL;   // copy of leading matrix A
    double **B = NULL;        // r.h.s. vector in A.x = b
    double **C = NULL;        // product of A.A^-1 = I
    double **E = NULL;        // error matrix

    cout << "\n PrepareMatrixInversionLargeSystem()\n";

    // MEMORY ALLOC
    A = new double *[nrowsA];      // allocate an array of ptrs-to-double
    for(i=0;i<nrowsA;i++)
    {
        A[i] = new double[ncolsA];        // allocate an array of
          doubles, return & to matrix[i]
    }

    A_copy = new double *[nrowsA]; // allocate an array of ptrs-to-double
    for(i=0;i<nrowsA;i++)
    {
        A_copy[i] = new double[ncolsA];      // allocate an array of
          doubles, return & to matrix[i]
    }

    B = new double *[nrowsB];      // allocate an array of ptrs-to-double
    for(i=0;i<nrowsB;i++)
    {
        B[i] = new double[ncolsB];          // allocate an array of
          doubles, return & to matrix[i]
    }

    C = new double *[nrowsA];      // allocate an array of ptrs-to-double
    for(i=0;i<nrowsA;i++)
    {
        C[i] = new double[ncolsA];          // allocate an array of
          doubles, return & to matrix[i]
    }

    E = new double *[nrowsA];      // allocate an array of ptrs-to-double
    for(i=0;i<nrowsA;i++)
    {
        E[i] = new double[ncolsA];          // allocate an array of
          doubles, return & to matrix[i]
    }
```

```
// Seed the random no. generator with time value to get truly
  random nos.
srand( (unsigned)time(NULL) );

// Setup A and B
for(i=0; i<nrowsA; i++)
{
    for(j=0; j<ncolsA; j++)
    {
        random_no = rand();
        uniformly_rand = double(random_no)/double(RAND_MAX);

        A[i][j] = uniformly_rand;
        A_copy[i][j] = A[i][j];
    }
}

for(i=0; i<nrowsB; i++)
{
    random_no = rand();
    uniformly_rand = double(random_no)/double(RAND_MAX);
    B[i][0] = uniformly_rand;
}

// Print A and B
cout << "\n A:\n";
PrintMatrix(A, nrowsA, ncolsA);

cout << "\n B:\n";
PrintMatrix(B, nrowsB, ncolsB);


// -- COMPUTE THE INVERSE AND THE SOLN VECTOR
GaussJordanEliminationFullPivoting(A, nrowsA, B, ncolsB);


// Print A^-1 and the soln vec. x = A^-1.b
cout << "\n A^-1:\n";
PrintMatrix(A, nrowsA, ncolsA);

cout << "\n x = A^-1.B\n";
PrintMatrix(B, nrowsB, ncolsB);


// -- COMPUTE THE ERRORS

// Check the inversion: A.A^-1
MatrixMult(nrowsA, ncolsA, ncolsA, A_copy, A, C);        // A.A^-1 = C

cout << "\n I = A.A^-1\n";
PrintMatrix(C, nrowsA, ncolsA);

// Determine the differences bw. the identity I, and the recovered C,
  i.e. A.A^-1 = C
for(i=0; i<nrowsA; i++)
{
    for(j=0; j<ncolsA; j++)
    {
        if(i == j)
        {
```

```
                    E[i][j] = 1.0 - C[i][j];           // I - C = 1 - C
                }
            else
                {
                    E[i][j] = 0.0 - C[i][j];           // I - C = 0 - C
                }
            }
        }

    // Check the matrix norm of the difference bw. the identity and C
    norm = MatrixNorm(nrowsA, ncolsA, E);
    //printf("\n norm = %7.4lf\n", norm);

    // MEMORY DELETE
    // Delete A
    for(i=0;i<nrowsA;i++)
    {
        delete [] A[i];
    }
    delete [] A;

    // Delete A_copy
    for(i=0;i<nrowsA;i++)
    {
        delete [] A_copy[i];
    }
    delete [] A_copy;

    // Delete B
    for(i=0;i<nrowsB;i++)
    {
        delete [] B[i];
    }
    delete [] B;

    // Delete C
    for(i=0;i<nrowsA;i++)
    {
        delete [] C[i];
    }
    delete [] C;

    // Delete E
    for(i=0;i<nrowsB;i++)
    {
        delete [] E[i];
    }
    delete [] E;

    return 0;
}


void GaussJordanEliminationFullPivoting(double **A, int n, double **B, int m)
{
    // THIS MATERIAL FOLLOWS CLOSELY THE WORK OF:
    // Numerical Recipes in C: The Art of Scientific Computing (2nd Ed.),
        sections 2.0 - 2.1.
```

```
// by, W.H. Press, S.A. Teukolsky, W.T. Vetterling and B.P. Flannery.
// Only minor syntactic changes are made here to the original,
   e.g. array indexing
// (0 to n-1 is used here, rather than the original 1 to n).

/* GaussJordanEliminationFullPivoting() solves the systems of
   equations represented by, e.g.,

     [A].[x_1, x_2, x_3, Y] = [b_1, b_2, b_3, I]

     where
     A.x_1 = b_1,
     A.x_2 = b_2,
     A.x_3 = b_3,

     and

     A.Y = I
=> Y = A^-1

     A:nxn = input matrix.
     This is overwritten with A^-1.

     B:nxm = input matrix containing the m r.h.s. vectors (of length n).
     This is overwritten with the corres. set of soln. vectors. That is,
     x_1 = A^-1.b_1,
     x_2 = A^-1.b_2,
     x_3 = A^-1.b_3.
*/

// Declaration
int i;
int icol;          // col index
int irow;          // row index
int j;
int k;
int u;
int v;
int *index_c = NULL;        // col index used for pivoting
int *index_r = NULL;        // row index used for pivoting
int *ipiv = NULL;           // pivot index array
double big;
double dum;
double pivinv;
double eps = 1.0e-6;        // ALTERATION: epsilon value to check for
   a "zero" on the diagonal

// MEMORY NEW
// Integer arrays used to manage the pivoting
index_c = new int[n];
index_r = new int[n];
ipiv = new int[n];

// Nullify the ipiv array
for(j=0; j<n; j++)
{
    ipiv[j] = 0;
}
```

```
// Main loop over the n columns to be reduced.
for(i=0; i<n; i++)
{
    big = 0.0;                      // init big == 0.0

    // Outer loop of the search for a pivot element
    for(j=0; j<n; j++)
    {
        if(ipiv[j] != 1)        // if the pivot array element != unity
        {
            for(k=0; k<n; k++)
            {
                if(ipiv[k] == 0)                // if the pivot array
                  element == nullity
                {
                    if(fabs(A[j][k]) >= big)    // floating point
                      absolute value
                    {
                        big = fabs(A[j][k]);    // update big with the
                          double-type abs value of A[j][k]
                        irow = j;
                        icol = k;
                    }
                }
            }// end for k
        }// end if ipiv[j]
    }// end for j

    ++(ipiv[icol]);

    // Now the pivot element is found, rows need to be intechanged,
      if rqd. to put the pivot element on the diag.
    // The cols are not physically interchanged, only relabelled:
    // index_c[i] the col of the ith pivot element is the ith col
      that is reduced
    // index_r[i] the row in which the pivot element was originally
      located.
    // If index_r[i] != index_c[i] there is an implied column
      interchange.
    // With this form of pivot management, the solutions x = A^-1.b
      which overwrite B, will end up in the correct order,
    // and the inverse matrix will be out of column alignment.

    if(irow != icol)
    {
        for(u=0; u<n; u++)
        {
            Swap(A[irow][u], A[icol][u]);
        }

        for(u=0; u<m; u++)
        {
            Swap(B[irow][u], B[icol][u]);
        }
    }
```

```cpp
        // Pivot element indexing
        index_r[i] = irow;
        index_c[i] = icol;

        // Warn if there is a zero on the diag. implying a singular
        //   (non-invertible) matrix: was "if(A[icol][icol] == 0.0)"
        if( (A[icol][icol] >= -eps) && (A[icol][icol] <= eps) )
        {
            cout << "\n GaussJordanEliminationFullPivoting(): Singular
            Matrix\n";
        }


        // Now the pivot row can be divided by the pivot element, located
        //   at irow and icol.
        pivinv = 1.0/A[icol][icol];
        A[icol][icol] = 1.0;

        for(u=0; u<n; u++)
        {
            A[icol][u] *= pivinv;
        }

        for(u=0; u<m; u++)
        {
            B[icol][u] *= pivinv;
        }


        // Now the rows are reduced, except for the pivot one.
        for(v=0; v<n; v++)
        {
            if(v != icol)
            {
                dum = A[v][icol];
                A[v][icol] = 0.0;

                for(u=0; u<n; u++)
                {
                    A[v][u] -= A[icol][u]*dum;
                }

                for(u=0; u<m; u++)
                {
                    B[v][u] -= B[icol][u]*dum;
                }
            }
        }
    }// end for i
    // The end of the main loop over columns of the reduction.

    // Realign the soln given the column interchanges. This is done by
    //   interchanging pairs of columns in the
    // reverse order to that in which the permutation was built.
    for(u=(n-1); u>=0; u--)
    {
        if(index_r[u] != index_c[u])
        {
            for(k=0; k<n; k++)
```

```
                    {
                            Swap(A[k][index_r[u]], A[k][index_c[u]]);
                    }
            }
    }

    // MEMORY DELETE
    delete [] index_c;
    delete [] index_r;
    delete [] ipiv;
}
```

E.4 SUMMARY

The Win32 Console Application, MatrixInversion, presents exploratory code to compute the inverse of a matrix and the solution to a system of linear equations using the "Gauss–Jordan elimination with full pivoting" method of Press et al. [1]. The key functions used are GaussJordanEliminationFullPivoting(), MatrixMult(), MatrixNorm(), PrepareMatrixInversion(), and Swap(), which compute a system of equations, perform matrix multiplication, determine the matrix norm, prepare the system to be computed, and swap values, respectively.

REFERENCE

1. Press, W. H., Teukolsky, S. A., Vetterling, W. T., and Flannery, B. P., *Numerical Recipes in C: The Art of Scientific Computing*, 2nd edn., Cambridge University Press, Cambridge, U.K., 2002.

Appendix F: Using DiagramEng

F.1 INTRODUCTION

The DiagramEng software application provides users the means to efficiently represent mathematical equations, perform interactive and intuitive model building, and conduct control engineering experiments. The software incorporates block icons, representing model components and adjoining connections, signifying a relationship between them.

DiagramEng has been built with Microsoft Visual C++ 6.0 [1] using the Microsoft Foundation Classes (MFC) and the Standard Template Library (STL). The graphical user interface involves menus, toolbars, a block library tree-like browser for block selection, and a palette upon which a diagram, consisting of blocks and connections, can be drawn. The computation of a system model is performed either directly or iteratively through the use of a Newton-method-based nonlinear solver. A range of blocks, including the Derivative and Integrator blocks, used for numerical differentiation and integration, respectively, allow the user to model time-based linear and nonlinear differential equations.

The remainder of this Using DiagramEng document discusses functionality provided in the menus and toolbars and provides examples of how to model typical real-world engineering problems and compute results that may be visualized or saved to an output data file.

F.2 MENUS

There are two frame-based sets of menus used in the DiagramEng application: (1) the Main frame–based menus, which include the File, View, and Help menus (Figure F.1), and (2) the Child frame–based menus (Figure F.2) which include the File, Edit, View, Model, Simulation, Format, Tools, Window, and Help menus. A listing of menu-based functionality is presented in Tables F.1 through F.13.

F.2.1 MAIN FRAME–BASED MENUS

Tables F.1 through F.3 present information on the Main frame–based menus, File, View, and Help, as shown in Figure F.1.

F.2.2 CHILD FRAME–BASED MENUS

Tables F.4 through F.12 present information on the Child frame–based menus, File, Edit, View, Model, Simulation, Format, Tools, Window, and Help, as shown in Figure F.2.

F.2.3 CONTEXT MENU

The Context menu is invoked by right-clicking on a diagram entity, e.g., a block or block port, or upon the palette, and an item may be chosen from the list to perform some action. The location of the cursor at which the Context menu is invoked is used to determine the applicability of the selected action for the object concerned. Some of the invoked functions need to be preceded or followed by other necessary steps to complete the whole interactive action. For example, to perform fine movement of a diagram entity, the Fine Move Item entry should first be selected, followed by the usage of the arrow keys to move the item. The Context menu entries and their function are listed in Table F.13.

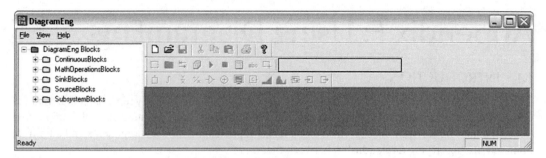

FIGURE F.1   Main frame–based menus: File, View, and Help.

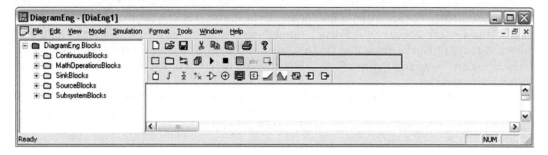

FIGURE F.2   Child frame–based menus: File, Edit, View, Model, Simulation, Format, Tools, Window, and Help.

TABLE F.1
Main Frame–Based File Menu Entries and Function

File Menu Entry	Function
New	Creates a new empty child document
Open	Opens an existing document previously saved to a model data file
Print Setup	Sets up the printer properties
Recent Files	Lists the four most recent files
Exit	Exits the application, prompting the user to save unsaved files

TABLE F.2
Main Frame–Based View Menu Entries and Function

View Menu Entry	Function
Toolbar	Shows or hides the Toolbar
Status Bar	Shows or hides the Status Bar

TABLE F.3
Main Frame–Based Help Menu Entry and Function

Help Menu Entry	Function
About DiagramEng	Displays program, version number, and copyright information

TABLE F.4
Child Frame–Based File Menu Entries and Function

File Menu Entry	Function
New	Creates a new document in a new child document window
Open	Opens existing document, prompting the user to save the current document if it already exists in the child document window
Close	Closes a document, prompting the user to save if the document content has not already been saved
Save	Saves the active document to a file
Save As	Saves the active document to a new file
Print	Prints the active document
Print Preview	Previews the active document prior to printing
Print Setup	Sets up the printer properties
Recent File	Lists the four most recent files
Exit	Exits the application, prompting the user to save unsaved files

TABLE F.5
Child Frame–Based Edit Menu Entries and Function

Edit Menu Entry	Function
Undo	Undoes the last system model–based editing action
Redo	Redoes the last system model–based editing action
Cut	Cuts the selection and places it on the Clipboard
Copy	Copies the selection and places it on the Clipboard
Paste	Inserts Clipboard contents onto the system model diagram
Delete Grouped Items	Deletes items grouped by an enclosing rectangular region
Select All	Selects all document content with an enclosing rectangular region
Add Multiple Blocks	Presents a block library dialog window for multiple block selection

TABLE F.6
Child Frame–Based View Menu Entries and Function

View Menu Entry	Function
Toolbar	Shows or hides the toolbar
Status Bar	Shows or hides the status bar
Common Ops. Toolbar	Shows or hides the Common Operations toolbar
Common Blocks Toolbar	Shows or hides the Common Blocks toolbar
Block Directory	Shows or hides the block directory tree
Auto Fit Diagram	Automatically fits diagram to view
Zoom In	Zooms into detail, enlarging the size of the diagram
Zoom Out	Zooms out of detail, reducing the size of the diagram
Reset Diagram	Resets diagram to original size prior to zooming operations

TABLE F.7

Child Frame–Based Model Menu Entries and Function

Model Menu Entry	Function
Build Model	Builds the active model
Build Subsystem	Builds the selected model subsystem (not functional)

The shaded entry denotes a nonfunctional item.

TABLE F.8

Child Frame–Based Simulation Menu Entries and Function

Simulation Menu Entry	Function
Start	Starts the simulation, invoking Build Model if model not already built
Stop	Stops the simulation
Numerical Solver	Sets the numerical solver parameters (not all fields are functional)

TABLE F.9

Child Frame–Based Format Menu Entry and Function

Format Menu Entry	Function
Show Annotations	Shows or hides diagram annotations if present

TABLE F.10

Child Frame–Based Tools Menu Entry and Function

Tools Menu Entry	Function
Diagnostic Info.	Presents process and system memory utilization statistics

TABLE F.11

Child Frame–Based Window Menu Entries and Function

Window Menu Entry	Function
New Window	Opens another window for the active document
Cascade	Arranges windows so they overlap
Tile	Arranges windows as nonoverlapping tiles
Arrange Icons	Arranges icons at the bottom of the window
Close All Documents	Closes all documents and prompts the user to save if necessary
Name of child windows	Shows names of windows and activates the selected window

---

TABLE F.12

Child Frame–Based Help Menu Entries and Function

Help Menu Entry	Function
About DiagramEng	Displays program, version number, and copyright information
Using DiagramEng	Displays information about using the DiagramEng application

---

TABLE F.13

Context Menu Entries and Function

Context Menu Entry	Function
Delete Item	Deletes selected block, connection, or connection bend point
Delete Grouped Items	Deletes items grouped by an enclosing rectangular region
Fine Move Item	Moves an item using the arrows keys
Format Annotation	Formats an existing annotation or inserts a new one
Insert Bend Point	Inserts a bend point upon a connection object
Reverse Block	Reverses the direction of a block
Set Output Signal	Sets block output connection-based signal
Set Properties	Sets block, port, and numerical solver properties

---

F.3 TOOLBARS

The three application toolbars are (1) the standard Main frame–based toolbar and the Child frame–based toolbars, (2) Common Operations, and (3) Common Blocks, as may be seen in Figure F.2. Tables F.14 through F.16 present information about the toolbar buttons and their associated functionality.

F.3.1 MAIN FRAME–BASED TOOLBAR

The standard Main frame–based toolbar is that shown in Figure F.3: as a child window is not open, the Child frame–based toolbars are not visible and only the Main frame–based functionality for the toolbar is enabled.

TABLE F.14

Standard Main Frame–Based Toolbar

Toolbar Button	Function
New	Creates a new, empty child document
Open	Opens an existing document previously saved to a model data file
Save	Saves the active document to a file
Cut	Cuts the selection and places it on the Clipboard
Copy	Copies the selection and places it on the Clipboard
Paste	Inserts Clipboard contents onto the system model diagram
Print	Prints the active document
About	Displays program, version number, and copyright information

The shaded entries are inactive since they relate to the Child frame–based document (in the order displayed on the toolbar from left to right).

TABLE F.15

Common Operations Toolbar Buttons and Their Associated Functionality

Toolbar Button	Function
Select All	Selects all document content with an enclosing rectangular region
Add Multiple Blocks	Presents a block library dialog window for multiple block selection
Auto Fit Diagram	Automatically fits diagram to view
Build Model	Builds the active model
Start Simulation	Starts the simulation, invoking Build Model if not already built
Stop Simulation	Stops the simulation
Numerical Solver	Sets the numerical solver parameters (not all fields are functional)
Show Annotations	Shows or hides diagram annotations if present
Track Multiple Items	Selects and moves multiple items
Edit Box Control	Displays the current simulation time and final execution time

In the order displayed on the toolbar from left to right.

TABLE F.16

Common Blocks Toolbar Buttons and Their Associated Functionality

Toolbar Button	Function
Derivative Block	Adds a Derivative block to the system model
Integrator Block	Adds an Integrator block to the system model
Transfer Function Block	Adds a Transfer Function block to the system model
Divide Block	Adds a Divide block to the system model
Gain Block	Adds a Gain block to the system model
Sum Block	Adds a Sum block to the system model
Output Block	Adds an Output block to the system model
Constant Block	Adds a Constant block to the system model
Linear Function Block	Adds a Linear Function block to the system model
Signal Generator Block	Adds a Signal Generator block to the system model
Subsystem Block	Adds a Subsystem block to the system model
Subsystem In Block	Adds a Subsystem In block to the system model
Subsystem Out Block	Adds a Subsystem Out block to the system model

The shaded entries are nonfunctioning blocks.
In the order displayed on the toolbar from left to right.

FIGURE F.3 Main frame–based toolbar with the enabled buttons (no child document is present).

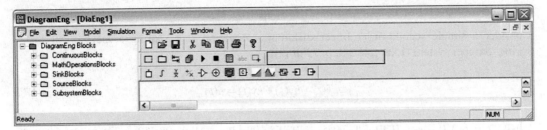

FIGURE F.4 Child frame–based toolbars: Common Operations toolbar (second from the top) and the Common Blocks toolbar (third from the top), where the top Main frame toolbar is still shown.

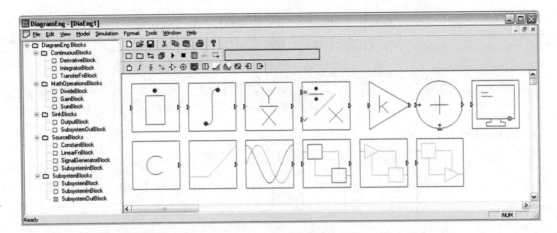

FIGURE F.5 All blocks of the Common Blocks toolbar displayed on the palette.

F.3.2 Child Frame–Based Toolbars

The Child frame–based toolbars, visible in Figure F.4, are the Common Operations and Common Blocks toolbars, second and third from the top, respectively, where the Main frame–based toolbar is still present since some of its functionality becomes active in the presence of a child document, in particular, the Save, Cut, Copy, Paste, and Print items (shown disabled in Figure F.3). The Common Operations and Common Blocks toolbar-based buttons and their function are shown in Tables F.15 and F.16, respectively.

The blocks available on the Common Blocks toolbar are shown placed on the palette in Figure F.5. The user may double-click the center of a block and enter block-specific parameters through the use of a block-parameter-input dialog window.

F.4 EXAMPLES

Real-world engineering problems typically involve second-order linear differential equations that need to be converted to first-order equations using order reduction, prior to their numerical integration, to obtain the trajectories of the dependent variables and their time derivatives. In addition, non-linear dynamical systems often possess coupling and oscillatory dynamics that can be conveniently modeled using feedback loops and computed with the Newton-method-based nonlinear solver and the Integrator block. The following examples show the user how to model differential equations and nonlinear dynamical systems.

F.4.1 SECOND-ORDER LINEAR ORDINARY DIFFERENTIAL EQUATIONS

Consider a simple second-order linear differential equation representing a mechanical mass–spring–damper system (Example 3-3, p. 73 of [2]):

$$m\ddot{y}(t) + b\dot{y}(t) + ky(t) = u(t) \tag{F.1}$$

where m, b, k, $y(t)$, and $u(t)$ are the mass, damping constant, spring constant, output mass displacement from the equilibrium position, and external force input to the system, respectively. An order reduction is used to reduce the second-order system to two first-order equations, where $x_1(t) = y(t)$ and $x_2(t) = \dot{y}(t)$ and results in the following system:

$$\begin{bmatrix} \dot{x}_1(t) \\ \dot{x}_2(t) \end{bmatrix} = \begin{bmatrix} 0 & 1 \\ -k/m & -b/m \end{bmatrix} \begin{bmatrix} x_1(t) \\ x_2(t) \end{bmatrix} + \begin{bmatrix} 0 \\ m^{-1} \end{bmatrix} u(t) \tag{F.2a}$$

$$y(t) = \begin{bmatrix} 1 & 0 \end{bmatrix} \begin{bmatrix} x_1(t) \\ x_2(t) \end{bmatrix} \tag{F.2b}$$

where (see Ref. [2])

$$A = \begin{bmatrix} 0 & 1 \\ -\dfrac{k}{m} & -\dfrac{b}{m} \end{bmatrix}, \quad B = \begin{bmatrix} 0 \\ m^{-1} \end{bmatrix}, \quad C = \begin{bmatrix} 1 & 0 \end{bmatrix} \quad \text{and} \quad D = 0$$

Students of control engineering will recall that the state and output equations in linear form are

$$\dot{x}(t) = A(t)x(t) + B(t)u(t) \tag{F.3a}$$

$$y(t) = C(t)x(t) + D(t)u(t) \tag{F.3b}$$

where
   $x(t)$, $u(t)$, and $y(t)$ are the state, control, and output vectors, respectively
   $A(t)$, $B(t)$, $C(t)$, and $D(t)$ are the state, control, output, and direct transmission matrices, respectively [2]

One will notice on comparing Equations F.2 and F.3 that (F.2a) and (F.2b) are the state and output equations, respectively. The corresponding block diagram representation of the state and output equations (F.3) is shown in Figure F.6 [2].

The integration in the earlier diagram concerns that of $\dot{x}(t)$ to yield $x(t)$, and since $x(t) = [y(t), \dot{y}(t)]^{\mathrm{T}}$, the initial condition for the Integrator block is $x(0) = [y(0), \dot{y}(0)]^{\mathrm{T}}$ (e.g., if the mass is initially at rest with displacement 2.0 m, then $x(0) = [2, 0]^{\mathrm{T}}$).

The engineer can draw Figure F.6 using the DiagramEng application, as shown in Figure F.7, and enter various selections of mechanical properties, m, b, and k and forcing functions $u(t)$, to generate different displacement outputs $y(t)$ and to analyze the physical response behavior of the mass–spring–damper system.

The general analytic solution $y_g(t) \equiv y(t)$ to (F.1) is the sum of the homogeneous solution $y_h(t)$ and the particular solution $y_p(t)$, i.e.,

$$y_g(t) = y_h(t) + y_p(t) \tag{F.4}$$

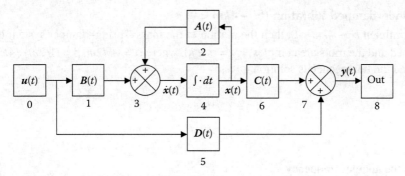

FIGURE F.6 Block diagram representation of the state and output equations (F.3). (From Ogata, K., *Modern Control Engineering*, 4th edn., Prentice Hall, Upper Saddle River, NJ, 2002.)

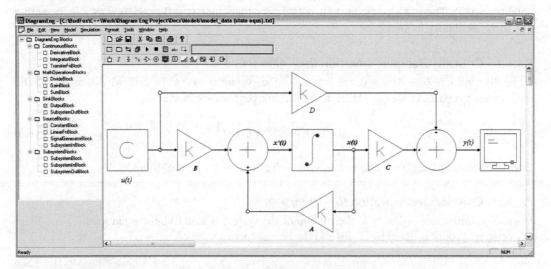

FIGURE F.7 Block diagram model of the state and output equations (F.3) drawn with DiagramEng.

The homogeneous solution is obtained by setting the right-hand side of (F.1) to zero, as follows:

$$m\ddot{y}(t) + b\dot{y}(t) + ky(t) = 0 \tag{F.5a}$$

$$\Rightarrow \ddot{y}(t) + \frac{b}{m}\dot{y}(t) + \frac{k}{m}y(t) = 0 \tag{F.5b}$$

and letting $y(t) = e^{rt}$ results in the characteristic equation

$$r^2 + \frac{b}{m}r + \frac{k}{m} = 0 \tag{F.6a}$$

with roots

$$r_{1,2} = \frac{1}{2m}\left(-b \pm \sqrt{b^2 - 4km}\right) \tag{F.6b}$$

F.4.1.1 Underdamped Vibration ($b^2 - 4km < 0$)

If the discriminant $b^2 - 4km < 0$, then the motion of the mass–spring–damper system is said to be underdamped and the roots are complex, $r_{1,2} = \alpha \pm j\beta$, where $\alpha = -b/2m$, $\beta = (1/2m)\sqrt{4km - b^2}$, and $j = \sqrt{-1}$, and the homogeneous solution is

$$y_h(t) = C_1 e^{\alpha t}(\sin(\omega t) + C_2) \tag{F.7}$$

where
  $\omega = \beta$ is the angular frequency
  C_i, for $i = 1, 2$, are constants [3]

Values for the constants may be determined with knowledge of quantities b, k, m, $u(t)$ and the initial conditions $x(0)$. The mathematician will notice here that since $\alpha < 0$, $y_h(t) \to 0$ as $t \to \infty$, with a decaying oscillatory motion.

F.4.1.2 Critically Damped Vibration ($b^2 - 4km = 0$)

If the discriminant $b^2 - 4km = 0$, the motion of the system is said to be critically damped [3] and there exists a repeated root $r = -b/2m$, and the homogeneous solution is

$$y_h(t) = C_1 e^{-bt/2m} + C_2 t e^{-bt/2m} \tag{F.8}$$

Both exponents are negative, and hence, $y_h(t) \to 0$ as $t \to \infty$, without oscillation.

F.4.1.3 Overdamped Vibration ($b^2 - 4km > 0$)

If the discriminant $b^2 - 4km > 0$, the motion of the system is said to be overdamped [3] and there exist two real roots as given by (F.6b) and the homogeneous solution

$$y_h(t) = C_1 e^{r_1 t} + C_2 e^{r_2 t} \tag{F.9}$$

Both roots are real but negative, and hence, $y_h(t) \to 0$ as $t \to \infty$, without oscillation.

The particular solution of (F.1) may be found by the Method of Undetermined Coefficients, and given initial conditions, the coefficients may be determined and a general solution found.

Figure F.8a through c illustrates the three different damping conditions where the homogeneous solutions ($y_h(t)$) are those provided by (F.7 through F.9) and $y_p(t) = 1/k$ (given $u(t) = 1$) for the initial conditions $x(0) = [2, 0]^T$: (1) Figure F.8a shows underdamped oscillatory vibration, where $y_g(t) \to 1.0$ as $t \to \infty$, for $u(t) = 1$, $m = 1 = k$, and $b = 0.5$; (2) Figure F.8b shows critically damped nonoscillatory vibration, where $y_g(t) \to 1.0$ as $t \to \infty$, for $u(t) = 1$, $m = 1 = k$, and $b = 2$; and (3) Figure F.8c shows overdamped nonoscillatory vibration, where $y_g(t) \to 1.0$ as $t \to \infty$, for $u(t) = 1$, $m = 1 = k$, and $b = 3$.

F.4.2 Nonlinear Dynamical Systems

A coupled nonlinear system involves equations that are nonlinear in the variables for which the system is to be computed. Consider the Lotka–Volterra system consisting of two coupled first-order nonlinear differential equations, describing the population dynamics of predator–prey interaction, presented in Ref. [4], where $x(t)$ and $y(t)$ are the populations of the prey and predator, respectively:

$$\frac{dx}{dt} = \alpha x - \beta xy \tag{F.10a}$$

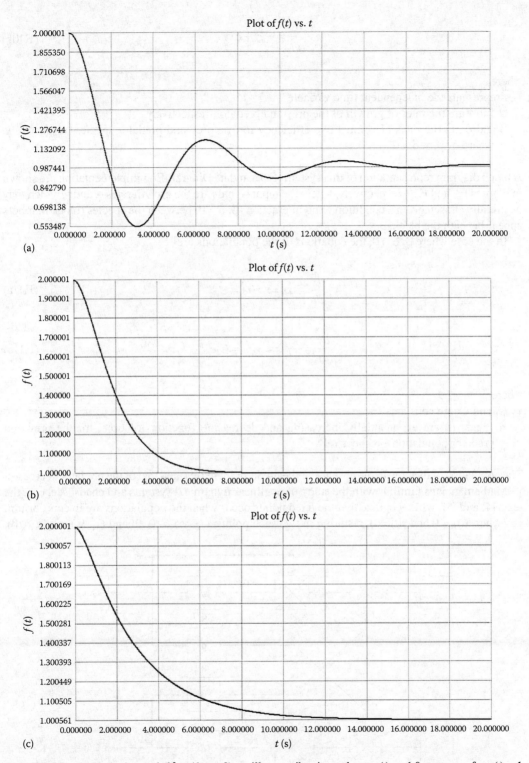

FIGURE F.8 (a) Underdamped ($b^2 - 4km < 0$) oscillatory vibration, where $y_g(t) \to 1.0$ as $t \to \infty$, for $u(t) = 1$, $m = 1 = k$, $b = 0.5$, $\boldsymbol{x}(0) = [y(0), \dot{y}(0)]^T = [2, 0]^T$, and $\delta t = 10^{-3}$ s. (b) Critically damped ($b^2 - 4km = 0$) nonoscillatory vibration, where $y_g(t) \to 1.0$ as $t \to \infty$, for $u(t) = 1$, $m = 1 = k$, $b = 2$, $\boldsymbol{x}(0) = [y(0), \dot{y}(0)]^T = [2, 0]^T$, and $\delta t = 10^{-3}$ s. (c) Overdamped ($b^2 - 4km > 0$) nonoscillatory vibration, where $y_g(t) \to 1.0$ as $t \to \infty$, for $u(t) = 1$, $m = 1 = k$, $b = 3$, $\boldsymbol{x}(0) = [y(0), \dot{y}(0)]^T = [2, 0]^T$, and $\delta t = 10^{-3}$ s.

$$\frac{dy}{dt} = -\gamma y + \delta xy \qquad \qquad (F.10b)$$

where

t represents the independent time variable

α and γ are the rates of growth of the prey and predator, respectively

β and δ are the rates of competitive efficiency for the prey and predator species, respectively, where $\alpha, \beta, \gamma, \delta > 0$

A block diagram representation of this system (F.10) and its DiagramEng implementation are shown in Figures F.9 and F.10, respectively, where the input signals are the growth rates α and γ, which may be initially chosen given a condition of no interaction ($\beta, \delta = 0$) between the species (block numbers appear beneath the blocks).

In the case where $\beta, \delta = 0$, the equations of the populations are

$$\frac{dx}{dt} = \alpha x \Rightarrow x(t) = C_1 e^{\alpha t} \qquad \qquad (F.11a)$$

$$\frac{dy}{dt} = -\gamma y \Rightarrow y(t) = C_2 e^{-\gamma t} \qquad \qquad (F.11b)$$

where

C_1 and C_2 are constants

$x(t)$ and $y(t)$ are exponentially increasing and decreasing functions of time, for the prey and predator populations, respectively

The population of the prey in the absence of the predator increases, and that of the predator decreases.

Mathematicians familiar with the study of nonlinear dynamical systems and chaos (see, e.g., the texts [4] and [5]) will recognize that the fixed points occur when the populations are in equilibrium, i.e., when $\dot{x}(t) = 0$ and $\dot{y}(t) = 0$, resulting in two such points: $(x_0, y_0) = (0, 0)$ and $(x_1, y_1) = (\gamma/\delta, \alpha/\beta)$.

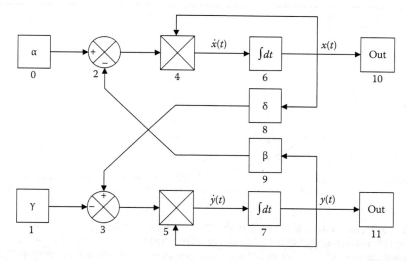

FIGURE F.9 A block diagram representation of the Lotka–Volterra system of two coupled first-order nonlinear differential equations (F.10).

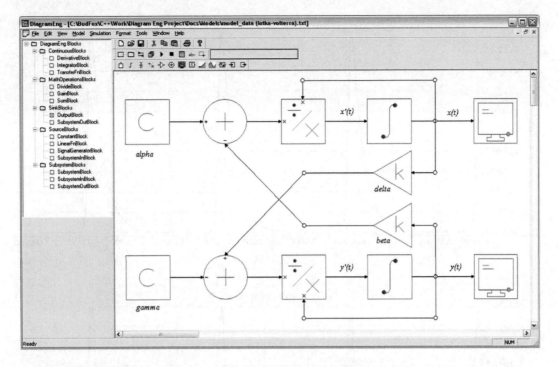

FIGURE F.10   The block diagram representation of the Lotka–Volterra system made using DiagramEng.

The stability of these points may be determined by observing the eigenvalues of the Jacobian matrix of the system (F.10), i.e.,

$$J(x, y) = \begin{bmatrix} \partial\dot{x}/\partial x & \partial\dot{x}/\partial y \\ \partial\dot{y}/\partial x & \partial\dot{y}/\partial y \end{bmatrix} \tag{F.12a}$$

$$= \begin{bmatrix} \alpha - \beta y & -\beta x \\ \delta y & \delta x - \gamma \end{bmatrix} \tag{F.12b}$$

For $(x_0, y_0) = (0, 0)$, the eigenvalues of $J(x, y)$ are $\lambda_1 = \alpha$ and $\lambda_2 = -\gamma$, with corresponding eigenvectors $v_1 = [1, 0]^T$ (the unstable manifold, x axis) and $v_2 = [0, 1]^T$ (the stable manifold, y axis), respectively, and hence, the critical point is a saddle point and the system is unstable, implying that the extinction of both species is unlikely.

For $(x_1, y_1) = (\gamma/\delta, \alpha/\beta)$, the eigenvalues of $J(x, y)$ are $\lambda_{1,2} = \pm i\sqrt{\alpha\gamma}$, i.e., they are purely imaginary $(\text{Re}(\lambda_{1,2}) = 0)$, indicating the presence of a center (in the positive quadrant) rather than a spiral, and Kibble states that as a result, there are cyclic variations in $x(t)$ and $y(t)$ which are not in phase [4] (the population of the predators grows while that of the prey declines and vice versa).

A simulation of the Lotka–Volterra system (F.10) was made with the parameters $\alpha = 2$, $\gamma = 2$, $\beta = 1$ and $\delta = 0.5$, where the initial conditions of integration were $x(0) = 20$ and $y(0) = 10$, the initial output signals for the Divide blocks (which must be set since the Divide blocks are involved in two feedback loops) were $x_4(t_0) = -8$ and $x_5(t_0) = 8$, and a time-step size of $\delta t = 10^{-4}$ s was chosen. The cyclical variations in the populations of the prey and predators are shown in Figure F.11a and b, respectively, where the population of the prey leads that of the predator, i.e., the variations are in fact not in phase.

The phase portrait of the population of the predator vs. the prey, i.e., $y(t)$ vs. $x(t)$, may be generated by saving the output data through the Output blocks and plotting the two population values

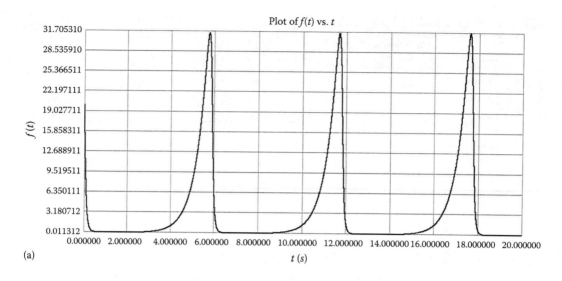

(a)

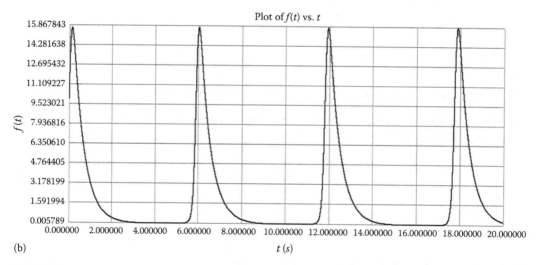

(b)

FIGURE F.11 Computation of the Lotka–Volterra system (F.10) with parameters, $\alpha = 2$, $\gamma = 2$, $\beta = 1$, and $\delta = 0.5$, where $x(0) = 20$ and $y(0) = 10$, and $\delta t = 10^{-4}$ (s): (a) cyclic variations in the prey population; (b) cyclic variations in the predator population.

against each other as shown in Figure F.12 (using a third-party graphical application). A saddle point resides at the origin $(x_0, y_0) = (0, 0)$, and a center is present at $(x_1, y_1) = (\gamma/\delta, \alpha/\beta)$. As the prey declines in number, the predator grows, and vice versa, and neither species becomes extinct. As $t \rightarrow \infty$, it is observed that the trajectories do in fact form a center.

F.5 OUTPUT

The output shown in Figures F.8 and F.11 is obtained by double-clicking the Output block and selecting the Show Graph button on the OutputBlockDialog dialog window (Figure F.13). If the underlying numerical data are desired, then these may be saved by selecting the Save Data button and specifying the appropriate file name and location. Then, a third-party application may be used to plot the data of different Output blocks against each other, as has been done to produce the phase portrait of Figure F.12.

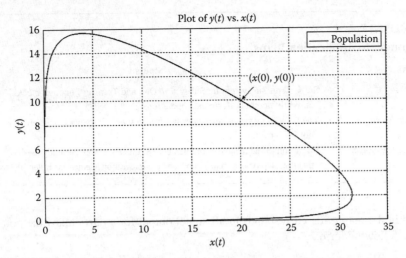

FIGURE F.12 Phase portrait of $y(t)$ vs. $x(t)$ showing the change in population of the predator vs. the prey, where $(x(0), y(0) = 20, 10)$: the saddle point is at $(0, 0)$ and the center at $(\gamma/\delta, \alpha/\beta)$.

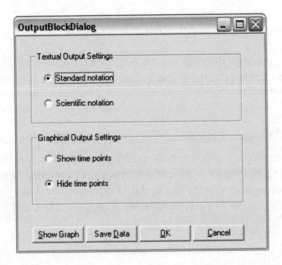

FIGURE F.13 Output block dialog window allowing the user to view the graphical results (Show Graph) or save the underlying data (Save Data).

F.5.1 OUTPUT BLOCK DATA FILE

Consider an Output block–based recorded data matrix of the following form:

$$M = \left[\begin{bmatrix} f_1(t_0) & f_2(t_0) \\ f_3(t_0) & f_4(t_0) \end{bmatrix} \begin{bmatrix} f_1(t_1) & f_2(t_1) \\ f_3(t_1) & f_4(t_1) \end{bmatrix}, \dots, \begin{bmatrix} f_1(t_n) & f_2(t_n) \\ f_3(t_n) & f_4(t_n) \end{bmatrix} \right] \tag{F.13}$$

where $f_s(t)$, for $s \in \{1,\dots, 4\}$ (four signals are used here for simplicity), are the individual signals being recorded for each time point $t_i \in [t_0, t_n]$, for initial and final simulation time points, t_0 and t_n, respectively. The data are written to an output file, with default name "output_data.txt" where each

TABLE F.17

Incomplete Application Items

Item	Status
Blocks	Subsystem, Subsystem In, Subsystem Out, and Transfer Function blocks currently do not perform data operations
Model Menu	The Build Subsystem entry does not function as subsystem blocks are not implemented
Numerical Solver	The absolute and relative error tolerance parameters are not currently used, the time-step type is "fixed-step", and the Integration Method is "Euler (1st Order)"

row of data in the output file corresponds to all signal output for a particular time point t_i and the file is of the following form:

$$t_0, f_1(t_0), f_2(t_0), f_3(t_0), f_4(t_0)$$

$$t_1, f_1(t_1), f_2(t_1), f_3(t_1), f_4(t_1)$$

$$\vdots$$

$$t_n, f_1(t_n), f_2(t_n), f_3(t_n), f_4(t_n)$$

(F.14)

If there are no data in the output matrix, then the number of rows and number of columns are zero, and only the time points corresponding to the system model simulation parameters will be written to the output file.

F.5.2 Model Data File

The model data file used to record all system model elements that specifies the geometry of the model and its underlying properties is different to the aforementioned numerical output data file. The user need not be concerned with the model data file format but should be aware that the saving and restoring of a system model is performed using a user-specified text file, which has a default name "model_data.txt".

F.6 NONFUNCTIONAL ITEMS

The current initial version of the DiagramEng software application allows the user to perform general modeling and simulation activities with the essential mathematical features. However, some functional elements exist that require additional work for their completion and are left till the second version of the software. The incomplete application items are shown in Table F.17.

F.7 SUMMARY

The topics covered in the "UsingDiagramEng.pdf" document include (1) the Main frame–based menu, Child frame–based menu, and Context menu; (2) the Main frame–based toolbar and the Child frame–based Common Operations and Common Blocks toolbars; (3) two examples concerning ordinary differential equations and nonlinear dynamical systems; (4) forms of output data including numerical simulation data ("output_data.txt") and system model data ("model_data.txt"); and (5) nonfunctional elements that will be completed in the next version of the software.

REFERENCES

1. Microsoft Visual C++ 6.0, Microsoft® Visual Studio™ 6.0 Development System, Professional Edition, Microsoft Corporation, 1998.
2. Ogata, K., *Modern Control Engineering*, 4th edn., Prentice Hall, Upper Saddle River, NJ, 2002.
3. Salas, S. L. and Hille, E., *Calculus: One and Several Variables (Complex Variables, Differential Equations Supplement)*, 6th edn., John Wiley & Sons, New York, 1990.
4. Kibble, T. W. B. and Berkshire, F. H., *Classical Mechanics*, 5th edn., Imperial College Press, London, U.K., 2004.
5. Strogatz, S. H., *Nonlinear Dynamics and Chaos: With Applications to Physics, Biology, Chemistry, and Engineering*, Addison-Wesley, Reading MA, 1994.

Index